RESOURCES FOR TEACHING CHILDREN WITH DIVERSE ABILITIES

●

BIRTH THROUGH EIGHT

Penny Low Deiner

UNIVERSITY OF DELAWARE

HARCOURT BRACE JOVANOVICH COLLEGE PUBLISHERS

Fort Worth Philadelphia San Diego New York Orlando Austin San Antonio
Toronto Montreal London Sydney Tokyo

Publisher: Ted Buchholz
Acquisitions Editor: Jo-Anne Weaver
Project Editor: Barbara Moreland
Production Manager: Kathleen Ferguson
Designer: Linda Miller

Address Editorial Correspondence to: 301 Commerce Street, Suite 3700, Fort Worth, TX 76102

Address Orders to: 6277 Sea Harbor Drive, Orlando, FL 32887
1-800-782-4479 or 1-800-433-0001 (in Florida)

Printed in the United States of America

ISBN: 0-15-500024-1

2 3 4 5 6 7 8 9 0 1   085   9 8 7 6 5 4 3 2 1

DEDICATION

To my husband, John, my most critical editor, and the marriage that survived this writing process. And to our daughter, Paige, who provided a real values clarification experience.

Preface

This is both a textbook and a resource book for teachers who are including or will include children with disabilities in their classes. The book acknowledges and identifies the role of theory in the field and then translates this theory into practice. The book provides information about growth and development, program planning, and working with families. It contains over three hundred activities to facilitate individualized programming.

The book is written in a nontechnical style and is designed to increase knowledge about children with disabilities and to demonstrate how to apply this knowledge in a teaching situation. The scope of this book is broader than that of most books in the field. In addition to traditional information about disabilities, it assumes that appropriate programming requires a knowledge of how all children grow and develop, and it provides this information. Families are an integral part of early childhood special education, and to work with families one needs knowledge about how families operate and techniques for working with them. The philosophy of the book strongly supports "best practice." It is written with the expectation that children with disabilities will be included in all settings.

The book is divided into four parts. Part I, "Early Childhood Intervention," introduces the text and the field of early childhood special education, then details the theoretical bases for early childhood special education. It also provides an overview of typical and atypical development, early identification, diagnosis and assessment, how to use that information in individualized program planning, and how to include these individualized program plans in general planning for preschoolers and infants and toddlers. It concludes with a discussion of different types of service delivery systems.

Part II, "Including Children with Diverse Abilities," focuses on the needs of children with disabilities: communication disorders, hearing and visual impairments, learning disabilities, physical disabilities, emotional/behavioral disorders, health impairments, and mental retardation. Part II also includes a chapter on infants and toddlers with disabilities. Each chapter in this part briefly defines the disability and its major characteristics, then focuses on general teaching goals. Guidelines are given for working with the children, and information on curriculum adaptations is included by curriculum area. A glossary follows each of these chapters and a section on teaching resources lists organizations that can give additional information about a disability. Each of these chapters has a reference and bibliography section that includes additional readings for teachers (which can also be shared with parents) that provide more detailed information about the disability. This list is followed by a fiction and biography section, which is designed to expand knowledge of the ways families and individuals have coped with disabilities.

At the end of Part II is a bibliography for children. This is an annotated bibliography that contains books about children with disabilities or books that are particularly relevant to these children and classrooms where they are included. The books are arranged by topic.

Part III is titled "Working with Families." It provides a basic foundation on family interactions and styles and looks at the impact of a child with a disability on the family. It also focuses on families and children at risk, ways of assessing families, and family differences, as well as techniques for working with families.

Part IV, "Integrating the Curriculum to Meet Children's Needs," consists of activities designed **v** to help children gain needed skills. These activities are grouped into chapters by curriculum area and are also indexed at the beginning of each chapter by the goals the activities are designed to meet. The beginning of each chapter provides a developmental base for the area and discusses how the activities fit in with the total program. The activities described in the book—although applicable for all children—are particularly appropriate and effective for children with disabilities.

The book is designed to be used flexibly. Each of the four parts of the book, although supporting each other, are independent. Course sequences, the availability of practicum settings, the option of observing different service delivery systems, or instructor preference may influence the order in which the chapters are read.

The activities and resource material provided in the book are just that, resources for current and future use. As such, they are designed to be useful in classroom and child care settings, in field and student teaching experiences, and also as a resource for ongoing program planning. The book is designed to be referred to, used, and modified throughout one's teaching career.

I want to acknowledge the contribution of students who took my courses and who, instead of just taking notes, asked questions that jogged my thinking and forced me to clarify my ideas. Supervision of students in the field has connected me with two realities that are reflected in the book. First was the need to qualify, quantify, and package material for inexperienced preservice teachers. The second was an increased appreciation of the concerns expressed by practicing teachers who shared their ideas about what they wished they had been taught and what they currently needed to know.

I want particularly to acknowledge the teachers who allowed me to take pictures. Although I am obviously grateful for the pictures, I also want to express appreciation for the information gained and the support that went beyond the pictures themselves. The University of Delaware Laboratory school, directed by Alice P. Eyman, was a valuable resource, and particularly its teachers Jane Davidson, Nancy Edwards, and Nadine Heim. Especially valuable support was provided by: The Meadowood Program Preschool and its head teacher Lynne Meyer-Berlin; the Leach School at Castle Hills and its head teacher Melanie Chadwick; the Delaware Curative Workshop and its head teachers Maryann Koziol, Valerie Martin, and Celeste Ryan; and Joanne P. Gichner's family day care home. I also want to thank Maria and Tom Armington and Kate Conway-Turner and their families for allowing me to take pictures in their homes. Two graduate students, Jennifer Wallitsch and Faith Lawton, deserve special recognition. I would like to note Ginger Biasotto's contribution to my understanding of dyslexia and some of the activities that are useful in building skills for children in this area. Also, Madeline Anduz, who gave me the first threads of what consistency meant in a book of this length, was more helpful than she knows.

While rewriting this book I served as chairperson of the Delaware Developmental Disabilities Planning Council. Because of this position and the people I worked with on the council, I became more keenly aware of the broader concerns of developmental disabilities, family needs across the life course, and the long term implications of developmental abilities.

Two grants for which I was the principal investigator were strongly influential in my thinking: Grant #G008630267 from the U. S. Department of Education, Handicapped Children's Early Education Program and Grant #88-01-23-02 from the Delaware Department of Public Instruction through P.L. 99-457, Part H. Although work on this book was not even begun when I directed these grants, the people I worked with and the problem solving that was done have had a profound effect upon my thinking. Linda C. Whitehead was an inspirational colleague, as were Catherine M. Prudhoe, Donald L. Peters, Celeste Ryan, James J. Lesko, Deborah Ziegler, and Karen Reif. I am indebted to Grace Lowe, who stepped in at the eleventh hour and provided invaluable help with the children's bibliography. In addition, she provided emotional support and soup when it was most needed.

I want to acknowledge Patricia A. Childs, who had progressive ideas ten years ago that influenced the book, and who continues to influence my awareness of the challenges people with disabilities face and the skills children with disabilities need to meet these challenges.

I owe a special thanks to the reviewers of this manuscript: Alice Sterling Honig, Syracuse University; Jan Blaxall, Fanshawe College; David Sexton, University of New Orleans; Harleen Vickers, University of Delaware. They provided not only constructive criticism, but encouragement that the book was worth the investment of both their time and mine. The editors that I worked most closely with at Harcourt Brace Jovanovich, Barbara Moreland and Jo-Anne Weaver were not only competent, but pleasant and interesting to work with.

I also wish to acknowledge my family and their support: my mother, Myrtle Haag's, encouragement, Jamie and Michael, now adults living independently, who still asked how it was going, and my husband John and our youngest daughter Paige, who dealt with all the things that had to be "put off" until the book was completed.

Finally, I owe a great deal to the children I have taught, who in reality taught me—not so much the easy ones, but those who wouldn't learn.

Contents

PART ONE

Early Childhood Intervention

Chapter 1

Teaching Children

I teach children. For some children I individualize my programming all the time, others only require minor modifications. How do I teach all these children? That is the question this book answers. It is intended to provide guidance for all those who plan to teach young children and to be a resource for those who are already working in the field. The book assumes that whether or not one plans to teach children with disabilities, they at some time will be in every classroom.

Children with disabilities are those who require adjustments to their programming or classroom. For example, a child with spina bifida who is in a walker requires long-range planning: Has enough time been allotted for changing to a new activity? Is the furniture spaced far enough apart to allow the walker to pass through easily? Will the motor requirements of large group activity present problems? Another child, unhappy about a new baby sister, may need to express his feelings through play. The intensity of the need may result in his spending most of his time over several days in the free play area, while his work on readiness skills is postponed. Responsive programming is flexible; it allows "additional free play" to become temporarily the child's regular program.

All children have needs. Some children have specialized needs some of the time; some children have specialized needs all of the time. My goal is to help teachers program for the needs of *all* the children in their classrooms, including those with disabilities. To accomplish that goal, this text provides basic information on disabilities (supplemented with numerous resources) and a wealth of flexible methods and activities for teaching children with disabilities.

About You

I assume, since you, the reader, are or plan to be a teacher, that you already know some general **3**

You are a model for the children.

techniques of teaching, and you understand how children develop and learn. You can recognize the rate at which a child is learning and identify where in the learning process a child is having problems. Changes in educational philosophies now call for the inclusion of children with disabilities in the regular classroom. Consequently you now need additional knowledge about disabilities and their effect on children's growth and learning. You need to know how to program for the individualized needs of these children. You may have mixed feelings about meeting this challenge.

What you require, at least initially, is not in-depth expertise, but a basic understanding of various disabilities.* You need new or adapted methods and activities that are not only designed to meet the needs of children with disabilities, but are good for all children. In short, you need a guide on how best to teach, cope with, and enjoy children with disabilities while you meet the needs of all the children in your classroom.

In addition to being their teacher, you are a model for the children in your class. Both your verbal and nonverbal behavior indicate to the class your feelings toward children with disabilities. If you view those children as odd or as needing too much extra help or as requiring that exceptions be made for them, the children will also. Being a positive role

model may be more important than having the latest information about disabilities.

As children are now being viewed as part of a family-centered unit (Dunst, Johanson, Trivette, & Hamby, 1991), you can expect to have many interactions with the families of the children you teach. Usually it is necessary to have frequent contact with parents of children with disabilities. Developing techniques of communicating with parents on a regular basis, viewing the child within the context of the family system, and generating solutions that work for families and children are additional skills this book will help you develop.

About Children

All children are individuals, yet all have much in common. They all have strengths as well as needs. In some cases the strengths may be elusive, but they can be found. All children have specialized needs some of the time. One child may have a cast on his broken leg for several months, while another may forget her toilet training because of stress at home. Are they disabled? No, they simply have special needs during a crucial period in their lives.

When children have disabilities, there is a danger of considering only how different those needs make them; a teacher may lose sight of how much they resemble other children. When that happens,

*For additional information on specific disabilities, see Chapters 10–18 and the references at the end of each chapter.

she forgets these children have the same needs as their classmates. All of a child's needs must be taken into account, not just those related to a disability. A child with a hearing loss needs to learn to speech read and use residual hearing. However, she also needs to learn how it feels to wear a firefighter's hat and how to roll out clay.

School may be a new and possibly frightening experience for many children. A child with a disability has an added fear—fear of rejection by the teacher or by peers. The child may have had few experiences away from the family, and those may have been painful. More than other children, this child may need reassurance and may take some time to develop a trusting relationship.

The teacher can help classmates accept this child by developing in them an awareness of the strengths and needs of others. As their understanding of other children grows, so will their self-awareness. Through the awareness of others and themselves, children can learn strategies for dealing with people who are different from them—a valuable skill, for all individuals are different.

Labels and Labeling

The practice of categorizing or labeling children based on their primary disability evolved gradually; no one planned it. It comes out of the traditional medical model; a professional diagnoses an "illness" and labels it. Labeling has also been encouraged through federal law. In 1958 the federal government allocated money to improve the education of the mentally retarded. Funding was extended in 1963 to include the hearing impaired, speech impaired, visually impaired, emotionally disturbed, and crippled or health impaired; the learning disabled were added to this list in 1970. In order to receive federal money, educators were, and still are, required to label children. A child's disability must be diagnosed and classified under a traditional set of categories in order for the child to obtain services. These categories are established by law (Public Law 94-142). Unfortunately, the practice of labeling is carried into the children's daily lives. Changes in the law (Public Law 99-457) now allow children under the age of three to be labeled developmentally delayed when a specific diagnosis is not obvious. This label is replaced by a more specific one (for example, learning disabled) as the child gets older, or dropped altogether if the delay is "outgrown."

Leaders in the field are now questioning labeling. They argue that the challenge for both research and implementation is for delivering effective, comprehensive services for all children based on their individual educational needs rather than their labeled disability. They are hopeful that there will be no more "special" education, but rather an education system that serves *all* children.

Labels pick out a single characteristic of a child (usually not a strength) and call attention to this characteristic. A physically impaired child, for example, may be viewed as "a pair of legs" rather than as a child with all the feelings, wants, and needs of a normal child. A picture of the child as a whole is lost.

Another problem is that diagnostic tools are not completely accurate, and children may in fact be mislabeled. Of special concern are young children, as a label is given at age three may be on a child's record for his entire educational career, whether or not the labeled condition still exists. Future teachers may be biased by the label before they even meet the child. The expectations of both the teacher and the child may be lower because the child is labeled. Children may miss opportunities because it is assumed (because of the label) that they cannot do something.

In addition to having a stigmatizing effect, the use of labeling actually keeps many young children who need intervention from obtaining the services they need. Preventive actions are made difficult and helping children who are at risk is not supported. Under the labeling system, educators must wait until the disability is great enough to be diagnostically verifiable before intervention can begin.

In an attempt to be more descriptive and more accurate, labeling often includes the level of severity of the child's problem. For example, a child who has what is called a "situational, short-term adjustment problem" (perhaps due to divorce, the death of a grandparent, moving, or starting school) would be labeled *mild*. A more tenacious problem (such as school phobia, persistent acting out, or withdrawal) would be labeled *moderate*. A behavior disorder such as autism would be labeled *severe*. Children with mild and moderate impairments will be in the classroom; increasingly children with severe disabilities are being included for all or part of the day. Identifying the level of severity is helpful, but it is only a starting point.

Despite personal feelings about labeling, I have used conventional labels for subjects covered by this book. They are also used for chapter titles for those disabilities labeled in the law. Every teacher encounters and uses labeling early in the process of screening children to determine eligibility and for reporting purposes. The kind of disability and its degree of severity may indicate to the teacher general areas in which to check for needs. These labels, however, are too general; I cannot program for a label. I can program for a child.

The most useful and positive approach is to identify each child's needs and then to build programming to meet these needs. Saying "John has a visual impairment and can distinguish only light and dark" will not help me design an appropriate program, but only to label the disability. But when I describe the needs—"John will need an alternative method for handling projects that require visual skills"—I imply several possible actions. I can adapt the approach John must use or expand the project so that all the children can enjoy it and learn from it. With a simple statement of need, effective programming has already begun. The process of translating needs into program goals and then into activities is demonstrated throughout this book. The process of programming for needs is a dynamic one. A child who is labeled visually impaired may in fact be visually impaired for life, but that child's needs will change—not merely each year, but perhaps each week or day. Programming must be responsive to the changes.

Terminology

The terminology in the field of early childhood special education is changing. Some of the changes are dramatic, others more subtle. However, the intent of all of the changes is to focus on people first and disabilities second. The words people choose to use can convey messages of value, equality, and respect, or they can devalue individuals.

The terms "handicap" and "disability" are not synonymous. A handicap describes a condition or barrier to completing a task; a long flight of stairs is a handicap to a person using a wheelchair. A disability is a general term referring to a functional limitation that interferes with major life activities such as walking, hearing, or learning. Beginning in 1990, the term "handicapped" has been replaced by the term "disability." This change is reflected even in the names of the laws passed. The Education of the Handicapped Acts (EHA) were replaced by a new law in 1990, the Individuals with Disabilities Education Act (IDEA). All references to "handicapped children" were changed to "children with disabilities." The word handicapped is still used in citing laws or environmental barriers, but not in reference to people.

Another important change focuses on "people first" language. That is, descriptions of disabling conditions should not be used as preceding adjective phrases (thus one should say, "a child with a hearing impairment," not "deaf child" or even, "hearing-impaired child"). The term "special" has also come under scrutiny. Why should there be "special education"? Why not just "education" that meets the needs of all children? The same thinking applies to "special needs." Don't all children have needs? When comparing children with disabilities to children without disabilities, talk about the latter as "nondisabled." If one refers to them as "normal," the obvious implication is that children with disabilities are "abnormal."

The words "mainstreaming," "integration," and "inclusion" are also used interchangeably by some. They, too, have different meanings. Consider the concept of mainstreaming; if children are to join the mainstream, then obviously they were not part of it to begin with. They are being added to an existing group. Likewise, integration is another term that allows children to be integrated based on some criteria. Integration provides the opportunity for children with disabilities to participate in academic, physical, or social activities with their nondisabled peers. "While integration is considered to be philosophically and educationally superior to segregation, such 'push in' arrangements remain inherently hierarchical and

unequal" (Salisbury, 1991, p. 147). Inclusion is a value term indicating that all children belong in the classroom they would attend if they did not have a disability. Inclusive programming is concerned with meeting the diverse needs of *all* children within the regular classroom. Inclusion requires teachers, parents, and administrators to examine their value systems and to develop creative, effective programming for all children. This text is about inclusion.

About the Text

This book is divided into four parts. In the first part, "Early Childhood Intervention," Chapters 1 and 2 introduce the text and the field of early childhood special education. Chapter 3 details the theoretical bases for early childhood special education. Chapter 4 provides an overview of typical and atypical development. Later chapters focus on the early identification, diagnosis, and assessment of children; how to use that information in individualized program planning; and how to include these individualized program plans in general planning for preschoolers, infants, and toddlers. The final chapters in this section focus on different types of service delivery systems.

Part Two is on "Including Children with Diverse Abilities." Chapters 10–18 focus on the needs of children with disabilities: communication disorders, hearing and visual impairments, learning disabilities, physical disabilities, emotional/behavioral disorders, health impairments, and mental retardation. The section ends with a chapter on infants and toddlers with disabilities.

In each of Chapters 10–18, a disability is briefly defined and its major characteristics given. Each chapter gives information on the characteristics of children by listing their greatest needs, which then become the focus for teaching goals. Guidelines are given for working with the children and ways to adapt curriculum to fit their needs. These adaptations are arranged by curriculum area.

These guidelines are followed by reference to a children's bibliography located at the end of Part Two. Activities particularly relevant to the disability just discussed are highlighted.

A glossary follows. When possible, nontechnical terms are used in the text. However, as one reads technical reports and talks with specialists, the need to learn the terminology of the field becomes important. These terms are defined in the glossary.

The next section, on teaching resources, lists national and some regional organizations that can give additional information about a disability. Also listed are sources of specialized materials that may be helpful in the classroom.

Each of these chapters is followed by a section on references and bibliography. This contains the references used to write the chapter and additional readings for teachers and parents. The books listed provide more detailed information about a particular disability or programming area. I encourage any teacher to read them if he has a child with that disability in his classroom. This list is followed by a fiction and biography section designed to increase awareness of the ways families and individuals have coped with disabilities.

At the end of Part Two is an awareness bibliography for children, an annotated list that contains books about children with disabilities. This list is followed by books that meet the needs of children with the disability (for example, books about death and dying, books without words, and so on). The books are arranged by topic.

Part Three, Chapters 19–22, concentrates on "Working with Families." Chapter 19 provides a basic foundation for how families work and looks at the impact of a child with a disability on the family. Later chapters focus on families and children at risk, ways of assessing families and family differences, as well as techniques for working with families.

Part Four of the book consists of activities designed to help children gain needed skills. These activities are grouped into chapters by curriculum area and are also listed at the beginning of each chapter by the goals the activities are designed to meet. At the beginning of each chapter is a description of the developmental base for the area and how the activities fit into the total program.

The activities described in the book—although good for all the children—are particularly appropriate and effective for meeting the needs of children with disabilities. All activities are presented in the following format:

Specific programming area provides a more specific designation for activities. For example, within Language Arts, a specific area would be Reading Readiness.

Goal states what the activity does. For example, a goal might read, "To increase body awareness." This statement is similar to the annual goal in an Individualized Education Program (IEP).

Objective is a statement in behavioral terms of what the child is expected to do at the end of or during the activity: The child will point to at least five body parts on request. This step is similar to the objectives needed to carry out the annual goal in the IEP.

Materials provides a list of the materials necessary to perform the activity.

Procedure tells the teacher or student how to carry out the activity.

Increase level of difficulty:
  Materials
  Procedure
This section gives ideas for making the original activity more difficult for all the children or for a particular child. Increasing the level of difficulty is usually done by varying the materials used (using a two-inch instead of a four-inch balance beam) or by varying the procedure (having children walk the balance beam backwards or blindfolded).

Decrease level of difficulty:
  Materials
  Procedure
This section gives ideas for making the original activity easier for all the children or for a particular child. This change is again usually accomplished by varying the materials used (using a six-inch line taped on the floor instead of a four-inch balance beam) or the procedure (having children walk the line while holding your hand).

Comments are additional remarks, such as how to adapt this activity for children with different disabilities, what parts of the activity to emphasize, and why it is useful for particular groups of children.

Using the Book

The book may be used flexibly to fit each teacher's needs. Although supporting each other, each of the four parts of the book are independent. Course sequences, the availability of practicum settings, the option of observing different service delivery systems, or instructor preference may influence the order in which the chapters are read.

The activities and resource material provided in the book are just that, resources for future use. The activities and discussion of the developmental base for each curriculum area are designed to help students and teachers in the field. As such, they will be useful in student teaching experiences and also as part of regular program planning. They may well be shared with families. They can be referred to, used, and modified throughout one's teaching career.

References and Bibliography

Derman-Sparks, L. and the A.B.C. Task Force. (1989). *Anti-bias curriculum: Tools for empowering young children.* Washington, DC: National Association for the Education of Young Children.

Dunst, C., Johanson, C., Trivette, C., & Hamby, D. (1991). Family-oriented early intervention policies and practices: Family-centered or not? *Exceptional Children, 58*(2), 104–112.

Salisbury, C. (1991). Mainstreaming during the early childhood years. *Exceptional Children, 58*(2), 146–155.

Chapter 2

Early Childhood Special Education: A Blend

Early childhood special education is a new field and a new profession. As short a time ago as twenty-five years things were very different. If a child were born severely disabled, institutionalization was usually recommended. If that were not done, the child was kept at home and made comfortable. No effort was made to teach these children because such efforts were thought to be a waste of time. The only concentrated effort was made in the area of self-help skills, in the hope that these could ease the family burden and perhaps make the child eligible for school.

Children whose disabilities were not apparent at birth, but who did not meet the appropriate developmental milestones, were typically dealt with by a physician using a medical model. Advice was usually to "wait and see," or "let's keep it under observation." Parents were typically labeled "overanxious," or especially in the case of a first child, "inexperienced." If it was a later child they were told that all children develop differently at their own pace. They were not to worry but to bring it up at the next well baby checkup. Given such an approach, it was frequently not until the child reached school age that a concerted effort was made to diagnose a specific problem and to develop an intervention program. Obviously, the critical preschool years were wasted.

Historical Overview

The history of early childhood special education is a relatively short one. The mood of the 1960s began to change attitudes. Initially, these changes were small and isolated. The mandate for Head Start first made in 1965 publicly acknowledged the value of early childhood education and the whole concept that education begins before public school. As education was being offered to children who were "disadvantaged," parents of children with disabilities began to ask if their children, too, could not profit from early education.

The concept of early childhood special education was launched. Federal initiatives were designed to stimulate interest and activity in early childhood special education. As part of this initiative, in 1968 Congress passed Public Law 90-538, which created the Handicapped Children's Early Education Program (HCEEP). (This has been renamed Early Education Program for Children with Disabilities.) This was the first federal program exclusively for young children with disabilities (Hebbeler, Smith, & Black, 1991). The intent was not to provide services for children, but to stimulate activity and to provide model demonstrations. The act acknowledged the fact that experts did really not know how best to educate this population.

The joining of early childhood and special education to develop models for working with young children with disabilities emphasized the importance of both early childhood and special education. However, the union goes beyond applying traditional special education techniques to an earlier age and acknowledging developmentally appropriate practices; rather, it is a unique blend that began emerging into a field of its own.

The HCEEP demonstration projects were so successful that outreach projects were funded, enabling the results of the projects to be shared more widely. Technical assistance was established to provide connections among the projects and also to assist in program development. Federal funding moved onto the state level, but to get this money states had to agree to more stringent requirements in the area of providing parents with guarantees of due process protection if they disagreed with the system, the movement to "least restrictive environment" (LRE), nondiscriminative evaluation and testing, and actively searching for children with disabilities (Hebbeler, Smith, & Black, 1991). Those were events of the "early years" (late 1960 to early 1970). They set the stage for the middle years.

The passage of Public Law 94-142 has had a tremendous effect on the education of the traditional school-age child with a disability. It had much less effect on young children. Although children three to five "could" be included, it was not part of the mandate. Overall, the energy of special education was devoted to coping with the changes this law made for school-age children. Educators had their hands full, and little energy was left over for concerns about younger children. P.L. 94-142 made a significant yet little known (outside the discipline) change in the way funds were allocated. Previously, federal money was allocated based on the census count, which is based on prevalence figures, given in each chapter on disability. The assumption was that all children were being served and that disabilities were distributed equally across the states; therefore, population statistics were all that were necessary. Now, under P.L. 94-142, allocation is based on a "child count,"

obviously encouraging states to find and serve more children.

The government did create a Preschool Incentive Grant Program as part of P.L. 94-142 that encouraged states to serve children three to five. It even authorized money; in 1977 the amount was $63 per child (Hebbeler, Smith, & Black, 1991). Few states chose to participate as the $63 obviously did not cover the cost of serving these children. The money gradually increased. Additional state grants were added and Early Childhood Research Institutes were funded to address long-term research interests for young children with disabilities. The HCEEP projects continued. The Council for Exceptional Children established the Division for Early Childhood. The "middle" years lasted from early 1970 to early 1980; now early childhood special education is moving into the later years with more knowledge, but without a state-level system of services.

The need for interagency coordination became apparent as did the push to serve all eligible children (Hebbeler, Smith, & Black, 1991). Congress recognized that in any given state there were a variety of programs that served children from birth to age five, and some did not know the others existed. All states that applied were awarded State Plan Grants (SPGs) in an effort to facilitate the communication of existing programs and as a first step in providing a comprehensive service delivery system. The passage of Public Law 99-457 increased funding for preschool children and established programs for children from birth to age two.

With a history that began in the late 1960s, early childhood special education is no longer new, but it is certainly a field still struggling with issues of identity. What is "early childhood special education"? It derives some of its characteristics from special education, and others from early childhood education and child development, but it also includes aspects of family relations and family therapy, the creative arts, new branches of psychology and sociology, and the knowledge gained from compensatory education approaches. The field continues to change and expand in response to emerging information and innovative techniques.

Professionals in early childhood special education are committed to working with young children who are disabled, or at risk of becoming disabled, and their families. The goal is to remediate deficits where possible, or at least acknowledge biological limitations, permit optimal growth, and prevent at-risk conditions from developing into disabilities. There is an additional concern about the prevention of secondary handicapping conditions such as negative self-concept. However, and this is a big "however," these goals are to be achieved in alliance with families. Families are in charge of their children, and in charge of the priorities and goals for their children. The educator's role is to implement what families want for themselves and their children. These objectives may or may not be what the teacher wants, but if early childhood special education is to be effective, the work will be done in the context of the family. (Relative laws and their specific implications are detailed in Chapter 4.)

An Emerging Profession

Working in early childhood special education today mixes the excitement of helping mold a new profession with the unsettling position of having very few "knowns." In any "blend" it is difficult to sort out the exact source of any particular information. However, one can trace some of the roots of this emerging profession. It emerged because while working separately neither special education nor early childhood education practitioners were able to make an impact in the lives of young children with disabilities. Professionals from both groups found they were more effective when they blended their expertise.

Early Childhood Education

Early childhood education is a field of study that concentrates on the development and education of children from birth through age eight. It is concerned with practice, research, and theory in the field. It includes such areas as parenting and teaching young children, child care, curriculum, administration, discipline, and age-based topics focusing on infants, toddlers, preschool, and early elementary school children. The field has a strong child development base, although it adheres to no single philosophy of teaching children. It is committed to the principle that birth through age eight are critical years for development and that good programs and programming are imperative during those years. The focus of early childhood educators is typically on the whole child, with a balanced program taking into account the children's developmental characteristics in a setting that is designed for children. Initially, the concern was the "all children are children" approach, and the need for individualized programming might not have been met.

Special Education

Special education as a field is generally concerned with particular aspects of development, especially those that are atypical. Based on this focus, specific techniques to remedy those deficits have been

Working with families is an integral part of early childhood special education.

developed. In addition, to show that the techniques are effective, there is an emphasis on precision in record keeping and assessment. In the past, the focus has been on "difference," and the view of difference has typically been to give attention to what is exceptional rather than what is the same.

As the name implies, the focus in special education is on one particular aspect of the child's environment: education. It also traditionally focused on a particular age range, usually six to eighteen years. The orientation was primarily toward public schools with the expectation of separate classes for children with disabilities. In many cases special education was further broken down into separate sub-fields such as mental retardation, learning disabilities, and so on. The challenge for special educators is to learn about these younger children and how to program for them in a developmentally appropriate way. Those in early childhood must learn more about specific developmental disabilities and how to adapt developmental programming for children with these disabilities; they must increase their repertoire of techniques in individualized programming and record keeping. If *all* children are part of regular settings then *all* educators need to learn techniques for inclusion.

Related Fields

Related fields include child development, family relationships, and compensatory education. Most early childhood education programs are built on a child development base. Norms and developmental principles based on child development research are used to design programs. Theories of how children develop and learn influence curriculum. With educational programming beginning earlier and earlier, the importance of the family in the educational process has become apparent. The child is viewed as part of the family unit and is no longer seen as an entity to be dealt with in isolation. Obviously, one needs to have some understanding of how family units function to work effectively with them. Likewise it is necessary to view the family in a social/cultural context.

Although not truly a field in itself, compensatory education programs, which have focused primarily on the economically disadvantaged, have shown that early intervention can make a difference in a child's success. Many principles applied to these children through programs such as Head Start have been incorporated into early childhood special education.

Finally, the medical profession has had an important impact on the field of early childhood special education. Many children who are considered disabled would not have survived the birth process or the illness or accident they faced without advances in medical science. In the past the medical model usually focused narrowly on what was physically wrong with the individual child, especially with more severely affected younger children. It has not been concerned with more general environmental factors.

The Effects of Change

Many people feel sorry for individuals with impairments and often feel somewhat uncomfortable around them. As teachers looking at including children with disabilities, one may sometimes ask: What would I do if Sarah had a convulsion and I was the only adult around? David got lost and couldn't hear me calling him? Jane fell and hurt herself on something she didn't see?

These are disconcerting thoughts. For many people the easiest way to cope with such possibilities is to avoid situations where they are likely to occur. They tend to avoid children with disabilities if they feel inadequate around them. Given the tenor of the time, such behavior must be confronted and replaced with actions based on accurate knowledge about strengths and needs.

Such knowledge not only gives the confidence to work with children's needs, it enables the teacher to help all children accept their classmates. If knowledge about strengths and needs is passed on to them, young children can learn to interact with their peers as individuals: "Hey, if Sam isn't looking at you, he can't hear you." Inclusion of children with disabilities in the classroom provides children with the opportunity for positive experiences that build a good foundation for lifelong learning about others. Inclusion is intended to decrease isolation from and prejudice toward those who are different. However, its effects are more complex than that. It has changed the roles of teachers, children, and parents. Children are challenged to deal with issues of equality and to identify obstacles to inclusion. There is research to suggest there are positive social and academic outcomes for all when children with disabilities are included (Salisbury, 1991).

On Teachers

You are probably the most important element in including children with disabilities. You are expected to be able to teach all children. You cannot specialize in "regular education" or even one particular disability, but must be prepared to teach any child who comes to your classroom.

Your attitude as much as any other single variable will determine whether children with disabilities are successfully included in your classroom or not (Raver, 1980). The emotional climate you set not only influences the classroom for the children, but it also affects how comfortable parents of children with disabilities are having their child in your classroom (Edgar & Davidson, 1979).

Including children with disabilities in your class may not only be a challenge to teaching skills, but also your beliefs:

> Although my staff and I expected to learn and
> understand a great deal more with experience,

we were surprised to spend so much time and energy on our *feelings* about our work with the children and their families. We were not ready for the challenge to our emotions. (White & Phair, 1986, p. 44)

It is not possible to anticipate what types of disabilities the children you teach will have or with what frequency they will occur, or even if they will be identified as having a disability. You will have to learn about each disability as you encounter it. Your general knowledge base and observational skills will play an important part in the process of identifying and assessing young children with disabilities and those at risk. You, with the help of the child and his family, will also need to explain disabilities and their implications to the other children in the class (and to their parents) in terms that are accurate and easily understood.

You must be familiar enough with the terminology of a disability to understand technical written reports, to participate with specialists on a multidisciplinary team, and to work with families of the children in your class. You will have to participate in writing and carrying out an individualized program for children in your class identified as having disabilities. To create such a program you must know the particular forms and requirements for individualized planning. All of the above will be discussed in more detail in Chapters 5 through 8.

The law calls for equal opportunity for all children. The teacher serves as a model for interacting with a child who has a disability. If you accept, understand, and are sensitive to the needs of that child, the other children will follow your lead. Your attitude toward children is as important as your ability to plan and carry out individualized programs.

One way to demonstrate acceptance of children is to focus on their positive characteristics. Children need to be encouraged to do what they are able to do, not reminded about those things they cannot. Encouraging children effectively requires setting realistic goals and planning activities to meet those goals, combined with daily or weekly record keeping. Information about where a child is in the learning process is necessary for further planning.

In addition to being familiar with federal laws and their implications, you will need to become familiar with state laws concerning the education of children with disabilities. The need for keeping up with current laws and research is partly met by reading the newspaper and some professional journals, such as those published by the Division of Early Childhood of the Council on Exceptional Children and the National Association of the Education of Young Children. These groups also have annual conferences that are informative. In addition, many employers provide relevant in-service programs or help fund further education at a college or university. Informal conversations with colleagues are informative and give you a chance to discuss pertinent issues.

On Administrators

In general, administrators are concerned with coordinating and running service delivery systems. They are responsible for statistical descriptions of the children, priority setting, making sure the intent of the law is carried out, and other systems-related issues, like hiring personnel and structuring a personnel development plan.

Administrators must coordinate the activities of special service personnel in order to ensure the best education for the children. They need to understand enough about disabilities and how these are handled in the classroom to be supportive of teachers and helpful to parents. In most cases they are not involved with individual children or families unless something in the system goes awry.

On Children

The children in your class will see a child who is different from them. This encounter can be frightening, as they commonly wonder if an exceptionality is contagious. On the other hand, children with disabilities may feel hurt or discriminated against when they cannot participate in all the activities or when other children say unkind things. If these children are to be included, your goal is to help all children casually accept differences and think about *solutions* to problems rather than problems.

Children may need to modify their play to accommodate a child with a disability. They may have to learn new skills in order to interact with this child. These tasks are an expansion of their skills; they are part of lifetime learning and should be viewed that way.

On Parents

Parents of nondisabled children in your class may have to overcome initial feelings of pity for a child who is different. They may be concerned that their child will be negatively affected by the children with disabilities. You need to be clear with them about the value of including children with disabilities (if you are not clear, they will not be either).

Some children can and do pick up maladaptive behaviors. These behaviors need to be acknowledged. Some can be ignored and will then disappear. Others, such as aggressive behaviors, will have to be handled as you might handle any behavior problem. Other children laughing or responding to the inappropriate behavior may help sustain it.

Parents may fear that a child with a disability will invite their child to play after school or that their own child may want a child with a disability to play at their house. Some parents will not want to be responsible for such a visit. They may feel inadequate to meet the child's needs or worried about what they would do in an emergency. Parents may feel they cannot answer questions their children might ask about a child with a disability. Parents may also be concerned about how time-consuming such a child is for a teacher and whether their own child will get a fair share of the teacher's time.

Parents of a child with disabilities may wonder how well qualified you are to teach their child. They may worry about how their child fits in, whether the other children tease him, and how you feel about having their child in the classroom. It is important that you know your own feelings.

All parents should be encouraged to discuss their fears and, if possible, to participate in the classroom for firsthand experience. Part Three will give you more insight into the family and techniques for working with parents.

Teachers' Roles

Teachers' roles have changed tremendously over time—from adding wood to the furnace and teaching grades one to eight in one classroom, to being part of an educational team that includes children with disabilities in a regular classroom. New roles require new knowledge and new abilities. No longer is basic information about child development or special education and the materials and methods of teaching that goes with each of these professions enough.

Teachers today must have or develop skills for all the following:

1. Programming both for children with and without disabilities in one classroom.

2. Holding individual conferences with parents about their children and cooperating with them to design an individualized program.

3. Conducting parent meetings that parents of all the children in their class will attend.

4. Participating in the early diagnosis of children with disabilities and interpreting the diagnostic and assessment reports that come from both educational and noneducational sources.

5. Working with other professionals such as the school psychologist, physical therapists, occupational therapists, speech and language therapists, social workers, and others to develop programs for children.

6. Writing (with input from parents and other professionals) and implementing individualized educational programs (IEP) for children over three years and individualized family service plans (IFSP) for children below three years.

7. Evaluating both the progress of the children and the program itself to make changes and to determine its effectiveness.

8. Becoming a child's advocate when a child's needs are not being adequately met.

9. Keeping abreast of legislation and litigation that pertain to teaching.

The necessary skills listed above are in addition to others that it is assumed you already possess (that is, you are competent at general classroom management and program planning and you have developed your own philosophy of teaching).

How can you teach children with disabilities and those without disabilities in the same classroom? In fact, you already have, even if you have taught only a few classes. Since many young children have not had their disability diagnosed, chances are you have already had one or more unlabeled children. If you trace the careers of the children you have known, you may well discover that some of them were eventually diagnosed as having a disability. It is unlikely that their disability suddenly occurred after these children left your class unless they experienced a particular trauma. So, in reality, you have probably taught children with disabilities.

Since you will be teaching children with a wide variety of needs, you must be able to teach in a way that is beneficial to all. It takes careful planning to develop activities and materials that can meet specified goals and that can be useful on many levels at one time. Using fingerpaint, for example, you can plan to:

Strengthen the weaker arm of a child with cerebral palsy

Teach color mixing to a gifted child

Add sand to one color to give a visually impaired child a tactile experience

Teach vocabulary (colors, shapes) to a child with language delays.

All children will learn the feel of the paint and the effect of using different body parts to make a mark, and they will all have participated in a creative art experience. Such programming allows the children to work together while each child learns what is appropriate for him. All the fingerpaint pictures may look similar, but each child benefits differently from the process of doing them. Developing a *process orientation,* as this type of programming is called, is not difficult and will help you with a mainstreamed class. You will need two skills: the ability to choose good, flexible activities that will allow you to program for differences and the ability to adapt those activities to different needs. As you will soon learn, the activities need not be part of expensive kits, use exotic materials, or require an entirely new repertoire of skills. With practice, a process orientation becomes habit. You will even forget there was a time when you could not do it. Part Four of the book is devoted to "Integrating the Curriculum to Meet Children's Needs" and will supply you with the techniques and activities you need to teach children with diverse abilities.

Parent-Teacher Conferences

While you are programming for a child, you need to seek information from, coordinate activities with, and share information with the child's parents. Parental knowledge and values are ultimate. Parents live with the child. They know the child's likes and dislikes as well as her strengths and needs. Parents' support at home is equally valuable. As the child is with you only part of the day, it is imperative that you and the parents work together to achieve goals.

There are at least three occasions on which you traditionally will have parent-teacher conferences. The first occurs near the beginning of the year. Usually all of the parents are given an opportunity to schedule an individual conference. These are usually routine; the basic technique is frequently known as the "sandwich":

1. Talk about the child's positive qualities and how much progress the child is making.

2. State any concerns about the child and give concrete examples.

3. Conclude on a positive note.

The second routine conference occurs about the middle of the year and the final one at the end of the year.

On other occasions you will request a conference with the parents, or they with you, to discuss a particular concern. These conferences are different from the routine ones in that they are problem-related and usually have one definite topic. You need to schedule a parent-teacher conference when you notice a consistent change in a child's behavior

that interferes with learning, in other words, when a child deviates far enough from the norms of developmental and social behavior to come to your attention. You will need a different, although overlapping, set of techniques for conducting these conferences. These techniques are detailed in Part Three, "Working with Families."

Meeting with the parents of children with disabilities and the nondisabled in a large group requires different skills than does dealing with one child's parents, particularly if this is the first time the parents are encountering inclusion. Be prepared to make some initial statements about your personal philosophy of teaching, what you expect to have happen in your classroom, what inclusion is, and why it is happening. Think through beforehand some statements you will make at the meeting.

Although what you say will be affected by your own circumstances, the tone and content might resemble the following:

As we continue to study how children learn, we are discovering that it is beneficial to have a variety of children of this age in the same classroom, rather than to match similar children. This variety encourages children to learn about their own and others' strengths and needs.

In our class there is a child who prefers to play alone most of the time, who rarely joins the group. The other children are learning skills for approaching her as well as an appreciation of the fact that there are times when all of us want to be alone. When I require them to participate in group time yet don't require her to be part of the group,

The team approach requires teachers and therapists to work together to develop programs for young children.

the children are learning to be flexible and to allow exceptions to rules when appropriate.

These are difficult concepts for young children to learn, yet their efforts will be rewarded, for children's appreciation of individual differences in other children helps them learn more about themselves.

Try to avoid labeling children or citing children by name unless you do it while discussing many children. This approach becomes easier as you habitually learn to view a disability as one aspect of individual differences.

You need to be prepared for questions parents will ask. The following are some typical questions with possible answers.

Parent: Why doesn't *my* child get an IEP/IFSP?
Teacher: I take the individual needs of all the children into account when I plan my program. In some cases the exact form of programming that I use is dictated by law. In other cases I use a system of my own. I'd like to share this with you during an individual conference.

Parent: Do you have enough time to teach all the children in your class when some of them have disabilities?
Teacher: I think all the children in the class have special needs some of the time, so on a particular day or week I may spend more time with one child than others, but overall I think it evens out. I'm lucky to have Mrs. C. as a paraprofessional in the class. Her presence allows us far greater flexibility in programming. We can always use more help, so if any of you have time on a regular basis, I'd enjoy having your help in the room as well.

Parent; Isn't it hard to teach children at so many different levels of ability?
Teacher: I think the key to teaching children with varying abilities and interests is to plan activities that can be used at several different levels by children who are playing together. Many of the materials I use fall into this category. The playdough, for example, can be manipulated by all the children. Some children make specific shapes and then count them, others make impressions with cookie cutters, and some even make a "tea set." For some children, using playdough is primarily a creative activity; for others the main benefit lies in developing motor skills or in having a sensory experience. There are many other activities like this that I use for multilevel teaching.

Parent: My child says there is a child who cannot walk in his class. How does this affect the class?

Teacher: Yes, we do have a child in our class who uses a wheelchair or a creeper in the classroom. We have added ramps to make it easy for him to get outside. He needs some help getting out of the wheelchair and down on the floor, but in the same way that your child is working on tying his shoes, this child is working toward independence in movement.

Answers like those above help parents see the process you use in teaching as well as the product. More detailed techniques for working with parents are given in Chapter 22.

The Team Approach

As part of the process of diagnosing and implementing individualized planning you will participate as part of a team that includes the family and specialists who may work with the child outside the classroom on a regular basis, or who may be consulted only when their specialized expertise is necessary. The exact role you will play will vary with the type of team approach used.

In general, to benefit from your interactions with families and specialists, you should develop three sets of skills. First, learn enough of the specialists' jargon to talk with them about a child and to interpret their technical reports. Second, learn to use their reports in your programming and to support parents in participating in and understanding the team approach. Third, you need to establish an ongoing communication system to keep you, the specialists, and the family informed of progress and changes that need to be made.

In general, if a child needs therapy, it will be done in your classroom. That way both you and the other children have the opportunity to learn about the therapy and to ask questions of the therapist. In cases where the therapy is not done in your classroom, try to observe the child in therapy, if you can, or ask for a brief description and explanation of the activities that occur during therapy. The specialist can help you understand how a child's therapeutic needs will affect classroom behavior. Ask how you can carry out the therapist's goals in your classroom, and be sure to invite the therapist to visit your class.

Conversely, help the specialist understand what you are doing with the child and why. (For example, she may not have any idea why a housekeeping corner could be important.) Remember that a specialist is also a consultant. A child does not have to be in therapy to benefit from a specialist's knowledge.

The jargon specialists use is often difficult for others to understand. Prepare yourself ahead of time by reading the latter part of this chapter so that you are clearer about which professionals are responsible for which fields, so that you do not address a question to an occupational therapist that should be directed to a physical therapist. Look up terms in the glossaries of this book so that you are familiar with the terminology. If you have a report to decipher, use a medical dictionary or talk with a friend or colleague who knows the terms. If the meaning of some words or concepts is still obscure, ask the specialist. Although specialists are experts in their fields, their jargon is so much a part of their everyday vocabulary that their explanations are sometimes difficult to understand. To confirm or clarify points, restate (in your own words) what you think the specialist said and ask if that interpretation is accurate. You will sometimes want to ask questions to which you already know the answers, particularly on behalf of parents. If a specialist's explanation is still unclear, you might ask for a demonstration of the concept.

Once you understand the report, you must be able to translate it into needs for which you can program. In practice the two skills might work like this: The occupational therapist reports that a child "fell off the nystagmus board following rotation." You, after doing some research, decide that the child was probably dizzy! This child probably needs practice in changing directions and starting and stopping to better develop her vestibular sense (the sense of balance which is located in the inner ear). You might plan some creative movement with initial slow turns, as well as some work on body awareness and flexibility.

The role of the specialist is to be concerned about a particular aspect of the child's development. Your role is to plan a program for the whole child that is responsive to the specialist's input. You need to look at the child's needs in physical therapy from a developmental framework. You might have the child sit in a way that strengthens certain muscles during group story time; however, if the posture is so uncomfortable the child cannot concentrate on the story, inquire about alternatives or have the child use the posture when it is more appropriate. Regardless of any therapeutic benefits, group time is not a good time for a child to be alone at a standing table when all the other children are sitting on the floor.

Writing and Carrying Out an Individualized Program

In the past, teachers were generally accountable for preparing children to enter the next grade level. They made weekly plans for class activities but were rarely asked to plan for individual children or to plan with parents. Parents usually asked about the curriculum only when children's needs were blatantly not being met. Individualizing Programming may be a new task for both you and the parents.

With school-age children, too often the teacher and specialists write the Individualized Program, then present it to the parents, who are asked to glance at it and sign it. The conference is then over. In addition to violating the spirit of the law, this approach misses an opportunity for getting useful programming information about the child from parents' and finding out what they want him to learn. The

step-by-step writing of Individualized Programs for children is covered in Chapter 6.

Once both individual and class programs are in place, it is necessary to determine whether or not they are effective. In the past it was assumed that if children went to school they were learning. Now it is important to be more specific about what a child is learning. Many programs have critical objectives or levels of mastery that are required for children to pass on to the next level or grade. To ensure that children are learning, it is necessary to develop a system of record keeping and to plan for accountability within the program. This planning can no longer be a haphazard flurry of note-taking just before a parent conference; rather it needs to be an integral part of the program that provides information throughout the school year that is useful both for modifying programming for increased effectiveness as well as arriving at year-end evaluation. Chapter 9 discusses record keeping and evaluation and how to include them in your program.

Child Advocate

Your teaching role these days includes being an advocate for children, which means more than programming for them in your classroom or participating in their diagnosis where appropriate. Part of your job is to make sure that children get the services they need. You may have to take the initiative to find out from parents or specialists how best to serve this child in your class. The parents may need your knowledge of who provides services their child needs and how those services are best acquired. As an advocate, you may find yourself confronting bureaucrats and fighting to cut red tape. See yourself as an active "doer" rather than as one who waits to be told what to do. Young children cannot be advocates for themselves; they need your help.

Service Coordinator

As early intervention has become a more complex process, the need to coordinate services in an efficient way has become apparent. There needs to be someone to coordinate roles and information. The term "case manager" has been replaced by "service coordinator" in the last reauthorization of IDEA. A service coordinator is the person designated both to coordinate the professionals involved with the family and to act as the primary contact for the family. The service coordinator is often chosen based upon the child's most overriding problem; however, the role of service coordinator is primarily an administrative one independent of a discipline. All professionals must now be trained to assume the role of service coordinator as well as to function in their role of specialization.

The service coordinator typically functions as the leader of the group when her families participate and as a group member representing her specialization when other families are on the team. The service coordinator's task is to make sure that the team functions adequately. She needs to be sure that the other team members know when the meeting is scheduled, that the necessary assessments and observations have been completed and written up and are available for all members, and so forth. During the meeting the service coordinator will preside and use the skill necessary to help the various people there to listen and respect the views of others in a task-related situation so that some conclusion can be reached in the best interest of the family and child. Without coordination it is unlikely the family will get an integrated service delivery system, and the child might "slip through the cracks."

Major Specializations

Following are brief descriptions of specialists who provide some services you may encounter while teaching young children with disabilities.

Child Development Specialist. A child development specialist is usually trained in developmental principles and in the use of assessment measures for very young children. This specialist often works in a home-based setting and provides consultation to families.

Developmental Psychologist. A developmental psychologist knows about various aspects of child development and usually has a doctorate degree. Assessments are conducted that use observational techniques, especially of the child and the family, and can use educational and psychological tests to aid in the diagnostic process. Today developmental psychologists are trained to work with other professionals and families as part of an assessment team. The developmental psychologist is also usually knowledgeable in areas such as behavior management, counseling, and intervention strategies. In general, a developmental psychologist is most likely to be on the multidisciplinary assessment team of young children and the school psychologist takes over as children reach school age.

Early Childhood Educator. The early childhood educator teaches young children. She often informally assesses the child's development, particularly in the cognitive and social domains. She plans developmentally appropriate activities to help children's skill development, skills in thinking as well as social interaction. Behavior management issues also are often addressed by the early childhood educator. She may teach alone or with an early childhood special educator.

Early Childhood Special Educator. A specialists in early childhood special education has had training in child development, early childhood materials and methods, and special education. Increasingly there is state certification for this position. This specialist, either alone or as part of a team teaching situation, is typically in charge of the child's educational setting.

Family Practice. A doctor specializing in family practice is one who serves the whole family. The physician in family practice plays the same role as the pediatrician would in other families.

Nurses. Nurses are often part of an early intervention team. They may make home visits to address medical needs, screen or assess development, and recommend specific developmental activities. They also may refer the family to community resources and may be responsible for coordinating services for the family with a child who has a disability. In addition, "Since the nurse's base of knowledge crosses many disciplines and problems, this individual is often the appropriate professional to provide parents with follow-up education in health care, growth, and development, to support parents as they learn to adapt to and care for their handicapped child" (Garwood & Fewell, 1983, p. 332).

Occupational Therapist. Occupational therapists work from a developmental rather than a medical base. They hold a degree from a school accredited by the American Occupational Therapy Association and the American Medical Association. Course work for this degree includes biological and psychosocial sciences, foundations of medicine, sensory integration, psychiatry, and prevocational skill development. Therapy is based on the age of the child in order to enhance his potential for learning. It emphasizes vestibular (balance as determined by the inner ear), tactile, kinesthetic (sensory knowledge of one's body movements), and perceptual motor (mental interpretation of sensation and movement based on these sensations) development, gross and fine motor coordination, and self-help skills. Her role includes assessment, intervention, and consultation in the areas of self-help skills, adaptive behavior and play, and sensory, motor, and postural development. These skills help the child's functioning at home and in other community settings. The occupational therapist's role includes adapting the environment (e.g., limiting distractions, combining gross and fine motor activities, making a task achievable), providing devices to help develop functional skills (e.g., eating, dressing, and playing), and minimizing the impact of the disability. An occupational therapist may see children with the same needs as are seen by a physical therapist and a speech and language therapist.

Pediatric Nurse. A pediatric nurse is a registered nurse who specializes in young children. She has training in using developmental screening tools as well as additional training in family counseling and evaluation and child care. With infants, the pediatric nurse is frequently selected as the service coordinator.

Pediatric nurses can work out of a hospital or community-based setting or from a state department of public health. For young children with disabilities the pediatric nurse often makes home visits to help parents learn to better care and program for their child, in addition to monitoring the health status of the child.

Pediatrician. A pediatrician is a medical doctor specializing in the medical treatment of children from birth to about age twelve. The pediatrician is probably the most familiar professional to families of all young children, but especially to those who have developmental delays. Pediatricians may be the first to express concern about a condition or may be the first person to whom parents turn to express their concern.

Pediatricians know much about growth and development and, especially when children are young, play a major role in teaching parents what to look for in their children. They are also frequently consulted about child caring and rearing problems. Children are seen by pediatricians both for well baby checkups and when the child is sick.

When children have disabilities, medical specialists are frequently consulted. The exact nature of the problem and the complexity of it will determine the specializations required and the number of them. Specializations that are frequently used are those in the fields of otolaryngology (ear-nose-throat); ophthalmology (eyes); allergy; neurology; orthopedics; and genetics.

Physician. This person may be a pediatrician, neurologist, or other specialist. The physician may be the first to detect a disability or a specific handicap, such as spina bifida, heart defect, or hydrocephalus. The physician's role includes determining medical needs and referring the family to programs that can provide appropriate intervention services. She may oversee the case initially, when medical needs may be the greatest. She also needs to be kept informed of the child's progress developmentally, as the medical and developmental areas often influence each other. For instance, the physical therapist may need to collaborate with an orthopedist to recommend a piece of adaptive equipment for a child who has high muscle tone.

Physical Therapist. The physical therapist is a state-licensed health professional who has completed an educational program accredited by the American Physical Therapy Association. The program, largely medically based, includes the study of biological, physical, medical, and psychosocial sciences, as well as more in-depth course work in neurology, orthopedics, therapeutic exercises, and treatment techniques.

Physical therapy is actually directed toward preventing disability, that is, developing, improving, or restoring more efficient muscular functioning and maintaining maximum motor functioning for each person. A physical therapist would most likely work with any child requiring prosthetic management training, wheelchair mobility training, or measurement for or use of other medically prescribed mobility devices. The physical therapist evaluates the child's range of motion, posture, muscle tone, strength, balance, and gross motor skills. Treatment usually focuses on increasing strength, improving balance skills, and facilitating gross motor development. The therapist is also responsible for monitoring the child's orthopedic needs and assisting the family in obtaining adaptive equipment, if appropriate. Most importantly, he provides the parents with suggestions for positioning and carrying for different activities during the child's day.

School Psychologist. A school psychologist is state certified and has completed either a bachelor's, master's, or doctoral degree in school psychology. Course work varies from state to state, but may include psychology, counseling, standardized testing and its interpretation, child development, children with disabilities, and education. Most psychologists must complete an internship or practicum under a practicing psychologist. The duties of a psychologist in a school setting vary with the number of psychologists in the district and their individual skills.

Most school psychologists spend a great deal of time testing and observing children referred to them because of a suspected disability. They must write the formal reports that are usually required to place children into any special education program. The psychologist may act as a consultant to the teacher or parents, which includes discussing test results or observations. Some psychologists emphasize individual therapy; they counsel either a child or a parent. Others make family therapy their primary function; they work with the child as part of the family unit.

Testing school-age children usually occurs in a small, quiet room where the child and psychologist are alone. If possible, the psychologist and child may get to know each other in the classroom prior to testing. Information provided by both parents and teacher is essential for the psychologist's evaluation.

Federal law requires new testing and documentation of children with disabilities every three years. These test results are helpful in measuring growth and planning programs for individual children as well as in writing the IEP.

Social Worker. A social worker is a member of the team who usually concentrates on the adults in the family. She may well look at family needs in relation to child rearing or coordinating the social service network. Social workers are trained in family relations, counseling and advocacy skills, and working with agencies. They are also knowledgeable about resources and referral to community services (Medicaid, respite care). Social workers usually work in the home and are often the best source of information about the types of intervention families are most likely to use.

Speech and Language Therapist. A speech and language therapist is state licensed and has completed a degree program with a college accredited by the American Speech and Hearing Association (ASHA). A therapist working in the schools may or may not also hold a Certificate of Clinical Competency (C.C.C.), but a therapist in private practice is required to have this certificate in most states. The certificate is earned by working approximately three hundred clinical hours and passing a test. Course work includes psychology, education, and anatomy, with an emphasis on speech and language development. The roles of the speech and language therapist in early intervention includes assessment and intervention with oral-motor disorders (difficulties in feeding and swallowing as well as speech production) and communication delays and disorders. More specifically, the communication delays and disorders with which they work include socio-communicative competence during preverbal and verbal areas of development; receptive and expressive language (both speech and non-speech means of communication), and speech production and perception.

When infants and young children have difficulties with speaking or expressing themselves, hearing or understanding language, these difficulties can interfere with their ability to communicate. Many young children with disabilities have associated problems with muscle tone, which may be too high or too low for normal motor patterns. The muscle tone affects not only gross motor movement needs for crawling and sitting, but also finer movements needed for feeding and speech.

One theory in speech and language development proposes that a relationship exists between the movements made in feeding and the movements used to make speech sounds. However, the exact relationships are not known and research in the area is lacking. While working on feeding alone does not mean a child will produce sounds normally, it may give the child opportunities for better sound play, experiences in new oral–motor movements, and sensory-motor information related to auditory feedback.

While the field of speech and language pathology is generally thought to encompass the production of sounds and words and the understanding of language, the oral-motor area is a relatively new field that has particular significance for young children with disabilities.

Parents. Parents are the most important members of the team because they determine what the priorities are for their child and family once other team members have given them information about their child, support to obtain appropriate services, and options of ways to have their family's needs met. Parents are responsible for giving other team members information on how their child functions at home and what they see as needs for their family and child on an ongoing basis (Dunst, Trivette, & Deal, 1988).

Because of the wide range of professionals who provide services to young children with disabilities and their families, professionals need to know the range of services in their communities and when it is appropriate to refer a child to another service. In addition, with overlap in professional roles, communication and coordination of services is essential between professionals and parents. All professionals must develop competencies in working with young children with developmental delays and their families.

Professional Resources

Professional resources are any information, services, materials, or even people that you, the teacher, can use or suggest to someone else that will increase knowledge or skill. Realistically, no one can be expected to be an expert on every aspect of the field of early childhood special education; however, you can be expected to be knowledgeable about how to find appropriate information.

Literature

Written literature can be roughly divided into three categories: primary sources, secondary sources, and lay literature. Primary sources are reports of original research. This literature appears in professional journals such as the *Journal of Early Intervention* of the Division for Early Childhood, published by the Council for Exceptional Children's Division on Early Childhood. The journal has been published since 1979. Although there are some review articles, for the most part the journal publishes original research. These are articles that typically deal with some aspect of early childhood special education. This journal and others are typically available only at college and university libraries. Depending upon the interlibrary loan system, however, if you do not have access to these where you are, public libraries can get articles copied and sent to you for a relatively low cost. In addition to journals designed specifically for early childhood, such as *Topics in Early Childhood Special Education,* many individual disabilities also have journals devoted to them, such as *Journal of Speech and Hearing Disorders* and *American Journal on Mental Deficiency.* These journals have some articles on early childhood.

Secondary sources are reviews, as well as a synthesis of primary sources. Textbooks are an example of secondary sources. In this case you are dependent upon the person who wrote the article or book for accurate interpretations of the research. However, secondary sources are typically easier to read and cover a far greater range than primary sources. It is often useful to find the range of a topic in a good review article and then go to the primary literature for additional information or clarification.

Government documents are also a good source of written information. They are produced by the U.S. Government Printing Office, are usually inexpensive, and may provide information that is not available from other sources.

Lay literature is written for the public at large. It can be based on primary or secondary literature, but it rarely has the qualifications for generalizing or disclaimers that are present in primary literature. Also, it is frequently based on trends. This type of literature can be found in the newspaper, and in magazines such as the *Ladies Home Journal,* as well as in books. Books written by or about people who have a disability often fall in this category, such as *Life at My Fingertips,* the autobiography of Robert Smithdas, the second deaf-blind person to graduate from college.

Another way of locating books is to look at a volume called *Books in Print.* It provides a topical index of books. An additional resource for any field is the reference librarian. She is the expert in the library in helping you sort through the available literature and putting you in touch quickly and efficiently with the information you need.

Agencies, Professional Organizations, and Advocacy Groups

If your need is in the area of services available, it is important to know what agencies serve what particular populations. As with written literature, there are differences in level and complexity of services. You can contact national, regional, state, or local agencies depending upon what services you desire. For example, if you were concerned about the stereotypic presentation of the American Indian in your class you might write to the Indian Cultural/Curriculum Center in Tuba City, Arizona, which would provide you with a unit on Indian culture as well as a bibliography. On the other hand you might be concerned about local services available for the mentally retarded; if so you could write to the U.S. Department of Health, Education and Welfare in Washington, D.C., and ask for the Directory of State and Local Resources for the Mentally Retarded. Lists of national organizations that pertain to disabilities are presented at the end of all chapters in Part Three.

Local services vary greatly from one location to another. In general, most states produce some kind of a social services directory that lists available services. This list is not a judgment that the services are good or bad, only that they are available.

Professional organizations can also be on a national, regional, or state level. Many organizations, such as the Council for Exceptional Children and the National Association for the Education of Young Children, have a national organization and also state and local groups that hold meetings on a regular basis. These organizations are good places to exchange ideas and come in contact with others who are in the

same field. Because the time lag in what is being done in the field and when it gets into print is so great (often a year or two), organizations and meetings are often far more up-to-date in passing on information. In addition, if a point is not clear you have the opportunity to ask a question.

Professionals who work in the area are another resource. If you have a specific question you might ask a colleague. If that does not meet with success, calling professors at a local college or university can sometimes solve the problem. You could also call organizations of social workers, physicians, and other specialists to find contacts. Do not forget about the network of parents of children with disabilities who are often experts in their own way and may have more practical advice than the most esteemed of professionals.

Advocacy groups are often made up of parents or a combination of parents and professionals. These are usually local and vary greatly in areas. Some of the more common ones are Parents of Downs, Parents of Children with Learning Disabilities, and Parents of Preemies. Others are not as closely related to specific disabilities, such as Parents of Children with Developmental Delays. These groups are often a tremendous resource to both parents and professionals. They offer a different and enlightening perspective.

Before you can access these resources, however, you must reflect on what you need to learn.

1. For whom is the information intended? If it is just for you, then all of the sources listed are appropriate; however, if you plan to pass the information on to parents you are more likely to be successful searching in the lay literature or secondary sources rather than using primary sources. Before I suggest information to parents I would at least scan it to see if it were relevant and appropriate.

2. How much time do I have to find the information? This is often the determining factor. Here you need to make a decision: What exactly do I need to know in a hurry, and what can wait until later? It may be that you go to just one volume, such as the *Yearbook of Special Education,* as a beginning, and perhaps on the weekend take time to read more extensively. If you have a long time you can consider sending for information that may be relevant.

3. How much information do I need? If all you need is an overview of the subject, then a single review article might serve your purpose. However, if you plan to take a position and defend it, then you need to know both sides of the issue as well as the primary research in the field. If you, however, need programming information, you might consult a book such as this text or another activity book or call another teacher.

4. How crucial is it that the information be absolutely accurate? This is an extremely important

question. Any time you read secondary literature and lay literature you run the risk that someone has misinterpreted the results. This is not a common occurrence; however, if you need to be accurate, then you must go to the primary literature.

5. What will I do with the information after I get it? If you will use it informally in a verbal situation or just to give you ideas, you probably need only to take notes for your own information. However, if it is a more formal presentation, you need to take scrupulous notes about where the information comes from so that you can accurately reference it. Photocopying is helpful if you discover more information than you can easily remember or if you would like to share the information with someone else. In general it is good to keep a file of the information that you find; it may be helpful in the future.

Trends and Issues in Early Childhood Special Education

Some issues have remained constant over the short life of early childhood special education and even the older field of special education. These issues revolve around such things as how to define disabilities, how to train teachers, and how to pay for educational services. Other issues are relatively new and as yet unresolved. Many of the current issues and their resolutions affect the teacher directly.

1. Early intervention. Identifying children as early as possible and providing programming to maximize their potential for growth, to minimize the effect of the disability, to prevent secondary disabilities.

2. Normalization. Making the child and family's life as close to normal as possible, in school, in play, and in everyday living.

3. Inclusion. Teaching all children in the same schools and in the same classrooms. Not separating children based on ability groupings or other groupings that label children. Eliminating special education as a separate entity.

4. Family. Including families as equal, active participants in the team and system that make decisions about their child.

5. Transition. Preparing children to move from one service system to another (home to school, preschool to public school), as well as being sure the new (receiving) system is ready to meet the children's needs.

6. Cultural diversity. Recognizing and valuing differences and diversity and being aware of the influence culture makes in the area of assessment.

These issues are discussed in greater detail throughout the book.

Summary

Early childhood special education is a dynamic new field. It requires professionals to rethink many of the ways in which they have operated in the past and come up with new solutions for a younger population that includes families and is respectful of cultural diversity. It has changed the role of teachers and made them members of teams. It has brought specialists into the classroom. It is a field of growth and potential, and you will help shape the direction of that growth and fulfill the potential.

References and Bibliography

Allen, K. E., Holm, V. A., & Schiefelbusch, R. L. (1978). *Early intervention—a team approach.* Baltimore: University Park Press.

Dunst, C., Johanson, C., Trivette, C., & Hamby, D. (1991). Family-oriented early intervention policies and practices: Family-centered or not? *Exceptional Children, 58*(2), 104–112.

Dunst, C. J., Trivette C., & Deal, A. G. (1988). *Enabling and empowering families: Principles and guidelines for practice.* Cambridge, MA: Brookline Books.

Edgar, E., & Davidson, C. (1979). Parent perceptions of mainstreaming. *Education Unlimited, 1*(4), 32–33.

Fewell, R. R. (1983). The team approach to infant education. In S. G. Garwood & R. R. Fewell (Eds.), *Educating handicapped infants.* Rockville, MD: Aspen Systems Corporation.

Garwood, S. G., & Fewell, R. R. (Eds.). (1983). *Educating handicapped infants: Issues in development and intervention.* Rockville, MD: Aspen Systems Corporation.

Golin, A. K., & Duncanis, A. J. (1981). *The interdisciplinary team.* Rockville, MD: Aspen Systems Corporation.

Hebbeler, K., Smith, B., & Black, T. (1991). Federal early childhood special education policy: A model for the improvement of services for children with disabilities. *Exceptional Children, 58*(2), 104–112.

Marfo, K. (Ed.). (1991). *Early intervention in transition: Current perspectives on programs for handicapped children.* Westport, CT: Greenwood Publishing Group, Inc.

Peterson, N. L. (1987). Knowing your professional resources. In N. L. Peterson (Ed.), *Early intervention for handicapped and at-risk children: An introduction to early childhood–special education* (pp. 493–527). Denver, CO: Love Publishing Company.

Raver, S. (1980). Ten rules for success in preschool mainstreaming. *Education Unlimited, 2*(1), 47–52.

Salisbury, C. (1991). Mainstreaming during the early childhood years. *Exceptional Children, 58*(2), 146–155.

Weintraub, F. L., Abeson, A., Ballard, J., & LaVor, M. L. (Eds.). (1976). *Public policy and the education of exceptional children*. Reston, VA: Council for Exceptional Children.

Weintraub, F. L., & Ramirez, B. A. (1985). *Progress in the education of the handicapped and analysis of P.L. 98–199: The Education for the Handicapped Act Amendments of 1983*. Reston, VA: Council for Exceptional Children.

White, B., & Phair, M. (1986). It'll be a challenge! Managing emotional stress in teaching disabled children. *Young Children, 41*(2), 44–48.

Chapter 3

Social, Legal, and Educational Bases for Early Intervention

Inclusion is an ideal. The ideal is that children with disabilities will be reared like their nondisabled peers and will be educated as equal participants in society. This objective means that children with disabilities should be taught in their neighborhood schools in regular classes, that their lives should be as normal as possible, and that intervention should not interfere with individual freedom. However, what is usually added to these statements is "to the maximum extent appropriate." Some in the field believe that full inclusion is possible (Demchak & Drinkwater, 1992; Forest & Pearpoint, 1990); others feel this is inappropriate.

The Council for Exceptional Children made its position clear as early as 1976:

> . . . to the maximum extent appropriate, exceptional children should be educated with non-exceptional children; and that special classes, separate schooling, or other removal of an exceptional child from education with non-exceptional children should occur only when the intensity of the child's special education and related needs is such that they cannot be satisfied in the environment including non-exceptional children, even with the provision of supplementary aids and services (Council for Exceptional Children, 1976, p. 3).

The Council for Exceptional Children was not alone in its belief in inclusion. The Association for Persons with Severe Handicaps adopted a resolution calling for the education of all students in regular neighborhood schools. The Office of Special Education and Rehabilitative Services of the United States Department of Education has cited the inclusion of exceptional children into regular neighborhood schools as a top priority for the future (Stainback & Stainback, 1990).

Others, although acknowledging the challenges, go even further. They believe that *all* children can and should be educated in regular classrooms. They believe "the movement toward inclusive education is a process—a journey to create an educational system where excellence and equity walk hand in hand and where the highest values of the nation are respected, honored, and achieved" (Forest & Pearpoint, 1990, p. 187). They believe that inclusive education is for all; they even include "students who have or could potentially exhibit severe aggressive behaviors" (Forest & Pearpoint, 1990, p. 187). One state, Vermont, has acted on these ideas, and has had only inclusive education since 1991.

Interestingly, this concept has caused much controversy and concern for parents, teachers, and administrators. Parents are concerned that their children won't get the attention or services they need, that other children will be unkind to them, and that the teachers do not have enough training to teach their children. Many teachers agreed that they lacked appropriate training, and also felt that children with disabilities would detract from the needs of other children in the class. Administrators are concerned about the scheduling and management of such a broad-based system. Many are willing to believe that mildly involved children should be included; few believe that all should be included.

Given all these concerns, how did the concept of normalization become the dominant perspective? Why wasn't the solution more and better special classrooms, schools, and institutions? The answer lies in the events and changes that have occurred over the past thirty years. Separate forces—social, legal, and educational—created a favorable environment, and finally a demand, for normalization and inclusion.

Social Forces

In the United States, as in all countries, schools impart not only academic information but social values. To the extent that children are segregated from regular schools and classrooms, whether because of visual impairment or skin color, they are seen as deficient. Separate is not equal.

In the past, individuals sometimes opposed the philosophy of separation, but with little effect. In the 1960s some of the stigma of having a child with a disability was removed when such public figures as President John F. Kennedy and Vice President Hubert H. Humphrey openly acknowledged their affection for family members with disabilities. Perhaps encouraged by this, and acting within the context of the social activism of the 1960s, parents and professionals began to band together to form organizations and to take legal action. Parent organizations, such as the National Association for Retarded Citizens, and professional organizations, were founded in those years and actively promoted the cause of children with disabilities. They succeeded in making the general public (and eventually the legislatures) aware that "it can

happen to anyone." The first definition of developmental disabilities was written.

Society learned of the immediate and concrete need of the disabled for more trained professionals and teachers. Even more fundamentally, people began to realize that the disabled were being deprived of their constitutional and human rights. By the 1980s the movement to deinstitutionalize intensified and a movement to support families of the disabled increased. Early intervention emerged as a viable option for young children with disabilities at the same time that technological innovations opened new possibilities for helping people with disabilities.

A very different influence was also at work changing social attitudes and creating a demand for a solution. In the 1960s and 1970s the cost of general education was outstripping the funds available to pay for it. Constructing and maintaining separate buildings to provide programs for the disabled multiplied costs to parents and taxpayers. The cost of salaries for a separate set of teachers, administrators, custodians, and other personnel was an additional factor. As more children get closer to the mainstream, the need for residential and other separate facilities decreases. If we eliminate some of the special schools, the savings are tremendous.

Even after spending more money on support services, such as temporary foster care, family counseling, and the traditional therapies, society still benefits financially from inclusive education. Further savings are possible if, through early identification and appropriate programming, these children become contributing members of society. The personal and social gains to all of us are incalculable.

With increased knowledge about developmental disabilities, in the 1990s we have begun to realize that prevention of disabilities is a national priority. We know that risks to children are complex, cumulative, interactive, and compounding. Teen mothers who have not completed high school, and who have histories of abuse and neglect, are disproportionally becoming parents of children with disabilities. Poverty increases the odds of developmental disabilities. Many children born to mothers who abused drugs or alcohol are now entering the system, bringing increased legal and educational challenges.

Legal Forces

The legal basis for integration is a long and interesting one. The following highlights will help you understand the process.

The legal base has followed two paths, one in the area of civil rights, the other in education. The 1964 case of *Brown v. the Board of Education of Topeka, Kansas,* had little to do with disabilities, but much to do with segregation. Separate education was declared not equal. Whether the separation is based on race or disability, the principle is the same.

As parents of children with disabilities became increasingly dissatisfied with the education of their

In self-contained classrooms there is a high teacher-child ratio and instruction is typically more direct.

children, they too sought legal remedies to make the educational system more responsive to their needs. Encouraged by an increasingly receptive public and strengthened by better organization and cooperation among parent and professional groups, parents successfully pressed their cause in court.

In one classic case, *Pennsylvania Association of Retarded Children, et al. v. Commonwealth of Pennsylvania, David H. Kurtzman, et al.* (1971), a class action suit on behalf of the parents of thirteen children with mental retardation argued that the denial of a free public education for children with mental retardation was a violation of the Fourteenth Amendment of the Constitution of the United States. Education for some had to be education for all. In an out-of-court settlement, the state of Pennsylvania agreed to provide education to all school-age children with mental retardation living in the state (including those in state institutions) within one year. A parallel decision, *Mills v. The District of Columbia* (1972), added the stipulation that lack of funds was not an acceptable reason for excluding children.

Other decisions concerned children who had been misplaced by the system. In *Diana v. State Board of Education of Monterey County, CA.* (1970), the court ruled that children must be tested in their primary language. Previously, children whose primary language was not English had been tested in English and had sometimes been wrongfully declared

mentally retarded. The many court decisions were, in fact, so consistent and so consistently upheld in higher courts that litigation gave rise to legislation.

Legislators pass laws that are referred to as Public Law (P.L.), followed by two numbers separated by a hyphen. The first number is that of the congress that passed the law; for example, the 94th Congress passed P.L. 94-142. The second number refers to the sequential position in the laws that particular congress passed, in this case the 142d law.

The most significant laws for early childhood special education are detailed in the accompanying table. A discussion about their implications for teachers follows.

PUBLIC LAWS AFFECTING EARLY CHILDHOOD SPECIAL EDUCATION

Public Law	Title and Significance
90-538	Established the Handicapped Children's Early Education Program (HCEEP) to develop models to serve young children with disabilities.
93-112	The Rehabilitation Act of 1973 Section 504 of this law mandates equal opportunities for children with disabilities in preschools and schools that receive *federal* funds.

Public Law	Title and Significance
94-142	The Education for All Handicapped Children Act of 1975 (EHA) Mandates a free appropriate public education in the least restrictive environment for children and youth (5–21) with disabilities.
98-199	Amendments to the EHA passed in 1983 Supported the development of model demonstration programs for preschool special education, early intervention, and transition.
99-457	Amendments to the EHA passed in 1986 Established (Part B) mandated services for children 3–5 years. Established (Part H) an entitlement program for infants and toddlers 0–2.
101-476	Amendments to the EHA passed in 1990 renamed the law the Individuals with Disabilities Education Act (IDEA). Made language changes by replacing the term "handicapped" with "disability" and "people first" language. Includes services to children with autism, traumatic brain injury, serious emotional disturbances, and attention deficit disorder, as well as transition and assistive technology services.
101-336	The Americans with Disabilities Act (ADA) of 1990 Extends civil rights protection to people with disabilities in all settings.
102-119	Individuals with Disabilities Education Act Amendments of 1991 The terms "language and speech" have been replaced by communication, "psychosocial" by social or emotional, and "self-help skills" by adaptive development. "Case management services" are referred to as service coordination. Another important change is that "to the maximum extent appropriate," children are to be in natural environments, including the home, and community settings in which children without disabilities participate.

The move to educate children without discrimination was supported by Section 504 of the Rehabilitation Act of 1973. This civil rights law mandates equal opportunities for children with disabilities in institutions that receive *federal* funds, including Project Head Start. The Americans with Disabilities Act (ADA) of 1990 extends civil rights protection and nondiscrimination requirements to all settings (National Information Center for Children and Youth with Disabilities, 1991). The ADA opens all child care settings and private schools to children with disabilities.

The Education for Handicapped Children Acts

Legislation in this area has moved increasingly to mandate educational services for younger children (as opposed to simply providing incentives for states to do this), making it clear that children should be educated in the least restrictive environment.

P.L. 94-142, the Education for All Handicapped Children Act of 1975 (EHA), guaranteed a free appropriate education to children and youth with disabilities. As children move through public school, the relationship between Section 504 and P.L. 94-142 is important. All children who are eligible for services under P.L. 94-142 are also covered by Section 504. However, Section 504 includes disabilities that may not interfere with learning. For example, a child who has a missing hand may not have a learning problem or a child who tests HIV positive may have no symptoms that interfere with learning. Section 504 includes these children. If at some point their disability does interfere with their ability to learn, they will be covered under P.L. 94-142.

Public Law 99-457 (1986) lowered the age of eligibility to three years (Part B) and established the Infants and Toddlers Program (Part H). Amendments in 1990 renamed the law the Individuals with Disabilities Education Act (IDEA). The term "handicapped" has been replaced by "disability" and "people first" language, that is, a "child with a hearing impairment," not a "hearing impaired child." Children with autism and traumatic brain injury are now covered. Services for children with serious emotional disturbances and attention deficit disorder are included. Special programs on transition (moving from one placement to another, home intervention to public school or school to employment) and assistive technology are included. Together these laws are designed to provide more and better services for young children with disabilities and their families and to guarantee the rights of these children to equal educational opportunities. Additionally, these educational opportunities are to be provided in the "least restrictive environment," the setting that is as close as possible to where a child would normally be placed if he did not have a handicapping condition. The emphasis is on placing and educating young children with disabilities in their own homes, day care settings, preschools, and regular public school classrooms, not setting up separate segregated settings for them.

Because of the wide-reaching impact of IDEA and the specific terminology that is used, I have stated its purpose and defined the important terms in language taken directly from the public registry. The purpose of the Individuals with Disabilities Education Act is as follows:

Purpose It is the purpose (of this chapter) to assure that all children with disabilities have available to them, within the time periods specified, . . . a free appropriate public education which emphasizes special education and related services designed to meet their unique needs, to assure that the rights of children with disabilities and their parents or guardians are protected, to assist states and localities to provide for the education of all children with disabilities, and to assess and assure the effectiveness of efforts to educate children with disabilities.

The act carefully defines key terms and concepts, thereby setting minimum standards that must be met in order to achieve compliance. The following are the definitions I consider most important.

Children with disabilities means children—(A) with mental retardation, hearing impairments including deafness, speech or language impairments, visual impairments including blindness, serious emotional disturbance, orthopedic impairments, autism, traumatic brain injury, other health impairments, or specific learning disabilities; and (B) who, by reason thereof need special education and related services.

Children with specific learning disabilities means those children who have a disorder in one or more of the basic psychological processes involved in understanding or in using language, spoken or written, which disorder may manifest itself in imperfect ability to listen, think, speak, read, write, spell, or do mathematical calculations. Such disorders include such conditions as perceptual disabilities, brain injury, minimal brain dysfunction, dyslexia, and developmental aphasia. Such term does not include children who have learning problems which are primarily the result of visual, hearing, or motor disabilities, of mental retardation, of emotional disturbance, or of environmental, cultural, or economic disadvantage.

Special education means specially designed instruction, at no cost to parents or guardians, to meet the unique needs of children with a disability, including—(A) instruction conducted in the classroom, in the home, in hospitals and institutions, and in other settings; and (B) instruction in physical education.

Related services means transportation, and such developmental, corrective, and other supportive services including speech pathology and audiology, psychological services, physical and occupational therapy, recreation, including therapeutic recreation and social work services and medical and counseling services, including rehabilitation counseling, except that such medical services shall be for diagnostic and evaluation purposes only, as may be required to assist a child with a disability to benefit from special education, and includes the early identification and assessment of disabling conditions in children.

Free appropriate public education means special education and related services that—(A) have been provided at public expense, under public supervision and direction, and without charge, (B) meet the standards of the stated educational agency, (C) include an appropriate preschool, elementary, or secondary school education in the state involved, and (D) are provided in conformity with the individualized education program. . . .

Transition services means a coordinated set of activities for a student designed within an outcome oriented process, which promotes movement from school to post-school activities, including post-secondary education, vocational training, integrated employment (including supported employment), continuing and adult education, adult services, independent living or community participation. The coordinated set of activities shall be based upon the individual student's needs, taking into account the student's preferences and interests, and shall include instruction, community experiences, the development of employment and other post-school adult living objectives, and, when appropriate, acquisition of daily living skills and functional vocational evaluation.

Individualized education program means a written statement for each child with a disability developed in a meeting by a representative of the local educational agency or an intermediate educational unit who shall be qualified to provide, or supervise the provision of, specially designed instruction to meet the unique needs of children with disabilities, the teacher, the parents or guardians of such child, and whenever appropriate, such child, which statement shall include—(A) a statement of the present levels of educational performance of such child, (B) a statement of annual goals, including short-term instructional objectives, (C) a statement of the specific educational services to be provided to such child, and the extent to which such child will be able to participate in regular educational programs, (D) a statement of the needed transition services for students beginning no later than age 16 and annually thereafter (and, when determined appropriate for the individual, beginning at age 14 or younger), including, when appropriate, a statement of interagency responsibilities or linkages (or both) before the student leaves the school setting, (E) the projected date for initiation and anticipated duration of such services, and (F) appropriate objective criteria and evaluation procedures and schedules for determining, on at least an annual basis, whether instructional objectives are being achieved. In the case where a participating agency, other than the educational agency, fails to provide agreed upon services, the educational agency shall reconvene the IEP team to identify alternative strategies to meet the transition objectives.

The act goes on to define what is meant by the terms **excess costs, native language,** and **intermediate educational unit,** either directly or in terms of previous legislation.

The act further establishes a minimum level of compliance with regard to the rights of disabled children and their parents. The relevant section begins as follows:

> Procedural safeguards
> (a) Establishment and maintenance
> Any state educational agency, any local educational agency, and any intermediate educational unit which receives assistance under this subchapter shall establish and maintain procedures in accordance with subsection (b) through subsection (e) of this section to assure that children with disabilities and their parents or guardians are guaranteed procedural safeguards with respect to the provision of free appropriate public education by such agencies and units.
> (b) Required procedures; hearing
> (1) The procedures required by this section shall include, but not be limited to—(A) an opportunity for the parents or guardian of a child with a disability to examine all relevant records with respect to the identification, evaluation, and educational placement of the child, and the provision of a free appropriate public education to such child, and to obtain an independent educational evaluation of the child; (B) procedures to protect the rights of the child whenever the parents or guardian of the child are not known, unavailable, or the child is a ward of the State, including the assignment of an individual (who shall not be an employee of the State educational agency, local educational agency, or intermediate educational unit involved in the education or care of the child) to act as a surrogate for the parents or guardian; (C) written prior notice to the parents or guardian of the child whenever such agency or unit—(i) proposes to initiate or change, or (ii) refuses to initiate or change, the identification, evaluation, or educational placement of the child or the provision of a free appropriate public education to the child; (D) procedures designed to assure that the notice required by clause (C) fully informs the parents or guardian, in the parents' or guardian's native language, unless it clearly is not feasible to do so, of all procedures available pursuant to this section; and (E) an opportunity to present complaints with respect to any matter relating to the identification, evaluation, or educational placement of the child, or provision of a free appropriate public education to such child.
> (2) Whenever a complaint has been received under paragraph (1) of this subsection, the parents or guardian shall have an opportunity for an impartial due process hearing which shall be conducted by the State educational agency or by the local education agency or intermediate educational unit, as determined by State law or by the State educational agency. No hearing conducted pursuant to the requirements of this paragraph shall be conducted by an employee of such agency or unit involved in the education or care of the child.

The law further stipulates that if the hearing was conducted at the local or intermediate educational unit "any party aggrieved by the findings and decision" can appeal to the state educational agency for an impartial review. The following is specified:

> (d) Enumeration of rights accorded parties to hearings
> Any party to any hearing conducted pursuant to subsections (b) and (c) of this section shall be accorded—(1) the right to be accompanied and advised by counsel and by individuals with special knowledge or training with respect to the problems of children with disabilities, (2) the right to present evidence and confront and cross-examine, and compel the attendance of witnesses, (3) the right to a written or electronic verbatim record of such hearing, and (4) the right to written findings of fact and decisions (which findings and decisions shall be made available to the public . . . and to the advisory panel . . .).

The decision is usually final, although in some cases subject to appeal. If dissatisfied with the decision, but not (under the law) subject to appeal, a party may pursue the case further by bringing civil action in court.

What happens to the child during this process? After all, hearings and court cases may take a great amount of time. The act addresses the problem as follows: "The child shall remain in the then current educational placement of such child, or, if applying for initial admission to a public school, shall, with the consent of the parents or guardian, be placed in the public school program until all such proceedings have been completed." In other words, the child is not left in limbo.

The Infants and Toddlers Program was established by Part H of P.L. 99-457. This amendment requires states "to develop and implement a statewide, comprehensive, coordinated, multidisciplinary, interagency program of early intervention services for handicapped infants and toddlers and their families." Important aspects of P.L. 99-457 are detailed below.

1. States applying for funds through P.L. 94-142 will have to show that they are providing a free, appropriate public education to all children with disabilities, ages three through five.

2. With this law, a new state grant program was established for infants and toddlers, ages birth through two years of age, who are developmentally delayed or have a diagnosed condition which is likely to result in developmental delay. States may also decide to serve children at risk for developing delays. The grant program is designed to help states develop early intervention services for this population.

3. Early intervention services must include a multidisciplinary assessment and a written Individual Family Service Plan (IFSP) to be developed with the family. The IFSP is to include:

   a. A statement of the child's present developmental levels.

   b. A statement of family strengths and needs.

   c. A statement of major outcomes (goals) expected and methods and time line for measuring accomplishment.

   d. A statement of specific early intervention services necessary to meet individual child and family needs.

   e. Projected dates for starting and ending (if appropriate) services.

   f. Name of the service coordinator.

   g. Plan for transition into programs for three- to five-year-olds.

Each state has an Interagency Coordinating Council (ICC) whose members include parents of children with disabilities and representatives from various agencies serving this population. The ICCs in each state are currently working to develop plans for how P.L. 99-457 will be implemented in that particular state.

Legislation and Litigation

The relationship between legislation and litigation is an interesting one. In many ways the purpose of litigation is to determine the limits or interpretation of the law. The litigation then determines the minimum level of services that must be provided under the law. For example, the case of the *Board of Education of the Hendrick Hudson Central School District v. Rowley,* 453 U.S. 176 (1982) has provided guidelines on what the term "free appropriate public education" (FAPE) means. Amy Rowley is a child with a hearing impairment whose parents thought she would do better if she had an interpreter. Amy Rowley was functioning at the same level as her peers. The Supreme Court ruled against Rowley. Their interpretation was that the EHA was not intended to require any particular level of or intensity of educational services. The ruling was that maximizing a child's potential was too high a standard but also that providing only those services available to nonhandicapped children was too low a standard. The EHA requires the provision of a

"basic floor of opportunity" consisting of "access to specialized instruction and related services individually designed to provide educational benefit to the handicapped child." If the child is educated in the regular classroom, the program should be "reasonably calculated to enable the child to achieve passing marks and advance from grade to grade."

Additionally, they defined a Free Appropriate Public Education (FAPE) to be personalized instruction with sufficient support services to permit a child to benefit educationally from instruction, at public expense, that meets the state's educational standards and approximate grade levels used in the state's regular education and conforms with the IEP. They further felt that courts should not become overly involved in questions of methodology (adapted from Hartman, 1989).

In the area of related services, *Irving Independent School District v. Tatro,* 468 U.S. 883 (1984) expanded services to a child with disabilities. The Supreme Court determined that catherization for a three-and-a-half-year-old student, which can be provided by a school nurse or trained lay person, is a proper related service, not an excluded "medical service." The court approaches adoption of the "but for" test: "The Act makes specific provision for services, like transportation, for example, that do no more than enable a child to be physically present in class, . . . Services like catherization that permit a child to remain at school during the day are no less related to the effort to educate than are services that enable the child to reach, enter, or exit the school" (adapted from Hartman, 1989).

The *Education for the Handicapped Law Report* goes into much greater detail and many more cases. Determination of the law's meaning is an ongoing process. States, too, make decisions about how they will interpret the law. Some decide to provide the minimum required by law and are referred to as "floor of opportunity" states. States that provide services beyond those required by law are "maximizing" states. As you enter the job market or consider changing locations, be aware of a state's educational environment. It has a direct impact on your work. (See *Handicapped Students and Special Education* [1985] for more information on U.S. Supreme Court decisions dealing with special education.)

Theoretical Bases for Early Childhood Special Education

Interwoven with social and legal change is change in the field of education itself. Much of the change has come about as a combined result of research, experimentation, and law. For example, findings in psychology have affected our philosophy of what education is and how it takes place. As a result we have come to recognize the importance of individualizing our teaching. This has facilitated our providing the attention to individual needs that is essential when working with children with disabilities.

Most educational research has focused on how (and what) to teach rather than how children learn. After publication of the work of Swiss psychologist Jean Piaget in the early 1950s, educators began to focus on how children learn. According to Piaget, the teacher's role is to set up an environment that a child can actively explore. In addition, classroom activities, which are part of the environment, should incorporate both familiar and new aspects. From Piaget's work, we concluded that a child must actively interact with the environment and that the activities in the environment must be individualized to match and then expand the child's experience.

The work of Albert Bandura and others on how children learn by modeling other children has also affected the education of children with disabilities. Their separation at an early age meant that the only peers available as models were also disabled. This segregation effectively resulted in teaching children to imitate their disabled peers. Now we are finding

that with teacher support those children can learn to model nondisabled peers. Now all children are gaining experience from an early age in interacting with a wide range of people.

Piaget's work helped make integration possible by changing our philosophy and methodology of education. Bandura's work helped make inclusion imperative by demonstrating that segregation deprived children with disabilities and those without of a full education.

New teaching methods, support services, and technology used in the regular classroom have also prepared us for inclusion. For example, team teaching, now a common practice with young children, can help the teacher who has little experience with children with disabilities. The consultation model allows teachers access to specialists who can model behavior and provide technical assistance.

Inclusion is more than just placing children with disabilities in regular classes. For it to be done well

LEVELS OF INCLUSION

Most Inclusive - - - - - - - - - - ▶ - - - - - - - - - -▶- - - - - - - - - - - ▶ - - - - - - - - - - -▶- - - - - - - - - - ▶ - - - - - - - - - - -▶- - - - - - - - - ▶

Setting	Child care, preschool, regular kindergarten	Child care, preschool, kindergarten with consultation	Regular setting with itinerant teacher/therapist
Children typically served	Children who haven't been identified, children with mild speech and language delays, conductive hearing losses, mild behavioral and emotional disorders, and health impairments	Identified children with mild to moderate disabilities and some children with severe impairments	Children with visual, hearing, physical, or communication impairments
Teacher's role	Teach all the children in the classroom, make referrals	Teach all the children, receive some training in disabilities, are part of the intervention team, implement IFSP or IEP	Teach all children; accommodate and work with itinerant teacher/therapist on intervention team
Specialist	No specialist	Early childhood special educator (ECSE)	Itinerant teacher (for visually, or hearing impaired, and others)
Specialist's role	Child may receive therapy outside of setting	Model, demonstrate, and provide technical assistance, writes part of IFSP or IEP	Visits classroom, provides specialized materials and program, teaches child in regular classroom, may pull child out for specialized instruction, helps write IFSP or IEP
Features	Teacher meets child's needs; may be unaware of problem, rarely part of team for services outside the setting	Teacher teaches all children; ECSE provides technical assistant and consultation	Child is with peers: teacher can consult with and observe itinerant teacher, who is in a disability area, rarely early childhood

there must be support services for both the teacher and the child. When children with disabilities were channeled off into special schools, these services were primarily diagnostic. As soon as the child was identified as disabled the child was moved; the task of the regular school support services was finished. Despite their original limited function, school support services have grown to meet the needs of all children. The school psychologist no longer just gives intelligence tests, but also does group or family counseling. More speech and language therapists and more occupational and physical therapists work in schools. Social workers, adaptive physical education teachers, and home-school lessons may all be part of a school setting. Although some of these specialists have been around for a long time, their previous practice of pulling children out of class to work with them has changed. Now they perform some of their work within the classroom, and often consult with the teacher to develop a classroom program for a child that complements the individual or small group therapy that the specialist is carrying out.

Attempts at defining the characteristics of the least restrictive environment resulted in the concept of a continuum of services. The early concept of Deno (1970) showed a cascade system of services with "exceptional" children placed in regular classes with or without supportive services, moving to supplementally instructional services, part- and then full-time special classes, special stations or schools, homebound instruction, and hospital, residential, or total care settings. As Deno envisioned this model, one moved down the cascade only as far as necessary and then returned up "as rapidly as feasible" (Deno, 1970). This model has been expanded and augmented, but the essence of the model remains. The expectation is, however, that children with more severe disabilities will be placed in increasingly integrated placements until there is just one level of service.

The continuum of services not only affects the child with a disability, but the other children and teachers and therapists as well. When children with disabilities are included in the classroom setting the

- - - - - - - - - - →- - - - - - - - - →- - - - - - - - →- - - - - - - - →- - - - - - - - →- - - - - - →- - - - - - - → Least Inclusive

Resource room/pull out therapy	Special class/segregated intervention program in regular school	Special school or day setting	Residential school/institution
Children who need therapy (OT, PT, speech, etc.) or help in a subject area (reading, math, etc.)	Children with moderate, severe, or profound impairments	Children with severe or profound impairments	Children with severe/ profound impairments and those living where other services are not available
Teach all children, accommodate pull out schedule, consult with specialists, make accommodations for child	Help nondisabled children socialize (playground, lunch); support children mainstreamed for part of the day; support reverse mainstreaming for part of the day; increase awareness of disabilities	Increase other children's awareness of disabilities	Increase nondisabled children's awareness of disabilities
Therapist or special education teacher Teaches child part of the day and provides some technical assistance to teacher, writes and implements most of IFSP or IEP	Early childhood special educator Teaches children; writes and implements IFSP, EIP; supports regular or reverse mainstreaming	Early childhood special educator Teaches children; writes and implements IFSP, IEP	Special education teachers, therapists, nurses Teaches child; writes and implements IFSP, IEP; cares for child's needs and educational program
Child is with peers most of the day; a specialist/ teacher provides more individualized instruction in a segregated classroom	Child is integrated some of the day	Child is segregated for the school day	Child is segregated all day; has little contact with family

regular teacher plays the major teaching role, but she also needs skills to work with specialists as part of the early intervention team and to adapt her teaching style and programming for all the children she teaches. Likewise, therapists and early childhood special educators must take the needs of the regular teacher and the children in her classroom into account as they program for an individual child. This need for teamwork on the part of regular and special educators and therapists requires planning and cooperation that is new for both.

The following continuum of services is an example of how a system serving children from birth through eight years might work, the children you might find in each level, and the role of the teacher and of related specialists or therapists. It moves from most inclusive to least inclusive. It also serves as an historical view of the field. In the past, the norm was often institutionalization. We are moving toward the norm of inclusion.

In addition to deciding what is the least restrictive environment for a particular child, decisions around the role of related services have caused conflict. In general, parents want more help for their child from specialists than most school systems offer. Because we are identifying and serving more children earlier, available resources must be shared among more children than ever. Administrators must choose between the maximizing programming requested by parents and minimal compliance with the law. They must often make this decision based on the resources they have available as well as their personal value system.

In any given situation different people may have different ideas as to what is "appropriate." Sally's parents may think it is "appropriate" for her to have speech therapy five times a week. The school district sees that as "optimal," saying it is "appropriate" that she have speech therapy once a week. The teacher may well be caught in the middle—understanding both positions.

Specialists often have high case loads and are therefore unable to spend much time with any one child. One obvious solution is to hire more specialists. But that is expensive, and taxpayers are voting against tax referendums to give the schools more money. The shortage of specialists is even more acute in rural areas, for some specialists are reluctant to take jobs in areas where they may be the only specialist for miles. As we work toward inclusion, some of these problems may be solved. Instead of "pulling children out" for therapy, increasingly, therapy is being done in the classroom. This allows the teacher to observe the therapy and may increase the continuity of services for the child. It may also increase the teacher's awareness of how to better match programming for this child.

Because of the limitations and expense of specialists, some schools have invested in "hardware" as a means of individualizing and otherwise enhancing education. A computer, a talking typewriter, educational television, or some form of recently developed

A simple touch will make the bunny jump.

hardware may or may not be available to the teacher. Some of these items have applications for helping children with disabilities. Unless equipment is individualized to meet the needs of a particular child, however, it is not likely to be useful in program planning.

Assistive technology can help children participate in many activities that in the past would not have been available to them. Some technology items are expensive and complicated, others are not. For example, toys and other battery-operated devices can be made switch-activated with a $10 toy cable. The switch can be individualized to work with very slight pressure from a push of a thumb or even a puff of air. Some computers can be operated by having a child stare at commands (pictures) on a computer screen. We are just on the edge of assistive technology; it may solve problems beyond our wildest imaginations.

Family-Oriented Early Intervention

As services for children have become more normalized, the role of the family has changed, as has the relationship between families and professionals. Services for young children are now expected to be family-centered. As with previous examples, there are very different expectations about what "family-centered" really means. Dunst, Johanson, Trivette, and Hamby (1991) see six major categories or principles of family support:

1. Enhancing a sense of community. This involves bringing people together and building informal support networks between the family unit and the community. Interventions are then based on the needs of those who live in the community.

2. Mobilizing resources and supports. The necessary resources and supports should be responsive to the needs of the entire family unit, not just the child.

3. Sharing responsibility and collaboration. Parents and professionals should work in partnership to support and strengthen the family. The relationship should be based on mutual respect.

4. Protecting family integrity. Interventions should be provided in ways that accept and value a family's values and culture.

5. Strengthening family functioning. Interventions should build on strengths, not be designed to remedy weaknesses. Our goal is not to "fix" families.

6. Practicing proactive human service. Service delivery systems should be consumer-driven, not designed to meet the needs of the professional (Dunst, et al., p. 117).

In family-centered practices, the family determines the role of the service coordinator. The family decides what will or will not be in the Individualized Family Service Plan, if there is one, and family concerns are used to determine what areas of assessment are appropriate. Family priorities mobilize the system.

Just as many professionals have problems with including all children, many also have problems allowing parents to be "in charge" of their family and their children. Our profession is being stretched in new and different ways that require many and varied skills.

Summary

Inclusion has resulted from changing social, legal, and educational philosophies that have led to individualized programming for children. Of particular importance are the legal requirements that all children have a free, appropriate, public education. In addition to including all children with disabilities, their families are included as well, not just as sources of transportation and the like, but as equal decision makers whose priorities, values, and needs must be reflected in the educational process.

Inclusion in and of itself is neither good nor bad. Many people fear that inclusion will result in all children being "dumped together" in the rather arbitrary way they were separated out. And, if including children with disabilities is poorly done, that could happen. Inclusion involves placing children in an education setting and providing the support, both educational and social, they need to remain there. If this is not possible at the beginning, it should remain the goal. The purpose of inclusion is to help all children gain skills in interacting with each other that will be valuable throughout life, as well as to provide an appropriate education for all.

Crucial to the success of inclusion is your underlying support of equality for all. Inclusion depends, too, on your ability to measure and program for children's learning, for their strengths and needs, at many points along the developmental path.

References and Bibliography

Abramovitch, R., & Grusec, J. (1978). Peer imitation in a natural setting. *Child Development, 49*, 60–65.

Akamatsu, T., & Thelen, M. H. (1974). A review of the literature on observer characteristics and imitation. *Developmental Psychology, 10*, 38–47.

Bagnato, S. J., & Neisworth, J. T. (1980). The Intervention Efficiency Index: An approach to preschool program accountability. *Exceptional Children, 46*, 264–269.

Bailey, D. B. (1988). Assessing family stress and needs. In D. B. Bailey & R. J. Simeonsson (Eds.), *Family assessment in early intervention* (pp. 95–118). Columbus, OH: Charles Merrill.

Bailey, D., Simeonsson, R., Huntington, G., Cochrane, C., Crais, E., & Humphrey, R. (1988, November). Preparing professionals from multiple disciplines to work with handicapped infants, toddlers, and their families: Current status and future directions. Carolina Institute for Research on Infant Personnel Preparation. Paper presented at the International Early Childhood Conference on Children with Special Needs, Nashville, TN.

Benham, N., Miller, T., & Kontos, S. (1988). Pinpointing staff training needs in child care centers. *Young Children, 43*(4), 9–16.

Berk, H. J., & Berk, M. L. (1982). A survey of day care centers and their services for handicapped children. *Child Care Quarterly, 11*(3), 211–214.

Brown, C. (1979). *A naturalistic study of the characteristics and conditions promoting social integration of handicapped children in early childhood classes.* Unpublished doctoral dissertation, The Pennsylvania State University, State College, PA.

Council for Exceptional Children (1976). Delegate assembly issues mainstreaming challenge. CEC Update 7, No. 4.

Danielson, L. C., & Bellamy, G. T. (1989). State variation in placement of children with handicaps in segregated environments. *Exceptional Children, 55*, 448–455.

Data Research, Inc. (1985). *Handicapped students and special education* (2nd ed). Rosemount, MN: Author.

Deiner, P. L. (1987). Systems of care for disabled children and family members: New paradigms and alternatives. In M. Ferrari & M. Sussman (Eds.), *Childhood disability and family systems* (pp. 193–211). New York: Haworth Press.

Deiner, P. L., & Whitehead, L. (1988). Levels of respite care as a family support network. *Topics in Early Childhood Special Education: Alternative Caregiving, 8*(2) 51–61.

Deiner, P. L., Gold, B., Kaiser, M., Kontos, S., Widoff, E., & McNellis, K. (1988). *Successful models for mainstreaming disabled children into child care.* Paper presented at the Annual Conference of the National Association for the Education of Young Children, Anaheim, CA.

Deiner, P. L., Whitehead, L. C., Prudhoe, C. M., & Ziegler, D. A. (1988, November). *Issues in special needs day care for handicapped infants and toddlers.* Paper presented at the Annual Conference of the Division of Early Childhood of the Council for Exceptional Children, Nashville, TN.

Demchak, M., & Drinkwater, S. (1992). Preschoolers with severe disabilities. *Topics in Early Childhood Special Education. 11*(4) 70–83.

Deno, E. (1970). Special education as developmental capital. *Exceptional Children, 37,* 229–37.

Devine-Hawkins, P. (1981). *National day care home study final report: Executive summary* (DHHS Publication No. OHDS 80-30287). Washington, DC: U.S. Department of Health and Human Services.

Dunst, C., Johanson, C., Trivette, C., & Hamby, D. (1991). Family-oriented early intervention policies and practices: Family-centered or not? *Exceptional Children, 58*(2), 104–127.

Fewell, R. R. (1986). Child care and the handicapped child. In S. Gunzenhauser & B. M. Caldwell (Eds.), *Group care for young children.* Skillman, NJ: Johnson & Johnson.

Forest, M., & Pearpoint, J. (1990). Supports for addressing severe maladaptive behaviors. In W. Stainback & S. Stainback (Eds.), *Support networks for inclusive schooling* (pp. 187–197). Baltimore, MD: Paul H. Brookes.

Guralnick, M. J., & Bennett, F. C. (1987). Early intervention for at-risk and handicapped children: Current and future perspectives. In M. J. Guralnick & F. C. Bennett (Eds.), *The effectiveness of early intervention for at-risk and handicapped children* (pp. 365–382). Orlando, FL: Academic Press.

Harms, T., & Clifford, R. (1980). *The early childhood environment rating scale.* New York: Teachers College Press.

Harris, S. (1976). *An examination of social behavior between teacher-child and child-child in an integrated preschool setting.* Unpublished master's thesis, Pennsylvania State University, State College, PA.

Hartman, B. (1989, May). *Overview of special education case law affecting Delaware.* Presentation at Roles and Functions of Due Process Hearing Panel Members, Dover, DE.

Kostelnik, M. J. (1978). *Evaluation of a communication and group management skills training program for child development personnel.* Unpublished doctoral dissertation, Pennsylvania State University, State College, PA.

National Information Center for Children and Youth with Handicaps, (1988). *Questions parents often ask about special education services and Public Law 94-142.* Washington, DC: Author.

Nazario, T., with Blum, P., Hirshfield, S., & Maljanich, P. (1988). *In defense of children: Understanding the rights, needs & interests of the child—A resource book for parents and professionals.* New York: Scribner/Macmillan.

Peters, D., & Kontos, S. (1987). *Continuity and discontinuity of experience in child care.* Norward, NJ: Ablex.

Rubin, K. H., & Ross, H. S. (Eds.). (1982). *Peer relationships and social skills in childhood.* New York: Springer-Verlag.

Stainback, W., & Stainback, S. (1990). *Support networks for inclusive schools: Interdependent integrated education.* Baltimore, MD: Paul H. Brookes.

Zigler, E., & Balla, D. (1982). Selecting outcome variables in evaluations of early childhood special education programs. *Topics in Early Childhood Special Education, 1*(4), 11–22.

Chapter 4

Early Growth and Development

All children are unique, yet they share many commonalities in patterns of growth and development. Growth refers to the physical changes that occur in children over time, and can be measured in inches or centimeters, pounds or kilograms. Development is concerned with the acquisition of skills, such as walking and talking. Understanding the underlying principles of growth and development allows us to make predictions about whether or not growth and development will fall within the normal patterns. It also provides direction for intervention strategies.

Children come into the world "prewired" to grow and develop in a certain predictable pattern. Some children follow the pattern, but at a slower rate; others do not follow the pattern. Learning to plan for these children requires an understanding of growth and developmental processes. Knowing the pattern of development is a key component to successful early childhood programming and intervention.

Growth occurs in response to a genetic pattern unique for each person. The environment in which children are raised can also influence development. The environment for some children includes risk factors that reduce their probability for following normal growth patterns. For example, children who do not get enough calories for adequate nutrition may not reach their growth potential. Children who live in houses where lead-based paint was used are considered at risk for developmental delay even if at birth there was no reason to place them in this category.

There are many different ways to organize the study of child development. Some find a topical approach the best way, others an age-stage approach. This chapter uses an age-stage approach, with the topical approach used in specific chapters on disabilities and activities. For example, the chapter on visual impairment focuses on the development of vision; likewise, the chapter on motor development discusses the development of fine and gross motor skills and sensory **35** integration. This chapter is designed to give you an overview of developmental patterns.

It is important to remember, however, that even when ages and stages are highlighted, they are part of a continuous flow, and that the characteristics described in this book will be clearer and more distinct than you will find in the children you work with.

Developmental Patterns

Children develop according to a pattern. All children follow similar patterns in all areas of development. What makes children different are the ages at which specific skills are acquired.

Defining "normal" development is difficult. A skill one child begins to develop at one year, another may not accomplish until one, two, or even three months later. However, this does not mean that the second child is delayed. He is probably developing normally. There is a normal range of time during which these skills are acquired.

Acquiring the ability to walk provides a good example of this variation. Most children begin walking at about twelve months. Some begin to walk at nine months, while others do not begin until they are fifteen months old. This difference in age indicates only that some children walk early and some later, but they are within the normal range. When a child is not walking by sixteen months there may be some concern.

A related problem is defining the terms we are using. How far does a child have to walk for us to agree that the child can walk? Is six steps enough, or must the child walk six feet? If one person believes six feet and another believes six steps it is likely that the second person will see children walk "earlier."

Development, then, has a range of variation that is considered "normal." Although there is variation in development, there are some general parameters about when developmental milestones occur. Some children fall outside the normal range of variations in skill acquisition. Children who have not acquired certain skills by expected ages are "delayed" in their development. Other children who do not follow the usual pattern are considered atypical. Atypical development does not mean delayed. The child develops or has patterns of behavior that differ from the normal developmental pattern. To recognize delayed and atypical development it is necessary to first know what is considered normal growth and development. This chapter first covers normal growth and development and then delayed and atypical development.

Prenatal Development

The time from conception to birth is called gestation and usually lasts nine months. We divide these nine months into trimesters.

The First Trimester. The first three months are characterized by rapid growth and have tremendous developmental significance. The main organ systems (cardiovascular, neurological, digestive, and so on) are differentiated and established. By the end of the first trimester the fetus is about three-and-a-half-inches long and weighs about an ounce.

The Second Trimester. Growth continues during the fourth through the sixth month with the development of tissues and organs. Mothers can detect movement, the heart can be heard using a stethoscope or even placing an ear on the abdomen, and lung growth is significant. By the end of the second trimester the fetus is about twelve to fourteen inches long and weighs about one-and-a-half pounds. Some fetuses born at the end of this trimester are viable with the support of a neonatal intensive care nursery.

The Third Trimester. During the seventh month the fetus starts storing fat, and life support functions are more fully developed. The brain continues to develop rapidly. By the end of the ninth month the fetus is about twenty inches long, weighs about seven-and-a-half pounds, and is ready to be born.

External Influences on Pregnancy

Many factors influence the developing fetus. Generally, exposure to any risk factor during the first trimester of pregnancy poses the greatest risk to the developing fetus. During this time the organ systems are most vulnerable to drugs, viruses, radiation, infection, and poor nutrition. This exposure can have serious short- and long-term effects.

Teratogenic Substances. Teratogens are substances that can adversely affect the development of the fetus, causing death, malformations, growth deficiency, and functional deficits (Crain, 1984). Many of the effects of teratogens are known. Thalidomide, a drug used in the 1960s, primarily in Europe, caused defects in children such as missing or malformed limbs. The most devastating effects were during the first two months of pregnancy.

Alcohol. Alcohol is a common teratogen, which, when consumed by the mother, can lead to Fetal Alcohol Syndrome (FAS). Fetal Alcohol Syndrome is a major cause of mental retardation in the United States. Children born with FAS states range between one to three per 1,000 live births (U.S. Department of Health and Human Services, 1984). When a pregnant woman drinks alcohol, both her blood alcohol content and that of her fetus increase. They increase at the same rate, but the fetus's blood alcohol remains higher longer because the mother's liver must remove the alcohol from her own blood before it can remove the alcohol from the unborn baby. FAS is the result of heavy alcohol use—about six drinks a day. Pregnant women who drink less than this may have children with a condition known as Fetal Alcohol Effects (FAE). This condition has a milder impact developmentally, but the child's overall mental and physical growth is adversely affected (Warren, 1985).

Drugs. Drugs also can affect the development of the fetus. Drugs taken by the mother pass through her system to the infant via the placenta. Prescription medications indicated as sources of possible problems include anticoagulant, anticonvulsant, and antipsychotic medications.

Abused substances such as heroin and cocaine affect the central nervous system as stimulants and cause blood vessels to constrict. The fetus receives less oxygen and nutrients, which interferes with development. It is estimated that 375,000 babies each year are born to mothers who abuse drugs (Schneider, Griffith, & Chasnoff, 1989). Drugs are slow to be metabolized and excreted and remain in the fetus longer than in the mother (Schneider & Chasnoff, 1987). Some drugs can cause contractions of the uterus and a premature birth or spontaneous abortion.

Tobacco. Women who smoke have infants with lower birth weights. The carbon monoxide from the mother's blood stream crosses the placenta and reduces the amount of oxygen available to the fetus.

Radiation. Everyone is exposed to radiation. Low doses of radiation have not been found to cause harm, but excessive or repeated exposure to high levels of radiation have been shown to result in central nervous system damage. The greatest risk is for pregnant women whose occupations expose them to radiation and those who need radiation therapy.

Infection. Maternal infections can adversely affect fetal development, with exposure during the first trimester the most traumatic for the fetus. Exposure of pregnant women to rubella (measles) can result in possible disabling conditions to the fetus, depending on the gestational age and severity of the infection. If exposure occurs during the first eleven weeks of pregnancy, the risk of Congenital Rubella Syndrome (CRS) is almost 100 percent. CRS is characterized by blindness and heart defects. Other adverse effects include hearing impairment, microcephaly, mental retardation, and cataracts. The risks to the fetus are almost nonexistent after the sixteenth week (Miller, Cradock-Watson, & Pollock, 1982).

Other harmful infections include herpes, syphilis, toxoplasmosis, and cytomegalovirus. Again, the time at which a pregnant woman is exposed to the virus will have a direct impact upon the extent to which the fetus is affected. Even second and third trimester exposure can lead to problems in the fetus and later difficulties for the infant.

Blood Factors. In addition to the four major blood types—A, AB, B, and O—there is an Rh factor, involving a protein on the surface of blood cells. About 90 percent of the population have this protein and are Rh-positive. Problems only occur when the mother is Rh-negative and the fetus is Rh-positive. The mother's body may react to the Rh-positive blood cells as a foreign substance and develop antibodies to attack the fetus's blood cells, causing them to break apart and resulting in Rh hemolytic disease. This disease can result in brain damage or death. The first child is usually not affected because the blood of the fetus must mix with the mother's for the antibodies to be produced. This mixing frequently happens during delivery, but rarely before.

Genetic Influences

Heredity influences growth and development. Genetic make-up plays a strong role in dictating specific growth processes. Eye color, skin color, and whether hair is curly or straight are determined by one's genes, which are the components of chromosomes.

Considering the number of biological parts and processes controlled by chromosomes, it is not unlikely that some things may go wrong. A defect in any one of the genes can result in a developmental or biological problem. Problems can be the result of genetic defects or chromosomal abnormalities. Approximately 4 percent of infants experience some type of birth defect; more than half of these have unknown causes. Of the known causes, 25 percent are gene disorders, 12 percent are chromosomal disorders, and 7 percent are due to teratogens (Crain, 1984).

Genetic abnormalities can result in disorders such as Tay-Sachs Disease, phenylketonuria, and cystic fibrosis. Many, but certainly not all, genetic problems result in disorders that interfere with a child's ability to learn.

Chromosomal abnormalities are found in approximately one in six hundred live births. Down syndrome is a chromosomal disorder, the most common form of which is called Trisomy 21. In this disorder there is a rearrangement of the twenty-first chromosome; there are three parts instead of two.

Labor and Birthing

Labor is a dynamic personal experience, but technically it is the process of discharging the fetus, placenta, and umbilical cord from the uterus. Complications can affect the fetus during the birthing process. A prolonged labor, the umbilical cord wrapping around the neck of the fetus, or premature detachment of the placenta can cause loss of oxygen to the fetus. If this lasts for a significant period brain cell damage results.

One disability frequently associated with oxygen loss during the birthing process is cerebral palsy, which means brain cell paralysis. The site of the cell damage influences the disability in the infant. If, for example, the damage is in the motor cortex of the brain, the child will have problems with voluntary movements, whereas if the damage is outside the pyramidal tract the involuntary movements are affected (Batshaw & Perret, 1986).

Drugs administered during labor also affect the fetus. Analgesics and anesthetics are used to control or diminish the sensation of pain. Analgesics, such as Demerol, are most often used during the early part of labor. Their purpose is to relieve pain by depressing the central nervous system. Anesthetics such as the epidural block are used to numb the pelvic area and relieve the discomfort of contractions. A spinal or saddle block may be used during the delivery itself. Most doctors believe that the effects of these drugs are transitory. Others, however, disagree.

Postnatal Influences

After birth, the factors affecting the infant can be broadly grouped into three categories: injury, infection, and environmental influences.

Injury to the infant and young child is a common cause of disability in children. These injuries can be from accidental causes as well as from physical abuse. Injuries resulting in severe head trauma can lead to both physical and mental disabilities. Loss or damage to limbs, or any of the sensory organs, can lead to permanent disability.

Infection is another common cause of disabilities in young children, especially if accompanied by a high fever. Severe cases of meningitis, measles, and encephalitis, with associated high fevers, are commonly mentioned causes of disabilities. High fever has also been associated with the loss of hearing in young infants.

The environment in which children are raised is a major influence. Children raised in extreme poverty are at risk for developmental problems. Poverty itself does not directly lead to disabilities, but the related factors associated with poor environment, such as inadequate cognitive/language stimulation, poor nutrition, exposure to safety hazards, and poor health care can lead to disabling conditions.

Neonates

The infant is referred to as a "neonate" for the first four weeks of life. Neonates look very different from adults, and even their body content is different. Their initial energy is devoted to adjusting their body mechanisms such as respiration, maintenance of body temperature, food absorption, and elimination to independent living.

Physical and Motor Development

The neonate is wrinkled, with dry skin, and she may or may not have hair. A newborn's head is disproportionately large, about 20 to 25 percent of the total body length, and its circumference is greater than that of the chest. (In adults it is about 10 percent of the total length and markedly less than the chest.) Because of the molding of the head during the trip through the birth canal, the head may look asymmetrical. The two soft spots or fontanels at the top of the head and the one at the back are pronounced. The limbs are proportionately short and the fist closed. The arms and legs are typically flexed or curled up even when she is on her stomach (prone). Her body is primarily water; 75 percent of body weight is water. (Adults have about 50 percent of their weight in water.)

The neonate is about 20 inches long and weighs about seven-and-one-half pounds, with males being slightly longer and heavier than females. The neonate will grow about one-and-a-half inches and gain about two pounds during the first month. The neonate's motor development is dominated by reflexive behaviors.

Reflexes. The neonate has an amazing repertoire of innate, involuntary responses called reflexes. Some will disappear; others form the basis for coordinated, voluntary movement. The first observable reflexes are called primitive reflexes. They are present at or soon after birth and are predictable responses to specific stimuli. The sucking reflex occurs whenever a nipple, finger, or pacifier is placed in the neonate's mouth. It is unrelated to hunger or the nutritive value of what is being sucked. Reflexes have survival, protective, and adaptive value. Reflexive actions are used to help diagnose the infant's physiological and neurological status.

As the infant matures, these reflexes become integrated into overall motor movements. Many of the reflexes are overridden by more sophisticated voluntary motor skills.

Sensory Development

Neonates, although dependent, are amazingly competent beings. Though neonates do not have normal visual acuity (20/20), we know they are able to see and they prefer certain visual stimuli. The neonate's visual acuity ranges from 20/150 to 20/800, improves rapidly, and reaches close to normal by eighteen months. It is difficult for neonates to adjust their focus between close and distant objects. They are best able to focus on objects held about seven to eight inches directly in front of their faces. They prefer complex patterns over plain ones, and high contrast colors over gray.

The auditory system of the infant is one of the most well-developed bodily functions at birth. Research indicates that parts of the inner ear have grown to adult size by the fifth month of fetal development. Hearing provides important information to neonates. Although their hearing is not yet as sensitive as that of adults, they hear fairly well. They respond to sounds by blinking their eyes, arousing from sleep, crying, or total body movements.

Neonates have a remarkably developed sense of smell. They can discriminate between pleasant and unpleasant odors. They show a preference for fragrant odors and a displeasure for noxious ones.

Newborns can discriminate the mother's smell by the end of the first week.

The newborn has an adequate number of taste buds and can discriminate between sweet, acidic, salty, and bitter tastes. They much prefer sweet tastes and will spit out sour tastes; they like salty fluids also. They can discriminate between intensities of these tastes.

Cognitive Development

The neonate is in a reflexive action stage. When the corners of her mouth are stroked, the infant turns her head; when a finger or nipple is placed in her mouth, she sucks. Putting pressure on the palm of the hand causes it to close (Palmar grasp), likewise, the toes flex when pressure is put on the ball of the foot (Plantar grasp). Other reflexes relate to changes in position (tonic neck reflexes, startle, and Moro reflexes). Some of these reflexes become modified over the first month so that, for example, the sucking reflex becomes more efficient; the infant learns how much sucking is required for liquid to get into his mouth. He is adapting to the environment, but cannot differentiate between himself and the outside world.

Neonates can learn. In early work Lipsett and Kaye (1964) conditioned neonates using both classical and operant conditioning. In addition to learning, the neonate also becomes accustomed to repetitive stimuli and no longer responds to them; that is, he habituates. Habituation plays an important role in adaptation to the environment. The neonate learns not to awaken to familiar noises and can tolerate more stimuli.

Language Development

Language development begins at birth with the first cry. Parents learn to distinguish among the different cries of neonates. In addition to crying, babies can make gasping sounds and vegetative sounds (murmurs and gurgles) that often accompany feeding. Newborns are responsive to the human voice, regardless of the language of the speaker. They prefer vocal music over instrumental. They also move to the rhythm of adult speech—if the speech is fast, the infant's motion increases, and likewise, if the speech slows, the infant's motion slows (Barclay, 1985). At about three weeks the infant can turn her head and find her mother's eyes as she coos to her. This is communication.

Social and Emotional Development

The human infant is born helpless and remains that way for a relatively long time. The young infant comes with a repertoire of behaviors that allow him to summon his caregiver, keep the caregiver engaged once he has arrived, and eventually maintain proximity to the caregiver. Ethnologists believe that these

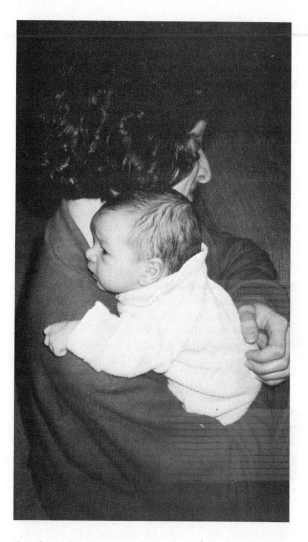

Gentle and responsive caregiving helps build attachment in the neonate.

behaviors have survival value to all species including human infants. These behaviors include crying and sucking, which the infant can do at birth, followed by the emergence of smiling and clinging, and, by the end of the first year, the ability to follow the caregiver.

Bonding is the process by which parents become emotionally tied to their newborn. Bonding is typically viewed as a one-way process—important for the establishment of adults' feelings but not reciprocated by neonates. Some believe that bonding can only occur during the neonatal period. They feel it is related to the sight, feel, and sound of the neonate as well as skin-to-skin contact (Barclay, 1985). Others see bonding as only a precursor to attachment. Attachment is the formation of a strong, lasting, reciprocal emotional tie between the infant and significant others that develops over time. Attachment is a broader concept and takes into account the infant's delight and preferences for grandparents and siblings as well as those who directly care for the infant.

Neonates are responsive to all adults. They like adult company, but have not developed preferences. Early social responsiveness for neonates often consists of behaviors such as mutual gazing. The adult looks at the infant and makes eye contact. If the infant looks away the adult may try to draw attention back by talking to the infant, making faces, changing the pitch or rhythm of her voice and so on.

States. Neonates are individuals who have different states and temperaments from birth. The neonate has at least six distinct states, the two most obvious being: *asleep* and *awake*. Within the sleeping state neonates can be in a regular sleep state, characterized by full rest, and irregular sleep in which the neonate stirs, may grimace and chew, and respiration is irregular. Drowsiness often appears when the neonate is waking up or going to sleep; the eyes open and close, the infant is not alert.

Waking states are characterized by alert inactivity with the eyes open and bright and the face relaxed and alert activity where the infant has spurts of motor movement. The last state is crying.

The neonate's ability to respond to the environment is influenced by the state she is in. Neonates differ in the amount of time they spend in each state. It is up to the caregiver to read the neonate's state and respond accordingly. The alert inactive state is the ideal one for learning and interaction.

Neonates at Risk

Birth weight and gestational age are the most widely used factors in determining neonatal risk. The neonatal period has the highest infant mortality rate with three times more deaths in the neonatal period than the remaining year of infancy. The highest number occurs the first day, followed by the first week (Rossetti, 1986). Prematurity and low birth weight babies account for about 50 percent of neonatal deaths and the death rate of this group of infants is three times that of normal-term babies for the first two years (Barclay, 1985). They also have a higher incidence of sudden infant death syndrome (SIDS), child abuse, and attachment problems (Glasgow & Overall, 1979).

Prematurity

A premature infant is one who is born before the completion of the 37th week of gestation, regardless of birth weight. Approximately 7 to 10 percent of live births in the United States are premature, with about 1 percent of these considered very premature (less than 30 weeks gestational age) (Harrison, 1983).

Prematurity occurs for a variety of reasons, most of which are unknown. Some known causes include toxemia, abnormalities related to the cervix and uterus, a placenta that implants low in the uterus and covers all or part of the opening to the birth canal (placentae previa), or a placenta that detaches too early (abruptio placentae).

Women who have had one pre-term infant have a higher risk of another premature infant. Those who smoke, are under 18 or over 35, and have multiple births are also at greater risk (Harrison, 1983). Being born too soon means that a neonate has to make the adjustment from a uterine to an extrauterine life with inadequately developed body systems.

Low Birth Weight

Neonates weighing less than five pounds and eight ounces (2500 grams) are considered *low birth weight*. Those weighing below three pounds and five ounces (1500 grams) are *very low birth weight*. The nutritional status of the mother has a direct impact on the size of the neonate. Mothers living in poverty, especially young mothers, are at greater risk of having low birth weight babies. When maternal nutrition is very inadequate there is jeopardy of children having underdeveloped brain cells as well as the complications of low birth weight. Low birth weight babies have a higher incidence of congenital malformations than do term or even preterm neonates (Barclay, 1985).

The relationship between gestational age and weight is an important one. Infants who are born small for their gestational age are particularly at risk. The smallness of the infant indicates fetal growth retardation.

Premature/Low Birth Weight Risks

Although distinct, the problems of neonates born prematurely and those with low birth weight are similar and often additive. They typically involve problems related to temperature control, nutrition, (both coordinating sucking and swallowing and the ability of the digestive system to absorb nutrients), respiration (immature lungs), and excess bilirubin (a by-product of breaking down red blood cells). These conditions are discussed in detail in Chapter 18.

Infants born at risk demonstrate more abnormal variation in their physical development. They are typically delayed in several areas in early infancy. Studies suggest that premature infants demonstrate motor delays through the first year of life. The relationship is less clear at later stages of motor development. Hanson (1984) suggests carefully watching and assessing these at-risk infants over time and working closely with their families. Risk factors are cumulative and interactive. One must evaluate not only the infant, but socioeconomic and familial factors that determine developmental outcomes. Without looking at both biological and environmental factors it is not possible to determine whether intervention will be helpful or inappropriate.

Infants

Infancy is a year of "firsts," the first tooth, the first step, and the first word.

Physical and Motor Development

Physical development progresses rapidly during the first year of life. Infants are expected to double their birth weight in five months and triple it in a year. Height increases by 50 percent. The first tooth emerges at about six months.

Motor development pervades all areas of development during infancy. It enhances social behavior and benefits from and supports cognitive development. It is important to know when different motor behaviors normally occur. If, for example, you did not realize that infants roll over as early as four months, then the infant could be endangered by leaving her alone on a raised surface (not that this is ever a wise idea).

Early motor movements are involuntary and reflexive. Motor development matures eventually to become controlled through voluntary responses on the part of the infant. Voluntary movements are deliberate motor responses that are a result of increased higher brain functioning.

Early motor development involves three interrelated aspects: gaining control of the gross or large muscles of the body, developing the fine or small muscles, and then integrating the developing motor skills with information from the senses.

Gross motor development refers to the maturation of the large muscles of the body such as those in the neck, trunk, arms, and legs. These muscles are necessary for all antigravity postures such as sitting, standing, and walking. They also are necessary to stabilize the body as finer movements are performed.

Fine motor development involves the child's ability to use the small muscles of the arms, hands, and fingers. The major goal is the precise use of the hands for reaching, grasping, and manipulating objects.

Motor skills are often used in conjunction with vision and hearing. In sensory motor integration both sensory and motor components are integrated in the brain to facilitate smooth movement and the ability to learn new skills.

Developmental Guidelines

Several principles govern how skills develop. The pattern of motor and physical development is consistent across cultures and races and most disabilities. The developmental pattern serves as a guide for matching activities to children.

- Motor development is sequential, and the sequences for development of motor behaviors are the same for all infants. Motor sequences are overlapping. Mastery of one skill is not necessary before others can begin, although it does need to

Rooting and Sucking

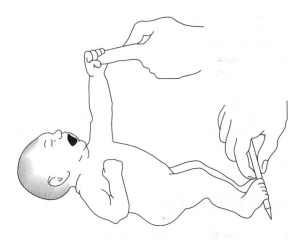

Palmar or Planter Grasps

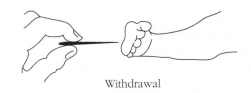

Withdrawal

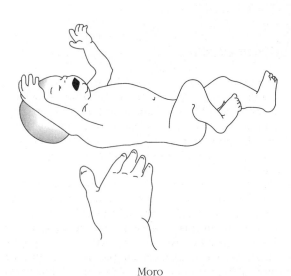

Moro

PROGRESSION OF INFANT MOTOR DEVELOPMENT

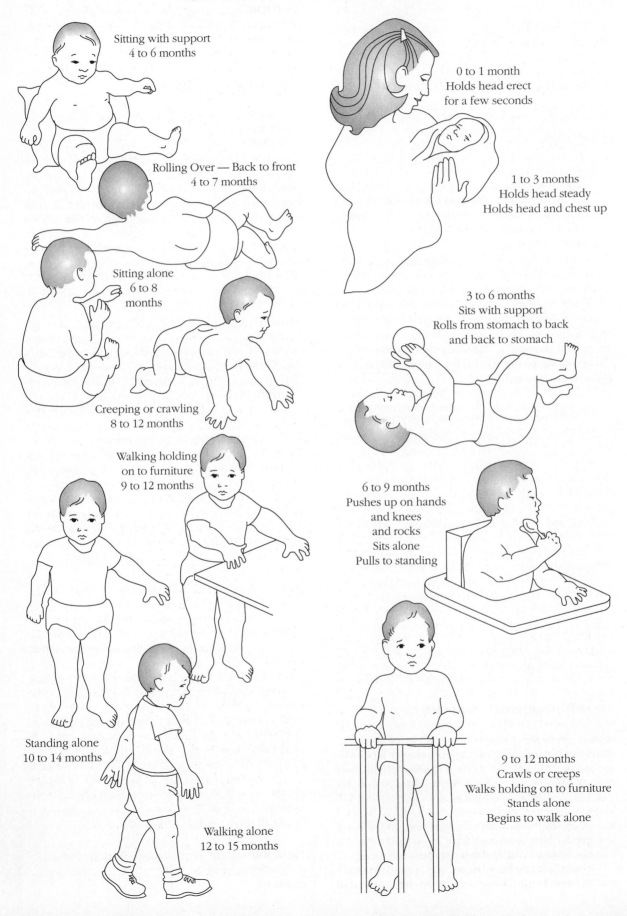

Sitting with support
4 to 6 months

Rolling Over — Back to front
4 to 7 months

Sitting alone
6 to 8
months

Creeping or crawling
8 to 12 months

Walking holding
on to furniture
9 to 12 months

Standing alone
10 to 14 months

Walking alone
12 to 15 months

0 to 1 month
Holds head erect
for a few seconds

1 to 3 months
Holds head steady
Holds head and chest up

3 to 6 months
Sits with support
Rolls from stomach to back
and back to stomach

6 to 9 months
Pushes up on hands
and knees
and rocks
Sits alone
Pulls to standing

9 to 12 months
Crawls or creeps
Walks holding on to furniture
Stands alone
Begins to walk alone

reach a functional level. Children begin to experiment with new motor skills as they are fine-tuning others.

- Children differ in the rate at which they acquire motor skills, but the progression of development is the same. The rate is influenced by both heredity and environment.

- Maturation of the motor system goes from gross activities to fine motor activities. It involves the breaking down of gross movements into finer, coordinated, and voluntary motor responses.

- Motor development, like physical development, proceeds from the head down to the feet (cephalo-caudal) and from the midline or spine outward to the extremities (proximal-distal). Infants gain head control first, then arm coordination, and finally control of their legs. Coordination of motor skills first develops close to the center of the body with control of the neck and the shoulders. Then body parts further away from the midline, such as the arms, develop coordinated movements, and eventually, the fingers.

- The acquisition of complex motor skills builds on simpler motor skills. A young child must acquire the ability to control his head before he acquires the ability to sit.

The development of fine motor skills is dependent on the prerequisite gross motor skills and is enhanced by vision. Though vision is not a prerequisite for fine motor development, visual abilities motivate reaching and grasping and allow children to direct their reaching more accurately.

The infant's early use of the hands is dominated by the grasp reflex, where everything placed in the hand causes the hand to close securely around the object. This reflex is visible until around the fourth month. About this time, the hand remains open and the child begins to attempt to reach voluntarily toward objects. Early reaching or swiping is seen in an arc pattern (Fetters, 1984). More directed reaching comes with better head and shoulder control. Voluntary grasping emerges next. When the grasp reflex is integrated, the child can concentrate on reaching and picking up objects. However, it is not until about the tenth month that the infant can voluntarily release objects with the hand.

The most important early motor skill is head control. The child can lift her chin up by four weeks, lift both her head and shoulders by three months, and can support herself on flexed elbows, chest off the surface, at four months. By six months the infant has the back strength to sit on the floor with arms forward for support, and by seven months can sit unsupported. The child eventually gains strength and equilibrium so that by the ninth month she can begin to securely manipulate items, rotate and pivot, and complete coordinated tasks while in the sitting position.

The infant can bear her weight around the sixth month. She begins bouncing when held at about seven months. By eight months she can pull herself up to standing and begins to take cautious steps while holding on. At the end of the first year the child begins to take steps unsupported.

Sensory Development

The infant's experiences and learning are based on motor and sensory skills. Each sense contributes information to the developing infant. Vision provides the infant with information about what is interesting. Seeing interesting objects and events motivates the infant to reach and locomote. Hearing provides the infant with speech and language information. Touch allows the infant to mold his body to that of his caregiver. Taste is part of mouthing, and the infant receives sensory information about objects by placing them in his mouth. The child develops associations with the sense of smell, particularly about mother and other familiar caregivers.

Visual Development. Though young infants do not have normal visual acuity, they can see (their acuity is about 20/50 at a year), and they prefer different visual stimuli at certain ages. Large, moving objects tend to catch young infants' attention. They focus on the corners or edges of objects, not the middle. At about two months visual skills begin to change. The infant attends for longer periods of time, particularly to the adult face, focusing mostly on the eyes, nose, and mouth. Infants have binocular vision, but they do not have stereopsis until about four months and depth perception (fear of heights) until they can crawl at about six months. They show a preference for novel and interesting events and objects. Initially the infant must move his whole head to track a moving object, but by five months he can track by moving only his eyes.

Hearing Development. The auditory system of the infant is among the best developed bodily functions at birth. As the infant matures she can localize the sound initially by turning her head to search for the sound and then by looking directly at the sound source.

Infants like low frequency sounds, and may show distress over high frequency sounds. They prefer the human voice to mechanical sounds, and by three months show a preference for their mother's voice. Until eight months infants cannot discriminate between individual sounds, rather, all the sounds come into their hearing field together. It is not until around the ninth month that the infant starts to be able to pick out human voices from other background noises. Subsequently, in about two to three months, the infant begins to speak several one-word utterances.

Taste and Smell. Development in taste and smell and preferences are basically the same as they are for neonates.

Tactile Development. Infants are born with sensitive tactile skills. Many early reflexes are stimulated through tactile sensations: rooting, Moro, sucking, and stepping reflexes. Through the combined integration of motor responses and reduction of immediate responses to tactile stimulation, the young child's reaction to touch decreases to mostly voluntary responses.

Tactile stimulation also plays an important role in the emotional development of infants. They crave tactile stimulation from others. They like hugs and affectionate responses. Touching is also important in the development of visual attentiveness and attachment behaviors.

Cognitive Development

Cognitive development is the growth of the child's thinking skills and abilities. It encompasses a complex variety of factors and variables that can affect development. There are many theories about the cognitive development process, the most notable one, which will be described here, was developed by the Swiss psychologist Jean Piaget.

Piaget believes that infants learn by actively engaging the environment. He emphasized that intellectual development, like motor development, occurs in a recognizable and predictable progression and that later development is based on the information the child received during earlier stages of development and interactions (Flavell, 1977; Piaget, 1952, 1970). He believes that the child's intellectual development begins at birth and that intellectual growth is a function of consistent interactions with the environment. The majority of early behaviors of infants are sensory-motor.

Piaget (1970) divided cognitive development into stages of intellectual growth which have learning processes. He described the key components in the learning paradigm as follows.

The young mind funnels all learning into the brain for processing **assimilation**; this is external information that is taken in. This information is treated as "old" knowledge. That is, the child will use the same grasping motion for a cube that he did for a rattle. **Accommodation** occurs when new information necessitates restructuring of what was already learned. If the child cannot grasp the block using the previous pattern, then the child will have to adjust. This is accommodation, an inner reality. One might think of assimilation as a process of generalization and accommodation as a process of discrimination. Assimilation and accommodation are separate and yet complementary processes that result in new levels of **adaptation**. Adaptation involves change.

Organization is the individual's interpretation of reality. It is concerned with systems of relationships among elements. Experience and knowledge are categorized, sorted into meaningful "bits," and complex, ordered relationships between these bits are established. Organization involves a stabilizing process as these bits become tied to one another.

Central to Piaget's theory is understanding that together, assimilation, accommodation, adaptation, and organization exist in a balanced state called **equilibrium**. Equilibrium is dynamic; it requires almost constant recalibration and adjustment. The process of building and maintaining equilibrium is called equilibration. The interaction of assimilation and accommodation that requires more complex organization also produces a new state of equilibrium. As the infant interacts with her environment, reality must be constantly reinterpreted in light of new adaptation. This is how Piaget sees the infant as successfully adapting to a more complex environment. The process of equilibration is discontinuous, as the child consolidates new learning before moving on to greater complexity in learning. This process has developed into a stage-related theory.

According to Piaget, all children progress through the stages or steps of cognitive development in the same order, but not necessarily at the same rates or ages. Intellectual development is hierarchically based, that is, what is acquired at a later stage is dependent upon what was learned in earlier phases of development. Each organized sequence or stage in development is a prerequisite to the next. Qualitative changes in the child's intellectual abilities occur as the child progresses through these developmental stages.

Children develop patterns of behavior or schemes that function as organizing responses to environmental interactions. Schemes are built by the process of assimilation and accommodation acting on reality. A **scheme** is an abstraction, or thought, from an organized behavior pattern that is repeated frequently. For example, when presented with a nipple, infants suck. These organized responses are repeated. The young infant will suck on a pacifier or finger also if placed in the mouth. As the infant adapts, the sucking scheme is modified. The infant abstracts the commonalities in the sucking, and this is the new scheme. As the infant is provided with greater and widening opportunities to interact with different materials and to practice skills already learned, he slowly progresses to higher levels of learning or cognitive activity. Infant schemes are based on sensorimotor actions.

Learning is a result of interaction with the environment. Infants acquire new information by actively experimenting with materials and objects. Active learning is essential for the child to practice and refine previously learned skills and to acquire new schemes. Children need appropriate materials to experiment with that are matched to their stage of sensorimotor learning.

Piaget divided the learning process of the child into four periods. Each period is identified and characterized by the occurrence of specific cognitive processes. The four periods are the sensorimotor period, the preoperational period, concrete operations, and formal operations. Piaget did not emphasize age levels, but rather emphasized the qualitative differences in intellectual abilities that occur in each period. The sensorimotor period and the preoperational period focus on the young child and are described in detail.

Sensorimotor Period

The period from birth to twenty-four months is the sensorimotor period of development. There are six individual stages in the sensorimotor period. Each stage has approximate ages. However, some children acquire skills quickly, and go through the stages rapidly; others develop more slowly, spending more time at each stage. Children do not skip stages. Characteristics of the sensorimotor stages and the individual skills acquired in each stage follow.

Stage 1 (0–1 month)—Reflexes. The first stage is primarily reflexive. The neonate practices and repeats these reflexes during the month. Reflexes such as sucking, rooting, and grasping undergo some assimilation and accommodation as the infant practices these skills.

Stage 2 (1–4 months)—Primary Circular Reactions. The infant's reflexes control the beginning of this stage. She gradually gains coordination and begins to turn her head toward interesting sounds and sights. Primary circular reactions begin; the infant's actions cause a reaction, and the infant does it again. These reactions are primary because they involve the infant's body; thumb sucking is an example. Infants at this stage are curious; they begin to imitate behavior and vocalizations of others. There is initial sensory integration; when the infant *hears* her mother, she also *looks* to see if she is there.

Stage 3 (4–8 to 10 months)—Secondary Circular Reactions. Infants become more goal-directed and repeat motor activities that are interesting over and over. Secondary circular reactions begin as infants purposefully explore objects to see what they do rather than for motor action itself. An infant shakes a toy and it rattles; the infant makes it rattle again and again. Secondary implies that the reaction is elicited from something in the environment other than the infant herself. When a new toy is offered, the infant tries out all her available schemes: the toy is sucked, banged, grasped, dropped, shaken, and so on. If the child becomes intrigued with one of these schemes it is repeated. (Dropping always seems to be most intriguing!) Children at this stage show abbreviated scheme; that is, if a child sees a rattle which he usually shakes in a certain way, he may shake his hand with that motion (Barclay 1985).

Stage 4 (8–10 to 12 months)—Coordination of Secondary Circular Reactions. Now the infant puts together two secondary circular reactions: the infant may combine pulling and dropping. The infant now shows true "means-end" behavior. The infant moves a toy out of the way (means) to get to a favorite doll (end). The infant's imitation skills improve. She can imitate new sounds, and by the end of this stage single words appear.

Signs of object permanence, the knowledge that an object still exists even when it cannot be seen, come into play during this stage. First, infants will search for a toy that is partially hidden. Then they search for objects they see being hidden. Yet if the object is not where they initially look, they stop searching. Their problem-solving skills are not fully developed. Object permanence is important for the acquisition of many later, higher level skills.

Stage 5 (12–18 months)—Tertiary Circular Reactions. This stage will be discussed in the section on toddlers.

Language Development

Language, too, develops through invariant stages that are not culture-bound. Infants cry to express discomfort; this is communication. The early communication processes and experiences form a basis for later communication development. Infants must first be able to produce simple sounds, such as cooing and babbling, before they will be able to coordinate the tongue and mouth to produce more complex sounds such as words. The skills are hierarchical, and children need repeated practice and opportunities to interact with the environment to develop them.

The cooing and laughing stage, which begins at about a month, is among the most pleasurable to adults. Although the pattern is established earlier, the turn-taking "game" that adults and infants play is satisfying to both. One vocalizes, the other actively listens, and then they switch. Toward the end of this period, at about three or four months, infants begin to exercise more control over their environment, and when they have had an overload of stimulation they will avert their gaze.

As the infant is awake more he begins to play with sounds. Vowel sounds are produced first. At first these sounds may appear irregularly, but this stabilizes. As children vocalize more, adults more frequently show them items and name them, especially toys and common household objects. The child may be offered those objects as they are named. Again, the reciprocity begins. At about six months infants will begin to offer objects to adults. This is typically followed by adults pointing out objects to infants and naming them: "Look, that's a cow!" "That's an airplane up in the sky. Can you see it?" The child's gaze is expected to follow. By about a year, the infant reciprocates and points things out to adults. This important prelanguage experience helps the child learn that a gesture or verbal communication can influence her environment. She can get something she wants.

Reduplicative babbling typically begins at about four months, but can begin as early as one month. The infant initially produces vowel sounds in the cooing stage. She next combines consonant and vowel sounds. This combination of sounds results in babbling. The initial consonant sounds used are those most easily produced, including /m/, /d/, /b/, and /g/. These sounds are easily produced by simple oral-motor manipulation, and the child eventually develops the ability to voluntarily produce sound-blend combinations—/ma/, /ba/, /ge/, /ga/, /da/, and so on.

During this early stage, the child can produce only sounds already in the vocal repertoire; new sound imitation is not yet possible. This is the reduplicative babble "ma-ma-ma," "la-la-la," and so on. Infants produce a large variety of sounds when they babble, some of which are part of their native language. Gradually, some sounds drop out, and both the tonal quality and the sounds produced seem more like language. At about eight months "da-da" appears. (This is unrelated to having a father in the household.) It is followed by "ma-ma," again, used without a referent. These sounds are used in reference to adults by about ten months. This more advanced babbling is call lallation. Jargon can begin at this point or later. Jargon is an entire "sentence" that has appropriate intonation patterns so that the intent is clear, yet it is made up of lalling sounds. Children are now fascinated by sound. Somehow, intuitively, adults understand that infants are more comfortable with nouns than pronouns and they alter their speech patterns appropriately: "Bring the cup to Mommy," and "Daddy will do it," as opposed to "I will do it." Typically, by the end of the first year a child has learned a word that actually refers to an object or event. As walking and talking emerge at about the same time, one or the other typically takes precedence, and the other is neglected for a time.

Social and Emotional Development

Social and emotional growth is an important process whose foundation begins early in children's development. The development of appropriate social responsiveness and emotional well-being in infancy lays the foundation for later social interactions and the development of healthy self-concepts and awareness. The development of attachment is the most important early social event to occur in the child's life (Connor, Williamson, & Siepp, 1978).

Attachment. Attachment is the development of a mutual relationship between infant and caregiver unlike bonding, which is a unidirectional relation from the adult to the child. The mother is the person with whom the infant most commonly first attaches. Attachment is not present at birth but develops over time and progresses through stages.

From birth until about five or six months infants enjoy being handled, approached by people, and engaged in social interactions. There is no special responsiveness to the primary caregiver; the young infant enjoys everyone. Although babies smile earlier, social smiling usually appears around the second or third month, increasing the social responsiveness of others. A baby's smile is an important social overture and one few adults can turn down.

Initial social behavior is often based on "turn taking." If the infant emits a sound, the adult often will repeat it—often exaggerated or slowed down. The infant then may take a turn making the sound. It is, however, the skill of the adult to match the infant in both timing and behavior that is crucial. This early turn taking provides the basis for communication and later social behavior.

Infants need adult involvement in play because motor skill limitations make them unable to play independently. Around the fifth month, reaching and trunk support develop, and infants can begin to explore materials independently. The length and quality of exploration increases as motor and cognitive skills develop.

Also around the fifth or sixth month infants show a marked change in social behavior. They develop a strong attachment to the primary caregiver. The infant visually follows the person, fusses when she leaves, and smiles more at that person. The infant can differentiate "mother" and some significant others from strangers. At about eight months strong stranger anxiety may be exhibited. The infant will fuss and cry in response to strangers, especially if they approach her and try to pick her up.

As attachment becomes more secure, the infant develops mobility and begins cautiously to explore the surrounding environment. She does so only when she feels safe and secure, which means having a familiar adult close by. The infant enjoys exploring materials sitting at the parents' feet.

The quantity and quality of early adult-infant interaction is important in the infant's attachment and social development. The quantity of early interaction can affect the security and temperament of the child. Mothers who have securely attached infants frequently cuddle and show affection. However, they do this in response to their infant's cues rather than adult desire. These infants smile more, fuss less, and are more easily comforted when distressed.

The progressive development of the interaction patterns between the infant and adult is the result of many factors: the infant's temperament and communication cues or signals, the adult's interaction style and personality, and the emotional investment in the child's upbringing. The development of social behavior results from the combination and interaction of these factors. A fussy infant with a calm and caring parent can develop into a relatively stable preschooler. A fussy infant with an intrusive, abrupt, and unaffectionate parent may develop into an older child with emotional difficulties and social behavior problems.

Temperament. Each child has a unique personality. Part of an individual's personality is his or her temperament. Thomas, Chess, and Birch (1968) collected data from parent interviews and child observations and identified nine characteristics of temperament. Soderman (1985) described these characteristics and observations in children.

1. Activity level. How active or inactive is the child? Does she get actively involved or sit passively on the sidelines?

2. Rhythmicity. How rhythmical or predictable is the child's internal time clock? Does the child have difficulty settling into a schedule?

3. Approach/withdrawal. What are the child's responses to new objects and people? Does the child confidently approach new situations or does he cling excessively in fear?

4. Adaptability. How does the child handle change? Does the child adapt quickly to changes or new situations or is he resistant?

5. Intensity of reaction. What is the child's response to the behavior of others? Does the child respond quickly and aggressively or does she hold all her emotions inside?

6. Responsiveness threshold. How sensitive is the child? Does the child become overstimulated by noise, touch, light, etc., or is he oblivious to such factors?

7. Mood. What is the balance between positive and negative feelings and behaviors? Does the child express a range of emotions or does he always seem to have bad days?

8. Attention span and resistance. How much time does a child spend at a developmentally appropriate activity? Is the child able to complete tasks or does she flit from activity to activity in a scattered way?

9. Distractibility. How does the child react to extraneous stimuli? Is the child able to block out distracting sights and sounds or does he easily lose concentration?

Thomas, Chess, and Birch (1968) have organized these nine characteristics into three basic temperament categories or types:

1. Easy. Children who were rated as moderate in intensity, adaptability, approachableness, and rhythmicity and had positive moods.

2. Difficult. Children who were slow to adapt, non-rhythmical, had intense reactions, and often had negative moods.

3. Slow-to-warm-up. Children who took a little longer to adapt than easy children and had low activity and intensity levels.

How children act or respond affects the way adults interact with them (Brazelton, 1978). Children who have difficult temperaments and need extra adult understanding may actually receive less positive responses if adults do not understand and know how to work with difficult children. Chess (1983) has suggested that there is a "goodness of fit" between adult style and expectations and what a child is capable of doing. She stresses that the interaction between the adults' expectations and the child's responses is a key factor in assessing the quality of adult-child relationships.

Overall, infants need physical care and protection, caregivers that can read the infant's signals of pleasure and displeasure, and the development of attachment between the infant and a significant other. Caregivers need to respond to the infant's changing developmental needs and signals.

Toddlers

The period from twelve to thirty-six months has many motor and language milestones. Social growth blossoms.

Physical and Motor Development

Physical development slows during these two years, with toddlers gaining only about ten pounds and growing about eight inches. By about thirty months children have their full set of twenty primary teeth.

The toddler has the wide stance of the beginning walker. As the toddler progresses, he obtains a smoother gait and walking becomes automatic. Toddlers add running, jumping, and climbing to their large motor repertoire. By the end of this stage, they can broad jump at least twenty-four inches, run on their toes, avoid obstacles in their path, walk down stairs using alternating feet, and climb jungle gyms and ladders. They can pedal a tricycle and play catch and also enjoy playing with large balls.

Preference for a particular hand may appear in infancy and by three most toddlers have a decided preference. About 90 percent will be right-handed. Toddlers can hold spoons and cup handles and find self-help skills pleasurable. By two, toddlers can not only make marks with a marker or large crayon, they can imitate vertical and horizontal strokes and circular scribbles. Spontaneous scribbling is just beginning.

Sensory Development

Toddlers' sensory organs are developed and well-used. Much play time is spent fine-tuning these skills. The senses are no longer a developmental concern as toddlers have almost the same abilities as adults in hearing, seeing, touch, taste, and smell.

Cognitive Development

A great many changes in the intellectual processes occur during the first three years of life. The child progresses from involuntary motor responses of early infancy to symbolized and abstract forethought—a giant leap for such a short period of time. This progress comes about as the child actively explores the environment. Only with the opportunity to explore, experiment, practice, and master skills will the child grow cognitively and intellectually during the early years of development.

Toddlers learn about themselves and their world by active exploration.

Sensorimotor Period

Stage 5 (12–18 months)—Tertiary Circular Reactions. This "what will happen if" is the wonderful stage of experimentation. The circular (repetitious) quality of the past continues, but it now involves first experimentation, and then variation. Entirely new ways of doing things are learned through *active* experimentation. This is a variation on repetition! Toddlers manipulate and explore materials to solve problems. They repeat actions and modify their behavior to see what happens in tertiary circular reaction. Problem-solving abilities develop, but involve trial and error rather than forethought. Causal thinking is developing. Object permanence development continues. Toddlers will search in new places for hidden objects, but they must still see the object hidden to look for it.

The toddler builds entirely new schemes during this stage. Mobility opens up new arenas for learning. Memory improves, and now children can learn from watching an event. With the advent of language, the toddler can and does ask questions.

Stage 6 (18–24 months)—Beginning of Thought. This is a transitional stage between the sensorimotor and preoperational period. It is the stage of symbolic representation. Toddlers are now able to solve problems in their mind, without going through the actual/external problem-solving process. The toddler can mentally represent objects and actions. She is free of

perception. She can invent new means to get objects, without using trial and error. She can imitate models that are not present; she can wave "bye-bye" even if no one is waving to her. She can begin to imitate gestures she cannot see herself make, such as facial gestures. She can play search activities without needing to see the objects hidden. Pretend play begins!

Preoperational Period

Toddlers move into the preoperational period about age two and stay in this period until they are about seven years old. Although children grow in predictable patterns, the rate of growth of an individual child and between groups of children is often irregular. Not all two-year-olds will automatically move into preoperational thought. Likewise, a child will typically have some thought patterns grounded in the sensorimotor period as she moves into preoperational thinking in others. Their irregularities are important to remember as you work with toddlers and preschool-age children.

The child in the preoperational period is present oriented. Although he might use words like "tomorrow" or "yesterday," he does not understand the concepts they represent. Children this age are beginning to work out causal relationships, but these connections are often imprecise. He can now think in mental representations, but these are more like mind pictures than the abstractions that characterize higher levels of thought. He uses symbols to represent the environment and words take on the form of signifiers of objects and events. The child's play skills now expand into more creative activities. Additional details of the preoperational period are given in the section on the preschool child.

Language Development

Toddlers start with only one or two words in their repertoire, and by eighteen months many will enter the transitional phase of two-word utterances. The young toddler is not able to produce all the sounds and accompanying sound blends when she begins speaking words. The ability to produce particular sounds depends upon oral motor coordination, vocal experience, and verbal modeling.

Around the sixteenth to eighteenth month the child begins to experiment with new sound blends, using sounds heard in the environment, combining them, and producing new words. By the second year, the child uses many new consonants. By the end of age two, the only sounds not mastered are /r/, /s/, /l/, /j/, /v/, and many blend combinations such as /ch/, /sp/. The late toddler has an expressive vocabulary of 300 to about 1,000 words (Furuno, et al., 1987).

As children make the transition into two-word utterances (about eighteen months), the word order is not fixed, so a child may say "little doll" or "doll little." This level is followed by two-word utterances that relate. With the few words that toddlers can put together they can convey an amazing amount of information. Children use these two-word sentences primarily to comment on situations and to make requests. Typically the adult has little problem understanding the meaning of the utterances ("Where Buba?" "Want cookie"). Sensitive adults tend to modify their speech in response to the toddlers' changing language style, using simplified adult speech (Barclay, 1985).

Although the age of the first word is fairly predictable, the acquisition of additional vocabulary is more varied and less useful in describing language maturity. The mean length of utterance (MLU) is probably the most useful measure. MLU measures morphemes or units of meaning. Morphemes are words as well as endings attached to words ("block" is one morpheme, but "blocks" is two). Older toddlers can repeat five-word sentences and use short sentences in spontaneous speech.

Language is not limited to vocal expression. It involves the total concept of communication—communicating ideas, wants, and needs through some mode: physical gestures, facial expressions, grunts, crying, words, and complex phrases. It is important that toddlers' communicative intents are responded to so that they continue to communicate with the world around them. Lack of reinforcement extinguishes behavior. Adult interaction is necessary for the development of the child's language abilities.

Social and Emotional Development

Toddlers begin to be attached to several familiar people. The toddler follows adults and begins to cautiously explore alone at ever greater distances. As they explore and suddenly realize the adult is not in sight they often cry. When children gain object permanence they can be comfortable exploring without the adult in their visual field.

There is little infant to infant interaction. Young toddlers are egocentric and think the world centers around them. They participate mostly in Parten's category of "Unoccupied Behavior." They look around the room and visually follow adults. As they are able to safely venture away from adults their social interaction increases. Beginning about two, toddlers watch other children play (Onlooker Behavior). They may talk with them, but they do not engage in play with them. By two-and-a-half the toddler engages in play by himself. He plays with his materials in his own way (Solitary Play). He is not involved with the play of others.

Soon after Solitary Play appears, Parallel Play is added. Toddlers still play independently, but these activities now occur in close proximity to other children using similar materials. Toddlers watch each other's play activities and imitation of play actions is common.

Toddlers notice other children, but interaction is still minimal. They see other children as objects rather than people. They may resort to pulling, pinching, hitting, and biting with little regret. This aggression comes from a combination of factors, including lack of appropriate language to express anger, inadequate social skills, egotism, and undeveloped self-control. As these skills are mastered, these aggressive behaviors are reduced. Arguments over possession of objects is common and desired objects are grabbed and taken from each other. Closely watching other toddlers play, the others' toys become more interesting than one's own. At two, toddlers do not understand the concept of sharing.

Preschoolers

The preschool years begin at age three and end at five. Actually, this term is gradually becoming obsolete, for most children have some school experience before five, and virtually all children go to kindergarten when they are five as it is part of the public school system.

Physical and Motor Development

Gains in height and weight continue to slow as children grow between two and three inches each year and gain between four and five pounds. Weight gain is primarily due to muscle development. Preschoolers

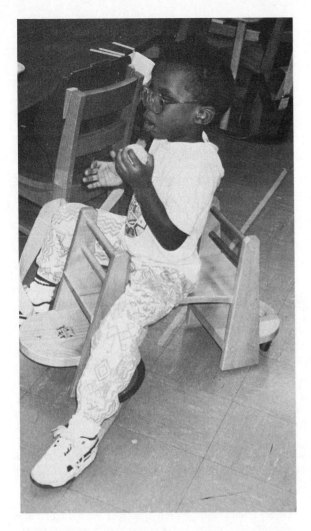

Moving toys such as this allow a child with a visual impairment to explore his surroundings safely.

begin to look more like adults in their body proportions.

Walking is automatic. The stride increases and becomes characteristically personal. Control over starting, stopping, and turning is developed and running is smoother. Children can climb stairs using alternating feet. They can throw, but do not step and transfer weight as the ball is released.

Fine motor skills improve, and preschool children can cut with scissors, paste, paint, draw, color, and by the end of this period, print. Their improved motor skills let them interact more accurately with their environment. As they can play with others, they learn about games with rules.

Cognitive Development

Preoperational Period

During this period from two to seven years thoughts remain egocentric, with symbolic imagery highly individualized. However, this egocentrism is different from the sensorimotor period, which is an egocentrism where the child cannot take a perspective other than his own. They assume that everyone likes what they like. Rules are changeable. They have trouble seeing how steps of a project fit together to make a whole; each step is a separate focus.

Although children in this period have advanced far above the sensorimotor-based learning of the previous period, their thought processes are still immature. Some of the significant changes that occur during this period are detailed below.

Egocentrism. The child is not able to view things from another perspective, and his language reflects this egocentrism. Children seem to believe that others know what they are thinking, and they leave out important pieces of information. On the other hand, they can't put themselves in another's place to figure out the strategies that someone else might use in a game or in problem solving.

Centration. To solve problems successfully children must be able to attend to many attributes of an object at the same time. The preoperational child's centration in thinking does not allow her to think of the attributes simultaneously. She cannot see that the volume in one glass is both lower and wider. She will center on one attribute or the other. Likewise, if the child is given ten wooden blocks, six of which are yellow and four are red, she will probably be able to name the color of the blocks and tell which color there are more of. However, she could probably not answer whether there were more yellow blocks or wooden blocks. She cannot focus on the attributes of both color and wooden.

Irreversibility. The preoperational child is not aware that all logical operations are reversible. The ball of clay made into a pancake can be "reversed" into the original ball of clay. Conservation requires that a children can focus on the transformation from state to state in relation to mass, length, number, volume, and area. Of these, number appears first. A simple number conservation problem might involve asking the child initially if the rows are equal (one-to-one correspondence). If the child does not agree to this, quit. Then one row is lengthened and the child is again asked whether the row has the same number. Until about age six, children will not think the number is the same regardless of the length of the rows.

Conservation of number experiment

```
a.  x  x  x  x  x
    x  x  x  x  x

b.  x  x  x  x  x
    x    x    x    x    x
```

Transductive Reasoning. Logical reasoning requires the child to use both inductive (generalize from specific instances) and deductive (using specifics to generalize) reasoning. This requires the child to recognize the stable commonalities of attributes despite perceptual changes. Higher order relationships are not possible.

Concept Formation. With the emergence of logical thought the child's problem-solving and decision-making ability change dramatically. Children can put events and objects in some useful order. They begin to understand classes and subclasses and the relationship between these.

Children do not conserve during the preschool years. That is, they cannot mentally understand that mass, quantity, and volume are unaffected by the appearance of containers. They tend to center on one aspect of an object, such as height or width, and not see the compensatory relationship between the two.

Language Development

The preschool years show a marked increase in the quantity, quality, and complexity of language. Children start this period with perhaps a 150-word vocabulary and end with about 5,000. They can count to ten or higher, correctly use all parts of speech, and even correct their own errors in learning to pronounce new words. They can name primary and secondary colors and follow three-stage commands. Their speech is understandable and they enjoy telling stories.

Social and Emotional Development

Children can initiate and complete appropriate reciprocal interactions with adults and peers. They begin to form attachments with non-family members and peers. The focus of the attachment building is often centered around play and the accompanying activities.

Play enables children to develop new skills and to practice existing skills. It is also the focus of early social interactions. The quality and type or level of interaction that occurs between children in play activities builds sequentially, increasing with age and maturation. To the previous skills of onlooker behavior, solitary and parallel play, the preschooler adds associative play, that is, children can begin sharing materials as they play together. They begin to show an understanding that materials may belong to others and will ask permission to use them. They also begin to decrease their hoarding of objects, allowing other children to use them. There is much creativity in associative play. Children are now playing together, but the play lacks leadership and often any purpose other than play.

Between four and five cooperative play becomes more common and children become more planful in their play, switching roles with a purpose in dramatic play activities or agreeing to build a castle and deciding who will do what.

We have seen that growth and development follow predictable patterns in all areas. Knowing the underlying principles allows educators to arrange an environment that matches a child's developmental level. With adult support it ensures that challenges and high interest activities will take place. An environment that is too easy not only wastes valuable teaching time, but may produce children who are bored and find outlets for this boredom that are not conducive to learning. Likewise, an environment that is too difficult may frustrate children.

But what happens to these developmental patterns when children have disabilities? The specific knowledge and skills in the area of growth and development required in early childhood special education are very similar to those required for teaching all children. It is important, however, that this understanding include patterns of delayed and atypical development.

Delayed and Atypical Developmental Patterns

Some children do not follow the typical pattern of growth and development. Their development may be delayed or it may follow a different pattern. It may be normal at the present time, but based on physical or environmental conditions, it seems likely that it will not proceed in the normal pattern.

Delayed Development

Delayed development is development that progresses slower than normal but follows the same developmental pattern. That is, the sequence and progression of skill acquisition is the same, the rate of development is slower.

Children may be delayed in only one area, such as language or gross motor development, or in all areas. Most children with mental retardation, for example, share the same developmental patterns as do normal children. However, they develop at an overall slower rate. Their growth is typically delayed as compared to their peers.

Atypical Development

Atypical development is different from typical patterns of development. The child develops or has patterns of behavior that differ from the normal patterns. These differences can be additional behaviors not usually seen or the omission of typical behaviors. For example, children with behavioral and emotional disorders often exhibit additional stereotypic behaviors such as rocking, verbal repetition, and hitting or biting oneself.

Developmental Risk

The term "at risk" or "high risk" does not mean that a child will inevitably be delayed, but rather that the probabilities are higher. Children can be placed in this category because of biological conditions, the family in which they live, or the environment in which they are raised.

Children with established biological problems (for example, Down syndrome) who may be functioning within the normal range at an earlier age are considered "at risk" for later developmental delays because experience has shown that their rate of development is slower.

Families have the potential for increasing or decreasing child risk both in and of itself as well as in interaction with other risk factors. Families that abuse or neglect children put them in a risk category medically, psychologically, and educationally. Children with disabilities are particularly vulnerable to abuse and neglect.

Environments can also cause children to be at risk. Some environments are more conducive than others for developing disabilities or patterns of behavior that make learning difficult. Living in substandard and crowded conditions, poor nutrition, and lack of medical treatment increase the likelihood that children will have developmental problems.

Delayed/Atypical Physical and Motor Development

Infants and toddlers explore their world through motor actions. These actions are seen not only as developmental milestones, but also as sources of knowledge about the world in which they live. The development of antigravity positions such as sitting offers new possibility for play, and independent mobility creates new horizons for exploration. These developments also allow the infant to have some control over his world.

Infants with motor impairments have more difficulty engaging in these experiences. They may be dependent upon adults longer and lack the varied experiences that the independently mobile toddler can enjoy. Not only can the child not go where he wants, he may not be able to reach out to be picked up when he wants to be. Once picked up he may not snuggle in, therefore, adults may not pick him up as frequently. Problems in the motor area are pervasive; they affect not only motor development itself, but cognitive, language and social/emotional development.

Some physical and motor impairments are obvious, the limitations are easily identifiable, and a pattern of intervention is obvious. However, most physical and motor problems are less clear and educators must learn to look for the signs of motor problems. Fetters (1984) groups atypical physical development into three categories that include normal variation, abnormal variation, and pathology. Normal variation in the age of acquisition of motor skills is common among children. Some children may add or complete motor sequences in a slightly different way. Some children develop skills early in one area and use that to compensate for another area. For example, a child who talks early with willing help may request objects and not walk at eighteen months. These are acceptable variations in the acquisition of motor skills. The developmental patterns may be somewhat atypical, but not dysfunctional.

A second category includes children whose motor development is observably abnormal, yet no pathology is identified. Many of these children are motor-delayed, or demonstrate a weakness in muscle strength. There may be no clear reason why they are having motor problems. Fetters (1984) indicates that the apparent motor dysfunction may be transient for many of these children and will disappear without intervention. The problem may also be a sign of more involved motor difficulties that will appear later.

This second category is the most complex and the one in which educators play the largest role. The following signs may be observed: the presence of abnormal reflex patterns, beyond the times they should have been integrated; the absence of expected reflexes such as the automatic reactions (eye blink, protective arm positions); poor coordination; lack of balance or equilibrium; unexplained weaknesses; unusual muscle tone that may include either extremely tight or exceptionally loose muscles. Signs of motor regression in which the child's motor skills appear to be deteriorating should be cause for alarm. Finally, children with prenatal and perinatal histories that put them at risk for later delays should be watched carefully for any signs of possible motor problems.

The third category Fetters (1984) identifies as motor problems associated with known pathology such as cerebral palsy or spina bifida. Children with pathological motor problems are frequently identified early; however, symptoms associated with disabilities vary among individuals.

Chapter 14 gives more detailed information on physical disabilities and planning programs for these children.

Delayed/Atypical Sensory Development

Perception is the part of cognition that gathers information from the various senses about the world outside and then organizes and interprets this information. Children with sensory impairments lack some of this perceptual information. Our knowledge of infant and toddler perception is scant, and what we know about the perceptual development of children with sensory impairments is even less. As children increase in age, so does our knowledge about them. We do not know what these children perceive or what can be done during infancy to substitute one perceptual modality for another. Nor is it clear what the role of motivation is in perception. We do know that young children who have sensory impairments miss some or all early sensory stimulation.

Visual Development

Infants who have total loss of sight due to structural damage to the eyes are usually identified at birth or soon thereafter. Lack of visual responsiveness to the environment is identified by parents and medical personnel. Fraiberg (1977) found that infants with severe visual impairments used their mouth for exploration, not their hands, and that they needed to be encouraged to use their hands. They also showed atypical behavior patterns such as body rocking, head banging, and arm waving. Although infants with visual impairments attained most motor milestones within the normal range, they were typically late in creeping and walking (about seventeen months).

Although infants with severe visual impairments can typically be identified, infants experiencing partial visual impairments are very difficult to identify. Many times these children are not noticed until they reach the public schools. By this time they may have missed out on much valuable perceptual information and had many fewer opportunities to organize and interpret this information. Decreased visual abilities affect a child's ability to receive vital information. A young child depends heavily on vision for later skill development. All other developmental areas are affected by a child's lack of visual skills.

More information on children with visual impairments is included in Chapter 12.

Hearing Development

Hearing loss is difficult to detect in infants unless there is a specific reason to suspect it. Infants often respond inconsistently to auditory stimuli depending upon their state. It is the consistent lack of response that serves as an indication. The young infant who does not startle at loud sounds or the seven-month-old who does not turn to the source of a sound is of concern. Infants with hearing impairments make noises and babble like other babies up until about six months of age. However, in infants with hearing impairments this noisemaking begins to diminish. The infant with a hearing impairment makes only vowel sounds and these are limited in variety and pitch. Her cry may be higher pitched.

Auditory impairments most severely affect the development of speech and language skills. Both speech and language depend heavily upon hearing in the early years of development. Language is acquired through listening, imitation, practice, and correction, if needed. As the vestibular sense is located in the inner ear, children with hearing impairments may also experience difficulties in balance.

Young children with less severe hearing impairments are difficult to identify early. Their overall development is typically within the normal pattern except for speech and language, and even here they may be following typical patterns, just more slowly.

More information on children with hearing impairments is included in Chapter 11.

Tactile Development

Children with atypical tactile development reflect a very diverse group. Some children display extreme forms of tactile defensiveness. For these children, it is unpleasant or even painful to be touched or receive any form of tactile stimulation. Eating can be a difficult task, as the defensiveness produces the bite or gag reflexes and can result in children who refuse to eat.

Children with some physical impairments, such as cerebral palsy, react with primitive reflexes when they are touched. These reflexes interfere with normal motor movements. Atypical tactile development is also part of some emotional impairments. Autistic children, for example, tend to find tactile stimulation from adults or peers very unpleasant, and in fact will try very hard to stay away from situations that may involve touching. Some children exhibit low sensitivity to touch. They do not feel pain. These children frequently have severe emotional problems or profound disabilities. Careful planning and safe environments are necessary to prevent serious injury.

Cognitive and social skills are affected in children experiencing early sensory impairments. Typically, children with sensory impairments have delays in cognitive skills. This delay is not necessarily due to intellectual problems but rather to diminished auditory, visual, or tactile stimulation, resulting in language/concept development problems.

There tends to be less social interaction between children with sensory impairments and other children. They may be excluded from activities by well-meaning adults, and the amount of physical interaction between children and adults may be limited. The combination of these factors can result in social isolation.

Delayed Cognitive Development

Delayed cognitive development is intellectual growth that does not follow the expected rate. Children with cognitive delays follow the same sequence of cognitive skill acquisition, but the rate of learning is slower. These children will rarely acquire higher level abstract thinking skills.

The type and severity of a child's cognitive delay varies greatly, based on what is interfering with the development of cognitive skills. Children with cognitive delays are individually different. Each child's development is influenced by a multitude of factors, including the individuality of each child. However, children with cognitive delays can be grouped according to the cause or associated factors involved in the delay:

Brain or neurological problems. These include damage to the brain, malformation of the brain, and absence of certain parts of the brain, as well as other neurological problems difficult to identify.

Medical syndromes. Some medical diagnoses have established risk for cognitive delays. These include Down syndrome, certain genetic abnormalities, and metabolic disorders such as PKU.

Unknown causes. These children usually demonstrate mild to moderate developmental delay and have no known etiology. Many of these children come from extremely impoverished environments with a lack of adequate early stimulation (Peterson, 1987).

It is not only the cause of the delay that affects the level of cognitive impairment, but the extent to which the child is able to interact with the surrounding environment, and the type and quality of that environment (Connor, Williamson, & Siepp, 1978). Young children exhibiting delayed development are diagnosed as developmentally delayed, older children as mentally retarded.

Children with mental retardation have a slower rate of learning, poor memory skills, problems in abstract thinking, poor generalization skills, and lack of learning strategies (schemes). They may have a short attention span, and some are highly distractible. Language skills are typically delayed. Articulation disorders are also more apparent. There are delays in the acquisition of basic, daily living skills. Children with more severe delays may lack social interaction skills and independent work behaviors.

Additional information on children with mental retardation appears in Chapter 16.

Atypical Language Development

The child's ability to communicate becomes a critical factor in development and functioning. Individuals transmit and receive information, needs, wants, knowledge, and emotions. Disorders in the area of communication therefore can affect cognitive, social, and emotional areas of development.

Many variables affect a child's speech and language development. Some appropriate questions include:

Are the child's sensory systems intact?

Is the child capable of processing information, understanding what was seen and heard, and remembering the important facts?

Does the environment provide adequate stimulation?

Does the environment reinforce the child and stimulate further interactions (Peterson, 1987)?

Children with sensory impairments that interfere with their ability to receive or process relevant information will have language and/or speech delays. Children with information processing problems may have difficulty developing a good language base. Processing problems include how the child perceives the information received; how he stores the information; and how he uses the information, that is, association, accommodation, and discrimination. Children with poor memory skills may not remember object label names, thus decreasing vocabulary.

The inability to communicate ideas and thoughts can be very frustrating to children. This is especially true for children with intact language systems but defective speech output. If children know what they want to say but are unable to express their message, extreme frustration and stress can result. Children may develop behavioral problems or withdraw from interactions.

The environment plays an important role in language development. An environment lacking appropriate materials and reinforcement may delay language development. The quantity and quality of social interaction children receive also contributes to language development. Environments that fail to respond to children's communicative attempts will result in children that do not attempt to initiate communication. Children left unattended for long periods of time have a tendency to be poor communicators. The failure of the environment to respond appropriately to children's interactions eventually results in children that are unmotivated to interact with others.

See Chapter 10 for additional information on communication disorders.

Atypical Social and Emotional Development

Some infants fail to develop appropriate attachment patterns with adults. They do not respond as expected to social stimuli. They may be irritable, not easily comforted, dislike affection, and may be withdrawn. They are frequently described as "difficult" or "slow-to-warm-up" children. These children may have difficulties in their signaling systems that interrupt the early attachment process. They may cry continuously, have a piercing scream, arch their bodies to physical touch, and show no response to soothing interaction from adults. They may have poor eye contact and imply no interest in social interaction.

The demonstration of one or more of these behaviors can cause parents or caregivers to think that the infant does not like them. They may also find it unpleasant to be around the infant because of these behaviors. The result is the failure of the adult and the child to develop a close attachment.

The detection and identification of atypical social and/or emotional development is difficult with young children. Diagnosis includes a subjective judgment of what is appropriate or inappropriate (Peterson, 1987). Cultural and child-rearing differences must be included in the evaluation.

Peterson lists seven factors to help distinguish between normal behavioral patterns and atypical behavior development. These include:

1. the situations in which the behaviors are exhibited;

2. the developmental ages at which the behavior appears and continues to be manifested;

3. the intensity of the behavior, either excessive or deficient;

4. the duration or persistence of the behavior;

5. the extent to which others can alter the behavior;

6. how much the behavior interferes with progress in other developmental areas; and

7. how much the behavior interferes with the lives of others (Peterson, 1987, p. 226).

In atypical development, behaviors are exhibited more frequently, persistently, and at ages that are no longer appropriate, typically past the stages at which these behaviors are expected.

The first signs of atypical emotional development are identified as children try to master basic developmental skills or social responses. When an infant cannot be comforted, when a toddler does not talk, or continues to show extreme anxiety around strangers, or when a young child does not demonstrate any responsiveness to adults, these responses indicate a danger signal in social emotional development.

Most young children have some undesirable behaviors. When these are extreme they are labeled behavior problems. Behavior problems are typically divided into two general categories: conduct disorders and personality disorders. Children with conduct disorders exhibit behaviors characteristic of aggressiveness, such as destructiveness, temper tantrums, inappropriate attention-seeking behavior, distractibility, impulsivity, irritability, hyperactivity, and disruptiveness. Children exhibiting personality disorders demonstrate behaviors such as withdrawal, anxiety, crying, depression, unresponsiveness, shyness, timidity, and isolation (Kauffman, 1981).

Behavior problems are typically learned behaviors that affect children's ability to participate in activities with adults and peers. Seriously disturbed behaviors characteristically involve pervasive changes in behavior and mood states. They typically involve problems in the development of interpersonal relationships and the establishment of meaningful interactive social behaviors. Disturbed behavior will likely interfere with development and learning. The behavior is exhibited across many situations and settings. Behaviors that are harmful to the child or others are included in these patterns or clusters of behaviors (Peterson, 1987).

Failure to develop appropriate attachment patterns will likely lead to children who are withdrawn and/or shun social interaction. They may exhibit cranky and whiny behaviors. Social responsiveness may be limited. The combination of these behaviors typically results in further isolation, as both adults and peers tend to ignore and/or dislike these children and refrain from interaction.

See Chapter 15 for additional information on emotional and behavioral disorders.

Summary

Growth and development follow predictable patterns. Infants come into the world dependent, but with sensory systems that are prepared to take in information and with enough communication skills to survive. Understanding patterns of development allows us to identify patterns that are delayed or atypical. It also allows us to plan activities and experiences that will stimulate growth and development in infants and young children. This understanding allows us to develop assessment tools that can ascertain the rate at which children are developing relative to the "average" child.

References and Bibliography

Barclay, L. (1985). *Infant development.* Fort Worth, TX: Holt, Rinehart and Winston.

Batshaw, M. L., & Perret, Y. M. (1986). *Children with handicaps: A medical primer.* (2nd ed.) Baltimore, MD: Paul H. Brookes.

Brazelton, T. B. (1978). "Introduction." In A. Sameroff (Ed.), *Organization and stability of newborn behavior: A commentary on the Brazelton Neonatal Behavior Assessment Scale* (pp. 1–3). Chicago: University of Chicago Press for the Society for Research in Child Development, *43,* 5–6.

Bricker, W. A., Levin, J. A., & Macke, P. R. (1984). Early language development. In M. J. Hanson (Ed.), *Atypical infant development* (pp. 281–312). Baltimore: University Park Press.

Caplan, F. (1978). *The first twelve months of life.* New York: Bantam Books.

Caplan, F., & Caplan, T. (1980). *The second twelve months of life.* New York: Bantam Books.

Chess, S. (1983). Basic adaptations required for successful parenting. In V. Sasserath (Ed.), *Minimizing high-risk parenting* (pp. 5–11). Skillman, NJ: Johnson & Johnson.

Connor, F. P., Williamson, G. G., & Siepp, J. M. (1978). *Program Guide for Infants and Toddlers with Neuromotor and Other Developmental Disabilities.* New York: Teachers College Press.

Crain, L. S. (1984). Prenatal causes of atypical development. In M. J. Hanson (Ed.), *Atypical infant development* (pp. 27–56). Baltimore: University Park Press.

Essa, E. (1983). *A practical guide to solving preschool behavior problems.* Albany, NY: Delmar Publishers, Inc.

Fetters, L. (1984). Motor Development. In M. J. Hanson (Ed.), *Atypical infant development* (pp. 313–358). Baltimore: University Park Press.

Flavell, J. H. (1977). *Cognitive development.* Englewood Cliffs, NJ: Prentice-Hall.

Fraiberg, S. (1977). *Insights from the blind.* New York: Basic Books.

Furuno, S., O'Reilly, K., Inatsuka, T., Hosaka, C., Allman, T., & Ziesloft, B. (1979). *Hawaii early learning profile.* Palo Alto, CA: VORT Corporation.

Furuno, S., O'Reilly, K., Inatsuka, T., Hosaka, C., Allman, T., & Ziesloft-Falbey, B. (1987). *HELP Chart: Cognitive and language.* Palo Alto, CA: VORT Corporation.

Garwood, S. G., & Fewell, R. R. (Eds.), (1983). *Educating handicapped infants: Issues in development and intervention.* Rockville, MD: Aspen Systems Corporation.

Glasgow, L. A., & Overall, J. C. (1979). The fetus and neonatal infant: Infections. In V. C. Vaughan, R. J. McKay, & R. E. Behrman (Eds.), *Nelson textbook of pediatrics* (11th ed.) (pp. 468–496). Philadelphia: W. B. Saunders.

Greenspan, S., & Greenspan, N. (1985). *First feelings: Milestones in the emotional development of your baby and child.* New York: Viking.

Hanson, M. J. (1984). Parent-infant interaction. In M. J. Hanson (Ed.), *Atypical infant development* (pp. 179–206). Baltimore: University Park Press.

Harrison, H. (1983). *The premature baby book: A parents' guide to coping and caring in the first years.* New York: St. Martin's Press.

Honig, A. S., & Lally, J. R. (1981). *Infant caregiving: A design for training.* Syracuse, NY: Syracuse University Press.

Kauffman, J. L. (1981). *Characteristics of children's behavior disorders* (2nd ed.). Columbus, OH: Charles E. Merrill.

Klass, C. S. (1987). Childrearing interactions within developmental home- or center-based early education. *Young Children, 42*(3), 9–13, 67–70.

Lamb, M. E., & Campos, J. J. (1982). *Development in infancy.* New York: Random House, Inc.

Lipsitt, L. P., & Kaye, H. (1964). Conditioned sucking in the human newborn. *Psychonomic Science, 1,* 29-30.

Lockman, J. J. (1983). *Infant perception and cognition.* In S. G. Garwood & R. R. Fewell (Eds.), *Educating handicapped infants: Issues in development and intervention* (pp. 117–164). Rockville, MD: Aspen Publications.

Menolascino F. J., & Eyde, D. R. (1979). Biophysical bases of autism. *Behavioral disorders. 5,* 41–47.

Miller, E., Cradock-Watson, J. E., & Pollock, M. (1982). Consequences of confirmed maternal rubella at successive stages of pregnancy. *The Lancet, 2,* 781–784.

Peterson, N. L. (1987). *Early intervention for handicapped and at-risk children: An introduction to early childhood special education.* Denver, CO: Love Publishing Co.

Piaget, J. (1970). Piaget's theory. In P. H. Mussen (Ed.), *Carmichael's manual of child psychology:* Vol 1 (3rd ed.). New York: Wiley.

Piaget, J. (1952). *The origins of intelligence in children.* New York: Basic Books.

Rosenblith, J. F., & Sims-Knight, J. E. (1985). *In the beginning: Development in the first two years of life.* Monterey, CA: Brooks/Cole Publishing Company.

Rossetti, L. M. (1986). *High risk infants: Identification, assessment, and intervention.* London: Taylor & Francis.

Schneider, J. W., & Chasnoff, I. J. (1987). Cocaine abuse during pregnancy: Its effects on infant motor development—A clinical perspective. *Top Acute Care Trauma Rehabilitation. 2*(1), 59–69.

Soderman, A. (1985). Dealing with difficult young children: Strategies of teachers and parents. *Young Children 40*(5), 15–20.

Thomas, A., Chess, S., & Birch, C. (1968). *Temperament and behavior disorders in children.* New York: New York University Press.

U.S. Department of Health and Human Services, National Center for Health Statistics (1984). *Health United States—1984.* (DHHS Pub. No. PHS 85-1232). Washington DC: U.S. Government Printing Office.

Warren, K. (1985). Alcohol-related birth defects: Current trends in research. *Alcohol World: Health and research, 10*(1), 4–5.

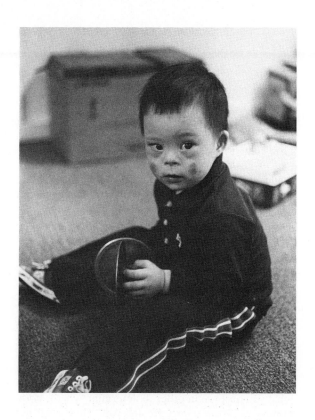

Chapter 5

Early Identification, Diagnosis, and Assessment

Young children are delightful, unpredictable, and difficult to make conclusive statements about. The child who "acts out" daily is angelic when you ask someone to come and observe; the child who is withdrawn cooperates beautifully during the observer's visit. Parents face similar problems when having their children examined. A child who shuts his eyes during an eye examination makes it difficult to determine accurately what he sees. If another cries when earphones are put on, it is difficult to determine what she hears. The difficulty in getting representative behavior from children on a scheduled basis makes the role of early childhood special education professionals important. These specialists can provide baseline information about whether the behavior observed is typical of the child, or is a reaction to the observation, the setting, or is perhaps caused by a physical condition such as coming down with a cold.

Until recently we lacked means to identify and diagnose children with mild to moderate disabilities at very young ages, nor did we see a great need to do so. Now there is a variety of diagnostic instruments that are designed to gain information about young children. In general, instruments are shortcuts for observation, and they have a variety of functions and formats. You will be expected to be familiar with some of them, although you will only have to use the results. Evaluation procedures can be further divided into formal and informal. Formal evaluation procedures use tests that have been standardized and are usually given by professionals such as psychologists or educational diagnosticians. They are often given in a "battery" that usually includes intelligence tests, criterion-based tests, and/or other specialized instruments. Informal evaluation is typically done by teachers as they systematically find out whether children know the names of colors, shapes, numbers, and letters. Sometimes informal evaluation is more global.

The scenario often goes something like this:

Natasha is one of the youngest children when she enters your class. She is not as advanced as the other children, but that is to be expected. As the weeks pass, you note that she doesn't seem to catch on as quickly as the other children, and she seems small for her age. Informal conversation with her family reveals that she was a preemie weighing in at only two pounds. You vaguely inquire if her parents have any concerns. They don't. They did when she was younger, but when she started to walk they knew that she had finally "caught up." Her behavior is still a puzzle to you, and your concern increases. You are now convinced that there is something different that you should be doing with Natasha, but you aren't sure what or whom to ask.

This is the first step in case finding. The teacher's role in case finding is usually an accidental one based on an informal evaluation. The next step is to talk with the parents to determine if they too see a problem and want follow-up testing. If so, children are then either given a screening to see whether or not a full battery of testing is necessary or that step may be bypassed because of the information you provide.

Case finding and screening are related, yet usually refer to different processes and use different tools. Screening is a much more organized, goal-directed process. The underlying assumptions behind screening are that children can be divided into two categories, those that are "at risk" and those that are "not at risk" for whatever it is that you are screening for. For example, at birth infants are screened for Phenylketurnia (PKU) by testing the level of phenylalanine in their blood. (PKU is a form of mental retardation that is preventable if a specific diet is followed, beginning within the first three or four weeks of life.)

We have all been screened at one time or another. Children are frequently screened when they enter kindergarten. Scheduled hearing, visual, and often dental screenings are done throughout the school years. Screening instruments vary. Some require highly trained professionals; others use trained volunteers. In general, the objective is to identify all the children who are at risk. In the process some children who are not at risk are mistakenly identified.

If the screening determines that a child is at risk, further diagnosis is designed to confirm or refute the existence of a problem. (This should sort out the children who were mistakenly identified.) Sometimes it is more a matter of degree rather than a "yes" or "no" answer. For example, a child with 20/30 vision may not profit from wearing glasses; a child with 20/100 probably would. The question really becomes, is the problem serious enough to require remediation? Diagnosis also is designed to clarify the nature of the problem. (That is, is a hearing loss the

result of fluid in the ear canal or nerve damage or both?)

The Teacher's Role

Your role varies depending on whether you are part of the case-finding diagnosis process or whether children come to you already diagnosed. You may be the first professional who sees young children for an extended period of time, therefore you may be the one to suspect that a child has a disability. The flow chart characterizes the decision-making process in assessment. When you are part of the case-finding process you begin at the top of the figure and participate in the decision making at all stages. When a child comes to you with a diagnosis, you are the teacher in the setting of choice (that is, you are at the bottom of the figure in "setting").

All of us have some expectations about what normal, or average behavior is. When you first suspect a problem in a child, you may have only a vague feeling of uneasiness. You may feel that something about this child is outside your category of "normal." Trust yourself. Watch the child more closely, noting down what you observe in order to determine what is bothering you. These notes are for you. They need not look beautiful and they might include questions your observations generate as well as the notes themselves. Your notes may resemble these:

Suzy often spills her milk (more often than other children?). She cannot (will not?) put simple puzzles together. She does not sit for an entire group time (bored? over her head?).

Does Suzy have a learning disability? Maybe she does, and maybe she doesn't, but it is unlikely that you will have a confirmation either way while she is still in your class. The formal diagnosis is a long process. You can contribute valuable information that will shorten this process.

In many cases it really does not matter whether or not Suzy is labeled learning disabled; you do not need a label to individualize programming. What does matter is how you program for her as a child who is displaying a particular need. Your observations can be translated into needs for which you can program. As long as two years may elapse between your officially expressed concern about a problem and medical or diagnostic confirmation. Those are two very important years. If a child appears to have a problem, the best time to start programming for it is now.

You now have two missions: (1) to gain enough information about the child to talk with the parents and (2) to learn how to program for the child until the diagnostic process is completed. You need to answer the following questions for yourself, "What do I need to know?" After that, "How will I use this information?" Then, "What is the most effective way to gather this information?" Your first goal probably is to

DECISION MAKING IN THE ASSESSMENT PROCESS

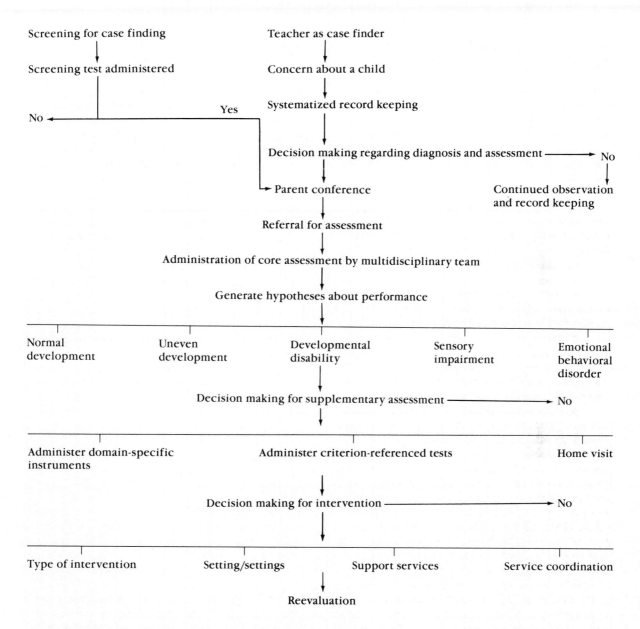

Screening for case finding

Screening test administered

No ←

Yes

Teacher as case finder

Concern about a child

Systematized record keeping

Decision making regarding diagnosis and assessment ———→ No

Parent conference

Continued observation and record keeping

Referral for assessment

Administration of core assessment by multidisciplinary team

Generate hypotheses about performance

Normal development   Uneven development   Developmental disability   Sensory impairment   Emotional behavioral disorder

Decision making for supplementary assessment ———→ No

Administer domain-specific instruments   Administer criterion-referenced tests   Home visit

Decision making for intervention ———→ No

Type of intervention   Setting/settings   Support services   Service coordination

Reevaluation

Adapted from McCune, Kalmanson, Fleck, Glazewski, & Sillari (1990).

gather the information that you need to feel confident in your own "hunch" and to talk with the parents. If you have a system of record keeping in place already, you may rely on it; if not, some suggestions for informal teacher assessments follow. Some simply consider this process record keeping. It is, but it is also an important part of the initial screening process.

Record Keeping

There are many different systems of record keeping. Older children have test scores and report cards.

Younger children provide more of a challenge. Especially at the beginning of the year, a combination of record keeping methods are most effective.

Anecdotal Records

Probably the most common form of voluntary record keeping is anecdotal notes. You might have a card for each child, a notebook with a page for each child, or a folder for each child. In a class of twenty-five, some teachers write notes about five children each day. There are some problems in this, in that significant

RECORDER _____

UNIT/THEME _____

TIME _____

DATE _____

RECORDS

CHILD'S NAME	AREA	DAY'S ACTIVITIES								
		ART	MANIPULATIVE	WATER/SAND TABLE	BOOKS	BLOCKS	DRAMATIC PLAY	LOCKERS	WANDERING	BATHROOM

This form is most useful at the beginning of the year. First survey your room and name each different area. Then add to the form those areas beyond the double line, that is, other places children might be. For example, in addition to being in the bathroom, wandering around, or in the locker area, children might be at the nurses' office or in therapy. If these events happen frequently, add them to the chart; if they are unusual, they are not worth including. Indicate the theme and place a brief reminder of the day's activity below each designated area. Use the form by placing a check in the box beside the child's name to indicate where each child is in the room. Use the form as frequently as you are free to do so. It helps to have them on a clipboard at various places around the room.

events often happen to children on days when you aren't writing about them, and one tends to write about interesting events as opposed to developmentally important information. If your order is random, on Friday you may have to write notes on five children about which you have nothing to write, and what you really want to do is go home. Frequently going home wins. It is useful to note on whom you have the fewest notes and try to figure out why. These may, in fact, be the children that you need the most information on.

Checklists

I like to use checklists. The first one I use looks only at where children are in the room, and can be filled out in less than a minute during free play. Often I will use it two or three times during free play. It also helps me learn the children's names. If there is a paraprofessional or a volunteer in the classroom, I encourage them to fill out the forms as well. Whoever is the recorder initials that line and fills in the time and date. I first divide the room up into areas. Then I write a brief description of what is in each area on a given day. (If the dramatic play area is a hospital, I would note that.) Then I write the first names of the children in alphabetical order on the side. Play with your version of the form for a while, then duplicate what you use all the time so you only have to make additions for daily changes. I have included a copy of the form I used. You would need to individualize it for your purposes.

In two weeks you have been able to fill out this form ten times. What can you do with the data you've generated? First you need to put it all on one form. Some of the implications will become apparent. Some children play in many areas, some in only one or two. You might identify small groups of children who play together. If you haven't noticed them yet, children who appear in the last three columns (lockers, wandering, and bathroom) frequently are of concern. These are children who are walking around without purpose and not engaging in activities. They probably need your help. At this stage you are asking more questions than generating answers. If you become interested in how long children are staying at activities, try to use the form at short intervals for a few days, and look at children who are in the same area of the room on at least two consecutive observations as well as those who are never in the same area twice. This allows you to generate some information about interest span. These data coupled with anecdotal notes begin to give you a foundation for looking at the children in your classroom in a more systematic way. You can do all this record keeping and teach at the same time. You may now decide that you need more specific data on children's skills.

Checklists can help focus attention on specific skills. Some you can more appropriately fill in after school is over. Examples and rationale for some of the ones I have found useful have been included.

I often add the children's age (in years and months) to a general skills checklist, as children in a given class have a range of twelve to eighteen months in age. For four-year-olds this is a fourth of their lifetime. It is my reminder that children are appropriately different. I try to add information to these charts a few times a week. Children that are inconsistent or need work in an area come to my attention. I must first decide if they need work in only one area or if the need is more general. I tend to observe these children more closely.

I find transitions a good time to collect information about children's skills. For example, it is easy as children move from a group situation to free play to dismiss them in a way that helps keep track of their learning. With planning, you can be sure that all children are successful, and yet have accurate records. If you are concerned with number and letter recognition, consider using the following record-keeping form. I include color and spatial concepts also. To do this effectively, you can use a calendar for number identification ("Put your finger on the 12 and then you may go to the block area") or recognition ("Tell me the name of this number [point to a number on the calendar] and you may go to free play"). If your calendar is magnetic or is designed in a way that something will stick to it (tape on the back of the object works), ask the children to put an object in different spatial configurations relative to a specific number on the calendar. ("Put the circle above the number 21.") This exercise allows you to tap both spatial and numerical concepts. You can modify these forms to gather information that is important to you. With an alphabet available, you can pose similar tasks. As children learn the capital letters, introduce the lower case ones.

The advantage of checklists is that they are quick and efficient to use. They can be used on your schedule, and they include all of the children. The disadvantage is that you have to prepare them ahead of time and it may take a few attempts for you to develop forms that fit your needs.

Work Samples

Work samples are another form of record keeping that is particularly applicable to young children. Examples of children's work can be art, writing, or anything that can be put in a folder. To be useful, the collection of samples needs to begin the first week of school so that you can see growth, and also so the children learn that putting some of their products in the folder is part of the system; both yours and theirs. Talk to the children about the folder and give them the opportunity to add items. Establish early that there are to be short- and long-term items for the folder. Long-term items would include children's first drawings and paintings of the year, as well as work that illustrates particular skills (or lack of them). Short-term items might be stories that are then replaced by other stories. Use the file with the

RECORDER _____   DATE _____

GENERAL SKILLS CHECKLIST

CHILD'S NAME	AGE YR./MOS.	LANGUAGE		APPROACH + OR –	SOCIAL		MOTOR	
		RECEPTIVE	EXPRESSIVE		ASSERTIVENESS INTERACTION CHILD	ASSERTIVENESS INTERACTION ADULT	SMALL	LARGE

Key

1 Above average/date
2 Average/date
3 Seems inconsistent/date
4 Needs work/date

The General Skills Checklist is just that. First decide what skills need to be monitored. Because language skills and motor skills have such widely available norms, I always include those. Then my focus is typically on the social skills that relate to inclusion. I am concerned about whether children approach each other and whether this approach is positive or negative. Another concern is that children have enough assertiveness to hold their own with peers. Often children with disabilities have learned this skill with adults, but are not as confident with peers. Become familiar with the norms in areas with which you are concerned before beginning to use the chart. At the beginning of the year include the children's ages by both year and months. Be aware of the ages of the children, which will vary by 12 months and perhaps by as many as 18. This span causes a significant difference in skill development.

RECORDER _____

TIME _____

DATE _____

QUALITY OF PLAY

CHILD'S NAME	UNOCCUPIED	ONLOOKER	SOLITARY	PARALLEL	ASSOCIATIVE	COOPERATIVE

Key: Write initials of playmates in space. For cooperative play, note the leader.

One goal of inclusive education is to have children play together. It is often useful to know the level at which children are playing to suggest playmates who are more likely to be compatible, and to see whether children can take leadership roles. In addition, the child's level of play is developmental and it is helpful in transition planning. Use a form such as this to make these observations more systematic. Unoccupied: Child is not participating in an activity or watching other children. Onlooker: Although not participating, the child is actively watching other children. Solitary: The child is playing alone with materials that are different from other children's. Parallel: The child is playing alone with materials that are the same as other children near by. Associative: Children are playing together but the play is not goal oriented and there is no leader. Cooperative: Children are playing together and the play is goal oriented and there is a leader.

CHILD'S NAME _____

GROUP TIME TRANSITIONS

NUMBERS

	Code	Date	Code	Date
0				
1				
2				
3				
4				
5				
6				
7				
8				
9				
10				
11				
12				
13				
14				
15				
16				
17				
18				
19				
20				

LETTER CONCEPTS/CAPITALS

	Code	Date	Code	Date	Code	Date
A						
B						
C						
D						
E						
F						
G						
H						
I						
J						
K						
L						
M						
N						
O						
P						
Q						
R						
S						
T						
U						
V						
W						
X						
Y						
Z						

LETTER CONCEPTS/LOWER CASE

	Code	Date	Code	Date	Code	Date
a						
b						
c						
d						
e						
f						
g						
h						
i						
j						
k						
l						
m						
n						
o						
p						
q						
r						
s						
t						
u						
v						
w						
x						
y						
z						

COUNTS OBJECTS

	Code	Date	Code	Date
1				
2				
3				
4				
5				
6				
7				
8				
9				
10				

SPATIAL CONCEPT

	Code	Date	Code	Date
ABOVE				
BELOW				
BETWEEN				
INSIDE				
OUTSIDE				
BEHIND				
UNDER				
AT THE TOP				
AT THE BOTTOM				
ACROSS FROM				
IN FRONT OF				
UP				
DOWN				
BESIDE				
BENEATH				
NEAREST				
RIGHT				
LEFT				

Key:
a - Recognition (point to the)
b - Identification (what is this letter called?)
+ - Correct
0 - Incorrect
⊕ - Correct with help
NA - Not attempted

This record keeping form is different from the previous ones. There is one form for each child rather than one form for the total group, and it is designed to be used over time to note individual skill development. First decide on the skills on which you must have specific information for each child. Then put these into a chart form and make one up for each child. Match the level of difficulty of the task to your expectation of the child's skill. For example, ask one child to point to the number 5 and another, "What is this number?" as you point to the 5. The latter task is more difficult. Use the key to code the child's responses.

GROUP TIME TRANSITIONS

CHILD'S NAME _____

COLORS:	RESPONSE	DATE	RESPONSE	DATE
RED				
BLUE				
YELLOW				
GREEN				
BROWN				
BLACK				
WHITE				

SHAPES:	RESPONSE	DATE	RESPONSE	DATE
△				
○				
▭				
▢				
⬭				

SIZE:	RESPONSE	DATE	RESPONSE	DATE
SMALL				
SMALLEST				
LITTLE				
LITTLEST				
MEDIUM				
BIG				
BIGGER				
LARGE				
LARGER				
LARGEST				

MATERIALS: THREE SIZES OF THE SHAPES

Key:
a - Recognition (point to the)
b - Identification (what is this letter called?)
+ - Correct
0 - Incorrect
⊕ - Correct with help
NA - Not attempted

BODY PARTS:	RESPONSE	DATE	RESPONSE	DATE
ANKLE				
ARMS				
BACK				
CHEEKS				
CHEST				
CHIN				
EARS				
ELBOW				
EYES				
EYEBROWS				
EYELASHES				
FEET				
FINGERNAILS				
FINGERS				
HAIR				
HEAD				
HIPS				
JAW				
KNEE				
MOUTH				
NECK				
NOSE				
LEGS				
LIPS				
TEETH				
TONGUE				
TOES				
THUMB				
WAIST				
WRIST				

	RESPONSE	DATE	RESPONSE	DATE
ONE-STEP DIRECTIONS				
TWO-STEP DIRECTIONS				

This variation on a chart that can be used to assess skills during group time transitions concentrates on shapes, colors, sizes, body parts, and following directions. Use these models to make charts to keep the information needed. Using naturally occurring transitions to note skills is more appropriate with young children than sitting them down and "testing" them on the same information.

children. Let them enjoy their personal growth by looking at work they have done earlier and comparing it with what they can do now. Talk about how much they have learned.

In addition to work that is the outcome of various activities, it is important to include work that helps you focus on specific areas. I like to make up a short story with some specific details in it at the beginning of the year and then have the children draw a picture about the story. (This is not an art project; it is an assessment project.) I then tell the same story about four months later and again at the end of the year. I look for personal growth and also at the level of detail in the drawing across the group. This story has details, familiar animals and modes of transportation, and a very simple plot. You might tell a story something like this:

One day a dog and a cat met. The dog said, "I like to run, I'll race you home." "Okay," said the cat, "One, two, three, go!" The dog raced past the cat. The cat saw a boy on a tricycle. "Can you go fast?" "Yes," said the boy, "Can you catch that dog?" "Sure." Off they went, up and down hills and across bridges. Finally, they caught up to the dog. The dog was mad. If the cat can play tricks, so can I. He met a horse and asked if the horse could go as fast as the bicycle. The horse said "yes." The dog jumped on his back, and off they went. They went through the woods, jumped a stream, and finally caught up with the boy on the bicycle. The boy on the bike hit a rock and the cat fell off. The dog raced by on the horse. The cat shook himself off. The dog said to the horse, "I'm glad we don't have to run as fast now." Just then they saw the cat go flying past on an airplane. "Oh, no!" said the dog. And when he got home he said to the cat, "Let's race again tomorrow." "Okay," said his friend the cat.

Feel free to use this story, modify it, or shorten it to make it more appropriate for younger children or add more details for older children. By having the children draw pictures about the same story over time, it is easier to see change. It is important that the story be original, as some children might know a published story and others not.

Other areas about which you may begin to gather some systematized data are fine and gross motor skills. The easiest way to do this is to set up an obstacle course that each child has to complete. Develop the items for the course from a criterion-based assessment such as the Hawaii Early Learning Profile (Furuno et al., 1987) or the Learning Accomplishment Profile (LeMay et al., 1978). For three-year-olds, an obstacle course might look like this:

1. Broad jump (mark off two feet) to the next line.
2. Push or pull a wagon to the next line (ten-foot distance).

3. Walk (ten feet) on a four-inch wide taped line.
4. Catch a ball thrown from five feet away.
5. Have the child put the ball down, take two steps, and kick it.
6. Finally, the child can gallop back to the starting line.

These are all skills that three-year-olds are expected to be able to do. You have made it fun and interesting as well as informative for you.

You now have some of the informal data you need to confirm or disconfirm your concerns about a particular child, as well as to monitor the growth of all the children in your classroom.

You use this information in two ways. One is to look at the growth of a particular child over time, the other is to compare children to a "norm" or what you consider average for the age level you are teaching. Next look at the birth dates of the children in the class. If there is a child you are concerned about, find other children who are within a month or two of her age and compare her work samples and observational results with theirs. The intention is not to make judgments, but to see the range of behaviors and to determine whether you feel a particular child is outside of this range. If the record keeping confirms rather than rejects your concern, the next step is to talk with the child's parents.

Parent Conferences

In a conference with the parents share both your concerns and the record-keeping information that shows the differences you found. Explain how you have reached your conclusions and why you believe the child will benefit from a formal diagnosis. You need the *information* a diagnosis provides (not the *label*) to meet this child's needs in your program planning. If the parents do not accept your knowledge and concern, this process may take several conferences and some structured observation. Some parents may never agree.

If the parents agree to diagnostic testing, the exact procedure depends on the age of the child, whether or not the child is in a public or private school, and the nature of the problem itself.

If the child is enrolled in a public school or is old enough (according to state and federal law), the parents can have the child evaluated at public expense. You would then refer the child to the school psychologist, educational diagnostician, the department of social services, or other organization functioning in this role.

If the parents choose private evaluation, your role would consist of telling them about the type of specialists that you feel would be the most helpful; sharing your written observations with the specialists of their choice (this may be on a referral form); allowing that person to observe in your classroom, if possible; and, with the parents' permission, obtaining a copy of the testing results and incorporating the child's strengths and needs into your programming. When the test results are obtained, use them to refine the plan you will have already put into action.

Diagnosis and Assessment

Early diagnosis is the key to progress for a child with a disability. The National Collaborative Infant Project (reported in Neisworth and Bagnato, 1987) found that most parents suspected a problem by six months of age, but the time lag between suspicion and medical confirmation for severe problems was six months, and for more subtle dysfunctions it was up to forty-five months. Beyond that the time lag between confirmation and early intervention often approached a year. Without early diagnosis, a child may experience years of failure, and the original disability may be compounded by a poor self-concept. Early diagnosis and good programming can allow a child with a disability to experience success instead of failure.

Many different approaches and techniques are used in assessment. All, however, are contingent upon the examiner's developing rapport with the child and her family. The assessment measures chosen are likely to reflect the theoretical perspective of the examiner or program. In general, how a person believes children develop and learn influences what they want to know about a child, the techniques they use to get this information, and how they interpret the results (Benner, 1992).

Assessment provides us with baseline data and the capacity for prediction. If one wishes to monitor change, the first thing that has to be established is change from *what*. The initial assessment provides this starting point. The second purpose of assessment is prediction. We not only want to know what the child is doing now, and at what rate he is learning, we also want to be able to predict how he will be learning when he enters public school or at some other future point in time. Prediction assumes continuity, representativeness, and a lack of external intervening factors (Cicchetti & Wagner, 1990). The assumption is that if the assessment is in fact representative of the child's behavior, then the child will continue to develop at a certain rate. If, however, an external force (such as early intervention, child abuse, or injury) impacts the child, then the principle of continuity would not hold and the assessment would not accurately predict behavior.

Regardless of the philosophy of the examiner or team, Benner (1992) notes seven strands to the assessment process. She sees these as a continuum and focuses on describing the end points of the continuum to provide understanding of the range.

1. *Formal to Informal Assessments*. Formal assessments use standardized tools and structured, systematized observation. Informal assessments are very similar to the record keeping and case finding described previously.

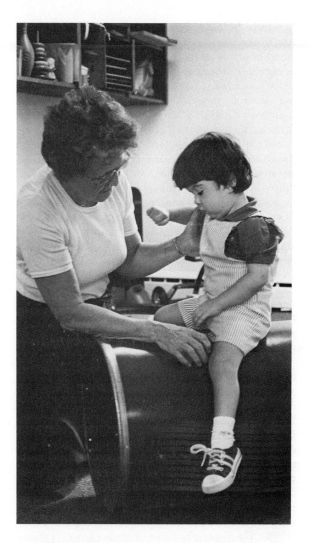

Assessment requires ongoing evaluation of skills.

2. *Norm-Referenced to Criterion-Referenced Assessments*. Measures that are based on comparing children within age groups with each other are referred to as norm-referenced. The question asked is "What does the 'average' child do at this age?" These criteria have limited usefulness in program planning, but provide useful information for placement and transition. For example, if a child with Down syndrome is being placed in a kindergarten classroom, a norm-referenced test might help you focus on the particular challenges that child will face. Criterion-referenced tests give information about the specific skills a child can perform within a developmental range. For example, you might learn that a particular child can jump from the bottom step with both feet together, but cannot jump forward a distance of two feet keeping his feet together. This type of information has application to program planning and gives useful information in knowing skill progression. One must be careful, however, to remember that the curriculum should be based on more than improving test scores.

3. *Standardized to Adaptive-to-Disability Assessment*. Standardized tests have specific procedures

that must be followed precisely for the administration of the test to be valid. These may be as subtle as whether or not you drop your voice at the end of a list of numbers. If the person giving the assessment varies these procedures, the test is no longer a valid measure. Some of the standardized procedures put children with disabilities at a disadvantage and may not measure their potential. Sattler (1988) recommends a technique known as "testing of limits" to explore the child's abilities. This is used only after the entire test has been given using the standardized procedures. The examiner can return to failed items and give additional time and/or provide additional help or cues. The examiner might probe for additional information, or ask the child to explain how he went about solving a particular problem. The examiner might change the modality from a written response to an oral one. The procedure allows you to gain some insight into the child's potential but does not produce a valid score for the test. Some tests are designed to be altered for use with children with disabilities and include information on adapting them to various situations (Benner, 1992).

4. *Direct to Indirect Assessment.* Direct assessment involves the examiner having face-to-face contact with the child. This typically involves both observing the child and using standardized assessment measures. Indirect assessment relies on others to provide information, primarily the parents or the teacher. If sources differ, it is important to explore the discrepancies. In many cases a combination of these techniques is used with young children. Observation and assessment of the child is supplemented by information gained from parents and teachers to develop an overall picture of the child's performance.

5. *Naturalistic to Clinical Observations.* Observation of children during their play interactions is naturalistic observation. Observers can look at the entire setting or focus in on specific types of behavior that are of interest (prosocial behavior) or concern (aggression). Although it is often interesting to know what is happening for the entire class time (and videotaping has taken the tedium out of this task), one often gets more material than is useful, and it takes time to quantify and categorize the information.

It is often more useful to decide what it is you specifically want to know and how to gather that information most effectively. If, for example, temper tantrums are a problem in your classroom, it would be more useful to focus on them than on the entire setting. You might use "event sampling" to note the time of day, physical setup of the classroom, people present, and the frequency and duration of tantrums. The goal would be to find the commonalities in these observations and begin to make changes.

Other methods of focused observation include time sampling, where you record what is going on in the classroom at specific time intervals, such as every five minutes. This method is useful for behaviors that occur frequently, such as child-to-child contact or teacher-child contact. (The *records* form given earlier in this chapter is a good form for time sampling

techniques.) Category sampling involves recording a number of different behaviors in a particular category (social initiations such as smiling, touching, verbal requests, and so on). These observations are all naturalistic. However, they are time-consuming, and the behaviors that are of interest to the observer may not occur.

Most clinical observations are done in settings where the examiner can control the environment. Typically the observation is set up to optimize the occurrence of the behavior that the professional wants to see. A combination of information from both the controlled environment and the naturalistic setting leads to the most complete and accurate diagnosis for a child.

6. *Product-Oriented to Process-Oriented Assessment.* A product-oriented approach to assessment produces scores or other final products much like a report card with grades. These test scores are usually easily understood, quickly communicated, and useful in transition planning. Process-oriented assessment is concerned with the child's ability to learn the task as well as the success or lack of success in completing the task. For children who are severely involved, this may be the only choice for assessment.

7. *Unidisciplinary to Team Approaches.* A unidisciplinary team is made up of professionals in a single field. The unidisciplinary approach is appropriate when children have a single specific presenting problem. However, when children have a variety of problems or when other services are needed, the unidisciplinary approach is less useful in handling the whole child. For example, if a child has an articulation problem, a speech and language therapist may be the only professional needed. If, however, the articulation problem is a result of a hearing loss, or if the articulation problem causes the child to be excessively withdrawn in social situations, then additional professionals may be needed.

There are many different team models, which are characterized in the next section of this book. In general, the professionals on the team are determined by the needs of the child. The way these professionals interact is based on differing philosophical frameworks. The multidisciplinary model attempts to bring together professionals from different disciplines to work as a team. Each discipline communicates specific findings, goals, and recommendations to each other, but team members primarily work independently rather than as a coordinated group.

In the interdisciplinary model there is a higher level of interaction. In this model all team members do their individual diagnosis, but they then meet to share information and observations. They may make suggestions to each other about additional information that might be helpful as well as intervention strategies for a particular child.

The transdisciplinary model has the highest level of cooperation and interaction. In this model, all the team members participate in the diagnosis at the same time. In the process each professional learns about the other fields represented, to the point where a single professional can implement the interventions and diagnoses of other fields.

Assessment Teams

It is unlikely that any one person has the ability or expertise to diagnose and assess all children with disabilities. Depending upon the specific disability or configuration of disabilities, some professionals will have more input than others. You may join an existing team of professionals, or you may be part of the initial team, especially if you were part of the diagnostic process. It is important to realize at this point that children and disabilities do not divide themselves nicely according to professional lines. There is frequently much overlap.

Any time more than one professional sees a child, one could consider it a team approach. However, the amount of collaboration varies greatly among teams. In some cases members of a team are not aware of who else is on their team, and they appear to lack a service coordinator. Consequently, parents often end up trying to coordinate and to figure out *whom* to consult about *what* problem *when*.

The role you as the teacher will play on the team is largely determined by how the team defines itself. Your role is extremely important. You have the opportunity to talk both formally and informally with families on a regular basis. Few other team members will have that contact.

As a multidisciplinary assessment is necessary, professionals choose to operate in one of three ways: as a multidisciplinary team, an interdisciplinary team, or as a transdisciplinary team.

Multidisciplinary Teams. The multidisciplinary team sorts the child's problem into component professional parts, the parents typically take the child to the various required professionals for diagnosis and intervention, and the professionals then funnel their input back to each other, the parents (and hopefully the service coordinator), who must sort it out. A strength for this model is that people from different disciplines are communicating and parents have more input into choice of team members (for example, they can choose the physical therapist or occupational therapist they like best). However, separate disciplinary assessments, reports, and goals written by each discipline may contribute to fragmented services and lack of coordination of services to children and their families (McGonigel & Garland, 1988).

It is not unusual for the professionals to present conflicting diagnostic and intervention strategies. As team members may not all get together, it is often left up to parents to decide what to do or whom to believe or what further information they need. Despite the obvious drawbacks, with strong, knowledgeable parents this type of team has the potential of providing good programming for children. In some cases, this is the only approach available to families, especially those that live in rural areas. For professionals this is the least time-consuming type of team. No time needs to be allocated for interacting with groups, and, for many privately employed professionals, that is an important consideration.

Interdisciplinary Teams. Traditionally, interdisciplinary teams have specified members as a core team and add additional members as needed. They meet on a regular basis (for example, once a month), and the designated service coordinator decides whether or not the families whose services she is coordinating need to be invited. With very young children who are severely involved the service coordinator is frequently a developmental or pediatric nurse. As children get older the service coordinator may be the early childhood special educator.

It is possible for such a team to function in an interdisciplinary fashion with some specialists who do not actually meet with the group but send in written reports. Drawbacks to this method include problems in communication and interaction when team members do not have comprehensive understanding of the expertise of other team members. Scheduling common, agreeable meeting times is a frequent problem.

Transdisciplinary Teams. Transdisciplinary teams have the highest level of coordination and integration. For example, a developmental psychologist may work with a child in the areas of occupational and speech therapy in addition to the type of therapy traditionally associated with developmental psychology. This does not mean that the developmental psychologist has become an instant speech therapist, but rather that the skills necessary to intervene with this particular child can be transmitted to the psychologist so that the child and family need interact with only one individual and yet receive three types of therapy in an integrated approach.

One major concept in the transdisciplinary approach is that of "role release." "Role release" is a conscious, carefully planned process that allows transdisciplinary team members to exchange information, knowledge, and skills across disciplines and to work as an integrated team (McGonigel & Garland, 1988, p. 14). Once the child is assessed, the team develops an integrated service plan and decides on one team member to carry out the plan with the family. To work effectively, the transdisciplinary team needs a full-team make-up and enough trust and respect for others to be able to use the "role-release" concept.

All members of the transdisciplinary assessment team, including the parents, provide information regarding the child's strengths and needs. Ideally this process helps each discipline see the interrelationships among developmental areas. What emerges is an individualized program based on the child as a whole. Because you are one of the professionals on the team, it is likely that this program can be implemented in your classroom following your regular routines.

The potential for more communication and a more accurate diagnosis exists because parents and professionals can question each other during the process of diagnosis and assessment rather than on the basis of written reports or recollections based on information gained earlier. As you might guess, this highly desirable approach is also a costly one. Considerable time needs to be allocated for sharing, planning, coordinating, and training team members. Coordinating schedules so that all are available at the same time almost necessitates an ongoing regular commitment. It also necessitates a high level of respect and trust among members of the team. However, more and more agencies are seeing the worth of this model. From a parent's perspective, one possible drawback is that once they choose the team they lose the ability to choose individuals, so that if there is one member of the team they do not like or respect they must adapt.

Being Part of the Team

As part of the assessment team you will often find yourself in the position of needing to get or give information about a particular child. Your comments and questions are particularly important as you have seen the child in a broader range of situations than most others, except the parents. Here are several points to remember when you take part in the assessment process.

Without meaning to, other professionals sometimes use terms which people without their particular background do not understand. Stop and ask them to define words that you don't understand. (Remember that there are probably terms from your background and training that they do not understand either.)

If you disagree with something that other professionals have written or said, ask them to talk a little more about it and ask why they said that particular thing. Often if you pair something that you like about what they did or said with something you are concerned about, they will be able to listen better. For example: "I'm very pleased with the progress Victor's been making since he began physical therapy, but I don't understand why it is so important for him to sit this particular way during group time. Can you tell me why it is so important?"

Remember that you know the child well. You certainly see the child more often than the specialist you are talking with, and you have important information to share. It is helpful to be specific when possible and to base your comments on direct observations of the child and your written records. For example:

- When you know that a child can perform some skills which specialists report he did not perform during the assessment or testing period, share that information with them. They may still want the child to perform the particular skill for them as well, but your input is helpful.

- Whenever you notice dramatic changes in a child, it is important to report them to the child's parents and other professionals on the team. For example, let the child's parents (or physician) know if you notice extreme changes in a child's behavior after a change in medicine. (Also, ask that others inform you if a child's medication is changed.)

- Keep other team members informed when you've observed that a child is able to master goals written on his IFSP or IEP. This will let others know that it may be time to write some new goals and suggest some new activities.

A child's needs are best met when all individuals working with the child, including parents, teachers, doctors, therapists, and child care providers are well informed.

Diagnostic and Assessment Instruments

Diagnostic and assessment tools are used to identify the developmental skills, strengths, and needs of the child that will have an impact on learning. Information gained through these assessment instruments should be supplemented by personal contacts with family members who can describe what the child does at home and indicate whether the child's behavior during the assessment was typical or atypical.

Many issues surround the assessment of young children with disabilities. One is that assessment

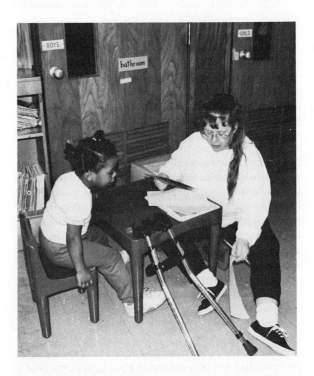

Direct assessment requires the examiner to work one-on-one with the child, but a quiet corner of the classroom is all that is necessary.

tools are usually standardized on nondisabled children, so the validity of using those same tests on children with disabilities is questioned. These tests assume that children have had equal opportunities to learn, which may not be accurate. Traditional assessments may also result in little information on functional skills. If all you are given are numerical data for test results, this is not useful for programming. Particular issues also occur with each disability. For instance, a child with severe motor problems may not be able to use his hands well in play. Since many items assessing development involve play, the child would not be fairly assessed. Assessments need to be given and used heeding these cautions.

The following pages list a variety of assessment instruments. The list is not exhaustive, but rather is intended to give you information about the types of assessment tools that are available in different categories.

Screening Instruments

The first group of measures are those that are designed to screen or categorize large groups of children into those who are at risk for developmental delay and those who are not.

The Denver Developmental Screening Test—Revised (DDST-R). Frankenburg, W., Dodds, P., & Fandal, A. (1975). Denver, CO: Ladoca Project and Publishing Foundation.

The DDST is used extensively in the medical community as a screening measure for children two weeks to six years of age. There is some question about its use with children from minority groups. It also fails to find children with disabilities and refers many children who are not experiencing problems. "Overall, the instrument proved to be less effective as a predictor of school dysfunction than was parent report" (Benner, 1992, p. 214). It is included here because, unfortunately, it is still used.

The Miller Assessment for Preschoolers (MAP). Miller, L., (1988). San Antonio, TX: Psychological Corporation.

The MAP was developed as a screening measure to identify children with mild and moderate disabilities and to look at children's strengths and needs relative to programming. It takes approximately thirty minutes to give. It is designed for preschool children and has five indices: the foundation index, the coordination index, the verbal index, the nonverbal index, and the complex tasks index.

Screening measures decide which children receive further testing and which ones don't. This is a crucial decision, and there are two types of errors that can occur during the screening process: false positives and false negatives. When screening results indicate children need additional testing, when in reality they do not, the results are considered false positives. This creates overidentification, concern and stress in families and children, and a workload problem for professionals. False negatives occur when children who are at risk pass through the screening and are not targeted for follow-up. This results in underidentification and hence lack of early intervention for children who could profit from it. Parents and professionals assume that the at-risk child is developing normally. The child is not likely to be monitored, and irrevocable damage may occur before the child's condition is diagnosed.

Norm-Referenced Tests

The next group of measures often forms the core of the diagnostic assessment. These measures are given to get an overall picture of the child and to determine whether further, more specialized assessment is necessary. Because of lack of high quality screening measures for young children, these measures may also serve that purpose. These measures are standardized and require a trained examiner.

Battelle Developmental Inventory (BDI). Newborg, J., Stock, J., Wnek, L., Guidubaldi, J., & Svinicki, J. (1984). Allen, TX: DLM Teaching Resources.

The battery includes a screening test that takes about twenty minutes. The total battery takes about two hours and covers five domains: personal-social, adaptive, motor, communication, and cognition. Assesses children from birth through eight years.

Bayley Scales of Infant Development. Bayley, N. (1969). New York: Psychological Corporation.

This scale includes assessments of mental, psychomotor, and social domains for children two to thirty months. It is often used as a screening tool, as children who receive low scores on the mental development area are usually at risk or identified as having developmental disabilities.

The Wechsler Preschool and Primary Scale of Intelligence—Revised (WPPSI -R). Wechsler, D. (1989). New York: Psychological Corporation.

The WPPSI -R is used for children three years to seven years and contains both performance and verbal scales with six subscales in each. It is an individually administered test of intelligence.

Criterion-Referenced Tests

Criterion-referenced measures are typically most useful in program planning and in measuring smaller increments of development. These are often used after screening and diagnosis has been completed.

Brigance Diagnostic Inventory of Early Development (Revised Edition). Brigance, A. (1991). North Billerica, MA: Curriculum Associates, Inc.

This scale is for children birth to age seven. It is based on a developmental task-analytic model and is very useful in program planning for a child with disabilities. It covers the following developmental domains: social and emotional development, pre-speech behaviors, fine motor skills, preambulatory motor skills, general knowledge and comprehension, written language, and math.

Learning Accomplishment Profile—Diagnostic Edition (LAP-D). LeMay, D., Griffin, P., & Sanford, A. (1978). Winston-Salem, NC: Kaplan School Supply Corporation.

The LAP-D is a developmental task-analysis instrument for children birth through six years. It contains five domains: fine motor, gross motor, language, cognition, and self-help. It is useful in program planning.

The Hawaii Early Learning Profile (HELP), Furuno, S., O'Reilly, K., Hosaka, C., Inatsuku, T., & Zeisloft-Falbey, B. (1979). Palo Alto, CA: VORT Corporation.

The HELP is a checklist divided into six developmental areas: cognitive (includes receptive language), expressive language, gross motor, fine motor, social-emotional, and self-help for children birth to three years. It is designed to be used as a practical tool for identifying needs, program planning, and monitoring individual progress.

In addition to the HELP, there is HELP at Home, a comprehensive set of developmental activities designed to emphasize a specific skill or behavior. It provides guidance to parents and professionals to support the child's development.

Help for Special Preschoolers Assessment Checklist: Ages 3–6. The Santa Cruz County Office of Education. (1987). Palo Alto, CA: VORT Corporation.

The Assessment Checklist is a broad-based, criterion-referenced assessment. Like the HELP, it is designed for early identification and program planning. It focuses on five skill areas: self-help, motor development, communication, social skills, and learning/cognition. The Help for Special Preschoolers: Ages 3 to 6 Activities Binder provides supporting developmental activities.

Specialized Measures

Other assessments are designed for particular populations that are difficult to test, such as the severely involved. Other assessment instruments look at particular areas of development or interaction patterns.

Carolina Record of Individual Behavior (CRIB). Simeonsson, R., Huntington, G., Short, G., & Ware, W. (1982). Chapel Hill, NC: Carolina Institute for Research on Early Education of the Handicapped, Frank Porter Graham Child Development Center, University of North Carolina at Chapel Hill.

The CRIB is designed to be used with children with severe disabilities who function below three

years of age. It is based on the Bayley and Brazelton scales. It is useful in organizing the environment to appropriately stimulate severely involved children.

The Vineland Adaptive Behavior Scales (Revised). Sparrow, S., Balla, D., & Cicchetti, D. (1985). Circle Pines, MN: American Guidance Service.

Several different versions of this scale are available; the Survey Edition is probably most appropriate in the area of early intervention. Its focus is on personal and social competence in children and adults. It assesses four domains: communication, daily living skills, socialization, and motor skills. It can be used from birth to age eighteen. This measure is useful for severely involved children as adults can answer questions about the child's abilities.

Parent/Caregiver Involvement Scale (P/CIS). Farran, D., Kasari, C., Comfort, M., & Jay, S. (1986). Available from Dale C. Farran, Center for the Development of Early Education, Kamehameha Schools/Bishop Estate, Kapalama Heights, Honolulu, HI.

The instrument measures the adult's involvement and the quality of that involvement in play interactions with the child from two months to five years. (Training manual and videotape also available.)

Multicultural Issues in Assessment

The impact of a child's culture cannot be overlooked in the assessment process. The devaluation of culture seems to have its greatest impact on young children (Benner, 1992). It becomes imperative for these children that a broad framework be used in their assessment process. Moving from a narrow concept of standard English language proficiency to communication competence changes views of children's abilities. Language barriers can be formidable. Even when interpreters are available, test results may be questionable, and the tests may not provide a picture of the child's abilities in the school setting. Viewing the child within the context of the family and environment, even at an informal level, may lead to insights that make placement and programming decisions more relevant and meaningful for all.

Summary

The United States is preoccupied with testing. We use tests to determine who is "gifted," "average," and "mentally retarded." Tests often decide who gets into college, who can become teachers, and who can deliver the mail. The validity of these tests depends to a great extent on whether or not the appropriate measures were selected, whether they were administered according to the guidelines, whether the scoring is accurate, and the skill of those interpreting the results. The testing, screening, and assessing process is crucial for young children with disabilities, because it has an enormous impact on their developmental progress.

References and Bibliography

Bagnato, S. J., & Neisworth, J. T. (1991). *Assessment for early intervention: Best practices for professionals.* New York: The Guilford Press.

Bayley, N. (1969). *Bayley scales of infant development.* New York: Psychological Corporation.

Benner, S. (1992). *Assessing young children with special needs: An ecological perspective.* White Plains, NY: Longman.

Brigance, A. (1991). *Brigance diagnostic inventory of early development* (rev. ed.). North Billerica, MA: Curriculum Associates, Inc.

Cicchetti, D., & Wagner, S. (1990). Alternative assessment strategies for the evaluation of infants and toddlers: An organizational perspective. In S. Meisels & J. Shonkoff (Eds.), *Handbook of early childhood intervention* (pp. 246–277). Cambridge, MA: Cambridge University Press.

Frankenberg, W. (1986). *Revised Denver prescreening developmental questionnaire.* Denver: Denver Developmental Materials.

Furuno, S., O'Reilly, K., Hosaka, C., Inatsuku, T., & Zeisloft-Falbey, B. (1987). *The Hawaii early learning profile.* Palo Alto, CA: VORT Corporation.

Gibbs, E. D., & Teti, D. M. (1990). *Interdisciplinary assessment of infants: A guide for early intervention professionals.* Baltimore, MD: Paul H. Brookes.

Johnson, B. H., McGonigel, M. J., & Kaufmann, R. K. (Eds.) (March, 1989). *Guidelines and recommended practices for the individualized family service plan.* National Early Childhood Technical Assistance System and Association for the Care of Children's Health. Washington, DC: Office of Special Education Programs.

LeMay, D., Griffin, P., & Sanford, A. (1978). *Learning accomplishment profile—diagnostic edition.* Lewisville, NC: Kaplan School Supply Corporation.

Linder, T. W. (1990). *Transdisciplinary play-based assessment: A functional approach to working with young children.* Baltimore, MD: Paul H. Brookes.

McCune, L., Kalmanson, B., Fleck, M., Glazewski, B., & Sillari, J. (1990). An interdisciplinary model of infant assessment. In S. Meisels & J. Shonkoff (Eds.), *Handbook of early childhood intervention* (pp. 219–245). Cambridge, MA: Cambridge University Press.

McGonigel, M. J., & Garland, C. W. (1988). The individualized family service plan and the early intervention team: Team & family issues & recommended practices. *Infants and Young Children: An Interdisciplinary Journal of Special Care Pediatrics, 1*(1), 10–21.

Miller, L. (1988). *Miller assessment for preschoolers manual* (rev. ed.). San Antonio, TX: Psychological Corporation.

Mott, S., Fewell, R., Lewis, M., Meisels, S., Shonkoff, J., & Simeonsson, R. (1986). Methods for assessing child and family outcomes in early childhood special education programs: Some views from the field. *Topics in Early Childhood Special Education, 6*(2), 1–15.

Neisworth, J., & Bagnato, S. J. (1987). *The young exceptional child: Early development and education.* New York: Macmillan Publishing Company.

Newborg, J., Stock, J., Wnek, L., Guidubaldi, J., & Svinicki, J. (1984). *Battelle developmental inventory.* Allen, TX: DLM Teaching Resources.

Parks, S. (Ed.), with Furuno, S., O'Reilly, K., Hosaka, C., Inatsuku, T., & Zeisloft-Falbey, B. (1988). *HELP . . . at Home: Activity sheets for parents.* Palo Alto, CA: VORT Corporation.

Powell, M. L. (1981). *Assessment and management of developmental changes and problems in children* (2nd ed.). St. Louis, MO: C. V. Mosby Company.

Rossetti, L. M. (1990). *Infant-toddler assessment.* San Diego, CA: Singular Publishing Group, Inc.

Santa Cruz County Office of Education. (1987). *Help for special preschoolers assessment checklist: Ages 3–6.* Palo Alto, CA: VORT Corporation.

Santa Cruz County Office of Education. (1987). *Help for special preschoolers assessment checklist: Ages 3–6. Activities Binder.* Palo Alto, CA: VORT Corporation.

Sattler, J. (1988). *Assessment of children* (3rd ed.). San Diego, CA: Sattler.

Simeonsson, R., Huntington, G., Short, G., & Ware, W. (1982). The Carolina record of individual behavior: Characteristics of handicapped infants and children. *Topics in Early Childhood Special Education, 2*(2), 43–55.

Sparrow, S., Balla, D., & Cicchetti, D. (1985). *Vineland Adaptive Behavior Scales.* Circle Pines, MN: American Guidance Service.

Wechsler, D. (1989). *Wechsler Preschool and Primary Scale of Intelligence—Revised.* New York: Psychological Corporation.

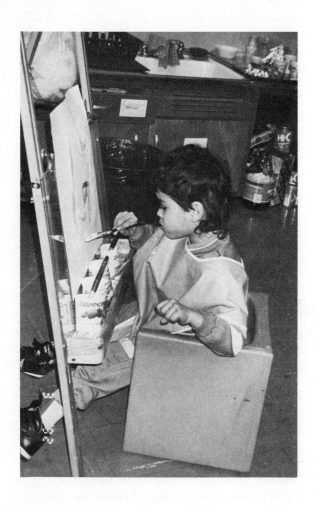

Chapter 6

Individualized Programming

When a child in your class has been identified as having a disability, certain procedures and requirements must be followed. We discussed the law in Chapter 3. In this chapter we will discuss some of its practical implications for individualizing programming. Although the intent of the law in many ways is the same, there are differences for programming for children from three and above and those from birth to three. Because all states are now required to individualize programming for children beginning at age three, we will deal with that group first.

The law requires that a specialized education program be designed *in writing* for each child with special needs. This program must be developed *jointly* by the teacher, specialists, the parents or guardians, and, if possible, the child. Many parents in the past felt that promises were not kept. Putting the program in writing is meant to ensure that it will be carried out and that agreement has been reached between parents and teachers about its content. Some parents believe the teacher knows best, and they are willing to agree with anything the teacher says. Others believe they know their children better than the teacher does; they would like to contribute to program planning. The law guarantees parents a voice in the education program designed for their child. Older children also may participate in their own program planning.

Parents have the right to examine all relevant school records regarding the identification, evaluation, and educational placement of their child. This right enables parents to examine the data that decisions are based on; they no longer simply have to accept the official verdict. Parents are now entitled, on request, to see test results and receive copies of reports.

The school district must provide the parents with information *in writing,* in a language they can understand, about the identification, evaluation, and placement of their child. The parents must be notified in writing of contemplated program changes as well. In the past, some parents were not informed when their children were placed in or removed from special education classes.

Individualized Education Programs

An individualized education program (IEP) must be developed for each identified child with a disability and must have the following components:

1. Statement about the child's present level of performance

2. Annual goals set for the child

3. Short-term instructional objectives

4. Specific educational services to be provided

5. Extent to which the child will participate in the regular education program

6. Dates on which special services will begin and end

7. Evaluation criteria to be used to determine whether or not the instructional objectives are being met

As you are learning the elements of an IEP, the fine points of writing good objectives, or how to work well with specialists, you may ask yourself, "Is this worth the effort for just one or two children?" In fact, in the process of learning to comply with these legal requirements, you can learn a great deal about individualizing instruction for all children and about getting the maximum benefit from the resources you have. For the other children in the class, especially any about which you have some concerns but who have not yet been officially identified, you can incorporate into your customary planning the principles used to design IEPs.

Introduction to the IEP Form

There are probably as many different IEP forms as there are school districts in the United States. All of them must conform to the guidelines stated in Public Law 94-142, but they may include information not required by law. The following IEP form was developed for illustrative purposes. You will be able to adapt without any difficulty the information it asks for to the particular form you are required to use.

This particular form was developed as a multipurpose form. The cover page is designed to meet both the requirements of the IEP and the IFSP. Increasingly, we are seeing the merits of the IFSP form and the fact that age 3 is an arbitrary age for children to move from one framework to another. Additional pages reflect the requirements of either the IEP or IFSP.

The IEP/IFSP Form: Cover Page. There are four major sections of the cover page. On the top, you will see space for *identification* of the child. Experience has shown that it is wise to have available two separate spaces for parents or guardians. The last piece of data in this section asks for information on past intervention. Increasingly, infants have participated in infant stimulation programs or some type of therapy or early intervention. Although not required by law, this is important information for you to know.

The second section provides information about the multidisciplinary team. This space should reflect that parent(s) are equal partners on the team, who is the designated service coordinator or contact person, and define the roles of other team members. So that members of the team are able to work efficiently together and to contact each other, phone numbers are also requested.

The third section provides information about the child's present level of performance. It includes space for both medical/clinical information and developmental/educational information. This is also the space to include a summary of the current test data. Information about strengths and needs—either of the child or the child and the family—can also be noted here.

You may encounter results from a variety of tests used by specialists. The most common tests are listed below. Note they fall into three categories— intelligence, achievement, and specialized. The results are usually stated in grade-level equivalents (1–5; first grade fifth month) or age equivalents (AE 4.7; four years seven months).

Intelligence (Ability) Tests

Battelle Developmental Inventory (BDI) (0–8)
Wechsler Preschool and Primary Scale of Intelligence—Revised (WPPSI -R) (3–7)
Stanford-Binet (2 to adult)
Slosson Intelligence Test (2 weeks to adult)
These tests generally yield an intelligence quotient (IQ) as well as a mental age (MA). Some yield a full-scale IQ that can be broken down into a verbal scale (VS) and a performance scale (PS). This breakdown can be useful in assessing relative strengths and needs.

Overall, IQ measures a rate of learning. An IQ of 100 has been agreed upon as the amount of information the "average" child learns. An IQ of 75 would mean that the child had only learned about three-fourths of the amount of information others his age had learned. This understanding is the same across this type of test. (Chapter 17 has more information about intelligence quotients.)

Criterion-Based and Achievement Tests

Brigance Diagnostic Inventory of Early Development (revised) (0–7)

INDIVIDUALIZED EDUCATION PROGRAM/
INDIVIDUALIZED FAMILY SERVICE PLAN

Child _____ Age _____ Birth date _____ Report date _____

Parents/Guardians _____ Address _____
street   city   state   zip

Parents/Guardians _____ Address _____
street   city   state   zip

Intervention to date _____

_____

Team members	Title/Role	Phone	Team members	Title/Role	Phone

Information for Program Implementation
Medical/Clinical information (including test results)

Developmental/Educational Information
(including test results)

Strengths

Needs

Disability Primary _____ Secondary _____

Services Required:

Child Care/Education   (hours)   Early Intervention/SpEd   (hours)   Special Services   (hours)

Necessary supports _____

_____

Placement recommendation _____

School district _____ Services to begin _____ Next review _____

INDIVIDUALIZED EDUCATION PROGRAM:
GOALS AND OBJECTIVES

CHILD _____

GOAL _____   Date _____ Page ____ of ____

SHORT-TERM OBJECTIVE	MATERIALS/METHODS ACTION/STRATEGY	CRITERIA/ EVALUATION	DATE	PERSONS RESPONSIBLE

| PARENT SIGNATURE | PERSON RESPONSIBLE SIGNATURE MD | | | |

Early Learning Accomplishment Profile (ELAP) (0–3)
Learning Accomplishment Profile (LAP-D) (3–6)
Hawaii Early Learning Profile (HELP) (0–3)
HELP for Special Preschoolers (3–6)
Wide Range Achievement Test (WRAT-R)
Diagnostic Achievement Battery (DAB)
Woodcock Reading Mastery Tests

Criterion-based tests for younger children and achievement tests are intended to test skills and knowledge. They are designed to reveal what skills children have learned relative to expectations for their age and/or grade level.

Specialized Tests

Southern California Sensory Integration Test Battery
Southern California Post-Rotary Nystagmus Test
Developmental Test of Visual Motor Integration
Illinois Test of Psycholinguistic Ability (ITPA)
Vineland Adaptive Behavior Scales (revised)
Adaptive Behavior Scale for Infants and Early Childhood
Adaptive Behavior Inventory for Children (ABIC)

These tests are typically given by specialists and the results are reported on the IEP form. The tests are designed to focus on specific aspects of an impairment (for example, auditory discrimination, language skills, eye-hand coordination). They are especially useful in determining learning strengths and needs of a child with an impairment.

In many cases the examiner's remarks indicating quality of the child's behavior are as helpful as the test results themselves. They will often tell you about

a child's strengths and needs, and usually give information about cooperation, motivation, response to failure, persistence, and so on.

The bottom section of the form includes information about both the primary and secondary diagnosis and services required by the child (and family). The first category looks at the need for child care or regular educational settings. The IEP requires that the extent to which the child will participate in the regular education program be stated. Put that information here. Information about preschool programs or child care settings is also placed in this area. The second space designates the specific educational services that will be provided. If appropriate, note the amount of time or particular areas designated. The third column provides space for listing the therapy the child requires. These are developmental, corrective, and supportive services necessary to provide the child with the adequate education the law requires. They include speech and language therapy, psychological services, physical therapy (PT), and occupational therapy (OT).

Some school districts also provide pediatric medical personnel, social workers, home-school visitors, and other special services. The available specializations and the amount of time specialists can devote to children vary from school to school.

The IEP cites the kinds of services required (such as occupational therapy), the type (group versus individual), and the amount of time to be spent with each service (a half-hour a week, for example).

The next section provides space to note the necessary supports for this child. For example, if the child will be in a child care setting, does an itinerant early childhood special education teacher need to provide some training and visit on a regular basis? Then a placement needs to be recommended. The school district in which the child resides must be written in and it must be designated when the services begin. The date of the next review must also be designated.

The IEP Form: Goals and Objectives. The tasks for the IEP's first page require compilation and interpretation. The second and following pages require synthesis, creativity, and perseverance. Here the teacher sets forth the actual programming for one child. The programming task involves stating annual goals, instructional objectives, and activities.

Writing Annual Goals. These are statements (one to a page) of long-range goals. They are based on the strengths and needs given on the first page of the form and your observations of the child, as well as on your general knowledge about the child's disability and appropriate developmental levels. Here are some examples of annual goals: to improve auditory discrimination skills, to improve math concepts, to improve eye-hand coordination, or to increase body awareness. Annual goals are too broad for practical application and must be broken down into instructional objectives.

Writing Instructional Objectives. Writing instructional objectives is not difficult after you have written a few. Some writing of objectives is based on common sense and trial and error, but for writing other objectives there are actually procedures, such as breaking the task into its component parts and sequencing these. The instructional objectives separate the annual goal into smaller, teachable bits of behavior. They are written in such a way that you, or anyone else, can tell whether the child has learned the behavior. To help satisfy this empirical requirement, there are rules for writing instructional objectives.

The first step is easy. You must decide who is going to do the action stated by the objective. The child, the teacher, or the parent may be the "doer." Second, determine what is going to be done. This is more difficult, as you must be able to measure (see) what is done. This means that some words—such as, *understand, know, appreciate, try, feel, discover,* and *think*—cannot be used. Teachers of young children have more difficulty with this step than other teachers because young children have such a small repertoire of behavior that traditional words—such as, *write, list, translate, read, predict,* and *compare*—represent skills the children in their class have not yet achieved. A starter list of "doing" words might include the following:

point to	order	name
match	say	pick out
select	label	choose
tell	repeat	find

color	locate	jump
copy	define	walk
dramatize	look at	cut out
dictate	draw	count
set up	circle	nod
state	hop	demonstrate
arrange	run	

In the third step of writing instructional objectives, state the object of the action. Fourth, impose conditions to make the task easier or more difficult. Here is what a sample objective might look like so far:

Tinea (doer)/will hop (action)/on left foot (object)/for ten feet (condition).

The conditions may also determine what will or will not be available to the child. They can be set forth at the beginning or end of the instructional objective. This is usually a matter of the writer's style and how the sentence best makes sense.

The fifth and final step is to develop an evaluation criterion. How well or how often does this objective need to be achieved for you as the teacher to decide that it has been mastered? Here are some examples of criteria: using at least two colors, within ten seconds, two out of three times, or 80 percent of the time.

Because of human variability it is unwise to decide on a 100 percent performance, even when you think this can be achieved. For a variety of reasons, children often decide not to comply with requests. You need to build flexibility into your evaluation criterion.

Putting it all together then, an instructional objective might look like this:

Given paper and crayons, the child will draw a picture using at least two colors.
  Condition: Given paper and crayons
  Doer: the child
  Action: will draw
  Object: a picture
  Evaluation: using at least 2 colors

For the purpose of illustrating the process of writing an instructional objective, I have used a concrete and somewhat over-specific example. In practice, your objectives can often benefit by being more general.

Objectives with enough flexibility to allow for individual differences lend themselves more readily to variety in programming. For example, in order to improve a child's social skills with peers, you may want to have that child interact with others. Your objective may read:

Given paper and watercolor paints, Cathy will paint a mural of a rainy day with two other children for ten minutes.

However, you have put a lot of wasted thought and time into Cathy's IEP if she happens to hate painting, and hates painting rainy-day scenes most of all. A more general objective that achieves the same purpose reads:

Given the appropriate materials, Cathy will participate in an art project with two other children for ten minutes.

This gives you and the child the option of using clay, paint, corn starch, playdough, fingerpaint, collage, or papier-mâché to fulfill the objective. There is room for experimentation, which makes the IEP more workable.

Several things may become apparent as you review this procedure. You may find that it is much simpler to write trivial objectives than important ones. Furthermore, some of the qualities you value most and want to teach are almost impossible to put into behavioral terms, for example, empathy, creativity, cooperation, joy, and interest. Finally, in order to determine whether or not these criteria have been fulfilled, you will have to develop some system of record keeping. Put such nagging thoughts aside for a while. The answers to these questions will become apparent to you as you grow familiar with the process of writing an IEP.

Try to order the objectives from simple to more difficult, as well as from high to low priority. For example, if your annual goal is to improve auditory discrimination, your objectives will concern listening skills. Perhaps you decide you want the child to distinguish between a bell and a siren. This is a relatively easy task—providing the child has the prerequisite skill of auditory identification; that is, the child can identify each sound by itself. To test the child on auditory identification, ring the bell and ask, "What is this?" Sound the siren and ask the question again. Repeat the sounds behind a screen. Can the child identify the sound without a visual cue? If so, the child can auditorially identify the bell and siren. This does not mean, however, that he can distinguish between the two sounds when played together. Once the child demonstrates the prerequisite skills, you may proceed with more difficult tasks. Be sure you have included enough objectives, in terms of both quantity and scope, to attain your goal.

Setting priorities, deciding what to do first, is often complicated. There is no one way to set them.

Parental concerns and the child's wishes influence your decision. If those are not apparent, ask yourself about each objective: How difficult will it be in the future if the child doesn't learn _____? The more the child will need this skill, the higher the priority you could assign the corresponding objectives to meet the annual goal.

Your priorities, as well as your assessment of the difficulty of the task, will be reflected in the dates you expect to initiate and complete the objectives. For example, your IEP might reflect the following progression:

Given an easel and paints in three primary colors, the child will point to the correct color when named.   Oct. 1–Dec. 1

Given an easel and paints in three primary colors, the child will name the colors on request.   Nov. 1–Feb. 1

Given an easel and paints in three primary colors, the child will mix two colors to make another color and name that color.   Jan. 1–May 1

The law requires you to state on the IEP form when an objective will be reached. This makes teachers more accountable for the child's learning. In most cases, the date you pick will be your best guess as to when the child will be able to perform that particular task. Some tasks are easier than others. If a child can already point to one color, you might expect that sometime in the fall the child will learn several others. If, however, you decide on June of the following year, a parent may well question your teaching ability. Setting dates requires you to think through what you will teach a child and how many opportunities in a day, week, or month the child will have to practice these skills. Obviously the dates you choose and the difficulty of the task will depend on the individual child.

Choosing Activities. The next step in the process is the most challenging. It involves choosing and adapting activities that meet the objectives you have set. You need to think in terms of the underlying principles of activities: Why do you use them in your program? As you implement the instructional objectives, remember:

1. Choose activities that use as many modalities as possible (vision, taste, touch, hearing, smell).

2. Choose several activities that reinforce the objective. Repetition helps children master a concept.

3. Use variety when presenting the same information. Color, for example, can be shown through clothing, painting, bingo, gelatin, and nature walks, to name just a few.

Implementing objectives with regard to different exceptionalities is discussed in Chapters 10–18 of Part Two.

Completing the Form. To complete the IEP form, you must write who is to carry out the objective. In most cases your name and your position (teacher) will be placed in those columns. Some objectives, however, will be the responsibility of specialists. Both you and the parents or guardian sign each page of the completed IEP.

Record Keeping

Good record keeping is indispensable for implementing an IEP for an exceptional child. You need accurate records documenting development or the lack of it in order to evaluate your program. Your record keeping will be partly informal—quick notes to yourself—and partly formal—a weekly or monthly report. This may sound like a lot of extra time and work, but once you establish a system, you will be amazed at your proficiency.

Notes kept throughout the week will help your memory, for example: *9/28 J. & Sally, blocks 5 min.* Weekly (or monthly) reports may be in outline or anecdote form. Outline form corresponds directly to the child's IEP. Numbers and key words identify the goals (1 Fine motor) and objectives (1.1 beads). The check, plus, and minus signs (see *key*) are also helpful shorthand for daily notes.

The second type of formal record keeping, anecdotal, is also based on the notes you take during the week or month.

There are advantages and disadvantages to each of these record-keeping methods and the decision to use or adapt one or the other will be based on personal preference. Of course, you may already have developed your own workable method. If so, use it.

Working with Specialists

In the process of writing and implementing an IEP, you will be expected to work as part of a multi-disciplinary team that includes specialists who may work with the child outside the classroom. Observe the child in therapy, if you can, or ask for a description and explanation of the activities that occur during therapy. The therapist can help you understand how a child's therapy needs will affect classroom behavior. Ask how you can support the therapist's goals in your classroom. Conversely, you can help the specialist understand what you are doing with the child and why. (For example, he or she may not have any idea why a housekeeping corner could be important.) Remember that a specialist is also a consultant. A child does not have to be in therapy to benefit from a specialist's knowledge.

The role of specialists and a brief description of each is given in Chapter 2. Methods for integrating the goals and objectives for an individual child into your on-going program are covered in Chapters 7 and 8.

Writing the IEP

Knowing in general how to fill out an IEP and actually doing it for a specific child are two different things. Full-time special educators and specialists who work only with children with disabilities may write anywhere from eight to ninety IEPs a year, depending on their case load. You may have to contribute only a page or two to an IEP. The specialists have usually received training in writing IEPs, and because they do it so often, they have developed techniques and aids that may include goal and objective checklists or computerized data banks. However, even if these are available to you, it is important to understand the logic of how you individualize programming.

		Evaluation criteria	
	9/15	10/15	11/15
Tinea B.			
1. Fine Motor			
1.1 beads	√ −	√ −	5 of 10 correct
1.2 copy forms	√ −	√ +	3 of 5 correct
1.3 5 block tower	√	√	4 blocks
2. Language Concepts			
2.1 colors	√	√	5 of 8 receptive
2.2 numbers	√	√ +	1-5 expressive
2.3 prepositions	√ −	√	on, under beside, in/recep.

KEY: NA   No attempt
    √ −   Attempted, little success
    √   Attempted, shows progress
    √ + Attained criterion

Weekly Report (Outline)

John H.   11/15/82
    Fine Motor: J. is still demonstrating needs in this area. He can now build a four-block tower and copy 3/5 (three out of five) forms, including _____, ○, □. Bead stringing is still very difficult for J.
    Language: J.'s language quality has improved since September. He is now speaking in 4-5 word sentences and nearly always expresses himself in full sentences. He can identify 5/8 colors and can recite the numbers 1-5. He can follow a one-step direction containing the following prepositions: on, under, beside, in.

Weekly Report (Anecdotal)

You are part of a team of specialists working together to develop programs for young children.

When preparing for the IEP conference, you must organize your thoughts and ideas in writing. Instead of shuffling through notes and reports, have one sheet of paper outlining the essential information you already have and pointing out information you need to obtain at the meeting.

A Sample Case

Our sources of information are three reports on tests, observations of a child, reports by a psychologist, an occupational therapist, and a team meeting for a child, Joanna P. The reports are typical of those you may receive about a child. They illustrate neither extremely good nor bad reports, but are average.

The team report consolidates the information obtained at a meeting of the specialists who have evaluated the child, the parents and teachers. Although the name of this group may vary, the functions of the team are to: (1) interpret test results, (2) relate its interpretations to observations and information about the child, (3) determine the significance of the data for the child's education, and (4) recommend teaching strategies.

Psychological Evaluation

STUDENT: Joanna P. DATE OF BIRTH: 8/2/87

EXAMINER: Mrs. F. DATE OF EVALUATION:

School Psychologist   2/10/92

AGE: 4.6

REASON FOR REFERRAL:

Unpredictable behaviors (varies between physical aggression and withdrawal). Poor peer relationships.

PROCEDURES USED:

Peabody Picture Vocabulary Test (PPVT), Form A
McCarthy Scales of Children's Abilities (MSCA)
Observational Data (classroom observation)

Background Observation:

This four-and-a-half-year-old girl was referred for a psychological evaluation by her Head Start teacher, who felt her behavior was "aggressive at times and withdrawn at other times." An occupational therapist's evaluation was also recommended by this examiner and has been scheduled. It is reported that Joanna is an asthmatic who has attacks when she is upset. It is also reported that she may feign attacks on occasion. The family has moved three times in the past two years.

A classroom observation by this examiner was conducted prior to testing. Some aggression noted by this examiner seemed to occur immediately following activities that may have been frustrating for Joanna. One example: After being unable to snap a doll's dress in the housekeeping corner, Joanna hit another child and proceeded to cry. A contrast to this behavior was seen on the day examinations were administered, when Joanna's mother brought her to this examiner's office.

Rapport was quickly established. She separated easily from her mother, offering her hand and a shy smile. The quality and intelligibility of her speech were good, but she spoke very little spontaneously. Near the end of the evaluation, she said "I want my mommy" several times. When allowed to see her mother, she immediately returned to the testing area quite happily. She did begin to tire, however, as the testing drew to a close. She became so tired that, when her mother was talking afterward, she fell sound asleep on the mother's lap.

Joanna was generally cooperative and attentive throughout testing.

Intellectual Functioning:

As measured by the PPVT, this child's receptive vocabulary is at a "high average" level, being equivalent to that of a child of 5.0 years. Her general cognitive ability, as assessed by the McCarthy Scales, is equivalent to that of a child of 4.0 years, a delay of six months. Her most highly developed skills are in verbal expression and understanding. Quantitative and memory skills fall within the average range. Her perceptual performance and motor skills are lower, falling in the borderline range. Her relational thinking ability is at a "high average" level as measured on the Opposite Analogies subtest, being equivalent to that of a child of five years ten months. Her ability to count and sort blocks is "average." Her memory skills and understanding of quantitative words are "average."

Conclusions and Recommendations:

Although this child's general level of functioning at the present time is only equivalent to the mental age of a child of 4.0 years, there is evidence that her intellectual potential may be higher. Her perception of spatial relationships and her manipulative skills, rated on the Block Building subtest are her least developed abilities. These learning disabilities could be dealt with in a prekindergarten program with occupational therapy included.

In addition, it is recommended that Joanna participate in counseling in order to enhance her peer relationships and help her deal with frustration more effectively.

Mrs. F.
Psychologist

Occupational Therapy Evaluation

NAME: Joanna P.   DATE OF BIRTH: 8/2/87
EXAMINER: Mr. M.   DATE OF EVALUATION:
Occupational Therapist   2/16/92
AGE: 4.6

Joanna P. was seen for an occupational therapy evaluation, as recommended by a psychologist. Scores from a recent psychological examination indicate weakness in motor skills and perceptual performance.

Joanna P. was brought to the evaluation by her mother. She went readily with the examiner. During the evaluation she tended to wander from the task and had to be repeatedly refocused to the testing. She exhibited some testing behavior, such as scratching her nails on the blackboard and then looking to the examiner for a reaction. Joanna worked best with manipulative materials.

The examiner administered a developmental assessment and the Developmental Test of Visual Motor Integration.

Results:

Joanna's performance on the tactile portion of the developmental assessment indicated that she has awareness of touch and pressure input and can localize tactile input (for example, she knows which finger is touched). Joanna was able to identify correctly four out of four basic textures.

Joanna's gross motor performance was found to vary from that of a three- to four-year-old. Response to vestibular input was within normal limits, but Joanna fell off the nystagmus board following rotation. This response suggests that Joanna has difficulty stabilizing her body in dynamic movement experiences. Joanna tended to use each hand on the same side of the body, suggesting inadequate postural flexibility or difficulty in crossing the midline. For drawing tests, Joanna preferred her right hand, and all graphic reproductions were shifted to the right side of the paper— further evidence of inadequate flexibility. Gross motor planning was found to be adequate.

Fine motor planning activities, such as tapping sequence, were stressful for Joanna. Joanna was able to use both sides of the body together in a coordinated fashion.

During block manipulation tasks, Joanna was able to build a cube bridge and a tower of nine blocks (36-month skills). She was unable to copy an oblique bridge (42-month skill).

Visual motor performance was at the 36-month level, a year-and-a-half below age expectancy. Visual-perceptual performance was also below Joanna's chronological age. She is beginning to use insight to nest and stack rings and blocks. She was unable to nest cans or tower blocks (36- and 42-month skills).

She was able to sort blocks according to big–little (42-month skill).

Joanna holds a pencil high on the shaft and does not have a refined, adultlike grasp.

Summary and Recommendations:

Joanna's sensorimotor needs include the following:

1. Improve postural stability and flexibility
2. Improve fine motor planning
3. Improve visual-perceptual performance

Occupational therapy is suggested to meet these needs.

Joanna can be easily engaged in an activity and just as easily distracted. It is recommended that she be placed in an extremely structured program that will provide firm behavioral controls.

Mr. M., O.T.R.
Occupational Therapist

Child Study Team Report*

Joanna P.

In attendance: Mrs. P., mother; Mrs. F., psychologist; Mr. M., occupational therapist; Ms. L., Headstart teacher; Mrs. R., Early Childhood Special Educator.

Joanna P. is a *four-and-a-half-year-old girl* who recently moved to this suburban area from a rural setting. Joanna's father has obtained a job as a salesman with a local firm. Prior to this, Joanna's *family moved quite often,* three times in the past two years, as Mr. P. was transferred frequently.

Records from Joanna's former preschool identify her as a problem child. Joanna also has *asthma.* Joanna does not have a current IEP, but testing was completed. The report in the file states that Joanna was referred because of extreme *moodiness* and frequent *physical aggression.* Observations by the school psychologist and by the teacher confirm this, reporting both *elation or withdrawal from day to day.* The psychological report notes that Joanna is *easily frustrated* and frequently *cries* and throws *temper tantrums* when she cannot do something. One example is a temper tantrum after Joanna could not snap a doll's dress in the housekeeping corner.

Testing was completed by the psychologist in one session, during which Joanna was cooperative and attentive. Aptitude testing identifies Joanna as being *average in ability* with some variation in test scores. *Pencil and paper tasks and those requiring concentration (such as block designs and motor skills) are more difficult for Joanna.* She seems to *enjoy* more *verbal* subtests, *such as vocabulary and even digit span* (repeating digits presented orally).

Joanna was referred by the psychologist for an occupational therapy evaluation. During this evaluation session, Joanna was *slightly more resistive. Tactile development and gross motor planning were adequate, while gross and fine motor performance and visual motor performance were below age level. Occupational therapy was recommended.*

Joanna, according to her former teacher's reports, was *frequently absent* from school. (She had several asthma attacks at school, which seemed to increase in frequency when Joanna learned the family was moving.) The *other children generally did not respond well* to Joanna due to her unpredictable behavior, and because they did not want to provoke an asthma attack. Joanna *feigned attacks when she didn't get her way* with the other children. Joanna *enjoyed one-to-one attention* from *adults* and *older children.* She worked best in a *small group* and needed a lot of *verbal praise and affection.* The teacher felt Joanna needed to learn ways to *express frustration, anger, and fear.* She also felt Joanna needed to develop *healthy peer relationships.* Based on the preschool teacher's observations as well as her own, the psychologist recommended family therapy.

Joanna lives at home with her father, mother, older sister, and younger brother. Mr. P. plans to remain in the area longer than his previous job allowed.

You now have a little more information about Joanna.

You can see that this child has as many nonclinical "special considerations" as she has tested clinical needs. And although you have a general idea of Joanna's low frustration level, you could benefit from information on what she specifically dislikes.

Looking back at the weaknesses under "Testing/Observation," you can determine some skills needing improvement. Your task is to translate the report's jargon into your own, for example:

Visual-motor skills: eye-hand coordination

Gross motor–fine motor: large and small muscle coordination

Easily frustrated: poor self-control/self-concept

You can assume two things about Joanna. First, she does not have good peer relationships; and second, because of the family moves and her illness, she feels she doesn't have much control over her environment. These can also be interpreted as:

Poor peer relationships: increase feelings of group belonging

Little control over environment: needs to increase awareness of feelings and to express feelings

The next step is to write the goals, which should reflect the needs. First, generate from five to ten goals for Joanna; second, try to consolidate them; finally, eliminate some and rank the remainder.

To improve large motor coordination

To improve eye-hand coordination

---

*The italicized comments in the Child Study Team Report are key words or phrases that apply to Joanna's IEP. Highlighting the report with a transparent colored marker will help you to locate pertinent data quickly.

To improve small motor coordination

To improve self-concept

To increase feelings of group belonging

To increase awareness of feelings

To express feelings

The grouped goals have similarities and can be consolidated. Eye-hand coordination and fine motor coordination may incorporate some of the same objectives.

The last four goals are all related to improving Joanna's social skills. Although your judgment may differ, I would eliminate "self-concept" and consolidate awareness and expression of feelings. My reasoning for this is that Joanna's needs seem to stem from her inability to express herself rather than simply from her poor self-concept, and that teaching her alternatives to temper tantrums and feigned asthma attacks will, in effect, help to solve the problem of poor self-concept. After Joanna becomes aware of her feelings, alternate ways of expressing those feelings can be more easily taught. therefore, the goal "To express feelings" is better added to the IEP later. In addition, I have chosen to eliminate "small motor" and "large motor" in order to concentrate on the three most important goals. Joanna will be given a more than adequate number of opportunities to practice small and large motor coordination in occupational therapy and with her peers.

Your goals for Joanna going into the IEP conference would be:

1. To improve eye-hand coordination

2. To increase feelings of group belonging/inclusion

3. To increase awareness of feelings

Now you are prepared for the IEP conference. The actual IEP should be filled out at the conference. An example of what might finally result is included.

What you have been given is the ideal way that the IEP should be developed. In reality, it is more frequently generated from a computer and you, the teacher, may be told that you can have only one goal, regardless of the needs of the child. After the form is filled out you may find that you hold the illegible sixth copy of the form.

Professionals rarely expect parents to play an active role in the process, and some of the IEPs are so filled with jargon and information specific to particular school practices that parents feel alienated from the process. A "poor" example of an IEP has been included on page 88, so you can better understand why some parents have been dissatisfied. Although the names have been changed, the report was done on an actual child and presented to the parents at an IEP meeting.

There are some specific elements to note. First, the annual goal is to improve reading skills. That is certainly valid. When you look at the Short-Term Objectives column you see that the objectives come from the critical objectives set up for the grade level in the

school district. The child is expected to master all of the critical objectives for the grade level with 75 percent accuracy. The first question that comes to mind is, "How is this different from the expectations for all the other children in that grade level other than the fact that the expectations are lower (not different)?" A second question arises: "How parent-friendly is this IEP? What does this page mean to a parent?" And again the question arises: "How is this individualized?" Essentially it is not. Interestingly, there was no teacher or parent participation in the development of this IEP; it was designed by the Educational Diagnostician. Also, note that of the four copies of the form, no regular teacher receives a copy. This district has no expectation that inclusion in a regular classroom is an option, and the standardized form has no place for this teacher. The pages that followed are similar. The parents refused to sign the IEP.

We learned from problems encountered in developing IEPs and have developed another instrument that individualizes programming for infants and toddlers, the Individualized Family Service Plan. Although it is similar in some respects to the IEP, it has different underlying principles. One assumes that it, too, will have problems, but it has not been used long enough for us to find out exactly what they are.

Individualized Family Service Plans

The Individualized Family Service Plan (IFSP) is one component of Part H of P.L. 99-457. Infants and toddlers (0–3) will have an IFSP. Changes in the law in 1991 mean that children three to five can have IFSPs or IEPs. The purpose of the IFSP is to identify, organize, and facilitate the attainment of families' goals for themselves and their children (Johnson, McGonigel, & Kaufmann, 1989). The process of interacting and joining with families in their exploration of their strengths and needs and goals for themselves and their children may be more important than the IFSP itself. The IFSP will require professionals to learn new skills and to go beyond the traditional boundaries of their disciplines. It requires a family-centered approach that not only acknowledges families but enables them to use or develop the competencies necessary to meet their own needs and those of their children (Dunst, Trivette, & Deal, 1988).

The whole idea of an IFSP is that services should be family-centered instead of child-centered. Every IFSP will look different in this regard. Many IFSPs will contain only child-focused outcomes, others will only contain family-focused outcomes, but most will have both. It is also expected that the IFSP will change as the family changes. The important concept here is that the process and resulting product are consumer (family)-driven. Families decide what they want as outcomes on the IFSP. They may make an informed decision to allow professionals to make this decision, but they *decided* to do that.

INDIVIDUALIZED EDUCATION PROGRAM/
INDIVIDUALIZED FAMILY SERVICE PLAN

Child _Joanna P._   Age _4-6_   Birth date _8/2/87_   Report date _2/20/92_

Parents/Guardians _Mr. & Mrs. P._   Address _14-C Holly Hill Apts. Madison Dr._
                                                    street   city   state   zip

Parents/Guardians _____   Address _Newark, DE 19711_
                                                    street   city   state   zip

Intervention to date _none_

Team members	Title/Role	Phone	Team members	Title/Role	Phone
Mrs. P.	Mother	(645-1922)	Ms. L.	Head Start Teacher	(227-1254)
* Mrs. R.	ECSE	(831-5429)			
Mrs. F.	Psychologist	(322-2130)			
Mr. M.	OT	(451-2304)			

* Service coordinator

Information for Program Implementation
Medical/Clinical information (including test results)

O.T. Eval. 2/16/92 Therapy recommended to improve postural & visual-perceptual and motor performance

Developmental/Educational Information (including test results)

MSCA 2/92 Some variation in test scores; strengths in verbal area - weakness in perceptual, visual, motor

Strengths

Verbal abilities, tactile skills attentive during one-to-one activity, vocabulary

Needs

Visual-perceptual skills, acceptable emotional responses, responding to change self-concept

---

Disability Primary _Emotional/Behavioral Disorder_   Secondary _Learning Disability (?)_

Services Required:

Child Care/Ed (hours)   Early Inter/SpEd (hours)   Special Services (hours)

Head Start   _____   _Occupational Therapy_
                                                Family Therapy

Necessary supports _The early childhood special education will go to Head Start and provide support and consultation_

Placement recommendation _Head Start continued with support_

School district _Cape_   Services to begin _2/30/92_   Next review _9/15/92_

INDIVIDUALIZED EDUCATION PROGRAM:
GOALS AND OBJECTIVES

CHILD _Joanna P._

GOAL _To improve eye-hand coordination_   Date _2/30/92_   Page ___ of ___

SHORT-TERM OBJECTIVE	MATERIALS/METHODS ACTION/STRATEGY	CRITERIA/ EVALUATION	DATE	PERSONS RESPONSIBLE
Given a choice of art medium (wire, clay, playdough, string, etc.) Joanna will use the medium	Salt putty beads, string mobile, string painting, wire sculpture, clay	5 minutes 1 time per week	2/30	
		8 minutes 1 time/wk 2 times/wk	4/30 5/30	Ms. L
Given a target 5' away, Joanna will hit the target with a ball or bean bag	Noisy toss, variations on throwing	2/5 trials 4/5 trials	2/30 5/30	Ms. L
Joanna will be able to build a block structure with 1" cubes	Cuisenaire rods, block play	stacked 5 high stacked 6 high	2/30 5/30	Ms. L
Joanna will be able to cut simple shapes from construction paper (▭, △, ▢, ○, ◯)	Letter collage, eye-hair collage, cutting cards — Put card in holder to keep it steady for her	using easy grip scissors using typical preschool scissors	2/30 6/30	Ms. L

PARENT SIGNATURE _Mr. P._   PERSON RESPONSIBLE SIGNATURE _Ms. L_

INDIVIDUALIZED EDUCATION PROGRAM:
GOALS AND OBJECTIVES

CHILD _Joanna P._

GOAL _To increase feelings of group belonging/inclusion_   Date _2/30/92_   Page ___ of ___

SHORT-TERM OBJECTIVE	MATERIALS/METHODS ACTION/STRATEGY	CRITERIA/ EVALUATION	DATE	PERSONS RESPONSIBLE
Joanna will participate in large group time	Music, storytime, parachute games, puppets, visitor	3/5 days per week 4/5 days per week	2/30 3/30	Ms. L.
Joanna will participate in structural games (inside and out) as requested with at least 2 other children	Team games, creative movement, noisy toss	1/2 of the time 3/4 of the time	2/30 4/30	Ms. L.
Joanna will participate in "freeplay" with 2-4 other children each day	Teachers will actively support this group initially in Blocks, Dramatic play, etc. whichever area Joanna chooses	5 minutes 10 minutes 15 minutes	2/30 4/30 6/30	Ms. L.

PARENT SIGNATURE _Mr. P._   PERSON RESPONSIBLE SIGNATURE _Ms. L._

INDIVIDUALIZED EDUCATION PROGRAM:
GOALS AND OBJECTIVES

CHILD _Joanna P._

GOAL _To increase awareness of feelings_   Date ___2/30/92___   Page ____ of ____

SHORT-TERM OBJECTIVE	MATERIALS/METHODS ACTION/STRATEGY	CRITERIA/ EVALUATION	DATE	PERSONS RESPONSIBLE
Joanna will be able to identify pictures of children and adults depicting the following feelings: sad, happy, angry, frightened, worried, surprised	matching expressions, matching faces, listen to stories about feelings	80% accuracy	2/30	Ms. L.
Joanna will create pictures that represent a designated feeling. She will talk about these pictures to adults and peers.	my book, my puzzle, best and worst, easy/hard, peek pictures	on request 80% of the time	2/30	Ms. L.
Joanna will name appropriate activities to do when given various feeling states (sad, happy, etc.)	Teacher will discuss feelings on a variety of occasions connecting feelings and behavior	80% accuracy	4/30	Ms. L.

PARENT SIGNATURE   _Ms. P._   PERSON RESPONSIBLE SIGNATURE   _Ms. L._

Although it is the process that is important, sometimes the product tells us about our process. Because infants and toddlers are not small preschoolers, the IFSP should not bring to it the behavioral, child-focused approach of the IEP.

Principles Underlying the IFSP Process

The following set of ten principles underlying the IFSP process have been adapted from those identified by Johnson, McGonigel, and Kaufmann (1989).

1. Infants and toddlers are dependent upon adults for survival; because of this dependency, a family-centered approach is essential.

2. The definition of "family" must reflect a diversity of family patterns and structures. We must expand our definition of family beyond biological ties.

3. Families are diverse; each must be respected for its structures, roles, values, beliefs, and coping styles.

4. Early intervention service delivery systems and strategies must respect and be congruent with the racial, ethnic, and cultural diversity of families.

5. Families are the decision makers. Families choose the early intervention program and how they want to be involved with it.

6. Professionals need to develop skills that promote mutual respect and partnerships with parents.

7. Service delivery systems must be flexible, accessible, and responsive to family needs.

8. Infants and toddlers and their families should have access to services that allow them to function in as "normal" an environment as possible; that is, they should be included in the neighborhood, school, and community as equal partners.

9. Partnerships and collaboration between families and professionals are necessary to successfully implement the IFSP process.

10. A team approach to planning and implementing the IFSP is necessary as no one agency or discipline can meet the needs of infants and toddlers with disabilities and their families.

Content of the IFSP

Much like the IEP, the content of the IFSP is determined by law, which specifies that the early intervention services must include a multidisciplinary assessment and a written Individual Family Service Plan (IFSP) to be developed with the family. The requirements for the IFSP include:

1. A statement of the child's present developmental levels. This includes physical, cognitive, speech

STUDENT _Charlene_   SCHOOL _West End_   Page _2_ of _____

ANNUAL GOAL _1.0 To improve reading skills_

SHORT TERM OBJECTIVE	CRITERIA AND EVALUATION PROCEDURES	SPECIFIC EDUCATIONAL SERVICES	DATES		STAFF RESPONSIBILITIES	
			Begin	End	Name	Position
1.0 Charlene will master the critical objectives for grade. Reading Vocabulary Comprehension VC 01 CM 01 02 02 03 03 04 04 05 05 06 06 07 Study/ References Sentences SR 01 SN 01 02	1.0 – Teacher Test ⎫ – Textbook Test ⎬ at least 75% accuracy – Observation ⎭ – Other Methods to include: – Structural Analysis – Phonics – Kinesthetic	Level I	9/91	6/92	Staff	

PARENT'S SIGNATURE   TEACHER'S SIGNATURE _Mo. Jones, E.D._

Copy 1 - Audit File, 2 - Parent, 3 - Cumulative Folder, 4 - Special Education Teacher

This is an example of a poor IEP. It was completed before the conference and is not individualized. There is no input from a regular teacher, nor is she designated to receive a copy. It shows lowered but not individualized expectations for the child.

and language, psychosocial development, and adaptive behavior (self-help skills).

2. A statement of family strengths and needs relative to enhancing the development of their infant or toddler.

3. A statement of major outcomes (goals) expected for the child and family, the methods for achieving them, and time line for measuring accomplishment or the degree to which outcomes are met, and whether or not revisions are necessary.

4. A statement of specific early intervention services necessary to meet individual child and family needs, including information about the frequency, intensity, and methods of service delivery.

5. Projected dates for starting and ending (if appropriate) services.

6. The name of the service coordinator who will be responsible for implementing and coordinating the plan.

7. A plan for supporting the child and family in the transition into programs for three- to five-year-olds.

The IFSP Process

Although all agencies will have slightly different procedures, eligibility criteria, and organizational frameworks, it is expected that there will be a similar overall process.

1. Families are referred by a physician, agency, or are self-referred to early intervention services.

2. Families then talk about their likes and dislikes, wants and needs, preferences and priorities. This may be first time some families have had any interaction with early intervention. It may also be the first time they have been asked what *they* want for their family as well as their child. This may be a new and different experience for some families, and they may have to be encouraged to think about the needs of the family instead of just the child. This process may take more than one meeting. As the families' preferences set the stage for the IFSP, it is vital.

3. Assessment planning then combines the information-gathering process. It requires clarifying the family preferences for involvement and their priorities for both the family and child. Information about the child's characteristics and additional information (if available) from other assessments should be included.

A service coordinator can help support the family in the level of participation and role they decide upon. They should have an active voice in the assessment process, giving input into when the assessment will be, the assessment measures to be used, and when and how the assessment information will be shared (Johnson, McGonigel, & Kaufmann, 1989).

It is important that parents ultimately make these decisions as their participation in the process will make the assessment itself more accurate. Planning the assessment around the parents' work, the child's most alert time, and the schedule of professionals can be a real challenge.

4. Before any formal assessment begins it is imperative to determine the parents' perceptions of their child. What do they consider the child's strengths and needs, the child's likes and dislikes, what are their specific areas of concern, and what do they want for their child? It is often useful to find out what a typical day is like in the family; be sure to include all family members to understand how they share roles as well as the role the child plays.

5. Child assessment serves different functions at various points in the process. Initially the assessment focuses on diagnosis. It is necessary to determine whether or not the child meets the eligibility criteria for the program. Information is also necessary to develop the IFSP.

6. Identification of family values and preferences involves clarifying with families what aspects of their family life they feel are relevant to helping their child grow and develop (Johnson, McGonigel, & Kaufmann, 1989). There are a variety of measures available to help families identify their strengths, needs, resources, and supports. These measures come in many different formats and are detailed in Chapter 21. The most efficient way to learn about what families want and how they want to participate is to ask them.

7. Developing outcomes to meet child and family needs requires the interpretation and synthesis of formal and informal assessment information in light of the families' priorities. It may involve some rethinking, and certainly will necessitate choices among strategies, activities, and services that will meet these outcomes. It is critically important to remember that there is far greater diversity within groups than between groups. Do not assume that all families with a child with Down syndrome have the same needs, wants, desires, or values.

Regardless of the specific requirements of the procedure you follow, Bailey (1987) recommends that IFSPs include the following information:

1. A statement of the child's strengths as well as needs

2. An emphasis on functional abilities rather than a compilation of test scores

3. A description of abilities within a developmental context

4. Inclusion of all the relevant developmental domains (physical, cognitive, language and speech, psychosocial, and self-help), not just the ones where deficits are noted

5. Information on behavioral and temperamental characteristics

6. A description of the functional limitations of the child that are relevant to intervention planning

The IFSP, unlike the IEP, does not require behavioral objectives. Its expected outcomes are the changes that families want for themselves or their child (Johnson, McGonigel, & Kaufmann, 1989). The IFSP requires a statement of what is going to occur to produce the desired outcome.

This collaborative development of the IFSP with parents requires new skills for professionals. Ideally, parents and professionals can negotiate a set of service priorities that both agree to; however, the IFSP should reflect the values and priorities of the families, not the professionals. The role of professionals is to look at families from a systems perspective to help families identify relevant needs. Professionals will need to use listening and interviewing techniques as well as negotiation skills. They also need to know the community resources they can match to family needs (Bailey, 1987).

Implementing the IFSP requires another round of decision making. Families need to know the range of options available to them and decide which of the options best fits their needs. Overall, this range should start with the options that the family would choose from if the child did not have a disability. If the parents' first choice is that the child be in a family day-care home that his older sister went to, then, that should be the first option explored. If this setting is chosen, the question for the team becomes how to support this child in that setting. Assistance might include the provision of necessary related and support services as well as training, technical assistance, and perhaps specialized equipment.

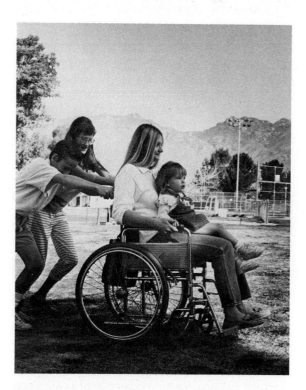

Families are different. They need to decide what services or settings best meet their needs.

Different families have different needs. For some placement in a child-care or preschool setting is most appropriate; for others a home-based program or even a segregated early intervention program will best fit family needs. The role of the professional, particularly the service coordinator, is to ensure that families make choices from the full range of options in both settings and service providers. Facilitating linkages among professionals, available resources, and program options is a major role. Creativity is required to meet the needs of today's families.

Young children change quickly. Informal IFSP reviews need to be made on an ongoing basis, and more formal ones should be called for when necessary. At the beginning, reviews need to be made early for trouble shooting if necessary. As placements stabilize a formal review in six months is appropriate.

Case Studies and IFSP

Families are very different. I have included two case studies to help to clarify these differences and the roles necessary for positive interaction. Because we are exploring the IFSP process and things are far less settled than in the IEP, rather than give one complete IFSP, I have used a variety of formats so you can see which ones most suit your needs and feel most comfortable. You might even ask families what format they would like to use, if any. These case studies are based on real families, but the names and identifying information have been changed.

The Dee Family

The Dee family consists of a single mother with six children. Four of the children have been classified as disabled and in need of special education services. Alvin is one year, eight months old and attends a child-care center full time, along with his two-and-a-half-year-old brother. Alvin was observed informally at the child-care center where staff was holding an inservice training. Upon learning about developmental norms, a child-care worker became concerned about Alvin and asked if she should talk to his mother. At one year, eight months Alvin was not walking, standing, eating independently, or talking. He exhibited strong temper tantrums. He had to be fed and used a bottle. He had limited social interaction skills and few purposeful play skills.

The mother, a full time homemaker, is pregnant with twins. The amount of child support payments make the family ineligible for the Aid for Dependent Children program; however, payments are at least six months late. While there is no money for utilities, heating bills are $400.00 monthly. The children experience frequent illnesses, but the mother cannot locate a doctor willing to treat the children because no local doctor will accept new Medicaid patients; therefore, illnesses go unattended.

Public Health nurses are involved with the family. They make appointments for the family, but the mother does not keep them (sometimes appointments conflict with one another, sometimes she forgets). The mother reports all children are behavior problems. The family lives in a rural area; therefore, transportation is sometimes a problem. The mother reports feelings of being overwhelmed. The father is available but reported not to live in the home.

A graphic outline of the coordination services facilitated by the staff between the family, day care, and service providers is shown. Initial involvement with this family required assisting the mother in meeting her priorities, including getting financial assistance for day care, food, and utilities. This assistance was gained through agencies listed under the economic category, and included accessing emergency utility funds and budgeting help, applying for special needs day-care funding, and accessing the regional food bank program.

Once some basic resource issues were attended to, the mother became more receptive to tackling child issues. Arrangements were made to have the two young boys assessed for intervention purposes. The family was channeled to the Early Childhood Center for an evaluation. Developmental evaluation results indicated Alvin was functioning at half his age expectations, and his brother had a significant language delay. The Early Childhood Center assisted in the provision of speech and language therapy and behavioral intervention. Therapy was provided at the day-care center to facilitate carryover. Behavioral intervention was provided at home with day-care consultation. The Public Health system was accessed in a coordinated fashion to attend to concerns for Alvin. This included the hearing clinic, vision clinic, and medical clinic. Transportation was arranged when possible, and efforts were made to prevent appointment conflicts.

Meetings were set up between the day-care center and service providers to facilitate a coordinated intervention program. The day-care center was able to implement activities involving language stimulation and behavioral management. The specialists encouraged the mother to attend those meetings. When she could not, the specialist made a home visit to share the information. The result of these efforts was a coordinated intervention system for Alvin.*

The sample first page given for the IEP is also designed to meet the requirements for the IFSP. If that were the first page, the following page could look like this. This form is similar to the second page of the IEP form with just slight variations. Because there is so much variation in IFSP forms, rather than offer any one form, samples of several different types have been included.

Service coordination for the Dee family was complex. It required an unusual variety of skills on the part of the service coordinator in addition to a broad knowledge of available community resources, far

*Adapted from Deiner et al., 1990.

NAME: _Alvin Dee_   DATE COMPLETED: _____

INDIVIDUAL FAMILY SERVICE PLAN

PRESENT LEVELS OF FUNCTIONING	STRENGTHS	NEEDS
CHILD		
Boyley Mental Age 13 months Motor Age 9½ months at 20 months CA Language 12 months receptive 8 months expressive Overall at 12 mo. level	Healthy	Improve motor skills, language, self-help and social behavior.
FAMILY		
Mother is in the home full time.	They have a car, house and washing machine.	Time for Mom Financial resources for basic expenses and info on money management Childcare financial assistance

This individualized Family Service Plan is a very simple one. Information about the levels of functioning of both child and family are noted, as well as statements about strengths and needs. This style is particularly good to use when the parent's reading level is low.

CHILD

CHILD'S NAME: _Alvin Dee_   DATE OF PLAN: _____

MAJOR OUTCOMES	STEPS TOWARD MAJOR OUTCOMES	PROCEDURES	TIMELINES STATUS				COMMENTS /STATUS
			Initiated	Made Progress	Modified	Achieved	
Alvin's receptive and expressive language skills will improve.	Receptive identify objects by pointing identify pictures by pointing identify body parts by pointing follow 1 step directions Expressive name familiar object name pictures name body parts	Talk with A. and then ask him to point to objects when he arrives Ask him to name objects he can point to					

PARENT SIGNATURE   **PERSON RESPONSIBLE SIGNATURE**

The heading child reflects that this page is for the child. This particular form is similar to more traditional IEP forms, however, the objectives have been replaced with outcomes, and the steps toward achieving those outcomes are identified along with the procedures. The timeline allows for noting progress and modifications as well as achievement.

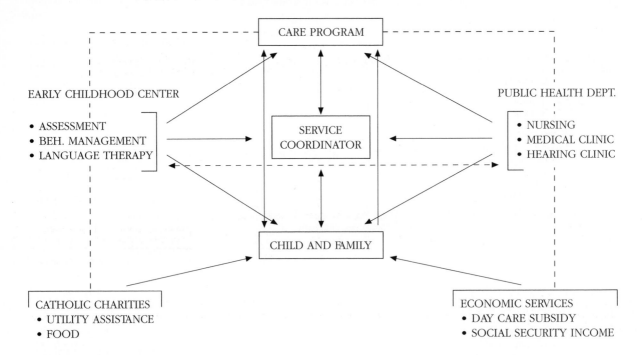

For some families service is complex. It requires the service coordinator to know not only about early childhood special education, but also about the available resources, public and private. When service needs are complex it is important that parents set the priority of what needs are more important. Until their basic needs are satisfied, it is unlikely that the child's needs will be a priority.

beyond that expected of most early childhood special educators.

The Monroe Family

The Monroe family consists of a dual-earner, professional couple and their two biological children and one daughter from the husband's previous marriage. Their youngest child has a tentative diagnosis of Down Syndrome (Mosaic Trisomy 18). Cathy was enrolled in the program in April of 1991 when she was twenty-five months old. She is severely delayed in all areas of development, currently functioning at levels of twelve to fourteen months in all areas. The Monroes heard about the early intervention program from another parent at a workshop sponsored by the Parent Information Center and contacted the program staff. When services were begun, the Monroe family had their daughter enrolled in a child-care center, but were not satisfied with the level of care she was receiving. They thought the center was too large. The Monroe family located a family day-care provider who agreed to participate in training and also enrolled their daughter in an early intervention program two afternoons a week. (Transportation provided by the early intervention program made this possible.)

This family is functioning well. The parents are aware of their daughter's disability and are seeking ways to provide her with the best opportunities possible. Their concerns have been to find the best public school option for Cathy and financially to plan wisely

for her future. Staff provided the family with information on financial planning for families with children with disabilities. The staff person also attended the family's IPRD meeting with the School District as part of the transition process to public school services.

The service coordinator made a few visits to the early intervention site to coordinate the services Cathy was receiving there with the care she received at the family day-care provider's home. She also arranged for Cathy's physical therapist to visit the family day-care provider to demonstrate positioning and carrying techniques. In the beginning, monthly home visits were scheduled, but once the program for Cathy was firmly in place, the visits were replaced by monthly telephone contacts.*

Some families might find an informal narrative statement of their strengths/resources and desired outcomes the most workable for them (Fewell, Snyder, Sexton, Bertrand, & Hockless, 1991).

Individualized Family Service Plan

Family Strengths/Resources/Desired Outcomes

Strengths:

The parents are aware of Cathy's disability and are actively planning for her present and future.

*Adapted from Deiner et al., 1990.

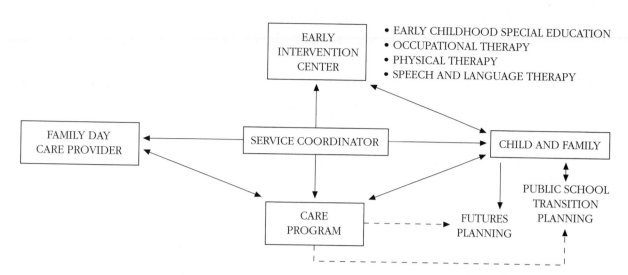

Some families need far less coordination. They are aware of their personal resources and those in the community. However, they, too, need to have a service coordinator available, especially as children transition from one setting to another.

Resources:

Parents are able to read and understand complex material and participate actively on both short- and long-term planning.

Desired outcomes (long term):

Find the best public school placement for Cathy. Sound long-term financial planning

Need from service coordinator:

Coordinate services between early intervention and child care. Help family day care provider understand the importance of positioning for Cathy. Provide some references on long-term financial planning.

Family Goals

Some families do not want to have family goals as part of the IFSP; others feel that having stated outcomes for the family can help them justify what they need for themselves but frequently neglect. The following are family goals for a mother who wants to return to work. Note another format different from the child's IFSP.

Individualized Family Service Plan

Family Goals—Sample

1. *Outcome:*   Lee and Joe will spend more time together as a couple

   Objective: They will be together alone for an outing 1 × /month

   Strategies:

   1.   Ask Joe's mom or friend to babysit

   Persons Responsible: Lee and Joe

   Criteria: They go out 1 × /month

   Review Date: 1 month

2. *Outcome:*   Lee will be provided with more information on prognosis of microcephaly

Objective: To obtain information on children with microcephaly

Strategies:

1.   Ask questions of medical personnel involved with Justin (i.e., pediatrician, pediatric neurologist, or Early Intervention Program)

2.   Provide reading material on specific disability

3.   Provide phone number of Parent Info. Center, where Lee may talk with other parents as well as get info. she wants

Persons Responsible: Lee and Celeste

Criteria: Parent is satisfied with information she obtained

Review Date: 3 months

Transition Planning

Moving from one educational setting to another can be stressful. Increasingly, kindergarten is not the first educational setting that young children have encountered. Most, especially those with a disability, have had previous experience with "school." Based on the requirements of P.L. 99-457 and common sense, we have begun to look more critically at the transition from one setting to another and what this means to children, parents, teachers, and program planning. Because the transition from preschool to kindergarten is the most common one, it will be used for examples in the text. However, the principles underlying transition planning are the same for transitions between other settings.

Smooth transitions require planning. This planning involves children, parents, and teachers from both educational settings. The critical goal for

FAMILY						
				OUTCOME		
DATE	OBJECTIVE	ACTION/STRATEGY	RESPONSIBLE PERSON'S RESOURCES	CRITERIA	RATING	DATE
	Get financial assistance for: daycare food utilities	Explore SSI, utility assistance, catholic charities	1. Service coordinator provides addresses and goes with Mrs. Dee. She does all talking Note: No phone.			

Evaluation Rating Scale

N/A	-	No Longer a Need, Goal, Aspiration, or Project
1	-	Unresolved or Worse; Unattainable
2	-	Unchanged; Still a Need, Goal, Aspiration, or Project
3	-	Resolved or Attained; But Not to the Family's Satisfaction
4	-	Unresolved or Partially Attained, But Improved
5	-	Resolved or Attained to the Family' Satisfaction

The heading family *reflects that this page is for the family. The form focus attention on what the family wants (objective), what kinds of actions or strategies are necessary to achieve this goal, and who is responsible for that role. In addition, this form has an evaluation rating scale that allows the family to decide whether or not the objective has been achieved to their satisfaction.*

children is to provide them the support and skills necessary for them to have a successful experience in the new setting. Children should approach kindergarten with self-confidence, motivation, and openness to a new experience that is a validation of their growing achievement and confidence.

If children are to approach this setting positively, parents, too, must feel confident about their child's ability and the ability of this setting to meet their child's needs. They need confidence in their ability to communicate with teachers and some feeling that they can influence the educational system.

For teachers to support the transition they need to know not only the individual child, but the differences and similarities between their program and the one the child will enter (or has been in).

The U.S. Department of Health and Human Services (1986) identified four key elements to successful transitions for children and families as they moved from preschool to kindergarten:

providing program continuity through developmentally appropriate curricula for preschool and kindergarten children,
maintaining ongoing communication and cooperation between preschool and kindergarten staff,

preparing children for the transition, and

involving parents in the transition. (p. 4)

In general, preschool and kindergarten children have similar learning styles. To the extent that both programs are developmentally based, the transition between the two is easier. It is also easier to meet the individual needs of children with disabilities because this type of programming allows for a wide range of developmental differences within the same class. To the extent that the kindergarten has a very academic orientation and the preschool a developmental one, the transition is likely to be more difficult.

Even kindergartens with a developmental base have some significant differences from most preschools. Because kindergarten children are older they are able to do more things. Increasingly they are interested in the broader community, they have better developed gross and fine motor skills, they are more interested in cooperative play, and play for longer periods. They are also more interested in the written aspects of language and numbers.

Other differences also exist. Kindergartens are likely to be part of the public school system and be located in community schools that also contain older children. The group size is typically larger and the number of teachers is smaller. Time schedules may

---

TRANSITION PLAN

Child: _____   Expected transition date: _____

Service Coordinator: _____   Target receiving site: _____

Reason for transition: _____

_____

Transition Event	Person Responsible	Dates Achieved
1. Parents informed of possible options	Service Coordinator	
2. Receiving agencies contacted	Parents Service Coordinator	
3. Parents visit agencies	Parents Service Coordinator	
4. Transition conference to determine appropriate placement	Parents/Service Coordinator Receiving Agency/ Intervention Team	
5. Transfer of records	Receiving and Sending Agencies	
6. Written transition plan developed	Parents/Service Coordinator Receiving Agency	
7. Placement	Parents/Child/ Receiving Agency	
8. Follow-up	Sending Agency/ Service Coordinator	

---

be more strictly adhered to as there may be only one time when kindergarten children can use the playground, or they may have a schedule for "specials" such as gym or music.

Transition planning begins in September and October, not June. To support children in transitions preschool and kindergarten teachers need open communication patterns throughout the year. If possible, teachers (as well as children) should visit the other program. Joint inservice workshops can facilitate the development of both informal networks as well as the exchange of information. If children are to be screened before entering kindergarten this might be done by the staff of the preschool since these teachers are familiar with the children and their abilities. At the least, these teachers should be asked for input.

As preschool teachers you can help children prepare by visiting kindergartens, perhaps eating lunch in a school cafeteria, or by showing a videotape of what happens in kindergarten. It is important that you show children several different kindergartens if you do not know the school or class they will be entering or if children will go to different schools. Because teachers often are moved or hired in August

this exposure is a good idea even if you feel confident you know exactly what will happen. Talk about the differences and similarities between kindergarten programs and between preschool and kindergarten.

Set up your classroom as a kindergarten for several days and have children role play the rules that may be unfamiliar to them (lining up, quietly walking through halls, asking to go to the bathroom). Support their learning and competence and make this fun, an adventure in growing, not an anxiety-producing experience. Invite some kindergarten children to come to your class and talk about kindergarten and how it is different from preschool. If your kindergartens are half day this exchange is easier, otherwise, consider a teacher inservice day when kindergarten children are not in school.

Effective transition planning needs to involve parents. Encourage parents to visit kindergarten classes in the school their child will attend. They may want to visit early in the year (October) to get a feel for the expectations teachers have of incoming children and then perhaps all the kindergarten classes during the latter part of the school year. Some schools are responsive to suggestions from parents about particular teachers with whom they feel their child would do well, others are not. Most are, however, willing to listen to why certain teachers might be a mismatch.

Talk with parents about what records they want forwarded and those they do not. Tell parents about the other children in your class or children that you know who will be attending the same kindergarten as their child. Encourage parents to invite that child over to play and perhaps arrange a time when parents could get together to talk as well. Encourage parents to find out what services the school has and will supply. Be sure that parents know what their rights are and help them stand up for them, if necessary. A formal transition plan that is part of the IFSP is included.

Summary

Over the past two decades we have learned much about individualized programming. We started by requiring the Individual Education Program to meet the specific needs of children with disabilities. This solved some problems, but did not succeed in getting the parental participation desired. Increasingly we saw the efficacy of including parents and the needs of the family instead of focusing solely on the needs of the child, especially with younger children. For younger children with disabilities an Individualized Family Service Plan is required. It is a family-centered plan that focuses on the strengths, needs, and resources of the family as well as the child. It is too early to determine whether or not our efforts are successful in including parents in this way.

As children are receiving intervention services earlier, they are moving from one program to another. Transition planning has become an important and vital part of the IFSP.

References and Bibliography

Bailey, D. (1987). Collaborative goal setting with families: Resolving differences in values and priorities for services. *Topics in Early Childhood Special Education, 7* (2), 59–71.

Bailey, D. (1988). Considerations in developing family goals. In D. Bailey & R. Simeonsson (Eds.), *Family assessment in early intervention* (pp. 229–249). Columbus, OH: Charles E. Merrill.

Bailey, D., Winton, A., Rouse, L., & Turnbull, A. (1990). Family goals in infant intervention: Analysis and issues. *Journal of Early Intervention, 14*(1), 15–26.

Bayley, N. (1969). *Bayley scales of infant development.* Cleveland, OH: The Psychological Corporation.

Bennett, T., Lingerfelt, B., & Nelson, D. E. (1990). *Developing individualized family support plans.* Cambridge, MA: Brookline Books.

Campbell, P. (1992). Enhancing parent participation in the individualized family service plan. *Topics in Early Childhood Special Education, 11*(4), 112–124.

Connor, F. P., Williamson, G. G., & Siepp, J. M. (1978). *Program guide for infants and toddlers with neuromotor and other developmental disabilities.* New York: Teachers College Press.

Deiner, P., Prudhoe, C., & Lesko, J. (1990). *Del Care: Final report.* Unpublished manuscript, University of Delaware, Newark.

Dunst, C., Johanson, C., Trivette, C., & Hamby, D. (1991). Family-oriented early intervention policies and practices: Family-centered or not? *Exceptional Children. 58*(2), 104–112.

Dunst, C. J., Trivette, M., & Deal, A. G. (1988). *Enabling and empowering families: Principles and guidelines for practice.* Cambridge, MA: Brookline Books.

Farran, D., Kasari, C., Comfort, M., & Jay, S. (1986). *Parent/caregiver involvement scale.* Honolulu, HI: Center for Development of Early Education, Kamehameha Schools, Kapalama Heights.

Fewell, R. R., Snyder, P., Sexton, D., Bertrand, S., & Hockless, M. F. (1991). Implementing IFSPs in Louisiana: Different formats for family-centered practices under part H. *Topics in Early Childhood Special Education, 11* (3), 54–65.

Hebbeler, K., Smith, B., & Black, T. (1991). Federal early childhood special education policy: A model for the improvement of services for children with disabilities. *Exceptional Children 58*(2), 104–112.

Johnson, B. H., McGonigel, M. J., & Kaufmann, R. K. (Eds.). (1989). *Guidelines and recommended practices for the individualized family service plan.* Washington, DC: National Early Childhood Technical Assistance System and Association for the Care of Children's Health.

Linder, T., Hall, S., & Anderson, N. (1988). Transdisciplinary Play-Based Assessment. Workshop at the *International Early Childhood Conference on Children with Special Needs.* Nashville, TN.

McGonigel, M. J., & Garland, C. W. (1988). The individualized family service plan and the early intervention team: Team & family issues & recommended practices. *Infants and Young Children: An Interdisciplinary Journal of Special Care Pediatrics, 1*(1), 10–21.

Nash, J. (1990). Public law 99-457: Facilitating family participation on the multidisciplinary team. *Journal of Early Intervention, 14*(4), 318–326.

National Association for the Education of Young Children and the National Association of Early Childhood Specialists in State Departments of Education (1991). Guidelines for appropriate curriculum content and assessment in programs serving children ages 3 through 8: A position statement. *Young Children, 46*(3), 21–39.

Neisworth, J., & Bagnato, S. J. (1987). *The young exceptional child: Early development and education.* New York: Macmillan Publishing Company.

Pearson, P. H. (1983). The interdisciplinary team process or the professionals' tower of Babel. *Developmental Medicine and Child Neurology, 25,* 390–395.

Shelton, T. L. (1989). The assessment of cognition/intelligence in infancy. *Infants and Young Children: An Interdisciplinary Journal of Special Care Pediatrics, 1* (3), 10–25.

Simeonsson, R. J. (1985). *Carolina record of individual behavior.* Chapel Hill, NC: Frank Porter Graham Child Development Center, The University of North Carolina.

Simeonsson, R. J., Huntington, G. S., & Short, R. J. (1982). Individual differences and goals: An approach to the evaluation of child progress. *Topics in Early Childhood Special Education, 1* (4), 71–80.

U.S. Department of Health and Human Services (1986). *Easing the transition from preschool to kindergarten: A guide for early childhood teachers and administrators.* Washington, DC: U.S. Government Printing Office.

Chapter 7

Program Planning

Developing a program that meets the needs of all the children in your classroom, falls within the guidelines of your current work place, follows the dictates of both state and federal laws, and fits your personal philosophy and beliefs is a difficult task at best. To do it on a daily basis, year after year, may seem impossible. Given the importance of the task, it is necessary not only to do it well, but also to do it efficiently, in a flexible manner that allows for both short- and long-term change, and to do it creatively, so that the classroom experience is enjoyable for you and the children.

With all the requirements, teaching could become like a car assembly line, with changes prescribed only for the different "options" as the cars come through. Joy and creativity could cease to exist. Teaching children with disabilities challenges the assembly line. Children with disabilities offer you the opportunity to work with not only new "options," but with entirely new "models," some you never knew existed. Some are race cars, and some need the care and expertise required by the early Model T. Some require only regular maintenance; others need fine tuning to run just right.

Children with disabilities find it more difficult to learn some concepts than their peers do. They need activities that are self-motivating within a prescribed set of goals. Additionally, planned activities must cover all the strands that are traditionally part of the developmental domain (cognitive, physical, social, and emotional) and, where possible, activities need to teach more than one skill at a time. For example, in order to print, children need to develop finger strength in their dominant hand, particularly in the thumb and index finger. You could require each child to open and close a pinch-type clothespin 100 times each day to develop this strength. You could probably even call it math if the child counted the number of times she opened and closed the pin. However, this activity is boring for both you and the child.

Washing doll clothes and hanging them on the line, or having a felt alphabet and placing letters on the line to spell words or to match a pattern or just for fun, develops the same finger strength and supports additional learning as well.

Program planning involves decisions about how children learn, when learning takes place, and what is to be learned. ". . . good curriculum must be individually appropriate to the needs and interests of the children in a program. In addition, it must be culturally salient and locally relevant and meaningful in the context of a specific community" (National Association for the Education of Young Children and the National Association of Early Childhood Specialists in State Departments of Education, 1991, p. 23).

Developing a Philosophy

Have you ever gone into a classroom, knelt down, and looked around? If not, give it a try. If you were a child, would you like to learn in this space? Does it look warm and inviting? Does it look cold and aseptic? What does the space tell children is important here? Is it safe? Does it invite them in? Can they be alone as well as with others? What do they do here?

You have a philosophy for working with children. It might not be well articulated, but it influences how you set up your room, the number and type of activities you choose, the amount of teacher-directed time versus child-directed time you allocate, and how you work with parents. There are no right or wrong philosophies, but it is important to know what your philosophy is, how it developed, and to evaluate and modify it continually with your personal growth. This is true whether this is your first teaching experience or if you have been teaching for thirty years.

Because your philosophy is such an important variable in how you teach, you need to bring it up to a conscious level so you can take a look at it. You need also to see where children with disabilities fit into it. By clarifying the dimensions of the philosophy, you can decide for yourself what you believe. The topics and illustrations in this book, for example, reflect the author's beliefs.

Begin thinking about your preparation for teaching. Who taught you? What did they believe? Your training experiences, in conjunction with the experiences and values that you brought with you, shaped your initial approach. As you interacted with children you began to evaluate your philosophy and modify it based on what worked for you and what didn't. Probably the more you became active in the work environment the more your philosophy and approach bumped up against others'. If the mismatch was great, you may have begun looking for a new job. In a job interview you may have decided that there were places you wouldn't want to work even if they offered you a job, while other places seemed well matched to your style. Over time you will probably adjust your philosophy to fit in with your work environment and,

with luck, modify the work environment to some extent as well.

The philosophy each of us has about teaching is obvious, whether or not it is directly labeled. For example, in the following statement Chenfeld's philosophy about teaching children comes through loud and clear:

We in education know the impossible is our everyday agenda.

There are many ways to reach our destinations. Sometimes, the way prescribed is not *the way that succeeds. We have our educational goals, our directives, our curriculum guidelines. Often, we are given preset ways to accomplish those goals. Sometimes those ways don't work. We mustn't think there is only one approach. But if goals, approaches, and curriculum grow out of children's ages, stages, interests, and feelings, they are more likely to work. Even so, we mustn't think there is only one approach (Chenfeld, 1987, p. 29).*

Issues in Program Planning

Many issues are involved in program planning. It is important for you to be aware of where you stand on these basic issues. As you will note, these areas overlap and influence each other.

Purpose of Education

What is the purpose of education? This important question is rarely asked. Is it to learn to read, write, and do arithmetic? Certainly cognitive development is an important component. But the purpose of education also is to prepare citizens to live in a democracy. What do children need to learn to be active members of this society? What you believe about the purpose of education influences how and what you teach. If education is about citizenship, then all citizens need to be represented, including those with disabilities, and everyone needs to be aware of the needs of all the citizens. How do the responsibilities of educating for citizenship influence your curriculum? Is your program congruent with these goals?

The Learning Environment

Young children, with disabilities or not, need to play in places where they are safe, feel secure, and can learn to master the skills they will need as adults. This environment must be designed with the children's biological needs in mind. Children should not be expected to sit, to listen to adults talk, or to do rote paperwork for long periods of time. They need periods of activity followed by periods that are more restful. They need to have their cultural values acknowledged and respected.

Content and Process

The relative importance of content and process has been debated for years. The conclusion is that they are both necessary and important. In reality, content and process support each other. If children are going to write (process) they need something to write about (content). Content defined as isolated skills learned through drill and practice is inappropriate at all ages. Relevant content integrated across a broad range of activities supports learning. This is not a new insight, but a reaffirmation.

The most crucial implication of Dewey's research and demonstration school at the turn of the century was that for reading, writing, and mathematics to be meaningful to children they must be built on a strong foundation of experiences, activities, and related language. The 3 Rs must be taught in a context relevant to the interests and understandings of the children. Subject matter cannot be digested well and easily by young children if it is broken down into isolated drill work that has no connection to children's lives and experiences at home, in the community, and at school. The less middle-class experience—which is what school work is based on—children have had, the more this is true (Borden, 1987, p. 15).

Child-Initiated and Teacher-Initiated Instruction

The proportion of time allocated to teacher-directed versus child-directed tasks is another area of concern. Children increase their own knowledge by acting upon their environment and reacting and organizing the feedback they receive. They also learn a great deal from adults. Obviously there is a relationship between content and teacher-initiated instruction and process and child-initiated instruction. The interaction is most supportive of learning, particularly in the area of early childhood special education.

Inclusion and Segregation

The move to include children with disabilities in regular classrooms has a legislative base. However, you need to look at your personal feelings about inclusion. Some feel that all children should be included; others feel that only children with mild disabilities should be in regular classes. Who do you believe should be included? Once you are clear about your

feelings you can then go to the next stage and look at how they will be included and consider the supports necessary for inclusion.

At a more personal level, there may be some disabilities that you find easier to plan for than others, and some children more appealing than others. This is reality. While all of us like to think we like all children equally, this is rarely true. I think we may treat all children equally, but personal feelings are different. Try to move yourself away from the specifics and figure out the "generic" aspect of the child or disability that influences you. That is the part that will be repeated with other children. Overall, "the goal for the teacher is to serve as a catalyst and to allow each child to feel that she is a capable learner" (Borden, 1987, p. 17).

Implications of a Philosophy on Programming

At this point you have examined your philosophy. What does it really mean on the first day of school? To the extent that you control how your day is scheduled, a great deal.

Time Allocation

Think about your day with children, whether it is a half day, a full day, or extended care. The first broad plans you develop divide the day into purposeful segments. The decisions that you make in time allotment reflect your philosophy. If one teacher in a two-and-a-half-hour program for four-year-olds designates an hour for free play and another fifteen minutes, that is a statement. Look at the length of group times. Are they appropriate for the age/developmental level of the children? How much time is allocated for individual versus group work?

Number of Activities

How many activities are available for children to choose from? Are all the children participating in art at the same time and making the same project, or are some at the easel, some working with playdough, and some building with blocks? Are some children in the hospital in the dramatic play area, while others are at the writing center, at the water table, or working on the computer? Do children choose their centers or are they assigned? Must they stay a specific amount of time or can they come and go at will?

Balance of Activities

Look at your activities to see the balance between active and passive times, and teacher-directed and child-directed activities. Do these match your philosophy? How complex are the activities you offer? Do children who are gifted as well as those who learn more slowly still have choices?

Being aware of your philosophy is the first step in program planning. It influences how you teach. That philosophy also influences the decisions you make about the curriculum you present to the children.

Curriculum Guidelines

The following curriculum guidelines have been adapted from those set forth by the National Association for the Education of Young Children and the National Association of Early Childhood Specialists in State Departments of Education for programs serving children ages three through eight (1991). These guidelines are broad-based and support developmentally appropriate curriculum and practices.

1. Program planning should be grounded in developmental theory and designed to teach the whole child. It should reflect what we know about child development, learning theory, and family studies. For all children to be included a narrow-based system such as one that is exclusively behavioral is inappropriate. Likewise, a curriculum that concentrates only on academics is also inappropriate. Programming must include all the domains: cognitive, physical, social, and emotional. In general, the younger the child the closer the curriculum must be tied to the child's experiential base.

2. Learning needs to be relevant, meaningful, and contextual. Children can learn to count by counting the number of children that sit with them at snacktime, or how many objects fit on a shelf. This is both relevant and meaningful. The underlying assumptions that "learning should hurt," and "the main job of education is to teach basic skills" (Roper, 1987, p. 12) are inappropriate. If children are to become lifelong learners the process has to be motivating. Using conceptual organizers such as themes or units is motivating and helps children learn information in context. Real life is not organized by subject matter areas, but rather applies appropriate knowledge to solve problems or learn about a particular area. Skills taught in context are more useful to children.

3. Program planning needs to be realistic, developmentally and age appropriate, reflective of the needs, interests, and abilities of the children being taught. Children are different. Young children need concrete learning experiences. It is unrealistic to expect them to understand higher level abstract concepts. These are learned more easily later. Since children with disabilities often display uneven development, it is important to support lower level skills in ways that are age appropriate, not just developmentally matched. Relevant curriculum decisions reflect the location of the program also. Children who live near the ocean might identify similarities and differences in sea shells they have collected. This would be inappropriate in other locations. Children's individual differences must be acknowledged

and supported. Their world needs to be expanded through using a broad range of learning strategies and experiences.

4. Programming moves from what children know to the acquisition and consolidation of new knowledge. Children come to learning experiences with different backgrounds; some have had a variety of experiences, others relatively few. It is important to meet all children where they are, therefore activities will have to be flexible and allow for different learning experiences with the same activity. You need the ability to make activities both easier and harder to meet the needs of a diverse group of children.

5. Program areas must have age and subject matter integrity. Although children are young, they need accurate information as a base for learning. Science is not magic. Language Arts includes literature, poetry, and plays. Music is more than "Where is Thumbkin?" It includes knowledge of instruments and an awareness of idioms from classical to jazz, from reggae to hard rock. This doesn't mean that you expect young children to memorize the type of music you play so they can raise their hand and identify it, but rather that they can relate to the music and identify a mood. That is appropriate for their age. As children get older, expectations change. Although some believe that you can teach children anything if you break the steps down into small enough parts, the question is "What is the point?" If they can learn it more efficiently at an older age and do not need the information now, why bother?

6. Children are active learners who can learn from errors as well as successes. Children must be active participants in the learning process. New concepts must be introduced in a hands-on, concrete way. Abstraction is possible when children have an experiential base to build from. To learn, children need the opportunity to make mistakes without being penalized. They need to be supported in taking cognitive risks. Often the mistakes children make are useful to teachers in guiding the learning process.

7. Programming emphasizes the importance of social interaction. Young children need to develop skills for being part of a group. Group inclusion is particularly important for children with disabilities. Just having children in the same room does not mean that they will necessarily interact; in fact, they frequently do not. Social interaction is dealt with in greater detail later in this chapter.

8. Programs need to be designed to support children's independence and develop competence. Children need to experience success and feel good about themselves as they learn. They need to become increasingly independent learners, decision makers, and problem solvers.

9. Programs need to be safe for children. Children need to feel safe in school both psychologically and physically. They should not be deprived of food or exercise as punishment for not completing tasks.

10. Programming needs to be flexible. Although guidelines are useful, they are just that, guidelines.

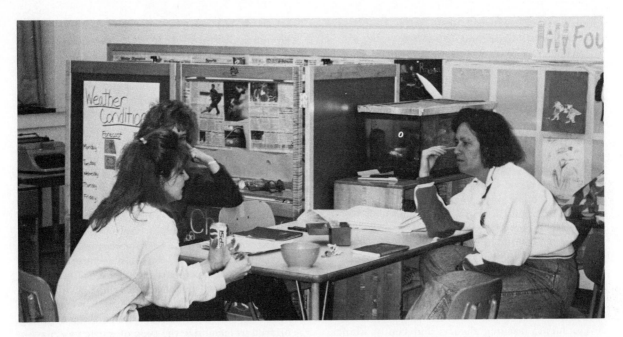

Program planning requires time. Teachers planning together can take into account the developmental needs of the children as a whole as well as individualize planning for specific children.

Teachers must be able to adapt programming to meet the needs of individuals and groups of children.

These guidelines are a useful foundation for making curriculum decisions for programs that serve children three through eight. In addition to using general guidelines, the ability to individualize the process of learning for particular children is important in program planning.

Interface of Developmentally Appropriate Practice and Early Childhood Special Education

Some feel that these guidelines are not enough for early childhood special education programs. They caution that the intent of these programs is intervention and the goal of preventing problems before they happen (Peterson, 1982).

Although the principles of developmentally appropriate practice are supported, some additional considerations include the fact that within a given classroom some children need more specialized services and planning than others. Some children may lack the prerequisite skills for child-based learning, and these may need to be taught and supported. Individualized planning, in addition to being based on the child's strengths and needs, must take into account the priorities of the family and the skills required for future school and nonschool environments (Carta, Schwartz, Atwater, & McConnell, 1992). Ongoing criterion-based assessment is necessary in order to monitor the child's progress toward these goals.

Teachers of young children with disabilities must have a wide range of teaching strategies to choose from. These strategies need to be matched to individual children to facilitate learning. Some children with disabilities may need support to be actively involved and participatory. Services for young children with disabilities are family-centered, and families must play an active role in home-school relationships. These principles broaden the expectations for teachers' skills, and assume that children will require more varied learning environments. The requirements, however, really represent a matter of degree of interpretation rather than an underlying philosophical difference.

"Programs serving young children with special needs must be outcome-based, with specific criteria, procedures, and timelines used to determine if individual children progress toward stated outcomes" (Carta et al., 1992, p. 7). This approach typically leads to teacher-directed programs. This outcome is probably the greatest inconsistency between the developmentally appropriate practice and the intervention philosophy. The accountability principle that came to the forefront with the passage of P.L. 94-142 seems still to be present.

Carta et al. (1992) question the efficacy of applying developmentally appropriate practice to young children with disabilities. At this time there is not, according to their review, a research base to support this approach. However, to date the approach has not been widely enough used to reach any conclusions.

I support the developmentally appropriate practices and the skills that teachers need to teach a wide range of children in their classes. I also feel that we need to develop a research base to show whether or not these practices can be supported empirically. This is an issue of which you need to be aware as you enter the field.

Strategies for Individualizing Learning

Regardless of content or age, there is a cycle of learning that takes place as new information becomes part of a child's repertoire. This learning framework has four broad aspects: awareness, exploration, inquiry, and utilization (National Association for the Education of Young Children and the National Association of Early Childhood Specialists in State Departments of Education, 1991).

Awareness. Awareness is the initial stage in the cycle of learning. Awareness grows out of experience. As children notice differences among themselves this awareness usually gives voice to questions: "Why can't Juan walk?" "Why is my skin black and Justine's white?" If children are at an awareness level they want a simple, straightforward answer. "Juan's legs aren't strong enough to hold him so he needs braces to help," may be all the child wants to know. Often we tell them more than they really want to know.

Exploration. Exploration is the next level and requires children to observe and try to make sense out of an event or experience by exploring the materials, gathering additional information, poking, prodding, or what ever seems to make sense to the child. Although it is tempting to "explain" the situation, it is rarely useful, as children need to find their own meaning for information. "Explaining" also fosters dependency. Asking open-ended questions is more useful.

Inquiry. Inquiry involves the understanding of classes of information, the ability to generalize information, or to call up previous learning for comparison. Adults can help children with more focused questions at this stage.

Utilization. Utilization is a functional level of learning where information can be used in a variety of situations and applied to new information and situations. Children who understand the concept of counting can not only count objects accurately but utilize that information to decide how many chairs are necessary for six children to sit on.

This cycle occurs again and again as children learn. It is important to know where individual children are in the cycle. When a child encounters information for the first time it is expected that he will begin at an awareness level. Children with previous experiences may be generalizing the information. Programs must be designed that allow children to profit from experience at all places in the learning cycle. With new knowledge the cycle begins again.

For a variety of reasons, children with disabilities may have less broad experiential backgrounds.

They need to be given time to experience and explore before they can be expected to participate in higher level skills. Young children encountering a wheelchair for the first time, too, will go through these stages. Initially, they will be curious about the wheelchair, then they might like to sit in it and see how it works. This is still exploration; they need this time. When they have their own understanding of the wheelchair, try to broaden and generalize this information so they can figure out what things are difficult or easy to do in a wheelchair and the relationship between the wheelchair, crutches, and walkers. As they integrate this information, have them think about the world outside the classroom, the utility of curb cuts, why bathrooms are so difficult, and the problem with table heights.

Theme/Unit Based Planning

Planning around a theme or unit helps focus activities. Themes provide a structure that supports concept development. However, like all good ideas, themes can be reduced to the trivial and mundane. As you think about long-range planning, start with brainstorming, not holidays. Be wild, include parents and children if this is comfortable for you. Gather ideas; you will focus and narrow them later. If you are comfortable with more structure, start with the seasons as a foundation and build from there. Traditional themes for young children include the senses, transportation, community helpers, and so on. There is nothing wrong with these themes, but sometimes it is fun to stretch yourself. Whatever the theme, be sure it has internal validity. (Don't have children plant seeds in the fall!)

The next step in planning is to decide how to implement the theme. It requires "deciding upon theme goals, listing the vocabulary associated with the topic, agreeing on a 'main event,' listing materials needed, describing parents' and children's involvement, and planning evaluation" (Nunnelley, 1990, p. 25). If you are excited about a theme, the children will be as well.

Implementing an IEP/IFSP in a Theme Plan

There are a variety of ways to incorporate individualized planning in a theme or unit. I find the easiest way is to make a chart. I put the annual goal in the middle and the areas around the room at the sides. If the theme was transportation and the annual goals were to improve both receptive and expressive language, my chart would look something like the following for four- to five-year-olds. I purposefully chose something that is common to illustrate the point that it is not difficult to incorporate individualized planning in a theme.

In many ways the theme makes some of the planning easier. The vocabulary to stress is more obvious and is more easily reinforced as it is maintained for at least a week. As children expand their concepts, use analogies from one form of transportation to another to help them learn. If parents want to work on language concepts at home, help them focus. Sometimes having parents decide what they will do in each room of the house helps children learn contextually. Make a chart similar to the one illustrated, but instead of having areas of the classroom have rooms of the house. In the bedroom children might learn the names of various parts of clothing; in the kitchen, eating utensils and foods; in the living room, furniture and so on. Parents are more likely to participate if they can put the sheet of paper on the refrigerator instead of in a notebook. If the charts are changed frequently and parents are aware of your themes, the possibility for language learning increases.

In program planning, there are certain events or times that are often forgotten or ignored which are crucial for the success of a program. Some of these are highlighted.

MATH

Identify and classify modes of transportation
Compare size of modes of transportation
Count and order different modes
(by speed, number of passengers, and so on)

LANGUAGE ARTS

Use a Language Experience story
Read books on various types of transportation
(Go on a field trip to see one mode of
transportation and do a Language Experience
Story when you return)

SCIENCE

Floating and sinking in water table (boats)
Wheels

To improve language skills
(Receptive and Expressive)

MANIPULATIVE

Small train, bus, cars, traffic signs

ART

Train mural
Car-shaped paper at easel

DRAMATIC PLAY

Sell tickets at the train station,
Bus station, Airline terminal
Boat marina
Have travel brochures

MUSIC

"The Wheels on the Bus"
"I've Been Working on the Railroad"
"Row, Row, Row Your Boat"

BOOKS

Richard Scarry's Book of Transportation
The Big Book of Trains
The Big Book of Boats
The Little Engine that Could

LARGE MOTOR

Train of cardboard boxes
Tricycle with wagons

BLOCKS

Add trains, buses, airplanes, cars, boats, to unit blocks

Vocabulary
Types of transportation
Train (station), bus (station), airplane (terminal, hangar), car (garage), boat (marina, slip, dock)
Freight train, passenger train
School bus, city bus, long distance bus
Sedan, station wagon, convertible
Speedboat, tanker, tugboat, sailboat

Transitions

Some times of the day have unique opportunities for growth as well as challenges to the system; arrival and departure times and other transitions fall in this category.

Transition is the label given to the time between the end of one event and the beginning of another. This can be the time between activities, the beginning and end of the day, before and after lunch, moving from inside to outside, and vice versa. Transitions are particularly difficult times for children and adults as well. At home, the times before meals, bedtime, and the like are also stressful. As there are many transitions in a single day, and the stress created in these transitions can carry over into the next event, it is important to carefully plan transitions to both increase learning and decrease stress.

The younger the children, the wider the age group of children, or the more severely disabled the children are the more likely it is that transition periods will be longer. (Compare the time it takes for a five-year-old versus a three-year-old to put on boots and a snow suit.) With younger children, the transitions may be more obvious to the adult than to the child.

Transitions are difficult for a variety of reasons:

Boredom. Transitions often involve waiting. Children who have "nothing to do" will usually find something to do, and it is rarely what you would choose.

Combat boredom. Eliminate as much waiting time as possible. When you can't eliminate it, help children by singing a song with them, doing a finger play, telling or reading a story. Do not move from an activity until you have the next one prepared. That is,

do not dismiss children from group time until the activity centers are prepared. Don't always wait until all the children are present before starting an activity. Often slower children speed up if they think they are missing something. Know your children; if some children are perpetually slow, start them first.

Change. Children, like adults, like to change activities when they are finished, not by the clock. They may feel uncertain about what will happen next.

Make change easier. Be sure to warn children before they are expected to make a change. "In five minutes it will be clean-up time." Have a schedule that you follow. As young children cannot tell time, it is not important whether you allow activities to run a little longer or shorter, but rather that you follow the same sequence of events. It is also important to have a simple picture schedule to show children the order of events. This is particularly helpful for children who are having problems adjusting, as they can see that the final picture is going home. Encourage children to think about what will happen next. Make a sequencing task out of schedule so children know what is happening. (Have children arrange the pictured events in sequence.) It is particularly important to do this at the beginning of the year and when schedules change or if your daily schedule is variable.

Rules. Children may feel uncertain about the "rules" or expectations for them during transition times.

Makes rules easy to follow. Help children understand exactly what you expect of them during transition times. When cleaning up, you may even want to have a picture or outline of the item on the shelf where it belongs if it is important that it be returned to the right place. Expect some testing behavior at transition

| Children arriving | Small manipulations | Group time | Free play | Snack | Outside | Children going home | Individual pieces with Velcro on the back |

Velcro strip

If you have activities (specials) that rotate, put those in the schedule, too, as well as unusual events such as a visitor or going on a field trip.

| music | gym | visitor (firefighter) | field trip |

time. Children need to feel secure and know that there are rules and that an adult is in control. A calm but firm response to children is reassuring.

Lack of planning. Transitions are an important part of the day and need to have a purpose as well as advanced planning to make them work.

Plan for transitions. Transitions are a great opportunity for learning as well as a necessary part of the day. Help increase body awareness by having "children with long hair" or "children with brown eyes" or "children with stripes" and so on leave first. Be creative and have children pretend they are cleaning up for a party, or as they move between activities have them jump like kangaroos, move as softly as a feather in the wind, march, or tiptoe (ideas adapted from Davidson, 1988).

Inclusion

Interpersonal competence is established in the first few years of life (Guralnick, 1988). Children with disabilities are often expected to have this interpersonal competence because of their experience with a wide variety of adults. However, these children may be competent with their parents and adults on a one-to-one basis because adults do the compensating and adapt their expectations. The same compensating may not occur with peers (Guralnick, 1988).

Competence with peers is important. Success with social tasks such as making friends and gaining entry into groups is imperative not only now but to later adjustment. Inclusion of all children in the same classroom makes this more of a challenge, yet integrated settings provide opportunities for many levels of play, including more complex play behavior (Guralnick & Groom, 1987). The predictive value of peer relations over the long term is true for nondisabled children as well as children with disabilities (Guralnick, 1988).

Social competence is the key to social acceptance. Peers make judgments based on data (Johnny can't climb, looks funny, and so on). Children enter a new group with a "clean slate," but develop a personal social history within the group. Children with disabilities often use strategies of approaching other children that make it difficult to make friends. They are often less socially competent. As clusters of children form, more complex entry skills are required to join groups; for children lacking these skills a reputation for lack of social competence is established, and a pattern of social separation and reduced social status results (Guralnick & Groom, 1987). Social networks become even narrower and more difficult to enter as children get older, therefore, it is imperative that children learn these skills early.

Intervention aimed at supporting the social integration of children with disabilities has been approached from two very different frameworks. Teachers with strong developmental backgrounds have assumed that physical proximity to other children, plus using more open-ended, process-oriented activities in a free play setting would result in social integration. This has not been the case.

Others, from a more behavioral orientation, have observed the lack of social competence and have developed very structured skits and specific exercises for children to repeat (Strain, 1990). Children might be paired, and one child would say, "Hello, my name is Dayonn. I like your shirt." The other child would respond, "I'm glad to meet you. My name is Min." "I'm glad to meet you." Other than using different names, all of the children in the class would use the same procedure and the same words. The exercise might be repeated several times. This activity has resulted in increased integration, but it has some limitations.

The problem is that the structured behavioral approach is an overly narrow solution to a complex problem. It is viewed as developmentally inappropriate by some preschool and kindergarten teachers. They find it stilted and not easily incorporated into their existing teaching style. It is not likely to be widely used outside of research settings.

Inclusion of children with disabilities probably will not happen without thoughtful planning and programming, yet we rarely think about this particular area when we program plan. One strategy is to start by increasing the awareness of all children to different disabilities. Using the conceptual framework of the learning cycle discussed earlier in the chapter has potential. Work from awareness to exploration to inquiry to utilization. Start with awareness. Some of the activities in Part Four of this book are designed to increase other children's awareness of disabilities. Then allow children time to explore and experiment. If this involves a simulation, do not have the child with a disability play the part of the child with a disability. Such casting reinforces the label, and the other children need to construct and test out their own knowledge. They are learning what it might be like to have a particular disability; the child with a disability already knows this.

Have the children discuss the feelings they had during the simulation and have them evaluate the strategies they used to cope. Help them decide what was easy and what was difficult in the classroom, at home, and in the community. Repeat the process on another day, helping children generalize and use the information they learned from before. At this stage your child "expert" has a role. Help children generate additional options as well as alternative explanations for behaviors. Again, try to encourage children who are ready to think in a broader context.

Teacher-Supported Learning

You, as the teacher, play a vitally important role in supporting the learning of children. It is often tempting to let children play by themselves or together with other children without being directly involved yourself. While it is good for children to learn to play independently and with other children, they will learn more if they spend some time with a supportive adult (Hohmann, 1988). Remember that it is through play that children learn. Play is really the "work" of childhood and is more than "just play."

In general, there are three kinds of support you can offer to children: environmental support, nonverbal support, and verbal support:

Environmental support. Set up the space to allow all children to participate in activities. This may mean adding pillows and bolsters to the rug to help a child sit, putting a block under a chair, or even adding a seat belt so all children can participate. Your support requires providing a sufficient quantity and variety of materials to meet children's needs. In addition to traditional materials you may need to include books that describe children with disabilities, contradict gender stereotypes, and accurately represent cultural and ethnic groups. Your support includes providing adaptive equipment that can be explored and used by children. You support children by planning an environment that stretches children's understanding of their world.

Nonverbal support. You can encourage children's play by watching what children do with materials and listening to what they say. Place yourself at the children's eye level. If the child is sitting on the floor, then you sit on the floor, too. If the child is standing, kneel down to be at her level. Use materials yourself, but don't get so involved that you are no longer paying attention to the children. Imitate children's actions. Watch, however, that you do not make things that might frustrate children when comparing their creation to yours. Use your body to express interest. Accept children's statements and explanations even when they appear to be blatantly out of line. Young children rarely consciously lie, their concept of reality is simply different from adults'. Remain calm in the face of children's "mistakes" and support the next steps of following through (cleaning up or picking up the pieces if necessary).

Verbal support. Verbal interactions encourage children's language, self-concept, and problem solving as well as social skills. Talk with children about what they are doing, acknowledge their actions and choices. Ask children questions that relate to their play. Refer children to one another for problem solving and additional conversation. Encourage children to answer their own questions by saying "What do you think?" Converse with nonverbal children whether or not you receive a response from them.

Children are curious about each other. It is important to encourage and verbally support this curiosity even if it feels uncomfortable by adult standards. You can stop children from asking questions, but not from being curious. Talk to children about differences as well as similarities and support their exploration of these differences. When children express concerns respond to them as real.

Children who receive support from adults during their play are likely to learn more. Children will greatly benefit from your support and attention (adapted from Whitehead, 1989).

Teachers support children's learning by encouraging and supporting them as they work together.

Praise versus Encouragement

A positive, appreciative atmosphere is more helpful for children's growth than is a setting where negative, blaming comments are made frequently. Children with disabilities, in particular, have already heard so much about what they can not do, making a positive approach all the more necessary. Praise is one way of doing this, although recently this approach has come into question (Hitz & Driscoll, 1988). We usually think about praise as being positive, general, and implying some judgment or evaluation of the individual's performance. Some examples of praise are, "Nice job, Alexis" or "Charday is being a good listener." Most of us use praise because we want children to feel good about themselves, to encourage them to learn, and to promote appropriate behavior. Recent research, however, shows that praise does not always have these effects (Hitz & Driscoll, 1988). Praise can sometimes have negative effects if not used appropriately. The technique of praising one child in order to get others to behave similarly is often not effective and may cause the other children to resent the praised child. Inappropriate praise may also influence children to rely on others' opinions rather than judging for themselves (they have become externally motivated rather than internally motivated), thus encouraging dependence on adults rather than independence (Hitz & Driscoll, 1988).

What are the alternatives? Certainly a positive climate is still most important for children. Encouragement may be more appropriate than praise. Encouragement refers specifically to responses to children's efforts and/or specific aspects of their work or play. Encouragement does not place judgment. ("You used a lot of colors in your painting.") Encouragement also focuses on the child's efforts rather than on an evaluation of a finished product ("I noticed that you played for a long time with the dress-up clothes today" or "You look like you enjoyed digging holes in the sand"). Encouragement is designed not to compare a child with other children but rather to note improvement and progress for that individual child ("You stacked more blocks today than you've ever done before").

If our goals are to have independent, self-motivated, happy children, it appears that encouragement, rather than inappropriate praise, may best foster the desired positive growth and development (adapted from Whitehead, 1989).

Discipline

Conflict and its resolution is at the core of many of society's problems. The conflict between the child's growing need for autonomy and the adult's need to inculcate values and socially acceptable behavior is classic. The methods that most adults use to accomplish this are discipline, guidance, or punishment.

This inherent conflict may be viewed as a continuum. Individuals often feel very differently about where on this continuum one should interact with children.

Complete autonomy ——————— Complete submission

This conflict appears first in toddlerhood, and parents and caregivers make a conscious or unconscious choice about where they stand on this issue. The issues that need to be resolved in toddlerhood are the forerunners of the conflicts in adolescence and perhaps even in later adult life. When put in perspective, and if one believes that conflict resolution with toddlers sets the groundwork for adolescence, then some solutions become more useful than others.

Many of us use the words discipline, guidance, or punishment as though they were interchangeable synonyms. However, each means something slightly different, and their use affects children differently. Gartrell (1987) defines discipline as behavior which is designed to encourage self-control. That is, any actions or words that help children learn to self-monitor their own behavior so that it is appropriate and acceptable is discipline. Discipline is a form of teaching. One assumption is that young children misbehave out of lack of knowledge. Discipline is designed to supply information on appropriate actions.

Punishment and guidance are two forms of discipline. Punishment involves the infliction of negative consequence for a behavior that is inappropriate or wrong (Gartrell, 1987). Punishment usually succeeds in stopping behavior that is unwanted, but it may have negative effects on some children. Children may learn that they can "get away" with negative behavior without the presence of the controlling adult. Alternatively, they may come to fear adults as harsh and uncaring.

Guidance or positive discipline facilitates the development of good self-concepts, prosocial behaviors, and an ability to control one's own behavior (Gartrell, 1987). It is a process-approach to guiding children's behavior rather than an isolated act of punishment. Positive discipline involves awareness of children's feelings, developmental levels, and the ability to set and keep sensible limits. When children do something that is unacceptable, they are presented with the logical consequences of their behavior in a way that preserves their self-esteem. As children learn there are consequences for their behavior—positive ones when they are acting appropriately, and negative ones when they act inappropriately—they begin to learn to act responsibly and control their own behavior.

The goal of discipline is to help children learn socially acceptable limits and develop internal controls to implement these limits. As such, discipline involves facilitating children's social development and prosocial skills (Lawton, 1988).

Typically, adults begin to discipline children at the end of the first year, when a child becomes mobile. Toddlers behave—they don't misbehave. Misbehavior is an interpretation by adults. Morrison

(1988) has noted some characteristics of toddlers that prompt adults to provide discipline. He includes:

1. The child's growing independence
2. The child's need to "do it myself"
3. The toddler's high activity level
4. The child's active learning style

Setting limits is part of an adult's commitment to a child, not just a reaction to the immediate behavior. The discipline should fit the child and should be accompanied by a conviction that setting limits is an important part of caring for young children. When caring accompanies discipline it is guidance; when there is no caring it is just punishment.

The goals of discipline are two-fold. One is an immediate: to stop inappropriate behavior as it occurs. The second goal involves the development of inner controls for behavior. Adults can facilitate the development of these inner controls in children if they use positive discipline effectively. The following suggestions are techniques that teachers and parents have found useful.

- Respond positively when children are acting appropriately, or making attempts to please. For example, "You did a good job putting away your toys today. That makes me happy."

- Set up physical space which encourages appropriate behavior. Avoid long running areas and tippable shelves.

- Help children label their feelings verbally when they are upset, angry, or hurt. You might say, "Sarah, you're really angry because Justin took your doll."

- Provide reasons for the limits you set for children. For example, "Bobby, you need to walk carefully inside. The floors are slippery."

- Help children solve their problems themselves. You may need to assist younger or more inexperienced children with the words to say at first, but eventually they will learn how to "talk out" their problems. An example, "Jimmy, tell Reneé you don't like it when she hits you."

- If a child is having a "bad day," give him or her some space to work out those feelings. Adding playdough or water play to the day's activities often provides a good outlet.

- Be consistent in setting limits, so children will learn what is expected of them. For example, if children need to stay at the snack table while eating, remind them and reinforce that behavior with all the children.

- If a child has a tantrum, allow him or her to calm down in a safe place. Being out of control is scary for the child, so an adult should be nearby. Tell the child, in a soothing voice, that as soon as he is calm the two of you can talk about the problem.

Do not try to reason with a child while he is screaming and thrashing. You might say, "When you are calm, we will talk about the problem."

- Let children know that you care for them and are proud of who they are and what they can do. For example, "Byung, I'm so proud of you. You put the blocks away all by yourself."

- Provide enough interesting activities and smooth transitions to keep children actively involved in constructive play with minimal time wasted in waiting. Give warnings before interrupting children's play and have the next activity ready so they aren't waiting idly while you set up.

- Let children know when you are angry and model appropriate ways to handle that anger. For example, "Rosa, it makes me angry when you hurt Shauna. You need to go to another activity."

- Help children realize that their actions and words affect others. For example, "Peter, did you see Mark's face? He was really angry when you knocked down his blocks."

Discipline is influenced by several factors, including what the adult knows about how the child usually acts or responds to social situations. Children's temperaments and the "goodness of fit" between adult and child may be particularly important when considering young children with disabilities (see Chapter 4 for additional details). Keogh (1982) found that teacher perceptions of the teachability of a child with a disability was significantly related to the child's temperament. That is, those children whose temperaments were rated as easy were more likely to be rated by teachers as successful in the preschool environment. She suggests that the child's temperament may influence the teacher's expectations of the child, and thus influence instructional and disciplinary decisions.

In addition to the child's temperament, other characteristics such as diagnostic category, care demands, behavior problems, and social responsiveness play a part in how adults handle discipline situations (Beckman-Bell, 1981). Those children whose care involves more demands usually cause more stress for caregivers (Beckman-Bell, 1981).

Program Evaluation

Once both individual and class programs are in place it is necessary to determine whether or not they are effective. In the past it was often assumed that if children went to school they were learning. But teaching, like other professions, must be accountable. Accountable not to only principals and other administrators, but to children, their parents, and the legal system as well. Evaluations are an integral part of teaching.

Program evaluation has three major issues: the purpose of the evaluation, the process of doing the evaluation, and the ways of going about the evaluation.

Purpose of Program Evaluation

The major reason for evaluating a program is to provide information to those involved with the program about what it is doing well and what needs attention (Barnard, 1986). One obvious question is, "Does the program meet the needs of the people it serves?" The answer to this question requires information. What are the characteristics and needs of the children and families served in the program? Different children in different types of families have different needs, although they may all be in the same program or classroom. Program evaluation needs to be sensitive to both group and individual differences.

Sometimes program evaluation is used to help solve a particular problem a program or class is having. This type of evaluation focuses on a single aspect of a program or a classroom that has been identified as a problem. Although the problems may vary, the procedure for evaluation is frequently similar.

- Identify the problem in a way that it can be solved. "They should not have violence on children's television shows" is not a solvable problem. It is a value judgment. On the other hand, "Some children watch 'superheroes' on television and come to school and play out what they have seen. How can I set up my classroom to discourage superhero play? What rules do I need to develop to regulate this play?"

- Review the relevant literature and talk to people in other programs or classes to see how they have dealt with similar problems. (Although problems may seem unique, it is unlikely that you are the first person to encounter the problem.)

- Develop a system for dealing with the problem. Share this system with all those involved (especially parents) and gather their input. Modify the system.

- Field-test the system for an appropriate period of time (perhaps two to four weeks).

- Evaluate the results, modify the system if necessary, and retest or decide to keep the system in place.

You may have used this procedure informally when you were coping with "superhero play" and not realized that in reality you evaluated your program as having a problem, explored the dimensions of the problem, looked at what others had done and developed a system to solve the problem, evaluated that solution, and modified your approach.

Some program evaluation is extensive and ambitious. You may be asked to support evaluation projects like that with specific input. Some evaluation projects are long-range as well as short-range. It is important to know at the beginning the purpose of the evaluation. When the evaluation is being done to decide whether to continue a program or eliminate it, those involved may have very different views of the process.

If the purpose of the evaluation is to determine whether or not early intervention decreased the number of children requiring special education services, then the data necessary for evaluation is very different than if the purpose of the evaluation is to decide which is more effective, full- or half-day kindergarten. Without having decided on the purpose of the evaluation, one cannot proceed in any meaningful way.

Sometimes evaluation is very long-term. Knowing long-term goals for children can help focus a curriculum in early childhood. United Cerebral Palsy cites a number of long-term goals for children with disabilities and their families. Programs for early childhood might evaluate their program planning in light of these goals:

1. independence;

2. a sense of self-worth, including adjustment to the disability, use of talents and abilities and constructive ways of dealing with feelings of helplessness and frustration;

3. integration of the disabled individual into the community;

4. positive integration into the family;

5. parental ability to deal constructively with their feelings about the child;

6. a parental sense of competence (Barnard, 1986, p. 6).

The Process of Program Evaluation

Program evaluation is "in." People who fund programs want to know how effective they are, and administrators may need the information to defend programs or to get additional programs or classrooms. Teachers, however, may feel threatened by the evaluation process or feel that it is not relevant to them. You may feel that the obligations of teaching are enough. "You hired me to teach, leave me alone and let me teach!" Program evaluation is not likely to succeed if teachers do not support it.

The process of evaluation at the least describes the population you serve and exactly what you are doing. At a minimal level, all programs and individual classrooms need this information. If you are not clear about what you are doing and why you are doing it, you cannot effectively present your classroom to parents or administrators.

Evaluation is essential for improving programs. It is important for administrators to know how you evaluate your program and how satisfied you are with your job. To the extent that you are not an active participant in the process, changing those things that do not satisfy you, you are unlikely to be happy in your job. You are one of the stakeholders; you have a vested interest, and you need to know enough about the evaluation process to make it work for you and the program. You also need to be sure the evaluation process does not interfere with your teaching.

The less intrusive and less burdensome to teachers the evaluation process is, the more likely it is to go smoothly and to be completed (Barnard, 1986). You need to remind others that this is a primary consideration, not a secondary one. It is also important that data collected is used, and that the people who collect the information are informed of its use. If you perceive the information you collect going into a "black hole," you are unlikely to continue collecting it in a careful manner, if at all.

To the extent that children have individualized programs with goals or outcomes that can be measured, it is important that these be evaluated as well. According to Barnard (1986), individualized plans should be grouped, and you should aim for an 85 percent achievement rate. A higher rate may show that you aren't stretching yourself or the families; a rate of 50 percent or less means that expectations are not realistic or the program is not effective.

Ways of Doing Program Evaluation

The most commonly asked question of programs is, "Are children different because they received this service or participated in this program?" This was the question asked of early intervention years ago, and researchers developed experimental designs to try to answer that question. Overall, the conclusion was that early intervention was effective economically and as a method for improving the quality of life of the children served.

Today we need to ask different questions because we no longer must "prove" the efficacy of early intervention. We are now into fine-tuning the system. We need to learn about the effectiveness of different models of programming for different populations: "What types of services, in what combinations, using what models are most effective?" Action research asks why a program works or fails to work and for whom it works best (Seitz, 1986).

Summary

Program planning is complex and challenging. It requires examining one's philosophy about teaching and where children with disabilities fit into that philosophy. It requires looking at the relationship between one's personal philosophy and how this philosophy is reflected in the classroom setting. Bumping up against these personal issues are the ones in the field at large. That is, "Is there a workable compromise between developmentally appropriate practice and the individualized needs of children with disabilities for intervention and prevention?"

Program evaluation grows also out of these concerns. In the past we asked whether or not children with disabilities should be part of regular classrooms. Now we are asking questions about the most effective way to plan programs to include all children.

References and Bibliography

Barnard, K. (1986). Major issues in program evaluation. In *Program evaluation: Issues, strategies and models.* (pp. 4–7). Washington, DC: National Center for Clinical Infant Programs.

Beckman, P. J., Robinson, C. C., Jackson, B., & Rosenberg, S. A. (1985). Translating developmental findings into teaching strategies for young handicapped children. *Journal of the Division for Early Childhood, 10*(1), 45–52.

Beckman-Bell, P. (1981). Child-related stress in families of handicapped children. *Topics in Early Childhood Special Education, 1*(3), 45–53.

Bishop, B. M. (1951). Mother-child interaction and the social behavior of children. *Psychological Monographs 65* (11).

Borden, E. (1987). The community connection—It works. *Young Children, 42*(4), 14–23.

Brazelton, T. B. (1976). How to set limits for toddlers. In T. B. Brazelton, *Doctor and child* (pp. 111–127). New York: Dell Publishing Co.

Brazelton, T. B. (1978). Introduction. In A. Sameroff (Ed.), *Organization and stability of newborn behavior: A commentary on the Brazelton neonatal behavior assessment scale* (pp. 1–3). Chicago: University of Chicago Press for the Society for Research in Child Development, 43 (5–6).

Carta, J., Schwartz, I., Atwater, J., & McConnell, S. (1992). Developmentally appropriate practice: Appraising its usefulness for young children with disabilities. *Topics in Early Childhood Special Education, 11*(1), 1–19.

Chenfeld, M. (1987). The first 30 years are the hardest: Notes from the yellow brick road. *Young Children, 42*(3), 28–32.

Chess, S. (1983). Basic adaptations required for successful parenting. In V. Sasserath (Ed.), *Minimizing high-risk parenting* (pp. 5–11). Skillman, NJ: Johnson & Johnson.

Davidson, J. I. (1988). Dealing with transitions. Paper prepared for Delaware Department of Services for Children, Youth and Their Families, Day Care Licensing Services.

Eheart, B. K., & Leavitt, R. L. (1985). Supporting toddler play. *Young Children, 40*(3), 18–22.

Gartrell, D. (1987). Punishment or guidance? *Young Children, 42*(3), 55–61.

Guralnick, M. (1988, November). Keynote address, presented at the International Early Childhood Conference on Children with Special Needs, Nashville, TN.

Guralnick, M. J., & Groom, J. M. (1987). The peer relations of mildly delayed and nonhandicapped preschool children in mainstreamed play groups. *Child Development, 58,* 1556–1572.

Hitz, R., & Driscoll, A. (1988). Praise or encouragement? New insights into praise: Implications for early childhood teachers. *Young Children, 43*(5), 6–13.

Hohmann, M. (1988). Children get along fine without adults . . . Or do they? *High Scope Resource,* (Spring/Summer). Ypsilanti, MI: The High Scope Press.

Hunt, J. McV. (1961). *Intelligence and experience.* New York: Ronauld.

Johnson, J. E., Christie, J. F., & Yawkey, T. D. (1987). *Play and early childhood development.* Glenview, IL: Scott, Foresman & Co.

Johnson-Martin, N., Attermeier, S. M., & Hacker, B. (1990). *The Carolina curriculum for preschoolers with special needs.* Baltimore, MD: Paul H. Brookes.

Keogh, B. K. (1982). Temperament: An individual difference of importance in intervention programs. *Topics in Early Childhood Special Education, 2*(2), 25–31.

Lawton, J. T. (1988). *Introduction to child care and early childhood education.* Boston: Scott, Foresman/Little, Brown College Division.

Leavitt, R. L., & Eheart, B. K. (1985). *Toddler day care: A guide to responsive caregiving.* Lexington, MA: D. C. Heath & Co.

Morrison, G. S. (1988). *Education and development of infants, toddlers and preschoolers.* Boston: Scott, Foresman & Co.

National Association for the Education of Young Children and the National Association of Early Childhood Specialists in State Departments of Education. (1991). Guidelines for appropriate curriculum content and assessment in programs serving children ages 3 through 8: A position statement. *Young Children, 46*(3), 21–39.

Nunnelley, J. (1990). Beyond turkeys, santas, snowmen, and hearts: How to plan innovative curriculum themes. *Young Children, 46*(1), 24–29.

Odom, S. L., McConnell, S. R., & McEvoy, M. A. (1992). *Social competence of young children with disabilities: Issues and strategies for intervention.* Baltimore, MD: Paul H. Brookes.

Peterson, N. L. (1982). Social integration of handicapped and non-handicapped preschoolers: A study of playmate preferences. *Topics in Early Childhood Special Education, 2*(2), 56–69.

Piaget, J. (1951). *Play, dreams and imitation in childhood.* London: Heinemann.

Roper, S. (1987). Viewpoint: Secondary school specialist says ECE people are resisting the harsher voices of "reform" better than their colleagues who teach older children. *Young Children, 42*(4), 12–13.

Ross, D. D. (1982). Selecting materials for mainstreamed preschools. *Topics in Early Childhood Special Education, 2*(1), 33–42.

Rubin, K. H., Fein, G. G., & Vandenberg, B. (1983). Play. In P. H. Mussen (Ed.), *Handbook of child psychology: Vol. 4. Socialization, personality and social development.* (4th ed.), (pp. 693–774). New York: Wiley.

Seitz, V. (1986). Evaluation strategies. In National Center for Clinical Infant Programs. *Program evaluation: Issues, strategies and models* (pp. 4–7). Washington, DC: Author.

Sponseller, D. (1974). Toddler play. In D. Sponseller (Ed.), *Play as a learning medium.* Washington, DC: NAEYC.

Strain, P. S. (1990). LRE for preschool children with handicaps: What we know, what we should be doing. *Journal of Early Intervention,* 14, 291–296.

Thomas, A., Chess, S., & Birch, C. (1968). *Temperament and behavior disorders in children.* New York: New York University Press.

Whitehead, L. (1989). Praise Vs. Encouragement. In Deiner, P., Whitehead, L., & Prudhoe, C. *Technical assistance: Information sheets of day care providers and families of children with special needs.* Unpublished manuscript. University of Delaware, Newark.

Whitehead, L. (1989). Adult-supported learning. In Deiner, P., Whitehead, L., & Prudhoe, C. *Technical assistance: Information sheets for day care providers and families of children with special needs.* Unpublished manuscript. University of Delaware, Newark.

Chapter 8

Programming for Infants and Toddlers

Education begins at birth. That does not mean that infants and toddlers need a "curriculum" with objectives to master. It means they need the planning of responsive, sensitive, consistent adults. These adults can be parents, caregivers, or teachers. Because of the age of the child, in many ways the adult *is* the curriculum. The timing and approach of the adult is as important as appropriate planning. Planning for infants must be flexible, individualized, and dependent upon the children themselves.

Infants and toddlers are not simply younger preschoolers any more than preschoolers are miniature adults. When teaching preschool children many professionals believe that teachers should leave close, intimate, or physical contact with these children to their parents (Furman, 1986); however, ". . . for babies, such relations are integral to their care" (Honig, 1989, p. 5). These close relations and physical contacts that support intellectual, and social/emotional development, include "tender, careful holding in arms; feedings that respect individual tempos; accurate interpretation of and prompt, comforting attention to distress signals; giving opportunities and freedom to explore toys on floor; and giving babies control over social interactions" (Martin, 1981, in Honig, 1989, p. 5).

With the increased number of working mothers, almost half of the infants in the United States are in out-of-home care. Family day care is the most common form of out-of-home care, but the number of infants in centers is increasing (Howes, 1989). One concern is whether "children enrolled in out-of-home child care as infants are at risk for later social and emotional development" (Howes, 1989, p. 24). The conclusion is that this concern may be unwarranted. "The research evidence does not suggest that infant child care per se is detrimental to the child's future social and emotional development. It does raise concerns for the child who experiences insensitive care both at home and in child care" (Howes, **113**

1989, p. 27). The findings raise hope that there is some compensatory nature between home and out-of-home care environments. However, the research also shows that parents with more complex lives and less secure attachments, even though they have the ability to pay, choose lower quality child-care settings (Howes, 1989). Overall, infants in high-quality child care from families that use developmentally appropriate practices adjust well to future challenges. Children in lower quality child care and troubled family histories do not fare as well.

There is a great deal of unease about the quality of care for infants. Out-of-home infant care is a relatively new phenomenon. Some fear that infants will receive only custodial care, that is, care that responds only to basic needs such as being fed, changed, and safe. Infants are vulnerable. They need sensitive, responsive caregivers who provide developmentally appropriate programming. Infants and toddlers with disabilities also require care and early intervention.

This chapter is devoted to helping you learn the skills to provide developmental care to infants and toddlers. Developmental care responds to the infant's needs "to be held, loved, and talked to; to be given things to look at and listen to; to play outside of the crib and be given help to do more things on his own" (Cryer, Harms, & Bourland, 1987a, p. 1). Like infants, toddlers, too, need programming to learn to get along with each other and develop both their minds and their bodies. The whole child needs to grow and develop.

Caring for Infants

Infant care and programming is a challenge. Infants are vulnerable and needy and dependent on adults. They offer cues to those who can read them, but the cues often need interpretation. The caregiver needs keen observational skills, a style that while calm, is flexible, creative, and comforting despite the distress of the infant. Further, the caregiver needs to react promptly, smoothly, and efficiently to comfort infants (Honig, 1985). This is particularly true for infants with disabilities who may lack the ability to comfort themselves and take a long time to quiet.

Crying is the main way infants have of letting you know something is wrong. Although some feel that babies should be left to cry, research has shown that babies whose cries are answered quickly actually cry less and are happier (Cryer, Harms, & Bourland, 1987a). When you answer infants' cries quickly, trust builds. They also cry less when you are calm. When you are anxious or upset, these emotions are conveyed to the infant. Each infant is unique; different things soothe or upset different infants. Sometimes you almost need to be a detective. When you have checked out all the obvious reasons why the baby might be upset, expand beyond caregiving. Think about yourself. Have you changed your routine? Is he overstimulated or bored? Is it possible she's getting sick? If some extra hugging and holding

are necessary, do it. This attention does not spoil infants.

Communicate your liking for the infant. Infants need to know you care about them. Let the infant know that you enjoy just being with her. Look into her eyes when you talk to her, use her name, and hold and cuddle her often. Have conversations by taking turns with infants as they talk. Smile and delight in them.

As infants grow and develop they get a clearer idea of to whom they belong. This awareness often results in infants' having a hard time leaving their parents. Separation problems usually occur between six and twelve months. Before and after this time infants have less trouble separating. Share this knowledge with parents to lessen their concern. To make it easier, try to have time to spend with the infant when she arrives, be sympathetic, and support her with a favorite blanket or toy if this helps.

If you are the only teacher, you will represent a stable figure in the infant's life. If there are several teachers it is best for each teacher to be responsible for a small group of children. This arrangement does not mean that teachers do not cooperate, but rather that it is important for infants to get to know one caregiver well and vice versa. Infants run on their own schedules. One caregiver can learn the idiosyncrasies of particular children and respond in a more consistent manner.

Stability and consistency are a primary consideration. If staff turnover is high, stability is problematic. The development of attachment is particularly important for children at risk. Infants and toddlers

Infants are vulnerable. They are dependent upon you for care and programming.

who live with families that are abusive, homeless, or in poverty are often in group care by court order as a respite for parents and for infant stimulation (Honig, 1985). These infants need comfort, stability, and security in their programming. Without these they may shut down and sleep a great deal, become hyper-alert and tense, or suck and rock (Honig, 1985). One caregiver usually can meet the needs of three or four infants.

Planning for Infants

Planning for infants is flexible. Routine care (diapering and feeding) can be used to give infants individualized attention. Be sure to plan other activities that can be done as you care for them. Routine care constitutes a large part of an infant's waking time. Look at the area where this care takes place. In addition to your face, what does the infant have to look at or play with? Can you add a picture or a mobile?

Choose an area where your activities will take place. Cribs are for sleeping. Infants who do not walk can be in infant seats with a mobile, on a rug or blanket. If necessary use pillows, rolls, bolsters, or wedges to prop the infant while on his stomach to make his arms more available for exploration. It is wise to separate infants who crawl or walk from those who do not, especially if you are not right there.

Be sure infants have enough toys available so they do not get bored (and probably fussy). New toys should often be used, but infants like to use the same toy many times as they explore its properties. Practice variations on a "theme." Similar toys that have slightly different properties, or the same toy with the infant in a different position challenge learning. Put materials on low shelves for infants who crawl or walk.

It is important that you decide ahead of time what you are going to do for the week or at least for the day. Plan both for the morning and afternoon (if infants are there for both). These plans need not be detailed, but they should be written, and they must cover the major

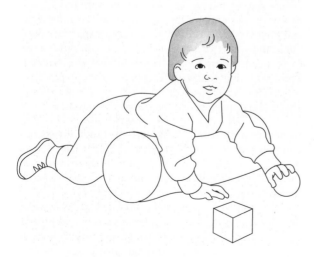

A bolster helps children free their hands for playing as it holds the weight of the child's trunk.

domains: communication, cognition, motor development (large, small, and sensory-motor), social, self-help, and creative arts.

Your role in planning for infants who are not independently mobile from planning for those who are is different. Since many children with disabilities are not mobile as soon as others, this issue is particularly important in their programming. They cannot get to materials independently to make choices, so you must choose toys or activities for them and put them in an accessible place. If the child does not seem to be interested in the toys you offer, you need to demonstrate how the toy works or in some way call attention to the toys; the infant then decides how to play with it. You can support this play by something as simple as eye contact or making statements about what the child is doing, "I like the noise you make with that rattle. Can you make it again? Great!" When the infant is finished your role changes. You may try to interest the child in a new toy, "Look at this rattle (demonstrate), it makes a different noise." You may show a variation with the same toy, "Let's see what happens when we bang this rattle" (demonstrate). Or, you may evaluate the state of the infant and pick up the baby to change the setting. The relationship between the materials and methods is shown in the diagram on page 116. This pattern is repeated frequently during the day with a variety of toys and activities.

Planning is very individualized at this age. What is appropriate for a three-month-old is not appropriate for a six-month-old. You will need to plan for each child if they are of different ages and/or developmental levels. Especially with young infants, theme-based planning is helpful.

Theme Planning

It is important to have a general plan in mind each week. Having a theme helps you decide on the materials you need, the books you read, the fingerplays you use, and the songs you sing. It is also helpful in focusing the infant's learning.

By using several toys and activities organized around a related theme, the "integrated" learning approach is supported. Playing with a pretend farm, singing songs about animals, and reading farm-related books is more productive than teaching isolated skills. Everyday themes help children relate many direct learning experiences to the activities. Themes such as "My Body," "Home," "Outdoors," or "Farm Animals" work well. The materials and activities you might use for a theme like "My Body" might look like this with materials for infants three to twelve months.

Theme: My Body
Materials

Lion wrist rattle (any animal rattle that can be attached to the child's wrist or ankle)

This is Raggedy Ann book (any book that has large simple illustrations of a body)

MATERIALS—METHOD INTERACTION

MATERIALS   METHODS

Teacher chooses materials and places them near the child.

She draws the infant's attention to the materials and/or demonstrates (visually, auditorially, or motorically) how the materials can be used.

Infant chooses materials to play with.

Teacher supports exploration through language and eye contact.

Infant plays with the materials in her own way until finished.

Teacher introduces a variation for play using the same materials or demonstrates a new material, or she responds to the infant with physical changes depending upon the infant's state.

Red foot teether (any teether that is made in the shape of a body part)

Large doll with sweater, pants, and hat

Plastic baby bottle

Cloth doll

Yarn ball (any ball made of yarn) and/or Koosh ball

Mirror rattle (any unbreakable mirror)

Face masks

Dressing book (any)

Cassette tape "Self-Concept," favorites

Vocabulary Words

eye	nose
mouth	foot
hand	leg
ear	hair
tummy (belly)	arm

Fingerplays

1. Two little feet go tap tap tap.
    Two little hands go clap clap clap.
    A quick little leap up from the chair;
    Two little arms reach up in the air.

2. Roll them and roll them
    and give your hands a clap.
    Roll them and roll them
    and lay them in your lap.

3. I have ten little fingers (show fingers),
    And they all belong to me.
    I can make them do things.
    Would you like to see?
    I can shut them up tight (make fists)
    or open them wide (open hands).

I can put them together (put hands together)
or make them all hide (put behind back).
I can make them jump high (high jumping motion).
I can make them jump low (low jumping motion).
I can fold them up quietly (fold hands)
and hold them just so.

Sensory Play

Give infants an ice cube to explore on the tray of their high chair or just add a little water to the tray for them to play in. Use pudding for finger paint, so that if they eat it, there is no problem. If chocolate, be sure to show them how they look in a mirror before the clean-up process begins.

Caregiving

Much of the infant curriculum revolves around caregiving, which can be quality time with the opportunity for one-on-one interactions. Talk to infants as you change them. Tell them you are taking their arm out of their shirt or that you are lifting their bottom up so you can put on a dry diaper. Infants are changed over 7000 times before toilet training is accomplished. It is a learning opportunity you cannot pass up. Eating also offers opportunity to be responsive to infants.

In addition to using these activities and ideas, remember that *how* you play with an infant is very important. Using basic materials such as these, you can plan for several infants with interactions that expand the age range of the materials selected.

In addition to planning, two other areas of programming you need to consider are safety and prosocial behavior. Safety is always an issue with young children, especially in multi-age groupings. Materials that are appropriate for older children could cause choking if an infant swallows them. If you are not actively supervising play, do not allow materials like this to be used where young infants are. Gather up materials such as crayons and small objects if you leave the area.

We are just learning the results of group care on children as they grow older. One particular area of concern is prosocial behavior. Teachers and parents must consciously build prosocial behavior by not only modeling such behavior but showing disapproval of aggression and explaining why it is inappropriate (Honig, 1989). This demonstration must be coupled with adults who are loving and sympathetic, and who comfort children who are upset. Prosocial behavior does not happen naturally. Aggression, on the other hand, appears to do so for children who have experienced child care since infancy.

Programming for Toddlers

The toddler curriculum is play; a simple statement, but one that carries important meaning in the life of a toddler. Through play, toddlers learn cognitive, social, language, physical, and self-help skills. Toddlers learn with their whole body. They learn by doing and take joy in experimenting with movement. While the play may at times seem random, with only short times spent at activities, at other times the same children could spend the entire morning in the bathroom washing their hands (if you would let them).

Toddlers learn about cause and effect relationships by playing with objects, exploring their different uses, and thinking about them. Understanding and knowledge develop when the toddler discovers "new" ways to accomplish something through manipulating the objects in her world. The child who uses two blocks as a telephone is playing rather than exploring the properties of blocks.

Play is pleasurable and enjoyable. The motivation to play comes from within the toddler. Their play is not goal-oriented as that of older children, but rather process-oriented; play for the sake of play. Play involves free choice.

Play is the central aspect in planning programs for toddlers. The primary role of adults is to set up the environment, support the children, and respond to invitations from toddlers. "Activities are only valuable to the degree to which they are appropriate for the age group" (Gonzalez-Mena, 1986).

To find out what is appropriate, observe toddlers at play. Adults support play by being interested in what the children are doing, avoiding interruptions, and giving children warnings before routine transitions. "A responsive caregiver is one who knows how to respond to a toddler's initiatives in play, expanding the scope of his play, while still allowing the toddler to take the lead" (Eheart & Leavitt, 1985, p. 18). Adults can expand toddler play by suggesting new ideas or by adding props to the play situation. Independent play and exploration allow toddlers to control and master their environment. However, it is important to be available to help children when

needed. It is often difficult for toddlers to play with peers for extended times.

To provide quality play experiences for children, adults must plan the time and provide space, materials, and preparatory experiences (Johnson et al., 1987). Toddler play needs to be scattered in blocks of time throughout the day. A good toddler schedule includes time for free play, time spent indoors and outside, and routine events such as eating and napping.

Toddlers need space to play: areas for messy art work, dramatic play, a block corner, a cozy area, a manipulatives area, and a sensory area. They also need materials to play with. Toys should be selected for all the areas listed. The actual materials will depend on the age and developmental level of the group. Toys for toddlers should be safe, durable, cleanable, appealing to children, realistic, versatile, and developmentally appropriate (Johnson et al., 1987).

Having a theme helps you decide which words and ideas to focus on with children during a particular activity. Most themes are selected because they reflect differing aspects of the everyday experiences of children. Not all children will be able to do all of these thematic activities. Some children may only be able to do the simplest activities with your help.

Children, especially those with disabilities, may need help to understand certain aspects of your themes. A toddler who has never been to the grocery store may use items in a home-oriented sense instead of understanding how the items relate to the grocery store. Field trips and class visitors can expand children's experiential base. A good "toddler teacher" enjoys working with toddlers and understands their behavior from a developmental perspective. Understanding why toddlers behave the way they do makes dealing with their behavior easier and even enjoyable.

Including Toddlers with Disabilities

Including toddlers with disabilities can be a positive learning experience for all. Peterson (1982) has found teachers who consciously support social interactions and find ways to facilitate positive social interactions between children with disabilities and others are successful. Ways of encouraging positive interactions include: highlighting the achievements of all children, pairing children for short time periods or tasks, modeling appropriate play behavior, and encouraging empathy and prosocial behaviors in all the children.

In addition to providing for the inclusion of a child with a disability, the teacher must also facilitate that child's educational goals. Beckman et al. (1985) suggest that adults who work with young children with disabilities need to:

- Be responsive to cues that indicate the child's understanding, interest, frustration, or fatigue.

- Verbally highlight relevant information about the child's attempts and positively reinforce the child's successes.

- Maximize the child's opportunities to manipulate and explore objects and materials. The adult is responsible for helping the child discover adaptive skills when necessary. Sometimes special toys or materials will be needed to give children the opportunity to learn new skills.

- Provide developmentally appropriate activities for the skills and goals for each child.

Materials and Equipment for Infants and Toddlers

Infants and toddlers require different equipment than preschool children. However, the same toys can be used by children these ages, including those with disabilities. All children need opportunities to play with fantasy or dramatic play materials. Through dramatic play, children learn social, cognitive, and language skills. Teachers may need to adapt paint brushes or put manipulative toys on surfaces such as Dycem (a nonslip plastic) so they do not move around inadvertently, but there are more similarities than differences in curriculum planning for the inclusive classroom.

Toy selection should be mindful of safety and the age and skills of the child. Some basic toys are good for all toddlers: balls (plush, soft rubber), musical toys, noise-making toys, construction toys, shape sorters, wheel and riding toys, cuddly toys, books, and records or tapes.

Major considerations when selecting toys are:

- Is the toy safe? Avoid toys that have sharp edges or points that can be jabbed in a child's eye or small parts which infants could swallow or choke on. Select toys with rounded edges, smooth surfaces, and parts large enough not to be swallowed. Check for splinters or nails that might scratch a child.

- Is the toy durable? Avoid toys that are poorly constructed and that could break easily. (Before giving toys to infants or toddlers, beat up on it yourself: throw the toy across the room, dunk it in water for five minutes, try to pull the eyes off. If you can do it, they can do it.) Avoid toys that have detachable parts like button eyes or noses. Be cautious of baby rattles that contain small items that could be swallowed. Consider whether the toy will stand up to banging, chewing, and so on.

- Is the toy washable? Young children enjoy and learn from putting toys in their mouth. Washability is a must to prevent spread of germs.

- Are the size, weight, and shape of the toy appropriate for the age and developmental level of the child? Consider how easy or difficult it will be for a child to hold and manipulate the toy. If the toy is heavy and hard to grasp, a child is less likely to play with it. If it tips over easily, the child may become frustrated. Children need successful play experiences with toys. They also benefit from being challenged by toys and activities slightly above their current level.

- Is the toy bright, colorful, and appealing? Does it stimulate more than one sense? Is the toy soft and textured *and* noise-making?

- Can the toy be used in many ways by children at different developmental levels? This is particularly important with expensive toys. Some toys allow children at different developmental levels to play together. Blocks, for example, are good because children play with them in different ways as they grow and develop. Infants grasp, mouth, and bring the blocks together. Toddlers place them in and take them out of containers. With increasing age, children stack blocks and begin "pretend" play. Blocks also encourage more than one child to become involved in the play.

- Does the toy encourage independence or dependence? Although adults can enhance play, *always* requiring adult help to play with a toy does not encourage independence.

Following is a list of basic toys all programs for infants and toddlers should include.

Basic Toys for Infants and Toddlers

Under six months:

rattles

teethers

unbreakable mirrors

soft dolls or animals

Six to twelve months:

musical rattles

drums

blocks

balls (soft, textured, clutch)

busy box

nesting cups or drums

Twelve to twenty-four months:

pull toys

riding toys

toy telephones

large cars and trucks

soft vinyl books or cardboard books

Twenty-four to thirty-six months:

puzzles

basic house or farm set

large plastic blocks that fit together

shape-sorting toys

kitchen or housekeeping toys

musical toys

pounding bench or work bench

Individualized Programming

While children with disabilities are more similar to those without disabilities than they are different, they still have unique needs. The following guidelines are helpful when adapting activities.

Selecting activities for an IFSP: Once you have an infant or toddler's IFSP with its goals and outcomes, you need to select activities to meet those goals. The IFSP should be written so that activities can be carried out within the regular routine of the child's program. Most of the needs of infants and toddlers with disabilities can be met with minimal rearrangements of daily routines and schedule. Many toys can be used effectively without any adaptations.

- Suction cup toys are valuable because they stay put more easily when a child with poor eye-hand coordination tries to manipulate them.

- Velcro wrist bracelets can aid a child who is unable to hold a rattle on her own.

- Pop beads or "bristle blocks" are usually thought of as being good for putting things together, but

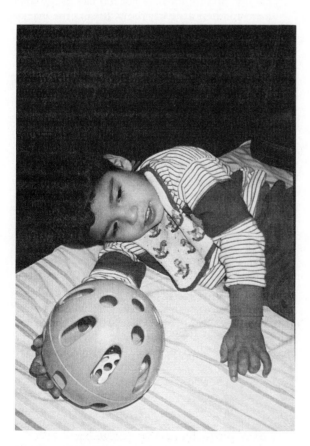

Toddlers' IFSP goals can easily be incorporated into the infant-toddler programming.

for a child who needs to work on strength, pulling them apart is great.

- Inflatable toys which haven't been inflated all the way are easier to grasp.

- Place Dycem (a non-slip plastic) on the table so toys don't roll away and cups and plates stay anchored. You can also put Dycem on chair seats to keep children from slipping off. (Dycem is available from Kapable Kids; see resources for address.)

Minor adaptations such as adding Velcro, handles, magnets, and so on to toys may make them easier to manipulate. For example, magnetic strips could be glued to the back of simple puzzle pieces, which a child could then manipulate and arrange on a cookie sheet (Langley, 1985).

Additional questions include:

- Is this toy appropriate for children who are functioning like infants, toddlers, or both?

- What skills can you facilitate/encourage with this toy?

- What kinds of activities can you do with this toy?

- How can you adapt this toy (if necessary) so a child with a disability can use it?

Sometimes major adaptations are necessary from a specialist. Other times what appear to be major adaptations can actually be just a matter of hooking up a toy to a capability switch. A capability switch is a device which the child uses to manipulate something. The child activates the switch and something happens (cause and effect reasoning). Capability switches are very sensitive and will respond to slight movements from any body part. Switch selection should be based on the infant's or toddler's most consistent and reliable body movement. There are switches that will respond to sipping or puffing, voice, sideswipes, pinches, touch, tongue movements, chin, nose, and so on. Some switches are lighted for children with hearing impairments, others are gravity sensitive so tilting by any body part will activate them. Photosensitive switches are activated by any body movement that creates a shadow. Switches can control robots, trains, fire engines, pigs, bears, and rabbits. They can be attached to music boxes, toy radios, toy TVs, and tops. They allow children with disabilities to gain control over their world (Toys for Special Children, 1991).

Evaluation

When you complete an activity, it is important to evaluate it either formally or informally. Think about what went well and what didn't. Does the child need more work on this skill? Is she ready to move on to the next step? How will having done this activity influence future activities? Observational skills will assist you in evaluation. Your evaluations of individual activities will also assist the team working with the child to decide when new goals need to be written.

Individualized planning is a circular process. It starts with a designated outcome—what is it you want the child to be able to do. For example, you might want a toddler to increase his receptive vocabulary. You then incorporate the words you want the child to identify into a theme to increase contextual learning. If you are interested in children learning household words you might set up the dramatic area as a house, choosing the specific household items based on the vocabulary you plan to teach. Then consider how you will incorporate the teaching into the play. You might begin by labeling the objects for the child and demonstrating what each does. Support the child using the objects and again verbally labeling the objects and what the child is doing. Finally request the child to discriminate between the desired object and others: "Show me the blanket." "Can you wrap the baby in the blanket?"

Based on your observations you either continue this procedure or modify it. When you have reached some conclusion about the technique, you tell the team that you are making progress toward the desired outcome or that you need ideas from the team as to how to change your procedure or reevaluate the outcome because it is not appropriate. The diagram depicts this process.

When discussing overall program planning there are certain times or events that are often forgotten or ignored but are crucial for the success of a program. Many of these were addressed in the previous chapter. Those that are particularly relevant to infants and toddlers are highlighted.

Planning the Day

A well-planned day prevents many discipline problems and makes transitions run more smoothly. Having a written plan is important for your personal organization, when new teachers come, or when there are substitutes. If you are absent the children will miss you; they need the security of the day's proceeding on a familiar schedule. A schedule for infants and twos needs to be both predictable and flexible. As they can't tell time, it is the sequence that is important, not the amount of time allotted to activities. The amount of time can easily be changed.

- Plan your activities and daily schedule thoughtfully. Are your activities and schedule developmentally appropriate for your children? Toddlers can join groups for a short story, singing and fingerplays, or other activities. This is five to ten minutes at most. Don't press your luck!

- Plan your classroom environment to help children's play and independence. If possible, have duplicates of particularly popular toys. Sharing is not a strong point for toddlers. However, they are usually willing to be redirected to the source of an identical toy.

- Give toddlers the opportunity and time to be independent with self-help skills. Encourage children to try things for themselves, but be alert to step in before frustration causes problems.

- Separate areas of active play from quiet ones.

- Toddlers need to renew their energy frequently. Plan the timing of snacks and lunch to renew this energy. Be sure they are not too late in the day; many toddlers are early risers. Be sure the snacks are healthful. You are teaching food habits in addition to refueling the children.

- Toddlers are active. Take them outside or arrange space inside for active play.

- Avoid abrupt changes in routine schedules such as eating and sleeping. Try to incorporate each child's particular habits into routine, if possible.

- Have a variety of toys and activities and change them often. Rather than put all the toys you have out at one time, pick toys that support a theme and have them available plus a core of always

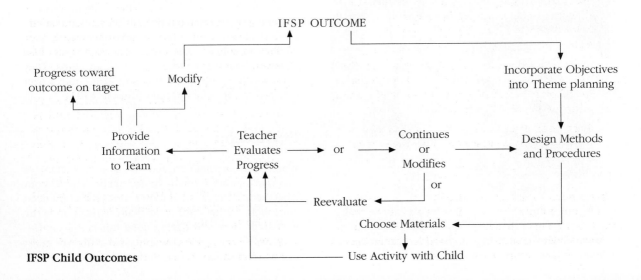

IFSP Child Outcomes

popular toys. As the theme changes, change the toys to support it.

Discipline

- Minimize rules. Strict environments cause more problems than they prevent. A simple rule to follow is: Children may not hurt themselves, each other, or the toys. You may not need any other rules. If you have additional rules, be sure the adults model appropriate behavior for children. If children are not permitted to sit on the tables, adults should not either.

- Show and tell toddlers what you want them to do if they are doing something that is not appropriate: "The fence is not for climbing. I'll walk you to the jungle gym."

- Move close to children who are having problems. Support your words with gentle physical prompts.

- Give positive attention to children when they are happily playing as well as when they are having problems. The more children trust and like a teacher, the more likely they are to respond to her suggestions and directions.

- Support toddlers in using words to solve problems. This may not occur to them, as language competence is relatively new.

- Give toddlers choices, but make sure they are choices you are willing to support.

- Step in early when things do not seem to be going well. Imagination and a "new" activity may solve the problem.

- Know your children. Keep a watchful eye on the child who hurts others. If he seems frustrated, intervene as quickly as possible.

- It is important to comfort a child who is hurt, but it is also important that the child who does the hurting has your support. He needs your guidance for his growth.

- Speak in a natural tone of voice using words children can understand. Maintain eye contact and be on the child's level when giving an imperative statement.

- Avoid long-winded explanations, but give children a reason for your direction: "Keep the sand in the sandbox. If you throw sand, it might get in someone's eyes and hurt them."

- State your directives positively. Tell children what they can do rather than what they can't.

SAY:	INSTEAD OF:
Walk inside, it's safer.	Don't run.
Sit on your bottom.	Don't stand on the chair.
Sarah is playing with that now. When she's done you can have a turn.	Don't grab that out of Sarah's hands. That's not nice.

Sometimes by telling children what not to do you actually give them ideas of doing things they've never thought of.

- Accept children's feelings: "If you are angry with Jasmine, tell her. It hurts when you hit her."

- Distract or divert children's attention when they are acting inappropriately. If a child wants another's toy, offer him a different one instead if you don't have an identical one. Make it sound special.

- Provide alternative appropriate behaviors. If a child is splashing water out of the water table, give him an egg beater to make waves.

- Avoid using labels such as "bad girl" or comparing children with each other. Comparing children leads to competition between them.

Transitions

Transitions are particularly problematic for toddlers. They do not wait well and see little sense in stopping an activity until they are ready. Plan at least one activity during transitions to help children wait. As children are dressing to go outside have a teacher to help dress and another who is doing fingerplays and songs with children who are waiting. If you have enough staff and it is safe, have an adult go out with the first children who are ready rather than waiting for all the children to be ready before you go out.

Transitions are important teaching times for toddlers, as many tasks involve self-help skills. Teaching these skills (dressing and undressing, toileting, handwashing, eating, and settling for a nap) consumes a large portion of the day. It is sometimes tempting to just do things for the children rather than support them in learning these activities. Learning skills is a legitimate part of the toddler curriculum and should be planned and valued in that light, not just as a daily necessity.

With the level of support most toddlers need with these activities, it is a time when you can be with an individual child and help him feel very special.

- Help newly enrolled toddlers become acquainted with classroom routines. If possible, assign one teacher to be responsible for supporting this smaller group.

- Use adults to help children during routine times. At least one adult should be sitting with the children while they eat. Several adults should be available to help children settle down to rest or sleep. Tucking in and back rubs make resting more personal in an impersonal environment.

- Prepare children for changes. Warn children a few minutes before a transition occurs so they can finish what they are doing and look forward to what is coming next.

- Reduce waiting time. Waiting is usually difficult and unproductive time that can lead to problem behaviors. If children must wait, involve them in a song or some other appropriate activity to help pass the time.

Implementing an IFSP in Infant and Toddler Programming

Because so much of infant and toddler programming is individualized, incorporating the goals of the IFSP into your daily plans is relatively easy. As you work from the IFSP, you may find it useful to develop your own format for planning.

Sometimes the easiest way to individualize programming is to work it into your daily routine on a regular basis. This process ensures that it is done and supports contextual learning. Serving a gelatin snack is an easy way to help children practice using a spoon. Likewise, talking about body parts and pointing to objects is easy when a child is arriving. "You needed to wear a sweater today to keep your arms warm. Please hang your sweater in your locker." "Show me what you have on your feet. What are these?" You can easily incorporate these steps in your planning, but you need to remain deliberate about what you are doing and why. Schedule when you will work on specific outcomes with a toddler. Short-spaced work is more effective than attempting to sit a toddler down for half an hour and "do it all."

A useful format is to write one or more daily activities to work on with each child on a calendar or plan book. A calendar is helpful because you can post it where you can see it. The illustration shows a sample calendar for toddlers for April. You can send a copy of your plan home to the parents so they are aware of what you are doing.

Some areas need particular attention for most young children with disabilities and frequently appear as goals on the IFSP. These include self-help skills and developing the senses.

Self-Help Skills

The development of self-help skills is important for the independence of the growing child and also to reduce the amount of time parents spend in caregiving. Parents often have conflicts regarding self-help skills. They want their children to be able to do more activities independently yet logical times for learning these skills are often stressful, especially in two–wage-earner households. Children could learn to dress themselves in the morning before going to school, but this is a high demand time for parents and, although they may value self-dressing, they may also find early morning time spent teaching dressing skills adds great stress to daily routines. This doesn't mean that parents don't value dressing skills. It means they need your help in finding another time and way to support dressing.

Self-help skills in general are repetitive and tend to be highly predictable in how they are done effectively. They might require adaptations for particular children, but overall the procedure is similar. Children with disabilities often find these tasks difficult and a time when someone is always trying to "hurry" them. It is helpful to have children experience success with each small part of a task rather than being expected to complete the whole task before feeling successful. One of the most effective ways of teaching these skills is through a task analysis. This breaks down a task into its component parts. Because self-help skills are so necessary and predictable, there are many commercially available sources for this information. One old standby is the *Guide to Early Developmental Training* (Wabash Center for the Mentally Retarded, Inc., 1977). Before going to a source such as this, it is useful to try to create one yourself. Pick an area such as handwashing and write down the steps involved. Number each step. Now, wash your hands using the steps. Did you forget anything? Does your chart look like this?

1. Turn on water.

2. Pick up soap.

3. Rub soap on hands.

4. Rub hands together.

5. Rinse hands.

6. Turn off water.

7. Dry hands.

8. Replace towel or throw paper towel away.

Knowing the parts of any task is the first step involved in teaching it. The next step is chaining.

Chaining refers to the process of taking a task analysis and deciding where to begin teaching. Chaining can be forward (start at the beginning of the task and work through it step by step to the end) or backward (start with the end of the activity and work backward through the steps to the beginning). With backward chaining, in particular, a child can feel successful after having to complete only the last step in the process. Gradually earlier steps are added until the child is able to complete the entire task. For backward chaining, then, you would *help* the child turn on the water, *help* use the soap, *help* rinse, and *help* dry her hands. You would then say something like, "Amie, now put the towel in the trash. Great job! You did that by yourself." Praise her for doing it well. To begin at step one is discouraging because the teacher, not the child, accomplishes the final step. Task analysis is useful in making you aware of the steps involved in a particular task. It also becomes clear what the prerequisite skills are. If a child lacks the prerequisite skills, it is doubtful that the task will be completed. Additionally, it is frustrating for both the child and you to continue working on a skill that is unlikely to be successful.

Child _____   Date _____

ROUTINES

Outcomes	Arrival	Morning Snack	Diapering	Play	Lunch	Special Time	Play	Outside
Point to or touch named objects	X	X		X		X		
Touch and name body parts	X		X		X	X		
Follow simple directions	X			X	X	X		X
Use a spoon		X			X			
Drink from a cup		X			X			

X indicates when you plan to work on the desired outcome behavior.
Progress toward attaining outcome:
AS - Attempted successfully
A - Attempted with some success
AU - Attempted very little success
NA - Not attempted
General Comments:

When individualizing programming it is often useful to take advantage of naturally occurring opportunities to facilitate skill development. As so much of infant/toddler programming revolves around routines, it is often useful to decide how to incorporate IFSP outcomes into these routines. A chart such as this one makes it clear when individual outcomes will be worked on.

April  Ideas for daily activities

Mon., Ap. 3	Tues., Ap. 4	Wed., Ap. 5	Thurs., Ap. 6	Fri., Ap. 7
stack and knock down large cardboard or milk carton blocks.	Find pairs of big & little objects (spoons, socks, trucks). Talk about big & little.	Use scarves while dancing to music.	Play with soapy water. Add small sponges & plastic dishes.	Play with nesting cups (or try boxes or cans).
Mon., Ap. 10	**Tues., Ap. 11**	**Wed., Ap. 12**	**Thurs., Ap. 13**	**Fri., Ap. 14**
Take a walk outside. How can you tell Spring is here?	Read a simple book about spring.	Tape record the children singing and talking. Listen to the tape.	Play with dirt! Use large containers & scoops, small shovels or large spoons.	Plant seeds in dirt.
Mon., Ap. 17	**Tues., Ap. 18**	**Wed., Ap. 19**	**Thurs., Ap. 20**	**Fri., Ap. 20**
Make an obstacle course for riding toys.	Talk about pictures or toys of farm animals. Make sounds of those animals!	Sing "Old MacDonald had a farm".	Brush paint with water outside on sidewalk or driveway.	Play with pots & pans & lids. See if children match lids to their containers or stack lids or pots.
Mon., Ap. 24	**Tues., Ap. 25**	**Wed., Ap. 26**	**Thurs., Ap. 27**	**Fri., Ap. 28**
Have children line up chairs to make a pretend train.	Whisper as you read a quiet story, such as "Goodnight Moon".	Sing "Open, shut them".	Finger paint with soap paint.	Have children make simple snack (spread peanut butter on cracker).

Sensory Stimulation

Infants and toddlers learn about their world through their senses—looking, hearing, touching, tasting, and smelling. The development of these senses increases the amount of input children receive. Children with sensory impairments and those who have not had rich environments because of restrictions due to chronic illness or their living conditions need many different daily experiences with sensory materials to encourage learning. With your support children with sensory impairments will optimize their use of a sense that is impaired and strengthen and adapt their other senses to compensate. Compensation is not an automatic biological response, it needs a lot of practice and adult support. Some children with sensory impairments avoid activities that are challenging to their disability. They need to be encouraged with warmth and caring to take part. It is important for their continued growth and development, but it is also difficult for them. Other children will need to refine their senses as a source of learning.

Include some sensory activities for infants and toddlers in your daily planning. Some ideas follow.

1. Put older infants in high chairs and pour a puddle of water on the tray. Encourage them to put their hands in the water; if necessary move their hands around and pat the water. Have some sponges around to wipe up messes. You can also add a wooden spoon to give a little variety. Place the high chair over a vinyl tablecloth or on a floor surface that can be mopped.

2. Toddlers enjoy playing in containers of water, a wading pool for several children or a dish pan for one child. Add a few inches of water and plastic measuring cups and spoons, or a few floating and sinking items such as a cork, a rock (small enough to handle, large enough so that it cannot be swallowed), styrofoam pieces, a clothespin. This is fun outside in warm weather or inside when it is colder. Vary the water temperature— cold water tends to be invigorating whereas warm water has a soothing effect.

3. Toddlers also enjoy painting with water. On a warm day, fill some buckets with water and add a couple of large paintbrushes. The children can harmlessly "paint" outside walls, sidewalks, fences, and so on.

4. Toddlers enjoy sand play. You can use the same container for sand play that you use for water play. Add cups, spoons, cars, and plastic dolls. You can add a little water to the sand to keep it contained and firm enough to mold. Watch to see that young children don't put sand in their mouths. For different textures, substitute corn-meal, oatmeal, beans, or rice and let the children play with the same items. This is often referred to as "dump and fill" with textures.

5. Good old-fashioned mud play is always a winner. If you have a corner where there is dirt to dig, add some water to make mud. On warm days, strip the children down to diapers/shorts and let them play. Mud washes off easily with soap and water!

6. Playdough is always good to have on hand. Whatever the children's ages and skill levels, they can squash, roll, pat, pinch, or shape playdough. Add cookie cutters and popsicle sticks. Watch for eating! Some children seem to prefer playdough to lunch.

7. A set of unit blocks is essential. Start with a small number of blocks; you can add to the set later. Blocks can be used in a variety of ways by children of varying ages. Infants may enjoy reaching for and grasping blocks, toddlers will like knocking down the towers you build, and preschoolers will enjoy building their own constructions (ideas adapted from Prudhoe, 1989).

Summary

Infants and toddlers are regularly appearing in group settings, and there is every expectation that this will continue. The challenge to teachers is to develop programming that is responsive to the needs of a group of young children that includes infants and toddlers with disabilities. Because much of the programming for this age group is individualized, inclusion is easier. As children grow up together aware of others' strengths and challenges, the inclusion of those with disabilities will seem to them to be natural. They will not realize that they are part of a new approach to education.

References and Bibliography

Beckman, P. J., Robinson, C. C., Jackson, B., & Rosenberg, S. A. (1985). Translating developmental findings into teaching strategies for young handicapped children. *Journal of the Division for Early Childhood, 10*(1), 45–52.

Cryer, D., Harms, T., & Bourland, B. (1987). *Active learning for infants.* Reading, MA: Addison-Wesley Publishing Company.

Cryer, D., Harms, T., & Bourland, B. (1987). *Active learning for ones.* Reading, MA: Addison-Wesley Publishing Company.

Cryer, D., Harms, T., & Bourland, B. (1988). *Active learning for twos.* Reading, MA: Addison-Wesley Publishing Company.

Developmentally appropriate curriculum. (1988, April/May). *Argus: The Journal of Family Day Care,* 20-21.

Eheart, B. K., & Leavitt, R. L. (1985). Supporting toddler play. *Young Children, 40*(3), 18–22.

Farran, D., Kasari, C., Comfort, M., & Jay, S. (1986). *Parent/caregiver involvement scale.* Honolulu, HI: Center for Development of Early Education, Kamehameha Schools, Kapalama Heights.

Furuno, S., O'Reilly, K. A., Hosaka, C. M., Inatsuka, T. T., Allman, T. L., & Zeisloft, B. (1985). *Hawaii early learning profile (HELP): Activity guide* (rev. ed.). Palo Alto, CA: VORT Corporation.

Gallagher, J. J., Trohanis, P. L., & Clifford, R. M. (1989). *Policy implementation and PL 99-457: Planning for young children with special needs.* Baltimore, MD: Paul H. Brookes.

Gonzalez-Mena, J. (1986). Toddlers: What to expect. *Young Children, 42*(1), 47–51.

Herb, S., & Willoughby-Herb, S. (1985). Books as toys. *Topics in Early Childhood Special Education, 5*(3), 83–91.

Honig, A. (1989). Quality infant/toddler caregiving: Are there magic recipes? *Young Children, 44*(4), 4–10.

Johnson, B. H., McGonigel, M. J., & Kaufmann, R. K. (Eds.), (1989). *Guidelines and recommended practices for the individualized family service plan.* Washington, DC: National Early Childhood Technical Assistance System and Association for the Care of Children's Health.

Johnson, J. E., Christie, J. F., & Yawkey, T. D. (1987). *Play and early childhood development.* Glenview, IL: Scott, Foresman & Co.

Johnson-Martin, N., Jens, K. G., & Attermeier, S. M. (1986). *The Carolina curriculum for handicapped infants and infants at risk.* Baltimore, MD: Paul H. Brookes.

Langley, M. B. (1985). Selecting, adapting, and applying toys as learning tools for handicapped children. *Topics in Early Childhood Special Education, 5*(3), 101–118.

Levine, M. H., & McColoum, J. A. (1983). Peer play and toys: Key factors in mainstreaming infants. *Young Children, 38*(5), 22–26.

Ostroff, E., & McGuinness, K. (1984, Summer). Adaptive environments: Classrooms for all kinds of children. *Beginnings,* 26–28.

Parks, S., (1986). *Make every step count: Birth to one*. Palo Alto, CA: VORT Corporation.

Peterson, N. L. (1982). Social integration of handicapped and non-handicapped preschoolers: A study of playmate preferences. *Topics in Early Childhood Special Education, 2*(2), 56–69.

Prudhoe, C. (1989). Sensory Play. In Deiner, P., Whitehead, L., & Prudhoe, C. *Technical assistance: Information sheets for day care providers and families of children with special needs*. Unpublished manuscript. University of Delaware, Newark.

Raver, S. A. (1991). *Strategies for teaching at-risk and handicapped infants and toddlers: A transdisciplinary approach*. New York: Merrill.

Rogers, S. (1984, Spring). Play in handicapped children. *Beginnings,* 14–16.

Rubin, R. R., Fisher, J. J., & Doering, S. G. (1980). How your toddler learns to talk. *Your toddler*.

Johnson & Johnson Child Development Publications. New York: Macmillan Publishing Co., Inc.

Segal, M. (1988). *In time and with love: Caring for the special needs baby*. New York: Newmarket Press.

Simeonsson, R. J. (1985). *Carolina record of individual behavior*. Chapel Hill, NC: Frank Porter Graham Child Development Center, The University of North Carolina.

Surbeck, E., & Kelley, M. F. (Eds.). (1990). *Personalizing care with infants, toddlers and families*. Wheaton, MD: Association for Childhood Education International.

Wabash Center for the Mentally Retarded, Inc. (1977). *Guide to early developmental training* (rev. ed.). Boston, MA: Allyn and Bacon, Inc.

What is curriculum for infants in family day care (or elsewhere)? (1987). *Young Children, 42*(5), 58–62.

Chapter 9

Service Delivery Systems

Service delivery systems, working singly or together, provide for the care and education of children with disabilities. In the early 1960s this chapter would have concentrated on institutionalization. Other service delivery systems increasingly have emerged over the past three decades. They can be distinguished by their location, level of inclusion, the focus (child or family), and whether the system is formal or informal. Children are increasingly being served by a combination of service delivery systems. These systems and their interactions are the focus of this chapter.

Depending on the child's specific disability, medical condition, family needs, the location of the community (especially rural versus urban), and available services, a range of delivery services is possible. Like the field itself, service delivery systems are struggling to find answers to questions such as:

1. Should service delivery systems be designed to meet the needs of the child or the total family?

2. What level of participation/cooperation can be expected between parents and service delivery systems?

3. How much power should parents have in the decision-making process?

4. How important is parent education and how actively should service delivery systems be expected to pursue programs in this area?

5. How is the role of advocacy divided between parents and service delivery systems?

6. What will adequate service delivery cost and who should pay?

Changing demographics are forcing service delivery systems to evaluate their policies in relation to their target population. Most men and women who have children work. Over half of the children born **127** since 1980 can expect to live part of their lives in a single-parent household. These changing demographic characteristics require interagency collaboration to ensure quality programming for children.

To meet the needs of the whole family, parents may develop complicated "packages" of care based on early intervention, therapy, and health concerns. Children with disabilities who attend school programs often need care before and after school as well as during the summer. This need extends past the time when other children can be left at home independently (Fewell, 1986).

As part of an interagency team, teachers must be aware of the support that child-care, health, and social service systems provide families. Many children come to school from child care and return there when school ends. Developing a communication system that includes parents and all child-care providers is essential.

As early childhood special education has grown and families have changed, so has the diversity of available service delivery systems. Varying theoretical differences influence the goals and supports that the delivery systems provide for children and their families. However, regardless of the diversity, several components contribute to successful service delivery systems. These include having a stated program and philosophy, appropriately trained staff, a program evaluation component, and parent involvement (Filler, 1983).

In many instances the program setting (home versus center versus institution) is also a reflection of the program philosophy mediated by the child's medical condition and disability.

Home-Based Service

Home-based service delivery systems involve an early interventionist (typically a nurse and/or early childhood special educator) visiting the child and family in their home. The specialist typically visits once a week or every other week and brings information to the family. While there, the specialist answers parental questions and models/demonstrates activities and behavior for working with the young child. Home-based service is frequently used for very young infants.

This system is based on the team member's building a relationship with the family by visiting at a scheduled time that is convenient for them. As most specialists work a typical daytime schedule, what frequently happens is that the mother is the one who is home and she then has the responsibility of carrying out the prescribed early intervention as well as interpreting for her spouse (if there is one) what the specialist said and why it is important to follow through. An additional assumption in this service delivery system is that there is a parent at home who is willing and able to deliver early intervention services.

Home-based intervention supports parents in developing the skills for early intervention. It uses

resources available in the home in demonstrating activities. Success for this type of system depends on the parents' understanding and following through on the intervention. There may be limited access to specialized materials and equipment (in some families there may be few toys and materials as well). For medically vulnerable children this may be the only viable system for service delivery, as exposure to other children (and their germs) may be contraindicated.

Center-Based Service

Center-based service delivery systems may be situated in a hospital, school, or public or private agency. The parents are usually responsible for bringing the child to the program, although some programs provide transportation. A center-based program often has a combination of early intervention specialists. Some programs are designed for one disability only, such as hearing impairment, while others serve children with a variety of disabilities. These programs have a wide variety of materials including specialized materials and equipment. Parents can meet other parents of children with disabilities at these

Home-based programs are the only viable system of service delivery for some children.

centers. Negative aspects are that the hours of the program may disrupt a child's daily routine and some children initially find it difficult to adjust to an unfamiliar setting. These programs are often only part-day programs, so they may represent only part of the service delivery system if the child needs full-time care. The New Mexico Developmental Disabilities Planning Council found that 40 percent of the children in centers were also in child-care settings before and/or after early intervention (Klein & Sheehan, 1987). They spent an average of twenty-six hours per week in child care. Within this dual-service perspective, the day-care provider was responsible for adapting activities to allow children with disabilities to participate and for supporting social integration. In this model the child-care provider was not responsible for the educational component of early intervention services.

The staff of early intervention centers is usually well trained in early childhood special education, and therapists not only make active contributions to the child's program but may provide needed therapy in the setting as well. This staff would also do assessments as needed. Parents often feel more comfortable leaving young children in a setting with specialists. For a variety of reasons, including both philosophy and funding, these center-based services are likely to be segregated programs.

Home/Center-Based Service

Some programs are a combination of home- and center-based programs. In these programs children go to the center but are served in an active home-based component as well. This service combines the advantages of both programs. Trained professionals are in charge of the programming, and parents can consult with them on a regular basis. Although parents participate in the programming, they are not solely responsible for it.

Public School Programs

Public schools play a major part in the service delivery system for children three and older and in some cases beginning in infancy. The intent of the Individuals with Disabilities Education Act is for children to be educated in the least restrictive environment (LRE). That is, children with disabilities should be educated in regular classrooms in neighborhood schools to the maximum extent possible.

States, and school districts within states, have differed greatly in their interpretation of "the maximum extent possible." Some suggest that every child with a disability should be in regular classrooms (Blackman, 1989); others feel that only mildly and perhaps moderately impaired children should be included. The cost of providing special services in many settings rather than a few often becomes an issue. Some proponents see inclusion as a cost saving since special schools will not be needed. There is little doubt that there are varying degrees of support for inclusion from administrators, teachers, parents, and the community (Tucker, 1989).

Within the public schools children can be placed in regular classes in neighborhood schools, in self-contained classrooms in the same or different schools, or can attend specialized schools. These options will probably continue to exist in most states. However, it is expected that higher proportions of children with disabilities will be included in regular classrooms. It is also likely that the move for more inclusion will begin at the youngest ages and move upward with the children.

Parents cooperate and participate in the education of their child at many different levels. These levels may change with the age of the child, the particular teacher the child has, or the school the child is attending. In general, parents are most active when their children are younger. Some parents are highly committed and choose to be actively involved in both the home and school. Other parents want to be involved in the decision-making processes. Still others are willing to volunteer in the classroom. A second group of parents participates less in the school setting, but supports school activities and actively monitors their children's progress. These parents support the value of education but are not active participants in the school itself. A third group is not involved in the education of their children nor do they seem to value it. When these are the parents of children with disabilities, the likelihood of follow-through is low.

These differences make it difficult to generalize about the public schools as part of the service delivery system.

Child-Care–Based Service

Placing children with disabilities in child-care settings is not a new idea (U.S. Department of Health, Education and Welfare, 1972), but it has recently received a great deal of attention in the United States because of changing demographics and a changing philosophical environment. Viewing families as dynamic parts of a larger social system has caused people to rethink service delivery systems (Deiner, in press). Empowering parents to make choices in the best interest of both their child and family has affected both delivery systems and the thoughts and actions of professionals in the field of early childhood special education.

Most mothers of young children are now in the work force. Some estimate that by the year 2000 nearly seven in ten mothers of preschool-age children will be employed outside the home (Children's Defense Fund, 1990). Between 5 and 10 percent of these children have disabilities (Salkever & Connolly, 1988). Fewell (1986) estimated that in 1990, there were already 1,475,303 children with disabilities under age six with mothers in the work force. This number will grow as more mothers join the work force.

Most mothers work because of economic necessity. Parents of children with disabilities face increased financial burdens (Hartley, White, & Yogman, 1989). Medical treatment, equipment, and supplies are expensive. A national survey of families with children who had physical disabilities (Harbaugh, in Seligman & Darling, 1989) found child care to be the largest single out-of-pocket expense. Parents of these children may hold additional jobs to make ends meet. Parents may have to change their plans to return to work (Fewell, 1986) or utilize child care that is less than satisfactory.

Service delivery systems have had to become more responsive to work/family issues. The necessity of child care is a reality for most families in the United States today, including families that have children with disabilities. Neither home- nor center-based services totally meet the needs of these families. For families who feel their children need the intensity of center-based services, children may be transported from a child-care setting to the center and then back again. Home-based services are tremendously valuable for very young infants, but as adults (or the only adult) re-enter the work force, home-based services become impractical and center-based services are not a total package for a child.

Family day care is the most common setting for children who are cared for outside the home, constituting 40 percent of child-care arrangements (U.S. Bureau of the Census, 1983). Family day care probably serves more disabled children than any other arrangement (Fewell, 1986).

Child care for children with disabilities is used in one of two ways by service delivery systems: child care before and/or after early intervention or as a primary site for the delivery of early intervention services. In the latter case, related services may be provided in the child care setting or elsewhere.

Programs which use child care as a primary intervention use consultation models. Professionals train the day-care provider to function as an early childhood interventionist with the support of a consultant who visits the site on a regular basis. Consultants provide a variety of technical assistance services ranging from specialized equipment to a selection of toys. The child-care provider then delivers the early intervention services.

The inclusion of children with disabilities in child-care placements is important to some parents. In addition to meeting their work/family needs they want their children to have the opportunity to play and socialize with children without disabilities (Karns & Kontos, 1987). Young children need the opportunity to learn to cope with and accept limitations in a supportive environment, to experiment and gain confidence in their strengths and abilities, and to be accepted by other children and adults (U.S. Department of Health, Education and Welfare, 1972).

An overarching issue is whether the amount and quality of individual attention provided in child care is enough to meet the needs of children with disabilities. This is actually part of the much broader issue addressing adequacy of care for all young children, particularly infants.

There are few objective measures of quality of care. The Family Day Care Rating Scale (FDCRS) developed by Harms and Clifford (1989) and the Early Childhood Environment Rating Scale (ECERS) for centers (Harms & Clifford, 1980) are the most widely used measures of quality. Both scales require that an outside observer rate about thirty-five items on a scale ranging from inadequate to excellent. The FDCRS focuses on the amount and appropriateness of the planning the provider does.

The directors of one project designed to include children with disabilities in family day-care homes initially decided to train only family day-care providers who had scores of 4.0 or better on the FDCRS. (This is one-half point above the average of the scale.) It was almost impossible to find providers who achieved such a score. The project revised its criteria. The scores did not cause them to question the validity of the scale, but rather raised concern about the quality of family day care (Deiner & Whitehead, 1988).

Hospital-Based Care

Most hospitals are designed for high-volume, short-term acute care. Their top priority is to preserve life. The focus is primarily on medical rather than social needs. The neonatal intensive care unit (NICU) certainly fits this description. (An infant is called a neonate for the first month of life.) When an infant is born prematurely or critically ill he is transported to a NICU. Not all hospitals have these units. They are staffed by neonatologists and neonatal nurses who are "approved to care for the critically ill and ventilator-dependent infants and to provide treatment for premature and sick full-term newborns during the most critical phase of their care" (Gilkerson, Gorski, & Panitz, 1991, p. 446). These are emergency medicine specialists. Infants may remain in the NICU for only a day or two for observation or up to a year or more for some of the most fragile infants. The biomedical focus is on the individual patient and the "disease," particularly in critical care.

When infants are medically stable they are moved to an intermediate unit. These units are designed to care for moderately ill infants. It is at this point, as the child is exiting the critical care section and going to community-based programming, that early intervention is usually considered. Some infants who remain in the NICU for extended times receive early intervention services there.

There are many different reasons why a child's medical condition may require that he be hospitalized (uncontrolled seizure disorder, machine-dependent, life-threatening symptoms). Specialists, such as physical and occupational therapists, may assist nursing personnel in special handling and positioning techniques, or in graded sensory stimulation or movement activities. Larger hospitals have Child Life staff who provide stimulation and intervention to young children while they are in the hospital. The length of the child's stay and the seriousness of the illness will determine to a great extent how much contact a child will have with the Child Life staff. They also work with children to prepare them for operations and other medical procedures.

Residential Care

A residential program is a treatment facility, which is not medical in nature, where young children live in order to receive early intervention services. Residential programs are being phased out for all children, but particularly very young children. Their use is primarily for disabilities such as hearing and vision impairment. The only way that children of rural families can attend these schools is to live there. Children as young as three and four live in the schools and may come home on weekends.

Respite Care

As families keep their children with disabilities at home they have found the need for services that had not previously been part of the service delivery system. All parents need a break from caregiving. However, few babysitters were willing or able to care for children with disabilities. Respite care has become part of the service delivery system. Respite care is one of the few services that is designed specifically for the *caregivers*.

Broadly defined, respite care is "the temporary care of a disabled individual for the purpose of providing relief to the primary caregiver" (Cohen & Warren, 1985, p. 26). That is, families need a break from the stress of caring for a child with a disability. Respite care is part of a support system that keeps children with developmental disabilities in the community (Powell & Hecimovic, 1981).

A young child with a disability often needs time-consuming and perhaps complicated physical caregiving. The demands on time and finances often lead to increased stress for the families. Often what families need is a break from care responsibilities to allow them time away from the child and time to focus, even if only briefly, on themselves (Gallagher, Beckman, & Cross, 1983).

Respite services can be either primary (designed specifically to provide respite care only) or secondary (primarily designed to provide other services such as early intervention, but at the same time incidentally providing respite) (Salisbury, 1986). Child-care services for children with disabilities are a good example of secondary respite services. Child care is a potential setting for the provision of respite care and early intervention services in one setting (Deiner & Whitehead, 1988).

In a national survey, Wikler (1981) found respite care to be one of the most needed and least available services for families. Understandably, respite care is used less when families have informal support networks available to them.

Service Coordination

Because young children with disabilities frequently require a variety of services, and often from different agencies, the law requires that a service coordinator be designated for infants and toddlers. The service coordinator is responsible not only for coordination with other agencies and persons, but also responsible for assuring the implementation of the Individualized Family Service Plan in concert with the family.

The impetus of the movement for a service coordinator was to help families obtain appropriate services for their child, and to coordinate those services within and between agencies. While service coordination has been identified as a need in the delivery of services to young children with disabilities and their families, many issues surrounding service coordination are yet to be resolved.

The initial term used in P.L. 99-457 law was "case management," with the interpretation that parents could *not* be their own case managers. Questions arose from both parents and professionals about the efficacy of this decision. Many believed that the family, not a professional, was the only appropriate case manager, and they should play the more active role in securing resources to meet the family needs (Dunst, Trivette, & Deal, 1988). Some felt that a dependency relationship was created when professionals played this role, and that the families would be unable to cope with the situation when the case manager left (when the child is three). Dunst, Trivette, and Deal suggested that part of the case manager's task should be to give families skills to help them use resources to meet their needs. This issue was resolved to some extent in the reauthorization of P.L. 99-457 in 1991 when the term was changed to service coordinator. This term was used to clarify the role of service providers as coordinators and families as decision maker-managers.

Interagency Coordination

Better planning and coordination to improve services to children with disabilities and their families is the overall goal of interagency coordination (Nordyke, 1982). Many agencies offer an array of services to families in a given community. Sometimes these services overlap; other times there are gaps in needed services. Some agencies are public, and some private. Some agencies serve families in many different capacities, others in only one. Services and personnel within agencies change.

The early interventionist and the family with whom she works may face serious challenges when agencies do not have current knowledge of each other's services and programs. Making an appropriate referral for a specific problem or concern becomes difficult.

Formal and Informal Social Support Networks

A social network is a group of people "who provide information leading the subject to believe he is cared for and loved, esteemed, and a member of a network of mutual obligations" (Cobb, 1976, p. 300). Research on social support for families of children with disabilities suggests that the presence of effective social supports can assist families in coping with stress and can enhance the well-being of these families (Dunst, Trivette, & Cross, 1986; Stagg & Catron, 1986).

While families with children with disabilities may benefit greatly from the existence of support networks, they are also less likely to have them available than are families with children without disabilities (Featherstone, 1980; Stagg & Catron, 1986).

Support networks can be formal or informal in nature. Formal networks are generally made up of professionals involved with service agencies. In contrast, informal social networks are made up of friends, neighbors, and extended family members. Families tend to utilize informal social networks more than formal networks (Unger & Powell, 1980), and this is particularly true for families of children with disabilities (Kazak & Marvin, 1984).

Networks offer three major types of support: (1) providing material things and services when needed; (2) providing emotional support by communicating the person's value and worth to them; (3) providing information about and referrals to other perhaps more formal support systems (Unger & Powell, 1980). In general, social networks work best when they are reciprocal in nature (although in some extreme situations the process of having to "pay back" support can itself add to stress) (Unger & Powell, 1980).

Support empowers families to strengthen and add to their already existing networks (Dunst, Trivette, & Deal, 1988). One relatively easy way for parents to increase the size of their support network is to meet parents of other children in their child's setting. These parents may or may not have children with disabilities.

Summary

Service delivery systems for young children with disabilities are changing in response to changing demographics and philosophies about how children with disabilities should be educated. Some service delivery systems, especially for very young infants or medically fragile ones, are home-based. Others are center-based, and some use a combination. Early intervention is increasingly only one of the settings that young children with disabilities need. They may go from a child-care setting to intervention and back. With the move toward educating children with disabilities in the least restrictive environment, intervention services are being incorporated into child care settings through the use of itinerant teachers and therapists. There are many excellent services available, however, little is being done to manage and coordinate the total system of services. More and more the needs of the total family are taken into account when planning and coordinating services needed by young children with disabilities.

References and Bibliography

Blackman, H. P. (1989). Special education placement: Is it what you know or where you live? *Exceptional Children, 55* (5), 459–462.

Children's Defense Fund. (1990). *Children 1990: A report card, briefing book and action primer.* Washington, DC: Author.

Cobb, S. (1976). Social support as a moderator of life stress. *Psychosomatic Medicine, 38,* 300–314.

Cohen, S., & Warren, R. (1985). *Respite care: Principles, programs, and policies.* Austin, TX: PRO-ED.

Deiner, P. L., & Whitehead, L. C. (1988). Levels of respite care as a family support system. *Topics in Early Childhood Special Education, 8,* 51–61.

Deiner, P. L. (in press). Family day care and children with disabilities. In D. L. Peters & A. R. Pence, (Eds.), *Family day care: Current research for informed public policy.* New York: Teachers College Press.

Dunst, C. J., Trivette, C. M., & Cross, A. M. (1986). Roles and support networks of mothers of handicapped children. In R. R. Fewell & P. F. Vadasy (Eds.), *Families of handicapped children: Needs and supports across the life span* (pp. 167–192). Austin, TX: PRO-ED, Inc.

Dunst, C. J., Trivette, C. M., & Deal, A. G. (1988). *Enabling and empowering families: Principles and guidelines for practice.* Cambridge, MA: Brookline Books.

Featherstone, H. (1980). *A difference in the family.* New York: Basic Books.

Fewell, R. R. (1986). Child care and the handicapped child. In N. Gunzenhauser & B. M. Caldwell (Eds.), *Group care for young children* (pp. 35–46). Skillman, NJ: Johnson & Johnson.

Filler, J. W. (1983). Service models for handicapped infants. *Educating handicapped infants: Issues in development & intervention* (pp. 369–386). Rockville, MD: Aspen Systems Corp.

Gallagher, J., Beckman, P., & Cross, A. (1983). Families of handicapped children: Sources of stress and its amelioration. *Exceptional Children, 50,* 10–19.

Gilkerson, L., Gorski, P., & Panitz, P. (1991). Hospital-based intervention for preterm infants and their families. In S. Meisels & J. Shonkoff, (Eds.), *Handbook of early childhood intervention,* (pp. 445–468). Cambridge, MA: Cambridge University Press.

Harbaugh, G. R. (1984) cited in Seligman, M., & Darling, R. (1989). *Ordinary families, special children: A systems approach to childhood disability.* New York: Guilford Press.

Harms, T., & Clifford, R. M. (1980). *Early childhood environmental rating scale.* New York: Teachers College Press.

Harms, T., & Clifford, R. M. (1989). *The family day care rating scale.* New York: Teachers College Press.

Hartley, M., White, C., & Yogman, M. (1989). The challenge of providing quality group care for infants and young children with special needs. *Infants and Young Children: An Interdisciplinary Journal of Special Care Practices. 8*(2), 1–10.

Healy, A. H., Keesee, P. D., & Smith, B. (1989). *Early services for children with special needs: Transactions for family support* (2nd ed.). Baltimore, MD: Paul H. Brookes.

Karns, J., & Kontos, S. (1987). Mainstreaming handicapped preschoolers into center care. *Child Care Center, 4*–6.

Kazak, A. E., & Marvin, R. S. (1984). Differences, difficulties, and adaptation: Stress and social networks in families with a handicapped child. *Family Relations, 33,* 67–77.

Klein, N., & Sheehan, R. (1987). Staff development: A key issue in meeting the needs of young handicapped children in day care settings. *Topics in Early Childhood Special Education, 7* (1), 13–27.

Nordyke, Nancy S. (1982). Improving services for young handicapped children through local,

interagency collaboration. *Topics in Early Childhood Special Education, 2*(1), 63–72.

Powell, T., & Hecimovic, A. (1981). *Respite care for the handicapped: Helping individuals and the families.* Springfield, IL: Charles C. Thomas.

Salisbury, C. L. (1986). Parenthood and the need for respite. In C. Salisbury & J. Intagliata (Eds.), *Respite care: Support for persons with developmental disabilities and their families* (pp. 3–28). Baltimore, MD: Paul H. Brookes.

Salkever, M., & Connolly, A. (1988). *Day care for disabled children.* Baltimore, MD: Maryland Committee for Children, Inc.

Stagg, V., & Catron, T. (1986). Networks of social supports for parents of handicapped children. In R. R. Fewell & P. F. Vadasy (Eds.), *Families of handicapped children: Needs and supports across the life span* (pp. 279–295). Austin, TX: PRO-ED, Inc.

Tingey, C. (Ed.) (1989). *Implementing early intervention.* Baltimore, MD: Paul H. Brookes.

Tucker, J. A. (1989). Less required energy: A response to Danielson & Bellamy, *Exceptional Children 55* (5), 456–458.

Unger, D., & Powell, D. (1980). Supporting families under stress: The role of social networks. *Family Relations, 29,* 566–574.

U.S. Bureau of the Census. (1983, November). *Child care arrangements of working mothers: June 1982.* Special Studies, Series P-23, No. 129. Washington, DC: U.S. Department of Commerce.

U. S. Department of Health, Education, and Welfare (1972). *Day care: Serving children with special needs.* DHEW Publication No. (OCD) 73-1063. Washington, DC: Office of Child Development.

Wikler, L. (1981). Chronic stresses of families of mentally retarded children. *Family Relations, 30,* 281–288.

PART TWO

Teaching Children with Diverse Abilities

Chapter 10

Children with Communication Disorders

Some children come to school as "talkers." They immediately want to know where the crayons are, why they are in school, why they can't go outside now . . . until you think you may change your profession if you hear one more question. These children stick in your mind from day one. Then there are the "slow-to-warm-up" children, who appear shy and immature and of whom you probably still won't have a clear picture even after a few weeks. This group is difficult to diagnose, as it is hard to determine whether these children choose not to communicate or do not have the ability to communicate. With them it is necessary to determine whether the speech and language skills are at an appropriate developmental level or whether the irregularities need assessment and educational planning. A third group is composed of children who actually have a diagnosed communication impairment.

The first question to ask when you suspect a problem is: Can this child communicate in an age-appropriate way that can be understood by others? Then think back over events of the week. When you dismiss the children from group time by the color of their clothes, does this child need to be prompted? When you give simple directions, can this child follow them? How about more complex directions? Does this child seldom volunteer comments to you? Does the child rarely speak up during group time? When this child speaks, can you understand most of the words or only some of them? Given free choice, does this child seek out activities requiring language, or does he avoid them? How can you tell whether the child falls in that wide range called average, or whether she has a disability?

Next consider: How typical is what I hear of the child's speech? Children are very adaptable in their language styles and use different language when talking with a peer or an adult, as well as adapting their speech to a variety of situations. Tizard (1981) found differences between young children's language in the school and home situation. When at home the child typically displayed more frequent, longer, and more **137** balanced conversations over a wider range of topics than at school. Children who were quiet at school were frequently non-stop talkers at home. Given this, it is important to talk with a child's parents about how representative the speech you are hearing is for the child.

Classification of Communication Disorders

Although it is difficult to determine the prevalence of particular disabilities at young ages, it is clear that children with communication disorders constitutes a large group. Depending upon the definitions used, children with communication disorders (including speaking, listening, reading, and writing) constitute about five to ten percent of the child population (Hallahan & Kauffman, 1991). Communication is frequently a secondary disability related to a wide range of other disabilities such as hearing impairment, mental retardation, and behavioral and emotional disorders. Language is rarely the only target for intervention in young children (Ensher, 1989). Young children can also have language delays because of a bilingual or multilingual background. This should not be confused with a communication disorder.

Communication has a developmental base. What is appropriate communication for one age is inappropriate and considered dysfunctional at other ages. Additionally, language does not develop in isolation, and the interaction between language and cognitive development is difficult to unravel. There are also many ways of classifying communication disorders. Some look at the rate and sequence in which language develops, others focus on the cause or related conditions, and still others break language down into subsystems (phonology, morphology, syntax, semantics, and pragmatics).

Overall, a child's communication is impaired when there are deviations in the formation, expression, or understanding of language. Characteristics of impaired communication include poor concepts, inability to follow directions, speechlessness, speech confusion, and poor word comprehension.

A child's *speech* is impaired when it deviates so far from the speech of other children that it calls attention to itself, interferes with communication, or causes the child to be self-conscious.

To determine the nature and extent of a suspected communication impairment, you must first be familiar with the stages of normal speech and language development. Then look up the child's birth date. This alone might resolve the problem. If this child is one of the youngest in the class and your basis for comparison is the older children, the difference between them may be a strictly developmental one that will disappear with time. In early childhood, even a few months has a considerable effect. As a further check, find out if this child was premature and is therefore developmentally younger.

If you are still concerned, assign the child to a small group with several others who are close in age. (Don't include children that have been designated as intellectually gifted or delayed.) While doing language activities with the children (choose activities from Part Four of this book), note who volunteers the most and least often. Take language samples from each child and compare them for sentence length, sentence structure, vocabulary and concepts, and articulation (note omissions, distortions, or substitutions of sounds). An easy way to obtain language samples is by recording small group time. Do this on at least two occasions to allow for a child's having a bad day. If the child you are concerned about is in the top to middle of this group, there is no cause for concern. If the child is at the bottom, continue gathering information.

As you continue your observation, note how the child uses materials not related to language. How many different materials are used? Are the materials used appropriately? This information will help you decide if the child is delayed in other areas. If so, the child's speech and language problems may have an underlying cause, such as mental retardation.

The next step is to determine the gap between the child's comprehension and production of language. All children at this stage have a greater ability to understand language than to speak it; you are looking for a significantly wider gap between the two than age mates have.

DEVELOPMENT OF CHILDREN'S ABILITY TO UNDERSTAND AND EXPRESS COMMUNICATIONS

Age	
0–12 months	**Understanding communications:** Responds to speech by looking at speaker. Responds differently to differences in speaker's voice (friendly versus unfriendly). Turns to sound source. Responds with gestures to words such as "Hi," "Bye-bye," and "Up." Stops action when told "No" firmly.
	Expressing communications: Makes crying and non-crying sounds. Smiles, coos, babbles, repeats syllable (ma-ma-ma-ma). Vocalizes after an adult vocalizes (takes turns). Communicates meaning through intonation. Attempts to imitate sounds.
12–24 months	**Understanding communications:** Gets familiar object on request: "Bring me the ball." Understands prepositions on, in, and under.

Understands simple commands: "Close the door."
Responds to simple "where" questions: "Where's José?"
Listens to simple stories.

Expressing communications:
Sound becomes more purposeful.
Uses first meaningful word.
Refers to self by name.
Uses my or mine to indicate possession.
Uses successive one-word utterances.
Begins to make two-word utterances: "All gone."
Answers some routine questions.
Asks "What" questions.
Has vocabulary of about 50 words.
Begins to use "me," "I," and "you."
Says the names of familiar objects in pictures.
Identifies body parts on a doll and own body.
All vowel sounds are learned, plus /h/, /p/, /b/, /m/, /n/.

24–36 months
Understanding communications:
Points to pictures of familiar objects when they are named.
Identifies objects when told their use.
Understands questions relating to what and where.
Understands negations "no," "not," "can't," "don't."
Enjoys simple stories, again and again and again.

Expressing communications:
Names many common objects.
Uses language as a way of communicating thoughts.
Uses "me" instead of proper name.
Enjoys using language, gains satisfaction from expressing self and being understood.
Understands and uses abstract words such as up, down, now, later.
Starts to use plurals.
Uses early forms of negation: "No," "No want," "Can't open it."
Starts asking primitive questions.
Combines words into short phrases.
Adds consonant sounds /k/, /d/, /f/, /ng/, /y/, /t/, /w/.
Has a vocabulary of 250 to 900 words.
Shows frustration when not understood.
Can state first and last name.

36–48 months
Understanding communications:
Begins to understand the vocabulary of time (tomorrow).
Understands size comparatives (large–larger).

Understands relationships "because," and contingencies "if" or "when."
Understands "pretend."
Can carry out a series of related directions (2 to 4 directions).

Expressing communications:
Vocabulary increasing rapidly.
Loves new words.
Has a vocabulary of about 1,200 words.
Talks to self while playing, but language is becoming more socially directed.
Begins to ask questions for information and for social contacts.
Begins to use the immediate future tense: "I will."
Uses simple sentences structures.
Begins using pronouns that refer to others (he, his, and so on).
Adds consonant sounds /g/, /s/, /r/, /l/, /sh/, /ch/.
Can repeat at least one nursery rhyme.

48–60 months
Understanding communications:
Follows three unrelated commands.
Understands three levels of comparatives: big, bigger, biggest.
Listens to longer stories.
Understands sequencing of events: "First we have group time, then free play, snack, stories, play outside, and then go home."

Expressing communications:
Explains why wants to do something a certain way.
Asks "when," "how," and "why" questions.
Talks a lot—not always to tell or ask something important, but to seek attention and companionship.
Loves silly language.
Uses a variety of sentence structures.
Uses almost all pronouns appropriately.
Adds consonant sound /th/.
Has a vocabulary of about 1,500 words.

60–72 months
Understanding communications:
Demonstrates pre-academic skills.
Except for understanding of complex vocabulary, functions at an adult level in understanding communication.

Expressing communications:
Is curious and asks many questions about things.
Uses complete sentences and gives full information; thus needs opportunities to talk with someone who is interested and who will listen attentively.

Adds consonant sound /v/.
Has a vocabulary of about 2,000
words.
Uses different verb tenses.

*72–96
months*

Understanding communications:
Demonstrates academic skills.
Functions at an adult level in
understanding communication.
Is understanding more complex
vocabulary.

Expressing communications:
Language structures are mastered
and are being refined for irregulars.
Adds consonant sounds /z/, /j/.
Has a vocabulary of about 2,600+
words.*

---

*The speech production sounds given are based on the age
at which 75 percent of the children master sounds. Information adapted from Herr & Libby (1990), Machado
(1990), Liebergott et al., (1978).

Analyze the child's speech carefully. If the child
is having trouble pronouncing words, note exactly
which sounds are difficult. Vowels and the consonants *p, b, m,* and *w* are easiest for a young child to
pronounce, followed by *t, d, n, k, g, f,* and *v.* The
more difficult sounds are *s, z, l, r, ch, th, sh, j, bl,* and
cr. If the child has problems with the last set of
sounds, which children normally take longer to
learn, reevaluate a few months later. Be sure to look
for the obvious. If the child doesn't have front teeth,
some sounds are not possible for him.

After carefully observing the child alone and
with others, if you still feel there is a problem, schedule a conference with the parents. Alert them to your
concerns, then accept whatever they say. Your goals
in the first conference are to gather more information
and to begin to make the parents aware of the problem. Schedule a class visit for them in about two
weeks. Have them observe their own child with an
age mate, just as you did. At your second conference
discuss and compare their observations with your
own.

Consider making a home visit. You will have an
opportunity to watch and listen to the family interact
more informally. You may learn that the child's
speech or language is modeled after the family pattern, which means you are unlikely to convince the
parents there is a problem. If you still feel the problem exists, discuss it, but be prepared for the parents
to not share your concerns. There is still much you
can do with classroom programming to foster this
child's speech and language development.

If you and the parents agree there is reason to
believe the child has a problem, you might suggest
that the child be tested. The family physician is probably the first choice, since there may be a medical
reason for the problem. The physician might then
refer the child to an audiologist to test hearing and to
a speech pathologist. You or the doctor might refer
the child to a psychologist for testing in social and

intellectual development. Some communities may
have a child diagnostic clinic or a counseling clinic.

No matter how the parents choose to obtain further information about the child's needs, there often
is a long lag between your initial concern and a final
diagnosis. Often as long as a year or two may elapse.
Young children can be difficult to diagnose. The test
results are often inconclusive, and many times the
decision is made to wait a while and try again. In the
meantime, you can develop ideas for helping this
child within your classroom.

Communication Disorders

The term communication disorder can refer to any
number of varying communication problems. The
specific label given to a disorder is generally attributed
to the characteristics of the disorder, such as language
delay.

There are many variables that can affect a child's
speech and language development. First, the child
must have an intact sensory system for extracting relevant information from the environment. Second, the
child must have the capabilities for processing the
information, understanding what was seen and heard,
and remembering the important facts. Third, the environment must be such that adequate stimulation is
provided for the child to learn. Fourth, the environment must be communicatively reinforcing to the
child to stimulate further interactions (Peterson,
1987).

Children with a disorder in their sensory system
that interferes with their ability to receive relevant
information from their environment will very likely
encounter language and/or speech problems. Children with hearing impairments may not be able to
differentiate between sounds nor learn language if
they are unable to hear those sounds or how words
are used. Children with physical impairments may
have difficulty developing language concepts if they
cannot interact with materials.

Children encountering difficulties processing
information they receive may also have problems developing a good language base. These processing
problems can include how the child perceives the
information received; how the child stores the information; and how the child uses the information. A
child with poor memory skills may be unable to remember object label names from one time to another,
resulting in a poor vocabulary.

The environment plays an important role in the
development of language. An environment severely
lacking in appropriate materials to facilitate development may have the secondary effect of delaying language development. Experience with a wide variety
of materials strongly contributes to children's overall
development, which includes language.

Language is essential in the learning of cognitive
skills. If the environment is causing the language
delay, then it will most likely have the secondary
effect of limiting cognitive development due to lack

of adequate early stimulation. The inability to understand and process what is communicated will interfere with learning. If brain damage is the cause of a language disorder, the damage to the brain may affect cognitive processing as well.

The quantity and quality of social interactions children receive also contribute to language development. Environments that fail to respond to children's communicative attempts will result in children that do not attempt to initiate communicative interactions. It is the consistent and repetitious socially reinforcing interactions children receive in response to their own communicative actions that motivate children to continue to communicate. Adults babbling back to infants who are babbling reinforce the communication interaction. The failure of the environment to respond appropriately to children's interactions will eventually result in children that are not motivated to interact with others.

An inability to communicate ideas and thoughts can be very frustrating for children. This is especially true for children with intact language systems but defective speech output. If children know what they want to say but are unable to express their message, extreme frustration and stress can result. This can lead to their developing behavioral problems or to withdrawal from interactions. In either situation, the children need to have available alternative means by which to communicate their messages.

Language

In order to program effectively for children with communication disorders you need to know the developmental sequence for children's capabilities at different ages (see table, pp. 138–140). Next you must have some understanding of the process of language development itself. Within the process there are four major elements: inner language, receptive language, integrative language, and expressive language. The processes are overlapping, and each can be broken down into small steps to be mastered in order from simple to complex. These steps are your teaching goals. Once you have defined your goals, you are ready to choose activities. Let us examine one way of looking at the process of language acquisition more closely.

Process	Characteristic	Criterion for Evaluation
Inner language	The ability to communicate with oneself. Developed by actively interacting and manipulating one's environment. Requires opportunity. Does not require adult intervention.	Given a ball, the child rolls, bounces, throws it. (The child doesn't eat it or sit on it.)
Receptive language	The ability to understand others. The child uses symbols to connect objects with their names.	Given the command "Show me the ball," the child does in fact show you the ball, not a hand or shoe.
Integrative language	The ability to synthesize information. After receiving information the child classifies it (coding, sorting, selecting, organizing, and retaining). Involves more than short-term memory. The child must hold the concept in mind while performing other tasks.	Given the command "Go get the ball" (from across the room), the child brings back the ball, not a crayon or eraser. (The child remembered the task while crossing the room.)
Expressive language	The ability to make oneself understood verbally: speech.	Given the question "What is this?", the child responds "ball," not "bell" or "hand."

The order in which concepts are introduced must correspond to the developmental sequence of learning. The child must first actively experience something, have it named, and then interact further with the named item before being expected to express the name and any ideas about it.

For each of the four processes described above, rate the child in overall language development. Is the child above, about the same, or below others of that age? If, for example, the child is average in inner and receptive language but below average in integrative language, the point in the sequence at which you start teaching skills is receptive language. Start from where the child is experiencing some success (or just a little frustration) and work toward gradually developing the next process.

Speech

The production of speech sounds involves the manipulation of the mouth, tongue, cheeks, and throat, along with the shaping and control of air, to produce specific vowel and consonant sounds. Problems with any one of these variables can result in atypical sound production or a speech disorder. Speech disorders fall into three categories: articulation, voice, and fluency. Articulation disorders are the most common.

Articulation involves the ability to appropriately produce, orally, any one of a variety of vowels, consonants and/or vowel-consonant blends. The inability to produce these sounds can be physiological; lack of tongue or mouth control, oral musculature difficulties, or a hearing loss.

Articulation errors occur when sounds are omitted, added, distorted, or substituted. Take, for example, *spaghetti:*

paghetti	(*s* is omitted)
spaghettiti	(extra *ti* is added)
spēghetti	(*a* is distorted to ē)
basaghetti	(*ba* is substituted for *p* and put at the beginning)

Articulation errors can happen at the beginning, middle, or end of a word. They may be the result of indistinct articulation. Slow, labored speech and rapid, slurring speech are both articulation problems. Some articulation problems are a natural part of a child's development. While children may, in fact, outgrow some problems, care must be taken to determine whether therapy is indicated.

One of the primary causes of articulation disorders is middle ear malfunction, resulting from chronic ear infections or ear blockages. This type of hearing loss prevents the transmission of higher frequency sounds, the consonants. This results in children who hear only the middle parts of words: "– able," "–irl," "–abbi–," "–o wha–." This hearing difficulty causes children to omit sounds when speaking. Some children also substitute sounds to make up for what is missing; "*d*irl-*g*irl," "*w*ell*wo*-*y*ellow," "*w*abbit-*r*abbit."

Voice disorders involve the pitch, volume, or voice quality of children's speech. The cause can be attributed to physical, learned, or psychological problems. Voice disorders occur less frequently than other speech problems. Children's pitch should be appropriate for their age, sex, and size. Mismatches can lead to social and emotional difficulties. Volume concerns the children's ability to monitor the loudness of their voices. Hearing losses can result in a child's using a louder voice than normal. Quality refers to the general character of the voice such as hoarse, nasal, breathy, normal. Extremely harsh or hoarse quality speech can be related to vocal cord nodules or excessive screaming. Nasal quality speech can be the result of cleft palate disorders. Most problems encountered in voice disorders are treatable through speech therapy.

Fluency disorders concern the child's inability to develop a regular flow or rhythm to speech. "Fluent speakers are those who speak easily (without much muscular or mental effort) and continuously (without interruption), at a rapid rate" (Gottwald, Goldbach, & Isack, 1985). The most common fluency disorder is stuttering. It involves abnormal repetitions, hesitations, and prolongations of sounds and syllables. Associated with stuttering are characteristic body motions such as grimaces, eye blinks, and gross body movements. Occasional dysfluency is common in children two through six.

The most common normal dysfluency is the repetition of whole words: "I want—I want the ball." These occur most frequently at the beginning of sentences. Boys show more repetitions than girls, but both sexes show fewer repetitions with increasing age.

Normal dysfluency is also situationally specific. It increases when children talk with someone who speaks rapidly, when language use is more formal, when they ask questions, use more complex sentences, or use less familiar words (Gottwald, Goldbach, & Isack, 1985).

Many children become stutterers during the preschool years. However, there are danger signs that teachers can detect before children have reached this stage. The first has to do with the frequency of dysfluencies. More than two sound or syllable repetitions or more than one sound prolongation per 100 words spoken is a danger sign (Gottwald, Goldbach, & Isack, 1985). Additional signs include part-word repetitions, especially if these repetitions are repeated more than twice and/or have an irregular rhythm: "Da-daddy," "Da-da-da daddy," or "Da———-ddy". Children who are tense and fearful are also at risk for developing stuttering. Ignoring stuttering is only appropriate with early dysfluencies. Maintaining eye contact and listening to the content of the message is helpful.

The cause of stuttering continues to be debated, between an organic versus learned behavior origin. Language therapy can help children overcome stuttering, as well as learn techniques to diminish the intensity of the stuttering. You can also enhance children's speech fluency by speaking slowly and clearly and not putting pressure on children for "on the spot" answers.

Augmented Communication

Some children have such severe communication disorders that normal spoken communication is not a long-range option for them. For some, manual communication is an option; others lack the motor coordination. In these cases a system of augmented communication needs to be developed. There are both "low-tech" and "high-tech" augmented communication systems. For young children a communication board is most likely the first step in communicating. For young children a communication board would consist of pictures of important caregiving events or activities that the child might want to do. The child then points to the picture of the activity he wants to do, or the teacher points to pictures of various activities until the child indicates his preference. Augmented communication must be designed on a personal level for each child involved in order to work effectively. The creative software that is being designed for microcomputers is greatly impacting augmented communication and has tremendous potential. Even for young children, the use of touch-sensitive control pads can facilitate communication. Voice synthesizers are relatively inexpensive and plug into the printer port of most computers. Rather than printing what is typed, it speaks it. For example, if the child touched the color "red" on an adapted keyboard the word red would be said (McWilliams, 1984).

Children's Needs: Teaching Goals

Related goals may be grouped under broad categories called "teaching goals." Although these goals are the same for most children, the amount of emphasis placed in each area and the levels of difficulty in the programming vary. Under each teaching goal below are the most important needs of children with communication disorders. A child may have some or all of these needs and additional needs as well. The exact configuration of goals and objectives is reflected in the IEP/IFSP for that child. Suggestions on what you might consequently teach them are included. Often, a course of action is implicit in the description of the need.

Communication Skills

Children with communication impairments may talk only when absolutely necessary because of the negative feedback they have received in the past: "You talk funny." Speaking in front of others may be a threatening experience for these children. When asked questions in a group situation, they may respond with a shrug or "don't know." It is easier for them not to know something than to risk ridicule by the other children. Start encouraging speech in one-to-one situations and in small groups before you work on large groups. Reinforce spontaneous language regardless of the quality of the speech. Respond to the *meaning* of children's communications. Which speech skills to emphasize will depend on the needs of each child. Skills include rhythm, volume, and articulation, especially as it relates to intelligibility of speech. Although the teacher will need to emphasize the skills related to expressive language, the interrelationship between expressive and receptive language and reading and writing must be acknowledged. For some children, writing with creative spelling might fill a needed communications outlet in a nonthreatening way.

As in speech, the focus in early writing is on the meaning of children's writing. If the initial focus on written work is on the spelling and punctuation, young writers can become very discouraged. Allowing children to spell creatively (how it sounds or looks to them, regardless of accuracy) increases their fluency and allows writing to serve as an outlet for children who are not comfortable speaking. Correcting children's spelling at this age results in the same problem as correcting their speech. If the task becomes onerous, the child may not participate.

Social Skills

Typically, children with communication problems do not seek out other children. They frequently play alone or near one other child. Encourage cooperative play so that children can learn to interact comfortably with peers. When they do play with others, these children are rarely leaders. They often receive instructions from classmates rather than give them, and as they are often reluctant to argue with the leader as others might, they may end up with the least desirable roles. Discourage, and if possible eliminate, teasing (this isn't always easy). As their self-concept improves, teach them ways to be assertive.

Under stress, these children may display tics, facial grimaces, unusual postures, or a characteristic gesture (head nodding, hair twirling). They may need to increase their body awareness. Help them to learn relaxation skills and to become aware of nervous mannerisms.

Guidelines

If the child has been diagnosed, read the child's file. It is sometimes useful to get copies of information sent to the parents as well as the more technical write-up that is frequently sent to other professionals. Talk with the speech and language therapist about the kinds of activities you can do in your classroom that would be helpful. Find out what the diagnosis means to the child's total development. (For example: Is the language delay a symptom of another disorder?) Whether the child is diagnosed or not, you must assess where in the language process the problem is, its severity, and how you will adapt your programming to meet this child's needs. As you listen to children throughout the day look for their most and least comfortable times with speech. Most children show a pattern. Support children's speech during the times and events when they are most likely to succeed. Although each child's situation will be different, the following guidelines will be helpful.

1. Simplify your grammar and vocabulary and use shorter sentences. The child will have fewer problems processing the information in this form. Also, slowing down your rate of delivery is helpful.

2. Ask few direct questions, especially during group time. This places high demands on a child for speech even when the response requested is just a short one.

3. Begin programming at the appropriate level (inner, receptive, integrative, expressive), where the child is just beginning to have problems.

4. Set aside a time each day for language development. (The activity may vary but the intent shouldn't.)

5. Increase the child's interest in himself and his environment. Encourage the child's desire to communicate.

6. Provide a secure and consistent environment.

7. Set up activities that provide noncompetitive peer interaction.

8. Include the child in group activities. The child need not have a speaking role if that is anxiety-provoking. Nonverbal group participation may be prerequisite to verbal participation.

9. Create a need for speech. If the child uses gestures instead of speech, deliberately (but not obviously) misunderstand briefly and name other objects. Before the child becomes frustrated, give the child what was requested, but use the word in one or two phrases or sentences. Gradually, over several encounters, increase the number of misunderstandings and incorrect guesses until the child is slightly frustrated by your "stupidity."

10. Do a lot of running commentary. Out loud, give a play-by-play description of what either you or the child is doing. Children learn to talk by listening.

11. Be a good listener. Give the child your undivided attention or explain that you can't listen then, but will soon. Arrange to do it as soon after as possible.

12. Reward the child for correct speech, but do not criticize or punish for lack of speech or incorrect speech.

13. Be a good speech and language model.

14. Differentiate between speech and language, and reinforce appropriately. For example, you might tell a child, "I'm glad you want to tell me about your picture, but I'm having trouble understanding what you are saying. Can you tell me with different words?" Therapists traditionally teach the child to understand the difference between "good language but poor speech."

15. Reinforce learning through visual and tactile experiences.

16. Structure lessons to provide children with more successes than failures.

17. Be aware that other class members may develop speech problems as a consequence of imitating defective speech and do not reinforce them.

The following guidelines will help you foster children's development in the four language processes.

Inner Language. Expand the child's awareness of the environment. Lack of stimulation may be a factor in underdeveloped inner language. Use field trips and many "hands-on" experiences that provide concrete learning experiences and materials to introduce and reinforce concepts. It is important that the children not be expected to talk about something they have no knowledge of. When providing opportunities to actively explore the environment, remember it often takes several experiences for a child to gain the necessary information.

Receptive Language. Provide varied listening experiences to help the child discriminate and associate sounds. Describe the child's behavior out loud: "Now you are going up the stairs." Use concrete examples or picture cues when possible, and reinforce learning through nonauditory experiences.

Integrative Language. Use simple one-step directions; gradually work up to more complex ones. If necessary, have the child repeat or verbally "walk through" the directions before actually doing an activity.

Expressive Language. Encourage the child to speak and reinforce attempts to do so. Don't rush the child when speaking or criticize the speech. If a child mispronounces a word, don't correct it. Instead, use it correctly in a sentence in response. Provide visual cues to speech sounds; if you are asking about a red shirt, point to it. Reinforce newly learned speech patterns (often done in coordination with the therapist).

Curriculum Adaptations

Children with communication impairments require few curriculum adaptations. Following are some general adaptations organized by curriculum area. This is not a complete list, but it will help you to begin programming for these children.

Language Arts: Speaking, Listening, Reading, and Writing

The language arts curriculum consists of speaking, listening, reading, and writing, and it is the area most emphasized for children with communication impairments. Communication skills cannot be viewed as isolated entities, but rather are related to the acquisition of all language skills. "Children who fail to acquire a complex sentence repertoire are considered at high risk for problems in reading and writing, which are language-based skills" (Garrard, 1987, p. 18).

In particular, these children need to develop and refine listening, attention, and memory skills. Language arts can be used to increase voluntary speaking as well as to develop readiness skills. Check with the child's speech and language therapist for more specific advice and additional activities.

Provide the child with firsthand experiences followed by discussions and opportunities for internalizing concepts and expanding key ideas. Using a farm as an example, you might:

Plan a trip to a farm.

Generate a language experience story about the trip to the farm.

Read a book about a farm at storytime.

Play farm animal lotto.

Discuss and imitate the sounds that farm animals make.

These suggestions are ordered on the principle that children learn the concrete before the abstract and that gradually increasing exposure to a concept increases learning.

Speaking. Children with communication disorders are often reluctant to speak. It is important that they have plenty of opportunities to practice in nonthreatening situations. Speaking requires practice and the need to communicate information. Provide opportunities throughout the day that encourage children to speak. Be sure to ask questions that involve answers beyond "yes" and "no."

1. Use puppets to encourage children to talk. Give the child cues to encourage speaking when necessary. As children become more confident have them play with each other using the puppets.

2. Have telephones available and encourage children to talk on the telephone with you and with each other.

Fingerplays are good for children with communication disorders. Although done with a group, fingerplays cause children to lose their self-consciousness, in part because they can participate in the motions without speaking. The motions also provide visual cues that help children understand the words. Fingerplays that rhyme are good for ear training. Those that have the sounds the child is working on are most useful.

1. Use fingerplays to stimulate body awareness. Those that involve the face and mouth area especially benefit the child.

Working with a speech and language therapist can be done in the classroom setting with only a few props.

2. Fingerplays such as "Teensy, Weensy Spider" facilitate eye-hand coordination as well as motor and manual control.

Listening. Stories expand the child's world as well as provide a fun opportunity to practice different sounds. Initially use stories about events familiar to the child. Books about children, family, and animals may fill this criteria.

1. Read stories that emphasize specific sounds, ones that are easy or hard for the child, depending on your objectives. *Sammy Snake* is an example of a story emphasizing the *s* sound.

2. Read stories that emphasize rhyming words (for example, *Each Peach Pear Plum*), voice control (*The Whispering Rabbit and Other Stories*), and listening skills (*What I Hear in My School*).*

3. To foster ear training, read stories and fingerplays that have rhymes until the children are familiar with them. Then read the stories with pauses to let the group fill in the rhyming word. The children will also enjoy nonsense rhyming games. You say a word and have the children call out real and made-up rhyming words for you to write on the board.

Reading. Young children with communication impairments are likely to have difficulty learning to read later (Kirk & Gallagher, 1979). While they are concentrating on pronunciation, their comprehension of the reading material suffers. Their reading rate will be slower than average and their phrasing will be poor. In fact reading may become so unpleasant they will avoid it whenever possible. Particular care should be taken to develop their reading readiness skills in order to forestall these problems.

When you teach reading readiness skills, you will most often use visual and auditory means. Children need to see and say a letter regardless of where it is positioned in the word. Ear training, the ability to listen well, is one prerequisite speech and language impaired children may find difficult to master. Yet it is essential to the development of reading readiness and the ability to communicate. Other skills include letter recognition, letter memory, and so forth.

Matching and sorting tasks are either perceptual or conceptual in nature or combine elements of both. Perceptual matching requires the children to match like letters to each other. They don't need to know what the letters stand for. When the task is a conceptual one, the children are required to abstract the idea and generalize it to another instance, for example, when going from small letters to capital letters or when going from script to printing. Conceptual matching can be used not only in reading readiness but also in other curriculum areas. Examples of both follow.

*Complete references as well as additional titles are given at the end of Part Two.

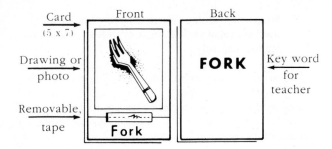

A picture file set up in a flexible format allows for later expansion. Divide the file into three sets: beginning consonant sounds, medial consonant sounds, and ending consonant sounds. Include the consonant blends (*bl*ouse, pu*mp*kin, sta*nd*) in each set. Vowels may be omitted because children rarely have problems with them. Organize the sets alphabetically and store them in three file boxes. Once you have developed the three basic sets, you are prepared for a variety of activities.

1. Have children find all the pictures with a specified beginning sound. (When ending an exercise, call out the sounds in alphabetical order. The pictures will automatically be organized for putting away.) Do the same thing for beginning consonant blends. Repeat the process for the middle and final position. When you introduce this activity you might have the name on the front of the card; the activity is easier when the child can match the initial letters as well as the sound. When the sounds are easier for the children, take off the word.

2. Set out four picture cards (three of which have the same ending sounds), say the words, then have the children identify the one that is different. Gradually give the children more responsibilities, thereby increasing the level of difficulty. You might have the children say the words, have them create sets for each other, and so on.

3. A more challenging and creative activity is making sound books. Introduce one sound at a time. Write the sound at the top of a piece of paper. Have the children find magazine pictures of objects that have that sound and have them paste the pictures on the page. When each child has a page for each sound, the pages can be made into books.

Lotto Card   Lotto Call Cards

A	F	W
J	O	C

A	a	🍎

Perceptual matching   Concept matching (sounds)   Concept matching (initial letter)

4. Letter Lotto (or variations of bingo) is a fun way to teach letter recognition. When children can match identical letters, add pictures as well as lower case letters to the game.

5. The development of letter memory can be facilitated by making two sets of the Lotto call cards and playing "Concentration." Start by turning four to six pairs of cards face down. If this is too easy add more pairs.

Writing. Writing provides both challenges and solutions for children with communication disorders. First they need to establish the connection between the written and spoken word. Do this informally by pointing out to children that you cannot see words if their hand is over them, or that you cannot read the book if it is upside down. Write what they say, but do not hesitate to ask them to slow down, pointing out that you can not write as quickly as they can talk. Use language experience stories and support all of children's attempts at writing, regardless of the quality of the letters or the spelling.

1. Write their names on papers and point out to children that you do this so they will not get mixed up. Compare two pictures and then explain that if you forget who made them you can look at the name.

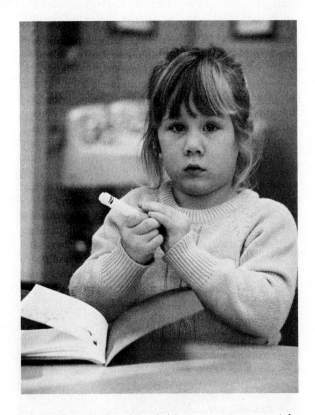

Watch how comfortable children are using materials not related to verbal language.

2. Support children's verbalizations by writing down what they say and then reading it back to them. Again, point out the advantage of a written language by reading what the children said at a later date.

3. Discuss writing as a symbol system and point out that the English language uses the alphabet they are familiar with but all other languages do not. Have the children write a syllabary—they can decide on the written configurations that stand for words or syllables. They can use this to write to each other. (In this instance spelling is irrelevant.)

4. Have a writing center and support writing as a process that involves authorship, illustration, editing, and publishing. Support children in each of these stages of the process.

Discovery: Mathematics, Science, Computers

For children with only speech problems the discovery area is not likely to be different from other children in the classroom. Those with other communication disorders need concrete experiences to learn best in this area.

Mathematics. Children with communication problems usually have math skills comparable to their classmates'. They often enjoy math, as it can be learned with a minimum of speech. Math, then, can give these children a feeling of achievement. When they count or discuss concepts, they are working through a strength (math) to meet a need (facility with language and speech).

1. Use math concepts that facilitate speech and language development. Have children count and sort objects that make sounds and objects that don't. Or, have them count the number of times a sound is made.

2. Make number books by having children cut out a specified number of pictures beginning with the same sound. You might have, for example, one *T,* two *R*s, three *S*s, four *TH*s, and so on.

3. Apply the math vocabulary (big/little, more/less, equal) to sounds and body awareness. Tell children to make their bodies as big as they can, then as little. Have them find pictures of an animal with a big tail and of one with a little tail. Do those animals make big/loud sounds or little/soft sounds?

4. Present pictures of geometric shapes and have children draw these shapes in the air with various parts of their bodies. Once they have shown they understand by tracing the shapes with their hands, have them outline the shapes with their jaw, head, tongue, and finally by moving only their eyes.

5. Compare the chest measurements of children after they inhale and after they exhale. This can be done with string or measuring tape, although string is more effective with younger children because they can see which string is longer.

Science. Science activities require few verbal skills. Therefore, the risk of failure by the speech and language impaired is minimized. Science topics, such as those outlined below, can enhance children's understanding of the mechanics of speech and language. Although fewer verbal skills are required by science than by some other subjects, interest is usually very high and stimulates language use.

1. Teach some anatomy, especially the organs that produce sound (lips, tongue, teeth, throat, diaphragm).

2. Use mirrors to help children see the articulatory organs while exploring the concept of mirror reversing.

3. Discuss the sounds different animals make and how they make them. (Crickets, for example, rub their legs together.) Have children experiment making sounds by using different body parts (clap, stomp, slap thighs). Make a tape recording of animal sounds; see if children can pair the picture of the animal with the sound.

4. Talk about how sound is made in nature (thunder, water moving, wind) and how humans make noise (music, talking, working). Discuss how noise cues us to what is happening in our environment. These sounds may be presented on tapes or on records. Use pictures when you first present the sounds; the visual reinforces the aural learning.

5. Discuss the properties of air and its function in speech. Use a balloon to make air more tangible.

Computers. Computers require no verbal input yet are capable of verbal output. Keyboards can be modified to simplify them for young children. Children who will later depend on computers for communication need to be interacting with them from the preschool years on. Most computers are designed with internal hardware features that we are unaware of. For example, symbols that take two strokes (hold down the shift key and press the designated letter to make a capital letter) usually can be reprogrammed to use only one key stroke. The manufacturers have this information and willingly share it.

1. Have a computer with a voice synthesizer in the classroom so children can become familiar with it.

2. Have a variety of keyboard modifications if this is possible, again, to match the child's needs.

3. Encourage children to learn that computers are part of their life, and that they are in control of them.

Sensory Motor: Large Motor, Sensory Motor Integration, Small Motor

Sensory motor activities support the communication process by increasing body awareness. They provide opportunities for communication, but the activities are not dependent upon this skill.

Large Motor. Large motor play is usually a pleasure for these children and should be encouraged. Because their language problem rarely interferes, this may prove one of their strengths.

1. Use large motor play to foster a sense of belonging to the group.

2. Help classmates see the child's strengths in this area.

3. Blocks are one activity where speech requirements are few but opportunities for speech are many. As cooperative play increases, children talk more to each other.

4. By telling children what they are doing, in a play-by-play commentary, large motor play can be made a language-enriching experience.

Sensory Motor Integration. Children with communication impairments need to develop their ability to listen in coordination with seeing and touching. Sensory integration and eye-hand coordination can be accomplished through small motor play.

1. Use activities that pair listening skills with visual or tactile skills: "Turn the page when you hear the tone."

2. Use activities that help establish a hand preference (coloring, turning nuts on bolts, eating). (It is irrelevant which hand is preferred.)

Small Motor. Children may need to focus on the small muscles of their body: eye movements are necessary for reading, the hand and fingers for writing, as well as the facial muscles for speaking.

1. Finger strength is necessary for holding a crayon or pencil. Start with large writing tools.

2. Encourage children to draw or scribble by providing a variety of paper and drawing utensils.

3. Have children use their breath to do things such as blow up balloons or make pinwheels turn to make them more aware of the output. See if they can make a pinwheel turn very slowly or fast.

Social Awareness: Social Studies, Inclusion, Health and Safety

Children with communication disorders may not have good skills at joining groups. Help them

develop the language necessary to be included. Think about the priorities in language development and work on the language skills that will increase the child's safety if lost and on auditory identification of warning signals.

Social Studies. Speech and language skills can be integrated into the social studies curriculum through conversation and role playing. Help the children identify similarities and differences throughout the immediate environment, the region, the country, and the world. Your goal is to promote the concept of diversity. At the same time you are promoting the children's awareness of differences and similarities in speech and language without their making judgments.

1. Names are different in other languages. Some common names can be discussed that translate well: John in Spanish is Juan; in French, Jacques; in German, Johann. However there are some names for which there are no equivalents. Discuss these as well.

2. Make a tape recording of people from different regions in the United States (with the characteristic accent). If possible have them all say the same sentences so that the children can more readily grasp the differences.

3. Act out situations that require the children to assume roles that have different speech patterns associated with them: for example, cowhand, police officer, father, mother, baby.

Inclusion. It is important for all children to feel they belong. Children need to know they are all similar in some ways and different in others. Language may be an area in which they are different.

1. Have children play with language, perhaps mispronouncing an unfamiliar word. Ask children how they feel and how they would feel if others criticized or made fun of them. Ask them whether they would try to pronounce the word again and how they would feel.

2. Discuss the importance of turn taking in language as well as on pieces of equipment. Point out that sometimes they will need to wait for others to have time to say what they want to communicate. It is important for them to wait as well as you.

Health and Safety. Speech and language production requires the coordination of muscles from the waist up, the speech organs, and the brain. It is one of the most complicated human processes. Children need to be made aware of the body parts involved while they learn how to take care of their body. Listening to someone who has a stopped-up head helps children learn the nose's function. A sore throat demonstrates the throat's contribution to speech.

Teeth. Discuss how to care for teeth. Invite a dentist to visit the class. As children begin to lose their baby teeth, discuss what sounds become difficult. Have them discover the role teeth play in making sounds.

Jaw. Use scissors to illustrate the hingelike action of the jaw. Have children use their fingers to feel the bones and muscles as they drop their jaw. Again, experiment with sound as the jaw lowers and rises.

Tongue. Do tongue exercises with the class. Let the children use mirrors to watch their tongue move. Have them pair off and watch each other.

Vocal Cords. Have children place their hands on their throat to feel the vocal cords vibrate. See if they can feel a difference in sounds. Use a rubber band to show how the vocal cords work, stretching it tight for high sounds and only slightly for low ones.

Creative Arts: Art, Music, Creative Movement, and Dramatic Play

Creative arts offer children the ability to develop skills with much less emphasis on the specific product.

Art. Children have the opportunity in art to develop fine motor skills. They also get satisfaction from having a product to show for their efforts. Art activities provide a constructive nonverbal way of expressing feelings and working off energy.

1. Children can learn to recognize differences in how a pencil, a crayon, paint, and chalk sound and feel.

2. Blow painting, or straw painting, develops the muscles of the mouth, gives practice in closing off the palate and throat, and teaches breath control.

3. Encourage children to talk about their pictures (not in response to "What is it?" or, as a naive graduate student once said to a three-year-old, "What does this picture represent to you?"). Start out with a comment such as "I like the way you use red in this picture." That's an invitation—you may have shown enough interest to get a response. You might ask, "Does your picture have a story?" Be prepared for the fact that it may not!

4. Make puppets to be used in dramatic play. Often shy children will vocalize more with puppets.

Music. Music offers many fun opportunities for nonthreatening speech and language training. Music requires children to develop and use different vocal patterns. Blowing instruments and singing stimulate the palate and musculature of the mouth. Because some speech problems don't carry over into singing, this is a vocal activity that can be rewarding for children who have communication disorders.

1. Have children make musical instruments to develop listening skills. Make paper plate tambourines filled with stones, beans, and rice. These can be played in a group as well as paired according to the different sounds they make. Also make balloon squeakers and rubber band whistles. Have children make musical instruments that emphasize mouth movements.

2. Children become more aware of their voices as they whistle, hum, and sing high and low, loud and soft. Help them note tension in the lips and the feel of air coming in and out. Help them relate what they learn to speaking.

3. Music is a natural way to teach the concepts of high and low. Reinforce the concepts by having the children stretch their bodies high for the high notes, crouch low for the low notes, and be somewhere in between for the middle notes.

4. Holding notes for long or short periods of time increases breath awareness and improves breath control.

5. Music with movement provides an avenue for interpreting or expressing moods.

6. The rhythm of music also applies to speech and language, especially for children who stutter. Interestingly enough these children can often sing things they cannot say. To create more awareness of rhythm you can have children brush teeth, lower jaws (as if chewing), or even click tongues to a rhythm pattern.

7. Songs with action allow children to participate whether or not they know the words. Actions provide visual cues for learning the words.

8. Records and tapes enhance listening skills, but they should be used with visual aids to help children comprehend the content.

Creative Movement. Use movement to increase body awareness (especially of speech organs) and to provide relaxation.

1. For relaxation have children be clothes fluttering on the line in the wind. To relax the throat and neck, have the children drop their heads forward (chin toward chest).

2. To improve articulation, put milk or juice in a bowl and have children lap it up, like a cat, with their tongues. Licking designs in ice cream will also exercise the tongue.

Dramatic Play. Dramatic play provides a safe outlet for energy and an opportunity for children to try out roles without fear of judgment. It also allows children to be a part of a group.

1. At the beginning of the year the dramatic play area should be an easy, familiar, nondemanding place. Children with communication disorders will often drift toward this area, as it represents a tie with home. (This is particularly true of three-year-olds.)

2. These children are often fearful of new situations, such as a field trip or moving to a new house. (The parents may tell you of a new experience the child is going to encounter.) Take advantage of dramatic play to have children rehearse the experience beforehand to gain knowledge of what to expect.

3. Puppets encourage speech in a nonthreatening way. Play a recording of Donald Duck or Mickey Mouse to reassure children that it is all right for puppets to sound different.

Transitions

As children end one activity and prepare to go on to another, there is often some confusion. Turn the confusion into opportunities for learning by taking advantage of transitions.

1. Combine movement and sound to help children get from one area to another: "Walk like a duck and quack as you go to the art area." Ask children to walk as quietly or to make as much noise as they can while going to the learning center of their choice.

2. Increase body awareness and sense of self. Dismiss children by hair and eye color.

Children's Bibliography

See the Children's Bibliography on page 286 for books to increase children's awareness of disabilities as well as books that are especially good for children with particular disabilities. Note especially:

Awareness of Communication Disorders

Picture Books

Rhyming and Sound Books

Glossary

Aphasia An inability to use words as a way of communicating ideas. This condition is usually the result of a brain lesion.

Apraxia A disorder that relates to the selecting and sequencing of speech.

Articulation The production of speech sounds.

Auditory skills Identification, discrimination, memory, closure, association, and comprehension of sounds. (See Part Four, Chapter 23.)

Augmented communication Alternative communication that does not rely on speech, such as manual communication, communication boards, computers, and so on.

Babbling An early stage of speech when the child uses meaningless sounds as though talking.

Cleft palate A disorder in which there is no closing between the mouth and the nasal cavity. This gap can vary in size and may include only a portion of the roof of the mouth or include the gum ridge and upper lip. Children with this problem usually have trouble with high pressure sounds, such as $/s/$, $/z/$, $/p/$.*

Cluttering A rhythm disorder sometimes confused with stuttering. The child speaks so rapidly that sounds are omitted or slurred.

Dysarthria A term used to refer to articulation problems that are caused by nerve disorders. The result is usually weak or uncoordinated muscles that affect articulation. These conditions cause slow, labored speech that has consistent articulation errors.

Dyspraxia A term used to refer to articulation problems involving the planning and carrying out of voluntary movements. Dyspraxic speech is usually inconsistent and unpredictable.

Echolalia The repetition of what is said by another person as if echoing them. (Teacher: "Hello, John"; Child: "Hello, John.")

Jargon When used to refer to speech and language impaired children, confused unintelligible speech sometimes called jargon aphasia.

Lisping An articulation problem in which /th/ is substituted for /s/.

Morphemes The smallest units of a language that contain meaning. They are usually words or meaningful word parts.

Morphology The study of linguistics that deals with the internal structure and forms of words, that is, the structure, classification, and relationship of morphemes (grammar).

Phonation The production of sounds and sound combinations, usually speech.

Phonemes The smallest units of a language that distinguish meaning. They are usually letter sounds. The meanings of c*at* and c*ap* are distinguished by the phonemes $/t/$ and $/p/$.

Phonology The study of the rules for using the sounds in a language.

Pragmatics The social use of language for communication.

Semantics The relationship between words or phrases and their meanings.

Stuttering A rhythm disorder characterized by repetitions, hesitations, and prolongations. As the child becomes aware of the disorder, grimaces or other movements not related to speech often appear.

Syntax The arrangement of words into phrases or sentences.

*When letters are referred to, they are written in italics. When the sound of a letter is being referred to, it is written thus: /s/.

Visual skills   Identification, discrimination, memory, closure, association, and comprehension of speech. (See Part Four, Chapter 23.)

Teaching Resources

In some situations you may want or need additional information. There are many national as well as regional, state, and local organizations that can help you. The following annotated list of national organizations should be useful in helping you decide where to get the information you need.

American Speech-Language-Hearing Association
10801 Rockville Pike
Rockville, MD 20852
   Professional society of specialists in speech-language pathology and audiology.

Center for Applied Linguistics
1611 North Kent Street
Arlington, VA 22209
   Serves as a national and international research and resource center in the application of linguistic science to social and educational problems.

Division for Children with Communication Disorders
Council for Exceptional Children
1920 Association Drive
Reston, VA 22091
   A division of the Council for Exceptional Children (CEC) that focuses only on communication disorders. It publishes the Journal of Childhood Communication Disorders *as well as a newsletter. CEC has divisions for all major disabilities and is committed to advancing the quality of education for all children with disabilities.*

National Association of Hearing and Speech Action
814 Thayer Avenue
Silver Spring, MD 20914

National Association of Hearing and Speech Agencies
919 18th Street, N.W.
Washington, DC 20006
   Makes referrals to member affiliates and conducts public education campaigns through its bimonthly magazine and films.

National Council of Stutterers
c/o Speech and Hearing Clinic
Catholic University of America
Washington, DC 20064
   Promotes programs and studies of interest or benefit to adult stutterers.

References and Bibliography

Bernstein, D., & Tigerman, E. (1989). *Language and communication disorders in children* (2nd ed.). Columbus, OH: Charles C. Merrill.

Butler, K. (1986). *Language disorders in children.* Austin, TX: PRO-ED.

Cantwell, D., & Barker, L. (1987). *Developmental speech and language disorders.* New York: Guilford Press.

Cazden, C. (Ed.). (1972). *Language in early childhood education.* Washington, DC: National Association for the Education of Young Children.

Eisenson, J. (1976). *Is your child's speech normal?* Reading, MA: Addison-Wesley.

Ensher, G. (1989). The first three years: Special education perspectives on assessment and intervention. *Topics in Language Disorders, 10*(1), 80–90.

Garrard, K. (1987). Helping young children develop mature speech patterns. *Young Children, 42*(3), 16–21.

Gottwald, S., Goldbach, P., & Isack, A. (1985). Stuttering: Prevention and detection. *Young Children, 40*(7), 9–14.

Hallahan, D., & Kauffman, J. (1991). *Exceptional children: Introduction to special education.* Englewood Cliffs, NJ: Prentice-Hall.

Herr, J., & Libby, Y. (1990). *Creative resources for the early childhood classroom.* Albany, NY: Delmar Publishers, Inc.

Kirk, S., & Gallagher, J. (1979). *Educating exceptional children* (3rd ed.). Boston: Houghton Mifflin.

Liebergott, J., Favors, A., von Hippel, C., & Needleman, H. (1978). *Mainstreaming preschoolers: Children with speech and language impairments.* Washington, DC: U.S. Department of Health and Human Services.

Longhurst, T. M. (Ed.). (1974). *Functional language intervention* (2 vols.). Edison, NJ: Mss Information Corp.

Machado, J. (1990). *Early childhood experiences in language arts: Emerging literacy* (4th ed.). Albany, NY: Delmar Publishers, Inc.

McWilliams, P. (1984). *Personal computers and the disabled.* Garden City, NY: Quantum Press.

Mecham, M., & Willbrand, M. L. (1979). *Language disorders in children: A resource book for speech-language pathologists.* Springfield, IL: Charles C. Thomas.

Murphy, J. F., & O'Donnell, C. A. (1975). *Developing oral language with young children: A parent-teacher inventory* (6 workbooks). Cambridge, MA: Educator's Publishing Service.

Oyer, H., Crowe, B., & Haas, W. (1987). *Speech, language, and hearing disorders: A guide for teachers.* Boston: Little, Brown.

Peterson, N. L. (1987). *Early intervention for handicapped and at-risk children: An introduction to early childhood special education.* Denver, CO: Love Publishing Co.

Rosolack, M. N. (1975). *Speech improvement in early childhood through auditory awareness and discrimination.* Danville, IL: Interstate.

Rousey, C. (1984). *A practical guide to helping children with speech and language problems.* Springfield, IL: Charles C. Thomas.

Sanders, L. J. (1979). *Procedure guides for evaluation of speech and language disorders in children* (4th ed.). Danville, IL: Interstate.

Schneider, M. J. (1979). *A guide to communication development in preschool children: Birth–five years.* Danville, IL: Interstate.

Terango, L. (1977). *Early recognition of speech, hearing and language disorders in children under six years of age.* Danville, IL: Interstate.

Tizard, B. (1981). Language at home and at school. In C. B. Cazden (Ed.). *Language in early childhood.* Washington, DC: National Association for the Education of Young Children.

Valletutti, P., McKnight-Taylor, M., & Hoffnung, A. (Eds.). (1989). *Facilitating communication in young children with handicapping conditions: A guide for special educators.* Boston: Little, Brown.

Van Riper, C. (1978). *Speech corrections: Principles and methods* (6th ed.). Englewood Cliffs, NJ: Prentice-Hall.

White, J. D. (1976). *Talking with a child.* New York: Macmillan.

Wilson, D. (1979). *Voice problems of children* (2nd ed.). Baltimore, MD: Williams and Wilkins.

Zwitman, D. (1978). *The disfluent child.* Baltimore, MD: University Park Press.

Chapter 11

Children with Hearing Impairments

When a child with a hearing impairment joins your class, you will suddenly become aware of the many times during the day that children must listen. They have to listen for roll call, opening exercises, and directions for activities and cleanup. They must listen for music, story time, and even fire drills. You may wonder whether the child will talk and, if so, whether you and the other children will be able to understand. How much can this child hear and how will this affect your classroom routine? How much individual time will this child require? What will you tell the other children (and their parents) about this child?

Hearing is important in developing communications skills. Children learn to talk by listening and imitating others and by hearing themselves. The hearing child enters kindergarten with a vocabulary of about 5,000 words. The child with a hearing impairment may understand and speak only a few basic words and even those few words may be hard to understand. Our society assumes that people can convey their wants and needs verbally. In school, children are expected to ask to go to the bathroom, to tell the teacher if they are hurt, and to talk with their playmates. They are also expected to put away their materials when told to, and to line up or come when called. Children with hearing impairments have trouble following instructions and discussion. They may be mistaken for children who daydream or choose not to listen, and they are sometimes seen as being stubborn, disobedient, or lazy.

Hearing allows a person to gain cognitive information about the world. We use hearing to monitor our physical and social environment. Children who cannot hear danger signals may find themselves in hazardous situations that others can avoid. Being out of touch with moment-to-moment ordinary sounds has a social-emotional impact of equal magnitude. Children with hearing impairments must be taught to use other cues to be in touch with their world. **153**

Classification of Hearing Impairments

Before you begin programming, it is important for you to find out more about the child's hearing. A child who is deaf cannot understand speech by using only his ears, even with a hearing aid. A child who is hard of hearing can understand speech (with difficulty) using only the ears, either with or without a hearing aid. The effects on the child vary according to the severity of hearing loss and can be summarized as follows (Neisworth & Bagnato, 1987; DuBose, 1979):

Severity of Loss	*Effects*
Mild/Slight (hard of hearing) 35 to 54 db.	Will have a more limited vocabulary than peers. If faced and spoken to within 3–5 feet, will probably understand. If in a large group and voices are faint, may miss as much as half of what is being said.
Moderate/Marked (hard of hearing) 55 to 69 db.	Will have a limited vocabulary and may have speech problems. Loud conversations, face-to-face, will probably be understood. Will have a great deal of trouble understanding large-group discussions.
Severe (deaf) 70 to 89 db.	Will have little comprehensible speech. May hear loud voices from one foot from ear. May hear warning signals (alarms, sirens).
Extreme/Profound (deaf) 90 db and greater.	Will have very little comprehensible speech. Will be more aware of vibrations than of speech itself. Will rely on vision rather than hearing.

Remember, the two ears can have different amounts of loss and, typically, the child can function at the level of his better ear. In other words, if a child had a 55 db loss in the right ear and an 80 db loss in the left, he may function as a moderately hard-of-hearing child.

However, the difference between hearing sound and hearing words is a big one. Consider the following sentence (Bryan & Bryan, 1979, p. 226):

"Let's go camping in a state park next August."

The child may hear:

"Le   o amp n   a   ar ne Au u ."

At the same time, the child may see by speech reading:

"Let's o ampi in a state par ne t Au ust."

Even using a combination of hearing and vision, understanding is still difficult for children with a hearing loss.

The prevalence of hearing impairment is difficult to estimate. The diagnosis varies somewhat according to the method of testing and criteria used by the audiologist. Mild hearing losses in particular are not easily detected and, consequently, the child is not even referred for testing. The same is true for children who have intermittent conductive losses.

Infants who are born with a hearing loss or acquire one before they acquire speech are also difficult to identify. Infants with hearing impairments make noises and babble like other babies up until about six months of age. They do not, however, respond to auditory stimuli out of their range of hearing. Parents may be concerned, but the problem is hard to pin down, and just when parents think they should be concerned the infant does something to make them think they are imagining things. Most parents don't want to appear overprotective and look foolish to their pediatricians. Horton (1976) found

An ear-level aid can help children keep in tune with their environment.

in a survey of parents who had children with hearing impairments, that it was the parents in 70 percent of the cases who suspected the hearing loss and in only 7 percent was it the physician who first noted the problem. Parents who note the problem usually do so because the child does not reach traditional milestones in the area of speech and language.

It has been estimated that between 3 and 5 percent of school-age children have hearing needs severe enough to profit from individualized programming (Bryan & Bryan, 1979). However, the U.S. Department of Education (1989) reported only .12 percent of school-age children having hearing losses. Because of definitional problems, it is difficult to reach conclusions about prevalence.

The Ear

The ear is the organ of the body that we think of when we think of hearing. However, it is rarely a problem with the outside ear that causes the hearing loss. The outer ear is one of three parts of the ear and the only one that is visible. It is connected to the middle ear and the inner ear (see illustration).

Sounds or vibrations travel through the ear canal and hit the eardrum, causing it to vibrate back and forth. The eardrum is attached to one of the small bones in the middle ear, the malleus (hammer), through which vibrations are transmitted to the incus (anvil) and stapes (stirrup), until they reach the oval window, the beginning of the inner ear. As the vibrations push the oval window (a thin membrane) back and forth, the fluid in the cochlea moves, sensitizing the tiny hair cells inside. These hair cells send electrochemical impulses through the nerve fibers, through the auditory nerve, and to the brain. The brain must then interpret the signals.

In addition to providing hearing, the ear serves two other functions: balance and responding

to differences in pressure. The inner ear has three loop-shaped tubes, the semicircular canals, that serve to maintain balance (vestibular sense). The eustachian tube, a slender tube that runs from the middle ear to the pharynx, equalizes pressure on both sides of the eardrum. When flying in an airplane or going to higher altitudes on the ground, it is the clearing of the eustachian tube by swallowing or chewing gum that keeps the eardrum from bursting. The ears essentially duplicate each other, with the major benefit of having two ears being the ability to localize sound.

Sound

A hearing impairment affects either the loudness (intensity) of the sound that can be heard or the pitch (frequency) of the sound that can be heard, or both. Decibels (db) are the measure of sound intensity. The higher the number of decibels, the louder the sound. People can hear sound from 0 db to about 120 db. Sounds louder than 120 db first produce a "tickle," then pain, and beyond that sensorineural damage. Ordinary conversation falls in the 50 to 80 db range. Pitch is determined by the number of cycles per second the sound wave has. These are measured in Hertz (Hz). People can hear sounds that are low (about 20 Hz) to those that are very high (about 12,000 Hz). The normal speech frequencies fall between 500 and 2,000 Hz. A loss above those frequencies (such as is common with increasing age) may affect one's appreciation of music but does not interfere with communications until it comes into the speech frequencies.

Hearing is assessed for each ear separately, as it is possible to have a severe loss in one ear and not in the other, or have a different configuration of loss in each ear. For education purposes, we are rarely concerned about losses that are very mild (5–30 db) or those in the higher frequencies (over 4,000 Hz) as they will have minimal effect on the child's education.

Once a problem is detected, referral is made to a medical doctor, an otologist, who is a specialist in the diagnosis and treatment of ear diseases, and to an audiologist. The medical specialist is concerned with looking at the physical conditions associated with the ears to determine whether or not any medical intervention is indicated. The audiologist is a professional trained in the identification and measurement of hearing impairments. The audiologist also aids in the rehabilitation of children with hearing impairments.

One of the first things that an audiologist does is to determine the level of hearing impairment. The child is placed in a sound-proof room. An audiometer is used to generate sounds electronically so that the intensity and frequency of tones can be controlled to determine how much or how little the child hears. The results of the testing are charted on an audiogram. The audiologist may also test the child's ability to comprehend speech at various intensities. In addition to working with an audiologist, most children who have

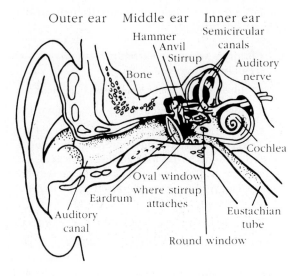

The Ear

hearing impairments serious enough to need hearing aids also work with a teacher of the hearing impaired or a specially trained speech/language therapist.

Causes of Hearing Impairments

The most common way to classify causes of hearing impairments is by their location in the hearing process. Knowing the exact type of loss has implications for treatment and education, and the long-term implications differ greatly.

Conductive Loss. A conductive loss is one in which the outer or middle ear prevents sound from getting to the inner ear. This can be caused by something lodged in the ear canal, excessive ear wax, or fluid in the middle ear (otitis media). Many young children who experience frequent ear infections have periodic conductive losses, typically running about 60 db or less. Conductive losses reduce the child's ability to hear speech sounds through air conduction. Sounds transmitted through bone conduction are heard normally. Most conductive losses can be corrected through surgery.

Impairments of the Middle Ear. Because of the frequency of middle ear disease in young children, its implication for language development, and your role in case finding, it is treated in detail here. Middle ear disease, middle ear effusion, middle ear dysfunction, or otitis media are all terms used to describe the same chronic condition: fluid in the middle ear. Most children have one or two ear infections during their early childhood years. However, there are usually few long-term implications from these. In fact, earaches are the second most commonly diagnosed disorder in young children during an office visit. It is estimated that over half of all antibiotics given to children are for otitis media (Hallahan & Kauffman, 1991). Children who have repeated bouts of otitis media, on the other hand, are at risk of acquiring language skills slowly and of displaying learning disabilities (Denk-Glass, Laber, & Brewer, 1982; Ralabate, 1987).

Middle ear disease (M.E.D.) is caused by thick fluid in the middle ear that does not drain through the eustachian tubes. Once the middle ear is stopped up, the child experiences a hearing loss. Additionally, this thick fluid is a prime target for bacterial growth. Antibiotics cure the infection, but the fluid may linger on for days or even weeks, causing a hearing loss.

It is difficult to accurately measure the prevalence of middle ear disease. However, some estimates are as high as 50 percent of young children (Denk-Glass, Laber, & Brewer, 1982). The problem is that middle ear disease is often undetected until the child shows signs of physical illness. Typically, irritability, lethargy, and inattentiveness are the most visible symptoms. Because of the intermittent nature of the problem even children who have their hearing checked can be missed. "Up to 60 percent of the children who have M.E.D. can be missed by the traditional school hearing screening" (Ralabate, 1987, p. 10).

Middle ear disease can be treated medically by inserting tubes in the child's ears to allow the fluid to drain. However, if it is not treated, a temporary loss could become a permanent one (Mollick & Etra, 1981). Many parents may not be aware of the implications of ear infections for hearing loss or the risk for learning disabilities. Sometimes physicians themselves are overcasual about frequent ear infections, making statements like, "Don't worry, spring is coming." That is an appealing idea, but not one that is necessarily useful to the child.

Sensorineural Loss. A sensorineural loss involves damage to either the inner ear, the nerve to the brain stem, or both. Perceptive impairment and nerve loss are synonyms. The loss may be congenital or occur due to illnesses that have high fever or some medicines that are used. Sensorineural losses cannot be treated surgically at this time. Typically a hearing aid is prescribed to make sounds louder. Even with amplification, however, sounds are unclear and distorted to the child.

Mixed Loss. In some cases children can experience both a sensorineural and a conductive loss. In this case, the conductive problem is typically treated surgically and the sensorineural problem with a hearing aid. These combined situations can be difficult to diagnose.

A new surgical procedure, a cochlear implant, allows some profoundly deaf children to hear sound they previously could not. Sounds are picked up by a small microphone and sent electronically to the inner ear. The implant enables children to hear many environmental sounds, such as the telephone and car horns, and makes speech reading easier. A learning process is necessary as the child needs to differentiate and identify sounds she hears for the first time (Hallahan & Kauffman, 1991).

Be aware of the following signs that indicate children are not hearing:

1. Children who are extremely attentive or extremely inattentive.

2. Children whose speech is delayed or immature.

3. Children with frequent colds or ear infections.

4. Children with allergies. (Signs of allergies vary. Red itchy eyes, a runny nose, and sneezing are typical signs.) Also look at the child's eyes. Children with allergies may look as though they have "black eyes," as there are often dark circles under the eyes.

5. Children who speak too loudly, or give inappropriate answers to questions.

6. Children who ask for information to be repeated or say "What?" a lot.

7. Children who have had diseases such as mumps, measles, or rubella or high fevers for a long period.

8. Children who have poor balance and seem clumsy (Mollick & Etra, 1981).

It is important that you as a teacher are alert to these signs. You may see the child more than the parents, and have more information about how she responds. Alert them if you are concerned.

Hearing Aids

The ears receive sound waves or vibrations in the air and convert them into electrical signals the brain can understand. When the ear is defective, it sends weak or distorted signals. A hearing aid amplifies sounds, and it magnifies all sounds, not just speech. Because it does not correct distortion, it is not useful for all types of hearing impairments.

Hearing aids are individually prescribed by audiologists and purchased from commercial dealers. Using the aids properly requires training. (The child must actually be taught how to listen; speech may be gobbledygook to someone who has never heard it before.)

Although a hearing aid is beneficial, that doesn't mean the child will willingly wear it. Parents and teachers are frequently frustrated by children who pull out their hearing aids. For young children especially, the aid may feel strange. They will try to make themselves feel more comfortable by taking it out. If children were previously unaware of most sounds and speech, the hearing aid may be delivering what to them is meaningless noise. Again, their solution is to remove the aid. Once children see the advantages of hearing with the aid they are usually willing to wear it. Until then, however, encouragement is needed. If you force the child to wear the aid, the child will associate you with the hated process, and you will become ineffective as a teacher. Don't be in awe of the hearing aid, the parents, or the audiologist. Work out a compromise with the parents about what to do about this problem.

You need to develop skills in working with a hearing aid. The child's parents can help you. You should be able to do certain things the child may not yet have mastered.

1. Put the earpiece back in when it falls out or is pulled out.

2. Check if batteries are dead and replace them. (Keep a supply in the child's locker or with the school nurse.)

3. Know how to manipulate the controls. When the hearing aid "whistles," turn it down.

4. Hearing aids should not be abused, but they are sturdy enough to allow the child to participate in most activities. Try to keep them from getting painted, soaked, or sandy.

The model of hearing aid a child has is determined by the type and amount of his loss. In general, the greater the loss the more powerful the hearing aid must be. Most young children will have a hearing aid that is worn on their chest with a Y-shaped cord going to ear molds in each ear. These body-worn aids are more powerful than ear-level aids, but they do not compensate for different losses in each ear. They are also conspicuous and a bit cumbersome. As children get older, Y-aids are often replaced with ear-level aids, much smaller hearing aids that fit behind the ear itself. Two aids may be required. However, the aids are almost unnoticeable, especially under long hair.

Hearing aids do not make a child hear perfectly. Be sure the other children understand this. A hearing aid works well for a radius of only ten feet. Even then it amplifies all sounds.

Communication. The *total communication* approach uses the auditory, visual, and tactile senses in combination to provide children with as much information as possible. In this system the sender of the message, or speaker, verbalizes the message while simultaneously signing or finger spelling the same message.

American Sign Language (Ameslan or ASL) consists of a set of standard hand signs used in relation to other parts of the body. Each sign represents an idea or concept. Grammatically and conceptually, ASL is a shorthand system. It also uses fingerspelling for verb tenses and words that do not have signs. Fingerspelling uses twenty-six different finger configurations, one for each letter of the alphabet. (See the Glossary for an illustration of this alphabet.)

Not everyone believes in total communication. *Oralists* favor using speech and whatever residual hearing there is. They fear that because signing is easier than speech reading or talking, children will not develop these skills and hence will be able to communicate only with people who can sign and not the majority of society. *Manualists* favor signing and finger spelling with less emphasis on speech reading or talking than is advocated by total communication. Although you should be aware of the issues, you will not have to take a side in the controversy as you will teach the child in accordance with the parents' choice.

Some people feel that *cued speech* is a better system than signing. In this system a hand motion depicts a particular sound and the speaker says the word as well as cueing it. As it is based on sounds in the English language, once those sounds are learned any word can be cued.

Children's Needs: Teaching Goals

Related annual goals may be grouped under broad categories called "teaching goals." Outlined under each teaching goal below are the most important needs of children with hearing impairments. A child may have some or all of these needs and additional needs as well. Suggestions on what you might consequently teach them are included. Often, a course of action is implicit in the description of the need.

Sensory Skills

Visual Skills. Children with hearing impairments need to replace some of the auditory skills they lack with visual skills. Speech reading depends on fine visual discrimination bolstered by visual closure, which fills in some of what speech reading misses. Interpreting signs and finger spelling is both a visual task and a reading readiness skill. Plan numerous activities that require fine visual discrimination. Introduce variety into activities by using three-dimensional objects, pictures, line drawings, and even people.

Auditory Skills. Hearing impaired children often have poor listening skills; they haven't developed what hearing they do have. They often listen with their head tilted, to favor the stronger ear. They have difficulty understanding the speech of others, especially when in groups, when the speaker is far away, or when the speaker is looking in another direction. These children need practice in using their residual hearing. Be sure the auditory tasks are presented clearly and loudly enough so that children can hear them.

Sensory Integration. Characteristically, when these children explore the environment, they rely more on vision and touch than do their peers. Their visual and tactile skills need to be refined so that they can gain as much information from the environment as possible.

Language Skills

Children with hearing impairments have limited or impaired speech. They often run words together and have a peculiar voice quality that might be described as a flat, high-pitched monotone. Even when they can speak, they often don't because of difficulties in being understood and their embarrassment. When they do speak, the volume may be inappropriate (e.g., shouting in church or whispering at a football game). They often use gestures to express themselves. Encourage these children to speak in small groups first where they feel safe. Be sure to reward their speaking even if it is labored and difficult to understand.

These children frequently lack experience compared to other children their age. Their lack is compounded if overprotective parents don't allow participation in certain activities (perhaps vigorous outdoor play, swimming, climbing, or riding tricycles) out of fear of worsening the hearing loss through falls or infections. Participation in new experiences will help them increase their inner

language. (See Chapter 10 for a discussion of inner language.) You must be concerned about the children's safety yet encourage participation as well.

Awareness

Because of difficulty in communicating with the outside world, children with hearing impairments often have developed self-feedback systems (e.g., teeth grinding, mouth breathing, masturbation). Such actions result from their need to receive information from other senses. You will need to teach them body awareness.

In general, these children have usually had more negative experiences compared to other children their age, both medically and personally. They need to learn to view themselves positively and to develop skills in dealing with others, especially when others are being unkind.

Feelings

These children need to increase their feelings of group belonging. Previous unsuccessful experiences in interacting with children and adults may cause children to withdraw or to avoid participating with others. When interacting, children with hearing impairments are further encumbered by their lack of experience. Because they are often not aware of the tone of the events taking place, they may have an inappropriate facial expression. When possible, they watch for cues and are often followers not leaders. Children with hearing impairments rarely reach out toward others and often feel rejected. When they do reach out, their approach may be physical and inappropriately vigorous. Help the children develop the skills to approach others and give them cues for roles that they might play.

Guidelines

Some children with hearing impairments know how to speech read and may depend on it to various extents. Others, with milder hearing loss, may not have learned speech reading, but will still benefit from picking up cues and by watching lips. Regardless of the type of communication system the child is using, and whether or not there is an interpreter present, it is important that you as a teacher be expressive and congruent in your spoken and body language. Hearing impaired children will watch you as a way of tuning into their environment.

1.   Face the child and, whenever possible, bring yourself to the same eye level. Sit in front of the child when helping him, not beside him. Don't talk to the child from another room, while looking in a closet, or while writing on the chalkboard. Don't walk around the room or pace back and forth when you talk.

2. Don't obscure your lips; wear lipstick; shave a beard or mustache. If your hair is long, tie it back so that it doesn't fall in your face while you talk. Don't talk with your hand over your mouth or anything in your mouth. Don't shout.

3. See that the light is not shining in the eyes of the child.

Once you are certain the child can see your face,

1. Attract the child's attention before speaking. Call his name and wait to make eye contact. (You may even use a prearranged signal for some events such as flicking the lights.) Otherwise you will have to repeat your first few words.

2. Speak in a normal voice without shouting or exaggerating. It is impossible to speech read when the mouth is distorted. Even if you whisper loudly, the sounds and lips are distorted.

3. Aid the child's understanding of your speech by using appropriate body language (use gestures, point).

4. Reduce background noise when carrying on a conversation. When this is not possible, realize that the child is likely to miss much of what you say. (Hearing aids pick up all noises not just relevant ones.)

5. Some words are more difficult to speech read than others. If you find different ways of saying something rather than merely repeating the sentences exactly, these children will have a better chance of getting the information. It is important to repeat concepts. However, until the concepts have been established be consistent on word usage (cat, not kitty or kitten).

Similar principles are reflected in the use of audio-visual aids.

1. Use as many visual aids as possible (e.g., picture cards or daily routines, charts, and hand gestures).

2. Remember that this child will miss much of what is said on TV, films, and videotapes, as the actors often turn their faces away from the camera.

3. Use an overhead projector instead of a chalkboard, if possible. Then you do not have to turn your back to the child.

4. Try not to talk in the dark during a filmstrip or slide presentation. If this is necessary, seat the child close enough to see you and try to use some spot illumination.

5. Don't expect the child to react to a tape recorder, record, radio, or intercom just because you turned the volume up. He still may not understand.

During group activities the following adaptations will help.

1. Let the child with a hearing impairment sit where he has the best view of the teacher and class. This is in front of, not beside, the teacher and not facing a window. It is best to seat the group in a circle.

2. Call names during a discussion so that the child will know who is speaking next and can follow the conversation. If the children have hand signs for their names, sign the speaker's name or if the child is using cued speech, cue them. Have other children raise their hand (not call out) so that the child can see at whom to look.

3. Remember that the child may be so intent on catching the main points of the discussion that he cannot think about the concepts at the same time. If you call on the child to participate, give extra time to think; don't demand an immediate answer.

4. Summarize and repeat points other children have made.

5. Encourage other children to use gestures, signs, and cues when they talk to this child. Ask them to show him what they want.

If the child knows how, signing, finger spelling, and cueing are aids to communication whether used individually or in groups.

1. Teach the other children some signs, especially the sign or cues for their name. Learn significant signs (drink, bathroom) and cues. Ask the help of the child and his parents or a teacher of the deaf in making up signs or cueing each child's name. To help yourself, draw these on the back of your roll cards.

2. Learn to sign, fingerspell, or cue depending upon the system that the child's family has chosen.

Finally, there are two points of caution. Remember that only about one-fourth of the speech sounds are visible on the lips. The best speech reader only gets about one word in four. Hearing impaired children are great bluffers. They may not want to ask you to repeat. If you ask if they understand, they will often say yes when in fact they do not. Learn to recognize when a child is bluffing, and when it is important, ask the child to demonstrate or repeat the instructions.

Generalization and Differentiation. Developing ideas about their world through generalization and differentiation is difficult for children with hearing impairments because they learn primarily from direct experience. If a child is shown an armchair labeled "chair," the child may not immediately make the generalization that a rocking chair also belongs in the "chair" class. Because of this, it is important that children with hearing impairments be given a larger variety of visual stimuli to help them generalize to an abstract concept. For "chair," you would want to compare many different chairs.

Introducing the Class. People disagree about the best way to introduce a child with a hearing impairment into the classroom. Some teachers have the child not attend until the second or third day of class. On the first day they tell the children about the child during group time. Others send letters home and have the parents tell their children before school starts. I recommend that you start school with all the children (having already allowed the child with a hearing impairment an advance visit to become familiar with the classroom). Then introduce the concept of differences. When warned in advance about a child with a hearing impairment, the others conjure up fantastic ideas about what the child will look like. Sometimes they expect the child to have no ears! As your first activity, plan a group time game emphasizing similarities and differences. For example:

"Will all the children with hair stand up?"
"Will all the children with brown hair stand up?"
"Will all the children with red shoes stand up?"
"Will all the children with hearing aids stand up?"
"Will all the children with blue eyes stand up?"

In the process, emphasize that all of the children have hair, some have brown hair, one has red shoes, one has a hearing aid, and a few (or some) have blue eyes.

Inclusion. If children ask questions, answer them simply and honestly. Encourage the child with the hearing loss to help answer the question if possible.

"What's wrong with John?"	"There's nothing wrong with John. He can't hear as well as others."
"Why does he wear that box?"	"To help him hear better."
"Does he sleep with it?"	"No."
"If I play with him can I catch that?"	"No, it isn't like a cold or chicken pox. John was born that way (or however it occurred)."
"Can I have a box, too?"	"No, ear doctors decide who needs these boxes just like eye doctors decide who needs glasses. We'll have a box in class someday that you can try out."
"I don't like it when John hits me."	"I can understand that. John is telling you in his way that he wants to play with you. What could he do that would be better for you?"
"Can't he talk?"	"He can only say a few words. It is hard to learn to talk when you can't hear other people talk."

"I hate John."	"Today that is true for you. Someday you might like him."

You might also give the children hints on how to communicate with the child, such as: "Be sure John is looking at you when you talk to him." "Can you show him what you want?" "What can he do that doesn't require talking?" "What kind of game do you think John would like?"

Curriculum Adaptations
Language Arts: Speaking, Listening, Reading, and Writing

Language arts is a difficult area for children with hearing impairments and requires the most adaptation. Nevertheless language is an area that is extremely important and deserves your time. After reading this section, be sure to refer to Chapter 10, "Children with Communication Disorders," and to consult the child's therapist for additional ideas and activities.

Speaking. Speaking is difficult for children with hearing impairments. Initially they need to develop inner language experiential concepts before spoken language is possible. Help them associate objects with words, the written word with the spoken one. Understanding and talking about abstractions is extremely difficult for people with hearing impairments.

1. Give children enough time to talk without feeling rushed.

2. Always respond to a child's communication. If you understand, reply, if not try to have the child tell you in a different way or show you.

3. To teach concepts, use materials that interest the child. If you are teaching number concepts to a football fan, you can put the numbers on checkers, set up a checkerboard as a football field with the checkers as players, and then call the plays: "Give the ball to number 3 and have him run around number 5 and then between 1 and 7." The child scores only if he follows the correct pattern. If the child cannot hear or speech read, use your fingers or cards to show the plays.

4. You can use the concrete to demonstrate the abstract. Use conceptual matching cards; shoe–slipper, clock–watch, lamp–flashlight, shirt–blouse, jacket–coat.

5. Point out objects in the room that are used in the same way but look different: crayons versus paint, short versus long brushes.

6. Show visual analogies and have the child choose the correct card. (See the activities in Part Four for a more complete description.)

7. Have children classify and reclassify objects in different ways. For example: Using small and

large shapes, some of which are black and the others white, ask the child to sort them into two piles; when the task is complete, ask the child to sort another way. Demonstrate what you mean, if necessary.

8. Teach situationally, describe verbally what is happening at that moment: "I'm sitting in front of you."

Fingerplays are excellent for children with hearing impairments; they can participate whether or not they can speak. The "choral" aspect of fingerplays sometimes reduces their self-consciousness about speaking. This is an excellent way to teach visual memory and sequencing.

1. Choose short, simple fingerplays at first.

2. Demonstrate the actions as you sing or say the words.

3. Encourage the children to imitate you; move slowly so the children can keep up.

Listening. The sequence of developing listening skills is the same for all children. Children with hearing impairments may need you to help more in matching their skill level. Initially children need to become aware of sound. They need to pay attention to sound and find its source. Then they need to make gross discrimination among sounds followed by finer ones. Finally, they have to attach meaning to sound. Children who can hear usually go through these stages within the first year of life. Children with hearing impairments may still be learning to distinguish sounds and attaching meaning to them during the preschool years.

Help children learn to check during the day that the volume of the hearing aid is at an appropriate level. Active play can change the volume or move the on/off switch.

1. Point out sounds to children when they might hear the sound and can have a visual association: "See the airplane. It went vrrrooom."

2. Emphasize some of the basic vocabulary words in each curriculum area. Post the words where they will best be seen or hang them on a string from the ceiling so that all teachers and aides use the same vocabulary. If you have a doctor's office in the dramatic play area, you might emphasize the following four words, backing the labels with pictures (avoid stereotyping by using several pictures).

3. Use as many visual aids and gestures as possible to help the child understand.

Stories help expand the child's world. Start with stories about familiar events before using more creative ones.

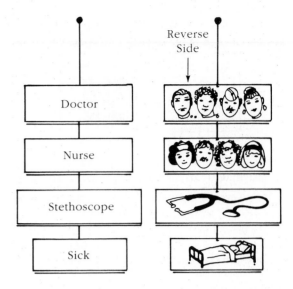

1. Choose books that depict familiar sights and actions.

2. Use illustrations that are simple, large, and uncluttered.

3. Choose scratch and smell, or touch books, which have extra olfactory or tactile appeal.

4. Provide the child with auditory cues and visual aids when reading. For example, during *The Three Little Pigs,* squeal, change rhythm, and huff and puff. You might even bring in straw, wood, and bricks and let the children huff and puff at them at the science table.

5. Use flannelboard stories, as these usually have simple, graphic plots.

6. Have the children act out simple stories.

7. Allow the child with a hearing impairment to preview the story.

8. Place picture books with a clear, sequential story line in the book corner.

9. Avoid using chalkboard stories. If you draw on the overhead projector, the child will have an unobstructed view of your face.

10. Choose books with realistic, not abstract illustrations when teaching language arts. Abstract illustrations are more appropriate for art time.

Reading. Early reading readiness skills include: habitually looking at words and letters from left to right, making fine visual discriminations, and recognizing a sense of pattern (letters versus spaces).

1. Demonstrate left to right progression. For example, point a marker or your finger at the left side before starting and move it to the right as you read.

2. When writing stories of the children's experiences, draw or paste in pictures illustrating significant words.

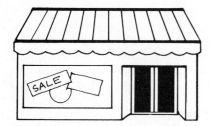

3. Use activities that require perceptual (visual matching) skills, such as lotto, bingo, and puzzles.

4. Label everything in the classroom (tables, chairs, lockers, crayons, paints, easel, and so on).

5. Emphasize activities that require fine visual discrimination (alphabet matching lotto) because this skill is needed for reading.

Writing. Give children a wide variety of writing tools and paper to work with. Children need to explore the media and develop the connection between the written and spoken word before writing will be meaningful. Because children with hearing impairments may be more dependent on writing for communication it is important that they have a positive view of writing from the very beginning.

1. Add stickers to the writing center as well as pictures that can be cut and pasted.

2. Encourage children to use creative spelling in their writing. Support all attempts at writing and illustrating.

That is, emphasize the meaning of writing, until children become fluent writers. Accept the children's spelling and do not correct it. It is extremely difficult for children who cannot hear accurately to spell accurately.

Discovery: Mathematics, Science, Computers

Math and science are areas of importance and potential strength for children with hearing impairments. The abstractions in math and science are more logical and data-based than in language arts. Children need to develop the skills of inquiry, problem solving, and cause-effect reasoning at this stage.

Mathematics. Math goals for children with hearing impairments are directed toward developing a concrete base of fundamental math concepts to prepare the child for abstract concepts that will come later.

1. Use three-dimensional materials (cubes, balls) before progressing to two-dimensional squares and circles.

2. Develop the language skills that serve as the foundation for math, such as understanding the relationships equal/more/less.

3. Use naturally occurring situations to teach math, such as the number of chairs at the table or the one-to-one correspondence between children and napkins. Cooking, sand play, and water play provide many opportunities for learning math concepts.

4. Use human three-dimensional illustrations. For example, have four children form a square; three, a triangle; and so on.

5. Measure with different instruments (ruler, metal tape, cloth tape). Compare relative amounts, using both conventional and nonconventional measures. Some nonconventional measures you might use are sponges and bottles for liquids, the children's feet or paces for length.

Science. Few other curriculum areas have the potential for discovery, satisfaction, and interaction with materials that science has. Provide children with hearing impairments with the right materials and offer well-timed visual hints, instead of asking questions as you normally would.

1. Help the child generalize by providing abundant materials.

2. Allow plenty of time to process hypotheses and conclusions.

3. Help the child understand that things can exist in more than one state. Compare corn on the cob, frozen corn, canned corn, creamed corn, and popped and unpopped corn.

4. Use visual demonstrations.

5. Have the child go through the action when there are directions to be followed.

6. Use a variety of media. For example, to teach about plants: visit a farm, nursery, or plant store; plant seeds, varying the water, light, and soil; look at books on plants; show a filmstrip on how plants grow; invite a florist to speak to the class.

7. Use regularly occurring natural events like seasonal change to teach a sense of predictability in the world.

8. Use items made of different materials, such as wood, cardboard, styrofoam, to broaden the child's understanding of the concept of matter.

Computers. Computers are very usable for children with hearing impairments. Both the input and output are visual and require no hearing. Computers can be used as an interactive teaching tool for children with hearing impairments.

1. A child can learn cause and effect reasoning easily on a computer. He presses a key and the computer does something—instantly. A different key causes something else to happen.

2. Encourage children to use computers. This may be one area where they can work with another

child and not be at a disadvantage. The words may be so obvious that they are understood regardless of the quality of articulation.

3. Computers are likely to play an important part in the lives of children with hearing impairment. Their hearing impairment hardly affects their ability to use a computer.

4. With the help of a modem and a computer, the telephone lines are available to members of both the deaf and hearing communities with computers. This may seem like a long way in the future to you now, as you look at a young child, but the computer skills and attitudes learned now will serve a child for a lifetime.

Sensory Motor: Large Motor, Sensory Motor Integration, Small Motor

Sensory motor activities help children learn skills to become more physically fit, be more aware of where their body is in space, and fine-tune the small motor skills that support reading and writing.

Large Motor. There are relatively few restrictions placed on children with hearing impairments when large motor activities are taking place, though concerns over safety may have limited large motor experience. If there is damage to the semicircular canals, the child will have problems with dizziness, with obvious implications. High climbing should be discouraged (falling on a hearing aid hurts). Rough tumbling may also cause damage. Remember, too, that the child's difficulty in hearing verbal instructions poses some safety concerns. The child should stay fairly near you, and you should have an unobstructed view of him if the child is in a relatively dangerous area (near the swings, seesaw, blocks, and so on).

1. Choose activities that help develop the child's sense of balance.

2. Choose activities that require stopping, starting, and changing directions. (Inability to do these without losing balance is related to the inner ear.)

3. Use activities such as obstacle courses to teach language skills (crawl *through* the tunnel, jump *over* the bar, run *around* the pole).

4. Help the child perfect the skills of running, leaping, jumping, skipping, and so on.

5. Have the children imitate animal walks (with pictures as cues) to help them identify different styles of walking.

6. Help the child use large motor skills to safely relieve pent-up energy and frustration.

7. Use props to help this child realize the intent of the group if it appears a change of plans has been missed by the child.

Sensory Motor Integration. The sense of balance (vestibular sense) is located in the inner ear, and children with hearing impairments often need more practice than others developing balance skills. They need practice at starting, stopping, and changing directions while maintaining balance.

1. Provide a variety of activities that help in processing movement information in the brain (running, hopping, skipping, swinging, sliding, and so on).

2. Add a ball to activities to help focus concentration, such as having children kick a ball to each other in a circle game, or while doing a crab walk.

3. Have children do various activities with a beanbag on their head.

4. Provide opportunities for the hands and fingers to practice working together such as cutting with scissors (one hand holds, the other cuts), mixing activities, using an egg beater, and so on.

Small Motor. Children with hearing impairments interact with the world primarily through vision, touch, smell, and the integration of these senses. It is particularly important to help them develop good fine motor control in conjunction with vision and smell.

1. Use activities that require both visual and fine motor skills (puzzles, assorted nuts and bolts to put together, wood working, bead stringing).

2. Use activities requiring only the sense of touch, such as sorting graded sandpaper or playing with a feeling box. In case the child is not able to name the feeling box objects, have a tray with a second set of the objects, so the child can choose the matching one.

3. Provide some relatively unsupervised activities to give the child with a hearing impairment opportunities to make discoveries on his own.

4. Use fingerplays to develop awareness of the hands and fine motor control, which are necessary for learning sign language.

5. Use tweezers or tongs to sort cotton balls, blocks, wooden beads, or small toys.

Social Awareness: Social Studies, Inclusion, Health and Safety

All children need to be part of the group. They need to realize they can support each other in many ways. Given information, young children can be incredibly adept at helping each other. Make sure that the child with the hearing impairment is not always receiving the help, but giving it as well.

Social Studies. The child with a hearing impairment has to learn the skills to cope with a hearing world.

1. When teaching these children to generalize, use illustrations of diverse families (those with single parents, working mothers, grandparent in the home, and so on).

2. Emphasize firsthand experiences but use follow-up activities as well. Take your class to a police station. Later, read stories about police and use police props in dramatic play.

3. Prepare children with hearing impairments for social situations they may encounter.

4. Use family celebrations and holidays to talk about similarities and differences.

5. Making maps is an excellent way to familiarize a child with a hearing impairment with a new situation. Start with maps of known places (the classroom, the play yard) before you branch out into less familiar places (the whole school).

Inclusion. Children need to learn skills for including others as well as skills for approaching others. They need to know that no matter who they are, skills do not mean that they will be accepted into the group each time they ask. Including children with disabilities takes a type of planning you may not have done before.

1. Play games where you whisper or talk to children so softly they have difficulty hearing you and then talk about how it feels to them.

2. Have children wear ear muffs when they play together. Keep them on long enough for children to feel the limitations, not just until the novelty wears off.

3. Discuss differences in families, races, and abilities.

4. Ask all children to talk about things that are difficult for them and what they would like others to do to help.

5. Help all the children understand how they might feel and behave if they could see people talking but not understand what they were saying. Have them decide what to do to include a child who might feel like this.

Health and Safety. Because children with hearing impairments may miss some warning signals, their safety is jeopardized more often than other children's. In addition, they often have fewer skills to deal with dangerous situations.

1. Use traffic warning signals outside with the tricycles, wagons, and so on. Teach the meaning of traffic lights (play Red Light–Green Light).

2. Practice crossing streets.

3. Discuss what to do if the child is lost or hurt, then dramatize the emergency (using dialogue) or pantomime it.

4. Use snack or lunchtime to instill good eating habits, and toileting to teach good hygiene.

5. Familiarize the child with a hearing impairment with the procedure for fire alarms. Incorporate a visual cue (flickering lights or a red flag) into your usual procedure. Try to keep the child with a hearing impairment in sight during a fire alarm to ensure that the child neither wanders off nor misses later instructions. With older children you might use a buddy system as well.

Creative Arts: Art, Music, Creative Movement, and Dramatic Play

Because the emphasis in creative arts is creativity, children with hearing impairments are not at a disadvantage. Use pictures and realistic props to set the mood.

Art. Art needs few adaptations for children with hearing impairments. Follow the general guidelines for communicating with these children.

1. Help the child with a hearing impairment learn to use art as an emotional release when necessary. An additional outlet is especially useful in bad weather, when large motor activities are restricted.

2. Post any rules, adding illustrations and the word NO or an X through the picture. Also, post pictures of some of the things the child is allowed to do. Visual reminders of how to carry scissors and put paint away will be helpful to the entire class.

3. Have three-dimensional art materials available.

4. The child may tend to overgeneralize as a result of limited experience. Know that this child will probably learn the qualities of materials (paint versus paste, for example) through trial and error as well as from your demonstrations and watching peers.

5. If the child has a Y-cord hearing aid, put it on his back or outside of the apron to optimize hearing during art. The noise made by an apron rubbing will make it difficult for him to hear.

6. Give simplified directions because following instructions is more difficult for a child with a hearing impairment.

Music. Accompanied by visual cues, music can be a positive experience for children with hearing impairments. Don't eliminate them from the group because they can't sing.

1. Use percussion instruments (children can feel vibrations and see the beat).

2. Take the front off the piano, so the children can see how and when the piano hammers strike.

3. Choose songs that incorporate motion, so the child can participate in the movement if not in the singing.

4. Show pictures to set the mood for songs and creative movement. If you want the children to pretend they are walking through leaves, use a fall picture with leaves. If they are to be flowers growing, show both buds and flowers in full bloom.

5. Use the piano with a mildly hearing impaired child to teach the concepts of high/low, fast/slow, and other types of auditory discrimination. For a child with a moderate to severe impairment use a more visual method—drums or clapping.

6. When you sing, use your hand to show when the song goes up or down in pitch.

7. Use rhythmic dance and free dance.

8. Learn to sign some favorite songs. The class may find this more challenging and fun than some fingerplays.

Creative Movement. Keep the focus on the process. If you are trying to convey a mood use visual props.

1. If children are taking turns, don't call on a child with a hearing impairment first, and as other children move point out the features of the movement that help set the mood.

2. Place the child so he can best see how others move.

3. Use mirror movement and allow the child to be the mirror first if there is a mood. If there is just movement, be sure the child has equal opportunities to lead.

Dramatic Play. Through dramatic play children with hearing impairments can express feelings and concerns. They can also try out roles (mother, father, teacher, and so on) without fear of being judged. Dramatic play provides some of the experiences necessary for developing inner language.

1. Include a traditional home living area in your classroom initially. (This fosters some sense of security.)

2. Use the dramatic play area to expand the child's environment.

3. Provide play props appropriate to the activities.

Transitions

Transition periods are not particularly fun for any child. They can be difficult for a child, who may not have grasped the verbal directions or the other children's intentions.

1. Be sure the child knows the daily sequence. Use a picture poster and point to what will happen next.

Dramatic play holds the potential for learning about the world while developing other skills.

2. Keep your schedule fairly standard once it is set. Knowing that some things are predictable gives the child with a hearing impairment a sense of security.

3. Use visual signs to announce upcoming changes. (One light blink for a five-minute warning, two blinks for cleanup time.)

4. Demonstrate what is going to happen (start picking up, get your coat, and so on).

Glossary

Air-conduction tests A measure of the child's ability to hear sound through the air. For testing, the soundwaves are delivered to the child's ear by earphones connected to a pure-tone audiometer.

Audiogram A graph on which levels of hearing are recorded. Frequency is plotted horizontally and intensity vertically. Each ear is plotted separately.

Audiologist A professional trained in the identification and measurement of hearing impairments. The audiologist also aids in the rehabilitation of the hearing impaired.

Audiology   The study of hearing and disorders of hearing.

Audiometer   An instrument that generates sound electronically. The intensity and frequency of tones can be controlled to determine how much or how little someone hears. The results of the testing are charted on an audiogram. Earphones are used to test air-conduction hearing. Bone-conduction hearing is tested with a vibrator that is attached to the head. The difference in hearing scores between air and bone conduction has diagnostic significance.

Bilateral (or binaural) hearing loss   Loss in both ears. The amount of loss in each ear may differ.

Bone-conduction test   A measure of the ability to hear through vibrations of the bones in the skull. These bones can directly cause movement in the fluid of the inner ear. The test is performed with a bone-conduction vibrator attached to a pure-tone audiometer.

Cycles per second (cps or Hz)   A measure of frequency (pitch). The greater the number of cycles per second, the higher the pitch.

Conductive impairment   A dysfunction of the outer or middle ear. Sound doesn't get into the inner ear.

Decibel (dB or db)   A measure of sound intensity (loudness). The higher the number of decibels, the louder the sound.

Eustachian tube   A slender tube from the middle ear to the pharynx. Its purpose is to equalize pressure on both sides of the eardrum.

Frequency   Cycles per second; pitch.

Hearing aids   Battery-operated mechanical devices that amplify sound over a limited frequency range. They are composed of three main parts: receiver, amplifier, and speaker. The sound always has some distortion. Hearing aids have volume and tone controls. A *body-worn aid* is usually worn in a sling around the neck and chest. *Ear-level aids* are worn behind the ears.

Hertz (Hz)   A measure of frequency (pitch). *See also* cycles per second.

Impedance Bridge Test   An audiometric test that measures pressure on either side of the eardrum. It does not require a verbal response and is often used with infants and young children.

Intensity   The carrying power of speech.

Manualists   People who believe that the deaf should be taught to finger spell and use conventional signs. They feel the effort required for learning speech shortchanges the child's overall academic and social development.

Nerve loss   Same as sensorineural impairment.

Oralists   People who believe that the deaf should be taught only to talk and speech read, not to use signs or finger spell. The deaf can then communicate with hearing people.

Otology (Otologist)   A medical specialty that deals with the diagnosis and treatment of ear diseases.

Perceptive impairment   Same as sensorineural impairment.

Pitch   Relative highs and lows as measured in cycles per second: frequency.

Semicircular canals   Three loop-shaped tubes of the inner ear that serve to maintain balance.

Sensorineural impairment   A type of hearing loss caused by a defect in the inner ear or the nerve to the brain stem (not curable by surgery). Perceptive impairment and nerve loss are synonyms.

Sign language   The American Sign Language, *Ameslan,* is a system of visual communications using the hands; see page 167.

Speech pathology   The diagnosis and treatment of people with oral language disorders.

Threshold (absolute)   The intensity at which someone can detect a sound at least half the time.

Tinnitus   A ringing or other sensation of sound in the ear not resulting from an external stimulus.

Total communication   Simultaneous use of oral and manual methods of speaking.

Unilateral hearing loss   Loss in one ear. Because of the duplication of the hearing mechanism this does *not* decrease hearing by half. It creates difficulty in locating sound and some difficulty in hearing.

Teaching Resources

In some situations you may want or need additional information. There are many national as well as regional, state, and local organizations that can be helpful to you. The following annotated list of national organizations should be useful in helping you decide where to get the information you need.

The Alexander Graham Bell Association for the Deaf
3417 Volta Place, N.W.
Washington, DC 20007
    Publishes many useful materials for parents and teachers.

American Annals of the Deaf
The Convention of American Instructors of the Deaf
5034 Wisconsin Avenue, N.W.
Washington, DC 20016
    The American Annals of the Deaf is a directory that lists schools and classes for the deaf, clinics, organizations, publications. Gives information about current research. Send $5.00 to above address.

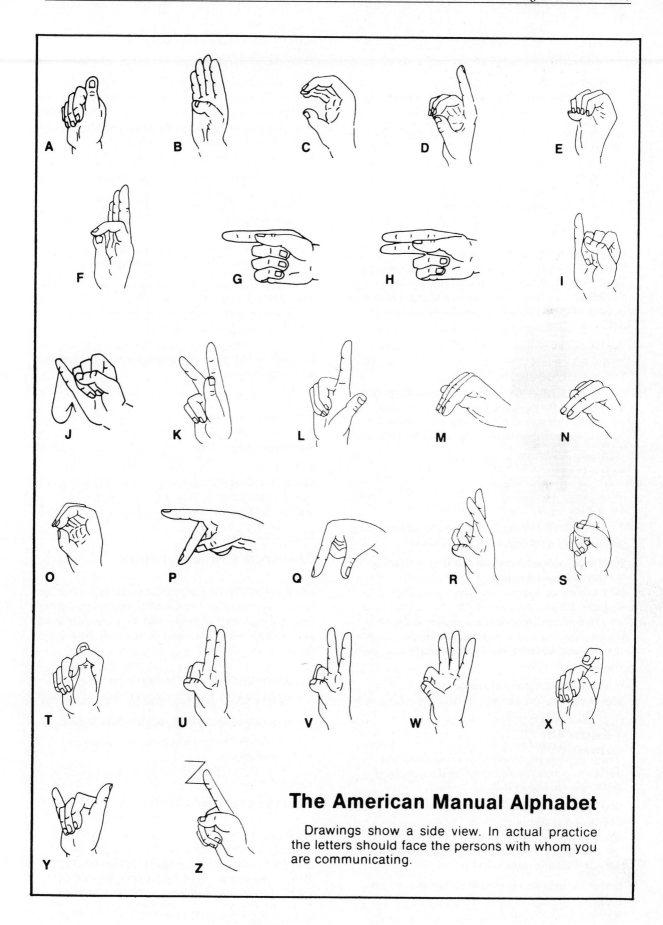

The American Manual Alphabet

Drawings show a side view. In actual practice the letters should face the persons with whom you are communicating.

American Society for Deaf Children
814 Thayer Avenue
Silver Spring, MD 20910
(301) 585-1788
Publishes useful information on the impact of a hearing impairment on children.

American Speech–Language–Hearing Association
10801 Rockville Pike
Rockville, MD 20852
800-638-TALK
Provides information as well as posters, buttons, and suggested activities.

American Tinnitus Association
P.O. Box 5
Portland, OR 97207
Includes physicians, audiologists, hearing aid dispensers, and individuals who suffer from tinnitus. Disseminates information about tinnitus; provides referrals; supports research; sponsors monthly workshops for testing and evaluating.

Ear Research Institute
256 S. Lake Street
Los Angeles, CA 91345
Develops conceptual and technically feasible approaches to resolving hearing and balance disorders through applied research. Conducts research; offers seminars; maintains library.

Gallaudet Bookstore
Kendall Green
P.O. Box 103
Washington, DC 20002
(202) 651-5380
Has catalog of curriculum materials designed for students with hearing impairments.

International Foundation for Children's Hearing Education and Research
871 McLean Avenue
Yonkers, NY 10704
Parents and professionals concerned with public awareness of hearing impairments. Supports research; seeks to improve educational facilities for the deaf.

International Parent's Organization
c/o Alexander Graham Bell Association for the Deaf
3417 Volta Place, N.W.
Washington, DC 20007
Encourages and supports parent group action and programs on behalf of hearing impaired children; works for auditory/oral teaching of hearing impaired children.

The John Tracy Clinic
806 W. Adam Avenue
Los Angeles, CA 90007
Specializes in stimulation programs for infants who are hearing impaired.

Junior National Association of the Deaf
Gallaudet College
Washington, DC 20002
Provides a resource directory.

National Association of the Deaf
905 Bonifant Street
Silver Spring, MD 20910
National headquarters works for improved educational and employment opportunities for the deaf. Serves as an information and referral center. Does not concern itself with the medical aspects of deafness other than to serve as a source of information in medical research.

National Foundation for Children's Hearing Education and Research
928 McLean Avenue
Yonkers, NY 10704
(914) 237-2676
Focuses on public awareness and improving educational facilities within the United States.

National Organization for Hearing and Speech Action
814 Thayer Avenue
Silver Spring, MD 20910
Political action group.

For specialized materials, request catalogs from the following companies.

Sign Language Store
8753 Shirley Avenue
P.O. Box 4440
Northridge, CA 91328

Joyce/Ideal
Ideal School Supply Company
11000 South Laverne Avenue
Oak Lawn, IL 60453

Children's Bibliography

See the Children's Bibliography on page 286 for books to increase children's awareness about disabilities as well as books that are especially good for children with particular disabilities. Note especially:

Awareness of Hearing Impairments

Picture Books (especially those without words)

Scratch and Sniff and Touch and Feel Books

Simpler Books (for teaching vocabulary and concepts)

References and Bibliography

Blackwell, P., Enger, E., Fischgrand, J., & Zarcadoulas, C. (1978). *Sentences and other systems: A language and learning curriculum for hearing impaired children*. Washington, DC: Alexander Graham Bell Association for the Deaf.

Bryan, J. H., & Bryan, T. H. (1979). *Exceptional children*. Sherman Oaks, CA: Alfred Publishing Co.

Denk-Glass, R., Laber, S., & Brewer, K. (1982). Middle ear disease in young children. *Young Children 37*(6), 51–53.

Garrard, K. R., & Clark, B. S. (1985). Otitis media: The role of speech-language pathologists, *ASHA (American Speech-Language-Hearing Association), 27*(7), 35–39.

Garwood, S. G. (1979). *Educating young handicapped children: A developmental approach.* Germantown, MD: Aspen Systems Corp.

Hallahan, D., & Kauffman, J. (1992). *Exceptional children: Introduction to special education* (5th ed.). Englewood Cliffs, NJ: Prentice-Hall.

Horton, K. B. (1976). Early intervention for hearing impaired infants and young children. In T. D. Tjossem (Ed.), *Intervention strategies for high risk infants and young children* (pp. 371–380). Baltimore: University Park Press.

Hull, R., & Dilka, E. (Eds.). (1984). *The hearing-impaired child in school.* Orlando, FL: Grune & Stratton.

LaPorta, R., McGee, D., Simmons-Martin, A., Vorce, E., von Hippel, C., & Donovan, T. (1978). *Mainstreaming preschoolers: Children with hearing impairment. A guide for teachers, parents, and others who work with hearing impaired preschoolers.* Washington, DC: U.S. Government Printing Office.

Ling, D., & Ling, A. H. (1977). *Basic vocabulary and language thesaurus for hearing impaired children.* Washington, DC: Alexander Graham Bell Association for the Deaf.

Martin, F. (1987). *Hearing disorders in children.* Austin, TX: PRO-ED.

McWilliams, P. (1984). *Personal computers and the disabled.* Garden City, NY: Quantum Press, Doubleday & Company, Inc.

Miller, A. L. (1980). *Hearing loss, hearing aids and your child.* Springfield, IL: Charles C. Thomas.

Mollick, L., & Etra, K. (1981). Poor learning ability . . . or poor hearing? *Teacher.* Reprinted in Annual Editions, *Educating exceptional children.* (1992). (pp. 178–179). Guilford, CT: The Dushkin Publishing Group, Inc.

Neisworth, J., & Bagnato, S. (1987). *The young exceptional child: Early development and education.* New York: Macmillan Publishing Company.

Nix, G. W. (Ed.). (1977). *The rights of the hearing impaired child.* Washington, DC: Alexander Graham Bell Association for the Deaf.

Peterson, N. L. (1987). *Early intervention for handicapped and at-risk children: An introduction to early childhood special education.* Denver, CO: Love Publishing Co.

Ralabate, P. (1987). What teachers should know about middle ear dysfunction. *NEA Today,* 10.

Rampp, D. L. (1976). *Classroom activities for auditory perceptual disorders.* Danville, IL: Interstate.

U.S. Department of Education. (1989). *Eleventh annual report to Congress on the implementation of the education of the handicapped act.* Washington, DC: U.S. Government Printing Office.

Awareness Bibliography for Adults

Brown, Helene. (1977). *Yesterday's child.* New York: Signet Books.

Karen is deaf, mentally retarded, and has cerebral palsy. The story tells of the struggles of Karen and her parents, how the problem breaks up the family, and how the mother then deals with Karen and a normal son.

Forecki, Marcia. (1985). *Speak to me.* Washington, DC: Gallaudet College Press.

The autobiography of a young mother's life with her son Charlie. Her initial refusal to believe there was anything wrong with him to her increasing independence from her parents and her coping.

Greenberg, Joanne. (1970). *In this sign.* New York: Holt, Rinehart and Winston.

The story of a deaf couple—their married life, their adjustments to living in a hearing society, and the difficulties they face in trying to raise two "hearing" children. It gives an excellent insight into the world of the deaf and the special problems of normal children reared by deaf parents.

Smithdas, Robert. (1958). *Life at my fingertips.* New York: Doubleday.

Bob Smithdas had spinal meningitis at age five. He lost his vision at once and his hearing by the end of the fourth grade. Through determination and perseverance, he became the second deaf-blind person to graduate from college (the first being Helen Keller). He went on to pursue a career and a fully independent life.

Tidyman, Ernest. (1974). *Dummy.* Boston: Little, Brown.

A deaf lawyer attempts to give legal assistance to a black deaf-mute, who's twice accused of murder. It raises philosophical and practical questions concerning the rights of an individual who lacks the means to communicate with others. Thought provoking and just plain good reading.

Chapter 12

Children with Visual Impairments

One of my memories of being in first grade is of Charles, whose mother once asked our teacher whether or not we teased him about his patch. The teacher's startled response was, "What patch?" Charles went out of the house each morning with a patch over his left eye, put it in his pocket, and arrived at school without it. He put it back on before he got home. I don't know if we would have teased him when he wore it, but the fear of being teased or different made him avoid the possibility. It is a very powerful concern that causes a six-year-old to do that kind of planning and remembering. Teaching children with visual impairments means dealing not only with those who have noncorrectable problems but also with those who refuse to wear glasses or corrective patches out of fear of ridicule and with those whose visual impairments have not yet been discovered. The child with glasses has a visual impairment, and so does the child who is blind.

You will have a number of important questions about children with visual impairments. First, of course, you will need to determine the extent of the impairment and what the needs of each child are. Can the child deal with everyday classroom tasks or should special methods and materials be used? How do the needs affect the child's development and the programing of the class? Should the room be rearranged to make it easier to get around? Should special care be taken in play areas to protect the child from injuries? How do you head off or deal with other children's jokes and taunts about glasses and patches and the inability to move as quickly and skillfully as they do? And how do you recognize a child with an undiagnosed visual impairment and discuss the issue with the child and parents?

Children with visual impairments can be classified in a variety of ways. Visual problems can be labeled according to the legal, medical, or educational implications of the impairment. The legal and medical definitions typically emphasize the acuity of the visual ability, or how clearly the child can see. The educational definition emphasizes the extent to which the child can use her visual abilities to read printed material for learning (Peterson, 1987).

The three professions identifying visual impairments use the same terms but have different definitions for the terms. By legal and medical definitions, children who are *blind* have visual acuity of 20/200 or less in the better eye, given the best possible correction. For educational purposes, children who are *blind* experience a visual loss severe enough so that it is not possible to read printed material and necessitates the use of alternate forms of communication such as Braille.

The legal and medical definition of partially sighted children are those with visual acuity between 20/200 to 20/70, in the better eye with the best possible correction. The educational definition for partially sighted is that these are children with enough residual vision to allow for reading large print, or regular print with special assistance.

Blindness is primarily an adult disability. Visual impairment is one of the least prevalent disabilities in children. The U.S. Department of Education (1989) identified only .05 percent of the school-age population as visually impaired.

The Eye

The visual system is very complex; however, a basic understanding is necessary. A brief discussion of the visual mechanism follows.

When light enters the eye it passes through the *cornea* (a transparent membrane), the *aqueous humor* (a watery fluid), the *lens,* and the *vitreous humor* (a jellylike substance that fills the eyeball). The amount of light that enters is controlled by the *iris,* a set of muscles that expands or contracts the *pupil,* the hole through which the light enters. The light focuses on the *retina,* a layer of nerves that transmits impulses to the brain through the *optic nerve.* The most sensitive part of the retina is the

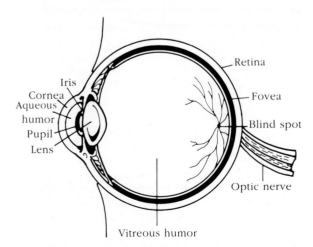

The Eye

fovea; the only insensitive part is the *blind spot,* where the nerve fibers come together.

The eye does not actually "see." It receives light, turns light into electrical impulses, and sends them to the brain. It's the brain that actually perceives visual images. If the part of the brain that sees is severely damaged, a child may not be able to see, even though the eye is completely normal. Damage in the brain or the optic nerve is not correctable. Defects in the eye itself, however, often are. The purpose of most visual aids is to compensate for defects in the eye so that a correct message can be sent to the brain.

Classification of Visual Impairments

Visual problems are classified into four major categories. These are injury to the physical mechanisms of the eye, problems with visual acuity, impairments to the muscular structure of the eye, and problems in visual perceptions or the message pathway between the eye and brain. Each problem category can be further broken down into specific areas. For many children, problems involving the physical mechanisms, acuity, and muscular structure can be corrected with medical techniques, glasses, and/or surgery. Problems involving the nerve pathways are difficult to remedy with medical intervention.

Damage to the *physical mechanisms of the eye* involves the cornea, lens, retina, the aqueous chamber, and the optic nerve. Damage to any of these parts can affect how light passes through the eye. Causes have been traced to infectious diseases such as measles, genetic disorders, prescription drugs, and environmental hazards.

Cataracts are caused by the clouding of the lens inside the eye, which results in blurred vision. If the lens is clouded, light cannot reach the back of the eye and cannot be sent by electrical impulses to the brain. Some children are born with cataracts. A primary cause of congenital cataracts is maternal infection such as rubella. Cataracts can be removed surgically. Children who have had cataracts removed will wear very thick glasses that help bend and focus light rays in place of the missing lens (surgical lens implants are also possible).

Cornea damage, usually punctures or scars, results in impaired vision. Known as "the window of the eye," the cornea protects the lens and the iris. It is possible in some cases to have a cornea surgically replaced. This is the only kind of eye transplant possible to date.

Detached retina is usually the result of an injury. The retina comes loose from the back of the eye. As a result, the retina loses its ability to function. This can be corrected by burning the retina back on to the eye with a laser beam. There will be a permanent blind spot where the laser beam reattaches the retina.

Eyeball damage, damage to the eye itself, can result in permanent loss of vision. This can be the result of infection or injury. Damage can result from

Larger objects may be easier to handle.

large particles getting into the eye. The longer a particle remains in the eye, the deeper it becomes embedded, and the greater the likelihood of permanent damage.

Glaucoma is a condition in which the fluid in the eye does not drain properly, causing pressure to build up. Without treatment, the pressure can result in the gradual destruction of the retina. Blindness results. If detected early, it can be prevented through the use of eye drops or surgery (an iridotomy puts an additional hole for the fluid to drain from). Glaucoma is primarily a disease of adults.

Optic nerve damage is usually associated with the incomplete development of the optic nerve or damage to it from disease or trauma. The optic nerve carries the electrical impulses from the eye to the brain for processing. If this nerve is not developed properly, it will not be possible for the signals to get to the brain so that the child can see. The effects on vision vary depending on the amount and place of the damage.

Retinopathy of Prematurity (ROP) (previously called Retrolental Fibroplasia) involves the formation of scar tissue behind the lens of the eye. Excessive tissue can result in detachment of the retina from the optic nerve. The greater the scar tissue, the greater the level of visual impairment. This problem is encountered in premature infants when very high levels of oxygen are necessary for the infant's survival as well as prematurity itself. Hospitals do monitor this, but cannot prevent it.

Impairments affecting *visual acuity* involve the inability of children to see objects at specific

distances. Normal visual acuity is 20/20. What a normal person can see at 20 feet, most people see at 20 feet. A child having 20/100 vision must be within 20 feet to see an object that a person with normal vision could see 100 feet away. In most cases, visual acuity problems are correctable with glasses. Types of visual acuity problems are discussed below.

Astigmatism is an error in refraction caused by the lens or cornea being slightly bumpy instead of completely smooth. The image is out of focus because it falls in the wrong place on the retina. Astigmatism can usually be corrected by glasses that compensate for the irregular shape. This condition can also occur with other visual conditions. A child can be nearsighted and have an astigmatism.

Hyperopia is the technical term for *farsighted*. The child can see distant things better than relatively close things. The eye is too short, and the focused image that should fall on the retina falls behind it. The shorter the eye the more out of focus the image and the more convex the lenses in the glasses will be.

Myopia is the technical term for *nearsighted*. This is the opposite of hyperopia. The child can't see

Hyperopia, myopia, and normal vision

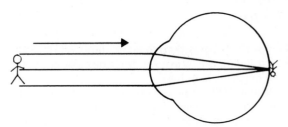

Normal vision

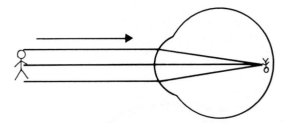

Myopia (nearsighted)

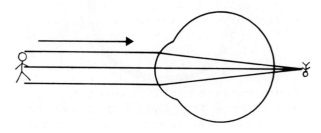

Hyperopia (farsighted)

things that are far away. The eye is too long, causing the image to be in focus before it reaches the retina. Myopia is corrected with the use of concave lenses.

Muscular problems involve the inability of the muscles controlling the eyes to work in coordination with each other to result in clear vision. Clear vision is produced by the action of the eye seeing two images, fused into one. Correct fusion of these images depends upon the eyes' being straight and moving in synchrony. Disruption in either causes visual problems. There are three common types of muscular problems including *amblyopia* (sometimes referred to as "lazy eye"), which is the reduction or loss of vision in one eye due to disuse. The cause is muscle imbalance. The weak eye may turn in toward the nose (*estropia*), away from the nose (*exotropia*), or upward (*hypertropia*). The brain, seeing a double image, will turn off the vision of the weaker eye to compensate. If this imbalance is not treated by the time the child is about six years of age, the vision in that eye will be poor for the rest of the child's life. Amblyopia is treated either by surgery or by wearing a patch over the stronger eye to force the weaker eye to work.

Nystagmus is the involuntary movement of the eye. It is not a disease but a symptom of another eye condition and is usually an indication of poor visual acuity. Nystagmus does not allow the child to see clearly. Contrary to popular misconceptions, the child will not see objects as being jerked back and forth. Rather, things will look blurry. Since nystagmus is only a symptom, it is important to diagnose the real condition.

Strabismus (sometimes referred to as "cross-eye") is an error of refraction where the eyes are not able to focus simultaneously on one point. One or both eyes squint all or some of the time. This is typically dealt with by corrective eye glasses and orthoptic training (exercise that works on developing the eye muscles).

Achromatopsia refers to a color deficiency or *color blindness*. Children who have it are unable to identify one or more of the primary colors. This deficiency is hereditary and is caused by a recessive gene that affects males. The term *color deficient* is technically correct and preferable to use because young children are often frightened by the use of the term *color blindness*.

Cortex damage results in loss of vision because of lesion in the visual area of the cerebral cortex. The exact location and size of the lesion determine the amount of vision lost.

All visual information received through the eye passes through the optic nerve and to the *optic centers of the brain*. There the messages are interpreted and action taken if necessary. For some children, the process appears to work accurately until the message gets to the brain, where a breakdown occurs.

Visual perceptual disorder is the inability of the child to identify, organize, and interpret what is perceived by the eye. This may not be noticed until children encounter learning tasks. These children have problems in the area of spatial relations. They are

often uncoordinated and clumsy. In visual discrimination tasks, they have difficulty classifying, sorting, and matching. The children also have difficulty recognizing objects when only a part of the object is visible.

Visual Acuity

Visual acuity is the resolving power of the eye. We usually measure this by having children identify or match letters or pictures in various sizes, a standard distance from the chart. That distance is 20 feet (6.1 meters). A person who can see at 20 feet what most people see at 20 feet has normal vision. Normal vision is expressed in a fraction: 20/20. For children below third grade, vision of 20/40 or better in each eye or vision of 20/30 or better when using both eyes is considered normal.

Low Vision (Partially sighted). Legally, a partially sighted person is one with a corrected visual acuity between 20/200 and 20/70. The American Foundation for the Blind, as well as most educators, prefer to use the term *partially sighted* for those with degrees of visual impairment, but with enough usable vision for learning through the help of magnification and large print books.

Blind. A person is legally blind who has a visual acuity no better than 20/200 in the better eye with correction. The legally blind person sees at 20 feet what people with normal vision can see at 200 feet or has a field of vision restricted to 20 degrees or less (tunnel vision). Educationally, a person who is blind will learn using the auditory and tactile modes.

It is unlikely that you will have a child who is blind in your class, given the prevalence rate of blindness in young children. However, it is very possible that you may help identify a child who has a correctable visual disorder. The estimates are that as many as 20 percent of children have this problem. Of every twenty-five children then, five are likely to have vision problems of some sort (Garwood, 1979).

In addition to accommodating programming to those with visual impairments, the preschool teacher plays an active role in early diagnosis. Unless we have a particular reason to suspect that a child has a visual problem, it usually doesn't occur to us to have the child's vision checked by an eye doctor. Children themselves are usually no help, since they assume that whatever vision they have is normal. There are, however, some things that you may observe or hear that will lead you to suspect a visual impairment. If your observations support your suspicion, point out the symptoms to the parents, state your concerns, and ask them to take the child to an eye doctor (ideally a pediatric or developmental ophthalmologist).

First, look at the child's eyes to see if they are red, watery, or appear to have a discharge; if they are not coordinated (one eye remains still while the other follows the object); if the eyelids are red, swollen, crusted, or droopy; if the pupil is white; or if there are frequent (recurring) styes. Any child with these symptoms should have an eye examination *soon*.

Other general signs of visual impairment include frequent frowning, squinting, or eye rubbing; shutting or covering one eye; tilting the head to one side or the other; and frequently complaining about headaches, stomachaches, or being unable to stand up because of dizziness.

In addition to these symptoms, there are behaviors and complaints that may indicate vision problems. When doing close work such as looking at books, puzzles, or games, a child with a visual impairment may blink continually, hold a book (or place himself) too close or too far away, keep changing the distance of the book, or over- or underestimate distance when working with puzzles or pegboards. When doing visual work at a distance (such as during group time, films, or slides) the child may seem inattentive or lose interest after a brief time. (This is, of course, more significant in a child who usually attends well during other activities.)

Other symptoms to look for during activities that require distance vision or when outside are the inability to identify parents, friends, or teachers at a distance; not noticing objects from across the room or playground; difficulty in such activities as calendar reading or chalkboard games; bumping into things; or misjudging distances in games.

One thing to watch for, however, is that the frequent complaint "I can't see" is usually unrelated to visual impairments. Sometimes it seems as if *no* child can "see" during group time. Keep in mind that, unless they are just chiming in with the others, children who really can't see are not likely to tell you that.

One of the most common screening tests with very young children is the Flash-Card Vision Test, which uses three symbols (apple, house, and umbrella) that can be either verbally or manually matched. Another common test, the Snellen (grades K–3), is a chart with the letter E in different spatial arrangements. These are relatively easy tests to give and are often used by the school nurse.

The question is, what can you, as a teacher, do to help children use the vision they have and the vision aids they need? When you are working with a child with correctable vision problems, the dilemma is that you want the child to wear the patch or glasses *and* to enjoy learning. You can't afford to be cast in the role of the villain who *makes* the child wear these things. First check with the parents or, if necessary, the ophthalmologist to be certain of what the child is supposed to do. Then the trick is to make the child *want* to do what he is supposed to.

Children's Needs: Teaching Goals

Related annual goals may be grouped under broad categories called "teaching goals." Outlined under each teaching goal below are the most important

needs of children with visual impairments. A child may have some or all of these needs, and additional needs as well. The greater the impairment, the more likely it is that teaching modifications will have to be made. Suggestions on what you might consequently teach these children are included. Often, a course of action is implicit in the description of the need.

Sensory Skills

All children with visual needs will benefit from practice in using what vision they have and from developing their other senses.

Visual Skills. Fostering visual skills means encouraging children to use their vision in a way most advantageous to them. This means encouraging children to wear their glasses or patch. Help children compensate for reduced vision by regulating the light levels in the room. Allow them to hold books and other visual material at the best place for them even if it seems odd to you. Remember, they will not hurt their eyes through use.

Within their ability to see, teach them visual discrimination. Start with gross discrimination paired with tactile reinforcement (shapes and sizes), then progress to finer distinctions. Because these children may miss details, work on visual closure. It will help them make better guesses about what is missing.

Auditory Skills. Children with visual impairments are more dependent on hearing to deal with their environment, to master (advanced) language skills, and to guard their personal safety. It is important that they learn to identify and discriminate between sounds. Help children develop better skills in this area through differentiating similar sounds and listening tapes. Tapes and records of stories and music are good for classifying sounds (long, short, high, low) and for identifying who or what might make that sound and in what situations; children also need practice locating sounds.

Language Skills

Children with visual impairments may rely more on auditory cues to learn speech, whereas other children can more easily see and imitate movements of the lips, mouth, and jaw. Encourage children to ask what things are and help them to broaden their understanding of labels used. When enhancing language skills, use real objects and field experience to help clarify points and build inner language. Encouraging feedback from the children about their perceptions will enable you to clarify misunderstandings and foster increased verbalization.

Following verbal directions is another important language skill. Start with simple one- or two-step directions. Remember to keep them concrete.

Thinking and Reasoning Skills

Children must develop many concepts, but most of these are useless unless they know when to use them. For example, children can learn to identify moving cars by ear and by sight, but this isn't much help unless they listen and look before crossing a street. Learning to make predictions about what will happen under a specified set of circumstances is important as a way of developing independence and creating a sense of predictability in their world.

Awareness

Children with limited vision tend to develop body awareness more slowly because of lack of confidence or having fewer examples to emulate. Exercises in naming body parts and the ways in which they move are helpful. Hold the child's hands in your own as you point and demonstrate, if necessary. Encourage children to explore a variety of methods of moving from place to place. Have them talk about when they could use these different methods. They need to become more aware of their body in relation to their surroundings. Provide an environment of acceptance and experimentation that will build these children's self-confidence.

Guidelines

The modifications that you will need to make in your classroom depend on the needs of the particular children you have. These guidelines are divided into two sections. The first deals with the techniques that you will use to encourage children to wear the glasses or a patch that allows them to use their vision. The second section provides guidance in how to modify your room for children whose corrected vision still qualifies them as being partially sighted or blind.

Corrected Visual Impairments

1. Find out when and for how long glasses must be worn. For example, are the glasses to be worn at *all* times? Sometimes the correction is for specific use only. A nearsighted child wears glasses to see at a distance, but because this correction may distort the child's vision for close work, it would be inappropriate to keep the glasses on during seat work.

2. Observe the child's behavior with visual aids. Does the child continually take the glasses off or look over them? Such actions may mean the correction is not helping and further consultation with the ophthalmologist or optometrist may be necessary. Young children can be difficult for the ophthalmologist to test and an incorrect prescription sometimes results.

Puzzles with knobs are easier for children with very low vision to use.

3. If a child refuses to wear glasses, try to create a situation in which the child needs to wear the glasses to succeed. How you actually do this depends on the problem. If, for example, a child is farsighted, find an intriguing book or game that requires close vision. Then, depending on the circumstances, say something like: "Before you got your glasses we couldn't have played this," or "I'd like to play this game with you, but you forgot your glasses. If you wear them tomorrow, we can play." You might also make appropriate statements like: "You've learned to do this so much faster since you got your glasses," or "I like the way you look with your glasses." The child will feel rewarded not only by the activity, but also by your attention.

4. Create a need to see. For example, if a nearsighted child will not wear glasses, you might have that child sit as far away from you as possible during group time. Then, when the child realizes that there is a need to see (in the middle of a story with pictures or during a fingerplay), have someone bring the child's glasses.

   This sounds like a manipulative thing to do and the child will have a harder time learning, but if you and the parents agree that it is important to wear the glasses, you must create a definite need and then reinforce the change in behavior that occurs. This process may be repeated many times before the behavior is established. You may have a farsighted child sit as close to you as possible during group time and then follow the procedure described above. Be careful to do this subtly and in a matter-of-fact way so as not to bring the attention of the group to the child.

5. A unit on feelings may be necessary to increase other children's awareness of visual needs, and the child involved might be asked to explain his reactions to taunting. At first, you may have to lead the discussion and state some typical reactions, but you should gradually help the child learn to speak up. Perhaps a session on assertiveness training will help. Children must learn to say, "I don't like it when you call me 'four eyes.'"

6. A unit on sight may also help all children better understand how they see. Discuss the sense of vision as well as a variety of visual problems. Simulating various visual needs creates awareness and is educational as well. Suggestions for appropriate activities are given in Part Four of this book.

7. Don't fall into the trap of saying, "I'll bet you can see much better since you got your glasses." A child who doesn't want to wear glasses will probably respond, "No, I can't," even when you know he can. Sometimes reality is irrelevant. Remember, if it is important that a child learn a particular thing, such as safety rules, make sure that he can learn it with or without glasses.

Uncorrected Visual Impairments

Partially Sighted. Children who are partially sighted need additional accommodations.

1. Be aware of lighting conditions and your source of light. Use shades to regulate the amount of natural light in your room. (Ideally, for all children, illumination should be between 70 and 100 foot-candles.) Light switches with dimmers can be helpful (but most cannot be used with fluorescent lights). Don't stand or sit with your back to the light source.

2. Arrange seating so that lighting conditions favor those who need it most. (Check the eye specialist's report. For some children maximum illumination is best, and for others lower-than-normal levels are optimal.)

3. Light-colored tables (or dishes) should have a dull finish; glare is fatiguing.

4. Where possible, paint the rims of bookcases, tables, and door frames with a lighter or darker color that will make the edges easier to see. Use a dark light switch against light-colored walls so that it will stand out.

5. Use a heavy black marking pen to outline the boundaries of the paper so that the child knows where the edges are. Look at the books you have in your reading area. Make sure that some of them have clear, simple pictures and large print.

6. Try to use materials with distinctive shapes and textures and bright, high-contrast colors.

7. Try to keep the general noise level down. A child with visual needs relies heavily on auditory cues, and these will be masked by noise. (If your room is beside the playground or cafeteria, you might try to have it changed.)

8. Avoid excessive detail on bulletin boards. Be aware of the child's vision when you display the children's work. The work of children with partial sight should be hung at their eye level. They can see it displayed and they can point it out to others.

9. Think about what you do to reinforce children's behavior. Do you rely on smiles, gestures, body cues, and eye contact? These are visual cues. With the partially sighted, you need to talk and touch for reinforcement.

Blind. Children who are blind need even more accommodations.

1. A well-arranged classroom is a great help to all children but especially to those with visual impairments. Eliminate clutter and confusion! Keep things neat and make sure that toys are picked up as soon as the children are finished with them and that chairs are pushed under the tables. Eliminate unnecessary obstacles in the classroom. Those that are necessary should have a consistent location. Consolidate items where possible. (For example, have one large wastebasket rather than many little ones.) Keep doors fully open or completely shut. Even children with excellent vision tend to run into partly opened doors. Round tables are safer than rectangular ones because there are no corners to bump into. If rectangular ones are all you have, pad sharp edges with foam. If you are a person who likes to arrange and then rearrange your classroom, *don't!* It takes a while for children with visual impairments to get their bearings and feel comfortable in a room. If possible, give these children the chance to become acquainted with the arrangement of the room before the other children come in.

   Use auditory, olfactory, and tactile cues to structure the room. The bubbling of an aquarium might identify the science area; a rug could mark the story area; wind chimes would indicate that the outside door is open, and so on.

2. Encourage independence. When you assign lockers or coat hooks, be sure to give this child one that is easy to locate—an end one that's out of the traffic pattern. Don't move objects around after this child has placed them. Moving something two inches may mean that it is "gone," since the child can't visually scan the area.

3. Encourage the child to find things without help. Use a label maker to put raised labels on materials

where possible. It is more important to label favorite toys with something easy to find than to make a descriptive label. (A puzzle of the Three Little Pigs might have just the raised number *3* on it rather than the entire title.) Make sure the materials are put away so that the label is facing out. Use rubber bands as labels on round objects. You might put one rubber band on the red paint, two on the blue, and three on the yellow. (This is good for children with color deficiencies also.)

Be careful not to give a child who is blind *unnecessary* special treatment. Before you give this child help that you would not give others, ask the child if he needs it. Do offer help, but don't take over or allow other children to do the task for the child.

4. Your teaching techniques will also have to be modified slightly. When you enter a room, especially if the child is alone, tell the child that you are there. Encourage the other children to do the same. Also make it clear when you leave, especially if you are wearing soft-soled shoes—it is rarely necessary with clogs! Use the other children's names during group time when possible. Have you ever talked to an unidentified person on the telephone who assumes you know who is speaking? It's disconcerting until you identify the person. It is important for the blind child to know who is present, especially at the beginning of the year. Use auditory cues—such as a short tune, a chord on the piano, or a song—to signal regular activities, such as cleanup time. Be consistent in using the signals, so the children learn to associate the activities and cues. Help out with an ongoing monologue about what is happening during an activity. If the class is making cookies, say "Susie has finished sifting the flour, and now Harry is going to beat the batter." This also helps the child learn to identify sounds.

5. When talking to this child, keep your voice within normal limits. (Some of us assume that those who don't see well also don't hear well.) When a child with a severe visual impairment is present, talk directly to the child, not about him. Don't ask Gloria's father if she wants to play in the block area, ask her. (Her father may answer, but that is a different problem.) Don't eliminate the words *see* and *look* from your vocabulary—use them when they are appropriate. When giving directions, use characteristics that can be felt or counted rather than seen.

Make sure that the instructions you give really help. "It's right over there" is not enough. You have to name places and specify ways of doing things. It helps if the child knows right from left. If not, have the child wear something (rings, bracelet, watch, ribbon) on one hand or arm so that you can say, "Reach up with the hand with the ribbon on it."

6. When walking with a child who is blind, you go in front, never behind. If you walk alongside, let the child hold your arm or wrist; don't hold his. This allows a greater sense of the movement of your body, especially when you turn or go up or down steps.

Curriculum Adaptations

The amount of visual acuity a child has will determine which, if any, curriculum modifications have to be made. The less vision the child has, the more the auditory and tactile channels must be used and the use of any residual vision encouraged.

Language Arts: Speaking, Listening, Reading, and Writing

Language arts is a challenging, yet essential area for children with visual impairments. Language is their major source of acquiring knowledge, of "seeing" the world, and of communicating with other children as well as herself.

Speaking. To develop fluent, precise language children need a variety of experiences and the words to talk about them.

1. Children with visual impairments depend more on words to express or understand feelings as they may not be able to see the nonverbal language, nor do they have eye contact. Be sure they have the vocabulary they need to express their feelings.

2. When the child learns the power of words to control his world he will repeat these words again and again.

3. Many young children talk to themselves; this is normal for all children. Children with visual impairments do this also. They may also talk to imaginary friends.

Fingerplays incorporate language as well as fine motor skills.

1. Begin with simple, short fingerplays that have more large than small movements. (In other words, teach "Head, Shoulders, Knees, and Toes" before "Thumbkin.")

2. For children who aren't picking up the details and sequence, try to teach the fingerplays to parents so the children can practice them at home or while traveling.

3. Children with low vision find fingerplays difficult because they can't see some of the finer details. When teaching fingerplays to these children, have someone help the child respond at the appropriate time so that the child begins to associate the movement with the words.

Listening. Children who are visually impaired have a greater need for understanding speech than their normally sighted peers since they are often dependent on verbal information to perform certain tasks. Even children with corrected vision problems don't always wear their glasses and may often be dependent on speech. They all need to be encouraged to use vision.

1. As the child with a visual impairment may not be able to see the speaker, she may not look at the person speaking, raise her head, or turn toward the speaker's face. This discourages communication. Teach children to look at the speaker even if this requires your physical help.

2. Play listening games. Make a sound and see if the child can locate the source of the sound. Once the source is located, the child needs to feel the object that makes the sound and tell how it is used.

3. Children will have to learn to listen and recognize many sounds. Describe and explain what the child hears but cannot see. Play this game with all the children in which you describe outside noises and their implications and the children try to guess the source from your description.

4. Where possible give children replicas of what you are talking about. Don't worry about size relationships at this point; you can describe those verbally.

5. "Where," "why," and "what" are difficult for all children to comprehend. Demonstrate where possible the meaning of these words. If possible, take the child to a location, or let the child feel "what" is making the sound.

6. The most difficult words for children to use and understand are those that cannot be experienced through the senses such as colors, the sky, and so on. Use these words in context so children have additional cues. Literature often does this well.

7. Use language to help children focus their vision, as well as to get feedback: "Can you see that wheel? Do you see what's inside the wheel? Those are spokes. Can you count them?"

8. Go from gross to fine discriminations, and from situations where you supply the language to those where you ask for the child to express language.

9. Use words that refer to things that can be smelled, touched, heard, seen, tasted, or experienced directly. Try to make the words you use as concrete as possible, using real examples whenever you can. Then move on to more abstract language concepts such as *time, friendship,* and so on.

10. Use functional definitions of objects as well as descriptive ones. "A ball rolls" or "a ball bounces" should be used in addition to the definition "a ball is round." Reinforce the concept by letting the child roll and bounce the ball.

11. In order to move freely, the child with low vision needs to be able to follow verbal directions. Words like *stop/go, high/low, big/little, in/out/on,* and *hard/soft* are useful. Games like "Simon Says" and "May I" work well for teaching directions.

Stories are a useful way of expanding the children's world, but it is important to start with themes children are familiar with. It is preferable to use pictures that illustrate the story's major points in a simple way. Point out to the children the relationship of the picture to the story. Create a need to see within their ability to discriminate. For children with low vision:

1. When you read stories, you might pass around small replicas of the major objects (rabbits, carrots, trains) for the children to feel. The same can be done with textures and smells. "Scratch and Sniff" books and "Touch and Feel" books are useful, but they tend to wear out quickly.

2. Use cassette tapes or records of books at a listening center. These allow more individualization and choice in the books available. You can make your own recordings of favorite books. You might even bring in blank cassettes so that the children can "write" their own books.

3. Have books with large type and in Braille. Even if the child does not require Braille, it broadens the range of experience and understanding to develop the idea that braille is a form of writing. "Talking books" may prove useful. (American Foundation for the Blind)

Reading. In the area of reading readiness, the emphasis is on developing and refining visual skills. If children are having problems developing these skills, you may suspect visual needs. It is not unlikely that you will find children who can't make the necessary distinctions to develop reading skills. Confer with the parents and refer those children for visual screening.

1. Start with large objects that have gross distinctions. Simple shapes are fine, such as circles, triangles, and squares. Encourage children not only to label and distinguish among shapes, but also to point out salient characteristics (a circle doesn't have any corners, a triangle has three). Have children trace the shapes with their index finger to gain a motor as well as a visual sense of these distinctions.

2. When children can make gross distinctions, work on finer ones. Even when you teach these, try to point out significant features. Use large letters and have the children trace them with their fingers. Teach that *A* has straight lines, *O* has curved lines, and *P* has straight and curved lines. Teach by contrasting *A, O,* and *P* and use other contrasting groups of shapes before you have the children attempt to differentiate among *A, K,* and *W,* for example, which have only straight lines.

3. Children with low vision may have to combine their usable vision with tactile skills to learn reading readiness. If the amount of usable vision

decreases, the need for more tactile discrimination will increase since this is a pre-Braille skill. Among the things that can be used to help these children are sandpaper letters and texture cards (for matching practice). Be sure the visual discrimination activities you employ are possible for the children. If not, find ways to adapt them, such as outlining significant features with a wide marking pen.

4. Use "Scratch and Sniff" books on a one-to-one basis with children.

Writing. All children need to develop the link between the ability to speak a word and the ability to write it so others can understand. The form this takes depends upon the child. Even if you don't think these children will ever write, they need the experience of working with writing tools.

1. For children who are partially sighted, choose wide black markers so they can easily see what they are marking.

2. If the child cannot get visual feedback, then you need to employ media with more tactile feedback. Start without tools. Have children write in the air. Encourage them to hold their two writing fingers together and then using their whole arm, write letters. (This gives them body feedback.) In this instance there is little use in teaching children to print, so I would begin with cursive; the flow is far easier.

3. Have children "write" on sand in a jellyroll pan, and mark clay that has been rolled flat, or, using their finger, "write" on black felt on which you have taped white lines (narrow masking tape is fine).

Discovery: Mathematics, Science, Computers

Discovery experiences need to start with the familiar and concrete and work toward the less familiar and abstract.

Mathematics. Number concepts are necessary for all children to learn. The fun is in using them creatively to help children explore and classify their world. For children with low vision, the tactile-motor aspect of learning these concepts can be added with a few modifications.

1. Teach children to tactilely discriminate and match materials of various shapes, sizes, and weights.

2. When teaching number concepts, start with real objects. Food works well because it can be used informally during snack time and eaten afterward. Everyone gets *one* carton of milk, *two* crackers, *ten* raisins, and so on. An abacus is also useful for counting. One can both see and feel the placement of the beads and check back if necessary. Encourage children to count. Have them count the days in the month, the number of children in the classroom, the number of boys, girls, children wearing pants, children with tie shoes, and so on. Have them even count the steps between places they are likely to go often.

3. Matching together large dominoes with indented dots is a good activity that teaches fine motor skills as well as number concepts.

4. Use actual objects for teaching geometric shapes and the concept of size. When the basics have been mastered, go on to pictures of these objects and then to finding specific shapes and sizes within complex pictures (a traffic signal light—three circles on a cylinder).

5. Have children use their body and other devices to measure. Record these measurements. Special modifications should be made to help low-vision children understand distances—an arm's length, two paces, three handspans. Glue pieces of string on the paper to make graphs with lines that can be felt.

Science. Science activities can help children learn about the sense of vision and the other senses. Emphasize creative problem solving and discovery.

1. Help children learn about the eye and how it works.

2. Talk about the purpose of lenses. Have magnifying glasses and binoculars available in the science area. Talk about the difference in the amount of detail that can be seen with the naked eye and with magnification. A field trip to visit a planetarium or observatory would also be interesting.

3. Have children participate in experiences in which materials change form, such as making butter or melting ice. Be sure to let low-vision children feel the changes as well.

4. Discuss the weather and appropriate dress for different types of weather. Talk about and feel fabrics used in warm versus cold weather clothing. Examine materials designed for use in the rain. Let children have time and opportunity to really handle these materials.

Computers. Computers may be difficult for young children with visual impairments because so much of computing is visual. For children who have enough vision to see the keyboard and the monitor the problems are fewer. Most visually impaired adults have learned touch typing and how to use a numeric keypad. This learning begins when children are young.

1. Obtain a voice synthesizer and hook it up so that what the child prints on the screen is fed back to him orally. The feedback allows a child to check his own work and is an aid in learning to type.

2. Use a 25-inch monitor so the letters displayed on the screen are large. Programs are also available that enlarge the type on the screen. Note: Many people with partial vision find it easier to read a video screen than a piece of paper because the light is coming from the letters on the screen and is not reflected light as is the case with printed material (McWilliams, 1984).

Sensory Motor: Large Motor, Sensory Motor Integration, Small Motor

The development and refinement of sensory motor skills provides additional feedback to the child with a visual impairment. Although vision may be limited, the coordination of hearing and tactile/kinesthetic senses provides an avenue of learning combined with available vision.

Large Motor. Using the large muscles of the body is one way for children to increase their knowledge of their own bodies, as well as a way to explore their environment. Children who have recently had visual correction and those with low vision will probably have less refined skills in this area than their age mates. They will need encouragement as well as practice.

1. Balancing "tricks" are especially useful. Start with static balance. The child stands or sits still and balances a particular object. (Bean bags are easier to start with than books.) For dynamic balance, have the children walk, jump, or crawl while balancing an object on their heads. As children become more skillful, see how long or how far they can balance things. Walking on a balance board or beam is also useful.

2. Relay races where children run, walk, jump, hop, or skip while holding hands with partners are great for developing both large motor skills and cooperating with peers. (Emphasize not speed and winning but completion of the task.)

3. Walking between the rungs of a ladder placed flat on the ground or floor helps children establish spacing, and they learn to realize whether or not they are walking in a straight line. As children become more skillful, have them do this blindfolded.

Sensory Motor Integration. If they do not have accurate visual feedback, children need to develop a motor memory for moving their bodies through space.

1. An obstacle course that requires children to crawl through, over, and under is a great way to teach (for some children you may have to demonstrate this).

2. Use audio tapes of music, people's voices, and the environment (even school getting-ready-to-go-home sounds). Audio reinforcement helps make the world more predictable, and children learn to associate sounds with activities.

3. Put together small bottles of "smells" and have the children identify the smell, talk about the function of the materials, and then, if possible, have the child use it (for example, put the hand cream on her hand).

4. Use the vision children have, but be aware that it may vary from day to day. Children who are anxious or tired may not have as much ability to focus their vision as they do when they are relaxed and rested.

Small Motor. The development and refinement of fine motor skills and eye-hand coordination requires extra practice for those with visual impairments. Start with experiences that are likely to be successful so that they don't get discouraged and quit trying. Success is especially important for those who are just learning to use corrective aids. They may tell you they can do it better without the aids and, if they have learned good compensatory skills, they may be right! Encourage the use of the aids and ensure success also.

1. Fit-in puzzles (those with large pieces that go into specific places) and knob puzzles are good for teaching fine motor skills.

2. Three-dimensional building toys are very helpful (but get the type that interlock in some way, so they won't fall apart when bumped). Encourage children to start with larger pieces and work toward using the smaller ones. Keeps the pieces in a tray so that children can keep track of them.

3. Sewing cards with large holes around the perimeter of the image allow a child to both feel and see the outline of the images. These cards can be easily made by pasting pictures on cardboard and using a hole punch.

4. Teach children to discriminate among textures. Begin with pleasant feeling textures such as satin and velvet. Then move on to wool, leather, cardboard, and so on. Teach children to discriminate among the textures. Do the same with various shapes, sizes, and weights.

5. Tactile skills can be developed with everyday materials (such as satin, felt, and cotton) that can be used for texture-matching games. Try different grades of sandpaper, which the children can try to arrange in order of fineness.

6. The pegboard offers opportunities for both fine motor and prereading activities, especially for those with vision that will decrease who will eventually need to learn Braille. It is also good for teaching simple geometric shapes and concepts like *straight*. Low-vision children should be taught to use their left hands for finding the holes and their right hands for manipulating the pegs (reverse this for left-handers). Start with large holes that can be easily located and low pegs so

that there is less likelihood of flipping the pegs out. Eventually children should be able to copy any uncomplicated pattern an adult makes.

7. Tracing shapes will help the child progress from using actual items to learning to represent them. Children can begin by tracing the actual shape (using a piece of very heavy cardboard) and can then fill in the space with colors.

Social Awareness: Social Studies, Inclusion, Health and Safety

All children need to be part of the group and learn about the strengths and needs of others. As adults, we are familiar with aids to vision such as glasses. Younger children may not be as familiar, and they need to learn.

Social Studies. All children need to learn about the world around them, and field trips are a pleasant and effective way to accomplish this. Children with visual impairments in particular can use many hands-on experiences in order to make accurate generalizations. Even children who have fully corrected vision have spent some large portion of their life without optimal vision. (If the corrective lenses were worn at age two and the child is now four, that is *half* of her lifetime.)

1. Try to plan many field trips with *small* groups of children so that all of them can participate in the experience. It isn't enough just to see a cow, especially if the child can't see it well. The child has to feel it and feel enough of it to avoid the classic errors of the blind men with the elephant.

2. Always provide follow-up activities with stories and dramatic play after field trips. Have the children describe with all their senses what they remember. Drink milk, smell and handle hay, make farm sounds, and sing farm songs.

3. Help children become aware of the role the medical profession plays in assessing visual acuity, as well as prescribing corrective lenses. This can be done with a field trip, a visit from an eye doctor, or both.

4. If you know a blind person who would be comfortable with the children, have the person visit. (A seeing eye dog always makes an impression.)

Inclusion. Your expectations of the child with a visual impairment will set the tone for the class. If you do not require the child to clean up, or if you are apprehensive or overprotective, the other children will quickly pick this up.

1. Teach children to identify themselves when they begin a conversation, otherwise the child's energy might be spent on trying to figure out who the speaker is, rather than what she is saying.

2. Sometimes children with visual impairments seem unresponsive and to lack curiosity, so other children do not approach them. Explain to other children the impact of having less vision.

3. Encourage children to bring toys to the child with a visual impairment to encourage play.

4. Children with low vision often learn about their environment through their tactile/kinesthetic senses. They may want to touch their classmates more than others. Help them find an acceptable way to work this out.

Health and Safety. Health and safety is an important and difficult area of learning for all young children. It requires them to consciously inhibit their spontaneous curiosity and think through the implications of actions *before* doing them. For children with low vision, the possibility of falling or bumping into things, or stooping over and hitting something, is far greater than for other children, yet the price of overprotection is great also. Greater coordination problems exist when learning skills because the children are more dependent on tactile cues for learning than on visual ones. Bear in mind that they need the confidence and esteem that come from learning self-help skills to motivate further exploration.

1. Help all children develop independence in self-help skills. Use buttoning, lacing, and snapping frames to teach these skills. Montessori materials are excellent, but you can make your own fairly easily. Keep soap, paper towels, and the wastebasket in the same places in the bathroom and at a level the child can reach.

2. Teach safety, looking, and listening skills. Make sure children can identify such sounds as cars, sirens, and fire bells, and that they know what they should do when they hear these sounds.

3. Teach all children to do deep knee bends as a way of getting down to pick things up. It is especially important when they lift heavy objects, and it decreases bumped heads.

4. When children are playing very actively, have those who wear eyeglasses use a safety strap to keep the glasses from falling off.

5. In outdoor play areas, fence in the swings, seesaws, or any other heavy moving equipment. Keep tricycles and wagons on specified paths. For low-vision children, add bells to any moving objects (tricycles, wagons, even balls) so the child can hear them and learn to avoid their path.

Creative Arts: Art, Music, Creative Movement, and Dramatic Play

Creative arts provide the child with the opportunity to explore his world in a safe way. He can gain experiences inside the classroom that prepare him for what will happen outside. As it is the process that is important, the child can participate without fear of doing it wrong.

Art. Although children with very little residual vision face limitations in some areas of art, there are many highly tactile materials (such as clay) that allow a great deal of manipulation. The potential that art activities and materials offer for the release of emotions make them doubly valuable experiences for all children with visual needs.

1. Use a variety of modeling materials to provide different tactile experiences. Among the most popular materials are playdough (made of salt and flour), clay (use the powdered type and let the children help mix it), cornstarch, papiermâché, and plastic-coated wire.

2. Have children fingerpaint right on the table if they are using actual fingerpaint. You can then print the picture when a child makes one he wants to keep. In addition, try fingerpainting with pudding, shaving cream, Ivory Snow Flakes (a clean feeling for those who are reluctant to get dirty), or laundry starch. Fingerpainting to music is another good variation.

3. Add textured materials such as sand or sawdust to easel paint and fingerpaint. Make the paint thicker so that it can be more easily felt and controlled.

4. Make textured boundaries for work areas. (This is a good idea for any child who tends to use too much space.) Use masking tape to divide the table into areas, depending on your needs.

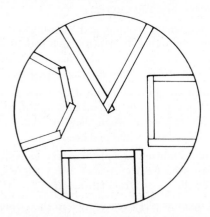

Use place mats to define each child's space. Put glue around the outside edge of a sheet of paper and sprinkle a little sand on it.

5. If you are using white paper on the easel, first cover the easel with dark construction paper so that the child can easily see where the paper ends. If the child cannot see, use a textured material for the board, such as coarse sandpaper or cork so the child can feel the boundaries.

6. Use a heavy lead pencil or a dark marking pen to print names on papers and, obviously, remember to *print big.*

7. Hang the child's artwork in a place where the child can find it easily, see it, and point it out to others. Hang it low and near the beginning or the end of the line.

8. If you have a child who is wearing a patch over one eye, have the class make patches and then decorate and wear them.

9. Make a texture collage with a specific theme: for *nature,* use feathers, pine needles, leaves, and grass.

Music. Music is usually a particularly enjoyable activity for children with low vision and, with the number of famous musicians who are visually impaired (such as Ray Charles, Stevie Wonder, and Joaquin Rodrigo), it is not difficult to find encouragement to do well in this area. However, don't assume that because children are visually impaired they will automatically be good at music. This may just be one of the few fields in which they are at less of a disadvantage.

Music study is a good way to develop finer auditory discrimination and to facilitate the development of memory skills—both of which are particularly important to the visually impaired. The best musical games to play are those in which none of the children are eliminated.

1. Play an instrument or ring a bell and have the children (who have their backs to you and eyes closed) guess what area of the room you are in. A variation of this is to have them search for a ticking kitchen timer, which you set to go off in a short time. A wind-up music box can be placed inside a small foam pillow and thrown or kicked and then found.

2. Teach the concepts of *high* and *low* with music pitch games. Have children practice using *loud* and *soft* volume as cues to distance (for finding a hidden object, for example). *Fast* and *slow* are also easily taught through musical games—the faster the music, the closer the child is to the hidden object.

3. Songs that have motions are often a great way to teach labels (especially those of body parts and actions). Extra time, however, must be devoted (at school or home) to teaching low-vision children the motions that go with songs.

4. Moving creatively to music is good because it encourages varieties of movement and gracefulness, and because there is no right or wrong. Dancing,

from the waltz to the twist to disco, is good exercise and great for developing coordination.

Creative Movement. Combining movement and an idea to move helps children learn abstract concepts. It is also a great way of finding out about a child's concepts of the world. If you ask the child to be a leaf blowing in the wind, you will see his interpretation of what this is like. It can serve as the foundation for some additional planning.

1. Start with ideas that are simple and familiar to children and provide props that support these ideas, but do not dictate how an activity is done. (Talk about being a group marching in a parade and play music to march by.)

2. When you ask children to move in a particular way, be sure to verbally discuss "how" this will happen and to give clear, precise details about the event the children are portraying. If we go back to the leaves, you might ask children what would make the leaves fall. Then talk about how they would move in response to falling off the tree versus being blown by a strong wind.

3. Talk about personal space and how to figure out where they can move without bumping into each other.

4. Provide props such as music, scarves, hats, and so on to make the experience more concrete. These props help set the stage for children who are visually impaired. They can expand on an idea that has been established.

Dramatic Play. Dramatic play allows children to learn about, experience, and control situations. They can make new experiences more familiar by playing through them first. Working through some frightening experiences will take the sting out of them.

1. Provide a lot of props. Be sure that at least some of them give obvious cues (tactile as well as visual) about the activity going on. For example, tea cups and saucers mean a tea party, but add a tea pot and appropriate clothing for the occasion to set the mood.

2. When children dress up, check to be sure there are no dangling belts or scarves that could cause tripping.

3. Set up an optometrist's office and have children test each other's vision. (The purpose is to teach a process, not to get accurate visual acuity results for each child.)

Transitions

Transition times are difficult for all children because a lot of movement and change occurs. You can slow the process down, make it more fun, and teach spatial awareness concepts such as *over, under,* and *around*

by having the children go over a chair, under the table, or around other children as they are dismissed from the group. Use nonvisual cues as one means of dismissal: for example, "Everyone with a shirt that buttons can get their coats." You can use types of clothing, fabrics, or the first letters of names. (Try not to use the girls/boys division very often.) It is a good idea to dismiss children with visual needs either early or late, when there will be the least amount of confusion.

Glossary

Achromatopsia   *See* color deficient.

Amblyopia   The dimness or loss of vision in one eye due to disuse of the eye. Correctable through surgery and/or wearing a patch over the stronger eye to prevent muscle deterioration and double vision.

Ametropia   Errors of refraction (hyperopia, myopia, and astigmatism). In all cases and for a variety of reasons, the best focal point is not on the retina.

Astigmatism   A visual impairment caused by variations in the curvature of the cornea or lens that prevent the light rays from coming to a single focal point on the retina. It can be corrected with glasses.

Braille   A system of touch reading. The characters are in combinations of six dots arranged in a cell, two dots wide and three dots high. The symbols are embossed on heavy manila paper and read from left to right. There are 63 possible dot combinations, and special notations for mathematics, music, scientific problems, and numbers make almost any academic subject possible.

Cataracts   A disease in which the lens of the eye becomes opaque. Vision can be restored only by an operation in which the lens is removed and rather thick glasses are prescribed.

Color deficient (blindness)   Achromatopsia. The inability to identify one or more primary colors. There is no way to correct this.

Cornea damage   The cornea is the "window" of the eye that protects the lens and iris. Scars or punctures of the cornea can obstruct vision, but it is possible to have the cornea replaced. This is the *only* kind of eye transplant possible to date.

Cross-eye (Strabismus)   The inability of the eyes to focus together because the muscles that control movement are not equally strong. One or both eyes may be affected, vertically and/or horizontally. An inward-turning condition is called *cross-eye,* an outward-turning one is called *walleye.* Because a double image is perceived, there is a tendency to use only one eye. Strengthening exercises are needed, and a patch is sometimes worn primarily over the stronger eye although occasionally over the weaker. If necessary, an operation can be performed.

Diplopia   Double vision in either one or both eyes.

Farsightedness (hyperopia) A defect in which things at a distance can be clearly seen but things that are nearby cannot. It is the result of a short eyeball or a lens problem that causes the image to focus beyond the retina. It can be corrected with glasses.

Glaucoma If the fluid in the eye does not drain properly, pressure will build up and impede the entry of blood. This can lead to the destruction of nerve cells in the retina. Special eye drops or an operation that uses a laser to put a hole in the iris for drainage can be used to control the pressure. The disease is extremely rare in children.

Nearsightedness (myopia) A defect in which images that are near the viewer can be seen clearly but things that are distant cannot. It is the result of a long eyeball or a lens problem that causes the image to focus in front of the retina. It can be corrected with glasses.

Nightblindness Less-than-normal vision in dim light. The eyes cannot adjust easily from light to dark stimuli. It is a symptom of vitamin A deficiency. If the condition continues to exist for more than a few months it becomes permanent.

Oculist A physician who specializes in eye problems and writes prescriptions for lenses (glasses).

Ophthalmologist Physician specializing in the anatomy, function, and diseases of the eye.

Optacon A device that scans print and converts it into patterns transmitted by 144 tactile pins that produce an image of the letter against a finger.

Optic nerve The second cranial nerve. It carries impulses from the retina to the occipital lobe of the brain.

Optometrist Specialist who can examine eyes and write prescriptions for lenses, but who does not have a medical degree.

Orthoptics The science of using exercises that use the eye muscles to correct faulty eye coordination.

Retina, detached One that has been torn loose from the next layer of the eyeball. It can be reattached surgically with very little loss of vision.

Teaching Resources

In some situations you may want or need additional information; there are many national as well as regional, state, and local organizations that can be helpful to you. The following annotated list of national organizations should be useful in helping you decide where to get the information you need.

Association for Education of the Visually Handicapped
919 Walnut Street, 4th Floor
Philadelphia, PA 19107

Teachers, administrators, and parents of children who are visually impaired. They are interested in the education, guidance, vocational rehabilitation, or occupational placement of the visually handicapped.

Better Vision Institute
230 Park Avenue
New York, NY 10017
Sponsors preschool screening programs by Junior Chamber of Commerce, primarily aimed at amblyopia: "To keep public aware of the need for more adequate vision care."

American Foundation for the Blind, Inc.
15 West 16th Street
New York, NY 10011
Serves as a consultant to local agencies and refers individuals to local agencies where they can receive direct help. Write the Foundation for addresses of regional offices.

National Society for the Prevention of Blindness, Inc.
79 Madison Avenue
New York, NY 10016
The National Society and its affiliates carry out a comprehensive program for service, education, and research dealing solely with blindness prevention.

The Talking Book Service Division for the Blind and Physically Handicapped
Library of Congress
Washington, DC 20542
The service provides talking books for those who need them.

Touch Toys
P.O. Box 2224
Rockville, MD 20852
Information on tactile toys and how to construct them.

Children's Bibliography

See the Children's Bibliography on page 286 for books to increase children's awareness about disabilities as well as books that are especially good for children with particular disabilities. Note especially:

Awareness of Visual Impairments

Books for Low-Vision Children (simple, high-contrast designs)

Body Awareness

Scratch and Sniff and Touch and Feel Books

Simpler Books (for teaching vocabulary and concepts)

References and Bibliography

A beginner's guide to personal computers for the blind and visually impaired. (1982). Boston, MA: National Braille Press.

Aiello, B. (1981). *The visually handicapped child in the regular class*. Washington, DC: Teachers Network for the Education of the Handicapped.

Alonso, L., Moor, P., Raynor, S., von Hippel, C., & Baer, S. (1978). *Mainstreaming preschoolers: Children with visual handicaps*. Washington, DC: U.S. Government Printing Office.

Bishop, V. E. (1978). *Teaching the visually limited child*. Springfield, IL: Charles C. Thomas.

Chapman, E. K. (1978). *Visually handicapped children and young people*. Boston, MA: Routledge and Keegan.

Gallagher, P. (1978). *Educational games for visually handicapped children*. Denver, CO: Love Publishing Company.

Garwood, S. (1979). *Educating young handicapped children: A developmental approach*. Germantown, MD: Aspen Systems Corp.

Harley, R., & Lawrence, G. (1984). *Visual impairment in the schools* (2nd ed.). Springfield, IL: Charles C. Thomas.

Jan, J., Freeman, R., & Scott, E. (Eds.). (1977). *Visual impairments in children and adolescents*. New York: Grune and Stratton.

Kukurai, S. (1974). *How can I make what I cannot see?* New York: Van Nostrand Reinhold.

Library of Congress. Division for the Blind and Physically Handicapped. (1970). *Sources of reading materials for the visually and physically handicapped*. Washington, DC.

Lowenfeld, B. (1977). *Our blind children: Growing and learning with them* (3d ed.). Springfield, IL: Charles C. Thomas.

Lowenfeld, B. (Ed.). (1973). *The visually handicapped child in school*. John Day Books in Special Education. New York: John Day.

Lowenfeld, B., Abel, G. L., & Hatlen, P. H. (1974). *Blind children learn to read*. Springfield, IL: Charles C. Thomas.

Mangold, S. (Ed.). (1982). *A teacher's guide to the special educational needs of blind and visually impaired children*. New York: American Foundation for the Blind.

Martin, G. J., & Hoben, M. (1977). *Supporting visually impaired students in the mainstream: The state of the art*. Reston, VA: Council for Exceptional Children.

Scott, E. (1982). *Your visually impaired student: A guide for teachers*. Baltimore, MD: University Park Press.

Scott, E., Jan, J., & Freeman, R. (1977). *Can't your child see?* Baltimore, MD: University Park Press.

Spungin, S. J. (1977). *Competency based curriculum for teachers of the visually handicapped: A national study*. New York: American Foundation for the Blind.

Stratton, J. (1977). *The blind child in the regular kindergarten*. New York: Charles C. Thomas.

Warren, D. (1984). *Blindness and early childhood development*. New York: American Foundation for the Blind.

Awareness Bibliography for Adults

Caulfield, Genevieve. (1960). *The kingdom within*. Edited by E. Fitzgerald. New York: Harper Brothers.

The autobiography of a woman who was accidentally blinded at the age of two and had only faint light perception in one eye through her life. She graduated from college as a teacher and traveled to both Japan and Thailand to work with the blind.

Hartwell, Dickson. (1960). *Dogs against darkness: The story of the seeing eye*. New York: Dodd, Mead.

Seeing eye dogs and their training.

Sullivan, Tom, & Gill, Derek. (1975). *If you could see what I hear*. New York: Harper & Row.

An autobiography on blindness from infancy to adulthood. Contrasted with his mother's overprotective attempts to isolate him and his father's equally extreme belief that his son could accomplish all that other boys could, if not more, are Sullivan's ongoing attempts to live a normal life and become a part of the mainstream.

Ulrich, Sharon. (1972). *Elizabeth*. Ann Arbor, MI: University of Michigan Press.

A brief description of the life of a preschool child who is blind. The first section of the book was written by the director of the child-development project Elizabeth participated in. The second section was written by Elizabeth's mother, who explains methods used in toilet training, learning to walk, and learning how to deal with basic problems.

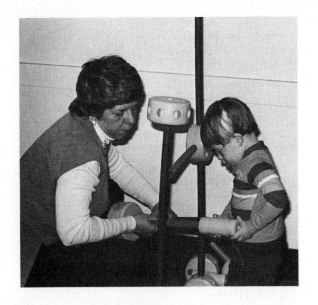

Chapter 13

Children with Learning Disabilities

My concern for children with learning disabilities started in the late 1960s when we thought in terms of children who *wouldn't* behave.

At the beginning of the school year, four-year-old Sam was "acting out." He hit other children without provocation. He would neither print his name nor remember where his locker was (despite the animal sticker on it). He wouldn't sit still during group time, but would wander around the room being disruptive. He was reminded so often that "it hurts when someone hits you" that by the end of the school year no matter where he was in the room, if a child cried, Sam would go up to that child and say, "I'm sorry I made you cry." He believed he caused others to cry even when he wasn't responsible.

Now I wonder if Sam was a child who *wouldn't* or *couldn't* behave. We didn't have a label for "learning disabilities" then; there were only "difficult" children who were "behavior problems." Sam was in fact diagnosed as learning disabled after he had repeated first grade and was having trouble in second grade. By then, he had not only a learning disability but also a poor self-concept. Sam is only one of the children I wonder about. I have had others; perhaps you have, too. This chapter is designed to help you find and teach the children who "can't" but who "should be able to."

Classification of Learning Disabilities

Learning disability is one of the newest areas of education and one with the least agreement over the terms used. All now agree that children with learning disabilities are more than children who "just aren't trying." There is, however, little agreement on the definition of what a learning disability is. The following four elements are part of all definitions:

1. The child has a discrepancy between his tested intelligence and his performance in the classroom. People have tried to quantify this "discrepancy," but there is no universal agreement about when the discrepancy is significant enough to be labeled as a learning disability.

2. The learning problems are not the direct result of other disabilities (such as sensory impairment, mental retardation, emotional disturbance, or the environment). This is an area of controversy. Some definitions preclude children with sensory impairments from being labeled as having learning disabilities. Experience in the field has shown that some of these children may also have learning disabilities.

3. Children with learning disabilities are not able to perceive or interpret information accurately—they have psychological processing problems. There is disagreement here as well. We do not have good methods of measuring "psychological processing," and children who have been trained to "process information" have not shown the expected gains in academic performance (Hallahan & Kauffman, 1991).

4. There is dysfunction in the central nervous system. Initially the assumption was that there was damage or injury to the brain. Medical (neurological) examination did not necessarily support this position. However, the child's behavior seemed similar to that of children who did have brain damage. What has become clearer is that there is probably some malfunction in the brain (not necessarily tissue damage) (Hallahan & Kauffman, 1991).

It is important that you know the federal government's definition of learning disabilities, since that definition governs academic programs and our estimates of children with learning disabilities.

"Specific learning disability" means a disorder in one or more of the basic psychological processes involved in understanding or in using language, spoken or written, which may manifest itself in an imperfect ability to listen, think, speak, read, write, spell, or do mathematical calculations. The term includes such conditions as perceptual handicaps, brain injury, minimal brain dysfunction, dyslexia, and developmental aphasia. The term does not include children who have learning problems which are primarily the result of visual, hearing, or motor handicaps, of mental retardation, of emotional disturbance, or of environmental, cultural, or economic disadvantage (Federal Register, 1977, p. 65083).

More than ninety terms have been used to describe the problems that we now call learning disabilities.

(Some of these are in the Glossary.) The label encompasses a broad spectrum of needs, but they can be summed up by the title of a book written by Louise Clarke: *Can't Read, Can't Write, Can't Talk Too Good Either*. Learning disabilities are far from being completely understood.

The U.S. Department of Education found during the 1987–1988 school year that 4.4 percent of school-age children were identified as learning disabled (U.S. Department of Education, 1989).

There are few estimates of how many preschool children fall into this category. No doubt the problem exists at this age; it just hasn't been diagnosed this early in most cases. You may be the first, then, to suspect an exceptionality. You may have to base your programming on your own diagnosis because as much as a year may pass before the diagnosis is confirmed.

In most cases, the causes of learning disabilities are not known. Learning disabilities seem to occur with greater frequency in some families than others, but the contributions of heredity and environment have not yet been determined. It is currently held that learning disabilities can be present at birth, can result from an accident, or can be caused by environmental factors.

As your role is most likely to be in the early identification of and planning for children with learning disabilities, knowledge of their characteristic behaviors are important. Many symptoms of learning disabilities relate directly to specific academic areas (reading, writing, spelling, and mathematics). Because of this, some experts feel that learning disabilities cannot be diagnosed during the preschool years; others disagree. You will not see some behaviors; however, other characteristics are observable at earlier ages. Regardless of labeling, children need to learn to control their body and to develop skills for learning. The behavioral characteristics typical of children with learning disabilities are described below.

Behavioral Characteristics of Learning Disabilities

Impulsiveness   In young children impulsiveness usually means acting quickly without planning and thinking about the consequences of actions.

Distractibility   The children cannot attend to a task. Their attention and even their bodies seem to be drawn elsewhere. They do not have the ability to redirect their attention back to the original task once it has wandered.

Short Attention Span   The children do not stay at tasks for long. They rarely finish tasks or get satisfaction from them.

Inability to Follow Directions   Some children do not seem to understand directions. Others seem to understand initially but forget what was asked.

Hyperactivity   Most young children are active. What separates activity from hyperactivity is that active children usually have activity that is purposeful (at least to them). They can typically stay at an activity for a period of time. Hyperactive children seem to be constantly in motion. Their motion is not goal-oriented, as they seem distracted by and need to respond to all environmental stimuli. Even when sitting these children are not quiet; they may twitch, jerk, or rock.

Hypoactivity   Other children with learning disabilities may be hypoactive. They appear to move in slow motion, if they move. They may seem listless, bored, or sleepy. Every movement seems to require a lot of effort.

Perseveration   The children start a task and can't seem to stop. For example a child rolling a playdough snake may roll the snake all morning if not interrupted. It is as if the child is not capable of refocusing his attention once it has been focused.

General Awkwardness   These children are awkward compared to other children their age. They frequently bump into things or people, knock things over and trip.

Handedness Not Established   Young children often use their hands inconsistently. However, by the time they are about five or six a preference is usually established. Children with learning disabilities are not ambidextrous, they are nondextrous—unskilled with both hands.

Conflict with Other Children   Given the above characteristics it is not surprising that these children may irritate others. They are more likely than other children to be in conflict with their peers (adapted from Hayden, Smith, von Hippel, & Baer, 1978).

The question now becomes, when does a child exhibit enough of these behaviors for you to talk with her parents? Before approaching parents, look at the cultural background of the family and learn something about their expectations for the child. Information about any child needs to be evaluated within the context of the family.

If further information sheds no light on the behavior, observe the child over a span of time to try to get a representative look at the behavior. Then construct a simple behavioral checklist that focuses attention on areas you are concerned about. First decide how much a particular behavior describes the child on a given day. Then note the behaviors that you observed to form that opinion. I would do this for several days and ask other adults in the classroom to do the same. I might also do this on another child just to check myself. My form would look something like the one on page 189.

Your observations should be systematic and the behavior observed should have necessary detail: "Sheila knocked over the juice while reaching for the crackers with her left hand." Write down the details as you see them. Keep your facts objective. The most important part of observing is to look for patterns. You will have to observe for several days to get enough data for patterns to emerge.

Whether or not you decide to talk with the parents about your observations, you will get a more accurate picture of the child. This information is useful in targeting program goals for him.

Children's Needs: Teaching Goals

Related annual goals may be grouped under broad categories called "teaching goals." Outlined under each teaching goal below are the most important needs of children with learning disabilities. A child may have some or all of these needs, and additional needs as well. Suggestions on what you might consequently teach them are included. Often, a course of action is implicit in the description of the need.

A learning disability is usually not a single problem but rather a combination of problems. Learning disabilities are diverse; two children may be labeled learning disabled and one's strengths might be the other's weaknesses. Be alert to "need clusters" that indicate areas to concentrate on. (For example: If a child is clumsy, has poor eye-hand coordination, and has balance and rhythm problems, concentrate on teaching this child motor skills.) It is also important to keep in mind the developmental level of the child. (Is the attention span really short for a three-year-old?) Look for uneven development characterized by average to above-average development in one or more areas, but noticeable developmental lags in other areas. (The child can discuss trains, the roles of the various people on the train, and how trains work, but cannot put a toy train beside, in front of, or above a block.)

Sensory Skills

Visual Skills. It is difficult for children with learning disabilities to interpret what they see (visual perception). A child may not be able to judge size, shape, location, movement, and color because to him these properties keep changing. Because of the difficulty they have in sorting out foreground and background, these children often focus on irrelevant details. It is difficult for children to recognize similarities and differences (visual discrimination). Their problems are magnified when they try to learn to recognize numbers and letters, as the differences are slight. The letters that are reversible are especially difficult (b,d), as are the ones with "tails" (p,q,j,g).

Visual tracking is the ability to focus the eyes on one point and then move them rhythmically from

Child's name _____ Date _____

Observer _____

	Actual Occurrence	Perception of Occurrence		
		Often	Sometimes	Rarely
Impulsivity				
Observation				
Distractibility				
Observation				
Short attention span				
Observation				
Inability to follow directions				
Observation				
Hyperactivity				
Observation				
Hypoactivity				
Observation				
Perseveration				
Observation				
General awkwardness				
Observation				
Hands used interchangeably				
Observation				
Conflict with other children				
Observation				

Comments:

Use a form such as this to quantify your observations and to add some qualitative comments. Use the first column to identify the number of times you actually observe the behavior happening, and your guess as to whether this behavior happens often, sometimes, or rarely. The space for observations is designed for you to report what you see. If you are inclined to write more, add more space in your form. It is important that you count as well as clarify when the behavior occurs. Any plan of action is dependent upon this information. In some cases you may think a behavior is a problem, but the data does not support your conclusion. This insight is helpful in deciding how to approach a situation.

side to side, up and down, and diagonally. Some children have jerky eye movements, or move their whole head instead of just their eyes. Part-whole relationships (visual closure) cause problems. Children have trouble identifying missing parts; a picture of a three-legged chair appears normal to them. They also have trouble remembering what they see (if you had four objects on the table, covered them, removed one, and asked them to name the missing object they probably couldn't). Poor visual memory also makes it difficult to remember sequences. Visual-motor integration or eye-hand coordination is often problematic. These children predictably have a difficult time drawing, pasting, and particularly cutting.

Have the children practice identifying and matching shapes and colors before they proceed to letters and numbers. Needed memory skills can be built by games that require children to remember the original order or objects that have been moved.

Auditory Skills. Auditory skills are also challenging. Auditory discrimination is the ability to tell the difference between sounds. Children with learning disabilities have difficulty recognizing differences in sounds or words; hence they often misinterpret meanings (*rat, rap*). They also have problems identifying the rhyming elements of words. They find classifying words next to impossible (for example, finding all the words that start with *a*). Hierarchical classifications are generally beyond their capability. As you might guess, these are children who do not enjoy sound and word games and who often cannot express thoughts and ideas clearly.

Auditory memory is the ability to remember what has been heard. Sometimes children forget the beginning by the time you get to the end of a long sentence. The second request in two-step directions may not be remembered. They may also have trouble locating the source of a sound (if you call their name they may search around the room and not find where you are).

Because it is important that the children develop auditory skills, choose topics that are of particular interest to them and reinforce their attempts at communicating. Don't avoid areas that are difficult, but keep the time spent on them short and praise the children's attempts. Work to increase concentration and attention span as well. Shorten your sentences and give directions one step at a time.

Thinking and Reasoning Skills

Children with learning disabilities may not have as much general knowledge as other children. This is especially true in the area of relationships. They may not understand that it is hotter in the sun than in the shade; that if you don't water plants they will die.

They need practice in logical reasoning. Demonstrate first with objects and then by drawing attention to the child's own behavior that it is possible to make predictions about what will happen. In this way they will gradually develop cause and effect reasoning skills. Start with short, obvious examples, such as putting weights on a balance. Work toward tasks requiring higher-level reasoning skills, such as figuring out the need plants have for water and sunlight. Include activities in which children can cause change—the harder they press their crayons, the darker the color. Then (in combination with the work on body awareness) help children learn how they cause their environment to change.

Motor Skills

Large Motor Skills. Children with learning disabilities may have been late (or at the end of the normal age range) in reaching developmental milestones such as sitting up, crawling, and walking. They tend to lack body control and rhythm. While walking or running, these children appear disjointed. They get where they want to go, but they appear inefficient and they don't move smoothly. They may lack the necessary coordination for hopping, jumping, and skipping and show an irregular rhythm when clapping or tapping.

They may exhibit some problems in tasks that require bilateral movement (using both arms and hands at the same time) such as lifting or throwing. Cross-lateral movements (using opposite arm and leg at the same time) such as crawling may be difficult. They may find it difficult to control their balance while moving and frequently trip, bump into things, or drop things. Some children have poor spatial orientation skills, that is, they do not understand their position in space relative to the objects around them. They may not recognize objects that are upside down if they have never seen them this way before. They may also find the relationship of objects to each other difficult to understand. They may not know how high to step to get over an object or how to fit their body under a rope. Tricycle riding may be difficult. Bicycles may be impossible! The children also have trouble catching a ball, especially if it bounces first. It is difficult for them to decide when the ball will reach them and how high the ball will be when it does. Hence, they rarely catch it. Use under-inflated beach balls as well as large balls to increase the possibility for success.

They may need your encouragement to participate in large motor activities, especially if others have teased them in the past. Plan opportunities both indoors and out for children to practice large motor skills in a noncompetitive way. Walking on a line or balance beam and stepping through the rungs of a ladder lying on the floor are both useful. Riding a tricycle and climbing a jungle gym provide opportunities to develop large motor coordination.

Small Motor Skills. Children with poor fine motor skills are clumsy handling small objects that require finger and wrist movement. They may not be able to button and unbutton, snap, or tie. An underdeveloped pincer grip may make it hard to pick up small items. Even speech, which requires the coordinated movements on the lips and tongue, may be challenging.

Coloring "inside the lines" and pasting in a specific area may be very difficult. Cutting with conventional scissors is often close to impossible. Provide scissors that work by squeezing a circular handle. Large crayons and large chalk and simple designs all help. Your concern is to ensure that these children experience success in this area so that they don't quit trying.

Communication Skills

Expressive Language. Sometimes children with learning disabilities have articulation problems until they gain control of the muscles in the face. They are sometimes unable to remember what it is they want to say, and may confuse items and call a chair a table. They may also have difficulty imitating sounds and words. They need a great deal of practice using speech and body language as well as positive feedback from you to keep at it. They also need your patience in listening to them when they have something to say.

Receptive Language. Children will have a difficult time understanding the meaning of language if they do not understand the meaning of prepositions of position such as *in, on, over, under, beside,* and so on. If they lack understanding of action verbs they also have problems understanding what is spoken. Give them plenty of practice following your directions using these words and showing you what they mean both with their own body and with a block or doll.

Feelings

They need to increase their awareness of their own feelings and those of others as well. They also need experience in differentiating between feelings and behavior: "It's OK to be mad at Chunga; it is not OK to hit her." Help them learn to express both positive and negative feelings in socially acceptable ways. They can run, poke playdough, or hit a punching bag. They need to consciously decide how they will deal with their feelings. They may also need to learn the expressions and gestures to show others that they are happy and like them. They need help making and keeping friends.

In general, these children dislike change. Special school events are often stressful. They have trouble handling feelings of anticipation, as will become apparent when you are preparing the class for a field trip. The anxiety often takes the form of questions: These children ask many more questions than their peers, and they ask the same questions over and over. Help them learn other ways of coping with anxiety.

Awareness

Body Awareness. Children with learning disabilities show poor knowledge of their own body whether they are asked to label parts on a doll or identify a body part of their own. They need to become more aware of themselves in relation to their surroundings. Help children learn to use spatial terms that define where they are—*near, far, in front of, behind, above, below.*

Self-concept. Identifying learning needs early benefits both you and the children. Once children have already experienced failure, you have to deal with a poor self-concept in addition to the learning disability. You can help them become aware of their individual strengths even while working on challenging activities.

Guidelines

The following guidelines should prove generally useful when teaching children with learning disabilities. Two key words to keep in mind are consistency and preparation.

1. Be consistent, not only in the class rules you set but also in the daily schedule of activities.

2. Prepare children for changes in routine. Announcement of a change will set off a flood of questions, which you may have to control. The third time you hear the same question, you might respond, "I understand your concern about the trip to the orchard. I'll answer the question this last time, but not again." From then on you can usually discourage the questions with one of those "teacher" looks.

It may be necessary to simplify the program and make it as concrete as possible. Work very gradually toward a more challenging program.

1. Eliminate as many distractions as possible when it is important that the child concentrate. For example, don't have a group activity in a place where this child can look out the window and see others playing on the playground.

2. Begin with simple activities dealing with one concept and move to more complex concepts as the child seems ready, for example, from *taking turns* to *friendship,* from *counting* to *estimating.*

3. Make directions simple, short, and clear; if necessary, give them a step at a time. "It's cleanup time" may not be enough. Try "Put the doll clothes back in the drawer" and when that is completed continue with "Put the dolls in their bed," and so on. When the child has done as you requested, be sure to reinforce the behavior: "I liked the way you folded the doll clothes and put

Outside play allows children to work off energy and learn important lessons in sharing and respecting personal property.

them away." A specific and concrete reinforcement is more effective than one as general as "That's a good job."

4. If a child has problems learning a particular task, check if he has mastered the prerequisite skills. For example, if a child can't pick out the square from a group of circles, he probably can't find the *p* among similar looking letters.

5. As young children begin to reason concretely, be sure to use concrete objects when teaching. For example, count children, fingers, boys, girls, windows, teachers, but don't just count.

6. All children have a preferred way of learning information (visual, auditory, or kinesthetic/tactile). It can be particularly helpful to know and use the child's preference. For example:

    Visual: Have a poster in the block corner demonstrating the proper and improper use of blocks.

    Auditory: Tell the child, "Blocks are to build with" or "You may not throw the blocks."

    Kinesthetic/Tactile: Take the child to the block corner and show the child what to do, then have the child demonstrate the appropriate behavior to you.

7. Provide numerous and varied learning experiences that teach the same idea in many different ways. For example, you can teach body awareness through art, movement, listening, music, and health activities.

8. Provide many activities that encourage movement, especially during large group times. Don't expect these children to sit as long as some of their peers might.

Discipline, or classroom management, is rarely easy; children with learning disabilities present an additional challenge. Because their behavior is inconsistent, it is difficult to know whether these children are refusing or are unable to behave as they should. (Parents have the same dilemma.) The traditional solution is *behavior modification*. This may involve token rewards for good or "on task" behavior and sitting in a "time out" area or loss of token rewards for inappropriate behavior. Others have successfully used *logical consequences*. For example, if a child knocks all the plastic blocks off a table, he needs to help pick them up. If she spills juice, she should help clean it up. (If the child spills juice persistently and purposefully, you might try not giving him any more. If he claims to be thirsty, you could give him water.)

A combination of the two methods works best. You want the child to learn internalized self-control in order to stop inappropriate behavior.

Ignoring inappropriate behavior (especially when you think that getting attention is the child's purpose) is ideal when it works. However, it doesn't always work in the classroom, particularly if the child is doing something dangerous or is disturbing the others. In those cases, removing the child from the situation is probably the best solution.

The use of "time out" for children with learning disabilities has its proponents and opponents. "Time out" is removing the child from the ongoing activities to a specified location off to one side of the room or playground. It is designed to give children time to regain their self-control. It is not a punishment. Space can be designated by placing a chair in a taped-off square. When the child is ready, she can easily rejoin the group.

Keep in close touch with the parents. Change can take place daily, and knowing that a child had a "good day" may be the support a parent needs.

I once taught a little girl who was particularly disruptive during group time. I had a student teacher take her out into the hall whenever she acted up. Instead of decreasing, the disruptive behavior increased, and it began to occur closer to the beginning of group time. I decided to trade roles to see what was happening. The next time Andrea created a disturbance, I took her out into the hall. Once there, she told me to sit down, plopped herself in my lap, and said, "This is the book I want to read today." She then hauled out her book, and I read it. Now I knew why this child disrupted my group! The next day Andrea went to the hall with *no* book, and the student teacher was instructed to ignore her. The following day she sat through most of group time! The point of the story is, make sure your consequence is not rewarding.

Satiation is another way of dealing with inappropriate behavior. The child is made to continue the behavior when he no longer wants to. This is particularly effective for something physical, like falling off a chair. In one case I required a child to sit down, fall off, and get up repeatedly for twenty minutes! As you might guess, this behavior lost its charm when I not only encouraged but also required it. To discourage acts that are likely to be contagious in a classroom, satiation is far more effective than ignoring.

An additional method of stopping a behavior is to set up *incompatible alternatives*. I used this technique successfully with a child who frequently masturbated in class. After all my attempts had failed in discussing the difference between private and public behavior, reviewing my program to see if he could be bored, checking to see if his pants were too tight, and asking his mother if he had a rash—I changed tactics. I planned a program of messy table activities requiring two hands. It really is difficult to finger paint with pudding with both hands and masturbate at the same time!

Curriculum Adaptations

Children with learning disabilities usually require few adaptations. However, if you adapt your programs to meet their needs in the preschool years, chances are their problems can be corrected or at least diminished.

Language Arts: Speaking, Listening, Reading, and Writing

Communication is important to all children. Children with learning disabilities will find this a challenging area. Make it a positive experience. However tempting, don't resort to drill and practice as a method of teaching.

Speaking. Encourage children to verbalize their feelings as well as to communicate ideas. Provide them with the language when they do not have the words.

1. When possible, support children in their verbalizations with picture cues. Ask children to tell you about specific items in a picture. This helps focus their attention as they talk.

2. Have children name pictures and/or discuss what is happening in pictures.

3. Give children a sequence of pictures that display a familiar action such as getting ready for bed and have the children tell you what is happening in the sequence.

4. Give children pictures of the sequence of your day at school and have children put these in order and describe the sequence.

5. Play a sentence completion game such as "I draw with a _____." To make it more difficult ask other children what else they can draw with.

6. Play "Say What I Say." You can make sounds, words, sentences or "nonsense."

7. Follow up a field trip with a language experience story in which the children contribute. (If you have more than one teacher you might divide the children into two groups so there is more for each child to say. It can be fun to compare the stories.)

Fingerplays are great for children with learning disabilities. They are actively involved and able to learn through the kinesthetic/tactile sense. Also, hands that are busy doing fingerplays are less likely to be bothering the person next to them.

1. Use fingerplays to teach concepts where appropriate.

2. Quiz the children in a way that is fun but that also makes them think about what they are saying: For example, sing "Where Is Thumbkin?"

but instead of holding up your thumb when you sing "Here I am" hold up your index finger. Ask them what is wrong with doing it that way. Ask them for another word for thumbkin (thumb), pointer (index finger), tall man (middle finger), ring man, and pinkie. Can the children tell you how the fingers got these nicknames?

Listening. Listening is difficult, especially for children who are ready to move. Be sure you have the child's attention before you begin to talk. Make your statements short and to the point. Give directions a step at a time until children can handle more than that. Keep group times short.

1. Play games such as "Find the _____."

2. Play direction-following games such as "Put the block under the table," "Simon Says," and "Mother, May I?" Add steps until children can follow three-step directions. Don't eliminate children who make mistakes; they are the ones that need the most practice.

3. Play "Musical Chairs." Don't eliminate any chairs; this is a listening game.

4. Use sound tapes and have the children identify the sounds.

5. With the child blindfolded or looking away, have the child guess who is talking or where in the room they are speaking from.

Stories can be entertaining and enlightening for children or they can become totally frustrating. Children with learning disabilities are often the ones who hit the person beside them and are eliminated from the group for not listening—an unpleasant experience.

1. Keep stories short. It is better to read a five-page story that the children sit through attentively than to read a twenty-page story with twenty interruptions.

2. During group times you may want to use physical signals to help children organize their bodies as they listen. A carpet square or X made with masking tape may help. As children become more competent, replace these with verbal reminders. It is important for children to learn to control their body without these cues, so you don't want them to become dependent upon them.

3. Use stories that allow participation. Children can move the flannel board characters to follow the story.

4. Sometimes read stories in small groups, where you can individualize the story and your attention.

5. Choose stories that deal with hostile or unhappy feelings as well as happy ones.

6. Choose stories that deal with individual differences. (For suggestions see the Children's Bibliography on page 286.)

Reading. Because many children with learning disabilities will have problems learning to read, it is imperative to make language arts a successful and enjoyable experience for them at the preschool level. To be motivated to overcome their problems in this area they need to know it can and *will* be fun. Begin by building strength in reading readiness skills.

1. Play visual tracking games by having children follow a flashlight or pointer with their eyes.

2. Hide objects or pictures so they are partially visible and have children find them.

3. Play memory games such as Concentration with increasing numbers of cards. Use matching colors or shapes or a combination.

4. Have a set of wooden numbers and letters for children to play with. Encourage children to feel the letters and numbers and match them to outlines of the same letters. Start with letters that look as different as possible or those that have some significance such as the letters in the child's name.

5. Play sequencing games using picture cards.

6. Help children learn to observe detail. While taking a walk, have children think about all of the characteristics of a flower. They can do this both while they are looking at it and then from memory back in the classroom.

7. Encourage children to read by having a wide selection of books available on all reading levels including those that have no words.

8. Have a soft, quiet reading area that has some private space for children to get away if they need to but also to encourage looking at books.

Note: Children are expected to be ready to read when they are about five or six years old. However, many children with learning disabilities don't seem to be ready when their peers are. If this is the case, check that they have the prerequisite skills necessary. Use the activities in Part Four to informally diagnose at what level the children are functioning. You might even devise for yourself an informal check sheet to ascertain what skills the children have acquired. This way you can match your teaching to the children's level of skill. Challenge but don't overwhelm children with the necessary visual and auditory skills that are prerequisites to reading.

Writing. Most young children love to write until someone tells them they aren't "really" writing, or that they can't spell. They become discouraged and often stop writing. Seeing oneself as an author during the preschool years provides some insulation for the future.

1. Set up a writing center and stock it with a variety of writing instruments and a variety of things to write on. Talk about writing.

2. When you read books, talk about the author who wrote the book and the illustrator who drew the pictures.

3. Show children books that other children have written. If children say they can only scribble, support their efforts and ask them if they would like to entitle their book *A Book of Scribbles* as Ricardo Sanchez did. (It is important to get children "hooked" on writing. It is a necessary but usually difficult skill for them.)

4. If children want to write a book with words, have them dictate it to you and write it for them. They could also "write" it verbally on a tape recorder to be transcribed later.

5. Encourage children to "read" their book to others. Let them know that writing is a process that includes writing, editing, rewriting, and publishing. When children are not pleased with their work, talk about editing.

Discovery: Mathematics, Science, Computers

Children need skills to understand and organize their world. They need to recognize relationships, classify items, compare and contrast objects, and solve problems.

Mathematics. Helping these children at this age develop a sensorimotor experiential awareness of math will help alleviate future problems. *Doing* math, not just looking or hearing about it, is the key.

1. Use concrete objects to teach number concepts, and employ as many variations as you can think of. Use food (raisins, cereal, small crackers) for teaching these concepts: *same/different, numbers, sets, equal, one-to-one correspondence,* and *more/less/same.* (Somehow, children learn faster when another child is going to get "more" than they are!)

2. Provide running commentary whenever possible: "You've had half of your juice." "You have one cookie yet to eat." "We have two empty chairs at this table."

3. Create situations where children must come up with mathematical solutions: "What if you run out of large blocks and you need to make another wall the same length as the first?" Discuss relative length.

4. Play size comparative games with children: "Give me the big ball." "Give me the biggest triangle."

5. Play number concept games such as counting objects, naming numbers when shown the number, matching numbers to groups of objects.

6. Play games that match, sort, and select numbers, colors, or pictures.

7. Help children identify, construct, and predict patterns of colors or objects (shoe, shoe, sock, shoe, shoe, sock).

Science. Science activities may create enthusiasm in children with learning disabilities if a basic discovery approach is taken.

1. Use science to teach general information to children, such as the different forms of water (liquid, steam, ice), the concepts of floating and sinking, and so on.

2. Help them learn about the environment they live in and how it works.

3. Let children examine items (orange, cup, mirror) and describe as many details of the item as they can (color, shape, size, texture, function, parts). This is a great way for children to learn comparison. Two items may be alike in some ways and different in others.

4. Cause and effect reasoning is important. It may help children develop inner controls and curb impulsivity. Encourage children to answer questions like: "What happens if . . . ?" "What could you do about . . . ?" "Is there anything else you could do?" And then, when practical, have them test out their answer.

Computers. Computers have infinite patience, their energy is inexhaustible, and they don't get upset with children who forget what we thought they had learned. Some programs are even designed to support children as they get closer to the right answer or have increased their scores no matter where they started. Computers are under the control of the children who use them. They can be turned off or their plug can be pulled. This is empowering to children who are in charge of so little.

1. Computers can provide personal instruction to children at a speed they are ready to learn at and in a time frame that accommodates the child's attention span. Children can participate at their own pace.

2. Choose software that is compatible with the child's learning needs and supports his interests.

3. Although older children might profit from some of the drill and practice software in the areas of spelling and math, with younger children the idea that it is interactive and that they can learn cause-effect reasoning is far more compelling.

4. If you have a computer available, consider using Logo, a computer language that uses a turtle to draw graphics that the children design. They can also move the turtle through an obstacle course. Logo requires children to plan, estimate, compare, sequence, and visualize as well as use commands. The turtle does what the child commands.

It is a powerful learning tool for children with learning disabilities.

5. Becoming comfortable with computers at a young age is critical for children with learning disabilities. Computers can compensate for poor handwriting, they can check spelling, and as children get older, there are even programs that can analyze their writing.

Sensory Motor: Large Motor, Sensory Motor Integration, Small Motor

Children need to refine the movements of both their large and small muscles in addition to coordinating these muscles with information they receive from their senses.

Large Motor. Children with learning disabilities use large motor activities as a means of releasing frustration, tension, and anger. Participating in these activities with minimal conflict will help children develop feelings of belonging to a group.

1. Help children develop concepts of space and direction by having them pace off distances or see how far they can run in five seconds compared to walking or crawling.

2. Have children do variations on skills that they already know, like walking, jumping, throwing, rolling, and crawling.

3. Include activities that develop the lateral muscles of the trunk: crawling, climbing, and crashing. It is generally believed that children can't develop fine motor coordination until these lateral muscles have been strengthened. Therefore, it is futile

The children are developing their tactile skills and spatial awareness. They can be successful at this first-hand experience because they don't have to deal with gravity or balance—both of which can be problematic for children with learning disabilities.

to expect a child to color within the lines until the lateral muscles are sufficiently developed.

4. Help the child with a learning disability learn to use large motor activities as a tension release.

5. In a doorway, hang up an old laundry bag stuffed with pillows, scrap materials, or anything soft. Encourage children who feel like hitting to hit the punching bag (not just to hit once or tap lightly but as hard and often as they can).

6. Provide a large rubber ball for kicking. Encourage children to kick the ball and then run after it and kick it again, or kick the ball and try to hit a target like a bowling pin.

7. Help children learn sequencing by using the large muscles of their body. Design an obstacle course that children must do in order. After the child can successfully navigate the two or three obstacles in sequence, add another obstacle.

Sensory Motor Integration. The child needs to get information from the senses and integrate that information into motor planning to execute motor skills. For some children this is easy and natural; children with learning disabilities require practice.

1. Play "Freeze." Play music, and when the music stops the children must hold the position they are in. Don't stop the music for long.

2. Play "Hot and Cold." Hide an object and have the child try to find it by telling her whether she is hot (close to object), hotter (even closer), or cold (going away from the object).

3. Play "Do What I Do." This is a variation on "Follow the Leader" sitting still. You do something (clap twice, tap your head with one hand, and hit your thighs with both hands). The children imitate what you do.

4. Play "Follow the Leader."

5. Include activities that require children to use both sides of the body together, such as throwing or catching a ball or balloon with both hands, hopping or jumping with both feet together, clapping, and doing jumping jacks. (An underinflated beach ball is easier for the child to catch.)

6. Include activities that require children to use both sides of the body alternately, such as going up steps with alternate feet on each tread, climbing a ladder, riding a tricycle, walking a line or balance beam, running, walking, and skipping. Place a string in various configurations (straight, curved, with angles) and have the children walk on this.

7. Include activities that require children to cross the midline (the imaginary line through the center of the body, which divides it into right and left sides). When playing "Simon Says" request children to put the *right* hand on the *left* shoulder and

so on. Have children throw balls or beanbags while standing sideways to the target. Have them touch the toes of the opposite foot while standing. Don't force a child to cross the midline, and when doing these activities, focus children's attention on the activity, not on whether or not they are crossing the midline.

Small Motor. All young children need practice in fine motor skills. Children with learning disabilities should receive extra attention in this area. Because they are often uncoordinated, they may avoid small motor activities.

1. Pick some activities that may especially intrigue the particular child. If the child likes cars, provide a car drawing to color. (This to me is not creative art, but rather practice in small motor skills.) Provide a maze for small toy cars to follow. Have the child practice lining the cars up in specified patterns. Magnets can be used to attach metal cars to one another.

2. Have children practice the self-help skills of buttoning, snapping, and tying. Discuss the pride of being able to "do it myself."

3. Avoid small motor play if a child is having a "bad" day or seems to have excessive amounts of energy. One sweep of the arm can scatter endless numbers of small items all over the classroom.

Social Awareness: Social Studies, Inclusion, Health and Safety

All children need to get involved and interact with others. They need to form relationships with other children and adults. They need to be aware of ways in which they are similar to and different from others.

Social Studies. Social studies can be used to create awareness of other people and the roles they play.

1. Try setting up a "society" in your class based on the strengths and needs of the individual children: "Gina will take the messages to others because she is a good runner. Barbara will print the messages. Kenzi will call us all together because he has a good strong voice."

2. Emphasize group belonging and the courtesy extended to other group members, property rights, space to play, including others, and so on. Discuss how people feel when they are not included, their toys are taken, or their space is intruded on. Also discuss ways of dealing with these feelings.

3. Explore varied occupations such as plumber, computer programmer, baker, physicist, producer, professional athlete, and pest exterminator. Let the children's interest guide your choices. Be sure

to give a nonsexist presentation of occupations. (Check the Children's Bibliography at the end of Part Two for useful books.)

4. Discuss where different foods grow and compare fresh foods with canned or frozen foods. Introduce some foods that are from other parts of the country or from other countries.

5. Cook foods as a group.

Inclusion. Children need to feel part of the group. Help all children appreciate their uniqueness as human beings.

1. Help children become aware of the situational aspect of socially acceptable behavior. In the classroom there are rules that all children need to abide by.

2. Help children develop skills to be part of a group some of the time. Also help them develop the skill to be and do things alone.

3. Teach children to view events from a variety of perspectives. Increase children's awareness of the uniqueness of "self."

Health and Safety. This is an important curriculum area for children with learning disabilities, who, even at this early age, may have seen a variety of specialists, perhaps had an EEG, taken medication, and who may have some fears about health professionals. Because these children must cooperate in testing and report their reactions to drugs they may be taking, developing good rapport between children and medical personnel is important. Increase body awareness so the children can successfully locate body parts and then respond about how specific parts feel.

Other important health and safety areas need work.

1. As these children are more likely than others to become lost, teach them to state their name, telephone number, and parents' names early in the year.

2. Work on traffic signs and try to teach the children to control impulsive behavior that may lead to accidents.

3. Help children see the relationship between actions and results (e.g., what may happen if someone runs in front of a car).

4. State and post class safety rules, especially those related to situations in which children could be hurt (standing on chairs and tables, walking with scissors, throwing blocks).

5. When children initially engage in some unsafe practice, such as climbing the fence instead of the jungle gym, make your limits clear, but situational: "*At school* you may not climb on the fence. If you want to climb, you may climb on the jungle gym." Be prepared to reinforce this statement physically if necessary: Help the child climb down from the fence and walk over to the jungle gym with him.

6. Integrate food preparation into the curriculum through snack and lunch. Discuss nutrition. Help children learn about the relationship between growth, food, and health. Be sure to include cultural variations of "good food." Use foods that are familiar to the children, as well as some that aren't.

7. Suggest a variety of eating situations (picnic, banquet, brown bag lunch, bedtime snack) and have children predict what foods might be served at each.

Creative Arts: Art, Music, Creative Movement, and Dramatic Play

Creative arts provide an opportunity to practice motor skills as well as sensory motor integration without concern about the quality of the product. Children can practice skills in a safe place before using them elsewhere and they can learn more about the world they live in.

Art. For children with learning disabilities, the focus of art should be on the *process,* not the product. Leave them free to be spontaneous and creative. When they begin to feel that their work should "be something" or look like something specific, and the emphasis is on a product, the potential for failure is greater.

1. Use three-dimensional materials (clay, playdough). They can be good for releasing tension, and because they are reusable and easily stored, they are available on short notice.

2. Use large paintbrushes and finger paint. They require less eye-hand coordination than small brushes.

3. Be sure to use some art materials that accommodate expansive work: Color or paint on very large paper without restriction or use finger paint on the table, then print the pictures.

4. Colored marking pens are easier for these children to use than crayons, since either light or heavy pressure leaves an impression and looks fine.

5. Use squiggle pens with the children. They are battery powered, and the design changes depending on the strength of the battery, where you hold the pen, and how quickly you move the pen. The result is always interesting. Because of the vibration they provide unique muscular feedback.

Music. Music can contribute much to a child's physical, aesthetic, and intellectual development. It provides pleasure and creative experience, develops auditory skills, encourages physical development, and increases range and flexibility of the voice. There should be a wide variety of musical experiences: listening, singing, moving to music, and playing instruments.

1. Have a variety of different instruments available. Help children explore and evaluate the sound of an instrument when it is held and played in different ways. See if they can identify the instruments they know in a recording.

2. Incorporate music and language experiences; have children make up new verses to old songs. Play unusual instrumental records and ask the children to describe what they imagined while listening.

3. Put stories to music. Have children choose background music for stories.

4. Paint to music.

5. Have children make musical instruments (cigarbox guitars, coffee-can drums, wax paper and comb). As they participate in this process, they will gain an understanding of how sounds are made, where they come from, and how to change them. See if they can make sounds with different parts of their body.

6. Introduce concepts of pitch, loudness, and length.

7. Use songs with motions: "My Bonnie Lies over the Ocean," "Hey, Betty Martin."

8. Use songs that create body awareness: "Put Your Finger in the Air," "Head and Shoulders, Knees and Toes."

Creative Movement. Movement that is not judged on quality, but rather on creativity, offers potential to children with learning disabilities. Children can experiment with movement and their interpretation of what it should be like without judgment. Movement provides an opportunity for sensory integration.

1. Have the children walk through imaginary substances, such as gelatin, deep sand, flypaper, a swamp, or quicksand. Have the others guess what the substances are.

2. Combine music and movement to give children the opportunity to translate an auditory stimulus (record, music) into movement. Be sure to discuss the mood of the music and what types of actions this mood evokes.

3. Music can be used to release energy. If bad weather has kept the children indoors, play salsa or a Sousa march. Music also helps children settle down. If the children are excited before a rest period, help them relax with some "easy listening" music.

4. Encourage a feeling of group belonging and, at the same time, foster creative movement. Have children "hold up the roof." Children strain together to hold up the roof. They gradually let it down and then push it back up again. They can be ice cubes melting in the hot sun or a balloon deflating. Play "people machines," with or without noises. The children can do this all together or one at a time, slowly or speeding up. Repeat such creative movement experiences until the children are comfortable enough to experiment with their bodies.

Dramatic Play. Dramatic play allows children to try out roles and perhaps work through fearful experiences. It gives children the chance to be in control.

1. Holidays and special events are particularly stressful; play through some of these.

2. Because children with learning disabilities often have as much trouble expressing pleasure as pain, have them practice being happy and sad. Discuss how others know you are happy. Have the children pretend to open a package that contains something they really want.

3. Help children play through field trips, visits to the doctor, and so on. Discuss what could happen as well as what behavior is expected of them.

4. Encourage children to build structures for various climates and uses. Ask them to suggest additions they need to the construction area, such as fabric, dowels, netting, and so on to build their structures. Have them design:

    a house where it is hot and rainy

    a school where it is almost always cold

    a store where the temperature changes

Transitions

Transitions provide another opportunity for helping children feel the same as other children yet be unique as individuals. Be sure children understand what you want them to do during transitions, especially at the beginning of the school year.

1. Without being obvious about it, dismiss the child with a learning disability early in the transition—this should be thought of as prevention, not favoritism.

2. Use transitions to increase body awareness and feelings of being part of the group: "All children with brown eyes and black hair may *jump* to their centers."

3. Play the "I'm thinking of someone" game to dismiss children: "I'm thinking of someone with brown hair, brown eyes, and a plaid shirt! Yes, Lisa, you can get your coat."

4. Encourage knowledge of full names and addresses by dismissing children by last name, address, or phone number. (Not all children necessarily have a phone number, so you may want to ask parents if

there is a phone number for them to learn. Have them learn an emergency number for your area.)

Glossary

Attention Deficit Disorder (ADD)   A chronic inability to focus on an activity or subject for a long period of time.

Agnosia   The inability to recognize objects.

Alexia   The inability to read.

Auditory Perceptual Disorder   The inability to identify, organize, or interpret what is heard.

Behavior modification   A systematic technique for changing someone's behavioral responses to specific stimuli. *See* Conditioning, Reinforcement.

Central Nervous System Disorder   A disorganization of the brain and spinal cord system that confuses the sensory impulses transmitted.

Conditioning   A technique for establishing a specific behavior. The most common type used in education is instrumental, or operant, conditioning. When an appropriate behavior occurs, it is reinforced.

Developmental aphasia   Inability from an early age to use or understand the spoken or written word.

Distractibility   How easily a person's attention is drawn to extraneous stimuli.

Dyscalculia   The inability to perform mathematical functions, usually associated with neurological dysfunction.

Dysgraphia   Extremely poor handwriting or the inability to perform the motor movements required for handwriting.

Dyslexia   The partial inability to read or to understand what one reads.

Echolalia   The parrotlike repetition of words, phrases, or sentences spoken by another person, without understanding the meaning.

EEG   Electroencephalogram. A graphic record of the wavelike changes in the electric potential observed when electrodes are placed on the skull. Irregular patterns in an EEG are used to locate lesions in the brain.

Enuresis   Bed-wetting.

Hyperactivity   An increased or excessive motor activity probably due to a neurological disorder.

Hyperkinesis   Extremely restless behavior, communication, body movements, and so on (sometimes used as a synonym for hyperactivity).

Hypoactivity   A decreased or extreme inactivity in motor activity.

Information Processing Disorder   An inability to organize, interpret, and store information.

Laterality   An internal awareness of the two sides of the body. Usually there is a dominant side (left-handedness, right-handedness). There is concern about the relationship of laterality to learning disabilities.

Minimal Brain Dysfunction (MBD)   A neurological dysfunction in children who display "learning disabilities."

Perceptual handicap   The inability to integrate sensory information.

Perseveration   The tendency to continue in any activity, once it is begun, beyond its logical conclusion. This is caused by relative difficulty in shifting from one task to another or in changing methods to suit a change in conditions.

Reinforcement   The giving or withholding of a reward in order to increase the likelihood of a response.

Reversal   The tendency to read or write backward (*was* for *saw,* for example).

Syndrome   A set of symptoms that occur together.

Underachievement   Educational attainment below one's evidenced ability.

Children's Bibliography

See the Children's Bibliography on page 286 for books to increase children's awareness about disabilities as well as books that are especially good for children with particular disabilities. Note especially:

Awareness of Learning Disabilities

Body Awareness

Feelings

Friendship

Scratch and Sniff and Touch and Feel Books

Simpler Books (for teaching vocabulary and concepts)

Teaching Resources

In some situations you may want or need additional information. There are many national as well as regional, state, and local organizations that can be helpful to you. The following annotated list of national organizations should be useful in helping you decide where to get the information you need.

Association for Children and Adults with Learning Disabilities (ACLD)
4156 Library Road
Pittsburgh, PA 15234
(412) 341-1515
   ACLD is a nonprofit organization whose purpose is to advance the education and general welfare of children of normal or potentially normal intelligence who have learning disabilities of a perceptual, conceptual or coordination nature. They have conferences and write Newsbriefs.

Council for Exceptional Children (CEC)
Division for Learning Disabilities
1920 Association Drive
Reston, VA 22091-1589
(703) 620-3660
   CEC politically advocates for children with disabilities. The Division for Learning Disabilities concentrates its efforts on learning disabilities. They produce a journal and newsletters. They also have state divisions.

Council for Learning Disabilities
P.O. Box 40303
Overland Park, KS 66204
(913) 492-8755
   Publishes the LD Quarterly, *a journal on learning disabilities.*

Foundation for Children with Learning Disabilities
99 Park Avenue, 6th Floor
New York, NY 10016
(212) 687-7211
   Writes FCLD Resource Guide: A State-by-State Directory of Special Programs, Schools and Services *and provides direct financial assistance to various programs that aid children with learning disabilities and their families academically and socially.*

Learning Disabilities Association of America
525 Grace Street
Pittsburgh, PA 15234
(412) 341-1515
   Provides information for parents and professionals.

Perceptions, Inc.
P.O. Box 142
Millboro, NJ 07041
   Publishes a newsletter that serves as an information source for parents wishing to develop expertise in meeting the educational, social, and emotional needs of their child with a learning disability.

Research and Demonstration Center for the
   Education of Handicapped Children and Youth
Box 223
Teachers College
Columbia University
New York, NY 10027
   Addresses itself to the identification of psychoeducational characteristics of the learner with a disability and the development of instructional methods and materials which will be effective in bridging existing gaps between these learners and school tasks.

References and Bibliography

Adamson, W. C., & Adamson, K. K. (Eds.). (1979). *A handbook for specific learning disabilities.* New York: Halsted Press.

Ayers, A. (1979). *Sensory integration and the child.* Los Angeles, CA: Western Psychological Services.

Bloom, J. (1990). *Help me to help my child: A source book for parents of learning disabled children.* Boston, MA: Little, Brown.

Bos, C., & Vaughn, S. (1988). *Strategies for teaching students with learning and behavior problems.* Boston: Allyn & Bacon.

Brutten, M., Richardson, S., & Manzel, C. (1979). *Something's wrong with my child: A parent's book about children with learning disabilities.* New York: Harcourt Brace Jovanovich.

Bush, C. L., & Andrews, R. C. (1978). *Dictionary of reading and learning disabilities terms.* Los Angeles: Western Psychological Services.

Crook, W. G. (1977). *Can your child read? Is he hyperactive?* (rev. ed.). Jackson, TN: Professional Books.

Cruickshank, W. M. (Ed.). (1979). *Learning disabilities in home, school and community.* Syracuse, NY: Syracuse University Press.

Durkin, D. (1980). *Teaching your children to read* (2nd ed.). Boston: Allyn and Bacon.

Faas, L. A. (1980). *Children with learning problems: A handbook for teachers.* Boston: Houghton Mifflin.

Fisher, J. (1979). *A parent's guide to learning disabilities.* New York: Scribner.

Franklin, B. (1987). *Learning disabilities: Dissenting views.* Philadelphia, PA: The Palmer Press.

Hallahan, D., & Kauffman, J. (1991). *Exceptional children: Introduction to special education.* Englewood Cliffs, NJ: Prentice-Hall.

Hayden, A., Smith, R., von Hippel, C., & Baer, S. (1978). *Mainstreaming preschoolers: Children with learning disabilities.* Washington, DC: U.S. Department of Health and Human Services.

Kavale, K., Fornes, S., & Bender, M. (1987). *Handbook of learning disabilities: Dimensions and diagnosis.* Boston, MA: College Hill Publications.

Levine, M. (1987). *Developmental variation and learning disabilities.* Cambridge, MA: Educators Publishing.

McWilliams, P. (1984). *Personal computers and the disabled.* Garden City, NY: Quantum Press, Doubleday & Company, Inc.

Mercer, C. (1989). *Teaching students with learning problems.* Columbus, OH: Charles E. Merrill.

Montgomery, D. (1990). *Children with learning difficulties.* New York: Nichols Publishing Company.

Osman, B. B. (1979). *Learning disabilities: A family affair.* New York: Warner Books.

Silver, A., & Hagin, R. (1990). *Disorders of learning in childhood.* New York: John Wiley & Sons.

Smith, D. D. (1981). *Teaching the learning disabled.* Englewood Cliffs, NJ: Prentice-Hall.

Stevens, S. H. (1980). *The learning disabled child: Ways that parents can help.* Winston-Salem, NC: Blair.

Szasz, S. (1980). *The unspoken language of children.* New York: W.W. Norton.

Velten, E. C., Jr., & Sampson, C. (1978). *Rx for learning disabilities.* Chicago: Nelson-Hall.

U.S. Department of Education. (1989). *Eleventh annual report to Congress on the implementation of the education of the handicapped act.* Washington, DC: U.S. Government Printing Office.

Awareness Bibliography for Adults

Browning, Elizabeth. (1973). *I can't see what you're saying.* New York: Coward, McCann and Geoghegan.

A mother's account of the medical and educational history of her son's language disability.

Clarke, Louise [pseud. for Thelma Purtell]. (1973). *Can't read, can't write, can't talk too good either: How to recognize and overcome dyslexia in your child.* New York: Walker and Co.

A mother writes of her son's struggle to overcome a handicapping condition characterized by difficulty in reading, writing, spelling, and speaking. Mrs. Clarke gives a vivid picture of what she considers to be the social and economic implications of the untreated dyslexic.

Cohen, Martin E. with Barbara Davidson. (1975). *Bets wishz doc: A dynamic approach to learning disabilities.* New York: Penguin Books.

An informative book concerned with the education of learning disabled children. The book itself is divided into four parts: (1) case histories; (2) the defining of learning disability and perception training, and the explanation of an educational program; (3) a daily account of the program in operation at a private school; and (4) a section designed for parents providing guidelines for dealing with their exceptional child in the home.

Rimland, Ingrid. (1984). *The furies and the flame.* Novato, CA: Arena Press.

The story of a Mennonite woman who travels from the jungles of Paraguay to the United States to find an education for her son who has a severe learning disability.

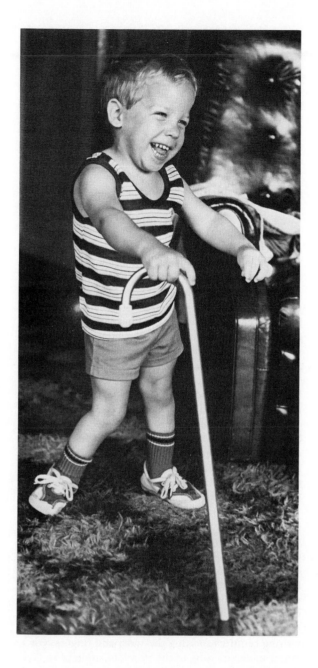

Chapter 14

Children with Physical Disabilities

All children want to move—for some it is easy, for others it is more difficult—but move they can and will in their own ways. While most preschool children can climb and run, children with physical disabilities may be limited to walking, crawling or scooting. Because of these limitations they may have different firsthand knowledge and experiences than their peers. They may show an unevenness in physical, sensory, mental, and social-emotional growth.

Each child with a physical impairment is unique. However, there are some common problems that affect all children with physical impairments, whether the impairments are long term—such as cerebral palsy, spinal cord injuries, and amputations—or short term—such as broken limbs. Obviously, the more severe the impairment and the longer it lasts, the more impact it will have on your programming. Physical limitations may interfere with school attendance and may require special equipment and educational services.

Classification of Physical Disabilities

In general, physical impairments are classified according to three considerations: severity of the impairment, the clinical type of impairment, and the parts of the body that are affected.

Children with a *mild* impairment can walk (with or without crutches, walker, or other prosthetic device), use their arms, and communicate well enough to make their wants and needs known. They may take more time to do things, but with adaptations, can in fact do what most other children can. Their problems involve mostly fine motor skills.

Children with a *moderate* impairment require some special help with locomotion and need more assistance than their peers with self-help and communication skills.

Children with a *severe* impairment are usually not able to move from one place to another without the aid of a wheelchair. Their self-help and communication skills are usually challenging.

According to figures from the U.S. Department of Education (1989) for the late 1980s, about 0.25 percent of school-age children, or about 100,000 children, have physical disabilities, some of whom have multiple impairments.

The actual name given to an impairment is often a partial description of it. The names and subcategories are usually only meaningful for those in the field. There are, however, some common terms that will be useful for you to know. Several are discussed later in this chapter; others appear in the Glossary.

Following are some terms often used to describe the areas of the body affected.

Hemiplegia: one side of the body is involved

Diplegia: legs more involved than arms

Quadraplegia: all four limbs are involved

Paraplegia: only the legs

Monoplegia: only one limb

Triplegia: three limbs are involved

Physical impairment can have a variety of causes—some of which are unknown. Lack of oxygen in the child's brain either while the mother is pregnant or during birth can cause physical impairment. Diseases that affect the brain, such as meningitis or encephalitis, or prolonged high fevers can also cause permanent damage. Poisoning and other conditions that lead to lack of oxygen in the brain, as well as head, neck, and back injuries, sometimes cause paralysis or abnormal movement patterns. Some chronic health problems like arthritis or muscular dystrophy may ultimately result in physical impairments, but, since such impairments usually occur only after repeated acute attacks, they are less likely to be apparent at the preschool level. (Chronic health problems are dealt with in the next chapter.)

Before explaining in detail the implications of various impairments, it may be helpful to look at movement in general. Knowledge of how we move and the importance of muscle tone in movement aids in the understanding of some of the problems encountered by children with physical disabilities.

In order to move, we increase the tension in specific groups, or patterns, of muscles. For example, if you are lying on your back on the floor and want to sit up, you will probably lift your head and shoulders first. You then bend your back and afterward your hips. (Try sitting up by raising your head and shoulders but keeping your back straight.) One reason why children with physical impairments have trouble moving is that various muscle groups do not function in coordination. These children need to learn to use alternate muscle groups as well as to gain more control over affected muscles.

With your back on the floor again, tense all of your muscles (make fists, squinch up your face, tense your legs, trunk, and back) and try to sit up. You will find that your movements are jerky and stiff and that you probably cannot sit up. Now relax. Let your arms become floppy as you pretend to be a rag doll. Try to sit up without tensing any of your muscles. That doesn't work either. The first situation will give you an idea of the problems *hypertonic* children have; the second will help you understand *hypotonic* children.

Some children (primarily those with cerebral palsy) have abnormal muscle patterns because of brain damage. The result is inefficient, uncoordinated movements. These children must learn compensatory patterns in much the same way that you discovered that when someone held your feet down you could still sit up by using other muscle groups.

Muscle tone is the amount of tension, or resistance to stretch, in muscles. "Normal" muscle tone is the condition of the muscles at rest. Children with high muscle tone (hypertonic) move with stiff, jerky movements. In some cases, depending on the exact area of the brain involved, a child's motor problems are compounded by faulty internal communications. The child may think, "Let go of the cup," but the brain does not send the appropriate message to the muscles in the hand for the child to let go.

Children with low muscle tone (hypotonic) may have problems picking up the cup in the first place. A child who did pick it up successfully may unexpectedly drop it later because it was held too loosely. Grasping very small objects is especially difficult for hypotonic children.

If children have high, low, or inconsistent muscle tone, you can expect that they have difficulty picking up and holding small, hard objects, screwing on paint-jar lids, turning the water off and on, and doing a different thing with each hand (for example, holding a music box in the left hand while winding it with the right). These latter skills require *rotation*, the ability to twist a part of the body. Rotation is of primary importance in learning to write because writing requires rotating the wrist and fingers. For a better understanding of the problem, attempt to take the lid off a container while keeping your fingers and wrists stiff. (Try handling all classroom materials and doing all classroom procedures with stiff muscles to check how difficult each task is for children with physical disabilities.) In general, hard objects are more difficult to handle than soft, small more difficult than large, and slippery more difficult than rough. Your awareness of the child's strengths and needs and your creativity and willingness to try things that are different are the key to good programming for children with physical impairments.

Common Physical Disabilities

Regardless of the exact diagnosis, general information on the child's muscle tone and ability to move is important both to your programming and your expectations. Here is some information on physical disabilities children may have.

Absent Limbs. Some children are born with deformed or absent limbs. These disorders can be the result of genetic or chromosomal causes, or environmental influences such as drugs or chemicals. When congenital, the insult usually occurs during the early gestation period when limb development occurs. Young children can also have limbs surgically removed because of injury or disease. Prosthetic devices are available to assist in replacing missing limbs. There is a difference in philosophy about the age at which children should be fitted with an artificial limb or prosthesis. Some believe that children should be fitted almost immediately. They feel that the younger a child gets an artificial limb, the easier and more natural the adjustment is. Others feel that children should not be fitted for devices until they are older, when they are better able to use the device, have better control, and can take better care of the device (Peterson, 1987). Regardless, fit is very important, in terms of both comfort and the ability to use the device. A prosthesis must be adapted as the child grows.

You need to have some basic understanding of how the prosthesis works in case the child needs help making adjustments, and so that you can plan activities that do not frustrate the child who must use one. Being accepted as a whole person is extremely important, so don't refer to this device as the child's *bad* arm or leg. If you notice abnormal postures or motor patterns developing, discuss them with the parent and physical therapist so that they can decide what to do. Exercising the joints nearest an amputation is important; ask for information about that as well.

Arthrogryposis Multiplex Congenita. Arthrogryposis is a condition that is present at birth and is characterized by stiffness of the joints. This usually affects both sides of the child's body and means that there may be little or no movement in the child's joints. This is caused by thickened joint capsules, shortened muscles, and decreased muscle bulk. The arms turn in from the shoulders and the elbow and wrist joints are very stiff. The fingers may also have little useful movement. The legs turn out from the hip and the hips are prone to dislocation. The knees and ankles have only a few degrees of movement. Long leg braces help the child who has adequate trunk control. A walker or crutches may be useful depending upon the child's upper body control.

Adaptive skills may be difficult for this child. Independent eating is hard because lack of movement in the elbows and wrists may make it difficult for the child to bring his hand up to his mouth. Some children become very adept and graceful at taking food from the plate directly with their mouth. When children use this technique, consider putting the child's lunch box or a plastic box on the table to

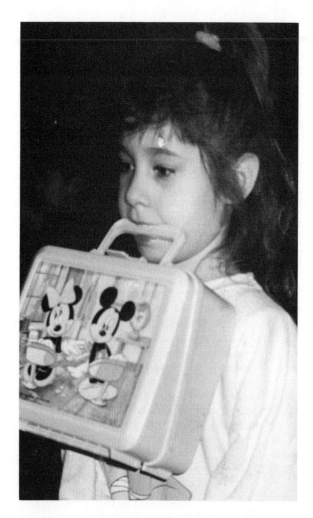

Adaptive skills are difficult for children with arthrogryposis; however, their creativity and persistence often supports their independence.

place the food at a more appropriate height. The child with arthrogryposis may also use her mouth to manipulate objects during play. Dressing and toileting skills may be difficult for this child.

As you assist these children, remember that not only are their joints stiff, their bones are osteoporotic—they tend to fracture easily. Keep handling to a minimum and when you do, do it gently (section adapted from Albert, 1991).

Cerebral Palsy. Cerebral palsy (CP) is a nonprogressive disorder, and there are no remissions. It is caused by damage to the brain before it is mature. Anoxia (lack of oxygen to the brain) and injury to the brain at birth are the most frequent types of trauma causing cerebral palsy (Peterson, 1987). Cerebral palsy, although primarily thought of as a motor impairment, is more complex than thought before and is more appropriately considered as a syndrome that can include motor impairment, psychological dysfunction, seizures, or behavior disorders all due to brain damage (Healy, 1984; Hallahan & Kauffman, 1991). Children are affected in different degrees, from very minimally so that it is hardly detectable to so severely the child has little control over his body.

Cerebral palsy is typically classified by the extremities involved (see page 220 of this chapter) and the type of brain damage with its subsequent motor disability:

Pyramidal (spastic). Children who are classified as spastic have limb muscles that are very tight and are difficult to move. Voluntary movements are often spastic and inaccurate. In this case the motor cortex or pyramidal tract of the brain was damaged. Spastic cerebral palsy accounts for about half of the population with CP.

Extrapyramidal (choreoathetoid, rigid, and atonic). Damage outside the pyramidal tracts results in abrupt, involuntary movement of the limbs. The muscle tone is variable. Some children have great difficulty maintaining posture (choreoathetoid), some have rigid, constantly tight muscles (rigid), and yet others have so little muscle tone they are described as "floppy" (atonic). About a quarter of children with cerebral palsy fall in this category.

Mixed. Some children have damage to both the pyramidal and extrapyramidal area of the brain and can have symptoms of both types (that is, rigidity in the arms and spasticity in the legs). Children with mixed types of CP also account for about a fourth of the population.

Cerebral palsy is classified medically based on the type and extremities involved; for example, a child might have "spastic quadraplegia." This means that the muscles in both the child's arms and legs are very tight and difficult to move.

New medical procedures are being developed that, in combination with physical therapy, have the potential for giving children more usable motion. For example, the selective posterior rhizotomy, a surgical procedure which cuts selected nerve roots below the spinal cord, allows some children to walk and others to walk more naturally (Dyar, 1988.)

Cerebral palsy, although difficult to determine accurately, occurs in about 0.15 percent of children (Batshaw & Perret, 1986). It thus affects about half of the children diagnosed with physical impairments. It is more likely in males than females, in whites than blacks, and in lower SES groups.

Many children with cerebral palsy also have sensory impairments, speech disorders, and mental retardation. Testing some of them requires sophisticated methods. Teaching can be a challenge. Consult with the parents and physical therapist to learn what activities the children can participate in, what kinds of

bowls and cups are easiest for them to use, and what special toileting procedures, if any, are required.

Because children spend a lot of time sitting, it is important that they sit in the most beneficial position. This is often not the easiest one. If you hold a child with cerebral palsy in your lap, have his legs straddle one of yours and hold him around the middle. If the child sits on the floor, cross-legged, or tailor-style sitting is not recommended. Have the child sit with his legs in front and together, bent at the knee if the child is athetoid, straight if spastic. The child with cerebral palsy already has abnormal patterns of movement that should not be exaggerated or reinforced. (See Finnie, 1975, for details and illustrations.) These children need a lot of practice to develop fine motor skills. You need to plan more time for them in this area than for other children.

Correctable Orthopedic Impairments. A variety of relatively short-term orthopedic problems must be dealt with during the preschool years to facilitate normal future growth. These conditions usually require surgery, bracing, casting, and physical therapy. The prognosis is generally good if the condition is treated at an early age. If not treated, orthopedic problems result in some degree of physical disability.

Bowlegs and inwardly rotated feet are common when a child first begins to walk. They are usually cured by normal growth. In extreme cases, however, braces and casts and/or surgery are used to correct the problem.

Clubfeet are usually treated with casts and splints and physical therapy, or surgery. Flat feet may be treated with arch supports.

Congenital hip problems result from improper fit of the femur in the socket joint of the hip. They are most often treated by a webbed brace, traction, cast, or surgery. Usually, hip problems are treated in infancy. In severe cases, they can have long-term implications.

The prognosis for these correctable orthopedic impairments is good, yet from the child's perspective the restriction of movement is frustrating and "mean." Some children need a lot of help expressing this anger. Prepare children for medical procedures; discuss their fears and feelings; help them express emotions while they are physically restricted; give them activities they can participate in; and try to explain the purpose of the medical treatment in terms they understand.

Muscular Dystrophy. Muscular dystrophy is an umbrella term for a group of chronic, progressive disorders that affect the voluntary muscles. The disease is inherited. The most common type is not usually detected until the child is a toddler and begins to fall down frequently due to muscle weakness. The muscles closest to the center of the body, those of the hip and shoulder area, are affected first, with the muscles in the fingers being affected later. The result is gradual weakness and decline in muscle strength and health. The child's intellectual functioning is not affected. The process, which can occur quickly or slowly, leads to increased disability and ultimately death (usually by age twenty).

We do not know how to correct the metabolic disorder or halt the progression of the disease. The earlier the symptoms appear, the more severe the disease is likely to be and the earlier death will occur. Toddlers will have a waddling gait, fall frequently and have trouble getting up, climb stairs with difficulty, and may walk on their toes. They will typically be able to walk during early childhood. As more muscles deteriorate and the child becomes weaker and more helpless, a wheelchair is necessary. The disease itself is painless. Once the disease has started there are no remissions and its progress over time is predictable. Patience and emotional support are an essential part of dealing with the everyday frustrations that face the child.

Children with muscular dystrophy have normal feeling in their limbs even though they cannot always move them (unlike a child with a spinal cord injury, who may have little or no feeling in the limbs). These children cannot hold on to you very well because of muscular weakness, so be sure you are holding them securely before you pick them up. Don't lift them under the arms. Because of weak shoulders the arms will fall through your hold. Remember that the neck muscles are often very weak, so support the head when going from sitting to lying. Make sure the child has side supports when sitting. These children often depend on armrests to help hold themselves upright. As children get older and heavier, get someone to help you move the child—a two-person transfer is almost always safer for a child with muscular dystrophy. Find out from the child's therapist the most advantageous way to move her (adapted from Temme, 1991).

Although too much exercise is painful, appropriate stretching exercises are helpful (be sure to consult the parents and physical therapist to find the right exercises). Because the child's physical activities are limited and added weight is an additional burden, a low-calorie diet is recommended.

Blowing and breathing activities maintain the chest muscles that are essential in coughing. Snacks and lunches should be planned with the child's diet in mind. At preschool age, this child looks weak, not ill, and hence may be made fun of. Work to develop both the child's self-image and peer relationships.

School, especially at an early age, is invaluable psychologically for both the child and the parents. The children pose few problems at this age.

Osteogenesis Imperfecta. Osteogenesis imperfecta is also known as *brittle bone disease.* The result of this condition is poor bone formation, that is, the bones do not form completely and as a result are short, thin, and prone to breaking. Frequent fractures exacerbate the condition, leading to additional shortening of the limbs compared to the trunk. Although the fractures heal quickly, there may not be good alignment, leading to the curving of long bones between the joints. Related problems may result, such as thinning of the skin, excessive joint mobility, and hearing loss (usually in adulthood). This condition is sometimes misdiagnosed as child abuse because of frequent hospital visits for fractures early in the child's life. The condition usually improves after puberty.

When these children are bright and verbal, ask for their input in how you can help them comfortably and safely. They will typically know and tell you. Encourage them to participate in as much activity as parents and therapists feel is safe. Emphasize fine motor skills, especially eye-hand coordination, and social skills. These children can have problems with constipation, so provide plenty of liquids. Excessive weight may also be a problem, so consider snacks wisely. The children may use some adaptive equipment with which you will need to become familiar (adapted from Albert, 1991).

Spina Bifida. Spina bifida is the common term for a condition in which the bones of the spine allow the nerves of the spinal cord to become tangled. The spinal cord is not closed or protrudes at birth or both; this looks like a bubble on the baby's back. Surgery is usually done within several days to remove the bubble and save as many nerves as possible. The severity of the condition depends upon the location of the opening on the spine. The higher the opening, the greater the area of the body that is affected. Higher spinal openings can affect bowel and bladder control. There are three types of spina bifida: in *myelomeningocele,* the most severe form, a cyst-like formation containing nerve roots and part of the spinal cord protrudes through the spinal cord into a sac at the spinal opening. Children with myelomeningocele frequently experience lower limb paralysis and do not have bowel or bladder control. In some instances the circulation of cerebrospinal fluid in the brain is blocked, putting pressure on the brain tissue itself. A shunt may be necessary to drain this fluid. A shunt consists of plastic tubing with a one-way valve that provides permanent drainage to relieve pressure on the brain. The shunt needs to be modified as the child grows since it may become too short or become infected. If you notice any changes in personality, if the child complains of headaches, stomachaches, or double vision, notify the parents. These may be signs of increased pressure on the brain.

Children with myelomeningocele are usually incontinent and, since they have no feeling, cannot tell when they are wet. Catheterization is the usual way to empty the bladder, which means the child may wear a bag and collecting device. When children are old enough, they learn to insert the catheter independently—but until that time, trained adults must perform the procedure.

During the preschool years, incontinence is not a significant problem because the child can usually just wear diapers. The parents and surgeons later make some decision about how to manage this problem.

Because of concern over urinary infection, it is often recommended that these children drink a lot of liquids. Children with spina bifida may have weight problems due to lack of movement, which must be kept in mind, along with the need for liquids, when choosing snacks.

The mortality rate of children with myelomeningocele is decreasing, which means you are more likely to see them in your classroom. Overall, it is estimated that they make up about 0.1 percent of the disabled population. This makes myelomeningocele one of the most common congenital causes of physical disability (Hallahan & Kauffman, 1991).

These children have decreased strength and feelings in their legs so special care must be taken to protect their lower limbs. Their bones are not as strong as they should be and prone to fractures. Be alert for things that might cause skin problems, such as water that's too hot, sunburn, insect bites, and so on. Socks should be worn in wading pools and shoes should be worn if the child is walking or crawling (adapted from Temme, 1991).

Meningocele is the term used when a spinal opening exists but the sac contains only the covering tissue (meninges). Generally, there are few motor-related problems. In *spina bifida occulata,* some of the arches to the spinal vertebrae fail to develop. There is no protrusion and no resulting motor problems. Spina bifida occulata may not be identified, or the problem may be identified only by X ray. These children require very little in program modification.

Head and Spinal Cord Injury. An increasingly frequent cause of physical disabilities is head and spinal cord injuries. This can occur from automobile accidents, falls off of a bicycle, gunshot wounds, or from other accidental causes. The effects of this injury vary widely and can include sensory, motor, emotional and intellectual impairments. This ranges from mild to profound and from temporary to permanent.

In cases where the cause was traumatic head injury it is important that the transition from hospital to school involves shared information. These children will typically have a difficult time attending for long periods, remembering information they had known before and learning new information. Their greatest difficulty seems to be in the area of the organization of information. They may also find abstractions and creative thinking challenging. The loss of skills that they could perform before, that other children their age are now easily doing, is a source of frustration. It is important to maintain very close contact with their parents and review their IEP/IFSP every month or six weeks during the early recovery period as rapid changes can take place.

Spinal Cord. Some infants are born with malformed spinal cords or conditions where the spinal cord deteriorates. If the spinal cord is not completely cut, some feeling may remain below the lesion, but in general, anyone who has a spinal cord injury is permanently paralyzed and unable to feel pressure or pain below the lesion. The ultimate effect of an injury usually cannot be ascertained with certainty for about two months.

The spinal cord is divided into three major areas (see illustration). Starting from the bottom, there are five lumbar vertebrae, twelve thoracic vertebrae, and seven cervical vertebrae—which are sometimes referred to as *L, T,* and *C.* The closer to the head, the more severe the injury. Each inch of spine or vertebra is important in bodily function (Travis, 1976).

If a child has movement in the arms and shoulders, work should be done to strengthen these, since future mobility may depend on them—ultimately the child has to learn to lift his own weight. Another important consideration is the prevention of pressure sores ("bed sores"). These seem innocuous, but pressure sore infections can cause death. Sometimes it takes weeks or months for them to heal, and they may have to be closed surgically. These children generally have poor blood circulation, therefore injuries are slow to heal and the children prone to infection.

Spinal atrophy is characterized by progressive degeneration of the motor-nerve cells, resulting in slow weakening of the body's muscle strength. The effects include skill decrease, fatigue, and decreased coordination. Congenital atrophy progresses rapidly, resulting in an early death. Acquired atrophy develops much more slowly, first affecting the legs and then progressing to the upper extremities. Because the child lacks feeling, be concerned about sunstroke, overheating, and frostbite. Insect bites may also occur and not be noticed.

Mobility

Regardless of the particular diagnosis, many children with physical disabilities use adaptive equipment for assistance in moving. Most children have a variety of mobility aids; some are very simple, others highly complex. It is important that you know the purpose of the equipment and the relationship among the pieces. Organizationally, the equipment starts with the child and what is necessary to implement independent mobility. It then goes on to short- and long-distance mobility aids. Because children use many different types of equipment an adult must often help them "transfer" from one to another or to the floor or toilet. (See the section on "Transferring.")

Braces. The purpose of braces is to support the joints in a functional position, that is, ready for use. In general, being upright is better for body growth, respiration, and circulation. Braces are all custom made by an orthotist (professional brace-maker). There are two basic types of braces: plastic and metal.

Plastic braces are lightweight and can be contoured to use on the trunk and legs and occasionally on the arms. (A child with scoliosis or cystic fibrosis may even have a plastic "jacket.") Plastic braces are

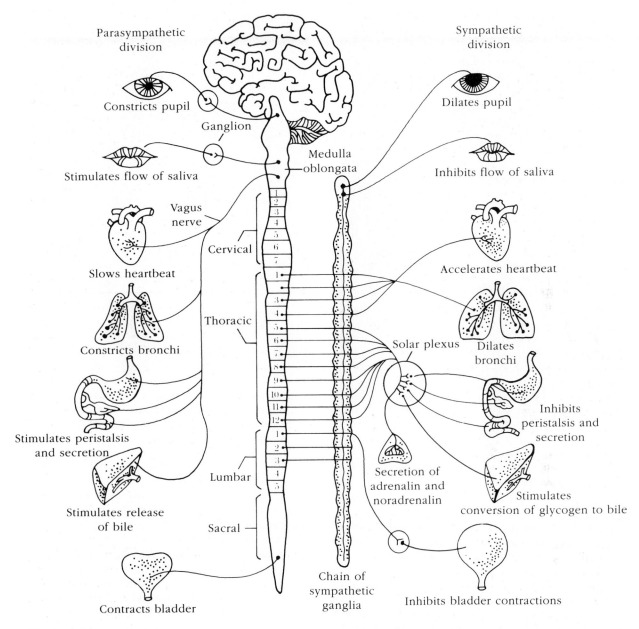

Parasympathetic
division

Constricts pupil

Ganglion

Stimulates flow of saliva

Medulla
oblongata

Vagus
nerve

Cervical

Slows heartbeat

Constricts bronchi

Thoracic

Stimulates peristalsis
and secretion

Stimulates release
of bile

Lumbar

Sacral

Contracts bladder

Chain of
sympathetic
ganglia

Sympathetic
division

Dilates pupil

Inhibits flow of saliva

Accelerates heartbeat

Solar plexus

Dilates
bronchi

Inhibits
peristalsis and
secretion

Secretion of
adrenalin and
noradrenalin

Stimulates
conversion of glycogen to bile

Inhibits bladder contractions

The Brain and Spinal Cord

molded to fit the body part and keep that body part in a position that is ready to function, as well as positioning it for better growth.

Metal braces for legs can be short or long. If they are long, they are hinged at the knee and have locks. Young children do not have the strength or dexterity to make these locks work. The first time you work with these locks you need to do it under the supervision of an occupational or physical therapist. (The locks require a lot of pressure to change. The pressure needs to be against the brace and not the child's body.) When the therapist demonstrates for you how the locks work, that is only the first step. *You* need to be able to work the locks. Ask the therapist to watch and coach you while you try. You need to be able not only to work the locks, but also to put the braces on

and off. (A child might get wet at the water table or have a toileting accident, and you would have to change him.) While the therapist is there, learn this too. Do it, and let the therapist coach you. Watching isn't the same as doing.

One of the things that you will notice is that the shoes of children in braces frequently look identical, and it may be difficult to tell the right shoe from the left one. Take your handy permanent marker and mark the right and left shoes. (Or ask the parents to do this.) Although the shoes look alike to you, they are individually fitted and feel very different to the child. If you have a child who is usually cheerful who is unhappy or crying, and you have gone through your usual repertoire of possible causes, check to see if the child's braces are on the appropriate legs. Molded

For children who wear long leg braces, the process of moving from a position where the knees are bent to one of walking is complex.

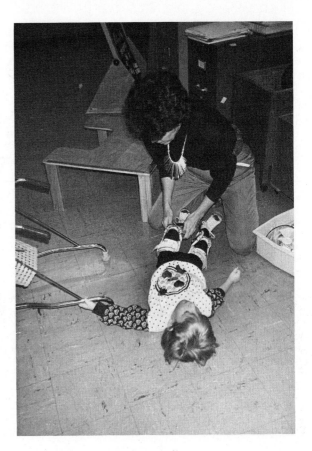

First the braces must be locked.

plastic braces are particularly uncomfortable for the child when placed on the wrong leg. On a hectic morning parents may make a mistake.

Short-Distance Mobility Aids. Walkers, scooters, and crutches are the most common mobility aids for short distances. Some or all of these may be in your classroom with the child, as they serve slightly different purposes.

Walkers are individualized to the disability, size, and functional level of the child. Young children often use walkers before they use crutches. Walkers provide a broader base of support. Children can use the walker for balance and get up to it independently before they can manage the same skills with crutches. The area inside the walker is almost a personal space for the child. If children need adult support to use the walker, place it out of the way when it is not being actively supervised.

If children can independently use the walker, it needs to be accessible to the child. You need to know the child's individual competence level with this, as with all pieces of equipment. Be sure to put a basket on a walker so the child can transport books, puzzles, and other items.

Crutches require much better balance than walkers. They are however, a more normalized system of transportation. They approximate a gait pattern that is similar to independent walking. Children might use crutches in therapy for a long time before they have them for general use.

Scooters are another set of wheels that children can use for independent mobility. Some are designed to be sat upon, others to lie on. Scooters provide children both independence and exercise when they don't have good sensation in their legs.

Long-Distance Mobility Aids. Strollers and wheelchairs constitute the most common long-distance mobility aids. For younger children, strollers are preferable. As children get older, strollers are typically replaced by wheelchairs.

When children are infants, it is fine to carry them. However as children get older, this is developmentally inappropriate, except for short distances or in emergencies. There may a period of time when children are too young for wheelchairs and too old to be carried. Specially made strollers are designed for this time slot. These strollers offer the child a little more positioning than regular strollers and are designed for larger children.

For young children a wheelchair can be thought of as a specialized source of assistance. It is necessary for fire drills, for long walks for which the child does not have enough stamina, and sometimes for seating. Wheelchairs are custom fitted to individual children

Then the child must move into a position behind the walker.

Then the walker itself can be used to help obtain an upright position.

by the occupational therapist, the physical therapist and a representative of the company that makes the wheelchair working together as a team.

Wheelchairs may be totally customized, or chosen from modular systems that are put together to meet the needs of an individual child. The wheelchair prescribed is based on the child's disability, the type of seating she needs, the level of independence, the child's age and cognitive ability, and how easy it is to get in and out of the wheelchair. Therapists are particularly concerned about the child's ability to position herself. If the child can't position herself well, the wheelchair will need more belts and padding.

All wheelchairs are different, and the expectations for the children who occupy these chairs differ also. There is however, one rule about wheelchairs that transcends types: Put on the brakes before anything else. And, when putting a child in a wheelchair, put on the child's seat belt before taking off the brakes. For your safety and the child's, get a lesson from the child's physical therapist on how to safely lift the child from a wheelchair, and where to put her after she is out. One obvious but crucial point: Before you take a child out of a wheelchair, you need to know where the child is going. The child can not stand there and wait for you to decide. In addition, you need to talk with the child before you move her. Say, "I'm going to take you out of the wheelchair and

put you on the floor" (if that is the destination). Except for very young children, you need to plan on two adults to transfer a child.

Young children should not be kept in wheelchairs in your classroom. They belong on the floor or in chairs like the others sit in (with modifications if necessary). Decide on a place to park the wheelchair, maybe in the hall outside. Use short-distance mobility aids in the classroom (walkers, scooters, or whatever meets the child's needs).

Transferring. Transferring is the term used when you move children from one piece of equipment to another. It might be from the floor to the toilet, the wheelchair to the floor, into or out of a cube or regular chair, and so on. In general, transferring requires two people. One person is in charge of the trunk area and stands behind the child, the other, the thigh area and stands in front of the child. In the case of *very small* children perhaps one person could do the transfer. In all cases, work with the therapists on transfers. The particular type of transfer that is most effective for the child and you will be determined and demonstrated by the physical and occupational therapists working with the child.

Warn children before you transfer them and tell them what you are going to do: "I'm going to lift you and put you in the wheelchair now." Enlist whatever

Once upright, the child positions herself and

walks to her destination.

assistance they can give you. A common request might be, "Keep your knees bent."

Transferring happens several times each day from different positions. Use the therapists' knowledge in this area.

Caution. It is imperative that you know a child's level of competence in mobility. If a child does not have protective reflexes, she needs the constant monitoring of a trained adult in all antigravity positions. Knowing the equipment is very different from knowing the child's ability to use such equipment (section adapted from Albert & Chadwick, 1991).

When you put children with physical disabilities with other children, you will find that the similarities are far greater than the differences. Other children will be astonished at their creative problem-solving skills.

Children's Needs: Teaching Goals

Related annual goals may be grouped under broad categories called "teaching goals." Outlined under each teaching goal below are the most important needs of children with physical disabilities. A child may have some or all of these needs, and additional needs as well. Suggestions on what you might consequently teach them are included. Often, a course of action is implicit in the description of the need.

Language Skills

Children develop language by interacting actively with their environment. To the extent that this first-hand experience has been limited, they may need more experiences to spur language development. Field trips followed by stories, both those written by the children about the experience and those written by others to expand the experience, may be necessary to develop a functional understanding of language.

Thinking and Reasoning Skills

Because children with physical disabilities are less mobile than others and may require more energy to carry out tasks, it is important that they learn to think about tasks before attempting them rather than use a trial-and-error approach. They must learn to predict how long it will take to cross the path to the swings if someone is approaching on a tricycle. They must develop cause and effect reasoning skills—for example, the sun may make their skin red even if they can't feel it. They can learn to prevent or slow down this process by using suntan lotion or by regulating the amount of time they stay in the sun. Help them develop problem-solving skills to compensate for things they may not be able to do. For example, have them think of how many different ways they can get across the room, paint a picture, or play with blocks. Encourage unconventional solutions.

Motor Skills

Most self-help skills as well as prewriting skills require small motor skills. These are essential for growing independence. Large motor skills and building up strength are necessary to learn to move from one place to another with crutches or a wheelchair. The children need more time to accomplish large and small motor tasks and they need practice, so be sure to schedule flexibly. Talk with the parents and physical therapist for help planning activities that will aid the child's development while staying within his capabilities.

Awareness

These children need awareness of their bodies not only to achieve a good self-concept but also to maintain health and safety. Children need to be able to assess what they can do physically. They must also be taught to notice sores on areas of the body that lack feeling. A full-length mirror in the classroom helps, and so do songs and fingerplays that use body parts.

Feelings

Children with physical impairments cannot do all the things other children can—or all the things they want to do—and this may result in frustration. Children need to become aware of these feelings and, since they have difficulties actively working them off, must learn ways of venting them. Help children learn the vocabulary to express their feelings. Talk about individual differences, stressing that differences are not good or bad.

All children need to feel that they are part of the group. This is especially true when physical distance from other children is sometimes required because of special equipment. Be sure to plan activities where children can move creatively as part of a group. Choose movements that the children are able to do, such as sitting on the floor, swaying to music.

Guidelines

School can provide a broader range of experiences for children with physical disabilities than they have had. Therefore, it is important to include these children in firsthand experiences when possible and to provide a wide variety of materials and equipment. Foster independence in any way you can.

1. These children learn early what others can do that they can't. To motivate them, give them tasks they *can* accomplish.

2. Be sure that they get to touch things as well as see them. Where necessary, bring things to them so that they too can explore.

3. If the child doesn't seem interested, demonstrate how things can be used. Some children really don't know what to do and are simply too shy to ask for help.

4. These children often have a self-concept that is in need of strengthening. Our society is a mobile one that values beauty and strength. Because body image greatly influences self-concept, these children need special help integrating body image into a healthy self-concept.

5. Work on developing language skills, especially those necessary to express feelings and to meet personal needs. Provide activities that help children release energy and work out feelings.

6. Help them establish a sexual identity. For some reason people with physical impairments are often treated as if they were asexual. An appropriate sex role identification is important to their development.

7. Keep in contact through get-well cards, audio tapes, and visits if the child is out of school for an extended period of time.

For children with physical impairments the classroom itself may need to be modified.

1. Provide ample space for activities, since crutches and wheelchairs often need extra room.

2. Use lighter equipment—this child may not be as strong as others of the same age.

3. Borrow a wheelchair or use a regular chair to determine how accessible classroom equipment is for the physically impaired. Check doors and passageways to be sure wheelchairs can get through.

4. Where possible, move sand and activity tables away from walls so that each child can get to them from all sides. Put materials on the floor; lower sand and water tables to floor level if necessary.

5. Be sure there are many different chairs a child can sit in. If necessary, modify a chair. Usually an abduction block—a chunk of something padded that the child's legs can straddle—will prevent the child from sliding onto the floor or add a seat belt. You may have to add a footstool so that the child's feet can be flat, but this should be done only at the recommendation of the child's therapist.

6. Temporary ramps may need to be added to help the child enter and leave the classroom.

7. Use nonslip floor coverings (no highly waxed floors or shag rugs). If you have carpets, be sure they are attached by a metal strip, so they won't slide and so children don't trip over the edges. Also make sure that toys are kept off the floor when not in use to prevent children from tripping over them.

8. Toilet cubicles may present a problem. They should be wide enough to accommodate the child in a wheelchair, with handrails to make the transfer an easy one. There are also many different types of potty chairs that are designed to solve a variety of problems. Parents and therapists will give you advice in this area.

9. Tables with legs that allow you to adjust the height of the table are particularly valuable. Some tables have tops that can be angled, which is also useful. If these are not available, a wooden wedge can serve the same purpose.

10. Shorten the handles on paintbrushes, rackets, and paddles to make them easier for the child with a physical disability to use.

11. For snacks, use deep-sided bowls instead of plates and two-handled mugs instead of cups. Serve a lot of finger foods.

12. Have bolsters, wedges, and beanbag chairs to provide a change for the children, as well as scooters to encourage movement.

13. Attach small bicycle baskets to walkers and provide around-the-neck carriers for children on crutches. (Knapsacks also work, but something in the front is handier.) Most wheelchairs can have their own trays.

14. Use larger versions of manipulative toys. Especially helpful are toys that have a built-in tolerance for error—blocks that fit together even if the child doesn't match them perfectly.

15. Remove equipment that is easily overturned.

16. Wagons are great for outside and field trips.

Curriculum Adaptations

The actual physical limitations a child has will determine the number and degree of adaptations necessary. In general, encourage the child to do as much as possible independently—but not to the point of frustration.

Don't forget that children change and grow. An adaptation that may be necessary at the beginning of the year may not be needed by the middle or end of the year. As you adapt equipment and programming for children, consider whether the adaptation is both developmentally and socially appropriate.

Language Arts: Speaking, Listening, Reading, and Writing

Language arts is a necessary and useful area for all children. It is a way of learning about other environments as well as participating in a group.

Speaking. Because children have physical limitations, they must rely on speaking to get some of what they need and to convey information to others. The ability to express oneself well helps compensate for lack of motor skills.

1. Use puppets to encourage expressive language. Have puppets that talk and move in many different ways. Finger puppets, as well as hand puppets, can encourage body awareness and the use of weak body parts. If the child favors one hand, encourage using a puppet on each hand and having them "talk" to each other. Sock puppets, or puppets on sticks that just need to be moved up and down, may be easier for some children to operate.

2. Expand children's utterances, especially when they use "telegraphic speech." If a child says "get doll," you might respond, "Which doll do you want me to get you? Oh, you want the one with the red dress." When children ask for objects by pointing, help them learn vocabulary by filling in the words they need. "That's the doll." However, if children are able to respond with only "yes" or "no," phrase your questions accordingly: "Do you want the blue one?" not "Which one do you want?"

Fingerplays are especially recommended because they encourage children to use both hands in a controlled fashion.

1. When you introduce a new fingerplay, encourage children to do only the actions at first, if they need a lot of concentration to follow those.

2. Keep the actions simple and slow enough for everyone to keep up.

3. Do variations, when you can, so that the children don't forget—and aren't always starting something new.

4. Many children with physical impairments have fine motor delays. Use fingerplays that allow the child to use the whole hand rather than just the fingers.

5. Remember that this child may need the help of a friend to make certain movements.

6. Fingerplays that require different motions with each hand are sometimes too difficult.

Listening. Be sure that books are stored in a place that is accessible to all children. Select stories that have a variety of characters, some of whom wear glasses and have disabilities.

1. Either have all children sit in chairs for group time or, if the class sits on the floor, and the child needs to sit a special way, be sure he does so at this time. Provide proper support for the child, if necessary.

2. Read stories and show pictures of children who are physically impaired, choose stories that

emphasize the senses the child can use. Present a balance of disabilities in your selections.

3. Use flannel board stories to help focus attention and to increase participation.

4. Add background music to stories to enhance the mood for children who haven't experienced the events described (circus music, waves breaking, and so on).

5. As you read stories, check the vocabulary for words children might not be familiar with. If possible add concrete examples to help children understand the story. For example, bring in types of seashells mentioned in the story to show the children.

Note: For children who have difficulty turning pages, get a specialized page turner. Also provide a listening center with headphones.

Reading. Reading skills involving listening and visual activities can easily be adapted for children with physical disabilities.

1. Field trips followed by language experience stories are good initial reading experiences. Help children establish the idea that you can learn about places by reading about them.

2. These children may lack experiences other children have had. Be sure that they can visually and verbally identify objects before you work on discrimination and other higher level skills.

Writing. Writing skills can present a challenge for children with coordination problems.

1. Children may need to start activities without tools. For example, have children draw with their fingers in the sand before giving them a stick. Have them write letters with their fingers before using a marker. Have children use two fingers, both their index finger and the one next to it, for these experiences.

2. The more variety you have in graphic materials and tools the more likely it is that children will find a match between what they want to do and what the medium will allow them to do. Also, children with physical disabilities may have had limited experiences, and the variety adds to their knowledge of the world. Use materials that have both dark on light and light on dark. Have a variety of sizes, shapes, and types of materials.

3. When teaching fine motor skills, have them use materials that create some resistance, such as a pencil used to draw on clay, so that the children can feel the resistance as well as see the results.

4. To teach prewriting skills, use activities that require finger and wrist movement, especially rotation. (Use, for example, activities requiring

children to lock boxes, screw bolts onto nuts, or twist jar lids.)

Discovery: Mathematics, Science, Computers

This area has potential for children with physical disabilities as the approach supports and encourages their development of skills for problem solving.

Mathematics. These children have been exposed to many concepts that are classified under the heading of math. They know something about time concepts: It may take them longer to do some things than it takes to do others. They know something about distance and how far they can go before they get tired. Math in school helps them quantify these experiences and build on them.

1. Children need to know something about the relationship between speed and distance: "I can go 20 feet (here to the door) as fast as I can and I'm tired. I can go 80 feet (the length of the room) slowly. It takes longer, but I can do it."

2. Measuring and weighing children helps them understand why braces no longer fit and need to be replaced.

3. Discuss shapes that roll and those that don't. Relate them to concepts like *brakes* and *moving*— round shapes are used for wheels; a triangular block of wood can be used to stop a wheel from moving.

Science. Science has great potential for children with physical impairments because it teaches cause and effect reasoning that is necessary for safety and encourages children to devise adaptations for their needs.

1. Magnets are fun and potentially useful. Attach a string to a stick, tie a magnet on the end of the string, and go fishing. Catch paper fish that have paper clip mouths. This activity is good for eye-hand coordination. Show children how they can pick up metal objects with a magnet attached to a stick. A child who is in a wheelchair can then pick up some things without needing help.

2. Work on simple casual relationships: "The faster I move my hands on the wheel, the faster the wheelchair moves. If I only move the right wheel forward, I turn left!"

3. Help children learn to use simple machines such as wheels and pulleys with ropes as a way of moving objects that they otherwise might not be able to move.

4. Use objects that vary in weight for sorting activities. Take a ping-pong ball, tennis ball, hard ball, empty cup, cupful of peanuts, and cupful of sand and see if the children can arrange them in

order. Discuss the relationship between an object's weight, the distance someone throws it, and the thrower's strength.

5. Use objects that vary in shape, size, and texture. Help children decide the easiest and most difficult to move.

Computers. Computers, too, hold tremendous potential for children with physical disabilities. Children need to be exposed to computers early and to think of them as part of their life. Computers can be used by any child who has control over one motor part, whether that is a hand, the big toe, or the tongue. Many computers are designed with adaptations that few are aware of. Call the manufacturer first to find out how easy adaptations will be.

1. Computers can and should be used by children with muscular, motor, and movement disabilities. Adaptations make computers accessible to these children. There are, for example, special plates that fit over regular keyboards. These plates provide a hole for each key, and a physical separation between the keys. This makes it more difficult to hit the wrong keys.

2. Computers can be equipped with foot switches and head switches. They can respond to the sip and puff straw or even the movement of an eyebrow. There are joysticks that can be operated by tongue or head movements. Because of the potential of computers for children with physical disabilities, they need to be part of their early environment.

Sensory Motor: Large Motor, Sensory Motor Integration, Small Motor

Children with physical disabilities must be given the opportunity to discover their abilities and challenges in the motor area. Allow children to use all equipment and participate in all activities normally provided in your setting, unless you have other directives. If there is any doubt, it's best to check with a child's parents and therapist to see if an activity is permissible. Specialists are one of your prime resources, too, for ideas on adapting equipment and activities.

Large Motor. Children need to develop good large motor strength, particularly upper body strength.

1. Supervise carefully. Children with poor muscular control are in danger of falling. Someone must be on hand to catch them.

2. In general, when climbing, children can climb down from the height they can climb up to. Don't assist children in climbing higher than they can climb independently.

3. If children can use equipment independently (get on and off a trike), encourage them to use it. However, don't assist them in using equipment beyond their skill level unless a therapist has requested this and gives you instructions on how to support the child.

4. Where possible have children work on vertical surfaces (chalkboard or easel) that are large enough so that children can use large muscles both standing and sitting. These are antigravity positions and are necessary for children to integrate the concepts high and low, up and down, and around.

5. If muscular control is unsteady, secure feet to tricycle pedals with giant rubber bands from an inner tube or with toe straps. (Check with therapist first!)

6. When you use toss games (beanbags, balls, ring throws), attach the objects to the child's chair with a string so that the child can retrieve them.

7. If the game cannot be otherwise adapted, allow the child to be scorekeeper with an abacus-like counter, attached to the chair if necessary. Instances in which a physical disability can't be accommodated should be rare.

8. A child with poor balance and motor coordination may increase his mobility if you have him push something as he moves forward, such as a toy carriage weighted with sandbags.

9. Mounting toys on walls at a child's height facilitates hand coordination, balance, and grasping. If a child needs practice standing, mounted objects provide the incentive and the opportunity.

10. The child in a wheelchair can participate with little or no difficulty in any game that requires sitting down. Tossing and catching are skills in which this child needs practice. Use soft balls of yarn or foam for safety. Balloons or underinflated beach balls are good, too. Scoopers for catching the balls in can be made easily from bleach bottles. You can use tossing games to teach concepts such as *over, under, low,* and *high.*

Sensory Motor Integration. Integrating information that comes in from the senses is critical. Try to give the children unusual stimuli as it helps them focus.

1. Use recipes for playdough that have different consistencies, smells, and even tastes. Support children in using their hands to poke, pull, and roll the dough before adding rolling pins and other tools. Have children use their whole arm to roll the dough. Encourage them to squish the dough between their fingers.

2. Make "Freddie the Frog" or "Katie Kangaroo" or some such animal from a large, limp beanbag. Putting this beanbag on the child's head and seeing how long it will stay there before it jumps off

Catching a ball improves sensory motor integration and helps children use both sides of their bodies.

is a fun way to strengthen neck muscles and to help children hold their heads erect.

3. Activities that require performing two separate motions or a different action with each hand are difficult. For example, a child's problems in holding a juice cup with one hand while pouring juice with the other hand can be avoided if you hold the cup while the child pours with two hands. Or have him hold the cup while you pour.

4. Buy or make a tetherball. Using a small table as a base, secure a thirty-inch pole in the center and attach a string. Attach a rubber ball to the string. The children try to wind the ball around the pole by hitting it with their hands or a paddle. This game can be played either sitting or standing. It develops the child's eye-hand coordination.

5. For children who have difficulty sitting, a sandbag shaped like a large worm placed around them (like the letter *c*) on the floor provides support.

Small Motor. For some children, traditional large motor activities are not possible. These children need to concentrate on fine motor skills as well as eye-hand coordination.

The ability to grasp, manipulate, and release objects is basic to using materials in the classroom and lifelong independence skills.

1. Magnetic toys are great. Use the front of a conventional teacher's desk for small group work, or for individual work give children cookie sheets with smaller toys.

2. Glue magnets to small toys and blocks such as one-inch cubes, parquetry blocks, and small "people" to make them easier for the children to manipulate. Use these on cookie sheets.

3. Blocks that snap together and those that are held together with bristles can be built into structures that are not easily knocked apart unintentionally by children with poor control of their hands.

4. Pegboard play improves the child's ability to grasp and aim, and to control involuntary motion. The size, number, and spacing of the pegs should vary according to the child's needs. Larger pegs are easier to grasp. Holes distantly spaced suit some children because children are less likely to knock over one peg when inserting another. Rubber pegboards are good for strengthening fingers because they offer some resistance.

5. Playing with popbeads helps develop coordination.

6. If a child has trouble holding a lacing card for stringing, you might use a stand-up pegboard or a piece of cardboard that is perpendicular to the table (and therefore does not require wrist rotation). (Pasting pictures on cardboard helps to make them sturdier.) Reinforce the end of the string with tape or glue so that it is stiff, or use colored shoelaces knotted at one end.

7. Use index cards or old greeting cards for cutting. They are stiffer and easier for children to handle.

8. Use flat, firm shapes such as cardboard or poster board with large holes for stringing. (The string comes through the hole faster and more easily.)

9. Clothespins that must be squeezed to open can be put around the edge of a can or used to hang up doll clothes. Their use develops necessary finger strength.

10. Puzzle pieces that have knobs are easier to insert and remove. Start with shapes that go in easily, for example, a circle before an octagon.

11. Get special scissors such as easy-grip loop scissors (they have a squeezable loop instead of finger holes) or scissors with four holes so that you can help the child cut.

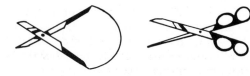

12. Have children stick objects in and take them out of clay and playdough—cookie cutters and rolling pins work well for this.

13. Use a pipe cleaner instead of a shoelace to string beads.

Social Awareness: Social Studies, Inclusion, Health and Safety

Children need to learn about the larger world and be part of it. They need both information and skills.

Social Studies. Community awareness is important for children with physical disabilities. Start by familiarizing the children with their immediate environment.

1. Get children out into the community so their knowledge is firsthand.

2. If you are doing a unit on transportation, include wheelchairs, crutches, walkers, and so on in your discussion.

3. Help children personalize their equipment. Wheelchairs can be decorated with license nameplates, bicycle bells, or horns and streamers. Walkers may be painted (with parents' permission) or wrapped with ribbon. Casts can be decorated with marking pens or paints.

4. Have appropriate community visitors (i.e., those who play a role in this child's life: osteopath, physical therapist, social worker, surgeon, neurologist).

Inclusion. Find out from the parents what they have told their child about her disability. Many parents do not talk with children about this, or give children the impression that there is a "cure" for what they have and that when they grow up the disability will be gone. It is important that children integrate their abilities and disabilities into their self-concept in a positive way.

1. Children need to talk about the feelings they have about their disability. Be a good listener.

2. Help children acknowledge obvious limitation, yet see other areas as challenges.

3. Talk about their role as part of the group, what they do to help others and what others do to help them.

Health and Safety. Health and safety are especially important for children with physical impairments, and can make a difference not only to them but to other children and to the teacher.

1. Teach children to put crutches or other aids in a place where others won't trip over them.

2. Help children learn to take care of bruises and scrapes and to spot pressure sores.

3. Be sure the child is familiar with the procedures and the routes to be taken during safety drills. Have your own drills in preparation for the official ones.

4. Keep extra boxes of tissues around for children to use and trash cans that are easy to get to. Distance makes a difference.

5. Children need to sit in chairs with their bottom at the back of the chair. At this point put the seat belt on, if necessary. It goes around the hips, not the waist. Check that the knees are at 90 degrees and the feet are on the floor also at 90 degrees. Elbows should rest gently on the table.

6. As a teacher you will do caregiving for these children. You need to practice good hygiene. Wash your hands after toileting, and so on.

Creative Arts: Art, Music, Creative Movement, and Dramatic Play

Creative arts offer a safe way to learn about the world. As the emphasis is on the process and creativity, all products are acceptable.

Art. Children with poor muscular control of arms and hands often find art difficult and discouraging. Others with better control may find it a release.

1. Choose activities that require two hands, like fingerpainting and modeling playdough. Encourage children to use both hands as a way of building strength.

2. Tape drawing paper to the table so that children can concentrate on what they are putting on the paper, not the paper itself. Or use Dycem. (Dycem is a plastic-like sheet that is tacky enough to hold objects where they are placed. (Put Dycem on the table at snack time so that plates and utensils stay where they are placed. Also use it to keep papers and other objects from moving around. When it becomes less tacky put it on the chair bottom to keep children from slipping off. (Source for Dycem at end of chapter.)

3. Use marking pens. They require little pressure, are easy to grip, and are colorful. Build up thin ones with masking tape or place sponge hair curlers around them so that they are easier to use.

4. Adapt other drawing materials where necessary. For easier gripping, use large pieces of chalk, push pens or pencils through rubber balls, and insert crayons wrapped in paper into roll-on deodorant bottles (with the ball removed).

5. Make paint jars easier to handle: Put a thick rubber band (or a thin sheet of foam or sponge) around them, and glue sandpaper on the lids.

6. Use extra large easels and paper. Adjustable easels allow children many options for working.

7. Paint large objects, like boxes.

8. Outside, have the child "paint" the sidewalk with a bucket of water and a broom (if the child is in a wheelchair) or large brush.

9. Make clay, varying the moisture to meet the strength and motor skills of the child (the moister the clay, the easier to manipulate). Encourage the use of a rolling pin or blunt knife as well as hands to mold clay. If you want, allow the clay to dry out, and fire it. It is then ready for painting. Be sure to allow adequate time for exploration. This activity will help build strength and coordination.

10. Don't make models for children. Support their attempts to control the medium, not the final product.

Music. Use music to increase body awareness and encourage movement. Music can also be used to teach concepts.

1. Sing the song "Put Your Finger in the Air" and substitute words for *finger* and *air*. Be sure to take into account the abilities of the children as you adapt this song. Some variations might be: nose on your shoulder, tongue on your lip, and wrist on your cheek. Other songs also teach body awareness.

2. Have children play rhythm instruments in an informal way to create a mood. This is a nondemanding way for children to be part of a group.

3. Activities that require two hands to be coordinated—such as clapping—are good practice, but may be difficult, so go slowly.

4. If a child has difficulty holding on to specific instruments, adapt them. On finger cymbals, have elastic attachments that go around the hand rather than knobs. If a child cannot hold a stick to tap a xylophone, have the child wear a mitten with Velcro in the palm and glue Velcro to the stick. Weight down objects like drums or xylophones with beanbags to help them stay in one place.

5. Use short, fat, round sticks to hit together or with the xylophone or triangle, or adapt the sticks as you did the paintbrushes.

Creative Movement. Creative movement is just that, creative. Help children see the creative quality to movement. This involves not judging the quality of the movement, but the right of individuals to interpret creatively.

1. Allow for individual differences and creativity. Make your suggestions in relation to the child's abilities.

2. Isolate movements, based on children's ability. Have them move their eyes creatively, or arms, or whatever you decide.

Dramatic Play. Children can use this type of activity to play different roles as well as to express fears and concerns. They need to learn to use dramatic play to acknowledge and act out their feelings. They cannot "run it off," and feelings that are denied eventually take a toll.

1. Help other children become more aware of the problems of being in a wheelchair or on crutches by having these available for the children to play with. These should be borrowed implements, not the child's.

2. Play hospital with casting tape (available in most drugstores). Have children cast dolls' legs or their fingers (use blunt-nosed scissors to cut the casts off).

3. Use a full-length mirror to encourage children to explore their individual characteristics. Be sure to show children how you use the mirror to see parts of you that are difficult to see otherwise. (Put a dot or a cutout on each child's back and have him try to see it in the mirror.)

4. You may have to demonstrate how to play some roles initially as children may not have been exposed to them and may not know what to do. Your role is a coach. You can't play the game for the children, but you can encourage them, spot them, model how to do it, and teach them techniques. In addition to having had fewer experiences, they process less visual and kinesthetic input. They need verbal support and feedback.

5. If children are likely to use equipment to pull up on, such as a stove in the housekeeping area, weigh it down with sandbags so it doesn't fall on the child.

Transitions

Transitions are often confusing. Be sure these children know where they are going and for what purpose.

1. Use transitions to teach simple concepts, such as color or clothing texture.

2. Because these children need more time to move around, dismiss them no later than the middle of the transitional activity.

3. Always tell the children what you are planning to do *before* you begin doing it. If you simply lift them onto the rug, for example, they may become frightened at suddenly being taken out of a secure position. Even if they have limited speech, talk to them, and make them aware of any change about to take place.

Glossary

Abduction   The movement of the limbs away from the middle (midline) of the body.

Adduction   The movement of the limbs toward the center (midline) of the body.

Asymmetry   Inequality of the two sides of the body. One side may be stronger and larger.

Ataxia   Primarily a balance and motor coordination problem. These children have a characteristic high-stepping walk, fall frequently, and are a bit unsteady (as if drunk). Eye coordination problems are common.

Athetosis   A condition in which the muscles move involuntarily. Thus children with athetosis are able to get their hand to their mouth, but they may go through a variety of unnecessary uncontrollable movements to get it there. During rest, these children show no abnormal behaviors. The more excited or upset the children become, the less control they have.

Atrophy   The deterioration of muscle or nerve cells. They become smaller and weaker through disuse. Atrophy may result from wearing a cast or from a child's desire for voluntary inactivity to avoid pain.

Cerebral Palsy   A condition that affects the motor system of the body as a result of lesions in the brain. There are many different types of cerebral palsy depending on the size and location of the lesion.

Chiropodist   A specialist in foot disorders.

Contracture   Permanent tightness of muscles and joints that limits their full range of motion.

Cyanosis   A bluish tinge to the skin caused by lack of oxygen in the blood. The tinge is most easily seen in the lips and fingernails.

Deformities   The body or limbs are fixed in abnormal positions.

Equilibrium   Sense of balance.

Extension   The straightening of any part of the body.

Flaccid   Body postures or movements lacking normal firmness. Also described as "floppy."

Flexion   The bending of any part of the body.

Hydrocephalus   A condition in which the buildup of spinal fluid in the brain causes pressure on the brain cells. Unless the fluid is drained, permanent damage will occur.

Hypertonic   Having high or increased muscle tension (similar to tightness and stiffness).

Hypotonic   Having low or decreased muscle tension. Standing and walking is difficult because the muscles are not tense enough to combat gravity.

Midline   An imaginary dividing line that runs vertically through the center of the body.

Neurologist   A physician who specializes in the nervous system.

Occupational therapy   Prescribed activities designed to restore, reinforce, and facilitate fine motor skills that are important in self-help.

Oral surgeon   A physician who specializes in surgery of the mouth.

Orthopedically impaired   Having a severe orthopedic impairment that adversely affects educational performance (as defined by PL 94-142). The term includes impairments caused by congenital anomaly, disease, and other causes, such as fractures or burns that cause contractures.

Osteopath   A physician who specializes in the musculo-skeletal system. He or she uses mechanical manipulation, medicine, and surgery to correct malfunctions.

Paralysis, forms of

Diplegia. The whole body is paralyzed, but the legs more than the arms. Diplegic children usually have some head control and moderate to slight paralysis of the upper limbs. Speech can be affected. This term is primarily used with cerebral palsy.

Hemiplegia. Paralysis of the upper and lower extremity on the same side of the body. In cerebral palsy, hemiplegics are usually of the spastic type.

Monoplegia. Only one arm, or, less frequently, only one leg is affected.

Paraplegia. Lower extremities are involved. Paraplegics are commonly found amoung spinal injuries and spina bifida and rarely found in cerebral palsy.

Quadraplegia. Paralysis of all four limbs. Head control may be poor and, in cerebral palsy, there is usually impairment of speech and eye coordination. With spinal cord injuries, speech is often not affected.

Triplegia. This condition involves three extremities, usually both lower extremities and one arm. It may also be a combination of paraplegia and hemiplegia.

Passive therapy   Therapy done without the child's help.

Physical therapy   Prescribed activities or exercises designed to restore, reinforce, and teach compensatory large motor skills.

Physiotherapy   The treatment of movement disorders by physical, mechanical, and electrical means. (Part of physical therapy.)

Podiatrist   A specialist in foot disorders.

Range of motion   The normal range, measured in degrees, within which any joint can be moved.

Righting   The ability to return one's head and body to normal and natural positions from abnormal or uncomfortable ones.

Rigidity   A condition in which the muscles involuntarily resist each other and the limbs become stiff and difficult to move.

Shunt   A plastic tube inserted in the brain that redirects excessive cerebrospinal fluid into the peritoneal cavity. This helps prevent retardation. The shunt must be lengthened as the child grows.

Spasticity Jerky, uncontrollable movements caused by an obstruction in the brain that suppresses certain nerve impulses, resulting in an imbalance between opposing muscle groups.

Spina bifida A condition in which the spinal cord is not closed or protrudes at birth. The degree of severity varies from bowel and bladder dysfunction to paralysis below the waist.

Tremor A type of cerebral palsy similar to the spastic type. While motor control is better, there is an involuntary, vibrating, rhythmic motion to the muscles. This is usually most obvious in the hands.

Children's Bibliography

See the Children's Bibliography on page 286 for books to increase children's awareness about disabilities as well as books that are especially good for children with particular disabilities. Note especially:

> Awareness of Physical Disabilities
>
> Body Awareness
>
> Doctors and Hospitals
>
> Feelings
>
> Friendship
>
> Simpler Books (for teaching vocabulary and concepts)

Teaching Resources

In some situations you may want or need additional information. There are many national as well as regional, state, and local organizations that can be helpful to you. The following annotated list of national organizations should be useful in helping you decide where to get the information you need.

March of Dimes Birth Defects Foundation
1275 Mamaroneck Avenue
White Plains, NY 10605
(914) 428-7100
   Sponsors research, but also provides current information on the latest research in the field.

The National Easter Seal Society for Crippled Children
   and Adults
2023 West Ogden Avenue
Chicago, IL 60612
   Administrative headquarters for Easter Seals affiliates that operate direct service programs for handicapped children and adults. They treat speech, hearing, and related disorders; learning disorders; and psychological disorders, in addition to physical ones.

National Head Injury Foundation
Turnpike Road
Southborough, MA 01772
   Provides information about teaching children who have had a traumatic brain injury.

National Rehabilitation Association
1522 K Street, N.W.
Washington, DC 20005
   Encourages an interdisciplinary approach. Interested in increasing public understanding of the physically and mentally handicapped.

Parents Campaign for Handicapped Children
   and Youth
Closer Look
Box 1492
Washington, DC 20013
   Provides information in a free newsletter about educational programs and special services to parents and professionals who work with physically, mentally, and emotionally handicapped children.

Services for Crippled Children
U.S. Department of HEW
Bureau of Community Health Services
Rockville, MD 20852
   Provides information about programs available for physically impaired children.

United Cerebral Palsy Association, Inc.
66 East 34th Street
New York, NY 10016
   National headquarters. Provides guidance and services to affiliates and supports extensive medical research programs.

References and Bibliography

Albert, R. (Personal correspondence, December, 1991).

Albert, R., & Chadwick, M. (Personal interview, December, 1991).

Batshaw, M., & Perret, Y. (1986). *Children with handicaps: A medical primer.* Baltimore, MD: Paul H. Brookes.

Blackman, J. (Ed.). (1984). *Medical aspects of developmental disabilities in children birth to three* (rev. ed.). Rockville, MD: Aspen.

Dyar, S. (1988). A step in the right direction. *Helex: The University of Virginia Health Sciences Quarterly, 6*(3), 5–11.

Finnie, N. (1975). *Handling the young cerebral palsied child at home* (2nd ed.). New York: E. P. Dutton.

Hallahan, D., & Kauffman, J. (1991). *Exceptional children: Introduction to special education.* Englewood Cliffs, NJ: Prentice-Hall.

Healy, A. (1984). Cerebral palsy. In J. Blackman (Ed.). (rev. ed.), *Medical aspects of developmental disabilities in children birth to three* (pp. 31–37). Rockville, MD: Aspen.

Temme, D. (Personal correspondence, December, 1991).

Travis, G. (1976). *Chronic illness in children: Its impact on child and family.* Stanford, CA: Stanford University Press.

National Head Injury Foundation. (1988). *An educator's manual: What educators need to know about students with traumatic brain injury.* Southborough, MA.

U.S. Department of Education. (1989). *Eleventh annual report to Congress on the implementation of education of the handicapped act.* Washington, DC: U.S. Government Printing Office.

Awareness Bibliography for Adults

Baker, Louise. (1946). *Out on a limb.* New York: McGraw-Hill.

A humorous and practical autobiographical account by an amputee of her adjustment problems and her experiences with crutches, an artificial leg, and a peg leg.

Brown, Christy. (1970). *Down all the days.* New York: Stein and Day.

A novel written by a man with cerebral palsy. He traces growing up as one of a family with twenty-two children living in a Dublin slum. He typed the manuscript of this novel with one left toe.

Carlson, Earl R. (1941). *Born that way.* New York: John Day.

The autobiography of Earl Carlson, who, despite his own cerebral palsy, became a doctor specializing in treating others with that disability.

Eareckson, Joni, & Musser, Joe. (1980). *Joni.* Grand Rapids, MI.: Zondervan.

Autobiography of a girl who becomes a quadraplegic from a diving accident.

Eareckson, Joni, & Estes, Steve. (1980). *A step further.* Grand Rapids, MI.: Zondervan.

A sequel to *Joni,* her further trials and triumphs.

Joel, Gil S. (1975). *So your child has cerebral palsy.* Albuquerque, NM: University of New Mexico Press.

Written by a man who has cerebral palsy, focuses on parent's reaction and feelings and gives advice.

Killilea, Marie. (1963). *Karen.* Englewood Cliffs, NJ: Prentice-Hall.

A mother's story of the life and upbringing of her cerebral palsied daughter.

Killilea, Marie. (1980). *With love from Karen.* New York: Dell.

Another book about Karen.

Marx, Joseph Lawrence. (1974). *Keep trying.* New York: Harper & Row.

This practical story, about and for the physically handicapped, is written by a man who had polio as an infant and who has since led a full and active life.

Neufield, John. (1970). *Twink.* New York: New American Library.

A story of a sixteen-year-old girl with cerebral palsy, told for the most part by her sister and mother.

Russell, Harold. (1949). *Victory in my hands.* New York: Creative Age Press.

A young man's adjustments after an explosion in which both his hands were blown off. It is an absorbing chronicle of the emotional obstacles he faced and conquered.

Viscardi, Henry, Jr. (1975). *The phoenix child.* New York: P.S. Eriksson.

The true story of Darren, a black orphan child with severe facial deformities, and the Human Resource Center on Long Island, which educates severely disabled children who cannot attend neighborhood schools.

HBO Video (1990). *My Left Foot,* 103 minutes.

The story of Christy Brown, who has cerebral palsy, and how he used his left foot to type and paint. It details his growing up and how the family coped.

Chapter 15

Children with Health Impairments

Everybody is sick some of the time. So what makes a health impairment different from a cold? A health impairment interferes with normal growth and development, it continues for a long time, and it is likely to have a prolonged convalescence.

Health impairment can be defined on two levels: categorical and functional. The categorical definition determines whether the condition falls within stated guidelines; the functional definition looks specifically at the child and how she is affected. In most cases the categorical definition is used for reporting purposes and the functional definition for programming.

Unlike other disabilities which directly affect the child's ability to gain or process information, health impairments interfere with the child's learning by decreasing the body's energy, its ability to remove waste, or its ability to grow. Some health impairments shorten the life span, others do not. All are potentially life-threatening. Almost all have periods of activity and remission. In some cases, the condition is progressive, getting increasingly worse, or it weakens other body systems, making the child more susceptible to other illnesses.

Estimates are that 1 to 2 percent of the children in the United States (at least one million children) have *severe* chronic illnesses (Hobbs, Perrinn, Ireys, Moynahan, & Shayne, 1984). This population appears to be increasing probably because of better identification procedures and medical services to selected populations. However, overall health programs designed to meet these children's ongoing needs are not increasing. Although their disabilities are different, children with health impairments have the following characteristics in common.

They will miss more school, spend more time convalescing at home, and be in the hospital more frequently than most other children. The repeated separation and trauma experienced during early childhood affect them both physically and emotionally. The **223** cycles of "good" and "bad" health are often related to stress. Stress may bring on an acute stage of the disease or make an existing acute stage more severe. Their family's physical, emotional, and financial resources may be severely taxed as they attempt to cope with the effects and limitations imposed by a child's long-term illness.

Parents are often expected to take on the role of clinician, or therapist-in-training, in addition to the traditional parental role. They perform daily much of the therapy that the specialists prescribe each week or month. They monitor the child's health, seeking medical help in acute phases. When medical treatment is required, they are the ones to chauffeur the child to and from the appointments. The extra work and responsibility places an added burden on the parent-child relationship.

Most health impairments are not covered under the Individuals with Disabilities Education Act; however, they are covered under section 504 of the Rehabilitation Act. This means that children with health impairments cannot be discriminated against in admission to child care settings and educational programming. Because of the progressive nature of some health impairments (such as AIDS and muscular dystrophy), children may require adaptive programming in the early years. Others will not need these adaptations until later. The implications of and concerns about the effects of health impairments are nevertheless present.

Classification of Health Impairments

Brief descriptions of the most common health impairments follow. Remember you will *not* be expected to be an expert on each impairment, but you need to be aware of typical characteristics and how they will influence your programming. (The impairments are discussed in alphabetical order.)

Acquired Immune Deficiency Syndrome (AIDS)

Acquired Immune Deficiency Syndrome (AIDS) is a communicable viral disease that is a concern for children and teachers alike. AIDS is a life-threatening disease, which as of 1991 has no known cure or vaccine. Forty-five percent of those with AIDS die a year after diagnosis, 85 percent in three years (Skeen & Hodson, 1987). Premature mortality is predicted for those who have the full syndrome.

The AIDS virus itself does not kill; rather, it makes the body unable to defend itself against other diseases. Let us look at the term more closely. Medically, *acquired* means that the disease is transmitted through contact. It is not genetically transmitted. *Immune* refers to the system of the body that is affected. (The immune system organizes defenses against harmful bacteria, viruses, and other invading organisms.) *Deficiency* implies that the immune system becomes unable to fight off the harmful organisms that are invading it. *Syndrome* refers to the group of symptoms and manifestations of the disease (Skeen & Hodson, 1987). Both males and females are affected by the disease, and all races have been affected. AIDS is not exclusively a disease of homosexuals.

From a teaching perspective, the most likely interaction you will have with AIDS is that the parent of one of the children in your classroom will have AIDS. The problem is a complex one. The child will be coping with the imminent deterioration and death of a parent at the same time as he or she is coping with the social complications of living in a family with AIDS. You can support the child in her efforts to cope with issues surrounding death and dying.

Beginning in the 1980s we realized that children could develop AIDS. The number of children with AIDS was increasing, and these children and their families were subject to discrimination (U.S. Department of Health and Human Services, 1987). Because of this discrimination, many states decided that teachers did not have the need to know whether or not a child in her classroom had AIDS. The rationale was that the risks to others are not great enough for a family's privacy to be violated. The risk assumption is based on such information as "No cases of AIDS to date have been attributed to skin contact or biting." Further, "Holding hands, social kissing, hugging, sharing a water fountain, and sitting on a toilet seat are thought to be safe" (U.S. Department of Health and Human Services, 1986, in Skeen & Hodson, 1987, p. 69).

The U.S. Centers for Disease Control estimate that by 1993, 450,000 cases of AIDS will have been diagnosed in the United States (Hallahan & Kauffman, 1991). As children born with AIDS live longer, they will be in educational settings.

Implications. If there is a child with AIDS in your classroom, you may not know, so that adaptive programming may not be possible. At one time we thought that AIDS only affected the immune system. However, especially in children, it appears to affect the brain as well. There is often a marked delay in developmental milestones, especially walking and talking (Schwarcz & Rutherford, 1989) in children with HIV infection. That is, in addition to fragile physical health, the disease may include psychotic behavior, mental retardation, seizures, and neurological impairments (Hallahan & Kauffman, 1991).

A major concern for a child who is HIV positive is that he may pick up a disease from one of the other children in the classroom that becomes fatal because the child lacks the ability to fight the disease. Good hygiene is crucial for everyone in the classroom.

Deciding what to tell young children about AIDS is difficult. Information should probably only be provided on a "need to know" basis. For children younger than eight it is generally felt that the information would be frightening and, with their cognitive capabilities, not useful. For those children who ask, the answers should be simple and direct and in response to what is asked. If children ask, "What is AIDS?", reply that it is a disease, a serious one, but not one that children usually get. It is caused by a virus.

Allergies

Allergies are the most common health impairment of children. They affect a child's development, behavior, learning, and relationships with others (Voignier & Bridgewater, 1980). Allergies account for one-third of all chronic health conditions that occur during the preschool years. Only about 35 percent of children with allergies have been diagnosed and treated. About 10 to 24 percent of the population has serious allergies; another 26 percent experience minor allergies. Most allergies begin before age fourteen (Travis, 1976).

An allergy is a sensitivity to something that most other people find harmless. In an allergic reaction caused by pollen, for example, the body acts as if it is being invaded and must defend itself. It produces antibodies, which stimulate (in the case of hayfever) the white blood cells to produce a chemical called histamine. Histamine causes the hayfever symptoms, and the drugs used to combat this reaction are called *anti*histamines. Allergenic substances fall into four categories. The most common items are listed below.

Air-borne (inhalants). These substances are taken into the body through the mouth and nose: plant pollen, fungi spores, mold, dust, feathers (down), and animal dander (Travis, 1976).

Foods and Drugs (ingestants). These substances are taken into the gastrointestinal tract. Early in the school year, before you have gotten to know your students, you may want to avoid using common problem foods for snacks. The following foods are responsible for 90 percent of food allergies: legumes (peas, beans, and nuts, especially peanuts), chocolate, citrus fruit (especially oranges), cereal and grain products (including corn, corn syrup, corn starch, and wheat), fish/shellfish, milk, eggs, cola drinks, berries, tomatoes, cinnamon, and food colors. Foods such as crackers and juice or water are good snacks. However, you still need to read the labels. Oral drugs such as these are common offenders: aspirin, sulfa drugs, and penicillin.

Contact (contactants). These substances come in contact with the surface of the skin: ingredients in cosmetics, starch, wool, and some detergents.

Some Drugs and Chemicals (injectables). These substances enter the body through the skin: penicillin (injected), mosquito venom, venom from bee stings. Insect bites can be fatal. A bee sting often results in localized swelling and redness, which indicates only a mild allergy. A serious allergic reaction causes more generalized swelling and/or hotness about the face and neck, followed by difficulty in breathing and more severe bodily reactions. A sting can result in death if treatment is not immediate.

Implications. You will play an important part in diagnosing allergies in very young children. Particularly difficult to spot are symptoms that seem to be related to the season or weather.

> Nose: Frequent runny nose, sniffling, rubbing the nose, frequent nosebleeds, frequent sneezing (four or five times in a row), wrinkling up the nose.
>
> Mouth: Dry hacking cough, wheezing, mouth breathing.
>
> Eyes: Red puffy eyes, rubbing the eyes, dark circles under the eyes.
>
> Skin: Skin irritations and rashes.

If a child is diagnosed allergic to common inhalants, you should have the classroom scrubbed and vacuumed frequently. (Dusting merely redistributes the dust.) If you have an air conditioner, be sure the filter is cleaned often. Do the same for the heating system filter. Consider adding a humidifier or air cleaner if necessary (Voignier & Bridgewater, 1980).

Be sure to ask all of the parents whether their children have known allergies. The information will help you screen lunch and snack menus, choose a class pet, and prepare in advance against insect bites and other potential allergens encountered during field trips. Find out what reaction the child is likely to have, what you should do if the reaction occurs, and what the side effects of the child's medication are.

Because a child's first allergic reaction may occur during school hours, it is important that you establish emergency procedures. (See the discussion under Guidelines.)

Asthma

Asthma is the leading cause of school absences in young children. It affects about 2 percent of the population and typically develops in early to middle childhood (Neisworth & Bagnato, 1987).

Asthma is a respiratory problem caused by an obstruction of the small bronchial tubes that occurs because of a swelling of the tubes themselves or the membrane linings. Asthma can also result from the contraction of the muscles around the tubes or by the plugging of the tubes with mucus. The symptoms are generally the same regardless of the cause—shortness of breath, coughing, wheezing, and choking. The lungs become enlarged because more air can be inhaled than can be exhaled. The chest expands, the neck muscles strain, and the veins tend to swell. This condition is twice as common in boys as girls.

Asthma has a variety of causes; the most common are allergies. Emotional excitement (good or bad) as well as overexertion or even ordinary activity can trigger an attack. Since these attacks occur without warning, they may be frightening to the child who is having one as well as to the other children. Attacks are most likely to come in the early morning hours. Children usually have prescribed medication (in pill or inhaler form) to take. You need to have it available and to know how to help the child use it. Generally, the most comfortable positions for the child having an attack are sitting backwards straddling a straight chair or planting the elbows on the knees. These positions are easiest to breathe in. Lying down is not helpful and in some cases may actually be harmful.

Implications. Young children with asthma are commonly allergic to dust. If possible, have the floor of your room damp-mopped and eliminate rugs or curtains. If not, have the room vacuumed at night so that dust can settle. Try to balance strenuous activities with less strenuous ones. You should arrange a way to keep in contact with this child at home, since he will frequently be absent. The severity of attacks will vary from time to time. The child will probably not "outgrow" asthma during the preschool years.

Cancer

Cancer is an umbrella term for a group of diseases, all of which produce malignancies in some part of the body (skin, muscle, nerve, lining of stomach, and so on). Most commonly affected in children are the nervous system, the genitourinary system, the system of connective tissues, and the blood-forming system.

Cancer is treated with surgery, radiation, chemotherapy, or a combination of those methods. The prognosis depends on how early the disease is detected, what type of cancer it is, and which system is affected. Although cancer occurs rarely, it causes more deaths in children between one and fourteen than any other disease (Travis, 1976). (Only accidents cause more deaths.)

Leukemia is the most common form of cancer found in young children. It accounts for approximately 40 percent of childhood cancer deaths. Boys outnumber girls, and the peak occurrence is between three and four years of age (Neisworth & Bagnato, 1987).

Although people think of leukemia as a blood disease, it is actually a disease of the tissues that produce the white blood cells. When affected by leukemia, these tissues produce copious abnormal white cells. The cells are ineffective in fighting infection, and they disrupt the production of red blood cells and prevent blood from clotting properly.

There are two types of leukemia—acute and chronic. Most afflicted children have acute leukemia. In the past that meant they would normally have only several months to live once the disease was diagnosed. Today a child may live an additional two to five years. Children with chronic leukemia may live

as long as ten years. Medical advances are continually increasing these predictions.

Because leukemia is not localized, surgery is not effective. Early diagnosis and treatment cannot prevent the disease from spreading. Various chemicals, hormones, and sometimes X rays are used to combat this disease. Platelet transfusions, gamma globulin, and other blood products are helpful in managing it. Being cured of leukemia is rare, although with new research there is new hope. Currently no way of preventing leukemia is known.

Although medical advances can increase the life span and even hold out the hope of an ultimate cure, leukemia is still a fatal illness in half of the cases (Neisworth & Bagnato, 1987). The decrease in red blood cells causes anemia, which results in the child's being lethargic, tired, and pale much of the time. Because of decrease in platelets, the child bleeds excessively and bruises from minor causes. Heavy nosebleeds are frequent. The low "normal" white cell count decreases the child's resistance to infection and makes getting well more difficult. Many children also have pain and discomfort from both the disease and the treatment. Often one side effect of the treatment is loss of hair; another is stiffness in the joints.

Implications. After the initial diagnosis, a period of intensive treatment follows and then a first remission in which the child looks well and has energy. This may be the time the child is in your program. Discipline should be "normal" at home and at school, but given the circumstances, disciplining this child will be hard to do. Adequate nutrition for growth is a problem because the drugs decrease appetite. (In some cases, the drugs must be reduced so that the child's appetite can improve.) Be sure your snacks and lunches are nutritious, as this child cannot afford empty calories. School, despite the dangers of infection and taunting by peers, has great psychological value to both the child and the family. Often hospitals or community agencies will offer seminars on death and dying which may be helpful for teachers and parents to attend.

Cystic Fibrosis

Cystic fibrosis is a hereditary chronic disease in which the mucus-secreting and sweat glands produce a mucus so thick and sticky that it interferes with the functioning of the respiratory and digestive systems. It affects boys and girls equally and occurs in about one in every 1,600 births. It is far more prevalent in whites than in black or oriental children (Neisworth & Bagnato, 1987).

Often cystic fibrosis is diagnosed in infancy by analyzing the concentration of sodium and chloride in the sweat. However, it is difficult to diagnose because it can be confused initially with asthma, food allergies, failure to thrive, and even maternal overanxiousness, to name but a few.

Symptoms vary, but some common ones are below-average height and weight despite a voracious appetite; frequent coughing (wheezing is common), throat clearing, sinus infections, and respiratory problems; foul-smelling stools, and gastrointestinal problems (upset stomach and diarrhea).

Currently, with improved treatment, about 75 percent of children with cystic fibrosis live until at least middle or late adolescence. Parents live with the constant knowledge of impending death. This psychological strain is accompanied by a financial one. Estimated costs of treatment range from $4,000 to $12,000 per year. Medication alone can cost $3,000 per year. The actual treatment and caring for the equipment often takes two hours a day. Children's lives depend on their family's ability to put them first.

Implications. Special arrangements have to be made. See that the child takes enzyme pills before snack and lunchtime. Develop a plan for maintaining contact when the child is home sick or hospitalized. See that the child is encouraged to bring up phlegm, not stigmatized for doing so. Some signs of emotional difficulty to look for in the child are depression and withdrawal, fear of death, fear of losing control (dependence), and acting out. Have an emergency plan (see Guidelines).

Provide matter-of-fact explanations for other children: "This child has trouble breathing, like you do when you have a cold, only Leroy has this all the time. He also has a tummyache a lot."

Juvenile Diabetes

Juvenile diabetes, by definition, begins before a child is fifteen years old. In young children it is almost always severe. (Diabetes causes the highest rate of hospitalization among white children.) Common symptoms are extreme thirst, frequent urination, constant hunger, loss of weight, itching, easy tiring, changes in vision, and slow healing of cuts and scratches. However, it is possible for a child to be a diabetic without having all these symptoms, and some children have no obvious symptoms.

Diabetes is a metabolic disorder in which the body either does not produce enough insulin (a hormone made by the pancreas that helps the body use glucose) or the insulin produced is not effective. In juvenile diabetes, the pancreas produces no insulin at all. Therefore the child cannot eat carbohydrates in great quantity. The goal is to manage the disease by developing a predictable relationship between the child's diet, insulin, and the amount of exercise. Diabetes can lead to many serious medical complications (kidney disease, blindness), as well as a shortened life span. Children typically live about thirty years from the time the disease is diagnosed (Neisworth & Bagnato, 1987).

Insulin injections are necessary for almost all children with diabetes. The injections must be given

Properly planned snacks allow the child with allergies and the child with diabetes to be part of the group. All the children can learn more about food and its effects.

daily and are probably the most hated part of the treatment. Urine testing (usually before breakfast and dinner) or blood testing may be necessary each day. This procedure is embarrassing for a child striving toward independence. Charting the test results provides the basis for changes in insulin dosage and gives clues to why some diabetics go out of control. Diabetic children are allowed to have slowly digestible sweets like ice cream, but are not allowed to eat candy bars and other carbohydrates that burn quickly. (An exception to this rule occurs when the child needs quick sugar to avert an insulin reaction.)

Brittle or "labile" diabetic children are those who are difficult to keep under medical control. In other words, it is difficult to determine the correct amount of insulin to prevent either shock or coma. These children are usually hospitalized until management techniques are worked out.

Although most juvenile diabetics are on a "free" diet, it is by no means unstructured. The "free exchange system" used by adults is often used with children. This system divides foods into six groups based on the calories and the grams of carbohydrates, proteins, and fats. Thus, if the child is allowed one bread exchange, the choice of any one of the following could be made: a piece of bread, one-half cup cereal, two graham crackers, one-half cup mashed potatoes, and one-fourth cup baked beans (Travis, 1976). The number of exchanges is determined by the individual's needs. The parents will tell you what exchanges the child requires.

Implications. You need to have snack and lunch at about the same times each day. Each should provide about the same food values every day. The child need not eat the same things every day, but the foods should be of equivalent groups and values.

Because of the possibility of insulin reaction (hypoglycemia), you must always have some quick-burning sugar on hand to give the child if you suspect a reaction is about to occur. Most children have some warning signs, but young children rarely can identify these. The child may be dizzy, shaky, trembling, or having an emotional outburst before the insulin reaction occurs. Find out in advance what the child's favorite sources of sugar are: You need to offer something especially tempting because the child may not feel like eating at this time. Some traditional quick sugar sources are orange juice, soda, a sugar cube, small chocolate bars. Always carry one of these on a field trip. If you miss the warning signs and the child becomes unconscious, do not try to get the child to drink, since choking might result. Discuss emergency measures with parents before the trip. (They will probably want to be informed and have the child taken to the emergency room of a hospital. You may even need to learn to give a shot of glucagon to the child.)

Too much sugar in the body for the amount of insulin is indicated by very frequent urination, thirst, hunger, weakness, drowsiness, vomiting, and finally coma. Call the parents when you notice any of the early signs. This condition can result from eating "forbidden foods," sleeping more, less active playing, or illness. If children know they have done something wrong to bring on the attack, they may be reluctant to tell. An unconscious child must be taken to the emergency room of a hospital.

The parents supervise and regulate the child's insulin and diet, and they can usually accommodate any situation if they know about it ahead of time. Send them a list of your snacks for the week or month, or at least post them on a bulletin board for the parents to check when they drop off or pick up their child. If another child will have a birthday party with cupcakes, tell the parents. The diabetic child can have one too, if it is planned.

The child should wear a Medic-Alert bracelet or locket at all times.

Being different is often a problem. Diabetic children often have low self-esteem and tend to be loners. Remember to work toward improving their self-concept.

Heart Problems

Defective hearts and rheumatic fever are the two major causes of heart problems in young children. In rheumatic fever, the child's heart often becomes enlarged and the pumping action weakened. Sometimes the valves (especially on the left side) become inflamed. If these heal with a scar, or if the enlarged heart does not return to normal, there is permanent damage. Healing can occur so that the child is able to lead a normal life. Rheumatic fever is only one-tenth as common now as in the past.

You may encounter a child with a heart murmur. Heart murmurs are unusual sounds produced by the blood as it circulates through the heart. This sound is caused by the incomplete closing of the heart valves. Heart murmurs are harmless for about half of the preschool children who have them. In other cases, restricted activity or heart surgery may be required.

About three dozen different heart defects have been identified. These may occur separately or in combination. Surgery is the usual treatment. Most heart conditions in children can be either completely or partially corrected by surgery, although some conditions are inoperable (Travis, 1976).

Preschool children with heart problems may show the following symptoms: poor physical development, frequent respiratory infections, squatting (this is a natural way of increasing circulation), clubbed fingers and toes, shortness of breath on exertion, and perhaps even fainting. Insufficient oxygen may sometimes cause these children to turn a bluish color around the lips and eyes, or cheeks and fingertips may become reddened. Young children with symptomatic cardiac defects may want to be held more, cry and whine more, eat poorly, and, with repeated serious illness, be difficult to establish a relationship with.

Implications. Although these children may need some limitations in their activity, there is generally not a problem if you alternate strenuous activities with restful ones and let children rest when they are tired. If you avoid strenuous competitive games, the children need not exert themselves unduly to win. Children who are subject to blackouts should be distracted from excessive activity that causes breathlessness. (Children may resist being distracted if they realize your intent, but their well-being may depend on it, so be creative.)

There is a tendency for families to overprotect these children, denying them the opportunity to build inner controls. It's important for you to be responsive to their needs within a framework that requires the children to learn responsibility. For example, if a child is too tired to help pick up the dolls he played with, the first time have the child rest. If you suspect the child is using his illness to avoid cleaning up, have the child rest the second time, but leave things to be put in their proper places later so that he learns that this is not a way to get out of cleaning up. If the child is genuinely tired, shorten the activity time.

Hemophilia

Hemophilia is a genetic blood disease that usually affects only males. It is transmitted by a recessive gene of the mother's. In hemophilia, the child's blood lacks one of the essential ingredients for clotting. The old fear was that the child would get a cut and bleed to death. The real threat is from internal hemorrhaging, with death resulting from bleeding into the brain, air passages, or other vital organs. This is now rare. Almost all children with hemophilia live into adulthood.

With early diagnosis and treatment using a clotting factor that can be isolated from blood plasma, many of the dangers of hemorrhaging are eliminated. However, this treatment is not a cure; it must be used whenever hemorrhaging from an injury occurs (Travis, 1976). Over the long term, bleeding into the joints can cause crippling. The more severe the disease (there are a wide range of clotting deficiencies within hemophiliacs) and the longer the time span between hemorrhaging and treatment, the greater the possibility of long-term crippling. As you might guess, surgery is not an easy solution to correct these deformities. Even dental work causes concern. This disease is very painful. Aspirin cannot be used in treating the pain since it further reduces the blood's ability to clot.

Implications. Parents and teachers should work out what equipment the child can safely use. If possible, tag the equipment this child cannot use as a visual reminder. Find out what the parents want you to do if the child is injured. Also decide how acting out and temper tantrums will be dealt with. If the child is experiencing a lot of pain or seems to be very tired, you might make arrangements for him to go home early. Use noncompetitive physical activities to reduce the dangers of overexertion and injury.

Juvenile Rheumatoid Arthritis

Rheumatoid arthritis is the most common crippling disease of childhood. It can appear as early as six months (although peak incidents occur between the ages of two and four, and eight and ten) and is more common in girls than boys. The joints are inflamed, which results in pain, fever, soreness, and stiffness.

The cause is unknown; one theory is that a virus causes the inflammation by triggering chemical reactions. Children experience flare-ups without warning as well as periods of improvement (remission). During a flare-up, the children feel pain and stiffness. Some wake up at night and cry from the pain. They may need a hot bath to relieve stiffness. Children are usually treated with drugs called salicylates, the most common of which is aspirin. In about one-third of children, the disease is active into adulthood. Rheumatoid arthritis stops in about two-thirds of the children by the end of ten years (Travis, 1976). In most children, growth is stunted. Some may have crippling, but with medical improvements this is becoming less severe. Physical therapy is used to prevent or rectify deformities. The prescribed exercises are repetitious, painful, and little fun. Ordinarily, the

parents and child do these activities at home on a daily basis.

The cause and cure are unknown. There is complete remission in about 75 percent of the cases (Hallahan & Kauffman, 1991).

Implications. This child will often be tired and lack muscular strength. Care needs to be taken to allow the child time to do things. Realize that the child is probably in some pain. (The drugs reduce inflammation and pain but don't cure.) The child should not participate in competitive sports, in activities that continuously use the same joints (typing, piano playing), or in jarring, twisting play.

Obesity

Obesity in young children is a serious problem. It affects their health, their self-concept, and the way others feel about them. Obesity is an excessive accumulation of fat; body weight exceeds "normal" by at least 20 percent. About 13 percent of preschool children are obese (Collipp, 1980). Obesity is commonly caused by eating too much. Overeating may result from poor dietary habits or from difficulties in coping with everyday problems. Rarely do inherited disorders or metabolic and endocrine abnormalities contribute to obesity. Few children are referred for medical advice at this age. It is assumed that they will outgrow their baby fat. However, in many cases they never stop being fat. Children who are classified as obese are likely to have one or two obese parents. It is difficult to tell if children become obese because of eating patterns in the home or because of a genetic tendency in the family or because of a combination of the two.

There is evidence that obesity in childhood is difficult to reverse (LeBow, 1984). Overweight children have a difficult time keeping up with their friends. They can't run as far or as fast or climb as high. The social and emotional costs are great. These children are also at risk for elevated blood pressure and, with increasing age, more susceptible to premature heart attack, diabetes, and arthritis (Epstein & Squires, 1988). Our society looks scornfully at obesity. Even from three-year-olds, the taunts of "tubby," "fats," and "fatso" are heard. These children are discriminated against by peers and teachers. They may grow up expecting rejection and usually get it. If they feel isolated and unhappy, they may react by eating more. Some children are obese from lack of activity and they need to be encouraged to participate in active play.

Implications. Children who are obese exercise less than other children. They seem to be able to do single, nonrhythmic activities like climbing, but have problems with repeated rhythmic activities like running. Playing loud music with a distinct beat during activities helps them improve this skill. To help burn calories and tone muscles, these children should be encouraged to participate in large motor play. As obese children may be loners, plan special activities to bring them into the group and foster a sense of group belonging.

They and their parents also need education on nutrition. Praise and other noncaloric rewards should be used, never sweets.

Sickle-Cell Disease

Sickle-cell disease is a painful, inherited blood disorder that primarily affects African Americans. There is a major distinction between sickle-cell trait and sickle-cell anemia. The trait exists when the child inherits the disease from only one parent, the anemia when it is inherited from both. The child with the trait is not ill, but instead is a carrier of the disease. The trait occurs in about one in ten African Americans, the anemia in about one in four hundred. The actual proportion of the sickle-shaped cells varies from child to child. The higher the proportion, and the earlier the symptoms appear, the more severe the disease is likely to be. Diagnosis is usually made between the second and fourth year. Characteristically, this child will be chronically sick with infections of one sort or another, be weak, and experience abdominal pain. He may also suffer from painful swelling of the hands and feet.

Red blood cells are normally shaped like a doughnut with a hole in the middle that does not go through completely. In sickle-cell disease, cells take on a crescent, or sickle, shape. This shape impairs the oxygen-carrying capacity of the cells and is also conducive to clogging. The result is pain and chronic fatigue. There is no known cure, and frequent blood transfusions are necessary to replace the destroyed red blood cells. Children afflicted with severe forms of the disease usually die in childhood or early adult life from a blood clot, which does not allow enough oxygen to reach the brain.

Implications. Toddlers and preschool children are more prone to crisis and, hence, hospitalization than are older children. Crises are precipitated by a variety of circumstances—infection, chilling, dehydration, strenuous exercise, sweating, cold (especially cold, damp weather). Use this knowledge to take preventive measures. This child needs a high-protein, high-vitamin, adequate iron diet. You can plan snacks and lunches to meet that need. He also needs to drink a great deal of fluid, especially water and juice. Encourage the child to drink more by having fluids readily available. The intake of liquids means the child frequently urinates. Make sure the child has easy access to the bathroom.

Fatigue is a major factor, as this child tires easily and a general lassitude is often present. Be aware of the balance of active and quiet activities in the classroom. Be sure to alternate these activities and to have available alternatives to those activities that are physically demanding. Stress cooperation, not competition. This is likely to be a small, fragile-looking child who needs help building a good self-concept.

Seizure Disorder (Epilepsy)

A seizure happens when there is an abnormal discharge of electrical energy in certain brain cells. The effect of the seizure depends on the location of the cells and how far the discharge spreads. Seizures reflect abnormal brain activity and occur more often in children under six and in old age. Seizures take many forms. However, there are two major types: generalized and partial or focal. Generalized seizures involve the discharge of cells in a large part of the brain, and as a result these seizures involve the whole body. Partial seizures begin in a localized area and only a small part of the brain and hence the body is involved (Hallahan & Kauffman, 1991).

There is great variation in seizures: They can last only a few seconds or for several minutes; they may occur every few minutes or once a year; they may be totally unexpected or be preceded by an internal awareness; they may cause major convulsive disorders or only minor motor symptoms (eye blinks) (Hallahan & Kauffman, 1991). Seizures may be completely controlled by drugs so the child does not have seizures or only partially controlled. Seizure disorders (not an isolated seizure) occur in about 0.5 percent of the population (Wolriach, 1984). They may be associated with other disabilities or unrelated to other medical problems.

Implications. Seizures are primarily a medical problem. The management of seizures that may happen in the classroom, however, involves educational decision making. The first thing to do is to talk with the child's parents and find out as much as you can about the type of seizures the child has, their frequency, length, if they are set off by identifiable environmental stimuli, and how the child reacts when he is having a seizure. The second most important thing to know is first aid for seizures. It starts with *stay calm*. You can't stop a seizure once it starts. If the child is upright, help move him to the floor, loosen clothing, and remove any nearby objects so he doesn't strike his head or body against them. Turn the child's face to the side so saliva can flow out of his mouth, but don't otherwise interfere with his movements. Don't be alarmed if the child stops breathing momentarily, and don't put anything in the child's mouth. When the movements stop and the child is relaxed, cover the child and allow him to rest or sleep until he is ready to get up. Notify the child's parents that a seizure has occurred. It isn't necessary to call a doctor unless the seizure lasts more than ten minutes or a second seizure follows (adapted from the Epilepsy Foundation of America in Hallahan & Kauffman, 1991).

In addition to knowing first aid procedures, you should note the length of the child's seizure, and what the child was doing when the seizure took place. (If the child is taking medication you should know the type and its possible side effects).

Again, you are the model; to the extent that you are calm and matter of fact, the children will be as well. If children ask you questions, answer them honestly, but simply: "Sometimes Sibyl's brain has too much energy. Her body shows this energy. Once the energy is gone she is tired and wants to rest."

Special Health Care Needs

Some children with health impairments have survived very serious medical experiences and may need specialized health care indefinitely. These children are sometimes called "medically fragile." Others are referred to as "technology dependent." In the past, they received their education in hospital or institutional settings. This is no longer the case for some children.

The problems of children with special health care needs raise many questions about the relationship between educational and medical services. Although there is general agreement that medical needs must be stabilized before educational needs can be met, there is disagreement about the proper setting for the children's education. In situations where the child is medically stable but ventilator dependent, oxygen dependent, needs nutritional supplements, is on an apnea monitor, or is dependent upon other specialized health care, the question of least restrictive educational environment arises.

These children may qualify for special educational services under "other health care impaired" (IDEA). However, many teachers and administrators are concerned about issues such as liability, medical support services, and educational barriers (Sirvis, 1988).

According to the Council for Exceptional Children (1988), "Medically fragile students require specialized technological health care procedures for life support and/or health support during the school day. These students may or may not require special education" (in Sirvis, 1988, p. 41).

Implications. Teachers of young children must be prepared to support children with special health care needs in the classroom. This may require in-service training and working with medical support staff. The classroom must be made hygienically safe, and adjustments (both individual and group) to the schedule must be made to accommodate learning needs. Teachers need to work closely with the parents to gain their input and knowledge as well as allay their fears about school. Clear plans must be in place for medical emergencies as well as school emergencies (fire drills, and so on). Working relations may have to be established between teachers in other settings (hospital- or home-based) to allow continuity. There is little doubt that these children will challenge the capacity of both the system and the teacher.

However, the potential for raising these children's quality of life is good.

Children's Needs: Teaching Goals

Related annual goals may be grouped under broad categories called "teaching goals." Outlined under each teaching goal below are the most important needs of children with health impairments. The child may have some or all of these needs, and additional needs as well. Suggestions on what you might consequently teach them are included. Often, a course of action is implicit in the description of the need.

Feelings

Children who are chronically ill may develop phobias; they may be fearful and anxious, always awaiting the next crisis situation, the next painful experience. They cannot even enjoy their periods of health because of the fear of doing something that will bring on an acute period. These children may suffer from loneliness, boredom, and depression.

Also, many of these children have shortened life expectancies, so the fear of death and dying is a major issue that may often be on their minds as well as on their parents'. (This seems to be true whether or not they have been told they have years ahead of them.) Teachers can help children become more aware of their feelings, help them learn to express them, and give them the skills to work through them.

Language Skills

Many of these children lack experience and hence a good inner language base. Especially in the case of terminal illness, parents are frequently overprotective both because of the disease itself and because most diseases weaken the child and bring increased susceptibility to contagious diseases. In addition to expanding their overall language base, these children need to develop the vocabulary to express their fears and concerns. They need to be aware of their symptoms and how to label them, know the body parts, and be able to put the two together to give more accurate information about their current state of health.

Awareness

These children need to become aware of their own uniqueness. Because they look normal, other children and adults may not understand or remember their problems. Because they have periods when they are fine and periods when they are not, others wonder if it is just a game they are playing. These children may be misunderstood at school. Often they cannot participate in some of the more strenuous activities. Because of frequent absences it is difficult for them to build relationships with other children and to complete projects. Especially if the child is experiencing pain or some side effects from drugs, the child may not be fun to be with. Teachers have to support the other children, remembering these circumstances. Emphasize quality, not quantity, and decrease the emphasis on speed. It's not how fast something is done that counts.

Guidelines

1. Use activities that allow children to be in control or adapt activities so that children have more control. For example, let the children decide what color paint to add to the shaving cream finger paint—and how much. Putting the paint in a large salt shaker allows children to shake out just the amount they want.

2. Encourage independence and allow the children to do as much as possible for themselves. Because it is very easy for these children to become dependent on adults, you must encourage age-appropriate independence.

3. Arrange the class schedule so that vigorous activities are followed by less strenuous ones, and, when necessary during strenuous activities, provide rest periods that are built in, not obvious.

4. Be flexible in scheduling the children's day so that if they have to leave for pills, shots, or therapy, this can become part of the routine. If you accept the children's therapy and its importance, it will be easier for them. Some children find a full day tiring, especially when they return after an illness. Allow them to come for part of the day.

5. Plan activities that are open-ended and do not require excessive amounts of time to complete, or plan ones that can be completed at home if necessary. Since these children often work more slowly and miss more school than others, they may decide not to start things they may never complete. If, for example, the class is doing wire sculpture, put the child's sculpture in a bag labeled *Sam's Wire Sculpture*. Ask the parents to put it in a place at home where the child can get it when ready. This will help him feel that he is still part of the group.

6. Learn about these children by being a good observer. Watch for mood changes, as these are often cues to well-being. Be aware of the children's body language. Often these children will grimace or give other signs that will alert you to possible pain. Young children have trouble recognizing and verbalizing their needs; you can help them.

7. Find out as much as you can about the illnesses children in your class have and how it affects them. Read books on the subject and talk to the parents, therapists, and doctors. Be informed about the children's diet, physical restrictions, medication, possible side effects of the medicine, and the behaviors that indicate when the chronic illness is turning acute. You also need to know what children have been told about their illness and its implications. Since the other children in your class may repeat things, you need to be prepared to respond to comments, such as: "I don't want to play with you. You have leukemia. You're going to die." You need to know how the parents are dealing with the concept of death and exactly what they call the illness. Even with that knowledge, handling the situation is not easy. Children at the preschool age are not capable of abstract thinking. Death to them is like going to sleep, and it is reversible. This doesn't mean, however, that they are any less fearful of it. While the child's classmates may seem unfeeling, they are only displaying curiosity and lack of knowledge.

8. Help children learn about the implications of their health problems. Verbalize for them what happens under certain circumstances: "You are allergic to peanuts. If you eat them, it will be hard for you to breathe. There are other things that are crunchy like peanuts that you can eat. These are sunflower seeds. I like them. Do you?" (Obviously, be sure a child is not allergic to the substitute.)

9. Provide an open atmosphere where children can discuss fears and problems freely. One thing that children know even at this age is that if it is "taboo" it is bad. Be honest when you do not know an answer; say you don't know and then find out the answer. In general, don't tell children more than they ask. They are the best guide about what they need to know.

10. Develop a plan for keeping in touch with absent children. You could send get-well cards through the mail. Another child could deliver an audio tape. The child could be called on the phone by other children. (Find out good times to call or let the child phone school.) Send home a "fun bag" or develop a lending library of books and toys. The best plan is one that is tailored to your situation and the child's needs.

11. Certain illnesses require adaptations such as free access to the toilet, extra time for task completion, special food for snacks, scheduling time to take medication, and so on.

12. Classroom stress can bring on crises in some chronic illnesses (asthma, diabetes), so play down competitive games and deadlines. Make the classroom as pressure-free as possible.

13. Special events (holidays, birthdays, field trips) may lead to flare-ups, as there is almost always some psychosomatic element in the timing or severity of acute bouts. Prepare children for events. Talk about what is likely to happen. This is a time to watch for stress-related reactions.

14. Learn to recognize warning signs that may signal an emergency. Discuss with parents what they want you to do in case of an emergency. If you are to call, call when you suspect something is wrong—do not wait for full confirmation. Tape the numbers near the phone you will use. Know the location of the nearest emergency room and the fastest way to get there. Take a first aid course. Be sure it includes the Heimlich hug and cardiopulmonary resuscitation.

Curriculum Adaptations

Children with health impairments require few curriculum adaptions as long as they are allowed to work at their own pace. While working in each curriculum area emphasize helping children feel part of the group and improving their self-concept. In addition, develop a means of communication and support to bridge long absences.

Language Arts: Speaking, Listening, Reading, and Writing

Language arts is important to these children because they need to learn to communicate.

Speaking

1. Use field trips to the grocery store, farm, post office, and so on to help the child gain the firsthand experiences that are often lacking in children with chronic health needs.

2. When the child is home for extended periods of time, exchange language experience stories. Have the parent and child write a story about "Going to the Hospital" or "Things I Can See Out My Window."

3. Send a "Get Well Soon" audio tape to the child. Have children who want to share send a message to this child on the tape. If you set this up as an activity area, you might put a picture of the child beside the tape and encourage the children to talk to the absent child. The child who is ill may wish to send an answer tape back.

4. Encourage children to learn a vocabulary and a life perspective that allows for differences by teaching concepts like *some, sometimes, often, frequently, rarely,* as well as *never* and *always.*

5. Encourage children to ask questions. Instead of showing children pictures of situations and asking them to describe what is happening in the picture, help them ask questions about what specific objects are, how they are used, and about what will happen next.

6. Show children pictures of scenes (the beach, a grocery store, a hospital, doctor's office, classroom, and so on) and ask them about how they would feel if they were part of the picture. Show pictures with varying moods that may be interpreted a variety of different ways. After one child has responded ask if others feel differently and have them describe their feelings. Ask children what they need to change in the picture to change a negative feeling to a positive one (have a parent present, a stuffed animal, and so on.)

Fingerplays can be used to teach concepts and are especially good for those who are in bed frequently. Fingerplays are active, yet not tiring. Parents can easily learn them and thus form another link with school.

1. Use fingerplays that are repetitive, so children only have to learn minor changes in order to participate: "Where is Thumbkin?"

2. Use fingerplays to increase body awareness: "I put my finger on my face."

3. Use fingerplays to teach concepts: "A Little Ball."

Listening. Children frequently are expected not only to listen, but to understand and follow through on adult requests, especially if they come from the medical profession. Children need skills in following directions, but also in asking for clarification when they do not understand what is required of them.

1. Play "Simon Says" and include requests that frequently occur in medical situations: "Say, 'ah',", "Take a deep breath," "Open your mouth wide," and so on.

2. Using similar phrases, put them together and have children perform a series of tasks involving their body: "Open your mouth, take a deep breath, and breathe out slowly."

3. If the child is likely to be hospitalized, make a listening tape of hospital sounds. This will make a strange place a bit more familiar. If the child has to stay in bed, do a listening tape of things one might hear from bed.

Stories are a great way to make the unknown a little more familiar, to help children know they are not the only ones with fears, and perhaps to help them put themselves and their situation into perspective. Choose stories that relate to the specific situation the children you are dealing with might face. (See the Children's Bibliography on page 286 for appropriate titles.)

1. Read stories about children in hospitals.

2. Read stories about children or animals who are different.

3. Have a listening center where you have appropriate books as well as tape recordings of those books. Help children develop the skill of independent listening, so that if they are out of school for an extended period they have a familiar

activity they can participate in. Some portable tape players have sound governors, so children can use headphones and safely listen while not bothering others. As your collection of tapes and books is likely to be more extensive than any family's, plan a system of loaning children their favorites.

4. Fatigue and illness can impair listening. If you notice children who are typically attentive listeners not paying attention, consider the appropriateness of what you are doing, but also consider health issues.

5. Read or tape a story that the children are familiar with. Make some obvious mistakes (change words, locations, outcomes, and so on) and have the children find your mistakes.

Reading. Reading requires not only cognitive readiness, but an experiential background so that reading makes sense. Part of your role is to develop creative ways to give children the experiential background they need to read.

1. Children with health impairments have limited experiences. When possible take them on field trips. When field trips are not possible, use the dramatic play area to extend their concepts. Some excellent videotapes are also available that bring experiences to children who cannot participate in field trips.

2. Listen to the child's spoken language. If children have not had the opportunities for speaking and listening that others have had, build these skills as part of your reading program.

3. Help children focus on the relationship between printed and spoken language.

4. Encourage children to gain some control over their world through sequencing activities, especially ones that hurt or are frightening: "First we go to the doctor's office, then I tell them my name, then I wait, then I get the shot, then I wait, then I get checked for a reaction, then I can go home." This makes the injection one of a series of events rather than the total focus.

5. Expose children to a wide variety of written materials. Include many different types of children's books, poetry, fingerplays, and so on. It is useful, especially if you are learning a new song or fingerplay, to have the words available in case you forget them. Point out to the children that you are doing this and why.

6. Give children opportunities to work with the perceptual skills necessary for reading.

7. Have children match line-drawing faces showing different expressions. Then talk about what these people might be feeling or doing.

8. Play hospital or medical Lotto.

Writing. The goal for writing at this age is to help children develop the small motor and eye-hand coordination necessary to write. Include a variety of writing materials (note pads, paper and envelopes, recipe cards, pens, pencils, crayons, markers, and so on).

1. Make writing part of the dramatic play area and encourage children to "write prescriptions for the dolls who are sick."

2. Have them keep a "chart" on what happens to the doll who is sick in the dramatic play area. Discuss with children why they might do this.

3. Have some of the children make a picture menu of what the choices are for snack and then let them find out from the other children what they want from the menu. (Be sure you have enough so that children can have what they request.) Each child can "write" his name on his menu, and it is placed at his place with his "order." Because of the quality of the writing it is likely that some of the "orders" will be wrong. Talk about that and the fact that mistakes happen in all restaurants.

Discovery, Mathematics, Science, Computers

Children need support in investigating the world around them and in making sense out of it. They need to sort, classify, and develop the vocabulary that allows them to express themselves in this area. They need to *do* this, not be told about it.

Mathematics. It is especially important for children who have had some physical limitations to start with a sensorimotor concept of mathematics. This involves active interaction with materials like blocks, cuisenaire rods, and pegs. Then move on to more abstract number concepts.

1. Use three-dimensional objects like unit blocks to teach basic math concepts; don't rely on rote memory.

2. Use music and rhythmic activities to reinforce math concepts (clap four times).

3. Make math relevant. Children need to know how many pills they must take and when. This is a

step toward independence as well as toward learning number concepts.

4. Have children sort and classify familiar pieces of medical equipment (cotton balls, tongue depressors, bandages [different sizes and shapes], gauze, and so on).

5. Have the child help draw and fill in a map of the route from his classroom to the nurse's office (if that is where he goes to take medicine). If hospitalized, remind children that they can learn about an unfamiliar place using the skill they have in map making. Include other significant places in the map.

Science. Since most of these children take medicine to alleviate symptoms, it is important to develop their cause-and-effect reasoning skills. They need to understand why they should take the medicine even when they feel well.

1. Plant seeds. Discuss conditions for growth. Put some plants in the dark. Do not water some. Discuss the implications of the various conditions and "treatments."

2. Use experiments that require children to make predictions. Help children apply this skill to their particular situation: "I have trouble breathing when I run fast. If I run slower, I can run farther."

3. Place a plastic tablecloth over an area (at home, this could be done in bed provided it also had a plastic cover under sheets so spilled water will not damage the bed), and let the child experiment with water play. Provide a variety of props (sponges, corks, small plastic tubs and measuring cups, pitchers, balls, spoons, and dippers). Be sure to include plastic syringes, plastic medicine droppers, and tongue depressors. Add food coloring or dish detergent to change the appearance of the water.

4. Help children learn about the seasons of the year, especially if they directly affect their state of health. Discuss with them how we prepare ourselves for seasonal change as well as how this happens in nature. Have children talk about its effect on them: "I can't walk as far in the winter when it is cold and windy." They need to develop this type of causal thinking.

Computers. The microcomputer has many applications for children with health impairments. It requires little energy to use. It is hygienic. It is self-paced. It is available when the child wants to use it, and it is potentially portable and interactive.

When children are comfortable with them, computers become a way they can play with their friends even when they are in separate locations.

1. Encourage children with health impairments to become familiar with computers. These children need to establish some control over their world, and they can do that with a computer. Regardless of how rudimentary their skills, the potential for cause-effect reasoning is present.

2. There may be times when children with health impairments cannot communicate. Computers equipped with a simple switch and a scanning program can allow children to make their needs known.

3. If children are absent from school, you might be able to loan or recommend to parents software that will help children learn some of the concepts you are teaching.

4. Computers have the possibility for helping children participate in interactive recreation. (Traditional "arcade" games typically require good fine motor coordination and are timed, which may not be helpful.) Computerized board games such as checkers and Monopoly are possible, as well as many other commercially available games.

Sensory Motor: Large Motor, Sensory Motor Integration, Small Motor

Many of the sensory motor activities that you do in the classroom are appropriate for children with health impairments. They, like all children, are individuals with differing needs. However, some children and some activities will require special planning. In general the child's functional level will determine what is best for that child. Children with health impairments may have less stamina than other children, so they may need periods of rest throughout the day.

Large Motor. Children with health impairments may find large motor play challenging. Be sure to consider how long you expect children to actively participate. Find ways of allowing different amounts of time for activities if they are not self-regulatory.

1. Keep activities noncompetitive and pressure-free.

2. Emphasize the quality of movement, not speed.

3. Modifications may need to be made to some games. Reduce the distance to be traveled. Slow the pace by having children walk, not run. Institute intermissions. (All children must clap ten times between events.)

4. Have children jump on a trampoline (or mattress with dust cover). This improves drainage of the respiratory tract.

Sensory Motor Integration. Children need experience coordinating their senses. If they have not had the opportunity to do this, then you need to provide more activities that make them aware of their body and where it is in space.

1. Give verbal directions for motor activities and see whether or not the child can follow them. Once you have ascertained that they can, change the directions slightly.

2. Games with balloons require little effort but a fair amount of coordination and integration.

3. Beanbags can be tossed, balanced, or caught. They are adaptable to the classroom as well as other settings.

4. Hand clapping is a simple but effective activity. When done to music or in a pattern (sequence)—especially when the hands cross the midline, the right and left hand take turns, and a partner is added—it is a challenging activity that can be used under a variety of circumstances.

Small Motor. Small motor play is not physically taxing and can therefore be a potential strength. Many activities that fall into this category use materials that can be placed in jellyroll pans. These can serve as storage trays and can also be used in a wheelchair, on the floor, or in bed.

1. Choose toys that are washable. If one child has a contagious disease, it may be passed to others if the toys cannot be disinfected.

2. Use a variety of fine motor toys. Children need much practice in this area and, without sufficient variety, they may become bored before they acquire the necessary skills.

Social Awareness: Social Studies, Inclusion, Health and Safety

Many children with health impairments have been hospitalized. They may have concerns about doctors, hospitals, and being separated from their parents. One of the most frightening aspects of hospitalization is the feeling of being out of control. Helping children learn about health and safety matters as a part of a group is useful. Giving them knowledge of the roles of various professionals in the medical profession is also empowering.

Social Studies. Although our concerns about children with health impairments focus on the medical profession and medical settings, the child spends most of his life in the community, not in the hospital. Children need to know and role play not only the traditional occupations but also variations.

1. Nurses—public health nurses who visit in homes.

2. Teachers—itinerant teachers who visit children who cannot attend school.

3. Social workers or others who may serve as a support system to the family.

4. Be sure to include cultural variations and the role of extended family as well as alternative medical sources if appropriate.

5. Help children understand the interconnectedness of the community in which they live. Include information about water, electricity, waste disposal, and the consequences if the community did not address these needs.

Inclusion. Children who have spent a long time in the hospital or at home convalescing have had little opportunity to learn how to play with other children. They may not function at an age-appropriate level in areas such as cooperating with others, sharing, and turn taking. They may have few skills in joining and being part of groups.

1. You are a model of the behaviors that are necessary for children to join groups. To the extent that you never join the children, others might decide that this is also behavior to be modeled.

2. Support inclusion of children with health impairments by joining groups, in suggesting roles that need filling, or parts that they could play. However, accept the reality that this sometimes doesn't work, and openly explain to the child that this is the way it is.

3. Your role should be one that changes over time. Children may initially need your active support. However, supporting them when they have the ability to act on their own creates dependency and decreases growth.

4. Emphasize ways of approaching others. Have the children practice introducing themselves to others.

Health and Safety. A major emphasis in programming for children with health impairments is health and safety. Children particularly need to learn about foods, those that are good for them and those they must avoid.

1. Work on the food groups, on what is in each, and how they are related.

2. Help all the children enjoy the foods that are allowed. Sharing is part of the fun of food.

3. Explain, using illustrations, what happens when people eat food they are allergic to.

4. Because these children should be protected from contagious diseases, it is important that all children cover their mouths when coughing and sneezing, wash hands after toileting, and follow all forms of good hygiene.

5. Emphasize body awareness. The child needs to be able to name body parts. If the children are older or gifted, you might include some of the internal body parts. Start with those they can feel (bones) and commonly known ones (stomach).

Creative Arts: Art, Music, Creative Movement, and Dramatic Play

Creative arts for children with health impairments is a process. They need to be rewarded for participating in the process whatever the product.

Art. Art is both a means of creative expression and a tension reliever. If children do not have the energy to participate in large motor activities or cannot do so for other reasons, art may be a primary channel for releasing tension.

1. Concentrate on the process. If you can convince children to use arms and fingers they might not otherwise use, you are succeeding. It really does not matter what the result is.

2. Use many three-dimensional art materials. Again, the goal is manipulation, not a final product.

3. Use art materials that do not require good fine motor skills. Coloring within the lines may promote good eye-hand coordination, but it doesn't serve to release tension.

Music. Music can contribute much to a child's physical, aesthetic, and intellectual development. It provides pleasure and creative experience, develops auditory skills, encourages physical development, and increases range and flexibility of one's voice. There should be a wide variety of musical experiences: listening, singing, moving to music, and playing instruments.

1. Have a variety of different instruments available. Help children explore and evaluate the sound of an instrument when it is held and played in different ways. See if they can identify the instruments they know in a recording.

2. Incorporate music and language experiences; have children make up new verses to old songs. Play unusual instrumental records and ask the children to describe what they imagined while listening.

3. Use music for exercise, self-expression, listening, and keeping time, not just for singing.

4. Introduce concepts of pitch, loudness, and length.

5. Teach some colors and numbers with songs: "Who Has Red On," "Ten Little Children."

6. Use songs that call children by name.

Creative Movement. Creative movement helps children internalize their ideas about the world and their ability to respond to it.

1. Have children toss balloons into the air and hum or sing one note until the balloon touches the floor.

2. Do movement exploration activities, especially those that emphasize relaxation skills: "Move like a rag doll." "Move like a flag blowing in the breeze."

3. Put stories to music. Have children choose background music for stories.

4. Paint to music.

5. Music that combines creative movement and stories is fun and mind expanding:

   The Story of Peer Gynt, with the recording of the *Peer Gynt Suite* by Grieg.

   Cinderella, with the recording of *Cinderella* by Prokofiev.

   Hansel and Gretel, with excerpts from the opera *Hansel and Gretel* by Humperdinck.

   Stories about troubadours and meistersingers, with excerpts from *Die Meistersinger* by Wagner.

   The fairy tale *Nutcracker King,* with Tchaikovsky's *Nutcracker Suite.*

   Mother Goose, with *Mother Goose Suite* by Ravel.

6. Use exercises, especially those done to music. Select a body part (or combination) and have the children move it back and forth at a slow tempo.

Dramatic Play. Dramatic play, given appropriate props, allows children to act out fears and gives them control over frightening situations. Set up situations chronically ill children may encounter.

1. Emergency room: Discuss and play scenes that might be going on in an emergency room, emphasizing the sense of urgency.

2. Doctor's office/clinic: Talk about routine visits and visits when children are sick.

3. Surgery: Discuss operations. Allow the children to operate on dolls to "fix" them. Make finger casts so that children can learn that this is not a painful process.

4. Hospital: Set up a hospital. Talk about being scared, about strange hospital sounds, about being left alone.

5. Encourage children to build a hospital, using blocks in conjunction with the dramatic play area.

Transitions

Transitions are often difficult times. Children who are wary of adults and who may not trust them have a particularly difficult time. Re-entries into the classroom require separation from important people, and after a period of being out of the classroom children may feel uncertain about their acceptance and about you. They need your support. This may be a time when children feel helpless or abandoned. They may

feel hurt that they are being left again or afraid that you will hurt them. A predictable routine helps this transition.

1. Have a predictable arrival schedule with one person assigned to be the "greeter." At least during difficult transitions, have that be the same person each day.

2. Have the same person help the child leave the setting and briefly talk about what will happen the next day with the expectation that the child will return.

3. As children become more comfortable, encourage more independence; however, *not* until the issue over separation has been resolved.

4. As the day is ending, try to make it positive. Find something that you can say about the day that is positive with the expectation that the next day will be even better.

5. If the child with a health impairment moves more slowly than the other children, remind her early about the transition to come. Dismiss her among the first few from the group.

6. Transitions may be a good time to have children take necessary medication. Other children are less likely to notice because there is a lot going on at this time.

7. This is a good time to emphasize similarities—all children with brown hair and blue eyes, all children with plaid shirts, all children with buckle shoes.

Glossary

Acquired   A condition that is not genetic, rather the result of some external trauma or influence after birth.

Allergen   Any substance that brings on an allergic reaction. What one is allergic to.

Allergist (pediatric)*   A physician who specializes in allergies of the skin and respiratory system.

Anesthesiologist   A physician specializing in drugs or gases that cause partial or complete loss of sensation or consciousness.

Arthogryposis   Children with this condition are born with stiff joints and weak muscles. The hips, knees, elbows, and wrists are the most commonly affected. The trunk is usually not affected.

Aura   A sensation that often precedes an epileptic attack. The nature of the sensation varies with each person.

---

*In addition to subject/area specialization, some physicians specialize in particular age groups. Those specializing in young children have the word "pediatric" before their specialization (Pediatric Allergist).

Benign   A growth that is nonmalignant and nonrecurring.

Cardiologist (pediatric)·   A physician who specializes in heart conditions, including heart defects.

Cerebrospinal fluid (CSF)   The fluid that surrounds the brain and spinal cord. (A spinal tap is used to test this fluid.)

Chronic health problems   According to PL 94-142: Health impaired means having limited strength, vitality, or alertness due to chronic or acute health problems, such as a heart condition, epilepsy, tuberculosis, rheumatic fever, asthma, nephritis, sickle-cell anemia, hemophilia, lead poisoning, leukemia, or diabetes, which adversely affect a child's educational performance.

Congenital   A condition that is present at birth.

Desensitization   Desensitization is a process designed to make children increasingly resistant to the substances they are allergic to. Some children with allergies receive desensitization injections, which are very weak solutions of the materials they are allergic to. The purpose is to make the child's body produce antibodies to prevent the allergy. Increasingly stronger preparations are injected over a period of months (years).

Endocrinologist (pediatric)·   A physician who specializes in endocrine (glands producing internal secretions) or metabolic disorders by means of dietary control and medication.

Enzyme   A substance that accelerates or helps the breakdown of certain chemicals. When enzymes are not present in the body, they must be supplied. (This would be done orally in the case of cystic fibrosis.)

Geneticist   A physician specializing in the study of genes.

Genetic counselor   A specialist in genes who talks with parents and others concerned about the likelihood of their offspring being born with a genetic defect.

Glucagon   A hormone that increases the concentration of blood sugar.

Hematologist   A specialist in the study of blood and blood-forming tissue.

Hereditary   A condition that is genetically transmitted from a parent or parents to the child.

Lead poisoning   Poisoning that results from eating lead or products containing lead, especially lead-based paints used to coat plaster, window sills, or toys. Abdominal cramps are the most common result. In chronic cases it eventually causes impairment of the nervous system and mental retardation.

Malignancy   A tumor that grows or spreads into other parts of the body; cancer. It can recur.

Nephritis   An inflammation of the kidneys that can be either acute or chronic.

Neurologist (pediatric)·   A physician who specializes in diseases and conditions of the brain, spinal cord, and nerves.

Orthopedist   A physician specializing in the skeletal structure, especially the joints and muscles.

Otorhinolaryngologist   A physician specializing in the ear, nose, and throat.

Pancreas   A gland that lies behind the stomach. It produces digestive enzymes and insulin.

Periodontist   A physician specializing in gums. (Children on some seizure-prevention medicine have periodontal problems.)

Platelet   A round disk found in the blood. Platelets help the blood coagulate by adhering to each other and forming a plug when an injury occurs.

Pulmonary specialist (pediatric)·   A physician who specializes in the diagnosis and treatment of lung diseases.

Radiologist   A physician specializing in the use of radiation for diagnostic and treatment procedures.

Systemic   A condition affecting the whole body.

Transplantation   The transfer of an organ or tissue from one person to another, or from one place within a person's body to another place.

Thrombosis   A blood clot that prevents oxygen from getting to vital body organs.

Children's Bibliography

See the Children's Bibliography on page 286 for books to increase children's awareness about disabilities as well as books that are especially good for children with particular disabilities. Note especially:

Awareness of Health Impairments

Body Awareness

Death and Dying

Doctors and Hospitals

Feelings

Friendship

Simpler Books (for teaching vocabulary and concepts)

Teaching Resources

In some situations you may want or need additional information. There are many national as well as regional, state, and local organizations that can be helpful to you. The following annotated list of national organizations should be useful in helping you decide where to get the information you need.

Allergy Foundation of America
801 Second Avenue
New York, NY 10017

Has national and regional programs to educate the public through printed literature. Gives lists of qualified, practicing allergists in any part of the country.

American Alliance for Health, Physical Education
 and Recreation
Room 422
1201 16th Street
Washington, DC 20036
 Provides information and materials on physical education and recreation for people with disabilities.

American Cancer Society
219 East 42nd Street
New York, NY 10017
 National Headquarters refers to its affiliates and prints literature. It does not operate medical or laboratory facilities, treat cancer patients, or pay physicians' fees.

American Dental Association
211 East Chicago Avenue
Chicago, IL 60611
 A professional service organization with informational and referral services for the public.

American Diabetes Association
18 East 48th Street
New York, NY 10017
 National headquarters is concerned with maintaining and expanding its five basic programs in patient education, professional education, public education, detection, and research. It will make referrals to affiliates and answer questions.

American Heart Association
44 East 23rd Street
New York, NY 10010
 The national office does not operate a direct patient service or referral program; however, inquiries and requests are forwarded to the appropriate affiliation which aids in maintaining or developing heart centers and clinics.

American Red Cross
1730 D Street N.W.
Washington, DC 20037
800-452-7773
 Writes and distributes information on a variety of health-related areas including AIDS.

Association for the Care of Children's Health
3615 Wisconsin Avenue, N.W.
Washington, DC 20016
(202) 244-1801
 A nonprofit organization that addresses the psychosocial and developmental issues in pediatric health care and seeks to promote health and well-being of children and their families in all types of health care settings.

The Arthritis Foundation
1212 Avenue of the Americas
New York, NY 10036

Offers grants to medical schools and hospitals to help support Clinical Research Centers. The local affiliates provide the complete spectrum of total care including diagnosis, treatment, orthopedic surgery, and rehabilitation services.

Association of State Maternal and Child Health and
 Crippled Children's Directors
Division of Maternal and Child Health
301 Centennial Mall S.
P.O. Box 95007
Lincoln, NE 68502
 Active in efforts to define health needs of mothers and children, including crippled children. Conducts studies; makes recommendations to U.S. Public Health Service, the Child's Bureau, and Congress.

Children in Hospitals
31 Wilshire Park
Needham, MA 02192
 Parents, educators, and health professionals who seek to minimize the trauma involved in a child's hospitalization by supporting and educating parents and medical personnel regarding the needs of children while hospitalized.

Cooley's Anemia Blood and Research Foundation
 for Children, Inc.
3366 Hillside Avenue
New York, NY 11040
 Maintains and distributes a blood credit; promotes means of obtaining funds for the blood credit program and research programs; and publicizes the nature of the disease and the needs of these children.

Epilepsy Foundation of America
1828 L Street, N.W.
Suite 406
Washington, DC 20036
 This foundation conducts programs in research, employment, public information, and patient services.

The Foundation for Research and Education
 in Sickle-Cell Disease
421-431 West 120th Street
New York, NY 10027
 Professional group concerned with making the public aware of sickle-cell disease. It assists in establishing special treatment clinics in the New York area, but accepts requests for referrals throughout the U.S.

Juvenile Diabetes Foundation
23 East 26th Street
New York, NY 10010
 This foundation funds research, provides counseling and support services, educates the public.

Leukemia Society of America, Inc.
211 East 43rd Street
New York, NY 10017

National headquarters conducts the research support program and public and professional education programs; it also makes referrals to local chapters, which provide many medical services.

Muscular Dystrophy Association of America, Inc.
1790 Broadway
New York, NY 10019

National headquarter services include direct payments for all authorized services for patients who don't live in areas with local chapters; education of the public, publishing of literature and films, and sponsoring of national research conferences.

National Coalition of Advocates for Students
100 Boylston Street, Suite 737
Boston, MA 02116

For the cost of postage and handling ($2) this organization will send you a copy of Criteria for Evaluating an AIDS Curriculum.

National Cystic Fibrosis Research Foundation
3379 Peachtree Road, N.E.
Atlanta, GA 30326

National headquarters: coordinates and funds Foundation programs for research, education, and care. Refers inquiries to their local chapters and Cystic Fibrosis Centers.

The National Hemophilia Foundation
25 West 39th Street
New York, NY 10018

This foundation stimulates and assists chapters in development of social service programs in the community. It makes referrals to treatment centers and provides publications.

National Kidney Foundation
116 East 27th Street
New York, NY 10010

This association gives referrals to affiliates; it also distributes public and professional educational materials.

National Tay-Sachs and Allied Disease
    Association, Inc.
200 Park Avenue South
New York, NY 10003

This association makes referrals to clinics for diagnosis and carrier and prenatal detection throughout the U.S. It provides information about social services and nursing care.

National Tuberculosis and Respiratory Disease
    Association
1740 Broadway
New York, NY 10019

This association makes referrals to affiliates and makes available literature and films.

U.S. Centers for Disease Control
1600 Clifton Road, N.E.
Atlanta, GA 30333

Has information on many contagious diseases that it will send free, including at least two on AIDS.

References and Bibliography

Anderson, G. (Ed.). (1990). *Courage to care. Responding to the crisis of children with AIDS.* Washington, DC: Child Welfare League of America, Inc.

Batshaw, M., & Perret, Y. (1986). *Children with handicaps: A medical primer.* Baltimore, MD: Paul H. Brookes.

Blackman, J. (Ed.). (1984). *Medical aspects of developmental disabilities in children birth to three* (rev. 1st ed.). Rockville, MD: Aspen.

Collipp, P. J. (Ed.). *Childhood obesity* (2nd ed.). Littleton, MA: PSG Publishing Co.

Cooper, I. S. (1976). *Living with chronic neurologic disease: A handbook for patient and family.* New York: W. W. Norton.

Council for Exceptional Children. (1988). *Final report: CEC ad hoc committee on the medically fragile.* Reston, VA: Author.

Debuskey, M. (1970). *The chronically ill child and his family.* Springfield, IL: Charles C. Thomas.

Epstein, L., & Squires, S. (1988). *The stoplight diet for children: An eight-week program for parents and children.* Boston, MA: Little, Brown.

Hallahan, D., & Kauffman, J. (1991). *Exceptional children: Introduction to special education.* Englewood Cliffs, NJ: Prentice-Hall.

Healy, A., McAreavey, P., von Hippel, C., & Jones, S. (1978). *Mainstreaming preschoolers: Children with health impairments.* Washington, DC: U.S. Department of Health and Human Services.

Hobbs, N., Perrin, J., & Ireys. H. (1984). *Chronically ill children and their families.* San Francisco, CA: Jossey-Bass.

Hobbs, N., Perrin, J., Ireys, H., Moynahan, L., & Shayne, M. (1984). Chronically ill children in America. *Rehabilitation Literature, 45,* 206–213.

Klinzing, D. R., & Klinzing, D. G. (1977). *The hospitalized child: Communication techniques for health personnel.* Englewood Cliffs, NJ: Prentice-Hall.

LeBow, M. (1984). *Child obesity.* New York: Springer.

Neisworth, J., & Bagnato, S. (1987). *The young exceptional child: Early development and education.* New York: Macmillan Publishing Co.

New guidelines on HIV infection (AIDS) announced for group programs. (1989). *Young Children, 44*(1), 51.

Oyemade, U., & Washington, V. (1989). Drug abuse prevention begins in early childhood: (And is much more than a matter of instructing young children about drugs!) *Young Children, 44*(5), 6–12.

Pless, I. B., & Pinkerton, P. (1975). *Chronic childhood disorder. Promoting patterns of adjustment.* Chicago: Year Book Medical Publishers.

Reinisch, E. H., & Minear, R. E., Jr. (1978). *Health of the preschool child.* New York: Wiley.

Schwarcz, S., & Rutherford, G. (1989). AIDS in infants, children, and adolescents. *Journal of Drug Issues,* Winter, 75–92.

Sirvis, B. (1988). Students with special health care needs. *Teaching Exceptional Children, 20*(4), 40–44.

Skeen, P., & Hodson, D. (1987). AIDS: What adults should know about AIDS (and shouldn't discuss with very young children). *Young Children 42*(4), 65–71.

Strauss, A. L. (1975). *Chronic illness and the quality of life.* St. Louis, MO: C. V. Mosby Co.

Sultz, H. et al. (1972). *Long-term childhood illness.* Pittsburgh, PA: University of Pittsburgh Press.

Tanen-Leff, P., & Walitzer, E. (1992). *Partners in caring: Parents talk to medical providers about their chronically-ill/disabled children.* Cambridge, MA: Brookline Books.

Travis, G. (1976). *Chronic illness in children: Its impact on child and family.* Palo Alto, CA: Stanford University Press.

U.S. Department of Education. (1989). *Eleventh annual report to Congress on the implementation of Education of the Handicapped Act.* Washington, DC: U. S. Government Printing Office.

U.S. Department of Health & Human Services, Public Health Service. (1987). *Report of the surgeon general's workshop on children with HIV infection and their families.* Washington, DC: DHHS Publication No. HRS-D-MC, 87-1.

Urbano, M. T. (1992). *Preschool children with special health care needs.* San Diego, CA: Singular Publishing Group, Inc.

Voignier, R., & Bridgewater, S. (1980). Allergies in young children. *Young Children, 35,* (4), 67–70.

Wolriach, M. (1984). Seizure disorders. In J. Blackman (Ed.), *Medical aspects of developmental disabilities in children birth to three* (rev. 1st ed.) (pp. 215–221). Rockville, MD: Aspen.

Awareness Bibliography for Adults

Baruch, Dorothy W. (1952). *One little boy.* Medical collaboration by Hyman Miller. New York: Julian Press.

An account of the emotional life of an asthmatic eight-year-old, written by his psychologist. As Kenneth works out his problems, his asthma all but disappears.

Deford, F. (1983). *Alex: The life of a child.* New York: Viking Press.

A story written by Alex's father. Alex has cystic fibrosis. This is the account of her life until she dies at age eight.

Gunther, John. (1949). *Death be not proud: A memoir.* New York: Harper & Row.

The struggles and triumphs of Johnny Gunther, who died of a brain tumor at age seventeen.

Lund, Doris. (1974). *Eric.* Philadelphia: Lippincott.

A moving account of a young man's struggle to live a fulfilling life despite the diagnosis of leukemia, written by Eric's mother after his death.

Massie, Robert K., & Massie, Suzanne. (1975). *Journey.* New York: Knopf.

The Massie family's struggle to deal with the hemophilia of Robert Massie, Jr. *Journey* dispels commonly held myths about hemophilia.

Chapter 16

Children with Emotional/Behavioral Disorders

"I wonder about Julie. She used to be such a happy, outgoing little girl, and now it seems like she'd rather sit in her locker than do anything else. Even the other children notice it. They ask me what's wrong with Julie. I'm probably overreacting; after all, what could be wrong with a four-year-old?"

That's a good question. What could be bothering a four-year-old? As you contemplate your own problems and worries, the things that might bother a four-year-old seem so inconsequential that you often decide the child's concerns are not worth worrying about. Therefore, you tell the child not to fret. That is like a millionaire telling you not to worry about your inconsequential rent, bills, and so on. Your response might well be a silent or spoken "you don't understand."

To go back to Julie, she has lost interest in everything, including playdough, which used to be her favorite activity. Trying to interest Julie in the playdough is one way you show you don't understand. Julie has been spending more time just sitting in her locker, and that worries you. Rather than enticing her away, show concern by saying, "Julie, *I'm* worried because you are sitting in your locker and not playing the way you usually do." Compare the preceding statement with this one: "Julie, *you* shouldn't be sitting here in your locker, especially when I put out your favorite activity." In the first instance, you make an *I* statement, which reflects your concern about the situation. It requires nothing of Julie, not even a response. In the second statement, you seem to be both judging and blaming Julie for her behavior. "You shouldn't" really means "she shouldn't because I don't want her to." You would be better off admitting your discomfort than blaming it on her. After expressing concern, give the child permission to talk about her feelings. "Sometimes when I'm sad I want to be alone. I wonder if you're sad about something now?" While still expressing concern, you can offer an opportunity, or invitation, for Julie to talk. **243**

Whether or not she responds, the next move is to tell her how you are willing to help, while giving her some control over the situation: "Would you like to talk about how you feel? (Pause) I can listen now. I'd like to come and sit beside you for a few minutes whenever I can. Is that OK with you?" Be careful not to make an offer you can't follow through on. Don't offer to sit beside the child all morning even if you think that would be helpful. Your duties as a teacher make an "all morning" offer impossible to fulfill.

The question is, is Julie just having a temporary bad time? Is this teacher's imagination or intuition? Is there, in fact, something wrong with Julie? Let's look at Julie to see what signs or characteristics are significant.

Children are different. Shortly after birth infants have identifiable personalities. Some people have labeled these personality traits and classified children as ranging from "easy" to "difficult." Although it is not particularly useful to label children as difficult, it is important to acknowledge that some children are easier to cope with than others. Some children have behavior that is not just difficult, but disordered. As early intervention is important, you need to be able to distinguish these children from others.

Before focusing on particular behaviors such as aggression or withdrawal, consider where a child is on the following range of behaviors. Make a chart and see where the child falls on each of these dimensions before you become too focused. Sometimes we fail to get a picture of the whole child and we reach the wrong conclusions. (I once had a four-year-old child who had daily temper tantrums. My charting showed these occurred about 10 o'clock every morning. I investigated a lot of alternatives and tried various interventions. With the help of his mother, we figured out that since he had breakfast at 5 o'clock maybe he was just hungry and didn't know how to express it. A substantial early snack eliminated the temper tantrums.)

The following characteristics are present in all children. It is the extremes in these areas that characterize children with emotional/behavioral disorders. Use caution and try to think about typical behavior. This is not a good thing to do at the end of a bad day. You might make a chart for two children, the one you are concerned about, and one that strikes you as representative of your class (choose a child who is the same sex for comparison). Place a hatch mark on the line where the child's behavior falls.

Activity Level. Activity level refers to the amount of time a child is active or not active. Children who are always on the go and can't sit still are at one end of the continuum; the child who just sits is at the other extreme. Children need a balance in themselves and their programming of both active and less active times.

High ————————————— Low

Rhythmicity. Children have an internal biological clock that can be either regular or unpredictable. For those children who are *very* regular (they get up at the same time, eat at the same time, and so on), it is important to look at the match between adult expectations and the child's typical pattern. To the extent these mismatch, this child can be more difficult than the unpredictable child.

Regular ————————————— Irregular

Approach/Avoidance. Children have a typical response to new experiences. The extremes are to approach without caution (no fear) or to avoid at all costs through crying or clinging to adults. For children who have had many or recent new encounters that were painful, the avoidance response is understandable, but still difficult.

Approach ————————————— Avoidance

Adaptability. Some children find it very difficult to adapt to change, such as new routines, a different child-care provider, or a new child. Especially when holidays and transitions occur these children need extra time.

Adaptable ———————————— Not adaptable

Intensity of Reaction. Many situations evoke reactions in young children. Some are happy; others are sad or angry. It is the intensity and length of the response in relation to the event that needs to be evaluated. The child who cries violently for twenty minutes when another child takes a toy and the child who shows little or no reaction when all toys are taken, are examples of extremes.

Very intense ———————— Little reaction

Responsiveness Threshold. The threshold indicates the amount of stimulation necessary to obtain a response. For one child being lightly touched will result in a cry of pain. Another child may have to be told the fire alarm is ringing.

Very responsive ———————— Not responsive

Mood. Children have a range of moods that are a balance of happy and less positive moods. Some children seem to be in a predictable mood most of the time; others vary considerably. Children who have predictable negative moods and frequently cry and fuss may make adults feel guilty or angry.

Predictable ———————— Not predictable
Positive ———————— Negative

Attention Span. Attention span indicates the amount of time a child attends to a task. Attention span increases with age. It is also related to how interested the child is in the task.

Long attention ———————— Short attention

Resistance. Resistance measures the ability of the child to return to an activity after an interruption. To be noted are momentary interruptions as well as longer breaks for such things as toileting.

Returns to task ———— Does not return

Distractibility. This dimension varies from the child who becomes so involved that he does not allow enough time to get to the bathroom, to the child who cannot become absorbed in any activity.

Highly distractible ———— Not distractible

Most children, and adults for that matter, have some "difficult" traits. The guidelines following this section are useful whether the behavior is typical of the child or just indicates a bad day. It is not appropriate to shame, compare, or coerce children to get them to do what adults want. In addition, it rarely works.

Classification of Emotional/Behavioral Disorders

There is no universally accepted definition for children with emotional/behavioral disorders. P.L. 94-142 uses the term "seriously emotionally disturbed." Today that term is criticized, as people feel the focus of attention should be on the child's behavior. This chapter acknowledges the emotional aspect but focuses on the disordered behavior.

As you might assume, if we cannot define the term we do not have a good idea of how many children fit the definition. Much of what is diagnosed is a matter of the degree to which behaviors occur. It is almost always subjective and falls in the category of "clinical judgment." The U.S. Department of Education (1989) finds only about one percent of school-age children fit the "seriously emotionally disturbed" category. Others have challenged this data, finding between 6 to 10 percent of school-age children in this category (Kazdin, 1989), which is designated "traditionally underserved" by the Department of Education.

The identification of *young* children with emotional/behavioral disorders is especially difficult. Peterson (1987) lists seven identifiers to help distinguish the difference between normal behavioral patterns and problem behavior development. Included are: (1) the situations in which the behaviors are exhibited; (2) the developmental ages at which the behaviors appear and continue to be manifested; (3) the intensity of the behavior (excess or deficiency); (4) duration or persistence of the behavior; (5) extent to which others can alter the behavior; (6) the extent to which the behavior interferes with progress in other developmental areas; and (7) the extent to which the behavior interferes with the lives of others (p. 226).

All children have emotional/behavioral problems sometimes; it is the length, severity, and unacceptableness of the behavior that determines whether or not it is a disorder. Some behavior problems are learned behaviors that affect children's ability to participate in activities with adults and other children. They are considered situationally specific responses; examples include attention-seeking behavior, pinching, and temper tantrums. Seriously disturbed behaviors involve pervasive changes in the child's behavior and mood states that are exhibited across many situations and settings. They interfere with the development of interpersonal relationships and with development and learning. They can be harmful to the child and others (Peterson, 1987).

Emotional/behavioral disorders are discussed first. Less severe emotional/behavioral problems follow.

Emotional/Behavioral Disorders

Disorders in this category for young children include psychoses and attachment.

Infantile Autism (or Autism). Infantile autism is considered a form of childhood psychosis. It is acquired very early, with the onset of symptoms during the first year of life. The infants are described as being unresponsive and unaffectionate. They engage in excessive repetitive body movements, including head banging and rocking. By the second year the lack of social responsiveness is more noticeable. Children with autism are usually diagnosed before thirty months. They do not make eye contact or initiate social interactions. There is no intelligible language, though they may use repetitive, jargony speech patterns. They often exhibit stereotyped behavior such as spinning objects, hand whirling, rocking, echolalic speech, or excessive orderliness. The symptoms are persistent. About a fourth of children with autism have epileptic seizures (Rutter & Schopler, 1987). The cause of infantile autism is not known.

Implications. Early intervention has been shown to be effective in dealing with early autism. It typically requires an intensive behavior modification program, individual attention, and a structured learning environment.

Childhood Schizophrenia. Childhood schizophrenia is another childhood psychosis. Children with this disorder typically have a period of normal development, and the symptoms do not appear until after thirty months. They exhibit behaviors such as delusions (strange ideas), hallucinations (seeing or hearing imaginary things), dramatic swings in mood states, and repetitive language. They may have normal intellectual abilities but demonstrate difficulties relating to current situations or events. There is often a lack of social responsiveness, but not to the extent of children with autism. They have psychotic episodes interspersed with periods of near normal behavior (Rutter & Schopler, 1987). Language skills are more developed than in the autistic child, but language is rarely used for communication.

Implications. Early intervention has been shown to be effective. Programming includes one-on-one behavior modification, usually in conjunction with medication.

Attachment Disorders. Some children fail to develop appropriate interaction patterns with adults. They are often irritable, not easily comforted, dislike affection, and may be withdrawn. They may cry continuously with a piercing scream, arch their bodies to physical touch, and show no response to soothing interaction from adults. They often have poor eye contact. They are frequently described as "difficult" children. The caregiver may find it unpleasant and stressful to be with the child. The result is a failure of the caregiver to bond to the child. These children may have inadequate signaling systems that interrupt the early attachment process.

Attachment problems can also be related to the caregiver. Caregivers who do not respond to their children's cues, or respond in inappropriate ways, may contribute to attachment problems. Separation of the child and caregiver during early infancy can also affect the attachment process. Children who have extended and/or frequent hospitalizations when young are at great risk for attachment difficulties.

Implications. Failure to develop appropriate attachment patterns leads to children who are withdrawn or are socially noninteractive. They may be "cranky" and "whiny" with limited social responsiveness. This combination results in further isolation, as both adults and other children tend to ignore and/or dislike these children and refrain from interaction.

Child Abuse

Although not technically an emotional/behavioral disorder, child abuse has such potential for developing behaviors in this area that it is addressed here. Child abuse is often used as an umbrella term to encompass all forms of child mistreatment. It includes behaviors such as physical abuse and neglect, emotional maltreatment and neglect and sexual abuse of children. Children under the age of five are the most frequent victims, but cases have been documented on children of all ages. In 1990, there were 1.5 million reported cases of child abuse and neglect, however, it is estimated that unreported cases could be 2 to 3 times that number (Bowdry, 1990).

Emotional abuse is the most subtle and often unrecognized form of abuse, however, it can be extremely damaging to a child's self-esteem. Sometimes this abuse is based on parents' perceptions that if they fail to degrade the child he will get a "big head." The child is perceived and portrayed negatively by the parents, and the child may see himself in the same light and describe himself as "bad." This attitude can result in behavioral problems and antisocial behavior. The child himself may become cruel or abusive

of younger children. These children often feel unwanted and unloved.

Physical abuse includes excessive corporal punishment, misguided attempts at teaching children, and battering children. Some parents use physical punishment rather than reasoning with children in the belief that it takes physical measures to make children into good people. These measures include whipping, face smacking, hitting with boards, belts, and cords. Injuries that result from this are typically bruises, welts, and cuts. Parents who discipline children in this way frequently report similar punishments in their childhood. They may agree that the punishment is excessive, but remain convinced that the child may grow up to be a delinquent if the child does not learn right from wrong in this way. Some people feel this is acceptable behavior, not child abuse.

Some parents harm their children as they attempt to teach their child certain behaviors. They might burn the child's fingertips as a way of teaching him that stoves are hot and he should not touch them. These parents will readily admit what they have done, but they do not see it as abuse and may be offended that you consider it as such.

Some children are battered. These are often children who are four or younger and have parents with very unrealistic expectations about children and parenting. For example, parents may expect an infant to quit crying when told to do so. Children with disabilities represent a disproportionate number of battering victims. These children have unexplained or inconsistent injuries. Injuries vary from bruises to severe trauma. Full body X rays are essential in assessing the extent of the damage. In addition to the person who actively participates in the abuse, some adults participate as passive abusers. They enable the behavior to continue by not preventing or reporting it.

Neglect is the most commonly reported form of abuse. Parents may not have the money to buy enough food and clothing for their children, or they have very different priorities in how the money they have is spent. Single mothers disproportionately fall into this category. Particularly when they are working or looking for work and cannot afford child care. They leave their children alone. In many cases neglect is the result of adult drug abuse. In these cases all the "family" income is used to buy drugs.

Children who have been neglected may have poor hygiene and personal care skills. They may have poor attention spans, related to hunger or lack of stimulation at home. They typically receive little encouragement, have low feelings of self-worth and lack interpersonal skills. They may be behavior problems in the classroom. Unfortunately, problems associated with abuse and neglect are frequently compounded by prenatal exposure to drugs and alcohol. This condition plus a neglectful or abusive environment increases the child's risk for multiple problems.

Often adult stress can be the trigger for child abuse. The stress can be either positive or negative—

a move, birth or death in the family, unemployment, divorce or remarriage (Meddin & Rosen, 1986).

Implications. Children who have been abused or neglected need a school environment that accepts the child, offers him emotional support and reassurance. It is important to make the child feel secure by providing a gentle, understanding, and consistent environment. Reframe the child in the school environment. That is, take a positive quality and stress that aspect of the child. Parents need to see this aspect of the child so they, too, can begin to build a more positive image of the abilities of the child. You need to model behavior for the parents. Because parents may lack knowledge of appropriate and effective forms of discipline, you might encourage them to observe in the class where you can demonstrate these. Parents can also see appropriate ways of teaching children. Unless you are a trained counselor, family therapy should not be attempted.

Child Sexual Abuse

Child sexual abuse is any activity between a child and an adult (or much older child) which sexually excites or satisfies the adult's needs or desires. Both boys and girls are the victims. While the child is *never* at fault, children often never tell what has happened. The perpetrator frequently tries to keep the secret by convincing the child that it is his or her fault and that no one would believe the child anyway. Sexual abuse is further complicated because the most frequent perpetrators are natural parents, step-parents, adoptive and foster parents (Faller, 1989). Abuse by nonfamily members is the least frequent type to occur.

There are some behaviors that can be used as warning signs of sexual abuse. These include play or conversation which suggests sexual knowledge unusual for the child's age, frequent masturbation, increases in hard-to-prove illnesses such as headaches and stomachaches, frequent crying or depression, extreme changes in behavior and eating patterns, and reluctance to return home.

Implications. Children who have been sexually abused may find it difficult to trust adults. They may have low self-esteem and many self-doubts. Show interest in the child and make encouraging supportive statements, but also allow the child space to join at her own rate. These children will not interpret adult behavior in the same way as other children. This child may interpret a supportive hug as having sexual overtones. Move very slowly and build trust through consistency and caring.

Note. Teachers of young children have many opportunities to help prevent child abuse and neglect. First, as a role model; second, in knowing the indicators and risk factors so you can spot potential danger; and finally, in helping families obtain the

supports they need to stop abusive patterns. Your first alliance is to the child. You must report patterns of circumstances or behaviors that indicate abuse and neglect.

Emotional/Behavioral Problems

Emotional/behavioral problems can be divided into two broad categories: externalizing and internalizing. Externalizing behavior involves striking out against others. Children often display aggressiveness, destructiveness, temper tantrums, attention-seeking behaviors (hitting and biting), and so on. Children exhibiting internalizing behaviors show withdrawal, anxiety, crying, depression, unresponsiveness, shyness, timidity, and isolation (Achenbach, 1985).

Some behavioral problems are common to certain stages of development. When they appear during expected periods they are considered normal behaviors. When these behaviors persist beyond expected ages and/or the behaviors become excessive in nature, they are considered emotional/behavioral problems.

As behaviors that are classified as externalizing are usually the first focus of attention, they are discussed first.

Externalizing Emotional/Behavioral Problems

Aggressive and Antisocial Behavior. Aggressive antisocial behaviors include hitting, biting, and throwing objects at others. Hurting others, non-sharing, swearing, name calling, bribery, and stealing are also in this category. In general, there is a victim as well as the child who is exhibiting these behaviors.

Implications. To stop aggressive behavior you must acquire some specific information. Take a few days to watch the child and plan a strategy. Delaying action is difficult because there is an urge to do something about it "now." However, what you have been trying has probably not been working, so the usual approach may not be the right one. You need the following information:

1. When and where does the behavior happen?

Look for a pattern. First try to see if there is any pattern to the timing of the behavior that is causing the problem.

Time of day. Does it happen when the child first arrives? When the child is leaving? Before snack or lunch time? During nap time? Randomly?

Activities or routines. Does it occur during specific activities or routines? If you get a "yes," do some additional thinking about the activities. Are they structured or free choice? Group or individual? Are the children sitting or active?

Place. Is there a particular place where the behavior occurs (outdoors versus indoors)? Is there a particular area or room, such as where the blocks are or the dramatic play area, that is the site of the behavior?

2. What causes or triggers the behavior? What happened immediately before the incident? Did another child take something away from the child or did the child ask for something to which another child said "no"? Did you say "no"? Was the child in an argument with another child? Were the children fighting or "pretend fighting" at the onset? Was the child tired?

3. Who is the victim? Is the victim anyone who happens to be there or is it usually a particular child or a certain few children? If it is a variety of children, check if they are mostly boys or girls or both. Are they bigger or smaller children? Are they older or younger children? Are they aggressive children or shy, timid children?

4. How does the child act after the behavior? Does the child deny the behavior or admit that it was done? Is the child upset by the victim's crying (if that is what happened)? Does the child get upset if the victim returns the behavior (e.g., bites or hits back)? Does the child look to see if an adult is watching before proceeding with the behavior? Does the child walk away? Does the child apologize and show concern for the victim?

The results of this information will focus your intervention. Use the guidelines at the end of this chapter for suggestions as well.

Temper Tantrums. Just about all children at one time or another display tantruming behavior. Tantrums are usually strong expressions of anger characterized by crying, screaming, and maybe hitting, kicking, or destroying materials. Older children may also hit others or use language to express frustration. Prior to developing adequate language abilities to express anger or frustration, children use tantruming as their way for venting pent-up tension.

Adults play an important role in helping children learn socially appropriate methods of releasing anger and tension. Modeling appropriate behavior is one way children learn. Teaching children what is acceptable without inhibiting their release of anger is necessary. As children develop language, they are better able to use speech as a viable way to express frustration and anger.

Children with tantruming behaviors often have delayed language skills. Physical outbursts of emotions are one of the few ways for them to express anger or frustration. The older the children, the more intense can be the tantruming behaviors. Tantrums can also be attention-seeking behaviors, especially for children raised in environments severely lacking in social stimulation.

Implications. Reinforcing appropriate behaviors while providing consequences for negative behaviors is the accepted method for treatment. Consequences can include loss of privileges, time-out, verbal reprimands. Reinforcement includes physical and social rewards for good behavior.

Biting. Most children go through a stage during which they bite or pinch others, whether children or adults. This is expected behavior of toddlers. They are egocentric and think only of themselves. They notice other children, but see them as objects, not real people. There is frequent tension over possession of objects. Children are learning to control their own lives, and saying "no" and biting can be used to get what one wants. Language skills are still developing and children do not yet have a good repertoire of words to express anger or frustration in acceptable ways.

Toddlers need verbal direction and support to redirect their anger in socially appropriate ways. Give them the verbal phrases to use. When children persist in biting and pinching past expected ages or when the biting is excessive, with breaking of the skin, the behavior is of concern.

Implications. Begin by looking closely at the environment and ensuring the setting is appropriate for children, including enough materials, correct structure and design, and appropriate curriculum. Prevent opportunities for biting by being alert to possible problem situations, reinforcing acceptable social behavior, and, if necessary, setting up a behavior program that informs the child the behavior is unacceptable, including possible use of consequence procedures (Essa, 1990).

Internalizing Emotional/Behavioral Problems

Withdrawal and Shyness. All young children exhibit withdrawal and/or shyness at some point in their early years. Young children develop stranger anxiety around the eighth month, and again around the eighteenth month. They cling to familiar adults around strangers, especially in unfamiliar environments. This anxiety eventually subsides as children develop a sense of security and trust. The failure to develop this security results in overanxious children who are unable to operate effectively in settings away from significant adults.

Excessive withdrawal, characterized by the inability to develop relationships with parents or peers, inactivity, excessive social isolation, and lack of affect, is of concern. Consistent lack of interaction will cause a child to miss experiences that lead to improved social competency, better self-esteem, and increased overall development.

Implications. Settings that emphasize warmth, caring, and consistency can help children overcome feelings of insecurity. Children may need to be taught social skill techniques, combined with social reinforcement for all social initiatives.

School can be a frightening experience for some children. Lacking adult language skills, these children often comfort themselves with infantile behaviors. Only when these behaviors persist for a long time is an emotional behavioral disorder indicated.

Eating. All children go through stages in which eating certain foods can be problematic, usually more a problem for adults than for the children. Typical eating problems involve "finicky" eating habits. Children may go through phases where they will eat only certain foods like hot dogs, peanut butter and jelly, and candy. They may refuse to eat most table foods, and eat on the run, grabbing an apple slice and cracker. For most children, these finicky habits are just phases that they experience and pass through.

For some children, eating problems are more severe and can lead to nutritional problems which affect development. Some infants develop a pattern in which they refuse to eat, turning their head away from nursing, the bottle, and cereal. Some of these children fall into a category of "failure to thrive" babies. They develop a pattern of refusing to eat or drink and refusing social interaction. Their weight can suddenly drop dramatically and necessitate medical intervention, including intravenous feeding. Treatment may include slowly enticing the child to begin eating again. This can be a long process.

Some children also develop a behavior identified as "pica," which is the eating of inedible substances. Young children naturally go through the stage of mouthing everything and tasting small objects. However, some children may actually search for objects and substances to ingest that are inedible, such as paint, chalk, paper, or other objects. The lead content in some paint can have severely damaging effects

on children and possibly result in mental retardation. Pica behaviors can be difficult to reverse, especially if left unattended for too long.

Implications. Reinforcing appropriate eating habits, ensuring the children are not hungry, consistent eating routines, and possible behavior modification techniques can help to overcome most eating problems.

General. At a more general level, before deciding a child has an emotional/behavioral disorder see if there are changes occurring in the child's life. Is there a new sibling, a grandparent visiting, a parent away? (Note: A child who is missing her parents may just need a lap to sit in.) If the behavior is unusual for that child, check to see if she is feeling well. Sometimes the first sign of an illness is a negative change in the child's behavior. Don't reach a conclusion too quickly. Be sure to talk with parents about how characteristic the behavior is. If possible have them come in and observe.

Children's Needs: Teaching Goals

Related annual goals may be grouped under broad categories called "teaching goals." Outlined under each teaching goal below are the most important needs of children with emotional/behavioral disorders. A child may have some or all of these needs and additional ones as well. Suggestions on what you might consequently teach them are included. Often, a course of action is implicit in the description of the need.

Feelings

Before children can learn to control feelings, they must become aware of their emotions and how they respond to them. It is important to ask a child how he feels: "When I see you sitting alone in your cubbie, I wonder how you are feeling." Don't tell a child, "You're lonely"; he may not be lonely—he may be sad or angry. Help the child learn that he is the only one who knows how he feels. Once a child is aware of feelings, he can be taught to express them. If you, as a teacher, accept the feelings and don't judge them, then the child will probably continue to talk. If children are told that it is silly or stupid to feel the way they do, they are likely to quit talking about how they feel.

More than others, these children need help in feeling they are part of the group. They need to be aware of individual differences, know the other children, and know that they too are accepted and belong even when they are isolated or have conflicts with others. Plan activities that don't demand a great deal of social interaction yet allow children to see themselves as part of the group. For example, have each child paint or color an area of a mural, or have each child contribute a page to a class book.

Language

Children who have emotional/behavioral disorders need to develop the language and vocabulary necessary to express their wants, needs, and feelings. Teach children words that facilitate this development: *happy, sad, tense, relaxed, tight,* and so on.

Awareness

Children need to become more aware of their body and the relationship between their feelings and what their body does. They need help learning how to recognize tension in their body and how to release that tension in a way that doesn't infringe on the rights of others. Children need to know how their body feels just before aggressive interactions and, once this knowledge is attained, you can help children learn to substitute other behaviors. (It is much like toilet training in that respect.) Children need to become aware of their body before they can control it.

Provide experiences in which these children are likely to be successful. Point out things that they do well. Look at the situational aspects of things that don't go well and verbalize these aspects to the child: "It is really difficult for *you and Joey* to play together in the block corner."

Guidelines

Children with social and emotional needs, whether temporary or long term, need a warm, relaxed, and secure environment. Accept the children as they are, not as you would like them to be, and gear your requirements accordingly. Allow children to work at their own pace. Until children can cope with the world, they may not have the energy to forge ahead academically, even if tests show they have the ability. You can still prod a bit, but keep the whole child in mind when you do.

Perhaps the most important thing you can do for these children is help them accept themselves as good people. The most effective ways to do that are to teach children to control the behaviors that cause other children to avoid them and to provide successful experiences for them in the various curriculum areas.

Set up your classroom in a way that is conducive to this child's learning.

Prevention. The simplest solution for preventing unwanted behavior is to arrange the environment to decrease the likelihood of such occurrences.

1. Remove objects or toys that cause problems. Make it a rule that if a child brings a squirt gun from home, it must stay in the child's locker until it is time to go home.

2. Consider restructuring the class day, especially if the child seems to have problems at the same times each day. If large group time is at 10:30 and this is a bad time for the child, consider rearranging the schedule so that the class is outside at 10:30 and in group time at 9:30 or 11:00.

3. If a child cannot cope with a situation, take him out of it early, before it worsens. If children are having problems playing together in the dramatic play area and your several solutions to sharing aren't working say, "There are too many children in the dramatic play area now. Who would be willing to play in another area?" If no one volunteers, ask a child. If that doesn't work, close down that area for the day. This is one way of preventing the need for more drastic measures.

4. Be sure the child understands what is expected of him. His definition of sharing the blocks may be very different from yours. You may have to ask questions to determine his perceptions. Be specific: "Which blocks are you sharing with Misha?" (The child points to three small blocks.) "You need to give him some of the big blocks too." (You may need to specify how many as well.)

5. As you learn more about the children in your class, be aware of who is sitting beside whom. Some combinations of children provoke trouble. You might place yourself between these children or ask another teacher to sit there or have one of the children move.

6. If you have planned a long story or listening time and some of the children are having problems listening for long periods, change the pace. Break for something active, such as having the children stretch as high and low as they can reach, then come back to your quiet activity.

7. Teach children to distinguish between feelings and behavior and provide them with socially acceptable outlets that are easily accessible. If the child feels like hitting something, then she can hit a punching bag or the playdough, or kick a ball.

8. Arrange your space to go along with your goals for positive behavior management. If you want to encourage more independence, arrange materials on low open shelves where the children can choose their own playthings. Have duplicates of the most popular toys when possible.

9. Keep waiting times to a minimum. Make waiting interesting by singing songs, doing fingerplays, and so on. Often behavior problems develop when children are unoccupied and expected to wait for long periods.

10. Change the environment: Look around. Can the traffic patterns be rearranged, the lighting made less harsh, toys that create problems removed, or duplicates purchased? Is there a good balance of active and passive activities? Are children being asked to sit too long for their age? Are they given choices? Are children being "warned" before changes?

11. Evaluate yourself and the children objectively: Are there particular behaviors that you don't

like? What is your temperamental style? What is the match or mismatch between the children you find most difficult and your temperament? What can you change about your own behavior?

12. Set limits and reinforce them: Children need to know what your expectations are for them. Write them down for yourself, tell the children, and post them both in writing and in picture form (you can draw a stick figure of a child with a block in a raised hand and put a large X over it). Try to keep your limits to as few as possible, but when children violate these there need to be natural and logical consequences to their behavior. For example, the child who throws blocks cannot play in the block area for the rest of the day.

13. Mediate: Children rarely think about how what they do affects others. Children need to be told that being hit with a block hurts and perhaps add that other children might not want to play with them if they do that.

14. Be patient: Changing is difficult, both for children and adults. When you become discouraged, try to think of *one* time when the desired response occurred. If even that doesn't work, pretend it did and think through the result. The struggle is long and hard, but the development of children is worth it.

Classroom Management. Your goals are to strengthen, or reinforce, appropriate behavior and to redirect inappropriate behavior. Let's start with the strengthening goal. It is easy to reinforce children who do the right things. Praise, a smile, a "thank you," a hug, or even a token reward works, but with children who don't do the right things, where do you start? Start with a principle called *successive approximation.* Reinforce the child at each step that brings him closer to the goal. For example, if a withdrawn child like Julie sits in her locker and cries during group time, praise her when she doesn't cry. Then praise her when she progresses (with your encouragement) to sitting on a chair beside her locker, a chair at a table, a chair nearer the group, a chair behind the group, a chair in the group, and then finally the floor in the group. Reward each stage, but don't expect her to go directly from the locker to the middle of the group. This process may take several days or weeks. You might try discussing with Julie where she'd like to sit. Then after you and she reach an agreement, reinforce behavior that conforms to the agreement. As children do things closer to what you want, keep rewarding that behavior until you achieve the goal.

Modeling—demonstrating behavior in situations—is also effective, but can be doubled-edged. Children tend to model meaningful people, which in a classroom means they will probably model you over classmates or volunteers (and model parents over you). You are always on display. If you combat aggression with aggression, you may then serve as an aggressive model for children regardless of your

Children should be allowed to approach new materials and situations in their own way. While some children are tentative and need support, others require limits.

intentions. Be a good model by behaving in a way you would like the children to copy.

Cueing—warning children before they are expected to do something—is another effective means of changing behavior. You use cueing when you flick the lights to tell the children it is cleanup time. More specifically, if Amy looks longingly at John's truck, warn her by saying, "Ask John if he is using the truck." Don't wait until Amy has clobbered John and then say, "John was using the truck. It hurts him when you hit him." If you can anticipate that the child is about to do something undesirable, act *before* it happens. When you sense trouble, just moving into the area will do a lot to prevent a child from misbehaving. (Observers comment that they can see children visually locating the teacher before carrying out some aggressive behavior.) Giving a child a "teacher look" is another way to cue a child that something the child is doing or plans to do is not appropriate. These nonverbal techniques (frowns, eye contact, throat clearing) are most effective when a child is just beginning to act out. To work, they typically require a relationship with the child.

When children have adjustment needs, it is important to fine-tune your classroom-management techniques. Be consistent, set clear limits, and state the necessary rules only as briefly as possible. However, be prepared to enforce those that you have. Make children aware of both positive and negative consequences. If you don't think you can enforce a rule, don't make it.

If a rule states that everyone who plays with the blocks helps to clean them up, you need to know who played with them. Then if one child is reluctant to help, you need to say, "Mae, you played with the blocks, so you need to help clean them up." If there is no response, you might make an offer: "It's time to pick up the blocks. Do you want to do it by yourself, or would you like me to help you?" If necessary, physically help Mae by opening her hand, placing a block in it, closing the hand, walking with her (or carrying her if need be) to the block shelf, helping her deposit the block in the right place, and then thanking her for helping. The rule was not that children had to clean up *all* the blocks. Time and physical limitations might make such a rule unenforceable. The children are only required to *help*, and even one block put away is a help.

When a child does do something that you want continued, by all means reinforce the child's behavior. Decide what specific behavior you want to reinforce (such as sitting through group time). Tell the children they can have or do something they value if they do the specific behavior you've decided on. The trick in using reinforcement is to discover what is rewarding to particular children. Praise, attention, being able to go outside first, a hug, or some time alone to read in the book corner may be the answers for different children. Make your best guess and then try it out. (If the behavior continues, you are doing something rewarding.) When dealing with adjustment needs, be cautious about being demonstrative at first. Some children find this frightening, and some find it difficult to handle praise. A child may not consider a hug or praise at all rewarding.

Some children will prefer rewards that you don't personally like. Start with their preferences until the behavior is established. Then decide how to change the reward system. For example, if the child finds candy rewarding and you want to use praise, use the following procedures. When Doyle does well, praise him, then give him candy. Gradually stop giving the candy. Present the new reward just before you present the old one that you know works but that you want to change.

Reward children's behavior each time only until the behavior becomes established, then reward randomly. This is the way to have behavior continue. If you *always* reward behavior then forget a few times, the child will decide you don't want that behavior to continue—if you did you would keep rewarding it as in the past. Random reinforcement is a proven method for establishing a new behavior. (Regretfully, the same principle works in reverse for setting limits. If you uphold the limits sometimes and not others, the children will *always* test them. It is important to always reinforce limits!)

If you think a child is acting out to get attention, purposefully ignore the behavior (providing the behavior isn't dangerous to the child or other children). Make a mental note to give attention when the child does something that is desired. Give the child cues for acceptable ways of getting your attention: "If you

want me to watch you build with the blocks, ask and I'll come over."

When these approaches don't solve the behavior problem, you need to take a more systematic structured approach to changing the behavior.

Write down the information that you gathered in the informal observation. Next, gather some baseline data on frequency and write that down. That is, if hitting is the problem, wear an apron with a pocket and keep a paper and pencil in it. Put a mark for each time the child hits during the day. (This can be adapted for whatever behavior is the problem.) You can get more elaborate and write down the time, place, victim, and reaction if you want. However, the first step is determining "How often does this behavior occur?" Do this for three days in a week and put it on a chart.

Mark where you begin to intervene. By using a chart like this you can tell if you are making a difference. If necessary, you can show the parents your documentation of the problem.

Intervention. All teachers and paraprofessionals must use the same procedure.

1. Quickly check on the victim. If possible, have another adult do this.

2. Tell the child firmly but quietly that you will not tolerate the behavior (think through this statement so you know exactly what you will say ahead of time): For example, say as you are walking with the child to a time out chair: "I will not allow you to hurt other children. You must sit here until I tell you you may get up."

3. Note the time or set a timer, turn your back on the child and walk away. Do not talk to the child or make eye contact with the child during this time. If other children approach the child simply state, "_____ needs to be alone for a few minutes."

4. Choose a time that is developmentally appropriate for the child. A definition of appropriate is

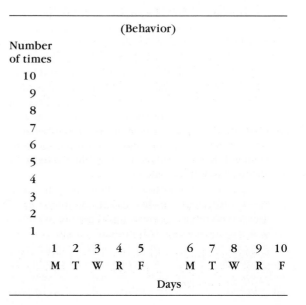

(Behavior)

Number
of times

10
9
8
7
6
5
4
3
2
1

  1 2 3 4 5   6 7 8 9 10
  M T W R F   M T W R F

Days

one minute for each year of the child's age. Two minutes for a two-year-old, four minutes for a four-year-old, and so on is appropriate. (Although this seems like a short time to adults, a child's perception is very different. It is far better to keep it short than to deal with the child's behavior during "time out.")

5. When the time is up, go to the child and say, "You may get up now." Help the child find an activity that is of interest. Don't discuss the incident; the child is aware of the reasons for being in "time out." At this point it is over, and feelings and behavior should go on as if nothing had happened (Essa, 1990).

If a particular child or children are especially difficult, remember that you can get help. You don't have to solve all problems on your own. Sometimes someone outside of your setting can be more objective about the situation. For example, ask another teacher or an administrator to watch the situation for a while and offer suggestions.

Positive behavior management requires respectful treatment of all children. Your consistent modeling of respect for the children in your care is probably the most powerful behavior management tool you have. Positive relationships between adults and children and between children themselves are the foundation of each person's feeling good about herself. Children who feel loved and respected are more likely to help and follow your rules.

Curriculum Adaptations

The number and degree of adaptations depend on each child's needs. Your awareness of short-term needs will do a lot toward the child's long-term adjustment.

Language Arts: Speaking, Listening, Reading, and Writing

The language arts area can help children develop the language skills to talk about situations they find difficult and the feelings these situations bring about. Through literature, children learn how other children have dealt with similar feelings and situations.

Speaking. Although children with emotional/behavioral disorders speak, they may not use speech to communicate with others. It is important that they learn to use speech for social interaction.

1. Teach vocabulary for expressing feelings. Use words the child can understand: *mad, sad, happy, tight, ready to hit, tense, excited.*

2. Encourage children to use words to solve problems: "May I play in the hospital with you? I could be the nurse."

3. Demonstrate words, especially those associated with feelings. Pretend to be a statue or fashion model. Have the children tell you how to arrange yourself to show a specific emotion. If necessary, give them some clues about the areas to address: "I'm angry. Should my hands be open or closed? Should I look up or down? How should my mouth be?"

Fingerplays are beneficial for children because they provide opportunities for peer-group acceptance and positive role modeling.

1. If a child has a characteristic behavior such as hand waving, incorporate it into a fingerplay or a set of motions done to music: Do this in a way that helps the child feel part of the group but doesn't draw attention to him: "Shake, shake, shake your hands, Shake your hands together." Then do something else that is incompatible with hand shaking: "Clap, clap, clap your hands, Clap your hands together." Ask for volunteers to do other motions.

2. Use fingerplays to "settle" children. Practice fingerplays ("Open Shut Them") that finish with the hands in the lap. Whether a fingerplay merely quiets the children or has them keep their hands in their lap, they will be less likely to poke their neighbors.

Listening. Use listening to increase children's awareness of their behavior.

1. Give children short, simple, and specific directions until they can predictably follow them.

2. Tell children what to do, not what not to do.

3. Reassure children with your words and the tone of your voice.

4. Give children feedback about their behavior: "You are walking too fast. Walk more slowly." (Put a hand on the child and walk with him.)

5. If children seem to listen but not understand, think about the content and whether the child has the internal language for understanding.

Groups. As many listening experiences happen during group time, be aware of some of the inherent problems for these children in groups.

1. Interestingly, aggressive children are often fearful of attack by others. This is particularly true when their personal space is invaded by sitting next to others. Try to seat these children between the most nonthreatening children in the classroom. However, keep a careful eye out for warning signs of aggression. Placing a child next to an adult externalizes their control and contributes to dependency.

2. Call on a child who is hyperactive frequently, or just mention her name; this helps focus attention.

Keep activities short, give directions frequently, and intersperse physical activities with those that focus on listening.

3. Children who are anxious may also find group experiences threatening. They should be seated by nonaggressive children. Although given the opportunity to talk, they shouldn't be forced to respond in front of the group.

4. Children who are withdrawn may not be able to participate in the group at the beginning. Initially they may need to watch and listen from the fringes. As children show signs of becoming part of the group encourage them as well as their participation.

5. Children who are psychotic may need an adult with them during group time. This is one of their weakest skill areas. Don't stop reevaluating their behavior. By the end of the year they may have contributions to make (adapted from Lasher, Mattick, Perkins, von Hippel, & Hailey, 1978).

Reading. Mastering reading readiness skills requires the child to make fine auditory and visual distinctions. Although here the needs of this child are similar to those of other children, try to use subject matter that is especially relevant to the adjustment needs of the child.

1. Distinguish and label facial features. Play Lotto by matching faces. Even in simple line drawings, focus attention on the face.

2. Have children discuss moods. Write language experience stories using these as themes. Discuss what might happen to make children happy or sad.

3. Cut pictures of people and situations out of magazines. (Those with obvious themes are easiest.) Have the children make up a story about what might have happened and how the people involved may have felt. Invent a variety of endings

and discuss which aspects of situations that could change.

Use stories to help children increase skills in dealing with themselves and others. (See the Children's Bibliography on page 286.)

1. Read stories dealing with angry feelings and peer conflict.

2. Select stories that have problem situations pertinent to the child's.

3. Tell stories about a child who learns to deal with feelings: "Once upon a time there was a girl named _____ who . . ."

Writing. Writing, like other fine motor activities, is problematical with these children. Again, focus on the process, not the product. Some children may find it is easier to convey ideas graphically than verbally.

1. Have a variety of materials available, especially large paper and large markers and crayons.

2. Help children focus on the communicative aspect of writing as opposed to fine motor or art.

3. Praise their efforts and call them authors and/or illustrators. Any attempts they make at communication in any media need to be encouraged.

4. Securing paper with a clipboard may be helpful.

Discovery: Mathematics, Science, Computers

Children need positive, successful learning experiences. Praise participation and the process regardless of the outcome. Break tasks down into small steps that can be done in a short amount of time.

Mathematics. Math skills can be taught for their own sake, but when taught as part of other activities, they can also be used to increase a child's general awareness.

1. Use math to point out likenesses and differences and to create a sense of group belonging: "There are *three* boys with brown hair, but only *one* boy with brown hair and a plaid shirt."

2. Incorporate math skills into turn taking and sharing: "You can play with the truck for five minutes, then it is Stan's turn." (Set a timer.) "You can ride the trike around the play yard four times, then give it to Finé."

3. Use simple card games like Fish to encourage peer interaction.

Science. A discovery approach has great potential for teaching science to children with adjustment problems. They can be doing what they prefer, yet still be part of a group.

1. Help children to understand cause and effect relationships as they learn the physical properties of materials: "Snow melts when it gets warm."

2. Help children make predictions about experiments before they actually do them: "What will happen to the balance when you put the cup on it? Let's try it and see." Eventually you can expand this skill to personal situations: "What might Brad do if you take this book?"

Computers. Computers offer the potential for communication without the need to cope with people. For some children this is much less threatening.

1. Start with simple programs where the children are in control and a single key stroke makes something happen. Talk with them about what they are doing. Help them begin to focus their behavior and make it more purposeful.

2. Make the computer an activity of their choice. They can come and leave at will. When they come, however, support their being there and try to make it intriguing.

3. This may be an opportunity for children to work together. They can actually work on the same software with little need for personal interaction.

Sensory Motor: Large Motor, Sensory Motor Integration, Small Motor

Children have the potential for developing gross and fine motor skills, the opportunity for peer interaction, and opportunities to learn spatial and temporal concepts. Help children learn to keep their level of activity under control.

Large Motor. Large motor activities should not be equated with being out of control.

Teach children to use large motor play to run off excess energy and frustration. The benefits are obvious to adults who clean house or jog or work out in a gym when angry. Children have yet to learn this. Rather than have them sit in time-out or read a book, help them learn to release energy. Encourage them to play hard until they are tired but not exhausted.

1. If children have a long ride to school, plan to do some large motor activities early in the day.

2. Actively encourage these children to participate. It is a good way to learn about oneself. It is also something the child might like and excel at.

3. Large motor play may let an aggressive child be part of a group and accepted in this role.

4. Consider adding a punching bag to your room. When children feel like hitting something, encourage them to hit the punching bag—hard. A duffle bag filled with old clothes and suspended from the ceiling works well. Comment positively on this behavior: "You really can hit that punching bag hard."

5. Use light, large, cardboard blocks. They are less of a problem when a conflict arises.

6. Have children throw Velcro-covered ping-pong balls at a bull's-eye or beanbags at a target.

Sensory Motor Integration. Children with emotional/behavioral disorders may not have good sensory motor integration. Obviously, a goal is to increase this, however, it must be done very gradually if children are hypersensitive in this area.

1. Some children are hypersensitive to touch. Allow children to wear a sweater or jacket when contact is likely. Designate personal space and be sure all children know the rules of the game.

2. Avoid competitive games, especially "chase" type games. Add a cooperative, or at least noncompetitive component to games.

3. Adapt games so children are not eliminated.

4. Be sure children have good control of their hands and fingers before expecting them to control tools. Build this strength through using dough, spray bottles, hole punches, holding on while swinging, and so on.

Small Motor. The timing of small motor tasks is crucial for children with emotional/behavioral disorders. If a child is already feeling frustrated, problems connected to small motor development may increase the frustration.

1. Encourage the use of small motor toys on children's good days or at good times of the day.

2. Use many varieties of toys, including some of the *large* small motor toys designed for younger children.

3. If a child appears frustrated by a toy or activity, remove the child, because usually his next step is to dump or throw the materials. Although rarely dangerous, the child's actions can create a real mess, with ensuing problems if you enforce clean-up rules.

Social Awareness: Social Studies, Inclusion, Health and Safety

For children with emotional/behavioral disorders this area is paramount. These children are not tuned into the world around them, and they need to be. They lack social skills, and because they do not deal with reality well, they are safety risks.

Social Studies. As children get into the preschool years, interaction with peers and the community at large becomes more important.

1. Adjustment problems may have their basis in the family. Talk about many different types of families: with one or two children, with many children, single parent, step or blended, with relatives living in the home, mixed racial, and with adopted or foster children.

2. Expand the concept of families by talking about the different roles: mother, wife, friend, daughter, teacher, sister. Help the children see their own various roles: son, friend, brother, pupil.

3. Be sure to acquaint the children with community helpers and their roles. Role play such situations as being lost, seeing a fire, and being sick.

4. Talk about the many roles of community helpers (some children may be frightened of police given their experience with them). They may need a neutral ground to learn about the variety of roles community helpers play.

Inclusion. It may seem clear to you by this point that including children with severe behavioral disorders will be a challenge. You are right. There may not be enough "nonaggressive" children to go between all the children who have behavior problems. Or, it may not seem fair to them. Teachers who have successfully included children with severe problems in this area have tried to build a circle of friendship for them.

1. Talk about children who are aggressive (or whatever specific problem you have) and what the child is like. Be sure that it is clear that it is not the child's fault.

2. Ask children what they think it would be like to be like that?

3. Then ask them how they would feel. (They will usually say lonely, angry, mad, and so on.)

4. Ask them how they behave when they feel that way.

5. Ask them what they really want from others when they feel that way.

6. Help them see how difficult it is to provide what they want, but challenge them to see if they are willing to help another child who feels like this.

7. Let them decide what they are willing to do as individuals and as a group to help another child become a member. Support their decisions as long as they are not counterproductive (they are far more willing to do what they decide than what you tell them).

8. Support their efforts, and reward their behaviors. Regardless of the result, they have learned about humanity and about themselves. They may even help a child become part of a group.

Health and Safety. Help the child learn to accept that the world is a basically safe place when you understand how to handle things and when to exercise caution.

1. Label "dangerous" things and discuss ways of dealing with them. Show children how to use the stove light to tell if an electric stove is on. (Use water to teach them the concepts *hot* and *cold* if they do not know them.)

2. Help the child gain independence and self-esteem by teaching self-help skills. To teach dressing, use buttoning and zipping frames as well as natural opportunities such as before and after toileting, coming and going home from school or outside, or playing with large dolls. Be sure children learn to wipe themselves, flush, and wash and dry their hands after using the toilet. Provide a variety of snacks or lunches to help children learn to use eating utensils correctly.

3. Use cleanup time to help the child feel like part of the group, and try to create a sense of responsibility for keeping the room neat.

Creative Arts: Art, Music, Creative Movement, and Dramatic Play

You need to be clear with children that the general behavioral expectations of the classroom apply to creative arts activities as well.

Art. Art can teach children about their bodies and how to express their feelings.

1. Use activities that incorporate the child's body or name.

    a. Make body pictures. Trace the outline of the child on a large sheet of paper. Have the child color and cut it out to make a life-sized paper doll.

    b. Use water to paint the child's shadow on the sidewalk.

    c. Use face- or body-shaped paper for painting or coloring.

    d. Make a "Name Book"—a book about the children and what each child does and likes.

    e. Make posters or books using pictures of the children in the class.

    f. Do foot or hand printing or painting.

2. Help children use three-dimensional art media such as clay to work through feelings. Let them pound, roll, and tear the clay.

3. Encourage children to paint their feelings and to use the paintings to talk about these feelings.

4. If children seem reluctant to try messy activities, try some "clean" messy activities. Use shaving cream for finger paint.

Music. Music can be used to teach the relationship between feelings and sound. Combined with movement, it is good for energy release.

1. If children are particularly wound up and you need to calm them down, start out with a vigorous tune and work toward a slow one. Make a tape of selections ranging from very loud and active to quiet and restful. Condense to save time. Tape only a part of each piece rather than the whole piece.

2. Once children have learned songs, use them often to promote a sense of predictability in a changing world. Teach new songs after singing old favorites.

3. The motion of the record player and/or tape recorder is fascinating to some children. When not in use they need to be stored out of reach.

4. Music can be exciting to children. Be sure to use quiet music before ending the activity.

5. Particular rhythms can be very enjoyable to children with emotional/behavioral disorders. The child may be encouraged to request a particular song.

Creative Movement. Children need to learn to control their bodies, be aware of their internal feelings, and develop socially acceptable behaviors that respond to these feelings. Help children learn to tense their body like wooden soldiers or to relax like a rag doll, for example. An adult may have to move the child's body in some way that responds.

1. At the beginning these children may have to be "moved through" the activity. (Although this is not by most standards creative, it is a beginning for participation.)

2. Add movement to make music time more than just a listening experience.

3. Movement requires space. Music activities with movement are good for helping children learn how much space they require not to bump into each other.

Dramatic Play. Dramatic play can be used to help children build successful peer relations and work out fears about specific issues.

1. If a child wants to play with another child or a group of children but does not know how to join the group, you might join the group with that child, play until the child becomes involved, and then slowly lessen your own involvement.

2. If a child is afraid to join in the play when many children are present, arrange some special times when this child and a child he or she likes can do things together. Arrange some dramatic play time together inside when the rest of the class is outside. Plan a visit to the office or kitchen or other separate room where the two can play together for a while.

3. Let children see how they fit into the various roles and relationships in a family, school, store, hospital, or fire station. Let them try different roles.

4. Help children re-enact fearful experiences in the more supportive class atmosphere, where they can come to grips with the experience.

5. Encourage the children to try on animal roles or roles of things they are afraid of, such as ghosts, monsters, skeletons, and snakes. This helps children feel in control.

6. Use puppets as a way for children to talk indirectly about experiences.

7. Have telephones available. These children may talk more freely when not face to face with their partner.

Transitions

Transitions may be the most difficult time of the day. It may be necessary for you or a paraprofessional to walk with the child when activities change. Consider having a classmate be a partner during this time. Consider the number of transitions in the day. Could any of them be eliminated? (For example, could you have an "open" snack that is available to the children during free play rather than a time specified for it when all children must participate?)

1. Follow a regular routine for arrivals, departures, and moving among activities. If the adults are disorganized, the children will feel even more confused.

2. Gradually reduce the support you offer during routines to match the child's learning.

3. Some children, particularly psychotic ones, have a difficult time coping with noise and movement, and have little internal sense of time. For them transitions may be incomprehensible and overwhelming. Adult support is necessary during these times until the child adjusts.

4. Use transitions to single children out and build their self-esteem. When you dismiss children from large group time or while you wait for others to join the group, try:

   Singing the children's names.

   Writing the names on the blackboard.

   Calling last names and telephone numbers.

   Calling parents' names.

   Using initials. (Children often are not aware there are so many different ways of referring to themselves.)

   Calling the child who lives at _____ (address).

Calling the child who has two brothers.

Describing an important event or fact about the child.

Calling hair color, eyes, or clothes.

Glossary

Acting out   Behavior that is physically aggressive when it is not warranted by the situation.

Autism   A rare mental disorder characterized by extreme withdrawal, speech and language impairment, and perceptual problems, as well as an inability to relate appropriately to people and objects.

Behavior disorders   Behavior that deviates from cultural norms and hence is hard to define specifically. What might be labeled a behavior disorder in one culture or setting might not be so labeled in another.

Neurosis   A mild mental disorder that is characterized by generalized anxiety, usually treated on an outpatient basis. These children are often mainstreamed. The neurotic child may be anxious about any or all new experiences.

Phobia   A mental disorder that is characterized by specific fears that seem to have no rational basis. School phobia, death phobia, and fear of abandonment are most common in young children.

Projective test   A psychological test in which the responses of the standardized materials are open-ended so that the child's particular response can be used to diagnose inner feelings and personality. (Children's Aperception Test—CAT—is an example.)

Psychiatrist   A medical doctor specializing in the diagnosis and treatment of mental disorders. The psychiatrist can prescribe drugs when necessary.

Psychologist   A specialist in the treatment of mental disorders through analysis, testing, and therapy, but who cannot prescribe drugs.

Psychosomatic disorders   Physical symptoms of illness that are caused by, or at least triggered by, emotions.

Psychosis   A severe mental disorder in which the child is disoriented and out of touch with reality.

Regression   A return to an earlier, more immature behavior, usually related to stress. As a situational, short-term problem it is common in all children.

Schizophrenia   A common psychosis that is characterized by extreme withdrawal, inability to establish relationships with others, disorientation, and extreme emotional responses. Hallucinations or delusions often occur as well.

Self-abusive behavior   Behavior that is characterized by excessive hitting, banging, or biting oneself on purpose (also called self-mutilation or self-destructive behavior). May sometimes be extinguished by behavior modification.

Self-stimulation   Inappropriate behaviors, or mannerisms (hand flapping, masturbation, teeth grinding), which apparently provide some sensory input for the child and are continued for this reason.

Transient situational personality disorders   Adjustment problems that usually stem from a traumatic event in the child's life, such as the death of a parent; the most common problem you will encounter among adjustment needs children. The symptoms differ for each child. Whether or not the child needs special help depends on the length and severity of the reaction.

Children's Bibliography

See the Children's Bibliography on page 286 for books to increase children's awareness about disabilities as well as books that are especially good for children with particular disabilities. Note especially:

Awareness of Emotional/Behavioral Disorders

Body Awareness

Divorce/Separation/Remarriage

Feelings

Friendship

Growing and Changing

New Baby

Starting School

Simpler Books (for teaching vocabulary and concepts)

Teaching Resources

In some situations you may want or need additional information. There are many national as well as regional, state, and local organizations that can be helpful to you. The following annotated list of national organizations should be useful in helping you decide where to get the information you need.

American Academy of Child Psychiatry
3615 Wisconsin Avenue, N.W.
Washington, DC 20016
   Write for publications on children's mental health.

American Association of Psychiatric Services
   for Children
1133 15th Street N.W., Suite 1000
Washington, DC 20005

Provides information on diagnosis and services.

Center for Attitudinal Healing
19 Main Street
Tiburon, CA 94920
Offers help, free of charge, to children and adults suffering from life-threatening diseases or traumatic accidents. Program deals with peace of mind and elimination of fear. Pain and death are openly discussed.

Foundation for Child Mental Welfare
255 West 71st Street
New York, NY 10023
Initiated development of Children's Day Treatment Center and School in New York City, an institution which works with mentally afflicted children and their families; seeks to rehabilitate children and return them to community schools and to a happier family and social life after a three-year program.

International Society for Autistic Children
1A Golders Green Road
London, NW11 8EA
England
Stimulates understanding of autism; exchanges information; performs research.

National Consortium for Child Mental Health Services
1424 16th Street, N.W., Suite 201A
Washington, DC 20036
Serves as a forum for exchange of information on child mental health services.

National Society for Autistic Children
621 Central Avenue
Albany, NY 12206
The national headquarters makes referrals to local chapters, and works for programs of legislation, education, and research for all mentally ill children.

The National Association for Mental Health
1800 North Kent Street
Rosslyn Station
Arlington, VA 22209
The national office refers individuals to local affiliations; directs a research program and a public information program; and acts as a liaison with governmental and private organizations. Also a source of information on both public and private mental health facilities.

References and Bibliography

Achenbach, T. (1985). *Assessment and taxonomy of child and adolescent psychopathology.* Beverly Hills, CA: Sage Publications.

Bowdry, C. (1990). Toward a treatment-relevant typology of child abuse families. *Child Welfare, 49* (4), 333–340.

Crow, G. A. (1978). *Children at risk: A handbook of the signs and symptoms of early childhood difficulties.* New York: Schocken.

Essa, E. (1990). *A practical guide to solving preschool behavior problems* (2nd ed.). Albany, NY: Delmar Publishers, Inc.

Faller, K. (1989). Why sexual abuse? An exploration of the intergenerational hypothesis. *Child Abuse and Neglect, 13,* 543–548.

Garbarino, J., Brookhouser, P. E., Authier, K. J., & Associates. (1987). *Special children–special risks: The maltreatment of children with disabilities.* Hawthorne, NY: Aldine de Gruyter, a division of Walter de Gruyter, Inc.

Hayes, R., & Stevenson, M. G. (1980). *Teaching the emotionally disturbed-learning disabled child: A practical guide* (4). Washington, DC: Acropolis Books.

Hewett, F. M., & Taylor, F. D. (1980). *The emotionally disturbed child in the classroom: The orchestration of success* (2nd ed.). Boston: Allyn and Bacon.

Kauffman, J. (1989). *Characteristics of children's behavior disorders* (4th ed.). Columbus, OH: Charles E. Merrill.

Kazdin, A. (1989). Developmental psychopathology: Current research, issues, and directions. *American Psychologist, 44,* 180–187.

Kazdin, A. (1989). *Conduct disorders in childhood and adolescence.* Beverly Hills, CA: Sage Publications.

Lasher, M., Mattick, I., Perkins, F., von Hippel, C., & Hailey, L. (1978). *Mainstreaming Preschoolers: Children with emotional disturbance.* Washington, DC: U.S. Department of Health and Human Services.

Meddin, B., & Rosen, A. (1986). Child abuse and neglect: Prevention and reporting. *Young Children, 41* (4), 26–30.

Menolascino, F. J., & Eyde, D. R. (1979). Biophysical bases of autism. *Behavioral disorders, 5,* 41–47.

Miller, D. (1990). *Positive child guidance.* Albany, NY: Delmar.

Mosier, D., & Pork, R. (1979). *Teacher-therapist: A text-handbook for teachers of emotionally impaired students.* Santa Monica, CA: Goodyear.

Newcomer, P. L. (1980). *Understanding and teaching emotionally disturbed children* (new ed.). Boston: Allyn and Bacon.

Reinert, H. R. (1980). *Children in conflict: Educational strategies for the emotionally disturbed and behaviorally disordered* (2nd ed.). St. Louis, MO: C. V. Mosby Co.

Rutter, M., & Schopler, E. (1987). Autism and pervasive developmental disorders: Concepts and diagnostic issues. *Journal of Autism and Developmental Disorders, 17,* 159–186.

Soderman, A. (1985 July). Dealing with difficult young children: Strategies for teachers and parents. *Young Children, 40* (5), 15–20.

Awareness Bibliography for Adults

Axline, Virginia Mae. (1964). *Dibs: In search of self.* Boston: Houghton Mifflin.

A bright boy who suffered from severe emotional deprivation. The book is based on Dr. Axline's records of the treatment and her later contacts with Dibs as he grew to adulthood. A bit dated, but a classic in the field.

Copeland, James. (1976). *For the love of Ann.* London: Severn House Publishers.

Within a year of her birth, Ann was demonstrating bizarre autistic behavior and turning her parents' lives into a nightmare. The book recounts the attempts made to alter Ann's behavior so that she could lead a normal life.

Greenfeld, Josh. (1972). *A child called Noah: A family journey.* New York: Holt, Rinehart and Winston.

The story in diary form of the thoughts and feelings of an autistic child's father, and what goes through his mind when he thinks about Noah's present and future.

Hundley, Joan. (1972). *The small outsider: The story of an autistic child.* New York: St. Martin's Press.

A mother's story about discovering autism in her son and the effects on herself and the rest of the family. The last part of the book tells about other autistic children and their families, and how they cope with the problems of living with an autistic child.

MacCracken, Mary. (1976). *Lovey, a very special child.* Philadelphia: Lippincott.

A teacher's account of a school year spent working with four emotionally disturbed children, ages eight to twelve.

Neufeld, John. (1969). *Lisa, bright and dark.* New York: S. G. Phillips.

The experience of a teenage girl who feels herself becoming increasingly mentally ill. Three girl friends try to help as her parents and teachers refuse to acknowledge her condition.

Park, Clara. (1972). *The seige: The first eight years of an autistic child.* Boston, MA: Little, Brown.

A mother's story of her autistic daughter's life from infancy through adolescence. She depicts the parents' frustrating search for professional help and counseling. The book contains numerous techniques and methods that Mrs. Park found useful with her daughter.

Phillips, Leon. (1975). *I love you, I hate you.* New York: Harper & Row.

Phillips writes about his daughter, Andrea, who has an emotional problem, tracing her antisocial behavior from childhood through adolescence. Parts of the book were written by Andrea herself, including passages from her diary, that show the inner torment of her life.

Rubin, Theodore Isaac. (1967). *Jordi/Lisa and David.* New York: Ballantine.

Two separate stories of psychotic children. *Jordi* is about a young autistic boy who suffers from severe anxiety attacks and hallucination, but who possesses superior intelligence. Reluctantly, his parents institutionalize the eight-year-old. He remained there for the next five years.

Lisa and David is about adolescents in a residential treatment center over a period of two years.

Autobiography of a schizophrenic girl, with analytic interpretation by Renée M. Sèchehaye. (1951). New York: Grune and Stratton.

The story of a young girl who went "mad" and was brought back to reality by a psychoanalyst, told in biographical form, with interpretation by the analyst. Good for anyone who has ever wondered what it is like to feel "split" or what analysts look for.

Smith, Bert. (1964). *No language but a cry.* Boston: Beacon Press.

Discusses the causes, types, and treatment of childhood mental illness. The author also deals with the needs of the parents and describes the facilities available to help these children find meaningful, useful lives.

Stehli, A. (1991). *The sound of a miracle: A child's triumph over autism.* New York: Doubleday.

The story of a family's frustrations and a mother's relentless quest for help for her autistic daughter Georgie. A French hearing specialist designed a program of music at frequencies where Georgie's hearing was supersensitive. She made tremendous progress following treatment.

Wexler, Susan Stanhope. (1955). *The story of Sandy.* Indianapolis: Bobbs-Merrill.

The struggles of a severely emotionally disturbed child, told by the boy's foster mother. At the age of three, Sandy came to live with foster parents after having been mistakenly diagnosed a "congenital imbecile."

Wilson, Louise. (1968). *This stranger, my son: A mother's story.* New York: Putnam.

The story of Tony, a beautiful child who grows increasingly difficult to handle, much to the concern of both his parents and siblings. The parents were blamed for Tony's problem. When they learned of theories of a biological basis for paranoid schizophrenia, they were relieved of their guilt feelings.

Chapter 17

Children with Mental Retardation

Watching André, you would guess him to be one of the youngest children in the class, yet he is actually one of the oldest. He rarely has much to say, and he seems to play at things rather than with them. Everything seems hard for him. And then, in certain areas it is as if a light goes on, and he can do things the others can't. His self-help skills are certainly as good as the other children's, but many things seem to be beyond him. I thought about referring him for testing, but I really can't decide if it is just the environment he lives in or if he is not as capable of learning as the others.

This vignette summarizes many of the concerns in the field of mental retardation today. A majority of children who are identified as mentally retarded are mildly retarded and look like other children. We do not have good methods for identifying children who are mildly retarded at early ages. Therefore, it is not until children enter an intellectually demanding environment that adults become concerned about their level of functioning. Because children don't become "retarded" until they enter school, and have apparently functioned satisfactorily until this time, many questions have been raised about the classification.

When children's intellectual growth does not keep pace with physical growth and chronological age, they are considered mentally retarded. As the children get older there will be some things they are not capable of learning. At this age, a watered-down kindergarten program is not the answer. You need a program designed to build on these children's strengths.

Classification of Mental Retardation

The label "mental retardation" significantly impacts the person being labeled and his family. The American Association on Mental Retardation has developed the most widely accepted criteria for classification. These criteria include:

1. Demonstration of significantly sub-average general intellectual functioning. This is generally regarded as at least two standard deviations below the mean on a standardized test of intelligence. On the Wechsler Intelligence Scale for Children–Revised, this would be an IQ of 70. (The AAMR also recognizes the possibility of error in testing and sees 70–75 as a cutoff, depending upon the circumstance.) An IQ less than 70 is no longer enough for a child to be classified as mentally retarded. Additionally there must be the following conditions.

2. Demonstration of impairments in a child's adaptive behavior. These behaviors include independence (walking, toilet training), self-help skills, social skills, skills of daily living, and so on. The behaviors included vary depending on the age of the child.

3. The age of onset of both of these conditions must occur during the developmental period.

4. The determination of mental retardation must be made by a qualified professional, experienced in assessment of cognitive and adaptive behavior. This is usually a psychologist (Grossman, 1983).

Two elements are important to note here. One is that a child must be well below average in *both* measured intelligence and adaptive behavior. The second is that we no longer regard mental retardation as irreversible, especially for those who are in the mild range. We now believe that with appropriate educational intervention some children will no longer be considered mentally retarded and with early intervention some children who would have been categorized as mentally retarded will not be (Hallahan & Kauffman, 1991).

As with many other disabilities, mental retardation is further divided into levels. These are based on the theoretical assumption that intelligence is normally distributed.

The level of retardation generally indicates the intensity of services that are needed for the child. The levels are assigned after formal assessment of the child's intellectual and adaptive functioning skills. Below is a breakdown of the levels of mental retardation.

Mild Mental Retardation. (IQ 50-55 to 70-75). The label of Educable Mentally Retarded (EMR) is also used for this group in educational settings. Children with this intellectual ability generally attend regular preschool or child-care settings and neighborhood public schools. Some are placed in special education classes; some have only occasional assistance. The learning process is slower then with other children, usually requiring concrete learning procedures. The focus is on learning basic academic skills. Most are able to live independently and hold jobs after schooling is completed.

Mild delays are often not noticed during the preschool years, although you may begin to suspect something as you watch these children. The most obvious signs are that they are slower to talk than other children, may seem immature, and may also have been slower to walk (after fifteen months). A four-year-old with a mild delay will act more like a three-year-old.

Moderate Mental Retardation. (IQ 35-40 to 50-55). Educationally these children are frequently called Trainable Mentally Retarded (TMR). Increasingly, they are in regular child-care settings. Some are in segregated classes or even special schools. This number is decreasing. The learning process typically focuses on self-help skills, functional academic skills, and prevocational skills. Adult living is usually in a supported living arrangement.

Even at a preschool age, *moderately* affected children show noticeable delays in both mental development, especially speech and language, and motor development. They may need assistance in self-help skills. These children may not be toilet trained at the preschool level, or if they are, may not be able to manage taking off and putting on their clothes alone. In some cases, these children will look different from other children (if, for example, they have Down syndrome). In other cases they won't. A four-year-old will act more like a two-year-old. Most likely, parents will know that their child is mentally impaired.

Severe Mental Retardation. (IQ 20-25 to 35-40) and *Profound mental retardation* (below 20-25). Children who are severely and profoundly retarded are delayed in all areas of development and require intensive services. Early intervention generally focuses on self-help skills, mobility, and basic cognitive development. These children are now being served within the public school system (Grossman, 1983).

Increasingly children with severe and profound delays are being cared for and educated in regular settings, particularly in child-care and preschool settings. Severely delayed children showed marked delays in all area of development, and, at the preschool level, have few communication skills. These children may be in regular settings for part of the day and in a setting designed for intensive early intervention for part of the day. They are least likely to be in regular classes in public schools.

Our basis for deciding how many children are mentally retarded is based partly on our definitional procedure; that is, those children who are two standard deviations below the average IQ, which is 100. The U.S. Department of Education (1989) reported 1.2 percent of the school age population as mentally retarded. This figure is below that predicted statistically. There are some explanations put forth for this discrepancy. First, because the criteria involves both IQ and adaptive behavior, the level of behavior may have moved children who were on the borderline out of this classification system. Alternative explanations are that because schools have been criticized for

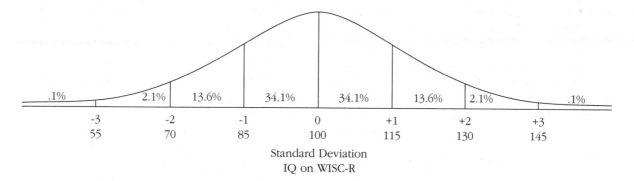

Theoretical Distribution of IQ

improperly identifying minority children as mentally retarded, they are now reluctant to identify any of the children as retarded. Or, as the term *learning disabled* is more acceptable to both parents and administrators, children are more likely to be placed in this category (Hallahan & Kauffman, 1991).

The concept of *mental age* is useful for teaching purposes. If you are given an IQ, you can figure out the mental age. You can estimate if you are given only a classification and know the chronological age. Ages should be converted to months to make the arithmetic easier.

$$IQ = \frac{\text{Mental Age}}{\text{Chronological Age}} \times 100$$

$$50 = \frac{?}{48 \text{ months}} \times 100$$

The mental age equals 24 months.

If you have a child who is four years old (48 months) and is classified as moderately retarded or trainable, this child is developing at about half the normal rate and will function much like a two-year-old. A child who is classified as having a mild delay is functioning at about three-fourths the normal rate. Such a four-year-old will be more like a three-year-old.

When children with mental delays are mainstreamed, they are often placed with younger children, which makes their delays less obvious. A mildly delayed four-year-old may be placed in a class with three-year-olds. Unless the child is unusually large, this is often a good solution for all, as this child will perform at a level closer to his mental age than his chronological age.

The environment in which a child is raised is a big factor in facilitating the development of his cognitive abilities. Some limitations may be present that prevent a child from acquiring specific intellectual skills, such as advanced abstract thinking abilities. However, limiting a child's experiences based on a diagnostic label is a serious and dangerous situation. Many children previously thought unable to function effectively in their environment have accomplished wonders, mostly due to individuals who did not let the label of retardation limit the type and range of opportunities and experiences they provided for the children. Appropriate stimulation is a key ingredient to a successful educational program.

In the past mental retardation that was present at birth was viewed as a given, a nonpreventable disability. Increasingly, the causes of mental retardation are preventable. Some prevention is based on health procedures that ensure that children receive inoculations in a timely manner. Others relate to accident prevention, that is, the use of car seats for young children, preventing drownings, and so on. However, the fastest growing prenatal causes of mental retardation are preventable. These are detailed below.

Fetal Alcohol Syndrome

Fetal Alcohol Syndrome (FAS) is a major preventable cause of mental retardation in the United States. Children born with FAS range from one to three cases per 1,000 live births (U.S. Department of Health and Human Services, 1984). FAS is the result of heavy alcohol use—about six drinks a day. Pregnant women who drink less than this may have children with a condition known as Fetal Alcohol Effects (FAE) or Alcohol Related Effects.

Fetal Alcohol Syndrome results in four types of anomalies: mental retardation (usually mild), growth deficiency, facial anomalies, and central nervous system dysfunction. FAS can be diagnosed on the basis of a clinical examination of the child. Knowledge of maternal drinking behavior is not essential.

Children with Fetal Alcohol Effects have only some of the characteristics of FAS. FAE is often broken down categorically into partial FAS, mild FAS, or possible FAS. Typically these children may function within the normal range of intelligence, however, they manifest a variety of maladaptive behaviors and more subtle central nervous system disorders such as learning disabilities, communication disorders, hyperactivity and attentional problems. FAE is probably far more prevalent than FAS, yet more difficult to isolate and attribute to alcohol consumption. Low birth weight, for example, could be caused by alcohol consumption, smoking, or inadequate nutrition. Without knowing the mother's drinking patterns during pregnancy it is not possible to know whether or not a child's problems are caused by alcohol (Warren, 1985).

Implications. Children with Fetal Alcohol Syndrome will be identified early, those with Fetal Alcohol Effects will not. These children might initially be identified as children with emotional/behavioral disorders. Beyond the physical effects of prenatal alcohol, these children may come from families who are alcoholics. Children of alcoholics are far more likely to be victims of child abuse and neglect than other children (Davis, Allen, & Sherman, 1989). Teachers need to view the child in the context of the family to focus on his needs.

Pediatric AIDS

Acquired Immune Deficiency Syndrome (AIDS) is a particular problem for early childhood special education because of the increasing number of infants and young children who are contacting the disease from their mothers. Pediatric AIDS is the fastest growing infectious cause of mental retardation. Somewhere between 20 and 65 percent of infants born to HIV-infected mothers will become infected before or during delivery. Infants can become postnatally infected through breastmilk (Schwarcz & Rutherford, 1989).

Young children face problems of frequent infections including recurrent bacterial infections, hepatitis, renal disease, gastrointestinal disorder and pneumonia (Widerstrom, Mowder, & Sandall, 1991). Additionally, for the pediatric population, there are a variety of cognitive, behavioral, and neurological symptoms. These include such things as mental retardation, neurological impairments that are similar to cerebral palsy, seizure disorders, and psychotic behavior (Hallahan & Kauffman, 1991). It is estimated that 50 to 90 percent of children with HIV infection have some form of central nervous system dysfunction (Schwarcz & Rutherford, 1989).

Implications. Children born with HIV infection are living longer and challenging the educational and medical service delivery systems. As of 1992, there is no cure for AIDS, nor any lasting treatment. Children with AIDS face death (not only their own, but probably also that of a parent). They may be ostracized by other children and even adults. As the disease progresses, the child will be separated from the family unit more and more frequently. For children with AIDS this separation may be the most devastating aspect of the disease.

With the increasing rate of HIV infection it is likely that you will have a child with AIDS in your classroom. The proportion of infants who will develop clinical AIDS is not known. The HIV antibody may exist in the infant for up to 15 months (or longer) in a passive state. For children who do progress to the disease, it usually develops around four to eight months of age. The prognosis for pediatric AIDS is poor. When compared with adults, the progression from HIV infection to ARC (AIDS-related complex) having the symptoms to full-blown AIDS is very rapid.

Because of the low probability of child-to-child infection (no siblings of AIDS children have yet contracted the disease), it is felt that these children have much to gain from early education and do not pose a substantial risk to the other children. Many feel that the greatest risk is to the child himself who increases the risk of infection through school attendance. That, however, is a decision for the child's parents and physician to make.

Pediatric AIDS poses a difficult dilemma for the profession, one with many more questions than answers. It is an area that is changing quickly, and what is considered "fact" when this book is published may no longer be true. Keep informed about both breakthroughs and risks.

Children's Needs: Teaching Goals

Related annual goals may be grouped under broad categories called "teaching goals." Outlined under each teaching goal below are the most important needs of children with mental retardation. A child may have some or all of these needs, and additional needs as well. Suggestions on what you might consequently teach them are included. Often, a course of action is implicit in the description of the need.

Language Skills

Language, both expressing and receiving, is probably this child's weakest area. This child has a smaller vocabulary, and uses simpler sentence structures than his peers. His language may be difficult to understand and used less frequently than that of other children in the class. As he is developing more language skills set aside time to repeat simple songs and stories. Use rhyming to develop vocabulary. Give the child practice following one- and two-step directions.

Thinking and Reasoning Skills

By definition children with mental retardation have fewer skills in this area than their peers as well as less resources to develop these skills. Begin with simple yet necessary concepts such as colors and numbers. Point out similarities and differences within classification systems (for example, cars and trucks both have wheels). Increase attention span by programming for what the child likes and praising the child for staying with projects to completion; initially this may require your staying with the child as well.

Motor Skills

These children are relatively better at large motor activities than small motor ones. However, motor activities in general often lack smoothness and flow.

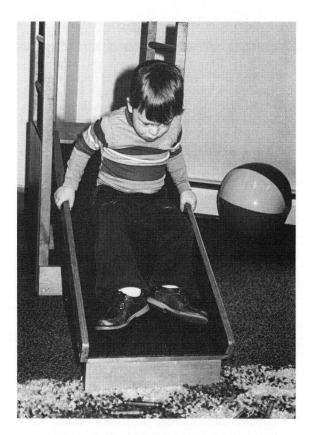

This child is hesitant to touch the slide and even more reluctant to go down it. The child needs more time to process sensory input.

These children need practice with activities that require stopping, starting, and turning corners—for example, running an obstacle path. Activities that require the use of alternating sides of the body such as riding a tricycle or marching are difficult, but also need practice. Fine motor skills can be practiced in conjunction with eye-hand coordination activities, which are necessary prewriting skills.

Awareness

All children need to learn about themselves. These children will take more time to learn the labels of their body parts. Use songs as well as direct questioning to teach this. Develop a more positive self-concept by pointing out to this child and others in the room what this child *can* do and how much he *has* learned.

Guidelines

Because it is more difficult for children with mental delays to learn, it is important that you become aware of how children learn in order to meet the needs of these children.

1. Use as many of the senses in teaching as possible. Even if you are teaching concepts that are primarily visual, like colors, have children reinforce the visual with other sensory experiences.

   See the red ball.

   Sit on the red square.

   Add red food coloring to the fingerpaint.

   Eat a red tomato.

   Listen to a red fire truck.

   These children, like most children, don't learn the first time around, so teach the same concept in different contexts.

2. Keep going over the same concept until they have *overlearned* it. Because these children may easily forget, review information until it is firmly established.

3. Teach a concept for a short time each day for many days, rather than for a long period of time on fewer days. Spaced practice is always more effective than massed practice as those who "cram" for an exam know.

4. Because it is difficult for these children to learn, determine the learning value of specific materials and use those which are most efficient or those that teach two necessary skills at one time. For example, buttoning sequences where children must duplicate a pattern of colors teaches both buttoning, a necessary self-help skill, and color concepts.

5. Generalizing is usually very difficult for these children. When you teach concepts try to make them as close to the setting where they will be used as possible and as real as possible. Keep activities relevant, short, and to the point. Be wary of cute shortcuts. One school I visited decided to teach children to say "three-teen" instead of thirteen because it was easier. Some of those children are now about "three-teen," and their peers make fun of them when they tell how old they are.

6. When teaching these children, use many examples. If you use only one example when teaching the concept *red,* it is likely that the children who learn this one particular "red" will deny other "reds."

7. In general, teach from simple to complex. Where appropriate, simplify information, but not to the point that it loses its meaning. If children are still having problems, do a task analysis. A task analysis is breaking a task down into its component parts, sequencing these, and then teaching them. A great deal has been written on the use of task analysis. However, if you understand the basic principles involved in a task, you can do the task analysis yourself. Start with something the child must do frequently, like putting on a coat. If the children still have problems, review your

analysis for both order and possible missed steps. Change a few things and try again.

Following is a sample task analysis, including a filled-in chart that shows the child's progress.

Task Analysis and Tracking Chart

	M	T	W	TH	F	M	T
1. Take coat off hook.	PH	VH	VH	VH	NH	NH	NH
2. Put coat on floor inside up.	PH	PH	VH	VH	NH	NH	NH
3. Stand at neck of coat.	PH	PH	VH	VH	VH	NH	NH
4. Bend over.	PH	PH	PH	VH	VH	NH	NH
5. Put hands in armholes.	PH	PH	PH	VH	VH	NH	NH
6. Flip coat over head, pushing arms into arm holes.	PH	PH	PH	PH	VH	VH	VH
7. Start zipper.	PH	PH	PH	PH	VH	VH	VH
8. Zip up coat.	PH	PH	VH	VH	VH	NH	NH

Be sure to praise the child for his efforts.

Key: PH = physical help
VH = verbal help
NH = no help

8. In some cases, the technique of backward chaining is useful. Using the example of putting on the coat, you would offer the most help with the first steps and the least help with the last. The first thing you would expect the child to do by himself is Step 8 (zip up the coat). This means the child gets some satisfaction for task completion instead of needing help to finish. (Backward chaining is easier when the component parts are of equal difficulty.)

9. Be sure to reinforce appropriate behavior. Set your sights realistically. Reinforce effort and steps accomplished toward a goal. Don't wait until the goal is accomplished or the child may lose motivation.

10. Avoid a watered-down program. Don't try to teach these children the whole curriculum at a lower, simpler level. Rather, concentrate on what is important for them. What skills will be essential later for the children that need a base developed now?

11. Let children who are mentally retarded progress at their own rates, not those of the other children in the class. Gear the rate toward the mental age rather than the chronological age.

Curriculum Adaptations

Adapting the curriculum, in general, consists of simplifying tasks, focusing on essential tasks and omitting others, and including tasks that other children may learn at home.

Language Arts: Speaking, Listening, Reading, and Writing

Children who are mentally retarded need firsthand experiences to translate into language arts experiences. They will need more time than other children to build the inner language base that is necessary for use in language arts. Start with the concrete and gradually work toward the more abstract.

Speaking. Like all children, those with mental retardation depend on communicating with others to have their needs met. They need to develop language skills to make this possible.

1. Work on vocabulary. Start with a nucleus vocabulary that focuses on the child. Teaching body parts teaches not only vocabulary but body awareness as well. Next focus on the family, followed by clothing, health care (toileting, food, safety), and some aspects of both the school and home environments. Emphasize nouns and verbs first. They are essential for communicating needs.

2. Encourage these children to talk. It sometimes helps to give the cues for subjects to talk about. Pictures taken during field trips can be used later to help children talk about what happened on the trips. The children can also sequence these pictures. A sequence of a trip to the apple orchard might look like this:

   Picture 1: Getting into the cars

   Picture 2: Arriving at the orchard

   Picture 3: Eating apples at the orchard

   Picture 4: Taking off coats back at school; with the apples in the picture.

3. Start with firsthand experiences. Add additional pictures when children can do this much. If you are going to set up a grocery store in the dramatic play area, take a field trip to a grocery store so they have this first experience to build on.

Fingerplays can help teach concepts, can improve fine motor coordination, and can keep children interested and occupied. Using fingerplays also engages the tactile mode for learning and may make the necessary repetition less monotonous.

1. Use fingerplays to teach basic concepts, such as numbers: "Counting Kittens," "Ten Fingers," "Five Little Girls," "One, Two, What Shall I Do?"

2. Use fingerplays to follow stories, field trips, and other activities: "Roly-Poly Caterpillar," "Elephant Song," "The Wheels on the Bus."

Listening. Listening is difficult. Where possible use props. Make statements that are slow, simple, and direct.

1. Provide concrete examples of the items that you are talking about so children can both see and hear the information.

2. Start with one-step directions.

3. Be sure that children understand the interactional quality to listening and speaking and that they don't see it as a passive experience (as they might with television.)

At the beginning, use short, simple stories that have a familiar theme. Remember, the group experience may be new to the child.

1. Animal stories with big pictures and few words, alphabet books, and those with simple rhymes are good.

2. It may be helpful to cue the child into a specific concept by asking her to listen for the item while you read the story. For example, before reading the story *Caps for Sale,* ask the child to listen for who sold the caps. It may also be helpful to discuss the meaning of some words beforehand. Establish that caps are hats, for example, since

By using a flannel board story to teach the names of animals, the teacher can vary the complexity of the story to meet the child's ability and can invite the child to participate in the process.

many of these children have generalization difficulties.

3. Use flannelboard stories.

Reading. These children usually need a longer period of "readiness" before they can apply skills. It is important to build a solid base. This requires patience on your part. You can't push them before they are ready, and you must not quit because you decide they will never learn. First establish basic skills, then use these skills to teach integration or higher level skills.

1. Concentrate first on auditory and visual identification. Don't assume that these children can label all the sounds and objects in their environment. Then work on discrimination skills. Once identification skills have been established, work on visual and auditory memory. For example, have children first match alphabet letters, then label them by name or sound.

2. Once some concepts have been mastered, move on to higher level skills. For example, have children classify objects by color once they understand the colors.

3. Sitting for the sake of sitting, although helpful to the teacher, is not a useful skill for the child. Teach the child to use readiness materials while they are waiting. This will also alleviate the long-term problem children with developmental delays typically have with leisure time.

Writing. Writing begins with marks on the page and ends with the understanding of a complex symbol system. Work initially with the fine motor aspect, as understanding the symbol system will take time.

1. Help children enjoy the process of making marks on paper. Give them a variety of tools to mark with.

2. Have large wooden alphabet letters available. Spell out the child's name and have the child trace the letters with two fingers.

3. Have children imitate you as you make large arm circles in both directions (encourage children to use their dominant arm). As children can make circles, begin to make letters with your arm (it is important that this is initially a large motor activity). Tell a story as you make the letter (the letters will all be cursive): "I am the letter *a*. I start on the line and I love to look up. Let's go on a picnic on a hill (move arm up). Whoops, I forgot the picnic lunch; we better go back and get it (arm returns). It's boring to go the same way. Let's see if there is another way to get back, a steeper hill (move arm down and around up to the peak). Great, and now we have to climb back down the hill" (move arm down to the initial level). Make up stories for each letter. You might want to write them down. You

may be very willing to change the story, but children rarely are.

Discovery: Mathematics, Science, Computers

This curriculum is challenging, but if the discovery approach is used with supporting verbalizations about the process, it holds tremendous potential for learning.

Mathematics. Although children with mental retardation may never learn calculus, they do need a foundation in basic mathematical skills to function in society.

1. Teach number concepts, such as counting, with real objects that can be moved or touched. Count children, blocks, chairs, and tables. Use an abacus.

2. Try to choose math experiences that also teach other skills. (Using real objects will help the child's motor development.) Pegboards are useful for facilitating small motor skills while teaching counting and one-to-one correspondence. They can also be used to teach sequential patterns and design duplication.

3. Use real objects such as socks to teach one-to-one correspondence. This is also a good activity for snacktime (children without something to eat or drink usually make this known).

Science. Science for children with mental retardation should be basic. It should focus on firsthand knowledge and give information that is relevant for their future learning and well-being.

1. Use field trips, especially those dealing with nature and the environment.

2. Discuss the seasons and the predictable changes that occur with the changes in nature. Discuss how the seasons affect clothing and activities.

3. Encourage these children to test simple cause and effect reasoning. State a relationship and have the child test it. "The color is darker if you press harder" may be obvious to you, but these children may not realize they cause the change systematically.

4. Plant a garden for firsthand experience with growth and the necessary conditions for growth.

Computers. Computers are often a challenge. However, because of the potential they hold for cause-effect reasoning, and their "patience," they are an absolute must.

1. Look at the keyboard options and choose one that best meets the child's needs.

2. Choose software carefully. It needs to be both developmentally appropriate and simple to operate.

3. Encourage independent use of the computer itself. This is tremendously impressive to others. Parents may be encouraged and surprised that their child can turn on and operate a computer. The skills are easy and sequential, and some software (especially those with picture menus) is very "user friendly."

Sensory Motor: Large Motor, Sensory Motor Integration, Small Motor

Children with mental retardation need many experiences in this area.

Large Motor. Large motor skills help develop stamina and increase body coordination and awareness. Game skills (kicking, running, throwing, catching, jumping, batting) involve the necessary large muscles. It is probably unwise, however, to expect these children to participate in organized games. The stress of winning and losing may only point out lack of skill rather than encourage skill development.

1. Emphasize basic skills and the variations: walking forward, backward, sideways, fast, slow.

2. These children are often below average in physical stamina. They tend to just sit or stand and watch. They need to be strongly encouraged daily to participate in active games.

3. Use large, light-weight blocks, which are easier to manipulate.

4. Some children with mental retardation (such as Down syndrome) are hypotonic, or have floppy muscle tone. This directly affects both large and small motor skills. To accommodate this, use a variety of activities at different levels of difficulty, such as walking sideways and skipping.

Sensory Motor Integration. Provide many opportunities for children to use motor skills in coordination with their senses.

1. Provide materials and activities that require the use of two hands: clapping, lacing beads onto string or pipe cleaners, lacing cards with various sized holes (some large and easy to string, others small), snap-construction toys.

2. Provide puzzles at different levels of difficulty. Children with mental delays often have trouble putting pieces in the corresponding holes because of delayed eye-hand coordination. Puzzles with pegs attached to individual pieces are easier to manipulate.

3. Provide activities that require different motions of each hand. (One example is Jack-in-the-Box, where a child must hold the box with one hand while turning the knob with the other.) Many times children with cognitive delays have difficulty with this task. It is easier for children to do the same thing with both hands or to use only one hand. They will naturally gravitate toward easier tasks.

Small Motor. When you plan for small motor play, you need to think of the skills this child is going to need to find a job and work, even though that may seem too far off in the future to worry about. It takes these children longer to learn skills. Since abstract reasoning is difficult for them, it is important that you build on other, more concrete skills. Because fine motor skills are necessary for most self-care, more time and space needs to be devoted to them.

1. Start with beginning grasping and manipulation. Be sure to use a variety of objects so that the child can practice many styles. Encourage the child to use the pincher grasp (thumb and forefinger apposition).

2. Use many different activities that require fine motor skills (form boards, pegboards—rubber ones for strengthening finger muscles—plastic

blocks that fit together). Start with relatively large, preschool-size objects. Gradually add more pieces and smaller objects. Use this opportunity to teach color and number skills also. Have children sort and group various materials.

3. Code your sorting and matching tasks by number. (Use *1* for easy tasks, *2* for more difficult, and so on.) This means that all the children can do the same activity but at different levels.

1 Sort identical objects out from a mix, round beads from crayons or paper clips from rubber bands.

2 Group the same objects by size, big from small paper clips or big nuts and bolts from small ones.

3 Sort the same objects in different colors, red from green beads or red from white Leggos.

4 Group the same objects with differing shapes, round from square from cylindrical red beads.

5 Have a mix of objects that can be grouped in two or more ways. At first demonstrate the system and have the child follow it. Later let the child group and regroup on his own. A mix of large and small paper clips, large and small rubber bands, and large and small beads (of varying colors, and shapes) may all be sorted into two containers, as large and small.

Within each step you can make the task more difficult by adding more objects, colors, sizes, and shapes. Start with two items and work up to perhaps ten. A more difficult version would be grouping different objects by color, size, and shape.

4. Often it is hard for children with delayed development to hold a pencil or crayon. Larger ones are easier to grip. Provide a variety of pencils, crayons, and brushes of different sizes. Add grips, tape or foam curlers to make them easier to hold.

Social Awareness: Social Studies, Inclusion, Health and Safety

Children with mental retardation need to be aware of the world around them and how it works. Start with the familiar, and begin with field trips. Focus on making these children part of the group and teaching them social skills that will be appropriate throughout their life.

Social Studies. Like all children, those with mental retardation need to learn about the community in which they live. When you teach units in this area,

Children need many opportunities to practice self-help skills. Providing small pitchers for pouring juice and snack foods with interesting textures integrates these skills into the school day.

concentrate on roles the children may need to know or can readily identify with.

1. Discuss the roles of police, firefighters, and mail personnel. Go on field trips to see them at work, then follow up with role playing.

2. Inevitably these children are tested by psychologists or educational diagnosticians. Help them learn about these roles. Have them play games in a one-on-one situation with a teacher or paraprofessional.

3. Be sure to value *all* occupations and jobs, not just prestigious ones. These children may eventually have a nonprestigious job.

4. Explore varied occupations. Be sure to include practical occupations and *some* that require limited skills (teacher, farmer, baker, factory worker, janitor, clerk, and so on). It is important that these occupations be included and that they be valued.

Inclusion. All children need to be part of the group. These children may challenge your creativity for inclusion. As you help them join groups, be sure they are not always the "baby," or that they do not have socially undesirable roles.

1. Teach children the courtesies of everyday living. Be sure children know how to greet you (say "Hello" and look at you while they say it). They also need to learn to use "please" and "thank you" appropriately.

2. They need to be contributing members of the class. Give them tasks they can do and praise their accomplishments.

3. Be sure to have easy, but age-appropriate options available so they can easily participate in group play.

Health and Safety. It is important for children with mental retardation to make good health habits part of their routine. They may have to be taught some of the things that seem obvious: (toileting, washing hands, blowing and wiping their nose, eating, grooming).

1. Teach safety skills. Emphasize dangers with the greatest likelihood of occurrence and those that are most dangerous, such as traffic or poison.

2. Concentrate on building good food habits. Help children learn about healthy snacks.

3. Role play with the children about what to do if they get lost.

4. Break complex skills down into simple tasks that the child can do. Teach the necessary skills in different curricula. Toileting, for example, involves the ability to dress and undress oneself, so be sure to teach buttoning and snapping as part of fine motor skills.

Creative Arts: Art, Music, Creative Movement, and Dramatic Play

As long as there is no competition and children are not required to do the "same" thing, children with mental retardation need little accommodation in this area.

Art. Art for children with mental delays should focus on the process not the product. It is important to keep in mind that, especially for these children, the final product may be inconsequential.

1. Use a variety of art media.

2. Cutting is often difficult—it may be helpful to use "easy grip" or "training" scissors with a loop or a spring handle. These can be obtained from many school supply companies. As alternatives, have children tear materials or consider using precut materials.

Music. Music can be used in a variety of ways. Repetition makes it easier for children to learn songs. Teach the parents the songs so the child can hear and sing them at home as well as in class.

1. Use music to teach basic concepts, such as numbers and colors.

2. Music can be used to expand a child's vocabulary and to increase auditory memory.

3. Music paired with movement encourages children to move and releases energy. In creative movement, there is no right or wrong. You may have to discuss the necessary elements first. (Quiet music means move slowly.) Don't expect a lot of interpretation.

4. Music can also be used to help children establish a rhythm pattern. However, be careful *not* to encourage a rhythm pattern if the child has a habit of swaying or rocking.

5. Using songs that call children by name, you can increase self-esteem and a sense of group belonging.

6. Songs may need to be sung slower than usual (especially those with movements) so that these children can participate, but increase the speed once they are known.

Creative Movement. Movement is a must for all children. Nonjudgmental movement is an added plus for children with mental retardation. They need to be supported in their attempts at movement.

1. Encourage children to move to music that has an obvious beat.

2. Encourage children to move specific body parts. Be sure to have these parts moved long enough so

you are sure the children know the part indicated: "Everybody move your arms in circles." Then you might comment on the size of the circles and whether they are forward or backward.

3. Help children recognize speed by having them move something quickly or slowly. Children gain sensory motor integration as well as necessary concepts through movement.

Dramatic Play. Dramatic play allows playing without judgment. It is a way to make strange experiences more familiar and is a good way to teach appropriate behavior.

1. Visit a real store, then set up a play store (department, grocery, pet). Play through the essential features. Use it for a week or more. Setting it up for one or two days isn't enough for these children. Add features throughout the week.

2. Playing with other children in this area might also provide the child with information about how roles are played in society. Some children with disabilities are assumed to have few demands beyond their physical needs. They are given little realistic feedback. Feedback is necessary for their development. It can be realistic without being judgmental.

3. Play usually should be fairly concrete with realistic props. These children are less imaginative than their peers. Have a lot of props available to facilitate play: (a garage, for example, needs cars, trucks, a block structure, rope, hose, gas pumps, and so on).

Transitions

Transitions can be used to teach colors, numbers, and body awareness. This time can also be used to promote independence and prevocational skills.

1. Have a sign in–sign out board. Use this for roll call some days. Either have the children find their own name tag and put it on and take it off the board, or have them move cards from one side to the other. This reinforces name recognition and independence as the children learn to do it more fully.

2. These children are likely to need more help with toileting and dressing. Dismiss them at a time when they can get the maximum amount of help.

3. Use this time to reinforce concepts the child has learned.

4. Allow enough time for self-help activities, so the child can be successful. It is easy for this child to get distracted and for you to feel rushed when others are waiting.

Glossary

Acquired Immune Deficiency Syndrome (AIDS) A fatal, communicable, virus-caused disease characterized by a breakdown in the immune system.

Adaptive physical education   Physical education activities that are changed to meet the needs of the child who is delayed or impaired.

AIDS-Related complex (ARC)   A stage that has some but not all of the symptoms of AIDS. In most cases this is a step in the progression toward AIDS.

Down syndrome   A form of mental retardation present at birth. Can be visually identified by characteristic "Asian" eyefolds and the simian crease in the palms of the hands. This diagnosis is confirmed by a genetic workup.

There are basically three different types of Down syndrome. In *trisomy 21* there is an extra chromosome; in *mosaicism* some cells have an extra chromosome and others do not; in *translocation* all or part of the extra chromosome of the twenty-first pair is attached to another chromosome pair.

Encephalitis   A viral infection of the brain that can cause permanent damage.

Fetal Alcohol Syndrome (FAS)   A syndrome that includes mental retardation and physical deformities in children of mothers who were alcoholic during pregnancy.

Human Immunodeficiency Virus (HIV)   One of the first retroviruses to be identified in humans.

Hydrocephalus   The condition of having excessive cerebrospinal fluid within the brain that can permanently damage brain tissue. This condition can result from a spinal injury or may be present at birth.

Karyotype   The process of analyzing the chromosome number and composition. This is used to determine the diagnosis and whether the cause is genetic.

Meningitis   A bacterial infection of the brain and its covering membranes. Severe cases can result in mental retardation.

Microcephalus   A condition in which the brain itself is underdeveloped (fewer brain cells), characterized by a small head and a forehead that slants away from the face.

Multihandicapped   A person who has several major disabilities (e.g., cerebral palsy and blindness that are not part of a specific syndrome).

Pediatric AIDS   The presence of HIV in children under 13. In addition to problems in the immune system, children have cognitive, neurological and behavioral symptoms.

Phenylketonuria (PKU)   A hereditary metabolic disorder in which a child lacks the specific enzyme to break down phenylalanine, causing mental retardation. With early detection and a special diet, this retardation can be prevented.

Prevocational skills Basic skills (self-help, fine motor, social skills) necessary for admission to a vocational program.

Primary disability A disability designated as the major one when children have several. (Such a designation is often required by programming guidelines.) When mental retardation is one of several disabilities, it is usually considered to be the primary one.

Task analysis Breaking down tasks into their component parts and ordering those parts.

Tay-Sachs disease A genetic disease which results in progressive brain damage and eventual death.

Teaching Resources

In some situations you may want or need additional information. There are many national as well as regional, state, and local organizations that can help you. The following annotated list of national organizations should be useful in helping you decide where to get the information you need.

American Association on Mental Retardation
1719 Kalorama Road, N.W.
Washington, DC 20009
(202) 387-1968
    Physicians, educators, administrators, social workers, psychologists, students, and others interested in the general welfare of mentally retarded persons and the study of cause, treatment, and prevention of mental retardation.

Association for Children with Retarded Mental
    Development
162 Fifth Avenue, 11th floor
New York, NY 10010
(212) 741-0100
    Write for information about children with mental retardation.

Association for Retarded Citizens
P.O. Box 6109
Arlington, TX 76005
(817) 640-0204
    A strong advocacy group for the needs of the mentally retarded population.

Children of Alcoholics Foundations, Inc.
P.O. Box 4185, Department O
Grand Central Station
New York, NY 10163
(212) 351-2680
    A voluntary nonprofit organization designed to increase awareness of the problems of children of alcoholics and to promote dissemination of this information.

Council for Exceptional Children
Division on Mental Retardation
1929 Association Drive
Reston, VA 22091-1589
    Publishes a newsletter and a journal, Education and Training in Mental Retardation. *Also a strong advocacy group. The only professional organization that is concerned about the quality of education of all exceptional children.*

Down Syndrome Congress
1640 West Roosevelt Road, Room 156E
Chicago, IL 60608
    Parents, educators, and health professionals interested in promoting the welfare of persons with Down syndrome. Advises and aids parents with possible solutions to needs of the Down syndrome child. Acts as a clearinghouse on Down syndrome information.

Directory of State and Local Resources for the
    Mentally Retarded
Secretary's Committee on Mental Retardation
U.S. Department of Health, Education and Welfare
Washington, DC 20201
    A directory of resources available on the state and local level.

National Association for Retarded Children
2709 Avenue E
East Arlington, TX 76011
    Does not make referrals but supplies general information about programs, facilities, institutions, and careers for the retarded.

National Association for Children of Alcoholics
31706 Coast Highway, Suite 201
South Laguna, CA 92677
(714) 499-3889
    A nonprofit organization for children of alcoholics in all age groups. It publishes a quarterly newsletter and holds an annual convention.

National Clearinghouse for Alcohol and Drug
    Information
P.O. Box 2345
Rockville, MD 20852
(301) 468-2600
    The clearinghouse is a service of the office for Substance Abuse Prevention of the Alcohol, Drug Abuse and Mental Health Administration. It provides information about publications, audiovisuals and organizations in the area of alcohol and drugs.

National Council on Alcoholism, Inc.
12 West 21st Street
New York, NY 10010
(212) 206-6770
    A voluntary health agency that provides information about alcoholism and alcohol problems through local affiliates. Some affiliates provide counseling for alcoholics and their families.

National Association of Private Residential Facilities
    for the Mentally Retarded
6269 Leesburg Pike, Suite B-5
Falls Church, VA 22044
    Facilities that serve mentally retarded and other developmentally disabled persons. Includes other groups interested in the field of private residential programming.

One to One
1 Lincoln Plaza
1900 Broadway
New York, NY 10023
    Develops community-based alternatives to institutions for the retarded and disabled. Provides grants, interest-free loans, technical assistance, and support to nonprofit agencies.

Retarded Infants Service
386 Park Avenue South
New York, NY 10016
    Service agency devoted to the physical well-being and development of the retarded child and the sound mental health of the parents. Helps families with retarded children with all aspects of home care, including counseling, Home Aide Service, and consultation.

Share, Inc.
P.O. Box 1342
Beverly Hills, CA 90213
    Individuals organized to raise funds for the mentally retarded under the direction of the Exceptional Children's Foundation. Projects include preschool training and special education classes for mentally retarded children not accepted by public schools; an infant development program; and a residential home for the retarded.

Children's Bibliography

See the Children's Bibliography on page 286 for books to increase children's awareness about disabilities as well as books that are especially good for children with particular disabilities. Note especially:

Awareness of Mental Retardation

Body Awareness

Growing and Changing

Picture Books

Starting School

Simpler Books (for teaching vocabulary and concepts)

References and Bibliography

Beyers, J. (1989). AIDS in children: Effects on neurological development and implications for the future. *Journal of Special Education* (Spring), 5–16.

Buscaglia, L. (1975). *The disabled and their parents: A counseling challenge.* Thorofare, NJ: Slack.

Davis, R., Allen, T., & Sherman, J. (1989). The role of the teacher: Strategies for helping. *National Association for Children of Alcoholics,* 11–14.

Dempsey, J. (1975). *Community services for retarded children: The consumer-provider relationship.* Baltimore, MD: University Park Press.

Grossman, H. (Ed.). (1983). *Classification in mental retardation.* Washington, DC: American Association on Mental Deficiency.

Hallahan, D., & Kauffman, J. (1991). *Exceptional children: Introduction to special education.* Englewood Cliffs, NJ: Prentice-Hall.

Isaacson, R. (1974). *The retarded child: A guide for parents and friends.* Niles, IL: Argus Communications.

Karnes, M. B. (conference chair), Jordan, J. B., Dailey, & Fewell, R. (Eds.). (1973). *Not all little wagons are red—the exceptional child's early years.* Arlington, VA: Council for Exceptional Children.

Koch, R., & Koch, K. J. (1975). *Understanding the mentally retarded child: A new approach.* New York: Random House.

Koch, R., & Dobson, J. C. (1976). *The mentally retarded child and his family: A multidisciplinary handbook.* New York: Brunner/Mazel.

Love, H. D. (1973). *The mentally retarded child and his family.* Springfield, IL: Charles C. Thomas.

Molloy, J. S., & Matkin, A.M. (1975). *Your developmentally retarded child can communicate.* New York: John Day.

Nichtern, S. (1974). *Helping the retarded child.* New York: Grosset and Dunlap.

Noland, R. L. (Ed.). (1970). *Counseling parents of the mentally retarded: A sourcebook.* Springfield, IL: Charles C. Thomas.

Perske, R. (1973). *New directions for parents of persons who are retarded.* Nashville, TN: Abingdon.

Schwarcz, S., & Rutherford, G. (1989). AIDS in infants, children, and adolescents. *Journal of Drug Issues* (Winter), 75–92.

Skeen, P., & Hodson, D. (1987). AIDS: What adults should know about AIDS (and shouldn't discuss with very young children). *Young Children, 42* (4), 65–71.

U.S. Department of Education (1989). *Eleventh annual report to Congress on the implementation of the education of the handicapped act.* Washington, DC: U.S. Government Printing Office.

Warren, K. (1985). Alcohol-related birth defects: Current trends in research. *Alcohol World: Health and Research, 10* (1), 4–5.

Widerstrom, A., Mowder, B., & Sandall, S. (1991). *At-risk and handicapped newborns and infants: Development, assessment, & intervention.* Englewood Cliffs, NJ: Prentice-Hall.

Awareness Bibliography for Adults

Buck, Pearl S. (1950). *The child who never grew.* New York: John Day.

Buck's own struggle to live with having produced a mentally retarded child, her decision to institutionalize the child, and her experience with how societies differ in treatment of the exceptional individual.

Burke, Christopher, & McDaniel, J. (1991). *A special kind of hero.* New York: Burke & Burke, Inc.

This is the story of the life of Chris Burke, the star of the television show "Life Goes On." Chris has Down syndrome. The book looks at his struggles and triumphs.

Dorris, Michael. (1989). *The broken cord.* New York: Harper Perennial, A Division of Harper Collins Publishers.

The story told by Michael Dorris of his adoption of Adam, a Native American with fetal alcohol effects. It details Adam's life and Michael Dorris's search for understanding of FAE. It also talks about the adoption of two additional Native American children, and his marriage.

Frank, John Paul. (1952). *My son's story.* New York: Knopf.

A father's story of his first child, John Peter, the problems that lead to a diagnosis of mental retardation, and the child's institutionalization. The story tells of the effects on the family, the financial and emotional demands, and the search for a suitable institution. Several chapters by the mother round out the book.

Jablow, M. (1982). *Cara: Growing with a retarded child.* Philadelphia, PA: Temple University Press.

Cara is a high functioning child with Down syndrome. It is the story of her early life including the early intervention programs she participated in.

Mantle, Margaret. (1985). *Some just clap their hands: Raising a handicapped child.* New York: Amada Books.

The story told by a mother about how she copes with the diagnosis of her daughter as being mentally retarded. It includes excerpts from interviews with other parents and professionals.

Meryman, R. (1984). *Broken promises, mended dreams: An alcoholic woman fights for her life.* Boston: Little, Brown.

Describes a woman's gradual recovery from alcoholism and how it affects her family. The thinking patterns and behavior of the woman are useful information for those working with children.

Murray, J., & Murray, E. (1975). *And say what he is.* Cambridge, MA: The MIT Press.

The parents' story of raising a child who is developmentally delayed and their decision to adopt two other children. They talk about caregiving and financial strains.

Rivera, Geraldo. (1972). *Willowbrook.* New York: Vintage Books.

The story of an institution for the mentally retarded in New York state; explores the thoughts of the parents who have children in that institution and the plight of misplaced children. The book points out how parents are actively fighting for their children's rights.

Rogers, Dale Evans. (1977). *Angel unaware.* New York: Jove Publications.

The true story of the actress's mentally retarded daughter born with Down syndrome, who lived only two years. It is a religion-based explanation of why children are born with this defect.

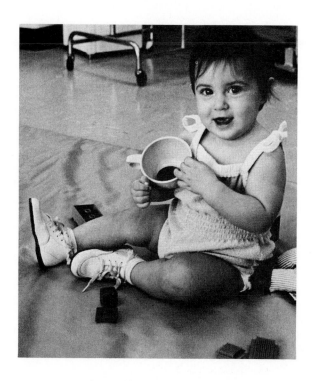

Chapter 18

Infants and Toddlers with Developmental Delays

The focus for infants born with disabilities, although initially a medical one concerned with survival, moves quickly to one concerned with long-range developmental outcomes. Early intervention with very young children requires a variety of services from different disciplines. Teachers play a very important role in these services, not just in their role as an infant-toddler interventionist, but as an important member of an interdisciplinary team. The concept of early intervention for infants and toddlers with developmental delays is new. It is very proactive in that it is designed to eliminate or minimize the effects of delays.

Early intervention is family centered. For both philosophical and practical reasons, very young children must be viewed and taught in ways that are congruent with family values and concerns. Families are the decision makers for their children. Professionals facilitate and help implement the decisions made.

Classification of Developmental Delays

It is difficult to assess accurately whether a young child's development is an uneven growth pattern or a developmental delay. As signs of delay become clearer, there is a need for intervention; however, a specific diagnosis (such as cerebral palsy) may not be warranted. In the past, in the interest of getting services for children, they have been mislabeled. The ability to use the term "developmental delay" allows children to receive services, yet eliminates concerns about inaccurate labels.

The law (P.L. 99-457) requires each state to decide upon its definition of a "developmental delay." There is therefore no single definition. However, there is agreement that the child must be evaluated by a multidisciplinary team and that a variety of assessment instruments must be used. There is less consensus in interpreting the results. Some feel that a **275** child must be delayed in more than one area of development, others that the delay must be great to be considered significant (at least two standard deviations below the mean) (Weiner & Koppelman, 1987).

Infants and toddlers with developmental delays, then, is a broad category that can contain at least three groups of children:

1. Children who are born with obvious identifiable disabilities, and who will later be identified as having specific disabilities. This is the smallest of the three groups.

    The next two categories include children who are considered "at risk" for developmental delay. Some of these children will have disabilities, others will not.

2. Children who are biologically at risk. These include low birth weight babies as well as those born with complications such as alcohol or other drug-related problems.

3. Children who are environmentally at risk. This is by far the largest group and includes children born to adolescent mothers and/or into poverty.

It is difficult to decide if some infants and toddlers are displaying uneven growth patterns or if their development is delayed.

Estimates for the size of this group range from 3 to 10 percent of the population (Weiner & Koppelman, 1987).

Note that the groups are not mutually exclusive. (A child born with fetal alcohol syndrome may have an adolescent mother who uses drugs and alcohol and lives in poverty.) In many ways the children in the latter two categories may be at far greater risk for problems than the children who have identifiable disabilities. In reality, within each category there are children with greater and lesser needs. The child must be viewed within the context of the family and environment within which he lives to determine need. It is neither a simple nor a straightforward process.

Public Law 101-496 (1990) includes children "who have substantial developmental delay or specific congenital or acquired conditions with a high probability of resulting in developmental disabilities if services are not provided."

Public Law 102-119 (Oct. 7, 1991) expanded this concept to include older children thus:

(B) The term 'children with disabilities' for children aged 3 to 5 inclusive, may, at a State's discretion, include children -

(i) experiencing developmental delays, as defined by the State and as measured by appropriate diagnostic instruments and procedures, in one or more of the following areas: physical development, cognitive development, communication development, or adaptive development; and

(ii) who, by reason thereof, need special education and related services.

Some definitions of developmental delay include only the first children as developmentally delayed and serve only these children. Others see the later groups as "at risk for developmental delay" and they are served as well.

Common At-Risk Conditions

Brief descriptions of the most common at-risk conditions follow. Remember, you will not be expected to be an expert on each condition, but you need to be aware of typical characteristics and how they will influence your programming. The infants and toddlers with these conditions do not necessarily have delayed development, but your observations and experience with the child will provide valuable input into any such determination.

The purpose of this chapter is to describe the unique characteristics and guidelines necessary to work with infants and toddlers with disabilities. In most instances we do not have a specific diagnosis. In cases where there is a diagnosis, for example a hearing impairment, read the chapter on hearing impairments for information about the disability. However, use this chapter for specific information on how to intervene with infants and toddlers.

Failure to Thrive. Some infants fail to gain weight at the expected rate. It may be because the mother does not have enough breast milk or that the baby has digestive problems or a variety of other related problems. Some failure to thrive symptoms are life-threatening, such as severe dehydration, seizures, low body temperature, and slow heart rate. Other general symptoms include inappropriate height and weight gain, listlessness or placidity, and infrequent bowel movements. Undiagnosed and untreated failure-to-thrive symptoms can lead to death or developmental delay.

Feeding Problems. Frequently infants who are at risk or who have disabilities have problems eating enough to provide a steady weight gain. They may have problems with the suck-swallow pattern necessary or such a weak suck that they waste energy and become tired before they get enough milk.

Some infants have gastroesophageal reflux (GER), a condition that causes vomiting and aspiration of food into the lungs. The infants gag and vomit, and the milk does not reach the stomach. This happens when the muscle sphincter of the lower esophagus is weak (Widerstrom, Mowder, & Sandall, 1991). These infants may have to be tube-(gavage) fed. They should suck a pacifier to help the suck reflex to mature, thus speeding the transition to oral feeding.

Prematurity. When babies are born prematurely neither they nor their parents may be ready for the transition. Prematurity, or preterm is the word used to describe infants who are born before thirty-eight weeks gestational age. The fetus becomes capable of living outside the womb sometime between the twenty-fourth and twenty-eighth week. Babies born before thirty weeks are considered to be *very* premature. (An infant born at twenty-five weeks usually weighs between two to three pounds and is between 11 and 18 inches in length.)

In addition to gestational age, weight is an important variable. Approximately 7 percent of babies born in the United States weigh 2,500 grams (5 pounds, 8 ounces) or less at birth. These babies are identified as having low birth weight. Slightly over 1 percent of low birth weight babies are identified as very low birth weight (1,500 grams or 3 pounds, 5 ounces or less) (Semmler, 1989c). Babies weighing two pounds or less have about a 50–50 chance of survival (Harrison, 1983).

Using gestational age and weight together provides additional information. We would be far more concerned about an infant born at forty weeks gestational age weighing 4 pounds, 8 ounces, than one who was born at thirty-two weeks with the same weight.

That weight is within the normal range for thirty-two weeks, but it is very low for a full-term infant.

Socioeconomic factors have a significant interaction with the predicted outcome for these at-risk infants. The substantial problems of coping with them are exacerbated by limited parental resources (money, transportation, education, and so on). The rate of developmental delay and neurological problems is much greater for very low birth weight infants whose mothers are seventeen years old or less, have less than a high school education, and are not married than it is for premature babies born to middle-class families (Heyne, 1989).

Overall, there appears to be a correlation between birth weight and developmental delay. The lower the birth weight the greater the probability of a developmental delay. Delays appear more likely in the perceptual-motor areas than in verbal areas (Bird, 1987). The low birth weight itself does not seem to be the major factor, but complications such as hemorrhaging and other medical risk conditions frequently corollary to it put the infant at risk.

Some unique medical problems relate to prematurity. Typically, infants weighing 1,500 grams or less stay in the hospital two to three months. Approximately a third to a half of these neonates have intracranial hemorrhage, which is the primary cause of death in these infants (Semmler, 1989c). These very low birth weight neonates account for approximately half of neonatal deaths.

The more severe hemorrhages result in a greater incidence of porencephaly, seizure disorders, cerebral palsy, retinopathy of prematurity, and developmental delays (particularly in language and cognition) (Semmler, 1989a). (The lower the birth weight and the earlier the gestational age the greater the probability of hemorrhaging.) A major concern upon discharge from the hospital is the implication the hemorrhaging will have on the infant's long-term development. Infants who have had grade III and IV hemorrhages are at very high risk for developmental delay and should receive frequent developmental assessments (Semmler, 1989c). They may profit from early intervention and therapy.

The ability to classify hemorrhages is relatively new, somewhat arbitrary, and constantly changing as new technology provides more accurate information. In general, the higher the number the more severe the hemorrhage. Ultrasound is the most widely used method for diagnosing intracranial hemorrhage.

It is difficult to tell which premature infants are most likely to need early intervention. It seems that medical risk factors are the best predictor during the first year and that environmental risk factors seem to be more useful at older ages (Bird, 1987). In general, developmental testing overpredicts those who will have problems.

However, it is important to note that a disproportionate number of low birth weight babies who have normal IQs are also diagnosed as having reading problems or learning disabilities. Note also that premature and low birth weight babies have a three times greater risk of being abused by parent or caregivers during infancy and early childhood (Schmitt & Kempe, 1979). This is true even when social class is held constant.

A common form of abuse of infants is shaking. Parents shake the infants by the shoulder, usually in an attempt to get the infant to stop crying. This may cause intraventricular hemorrhaging resulting in brain damage (Widerstrom, Mowder, & Sandall, 1991).

Children's Needs: Teaching Goals

Related annual goals may be grouped under broad categories called "teaching goals." Outlined under each teaching goal below are the most important needs of infants and toddlers with developmental delays. An infant or toddler may have some or all of these needs, and additional needs as well. The greater the impairment, the more likely it is that teaching modifications will have to be made. Suggestions on what you might consequently teach these children are included. Often, a course of action is implicit in the description of the need.

Sensory Skills

Infants support attachment behaviors and positive feelings through eye contact, visual fixation, and smiling. When infants do not display these behaviors, or display them at a lower rate than other infants, adults need to use other cues for their own reinforcement and also to respond appropriately to the infant (Hanson, 1984). Some early intervention programs, particularly for low birth weight infants, concentrate in the sensory area and encourage caregivers to massage or stroke the child's body or rock the child as a means of vestibular stimulation.

Language Skills

Infants and toddlers who show developmental delays are less skillful in entertaining themselves at an early age and need active mutual participation to stimulate optimal development. Reading to children and pointing out the pictures, using toys while talking to them, and being verbally responsive to children's overtures regardless of the content are important in developing language skills.

Motor Skills

Often infants and toddlers with developmental delays have problems in the area of motor development, particularly muscle tone. This can be the main characteristic (such as in cerebral palsy) or a related condition (infants with Down syndrome are often hypotonic). Hypotonic (floppy) infants have low muscle tone whereas hypertonic infants have high muscle tone. In

Motor skills require practice. Some children need support in safely practicing antigravity positions.

both cases problems in tone can be an indication of damage to the nervous system. There is some controversy in this area. Some feel that an infant's motor skills need to be assessed to determine whether the problems are transient or will remain constant. If they will remain constant, then intervention should focus on emphasizing what motor strengths the child has and concentrate on social-emotional, communication, and sensory-motor skills rather than trying to remediate deficits in motor development. The feeling is that these skills will have more of an effect on the child's adjustment and that technology can be used to compensate for the lack of motor skills. If, however, there can be long-term improvement in motor function, the approach is for therapeutic intervention. The question is, when can we accurately make these distinctions? By twelve to fifteen months most long-term motor problems have been identified.

Social Skills

Early learning is primarily social in nature. Positive feelings toward an infant or toddler with a disability and the development of strong mutual attachment bonds are imperative for the child's growth and development. This bond often grows and develops through contingent responsivity, that is, the interaction between an infant's behavior and a consistent response by the caregiver. Children need a warm, responsive relationship involving give-and-take social games.

Guidelines

For infants:

1. Flexible scheduling is imperative. The younger the infant the more necessary it is to respond to the child's biological clock rather than preset schedules.

2. Although flexible, a predictable schedule helps young children know what will happen next.

3. Infants change and grow quickly, so there is a constant need to evaluate and re-evaluate the curriculum to match the infant's changing skills.

4. Planning needs to be individualized for *all* infants, not just those with developmental delays.

5. Look into the infant's eyes when you talk and call him by name. Talk to infants. Talk about what you see and hear and what you are doing. Have the tone of your voice match what you are talking about.

6. Answer an infant's cries quickly. This is part of building trust. Infants will cry less and begin to wait for you to respond once they know that you will do so as quickly as you can.

7. Allow infants to adjust to new people or situations in their own way. They need both time and space.

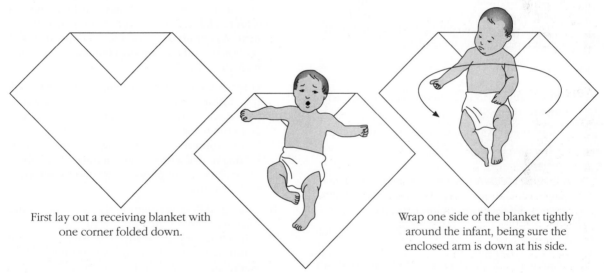

First lay out a receiving blanket with one corner folded down.

Place the infant on the blanket with his head on the folded corner as illustrated.

Wrap one side of the blanket tightly around the infant, being sure the enclosed arm is down at his side.

Tuck the blanket under the infant leaving the other arm out.

Now place this arm at the infant's side and fold up the bottom of the blanket. Wrap the remaining blanket snugly around the infant.

The infant is now swaddled.

Swaddling an Infant

8. Cribs are for sleeping. Have infants on the floor, in infant seats, or propped up so they can play. Provide a variety of activities within their reach so that they can get to them easily.

9. Use the infant's repertoire of skills to teach additional skills. Because infants with delayed development may have a limited repertoire, reinforcement is particularly important.

10. The cues that infants with developmental delays give are often subtle. With practice these can be interpreted and responded to. The task of interpretation and response, however, may not be an easy one.

11. Infants have individual differences in their tolerance for stimulation and ability to adaptively respond to such stimulation. Caregivers must match the amount and timing of stimulation to the infant's tolerance.

12. Sometimes swaddling an infant helps quiet him and helps him get himself under control. The basic technique for swaddling is illustrated on the previous page. A receiving blanket works well.

For toddlers:

1. Allow toddlers to talk about and play with what interests them.

2. Guide the learning and concentration of toddlers, don't force it. Provide help only when necessary.

3. Allowing toddlers to control what they choose to play with and how long they choose to play increases the development of internal controls.

4. Give toddlers many opportunities to be successful.

5. Sequence tasks from easy to hard. Break down more difficult tasks.

6. Toddlers need to participate actively in the learning process.

7. Use repetition with slight variation to keep interest.

8. Help toddlers organize their activities. For example, say, "What will you do first? . . . What comes next?"

When teaching multi-age groups that include toddlers it is important to adjust your expectations to their developmental level.

1. Don't expect toddlers to sit for a long time in a group situation. If you are doing a long activity, allow toddlers to come and go as they please.

2. When undesirable behavior cannot be prevented, anticipate when it will happen. (If a child typically has a difficult time leaving her parents, plan to have an adult available who can give her undivided attention to help this transition go more smoothly.)

3. Remember age-appropriate expectations. Different strategies are effective with different age groups. For example, younger children are more easily distracted than older ones.

4. Match children's developmental level in an age-appropriate way. Even if a toddler is functioning at a much younger level try to find toys and materials appropriate for a toddler, not a young infant.

5. Re-direct misbehaving children to more appropriate activities when possible. This may be difficult with a persistent toddler who is fascinated by a particular object and can't be distracted. You might find a special time when you can give the child your full attention and let her touch the forbidden object with your close supervision. This approach will often decrease rather than increase the fascination with the object.

6. Expect children to alternate between dependence and independence. They may be clingy one minute and saying "I want to do it myself" the next. As children try out their independence, it is normal for them to want a cuddly spot to come back to.

7. Offer limited choices whenever possible, and then follow through on allowing the children to have their choice. For example, "Do you want to go to the bathroom alone or with me?" However, before you offer a choice, be sure that you are willing to live with the option the child chooses. (That is, don't simply ask if the child wants to go to the bathroom.)

8. Allow toddlers the option of not participating. They will often watch for a while and then join you when they are ready. Everyone, including children, needs to have control over his environment, and letting children choose when they will participate is one way of ensuring this. Watch, on the other hand, for an older child who often doesn't want to participate. Find ways of regularly including this child.

9. A well-managed setting is not always quiet and neat. Decide what level of noise and mess you are comfortable with, and try not to go much beyond that level. Keep in mind that a quiet, immaculate setting may mean that children are not getting the experiences they need.

10. Toddlers do things fast; they get hungry fast, angry fast, or tired fast. However, they also bounce back fast. They are not good at waiting, so keep waiting times to a minimum and try to respond FAST.

Because very young children cannot tell parents about their day, communication with parents serves various functions.

1. Parents need information about the daily experiences of the infant and young toddler.

2. Develop a consistent system of recording information to give parents daily. This may be a message board, a notebook that travels with the child, or any system that works for you. It is important for parents of young children to know such things as when and how long the infant has slept, eaten, and so on. (You will find also that getting such information from the parents will help you plan your day.)

3. Parents want to know that you accept and like their child. For parents whose child has a disability it is imperative that you show warm feelings to both the child and the parents. You are a source of emotional support for the child and for the parents.

4. Young children are more interrelated in their physical, social/emotional and cognitive development than adults. Although it is convenient to single out one area of development, it is important to view its interrelationships with the other areas as well.

5. Young children are very vulnerable and are dependent upon adults to provide consistency in their development. Children with disabilities have greater vulnerability and are in dependent circumstances for longer periods than children without disabilities.

6. When you make a breakthrough in reading an infant's cues or finding the optimal amount of stimulation, share this knowledge with the family and other team members. They can make use of what you have learned and can provide you with feedback and modifications.

7. Parents of infants and toddlers with developmental delays need to hear positive information from you about their child and his accomplishments on a regular basis, no matter how small his achievements may seem.

Curriculum Adaptations
Language Arts: Speaking, Listening, Reading, and Writing

Learning the underlying concepts of language and its usefulness occurs during these early years. Infants and toddlers need to learn that communication is a useful skill. This learning requires responsivity.

1. Respond to the infant's language initiations to increase the likelihood of his continuing and increasing such activity.

2. Initiate language with infants with the expectation that they will respond whether or not they do.

3. Choose cardboard and plastic books for young children and encourage them to hold the books and turn the pages. Point out familiar objects. Pair the actual object with the picture and then encourage the child to use the object.

4. Use books individually with children or in groups of two or three. Choose books for the pictures and plan to tell the story rather than read it. You will probably need to shorten the story and individualize it so children can attend to the end.

5. Talk to infants and toddlers and offer praise and encouragement for their efforts to respond.

6. Model language in addition to extending and expanding children's language. Label experiences and pictures for children.

7. Some young children may be overly sensitive to noises. Be aware of this and try to eliminate these sounds.

8. Encourage children to label their body parts on their own body and to first point to and then name these parts on dolls. Talk with children about the function of these parts.

9. Say or read nursery rhymes, use simple fingerplays, and play easy rhyming games.

10. Give toddlers time to respond to your requests. Language is new to them.

11. Infants and toddlers understand many more words than they can speak. Give them the vocabulary they need, but also see yourself as a language model.

Discovery: Mathematics, Science, Computers

Young children construct knowledge by actively using materials. This activity can be supported with language, but language alone is not a substitute.

1. Provide opportunities for children to actively learn about their environment.

2. Provide a variety of materials to facilitate self-discovery so children can construct their own knowledge.

3. Young children learn competence when their behavior has a predictable outcome. They need practice discovering this in relation to objects as well as by people's behavior.

4. Being outside regularly helps children learn about nature and the environment in which they live. It provides both freedom and a challenge to understand nature. It is a way of checking out reality.

Sensory Motor: Large Motor, Sensory Motor Integration, Small Motor

Infants and toddlers are very active. They want to practice skills. Know and encourage the movements

Toddlers often need to look at a group from the security of their mother's lap before venturing out to join it.

markers you should talk with the parents. (Occupational therapists are your best source of knowledge in this area.).

7. Verbally label what the children do so they have the vocabulary as well as the skill.

Social Awareness: Social Studies, Inclusion, Health and Safety

1. The development of a secure relationship with the primary caregiver (or the primary caregiver and significant others) is critical to the development of the infant's health and competence.

2. The role of the caregiver in particular and the overall environment in general is transactional. The infant influences it and is influenced by it. Caregivers must create a positive, inviting environment for the infant, even if the infant does not seem to respond.

3. As young children are not concerned about issues of health and safety, it becomes the responsibility of adults to assure that the environment is both safe and healthy. Safety requires looking at toys to determine whether or not they are small enough to swallow or choke on, as well as to consider other health-related issues. You may wash your hands so often that you want to take out stock in a soap factory, but good health practices are extremely important. Keep washing, and have the children wash also.

that children are capable of. Be sure these movements are safe.

1. Be alert to the subtle movements of children to communicate thoughts or feelings. Each child has a unique signaling system. It is important to learn this.

2. Allow children to observe other children practicing motor skills at the next higher level. Then support them in their efforts to accomplish such skills.

3. Use large versions of manipulative toys, such as large Leggos, Tinker toys and blocks.

4. Be aware of equipment that may tip or roll.

5. Encourage children to use the motor skills available to them regardless of competence. They need the most practice in areas in which they are the least able, so emphasize process over product.

6. Some children are hypersensitive to touch. They may avoid messy projects or sand play because of tactile discomfort. Never force a child who complains about tactile stimuli to participate. However, if this tactile problem seems to be interfering with peer relationships, or is so pervasive that the child will not use tools such as crayons and

Creative Arts: Art, Music, Creative Movement, and Dramatic Play

1. Older infants and toddlers enjoy messy activities like water play and fingerpainting. Because of the probability of its going into their mouths, consider using pudding or other edibles to paint with.

2. Playdough (again a homemade "eatable" variety is recommended) provides the opportunity to practice developing fine motor skills.

3. Toddlers need to be supported and admired for their creative activities. By any objective standard they are rarely good, but the importance of a creative style of thinking is imperative.

4. Toddlers learn about what grownups do by playing at being "grownup." Role play also helps them learn about children with disabilities and think about creative solutions to their problems.

5. Creative activities are typically process-oriented at this age, thus they present the opportunity for learning about oneself as well as learning to use materials involved.

6. Pairing music and movement encourages toddlers to move in different ways and explore body awareness.

Transitions

Changing activities is often difficult for young children. The following suggestions will help manage this daily occurrence.

1. Have a routine and stick to it so children will have a sense of what comes next on a regular basis.

2. Give a warning when the group is close to the end of an activity: "We will be cleaning up in five minutes." Even without an accurate sense of time, this helps children know that an activity is about to end and they should finish what they are doing.

3. Have a few clear rules and enforce them.

4. Part of the transition requires learning adaptive behaviors or self-help skills. Rushing the transition puts pressure on toddlers as they are mastering emerging skills, often resulting in resistance and the word "no." Allowing additional time is an asset to all.

5. Giving toddlers choices, allowing control over some decisions, often helps transitions. Be sure they are choices you are willing to live with. The child can decide which book she wants to look at during rest time, not whether or not she will rest.

6. If children have to wait, make it an enjoyable experience by singing or by providing activities for them to do as they wait.

Children's Bibliography

See the Children's Bibliography on page 286 for books to increase children's awareness about infants and toddlers and books that are especially suitable for infants and toddlers. Note especially:

Picture Books (especially those without words)

Scratch and Sniff and Touch and Feel Books

Simpler Books

Glossary

Adjusted, corrected, or conceptual age   The age of the child calculated from conception. (Typically this is used to compensate for prematurity.)

Apnea   The absence of breathing for more than 15 seconds.

Bradycardia   A lower than normal heart rate (often accompanies apnea).

Chronological age   The age of the child calculated from birth.

Gestational age   The length of time the infant was in utero.

Large for dates (or gestational age)   Weight that is above the 90th percentile for the infant's gestational age.

Low Birth Weight (LBW)   A birth weight of 2,500 grams (5 pounds, 8 ounces) or less.

Neonatal period   Birth through the first twenty-eight days.

Preterm   An infant born at thirty-six weeks gestational age or less.

Small for dates (or gestational age)   Weight that is below the 10th percentile for the infant's gestational age.

Term   The average length of a pregnancy is forty weeks. An infant born between thirty-eight and forty-two weeks is considered born at term.

Very Low Birth Weight (VLBW)   A birth weight of 1,500 grams (3 pounds, 5 ounces) or less.

Teaching Resources

Association for the Care of Children's Health (ACCH)
3615 Wisconsin Avenue, N.W.
Washington, DC 20016
(202) 244-1801
   A multidisciplinary association of professionals and parents to promote quality health care. Publishes material on early intervention, health-related issues, and hospitalization of young children.

The Centering Corporation
P.O. Box 3367
Omaha, NE 68103
   Has a catalog of pamphlets on low birth weight babies, the neonatal intensive care unit, infant death, and so on. Some of these are written for siblings and grandparents.

Compassionate Friends Headquarters
P.O. Box 3696
Oak Brook, IL 60522
   Provides information on coping with the death of a child.

Federation for Children with Special Needs
312 Stuart Street
Boston, MA 02116
(617) 482-2915
   An organization of parents and health professionals to encourage partnership and involvement between parents and health care professionals.

Infant Stimulation Education Association
UCLA Health Science Center
Los Angeles, CA 90024
   Provides both written material and workshops on neonatal practices.

March of Dimes Birth Defects Foundation
1275 Mamaroneck Avenue
White Plains, NY 10605
(914) 428-7100
   Funds research, education, and service projects on high-risk infants. Local chapters may

have sources of audio-visual materials and other resources.

National Center for Clinical Infant Programs
733 15th Street, N.W., Suite 912
Washington, DC 20005
   Publishes a newsletter, Zero to Three, *and holds biennial national meetings as well as sponsoring research.*

National Center for Education in Maternal and
   Child Health/National Maternal and Child
   Health Clearinghouse
38th and R Streets, N.W.
Washington, DC 20057
   Provides information on services for children with disabilities and parental concerns.

National Center for Networking Community-Based
   Services
Georgetown University Child Development Center
3800 Reservoir Road, N.W.
Washington, DC 20007
(202) 625-7033
   Provides technical assistance and training to states to enhance interagency collaboration and improve services.

National Maternal and Child Health Resource Center
College of Law Building
The University of Iowa
Iowa City, IA 52252
(319) 335-9046
   Promotes the improvement and expansion of maternal and child health services through dissemination of information and training materials and technical assistance.

Parent Care
101 1/2 S. Union Street
Alexandria, VA 22314
(703) 836-4678
   Focuses on information for parents of infants who have been in the neonatal intensive care unit.

Parents of Premature and High Risk Infants
   International, Inc.
The National Self-Help Clearinghouse
33 W. 42nd Street
New York, NY 10036
   Provides information and other services to families, support groups, and professionals.

Perinatal Association
101 1/2 S. Union Street
Alexandria, VA 22314
(703) 549-5523
   Has a special interest section on developmental intervention.

References and Bibliography

Batshaw, M., & Perret, Y. (1986). *Children with handicaps: A medical primer.* Baltimore, MD: Paul H. Brookes.

Bender, M., & Baglin, C. A. (1992). *Infants and toddlers: A resource guide for practitioners.* San Diego, CA: Singular Publishing Group, Inc.

Bird, A. (1989). Cognitive and language development. In C. Semmler (Ed.), *A guide to care and management of very low birth weight infants: A team approach* (pp. 190–215). Tucson, AZ: Therapy Skill Builders.

Blackman, J. (1990). *Medical aspects of developmental disabilities in children birth to three* (2nd ed.). Rockville, MD: Aspen.

Brown, C. (Ed.). (1981). *Infants at risk: Assessment and intervention: An update for health care professionals and parents.* Skillman, NJ: Johnson & Johnson.

Connor, F., Williamson, G., & Siepp, J. (Eds.). (1978). *Program guide for infants and toddlers with neuromotor and other developmental disabilities.* New York: Teachers College Press, Columbia University.

Cortez, J. (Ed.). (1991). *Infant/toddler caregiving: A guide to culturally sensitive care.* Sacramento, CA: Far West Laboratory and California State Department of Education.

Dombro, A., & Wallach, L. (1988). *The ordinary is extraordinary: How children under three learn.* New York: Simon & Schuster.

Filler, J. (1983). *Educating handicapped infants: Issues in development and intervention.* Rockville, MD: Aspen.

Garwood, S., & Fewell, R. (Eds.). (1983). *Educating handicapped infants: Issues in development and intervention.* Rockville, MD: Aspen.

Graham, T., & Camp, L. (1988). *Teaching terrific two's and other toddlers.* Atlanta, GA: Humanics Learning.

Hanson, M. (Ed.). (1984). *Atypical infant development.* Baltimore, MD: University Park Press.

Hanson, M. (1987). *Teaching the infant with Down syndrome: A guide for parents and professionals.* San Diego, CA: Singular Publishing Group, Inc.

Hanson, M. (1989). *Early intervention: Implementing child and family services for infants and toddlers at-risk or disabled.* San Diego, CA: Singular Publishing Group, Inc.

Harmes, T., Cryer, D., & Clifford, R. (1990). *Infant/toddler environmental rating scale.* New York: Teachers College Press, Columbia University.

Harrison, H. (1983). *The premature baby book.* New York: St. Martin's Press.

Healy, A., Keesee, P., & Smith, B. (1985). *Early services for children with special needs: Transactions for family support.* Iowa City, IA: University of Iowa.

Heyne, E. (1989). Low birth weight infant follow-up at Children's Medical Center, Dallas. In C. Semmler (Ed.), *A guide to care and management of very low birth weight infants: A team approach* (pp. 124–135). Tucson, AZ: Therapy Skill Builders.

Odom, S. L., & Karnes, M. B. (Eds.). (1988). *Early intervention for infants and children with handicaps: An empirical base.* Baltimore, MD: Paul H. Brookes.

Schmitt, B., & Kempe, C. H. (1979). Abuse and neglect of children. In V. C. Vaughn, R. J. McKay, & Behrman (Eds.), *Nelson textbook of pediatrics* (11th ed.) (pp. 120–126). Philadelphia: W. B. Saunders.

Segal, M. (1988). *In time and with love: Caring for the special needs baby.* New York: Newmarket Press.

Semmler, C. (Ed.). (1989a). *A guide to care and management of very low birth weight infants: A team approach.* Tucson, AZ: Therapy Skill Builders.

Semmler, C. (1989b). Introduction. In C. Semmler, (Ed.), *A guide to care and management of very low birth weight infants: A team approach* (pp. 1–7). Tucson, AZ: Therapy Skill Builders.

Semmler, C. (1989c). Intracranial hemorrhage. In C. Semmler (Ed.), *A guide to care and management of very low birth weight infants: A team approach* (pp. 77–98). Tucson, AZ: Therapy Skill Builders.

Stewart, B., & Vargas, J. (1990). *Teaching behavior to infants and toddlers: A manual for caregivers and parents.* Springfield, IL: Charles C. Thomas.

Thurman, S., & Widerstrom, A. (1990). *Infants and young children with special needs: A developmental and ecological approach.* Baltimore, MD: Paul H. Brookes.

U.S. Department of Labor. (1988). *Child-care—A workforce issue.* Executive summary report of the secretary's task force. Washington, DC: U.S. Department of Labor.

Weiner, R., & Koppelman, J. (1987) *From birth to 5: Serving the youngest handicapped children.* Alexandria, VA: Capitol Publications.

Weiser, M. (1991). *Group care and education of infants and toddlers* (2nd ed.). Riverside, NJ: Merrill/Macmillan Co.

Widerstrom, A., Mowder, B., & Sandall, S. (1991). *At-risk and handicapped newborns and infants: Development, assessment, & intervention.* Englewood Cliffs, NJ: Prentice-Hall.

Children's Bibliography

Awareness of Communication Disorders

Lemke, Deborah. (1988). *The way it happened.* Boston, MA: Houghton Mifflin.

A variation on the old gossip game is this story of Sarah's fall from her bicycle and how it changes with humorous results as it is relayed from person to person.

Awareness of Cultures

Mahal, T. (1988). *Shake sugaree.* Redway, CA: Music for Little People.

Traditional folk tunes from around the world. They will add cultural diversity to programming.

Spier, Peter. (1980). *People.* Garden City, NY: Doubleday.

"A picture book for the ages" emphasizes the differences among the five billion people on earth.

African-American and African

Aardema, Vera. (1981). *Bringing the rain to Kapiti Plain.* New York: Dial Books, NAL Penguin.

A cumulative rhyme relating how Ki-pat brought rain to the drought-stricken Kapiti Plain.

Adoff, Arnold. (1973). *Black is brown is tan.* New York: Harper & Row.

Poetically phrased picture of a white-black marriage and family.

Baldwin, Anne Norris. (1973). *Sunflowers for Tina.* New York: Scholastic.

Tina, an African-American girl, is determined to grow a garden in the middle of New York City.

Bang, Molly. (1983). *Ten, nine, eight.* New York: Greenwillow Books.

A happy counting game by a loving father enticing a little girl to bed.

Bogart, JoEllen. (1990). *Daniel's dog.* New York: Scholastic.

A young boy adjusts to the arrival of his new baby sister with the help of his imaginary dog Lucy.

Bond, Jean Carey. (1969). *Brown is a beautiful color*. New York: Franklin Watts.

A story in simple rhyme that calls attention to all the things around us that are brown.

Carlstrom, Nancy. (1987). *Wild, wild sunflower child Anna*. New York: Macmillan.

Spending a day out of doors, Anna revels in the joys of sun, sky, grass, flowers, berries, frogs, ants, and beetles.

Cavin, Ruth. (1973). *Timothy the terror*. New York: Harlin Quist.

A story about an African-American boy's revenge on his three sisters.

Crews, Donald. (1991). *Big mama's*. New York: Greenwillow Books.

Visiting Big Mama's house in the country, young Donald Crews finds his relatives full of new and old stories. The place and its surroundings are just the same as the year before. A good book to read to younger children.

Elkin, Benjamin. (1968). *Such is the way of the world*. New York: Scholastic.

A young African boy, while minding his father's cattle, loses his pet monkey and goes in search of him.

Feelings, Muriel. (1971). *Moja means one: The Swahili counting book*. New York: Dial Books.

A Swahili counting book that describes East African culture.

Gray, Nigel. (1988). *A country far away*. New York: Orchard Books.

Side-by-side pictures reveal the essential similarities between the lives of two boys, one in a western country, one in a rural African village.

Greenfield, Eloise. (1976). *First pink light*. New York: Thomas Y. Crowell.

Tyree is a young African-American child whose father has been away for a month. Tyree and his mother wait up together for Father, whom they have missed.

Hill, Elizabeth. (1967). *Evan's corner*. New York: Holt, Rinehart and Winston.

Evan, a young African-American boy, tries to find privacy by creating his own special corner.

Howard, Elizabeth. (1974). *Jambo means hello: Swahili alphabet book*. New York: Dial Books.

An alphabet book that also describes East African culture.

Howard, Elizabeth. (1991). *Aunt Flossie's hats (and crab cakes later)*. New York: Clarion Books.

Sarah and Susan share tea, cookies, crab cakes, and stories about hats when they visit their favorite relative, Aunt Flossie.

Johnson, Angela. (1990). *When I am old with you*. New York: Orchard Books.

An African-American child imagines being with Granddaddy and joining him in such activities as playing cards all day, visiting the ocean, and eating bacon on the porch.

Johnson, Angela. (1989). *Tell me a story, Mama*. New York: Orchard Books.

A child and her mother remember together all the girl's favorite stories about her mother's childhood.

Johnson, Dolores. (1991). *What kind of baby sitter is this?* New York: Macmillan.

Kevin intensely dislikes the idea of having a babysitter until the unconventional baseball-loving "Aunt" Lovey arrives to change his mind.

Keats, Ezra Jack. (1962). *The snowy day*. New York: Viking Press.

Delightful story of an African-American child's adventures in the snow.

Keats, Ezra Jack. (1969). *Goggles*. New York: Macmillan.

Two African-American children find a pair of motorcycle goggles but have to outsmart a gang of "big guys" in order to keep them.

Keats, Ezra Jack. (1972). *Hit cat*. New York: Macmillan.

Archie, an African-American city boy, makes friends with a stray black cat. A humorous tale of how the cat follows Archie around.

Keats, Ezra Jack. (1977). *Whistle for Willie*. New York: Penguin Books.

An African-American city boy named Peter finds it difficult to learn to whistle for his dog Willie.

Lexau, Joan M. (1970). *Benjie on his own*. New York: Dial Books.

Benjie, an African-American boy in a ghetto neighborhood, must walk home from school alone one day when his grandmother doesn't meet him. On the way, he encounters a big dog and some big boys who threaten and tease him. At home, he finds that his grandmother is sick. He finds some people to help, and a friend's mother takes him into her home while his grandmother is in the hospital.

Lexau, Joan M. (1971). *Mandala*. New York: Harper & Row.

The story of an African family (MA is mother, DA is father, LA is singing). These sounds and others join over and over in a tuneful way that celebrates the circle of the family and the cycle of life.

Radlaur, Ed, & Shaw, Ruth. (1967). *Father is big*. Glendale, CA: Bowmar.

Close-up photographs by Harvey Mandlin show how a black child looks up to his father.

Ringgold, Faith. (1991). *Tar beach*. New York: Crown.

Cassie, an African-American girl, in her imagination flies over Tar Beach, which is really the roof top of her New York apartment house, and corrects all the family's problems, which include lack of money, discrimination, and job problems for Dad.

Scott, Ann Herbert. (1967). *Sam*. New York: McGraw-Hill.

Sam, a little boy, has nothing to do and causes his whole family to be mad at him.

Seeger, Pete. (1986). *Abiyoyo*. New York: Macmillan.

Banished from the town for making mischief, a little African-American boy and his father are welcomed back when they find a way to make the dreaded giant Abiyoyo disappear.

Sonneborn, Ruth A. (1970). *Friday night is papa night*. New York: Viking Press.

The tender story of an African-American family's looking forward to having Papa come home on Friday night.

Steptoe, John. (1974). *My special best words*. New York: Viking Press.

A little girls uses African-American dialect to describe her daily life with her family (her brother and father) and her babysitter.

Stone, Elberta H. (1971). *I'm glad I'm me*. New York: G.P. Putnam's Sons.

A little boy, when he is lonely, dreams of all the things that he would like to be. Finally he realizes that he is glad to be himself because he has two arms to hug people with and two legs to walk with. Most important, he will grow up to be what he wants to be.

Udry, Janice May. (1968). *What Mary Jo shared*. Chicago: Albert Whitman.

A little African-American girl shares her father during "show and tell."

Van Leeuwen, Jean. (1966). *Timothy's flower*. New York: Random House.

A sensitive story of a small African-American boy who starts a garden in the middle of a city.

Van Leeuwen, Jean. (1968). *What Mary Jo wanted*. Chicago: Albert Whitman.

Mary Jo, a young African-American girl, gets her wish: a puppy. She soon discovers that this is a twenty-four-hour-a-day responsibility.

Yolen, Jane. (1969). *It all depends*. New York: Funk & Wagnalls.

An African-American boy becomes more aware of himself by asking his mother questions: "How tall am I?" "It all depends—to an ant, you are immense, to a whale you are small."

Asian-American and Asian

Ayer, Jacqueline. (1962). *The paper flower tree*. New York: Harcourt Brace Jovanovich.

When a traveling peddler in Thailand presents little Miss Moon with a blossom from his paper flower tree, she plants its one seed and patiently waits for it to bloom.

Behrens, June. (1965). *Soo Ling finds a way*. Chicago: Childrens Press.

Fearing her grandfather's ruin from a laundromat's going up across the street from his hand laundry, Soo Ling tells Grandfather to iron in front of the window since he has a magic hand at ironing. Grandfather Soo is so good at the iron, the new owner asks Grandfather to be his partner!

Flack, Marjorie, & Wiese, Kurt. (1933). *Story about Ping*. New York: Viking Press.

An old favorite about a little duck who lives on a boat on the Yangtze River and his adventures when he hides from his master in order to avoid getting a spank on the back.

Handforth, Thomas. (1938). *Mei Li*. New York: Doubleday.

The story of a young girl in China.

Issa. (1969). *A few flies and I*. New York: Pantheon. Collection of Japanese haikus.

Johnson, Doris. (1968). *Su An*. Chicago: Follett.

This charming little book presents death, adoption, and leaving one's homeland in a very touching way. After her mother's death, Su An arrives in America from Korea, her home. She is going to join a new family, but her heart still longs for her mother.

Liang, Yen. (1953). *Tommy and Dee-Dee*. New York: Walck.

A simply written story illustrating how two boys living in different parts of the world, one in America and the other in China, are alike in many ways.

Martin, Patricia Miles. (1962). *The rice bowl pet*. New York: Thomas Y. Crowell.

Jim lives in a crowded apartment in San Francisco's Chinatown. He roams the street looking for a pet small enough to fit in his rice bowl.

Martin, Patricia Miles. (1964). *The greedy one*. New York: Rand McNally.

Tells the customs of the traditional Japanese "Boys' Day" and what happens when a greedy boy eats the fish being saved for the festival. Red and white ink illustrations.

Politi, Leo. (1960). *Moy Moy*. New York: Scribner.

A story about life in the Chinese section of an American city and the celebration of the Chinese New Year told through the eyes of Moy Moy, an American-Chinese girl who lives in Los Angeles.

Riwkin-Brick, Anna. (1961). *Mokihana lives in Hawaii*. New York: Macmillan.

The story of four Hawaiian children and how they spend one day.

Slobodkin, Louis. (1963). *Moon Blossom and the golden penny*. New York: Vanguard Press.

A poor child in Hong Kong receives a lucky penny when she helps an old woman.

Yashima, Taro. (1955). *Crow boy*. New York: Viking Press.

The moving story of Chibi, a shy Japanese boy, whose classmates are helped by their teacher to understand him. This book points up the problems of young children from different backgrounds.

Yashima, Taro. (1977). *Umbrella*. New York: Penguin Books.

    Momo, a Japanese girl, wants it to rain so that she can use her new birthday umbrella and her beautiful red boots. When it finally rains, she has a marvelous time playing.

Hispanic

Archuleta, Nathaniel, et al. (1975). *El perrioto perdido; Una luminaria; Para mis palomitas; Ya perdiste tu Colita, Tita; Perlitas de ayer y hoy*. Available from Dr. Nathaniel Archuleta, University of New Mexico, Albuquerque, NM.

    These five books of stories, poems, rhymes, songs and activities are written in Spanish with an English version in the back. They highlight the Hispanic culture.

Atkinson, Mary. (1979). *Maria Teresa*. Chapel Hill, NC: Lollipop Power.

    Maria and her mother move to a new town where no one speaks Spanish. With the help of her puppet, Maria helps the other children in the class learn the language.

Blue, Rose. (1971). *I am here. Yo estoy aquí.* New York: Franklin Watts.

    A young girl from Puerto Rico makes friends and begins to learn English in her new surroundings.

Brenner, Barbara. (1961). *Barto takes the subway*. New York: Knopf.

    A Puerto Rican boy explores the sights and sounds of New York's subway.

Brunhoff, Laurent de. (1965). *Babar's Spanish lessons*. New York: Random House.

    Babar gives Spanish lessons to his elephant friends. The text is written in English with Spanish after each English sentence.

Ets, Marie Hall. (1963). *Gilberto and the wind*. New York: Viking Press.

    This Mexican boy makes the wind his playmate. The book shows the many things the wind can do. (Also available in Spanish.)

Ets, Marie Hall. (1967). *Bad boy, good boy*. New York: Thomas Y. Crowell.

    The story of a large Spanish-speaking family. The little boy is always getting into trouble because he has nothing to do. When the mother leaves after a fight with the father, the father is forced to take the little boy to a day-care center. At first the little boy hates it there. After a while, he learns to speak English and writes his mother a letter begging her to come home. She does.

Freeman, Don. (1968). *Corduroy*. New York: Viking Press.

    This book shows a young Hispanic girl's feelings of loneliness, companionship, and love for a very special teddy bear.

Hautzig, Esther. (1968). *In the park: An excursion in four languages*. New York: Macmillan.

    Written in four languages (English, French, Russian, and Spanish), this book shows pictures of things seen in parks in New York, Moscow, Paris, and Madrid.

Keats, Ezra Jack. (1960). *My dog is lost*. New York: Thomas Y. Crowell.

    Juanito, who speaks only Spanish, comes to New York from Puerto Rico and loses his only friend, his dog. His search takes him to Park Avenue, Chinatown, and Harlem. The text introduces some simple Spanish phrases.

Kesselman, Wendy, & Holt, Norma. (1970). *Angelita*. New York: Hill & Wang.

    Angelita loses her treasured doll as she moves from Puerto Rico to New York City. Photographs depict the land and scenery of each place.

Morrow, Elizabeth. (1930). *The painted pig*. New York: Knopf.

    Pedro is a young Mexican boy whose greatest wish is to own a china pig. The story of his determined efforts to get his pig gives the readers an understanding of the children and customs of Mexico.

Nielson, Virginia. (1971). *Adassa and her hen*. Toronto: McKay.

    A little girl in Jamaica has an unusual pet hen.

Politi, Leo (1963). *Rosa*. New York: Scribner.

    Rosa is a little girl who lives in San Felipe, Mexico. Her wish for a doll comes true in a special way when a baby sister is born on Christmas Eve. This book, also available in Spanish, shows the toys and games Rosa plays with as well as the customs of her country.

Politi, Leo. (1973). *The nicest gift*. New York: Scribner.

    Carlito's dog has disappeared, but reappears on Christmas Day. Fantastic illustrations of a Mexican neighborhood near Los Angeles.

Roe, Eileen. (1991). *Con mi hermano (With my brother)*. New York: Bradbury Press.

    A little boy admires his big brother and aspires to be like him when he is older. Done with simple, beautiful, watercolor illustrations and text in both English and Spanish.

Schweitzer, Byrd Baylor. (1973). *Amigo*. New York: Macmillan.

    A Mexican boy wants a pet, but his family cannot afford to feed one. He decides to tame a prairie dog as a solution.

Serfozo, Mary. (1969). *Welcome Roberto! Bienvenido Roberto!* Chicago: Follet.

    A Mexican-American child's first experience in school.

Sonneborn, Ruth. (1968). *Seven in a bed*. New York: Viking Press.

Mama, the baby, and seven children come from Puerto Rico to join Papa, but they have a sleeping problem the first night.

Williams, Letty. (1969). *The little red hen: La pequeña gallina roja*. Englewood Cliffs, NJ: Prentice-Hall.

The story of the little red hen told in both English and Spanish.

Native American

Andrews, Han. (1986). *Very last time*. New York: Atheneum.

Beautiful, full-color pictures illustrate this exciting story of a Canadian Inuit girl's adventure on the bottom of the seabed looking for mussels.

Baker, Betty. (1962). *Little Runner of the longhouse*. New York: Harper & Row.

Little Runner is envious of his older brothers who are allowed to participate in the Iroquois New Year's ceremonies.

Blood, Charles L., & Link, Martin. (1978). *The goat in the rug*. New York: Scholastic.

Geraldine tells a story of a Navajo rug and the goat hair that was used to make it.

Goble, Paul. (1989). *Iktomi and the berries*. New York: Orchard Books.

Beautifully illustrated story of Iktomi, a Plains Indian boy who has some amazing adventures in his search for berries.

Hayes, Joe. (cassette, 1983). *Coyote and Native American folk tales*. Santa Fe, NM: Trails West Publishing.

These are tales of survival. Coyote is a Native American who has great adventures because his life is in danger. This is an introduction into a discussion of value clarifications. It is best listened to with an adult and with discussion.

Hoyt-Goldsmith, D. (1990). *Totem pole*. New York: Holiday House.

Beautiful color pictures of a Northwest Coast Indian boy who works with his father to make a totem pole for a tribal reservation.

Martin, Bill, & Archambault, John. (1987). *Knots on a counting rope*. New York: Holt.

A story about a Native American boy who is born blind and how he learns to cope. Captures the interdependence between Native Americans and nature.

Parish, Peggy. (1968). *Little Indian*. New York: Simon & Schuster.

In search of a name, the little Indian goes into the forest to catch an animal so that he can be called by the animal's name. Eventually, a turtle catches him, so he is called Snapping Turtle.

Perrine, Mary. (1970). *Nannabah's friend*. Boston: Houghton Mifflin.

A young Navajo girl copes with loneliness while taking her sheep to pasture.

Perrine, Mary. (1973). *Salt boy*. Boston: Houghton Mifflin.

The story of a Navajo Indian boy's feelings for his father.

Rogers, J. (1988). *Runaway mittens*. New York: Greenwillow.

Pica, a young Alaskan boy, has a pair of red mittens that keep running away. A sled dog uses the mittens as a bed to bear nine puppies. Depicts a native Alaskan lifestyle.

Sleator, William. (1970). *The angry moon*. Boston: Little, Brown.

Tlingit Indian legend from Alaska.

Stuart, Gene S. (1974). *Three little Indians*. Washington, DC: National Geographic Society.

The stories of a Cheyenne boy, a Greek girl, and a Nootka boy.

Wiseman, Bernard. (1977). *Iglook's seal*. New York: Dodd, Mead.

Iglook is an Eskimo who can't bring himself to harpoon a baby seal, so he brings it home as a pet. The seal ultimately catches fish for him.

Other Cultures

Alder, David A., & Hirsh, Marilyn. (1976). *The house on the roof—A Sukkot story*. New York: Bonim Books.

A gentle, warm, and humorous story about an old man getting ready for a special Hebrew holiday. Eventually, he must explain his actions to the neighbors.

Evans, Eva Knox. (1957). *All about us*. New York: Golden Press.

Explains simply the reasons for similarities and differences among children around the world.

Floethe, Louise, & Floethe, Richard. (1955). *The new roof*. New York: Scribner.

A Tahitian family needs a new roof on their palm-thatched house. When none of the men has time to do it the women decide to do it, and the next day the men decide to finish the project.

Goldin, Augusta R. (1972). *Straight hair, curly hair*. New York: Thomas Y. Crowell.

This is a science book with colorful illustrations that answers questions about hair.

Green, Mary McBurney. (1967). *Everybody eats, everybody has a house*. Reading, MA: Addison-Wesley.

Tells what boys, girls, and animals eat, and about the houses they live in.

Keats, Ezra Jack. (1979). *Louie*. New York: School Book Services.

Louie, an alienated little boy, joins his friends Susie and Robert at a magical moment in a puppet show.

May, Julian. (1971). *Why people are different colors*. New York: Holiday House.

Pictures of people of the three major races (Mongoloid, Caucasian, and Negroid). Discusses physical adaptations and their usefulness today.

Miles, Betty. (1975). *Around and around—love.* New York: Knopf.

A photographic expression of love among people. The text uses many different words to describe love. Photographs depict many different races and ages.

Paola, Tomie. (1959). *Watch out for the chicken feet in your soup.* Boston: Houghton Mifflin.

Joey takes Eugene to visit his old-fashioned Italian grandmother.

Simon, Norma. (1976). *Why am I different?* Chicago: Albert Whitman.

This story portrays everyday situations in which children see themselves as "different." The book says that it is all right to be different.

Wim, Marie. (1974). *The fireside book of fun and game songs.* New York: Simon & Schuster.

A good book for children of all ages. It offers songs of entertainment from a variety of cultures.

Awareness of Disabilities

Brown, Tricia. (1984). *Someone special like you.* New York: Holt, Rinehart and Winston.

A book for preschoolers about children with disabilities. It has black and white photographs and an easy to read text.

Awareness of Emotional/ Behavioral Disorders

Nemiroff, M., & Annunziatia, J. (1990). *A child's first book about play therapy.* Washington, DC: American Psychological Association.

This book, published by the APA, is designed to help families and children learn about the therapy process and how it works.

Awareness of Health Impairments

Corbin, William C. (1971). *The day Willie wasn't.* New York: Coward, McCann and Geoghegan.

A light-hearted look at the problem of juvenile obesity. After Willie's weight is made fun of, he goes on a starvation diet until he can't be seen anymore.

Gaes, Jason. (1987). *My book for kids with cansur: A child's autobiography of hope.* Aberdeen, SD: Melius.

The subtitle describes Jason's battle with Burkitt's lymphoma in his own words, writing, and eight-year-old spelling.

Silverstein, Alvin, & Silverstein, Virginia B. (1978). *Itch, sniffle & sneeze: All about asthma, hay fever and other allergies.* New York: Four Winds Press.

A serious and informative discussion about allergies and their causes.

Awareness of Hearing Impairments

Aseltine, L., & Mueller, E. (1986). *I'm deaf and it's okay.* Chicago: Albert Whitman.

A child's coming to terms with a hearing impairment.

Bahan, Ben, & Dennis, Joe. (1990). *Signs for me.* Berkeley, CA: Dawn Sign Press.

Very expressive black and white pictures give the basic sign vocabulary for children.

Baker, P. (1986). *My first book of signs.* Washington, DC: Gallaudet University Press.

In a dictionary format, this book shows the signs for common words that children use.

Bornstein, Harry, & Saulnier, Karen. (1990). *Little red riding hood.* Washington, DC: Gallaudet University Press.

Beautifully illustrated version of this old story has the signed version on a section of the page.

Castle, Sue. (1977). *Face talk, hand talk, body talk.* Garden City, NY: Doubleday.

This text, with accompanying photographs, shows children communicating through facial expressions and gestures.

Chaplin, S. (1986). *I can sign my ABC's.* Washington, DC: Gallaudet University Press.

Illustrates the sign for each letter of the alphabet and also the sign for a word that starts with that letter.

Charlip, Remy, Miller, Mary Beth, & Ancona, George. (1987). *Hand talk birthday.* New York: Four Winds Press.

Words and sign language depict friends helping a child with a hearing impairment celebrate her birthday.

Hill, Eric. (1987). *Where's Spot?* New York: G. P. Putnam's Sons.

Sturdy board book is also a lift-the-flap book with signs at the top of the page.

Levine, Edna S. (1974). *Lisa and her soundless world.* New York: Human Sciences Press.

Lisa's life changes dramatically after she gets a hearing aid.

Litchfield, Ada B. (1976). *A button in her ear.* Chicago: Albert Whitman.

A little girl relates how her hearing deficiency is detected and corrected with the use of a hearing aid.

Miller, Mary Beth, & Ancona, George. (1991). *Hand talk school.* New York: Four Winds Press.

Words and sign language depict a group of children involved in putting on a play at school for children with hearing impairments.

Miller, Mary Beth, & Ancona, George. (1991). *Hand talk zoo.* New York: Four Winds Press.

Words and sign language depict children at the zoo discovering how to sign the names of various animals and how to tell time.

Peter, Diana. (1977). *Claire and Emma.* New York: John Day.

This story of two girls, ages two and four, who were born deaf is written by their mother.

Peterson, Jeanne W. (1977). *I have a sister, my sister is deaf.* New York: Harper & Row.

An account of what a deaf child can and cannot do and how she experiences everyday events.

Saulnier, Karen Luczak. (1973). *Mealtime at the zoo.* Prepared under the supervision of the staff of the Preschool Signed English Project. Washington, DC: Gallaudet College Press.

A description of what various zoo animals eat is accompanied by diagrams showing how to form the sign for each word of the text.

Sesame Street. (1980). *Sign language fun.* New York: Random House.

Sesame Street characters introduce the reader to sign language with words, pictures, and signs.

Walker, Lou Ann. (1985). *Amy, the story of a deaf child.* New York: Lodestar Books, E. P. Dutton.

The true story of a child with a profound hearing impairment born to parents who are also hearing impaired, and the adjustments the family (which includes a hearing brother) and the school made to include her. A good story for adults to read to children.

Wolf, Bernard. (1977). *Anna's silent world.* Philadelphia: Lippincott.

Anna, a deaf child, learns to talk and is eventually able to attend school with hearing children.

Awareness of Learning Disabilities

Cohen, Miriam. (1977). *When will I read?* New York: Greenwillow.

A good book for children who are anxiously awaiting the time that they will learn to read.

Cohen, Miriam. (1980). *No good in art.* New York: Greenwillow.

A first-grader is convinced he can't draw, but when encouraged, he finds he can.

Fassier, Joan. (1969). *One little girl: A "slow child" finds her strengths.* New York: Human Sciences Press.

While Laurie is slow at doing some things, she is fast at doing others. When the adults realize this, Laurie is at last happy to be herself.

Hatch, Jean. (1980). *School makes sense sometimes.* New York: Human Sciences Press.

The author covers every aspect of early education as she helps children to appreciate many of the confusing experiences of school.

Lasker, Joe. (1974). *He's my brother.* Chicago: Albert Whitman.

A young boy sensitively describes the experiences of his slow-learning younger brother at school and at home.

Awareness of Mental Retardation

Anders, Rebecca. (1976). *A look at mental retardation.* Minneapolis: Lerner Publications.

The book touches lightly on the facts of mental retardation while focusing on the problems and feelings of the retarded and the importance of acceptance.

Bergman, Thomas. (1989). *We laugh, we cry.* Milwaukee, WI: Gareth Stevens.

A book to be appreciated on three levels: the remarkable photographs of Asa and Anna Karin, the text for the mature reader, and the six-page appendix on mental retardation.

Clifton, Lucille. (1980). *My friend Jacob.* New York: E. P. Dutton.

The relationship between seventeen-year-old, mentally retarded Jacob and eight-year-old Sammy is sensitively portrayed. This book is a must for children and adults to better understand the feelings of the mentally disabled.

Grollman, Sharon. (1977). *More time to grow. Explaining mental retardation to children: A story.* Boston: Beacon Press.

About Carla and her brother Arthur and their family's acceptance of children's different rates of development. It suggests activities for children, and provides guidelines and annotated resources for adults.

Hirsch, Karen. (1977). *My sister.* Minneapolis: Carolrhoda Books.

The narrator expresses mixed emotions of happiness and jealousy as she describes her mentally impaired sister's individuality and capabilities.

Larsen, Hanne. (1974). *Don't forget Tom.* New York: Thomas Y. Crowell.

Tom, a mentally handicapped child, is usually happy. But when he can't do all of the things his brothers and friends manage to do, he becomes jealous and angry.

Ominsky, Elaine. (1977). *Jon O.: A special boy.* Englewood Cliffs, NJ: Prentice-Hall.

Although the introduction is inaccurate, the rest of the book portrays a Down syndrome boy's joys and frustrations while coping with daily life.

Rodowsky, Colby F. (1976). *What about me?* New York: Franklin Watts.

Dorrie begins to understand her feelings about her younger brother, Freddie, who has Down syndrome.

Smith, Lucia B. (1979). *A special kind of sister.* New York: Holt, Rinehart and Winston.

Sarah's mixed feelings toward her mentally retarded sibling.

Sobol, Harriet Langsam. (1977). *My brother Steven is retarded.* New York: Macmillan.

Beth tells about herself and her brother Steven—about the good times they have together and the times when she is angry or upset or sad because of Steven. She explains what it is like to be a part of a family where one person is retarded.

Wright, Betty Ren. (1981). *My sister is different.* Milwaukee, WI: Raintree Publishers.

Read to children every day.

Carlo resents that he has to take care of his mentally retarded older sister; he realizes that he loves her as much as she loves him when he almost loses her in a store.

Awareness of Physical Disabilities

Adams, Barbara. (1979). *Like it is: Facts and feelings about handicaps from kids who know.* New York: Walker and Co.

A group of six children talk about how they learned to deal with their disabilities and have full, satisfying lives. The photographs may be useful for starting a conversation with younger children.

Anderson, Hans Christian. (1968). *The ugly duckling.* Minato-tu, Tokyo: Zokersha Pub.

The classic story that deals with being different.

Bergman, Thomas. (1989). *On our own terms, children living with physical disabilities.* Milwaukee, WI: Gareth Stevens.

Sweden's best-known children's photographer's black and white photographs show children in therapy while the text for the mature reader explains the disabilities and the therapy. A six-page appendix provides additional information.

Burger, G. (1979). *Physical disabilities.* New York: Franklin Watts.

Describes specific disabilities and the treatment used for them. Attitudes toward handicaps are also discussed.

Ets, Marie Hall. (1965). *Just me.* New York: Viking Press.

A little farm boy tries to walk like the different farm animals. He finds the best way to get around is to run just like himself.

Fassler, Joan. (1975). *Howie helps himself.* Chicago: Albert Whitman.

Howie has cerebral palsy and more than anything wants to be able to move his wheelchair by himself.

Greene, Laura. (1980). *Help.* New York: Human Sciences Press.

Through a simple text and colorful illustrations, this book portrays the many ways we give and receive help and confirms that it is all right to need help.

Henriod, Lorraine. (1982). *Grandma's wheelchair.* Chicago: Albert Whitman.

Four-year-old Thomas spends his mornings helping his grandmother, who is in a wheelchair.

Kamien, Janet. (1979). *What if you couldn't . . . ? A book about special needs.* New York: Scribner.

Encourages children to imagine themselves with different disabilities and discusses ways to overcome the problems that go along with each disability.

Krasilovsky, Phyllis. (1969). *The very tall little girl.* New York: Doubleday.

Upset in the beginning of the story because she is six inches taller than most girls her age, a girl soon finds lots of reasons for being glad she is tall.

Lasker, Joe. (1980). *Nick joins in*. Chicago: Albert Whitman.

When Nick enters class in a wheelchair he and his new classmates must resolve their initial feelings and apprehensions about inclusion.

Litchfield, Ada. (1977). *A cane in her hand*. Chicago: Albert Whitman.

Valerie longs to be treated normally by others.

Mack, Nancy. (1976). *Tracy*. Chicago: Childrens Press.

Tracy, who has cerebral palsy, talks about school and activities and how she overcomes her handicap in every way she can.

O'Reilly, Edward. (1979). *Brown pelican at the pond*. San Rafael, CA: Manzanita Press.

Children discover a pelican with a broken wing and nurse it back to health. This book is sensitively written and very appealing to children.

Powers, Mary Ellen. (1986). *Our teacher's in a wheelchair*. Niles, IL: Albert Whitman.

Text and photographs depict the actions of Brian Hanson, who leads an active existence as a nursery school teacher.

Pursell, Margaret Sanford. (1976). *A look at physical handicaps*. Minneapolis: Lerner Publications.

This factual, photographic book about physical handicaps provides a simple, honest introduction to the subject.

Rudolph, M. (1988). *Grey Neck*. Owings Mills, MD: Stemmer House.

Adapted from an old Russian tale, this is the story of a duckling who is crippled by a fox and can't fly. The family migrates, leaving Grey Neck to cope. As winter progresses and the water freezes over, Grey Neck is concerned. A hunter finds Grey Neck and brings him to his home. The story needs sensitive discussion, but points out that there are events beyond our control.

Stein, Sara Bonnet. (1974). *About handicaps*. New York: Walker and Co.

Vivid photographs and a simple, direct text characterize the child's version of the story, while the parents and teachers can follow in a more detailed accompanying text.

Sullivan, M. B., Brightman, A., & Blatt, J. (1979). *Feeling free*. Reading, MA: Addison-Wesley.

A group of children get together to explore what it would be like to be disabled.

White, Paul. (1978). *Janet at school*. New York: Thomas Y. Crowell.

Five-year-old Janet has spina bifida; she has no movement in her legs. Although at school she can't do everything the others can, she finds her own way to join in.

Wittman, Sally. (1978). *A special trade*. New York: Harper & Row.

Nelly and Bartholomew have a special friendship. Bartholomew pushes Nelly in her stroller. They trade roles when Bartholomew comes out of the hospital and Nelly pushes him in his wheelchair.

Wolf, Bernard. (1974). *Don't feel sorry for Paul*. Philadelphia: Lippincott.

Paul rides a bike, plays football, goes to school, and loves baseball games. Some people feel sorry for Paul; others laugh at him and call him Captain Hook. Paul has artificial feet and a hand that is a two-part hook. Even though the text is advanced for preschool, the incredible photographs will capture the children's interest.

Wolff, Angelika. (1969). *Mom! I broke my arm!* New York: Lion Press.

About bones, X rays, casts, and how it feels to have a broken bone.

Awareness of Visual Impairments

Brown, Margaret Wise. (1939). *The noisy book*. New York: Harper & Row.

A classic story about Muffin, a dog who got a cinder in his eye and all the noises he heard when he couldn't see.

Brown, Margaret Wise. (1950). *The quiet noisy book*. New York: Harper & Row.

Another book about Muffin and the sounds he hears while waking up.

Hale, Sarah. (1990). *Mary had a little lamb*. New York: Scholastic.

This old story (first published in 1830), as updated by artist/illustrator Bruce McMillan, features Sarah (Mary), a black girl who wears glasses.

Hartwell, Dickson. (1960). *Dogs against darkness: The story of the seeing eye*. New York: Dodd, Mead.

Seeing eye dogs and their training. (May be paraphrased for younger children.)

Heide, Florence Parry. (1970). *Sound of sunshine, sound of rain*. New York: Scholastic.

The experiences and sensations of a blind black boy as he maneuvers in his small world.

Hoban, Tana. (1972). *Count and see*. New York: Macmillan.

A black-and-white photograph book with numbers, dots, and corresponding objects.

Kalan, Robert. (1978). *Freight train*. New York: Greenwillow.

Kalan, Robert. (1978). *Rain*. New York: Greenwillow.

Both books use vibrant colors to portray the train tooting through city and country, the motion of rain, and the following rainbow.

Keats, Ezra Jack. (1971). *Apartment three*. New York: Macmillan.

Two young brothers develop a friendship with a blind man who plays the harmonica, and they develop an understanding of the meaning of visual impairment.

Keats, Ezra Jack. (1973). *Skates*. New York: Franklin Watts.

A simple story of two colorful dogs who find some skates and try them out.

Kunhardt, Dorothy. (1962). *Pat the bunny*. New York: Golden Press.

A touch-and-feel book with a simple verse.

MacLachlan, Patricia. (1980). *Through Grandpa's eyes*. New York: Harper & Row.

John's grandfather is blind, but he can see things in a special way.

Peterson, P. (1974). *Sally can't see*. New York: John Day.

Twelve-year-old Sally uses a cane and Braille to help her lead an active life swimming, riding horses, and playing the organ, among other things.

Showers, Paul. (1961). *Find out by touching*. New York: Thomas Y. Crowell.

A variety of objects to touch.

Thomas, Anthony. (1976). *Things we touch*. New York: Franklin Watts.

More objects to touch.

White, Mary S. (1962). *Touch and tell*. Nashville, TN: Broadman.

Identifying objects by touch.

Witte, Pat and Eve. (1961). *Who lives here?* New York: Golden Press.

Identifying animals by touch.

Being Sick

Ardizzone, Edward. (1979). *Diana and her rhinoceros*. New York: Oxford University Press.

Diana nurses a sick rhinoceros that has escaped from the zoo and then fights off armed men who come to take it back.

Brandenberg, Franz. (1976). *I wish I was sick, too!* New York: Greenwillow.

When Edward gets sick and the family waits on him, Elizabeth wants to be waited on, too. When she does get sick, she realizes that it is more fun being well.

Buckley, Helen. (1985). *Someday with my father*. New York: Harper & Row.

A little girl with a cast on her leg plans what she and dad will do when she is well. She knows she and dad will do all those things because "he promised me."

Lobel, Arnold. (1970). *Frog and toad are friends*. New York: Harper & Row

Toad and Frog take care of each other.

MacLachlan, Patricia. (1979). *The sick day*. New York: Pantheon.

Emily and her father trade roles as they take turns getting sick and caring for each other.

Wiseman, Bernard. (1978). *Morris has a cold*. New York: Dodd, Mead.

A delightful story of Boris the Bear's attempts to help Morris the Moose get well. Children with colds or allergies will find this book fun to read.

Body Awareness

Brenner, Barbara. (1973). *Bodies*. New York: E. P. Dutton.

This book looks at all kind of bodies—all shapes, colors, and sizes. It shows the differences and similarities in all of them and stresses the uniqueness in everyone.

Corey, Dorothy. (1962). *How many teeth?* New York: Thomas Y. Crowell.

Every child loses teeth and wonders what has happened.

Corey, Dorothy. (1977). *Tomorrow you can*. Chicago: Albert Whitman.

An understanding book about growing up and all the things that children may be ready to participate in later on.

Curry, Peter. (1984). *I can hear*. Los Angeles, CA: Price/Stern/Sloan.

Beautifully simple painted illustrations show what the little boy can hear with his two ears.

Harris, Robbie H., & Levy, Elizabeth. (1977). *Before you were three: How you began to walk, talk, explore and have feelings*. New York: Delacorte Press.

Children and adults can read this book together and explore the process of growing during the first three years of life.

Ingoglia, Gina. (1989). *Look inside your body*. New York: Grosset & Dunlap.

Sturdy board books with cut holes. Poke and look learning books introduce youngsters to the world about them. This one is about the body. Others in the series are: *Let's look at dinosaurs, Look inside a house, Look inside a ship, Look inside a tree*.

Maguire, Leslie. (1974). *You: How your body works*. New York: Platt and Munk.

Working from the outside in, it illustrates sneezing, jumping, climbing, and more, then explores the internal hows, whys, and whats. There is also a lesson on how to take care of your body.

Showers, Paul. (1963). *Follow your nose*. New York: Thomas Y. Crowell.

This book carefully gives young readers an understanding of smelling and other functions of the nose.

Showers, Paul. (1976). *Hear your heart*. New York: Thomas Y. Crowell.

In simple yet precise language, the structure of the heart and what it does are discussed. It contains light-hearted yet scientifically accurate pictures.

Books for Children with Low Vision

Cousins, Lucy. (1991). *What can rabbit hear?* New York: Tanbourine Books.

What can rabbit hear? Lift the flap and find out.

Fowler, Richard. (1990). *Mr. Little's fire house*. New York: G.P. Putnam's Sons.

Lift the flap and find out where the noises are in Mr. Little's fire house.

Henson, Jim. (1988). *Sesame Street fire trucks*. New York: Random House.

This fire truck-shaped book rides on yellow wheels and inside Ernie and Bert go to a fire.

Pelhan. (1990). *Sam's sandwich*. New York: Dutton's Children's Books.

A book almost good enough to eat has lettuce, meat, vegetables, ketchup, onions, and eggs popping out of two thick slices of brown bread.

Cities and Country

Bozzo, Maxine. (1982). *Toby in the country, Toby in the city*. New York: Greenwillow.

One Toby lives in town and one in the country. While comparing their environments, they become friends.

Burton, Virginia Lee. (1978). *The little house*. Boston: Houghton Mifflin.

A tender tale about a house built in the country and how the city grows up around it.

Clymer, Eleanor. (1968). *The big pile of dirt*. New York: Holt, Rinehart and Winston.

A group of city children make a playground out of a lot full of junk. After the lot becomes piled with dirt, the children are told they can't play there. With the help of grownups, the children take a stand and get a playground.

Getz, Arthur. (1979). *Tar Beach*. New York: Dial Books.

In a blistering hot city, children play in the spray of the fire hydrant and use other ideas to stay cool. City summers come to life in this story.

Himler, Ronald. (1976). *The girl on the yellow giraffe*. New York: Harper & Row.

The sights of the city become a fantasy world for one little girl.

Hoban, Tana. (1973). *Over, under and through*. New York: Macmillan.

Great black and white photographs depict children going over, under, and through different objects found in a city. Stimulates discussions about going over, under, and through things at school and in the child's immediate environment.

Howell, Ruth Rea. (1970). *A crack in the pavement*. New York: Atheneum.

Growing things are everywhere—even in the cities. Grass and dandelions grow in cracks of the sidewalk, and pigeons nest on window sills.

Keeping, Charles. (1969). *Joseph's yard*. New York: Franklin Watts.

A poignant story about a boy who wants his ghetto backyard full of things of nature. When he grows a rose and almost kills it trying to protect it, Joseph learns how too much can be as bad as too little.

Merrill, Jean, & Scott, Frances. (1970). *How many kids are hiding on my block?* Chicago: Albert Whitman.

Great hide-and-seek story written in prose style. Many children from different cultures are shown hiding in unique places.

Merrill, Jean, & Scott, Frances. (1970). *Uptown*. New York: Harper & Row.

A realistic and hard-hitting story of two young African-American boys in Harlem who sit and discuss all the things they can be when they grow up. Their choices are based on the limited things they have seen in their own community.

Ventura, Piero. (1975). *Book of cities*. New York: Random House.

A book about cities—what you would find in a city, different ways of getting around, and what things there are to do. It also talks about some unique features of various big cities.

Creative Thinking

Adler, David A. (1976). *A little at a time*. New York: Random House.

A grandfather and his grandson take a day's outing to the museum and take everything "a little at a time." This book could greatly enhance a child's concept of time.

Anno, Mitsumasa. (1970). *Topsy turvies: Pictures to stretch the imagination*. Salem, MA: John Weatherhill.

Intriguing picture book without words that has intricate as well as incongruous pictures.

Baldwin, Anne Norris. (1973). *Sunflowers for Tina*. New York: Scholastic.

Tina, an African-American, is determined to grow a garden in the middle of New York City.

Castle, Sue. (1977). *Face talk, hand talk, body talk*. Garden City, NY: Doubleday.

Discusses nonverbal communications. Photographs of children show alternate ways to express words and feelings.

Cauley, Lorinda Bryan. (1978). *The bake-off*. New York: G.P. Putnam's Sons.

Mr. Hare tries to find a delicious and nutritious dish that will beat Mrs. Beaver's chocolate cake, and you can help. Mr. Hare's recipe is included in the end.

Conford, Ellen. (1971). *Impossible possum*. Boston: Little, Brown.

Little boy possum's older sister uses her wits to help him overcome a weakness.

DePaola, Tomie. (1973). *Andy that's my name*. Englewood Cliffs, NJ: Prentice-Hall.

Andy carries his name in a wagon. His friends get together and rearrange the letters to make new words. Encourages flexible thinking.

dePoix, Carol. (1973). *Jo, Flo and Yolanda*. Chapel Hill, NC: Lollipop Power.

Three girls have a true adventure.

Freeman, Don. (1969). *Tilly Witch*. New York: Viking Press.

Tilly goes back to school for a refresher course in scaring people.

Galdone, Paul. (1975). *The little red hen*. New York: Scholastic.

This brave hen takes the role of leader among her animal friends.

Gauch, Patricia Lee. (1980). *Christina Katerina and the box*. New York: Coward, McCann and Geoghegan.

Christina takes a box that is intended for trash and turns it into a clubhouse, a dance floor, and a racing car.

Gill, Joan. (1969). *Sara's granny and the goodle*. Garden City, NY: Doubleday.

Sara goes on an incredible imaginary trip.

Hoban, Lillian. (1972). *Arthur's Christmas cookies*. New York: Harper & Row.

Arthur the chimp makes surprise Christmas cookies.

Kahn, Bernice. (1976). *The watchamacallit book*. New York: G.P. Putnam's Sons.

Children who read this book will have fun trying to identify and read words that are scrambled over the pages.

Kent, Jack. (1971). *Wizard of Wallaby Wallow*. New York: Scholastic.

A delightful story about a little mouse who visits the Wizard of Wallaby Wallow and receives a bottle saying that it will turn him "into something else." The little mouse finds something wrong with each creature he imagines himself as becoming.

Kroll, Steven. (1977). *Gobbledy-gook*. Northville, MI: Holiday House Press.

The humorous story of a boy getting up in the morning. It is told in mixed-up language. (He squashes his laces; he flushes his teeth.) Great fun to decipher.

Lasker, Joe. (1976). *Merry ever after: The story of two medieval weddings*. New York: Viking Press.

This book provides a fascinating way to compare medieval life with today's life. It may encourage imaginative dramatic play.

Lewis, Stephen. (1976). *Zoo city*. New York: Greenwillow.

This book contains pictures of animals and also pictures of objects you might find in a city that look like these animals. The children can match the real animal with the inanimate lookalike.

McCloskey, Robert. (1976). *Blueberries for Sal*. New York: Penguin Books.

A mother and daughter encounter a mother bear and cub while picking blueberries on a hill.

Mayer, Mercer. (1972). *A silly story*. New York: Parents Magazine Press.

A clever and comical story about a child's search for his identity. A young boy thinks "perhaps I am not me!" All the while he's wondering about who he really is, he fills his mind with all the silly things he might be.

Miller, Barry. (1971). *Alphabet world*. New York: Macmillan.

This book is made up of transparent pages with a letter of the alphabet on each one overlaying a page with a photograph of an everyday object in which the letter is to be found. (Look at the traffic light sideways and it forms an *E*.)

O'Neill, Mary. (1961). *Hailstones and halibut bones*. New York: Doubleday.

Twelve poems about color, written as though color can be heard, touched, and smelled as well as seen.

Rockwell, Anne. (1977). *Albert B. Cub and Zebra: An alphabet story book*. New York: Thomas Y. Crowell.

An alphabet book that has hidden pictures of many items starting with one letter of the alphabet. Although wordless, the pictures weave a story.

Ruchlis, Hy. (1973). *How a rock came to be a fence on a road near a town*. New York: Walker and Co.

This "story" of a rock starts 300 million years ago at the bottom of the sea and continues until the rock is where we find it today. An interesting way to look at changing geography and terrain.

Sandberg, Inger, & Sandberg, Lasse. (1965). *What little Anna saved*. New York: Lothrop, Lee and Shepherd.

Anna makes all sorts of things out of odds and ends.

Segal, Lore. (1970). *Tell me a Mitzi*. New York: Farrar, Straus and Giroux.

Imaginative Mitzi tells three delightful stories about her family life.

Sendak, Maurice. (1963). *Where the wild things are*. New York: Harper & Row.

The story of a boy who is sent to bed without supper. He dreams he goes to an island of monsters who make him King of the Wild Things.

Shulevitz, Uri. (1969). *Rain rain rivers*. New York: Farrar, Straus and Giroux.

While listening to the rain, a little girl looks forward to playing in the puddles.

Skarpen, Liesel Moak. (1969). *We were tired of living in a house*. New York: Coward, McCann and Geoghegan.

Imaginative story of kids tired of living in a house, so they try living in a tree, a pond, a cave, and at the seashore. In each place something unusual happens to make them move on to the next place and finally home.

Spier, Peter. (1978). *Bored, nothing to do*. New York: Doubleday.

Two bored brothers decide to make an airplane from scraps. Encourages divergent thinking.

Thompson, Susan L. (1980). *One more thing, Dad*. Chicago: Albert Whitman.

An ingenious counting book in which Caleb packs a healthy lunch. This book has many possibilities for activities and discussions.

Van Woerkom, Dorothy. (1979). *Hidden messages.* New York: Crown.

Shows how ants give messages to one another in order to find food, attract mates, and warn others. Good lead into nonverbal communication.

Vreeken, Elizabeth. (1959). *The boy who would not say his name.* Chicago: Follett.

A boy who won't answer to his real name because he likes to pretend he is someone else. One day he gets lost and has to tell his real name so that his parents can come find him. Helps teach children to differentiate reality from fantasy.

Wahl, Jan. (1969). *Wolf of my own.* New York: Macmillan.

A little girl thinks her birthday puppy is a "wolf friend."

Death and Dying

Aliki. (1979). *The two of them.* New York: Greenwillow.

One of the finest books available for children about grandparents and the aging process. Adults may find this book meaningful also.

Bartoli, Jennifer. (1975). *Norma.* Waterside Plaza, NY: Harvey House.

A beloved grandparent's death portrayed from the child's viewpoint.

Bernstein, Joanne E., & Gullo, Stephen. (1977). *When people die.* New York: E. P. Dutton.

What happens when people die, why people die, and how a child responds to death (black and white photos).

Borack, Barbara. (1969). *Someone small.* New York: Harper & Row.

A low-keyed story about a new sibling and a new pet growing together and the death of the pet.

Brown, Margaret Wise. (1958). *The dead bird.* New York: W. R. Scott.

Children find a dead bird and bury it in a quiet spot.

Buscaglia, Leo. (1982). *The fall of Freddie the leaf.* New York: Holt, Rinehart and Winston.

A common-sense explanation of the death of the leaves in the fall. A good book for a grownup to read to a child who has suffered a permanent loss.

DePaola, Tomie. (1978). *Nana upstairs and Nana downstairs.* New York: Puffin Books.

A child's love for her grandmother and her adjustment to the grandmother's death.

Dobrin, Arnold. (1971). *Scat!* New York: Four Winds Press.

A story of a small African-American boy growing up in a house full of adults. When his grandfather dies the young boy serenades his grandmother with a harmonica, hoping to ease the pain. The boy describes all the sadness around him.

Fassler, Joan. (1971). *My grandpa died today.* New York: Behavioral Publications.

A boy talks about his grandpa, what they did together, and his feelings about the death.

Gackenbach, Dick. (1975). *Do you love me?* New York: Seabury Press.

A boy accidentally kills a bird while trying to catch it.

Gauch, Patricia Lee. (1972). *Grandpa and me.* New York: Coward, McCann and Geoghegan.

A young boy remembers his grandfather and how they loved to do things together.

Hammond, Janice M. (1980). *When Mommy died: A child's view of death.* Ann Arbor, MI: Cranbrook.

This commendable book emphasizes the need for understanding the emotions a child feels toward the deceased and makes suggestions for guiding the child through the experience.

Harris, Audrey J. (1965). *Why did he die?* Minneapolis: Lerner Publications.

Poetry explaining the death of a grandfather.

Lamorisse, Albert. (1956). *The red balloon.* Garden City, NY: Doubleday.

A boy becomes attached to his balloon. The other boys tease him, throw rocks, and it breaks. (Many children see the balloon as dying.)

Little, Jean. (1965). *Home from far.* Boston: Little, Brown.

When Jenny's twin brother is killed in an automobile accident, she must deal with the loss. Her emptiness is filled when her family takes in a foster brother and sister.

Miles, Miska. (1971). *Annie and the old one.* Boston: Little, Brown.

Annie's grandmother tells her she, the grandmother, will die before the rug they are making is completed. When Annie tries to stop the completion of the rug, her grandmother explains that natural events cannot be changed.

Silverstein, Shel. (1964). *The giving tree.* New York: Harper & Row.

A beautiful tree gives its parts to a boy. As the boy gets older he wants more from the tree. Eventually there is just a stump left and the now old man rests on it.

Smith, Doris B. (1973). *A taste of blackberries.* New York: Thomas Y. Crowell.

A boy's best friend dies and he feels guilty when he thinks he might have prevented it. The boy successfully works out his feelings.

Stoddard, Sandol. (1969). *Growing time.* Boston: Houghton Mifflin.

Jamie mourns the death of her collie.

Tobias, Tobi. (1978). *Petey.* New York: G.P. Putnam's Sons.

Emily's parents help her deal with the illness and death of Petey the gerbil.

Tresselt, Alvin R. (1972). *The dead tree.* New York: Parents Magazine Press.

After a tree dies and falls, animals come to live in it. In the spring a new tree grows from a fallen acorn. A good introduction for kindergartners to the concept that everything dies eventually.

Viorst, Judith. (1971). *The tenth good thing about Barney.* New York: Atheneum.

A boy mourns the death of his cat, and at the funeral he tells his friends ten good things about Barney.

Wilhelm, Hans. (1985). *I'll always love you.* New York: Crown.

A child's sadness at the death of a beloved dog is tempered by the remembrance of saying every night, "I'll always love you."

Zim, Herbert S., & Bleeker, Sonia. (1970). *Life and death.* New York: Morrow.

A well-written book for all ages that discusses the physical facts, customs, and attitudes surrounding human life and death.

Zolotow, Charlotte. (1974). *My grandson Lew.* New York: Harper & Row.

Lew and his mother find they are less lonely when they share their memories of grandfather.

Divorce, Separation, Remarriage

Abercombie, Barbara. (1990). *Charlie Anderson.* New York: Margaret K. McElderry Books.

A cat comes out of the night to steal the hearts of two sisters, who look forward to his sleeping on their beds until one day Charlie doesn't come home. They discover that he has two homes, as do these girls of divorced parents.

Amos, Janine. (1991). *Annie's story.* Milwaukee, WI: Raintree Publishers.

Annie's story tells of Annie's feelings about her dad's not coming home any more and having to visit him. Discussion questions are included to explore further the hurt of divorce.

Brown, Laurene, & Brown, Marc. (1986). *Dinosaurs divorce: A guide for changing families.* Boston: The Atlantic Monthly Press.

"Divorce words and what they mean" begins this cartoon book that takes the reader from why parents divorce to adjusting to living with a single parent and then remarriage and having stepsisters and stepbrothers.

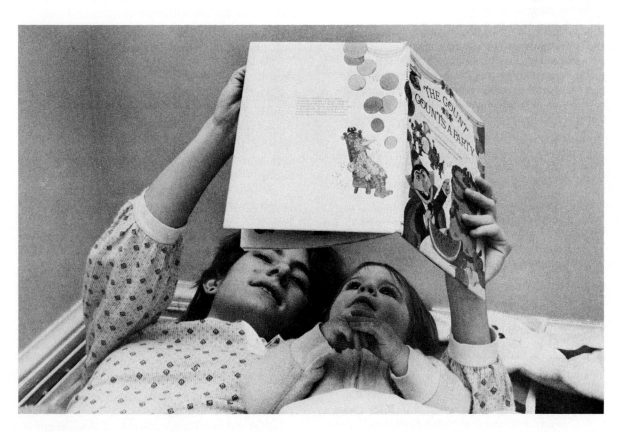

Encourage families to read to children at home.

Caines, Jeannette. (1977). *Daddy*. New York: Harper & Row.

A little girl's relationship with Daddy on their weekend get-togethers is highlighted.

Christianson, C. (1989). *My mother's house, my father's house*. New York: Atheneum.

A positively written book about the realities of children's lives including divorce, child care, and working mothers.

Clifton, Lucille. (1977). *Everett Anderson's 1-2-3*. New York: Holt, Rinehart and Winston.

When Everett's mother decides to marry the neighbor, Everett wonders what it will be like to have three people in the house.

Gardner, Richard. (1971). *The boys and girls book about divorce*. New York: Aronson.

A very useful, encyclopedic work that discusses all aspects of divorce clearly and rationally. It can serve as a reference for both parents and children.

Goff, Beth. (1969). *Where is Daddy? The story of divorce*. Boston: Beacon Press.

The fears and adjustments that children will go through if their parents are going through a divorce are explained. The illustrations are done from a child's point of view.

Hazen, Barbara Shook. (1978). *Two homes to live in: A child's-eye view of divorce*. New York: Human Sciences Press.

A little girl explains how she came to terms with her parents' divorce.

Hogan, Paula. (1980). *Will Dad ever move back home?* Milwaukee, WI: Raintree Press.

When a child is bitterly unhappy that her divorced parents no longer live together, she and her family discover the importance of her directly expressing her feelings. A good book to recommend for parents to read with children.

LeShan, Eda J. (1978). *What's going to happen to me? When parents separate or divorce*. New York: Four Winds Press.

Children's concerns about themselves during a time when families are separating.

Lexau, Joan M. (1971). *Me day*. New York: Dial Books.

A young African-American boy wakes up on his birthday with one wish—to see his father.

Perry, Patricia, & Lynch, Marietta. (1978). *Mommy and Daddy are divorced*. New York: Dial Books.

Young children's feelings about, and adjustment to, their parents' divorce. Explains that reasons for divorce often don't make much sense to young children.

Stein, Sara Bonnett. (1979). *On divorce: An open family book for parents and children together*. New York: Walker and Co.

A group of children are "playing divorce." A girl who hears the play becomes frightened that her parents will get a divorce. The parents explain that they disagree but are not getting a divorce.

Stensen, Janet Sinberg. (1978). *Divorce is a grown-up problem: A book about divorce for young children and their parents*. New York: Avon.

Parents explain to a child why they are getting a divorce, and the child talks about how it feels to have parents who are getting a divorce.

Doctors and Hospitals

Berry, Joy. (1986). *Teach me about the doctor*. Sebastopal, CA: Living Skills Press.

A combination of large, easily understood cartoon pictures, easily read text, and a seven-page appendix for parents makes this the complete book on a visit to the doctor.

Rockwell, Harlow. (1973). *My doctor*. New York: Macmillan.

A doctor's office from a child's viewpoint. The doctor is female.

Rogers, Fred. (1974). *Mr. Rogers talks about going to the doctor*. New York: Platt and Munk.

Addresses fears a child may have before going to the hospital or doctor's office. Introduces common medical procedures.

Sharmat, Marjorie Weinman. (1974). *I want Mama*. New York: Harper & Row.

A little girl's mother goes to the hospital. Helps children realize that anyone may have to go to the hospital, and although the stay may seem to last forever, the patient will eventually return home.

Shay, Arthur. (1969). *What happens when you go to the hospital?* Chicago: Reilly and Lee.

Karen cries and expresses her fears about her tonsillectomy.

Sobol, Harriet. (1975). *Jeff's hospital book*. New York: H. Z. Walck.

A young boy has eye surgery; a realistic portrayal of the operation.

Sonneborn, Ruth. (1971). *I love Gram*. New York: Viking Press.

Ellie, a little black girl, is waiting impatiently for her grandmother to come home from the hospital.

Stein, Sara Bonnett. (1974). *A hospital story: An open family book for parents and children*. New York: Walker and Co.

A young girl's tonsillectomy. Covers many hospital procedures.

Tamburine, Jean. (1965). *I think I will go to the hospital*. Nashville, TN: Abingdon.

Susie doesn't want to go to the hospital, but after a preadmission visit where she practices procedures on a pet, she feels much better.

Weber, Alfons. (1970). *Elizabeth gets well*. New York: Thomas Y. Crowell.

Fear and pain are acknowledged as Elizabeth prepares for her appendectomy.

Williams, Peggy. (1986). *Holli and Pandi's hospital adventure*. Pompano Beach, FL: Exposition Press of Florida.

This quite long black and white picture book has a detailed text of Holli's real visit to a hospital and Pandi's fanciful adventures with her.

Wolde, Gunilla. (1978). *Betsy and the doctor*. New York: Random House.

Betsy's feelings before and after she goes to the doctor for the first time.

Families

Barrett, John M. (1979). *No time for me: Learning to cope with busy parents*. New York: Human Sciences Press.

Eight-year-old Jimmy feels rejected because his parents seem to have no time for him. This is a helpful book for a child whose parents are both working and for the parents, too.

Bauer, Caroline Feller. (1981). *My mom travels a lot*. New York: Frederick Warrie.

The main character balances the good and bad things about having a mother who is gone a lot, but concludes that the best thing is that "she always comes back."

Blue, Rose. (1972). *Grandma didn't wave back*. New York: Franklin Watts.

Debbie feels very special: She has Grandma right at her apartment. However, one day she notices that Grandma is acting in a strange manner and forgetting things. Debbie thinks it is temporary but soon discovers she is mistaken. It is a traumatic experience for youngsters to see the signs of aging and the changing of someone special.

Brownstone, Cecily. (1969). *All kinds of mothers*. New York: McKay.

There are many different types of mothers and there are many options open to them. Questions put to the reader throughout the book involve children in the story. The detailed illustrations aid in comprehension.

Buckley, Helen E. (1959). *Grandfather and I*. New York: Lothrop.

A story about the relationship between a child and his grandfather. Ideal for ages three to six, it illustrates the closeness that can develop between a grandparent and grandchild.

Calmenson, Stephanie. (1987). *Babies*. New York: A Golden Book.

This sturdy, glossy board book shows a group of multicultural babies in a wide variety of daily activities.

Charnley, Nathaniel, & Charnley, Betty Jo. (1973). *Martha Ann and the mother store*. New York: Harcourt Brace Jovanovich.

A little girl tries out different kinds of mothers and realizes that her own is best, even if she does make rules, scold, and require some obedience.

Drescher, Joan. (1980). *Your family, my family*. New York: Walker and Co.

A clever look at many different types of families in a variety of settings. Children can recognize their own family group and learn about other people.

Girard, Linda. (1983). *You were born on your very first birthday*. Niles, IL: Albert Whitman.

Describes the life of a tiny baby in his safe, warm, floating place during the nine months before he was born.

Hines, Anna. (1986). *Daddy makes the best spaghetti*. New York: Clarion Books.

Daddy picks Corey up at day care and makes the evening fun as Mommy, Dad, and Corey do routine family chores. Depicts "family life at its best."

Lapsley, Susan. (1975). *I am adopted*. Scarsdale, NY: Bradbury Press.

A simple book in which two children describe what it means to be adopted. It means security and belonging.

Leifert, Harriet. (1988). *Daddy, can you play with me?* New York: Puffin Books.

This lift-the-flap book with easy to read text is about little Hippo and his stay-at-home Dad. A companion book is *Mommy, where are you?*

Lionni, Leo. (1991). *Matthew's dream*. New York: Alfred A. Knopf.

This new book by Lionni again uses his collage technique so enjoyed by his readers to illustrate the story of Matthew, the mouse who became a painter.

Lundgren, Max. (1972). *Matt's grandfather*. New York: G.P. Putnam's Sons.

Matt's parents take him to visit his eighty-five-year-old grandfather. They prepare him to see an old and feeble man. Matt and his grandfather take a walk, and the grandfather turns out to be not as old and feeble as Matt expected.

Merrian, Eve. (1989). *Daddies at work*. New York: Simon & Schuster.

Portrays daddies in different jobs, including sailor daddies, tailor daddies, and lawyer daddies with egg-salad sandwiches in their briefcases.

Merrian, Eve. (1989). *Mommies at work*. New York: Simon & Schuster.

Examines many different jobs performed by working mothers, including counting money at banks and building bridges.

Miziemuru, Kazue. (1968). *If I were a mother*. New York: Thomas Y. Crowell.

Animal mothers provide examples of ways of mothering. Each animal treats its baby a certain way, like the mother horse who helps its baby until it can stand on its own feet. The little girl and little boy end the story wanting to be like her or his own mother.

Radlauer, Ruth Shaw. (1960). *Mothers are that way*. London: Abelard Schuman.

This book tells from a child's point of view what the difference is between mothers and children. It explains how mothers use water not for making mud pies, but for cleaning. It shows children the difference in the way they and their mothers think.

Rappart, Doreen, et al. (1981). *A man can be . . .* New York: Human Sciences Press.

Through a glimpse into a day shared by a father and his son, this delightful book discusses the ever-changing roles and emotional responses of men.

Richardson, Judith. (1991). *The way home.* New York: Macmillan.

Savi's mother finds a creative way to handle a conflict between elephant mother and child that will delight readers, as will the colorful fabric relief illustrations.

Sheffield, Margaret. (1984). *Before you were born.* New York: Alfred A. Knopf.

Describes what life is like for a baby growing inside its mother's womb during the months before birth, and what it is like to be born. Sheffield also wrote *Where do babies come from?*

Simon, Norma. (1975). *All kinds of families.* Chicago: Albert Whitman.

The book reflects the many patterns of traditional and nontraditional families. It stresses the supportive function of a family and the child's joyous place in it.

Simon, Norma. (1980). *I'm busy, too.* Chicago: Albert Whitman.

A book about the diversity of families both within them and among them. Especially useful for the child who is new to day care, since it discusses three families who attend the community care center.

Sonneborn, Ruth A. (1971). *I love Gram.* New York: Viking Press.

A little girl's grandmother, who lives with her family, is taken to the hospital. The girl is very upset and afraid that her Gram will die like her friend's grandmother. Finally her grandmother comes home.

Surowiecki, Sandra Lucas. (1977). *Joshua's day.* Chapel Hill, NC: Lollipop Power.

Joshua lives in a one-parent home. His mother, who is a photographer, takes him to a day-care center where he interacts with both boys and girls.

Timmons, Christine. (1974). *The me and you book.* Chicago: Encyclopedia Britannica.

The book talks about different kinds of families and how hard it is to share feelings.

Waber, Bernard. (1977). *Good-bye, funny dumpy lumpy.* Boston: Houghton Mifflin.

Five vignettes reveal how a mother, father, and their three children negotiate common family problems.

Young, Eleanor R. (1971). *Mothers, mothers, mothers.* Minneapolis: T. S. Denison.

By showing children the universal aspects of a mother's role, this book helps a child understand that all people are basically similar. The simple illustrations make the point by showing mothers of different races and nationalities.

Zolotow, Charlotte. (1963). *The sky was blue.* New York: Harper & Row.

A tender story of a little girl who looks through the family album with her mother. As they look back over the years at the pictures of her mother, grandmother, and great-grandmother when they were little girls her age, the little girl wonders what it felt like to be a little girl back then. Her mother tells her the really important things don't change. The sky is always blue, the grass always green.

Zolotow, Charlotte. (1972). *William's doll.* New York: Harper & Row.

William wants a doll. His father buys him "boy" toys: a basketball, a train, and so on. He likes them but still wants a doll. His grandmother buys him one and explains to his father how important a doll is in helping him become a caring father.

Feelings

Amos, Janine. (1991). *Jealous.* Milwaukee, WI: Raintree Publishers.

Three stories of children who were jealous and how their parents helped them understand their feelings. Excellent discussion questions at the bottom of the page and at the end of the stories for use by the teacher or parent. Additional books in this series include: *Angry, Afraid, Hurt, Lonely,* and *Sad.* All were published in 1991.

Alexander, Martha G. (1973). *I'll protect you from jungle beasts.* New York: Dial Books.

Through a child's daydream, we learn of his fears in a dark jungle. He protects his teddy bear from the beasts, and later the bear protects him.

Bacigalupi, Marcella, et al. (1978). *It's scary sometimes.* New York: Human Sciences Press.

Discusses children's fears, both rational and irrational. Includes anecdotes and drawings by children.

Berger, Terry. (1971). *I have feelings.* New York: Human Sciences Press.

Through photographs and stories, this book discusses different feelings a child may experience in one day.

Berry, Joy. (1988). *Being selfish.* Danbury, CT: Grolier Enterprises Corp.

Joy Berry uses a cartoon format sure to appeal to children to tell how Katie and Sam learn to be unselfish. The accompanying text gives suggestions on understanding and dealing with selfishness.

Berry, Joy. (1988). *Complaining.* Danbury, CT: Grolier Enterprises Corp.

Reading about Amy and Tami and looking at the cartoons will help children understand and deal with complaining.

Hazen, Barbara Shook. (1979). *If it weren't for Benjamin (I'd always get to lick the icing spoon).* New York: Human Sciences Press.

A sympathetic look at both the older and younger brother's feelings.

Hazen, Nancy. (1973). *Grownups cry too*. Chapel Hill, NC: Lollipop Power.

Grownups are human. Men and women are shown as both sad and happy.

Jones, Penelope. (1977). *I didn't want to be nice*. Scarsdale, NY: Bradbury Press.

Nettie, a squirrel, didn't want to go to a birthday party at her friend's house, then her mood changes.

Kantrowitz, Mildred. (1971). *I wonder if Herbie's home yet?* New York: Parents Magazine Press.

A young boy is angry that his best friend has made plans to play with someone else one day. The colorful illustrations are cartoon style and match the story well.

Krahn, Fernando. (1982). *The creepy thing*. New York: Clarion Books.

Readers and nonreaders can enjoy this wordless book about a green hairy thing on an adventure in a black and white world.

Krahn, Fernando. (1983). *The secret in the dungeon*. New York: Clarion Books.

Readers and nonreaders can enjoy this wordless book about a girl's adventure lost in an old castle.

Kraus, Robert. (1977). *All the mice came*. New York: Windmill and Dutton.

The story of friendship and trust that was built up between a cat and mouse.

Kraus, Robert. (1977). *The little giant*. New York: Windmill and Dutton.

A small person makes himself feel he is a giant.

Lionni, L. (1986). *It's mine! A fable*. New York: Alfred A. Knopf.

Children are shown that sharing is better.

Mayer, Mercer. (1968). *There's a nightmare in my closet*. New York: Dial Books.

A boy conquers his fear of the nightmare in his closet by making the nightmare scared of him.

Memling, Carl. (1971). *What's in the dark?* New York: Parents Magazine Press.

Helps the child cope with fears of sleeping in the dark by showing the child where objects were left: pants, tee shirt, crayons, and other things the child can identify with that will help to make him feel safe and secure.

Meyers, Bernice. (1970). *My mother is lost*. New York: Scholastic.

A boy lost in a store finds another lost boy. When they finally reach Lost and Found, their mothers are there.

Ruffins, Reynold. (1979). *My brother never feeds the cat*. New York: Scribner.

Anna's brother never helps with chores around the house. A good book for talking to children about the things they can do, which helps in developing a positive self-concept.

Schick, Eleanor. (1973). *Peter and Mr. Brandon*. New York: Macmillan.

Deals with a child's fear of being away from home overnight.

Sendak, Maurice. (1963). *Where the wild things are*. New York: Harper & Row.

A humorous book about a little boy named Max who gets carried away the night he wears his wolf suit. A novel way to deal with those monster fears.

Sherman, Ivan. (1973). *I do not like it when my friend comes to visit*. New York: Harcourt Brace Jovanovich.

When her friend visits, everything she does is right and everything our heroine does is wrong. The situations are reversed the next day when our heroine visits her friend's house and gets to play with all of *her* toys.

Shortall, Leonard. (1972). *Tony's first dive*. New York: Morrow.

Tony's mother enrolls him in swimming lessons. He learns to overcome his fears through the aid of a lifeguard and a face mask and finds a woman's bracelet at the bottom of the lake.

Showers, Paul. (1977). *A book of scary things*. Garden City, NY: Doubleday.

The book focuses on both real and imaginary fears of children.

Silverman, J. (1988). *Some time to grow*. New York: Addison-Wesley.

Poems about feelings and problems some children face.

Simon, Norma. (1989). *I am not a cry baby*. New York: Puffin Books.

A multicultural group of children describe their worst fears and hurts, which include a broken leg, bad dreams, divorce, first day at school, death of a pet, getting a hearing aid, and parents fighting.

Skorpen, Liesel Moak. (1971). *Plenty for three*. New York: Coward, McCann and Geoghegan.

The contrast between the fun of doing something with a friend and the aloneness of doing it by yourself. At the end of the book the pair of friends invites the one who is alone to join them.

Smaridge, Norah. (1969). *Scary things*. New York: Abingdon Press.

The author touches on almost every circumstance that could be frightening for a child—great for helping a child overcome all kinds of fears.

Stanton, Elizabeth, & Stanton, Henry. (1978). *Sometimes I like to cry*. Chicago: Albert Whitman.

Several real-life situations are portrayed as Joey learns about crying.

Strauss, Joyce. (1981). *How does it feel . . . ?* New York: Human Sciences Press.

Thought-provoking questions explore the many feelings and emotions experienced in memory, fantasy, and everyday situations. This enlightening book will enable children to understand and express their emotions more effectively.

Udry, Janice. (1961). *Let's be enemies.* New York: Harper & Row.

The simply phrased pages explain the trials of friendship and an argument with a friend.

Vigna, Judith. (1978). *Anyhow, I'm glad I tried.* Chicago: Albert Whitman.

A witty, sensitive story of a child who treats a disagreeable classmate with kindness even though she feels her effort is in vain.

Viorst, Judith. (1972). *Alexander and the terrible, horrible, no good, very bad day.* New York: Atheneum.

The book describes the events that make Alexander's day horrible and how he deals with it in the end.

Waber, Bernard. (1972). *Ira sleeps over.* Boston: Houghton Mifflin.

Two children debate whether or not to share their fears. This story identifies fears of staying away from home at night and at the same time deals with sharing problems.

Webster-Doyle, T. (1990). *Fighting the invisible enemy, Understanding the effects of conditioning.* Ojai, CA: Atrium Publications.

A realistic, yet practical book about dealing with feelings in a world of conflict. Probably best read with an adult as the basis for discussion for kindergarten children and above.

Webster-Doyle, T. (1990). *Tug of war. Peace through understanding conflict.* Ojai, CA: Atrium Publications.

Another book that helps give words to feelings of conflict and violence. Best read with an adult as the basis for discussion.

Winthrop, Elizabeth. (1977). *That's mine.* New York: Holiday House.

Two children fight over blocks, only to find that with some cooperation they can build a more beautiful castle.

Wiseman, B. (1970). *Morris goes to school.* New York: Harper & Row.

A humorous story about a moose who goes to school. Despite his mistakes and differences, the class still likes him.

Wolde, Gunilla. (1975). *This is Betsy.* New York: Random House.

Betsy gets in touch with her body parts and her emotions.

Zolotow, Charlotte. (1963). *The quarreling book.* New York: Harper & Row.

Friends can quarrel, too.

Zolotow, Charlotte. (1969). *The hating book.* New York: Harper & Row.

A little girl decides her friend hates her and doesn't know why until she asks.

Zolotow, Charlotte. (1975). *The unfriendly book.* New York: Harper & Row.

Bertha criticizes everyone. Judy has something nice to say about everyone. They discuss their friends while walking their dogs.

Friendship

Asch, Frank. (1985). *Bear's bargain.* Englewood Cliffs, NJ: Prentice-Hall.

Bear wants to fly and Bird longs to grow big; the two become friends and help each other achieve their ambitions in a surprisingly creative way.

Boyd, Selma, & Boyd, Pauline. (1981). *The how: Making the best of a mistake.* New York: Human Sciences Press.

We all make mistakes and there is no reason to feel ashamed. The young hero turns a threatening situation into an opportunity to understand himself better and to make new friends.

Browne, Anthony. (1991). *Willy and Hugh.* New York: Alfred A. Knopf.

Willy the chimpanzee is lonely until he meets Hugh, an ape in the park, and the two become friends.

Carle, Eric. (1971). *Do you want to be my friend?* New York: Thomas Y. Crowell.

A child looks for and finds a friend.

Cohen, Miriam. (1971). *Will I have a friend?* New York: Macmillan.

Jim wonders if he will have a friend at his new school. The school setting of the book will be very familiar to kindergarteners or preschoolers.

Cohen, Miriam. (1973). *Best friends.* New York: Macmillan.

Jim and Paul are best friends. While doing an errand for their kindergarten teacher, their friendship is ruptured; it is eventually mended.

Delton, Judy. (1976). *Two is company.* New York: Crown.

Duck and Bear were very close friends until a newcomer joined them.

Ets, Marie Hall. (1955). *Play with me.* New York: Viking Press.

An inquisitive little girl finds many animal friends by a pond.

Gackenbach, Dick. (1976). *Hound and Bear.* New York: Seabury Press.

Practical jokes and friendship are given a light-hearted twist.

Heine, Helme. (1982). *Friends.* New York: Atheneum.

"Good friends always stick together" says Charlie Rooster, Johnny Mouse, and fat Percy, and their friendship leads to some exciting adventures.

Hoban, Russell. (1969). *Best friends for Frances.* New York: Harper & Row.

Frances, a badger, has to convince Albert that he values her friendship. In the process she learns sisters can also be friends.

Ichikawa, Satomi. (1977). *Friends.* New York: Parents Magazine Press.

Freddy has just moved into a new neighborhood and wonders who his friends will be. His ability to throw and catch win him the friendship of boys who need a good baseball player.

Tobias, Toby. (1976). *Moving day*. New York: Alfred A. Knopf.

A child's point of view about moving. The same feeling of being uprooted is often felt by a child who is hospitalized—especially far from home.

Viklund, Alice R. (1967). *Moving away*. New York: McGraw-Hill.

It can be sad leaving familiar things, but there is some excitement in facing something new and different.

Wise, William. (1961). *The house with the red roof*. New York: G.P. Putnam's Sons.

Jimmy likes his house with the red roof and all the familiar things about his life. After moving, he discovers he doesn't mind his new house with the brown roof after all.

Zolotow, Charlotte. (1973). *Janey*. New York: Harper & Row.

A young girl's best friend moves away.

Growing and Changing

Ahlberg, Janet, & Ahlberg, Alan. (1988). *Starting school*. England: Viking Kestrel, Penguin Group.

A preschooler's guide to everything that will happen in school up to winter vacation, done with detailed pictures and text.

Baer, Edith. (1990). *This is the way we go to school*. New York: Scholastic.

Describes, in text and illustrations, the many different modes of transportation children all over the world use to get to school.

Baum, Arline, & Baum, Joseph. (1973). *One bright Monday morning*. New York: Random House.

A picture book tale of what a child sees on the way to school. Helps children realize that, even if all they can do is look, there is a lot that is interesting.

Berry, Joy. (1984). *Separation*. Sebastopal, CA: Living Skills Press.

A combination of large, easily understood cartoon pictures, easily read text, and a seven-page appendix for parents makes this a good book for parents and children dealing with parent-child separation due to child care, and so on.

Jabar, Cynthia. (1989). *Alice Ann gets ready for school*. Boston, MA: Little, Brown.

Alice Ann experiences both fun and anxiety as she gets ready for the biggest event of her life.

Koulouras, K., & McCaig, G. (1987). *When someone takes care of you*. Southfield, MI: K & M Resources.

Encourages children to talk about the adults that care for them.

Krauss, Ruth. (1947). *The growing story*. New York: Harper & Row.

Tells how each animal, flower, and child grows and changes in its own special way.

Kuskin, Karla. (1961). *The bear who saw the spring*. New York: Harper & Row.

Illustrates the regular changes in the seasons.

Magorian, Michelle (1990). *Who's going to take care of me?* New York: Harper & Row.

Eric and Karin enjoyed day care together, and when Karin went to school Eric was lost until he found a scared new boy to take care of.

McCloskey, Robert. (1957). *Time of wonder*. New York: Viking Press.

The changing seasons.

McCully, Emily. (1987). *School*. New York: Harper & Row.

Little mouse is left behind when the older eight mouse children go off to school, so he slips off to see what his siblings are doing. A wordless picture book.

Tresselt, Alvin R. (1947). *White snow, bright snow*. New York: Lothrop, Lee and Shepherd Co.

Seasonal change.

Viorst, Judith. (1988). *The good-bye book*. New York: Atheneum.

A child on the verge of being left behind by parents who are going out for the evening comes up with a variety of excuses and requests.

Zolotow, Charlotte. (1978). *Someone new*. New York: Harper & Row.

An especially sensitive book about a child's changing and growing—a book of self-discovery.

New Baby

Alexander, Martha G. (1971). *Nobody asked me if I wanted a baby sister*. New York: Dial Books.

Oliver tries to give his sister away because she cries all the time.

Arstein, Helene S. (1973). *Billy and our new baby*. New York: Behavioral Publications.

The new baby takes up most of Mom's time. Billy wants to act like a baby, but Mom shows him it is more fun to be big and do things. Billy accepts the baby though he still doesn't like him part of the time.

Byars, Betsy. (1982). *Go and hush the baby*. New York: Puffin Books.

Before he can play baseball, a little boy must try many antics to hush the crying baby.

Clifton, Lucille. (1978). *Everett Anderson's nine months long*. New York: Holt, Rinehart and Winston.

Everett's parents take an understanding view of his feelings as the family welcomes the new baby.

Gewing, L. (1989). *Mamma, Daddy, baby and me*. Emeryville, CA: Spirit Press.

The story of a family's preparations for a new baby.

Greenfield, Eloise. (1974). *She came bringing me that little baby girl*. Philadelphia: Lippincott.

A little boy hates his new sister and everyone else because they play with the baby and not him.

Harper, A. (1986). *It's not fair!* New York: G.P. Putnam's Sons.

First the baby gets all the attention, and as the baby gets bigger he wants to do things he can't. The perennial struggle.

Helmering, Doris, & Helmering, John William. (1978). *We're going to have a baby*. Nashville: Abingdon.

Jimmy looks forward to a new baby in the family until his friends advise him that babies are no fun. Good for discussing the pros and cons of new babies.

Hoban, Russell. (1964). *A baby sister for Frances*. New York: Harper & Row.

Frances isn't sure she wants a new sister because no one seems to have time for her.

Holland, Viki. (1972). *We are having a baby*. New York: Scribner.

At first, four-year-old Dana is happy about having a baby sibling, but when the baby comes home she feels hurt and abandoned. Photos capture the emotions of that phase in a child's life.

Jordan, June. (1975). *New life: New room*. New York: Thomas Y. Crowell.

Rudy, Tyrone, and Linda work together rearranging furniture, painting their room, and weeding through toys. They are making room for the arrival of the new baby.

Keats, Ezra Jack. (1967). *Peter's chair*. New York: Harper & Row.

An African American boy experiences feelings of neglect after the arrival of a new baby—until he gets a chair of his very own.

Knotts, Howard. (1978). *Great-grandfather, the baby, and me*. New York: Atheneum.

A young boy feels sad about the arrival of a new sister. Great-grandfather tells the child a story and comforts him. They leave together to greet the new baby.

Levinson, Riki. (1991). *Me baby*. New York: Dutton Children's Books.

"Me baby," yells Danny to get attention when he feels the new baby has displaced him as the center of family affection.

McCully, Emily. (1988). *New baby*. New York: Harper & Row.

A wordless picture book explores the youngest mouse's feelings when a new baby is born.

Peek, Merle. (1985). *Mary wore her red dress and Henry wore his green sneakers*. New York: Clarion Books.

This beautifully illustrated animal book is a new version of an old folk song from Texas; a note from the author suggests ways for children to improvise further.

Skorpen, Liesel Moak. (1978). *His mother's dog*. New York: Harper & Row.

Both the dog and the boy feel rejected when mother comes home from the hospital with a baby. In despair they turn to each other for comfort.

Tester, Sylvia Root. (1976). *Feeling angry*. Elgin, IL: Child's World.

A little girl is jealous about the arrival of a baby.

Thompson, Carol. (1991). *Baby days*. New York: Macmillan.

Writer-illustrator Thompson chronicles busy days of babies and toddlers with lively pictures and simple captions.

Picture Books

Anno, Mitsumasa. (1975). *Anno's alphabet*. New York: Thomas Y. Crowell.

An alphabet book with large colorful pictures. No words.

Bang, Molly. (1991). *Yellow ball*. New York: Morrow Junior Books.

During a beach game a yellow ball is accidentally tossed out to sea, has adventures, and finds a new home in this large picture book with simple captions.

Boon, Emilie. (1984). *Peterkin meets a star*. New York: Random House.

Peterkin catches a star, takes it home to the star's dismay, and finally puts it back in the sky where it watches over him every night.

Carle, Eric. (1971). *Do you want to be my friend?* New York: Thomas Y. Crowell.

A mouse searches for a friend. The book helps teach right-left progression, and that not everyone wants to be friends.

Crews, Donald. (1980). *Trucks*. New York: Greenwillow.

Crews's double-page, colorful pictures take the reader on a wordless cross-country trip on a big red truck.

Crews, Donald. (1982). *Carousel*. New York: Greenwillow.

Crews's illustrations and simple captions capture the speeds of the merry-go-round from still, to horses racing, to slowing down.

Crews, Donald. (1984). *School bus*. New York: Greenwillow.

Every child will love these big yellow school buses that are so much a part of many children's daily school life.

Garland, Michael. (1989). *My cousin Katie*. New York: Thomas Y. Crowell.

Life on a farm is beautifully illustrated by award-winning illustrator Michael Garland, featuring Katie, who lives there.

Handford, Martin. (1989). *The great Waldo search*. Boston, MA: Little, Brown.

Looking for details is a skill delightfully learned by Waldo-seekers as they search the large pages for Waldo and numerous other characters and objects.

Harrison, Sarah, & Wilkes, Mike. (1980). *In Granny's garden*. New York: Holt, Rinehart and Winston.

The nonreading child will love the fantasy world created by illustrator Mike Wilkes on double page pictures, and the reader will enhance the pictures by enjoying poet Sarah Harrison's accompanying poem.

Henriett. (1991). *A mouse in the house*. New York: Dorling Kindersling, Inc.

Subtitled "A real-life game of hide and seek." Children will love searching for the mouse on each of the large double-page illustrations.

Henstra, Friso. (1983). *Mighty mizzling mouse*. New York: J. B. Lippincott.

A mouse wearing sneakers and a large cat chase each other with hilarious results in a charming picture book.

Henstra, Friso. (1984). *Mighty mizzling mouse and the red cabbage house*. Boston, MA: Little, Brown.

Mouse finds a mate and builds a red cabbage house which is eaten by a rabbit in a beautifully illustrated adventure story.

Isadora, Rachel. (1990). *Babies*. New York: Greenwillow.

A perfect book for a baby and adult to enjoy together. It chronicles baby's day with large, beautiful pictures and one-word captions.

Hutchins, Pat. (1971). *Changes, changes*. New York: Macmillan.

In this brightly colored book, blocks become various things (boat, house, and so on). No words.

Jones, Carol. (1990). *This old man*. Boston, MA: Houghton Mifflin.

Children will enjoy pulling their way through the hole on this rhyming song book.

Kent, Jack. (1974). *Jack Kent's hop, skip and jump book: An action word book*. New York: Random House.

Illustrations of children jumping, skipping, waving, and so on, with the word describing the action printed below.

Kent, Jack. (1975). *The egg book*. New York: Macmillan.

A chicken watches another chicken sit on an egg and hatch a chick. The first chicken sits on different eggs and hatches a turtle, an alligator, an ostrich, and finally a chick. No words.

McCully, Emily. (1984). *Picnic*. New York: Harper & Row.

A wordless picture book celebrates the mouse family picnic in lush summer-drenched watercolors.

McCully, Emily (1985). *First snow*. New York: Harper & Row.

In this wordless winter companion to *Picnic*, the mouse family has many winter adventures.

McMillan, Bruce (1988). *Growing colors*. New York: Lothrop, Lee and Shepard Books.

Large, colorful photographs of vegetables and fruits. Teaches colors in a new way. One-word captions.

Newton, Laura. (1980). *William the vehicle king*. New York: Bradbury Press.

Most children like vehicles, and those who do will love the colorful book about William's toys and his cat who stays close by.

Patent, D. (1988). *Babies*. New York: Holiday House.

Great pictures of babies and information about what they can do at a young age. Designed for preschool children.

Sears, Nancy. (1977). *Farm animals*. New York: Random House.

This pop-up book about a farmer and the different jobs he has to do is good for cause and effect reasoning.

Sloat, Terri. (1991). *From one to one hundred*. New York: Dutton Children's Books.

Terri Sloat wanted "to do a book with numbers of things in common scenes to help make children aware that groupings of objects are all around them" and succeeds with a beautifully illustrated no-word book.

Turkle, Brinton. (1976). *Deep in the forest*. New York: E. P. Dutton.

The Goldilocks story is turned around, making the little bear the intruder. No words.

Wilkes, Angela. (1991). *My first word book*. New York: Kindersley.

The bright pictures will delight the young child, and the one-word captions will challenge the young reader.

Rhyming and Sound Books

Ahlberg, Janet, & Ahlberg, Allan. (1978). *Each peach pear plum: An "I-spy" story*. New York: Viking Press.

Uses rhyming phrases based on Mother Goose. "Tom Thumb in the cupboard, I spy mother _____."

Alexander, Anne. (1956). *ABC of cars and trucks*. Garden City, NY: Doubleday.

Contains the alphabet and also many repetitive sentences and rhyming words.

Degen, Bruce. (1983). *Jamberry*. New York: Harper & Row.

A little boy and a bear find berries everywhere, and the bear converts their adventures to rhyme. Sure to invite repetition, such as "Quick berry! Quack berry! Pick me a blackberry!"

Latham, Jean L. (1974). *Who lives here?* Champaign, IL: Garrard.

As they approach each dwelling, animals try to guess from a rhyme who lives there.

McCord, David. (1967). *Every time I climb a tree*. Boston: Little, Brown.

A book of poetry and rhyme.

McMillan, Bruce. (1990). *One sun*. New York: Holiday House.

"A book of terse verse" aptly describes this photo-illustrated book, which will encourage children to make up their own verse after enjoying "pink drink" and "whale pail." Contains 25 verses with a lot of rhyming and repetition.

Mosel, Arlene. (1968). *Tikki Tikki Tembo.* New York: Holt, Rinehart and Winston.

Great for kids having trouble pronouncing /t/ as an initial consonant. Fun play with nonsense words. Adaptation of a Chinese folktale.

Spier, Peter. (n. d.). *Gobble, growl, grunt.* New York: Scholastic.

A picture book of animals and the sounds they make.

Supraner, Robyn. (1978). *Higgly-wiggly, snickety-snick.* New York: Parents Magazine Press.

Nonsense words, rhymes, and collages are combined to produce a book that children will want to hear many times.

Thackray, Patricia. (1975). *Big Bird's rhyming book.* New York: Random House.

This colorful pop-up book uses simple (three- and four-letter) rhyming words such as *cat* and *bat.* The pull tabs make it gamelike.

Tremain, Ruthven. (1976). *Fooling around with words.* New York: Greenwillow.

The riddles, stinky pinkies, and other word games are an entertaining way to learn language.

Tudor, Tasha. (1944). *Mother Goose: Seventy-seven verses.* New York: Oxford University Press.

Traditional children's stories and poems. Lots of rhyming words.

Wiseman, Bernard. (1979). *Morris tells Boris Mother Moose stories and rhymes.* New York: Dodd, Mead.

A delightful book of Mother Moose stories that will bring giggles to many children and adults.

Roles

Babbitt, Natalie. (1977). *Phoebe's revolt.* Garden City, NY: Farrar, Straus and Giroux.

Phoebe revolts against frills and lace and wants to wear her father's clothes.

Berenstain, Stanley, and Berenstain, Janice. (1974). *He bear, she bear.* New York: Random House.

Relates that both he and she bears can do anything they like. Shows a variety of occupational roles.

Blaine, Marge. (1975). *The terrible thing that happened at our house.* New York: Scholastic.

When a mother goes back to work, her children have to learn to cook and to care for themselves.

Burton, Virginia Lee. (1974). *Katy and the big snow.* Boston: Houghton Mifflin.

Katy, an old red tractor, rescues a snowed-in city.

Chapman, Kim W. (1976). *The magic hat.* Chapel Hill, NC: Lollipop Power.

Polly finds a magic hat that helps to make the fence disappear that separates boys' toys from girls' toys. The toys are for everyone, no matter what sex they are.

Eichler, Margret. (1977). *Martin's father.* Chapel Hill, NC: Lollipop Power.

Martin's father cares for him, and they perform everyday household tasks together.

Godden, Rumer. (1955). *Impunity Jane.* New York: Macmillan.

A young boy takes pride in his china doll.

Goffstein, M. B. (1970). *Two piano tuners.* Garden City, NY: Farrar, Straus, and Giroux.

Debbie decides that she would like to be a piano tuner just like her grandfather.

Goffstein, M. B. (1980). *Goldie the dollmaker.* Garden City, NY: Farrar, Straus, and Giroux.

Goldie makes wooden dolls for her living.

Goldreich, Gloria, and Goldreich, Ester. (1973). *What can she be? A newscaster.* New York: Lothrop, Lee and Shepard Press.

Photographs and text capture a day in the life of a black woman newscaster.

Goodyear, Carmen. (1972). *The sheep book.* Chapel Hill, NC: Lollipop Power.

A story of a farmer and her sheep.

Hazen, Nancy. (1978). *Grownups cry too: Los adultos también lloran.* Chapel Hill, NC: Lollipop Power.

Grownups are human and express their emotions. Men and women are shown as both sad and happy.

Kingman, Lee. (1972). *Georgina and the dragon.* Boston: Houghton Mifflin.

Ten-year-old Georgina is an early victim of job discrimination, but she overcomes this and makes life easier for girls in her neighborhood.

Klagsburn, Francine. (Ed.). (1974). *Free to be you and me.* New York: McGraw-Hill.

Jane is interested in dinosaurs and becomes a famous scientist.

Wolde, Gunilla. (1972). *Tommy and Sarah dress up.* Boston: Houghton Mifflin.

Tommy and Sarah dress up and act out many different roles.

Young, Eleanor R. (1971). *Fathers, fathers, fathers.* Minneapolis: T. S. Denison.

This story presents the father's role. It uses simple illustrations of men of differing nationalities and occupations.

Zolotow, Charlotte. (1972). *William's doll.* New York: Harper & Row.

William more than anything wants a doll, but his male relatives think that's "sissy." William's grandmother finally understands that he wants a doll to practice being a father and gives him a doll.

Scratch and Sniff and Touch and Feel Books

Scratch and Sniff and Touch and Feel books are great for young children as they learn to integrate their senses. These books bring sensory experiences to reading. Because the plots are typically simple and what will be touched is often obvious from the title, these books have not been annotated.

Awry, Rev. W. (1991). *James the fire engine.* New York: Random House.

Berenstain, Stan, & Berenstain, Jan. (1978). *Papa's pizza: A Berenstain Bear sniffy book.* New York: Random House.

Demi. (1992). *Cuddly chick.* New York: Grosset and Dunlap.

Fulton, Mary J. (1971). *Detective Arthur on the scent.* New York: Golden Press.

Hall, Susan. (1991). *Bunny tail.* New York: Golden Books.

Hays, Anna J. (1975). *See no evil, hear no evil, smell no evil: Sesame Street.* New York: Golden Press.

Hazen, Barbara S. (1973). *A nose for trouble.* New York: Golden Press.

Howard, Katherine. (1971). *Little bunny follows his nose.* New York: Golden Press.

Ikhlef, Anne. (1991). *Fuzzy little bear.* New York: Random House.

Kent, Jack. (1978). *Supermarket magic.* New York: Random House.

Long, Ruthanna. (1978). *Once-upon-a-time scratch and sniff book.* New York: Golden Press.

Mayer, Mercer. (1977). *Professor Wormbog's gloomy kerploppus: A book of great smells.* New York: Golden Press.

McHargue, Georgess. (1971). *What's in Mommy's pocketbook: A touch and feel book.* (rev. ed.). New York: Western Publishing Co.

McKie, Roy. (1978). *The sniff and tell riddle book.* New York: Random House.

Miller, J. P. (1980). *Sniffy the mouse.* New York: Random House.

Milne, A. A. (1975). *Winnie the Pooh scratch and sniff book.* Wayne, NJ: Western Publishing Co.

Ottum, Bob, & Wood, JoAnne. (1974). *Santa's beard is soft and warm.* New York: Western Publishing Co.

Scarry, Patricia M. (1970). *The sweet smell of Christmas.* New York: Golden Press.

Scarry, Richard. (1964). *Egg in the hole.* New York: Western Publishing Co.

Scarry, Richard. (1964). *Is this the house of Mistress Mouse?* New York: Western Publishing Co.

Smollin, Michael J. (1978). *Sweet smell of strawberryland.* New York: Random House.

Thackray, Patricia. (1978). *Big Bird gets lost.* New York: Golden Press.

Thackray, Patricia. (1977). *Raggedy Ann's sweet & dandy, sugar candy.* New York: Golden Press.

Walt Disney Studio. (1975). *Bambi's fragrant forest.* New York: Golden Press.

Walt Disney Studio. (1979). *Mickey Mouse and the marvelous smell machine.* New York: Golden Press.

Witte, Eve, & Witte, Pat. (1961). *Look, look book.* New York: Western Publishing Co.

Witte, Eve, & Witte, Pat. (1961). *Touch me book.* New York: Western Publishing Co.

Simpler Books

Aliki. (1962). *My five senses.* New York: Crowell.

A simple, informative book about the delight of discovery through seeing, hearing, smelling, tasting, and feeling.

Allen, Robert. (1968). *Numbers. A first counting book.* New York: Platt and Munk.

A book with big, clear photographs of familiar objects.

Alley, R. W. (1986). *Busy farm trucks.* New York: Grosset and Dunlap.

A truck-shaped board book that rolls on sturdy black wheels is fun to play with and to look at, as are all the trucks inside.

Bayer, Jane. (1984). *A my name is Alice.* New York: E. P. Dutton.

Alice and husband Alex from Alaska sell ants and start a parade of ABC animals who sell fascinating things. Based on a favorite playground game of the author.

Carle, Eric. (1986). *Papa please get the moon for me.* Saxonville, MA: Picture Book Studio.

Monica's father fulfills her request for the moon by taking it after it is small enough to carry, but it continues to change in size. Some pages fold out to display particularly large pictures.

Ginsburg, Mirra. (1972). *The chick and the duckling.* New York: Macmillan.

About a leader, the Duckling, and a follower, the Chick. Whatever Duckling does, Chick does, until he realizes that he can't do all that Duckling can do. Chick learns to be content to be himself.

Hoban, Tana. (1991). *All about where.* New York: Greenwillow.

"Look at the picture. What do you see?" The author invites the reader to apply descriptive words to the excellent photographs of people and things which can be enjoyed by the nonreader.

Johnson, John Emil. (1979). *My first book of things.* New York: Random House.

A short colorful book about a little boy and all the things he has. The drawings are large and realistic.

Johnson, John. (1980). *The sky is blue, the grass is green.* New York: Random House.

A delightful cloth color book with large bright pictures.

Krauss, Ruth. (1947). *The growing story.* New York: Harper & Row.

A little boy sees everything growing and wonders if he is growing, too. When his pants and warm coat are brought out again after being stored for the summer, he realizes that they are too small and that he has indeed grown.

Shortall, Leonard. (1980). *Zoo animals.* New York: Random House.

A colorful cloth book with large pictures and one-word descriptions.

Tafuri, Nancy. (1984). *Have you seen my duckling?* Greenwillow.

A mother duck heads her brood around the pond as she searches for one missing duckling in this picture book with simple captions.

Tafuri, Nancy. (1986). *Camping.* New York: Greenwillow.

The movements and actions of a family camping in the woods cause the forest creatures to move, scurry, and make noise in this beautiful wordless picture book.

Tafuri, Nancy. (1988). *Jungle wall.* New York: Greenwillow.

A little boy falls asleep after reading a book about animals in a jungle, and then he meets them in his dream.

Williams, Vera. (1990). *"More, more, more, said the baby."* New York: Greenwillow.

This Caldecott Honor book consists of gouache paintings with lettering done as part of the paintings, which should appeal to the younger child. The three stories are called "love stories" by the author and are about three toddlers from different cultures.

Wood, Don, & Wood, Audrey. (1991). *Piggies.* San Diego, CA: Harcourt Brace Jovanovich.

This new book by the Woods has the same outstanding large pastel pictures as their other award-winning books and is a delightful story about a child's finger.

Starting School

Amoss, Berthe. (1972). *The very worst thing.* New York: Parents Magazine Press.

A story told by a little boy who is new in school.

Barkin, Carol, & James, Elizabeth. (1975). *I'd rather stay home.* Milwaukee, WI: Raintree Editions.

A boy's first day at school is depicted.

Breinburg, Petronella. (1973). *Shawn goes to school.* New York: Thomas Y. Crowell.

Shawn's reaction to his first day at nursery school is shown.

Johnson, John E. (1979). *My school book.* New York: Random House.

The story explains what happens on the first day of school.

Kuklin, Susan. (1990). *Going to my nursery school.* New York: Bradbury Press.

A little boy describes in text and photographs what he does in his nursery school class.

Marino, Dorothy. (1970). *Buzzy Bear's first day at school.* New York: Franklin Watts.

Buzzy Bear is anxious to go to school, but when he gets there the other animal children are doing things that Buzzy feels he can't do. Finally he learns what he can do.

Mayer, Mercer. (1990). *Little Critter's this is my school.* Racine, WI: Golden Books, Western Publishing Co.

Little Critter's first day of school is fun but mouse is worn out. Children will enjoy looking for the mouse on each page.

Rogers, Fred. (1985). *Going to day care.* New York: G.P. Putnam's Sons.

Describes the typical activities and feelings children can experience at a day-care center, including conflicts and apprehensions involved in being away from home along with the fun and excitement.

Rockwell, Harlow. (1976). *My nursery school.* New York: Greenwillow.

A good book for a child who is either hospitalized or at home, because it demonstrates through the use of pictures what may be going on at school while the child is away.

Soderstrom, Mary. (1981). *Maybe tomorrow I'll have a good time.* New York: Human Sciences Press.

Marsha Lou finds the first day of school difficult. This story helps children confront their own feelings of separation and gain a sense of independence and self-confidence.

Solomon, Chuck. (1989). *Moving up.* New York: Crown.

Text and photographs detail for kindergarten children what they can expect in first grade.

Additional Resources for Teachers

American Dealers of Books in Spanish for Children

Aims International Books, Inc.
3216 Montana Avenue
P.O. Box 11496
Cincinnati, OH 45211

Baker & Taylor
Books in Spanish
380 Edison Way
Reno, NV 89564

Bilingual Publications Co.
1966 Broadway
New York, NY 10023

French and Spanish Book Corp.
652 Olive Street
Los Angeles, CA 90014

Hispanic Book Distributors, Inc.
1665 W. Grant Road
Tucson, AZ 85745

Iaconi Book Imports
300 Pennsylvania Avenue
San Francisco, CA 94107

Lectorum Publications, Inc.
137 West 14th Street
New York, NY 10011

Pan American Book Co.
4326 Melrose Avenue
Los Angeles, CA 90029

Spanish Books, Inc.
5963 El Cajon Boulevard
San Diego, CA 92115
(listed by Schon, 1991)

Allen, A. (Ed.). (1987). *Library services for Hispanic children.* Phoenix, AZ: Oryx.

Austin, M., & Jenkins, E. (1983). *Promoting world understanding through literature, K–8.* Littleton, CO: Libraries Unlimited.

Beilke, P., & Sciara, F. (1986). *Selecting materials for and about Hispanic and East Asian children and young people.* Hamden, CT: Library Professional Publications/Shoe String Press.

Schon, I. (1986). *Basic collection of children's books in Spanish.* Metuchen, NJ: Scarecrow.

Child Development

Berk, L. (1989). *Child development.* Boston: Allyn & Bacon.

Black, J., Puckett, M., & Bell, M. (1992). *The young child: Development from prebirth through age eight.* Riverside, NJ: Merrill/Macmillan Co.

Charlesworth, R. (1987). *Understanding child development* (2nd ed.). New York: Delmar.

Greenspan, S., & Pollock, G. (1989). *The course of life. Vol. 2: Early childhood.* Madison, CT: International Universities Press.

Morrison, G. (1990). *The world of child development: Conception to adolescence.* Albany, NY: Delmar.

Assessment

Abbott-Shim, M., & Sibley, A. (1987). *Assessment profile for early childhood programs.* Atlanta, GA: Quality Assist.

Bagnato, S., & Neisworth, J. (1991). *Assessment for early intervention: Best practices for professionals.* New York: The Guilford Press.

Love, D. (1990). *Assessment of intelligence and development of infants and young children with specialized measures.* Springfield, IL: Charles C. Thomas.

Early Childhood Education

Beaty, J. (1992). *Skills for preschool teachers* (4th ed.). Riverside, NJ: Merrill/Macmillan Co.

Feeney, S., Christensen, D., & Maravcik, E. (1991). *Who am I in the lives of children? An introduction to teaching young children* (4th ed.). Riverside, NJ: Merrill/Macmillan Co.

Hendrick, J. (1992). *The whole child: Developmental education for the early years* (5th ed.). Riverside, NJ: Merrill/Macmillan Co.

Katz, L., & Chard, S. (1989). *Engaging children's minds: The project approach.* Norwood, NJ: Ablex.

Marion, M. (1991). *Guidance of young children* (3rd ed.). Riverside, NJ: Merrill/Macmillan Co.

McKee, J. (Ed.). (1986). *Play: Working partner of growth.* Wheaton, MD: Association for Childhood Education International.

Morrison, G. (1991). *Early childhood education today* (5th ed.). Riverside, NJ: Merrill/Macmillan Co.

Raver, S. (1991). *Strategies for teaching at-risk and handicapped infants and toddlers: A transdisciplinary approach.* New York: Merrill.

Read, K., Gardner, P., & Makler, B. (1987). *Early childhood programs: Human relations and learning.* New York: Holt, Rinehart & Winston.

Roopnarine, J., & Johnson, J. (Eds.). (1987). *Approaches to early childhood education.* Columbus, OH: Merrill.

Early Childhood Education Administration

Decker, C., & Decker, J. (1992). *Planning and administering early childhood programs* (5th ed.). Riverside, NJ: Merrill/Macmillan Co.

Hewes, D., & Hartman, R. (1988). *Early childhood education: A workbook for administrators* (rev. ed.). Saratoga, CA: R & E Publishers.

Working with Parents

Berger, E. (1991). *Parents as partners in education: The school and home working together* (3rd ed.). Riverside, NJ: Merrill/Macmillan Co.

Cataldo, C. (1987). *Parent education for early childhood: Childrearing concepts and program content for the student and practicing professional.* New York: Teachers College Press, Columbia University.

McLoughlin, C. (1987). *Parent-teacher conferencing.* Springfield, IL: Charles C. Thomas.

Shea, T., & Bauer, A. (1991). *Parents and teachers of children with exceptionalities: A handbook for collaboration* (2nd ed.). Boston: Allyn and Bacon.

Swap, S. (1987). *Enhancing parent involvement in schools.* New York: Teachers College Press, Columbia University.

Differences

Neugebauer, E. (1987). *Alike and different: Exploring our humanity with young children.* Redmond, WA: Exchange Press.

Ramsey, P. (1987). *Teaching and learning in a diverse world: Multicultural education for young children.* New York: Teachers College Press, Columbia University.

Tobin, J., Wu, D., & Davidson, D. (1989). *Preschool in three cultures: Japan, China, and the United States.* New Haven, CT: Yale University Press. (Videotape available.)

Divorce

Shapiro, R. (1991). *Separate houses: A practical guide for divorced parents.* New York: Prentice-Hall.

Death

Blackburn, L. (1991). *The class in room 44: When a classmate dies*. Omaha, NE: Centering Corporation.

Culture

Comer, J. (1988). *Maggie's American dream: The life and times of a black family*. New York: Penguin Books.

Hale-Benson, J. (1986). *Black children: Their roots, culture, and learning*. Baltimore, MD: Johns Hopkins University Press.

MacMillan, D., & Freeman, D. (1987). *My best friend Duc Tran: Meeting a Vietnamese-American family*. New York: Julian Messner.

Peters, W. (1987). *A class divided: Then and now*. New Haven, CT: Yale University Press.

Saracho, O., & Spodek, B. (Eds.). (1983). *Understanding the multicultural experience in early childhood education*. Washington, DC: NAEYC.

Shalant, P. (1988). *Look what we've brought you from Vietnam: Crafts, games, recipes, stories and other cultural activities from new Americans*. New York: Julian Messner.

Warren, J., & McKinnon, E. (1988). *Small world celebrations*. Everett, WA: Warren Publishing House, Inc.

Designed as a "multicultural resource book for teachers of young children," the book contains easy suggestions for holiday celebrations for fifteen cultures.

Videotape Training Programs

(This list represents sample titles only. For complete listings request a catalogue.)

Infants and Toddlers with Special Needs and their Families

The "Year One" Materials from George Washington University

> The Family Experience (Part I, 25 minutes, Part II, 20 minutes)
>
> The Neonatal Experience (Part I, 25 minutes, Part II, 20 minutes)
>
> The Community Experience (30 minutes)

Infants and Young Children with Special Health Care Needs

> Promoting Cognitive, Social and Emotional Development (20 minutes)
>
> Promoting Motor Development (23 minutes)
>
> Promoting Family Collaboration (20 minutes)
>
> Working as a Team (20 minutes)
>
> Other Topics

Apnea Monitoring: Your Baby and You

Care of Children with Asthma in School Settings

Birth Crisis Intervention

Learner Managed Designs, Inc.
2201 K. West 25th Street
Lawrence, KS 66047
(913) 842-9088

Note: Learning Managed Designs, Inc. is a research and development organization in the design of training programs for care providers of infants, toddlers, school-age students, and adults with special needs and their families.

The Chapel Hill Training-Outreach Project Training series is available in a combination of slide-tape and VHS video cassette:

> "Transition to Preschool" (13 minutes)
>
> "PL 99-457: Family Involvement" (16 minutes)
>
> "PL 99-457: Placement in the Least Restrictive Environment" (12 minutes)
>
> "PL 99-457, A New Commitment" (12 minutes)
>
> "Mandate for Collaboration" (12 minutes)
>
> "The Local Interagency Coordinating Council" (12 minutes)
>
> "Joining Forces" (10 minutes, slide tapes only)

Chapel Hill Training-Outreach Project
800 Eastowne Drive, Suite 105
Chapel Hill, NC 27514
(919) 490-5577

Therapy Skill Builders has videos on normal growth and development and special needs:

> "Development of Reach and Grasp" (20 minutes)
>
> "Normal Infant Reflexes and Development" (30 minutes)
>
> "Learning about Learning Disabilities" (20 minutes)
>
> "Sensory Integration Therapy" (20 minutes)
>
> "A Neuro-postural Approach to Movement and Posture Disorganization in Learning Disabilities" (30 minutes)

Therapy Skill Builders
3830 E. Bellevue/P.O. Box 42050-C92
Tucson, AZ 85733
(602) 323-7500

Toys (Catalogues)

Kapable Kids (1991–92)
P.O. Box 250
Bohemia, NY 11716
(800-356-1564)

Pocket Full of Therapy, Inc.
P.O. Box 174
Morgantown, NJ 07751
Catalogue (send $4.50) on toys and materials for learning and therapy.

Toys for Special Children (1991) *I*(3)
385 Warburton Ave.
Hastings-on-Hudson, NY 10706

PART THREE

Working with Families

Chapter 19

Families and Children with Disabilities

Times are changing, families are changing, and schools are changing. The questions we ask about families and about how to educate children have changed. In the past the child was the focus of intervention, and professionals used theories related to growth and development when working with individual children. As the focus has changed to the child within the context of the family, new theories have emerged. These theories provide a different way of looking at families.

Parents' Roles

Over time we have viewed parents from many different perspectives (Turnbull & Turnbull, 1990). In the past, we believed that parents were the cause of their children's problems. We thought of parents as members of organizations. They might belong to the Parent Teachers Association (PTA), or perhaps they were "boosters" who help raise money for needed projects. They might be members of support groups.

Parents were also advocates for their children in the area of service development. Professionals *expected* parents to somehow find ways of obtaining needed services for their children. This was particularly true in areas such as accessibility of recreation activities, religious activities, and organizations such as scouting or 4H.

We saw parents as learners. Parents lacked skills and so had to be taught. We offered them parenting classes, or gave them information to read about discipline or disabilities. They sometimes had roles as adjuncts to professionals in that they were to carry out a "home program" to support what teachers and therapists were doing. We frequently thought of parents as recipients of professionals' decisions. That is, we as professionals, made educational decisions in the best interest of their children and interpreted those decisions to the parents.

Overall, the parental role was not to question decisions, but to appreciate the time and effort that went into the decision making for their child and to follow through. Although the law gave parents the right to make educational decisions for their child, professionals rarely expected parents to take on that role. And, in fact, parents frequently supported this position, saying "You're the expert," and abdicating their decision-making authority.

Today the focus is changing. Parents are people who, in addition to being parents, also have roles as husbands, wives, cousins, nephews, nieces, aunts, uncles, sons, and daughters. Likewise, they are employees or employers with long-term personal and professional goals. This view is considered "best practice" in the field today. It leads to new assumptions about families, new service options, and a need to understand the family as a system (Turnbull & Turnbull, 1990). This chapter includes information about the family system as a whole and about the many roles that all family members play both in the family and in society.

Few parents expect that their children will be disabled. Families with children with disabilities not only face the ordinary tasks of family life, but must also confront issues that are idiosyncratic to the specific disability and level of functioning of the child. Factors such as the child's personality, activity level, attractiveness, and others influence the family. Interactions among family members also influence the way the family unit interacts with society. The impact of the child on the family changes as the child grows. Learning about and adjusting to a child's disability impacts the entire family system (Deiner, 1987).

Family Systems Theory

The family systems framework is a theoretical umbrella that makes assumptions about how families work. Family systems theory focuses on the family as a unit as opposed to the child. The family is the larger social system within which the child functions (Karpel & Strauss, 1983). The emphasis is on the relationships

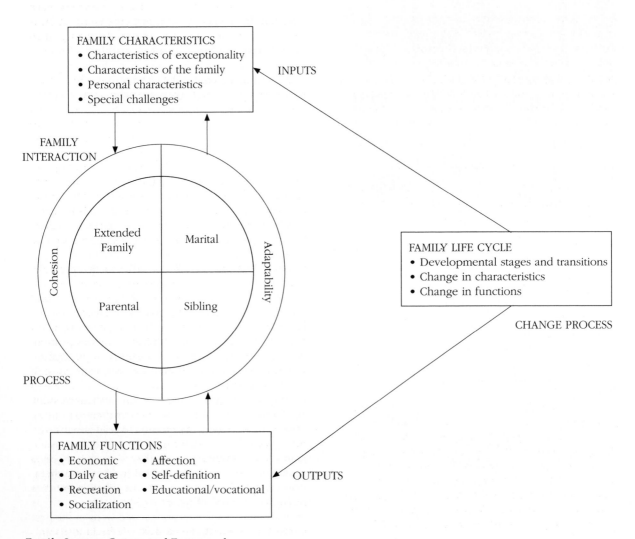

Family Systems Conceptual Framework

between family members rather than on the members themselves (Watzlawick, Beavin, & Jackson, 1967; Bateson, 1972).

Family systems theory posits that families operate under the same rules that govern all systems. (A system is a set of objects that interrelate with one another to form a whole.) The underlying assumption is that if one component of the system changes, the others will also change, which will in turn change the initial component through the process of feedback. Like families, early intervention settings and schools are also systems. One goal in learning about systems is to facilitate family and school in working together for the good of both the family and child.

For example, after observing a particular child you, at an intervention site, start to teach the child to drink from a cup. You send notes home about what you want the family to do and so on. To the extent that the family does not want or support this change and continues to feed the child from a bottle the child is unlikely to learn to drink from a cup and the family system will not change. It is imperative that families decide what is important to them and the areas in which they want to change.

Featherstone (1980) vividly reminds us of the parent's perspective as she talks about receiving a call from the occupational therapist at her son's school. The therapist relayed a request from a visiting nurse that she use an electric toothbrush on her son's teeth for about five minutes three or four times each day to help his gum overgrowth. Her response is something that all professionals should keep in mind.

Although I tried to sound reasonable on the phone, this new demand appalled me. I rehearsed angry, self-justifying speeches in my head. Jody, I thought, is blind, cerebral-palsied, and retarded. We do his physical therapy daily and work with him on sounds and communication. We feed him each meal on our laps, bottle him, change him, bathe him, dry him, put him in a body cast to sleep, launder his bed linens daily, and go through a variety of routines designed to minimize his miseries and enhance his joys and his development. (All this in addition to trying to care for and enjoy our other young children and making time for each other and our careers.) (Featherstone, 1980, pp. 77–78)

She concludes: *Well, it's too much. Where is that fifteen minutes going to come from? What am I supposed to give up? Taking the kids to the park? Reading a bedtime story to my eldest? Washing the breakfast dishes? Sorting the laundry? Grading students' papers? Sleeping? Because there is no time in my life that hasn't been spoken for, and for every fifteen-minute activity that is added, one has to be taken away (Featherstone, 1980, p. 78).*

We as professionals need to evaluate what we ask of parents in the context of their life and values, not our own. The nurse, in her effort to care for the child, did not take into account the reverberations in the system caused by her innocent suggestion.

Recognizing the needs of parents as family members has had a profound effect on the field. Turnbull and Turnbull (1990) have proposed a family systems framework that is specifically designed to aid in the understanding of children with disabilities and their families. They have four major components in their framework: family characteristics, family interaction, family functions, and the family life cycle.

The figure on page 316 shows the interactions of these components in this framework.

Family Characteristics

Families are diverse. In order to understand the impact of a child with a particular disability on the family system one first needs to understand the characteristics of the disability and of the family. Different disabilities have qualitatively differing impacts on different families. Involved are the nature and severity of the disability as well as the demands a particular disability requires in caregiving and the family's perception or definition of the situation.

Characteristics of the Disability. Disabilities make different demands on families. Some disabilities, such as chronic illness, are frequently episodic and require high levels of medical intervention at various times. Others, such as hearing impairment, require families to adapt their communication style permanently, whereas a physical impairment may necessitate physically altering the home. It is important to look at how the family perceives the impact of the disability. What might be viewed as a crisis for some is a minor inconvenience or even an asset for others, depending on how the family system is organized to cope with crisis.

The severity of the disability is an important variable. The more severe the disability the more difficult it will be for the family to care for the child (Schell, 1981). The family may actually try to avoid becoming attached to a severely involved infant for fear the infant will die. Typically, young children with severe disabilities require more caregiving for a greater length of time. They also need a wide range of services involving many specialists; necessitating more appointments, more waiting, and more bills. However, the effect is not linear, that is, one cannot necessarily assume that the more severe the disability the greater the impact on the family. Children with severe disabilities are more easily planned for and controlled (Turnbull, Summers, & Brotherson, 1984), whereas children with milder disabilities are less predictable, especially over the long term.

Characteristics of the Family. To be most useful, the family systems approach requires a variety of information about the family. This information includes the size of the family and its configuration, as well as the cultural, ideological, and personal style of its members (Turnbull & Turnbull, 1990).

Family Structure. Families differ in the number of parents, children, stepchildren, the sex of these children, and their position in the family. The traditional biological family unit is no longer the norm. In fact, as families divorce and then remarry, stepfamilies will probably become the most common family structure (Albert, in Turnbull & Turnbull, 1990). The complexity of the role of a noncustodial parent relative to the development of the child's IEP/IFSP is both a practical one and an ethical dilemma. The stepparents' roles also lack definition at this time. The general thrust is to involve as many caring adults as possible.

Cultural Background. One's cultural background, in combination with ethnic and religious differences, determines foods eaten, rituals and celebrations, and values and perspectives. Increasingly the United States is becoming a nation of color. In many large cities people of color are the majority of the population. A disproportionate number of children of color are represented in special education programs (Reschley, 1988). Early childhood special educators need to be aware of and value cultural differences, be cognizant of family values, and use culturally sensitive communication.

Socioeconomic Status. A family's economic resources, education, and occupation combine to form a family's socioeconomic status. Families with a high SES frequently have more options in obtaining services; however, within limits, this does not mean that these families necessarily cope better. Concerns about poverty are dealt with in the next chapter.

Geographic Location. There is little doubt that metropolitan areas offer a wider range of services than rural areas. Needed medical care frequently necessitates long drives for those in rural areas. Medical expertise and equipment may simply be too far away to meet some emergencies. When a child with a disability lives in an area where services are lacking, the family's choices may be to relocate, put the child in a residential placement, or be classified as part of the "unserved or underserved" population.

Personal Characteristics. The diversity of families as a unit is multiplied when one looks at the characteristics of family members. All people have characteristics which can be either strengths or challenges when coping with children with disabilities.

Overall health status is an important variable. To the extent that family members have repeated or chronic physical or mental illnesses, their abilities to cope are reduced.

Most researchers have found that having a child with a disability increases family stress (Beckman-Bell, 1981). Some see chronic stress in caring for a family member with a disability (Wikler, 1981). Individuals within families have different ways of reducing stress and coping with situations. Some members are more skillful than others, but all family members need to learn methods of coping. Some find religion an aid in coping, others reframe the problem to make it more positive and solvable, others rely on formal or informal support networks, and still others simply ignore the problem in the hope that it will go away or cure itself. If possible, information about a disability should be conveyed to a family in a way that is harmonious with its coping style.

Family Interaction

Like most systems, families are divided into subsystems, which are in fact systems within systems. Boundaries define who is part of the system and who isn't. Boundaries vary on a continuum from very rigid to very diffuse. At the one extreme are "rigid" boundaries, so inflexible that people cannot join or leave the system and where even communication cannot move between subsystems. The other extreme is "diffuse," where it is difficult to figure out where one system ends and the other begins and who belongs to what system. Optimally, there are clear boundaries where the rules of the relationships are spelled out, good communication between subsystems, and functional subsystems that do not interfere with each other.

Within the family system, the husband and wife, or couple, constitute the marital subsystem. This executive subsystem should be in charge of the family. These same people also constitute at least part of the parental subsystem. In a blended family there might be three or four people in the parental subsystem, which adds considerable complexity to the system. The following genogram may make this clearer. A *genogram* is a graphic picture of how people are legally and biologically related.

The "word picture" of the genogram is: "Joe and Myrtle have two natural children, Mary and Charlie. Joe and his first wife Eva have two children, Clarence and Marge. Eva is remarried to Jim, and they have Steve. Sometimes Clarence and Marge stay with Joe and Myrtle and sometimes with Eva and Joe. Myrtle was previously married to Charles, who is deceased. They had two children, Norma and Grant. Grant died at age ten. Norma is a young adult who lives independently."

Several different child subsystems exist in the above genogram: all the children, all the boys, all the children from the same biological father or mother, and so on. A gender-based subsystem could also be composed of all the males or females in the family.

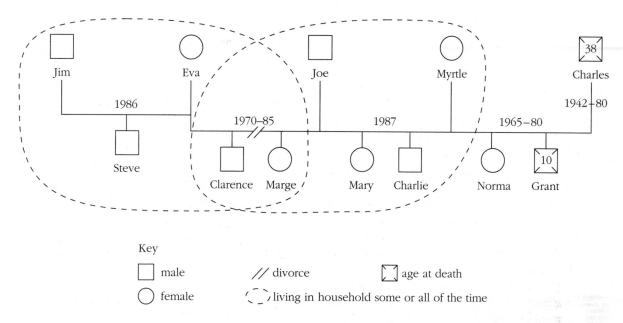

Genogram of a Blended Family with Joint Custody of Two Children

Interest-based subsystems could be composed of all the people who share a certain activity such as swimming, listening to music, reading, and so on. Each person is part of many different subsystems and, depending upon the occasion, can feel very much part of what is happening and at other times not. Think about a marital subsystem which is currently very involved deciding whether or not to take a promotion that would require the father to be out of the country for a year. The child subsystems may feel very left out. On another occasion when the mother takes the children camping and their father is left home alone, he is the one who feels isolated.

A hierarchical structure operates as the subsystems interact with each other and relate to the educational system. Most therapists believe that the most important subsystem bond is that between the marital couple. The ability to establish a clear boundary around the marital subsystem allows the parents to run the family effectively. When the bond across generations (for example, the mother-child bond) becomes stronger than the marital bond, the marriage is at risk. The following scenario is an example of why this is a concern.

Margie and Charlie are married and have a daughter Diana. The marriage is stable yet volatile. As the partners are actively trying to solve problems about which they disagree, Diana has an asthma attack. The argument is off; the problems are not resolved. It happens again. Just at the height of an argument, Diana needs to be taken to the emergency room for adrenalin. Again, no solutions. To the extent that the child can pull this much energy away from the marital subsystem and does it consistently (even

unconsciously), the system is at risk. And, to the extent that she systematically does this she is, in fact, in charge of the family. The diffuse boundaries between the parents and child call into question who is in charge of what in this family.

Let us further assume that Diana has respiratory problems and allergies and misses a lot of school. Diana's teachers think Margie is wonderful. She works with Diana at home and does it well, not pushing, but stimulating. Teachers applaud and support Margie's work. They tell her how great it is that she spends so much time with her daughter, that she cares so much. They encourage her to do more, to volunteer at the school, and so on. She does. As a result, the child is functioning at age level, but the dominant relationship in the family becomes the mother-child relationship, leaving Dad outside the important process at home. He files for divorce.

Is that a success story? What part did teachers unwittingly play? To the extent that we as professionals don't evaluate our behavior within the family context we may be contributing to problems when we think we are solving them. We need to include fathers in our educational planning for children and not assume children have only mothers.

Communication within the System. Communication drives the system and makes change possible. Communication is a process. Communication within a system often takes on a predictable form or pattern. Communication is both verbal and nonverbal, and in families, is governed by *rules*. Rules generally evolve over time and usually are not made at a conscious level. An example of a simple rule and how it evolved follows.

A three-year-old asks her mother, "Are you mad at me, Mommy?" The mother replies, "No. I'm mad, but I'm not mad at you" or "Yes." Mother becomes curious, especially if her answer was "No," as to why her daughter chose that particular time to ask. So the next time she answered "No," the mother said to her daughter, "What did I do that made you ask me if I was mad at you?" The daughter replied, "You called me Christine." "That's your name," the mother pointed out. Her daughter replied that she was usually called Christy or Sissy, and when she was called Christine she thought her mother was mad at her.

Christine had developed a family communication rule based on her experience. However, she had overgeneralized the rule. She had also developed one of the most important skills in family communication—"checking it out." People of all ages need that skill, and it is one that can save a lot of pain.

Rules determine what one is allowed to talk about, how it can be talked about, and to whom it can be talked about. When you talk to families and run into a blank wall, it may be that you have violated a family communication rule. Usually you find out about the rule only when it is broken or when it is questioned. Sometimes you never know about it.

Families have rules about *what* can be talked about. All families have subjects that are taboo; for some it is death, for others sex, drugs, or the family "skeletons." Some families do not talk about disabilities. Teachers need to know what families do not talk about.

Families also have rules about *how* subjects can be talked about. The issue of how one talks about things is another aspect of communication. This "how" issue includes information on the time (after the children have gone to bed) and place to talk (in the kitchen) and what language is acceptable. Again, an example for clarification:

When Shana was about three years old, her thirteen-year-old brother babysat her one Saturday afternoon. Things appeared to have gone well when the parents returned, although the brother had a friend visiting during the time. Monday morning as Shana was waiting for the car pool, she said, "Matthew isn't here, damn it." Her mother said "What?" She repeated, "Matthew isn't here, damn it." "Where did you learn that?" her mother asked. Shana's response was, "My brother." A family rule about "how" you can talk had just been broken. The rule evidently was that children could not swear in front of their mother. Shana had unwittingly broken that rule.

To whom can it be talked about is significant: "Don't tell Grandma; she'd have a heart attack." The question is, who within a family is privileged to what information? Some rules are age-related and some are dependent upon specific personal characteristics. Sometimes these rules do not change even though circumstances change, and important information may not be passed on because of a past set of practices.

For example, some families will not talk to a child who has a terminal illness about death. That decision may have been made when the child was at the beginning stages of a terminal disease. However, communication rules are difficult to change, and if this decision is not re-evaluated when death becomes inevitable, the family is less of a support system to the child.

Determining family rules is a particularly difficult task as couples join, especially for blended families. Both partners have established, usually unconsciously, rules to live by in their respective households. When these rules are very different, adjustment is difficult. Because the rules usually are not stated, children experience tremendous confusion in trying to sort out the working set of rules, especially if they don't have the skill of "checking it out."

Families, particularly blended families, may use one person as a "switchboard" because of rules about who can be talked to, about what. The assumption is that the person who is the "switchboard" will convey the information to others.

In addition to looking at which subsystems interact, one can also attend to how they interact. The levels of cohesion and adaptability in a family describe how the subsystems interact.

Circumplex Model of Family Systems. In an attempt to more clearly define and measure family systems, Olson, Portner, and Levee (1985) developed and continue to update measures for evaluating the cohesion and adaptability of families. The Family Adaptability and Cohesion Evaluation Scale (FACES III) is now in its third revision. This model is concerned with overall family functioning, or *how* people interact.

Cohesion. Cohesion as defined by Olson, Portner, and Levee (1985) has to do with the emotional bonding family members have with one another; that is, how they handle distance and closeness and the degree of autonomy a person has in the system. When looking at the dimension of cohesion, questions are asked about emotional bonding, how much independence family members have, how decisions are made within the family, the amount of time families spend together, whether family members share interests or hobbies, and so on.

Families that are extremely high on cohesion are often referred to as enmeshed; that is, the bonds are so close that there is little individual autonomy, and family goals and needs are put before individual goals and needs. These families are characterized by over-involvement and overprotection. The other extreme of cohesion is called "disengaged." Disengaged families have high autonomy and individuality but experience very little closeness and are not high on family solidarity. In such a family a child with a disability might feel lonely and isolated. The family may be underinvolved in the child's education. A family unable to accept a child's disability is often characterized as disengaged.

Most families fall somewhere between enmeshment and disengagement, with healthy families with young children being closer to enmeshment and moving more toward disengagement as adolescence approaches. Early intervention professionals need to be aware of the cohesive aspect of families so they do not contribute to the enmeshment of the mother and the child at the expense of other family members, or as adolescence approaches.

Adaptability. Adaptability refers to the ability of the family system to change or modify its power structure, role relationships, and rules in response to differing situations (Olson, McCubbin, Barnes, Larsen, Muxen, & Wilson, 1983). All families differ in their ability to handle change and stability, and most systems need periods of both change and stability in order to function.

Families that demonstrate little control and structure may be viewed as chaotic. These families have few rules, and even these change frequently and are rarely enforced. It may not be clear who is part of the family and who is not, and there may be no one in charge. Family members come and go apparently at will with little notice or planning. These families are unpredictable and sometimes stressful; they have little opportunity to develop relationships and common meaning. Family members cannot count on each other nor do they plan together for the future of family members. Chaotic families frequently have trouble complying with complicated care routines for children with disabilities and may miss appointments.

At the other extreme are rigid families with a high degree of control and structure. They tend to repress change and growth. Little happens that is spontaneous. Roles are rigidly, and often traditionally, defined. The power hierarchy is clear, and there is little room for negotiation. Rules are handed down and enforced. However, rules that are appropriate for a preschooler may still be in place when that child reaches adolescence. In working with families who have children with disabilities, it is important to know who is in charge of the family and to work through that person; otherwise the likelihood of success is low.

Well functioning families function between chaotic and rigid. Knowing the attitudes of family members regarding change (adaptability) can help you pace change for families, especially during transition phases. Adaptability is important in a family's adjustment to a disability, as traditional role responsibilities may have to be changed and family members may have to interact with professionals and agencies they did not know even existed.

Communication is seen as the facilitating dimension in the circumplex model. It both characterizes families and helps them adjust their degree of adaptability or cohesion. Interventionists must have good communication skills also, as well as being able to recognize the communication patterns that characterize different types of families.

Family Functions

To survive, all families must perform certain tasks. These tasks are designed to meet the needs of all family members, and also have the long-range goal of helping young family members become self-sufficient and independent.

Economic Needs. Most families must generate income and pay bills. Children with disabilities may add additional expenses. These expenses can range from lost income because parents cannot work, to special food, extra telephone cost, transportation, and so on. Such expenses are not covered by medical insurance, but are just as real.

Daily Care Needs. All families must perform the daily tasks of living that include cooking, cleaning, laundry, and so on. Children with disabilities may require more care for a longer time. The source of much family stress falls in this area (Beckman-Bell, 1981). The burden of this care impacts parents' psychological, physical and financial well-being (Seligman & Meyerson, 1982).

Recreation Needs. All families need recuperation time; rest and relaxation. Frequently recreation is the family activity most often eliminated under stress. Sometimes families don't meet recreational needs because of lack of finances; at other times because including a child with a disability makes the activity too difficult. It is important to help families find recreational activities they can enjoy as families as well as individually.

Social Needs. Most families find their social life and outside leisure activities affected by having a child with a disability. Yet families need to be part of the larger social system. They need an informal support network of friends and neighbors to provide opportunities for children to develop and practice social skills. Some parents get so involved in the education of their child that they forget the importance of this area. Overall, families with good social support networks make it through crises better than those who lack such a system.

Self-Image Needs. A positive self-image is important for everyone in the family. All family members need to see themselves as having competence and worth. Parents of children with disabilities may have difficulty seeing themselves as competent parents. Siblings may be at risk regarding self-image if the family revolves around the child with a disability. The child with a disability may have problems in this area also.

Affection Needs. Families meet the needs of their members for physical intimacy as well as support and love. A disability may make unconditional love a challenge, and family members may not establish these bonds with children who are terminally ill because of the fear of pain when they are broken. As children grow older the concept of sexuality often becomes confused and confounded with needs for affection.

Educational/Vocational Needs. It should be noted that meeting educational needs is only one of many functions of families. Even though it is probably the one in which your interests overlap with families the most, and where you have the greatest interest, this is not necessarily the most important function to the families. Before making an assumption about this, "check it out" with the family.

Family Life Cycle

Families change over time. Sometimes they change in ways that are predictable (normative change), as when family members grow up and leave the home. Sometimes the changes cannot be predicted, such as an untimely death from an accident.

Family life cycle theorists try to organize and understand the predictable changes in families over time. The family life cycle highlights the different types of responsibilities and concerns families have at different times. Theorists believe in a stage-based theory, but disagree on the number of stages in the life cycle (somewhere between six and twenty-four). Although initially conceptualized as linear, it is clear (with blended families in particular) that families can be in several stages at the same time. Although briefly alluding to seven stages, the following discussion will concentrate on the stages affecting early childhood.

During each stage there are developmental tasks to be completed. A developmental task arises when an individual within a family has needs that converge with societal expectations. For example, one developmental task in the United States is for a child to enter school at about age five. When developmental tasks are not met, stress is produced in the family. Something as simple as a child who is not walking at about a year, or a five-year-old who is not toilet trained are considered "off time" problems and often create stress. Today, the family life cycle emphasizes the three-generational family system as it moves through time.

The Newly Married Couple. A new marriage, whether it is a first or later marriage, involves renegotiating personal issues that have been decided individually. Major issues, such as deciding whether to have children or not, and minor issues, such as putting the cap on the toothpaste, are important. The couple must develop a mutually satisfying relationship. Assuming they decide to have children, they must then make adjustments to pregnancy and the anticipation of parenthood.

The Family with Young Children. This family life cycle stage requires that people add the role of parent to role of adult. They must move up a generation and perform the role of caregiving to the infant and young child. This stage is often stressful as there are few support systems available to help people set intergenerational boundaries (McGoldrick & Carter, 1982).

Transition to Parenthood. All family life cycle transitions, such as marriage or retirement, bring some accompanying stress, and the transition to parenthood is no exception (Belsky & Rovine, 1984). The transition to parenthood is particularly stressful for a variety of reasons, including the abruptness of the transition and the radical changes in lifestyle, including changes in sleep, career, contacts with extended family members, and finances. Some feel the birth of later children requires less change than first-born children (Grossman, Eichler, & Winickoff, 1980). Others feel that each birth brings its own unique stressors. With later-born children, you must cope

Families provide love and support for their members.

with siblings' reactions to the new baby in addition to caring for the siblings themselves.

Becoming parents causes adults to clarify their values. Most parents make decisions about what they will or won't do when the baby comes. The reality of the baby may be different from the expectation. A mother who initially planned to take a six-week leave from work and then place the baby in child care may decide that she doesn't want to do that. Likewise, a mother who quit her job may decide that infants aren't as much fun as she thought, and so she again seeks a job. As with all joint decisions, the partner may not have changed his thinking or may have changed in different areas. This amount of change is stressful in families.

The Premature Infant.   Children who are born prematurely are not what families expect. Parents may move from wondering if the infant will live to wondering what to tell people. They are concerned about the long-term implications for the infant's quality of life. Yet at this early stage there are usually too many unknowns to make accurate predictions. For infants who are critically ill, long hospitalizations and separations from parents cause additional problems. Parents may have other children at home that need care. If the infant requires the Neonatal Intensive Care Unit he may have to be moved to a large metropolitan hospital where there is more technical support. This may or may not be near by.

In addition to anxiety about the obvious problems for the infant, the couple may not have been physically or emotionally prepared for the early birth. Preterm infants often do not respond well. They offer unclear signals (Field, 1982), and families have to work harder or modify their interaction to get a response. Barnard (1981) reported that with preterm infants having these characteristics, parents showed signs of burn-out by the time the child was one year old.

Discovering the Disability.   The extent to which the newborn is divergent from the family's hopes and expectations is stressful. Reactions to having a child with a disability both within and between families are highly individualistic and depend on the severity of the child's handicap, supports available to the family, and the cultural context of the family as well as other factors (Gabel, McDowell, & Cerreto, 1983). Children both affect and are affected by the systems in which they develop. The characteristics of the child and the interaction of these characteristics with parenting styles are particularly important factors.

Parents have a variety of reactions when they are told that their child has a disability. Most professionals see some type of "grief cycle," in which parents move through stages on their way to acceptance of the child. The exact stages, sequences, and time spent in each are individualistic.

Most parents report feeling a sense of shock. They feel emotionally "numb." They may even show physical signs of shock. Shock often turns to denial;

parents may deny the disability or the severity of it. For children who look "normal," this denial is easier. Parents may "shop around" for another opinion that is more optimistic. These reactions may be a way of buying time to adjust. To the extent that reality is acknowledged then, everything must change.

Parents may feel angry at doctors, professionals, and even the child himself. This, too, is part of the grieving cycle. Some feel a kind of mourning, feeling sad about the child they had expected but didn't get; in reality, mourning the death of the normal child. Featherstone (1980) compares the death of a child and the birth of a child with a disability:

The most important difference between mourning a death and mourning a disability is that the child in question is not dead at all. . . . While death provides a moment's respite from ordinary demands, disability generates new tasks and necessities (Featherstone, 1980, p. 234).

Chronic sorrow may continue off and on throughout the child's life. The cyclical process becomes especially strong at normal transition times such as birthdays, school entry, and at traditional times when families join for reunions. Seeing how easy it is for other children to do certain things and how difficult it is for their child to do the same thing can bring back the tears or the anger. Even explaining the child's disability may activate the cycle for some parents. Rather than endure this, the family may reduce its social life and withdraw from all but medical associations with the community.

Parents may feel that the child's disability was their fault. The mother may think she has done something she shouldn't have. She didn't drink enough milk, get enough sleep, gained too much or too little weight. She thought angry thoughts or she and her husband had a fight. If parents think long enough there is always something they might have done to cause the disability, at least in their own minds. In some cases it is a genetic or biological reality, but not necessarily one they had any control over. It is not, however, useful to get "stuck" in self-blame.

Hope provides strength even when the hope is unrealistic. Sometimes having some degree of unrealistic hope may actually be helpful to the family if it is all they have to go on.

These reactions are normal and are typically seen in parents of children with disabilities. Parents have all these feelings at some time. Some of them are only momentary, others long-lasting.

There is disagreement about whether the goal of families' accepting a disability is realistic. DeLuca and Salerno comment that ". . . families do not accept the child's handicap, nor should this be a goal for them; rather, families adjust to the reality of the handicap in diverse and unique ways" (DeLuca & Salerno, 1984). One parent told me that you never reach "acceptance." You love your child, but you never quite accept the disability.

The timing of the grief cycle is an important variable. Parents go through the stages in the cycle individually and in their own time frame. Often the person who spends the most time with the child reaches a level of acceptance before others. It adds to family stress when one parent wants to make adaptations to accommodate the child's disability and the other parent is in a stage of denial and refuses to allow the adaptations. Most families eventually reach some degree of adaptation.

Rather than reaching and remaining at a level of acceptance, it appears that families re-experience these reactions across the family life cycle as a continuing, evolving reaction to the chronic stresses of caring for a family member with a disability (Olshansky, 1962; Wikler, 1981).

Later Discovery of the Disability. For children whose disability is not identified at birth, a diagnosis usually is made during early childhood. For the family, the process of identification is different. The family believes they have a normally developing healthy baby. Often one parent thinks something is wrong, but is not sure. There is a sense of foreboding that is sometimes worse than knowing for sure that the child has a specific disability, particularly when that parent shares her concern with her spouse or friends and they find her concerns ridiculous. Mothers are typically the first to sense some difficulties, if these weren't picked up by the physician at birth. Physicians may attribute mothers' concerns to lack of experience or being overanxious. Getting confirmation is often a long process. Mothers often have concerns for months or even years before they are confirmed medically. Sometimes learning that the child really does have a disability is a relief. For example, parents may be relieved to find their child has a learning disability when their greatest fear was mental retardation.

Although for some families having a child with a disability seems overwhelming, to others it is a challenge they look forward to meeting. Regardless of the outlook, it is important to consider the positive elements associated with disabilities, as well as the fact that child rearing has its strong and weak points whether or not the child has a disability. Many families report that having a child with a disability in their family increased family closeness, pride in working together through difficult times, and increased their sensitivity to the needs of others.

In addition to the child's being at risk, the family itself is at a crucial stage in the family life cycle. This is the "pressure cooker" phase of the family life cycle when a majority of divorces take place. Many of these are initiated by women (McGoldrick & Carter, 1982). The decision to get a divorce is a complicated one with many interrelated factors. The role that a child with a disability plays is not clear. One can make some assumptions based on the reasons typically given by men and women for divorcing. Men typically give sexual incompatibility and in-law problems as reasons, while women are more likely to complain of physical as well as verbal abuse, financial problems, drinking, neglect of home and children, and lack of love (Kitson & Sussman, 1982).

It is not difficult to see how a child with a disability could exacerbate these problems. However, there is conflicting evidence about the role of children with disabilities and divorce. An older study (Love, 1973) found divorce rates for parents of children with mental retardation to be three times as high as parents of children without mental retardation, and the suicide rate twice as high. Desertion rate by fathers was also above the national average. A later, better controlled study (Wikler, Haack, & Intagliata, 1984), did not find the divorce rate of parents of children with developmental disabilities to be significantly higher than the national level for divorce in general. However, the divorce rate generally had increased significantly at this time.

Some, but not all, families, experience marital strain (Gabel, McDowell, & Cerreto, 1983). The primary caregiver may form a very strong bond with the child, leaving considerably less time and attention for the spousal relationship. At the very least, most families find their social life and outside leisure activities affected by the birth of a child with a disability. Families may require tremendous creativity to continue as before.

The Family with School-Age Children. Some parents of children with disabilities have already encountered the public school system, others have not. In any case, families need to develop skills to communicate with the educational community to add to the skills they have in relation to the medical community and early intervention. In addition they often must find ways to get these two communities to communicate with each other.

All children, including those with disabilities, are now expected to attend schools, primarily public ones. The transition to school may be a major event. Teachers expect children to learn. If children are not making expected progress, teachers expect parents to help the children more. If parents are unable or unwilling to do this they may be labeled as uncooperative (Combrinck-Graham & Higley, 1984).

If you are teaching children at a transition time for families remember that the parents may re-enter the denial-acceptance cycle. They may initially appear to you as parents who do not acknowledge their child's disability. Most of them do know. They simply need time to work through their feelings and adjust to what the child's disability means in a new set of circumstances. They need some time to adjust to the demands of this new stage.

The Family with Adolescents. All families with adolescents must evaluate and establish qualitatively different boundaries than they used when children were younger. Children need freedom with guidance (McGoldrick & Carter, 1982). A stressful time is even more complex when families have children with disabilities who are adolescents. Adolescents want to be like their peers, thus parental authority is often challenged. Adolescents are less likely to stick to regimes that make them appear to be different.

In families where children require physical care such as lifting in and out of bed or the bath, the size and weight gain in adolescence is an added problem. Likewise, children whose behavior is not under control become more of a threat to families, as the potential damage to others is far greater now than in early childhood.

There are also the added complexities of sexuality at this time. Biologically most people with disabilities mature sexually at about the same time as their peers. A variety of concerns surrounds the issue of sexuality. For some it focuses around the genetic transmission of disabilities, for others, concerns about victimization.

Families Launching Young Adults. Young adults with disabilities may not be able to leave home. Families have to consider seriously plans to care for their child. They realize their caregiver role may be permanent. However, the current move to community living arrangements for disabled young adults is changing this reality.

Middle-Aged Parents. With families having fewer children, closer together, many parents can now plan on almost twenty years together without children at home before retirement. The goal of independence may be difficult for parents to attain if they have an adult-child with a disability. The responsibilities of caregiving may appear overwhelming at this stage, as, in addition to caring for an adult-child with a disability they may be responsible for their own parents as well. As a society we have far less experience in caregiving for adults than we do for children. Springer and Brubaker (1984) note, "No preparation is given to people for the kinds of stresses and duties they must deal with in the caregiving role" (p. 18).

The Family in Later Life. Adjusting to retirement is the major task of this stage in the life cycle. It is also a time when couples must cope with the loss of friends, relatives, spouse, and perhaps a child. They themselves may become dependent upon others for care.

Before concluding this discussion of families it is important to highlight two areas that were not adequately covered in the above presentation: grandparents and the effects of divorce.

Grandparents

For many families, grandparents play an important role. They frequently provide support for their children in a variety of ways; babysitting their grandchildren being a popular one. The birth of a grandchild with a disability is an emotionally draining experience for the grandparents. "The same

Grandparents play an important role.

event that creates the need for emotional support in parents also wounds grandparents and renders them less able to supply it" (Gabel & Kotsch, 1981, p. 32). Even when extended family are willing to help, the care of the child may be very complex and grandparents are less able to help without a lot of training.

Divorce, Single-Parenting, and Remarriage

At its current rate (about 55 percent), divorce has become more a norm than an exception to the norm. For many, divorce is the first in a series of changes from a two-parent family to a one-parent family and for many, with the remarriage rate, again a two-parent family. One result of the high divorce rate is an increase in the number of single-parent families. Approximately 90 percent of all children who live with a single parent live with their mothers. The proportion of children with disabilities living with their mothers may be even greater (Wikler, Haack, & Intagliata, 1984).

The needs of these mothers appear to be different both from two-parent families and single mothers of nondisabled children. ". . . single mothers with retarded children listed respite child care as their greatest need. They ranked financial needs second, and personal/social needs third" (Wikler, 1981). Single mothers of nondisabled children listed their priorities in the reverse order. Wikler (1981) found single mothers with children with disabilities to be socially isolated, with neither strong formal or informal support networks. Not surprisingly, children of single parents show up disproportionately in institutions (Wikler, Haack, & Intagliata, 1984).

Being a single parent for many is a transitional phase between marriages, with 60 percent of remarriages involving children. Although extensive data is not available, it appears that mothers of children with disabilities are less likely to remarry (Wikler, Haack, & Intagliata, 1984). It would appear that these children and families may need different types of service delivery system.

Summary

The unit of intervention has changed from the child to the family. This change requires teachers to be cognizant not only of individual cycles of growth and development, but also the family life cycle. The family is viewed as a system with the same rules that govern all systems. To interact with families effectively one has to acknowledge these rules. Having a child with a disability is a different experience for different families and can be expected to have different kinds of outcomes.

References and Bibliography

Barnard, D. E. (1981). An ecological approach to parent-child relations. In C. C. Brown (Ed.), *Infants at risk: Assessment and intervention. An update for health-care professionals and parents* (pp. 89–96). Skillman, NJ: Johnson & Johnson.

Bateson, G. (1972). *Steps to an ecology of mind.* New York: Ballantine Books.

Beckman-Bell, P. (1981). Child-related stress in families of handicapped children. *Topics in Early Childhood Special Education, 1,* 45–54.

Belsky, J., & Rovine, M. (1984). Social-network contact, family support, and the transition to parenthood. *Journal of Marriage and the Family, 46,* 455–462.

Brooks-Gunn, J., & Lewis, M. (1982). Affective exchanges between normal and handicapped infants and their mothers. In T. Field & A. Fogel (Eds.), *Emotion and early interaction* (pp. 161–188). Hillsdale, NJ: Erlbaum.

Carter, E., & McGoldrick, M. (Eds.). (1980). *The family life cycle: A framework for family therapy.* New York: Gardner Press.

Combrinck-Graham, L. (1985). A developmental model for family systems. *Family Process, 24,* 139–150.

Combrinck-Graham, L., & Higley, L. (1984). Working with families of school-aged handicapped children. In E. Coppersmith (Ed.), *Families with handicapped members* (pp. 18–28). Rockville, MD: Aspen.

Deiner, P. L. (1987). Systems of care for disabled children and family members: New paradigms and alternatives. In M. Ferrari & M. Sussman (Eds.). *Childhood disability and family systems* (pp. 193–211). New York: Haworth Press.

DeLuca, K., & Salerno, S. (1984). *Helping professionals connect with families with handicapped children.* Springfield, IL: Charles C. Thomas.

Duvall, E. (1977). *Marriage and family development* (5th ed.), Philadelphia: Lippincott.

Duvall, E., & Miller, S. (1985). *Marriage and family development.* New York: Harper & Row.

Entwisle, D. R., & Doering, S. G. (1981). *The first birth: A family turning point.* Baltimore: The Johns Hopkins University Press.

Featherstone, H. (1980). *A difference in the family: Life with a disabled child.* New York: Basic Books.

Filler, J. (1983). Service models for handicapped infants. In S. G. Garwood & R. Fewell (Eds.), *Educating handicapped infants: Issues in development and intervention.* (pp. 369–386). Rockville, MD: Aspen.

Field, T. (1982). Affective displays of high-risk infants during early interactions. In T. Field & A. Fogel (Eds.), *Emotion and early interaction* (pp. 101–125). Hillsdale, NJ: Erlbaum.

Gabel, H., & Kotsch, L. (1981). Extended families and young handicapped children. *Topics in Early Childhood Special Education, 1* (3), 29–38.

Gabel, H., McDowell, J., & Cerreto, M. C. (1983). Family adaptation to the handicapped infant. In S. G. Garwood & R. R. Fewell (Eds.), *Educating handicapped infants: Issues in development and intervention* (pp. 457–494). Rockville, MD: Aspen.

Gartner, A., Lipsky, D. K., & Turnbull, A. P. (1990). *Supporting families with a child with a disability: An international outlook.* Baltimore: Paul H. Brookes.

Grossman, F. K., Eichler, L. S., & Winickoff, S. A. (1980). *Pregnancy, birth, and parenthood.* Washington, DC: Jossey-Bass.

Jackson, D. (1967). The individual and the larger contexts. *Family Process, 6,* 139–147.

Karpel, M., & Strauss, E. (1983). *Family evaluation.* New York: Gardner Press.

Kitson, G., & Sussman, M. (1982). Marital complaints, demographic characteristics, and symptoms of mental distress in divorce. *Journal of Marriage and the Family, 44,* 87–101.

Love, H. (1973). *The mentally retarded child and his family.* Springfield, IL: Charles C. Thomas.

McGoldrick, M., & Carter, E. (1982). The family life cycle. In F. Walsh (Ed.), *Normal family processes* (pp. 167–195). New York: Guilford.

Minuchin, S. (1974). *Families and family therapy.* Cambridge, MA: Harvard University Press.

Olshansky, S. (1962). Chronic sorrow: A response to having a mentally retarded child. *Social Casework, 43,* 190–193.

Olson, D., Portner, J., & Levee, Y. (1985). *FACES III.* St. Paul, MN: Family Social Science, University of Minnesota.

Olson, D., McCubbin, H., Barnes, H., Larsen, S., Muxen, M., & Wilson, M. (1983). *Families: What makes them work.* Beverly Hills, CA: Sage.

Ramey, C., Trohanis, P., & Hostler, S. (1982). An introduction. In C. Ramey & P. Trohanis (Eds.), *Finding and educating high-risk and handicapped infants* (pp. 1–18). Baltimore, MD: University Park Press.

Reschly, D. (1988). Minority MR over representation and special education reform. *Exceptional Children, 54,* 316–323.

Roberts, J. (1984). Families with infants and young children who have special needs. In E. Coppersmith (Ed.), *Families with handicapped members* (pp. 1–17). Rockville, MD: Aspen.

Sandler, A., Coren, A., & Thurman, S. (1983). A training program for parents of handicapped preschool children: Effects upon mother, father, and child. *Exceptional Children, 49,* 355–358.

Schell, G. (1981). The young handicapped child: A family perspective. *Topics in Early Childhood Special Education, 1,* 21–27.

Seligman, M., & Meyerson, R. (1982). Group approaches for parents of exceptional children. In M. Seligman (Ed.), *Group psychotherapy and counseling with special populations* (pp. 99–116). Baltimore: University Park Press.

Springer, D., & Brubaker, T. (1984). *Family caregivers and dependent elderly: Minimizing stress and maximizing independence.* Beverly Hills, CA: Sage.

Turnbull, A.P., Summers, J. A., & Brotherson, M. J. (1984). *Working with families with disabled members: A family systems approach.* Lawrence: University of Kansas, Kansas University Affiliated Facility.

Turnbull, A. P., & Turnbull, H. R. (1990). *Families, professionals and exceptionality: A special partnership* (2nd ed.). Columbus, OH: Merrill Publishing Company.

Watzlawick, P., Beavin, J., & Jackson, D. (1967). *Pragmatics of human communication: A study of interactional patterns, pathologies, and paradoxes.* New York: W. W. Norton & Company.

Wikler, L. (1981). Chronic stresses of families of mentally retarded children. *Family Relations, 30,* 281–288.

Wikler, L., Haack, J., & Intagliata, J. (1984). Bearing the burden alone? Helping divorced mothers of children with developmental disabilities. In E. Coppersmith (Ed.), *Families with handicapped members* (pp. 42–62). Rockville, MD: Aspen.

Chapter 20

An Ecological View of the At-Risk Family

Looking at the child as an individual without considering the child's family has not been useful. Likewise, looking at all families as if they were the same leads to fallible decision making. To plan appropriately for children we need to view the child within the context of the family and the family within the broader context of the environment in which he lives. Risks to children and families are complex, cumulative, interactive, and compounding. Children face varying challenges and risks for development because of their biological makeup and because of the environment in which they live.

One must start with the child himself as a biological organism, then look at the child's immediate social environment (usually the family), and then look farther outward at the systems that affect the child and family. Without looking at the interplay and interactions of these levels of the system one cannot appraise risk. An ecological perspective helps organize this information.

This chapter uses an ecological systems framework to organize the complexity of biological, psychological, social, cultural, and economic information to better understand families and children with disabilities as well as those "at risk" for developmental disabilities.

The use of the concept "at risk" is currently much discussed in the literature. "At risk" does not mean that something is inevitable, but rather that the probabilities are high. It is much like having chicken pox break out in a school. The outbreak does not mean that all the children in that school will get chicken pox, but rather that more children in that school are likely to get chicken pox than are children in another school who have not been exposed to chicken pox.

Ecological Systems

Ecology is the study of relationships between organisms and environments. This chapter specifically concerns the relationship of children with disabilities to their family, their neighborhood, their schools, and the social/legal system. (For further information about the ecological systems theory itself see Bronfenbrenner, 1979, 1986.)

Microsystems

A microsystem is the smallest unit of the ecological system. It is the immediate setting in which individuals develop. Children typically develop in family settings. The quality of the setting or family is dependent upon "its ability to sustain and enhance development, and to provide a context that is emotionally validating and developmentally challenging" (Garbarino, 1990, p. 81).

The microsystem is continually changing, so it is not useful to look at single events, but rather at the pattern of events over time. What patterns of behavior characterize a microsystem? Do the patterns reflect warmth, love, and support, or stress, abuse, and neglect, or some less clear-cut pattern? Are the patterns similar for all family members?

Mesosystems

Mesosystems are the relationships between the microsystems in which the individual acts and reacts. These relationships, too, form a system. This system is often referred to as a support network. Having a strong support network can ameliorate some of the more challenging aspects of having a child with a disability. Conversely, not having a support network can increase the perceived burden. Typically support networks are evaluated by the number of linkages within the system, whether or not the people in different microsystems know each other, and how helpful the network is.

The mesosystem might include a child-care setting for some children. The system gets stronger if the parents of the children in the child-care setting know and interact with each other. For a child with a disability an early intervention setting might also be included. The network would be stronger if those in the setting see each other regularly in other settings. If the child provides the only linkage between systems, the network is less strong.

Because the relationship between the child's school and the child's home is central to this book, the relationship between how parents view children and how teachers view them is explored in some depth.

Parents' Views and Teachers' Views. Parents and teachers view children from different perspectives. Because of the opposition of some of these views it is important that you be aware of them, and consider how your view might bias your perceptions of parents' priorities. When parents and teachers see behavior very differently it is not necessarily because they disagree on the behavior per se, but rather because they approach the situation from different orientations. In order to work together effectively, it is important that each is aware of the other's perspective.

Parent goals are universal. They are the same in all cultures and across diverse groups within the same culture. Parents are concerned about the physical health and survival of their child. They are also concerned that their child, over time, will develop the skills and capacity for being increasingly more independent. They are concerned that these necessary self-help skills, decision-making strategies, social, and cognitive skills are developing in a timely manner. Additionally, parents want children to learn about their culture and develop a system of values that will help guide them in decision making.

Teachers' goals vary considerably depending upon the age of the child, the type of program the child is enrolled in, and the philosophy of both the teacher and the program. Initially, most teachers are concerned about children's separating from their parents, joining the group, and observing some ground rules and routines set up for all children.

Parents are concerned about the whole child, and tend to evaluate feedback based on its impact on the child's total development rather than on just one aspect of development. They may evaluate as irrelevant a particular aspect of behavior such as an inability to pick up a pea using finger-thumb apposition.

Families are part of school celebrations.

Teachers tend to focus on a specific aspect of behavior or development about which they are concerned. For example, teachers may be concerned with a child's unwillingness to use messy sensory materials, such as water or finger paint.

Parents typically focus on broad, long-range goals that they have for their child, such as learning to talk or becoming more independent. Teachers tend to concentrate more on short-range goals that can be accomplished and even documented, such as learning color names.

Parents view education at all ages from a very personalized perspective and focus on how it affects their child and how their child is progressing. Teachers are concerned about all the children in the group. They may discuss relationships between children and how a child relates to the group.

Parents often have convictions about how their children should be raised or taught, and these feelings may be based on how they were taught or not taught, but the feelings are rarely strongly influenced by particular theories about how children learn and develop.

Teachers often have strong opinions about how children should be taught. These are sometimes based on requirements set up by licensing agencies and other regulations that govern education and early intervention. Additionally, educational programming is often based on a particular theory about how children learn. These developmental or educational theories are important for the teacher who is guiding the program.

It is not unusual, then, to discover that what parents and teachers want for children is different. Teachers need to think through these differences before approaching parents.

Exosystems

Exosystems, in this context, are settings that influence the development of children, but in which children play no direct part. School boards who set school policy are an example. The parents' workplace is another. The exosystem directly affects children by the policies that are set and indirectly affects children through their parents. For example, a school district might close its special schools and include children with disabilities in neighborhood schools. The parents' workplace usually sets policies regarding parenting leaves, sick child care, family transfers, and so on. Likewise, the parents' salaries and, importantly, the level of medical and dental benefits provided, have a tremendous impact on their children. These policies can increase risk or they can decrease it.

Macrosystems

Macrosystems are the broad ideological and cultural patterns within which mesosystems and exosystems operate. In the United States the change in practice from the separation of children with disabilities to

their inclusion has had a profound effect upon all the other systems.

Some see ecosystems as a series of ever-widening concentric circles going from the microsystem to the mesosystem to the exosystem, with the largest circle being the macrosystem. Using an ecological framework helps us understand the range of situations affecting children. It also clarifies our thinking about the levels and types of intervention that have the greatest probability of succeeding.

Microsystems at Risk

Child Risk

Children who are categorized as "at risk" have no identified disability at the time of categorization. They are, however, in a situation that is conducive for developing disabilities or patterns of behavior that make learning more difficult. For example, a child with serious otitis media, an infection of the middle ear, may experience a temporary hearing loss. If this happens once or twice, there is little risk to the child. If this is a chronic condition, then the child is at risk. He may not trust his hearing and may not develop good listening skills. If the child has tubes placed in his ears as a medical intervention, and his educational program isolates and teaches auditory skills, that child will probably have few, if any, long-term effects even from a chronic condition.

However, if there is no intervention, recurring bouts of otitis media have a two-fold effect. Pressure from the infection can cause the tympanic membrane to rupture repeatedly and possibly leave scars which permanently impede hearing. Additionally, the child is likely to have had fluid in his ears for several days which, even without infection, can cause a hearing loss. The young child with little basis for comparison does not mention that he has a hearing loss. As the child experiences more time with the hearing loss, he becomes less dependent upon that sense and, literally, quits listening. Thus, without treatment, the child with chronic otitis media is at risk for a mild to moderate hearing loss and perhaps a learning disability most likely classified as an auditory processing problem. However, with appropriate medical and educational intervention it is likely that the child will suffer no long-term effects from this condition.

Biological risks may be associated with one or more of several possible conditions. The child may be dependent on complex medical technology. (For example, an infant might be on an apnea monitor.) The infant might have had an illness or trauma that is associated with developmental delays. He might have been shaken. He might have been exposed to drugs in utero. He might have been in the Neonatal Intensive Care Unit. He might have been born to a chronically ill mother with conditions (maternal diabetes, anemia, and malnutrition) that are associated with delays. Infants weighing 1,000 to 1,500 grams are at risk and those weighing 1,501 to 2,000 grams who are born with complications are also considered at risk. There are socioeconomic factors such as poverty that can affect developmental progress and put children at risk.

Children who live in older houses with lead-based paint are at risk. Childhood lead poisoning is one of the most common pediatric health problems in the United States today. It is preventable. Lead poisoning, for the most part, is silent; children rarely show obvious symptoms. Universal screening is recommended because, without screening, a majority of the cases go undiagnosed and untreated. A current report states: "Lead poisoning is widespread. . . . No socioeconomic group, geographic area, or racial or ethnic population is spared" (Centers for Disease Control, 1991, p. 1).

Death from lead poisoning is now rare. However, it does contribute to mental retardation and reduced mental functioning. It is expected to take at least twenty years to remove this threat society-wide (Centers for Disease Control, 1991).

Family Risk

In addition to biological and socioeconomic factors which may put children at risk, families can also be a risk factor. The family has the potential for increasing or decreasing child risk both in and of itself as well as in interaction with other risk factors. Families that have a history of abuse or neglect or of violence in the home put children in a risk category medically, psychologically, and educationally. Children with disabilities are particularly vulnerable to abuse and neglect. In Florida, low birth weight babies represent 7.7 percent of all births but 20 percent of abused children (The Task Force for Prevention of Developmental Handicaps, 1991).

Few educational programs target preventable injuries, a leading cause of disability and death in infants and young children. Preventable injuries account for almost half of all deaths in young children (The Task Force for Prevention of Developmental Handicaps, 1991). Preventable injuries include such things as automobile accidents, drowning, gunshots, choking, child abuse, burns, lead and other poisoning, and falls. Prevention in this area needs to be a part of all educational programming.

By law, teachers and child-care workers are required to report suspected cases of child abuse and neglect. You, as an early childhood education teacher, are a most important link in the detection and prevention of child abuse and neglect. It is imperative that you know the warning signs that may indicate that a child has been abused or neglected and the steps to follow for reporting cases.

The causes of child abuse are complex. Often parents who were themselves abused, neglected, or abandoned may continue this cycle with their children. It is difficult to determine the exact contribution of a disability to abuse and neglect. Research studies have found that between 8 and 55 percent of

abused children have disabilities (Frodi, 1981). Further, it is not possible to determine if a developmental delay is the cause or the result of abuse. Additional information about child abuse and neglect appears in Chapter 16, Children with Emotional/Behavioral Disorders.

Early, unprotected sexual activity has the obvious risk of pregnancy but also of producing an infant with a disability. Teen mothers who have not completed high school put their children at risk. This risk is compounded if they do not seek prenatal care in the first trimester. Births to unwed mothers are also in the risk category. Risk is compounded if these mothers drop out of school and/or have additional children.

For a variety of reasons it is difficult to identify women at risk of transmitting sexually transmitted diseases. Poverty, multiple sex partners, and drug abuse contribute to this problem. Congenital AIDS is the fastest growing birth defect in the United States. A report from Florida affirms that "Most children born to HIV-infected mothers will test positive for HIV for maternal antibodies for up to 18 months. About one-third of these children will contract the disease. . . . Approximately 80–90 percent of all children with HIV infection will experience significant developmental delays" (The Task Force for Prevention of Developmental Disabilities, 1991, p. 38).

Children with HIV need unique programming, yet they generally will receive no intervention until they experience delays and can hence be categorized. Confidentiality with HIV is a very difficult problem. Decisions are probably best made on a case-by-case basis rather than by legislation.

Some children are at risk because of the life style of the mother. Smoking, poor nutrition, and the use of drugs and/or alcohol put infants at risk. Women who use drugs fear they will be treated as criminals if they seek help. This does not promote prenatal care, nor does it increase their likelihood of getting into treatment. Rather, it increases the probability that they will deliver their infant at home to avoid detection. Infants who are exposed to drugs in utero may appear normal, but they are often irritable, overstimulated, and difficult to console. Additionally, risk signs may be delayed. An infant born to a mother addicted to cocaine, for example, may not show the signs of sudden interpersonal violence until some time after birth.

When mothers remain addicted they often ignore their infant's needs and are overwhelmed by them. The inability to stop a child from crying is the reason most cited for child abuse (Governor's Drug Policy Task Force, 1990).

A mother who drinks alcohol during pregnancy puts her infant at risk for either Fetal Alcohol Syndrome (FAS) or Fetal Alcohol Effects (FAE). Fetal Alcohol Syndrome occurs in about 2 of every 1,000 live births. FAS is a leading cause of mental retardation in the United States today. The less severe response, Fetal Alcohol Effects, occurs three times as often as

FAS. Smoking by pregnant women increases the risk of having a low birth weight infant.

Pregnant women who are over forty or under seventeen, as well as those with little or no prenatal care, are at risk for bearing a child with disabilities. Women who have had multiple miscarriages or pregnancies close together are also in this category.

There are additional family stressors that place children at risk. These include such diverse circumstances as parents who have separated or divorced, those with a recent death in the family, families who have moved twice in the past year, and those who have a family member who is mentally retarded, seriously ill, or incapacitated.

Parents who have low educational attainment, those who are poor, and those who are medically underserved are at risk. Parents who themselves were abused, neglected, or abandoned as children are a concern. Parents who use drugs or have been exposed to excessive radiation or industrial pollutants are at risk.

Additionally, those who have had a family member under eighteen who has been pregnant in the last three years, or a family member who has been the victim of a serious crime in the past year also have risk factors. Young children who are often left unsupervised are also at risk (The Task Force for Prevention of Developmental Handicaps, 1991).

Children who are normal at birth can grow up under conditions that cause them to be at risk. One of the most encompassing harmful environmental conditions is poverty. A demographics study states that "Preschool children are America's poorest age group" (Edmunds, Martinson, & Goldberg, 1990, p. 4). Families with young children are the poorest families in the United States. As early childhood experiences form the foundation for future medical and educational experience, this poverty has a crucial impact. Who are these poor preschool children? Statistically, they are most likely children of color, living in inner cities, and having single mothers. The cycle of poverty is associated with poor maternal nutrition, low birth weight in babies, and increased substance abuse by pregnant women. These are all potential causes of disabilities (Minority Issues in Special Education, 1987).

Children raised in extreme poverty are at risk for developmental delays. The causes are complicated, but include poor cognitive/language stimulation, poor nutrition, exposure to safety hazards, and poor health care. The poor quality of the environment itself does not directly lead to disabling conditions. It is the related factors associated with the poor environment that many times lead to disabling conditions. Statistically, "Twenty-five percent of people with developmental disabilities live in families which exist below the poverty level" (Massachusetts Developmental Disabilities Council, 1990, p. 46). Additionally, "child poverty and adverse health outcomes are disproportionately found among non-white populations" (Massachusetts Developmental Disabilities Council, 1990, p. 48). The following table highlights this concern.

Substandard housing and crowded conditions increase the probability of infection, which may be compounded by poor nutrition and lack of medical treatment so that conditions that respond easily to medication at an early stage may become serious or chronic. Families who are forced to spend their resources and energy on mere survival often do not have additional time or energy to encourage their children to develop language and other cognitive skills. Under circumstances such as these children are more likely to ingest poisons, to experience emotional trauma, and to sustain accidents.

PERCENT OF CHILDREN WHO ARE POOR (1988)

Age of Child	Total	White	Black	Hispanic
Younger than 3	23.3	17.3	50.4	43.6
Younger than 18	19.2	14.1	43.5	37.6

U.S. Census Bureau. October 1989. (In Edmunds, Martinson, & Goldberg, 1990, p. 3).

Increasingly there are large numbers of "couch people," people who live with others because they do not have a home of their own. These people and their children are at risk of becoming homeless, reduced to living in shelters or in cars on the street. Homeless or migrant families are at risk, as well as families that live in shelters or in situations where children have been placed in foster care. These families are living on the edge of society and struggling to survive. They have difficulty securing the basic necessities of life and rarely have enough energy left over to provide early stimulation for a child with a disability.

At-risk conditions are not mutually exclusive, in fact, they often appear in combination, and this interaction or additive quality increases the probability of creating a developmental disability. In addition, the interactive quality confounds early diagnosis and makes specific appropriate intervention more difficult. It is difficult to determine if a child with poor language skills is suffering from a conductive hearing loss due to serious otitis media, whether he is distrustful of adults because of his past experience with them and chooses not to talk, whether he has received so little language stimulation that he does not have an adequate vocabulary, or whether he lacks the expectation that language is a useful tool for getting what one needs.

Even assuming one can isolate the problem as a chronic ear infection, the child who does not receive medical treatment, who has experienced physical abuse, and is living below the poverty line is far more likely to have delays. A child with the same ear condition who grows up in a family that has and uses its resources for medical treatment of this condition has a different experience. If they send the child to a nursery school where he can interact with other children and develop good auditory skills, he makes additional gains. If the parents have a record player or tape recorder at home and use it, or if they carry on interesting and stimulating conversations with the child and expect he will be an active participant, the expected outcome is quite different from that of the neglected child living in poverty. For this latter child solutions to the medical problems may not be sufficient to remediate and overcome the negative factors. Even if the child's hearing condition is reversed, to develop language and listening skills he needs to hear people talk and use words in a meaningful way.

Although you do not have the ability to prevent or cure all at-risk conditions, you, more than other professionals, see the child at an early age, on a continuing basis. With appropriate planning and caring you can make a long-term difference in a child's life. Parent education is an integral part of all good early childhood programs. You have the opportunity to not only support good practices, but to teach parents alternative nonpunitive methods of child rearing. However, often the parents you most want to reach do not come to meetings.

Cultural Diversity

The analogy of the United States as a "melting pot" has been replaced by that of a "salad bowl." The growth of ethnolinguistically diverse groups has increased to the point that the term *minority* is no longer accurate (Hanson, Lynch, & Wayman, 1990). This is particularly true for families and children at risk for disabilities. Hanson, Lynch, and Wayman present some interesting information about the changing demographics of the American population. The overall percentage of children in the United States is decreasing; however, the proportion of children from culturally diverse populations is increasing. They state: "In the years between 1985 and 2030, the total number of ethnolinguistically diverse children will have increased by 53 percent, and the proportion of children in those groups compared to all children will have risen from 28 percent to 41 percent" (Hanson, Lynch, & Wayman, 1990, p. 115). The causes are increased immigration, higher birth rates, and earlier ages of child bearing in these populations. It is also likely that this population will have a greater proportion of children "at risk," as these figures interact with environmental risk factors, particularly poverty and its concomitant lack of early medical support.

It is likely that these families will not have a great deal of experience interacting with professionals when intervention begins for their child with a disability. Also, because of the age of the child, many of these programs will be home-based or have an element of the program that involves programming in the home, making cultural differences more relevant.

It is important to know the family's view of child rearing and their expectations, both personally and culturally, for children of various ages. For example, to set up programming that promotes independent functioning and adaptive skills with a family that values dependency is almost sure to fail. You also need to know how the family views having a child with a disability. Some families see it as fate, viewing themselves as being chosen for their strengths or being punished for previous sins. The family can view itself as responsible for the situation, resulting in a sense of shame and stigma (Seligman & Darling, 1989).

A family's cultural belief system influences whether or not they will seek intervention services for the child and to whom they would go for this intervention. For some, extended family members or a folk healer would be chosen over a medical doctor.

Appropriate intervention requires gathering information. When the person gathering the information and those giving it are not proficient in the same language, the process can be very difficult. Even when information is translated there can be confusion, especially if there is conflict between the verbal and nonverbal messages. To be ethnically competent teachers must learn four tasks:

First, they must clarify their own values and assumptions. Second, they must gather and analyze ethnographic information regarding the cultural community within which each family resides. Third, they must determine the degree to which the family operates transculturally; and finally, they must examine each family's orientation to specific child-rearing issues (Hanson, Lynch, & Wayman, 1990, p. 126).

Exosystem Risk

Decisions about service delivery systems and families come together at the exosystem level. In general (in the United States), the highest risks are the medically underserved populations such as rural residents, migrant workers, and families who are poor but ineligible for Medicaid. (Some physicians will not take Medicaid patients because of reimbursement problems.)

Risk can be prevented or minimized by having family planning services, quality prenatal care, and education available. The availability of child health care and early intervention services, including routine screening for early detection of conditions not identified at birth, reduces risk.

Macrosystem Risk

Decisions at the macrosystem level (state and national) affect a vast number of people and have broad-reaching effects. It is at this level that laws are made. However, if money is not allocated to implement or enforce those laws, they are meaningless. At this point (1992) the United States does not have an effective national policy to support families nor is there an adequate system of health care and insurance.

As there are budget cuts and money is reallocated, children with disabilities may lose services or be placed on waiting lists. Less money may be allocated for prevention. Without family supports in place, children who could be cared for in the home will have to be placed in more expensive residential programs. This particular policy at the macro level is easy to evaluate in terms of families and children with disabilities. Some public policies that are general in nature, such as the minimum wage, also have profound effects on people with disabilities.

In 1979 the minimum wage was high enough for a family of three with one wage earner to live above the poverty line. In 1991 the minimum wage was raised to $4.25 an hour, which puts families of three with one wage earner at 80 percent of the poverty level (Children's Defense Fund, 1991).

Summary

The educational system is not expected to solve the problem of children and families at risk, but educational solutions can contribute to strengthening families. The expectation is that teachers will be knowledgeable about the larger context within which children and families grow and develop and will temper their expectation with realism, as well as working toward new and innovative solutions to problems. Systems at all levels need to interact to support families and their children.

References and Bibliography

Centers for Disease Control. (1991). *Preventing lead poisoning in young children*. Washington, DC: U.S. Department of Health and Human Services.

Children's Defense Fund. (1991). *The state of America's children*. Washington, DC: Children's Defense Fund.

Edmunds, P., Martinson, S., & Goldberg, P. (1990). Changing demographics. In *Demographics and cultural diversity in the 1990's: Implications for services to young children with special needs, 1–5*. National Early Childhood Technical Assistance System: PACER Center.

Frodi, A. (1981). Contribution of infant characteristics to child abuse. *American Journal on Mental Deficiency, 85*, 341–349.

Hanson, M., Lynch, E., & Wayman, K. (1990). Honoring the cultural diversity of families when gathering data. *Topics in Early Childhood Special Education, 10*, (1), 112–131.

Massachusetts Developmental Disabilities Council. (1990). *A challenge for the 90's: Creating open communities*. Boston, MA: Developmental Disabilities Planning Council.

Minority issues in special education: A portrait of the future (Special issue). (1987). *News Digest,* No. 9. Washington, DC: National Information Center for Handicapped Children and Youth.

Seligman, M., & Darling, R. (1989). *Ordinary families, special children: A systems approach to childhood disability*. New York: The Guilford Press.

The Task Force for Prevention of Developmental Handicaps—1991 Update. *Florida's children: Their future is in our hands. Preventing and minimizing disabilities: A focus on the first 60 months of life*. Tallahassee, FL: Developmental Disabilities Planning Council.

Chapter 21

Family Assessment and Family Differences

The assessment of families is relatively new to many professionals in early childhood special education. As programs strive to meet the mandates of the law, more information is needed on the identification of family strengths and needs and the role of family goals in the Individualized Family Service Plan (IFSP).

Theories about the family life cycle, viewing the family as a system, and looking at the impact of a child with a disability on the family have all increased our understanding about the family unit. These theories are also influencing how we work with families. Families are partners in the educational process. Families have rights that are in many cases now dictated by law.

This change in focus has made it necessary for teachers in early childhood special education to have knowledge about families and how they work, as well as being familiar with family assessment tools, including family needs assessments. These measures are designed to help families focus on what is important to them and identify areas in which they would like additional information or help.

The role of the early childhood special educator in family assessment is evolving and varies among programs. In some programs, the early childhood special educator would have the lead role with the family and be expected to conduct interviews and family assessments. She would be the "service coordinator." She would then be responsible for reporting information back to the team and, with the family, write the IFSP. In other programs another professional would be the "service coordinator" and she would be a team member. Early childhood special educators need the skills for both roles. They need skills in interviewing families and using family assessments; they also need to interpret the results of these interviews and assessments. This chapter is designed to help the educator perform these roles.

Family Assessment

Family assessment must play an integral role in service delivery to young children with disabilities and their families or it has no place in the system. If knowledge gained will not be used, there is no point in gathering the data. In assessing children and families certain principles must be considered. These principles are underlined.

- Families have varying reactions to the assessment process. While most are willing to participate, some do not see the relevance of family assessment to services for their child. The purposes and usefulness of measures for families need to be made clear and *the process itself must be, over all, respectful and useful to families.*

- If the system is to be responsive, *families must be listened to and their input valued.* There is variability in the usefulness of assessment measures in generating family goals for the IFSP. If the IFSP is to be developed from assessed family needs tools not contributing to the self-assessment of family needs should not be included in the process (Deal, Dunst, & Trivette, 1989; McGonigel & Garland, 1988). Assessment tools can be viewed as a menu of choices. Only those items that are necessary and appropriate for a particular family should be chosen from a menu of formal and informal measures.

- *Family assessment appropriately follows child assessment.* Families of children who are not eligible for programming would not be included in the assessment process.

- *The process of identifying family needs may be a goal in and of itself,* rather than simply being a process leading towards a goal. For many families identifying needs is a very new process offering great potential for them to learn about themselves. Initial family IFSP goals might be thought of as a "process IFSP" that focuses on *how* the family will go about selecting goals rather than the goals themselves. This may avoid determining goals too early in the process that are later found to be inconsistent with family needs (Whitehead, Deiner, & Toccafondi, 1990).

- Professionals administering family assessment tools generally have had training in Early Childhood and/or Special Education. This training often includes only minimal emphasis on the family and family assessment. While skilled, experienced professionals find informal assessment to be the most effective mode of data collection, most of these same professionals gained this expertise in informal assessment by first having experience with the administration of formal family assessment measures. *It is important that new professionals are trained and understand the purpose and usefulness of the measures.*

Select family assessment measures that are sensitive to family values and changing family needs.

- We are less skillful at measuring family strengths than needs. However, the importance of utilizing family strengths in meeting needs is obvious (Deal, Dunst, & Trivette, 1989). *Assessment of family strengths should be part of the evaluation process.*

- *Families need to be informed of the results of the assessment.* A structured, if informal, system of feedback to families, which is responsive to their needs and desires, is essential.

Identifying Family Strengths and Needs

Bailey and Simeonsson suggest five domains that are important in the process of family assessment. These include: (1) child needs and characteristics, (2) parent-child interaction, (3) family needs, (4) critical events, and (5) family strengths (Bailey & Simeonsson, 1988, p. 10). While P.L. 99-457 requires only a statement of family strengths and needs, it may be useful to look at additional domains in some cases.

Selecting Family Assessment Measures

The philosophy and scope of your program will determine the appropriateness of various family assessment measures. The questions all programs need to ask are: "Why are we assessing families?" Is it solely to develop the IFSP? Are you thinking of starting a fathers' or siblings' group? Is the school's policy on inclusion being expanded? The answer to these questions will help determine the instruments that are used. (A list of some of the measures with a brief description of each is included at the end of this chapter.)

As you think about selecting a family assessment measure consider the following issues:

1. Does the instrument provide useful information to the family as well as the program?

2. Does the instrument identify strengths as well as needs? Can parents prioritize these needs?

3. Is the content sensitive to cultural differences?

4. Is the content sensitive to changing family needs and priorities?

5. Is the reading level of the instrument appropriate for the family?

6. How long will it take the family to complete the instrument?

7. Who will interpret the results and bring that information back to the parents?

8. Is the information necessary for program planning?

9. Is the instrument itself technically sound? That is, does it have known reliability and validity that is available?

Knowledge about the available measures can be gained by reading published review articles (Forman & Hagan, 1983; Mott et al., 1986; Bailey et al., 1986), or by reviewing the measures themselves.

In reality, most family assessments are a combination of formal and informal measures, including observations and interviews. An initial family visit might begin with a general interview to determine overall family strengths and needs. That interview might be followed at a later visit with formal or informal measures addressing areas of expressed family need. These needs can relate only to the family's ability to optimize the development of their child or be more broadly based. The goal is to tailor assessments to the family and planned intervention (Bailey, 1987; Johnson, McGonigel, & Kaufmann, 1989).

Informal Assessment

As adults we do not expect to be "tested" and usually feel that we have the right to raise our children as we choose. We are not necessarily happy to have a sometimes younger, perhaps single, person come and "assess" us. This may not be how it seems to you, but it frequently is a parent's perception. For this reason, informal assessments often are useful, especially as you are building rapport with families. What is important is that you must focus on what you want to know.

The Family-Focused Interview

An interview may be the only way to obtain necessary information. To discover the family's perception of what they want it is necessary to ask. Given the complexity of family life today, standard forms may not cover a particular family's situation, that is, the "fill in the blank" form may not have had a blank to state that Dad's sister Rosy lives with the family. This is important information which can be generated from an interview.

An interview is more than just sitting down for a chat with a family. There are two essential elements: establishing rapport and gathering information. Winton (1988) describes five specific phases in the focused interview process. The **preliminary phase** is a planning one and happens before the interview. Any assessment data that has been gathered needs to be organized and evaluated for discrepancies or areas that need further clarification. Interviewers often go in with a list of items about which they want further information. During the **introductory phase** of the interview information about the purpose of the interview, and its format and structure, are clarified with the family and their permission is requested. It is useful to clarify the time frame as well. It is important that the interview be scheduled at a time that is convenient for the family. This is the time to establish rapport and a sense of trust.

The **inventory phase** is the needs assessment itself. Listening skills are important. The role of the interventionist is to be sure that all relevant topics are covered. Although the major role is one of listening so that it is clear that these are the family's goals, families may have had little experience in this area and may need some guidance. It may be useful to make some suggestions to families based on what you know about the field in general and this family in particular. You might say, "Some families want all the information they can get about cerebral palsy. Others decide that they would rather learn just a little at a time." Depending on what they say you might inquire about how they want to acquire that information: "Some families like to go to the library and take out books on cerebral palsy. Others would rather talk to the parents of a child who has cerebral palsy. Some find watching a videotape the most useful way. And some want to do all those things." Note that the interviewer doesn't show a preference or even follow up with a "What do you want to do?" The family may not be ready to decide yet. Listing options lets them learn what is available.

The fourth phase is the **summary, priority,** and **goal-setting phase**. This stage is characterized by the interviewer's summarizing what has happened and framing the needs into goals that are attainable. The beginning of this phase involves the interviewer's asking the family for clarification on what the needs really are, then talking about which ones are the most important. These priorities then need to be translated into goals (see Chapter 6). The final phase is **closure**. The interviewer expresses appreciation to the family for its time and effort. This is the time to clarify times for future meetings and so on. It is important in your planning to allocate time for this phase. Additional important information may be brought up as parents themselves pull information together. For example, a family who had decided not to discuss the terminal illness of a child with her brother and sister may ask, "Do you think it is important that we talk to Shana and Mica about their sister?" They are not purposefully detaining you; it just took time for the implications of what had been said to be focused. Their question is important and one that needs to be answered. An appropriate response might be, "I want to support you in giving Shana and Mica information, if that is what you decide to do. Let's think more about it and the different ways that are available for conveying this information."

If the interview was difficult, a **follow-up** phone call may help. Families may have shared very personal information with you and begin to wonder if this was a good decision (Winton, 1988). A brief phone call can offer them the reassurance they need.

In family assessments it is important that all family members have some input; otherwise, we are simply assessing the parents. Siblings play an important role in the family and how it functions. There are few formal measures that assess siblings, yet their involvement is important both for their own well-being and that of their sibling who has a disability. If possible, always speak with both parents. The particular and unique needs of fathers is missed if mothers are the ones filling out the forms. Sometimes the differences in perception of husbands and wives is the most interesting aspect of the assessment process.

Siblings

Until recently we have focused our interest on children with disabilities and their parents, particularly the mother. As we have broadened our interest to include fathers and siblings, we have discovered that some siblings may be at psychological risk (DeLuca & Solerno, 1984). Children with disabilities often require a greater amount of time, supervision, and attention than other children. Parents may need to spend time driving back and forth to doctor and therapy appointments, participating in early intervention programs, and working with the child at home. While all of this is good and very necessary, it is also important to consider the needs of any brothers or sisters in the family.

Seligman and Darling have noted that "sibling relationships are usually the longest and most enduring of family relationships" (1989, p. 111). Experiences of siblings of children with disabilities show that they have many of the same feelings about the child with a disability that parents do. Brothers and sisters may be very proud of each accomplishment their sibling makes. Or, they may wonder why this has happened to them, and be sad or angry about it. There may be times when they are embarrassed by their sibling.

They may feel jealous of the extra attention he receives and yet, at the same time, feel guilty for having those feelings. All of these feelings are normal and expected. While there will continue to be times when they are frustrated with their brother or sister (as children are with *any* brother or sister!), most children will reach acceptance and feel love for a sibling with a disability.

It is likely that you will find some of the following needs expressed by siblings or by parents about siblings:

Brothers and sisters of children with disabilities need information. They want to know what's going on. Parents, in an effort to "protect" them, often don't tell them very much. Limited or poor information adds to their confusion. If the child wears a hearing aid, for example, siblings need to know what it is for, how it works, and what it does and does not do to aid hearing.

They need specific information about whether the disability is transmittable, how to talk to their friends about it, how to relate effectively to their sibling, and what family expectations are for the role of the sibling with a disability in the future.

Despite what siblings are told, many have a private version of why their sibling has a disability and may feel that in some way they are the cause of it (Seligman & Darling, 1989). It is important that someone learn about this private version and help siblings gain more accurate information about the cause of disabilities.

While brothers and sisters are often involved in the care of their sibling, overburdening the child with responsibility can result in anger and resentment rather than acceptance. All children in a family need time to develop friendships with other children close in age outside the family. Children also need time with parents which is for them alone. If there are two parents in the family, *each* parent needs to spend some time alone with each child. For the most part, siblings don't expect the situation to be "fixed"; they do, however, need a safe time and place to express their feelings and still be accepted. A child's sense of obligation for a disabled sibling can be a major concern and may require professional counseling.

Siblings may need specific support in developing their own identity. They may need the opportunity to talk with other siblings of children with disabilities. If one is available, they may want to join a support group. Parents often think that siblings are coping much better than the siblings see themselves coping (Wallinga, Paquio, & Skeen, 1987). It is important that parents are aware of possible differences in perception about how well siblings are coping. It also means that if you want to find out how siblings are coping you need to ask them, not their parents.

Fathers

Because much past research focused on the child herself or the mother and child, we know less about

Siblings, especially older ones, are often involved in the care and entertainment of their younger sibs.

fathers and their role in families with children with disabilities. Even today, if we give a family an assessment form to fill out, it is usually the mother who does this. Mothers are frequently the spokesperson for the family. In these situations valuable information is lost, and we don't truly have an individualized *family* service plan.

Fathers play an extremely important part in their child's development. This is equally true for fathers of children with disabilities. (While I refer to fathers, most of the information is true for any male caregiver in the home.) Because of work schedules and other factors, traditionally fathers usually do not get to spend as much time with their child as mothers or other caregivers. Some men were taught directly or indirectly that caring for and nurturing children was not part of their job and was somehow "unmanly." While many fathers are overcoming this stereotype and taking a more active role in parenting, traditional attitudes about male roles still prevent some fathers from being as involved as they might otherwise be.

Fathers and mothers respond differently to being told their child has a disability. Usually fathers are less emotional and focus on long-term concerns, whereas mothers are more emotional and are involved with more immediate concerns about child care (Seligman & Darling, 1989). Males are also less likely to participate in formal or informal support groups because they are often composed totally of women, they may be held during the day when the father can't attend, or because sharing feelings is uncomfortable. This leaves fathers out of one of the most common support systems available to mothers of young children with disabilities.

Fathers play and interact with young children in different ways than mothers do. Mothers tend to spend more time in routine caregiving behaviors while fathers tend to play more often in physical ways. Some fathers see their role as discretionary, that is, the child requires the care of the mother but the play of the father is an extra. The father's attitude can set the tone of acceptance or withdrawal for the entire family. However, when fathers withdraw (either psychologically or physically), the system is affected and mothers must assume additional duties.

Some areas have developed fathers' groups in an effort to support fathers in their need for information and emotional support (Vadasy, et al., 1986). The groups have proved to be helpful not only for the fathers, but for the entire family. A handbook has been developed that details how to start such a group (Meyer et al., 1985).

Cultural Diversity in Families

Families' views are influenced by their cultural background. Different cultural groups have very different views about the meaning of a disability, appropriate child rearing practices, and their feelings toward medicine and health care (Hanson, Lynch, & Wayman, 1990). Because of the increased attention to families, it is important that early interventionists and teachers recognize and respect the diversity of views that families express.

The following brief sketches provide some information on the concerns that will be most relevant to your teaching. The resources and bibliographies at the ends of chapters can help you locate additional information.

African-Americans

African-Americans are currently the largest distinct cultural group in the United States; they number about thirty million or about 12 percent of the population according to the 1990 census data (Bureau of the Census, 1991). Much of the research on black families has focused on socioeconomic issues. African-American families are more similar to than different from white families of the same social class. However, a disproportionate number of blacks live below the poverty line. Because so many black families are poor the incidence of poverty-related disability (poor nutrition and poor prenatal care resulting in low birth weight) is disproportionately high. African-American children constitute 45 percent of those enrolled in classes for the educable mentally retarded (Moore, 1981).

To gain a perspective on African-Americans today it is important for you to study their history and how it has contributed to their culture. Although black families are primarily nuclear families, they have a much stronger social support network than whites. The significance of such a support system is extremely important to families with children with disabilities. African-Americans at all social levels have more significant others than whites (Manns, 1981). Relatives form a significant part of this support network. The relative importance of religion in family life at all social levels is another difference between African-American and white populations. The religious community can provide a social life for the African-American family as well as giving emotional support and help in caring for a child with a disability (Manns, 1981).

Within nuclear families the typical pattern appears to be egalitarian relationships where roles are flexible and tasks are often interchanged. Parents, males in particular, seem to be more authoritarian than in white families and encourage independence and responsibility earlier (Seligman & Darling, 1989). For children with disabilities who cannot live up to this expectation this might provide added stress.

African-American women may have relatively more power than in other cultures, but the female dominance often portrayed is rarely true, except for single-parent families with a female head of household. Education is valued for upward mobility. Most women work either out of necessity or out of desire to enhance family income. About half of the children between three and five years of age are in preschools or day-care centers (*Statistical Abstracts of the United States,* 1980).

Although most teachers are aware of economic and cultural differences between African-American and white children, to date the most prevalent way of educating African-American children is to assume they are white children who "happen to be painted black" (Wilson, 1978). We have done little to enhance the children's understanding of their culture. African-Americans are now asking for separate facilities and for some of their differences as well as their similarities to be acknowledged and encouraged. Because the tests that are used to determine learning ability and achievement are standardized on white populations, we don't know how black children learn best. Perhaps because of fear of discriminating, we have been so afraid to teach these children differently that we have not reached them. Remember, when you teach them, these children have individual strengths and needs.

Examine your teaching materials. Do you have stories about African-American children and representative dolls available in the doll area? When you discuss families, include families that have others living with them, single-parent families, and those with working mothers. Emphasize role flexibility in the family. Learn about the African-American culture and incorporate this knowledge in your teaching. If children use black dialect, show you value it as a valid method of communication while you also encourage children to use standard English at school. Stress the situational aspect of language usage.

Hispanics

Hispanics constitute the second largest ethnic minority in the United States. The Hispanic population in the United States is increasing rapidly and may soon be the largest minority. There are approximately twenty-two million Hispanics (about 9 percent of the population) in the United States today (U.S. Bureau of the Census, 1991). Most are American citizens; some are not, but are legal residents; some are here illegally. Although diverse, a majority of this population comes from Mexico and Puerto Rico, with about 20 percent coming from other countries in Latin America.

The overall Hispanic population is young and primarily urban. Mexican-Americans, however, are concentrated in the southwestern part of the United States. Like African-American families, they too are overrepresented in families in poverty, and their children are disproportionately placed in classes for children who are educationally mentally retarded. (Bias in assessment instruments may be contributing to this, as well as language differences.)

Schools and medical settings may be intimidating to Hispanic parents. Hospitals may be thought of as places where people go to die. Visiting rules which are time-bound and exclude some family members may make families feel even more alienated. If a language barrier is added to these conditions the situation becomes almost lethal.

The extended family plays an important role in Mexican-American families. Siblings, cousins, and other relatives provide a support network that is helpful to families with children with disabilities. Their overall attitude toward children is one of acceptance, and they put less pressure on children to achieve milestones early. This attitude may make it easier to cope with a child who is developmentally delayed. However, concern with socialization and showing respectful well-mannered behavior may be difficult at later ages.

Depending upon their degree of identification with the traditional culture, some Hispanics may see disease and disability as punishment for wrongdoing. A diagnosis or permission for testing may not be signed when it is initially proffered, as the mother may want to go home and talk with the entire family about the advisability and implications of testing or treatment.

Because of family values, it is not likely that you will have many very young Hispanic children in preschool programs. Mothers are generally expected to stay home and raise children. When this is not possible, the extended family frequently takes over the care of the young children. Some families may see sending children to school before kindergarten as a sign of deteriorating family values. Within the family itself there may be more stringent role requirements. The father is the head of the household; he earns the money. The mother traditionally raises the children. The children are respectful and obedient to adults.

Communicating with Hispanic families may be a challenge. Spanish may or may not be the only language spoken in the home. Children may come to school with good language skills in both Spanish and English or with only rudimentary knowledge of English or Spanish.

Families who choose to send their children to preschool need your support. Help them see preschool as an alternative to extended family care. They should not be made to feel that you judge them or that they are not fulfilling their roles as parents. If the parents speak little or no English, it is important to have bilingual/bicultural support for parent-teacher conferences and to translate forms that are to be sent home. If possible, use the parents as a resource to learn about the culture and enrich the class curriculum. Learn about traditional holidays and how they are celebrated. Help children develop their skills in both languages by labeling objects and teaching songs and fingerplays in both languages.

Asian-Americans

Today there are over seven million Asian-Americans (about 3 percent of the population, Bureau of the Census, 1991). This number is increasing with new immigrants, primarily from Japan, China, the Philippines, Vietnam, and Korea. Although all Asian subcultures have some similarities, the differences are important as well. Overall, Asian-Americans value family very highly and tend to solve problems initially within private family settings. Family needs often have precedence over individual needs. Family ties are close. As a culture they avoid open confrontation, therefore they are unlikely to challenge professionals even when they may disagree. Communication is often indirect.

Asian-American families place a high value on education. The parents generally show teachers respect and expect their children to do the same. As you are an authority figure, children are expected to obey and not question what you say. It is important to teach these children the skill of asking questions of adults without questioning the authority that adults have. As these children are very family oriented they may need to learn skills for getting along with peers. Stress the value of cooperation and helping others rather than one child's winning and others' losing. Talk about the differences between feelings and how these feelings can be expressed. Children will need your help in learning to express themselves in ways that do not conflict with family values. As you work this out, consult with the parents for their ideas. In addition, the parents are a resource for expanding your knowledge of the Asian culture. Encourage children to use and develop their native language in addition to English.

In order to facilitate learning and to be more relevant, materials and programming need to take the child's culture into account. Be aware, however, of the differences among Asian cultures. Japanese and Chinese people have both similar and different values. Even among members of one group, there is great variation. Learn about the particular families that you will interact with. Then decide which generalizations apply and which do not.

Typically, the Asian family is very structured with clear roles and authority. The father is the head of the family. Children are expected to be obedient and respectful to their parents, specifically, and to anyone older than they are, generally. Family interactions may be verbally limited and involve few direct confrontations. The family is seen as a harmonious group and anything, such as strong emotions, that might disrupt this harmony is expected to be suppressed. Children are expected to conform. In order to develop these values in children, parents may teach children that disobedience brings ridicule on the child and shame on the family (Kitano, 1980). Traditional cultural values of patience and persistence are handed down as well. Family dependency is valued over independent achievement and cooperation over competition. Many of these children are bilingual.

Native Americans

It is strange to think that the people native to America could be considered culturally distinct and need specially tailored educational programs, but this is nonetheless true. There are about two million Native

Americans in the United States, less than 1 percent of the population (Bureau of the Census, 1991). About half of them live on reservations and the other half dwell mostly in urban areas (Thompson, 1978). It is important to know the characteristics of the particular tribe the family belongs to, as there is much intertribal variation. There is always danger in overgeneralization. Overall, Native Americans stress cooperation over competition and harmony with nature as opposed to trying to control nature. They are adult centered as opposed to child centered, and their time orientation is present instead of future.

Education for Native American children has often been run by the federal Bureau of Indian Affairs. Traditionally, the schools have been boarding schools, located far from the children's homes, with white teachers. The focus of this education was to "de-Indianize" the Native Americans. It hasn't worked. Native Americans have in many instances not wanted to have their children included, but instead have wanted to foster close ties with the tribe. They want to improve the quality of education for their children by changing the standard curriculum to be more responsive to another view of American history.

Some feel that one reason the drop-out rate for Native American children is 50 percent higher than for the rest of the population (Beuf, 1977) is because of the biased view that teachers and textbooks present. For example, many Native Americans view Thanksgiving as a day of mourning, not one of cooperation, celebration, and feasting. Look at the ways in which you celebrate holidays and try some nontraditional approaches.

Other children's ideas of Native Americans may be influenced by traditional "Cowboy and Indian" movies. Replace these ideas with more realistic ones and have children do more than make Indian headbands and give war whoops. Giving an in-depth view of Native Americans will help other children increase their knowledge and decrease their prejudices.

Of all cultures, we tend to misrepresent this one to the detriment of the people. Consider the following quotation:

. . . I come to get my older son at his day care. I am very tired. It is one day after another of many pre-Thanksgiving hooplas. My son is in the back, reading, not participating in the class art project. I look over at it, and tears sting my eyes. The children are creating masks of "Indian" faces. I look at my son, brown, beautiful, and alone, and I want to protect him from the whole racist world and the destruction of our values, of our People. On the way home, we talk about it briefly. I lay my hand on his shoulder, and then let it go.

The next day, I pick up my younger son at his school, and see another "art" project—paper plates with "Indian" braids and faces. I feel overwhelmed at what my children have to endure. I speak to the teacher, who stares at me blankly, uncomprehending. "I didn't mean to offend

anyone." she says, and besides, the pictures are not of Indians, but of "Native Americans." I take my son by the hand and walk out. At home I tell him that he does not look like those paper plates. I hold him up to the mirror. I say, "Our people are beautiful" (Gonzales, 1991, pp. a, b).

Summary

Professionals in early childhood special education have a great responsibility to both children and their families. In order to provide appropriate service they need to find out what services families want and need. They need to coordinate these services in a useful fashion and help deliver the services in a way that is respectful of families, including those from diverse cultures. If at all possible professionals should speak the same language as the family. Although interpreters are useful, important information is missed. Language is only one dimension of culture. Resource people from the same culture or subculture often acquire more useful information than other professionals. Professionals need to be supportive of the family's values and work to provide services in an acceptable way. Intervention must be based on the family's definition of the situation, not the professionals'.

References and Bibliography

Abidin, L. (1983). *Parenting stress index.* Charlottesville, VA: Pediatric Psychology Press.

Bailey, D. B. (1987). Collaborative goal-setting with families: Resolving differences in values and priorities for services. *Topics in Early Childhood Special Education, 7*(2), 59–71.

Bailey, D. B. (1988). Assessing family stress and needs. In D. B. Bailey & R. J. Simeonsson (Eds.), *Family assessment in early intervention* p. (pp. 95–118). Columbus, OH: Charles Merrill.

Bailey, D. B., Simeonsson, R. J., Winton, P. J., Huntington, G. S., Comfort, M., Isbell, P., O'Donnell, K. J., & Helm, J. M. (Eds.). (1986). Family-focused intervention: A functional model for planning, implementing, and evaluating individualized family services in early intervention. *Journal of the Division for Early Childhood, 10*(2), 156–171.

Beuf, A. (1977). *Red children in white America.* Philadelphia: University of Pennsylvania Press.

Deal, A. G., Dunst, C. J., & Trivette, C. M. (1989). A flexible and functional approach to developing individualized family support plans. *Infants and Young Children, 1*(4), 32–43.

DeLuca, K., & Solerno, S. (1984). *Helping professionals connect with families with handicapped children.* Springfield, IL: Charles C. Thomas.

Dunst, C. J., Jenkins, V., & Trivette, C. M. (1984). The Family Support Scale: Reliability and validity. *Journal of Individual, Family, and Community Wellness, 1* (4), 45–52.

Dunst, C., & Trivette, C. (1986). *Child Expectation Scale: Support and family behaviors.* Chapel Hill, NC: Technical Assistance Development System.

Dunst, C., Trivette, C., & Deal, A. (1988). *Enabling and empowering families: Principles and guidelines for practice.* Cambridge, MA: Brookline Books.

Featherstone, H. (1980). *A difference in the family.* New York: Basic Books.

Forman, B., & Hagan, B. (1983). A comparative review of total family functioning measures. *The American Journal of Family Therapy, 11* (4), 25–40.

Gonzales, R. (1991) Notes from an Indian teacher. In F. Slapin & D. Seale, *Through Indian eyes: The native experience in books for children,* excerpted in *Books to build a new society,* Philadelphia: New Society Publishers.

Johnson, B. H., McGonigel, M. J., & Kaufmann, R. K. (Eds.). (1989). *Guidelines and recommended practices for the individualized family service plan.* Washington, DC: National Early Childhood Technical Assistance System and the Association for the Care of Children's Health.

Lynch, E. W., & Hanson, M. J. (1992). *Developing cross-cultural competence: A guide for working with young children and their families.* Baltimore, MD: Paul H. Brookes.

McGonigel, M. J., & Garland, C. W. (1988). The individualized family service plan and the early intervention team: Team and family issues and recommended practices. *Infants and Young Children, 1* (1), 10–21.

Mott, S., Fewell, R., Lewis, M., Meisels, S., Shonkoff, J., & Simeonsson, R. (1986). Methods for assessing child and family outcomes in early childhood special education programs: Some views from the field. *Topics in Early Childhood Special Education, 6* (2), 1–15.

Meyer, D. J. (1986). Fathers of handicapped children. In R. R. Fewell & P. F. Vadasy (Eds.), *Families of handicapped children: Needs and supports across the life span* (pp. 35–73). Austin, TX: PRO-ED.

Meyer, D., Vadasy, P., & Fewell, R. (1981). *Living with a brother or sister with special needs: A book for sibs.* Seattle, WA: University of Washington Press.

Meyer, D., Vadasy, P., Fewell, R., & Schell, G. (1985). *A handbook for the fathers program.* Seattle, WA: University of Washington Press.

Olson, D. H., McCubbin, H., Barnes, H., Larsen, A., Muxen, M., & Wilson, M. (1985). *Family inventories: Inventories used in a national survey of families across the family life cycle.* St. Paul, MN: Family Social Science, University of Minnesota.

Olson, D. H., Portner, J., & Lavee, Y. (1985). *FACES III.* St. Paul, MN: Family Social Science, University of Minnesota.

Sawin, D. B. (1981). Fathers' interactions with infants. In B. Weissbourd & J. Musick (Eds.), *Infants: Their social environment* (pp. 147–167). Washington, DC: National Association for the Education of Young Children.

Seligman, M., & Darling, R. (1989). *Ordinary families, special children: A systems approach to childhood disability.* New York: Guilford Press.

Simeonsson, R. J., Huntington, G. S., & Short, R. J. (1982). Individual differences and goals: An approach to the evaluation of child progress. *Topics in Early Childhood Special Education, 1* (4), 71–80.

Solnim, M. B. (1991). *Children, culture, and ethnicity: Evaluating and understanding the impact.* New York: Garland Publishing, Inc.

Statistical Abstracts of the United States, 1980. 101st Edition. U. S. Department of Commerce, Bureau of the Census. Washington, DC: U.S. Government Printing Office.

Turnbull, A. P., & Turnbull, H. R. (1985). *Parents speak out: Then and now.* Columbus, OH: Merrill.

Vadasy, P., Fewell, R., Greenberg, M., Desmond, N., & Meyer, D. (1986). Follow-up evaluation of the effects of involvement in the fathers program. *Topics in Early Childhood Education, 6,* 16–31.

Wallinga, C., Paquio, L., & Skeen, P. (1987). When a brother or sister is ill. *Psychology Today, 42,* 43.

Whitehead, L. C., Deiner, P. L., & Toccafondi, S. (1990). Family assessment: Parent and professional evaluation. *Topics in Early Childhood Special Education, 10* (1), 63–77.

Wilson, A. (1980). *The developmental psychology of the black child.* New York: United Brothers Communications Systems.

Winton, P. (1988). The family-focused interview: An assessment measure and goal-setting mechanism. In D. Bailey & R. J. Simeonsson, *Family assessment in early intervention* (pp. 185–205). Columbus, OH: Charles Merrill.

Teaching Resources

National Sibling Network
5112 15th Avenue South
Minneapolis, MN 55417
   The committee of the National Alliance for the Mentally Ill publishes a newsletter that provides information and essays written by siblings. It is called *The Sibling Bond.*

Sibling Information Network
School of Education
Box U-64, Room 227
University of Connecticut
Storrs, CT 06268

The network provides information and publishes a newsletter in which siblings share their feelings.

Siblings for Significant Change
105 East 22nd Street
New York, NY 10010

Has available a videotape, *The other children: Brothers and sisters of the developmentally disabled,* in which a group of siblings express their views about living with a sibling with a disability.

Family Measures

Child Expectation Scale

Dunst, C., & Trivette, C. (1986)
Family, Infant, and Preschool Program
Western Carolina Center
Morgantown, NC 28655

This is an eight-item self-report scale that measures parental perception of the future capabilities of their preschool child in the areas of academic, financial, community, and social independence.

Family Adaptation and Cohesion Evaluation Scales (FACES) III

Olson, D., Portner, J., & Lavee, Y. (1985)
Family Stress and Coping Project
290 McNeal Hall
Department of Family Social Science
University of Minnesota
St. Paul, MN 55108

FACES III is a self-report 20-item scale which measures family adaptability (flexibility) and cohesion (emotional closeness), both as they are and as family members ideally would like them. The difference between the perceived and the ideal provides a measure of family satisfaction.

Early Intervention Research Institute
Utah State University
Provo, UT

A number of family scales and inventories have been developed from this project.

Family Inventory of Life Events and Changes

McCubbin, H., Patterson, J., & Wilson. L. (1983)
Family Stress & Coping Project
290 McNeal Hall
Department of Family Social Science
University of Minnesota
St. Paul, MN 55108

This 71-item self-report questionnaire assesses life events and changes experienced in families. The dimensions include: intra-family strains, marital strains, pregnancy and childbearing strains, finance and business strains, work-family transitions, illness and family "care" strains, losses, transitions "in and out," and legal strains.

Family Needs Survey

Bailey, D., & Simeonsson, R. (1985)
University of North Carolina at Chapel Hill
Frank Porter Graham Child Development Center
Chapel Hill, NC 27514

The survey consists of 35 statements. Family members decide if they need help with a particular topic, do not need help, or are not sure. Needs are assessed in six major categories including needs for information, support, explanation of child's handicapping condition to others, community services, financial help, and family functioning. There is an opportunity for the adults to rank their most important needs.

Family Resource Scale

Leet, H., & Dunst, C.
Family, Infant, and Preschool Program
Western Carolina Center
Morgantown, NC 28655

This thirty-item self-report questionnaire measures the adequacy of resources available in households with young children. Factors include: general resources, time availability, physical resources, and external support.

Family Support Scale

Dunst, C., Trivette, C., & Deal, A. (1988)
Family, Infant, and Preschool Program
Western Carolina Center
Morgantown, NC 28655

One of several instruments that have been developed by this group of researchers. This instrument measures the availability of eighteen possible sources of social support as well as the family's judgment of the helpfulness of each support available.

Impact-on-the-Family Scale

Stein, R., & Riessman, C. (1980)
Department of Pediatrics
Albert Einstein College of Medicine of Yeshiva
   University
Bronx, NY 10461

The instrument assesses the change in family behaviors that may be attributable to having a child with a chronic illness. It measures financial burden, familial social support, personal strain, and mastery.

Impact-on-the-Family Scale Adapted for Families of Children with Handicaps (IFS)

McLinden-Mott, S., & Braeger, T. (1988)
The impact-on-the-family scale: An adaptation for families of children with handicaps. *Journal of the Division for Early Childhood, 12*(3), 217–223.

This is a report on the adaptation of the Impact-on-the-Family scale for children with disabilities. The article does not contain the instrument. (Write to the authors for further information.)

Parent Role Scale

Gallagher, J., Cross, A., & Scharfman, W. (1980)
Carolina Institute for Research in Early Education
    for the Handicapped
Frank Porter Graham Child Development Center
University of North Carolina at Chapel Hill
Chapel Hill, NC 27514

This twenty-item self-report questionnaire describes roles in the family and how labor and responsibility are divided. Scores are for the general family, child care, and total family roles in the areas of current role status, ideal roles, and degree of current satisfaction.

Parenting Stress Index (2nd ed.)

Abidin, R. R. (1983)
Pediatric Psychology Press
2915 Idlewood Drive
Charlottesville, VA 22901

The instrument contains 101 statements divided into child and adult domains. It measures stress related to the child's characteristics and stress related to the parents' functioning. It is designed to measure the amount and sources of stress parents are feeling. It also provides guidelines for levels of stress.

Chapter 22

Techniques for Working with Families

Children with disabilities are children first. In the same way, the families of the children are families first, and families of a child with a disability second. You probably don't need special techniques for working with these families—you will use the techniques that are a part of your repertoire already. However, some additional techniques may be helpful when you encounter new situations, such as asking parents for permission to have their child assessed or when you need to discuss particularly difficult issues. These special techniques, however, are applicable to all families, whether or not they have children with disabilities.

Communication is the process we use to get and give information. It may be nonverbal as well as verbal and involves the social context in which it occurs. Communication is an indicator of interpersonal functioning. If you are going to get and give information, clear communication is essential.

The meaning of words is complex, as the same word can have more than one meaning. The word orange is an obvious example; it can be a fruit or a color. The context typically allows us to distinguish between the two. However, as words get more abstract, clarity is more difficult. I may consider myself to have been a "little" late for our meeting. You may have considered me "very" late. The different meanings of "family," both within and among cultures, can create a problem.

The same word can also have different associations. The word "baby" denotes a young child; however, for some the word brings up a picture of a cuddly, smiling, cooing, healthy infant, for others it depicts a fussy, rigid, crying being who cannot be comforted. Words are abstractions that stand for ideas. They make communication possible but also confound it. Clarity is especially difficult when people from different cultural backgrounds communicate. Non-native Spanish speakers sometimes compound their mistakes by an apology saying, "Lo siento, estoy embarazado." It sounds appropriate, but what the speaker has actually said is, "I'm sorry, I'm pregnant" (Sullivan, 1991).

Parent-Teacher Conferences

When you are programming for a child, you need to seek information from and share information with the child's parents. Parental knowledge can be invaluable. Because parents live with the child, they know the child's likes and dislikes as well as strengths and needs. Parents' cooperation at home is equally valuable. As the child is with you only part of the time, it is important that you and the parents work together to achieve goals.

There are at least three occasions on which you traditionally will have parent-teacher conferences. The first occurs near the beginning of the year. Usually all parents are given an opportunity to schedule an individual conference. Conferences are usually routine. The basic technique used is frequently known as the "sandwich":

1. Talk about the child's positive qualities and how much progress the child is making.

2. State your concerns about the child and give concrete examples.

3. Conclude on a positive note.

The second routine conference occurs about the middle of the year and the final one at the end of the year.

On other occasions you will request a conference with the parents, or they with you, to discuss a particular concern. These conferences are different from the routine ones in that they are problem related and usually have one definite topic. You need to schedule a parent-teacher conference when you notice a consistent change in a child's behavior that interferes with learning, in other words, when a child deviates far enough from the norms of academic and social behavior to come to your attention. This deviation is more than just having a bad day. You need a different, although overlapping, set of techniques for these special conferences.

Techniques for Translating Priorities into Goals

As you work with parents, especially in the process of writing up an Individualized Family Service Plan, you will discover that, in addition to using interviewing techniques necessary to establish trust and obtain information, it is frequently necessary to frame this information in a particular way. This frame makes it more useful to both you and the parents.

Needs or priorities are typically stated in broad and far-reaching terms. These priorities need to be fine-tuned to be attainable goals. The family might have as their top priority that "Jeremy's siblings understand his disability better." Although some might see this as a goal, it is difficult to take steps toward implementing it without further clarification. (We will assume that the siblings are six and ten, and that Jeremy is one year old.) The first thing that must be determined is what the parents mean by "understand." Do they want the children to know more about the disability, more about what Jeremy can and cannot do, or do they want the children to get along better? It is often useful to ask parents such questions as: "In what ways will the siblings be different when they understand Jeremy's disability?" "How will we know when we have accomplished this goal?" Without this level of clarification you might consider a goal accomplished while the parents may think you have not started working toward it.

It would be useful to talk with the siblings to see how they feel about the goal. They may have different insights from their parents about what they do or don't "understand" and what is expected of them.

Once you have established a common meaning of the goal, the next step is to determine *how* to go about implementing the goal. This again requires further clarification. What mode of input is most appropriate? Typically, it takes a variety. You might find a story about a child with a similar disability that the ten-year-old could read, and one that could be read to the six-year-old. If this is not possible, you might consider using an interesting book that provides the opportunity for bringing up the subject naturally. Videotapes may be used in the same way. Siblings might go along on doctor's visits and talk with the doctor or others in the medical profession if this seems feasible. Again, if it is the siblings who are the object of this goal, they should be included in the discussion. (If the ten-year-old hates to read, giving her a book is not a good solution.)

Who is to carry out the program? In this example, I feel strongly that it should be the parents. For you or someone else to do it creates dependency. (Obviously, if the parents found this easy to do it probably wouldn't be a priority problem for them.) Therefore they will need your coaching and your expertise in locating materials. They may even need to role play answering questions that the children might ask. Help them find the words they need. You may need to share with them information about typical responses and concerns of siblings in general. Depending upon your location, you might give them information on sibling support groups or provide them with a telephone number for further information. You might give them the address of a newsletter designed for siblings (see section on additional resources). Your role is to help translate priorities into attainable goals. You will provide resources and support, but not solutions.

Although the following techniques are applicable to all conferences, they are vital in ones where problems are broached.

Gathering and Sharing Information

If someone told you your new car had just been hit in the parking lot and was now on fire, what would you say? "It can't be my car. Are you sure? How can this happen to me?"

Such reactions are not unlike those of parents when they learn something may be wrong with their child. Their first response is a denial: "That can't be true. He'll grow out of it. I'd like another opinion." These responses are normal and natural. They are our way of gaining time to absorb the information and to prepare ourselves to deal with the problem. Such a pattern of parental response has special meaning to you, the teacher. Some parents deny information longer than others. You will have to work differently with parents who deny their child is impaired or potentially impaired than with parents who have accepted the exceptionality. To complicate the situation, each parent may react differently to the information. You need to be very careful not to get in the middle or to appear to be taking sides. You are not a trained psychological counselor. Your goal in working with parents is to get the best possible education for their children, not to help the parents emotionally accept a diagnosis.

No one wants to be the bearer of bad news, but your role in the early diagnosis of children is a crucial one. You need to develop confidence in your ability to determine when a child's needs require special techniques. You then need to convince the parents of the validity of your concerns in such a way that they will seek a formal diagnosis. A delay in detection and programming penalizes a child. Teachers have an awesome responsibility both for obtaining a diagnosis and informing the parents.

When the reality of the problem can no longer be denied, most parents go through a stage where they want more information. If we go back to the car: "How did it happen? Who is going to pay for the repairs? Who did this?" Again, parents ask the same kinds of questions. They are concerned about why and how the child became impaired. They may be especially concerned if they have or plan to have other children. They are also very much concerned about the impact their child's disability will have on their lives and other members of the family. As with any new experience, their first attempts at coping with the situation may go badly. We don't train people to be parents, let alone the parents of children with disabilities.

Once parents accept that their child has a disability, they usually look at this cognitively. The parents seek information about the disability and its long- and short-term effects. They may also actively participate in therapy with their child. This is usually an active phase, where people try to adjust their roles and expectations.

Parents may ask you about special programs, developmental norms, long- and short-term expectations for their child, how he fits in with his peers, and so on.

You don't need to be an expert on each disability, but you do need to be able to get relevant information. Once you've mastered the skill of information getting, you will want to share your techniques with parents. Techniques that are especially useful follow.

Fathers play and interact with their children in different ways than mothers do.

Gathering Information Techniques

Gathering information techniques first requires that you sort out content and process: Where are you going? How are you getting there?

Process words used in conversation are verbs, adjectives, and adverbs.

People experience their world through their senses: you *see* a friend in class; you *hear* someone talking; you can *feel* the texture of the seat; you might have *smelled* and *tasted* a cup of coffee this morning as I did. In addition to information, according to Neurolinguistic Programming (Bandler & Grinder, 1975), these experiences are stored in your brain with these tags on them. In order to access the system most efficiently you need to know how the information was stored. People are rarely conscious of exactly how they store information. However, one can almost always find out by listening to them.

Listening to cues gives you some insight into how someone is either storing or retrieving information. The following words are good indicators of how people are representing information. Use this list both to decide on their representational system and to match it in your conversation.

Representational Cues

Visual	*Auditory*	*Kinesthetic*	*Smell/Taste*
see	hear	feel	bitter
clearly	sound	coolness	salty
image	rustling	brushes	fragrant
colors	listen	catch	pungent
shapes	whispers	warm	smells
watch	scream	touch	stale
picture	shout	handle	fresh
vague	amplify	grasp	taste
bright	tune	soft	sweet
flash	tone	smooth	sour
blue	harmonize	rough	stinks
focus	screech	hard	
perspective	loud	gut	
blurry			

Unspecified

think

know

understand

learn

change

consider

remember

believe

Verbal Cues

Most of us have a preferred way of gathering information (Cameron-Bandler, 1978). For some people, this is visual; for others, auditory; and for some, tactile. In other words, we prefer to receive information through one of our senses rather than others. These preferred modalities are important in communicating with people, especially under stressful conditions, as people will often stay in their preferred modality under stress. If you do not match the modality of the people you are communicating with,

Auditory people may tune you out.

Visual people will not picture what you are discussing.

Tactile people cannot get a feel for what is going on.

To reach people effectively, you need to develop an awareness of their preferred way of communicating and to match yours to theirs. Some complex ways of doing this are quite successful, but they require training. There is a simplified approach that may work for you.

Listen to the parents as they talk and note mentally key words that may give you some indication of which sense they favor in receiving and giving information. Words like *think* and *know* are not useful indicators.

After you have made a guess about the preferred modality, match your choice of words to the parents'.

Visual:

Parent: I can't really *picture* Stan as having a disability.
Teacher: How do you *see* him?

Auditory:

Parent: I just get tired of *listening* to these doctors go on and on.
Teacher: After a while it is difficult to *hear* what they're *saying*.

Tactile:

Parent: I *feel* so out of *touch* with the world right now.
Teacher: It's *hard* to *feel* that way.

By matching the modality that people use and using similar terminology, you make it easier for them to talk to you. Remember, too, that each parent may well have a different preferred modality—good communication is a challenge.

"All the boys in our family talk late."

"Oh, she can do all those things; she's just stubborn."

Such statements in and of themselves may be true, or they may indicate that parents are not yet ready to cope with your information. You can probably get them to agree to further observation and consideration. In the meantime, start programming for the child's needs and schedule another conference!

Embedded Questions. One of the initial goals in a conference is to establish rapport. Once this has been established (with some families this may be a five-minute process, for others it will take several conferences), it is important to gather the information that you need from parents. One effective way of doing this is through embedded questions. The wording carries the impact of a question but is delivered as a statement. Some examples of the questions you might ask as embedded questions versus regular questions follow:

"I wonder what Chunga likes to do at home." versus "What does Chunga do at home?"

"I'm curious how you chose this particular school for Chunga." versus "How did you choose this particular school for Chunga?"

"I'm wondering what Chunga tells you about school." versus "What does Chunga tell you about school?"

The first statement is actually a "soft" question. People answer these questions readily and they flow easily. Note that all of the questions begin with "I" statements. The more obvious questions may seem like an interrogation and parents may respond defensively. Because you ask, they may automatically decide that they are doing something wrong at home. (Their reaction to your asking questions about what happens at home may be to challenge your "need to know.")

Request Specificity. Once parents begin to answer your embedded questions you will discover that they typically do it vaguely and that you will need to ask them to be more specific. In response to the first question:

"I guess Chunga likes to do what all kids like to do at home, you know, play." (That isn't useful information.)

"Tell me more SPECIFICALLY what she likes to play."

"Well, she likes to play with her sister."

"What kinds of games do they play?"

"Well, you know, they play what little kids play."

"Tell me what they like to play best."

"Well, Chunga likes to be the mother and order her sister around." (Now you are beginning to get useful information.)

"What happens then?"

"Well, her sister doesn't like that and so she won't play with Chunga."

"What does Chunga do then?"

"Well, Chunga comes to me crying and says that Min won't play."

"What happens next?"

"Well, I go talk with Min and get her to play."

"How frequently does this happen?"

"Every day."

"Do you do the same thing each time?"

"Yea, I used to try to make her take turns, but after a while it wasn't worth it. You know how Chunga is." (Additional useful information.)

You need to continue asking questions that are more specific until you get information that is useful.

Ask in a Different Way. If you are requesting information from parents that they have been asked frequently one of the things you will discover is that they will answer your question without affect. That is, whatever experience the event had been for them (and typically it was an emotional experience) is not there. It is almost as if there is a tape recorder in their head that turns on and answers. This is typical when you ask parents about when they learned that their child had a disability, or what the doctor said, or even the predictions for long-term outcomes. Parents have been asked these questions so frequently that they don't want to be part of the answer and to protect themselves they turn on the "tape."

It is often necessary for you to know what past experiences mean to parents. To get the affect as well as the information it is often necessary to ask for information in a way the parents have not been asked for it before. This causes them to go back to their feelings as well as the event. (If you don't truly need the information, don't ask.)

Some suggestions for learning about families would include: "How did you tell *your* parents about Taylor?" "How would *you* tell someone their child had (name of disability)?" I find it useful to ask parents what a typical day is like. They initially respond, "Well, I get up." I inquire, "How do you get up?" "Well, the alarm rings, I get up, and then I put on the coffee, I call my husband, I fix breakfast for the children, and then I get them up." Obviously, she is responsible for getting the family up. "Then what happens?" She will continue, but at this point it is useful to create a problem. "What happens if you think one of the children is sick?" Again, you have learned about how this family works.

Overgeneralizations. Sometimes we overgeneralize and use words as if one instance stands for all instances. This is particularly true with relation to the words that relate to questions of who, what, where, and when (Satir, 1967). The solution is to reconnect the image for the family.

Who:

The parent might remark, "*All* doctors are only in it for the money." You could reply, "*Is there a particular doctor* who you think is only in it for money?"

"*None* of the children in the neighborhood play with Ryan." "Is there *one child* in the neighborhood who plays with Ryan?" If the parent responds, "No, *none* of the children will play with him," consider trying, "If *someone* did play with Ryan, what would this child be like?"

Parents sometimes immobilize themselves by overgeneralizations such as these. Based on this view of the world, it is easy to see that Ryan's mother is unlikely to invite any of the neighborhood children in to play. When she can focus on the qualities in children that she is seeking she may discover that play is possible, if not in the neighborhood, maybe with someone from school.

What:

"*Nothing* ever turns out right." "*What* didn't turn out right?"

"*Everything* is a mess." "*What* is a mess?"

The goal is to connect the overgeneralization back to the specific instance that the parent is concerned about.

Where:

"This happens *everywhere.*" "*Where* did this happen before?"

"There is *no place* that will take her." "*Where* would you like her to go?"

"It is not safe *anywhere.*" "*Where* isn't it safe?"

When:

"This *always* happens to me." "*When* did this happen before?"

"Things will *never* be any different." (This one offers a choice). "What will *never* be different?" or "*When* would you like things to be different?"

Calling the Process. A special kind of "I" message is used when you begin to feel uncomfortable with the process that is occurring. It is typically used when you have repeatedly told someone something and they don't seem to get the picture. For example: "I feel that I have said that I am not willing to go to the store with you as clearly as I can, yet you keep asking." Or, "I think you really have a point. We could discuss it tomorrow after I have had some more time to think about it." This process moves the conversation out of the content area and focuses on the process of communicating.

Reinforcement

Reinforcement is more than saying nice things about people and what they do (Satir, 1972). As a technique it can help build good working relationships with parents. When parents who are separating tell you how they have explained this to their children, you respond, "I'm really glad you took the time to tell me how you have discussed the separation with the children. It makes it easier for me to answer the questions that arise in class." Your response does not mean you necessarily agree or disagree with what they have told their children. It means you are glad to know *what* they told them. You are reinforcing the sharing of information.

When you reinforce others, be specific about what it is you are citing. You might have said, "I'm really glad you took the time to tell me *this.*" Spell out what *this* is. You need to specify what the behavior is that you appreciate and want to continue.

If you had to persuade the person to give you information, you may now feel you should be thanked for your perseverance rather than expected to praise the other person! The technique may seem awkward or unnatural at first, but the results—warm, effective working relationships—are worthwhile.

Broken Record

Broken record is a technique of persistence that is especially useful when parents deny something is wrong (Smith, 1975). When paired with reinforcement, it is an effective way of gaining information or compliance. It involves coming back to an issue again and again until it is resolved.

A conversation using the broken record technique is illustrated below.

Teacher: *I have been watching Kenneth, and he seems like one of the youngest children in the class to me, yet he is really one of the oldest. He is often restless during group time, he has problems putting pegs in the pegboard, and he hasn't yet learned his colors and shapes. Have you noticed this at home?*

Parent: *Well, you know he's an only child and hasn't played with other children very much. He's probably just shy.*

(The parents just gave you an easy out that is tempting, but if you are really concerned, you need to keep pressing.)

Teacher: *Although Kenneth was shy at the beginning of the year, now he seems to be quite comfortable in the class. However, he still does not seem to be learning as fast as the other children.*

Parent: *Well, we've read that boys are always slower at things like school and he's "all boy."*

(Again, they have given you a way out. They don't want to hear what you are saying any more than you want to say it. Don't judge them as being unobservant, unconcerned, or negligent, but rather as being normal—persist.)

Teacher: *I agree that boys often have more small motor problems than girls do at this age; however, he has more problems than the other boys his age do as well. I would really like you to come in and observe your son. I am genuinely concerned about him.*

Parent: *You are the best teacher Kenneth has ever had. He likes you, and he likes school for a change. I'm not sure I really want you to change anything.*

(If at this point you feel that you are getting nowhere, you are right. You want the parents to be concerned about Kenneth's developmental progress. It is difficult for parents who think their child is actually developing normally, or even for those who think there may be something wrong, to absorb all your information in a short conference. Their behavior is healthy, not obstinate. You have just planted a seed; it needs time to germinate. But don't give up; take another approach.)

Teacher: *Thank you. I really like Kenneth too. Perhaps that is why I'm so concerned about him. Maybe at this point the best thing would be for the three of us to watch Kenneth carefully for two weeks. I'll watch him at school, where perhaps you could join me one day, and you can watch at home so that we can decide whether Kenneth is behaving about the same way in both places. Then we can meet again at the end of the two weeks to talk about our observations and see where we are. How does that sound to you?*

Parent: *OK, but I'm really not sure all this is necessary.*

Teacher: *I really feel it is necessary, and it would make Kenneth feel very special for you to come to class. He has often said that he wishes you could see what he does in school.*

Parent: *Well, I guess we can arrange it.*

Teacher: *Good, what day will be the best for you? We are going on a field trip Tuesday, but any other day next week is fine.*

Parent: *I'm not sure, maybe we should think about this a bit more.*

Teacher: *I agree we need to think about it, and I think careful observation would really help us*

make some plans. *Would next Thursday be a good day?*

Parent: *Well, maybe I should call you and let you know.*

Teacher: *Why don't we set the date for Thursday at 1:00, and then if you must change that, call me. And once we've observed Kenneth together, we'll meet to discuss our observations in two weeks.*

Parent: *I guess so.*

Teacher: *Thanks so much for coming. Kenneth is really lucky to have concerned parents like you.*

(It was a bit tedious, but you persisted and were a marvelous example of a broken record. When the parents backed off or avoided the subject, you continuously sought your goal, only modifying your responses according to their statements and current attitude.)

Accepting Responsibility

Accepting responsibility is a simple yet successful way to put people in a frame of mind that allows mutually effective interaction (Fensterheim & Baer, 1975). It consists of making "I" statements instead of "you" statements.

"I'm really glad you told me that today."
"I wish I had known that before."

versus

"You should have told me that before."

The latter statement is a blaming statement. The person that you blame often becomes defensive and responds with another blaming statement: "You weren't listening; I have told you before." This is a difficult cycle to break once it starts.

Despite the temptation to point blame, "you" statements are rarely useful.

Agree and Ask Again

Often when people are under stress, they stop taking in information. This may happen to parents when you tell them things they do not want to hear. It can also happen to you. If you feel that parents blame you for the situation, you may get defensive and quit listening. You may later realize that the information they can provide is essential to you. If you ask a question and they tell you that they answered it ten minutes ago, you should *agree* and *ask again*: "I agree that you did tell me that information, but I wasn't ready to hear it. I still need to know, and I'm ready to listen now."

In much the same way, parents may have been intimidated by doctors or specialists and have not followed up on information, or they may not have understood what was said. Ask the parents to get the information you need from the doctor, or, with parents' written permission, call the doctor yourself for the information. Ask them to give you a copy of the medical report to study. (You may need the doctor's help to interpret the results.) Parents may have been frightened of asking for copies of medical reports or may not have known they have access to them. It is not routine to send copies of reports to parents. Therefore, it may be easier at times to get the information directly from the doctor or specialist. After studying the report, talk with the parents again. It is unlikely that all of you will agree on all the interpretations and implications. That's fine, but you can help the parents make a list of questions that need amplification to take to the doctor or specialist on their next visit.

When this occurs, after a reasonable amount of persistence, it is often best to back up and re-evaluate the situation. Do you really need this information? Does anyone else have it? Is there another way of getting it? If I were this person, why wouldn't I want to give the information out? Then try another approach. If you have been asking to see test results without success, you might now ask, "I'm wondering if there is some reason why you don't want me to see these test results?" This will come as an abrupt change from your previous pattern and may result in a useful answer. You might then learn what the parents are willing to do that is acceptable to you. Might they summarize the results or discuss them? With a workable compromise both parties win.

Matching Style

Matching style involves watching the parents and matching your verbal and emotional style to theirs (Berne, 1961). Are they being ultrareasonable (calm, cool, collected) when you are talking about some potentially distressing topic? If the parents are dealing with the information in a clinical way, take that as a cue. It may be that they are very private people who do not show emotions in public, or they may be feeling vulnerable and using feigned calm to protect their private selves. For some it is less painful to adopt the role of an unemotional clinician than feel the emotional involvement of a parent. At this point, you should respect their right to be detached. Adopt the same style when you talk to them. Have data available to back up your points; show them records and charts. Appeal to their organizational abilities. (Prepare yourself ahead of time so that you are completely comfortable with any technical terms you must use.) Remember, your goal is not to provide therapy for parents but programming for a child.

Families will implement goals in different ways.

Self-disclosure

Self-disclosure involves revealing to the parents something about yourself that is of a personal nature, for example:

When I first learned that Jack was going to be in my class, I was really scared. I'd never taught a child with a physical disability before. Actually, I guess I thought more about the wheelchair than I did about Jack. I can't imagine how I could have felt that way. Now he sometimes has to remind me of the things he can't do. Before, I hardly let him breathe without asking him if he was OK.

A self-disclosure statement can help parents see your emotional acceptance of their child. That is useful for developing a good working relationship.

Workable Compromise

There will be occasions when, regardless of how persistent you are, you will not be successful in gaining the information you need or the services you want. In that case you must reach a *workable compromise* (Fensterheim & Baer, 1975). Perhaps you want the parents to sign a release form giving you access to their child's medical report, but they refuse your request.

Giving Permission

Giving permission allows parents to make comments to you that they might otherwise be unwilling to make.

Teacher: *I wonder if there is anything I could do in my room that might make it easier for Jack to get around?*
    Parent: *Well, if you moved his locker to the far end of the row, it would keep him out of the traffic pattern a little more.*

This technique is a bit more subtle than asking direct questions. It can be done in an open-ended way as well.

Teacher: *I really hope that if you think of some useful things that I can do in the classroom for Jack, you'll tell me. I may not be able to do all of them, but I would like to hear your ideas and learn what has been useful in the past.*

Statements like this do not force the parents to follow through, but do encourage them to make suggestions. In addition, you have reassured the parents that you will think carefully about what they say. Because you will not automatically do whatever they suggest, some of their burden of responsibility will be relieved.

Techniques to Avoid

There are some techniques that are almost guaranteed to be counterproductive in dealing with parents (or with anyone).

Avoid Judging or Blaming

Most of us don't like to be judged unless we have agreed to be in a formal competition. Words like *should* and *ought* that are commonly used to judge others evoke negative, defensive feelings (Berne, 1961). In a phrase like "you should have . . ." blame is implicit. Judging and blaming statements will not encourage others to cooperate with you.

Avoid Mind Reading

"Mind reading," as you might guess, is assuming what another person wants to know or should know, without their telling you (Bandler, Grinder, & Satir, 1976).

Teacher: *What do you want to know about your son's program?*
    Parent: *Whatever you think we need to know.*

After such an exchange, teachers may be led to talk about what they find interesting or what they would want to know if they were the parents. This may not be at all what the parents want to know! If the parents aren't interested, they may simply tune the teacher out. Unless you help the parents make clear statements about what they want, at the end of the conference you will sense they are dissatisfied, but you won't know why. Here is a more productive follow-up to the earlier exchange:

Teacher: *It is more useful to be able to tell you what you want to know. Not what I think you need to know. Do you want to know what the diagnosis is technically, do you want me to try to explain it to you, or both? Do you want the test reports? Do you want to know my best guess about the short- and long-term effects of this illness? I want to know what you want to know.*

Leading questions may still not get the results you want, but, you can start by making your requests clearly and then query points you are not satisfied about.

Avoid Giving Advice

Most parents don't want you to tell them how to raise their children. However, if you are going to offer positive constructive suggestions (which should be rare), first gain enough information about the situation to make the advice relevant (McMurrian, 1977). Suppose the problem is plate-throwing. The parents say that their three-year-old son, Bob, frequently throws his plate on the floor when he does not like dinner. First, get the facts you need: "What do you usually do when Bob throws his plate? . . . Have you tried other things? . . . What? . . . Have they worked?" Next, check your perception of the situation. (Just because something is a problem for you doesn't necessarily mean that it is a problem for the parents and vice versa.) "Is it OK with you that Bob does this, or is it a problem?" Then offer advice tentatively, in a nonjudgmental way, by suggesting some specific actions that might be taken: "Have you tried telling him that when he throws his plate, he will not get it back and will get no snacks? You might see if that works for you."

Avoid the Word Understand

Eliminate *understand* from your vocabulary (McMurrain, 1977). If a parent tells you about a problem, do not respond, "I understand exactly what you mean." Such a response is likely to trigger the following thoughts in a parent: "How can he understand? He is not me. He does not get up in the middle of the night. . . ." People who respond by "understanding" usually convey the impression to others that they really don't understand.

The alternative is an empathic response, such as: "It must be really hard to have to get up in the middle of the night."

Workable Relationships

It is difficult for people to find the right level of expectations for their child. Some people decide that a child with a disability has enough problems already. These people feel, therefore, that if the child likes TV and popcorn, the best solution is to allow this child to watch TV and eat popcorn as long as he is happy. Other parents view disabilities as something to be overcome. They may expect their child to excel beyond what even an average child is capable of. And to them the therapy, extra hours of work, persistence, and, perhaps, pain that are necessary to achieve that goal are worth the cost. Most parents are somewhere between those two extremes.

Knowing how the parents feel will help you, especially in adjusting your expectations regarding the parents' role. Thus, if you automatically expect parents to be actively involved in the education of their child, both in and out of school, a parent like the first one I described will not fulfill those expectations. On the other hand, you might find the second parent a bit pushy and at times more like a clinician than a parent. A home visit might be particularly useful in ascertaining the role parents are prepared for.

Developing a good working relationship with all parents is important, but it is crucial in an inclusive classroom. All parents have the potential to learn and grow with their children. Parents of children with disabilities are, more than most parents, forced to confront individual similarities and differences, and to re-examine their own value systems. Your goal is to reach these parents and support them as they become contributing members of your educational team.

References and Bibliography

Arnold, E. L. (Ed.) (1978). *Helping parents help their children*. New York: Brunner/Mazel.

Bailey, D., & Simeonsson, R. J. (1988). *Family assessment in early intervention*. Columbus, OH: Charles Merrill.

Bandler, R., & Grinder, J. (1975). *The structure of magic: A book about language and therapy*. Palo Alto, CA: Science and Behavior Books, Inc.

Bandler, R., Grinder, J., & Satir, V. (1976). *Changing with families: A book about further education for being human*. Palo Alto, CA: Science and Behavior Books, Inc.

Baruth, L., & Burggraf, M. (1978). *Readings in counseling parents of exceptional children*. Guilford, CT: Special Learning Corp.

Berne, E. (1961). *Transactional analysis in psychotherapy*. New York: Ballantine Books.

Berne, E. (1964). *Games people play*. New York: Grove Press.

Bronfenbrenner, U. (1979). *The ecology of human development: Experiments by nature and design*. Cambridge, MA: Harvard University Press.

Bronfenbrenner, U. (1986). Ecology of the family as a context for human development research perspectives. *Developmental Psychology, 22*, 723–742.

Buscaglia, L. (1975). *The disabled and their parents: A counseling challenge*. New York: Charles B. Slack.

Cameron-Bandler, L. (1978). *They lived happily ever after: A book about achieving happy endings in coupling*. Cupertino, CA: Meta Publications.

Chinn, P., et al. (1978). *Two-way talking with parents of special children: A process of positive communication*. St. Louis, MO: C. V. Mosby Co.

Fensterheim, H., & Baer, J. (1975). *Don't say yes when you want to say no*. New York: Dell.

Garbarino, J. (1990). The human ecology of early risk. In S. J. Meisels, & J. P. Shonkoff, (Eds.). *Handbook of early childhood intervention,* pp. 78–96. Cambridge, MA: Cambridge University Press.

Ginott, H. G. (1969). *Between parent and child*. New York: Macmillan.

Gordon, T. (1970). *P. E. T. Parent effectiveness training*. New York: New American Library.

Gordon, T. (1977). *T. E. T. Teacher effectiveness training*. New York: Longman.

Hanson, M. J., Lynch, E. E., & Wayman, K. L. (1990). Honoring the cultural diversity of families when gathering data. *Topics in Early Childhood Special Education, 10* (1), 112–131.

Henninger, M. L., & Neselroad, E. M. (1984). *Working with parents of handicapped children: A book of readings for school personnel*. New York: University Press of America.

Heward, L. W., Dardig, J. C., & Rossett, A. (1979). *Working with parents of handicapped children*. Columbus OH: Charles E. Merrill.

Kitano, M. K. (1980). Early education for Asian American children, *Young Children, 36* (2), 13–26.

Koth, R. L. (1975). *Communicating with parents of exceptional children: Improving parent-teacher relationships*. Denver, CO: Love Publishing Co.

McMurrian, T. T. (1977). *Intervention in human crisis: A guide for helping families in crisis*. Atlanta: Humanics Limited.

Meisels, S. J., & Shonkoff, J. P., (Eds.). (1990). *Handbook of early childhood intervention*. Cambridge, MA: Cambridge University Press.

Rutherford, R. B., Jr., & Edgar, E. (1979). *Teachers and parents: A guide to interaction and cooperation*. Boston: Allyn and Bacon.

Satir, V. (1967). *Conjoint family therapy*. Palo Alto, CA: Science and Behavior Books, Inc.

Satir, V. (1972). *Peoplemaking*. Palo Alto, CA: Science and Behavior Books, Inc.

Seligman, M. (Ed.) (1991). *The family with a handicapped child*. (2nd ed.) Boston: Allyn and Bacon.

Shea, T., & Bauer, A. (1990). *Parents and teachers of children with exceptionalities: A handbook for collaboration*. Boston, MA: Allyn and Bacon.

Smith, M. J. (1975). *When I say no, I feel guilty: How to cope—Using the skill of systematic assertive therapy*. New York: Dial Press.

Stewart, J. C. (1978). *Counseling parents of exceptional children*. Columbus, OH: Charles E. Merrill.

Sullivan, C. (November 27, 1991). Language differences in Latin America: A rose by any other name . . . may not be a rose. *Times of the Americas,* 11, Washington, DC.

Thompson, T. (Ed.) (1978). *The schooling of Native America*. Washington, DC: American Association of Colleges for Teacher Education.

United States Bureau of the Census, (April 1991). *Census and You,* 3. Washington, DC: Author.

PART FOUR

Integrating the Curriculum to Meet Children's Needs

Introduction

As diversity in the classroom has increased, you have been called upon to use more care in planning your work. In choosing activities for your class, you will have to analyze the needs, strengths, likes, and dislikes of each child. Although some of the children in your class will have particular needs and disabilities, you will want to choose activities that teach concepts, develop skills, and satisfy the needs and interests of *all* the children in your class.

Activities and Record Keeping

In addition to designing a curriculum and choosing appropriate materials for the children in your classroom, you will want to develop a record-keeping system that helps you identify children and chart their progress. When you think about developing or refining your record keeping, first decide *why* you need to keep the records. If, for example, your goal is to find out what activity areas your children like or dislike or which particular children play together, a checklist, like those illustrated on page 60 would be useful.

Such a record is also useful at the beginning of a parent-teacher conference. Because the record has nothing to do with quality of performance, it is nonthreatening to parents and provides information about their child's activities during the day. Use this type of chart at the beginning, middle, and end of the year to track how the children have changed. It is also useful in evaluating the interest level of the activities you have chosen.

Knowing where children are, how long they stay at various activities, and who they play with is useful, but it is only a beginning. From charts and other observations, you probably will have unconsciously labeled some children as "needs more observation." This may be because they do things better than or not as well as their peers, or because their skills seem to be uneven or to fluctuate greatly.

If you want to concentrate on the children's level of skill, a checklist may help you quantify and focus your observations. Start with general areas such as the major activity areas in the book and add or delete areas depending upon your focus.

At this stage, your memory and a little observation will sort children fairly well. This is an initial screen, and perhaps a reminder to you to observe all the children. Thinking about the activities you plan in these areas is useful for future programming. For example, if you play a ball game outside (motor) and decide that Cho appears uncomfortable, awkward, and doesn't **357** seem to know what to do, you would want to follow that up with additional observations. The major goals in the sensory motor area would provide the framework. The form would be more specific:

GENERAL CURRICULUM GOALS

Children's Names	Language Arts	Discovery	Sensory Motor	Social Awareness	Creative Arts
Cho					
Dene					
José					
Marsha					
Tom					

Key   1. Above average
      2. Average
      3. Needs work

a. Seems inconsistent
b. Needs further observation

SENSORY MOTOR GOALS

Child's Name _____

	Date	Activity/Area	Quality/Comment
Large motor coordination			
Body awareness			
Physical fitness			
Sensory motor integration			
Motor planning			
Small motor coordination			
Eye-hand coordination			
Adaptive skills			

Key   Date: The date on which you try the activity
      Activity: The name of the activity you used
      Area: The name of the curriculum area
      Comments: Additional information you note

Quality: 1. Activity done quickly, easily, accurately
          2. Activity completed accurately, but with some difficulty
          3. Activity completed with many errors
          4. Activity not completed
          5. Activity not attempted

Before you pick the activities you will use, review your information about where the child spends his time and what he likes to do. Choose activities that both provide information on the goals you are concerned about and are in an area the child enjoys. The trick is to figure out how to teach what the child needs to learn in such a way that he will want to learn it. Before reaching any conclusions about a particular child, use several different activities that include a range of skills. This is where the activities and the indexes come in. The indexes at the beginning of the curriculum areas list the activities within those areas by goal. The overall index at the end of the book lists all the activities in the book that are designed to meet a particular goal and specifies the curriculum area for each activity. Using these indexes effectively will help you plan your teaching program.

Organization of Activities

The activities in Part Four are organized by developmental/curriculum areas such as Language Arts and within each chapter these are broken down into smaller areas (e.g., large motor, sensory motor integration, and small motor). Activities are presented in terms of the particular needs they meet. Within curriculum areas they are organized by goals. This makes them easily accessible to your programming needs.

First is a developmental overview of the underlying principles in a particular area. The overview allows the matching of activities to the developmental level of the children. Thus:

CHAPTER 24 DISCOVERY

Before children can be expected to use standard units of measurement such as feet and inches or meters and centimeters, they need to understand that measuring involves describing something in smaller increments.

Next is a discussion of long-term goals that are most easily met. For example:

CHAPTER 27 CREATIVE ARTS

To encourage creativity
To improve self-concept
To express feelings

These teaching goals are followed by particular strategies that are most useful with children who have disabilities. For example:

CHAPTER 25 SENSORY MOTOR

Large motor activities allow children with learning disabilities *to release energy as well as to increase body awareness. Often children with* learning disabilities *have related sensory motor integration problems. It is critical that they develop trunk stability as a prerequisite for fine motor skills. As these children may not do well at these activities they may tend to avoid them. Practice at such skills as snapping, typing, and buttoning are practical self-help skills which also promote sensory motor integration.*

A list of activities appears next for each curriculum area. The activities are organized by the goals that they implement. When activities have more than one goal, they appear in the index under each goal. (An index for activities in a chapter is before the activities for that chapter, and an index for all the activities in the book is at the end of the book.) For example:

CHAPTER 23 LANGUAGE ARTS

Goal	Activity
To improve expressive language	My Shoes
To encourage creativity	My Shoes

The organization of the activities section is designed to aid you in record keeping as well as day-to-day programming. The activities have a standard format and include suggestions for both increasing and decreasing the level of difficulty of the activity. This can be done to adapt for individual children or to expand the age range of the activity. The standard format is:

Curriculum Area

ACTIVITY NAME

GOAL

OBJECTIVE

MATERIALS

PROCEDURE

Increase Level of Difficulty

Materials

Procedure

Decrease Level of Difficulty

Materials

Procedure

COMMENT

The final section in each chapter in Part Four includes references and a bibliography for additional reading. It provides suggestions of books that have additional activities in the area.

Using Activities in the IEP

If a child has an Individual Educational Plan (IEP/IFSP), look at the annual goals or outcomes in the plan, locate these goals and related ones in the index, and use the activities listed to implement the IEP.

If you are in charge of writing the IEP, use the goals and activities to help you write the plan. To adapt the specific activities to an IEP format use the following example:

Small Motor

BUTTONS

GOAL   To improve small motor coordination
To improve sensory motor integration

OBJECTIVE   The child will pair the buttons.

MATERIALS   12 pairs of buttons (tactile differences)   a bowl (bag)
an egg carton or ice cube tray   a blindfold

The goal is already stated as an annual goal. The objective and materials are combined to become an instructional objective. An appropriate evaluation is added: Given an egg carton, 12 pairs of objects, and a blindfold, the child will correctly match 10 of the 12 pairs of objects.

You have now reformatted the activity to meet the requirements of an IEP. Look up other activities that also improve small motor coordination. You now have not only the IEP but also a variety of activities you can use to implement it.

Using Activities in the IFSP

If a child has an Individual Family Service Plan, the activities are also useful for those outcomes that relate to the child. The format of the IFSP varies more than for the IEP. However, the same system of reformatting applies. Objectives can be written as can "Outcomes."

Many of the activities in the book can be used with younger children by using the section called "decreasing the level of difficulty." Share these activities with families if that is compatible with their wishes. The last chapter in this section has activities designed specifically for infants and toddlers. Most activities for an IFSP will come from this part of the book.

Using the Activities

Some of the activities in this book are familiar ones given a twist to make them especially useful for children with disabilities (e.g., Circus, Animal Families). Others are new activities designed to fulfill a specific purpose (e.g., Audiologist, Slings). However, if you refer to the goals at the beginning of the activities, you will see that each activity is designed to meet the needs and help develop skills in all the children in the class. Feel free to adapt these activities to suit your class, and use them as a springboard to make up your own. If you want more ideas for activities, a bibliography of activity books is given at the end of each chapter.

Activities are the building blocks of program planning. These activities alone are not a substitute for program planning but are designed to be part of an integrated curriculum. Chapter 7, Program Planning, covers this area in detail. However, a simple flow chart is a useful way to organize your thinking. Start with the child. Then add an idea. This can be a theme such as Farm Animals or as simple as a "feather" or even an "empty egg carton." Choose activities from the book or your own experience.

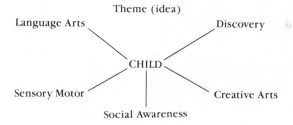

There are many by-products of a good activities program. While the main purpose of the activities is to teach specific concepts and skills, they also can increase the children's awareness of their own strengths and needs and the differences between themselves and others. If materials are stored conveniently, the children can learn independence by getting things and putting them back instead of depending on others to do these tasks. They also can gain practice in making choices, deciding what activities they want to participate in and for how long. As they put things away, they can practice sorting and classification skills. And since there are limits to how many children can participate in an activity at one time, children also can learn about sharing and taking turns.

As a teacher of young children you have much to keep in mind. Because you have the strengths and needs of all the children in your class to consider, you must find activities that meet the needs of children with disabilities, but are appropriate and enriching to all. You must use school as a world in which all children belong and have appropriate work to do. But, most of all, you must remember that you are a model for the children. Your behavior toward children—your acceptance, consideration, and respect—will speak louder to the class than anything you deliberately set out to teach. I hope these varied activities will be a stimulating resource for your teaching programs.

OCEAN (THEME)

Teachers read about the plants
and animals that live in the ocean.

Children read books about shells and
identify them.

They count and classify
different types of shells.

They use blocks to
create a gasoline
station that serves
362 both cars and boats.

The dramatic play area is a beach, and they are scuba divers and water skiers.

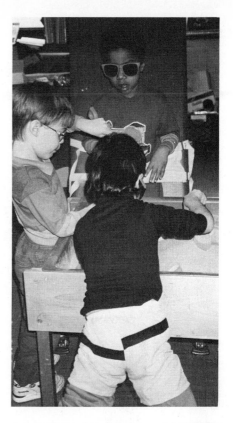

They find shells hidden in the sand.

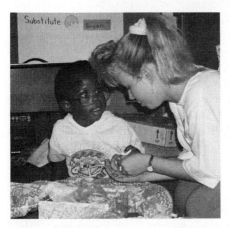

They explore shells tactily.

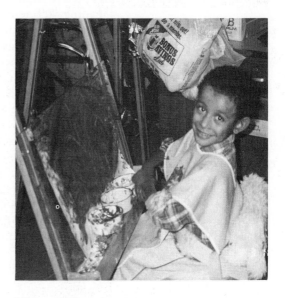

They make sea scenes with fingerpaint on the easel.

363

Chapter 23

Language Arts: Speaking, Listening, Reading, Writing

Learning to communicate is one of the major tasks facing all young children. Regardless of the language, the process of learning a language is the same. Infants first imitate sounds (phonemes) and gestures. Babbling puts these phonemes together and adds rhythm, stress, and intonation. Babbling is self-rewarding. The infant enjoys babbling. Sounds eventually get put together in patterns that resemble a simple word or morpheme. When adults hear a word they are usually delighted and reinforce it. More words emerge, or at least consistent morphemes. Meaning becomes consistently attached to these words. Finally, the words are put together to "telegraph" meaning. Refinements are added so sentences become longer and are more descriptive. Learning is cumulative.

Learning language is a dynamic process that is affected by the language heard in the environment and the way that adults respond to development of speech. In situations where children have rich language models and are supported in producing speech they are more open to new opportunities to expand their language skills. In addition to a strong base in experience, children need to feel the urge to communicate. If no one listens, they are unlikely to talk. Children who spend long hours in front of a television set have little incentive to talk since television is a noninteractive media.

Speaking, listening, reading, and writing are the major components of the language arts curriculum. These skills are interdependent. Although this chapter divides them into these components, overall program planning would see them as interrelated and interdependent. Likewise, although there are designated language arts activities, the language arts curriculum should be part of all program planning.

Speaking

Speaking, or expressive language, is a major component of the early language arts curriculum. In order to match language arts activities to the level of the children in your class it is important to know the child's present level of language functioning, what the average child of that age can say, and types of activities that are likely to help the child move from his current level to the next one. Each child will be at a different level. You can use standardized tests given by specialists to determine the child's level. (A child who comes to you diagnosed with a deficit in this area will usually come with these test results.) You can also use observation and teacher-made "tests" to help you program. See Chapter 4 for an overview of language development.

Children use more complex sentences with increasing age. During the preschool years children use simple infinitive clauses such as: "She went to get it." With increasing age the clause might read: "She is going to the store to get it." Children begin to use the conjunctive "if" and start to coordinate phrases with *and, so, but,* and *or.* They increase their use of adjectives and adverbs and can apply them to the subject or predicate. Their speech also includes the use of relative, comparative, and nonabsolute terms such as *near, slower, some.*

Expansion and extension are two techniques that encourage the use of more complex language structures. Expansion is the process of extracting the meaning of a child's utterance and putting it into a more complex form. With a younger child using telegraphic speech such as "Me go" the expansion might be "Where do you want to go?" or "Are you ready to go now?" The objective is to provide a language model, not just an answer that says "OK." As children get older, the expansion can help them be more specific in their word usage and structural complexity. If the child says, "I want that," respond with "Do you want the one with the red flowers or the one with the green stripes?" Your objective is to encourage the child to give you a more descriptive response in return.

Extension involves putting the child's statement in a broader context. That is, extending the meaning of the child's phrase. If the child says, "I want to go out," you might respond, "If you want to go outside and play you need to put your coat on." Using these techniques is particularly effective as the child is prepared to listen to the response because it is meaningful to him.

Sometimes it is helpful to rephrase what you say to a child if he does not appear to understand or comprehend what you ask. This is also useful if you didn't understand a child. Instruct him: "Tell me in different words." This way both you and the child have a second chance to process the information.

Young children need concrete language experiences to build their skills. They need firsthand experiences such as field trips to build the connection between words and objects or actions. Because of special concerns and logistic problems, children with disabilities may lack these experiences.

Remember that you are always a language model for your children, not just when you are teaching a language lesson. Whenever you are addressing a child, talking to his peers, or talking to other adults in the classroom you are a language model. The richer and more descriptive your language is, the greater the variety of syntactic forms you use, the better language model you will be for the children.

It is imperative that children have a vocabulary large enough to express their wants and needs and to enable them to understand the wants and needs of others, and also that they learn the rules that govern how language is used. Understanding language enables them to function effectively in their environment. They also need to learn that language can be both spoken and written.

Listening

Listening is a recent addition to the language arts curriculum. It was obvious to most people that children learned to talk and must be taught to read and write, but listening was taken as a "given." All children knew how to listen; they just needed to "pay attention."

Listening is a complex component of learning. It involves hearing that allows for auditory identification and discrimination. There is both a short- and long-term memory component. Listening or auditory processing is also a part of attending and sensory motor integration.

As with speaking, children are most likely to develop good listening skills if you are a good model. If you always repeat what you say, children learn *not* to listen the first time. When you are listening to a child, LISTEN.

Although we don't often think of listening as a subject in school, children spend more of their school time listening than doing any other single task. They listen to the teacher, they listen to peers, they listen to the intercom, and they listen to recorded sounds. For younger children we have fingerplays that help them "zip their mouths closed" so they can listen, or they put on their "listening cap." Despite the preparation for listening, our goal is usually having the children quiet; the focus is still on speaking rather than the skills involved in listening. One of the questions we as teachers must evaluate is, "How much of what we say is worth listening to?" Would we be willing to sit spellbound for several hours each day listening to boring information? For children to practice good listening skills, they need something stimulating to listen to. Interest helps them to focus on listening as a process.

Just as with other areas, it is helpful to develop rules for listening. For children to listen, they must pay attention. Teachers usually have a signal to focus children's attention on listening, such as a chord played on the piano, a particular fingerplay, or flicking the lights. That may be the first rule. Other common rules have to do with taking turns, not interrupting, raising your hand, and so on. You might add some speaking rules to this as well, like talking loud enough to be heard and speaking clearly. You don't want children not to participate, yet you can't expect them to listen when it is not possible to hear. Helping them fine-tune their listening skills means that children will get more useful information from their environment.

Auditory identification is the process of getting meaning from what is heard. Some of the first words the child learns to identify are his name and those of his family. Names of favorite toys and pets are also identified early. Later children learn to identify sounds in the environment such as a car horn, running water, and other familiar sounds. The ability to identify specific sounds and to attach meaning to these sounds allows the child to get more cues about his environment.

Auditory discrimination involves distinguishing likenesses and differences in sounds. The child learns to distinguish between a fire alarm and a jingle bell (gross discrimination) or the "p" and "b" sound (fine discrimination). Children learn from listening who is talking and even something about their mood based on their speech patterns, volume, and choice of words. Once children can identify a variety of sounds, they begin to make finer distinctions. They may know without concentrating that the teacher is calling roll, but they must listen carefully to know whether to respond to Kenny or Denny. Rhyming words help sharpen the child's ability to identify similar and dissimilar sounds in words and build vocabulary at the same time.

Auditory memory involves remembering what was heard a few moments ago, such as the directions for who could get their coats, as well as the story *Whistle for Willie* which was read last week and *your name,* unless you are willing to be called "Teacher" all year.

Auditory closure involves using grammatical rules (parts of speech, tense, pronouns, and so on) and picking out speech patterns and rhyming words. For example, "Sugar and spice and everything _____." Children learn what category of word is missing as well as the particular word. They know the sentence, "We swim in the _____?" might be completed by *pool* or *lake* but not *her,* as the sentence requires a noun, not a pronoun.

Auditory association and comprehension are higher level processing skills. *Auditory association* involves understanding what is heard in the context of past experience and knowledge. This is a high-level process that uses analogies (at night it is *dark,* in the day it is _____), categorization and classification skills, and the ability to associate behavior with words: "What do you do when you hear the fire alarm?" It also involves generalizing about how things are alike and different: "How are a bell and a siren alike? How are they different?"

Auditory comprehension requires children to bring together all the previously learned skills and use them to understand and focus on what is being stated. This involves being able to think up a title for a story or make up a relevant beginning or ending of a story. The more complex the material, the more difficult the task.

It isn't necessary for you to think about each of these processes as a separate entity, but rather to be aware of them and to be sure that your range of programming in the area of listening covers all of them. Good auditory processing provides a solid foundation for other language skills.

Reading

Educators are becoming more and more interested in and concerned about reading and reading readiness, although there is no general agreement on one particular method for teaching reading. There does seem to be agreement that the teacher is an important variable. Your enthusiasm for reading and valuing it as a skill are more important than the way you decide to teach it. Learning to read is a complex task, and although the formal teaching of reading is not part of the preschool curriculum, many of the readiness skills are. Developing reading readiness at the preschool level is a broad process that includes field trips, followed by stories dictated by the children to help them recall trips, and children's illustrations of their trip.

It can be difficult for some children to learn to read. Although many activities are given to make learning the small steps of reading more fun, it is your role to put the magic in reading. The best way to do that is to read to children. Read literature, poetry, and plays. As one bright son said to his father, "I don't want to learn to read. If I learn to read you'll stop reading to me." Read to children even after they can read. Their ability to read and what they enjoy as literature may be on a different level. My favorite fourth-grader announced after the first week of school that she liked all her teachers but one, the librarian. When I inquired why, she said, "She doesn't read to us."

In order to read children must learn to see small differences. Using *visual identification* skills, they must learn that objects have consistent labels and these labels stand for or symbolize the objects. More specifically, they must learn the names for the letters of the alphabet and know that these names are consistent. They must also distinguish among various objects by looking for similarities and differences (*visual discrimination*). In order to read, children need to be able to make fine distinctions between letters and patterns of letters and spaces between words. This is an extremely difficult task built on simpler tasks such as discriminating shapes and colors. Children must not only learn to discriminate letters, they must remember what the symbols stand for. Eventually, they not only need to remember the letter but the sound of the letter and, as they begin reading, the sequence of the letters and how this sequence influences sound. Because the sequence in which letters appear determines what word is formed (*mat* versus *tam*), remembering sequentially is an essential reading skill.

Visual closure involves recognizing objects or pieces of visual information without seeing the whole thing or through a quick scan. For example, it is possible to recognize a rabbit even if one ear is missing. A quick scan might not even pick up the missing ear but would register the rabbit. Eventually, children learn to look at word configuration instead of looking only at the individual letters in each word.

Higher-level skills, such as *visual association,* require children to understand what is seen in the context of past experience and knowledge. If you show children a snow scene and ask them about the temperature, they should tell you it is cold. If you place a girl in a swimsuit in the snow picture and ask what is wrong, the children should point out that her clothing is inappropriate. This skill includes the ability to abstract the function of things. Children can pair a lamp and a flashlight based on their function of giving light.

Visual comprehension involves bringing together previously learned skills and using them to interpret visual information. If you show children a picture and ask them, "What's happening in this picture?" they use visual comprehension to tell a story about it. This skill includes summarizing the main points or ideas of something that has been seen.

Most professionals in the field feel that children use their own language system to make guesses about words they cannot read. The more specific and complex their spoken language is, the better their guesses will be as they learn to read.

Writing

A classroom that provides the space, materials, time, and rewards for writing is a class in which children will write. Although we think of writing as beginning later than some of the other communication skills, such thinking is due more to our inability to interpret the writing of children than to a lack of interest in writing on their part. From the time a toddler picks up a marker and puts the first stroke on the page he has become an author. Over time, with appropriate materials and encouragement, that author will go from scribbling, to drawings that may contain letters or words or tell a story, to writing words using invented spellings, to fluent writing that may involve editing and publication.

One of the first things that children want to write is their name. However, even before children can write they need to see you write. As you write, verbalize for the children why you are writing: "I am writing your name on the paper so I know that it is yours." "I am making a list of the things we need at the store so I don't forget." "I am writing a note to your mother so that she knows why you have a bandage on your finger." Children need to be aware of the purpose of writing from an early age. If a friend is sick, suggest that they write a note so the other child knows she is being thought of. It is important in the age of the TV and the telephone that children learn the place that writing holds.

Writing, like most other skills, progresses through developmental stages. Thus, writing our name, for example, typically progresses as follows:

scribbling a name

writing a name in mock letters

copying a name

writing a name that is illegible

writing a first name legibly, but misspelled

writing a first name correctly with some letter reversals

writing a first name correctly

writing a first name with last initial

writing a first and last name legibly and correctly spelled (Lamme, 1985, pp. 48–49).

The requirements necessary for writing will vary with age. Very young children need both stand-up and sit-down places to write (Lamme, 1985). For young children, a chalkboard with large chalk, an easel with thick markers, or just large paper taped to the wall or any other flat surface can make a mural so that writing can also be a social event.

Although children can write almost anywhere, having a designated place in your classroom increases the likelihood that they will do so. Choose a table large enough for at least two and no more than four children. Tape on the alphabet letters which the children are using so that each child can see them as he writes. Think of writing as a social process, not an isolated experience. Children will ask each other questions related to what they are writing. After writing, children need an audience for their written work if they choose to share it. An author's chair, where children can read to others what they have written, is part of the process.

As children become more experienced writers the tools needed will increase. Designate one table in your classroom as the writing center. It should be equipped with a variety of paper: manila paper, wide-lined paper that covers the entire sheet as well as some that covers only half the sheet (which then allows for illustrations), plain white paper. Add paper which is folded in half, small note pads, paper cut into interesting shapes, colored paper, and even stationery. Rubber stamps allow children to print their own "stationery." Almost any light-colored paper will do; it is having a variety that is important. The writing tools need to be selected to match both the paper and the children using them. The youngest children (eighteen months to about three years) need water-soluble markers and large crayons or crayons with knobs on the top. They also need large paper. As children gain experience and proficiency, add thin markers and pencils that have erasers, as well as a supply of interesting erasers. Obviously, a pencil sharpener is a must. The small hand-held ones are fine if they don't "walk home." Colored pencils add interest also. As children get older you might add some of the writing and illustrating media that are more difficult to control, such as oil pastels, chalk used on paper, watercolors, and charcoal. One solution is to place the writing center near the art area so that children can freely use art materials to illustrate their writing.

Children need to think of writing as a process, and certain materials can help make that possible. Rewriting is often slow for children, so they need to have scissors and tape available for changes. Glue or paste is also helpful, as well as a stapler, hole punch, and brads to hold pages together. Add a ruler, gummed stickers, used cards, and other accessories.

Although you might have all of these materials available, it is not necessary to have them all out at any one time. The particular materials and accessories used can vary with the theme or unit that is being studied.

After children have completed a writing project, it is important that you show your

Children can be authors at a very young age.

appreciation of it and value it. Many children like to have writing folders where they keep all their work. Display some of it. Don't however, hang up only the work that has the neatest penmanship, as this may be more a deterrent than an incentive to writing for some children.

Language Arts Goals

To Increase Expressive Language

Create opportunities for children to talk. Be sure to ask questions that require more than a "yes" or "no" answer. Reinforce children when they use language appropriately. Be a good language model: Your speech should reflect a wide variety of verbs, nouns, adjectives, adverbs, and pronouns. Increase the specificity of words that depict what is happening in the environment: "He hobbled over to the table" versus "He went over there." Verbally label the environment.

To Improve Listening Skills

Children are most likely to develop good listening skills if you are a good model. Start off with brief periods when children are expected to listen. Vary your method of presentation to include some times of "listening." Tell a story instead of reading one, use a record or tape and give children verbal directions. It is important that children are exposed to situations that require active listening. We frequently pair listening with visual cues (reading a story with illustrations) and listening while doing something physical (dancing or movement). We also use listening as a cue for children that activities are changing or as background music to set a mood, perhaps at rest time. Listening skills need to be isolated and refined, as well as paired with other sensory inputs.

To Increase Comprehension

Expand the meaning of words that children already know (orange is a color and also a fruit). If you expand a child's speech, he learns new grammatical structures and vocabulary. Comprehension involves more than understanding what is said or read. It requires children to interpret nonverbal communication as well. Children need to become aware of the intonation patterns, tone, and rhythm of speech as a clue to its meaning. Children should become aware at an early age of their own body language and gain some skills in interpreting others' body language.

To Follow Directions

Following directions is an important aspect of education. Children need practice in following first one-step, and then two- and three-step directions.

To Improve Reading Readiness

Learning to read is a complex task. The foundation skills must be part of the early childhood curriculum for all children. Children must develop skills in the area of visual identification, discrimination, and memory as well as higher-level skills in association and comprehension. These skills must be paired with auditory skills involved in labeling, not only letters, but specific sounds of letters, and blending these into words.

To Improve Sequencing Skills

Understanding patterns or sequences is an important element in reading, science, and mathematics. Children need to identify a pattern, then repeat the pattern. Sequences can be simple repeating patterns such as a penny, a nickel, a penny, a nickel, or they can be as complex as those you might find in reading a word.

To Increase Writing Readiness

We don't expect children to write extensively at early ages, but the underlying skills must be developed. Early scribbling, the use of writing tools, and understanding that writing is a symbol system are precursors to writing. Allowing children to use inventive spelling and not pointing out letter reversals helps keep children writing until their skill level catches up with their interest in the power and process of writing. Supporting children's writing through illustrating, editing, and publishing are part of an early writing program.

Teaching Strategies

Children with *communication* disorders must concentrate on the development of underlying inner language skills by participating in many firsthand experiences. If children are reluctant to speak, create a need for them to talk: Instead of asking children yes/no questions ("Do you want to play with the blocks today?"), use forms such as "Where do you want to play today?" to elicit more speech. For children who need work on specific speech sounds, read stories and ask questions that require them to practice those sounds. Some children have articulation problems because they do not listen accurately or they don't have good speech models. Their speech reflects what they hear. It is important that you provide a good model for them. Children with few skills in listening and speaking may be reluctant to participate in reading and writing readiness activities. Negative feelings about language may carry over into these areas. These children need to be encouraged and rewarded for participation.

Children with *hearing* impairments may need support to practice talking; encourage them to attempt this even if their speech is not always understandable. Because they are more dependent on environmental cues than others, they need to fine-tune their ability to use this contextual information. They need many hands-on experiences to develop inner language. Children need to use any residual hearing that is available to them. Pair listening with visual or kinesthetic cues when necessary. When possible, help the child refine the auditory skills available. As reading and writing are not as dependent upon auditory skills as speaking, children may initially feel more comfortable in these language areas.

Children with *visual* impairments usually depend on verbal skills to communicate and also to learn about their environment. If they can't find a needed object, they may ask others for directions. They need practice in both giving and following directions. They are more dependent than others on using auditory cures, especially those skills related to auditory memory. Children who are blind miss some of the nonverbal qualities of attending and eye contact. They need help in focusing on intonation patterns, volume, and speed of language for additional cues. Children with visual impairments may require an individualized reading readiness program. Encourage children to refine the visual skills they can use. Have large-print books on your bookshelves for those who can learn to read print. For children who will use braille, emphasize the development of tactile skills. Use writing media which have different tactile properties.

Children with *learning disabilities* may find some aspects of language difficult. Particularly, sequencing activities and memory games may be difficult for them. For children with a high activity level, having to *just* listen may seem close to punishment. Since these children often have deficits in the listening area, be sure you are not competing with outside noises or an uncomfortable physical environment. These children are easily distracted and will need your support to listen. Both reading and writing are likely to be difficult skills to master for children with learning disabilities. They may need more practice than others in readiness skills. These skills are frequently difficult for them and they may try to avoid them. Emphasize activities that intrigue them while teaching the necessary skills at the same time.

Children with *physical* disabilities may not be as mobile as other children. They need practice in asking for what they want, especially if they cannot reach it. They particularly need to learn to give precise directions. To the extent that children with physical disabilities have been restricted in the variety of listening experiences that they have had, they may need help connecting sounds to possible sources and in comprehending the relationship. Reading can broaden the range of experiences available to these children. Writing may offer a particular challenge. Using materials that have some built-in resistance may be necessary, such as writing or drawing in sand or on clay.

Children with *health* impairments need to develop a vocabulary that will increase their understanding of the situations they may face and help them express their feelings. They may have consciously tried not to listen, or found that adults did not expect them to listen so they quit attending. Adults often forget that there may be so much attention to other areas of learning that listening is neglected, or that, although children listen, they may not understand what they hear. Reading offers the child with a health impairment an escape into other worlds of learning. Reading, and being able to write, affords an opportunity to express and share feelings even when those you want to speak with are not present. It provides a way of remembering important information.

Children with *emotional/behavioral* disorders require a vocabulary that helps them verbalize their feelings and communicate with others. These children may have learned to tune out their environment because it seemed negative, irrelevant, or scary. They will need your help in learning how to tune you in and listen again. These children may find reading and writing less threatening than field trips or oral language. They can expand their knowledge at a time when other options are not available. Be sure to allow them time to do these activities. Writing and illustrating are potential outlets for feelings and expression. Help children take advantage of these.

Children with *mental retardation* learn more slowly than other children, so they will need extra repetitions of vocabulary and extra help in generalizing words to apply to a variety of situations. They will spend most of their time in the preschool years mastering the concept of a symbol system and developing a functional vocabulary. They will require a lot of time to practice reading readiness skills. These skills may be learned in conjunction with such necessary small motor skills as patterned eye movement (left to right), following a line of print with a finger, and turning pages. Allow the children to work on these skills as long as necessary. Do this in short periods, and be sure prerequisite skills have been attained before going on to more difficult tasks. Children with mental retardation may just get to the initial stages of writing. If the prerequisite motor skills are not developed, it is useless to practice skills like name writing.

Children with *multiple* disabilities will require adaptations depending upon the area which is most involved. In general, follow the strategies given above and combine them to meet the child's needs.

Speaking, Listening, Reading, and Writing Activities

Goal	Activity
To increase expressive language	Sentences
	Synonyms
	Same and Different
	Never
	My Shoes
	Shoe Theater
	Ideas
	Divergent
	Bring Me
	Weekend News
	Peek Pictures
	Rhyming Words
	Telephone
	Object Hunt
	Interviews
	Body Sounds
To improve listening skills	Magician
	Sounds of Silence
	Whisper
	Say It
	Listening Walk
	Noisy and Quiet
	Sound and Tell
	Sound Cues
	Noisy Steps
	Sound Eggs
	Water Tones
	Number Tapping
	Where Is It/Who Is It?
	Tape It
	Same and Different
	Rhyming Words
	Telephone
	Flannel Board Stories
	Letter Day
	Sound Bingo
To increase comprehension	Imaginary Walk
	Word Associations
	Synonyms
	Bring Me
	Peek Pictures
	Rhyming Words
	Say It
	Listening Walk
	Noisy and Quiet
	Sound and Tell
	Sound Cues
	Going to the Beach
	Letter Day
	Title
	Mind Mapping
To improve sequencing skills	Listen Before You Move
	Going to the Beach
	Natural Sequencing
	My Shoes

Goal	Activity
	Changing Objects
	Books
To follow directions	Object Hunt
	Imaginary Walk
	Noisy Steps
	Listen Before You Move
	Color Graphs
	Books
To improve reading readiness	Alphabet Lotto
	Body Sounds
	Sound Bingo
	Flannel Board Stories
	Title
	Letter Day
	Changing Objects
	Color Graphs
	Alphabet Line
	Matrix
	Color Concentration
	Follow That Line
	What Is It?
	Sandpaper Letters
	Changes
	Natural Sequencing
	Going to the Beach
	Fishing for Faces
To increase writing readiness	Mind Mapping
	Booklets
	Air Writing
	Sand Writing
	Tickets
	Writing Center
	Book Making
	My Diary
	Written Languages
	Alphabet Line
To improve number concepts	Number Tapping
To improve observational skills	What Is It?
To improve classification skills	Same and Different
	Never
	Bring Me
To improve cause-and-effect reasoning	Divergent
	Natural Sequencing
	Sound Eggs
	Water Tones
	Follow That Line
To make predictions	Matrix
	Color Concentration
To improve generalization skills	Matrix
	What Is It?
To improve small motor coordination	Color Graphs

Goal	Activity
	Alphabet Line
	Tickets
	Writing Center
To improve eye-hand coordination	Fishing for Faces
	Book Making
To improve sensory motor integration	Object Hunt
	Imaginary Walk
	Noisy Steps
	Number Tapping
	Where Is It/Who Is It?
	Letter Day
	Sandpaper Letters
	Air Writing
	Sand Writing
To increase body awareness	Body Sounds
	Changes
To improve adaptive skills	Tape It
To increase inclusion	Never
	Shoe Theater
	Weekend News
	Peek Pictures
	Telephone
	Interviews
	Flannel Board Stories
	Follow That Line
	Changes
	Color Concentration
	Tickets
	Writing Center
To increase awareness of individual differences	Written Languages
To encourage creativity	My Shoes
	Shoe Theater
	Ideas
	Word Associations
To improve self-concept	Interviews
	Tape It
To express feelings	Weekend News
	My Diary
To encourage creative problem solving	Ideas
	Divergent

Speaking

SENTENCES

GOAL   To improve expressive language

OBJECTIVE   The child will respond to questions using complete sentences.

MATERIALS   None

PROCEDURE   At the end of group time tell the children that you are going to ask them questions and that, according to the rules for this game, they cannot use just the words "yes" or "no," but must answer with a complete sentence.

TEACHER: Is your name Susan?
SUSAN: Yes, my name is Susan.
TEACHER: Would you like to use the easel today?
SUSAN: No, I would like to play in the block area.

When the child has answered the question or completed a sequence, she is free to go.

Increase Level of Difficulty

Procedure   Ask these children questions that require more complex answers or a series of questions.

Decrease Level of Difficulty

Procedure   Ask these children simple questions. If they cannot answer in a sentence, provide a model for them to imitate. Call on these children when the group is small and you can give them more attention as well as when they have had the opportunity to hear others answer.

COMMENT   When children use only "yes" and "no" as responses they lose a chance to practice language. Often we, as teachers, are really only interested in the answer. This activity gives us an opportunity to concentrate on whether or not each child in the group really can answer in a sentence.

Speaking

SYNONYMS

GOAL   To improve expressive language
To increase comprehension

OBJECTIVE   The child will label an object or concept in at least two different ways.

MATERIALS   pictures or objects that have more than one name (see synonyms below)

PROCEDURE   Define synonyms—words that mean the same thing but sound different. Then present children with the objects or pictures of these objects, and see how many synonyms they can think of. It is not important that these be exact synonyms in a dictionary sense. The point is for the children to know that one object can have several different names. Start with familiar objects in your classroom and community:

rug/carpet/floor covering	store/shop
chair/seat	road/street
couch/sofa/davenport	bed/cot
scissors/shears	shirt/top
bathing suit/swimsuit	

Increase Level of Difficulty

Materials   Children's dictionary or thesaurus

Procedure   Encourage children to think up synonyms for more abstract words, for example, brave/courageous/fearless.

Decrease Level of Difficulty

Procedure   Use the analogy of nicknames to help children learn the concept. Give many different concrete examples.

COMMENT   Children need to know that objects often have several names even in the same language. Discuss how some names are different in different parts of the country. Subs, hoagies, and grinders or soda, pop, and soda pop all are regional variations.

SAME AND DIFFERENT

GOAL   To increase expressive language
To improve listening skills
To improve classification skills

OBJECTIVE   The child will state what is or is not his name.

MATERIALS   None

PROCEDURE   Go around the class and have each child state what is and is not his name: "My name is Jay. My name is not Lynn." When the children have the idea, begin to joke with them and have them correct you: "Sam is a chair!" "No, Sam is not a chair. Sam is a boy." Be sure to use the negations. Once children realize how the negation works and that there can be numerous names that are not theirs, add objects and other items: "Sam has blue hair," "These books are the same," and so on:

> is/is not
>
> has/has not
>
> does/does not
>
> same/not the same

Increase Level of Difficulty

Materials   books (different covers, different sizes)

markers, pens, pencils, crayons

chairs (child's, teacher's, doll house)

articles of clothing

children

Procedure   Use materials that are alike in some ways and not alike or different in other ways, then ask how they are not the same or how they are different. It is challenging to use objects that are conceptually alike and perceptually (visually) different, such as a red and a blue book, a flashlight and a lamp, and so forth.

Decrease Level of Difficulty

Materials   book/ruler   flashlight/crayon

paper/block   eraser/dish

yellow pencil/yellow pencil   cup/cup

Procedure   Use simple concrete objects that are the same and not the same. Choose objects that look different from each other. Be sure children have the idea of negation before introducing the idea that something is different. That is, teach the children the same/not the same before the same/different.

COMMENT   This language-based activity is difficult for those who do not have the prerequisite language skills. For children with *hearing* and *visual* impairments, establish the comparison first by using actual objects. Allow the children to handle the objects.

NEVER

GOAL   To increase expressive language
To improve classification skills
To increase inclusion

OBJECTIVE   The child will use opposites appropriately.

MATERIALS   None

PROCEDURE   After children are comfortable with negations introduce the concept of opposite and discuss how opposites are only part of the negation. Then introduce some of the other words that allow for comparison, such as:

Absolute		*Relative*	
always	often	rarely	sometimes
never	often	rarely	sometimes
all	some	few	many
none	some	few	many

Have children make up sentences using the absolute words. When appropriate, challenge the concept and encourage children to use a more relative word: "I *always* clean up the block corner." Question the child: "Has there been *one* day when you haven't?" Help the child choose another word that more accurately represents reality: "I *often* clean up the block corner."

Increase Level of Difficulty

Procedure   Helping children use the appropriate words in spontaneous speech is probably one of a teacher's greatest challenges. The need must be addressed as the occasion arises. Help children see the relationship between their language and their behavior.

Decrease Level of Difficulty

Procedure   Listen to children's speech patterns and their use of absolute terms. Choose one term that occurs frequently and begin to work on that specific word.

COMMENT   Although this may seem like belaboring a point, prejudicial statements are usually absolute ones: "John can't do *anything*." "All disabled people are *helpless*." The skill of using words that allow for exceptions needs to be developed as a language skill so that absolute, prejudicial statements can be avoided in social situations.

Speaking

MY SHOES

GOAL   To increase expressive language
To improve sequencing skills
To encourage creativity

OBJECTIVE   The child will tell a creative story about a familiar object.

MATERIALS   Common objects:

shoes	winter coat	roller skates
ring	tricycle/bicycle	seashell

PROCEDURE   During group time, discuss the difference between animate and inanimate objects and have children imagine what objects might feel if they had feelings. Give them an example:

Shoes

I have pretty buckles and I am red. This morning I was sleeping in a dark closet very peacefully when someone turned on a bright light and stepped on me. I creaked a little, but that didn't stop her. She wiggled her feet into me and then ran down a flight of stairs. I then was stood on in the kitchen for twenty minutes. Finally, there was some relief. . . .

Encourage children to tell stories in small groups.

Increase Level of Difficulty

Materials	brick	stone
	towel	cotton ball

Procedure   Use objects that have fewer visual cues and are less well known to the children. They may want to illustrate the story, record it on a tape recorder, or write it.

Decrease Level of Difficulty

Procedure   Use more familiar objects with numerous visual cues, such as a hat with flowers on it. Prompt the child with cues such as "What happened then?" or "How did you feel then?" or more obvious ones, such as "What color are you? What do you look like?" Expect only a sentence or two.

COMMENT   This activity can easily be adapted to most units and themes. For example, if you have a circus theme, have the children be the tightrope or the safety net or the lion tamer's shoes. Children can be autumn leaves falling or plants growing, a dog's dish, or any type of transportation. This is a good "game" for parents to play while they are waiting with children. They can pick an object in any room and have the children pretend they are that object. Items can range from the chair in a doctor's waiting room to the dentist's mirror or even his drill. Pretending to be the object may help a child to think about an object in a different way, especially if he is apprehensive about it.

Speaking

SHOE THEATER

GOAL   To increase expressive language
To increase inclusion
To encourage creativity

OBJECTIVE   The child will participate in a play using unusual objects as puppets.

MATERIALS   pairs of shoes (men's, women's, baby's)

pairs of socks (men's, women's, baby's)

PROCEDURE   Have the children pretend the objects are puppets. Use one hand for each shoe or sock and have a shoe or sock theater. Encourage children to make up a play and perform it.

Increase Level of Difficulty

Procedure   Children can develop a script for their play and dictate it into a tape recorder or have someone write it down. They can make props and scenery if desired.

Decrease Level of Difficulty

Procedure   Help less skillful children find roles that allow them to participate. If their language skills are not good they might choose the baby's shoes. They could be a visiting pair of shoes also.

COMMENT   Because shoes really suggest no particular theme, this game encourages creativity. Again, as the roles are undefined, it is easy to think of ways different children with varying skill levels can participate.

Speaking

IDEAS

GOAL   To increase expressive language
To encourage creativity
To encourage creative problem solving

OBJECTIVE   The child will name many uses for an object.

MATERIALS   Common objects with few details, such as:

block	plate	an article of clothing such as a scarf or a sock
book	chair	
cup/glass	table	

PROCEDURE   Choose an object and ask the children to identify it. First ask them to describe the usual uses for the object. Then ask them to think of different ways to use the object. (The block could keep the door open; you could paint a face on it and use it as a doll, step on it to reach something, and so on.) List the children's suggestions.

Increase Level of Difficulty

Procedure   Ask the children for more than three responses, or call on them after the easier answers have been given.

Decrease Level of Difficulty

Procedure   To make the task easier, call on children at the beginning and require only one response. Give hints for other uses. Reverse the procedure and create a hypothetical problem and ask the children for alternative solutions for the problem. Accept all solutions without judgment.

COMMENT   Use objects from traditionally threatening places, such as a doctor's office or hospital. Start with tongue depressors and flashlights, then work your way up to dentist's drills and needles for shots. Have children think of different uses for these objects.

Speaking

DIVERGENT

GOAL   To increase expressive language
To improve cause-and-effect reasoning
To encourage creative problem solving

OBJECTIVE   The child states at least two ways in which life would be different without a particular thing.

MATERIALS   None

PROCEDURE   Have a discussion related to a particular theme or topic (wheels, chairs, television, paper, and so on). Start off simply asking the children to name things they have or use. Then ask them to imagine what it would be like if we didn't have _____. Expand this concept to have children think about how life would be different if they didn't have hands, eyes, ears, and so on. Scrupulously avoid references that could hurt or offend a particular child or family situation. Pose questions as to how they could do certain things and learn ways of compensating. Where appropriate, have children demonstrate what they would do.

Increase Level of Difficulty

Procedure   Expand the examples into services such as medicine, electricity, water, and so on. Talk about natural events, asking what it would be like if the sun didn't set, for example. In situations where appropriate, ask what they could do instead or use as a substitute.

Decrease Level of Difficulty

Materials   paper   clothing   pencils

Procedure   Show children objects that they use in the classroom and then expand these into categories. For example, show them a piece of paper and then talk about all the paper used in the classroom and ask how it would be different not to have paper. Give children hints such as, "What would we write on if we didn't have paper?" and "What would we sit on if we didn't have chairs?"

COMMENT   This activity is particularly appropriate when studying cultures such as Native Americans or units that are in the past such as dinosaurs, or holidays such as Thanksgiving or President's Day. This is also a time for children with some disabilities to show off. Children with sensory impairments might share with others how they compensate. For example, "Joan has a great way of looking for things when her locker gets rearranged. Can you show the class how you search for things? What is she doing? Now, if there were no electricity and you were in the dark and wanted to find a special toy, how would you do it?" Perhaps even blindfold a child to demonstrate the search. Ask for new ideas. Build children's self-concepts by pointing out how they compensate either for disabilities or for situational conditions such as being too short to reach something they want. As children realize the principles behind their skill it will become easier to apply it in other situations.

BRING ME

GOAL   To improve expressive language
To increase comprehension
To improve classification skills

OBJECTIVE   The child will get a requested object or state that he can't bring it.

MATERIALS   None

PROCEDURE   The teacher requests various objects, and the child must either get the object or say, "I'm sorry I can't bring you _____ because _____."

CHILD COULD BRING	CHILD COULDN'T BRING
block	wall
shoe	sky
piece of paper	elephant

When children get the idea of the game, the child who can't bring the requested item can name something he can bring instead.

Increase Level of Difficulty

Procedure   Ask for objects that are either more difficult to find or more difficult to transport.

Decrease Level of Difficulty

Procedure   Make easy, obvious requests.

COMMENT   This request game requires some logical reasoning skills to play. It also offers a great opportunity to use a sense of humor.

WEEKEND NEWS

GOAL   To increase expressive language
To increase inclusion
To express feelings

OBJECTIVE   The child will share with others events that are important to him.

MATERIALS   None

PROCEDURE   During group time, give each child (or a designated smaller group of children) an opportunity to talk about things that happened to him over the weekend. Write down briefly what the children say and encourage them to look at it during the day. As you write be sure to include each child's name. For example,

Paige said, "Mary Beth slept over at my house."
"I saw a fire," Don said.

When children have gotten comfortable sharing what happened to them over the weekend ask them to talk about the best and worst things that they encountered. As children's time lines are not very well defined, they may relate events from longer ago than asked for. The variety of comments is likely to be tremendous:

Worst	Best
Coming to school	Going out to dinner
Falling down	Staying up later than usual
Hearing a scary noise at night	Having a special food
	Daddy's coming home
Being teased or yelled at	Playing with Mommy
A sibling's birthday	Getting my hair cut

As you might guess, these topics brought up by one or two children, can lead to general discussions about the concerns of all children. Children are surprisingly candid about and responsive to this. With the help of sensitive adults to make sure the children don't hurt each other's feelings, the activity provides a safe place for children to talk about the "worst" things without shame or ridicule. They learn that all people have best and worst things, including you, if you are willing to share these.

Increase Level of Difficulty

Procedure   Have the children "write" their weekend news and read it to the class.

Decrease Level of Difficulty

Procedure   Have the children draw pictures of what happened to them over the weekend, and if they are comfortable ask them to talk about their picture.

COMMENT   Having children talk about what has happened to them, especially when they discuss the best and worst events, can help others see that children with disabilities have many of the same problems they do. For those with communication disorders, drawings are useful.

Speaking

PEEK PICTURES

GOAL   To increase expressive language
To increase comprehension
To increase inclusion

OBJECTIVE   The child will label or describe at least one picture after two opportunities to look at it.

MATERIALS   shoe box with a hole 1″ × 1″ in one end and a 3½-inch slot in the lid (a 2″ × 2″ window may be added to the lid for additional light if necessary)

pictures pasted on 3″ × 5″ cards

PROCEDURE   Cut a small hole in one end of a shoe box and a slot in the lid at the opposite end. One child places a picture in the slot and the other child takes a peek and describes it. Each child can peek and add a statement about what he sees.

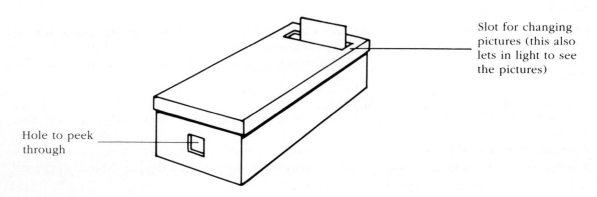

Slot for changing pictures (this also lets in light to see the pictures)

Hole to peek through

Increase Level of Difficulty

Materials   Pictures of more complex objects

Procedure   Use three children and make this a guessing game. One child puts the picture in the slot, one child describes the object but cannot tell what it is (e.g., it's something you drink out of), the third child guesses. Then the children rotate jobs.

Decrease Level of Difficulty

Procedure   Use the pictures without the shoe box. Choose simpler pictures.

COMMENT   Putting the pictures in a shoe box adds an element of surprise and a sense of secrecy to the activity. You might even put pictures of the children in the class on 3 × 5 cards and see if other children can identify their classmates. A good activity for the beginning of the year.

Speaking

RHYMING WORDS

GOAL   To increase expressive language
To improve listening skills
To improve comprehension

OBJECTIVE   The child will give at least one rhyming word for the one the teacher presents.

MATERIALS   None

PROCEDURE   Define rhyming words—words that end with the same sound. Give lots of examples before asking the children for words. Read a story or go over a familiar fingerplay that uses rhyming words. Start with familiar rhymes. List both real and nonsense words. Praise the children for finding a real rhyme, even if it is a nonsense word, but point out that it isn't a real word—look it up in a children's dictionary.

ACE	DARE	HEAD	BUMP
brace	scare	read	stump
trace	stare	bread	lump
pace	care	dead	jump
place	bare	tread	grump
COW	COT	IT	BED
now	hot	bit	fed
how	got	fit	led
pow	lot	hit	red
plow	shot	lit	sled

Without slowing the children down too much, use the opportunity to expand the children's vocabularies by asking them to define the words. Have the children repeat the rhyming words quickly and slowly.

Increase Level of Difficulty

Procedure   Encourage children to make a "Have You Seen a . . . ." book of rhyming words they can illustrate. Have you seen a

red bed	bare mare
plow cow	fake cake

Help children explore the structure of language using different parts of speech and longer words that rhyme.

Decrease Level of Difficulty

Procedure   Read a book such as Dr. Seuss's *Green Eggs and Ham* and point out the rhyming words to the children. See if they can generate some as well.

COMMENT   Rhyming is a good way to dismiss children. As each one leaves, ask the child to give a word that rhymes with yours: "José, give me a word that rhymes with cat." "Sat." "Sally, another word." "Hat." For children with *hearing* impairments, make cards with pictures of words that rhyme (red, bed, sled) and see if you can help children isolate the initial sound and add the rhyme.

Speaking

TELEPHONE

GOAL   To increase expressive language
To improve listening skills
To increase inclusion

OBJECTIVE   The child will talk to another child on the phone without seeing him.

MATERIALS   2 telephones

sets of pictures (at least 2 identical sets of 4 pictures each)

divider that stands on a table

PROCEDURE   Make telephones from string and tin cans or use those from the dramatic play area. Place the telephones on both sides of the divider and encourage children to talk with each other. If they do not talk spontaneously, you need to add some props or a procedure for encouraging them. When children are comfortable with the setup, give each child an identical set of pictures; have one child describe the picture he is looking at so the other child can find the picture. When children think they have found the correct picture have them check with the other child to verify this.

Increase Level of Difficulty

Procedure   Increase both the complexity and the similarity of the pictures so that it takes a very accurate description to distinguish among the pictures.

Decrease Level of Difficulty

Procedure   Take down the divider or use a lower one so the children can see each other. Use simpler pictures.

COMMENT   This activity isolates listening and requires the children to use verbal cues to obtain their information. It also encourages precision in language usage. For children with *visual impairments* use objects that can be felt and described rather than pictures.

Speaking

OBJECT HUNT

GOAL   To increase expressive language
To follow directions
To improve sensory motor integration

OBJECTIVE   The child will follow the directions and guess what the object is.

MATERIALS   None

PROCEDURE   Choose an object in the classroom. Tell the child who is giving the directions what the object is. He then gives directions to the searcher. The searcher can only ask questions that can be answered "yes" or "no."

DIRECTION GIVER: Go to the block area.
Stand beside the longest blocks.
Look up.
SEARCHER: Is it a window?
DIRECTION GIVER: No.
Turn around . . .

Increase Level of Difficulty

Procedure   Choose objects in difficult locations that require fine discriminations both on the part of the direction giver and the searcher.

Decrease Level of Difficulty

Procedure   You give the directions so that you can be sure they are easy to follow. You can hide an object such as a hat so the children know they are looking for a specific object (e.g., hat). They might then find the hat regardless of the accuracy of the directions.

COMMENT   Children can play this in pairs or small groups, inside or outside. It provides good feedback on how difficult it is to give accurate directions.

Speaking

INTERVIEWS

GOAL   To increase expressive language
To increase inclusion
To improve self-concept

OBJECTIVE   The child will answer questions in front of a group of children.

MATERIALS   a play microphone

PROCEDURE   Do a takeoff on some of the popular talk shows: "Good morning, today is Tuesday, February 2, and we are delighted to have as our guest today Miss Katie Ying. Katie, can you tell our listeners some of the things that you really like to do? Do you have any favorite foods? . . ."

Increase Level of Difficulty

Procedure   Encourage children to talk about particular interests they have and want to share.

Decrease Level of Difficulty

Procedure   Make the questions easy, and keep the interview short.

COMMENT   Be sure to have a "mike" as a prop. You might even explain that this is Katie's first appearance and she might be a bit shy.

Speaking

IMAGINARY WALK

GOAL   To increase comprehension
To follow directions
To improve sensory motor integration

OBJECTIVE   The child will walk following the directions given and do the appropriate movements.

MATERIALS   None

PROCEDURE   As the children take a walk around the room or outdoors, help them imagine they are somewhere else. Call out commands, such as:

Stop!
There is a big step. Go up it.
Oh, the sidewalk is hot. Tiptoe fast.
There is a little step. Go down.
Wait. Listen.
OK. Walk forward.
Stop. There is a wall. Walk sideways.
Oh, there is a small hole. Trace it with your hand. Now, wiggle through it.
Lean back against the wall and relax.

Take a deep breath.
Sit down.

Increase Level of Difficulty

Procedure   Make the walk longer, and ask the children how to circumvent various obstacles you invent.

Decrease Level of Difficulty

Procedure   The walk can be slower paced, shorter, and have one-step directions only.

COMMENT   This is an especially good activity for children with *visual* impairments who may be dependent on verbal directions to find things and move safely in their environment. It is also a good activity to use when children need to move during group time and yet remain in a group.

Speaking

WORD ASSOCIATIONS

GOAL   To increase comprehension
To encourage creativity

OBJECTIVE   The child will name an associated word and tell why it occurred to him.

MATERIALS   None

PROCEDURE   Teach the children the game of word associations. "I'll say a word and I want you to tell me what other words you think of." Start with something easy such as colors, for example:

red:	fire, hot, tomatoes, anger
blue:	water, cool
green:	grass, leaves
pink:	soft
white:	snow, uniforms
black:	night, cat
yellow:	sun, lemons

Increase Level of Difficulty

Procedure   Encourage children to say as many things as they can think of that they associate with the color. Use more obscure ideas and see what children come up with. Listen especially to their rationale for inclusion.

Decrease Level of Difficulty

Procedure   Have children look around the room for ideas if they are having problems.

COMMENT   If children don't say some of the obvious words you want to explore, say, "It reminds me of . . . " Then share with them your rationale.

Listening

MAGICIAN

GOAL   To improve listening skills

OBJECTIVE   The child will make the noise requested by the teacher and identify at least two noises made by classmates.

MATERIALS   None

PROCEDURE   The teacher plays the magician and "changes" a child into a noise-making object by whispering into the child's ear what object he is to be or gives the child a picture of the object. The child then pretends to be the object by making the noise, and the other children guess what the object is.

Increase Level of Difficulty

Procedure   Use sounds that are conceptually different yet sound similar, such as the tick of a clock, the click of a ball point pen, and the drip of water. Have the listening children shut their eyes.

Decrease Level of Difficulty

Procedure   Use sounds that are phonetically different yet conceptually related, such as vehicles, outside sounds, sounds of animals, or kitchen sounds. Have the objects, or pictures of the objects in sight. In addition to making the sound, have the child pretend to be or use the object, that is, if it is the hiss of a snake, have the child hiss as well as squirm on the floor if the sound is not initially guessed.

COMMENT   Use visual supports for the child with a *hearing* impairment; give him a picture of the object. Have the other children make the noises both in a regular voice and louder, supported with body movements and, if possible, pictures. Even though the child may not hear the sounds the other children make, the body language that accompanies the sound will be informative. By identifying sounds such as these the child gets feedback from her environment.

Listening

SOUNDS OF SILENCE

GOAL   To improve listening skills

OBJECTIVE   The child will listen and name one thing she heard.

MATERIALS   None

PROCEDURE   Ask the children to be quiet, then see if they can be silent. Explain that they are going to listen and figure out what they can hear when they are absolutely quiet. First help children relax their bodies, then have them listen for one minute. Make a list of what they heard. The list might include clocks ticking, heating sounds, blinds moving, birds chirping, and so on.

Increase Level of Difficulty

Procedure   Have a longer silent period. Help children write a poem or short story about the "Sounds of Silence." Talk about night and the sounds they hear while going to sleep. Encourage them to talk or write about this.

Decrease Level of Difficulty

Procedure   Keep the period of silence short. Call on children early to make the task easier for them.

COMMENT   The world is full of so much stimulation for children, they rarely concentrate on listening for very small sounds. This is a concentration and identification activity.

Listening

WHISPER

GOAL   To improve listening skills

OBJECTIVE   The child will act out the originally whispered task.

MATERIALS   None

PROCEDURE   This is a takeoff on the party game "Telephone." Pick a command such as "Touch your head." With the children sitting in a circle, whisper this to the first child, have the first child whisper to the second child, and so on around the circle until the child at the end performs the task requested.

Increase Level of Difficulty

Procedure   Increase the length of the task so that they must remember longer commands: e.g., "Go to the door and open it, then come back and sit down."

Decrease Level of Difficulty

Procedure   Have fewer people, simpler commands, and whisper louder.

COMMENT   Be sure to have a sense of humor about this. Whispering is a fun way for children to see the outcome of misarticulation.

Listening

SAY IT

GOAL   To improve listening skills
          To increase comprehension

OBJECTIVE   The child will correctly imitate the sound made by the teacher.

MATERIALS   None

PROCEDURE   During group time, say various words or sentences and have the children imitate you. Using the same words, change your voice pitch, intonation, speed, or stress.

SENTENCE	VARIATIONS
I like juice.	normal
	loud
	soft/whisper
	fast
	slow
	puckered mouth
I like juice.	stress
I *like* juice.	stress
I like *juice.*	stress
	raise your voice for a question
	hold your nose

As the children imitate you and change their voices, verbalize for them what you (they) did: "Great, you all said it as loud as I did." Explore with children the impact that tone and intonation pattern have for meaning. Discuss where you might use different voices. Ask children how they would say something at a sports event as compared to group time.

Increase Level of Difficulty

Procedure   Have children use longer and more challenging sentences. Have other children imitate them and give them feedback about different intonation patterns.

Decrease Level of Difficulty

Procedure   Start with the most obvious differences: loud and soft, fast and slow. Try to associate these with specific events.

COMMENT   Because so much of meaning is passed through the nonverbal aspect of language, it is important that children are aware of it from an early age.

LISTENING WALK

GOAL   To improve listening skills
To increase comprehension

OBJECTIVE   The child will identify a sound he hears on the walk, describe the sound, and what makes it.

MATERIALS   None

PROCEDURE   Before you take the children outside, ask them to listen carefully and identify sounds, but not to talk to each other during the walk. Tell them to try to figure out what is making each sound. When they return, have them describe and imitate the sounds they heard. The other children have to decide what might have made the sound. For example, the child might say, "I heard a peck, peck, peck. What is it?" rather than "I heard a bird."

Increase Level of Difficulty

Procedure   Take a small group of children and do the same walk again. Try to be quieter, pause more frequently, and walk more slowly. Compare what was heard on the first walk with the second.

Decrease Level of Difficulty

Procedure   Point out sounds on the walk. If possible, encourage children to pick up something to help them remember the sound when they return to the classroom.

COMMENT   Vary the walk by having the children first walk making a lot of noise and then very little noise and compare what they hear. Help children to stand or sit and listen.

NOISY AND QUIET

GOAL   To improve listening skills
To increase comprehension

OBJECTIVE   The child will identify sounds and events that are typically either noisy or quiet.

MATERIALS   None

PROCEDURE   Play the game "I'm thinking of something noisy," and have the children guess what you are thinking of. Respond to them in one of three ways: "Yes it is noisy, but not what I'm thinking of." "That is quiet; think of something noisy," or "Yes, that's it." Do the same thing with *quiet*. Make a list of the ideas the children generate on what is noisy and what is quiet. Ask children to think of noisy holidays, foods, animals, instruments, and so on.

Increase Level of Difficulty

Materials   construction paper   crayons   pencil

Procedure   Ask children to fold a piece of construction paper in half and draw a noisy picture on one side and a quiet one on the other or write a story using noisy or quiet words.

Decrease Level of Difficulty

Procedure   Help children use objects in the classroom and decide whether they are noisy or quiet. Point out times when the class is noisy or quiet.

COMMENT   It is important to point out that noisy and quiet are different, not to make judgments that noisy is "bad" and quiet is "good."

SOUND AND TELL

GOAL   To improve listening skills
To increase comprehension

OBJECTIVE   The child will identify the sound.

MATERIALS   a screen (could be a rectangular table on its side)

a paper bag for each child in the class

a noisemaker (an object from class or one brought from home, such as:

whistle	dishes	bell
two blocks	spoons	pen that clicks
timer	scissors	book (to close or drop)

PROCEDURE   Ask each child to bring a noisemaker from home or to find an object in the classroom that makes a noise and can fit in the bag. Give each child a bag in which to hide the noisemaker. Have each child go behind the screen and make the sound. The other children guess what it is. Then have the child make the sound so that all can see.

Increase Level of Difficulty

Procedure   Once the noises have been identified, have two children go behind the screen and make a pattern of noises that the children can identify.

Decrease Level of Difficulty

Procedure   Be sure the child knows how to make the noise. If not, help him.

Listening is an active process that can be both intense and fun.

COMMENT   Discuss the properties of objects that make noise and those that do not. Classify noises as loud, soft, sharp, and so on. Have children make noises with various body parts behind the screen (e.g., clap, stomp). The other children can then guess how the sound was made.

Listening

SOUND CUES

GOAL   To improve listening skills
To increase comprehension

OBJECTIVE   The child will identify the sound and the actions the sound describes.

MATERIALS   tape recorder   tapes of sounds

PROCEDURE   Record a variety of sounds. Have the children identify them. Then have them decide where they might hear each sound and what might be happening. Indoor sounds that might be used include the following:

mixer:	cooking
vacuum cleaner:	cleaning
toilet flushing:	going to the bathroom
washing machine:	washing clothes

This can also be done with street noises, such as

brakes:	stopping
engine:	starting
car door closing:	getting in the car
seat belt clicking:	putting on seat belt
horn:	attention

Increase Level of Difficulty
Procedure   Using the car noises as an example, see if the children can sequence them as they might normally happen in the act of coming to school in the car. Give the child a tape recorder and have the child record sounds in the classroom and outside and have others identify them.

Decrease Level of Difficulty
Materials   pictures of items making the sound
Procedure   Instead of asking the child to identify the sound from the auditory input alone, first give the child a choice of two possible pictures of objects, one of which actually made the sound. Increase the choices to three, then five, and then see if the children can discriminate without the visual cues.

COMMENT   Identifying different musical instruments provides a real challenge, but is a fun activity. Start with widely different instruments, such as a piano and a guitar, and add from there. At the beginning have some instruments available for the children to explore.

Listening

NOISY STEPS

GOAL   To improve listening skills
To follow directions
To improve sensory motor integration

OBJECTIVE   The child will step on the picture of the object in response to the sound.

MATERIALS   cassette and tape recorder (optional)

pictures of things that make sounds

PROCEDURE   Make picture cutouts and tape them to the floor or a piece of sturdy cloth. Use pictures of animals or sound makers (clock, tuning fork, bell, telephone). As the sound is made, the child steps on the picture of that object. As an activity for a single child, this can also be played like "Twister": that is, the child puts a different body part on each picture of an object as the sound of the object is made.

Increase Level of Difficulty

Materials   pictures of string instruments

Procedure   Use pictures that have sounds that are more difficult to discriminate such as musical string instruments. Or, instead of using sounds, use the initial letter or letter sound of the picture (check that only one picture starts with each sound). Have the children make the sounds while others move. Specify a body part that must touch the picture, that is, "Touch the picture that begins with *h* (helicopter) with your right hand."

Decrease Level of Difficulty

Materials   bell   miniature cow   tambourine

blocks   triangle   baby

Procedure   Put out the actual objects used to make the sound or a three-dimensional replica of them so the child can double check the answer. Decrease the number of different pictures used. Be sure that the pictures chosen have very different sounds. Increase the time allocated on the tape to find the picture, or have the child turn the tape off before finding the object. Give the child an additional hint; that is, if the cow is not chosen in response to "moo," add that it is an animal that gives milk, it lives on the farm, and so on until the child chooses the correct picture.

COMMENT   Use pictures that support specific themes (e.g., for transportation use a train, boat, car, ambulance, feet running, airplane). If a child has difficulty moving from place to place, have her throw beanbags to the appropriate picture.

Listening

SOUND EGGS

GOAL   To improve listening skills
To improve cause and effect reasoning

OBJECTIVE   The child will find the pairs of containers that sound the same.

MATERIALS   5 or 6 pairs of containers (these could be plastic eggs, orange juice or milk cartons, yogurt containers, and so on—nothing transparent)

materials that can be used to make a sound (enough for two containers):

rice	paper clips	pebbles
macaroni	bells	shells
dried beans/peas/lentils	ball bearings	

PROCEDURE   Partially fill each pair of containers with the chosen materials. Mark the bottoms of the pairs of containers with pairs of letters or numbers so the child can check to see if he has made a pair. Ask the child to shake the containers and match the pairs by sound.

Increase Level of Difficulty

Materials   cups with the materials (e.g., rice, macaroni) with plastic covers so children can see the materials

Procedure   See if the children can figure out what is inside the pairs of closed containers by looking at the possibilities. Help them make their own containers to check. Have them experiment. Does it sound the same when the quantity in each container is different? Does the sound change depending on how hard you shake the container?

Decrease Level of Difficulty

Procedure   Use fewer containers and materials that have very different sounds.

COMMENT   Children enjoy exploring the process of what makes sound and how they can control it.

WATER TONES

GOAL   To improve listening skills
          To improve cause and effect reasoning

OBJECTIVE   The child will state whether the tapped glasses sound the same or different.

MATERIALS   water glasses with varying amounts of water in them

PROCEDURE   Fill glasses with different amounts of water. Allow the children to examine the glasses and the sounds they produce. Help them discover the relationship between the amount of water and the pitch.

Increase Level of Difficulty

Materials   2 sets of water glasses

Procedure   Have children arrange the glasses by pitch. Talk with them about the relationship between the amount of water and the pitch. Blindfold the children and have them match the glasses and then put them in order of pitch from high to low. Encourage children to experiment by adding or subtracting water to make different pitches.

Decrease Level of Difficulty

Procedure   Start with three glasses, two nearly full and one almost empty. Help the children classify their sounds as the same or different. Gradually introduce more glasses. Encourage the children to experiment with making different pitches.

COMMENT   Children can both hear and see the differences produced. Help them make finer discriminations while talking about the underlying principles.

NUMBER TAPPING

GOAL   To improve listening skills
          To improve sensory motor integration
          To improve number concepts

OBJECTIVE   The child will state the number of taps made.

MATERIALS   piano   drum

               table   tambourine

PROCEDURE   Have a child tap a number or tap it yourself. Have the class state the number, hold up the right number of fingers, or call on one child to answer.

Increase Level of Difficulty

Procedure   Tap a nonrhythmic pattern or tap very quickly. Tap each rhythm on a different object or instrument. Have the children close their eyes. Ask the children to repeat the pattern back to you. Use different patterns.

Decrease Level of Difficulty

Procedure   Tap slowly on the same instrument in a steady pattern. Use only low numbers.

COMMENT   The activity requires the integration of auditory, tactile, and verbal skills to learn number concepts. For children with *hearing* impairments, tap dramatically so that the children can use visual as well as auditory skills.

WHERE IS IT/WHO IS IT?

GOAL   To improve listening skills
To improve sensory motor integration

OBJECTIVE   The child will point to the general area in which another child is walking.

MATERIALS   None

PROCEDURE   Have the children sit facing a wall with their eyes shut. Ask one child to walk to a specific area of the room. As he is walking, tell the children to listen and then point to the area where he has stopped. Then have them open their eyes and check if they are right.

Increase Level of Difficulty

Procedure   Instead of pointing, ask the children to name the area of the room where the walker is (e.g., the dramatic play area, the construction area). This is difficult because the children have to remember the various parts of the room and visualize their location. Children might also try to identify the walker by the sound of the footsteps. Help with some initial questions: "What kind of shoes is the child wearing? Is the walk heavy or light, fast or slow?" This is not a good variation with a rug.

Decrease Level of Difficulty

Procedure   Instead of just walking have the to-be-located child hit a tambourine or drum and stay in one place.

COMMENT   Children can learn to fine-tune their listening skills, but it requires practice.

TAPE IT

GOAL   To improve listening skills
To improve adaptive skills
To improve self-concept

OBJECTIVE   The child will identify his own voice and that of at least one classmate.

MATERIALS   a tape recorder

a blank cassette

PROCEDURE   Over the course of several days have children talk into the tape recorder for about a minute about what they are doing. When everyone in the class is on tape, have a small group listening time when the children try to guess who is talking.

Increase Level of Difficulty

Procedure   Children can try to disguise their voices. Also, children can identify the features in a voice that make it recognizable.

Decrease Level of Difficulty

Materials   Pictures of classmates

Procedure   Children can be given pictures of several classmates who might be talking and asked to choose which one it is.

COMMENT   Be sure to keep a list of the order in which the children speak so that you know for sure who is talking. Send this tape to a child who has been out of school for a while. If the parents are given the order in which the children speak, the child can practice identifying the voices at home. Encourage children to send tape messages to friends who are not in school and have them returned.

LISTEN BEFORE YOU MOVE

GOAL To improve sequencing skills
To follow directions

OBJECTIVE The child will follow at least a two-step direction.

MATERIALS None

PROCEDURE During transition times, dismiss the children with two- or three-part directions.

"If you are wearing blue, touch your nose and then get your coat."
"If you are wearing red shoes, jump twice, put one hand on your head, and get your coat."

Increase Level of Difficulty

Procedure Increase the complexity of the directions both in the number of steps and the tasks themselves.

Decrease Level of Difficulty

Procedure Give the directions one step at a time and model them as you say what the child is to do.

COMMENT It is important to use transitions as a time of learning. Vary the directions to keep up interest. For children with *visual* impairments use items that the child can recognize by touch (e.g., buttons, shoelaces, collars, belts). Use pictures to help children with hearing impairments.

GOING TO THE BEACH

GOAL To improve sequencing skills
To increase comprehension
To improve reading readiness

OBJECTIVE The child will remember at least three items that he is taking on a trip to the beach.

MATERIALS flannel board

pictures of objects drawn or glued onto Pellon that children would be likely to take to the beach

PROCEDURE Discuss the beach and what people do there. Then play the game "I am going to the beach and in my suitcase I'm going to take a *swimsuit.*" The child must repeat the sentence and add another item from the pictures available. As each child chooses, place the chosen picture on the board, which would look something like this:

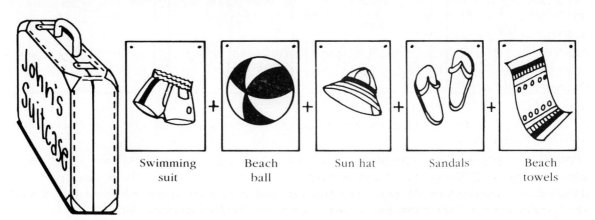

Swimming suit + Beach ball + Sun hat + Sandals + Beach towels

Write the name of each item below it. This is good for reading readiness and to compensate for lack of drawing ability. When the children have used up all the pictures, take the cards down in order and see how many they can remember.

Increase Level of Difficulty

Procedure   When this becomes easy, see if they can remember the pictures in the order in which they were hanging. As children become more adept, add more pictures or use no visual cues at all.

Decrease Level of Difficulty

Procedure   Have a suitcase and real items that the children actually pack. If children have trouble remembering the items give them functional cues (e.g., What will we sit on?).

COMMENT   This sequencing activity can be adapted to many situations. The class can go for a picnic and pack their lunches. Then see if the children remember to eat everything they brought. They can pack for a trip to the jungle, desert, North Pole, hospital, grandparents, and so on. Encourage children to discuss why certain items are necessary. Using actual objects allows children with visual impairments to participate.

Listening

NATURAL SEQUENCING

GOAL   To improve sequencing skills
To improve reading readiness
To improve cause-and-effect reasoning

OBJECTIVE   The child will put the pictures in order.

MATERIALS   pictures of a naturally occurring sequence

PROCEDURE   Make pictures of naturally occurring sequences. For example:

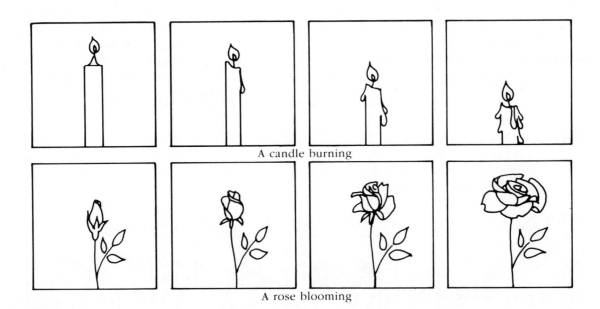

A candle burning

A rose blooming

Have the children order these pictures.

Increase Level of Difficulty

Procedure   Choose more complex but familiar sequences, such as getting dressed or brushing teeth. Then work into sequences that are less familiar but logical, such as going on a trip in a car or plane.

Decrease Level of Difficulty

Procedure   As these are naturally occurring sequences, have the actual objects there and match the stages with the sequences. That is, get a rose and put it in warm water and check how it opens, or burn the candle down and have the children match the sequence at each stage.

COMMENT   Be sure the pictures do not always show objects going from little to big. You do not have to be a terrific artist to make these, provided you pick concepts that are simple to illustrate (a pencil getting used up, a pine tree growing, and so on). However, pictures are available commercially. Natural sequencing is an especially good follow-up after a field trip. Children with limited experience often see events individually, without developing the connections that language and experience allow.

Reading Readiness

ALPHABET LOTTO

GOAL   To improve reading readiness

OBJECTIVE   The child will match the letters.

MATERIALS   alphabet game as described below

PROCEDURE   Divide pieces of poster board ($9'' \times 12''$) into six rectangles ($4'' \times 4^{1}/_{2}''$). Print a letter of the alphabet (not necessarily in order) in each rectangle. Make four cards with different letters on each.

D	N	A		Y	F	B		M	U	H		E	W	K
Z	Q	G		P	L	R		C	S	I		J	T	O

Cut twenty-four $4'' \times 4^{1}/_{2}''$ pieces, also out of poster board. Print a letter on each small rectangle to match the larger boards. Put the individual matching letters into a box to draw from so you can play a game of Lotto. (Note: As our alphabet has twenty-six letters, two will be missing. If you make two sets like this, omit different letters from each one.)

If children are having trouble matching particular letters, design cards to meet these problems. For example, with lower case letters, make a card with reversible lines and curves.

b	q	p
z	g	d

Increase Level of Difficulty

Materials   To expand the letter concept, make the following Lotto combinations:

Board

Printed upper case

Cards

Printed upper case

Printed lower case

Script upper case

Script lower case

Picture with initial letter sound

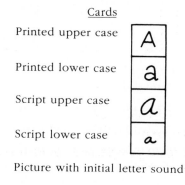

Procedure   Children can play this as a matching game alone. With all these combinations, there will be five cards for each letter on the board.

Decrease Level of Difficulty

Materials   Make a board out of letters that are very dissimilar (e.g., *A, W, O, S, T, D*). Don't have letters such as *M* and *W* or *O* and *C* on the same board as they might be confused initially.

Procedure   Initially work on letter identification using the boards. Then play Lotto.

COMMENT   Add the sign alphabet if children with hearing impairments are using signs. If a child with a visual impairment will become a Braille reader, the Braille alphabet can be used and matched to sandpaper letters. The sandpaper letters are helpful to the child with a learning disability as they provide sensory motor feedback as well.

Reading Readiness

BODY SOUNDS

GOAL   To improve reading readiness
To increase expressive language
To increase body awareness

OBJECTIVE   The child will decide which words for body parts have the same initial sound.

MATERIALS   None

PROCEDURE   Name a part of the body and then ask the children to name a part that has the same beginning sound or letter.

toe: teeth, tongue, throat, tendons

eye: elbow, eyebrow, ears, earlobe

hearing: hand, head, heart, hips

fingers: fingernails, foot, forearm, follicle

legs: lips, lungs

Increase Level of Difficulty

Procedure   Encourage children to think of less obvious body parts (internal ones) such as muscles, joints, and blood vessels. Give them functional clues.

Decrease Level of Difficulty

Procedure   Have children choose between two parts that you name. Allow children to name things in the room or anything they can think of that has the same initial sound.

COMMENT   This is a fun way of teaching children the names of body parts and the functions they serve. It is important for children to have the vocabulary to talk about their body with precision.

Reading Readiness

SOUND BINGO

GOAL   To improve reading readiness
To improve listening skills

OBJECTIVE   The child will identify the letter by its sound (/b/—/b/ as in ball).

MATERIALS   Bingo cards with letters rather than numbers

PROCEDURE   Using a regular bingo game format, call letter *sounds* instead of letters. A few letters will have to be eliminated, as they sound the same as others (e.g., /c/ and /k/), or give words that start with that sound as a clarifying clue. The children put a marker on the letter for each sound as it is called out. The winner is the first child to have a row, column, or diagonal. Continue to play until most children have completed a row.

B	I	N	G	O
a	u	r	p	o
s	h	b	c	i
w	x	free	v	g
m	j	n	l	d
e	f	g	t	z

Increase Level of Difficulty

Procedure   Instead of letter sounds, call out words and have the children mark the initial letter sound. This can also be done with the final letter sound, but you need to check the words for silent letters and those that are misleading, such as *penny,* where the *y* sounds like an *e.*

Decrease Level of Difficulty

Procedure   Play the game and ask children to identify the letters as you call them out. As you move to letter sounds, pair the children so they can work together.

COMMENT   As you work toward developing words for games such as this, you begin to appreciate the problems in learning a language like English that has so many exceptions to the rules.

Reading Readiness

FLANNEL BOARD STORIES

GOAL   To improve reading readiness
To improve listening skills
To increase inclusion

OBJECTIVE   The child will participate in the story telling process.

MATERIALS   flannel board   story

flannel board story pieces (trace figures from a coloring book or the storybook itself on Pellon and cut them out)

PROCEDURE   Pick a relatively simple story with a few central characters. (Animals work well.) Make felt or Pellon characters (they have more body if you use two pieces of fabric glued together). Tell the story and have the children put up the pieces as you talk about them.

Increase Level of Difficulty

Procedure   Allow children to play with the flannel board and pieces and encourage them to make up their own stories.

Decrease Level of Difficulty

Procedure   Give the child additional directions and support in putting up the pieces.

COMMENT   These stories are easy to follow and children can participate in the process. This sometimes makes listening easier.

Reading Readiness

TITLE

GOAL   To improve reading readiness
To increase comprehension

OBJECTIVE   The child will choose an appropriate name for the story.

MATERIALS   A made-up story or a printed story with the title hidden

PROCEDURE   Read or tell the story to the children. Explain that it has no title and that you want their help in deciding on the title. Ask them to suggest titles and write them down. Talk with the children about the list of titles and have them explain why they think the titles suggested would be good or not as good as others.

Increase Level of Difficulty

Materials   A more complex story

Decrease Level of Difficulty

Materials   A simple story or a paragraph from a story

COMMENT   Appropriate titles require high-level abstract reasoning skills. Children need to be challenged to think in this way.

Reading Readiness

LETTER DAY

GOAL   To improve reading readiness
           To increase comprehension
           To improve sensory motor integration

OBJECTIVE   The child will identify the letter through vision, hearing, and touch.

MATERIALS   letters of the alphabet made of sandpaper

                wooden cut-out letters

                objects that begin with each letter

PROCEDURE   Pick a letter of the alphabet. Expose the children to that letter in as many ways as you can. With the letter *P,* for example:

   Trace a sandpaper letter *P.*

   Feel your breath with your hand as you say */P/.*

   Point to *P* in a group of letters.

   Think of words that start with *P.*

   Make cookies or playdough in the shape of *P.*

   Eat *p*retzels for snack.

Increase Level of Difficulty

Procedure   Emphasize the sound of the letter as well as letter identification. This is particularly important for letters that have more than one sound such as *g* (*George* versus *Gary*) as well as long and short vowel sounds.

Decrease Level of Difficulty

Procedure   Concentrate on letter identification at first.

COMMENT   You can do any letter. Granted, *X* is a challenge! If you plan to do all the letters, start with the vowels and leave the most difficult consonants until last. Be sure to use both upper and lower case letters if you extend the activity.

Reading Readiness

CHANGING OBJECTS

GOAL   To improve reading readiness
           To improve sequencing skills

OBJECTIVE   The child will put three objects in their original order after they have been rearranged.

MATERIALS   objects   screen

PROCEDURE   Put three objects in a row and ask the children to look at them. Put a screen in front of the objects and rearrange them. Ask one of the children to put them in the original order. For variation, take one object away and have the children name the missing object.

Increase Level of Difficulty

Procedure   As the children improve, increase the number of objects and their similarity:

> easier: red block/blue airplane /green cup/orange crayon
>
> hard: red block/blue block /green block/orange block
>
> harder: red stocking cap/red baseball cap/red ski hat/red felt hat

Decrease Level of Difficulty

Procedure   Use objects that are less similar:

> *easy: cup/doll/block*

COMMENT   The objects that you choose can be based on the theme you are working on (hospital: tongue depressor, little flashlight, stethoscope, bandages) or as a way of introducing a topic that has unfamiliar materials or materials that children might be concerned about. Allow the children to touch and handle the materials.

Reading Readiness

COLOR GRAPHS

GOAL   To improve reading readiness
To follow directions
To improve small motor coordination

OBJECTIVE   The child will color the designated square a specific color.

MATERIALS   paper with squares drawn on it

crayons

PROCEDURE   Draw a pattern of squares on a piece of paper and duplicate it so each child has one. Then give the children directions:

Color the first two squares green. Color the next square red. Color the square below the second green square yellow . . .

It is a good idea to move from left to right in your directions. You can have children skip squares if that is useful. Have the children describe the pattern to you using both color and number.

Increase Level of Difficulty

Materials   Ditto with more squares in a particular shape

Procedure   Use left and right in the directions and don't have the children color adjacent squares in order.

Decrease Level of Difficulty

Materials   Squares in a line like a train

Procedure   Have the children color each "car" on the train in order. Make the first square somewhat different as a starting place. Give children additional time to color.

COMMENT   Vary your rate of presentation to match the skill of the children. If you are very creative, the design can be made to look like an object when it is colored correctly.

A teacher's desk is a good surface to use for magnetic toys. These boys are using it to practice reading readiness skills.

Reading Readiness

ALPHABET LINE

GOAL   To improve reading readiness
To improve writing readiness
To improve small motor coordination

OBJECTIVE   The child will find the designated letter and put it on the clothesline.

MATERIALS   clothesline   marking pen

paper   26 or more wooden clothespins

pictures

PROCEDURE   Print a letter of the alphabet on each clothespin. Have the children put the alphabet on the clothesline in the appropriate order or put up each letter you or another child requests. Print the letter on a separate piece of paper, and collect pictures that the children can sort by initial sound. Have the children match the paper letters to the clothespin, then hang the letters. The same can be done with pictures.

Increase Level of Difficulty

Procedure   Have children make words with the clothespins (for that you'll need additional letters) or copy words that you have printed on cards.

Decrease Level of Difficulty

Procedure   Use this as a letter identification task and have the child find the clothespin letter and put it on the clothesline.

COMMENT   Although simple, this activity is a useful way of developing finger strength while teaching a variety of skills relating to the alphabet.

MATRIX

GOAL   To improve reading readiness
            To improve observational skills
            To make predictions

OBJECTIVE   The child will state which piece is missing.

MATERIALS   flannel board

                       felt shapes, 1 large and 1 small of each of the following:

                            red triangle, circle, square, and rectangle

                            green triangle, circle, square, and rectangle

                            blue triangle, circle, square, and rectangle

                            yellow triangle, circle, square, and rectangle

PROCEDURE   Set up a 3 × 3 matrix on a flannel board.
Have the children close their eyes while you remove one piece. Ask them which piece is missing and how they know. If you remove the center piece, their reasoning should be "It has to be a circle because horizontally there are only circles, and it has to be green because vertically all the shapes are green." This is a thinking, not a memory game.

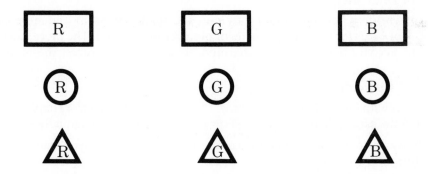

Increase Level of Difficulty

Materials   Work progressively from 3 × 3, to 4 × 4, to 3 × 6, to 3 × 8, to 4 × 8 matrices. The more complex 4 × 8 matrix (the eight columns are arranged into four groups of matching large and small shapes) looks like this:

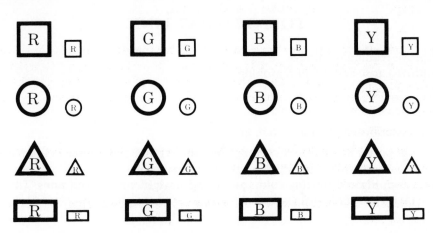

Procedure   After children learn the thinking, they can play with each other and create their own matrix.

Decrease Level of Difficulty

Procedure   Allow the children to use the pieces for color, shape, and size identification. When these are accomplished ask children to give you specific pieces. Then begin with a 2 × 2 matrix to work on the reasoning skills.

COMMENT   You can use different textures for children who cannot distinguish the colors. This is a thinking, not a memory game.

Reading Readiness

COLOR CONCENTRATION

GOAL   To improve reading readiness
To make predictions
To increase inclusion

OBJECTIVE   The child will remember where the matching color is.

MATERIALS   a set of cards with matching pairs of colors on one side

PROCEDURE   This is a variation of the game "Concentration." Lay out the cards face down. Each child takes a turn and chooses two cards. The objective is to turn over two cards that are the same color.

Increase Level of Difficulty

Procedure   As children become more proficient, add shades of colors and more cards. You can use a regular deck of cards for numbers, or pairs of pictures of any kind. The more cards you add, the more difficult the activity becomes. Also, the more detailed the pictures, the more difficult the game.

Decrease Level of Difficulty

Procedure   Start with four or five pairs of cards. Use primary colors and/or simple shapes. First have the children match the cards. Then demonstrate how the game is played. Gradually add more cards.

COMMENT   This can also be done with letters of the alphabet. You can even match capital and small letters, a more difficult variation.

Reading Readiness

FOLLOW THAT LINE

GOAL   To improve reading readiness
To improve cause-and-effect reasoning
To increase inclusion

OBJECTIVE   The child will make a pattern.

MATERIALS   poster board   markers (red, green, black)

PROCEDURE   Cut poster board into 3″ × 3″ squares and arrange these squares in a pattern on a large table or floor. (This is only for your ease in drawing.) Using black, red, and green markers, draw a pattern of lines, stopping and starting colors and using straight and curved lines. The children then can build a track with the cards in a variety of patterns, for example:

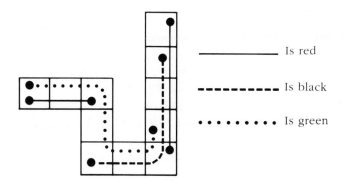

_____ Is red

- - - - - - - - - - Is black

· · · · · · · · · Is green

Increase Level of Difficulty

Procedure   The more squares you have available and the more colors and patterns, the more complicated the task is. It is also more challenging when children must make a designated pattern. Making the letter *H,* for example, requires a lot of problem solving. Children can also draw their own squares.

Decrease Level of Difficulty

Procedure   Use squares with only one color. When this is mastered, add a second color.

COMMENT   This is a good small-group project.

Reading Readiness

WHAT IS IT?

GOAL   To improve reading readiness
To improve observation skills
To improve generalization skills

OBJECTIVE   The child will identify the object.

MATERIALS   large (at least 5″ × 7″) pictures of familiar objects

large envelopes

PROCEDURE   Put a picture of a familiar object in an envelope. Pull it out slowly until part of the picture is exposed. Have the children guess what it is. Keep exposing more of the picture until it is correctly identified. Encourage the children to guess and give you the reasons for their guesses.

Increase Level of Difficulty

Procedure   Use pictures of less familiar objects or ones that have more ambiguous cues (an armchair and sofa look the same initially).

Decrease Level of Difficulty

Procedure   Be sure to start with pictures of simple, familiar objects (e.g., boats, cars, trains, people, animals). Pull about half of the picture out before you stop. You can use a screen and gradually push objects out as well.

COMMENT   Children need to develop skills in the area of visual closure. They need to be able to use partial information to infer what they cannot see. This also helps focus on relevant details.

Reading Readiness

SANDPAPER LETTERS

GOAL   To improve reading readiness
To increase sensory motor integration

OBJECTIVE   The child will trace the letter and name it.

MATERIALS   sandpaper   glue

cardboard   pictures

PROCEDURE   Cut the letters of the alphabet out of sandpaper and glue each on a cardboard square. Glue a picture of something that begins with that letter on the back. Have the child trace the letter with his index and middle fingers as you talk about the structure of the letter: "This is the letter *A*. It has three straight lines. One, two, three. The third connects the first two in the middle." Show the child the picture on the back to connect the letter with a sound.

Increase Level of Difficulty

Procedure   Have the children identify the letters blindfolded.

Decrease Level of Difficulty

Procedure   Start with the easiest letters based on the configuration of the letters and the child's knowledge.

COMMENT   The sensory integration aspect of learning the alphabet in this way is good for all children.

Reading Readiness

CHANGES

GOAL   To improve reading readiness

To increase body awareness

To increase inclusion

OBJECTIVE   The child will name or point to the change.

MATERIALS   None

PROCEDURE   Use a small group or have children pair up. One child turns around and closes his eyes while the child who is "it" changes something about his appearance (for example, unties shoe, rolls up pant leg, removes glasses, or unbuttons shirt). The first child must name or point to the change.

Increase Level of Difficulty

Procedure   As children improve, encourage them to make more subtle changes.

Decrease Level of Difficulty

Procedure   Help focus the children's attention by picking a category of change—for example, clothing—and have these changes be obvious. It may help if you are "it" first and give some clues.

COMMENT   This activity allows the child who is "it" to be in control of the change and to be part of the group, yet the child doesn't have to speak.

Reading Readiness

FISHING FOR FACES

GOAL   To improve reading readiness

To improve eye-hand coordination

OBJECTIVE   The child will match the face he catches to a face on a poster.

MATERIALS   matching pairs of pictures of faces   a shoe box

a poster-sized piece of paper   paste

construction paper   paper clips

a stick (fishing pole) with a string at the end, to which a magnet is tied

PROCEDURE   Paste one of each pair of faces on a small piece of construction paper and attach a paper clip at the neck. Put the faces in the shoe box. Paste the remaining faces on the poster. Have the children use fishing poles to fish for the faces in the box. Ask the children to match the face they have "caught" to the same face on the poster.

Increase Level of Difficulty

Materials   More faces with very minor differences

Decrease Level of Difficulty

Materials   Fewer faces with major differences

Procedure   Allow the children to hold the magnet in their hand.

COMMENT   Children can fish for numbers, letters, or even fish (then count the catch). If you want to put the fish in water, make them out of plastic and use waterproof marker for the face.

Writing

MIND MAPPING

GOAL   To improve writing readiness
To increase comprehension

OBJECTIVE   The child will participate in writing/drawing a mind map.

MATERIALS   paper   pencil/marker

PROCEDURE   After a topic has been chosen, encourage children to make a mind map before they begin to write. Start with the topic in the center of the page. Draw a balloon around it. Surround it with related ideas connected to it or to each other with lines. The lines show the relationship between the central theme and the topics mentioned. If there appear to be tangents, put these in the corners of the page. If they eventually become related attach them, if not they will not be part of the writing. Children's mind map might look something like this:

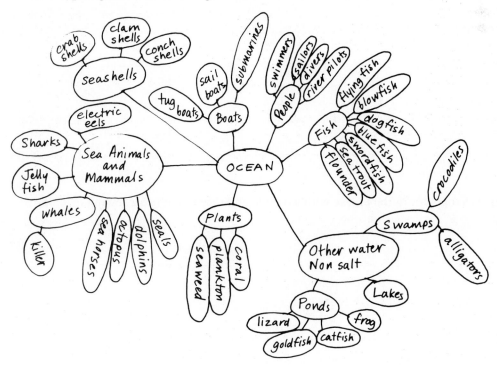

Mind Map or Webbing

The Ocean

This mind map was generated by a group of children, kindergarten to second grade, who live near the ocean. They needed help in differentiating between the animal and sea life that live in salt water and fresh water (tangent). However, their other ideas are very sophisticated.

Increase Level of Difficulty

Procedure   Have children make more complex maps on more difficult subjects.

Decrease Level of Difficulty

Procedure   Make the mind map as a group project with you as the teacher doing the writing.

COMMENT   Children need to organize their writing, but traditional outlines are rarely useful with young children. Mind mapping, or clustering ideas is more useful and helps set the flow for the writing. Initially, each balloon will probably be only a phrase or sentence.

Writing

BOOKS

GOAL   To improve writing readiness
To improve sequencing skills
To follow directions

OBJECTIVE   The child will write, illustrate, and publish a book with a hard cover.

MATERIALS   cardboard   cloth or wallpaperartists' spray dry mount
paper   needle and threadscissors

PROCEDURE   Decide how many pages you want in the book and add one additional page.

1. Fold paper in half for pages.

2. Sew pages together in the crease with a needle and thread (or use a sewing machine).

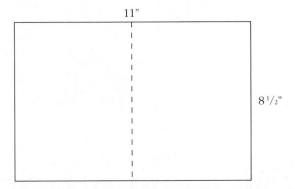

3. Cut a piece of cloth 1″ larger than book pages (open to measure).

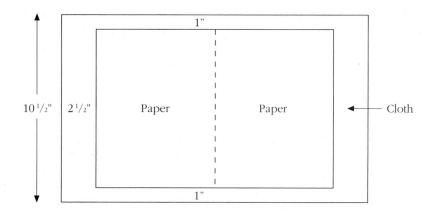

4. Cut two pieces of cardboard slightly larger than the folded pages.

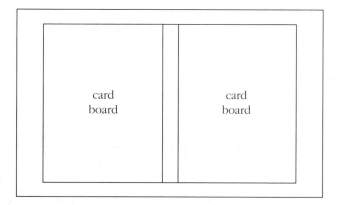

5. Lay cloth flat, wrong side up. Spray cardboard pieces with artists' dry mount spray. Leave a small space between the cardboard pieces to allow the book to open and close.

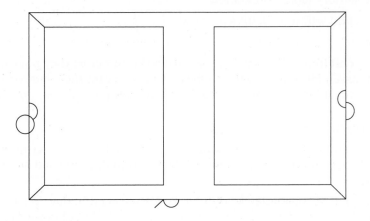

6. Fold corners in; then fold top down and hold.

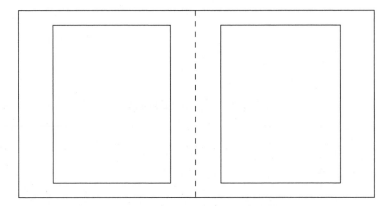

7. Spray side of cardboard facing up. Lay open page on cardboard; press first page then last page to the cover.

Note: You will need one extra page that will be part of the inside of the cover.

Children can now write and illustrate their book.

Increase Level of Difficulty

Procedure   Have children increasingly do more of the production with less supervision. Encourage them to choose different fabrics and to make books of different lengths and shapes and for different purposes.

Decrease Level of Difficulty

Procedure   Have more of the work completed so the child's major task is writing the book and choosing the cover.

COMMENT   Children like these books because they look like "real" books. They learn many of the steps of bookmaking in the process. Encourage them to look at some of their schoolbooks and notice how they are bound.

Writing

AIR WRITING

GOAL   To improve writing readiness
To improve sensory motor integration

OBJECTIVE   The child will write letters in the air.

MATERIALS   None

PROCEDURE   Have children write letters and words in the air before they put them on paper. Using the dominant hand, have children keep their elbow straight, point their index finger, and write the letter or word in the air. Be sure children use the large muscles of the arm, not wrist muscles. Write large letters.

Increase Level of Difficulty

Procedure   Encourage children to write words on the chalkboard afer writing in the air. If necessary, guide the child's arm through the motions or stand next to the child and model the motion while talking about the strokes.

COMMENT   As children become interested in writing, they need to develop a sensory motor base. For some children, this development comes easily; others will need help with activities like this, which require the use of the large muscles of the arms and shoulders. Children who have trouble writing with a pencil may need additional work with their large muscles before practice with a pencil and paper is useful. They need to write large letters in the air, then on chalkboards, and finally on large paper.

Writing

SAND WRITING

GOAL   To improve writing readiness
To improve sensory motor integration

OBJECTIVE   The child will write letters in the sand.

MATERIALS   jellyroll pan   sand

cards with an individual letter printed on each

PROCEDURE   Fill a jellyroll pan (cookie sheet with sides) about ¼″ deep with sand. Using the index finger of their dominant hand, have children write letters, their name, or words in the sand.

Increase Level of Difficulty

Materials   cards with simple printed words

Procedure   When children have written individual letters, encourage them to copy words in the sand from cards that you have written. Choose words that are important to the children, yet short.

Decrease Level of Difficulty

Procedure   Sort the letters into those that have straight lines, curved lines, or combinations. Start with either of the first two.

COMMENT   The sand provides some resistance and also leaves a mark so the children can see what they have printed. Sand writing is especially good for children who are working on fine motor control.

Writing

TICKETS

GOAL   To improve writing readiness
To improve small motor coordination
To increase inclusion

OBJECTIVE   The child will write and distribute tickets.

MATERIALS   markers   paper   press-on labels

PROCEDURE   Have the children make tickets for snack using the labels as a base. Tell children that today they need tickets to have snack and encourage them to make them. (Have a few extras and a marker for those who don't.) Be sure to collect and comment on the tickets as you distribute snacks.

Increase Level of Difficulty

Procedure   Have some children make two "identical" tickets (numbers are easiest) and have one ticket for snack and the other to mark where the child is to sit. Then have the children find their place at the table by matching the ticket to the place marker.

Decrease Level of Difficulty

Procedure   Support the children for any writing they do on the ticket. Even if it is a scribble, it qualifies.

COMMENT   Children need practice writing, especially numbers. Use an activity such as this in many different areas. Use it to support dramatic play and give out railroad and airline tickets. Give tickets for using an obstacle course or riding the tricycles. There can be tickets for puppet shows, group time, and stories. Children need to learn that writing is an important language arts activity, not a tedious small motor penalty.

Writing

WRITING CENTER

GOAL   To improve writing readiness
To improve small motor coordination
To increase inclusion

OBJECTIVE   The child will write and illustrate.

MATERIALS   variety of paper: manila paper, wide lined paper, plain white paper, paper which is folded in half, small note pads, paper cut into interesting shapes, colored paper, and even stationery

writing tools: thin and thick water-soluble markers, pencils and colored pencils, a supply of interesting erasers, a pencil sharpener

copy of the alphabet

writing folder with each child's name

PROCEDURE   Encourage children to think about an experience or feeling they would like to write about. Discuss writing as a process that involves writing, editing, and publishing. When you talk with children at the writing center use the terms author, editor, and publisher with them.

Increase Level of Difficulty

Procedure   Encourage children to write more detailed and longer stories; increase the variety of writing styles to include poetry and plays. Encourage children to read their work to others and to publish their work. Discuss the different, but related aspects of writing, editing, and publishing.

Decrease Level of Difficulty

Procedure   Emphasize the process of writing. Encourage children to work in small groups and distribute tasks. Discuss illustrating and differentiate it from "just drawing."

COMMENT   As children begin to think about themselves as authors their interest in writing increases. When they see writing as a process, and the details of editing as separate from writing, they can focus on the aspects of spelling and punctuation that are important in a final product but ought not to interfere with creativity.

Writing

BOOK MAKING

GOAL   To improve writing readiness
To improve eye-hand coordination

OBJECTIVE   The child will write, illustrate, and publish a book.

MATERIALS   poster board or cardboard   three-hole punch
notebook rings   written work

PROCEDURE   After children have written the text for their book, have them make a cover out of poster board and, using a three-hole punch, make holes in the paper and cover and put the book together. Encourage them to use a title page, and if there is more than one story, a table of contents.

Increase Level of Difficulty

Procedure   Talk with children about the parts of a book and the purposes they serve. Show them a copyright symbol and talk about the meaning of it. Show them a copyright page, dedications, acknowledgments, and indexes. Encourage children to use these parts in their own writing when appropriate. Help children add additional stories to their book or create new books on other topics.

Decrease Level of Difficulty

Procedure   Write a class book to which each child contributes. The contributions can vary with the ability and interest of the children.

COMMENT   Children like to think of themselves as authors who produce a product called a book that can be kept, read, and placed in a bookshelf.

Writing

MY DIARY

GOAL   To improve writing readiness
To express feelings

OBJECTIVE   The child will write and/or illustrate a diary.

MATERIALS   pencils and markers

notebook and sheets of paper stapled together

PROCEDURE   Talk with children about diaries and why people keep them. Tell them that diaries are personal and that they are usually kept over a long span of time. Include information that diaries are sometimes kept on trips or even about inventions. Ask the children to keep a diary for a week related to the theme that you are using. Have each child choose or put together the paper for his diary, label it, and put it in a particular place so he has access to it for at least a week. Encourage each child to spend some time each day writing or illustrating the diary.

Increase Level of Difficulty

Procedure   Continue to make the materials available for the diary and have children expand the content. Allow them to choose what they will write about, but support the writing process.

Decrease Level of Difficulty

Procedure   Support writing, not whether or not you can read what is written. Encourage children who are unsure about writing to illustrate their diary. Use the word *illustrate*.

COMMENT   Children need practice in writing. An activity that requires children to write for short periods over several days is useful. The emphasis in this activity is the process of writing itself. Inventive spelling and letter reversals are expected.

Writing

WRITTEN LANGUAGES

GOAL   To improve writing readiness
To increase awareness of individual differences

OBJECTIVE   The child will copy another written language.

MATERIALS   Samples of words written in other languages, some of which use different alphabetic symbols

Arabic

child   طِفْل ، ولد: إبن

Chinese

child　　孩子，儿童；胎儿，婴儿.

Japanese

child　　子供

Vietnamese

child　　Đứa bé con

Yiddish

child　　קינד || נאָ

PROCEDURE   Show children the written language of many different countries (choose the countries based on your school population as well as diversity of style). Talk about the importance of written languages to all people. Encourage children to try to copy some of the other written languages.

Increase Level of Difficulty

Procedure   Talk about some of the particular features of languages that you are familiar with, particularly the use of the accent symbols. Use a children's dictionary to show how vowels and accents are marked in English.

Decrease Level of Difficulty

Procedure   Help children appreciate differences in written language. Point out similarities and differences.

COMMENT   Help children realize the importance of a written language. Especially for children who find the motor aspect of language difficult, it is motivating to see the arbitrary yet unique aspects of written language.

References and Bibliography

Barron, M. (1990). *I learn to read and write the way I learn to talk. A very first book about whole language.* Katonah, NY: Richard C. Owen Publishers.

Butler, A., & Turkill, J. (1984). *Towards a reading and writing classroom.* Portsmouth, NH: Heinemann.

Carr, T. H. (Ed.). (1985). *The development of reading skills.* San Francisco, CA: Jossey-Bass.

Cazden, C. B. (Ed.). (1981). *Language in early childhood education.* (rev. ed.). Washington, DC: National Association for the Education of Young Children.

Chall, J. S., Jacobs, V. A., & Baldwin, L. E. (1990). *The reading crisis: Why poor children fall behind.* Cambridge, MA: Harvard University.

Chenfeld, M. B. (1987). *Teaching language arts creatively.* San Diego, CA: Harcourt Brace Jovanovich.

Franklin, M. B., & Barten, S. S. (Eds.). (1988). *Child language: A reader.* New York: Oxford University Press.

Gentry, J. R. (1987). *Spel. . . is a four letter word.* Ontario, Canada: Scholastic-TAB Publications, Ltd.

Goelman, H., Oberg, A., & Smith, F. (Eds.). (1984). *Awakening to literacy.* Portsmouth, NH: Heinemann.

Gould, T. S. (1988). *Reading: A practical guide for teaching reading readiness and reading.* Cambridge, MA: Educators Publishing Service, Inc.

Gregory, C. (1990). *Child-made: Awakening children to creative writing.* New York: Station Hill.

Hansen, J. (1987). *When writers read.* Portsmouth, NH: Heinemann.

Jalongo, M. R. (1988). *Young children and picture books: Literature from infancy to six.* Washington,

DC: National Association for the Education of Young Children.

Johnson, R. A. (1985). *Learning to communicate early in life*. Danville, IL: Interstate.

Lamme, L. (1985). *Growing up writing*. Washington, DC: Acropolis Books, Ltd.

Lass, B., & Davis, B. (1985). *The remedial reading handbook*. Englewood Cliffs, NJ: Prentice-Hall.

Peters, M. L. (1985). *Spelling: Caught or taught? A new look*. Boston, MA: Routledge & Kegan Paul.

Schickendanz, J. (1983). *Helping young children learn about reading*. Washington, DC: National Association for the Education of Young Children.

Schickendanz, J. (1986). *More than the ABC's: The early stages of reading and writing*. Washington, DC: National Association for the Education of Young Children.

Smith, F. (1985). *Reading without nonsense* (2nd ed.). New York: Teachers College Press.

Strickland, D. S., & Morrow, L. M. (Eds.). (1989). *Emerging literacy: Young children learn to read and write*. Newark, DE: International Reading Association.

Trelease, J. (1985). *The read-aloud handbook*. New York: Penguin.

Bibliography for Additional Reading

Adams, M. (1990). *Beginning to read: Thinking and learning about print. A summary*. Champaign, IL: University of Illinois at Urbana-Champaign Center for the Study of Reading.

Baker, A., & Greene, E. (1987). *Storytelling: Art and technique*. (2d ed.). New York: Bowker.

Commins, E. (1989). *Lessons from Mother Goose*. Atlanta, GA: Humanics Learning.

Conant, S., Budoff, M., & Hecht, B. (1990). *Teaching language-disabled children: A communication games invention*. Cambridge, MA: Brookline Books.

Dale, D. S. (1972). *Language development: Structure and function*. New York: Holt, Rinehart & Winston.

Devilliers, J., & Devilliers, P. (1978). *Language acquisition*. Cambridge, MA: Harvard University Press.

Fields, M., Spangler, K., & Lee, D. (1991). *Let's begin reading right: Developmentally appropriate beginning literacy* (2d ed.). Riverside, NJ: Merrill/Macmillan Co.

Garrard, K. (1987). Helping young children develop mature speech patterns. *Young Children, 42* (3), 16–21.

Holland, A. (1984). *Language disorders in children*. San Diego, CA: College-Hill Press.

Kamii, C., Manning, M., & Manning, G. (1991). *Early literacy: A constructivist foundation for whole language*. Washington, DC: National Education Association.

Kimmel, M. M., & Segel, E. (1991). *For reading out loud! From infancy to the teens*. New York: Dell Publishing, A Division of Bantam Doubleday Dell Publishing Group, Inc.

Language and Orientation Resource Center (1981). *Indochinese students in U.S. schools: A guide for administrators*. Washington, DC: Center for Applied Linguistics.

Lehr, S. S. (1991). *The child's developing sense of theme: Responses to literature*. New York: Teachers College Press.

Paley, V. (1990). *The boy who would be a helicopter: The use of story telling in the classroom*. Cambridge, MA: Harvard University Press.

Quicke, J. (1990). *Helping children understand disabilities: Disability in modern children's fiction*. Cambridge, MA: Brookline Books.

Raines, S., & Canaday, R. (1990). *The whole language kindergarten*. New York: Teachers College Press, Columbia University.

Rolginski, J. (1989). *Behind the covers: Interviews with authors and illustrators of books for children and young adults* (Vol. 2). Englewood, CO: Libraries Unlimited.

Smallwood, B. (1991). *The literature connection: A read-aloud guide for multicultural classrooms*. Reading, MA: Addison-Wesley Publishing.

Sutherland, Z. (Ed.). (1986). *The best in children's books: The University of Chicago guide to children's literature, 1979–1984*. Chicago: University of Chicago Press.

Chapter 24

Discovery: Mathematics, Science, Computers

Mathematics, science, and computers are taught as "hands on" experiences in the early childhood curriculum. Young children do not think either abstractly or logically at this age. Simply telling them about their world is rarely effective. They need to develop a solid base of internalized experiences as a foundation for later abstract scientific and mathematical thinking.

Mathematics

Mathematics is an area that causes concern for many people. When children have trouble remembering math "facts" at whatever level, adults usually try to intervene, perhaps by getting flash cards or writing numbers for children to count, copy, and add or subtract. Such an approach is rarely effective, even though the facts are reviewed "over and over again" (Parent Brochures).

Although younger preschoolers can often count up to 10 or higher, they rarely understand the relationship between the numbers that they are counting; that is, they do not realize that 6 is one more than 5 or that 7 is two less than 9. The names children give to numbers are referred to as tags. Children experience some predictable problems with counting and tags. The first relates to keeping track of the number of objects counted versus the number yet to be counted—a partitioning error (Schickedanz, York, Stewart, & White, 1990).

Children often forget where they started to count, especially when the objects are not in a straight line. Coordination errors involve having too many tags for the number of items counted, that is, counting objects more than once (Schickedanz, et. al., 1990). Although errors such as these are often declared carelessness, Kamii (1982) feels that it is more than a mechanical problem or one of not attending to the task. It really involves the child's lack of understanding of ordering items.

Many children understand the relationship among numbers up to 10 during kindergarten and can often count as high as 100. They may not understand, however, that in our base ten system there are eight 10s in 80, although they may be able to count to 100 by 10s. All of this is to say that understanding mathematical concepts is far more than arithmetic, and young children need many concrete mathematical experiences through the course of their day.

Children write numbers less frequently than they write letters or words, so their skill in this area may be less. Reversals of numbers in the preschool years are common, with the numbers 2, 3, 6, 7, and 9 the most frequently reversed. These numbers continue to be reversed even after children are consistently writing all of their alphabet letters correctly (Lamme, 1985). Left-handed children are more likely to have reversals than right-handed children.

In addition to signaling inadequate left-right orientation, reversals may be one sign of a sequencing problem. In this instance, before and after games with numbers are especially useful. Just playing "what number comes before or after X" is helpful, as is having children reproduce sequences or patterns. Patterning can be done with silverware, coins, markers, or anything that you have enough of to manipulate.

Children enjoy counting backward as well as forward, especially if it is tied to an event such as jumping off or "blasting off."

Board games which have children toss dice or spin to determine the number of spaces to move are helpful in sequencing, especially if one can be "sent back." Card games such as Fish, War, Hearts, Solitaire, Concentration, Skipbo, and Uno are also helpful. Having children put all the cards in order to see if there is a full deck is another useful activity, especially if the cards have fallen. Dominoes or Double Nines is another excellent way to teach matching and sequencing, and as children become older, addition.

Having a calendar can help sequencing, time, and number concepts. Children can count how many days until the weekend or their birthday. A calendar helps them to plan and sequence events as well as numbers. You can add family information as well as seasonal events.

Children learn basic geometric shapes during the preschool years. By kindergarten, children can usually identify basic shapes such as triangles, circles, squares, and rectangles, although the latter two are often confused. Although children can see differences in types of triangles they cannot usually articulate these differences. With experience, they can discover the relationships among these figures and what makes each unique.

Children need exposure to many different shapes, some plain, some colored, large and small, and even embedded in each other to sort out the qualities that remain stable. Understanding relative size and the vocabulary that goes with it is a necessary math skill. The vocabulary of size is part of all of our lives. We want a "little" more to drink and the "largest" piece of pie. Children are curious about how "big" they were when they were born and how "tall" they are now. All children like to see how they are growing by comparing their height over a span of months and years. Children, however, grow slowly compared to bulbs and seeds that can also be sized, measured, and charted. Have children predict whether things will be bigger or smaller than others and then have them check out their estimates.

Basic concepts of measurement is another focus of early mathematics. Children can measure length, weight, area, or volume. Before children can be expected to use standard units of measurement, such as feet and inches or meters and centimeters, they need to understand that measuring involves describing something in smaller increments. Children can use their hands, feet, books, popsicle sticks, blocks, or whatever is handy to measure length; scales and balances are used for weight; squares for area; and marbles or liquids to ascertain volume. Standard measures hold little meaning for children. It is only when two children measure the same item and get different results that the need for a standard becomes apparent. One child may claim that the water table is eleven hands long, another that it is really thirteen. Obviously, their hands are different sizes.

Intriguing children with measuring the dimensions of rooms and objects by a variety of means is also good. Encourage children to use a traditional yardstick, a meter stick, a ruler, paces, their feet, hands, and so on as tools of measurement. Getting the exact number of inches or feet is not the initial goal, but developing the skill of estimating and then checking is important.

Children need to learn number and measurement concepts before they can understand basic time concepts. (Telling time usually is not taught until early elementary school.) Children can begin to learn underlying time concepts by the use of a calendar and by using time sequences: "We will have a snack, go outside, and then it will be time to go home."

Money is another difficult concept for young children. They can, however, learn to recognize and name common coins and bills. Then they will learn the value of each. Somehow ten pennies seems like more than a dime, and the fact that a nickel is larger than a dime ought to make it worth more. These are difficult conceptual realities for young children. Again, it is not until the early elementary years that most will understand that four quarters and a dollar are the "same."

Mathematics for young children must be concrete and experiential. Adults can be a tremendous aid when they have an appropriate level of expectation for the children. They can expand math and make its usefulness in life apparent.

Some of the things you are already doing could make math learning part of children's daily lives. For example, having children "pay" for items at the "store" and count the change, learning about one-to-one correspondence during snack time, and writing down special events on a calendar are all important elements in mathematics. Count the chairs at the table and decide how many more are needed. Count the number of buttons yet to be buttoned on the shirt or the number of pockets in the skirt. Start with the child and then her near environment.

Since math requires few formal props, play math games while waiting or during transitions. Children can learn as much from activities that are fun as from those that seem "academic." The arithmetic problems that we so commonly associate with school are a formalization of experiences that relate to numbers, geometry, measurement, time, and money.

Science

Science is a process, a way of knowing about the world. Science "facts" may change at a fast pace, but the process of generating these facts is relatively stable. The first step in science involves gathering data. This requires observation. The next step requires that these observations be organized in some useful way so that information can be classified and hypotheses can be generated. These hypotheses need to be tested through experimentation and, typically, the results recorded in some way. The last step in the process is the application of the knowledge gained.

Think about a simple problem such as what sinks in water and what doesn't. First a child experiments and discovers that in fact some things float and others do not. The child then observes objects and tries to predict which will and which will not sink. There should be a place to list the sinkers. He may even note that some sink faster than others. He may try dropping them from different heights or laying them gently in the water. He may ask that the water be made deeper. Slowly, his guesses become more accurate. He might even be able to figure out that he could make a paper clip float by putting it in the middle of a piece of paper. Although he may not be able to articulate facts about density, he has started to use the scientific process to investigate sinking.

Although the major focus of science is on process, the learning process does not take place in a vacuum and some facts are important. The knowledge base works from the familiar to the unfamiliar. Science for young children moves from concrete to abstract. The content of science varies with the interest of the teacher, the children, and the setting. Children who live near the ocean may classify and learn about seashells. They may seine for sea life to put in their salt water aquarium. Such a marine theme would be inappropriate for young children in a school in South Dakota. Science activities need to be relevant to the children's interests and environment.

Children need to have a variety of experiences so that they can begin to generalize and learn from analogy. For example, "Do you remember why the sunflower died?" (No water?) "What do you think would happen to the hamster if he didn't have water?" (He would die.)

Children need the opportunity to explore materials on their own, with minimal adult supervision. Initially, children need questions like "What do you think will happen?", "What else could you try?", and so on. Such questions aid children in exploring materials and learning about their properties. Your goal is to have children discover as many properties as they can and to encourage their discovery of more subtle aspects of the materials. Your role is to give as little guidance as possible to promote the most learning. In this area, children are not just learning facts, far more importantly, they are learning how to learn.

Just exposing children to informal science and experiences is not enough to build the necessary concepts. But it is a necessary first step. This means that many activities in this area require at least two days and often more. The second time the materials are out, some children will continue to explore the materials, others will need more structure to expand their explorations. It is important that children view science as part of their world and that they see the cause-and-effect relationships rather than "teacher magic."

Computers

Computers are a fact of today's life. The question is how to make their use developmentally appropriate and an optimal learning experience for children. The computer offers children a potential source of communication and a way of exerting some control over their environment. Children can make a plan, carry it out, and see the outcome of their actions (Hurth, 1985).

Work in adapting computers to serve as a resource for children with disabilities is an important part of the field's growth. Computers can be customized for children with severe physical or sensory impairments using switches, voice and music synthesizers, robots, and other peripherals.

Whether or not you have computers available in the classroom or you use them only for administrative tasks, children can learn computing skills. All children learn to identify the letters of the alphabet. Teaching them using a bingo game that happens to be in the configuration of a keyboard enhances both reading readiness and computer skills. By providing children with a sensory motor understanding of prerequisite skills you can take much of the frustration out of learning to use a computer.

The key to using computers appropriately in early childhood is selecting appropriately designed software. The criteria for evaluating software set forth by Haugland and Shade (1990) offer some guidance in the selection process.

— Age appropriate. Think about the age of the children. Regardless of the computer, would you expect children to do these types of activities? The software should support your curriculum.

— Child control. Does the computer request responses from the child or does the child control the computer? The computer is only a tool. The control should be with the child.

— Clear instructions. How easy are the instructions? Young children do not read. To the extent that directions are dependent upon the teacher's reading to the children, the children are being taught dependence in a medium that should foster independence.

— Expanding complexity. Software should start where the child is and grow with her. It should be designed to provide increasingly challenging tasks, not solely repetition.

— Independence. The goal of computers is to make children independent of adults. The software must be selected to support this. Using a computer independently supports self-concept, confidence, and learning.

— Process orientation. Computers are discovery-oriented media; the reward is in the process. Printing a product should be a reminder of a pleasant process not a goal.

— Real-world model. In the real world houses are larger than children and eyebrows fit on faces. Look at the software to see if the illustrations on the screen reflect this orientation.

— Technical features. Graphics and sound should be designed to support the program. Cluttered designs and too much sound detracts. The program should load quickly, and the disks need to be sturdy.

— Trial and error. Children need the opportunity to make decisions and test them. They need a program that allows them to generate hypotheses and make their own decisions about what they like, not what is right or wrong.

— Transformations. Computers have the potential for making changes at the stroke of a key. Children can make designs and recreate them without the redrawing necessary in other media (adapted from Haugland & Shade, 1990, p. 21).

Much of the software that is on the market today for young children is not developmentally appropriate. The Developmental Software Criteria set forth by Haugland and Shade (1990) bring this issue into focus as well as evaluating specific software designed for young children.

To make traditional computers work, children need the ability to use a single key stroke. Without this skill typing looks like this—*pppppppppppp pppp*—and the computer cannot interpret it. Once children can make a single key stroke, they need to build keyboarding skills. These skills involve learning to locate keys, reading and selecting from a menu, and giving commands. Additionally, children need to learn about the computer itself and how to make it run (Davidson, 1990). They also must develop the necessary fine motor and sensory integration skills.

Computers have tremendous potential for positive change for children with disabilities. They need adult scaffolding to make the system work. Some children will be ready, others will not. Allowing children the choice is the most appropriate solution. Appropriately used, computers hold potential for helping all young children. Your role is to help children see computers as a natural part of everyday life.

Discovery Goals

To Improve Number Concepts

All children must learn to count, match numbers, and understand that numbers stand for quantities. Encourage children to count and to write numbers. By counting real things that have a purpose, such as the number of spoons to put on the table, the number of cookies baked, the number of stairs climbed, and so on, children learn the utility of math. As the opportunity arises, have children count out equal numbers of paper clips and piles of paper and put them together. Activities such as these provide a natural check on "one-to-one" correspondence.

To Improve Shape/Size Concepts

Recognizing and labeling shapes is a part of geometry, which is both a part of math and a reading readiness skill. The skill involves identification of what is relevant in symbols and learning that specific configurations of lines have names.

To Improve Measurement Concepts

Start by measuring the children themselves, not just their height, but the size of their feet, hands, and heads. Then measure familiar spaces. Much of cooking involves measuring both dry and wet ingredients. Children can easily learn the size of a cup and the resulting fractions that are common measures. Even if children don't actively participate in the cooking process, have them pour and measure substances such as dried beans, rice, or oatmeal.

To Improve Observation Skills

Observation is one of the most basic skills in science. Observing is more than looking. It requires children to describe information in detail, including subtle details as well as the more obvious. It requires the use of all the senses. If children find an earthworm, have them look at how it moves, watch its movements under a magnifying glass, listen to see if it makes any sound, set up a mark and see if it goes there, how long it takes, what happens to the dirt when it makes a hole, and so on. This is too much for one observation, but children must be supported in refining their observation skills.

To Improve Classification Skills

Classifying information makes order out of chaos. Children need to learn to classify in many ways, depending upon the properties involved. They need to learn that differing categories change what is included. They also need to be exposed to classification systems, although they are probably not ready for the logic that underlies the system. They can learn that animals include dogs, cows, and bears, and that in each category there are many different types. Distinguishing between mammals and reptiles may be beyond the scope of most young children.

To Make Predictions

Often the difference between exploration and just messing about is purposefulness. Making predictions focuses children's attention on what they expect to happen. It makes a project more goal directed and learning more direct. Children learn whether or not the prediction is accurate. When their prediction is not borne out, they need support in figuring out why. It is possible that the prediction was inaccurate or that some steps in the process were not completed. It is important that adults offer guidance at this stage.

To Improve Cause-and-Effect Reasoning

Children need to learn that they affect their world. Cups don't usually spill on their own—something causes the cup to spill. Children need to know about their actions and begin to learn how to manipulate change. At the beginning children usually use a trial and error approach, and may even need an adult to point out that they were responsible for the change. They need to establish a broad base of understanding before they can move into systematically testing hypotheses.

To Improve Generalization Skills

Generalization is actually the culmination of scientific thinking. It provides the basis for future learning. It allows children to have a base from which they can make more accurate predictions and structure their world. They can begin to make predictions based upon information.

To Improve Computer Skills

Children need to learn that computers are simply a more complicated tool than a pencil; good for some things and not for others. Children need to learn how to turn the computer on and off, the names of the parts of the computer and what they do, and how to care for and insert disks. They must develop keyboarding and menu-reading skills. Computer skills can be developed whether or not you have computers available in your classroom. None of the activities given in this book requires a computer.

Teaching Strategies

For children with *communication disorders,* in addition to working with naming numbers and shapes, emphasize the vocabulary that goes with the firsthand experiences of learning math and science: taller, shorter, more, less, the same, equal, one more, one less. Children can learn through science how sounds are made and which parts of the body are involved in making various sounds. They can learn to use objects such as a feather or pinwheel to observe the effect of their breath. Computers offer another opportunity for communicating without the need of speaking.

Children with *hearing impairments* can learn about the parts of the body concerned with hearing. Some children can explore how a hearing aid works by using microphones and by playing with the balance on a stereo and the volume on tape and record players. They need many firsthand opportunities to associate concepts with words and pictures. They need to use numbers, identify likenesses and differences, and group and classify objects using visual and tactile skills to reinforce the auditory. Because computers are primarily dependent upon small motor and visual skills, they are an asset to the child with a hearing impairment.

Children with *visual impairments* must learn math and science concepts with three-dimensional objects before they can be expected to generalize these concepts to two-dimensional ones. Use natural situations and real objects that are meaningful to the children: two crackers, ten raisins. Use pegs to count. Help children feel round balls and square boxes. Use sandpaper outlines of circles and squares. Help children pace off and count distances to and from various places in the room: five steps from the locker to the circle area compared with ten steps from the locker to the blocks. Provide additional time for children to touch the equipment and materials.

Be sure to include equipment that magnifies. Depending upon the degree of loss, computers can be an asset to these children or relatively unimportant. With a voice synthesizer they are more useful.

Children with *learning disabilities* can gain much in the way of first-hand experiences through varied sensory input. These children need a broad foundation in exploration without their products being judged. They need help learning how to learn and to develop some compensatory skills that will serve them as math and science become more formalized. Use real materials and situations. Give the children two crackers: they can count them, see them, touch them, hear you say there are two. Break one in half, count them again, and then consume them—one piece at a time. Once initial skills have been acquired, computers can be a tremendous aid to these children, but the initial skills acquisition may be difficult.

Concepts that relate to size, distance, and speed are especially important to children with *physical disabilities*. The children must be able to estimate distances and the time it will take them to travel a given distance. Size concepts help them understand where they can easily fit and still turn around. They also need to learn that like other children they are growing and they may get too big for some of their support equipment. Concentrating on some of the more mechanical aspects of science may help them learn to lift things using a pulley and to use a pole or magnet as a tool. Customized computers offer these children ways of communicating and moving that have not been possible before. They need to feel comfortable with this technology at an early age.

The lives of children with *health impairments,* perhaps more than others, are linked to medicine and scientific discoveries. Their understanding of the scientific process can help them look at the implications of taking medicine versus not taking it, for example. They can also explore and learn about their body and how it functions. Because children with health needs are often susceptible to many diseases they may have had fewer opportunities to interact with materials that form the base for later formalized science and math. As a safety issue, be sure children know the amounts of medication they need on a regular basis and the time sequence in which they take the medicine. Have them count sips of water, too. Make math real and relevant. Computers are a frequent aid in home study and may allow children to participate in the same experiences as their classmates.

Science and mathematics demand little social interaction yet they hold the potential for it. Children with *emotional/behavioral disorders* may be willing to participate in small groups in these areas. The emphasis on discovery may make this area less threatening for them. The use of water-based learning has the potential for quieting a disruptive child (have the water warm, not cold). Choose computer software that allows these children to control their environment.

For children with *mental retardation* be sure to allow time to repeat experiences and to do variations on themes. They will need special help generalizing knowledge. As activities become more difficult, plan some that can be done at different levels. These children will need concrete experience even after their peers are dealing with more abstract concepts. Use real objects that can be touched and manipulated. Count with pegs or an abacus, but also count children, tables, and blocks before you count dots. Be sure the prerequisite skills are developed before expecting children to interact with computers.

Children with *multiple disabilities* will require adaptations depending upon the area that is most involved. In general, follow the strategies given above and combine them to meet the child's needs.

Mathematics, Science, and Computer Activities

Goal	Activity
To improve number concepts	Abacus
	Matching Symbols
	Spacey Dots
	Half
	Number Line
	Number Squares
	Variations on Blocks
	Hidden Objects
	Variations on Cuisenaire Rods
To improve shape/size concepts	Areas
	Object Sizes
	Thinking Shapes
	People Shapes
	Sandwich Tricks
	Boxes and More Boxes
	Picture Shapes
	Shape Pictures
	Nesting Cups
	Big and Little Pairs
	Variations on Blocks
To improve measurement concepts	Measuring Tools
	Measure It
	Half
	Areas
	Boxes and More Boxes
	Maps
	Popcorn
	Cereal Balls
	Object Sizes
To improve observational skills	My Yard
	Goop
	Ant Farm
	Nature Board
	Sink or Float
	Color Changes
	Gelatin
	Pollution
	Popcorn
	Maps
	Bubbles
	Hidden Objects
To improve classification skills	Food Lotto
	Sorting
	Picture Shapes
	Big and Little Pairs
	Thinking Shapes
	Variations on Blocks
	Variations on Cuisenaire Rods
	Measuring Tools
	My Yard
	Nature Board
	Sink or Float
	Measure It
	Shape Pictures

Goal	Activity
To make predictions	Magnets
	Planting
	Scrambled Eggs
	Measuring Tools
	Variations on Cuisenaire Rods
	Gelatin
	Color Changes
	Pollution
	Measure It
	Number Squares
To improve cause-and-effect reasoning	Magnets
	Planting
	Gelatin
	Goop
	Popcorn
	Color Changes
	Nature Board
	Sink or Float
	Pollution
	Scrambled Eggs
	Robot-Controller
	Bubbles
To improve generalization skills	Spacey Dots
	Picture Shapes
	Planting
	Food Lotto
	Input-Output
	Port-Starboard
	Buried Treasure
	Sorting
	Ant Farm
To improve computer skills	Input-Output
	Robot-Controller
	Port-Starboard
	Buried Treasure
	My Keyboard
	Spell It
	Cereal Balls
	Fruit Kabob
	Alphabet Keyboard
	Computer Bingo
	Hidden Objects
	Scrambled Eggs
	Maps
To improve sequencing skills	My Keyboard
	Spell It
	Fruit Kabob
	Input-Output
To follow directions	Sandwich Tricks
	Shape Pictures
	Alphabet Keyboard
	Computer Bingo
	Cereal Balls
	Robot-Controller
	Port-Starboard

Goal	Activity
To improve reading readiness	Shape Pictures
	My Keyboard
	Spell It
	Alphabet Keyboard
	Computer Bingo
	Buried Treasure
To increase inclusion	People Shapes
	Number Line
To improve sensory motor integration	Boxes and More Boxes
To improve eye-hand coordination	Nesting Cups
	Shape Pictures
	Bubbles
	Fruit Kabob

Mathematics

ABACUS

GOAL   To improve number concepts

OBJECTIVE   The child will move a designated number of beads.

MATERIALS   a large abacus (or rods with nuts on them, suspended from a frame)

several small abacuses for individual work

cards with numbers on one side and a picture of the number of beads moved on the other

PROCEDURE   Give the children cards with the number side up. Have them count (move) the specified number of beads and then check their answer by comparing it to the drawing on the other side of the card.

Increase Level of Difficulty

Procedure   Children can be given higher numbers or more difficult math skills (simple addition and subtraction).

Decrease Level of Difficulty

Procedure   Use only the cards with lower numbers and use this as a teacher-directed activity.

COMMENT   The children must physically move the bead so they can visually check their work. The abacus can be used to progress to higher-level math skills if children are ready.

Mathematics

MATCHING SYMBOLS

GOAL   To improve number concepts

OBJECTIVE   The child will match a number card to the corresponding dot card.

MATERIALS   cards numbered 1 through 10

cards with up to 10 dots

PROCEDURE   Have the children match the cards.

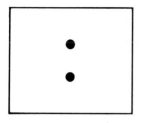
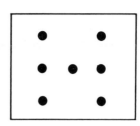

Increase Level of Difficulty

Materials   Add cards that have other shapes or pictures on them (small animal stickers, for example). Make cards that have different symbols on the same card (a dot, square, and a sticker).

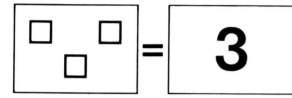
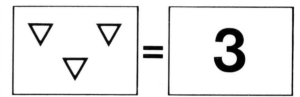

Procedure   Encourage the child to put all of the cards with the same number in a pile. Help the child learn that the number value doesn't change with the specific symbols or their arrangement on the card.

Decrease Level of Difficulty

Materials   Make cards larger. Use cardboard or laminated cards so they are easier to handle. Use only cards 1 through 5. Use sandpaper numbers and symbols.

Procedure   Initially use cards to count and identify numbers. Encourage children to point to or touch the symbols as they count.

COMMENT   Emphasize the language concept "equals." The activity uses visual cues to teach number concepts. For children with visual impairments use sandpaper or felt numbers and shapes.

Mathematics

HALF

GOAL   To improve number concepts
To improve measurement concepts

OBJECTIVE   The child will match the objects that are cut in half.

MATERIALS   Objects cut in half:

socks	plastic bottle	pencil
paper plate	piece of paper	crayon
glove	egg carton	straw
box or bag to contain objects		

PROCEDURE   The children will put the objects on the table and find the matching pieces.

Increase Level of Difficulty

Materials   Cut some objects in thirds or give the children whole objects and have them cut the objects into the desired number of pieces.

Procedure   Have the children match the objects blindfolded.

Decrease Level of Difficulty

Materials   Use fewer or more dissimilar materials.

Procedure   Let children use the pieces like a puzzle.

COMMENT   Use the vocabulary of whole and half or other fractions with the children to support the learning.

NUMBER SQUARES

GOAL   To improve number concepts
To make predictions

OBJECTIVE   The child will move the specified number of spaces in the fewest moves.

MATERIALS   graph paper   pencil   marker

1	2	7	6	1	2	6	7	8	6	2
5	9	3	2	9	8	1	9	3	5	1
4	3	7	7	1	2	5	6	8	6	1
5	1	2	3	5	9	8	7	6	4	2
6	8	9	7	8	5	2	4	3	1	2
2	3	4	1	9	✕	7	6	8	9	5
4	5	2	6	1	7	1	2	5	1	2
7	6	4	3	1	5	7	8	6	4	3
9	2	5	1	3	7	4	1	2	8	9
8	1	6	5	2	7	8	1	3	5	7

PROCEDURE   Use graph paper or make your own grid. Fill in each box with a number between 1 and 9. A grid of about ten lines up and ten across is a good starting size. Mark the center square and put a marker (button) on it. The object of the game is to figure out how to go from the center and land just outside the grid on the last move. You can move in any direction in a straight line (diagonal, left, right, up, down). Choose a number for the first move. The number that you land on is the next number of moves you will make.

Increase Level of Difficulty

Materials   Use a grid twenty across and twenty down, or larger.

Procedure   If children want to play this game alone, see how few moves they can make to land outside the grid.

Decrease Level of Difficulty

Materials   Use only numbers 1–5. Reduce the number of lines on the grid to six lines down and six across and make the grid itself larger.

COMMENT   It is useful to have several different sizes of grids and to have different number configurations so that children do not see this as a competitive game, but rather one of planning. If all the children have different grids it is more likely to be cooperative.

SPACEY DOTS

GOAL   To improve number concepts
To improve generalization skills

OBJECTIVE   The child will group together cards that are numerically equal.

MATERIALS   A set of three cards for each number between 1 and 10. Each card of the set has an equal number of dots, with different dots arranged in different configurations on each card.

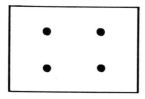  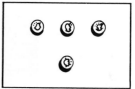

PROCEDURE   Have children match cards with equal numbers of dots.

Increase Level of Difficulty

Materials   Add two additional sets of cards. Add cards with numbers.

Procedure   Have the children tell you where the markings are on the card (e.g., center, right-hand corner, top half).

Decrease Level of Difficulty

Materials   Use only numbers 1–5. Start with two sets of cards.

Procedure   Ask the child to give you the card that has the same number of dots as the card shown. Count with the child. Encourage the child to touch the dots as he counts.

COMMENT   Spatial configuration sometimes distracts the child from the concept of numbers. It requires little verbal communication, and as children are mastering number concepts this is a good way to learn that spatial configuration is irrelevant. Children with visual impairments may need tactile cues. Use sandpaper shapes rather than dots or glue pennies to the cardboard.

NUMBER LINE

GOAL   To improve number concepts
To increase inclusion

OBJECTIVE   The child will move the specified number of spaces.

MATERIALS   a 20-foot length of fabric marked into 20 1-foot areas and numbered consecutively from 1 to 20

a spinner or dice

PROCEDURE   Spin the spinner or roll the dice and have children move on the cloth the designated number of spaces.

Increase Level of Difficulty

Procedure   Using the format of the board games, increase the complexity by having certain numbers be "wild cards" and have children who land on the same space send the other child back to "start." Ask children to read the number they are on.

Decrease Level of Difficulty

Procedure   Use only one die.

COMMENT   This is just a variation of a board game with the children as the playing pieces. Although this may initially be a teacher-directed game, once children learn the rules, encourage them to play independently.

Blocks are an integral part of the early mathematics curriculum. They can be counted, classified, and stacked.

Mathematics

VARIATIONS ON BLOCKS

GOAL   To improve number concepts
To improve shape/size concepts
To improve classification skills

OBJECTIVE   The child will perform the requested activity.

MATERIALS   A set of unit blocks

PROCEDURE   On specified days or during clean-up, the teacher will request that children follow specific directions relative to the blocks:

Pick up all the blocks that are the same as this one.

Pick up all the curved blocks.

Pick up blocks of three different lengths.

Pick up blocks in sets of twos, threes, or fours.

Pick up all of a certain type of block: rectangles, squares, cylinders, and so on.

Place blocks on the shelves in a certain order: top shelf, then middle, then bottom.

Count the number of different blocks in a structure.

Count how many blocks of a certain type were used.

Count the total number of blocks in a structure.

Increase Level of Difficulty

Procedure   Combine two or three of the above, such as requesting a child to put three cylinders on the top shelf.

Decrease Level of Difficulty

Procedure   Tell children about the specified information: "You've just given me three blocks. Let's count them. 1. 2. 3. Let's put them on the top shelf."

COMMENT   The block area is a great place to learn and reinforce math concepts. Children can learn much just through building and manipulating blocks, but adding the vocabulary increases the usefulness for understanding mathematics.

Mathematics

HIDDEN OBJECTS

GOAL   To improve number concepts
To improve observational skills
To improve computer skills

OBJECTIVE   The child will find the correct quantity of the designated object.

MATERIALS   familiar objects

pictures of the same familiar objects on numbered cards

cups or glasses   crayons

books   silverware

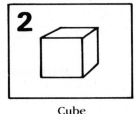

| Cube | Leaf | Rubber band | Key |

PROCEDURE   Hide a variety of familiar objects. Give each child a card and have him find a specific number of the object. Be sure that all the children connect the idea that a picture represents an object.

Increase Level of Difficulty

Materials   Give each child more than one card.

Procedure   Show the child the card but do not allow the child to take the card on the search. Increase the number and variety of objects searched for.

Decrease Level of Difficulty

Materials   Cards with fewer objects and objects hidden in more obvious places. Give the actual object to the child.

Procedure   Let the child carry the object or card in the search. Use low numbers. Encourage children to help each other and double-check the numbers. Have children work in pairs.

COMMENT   The activity requires children to translate visual cues into action, but does not require speech. Deciphering picture symbols is one of the skills children need to use computer menus. For children with visual impairments, glue an actual object on the card and use sandpaper numbers, or glue the actual number of objects requested on the card.

VARIATIONS ON CUISENAIRE RODS

GOAL   To improve number concepts
To improve classification skills
To make predictions

OBJECTIVE   The child will arrange the rods in the specified order.

MATERIALS   Several sets of cuisenaire rods. (Do not use with children under three; the small rods are easily swallowed.)

PROCEDURE   Initially, allow children to examine the rods. Encourage them to sort by length and color. Have them build flat designs as well as vertical structures. Have them count the rods used in various activities. Help children discover that the same length is always the same color. Support children working as a team to create a theme using the rods, such as building a farm, boat dock, or amusement park, and then tell what is happening in their creation. As children become familiar with the rods do the following activities:

Build a person.

Make flat designs (rods cannot be placed on top of each other).

Make a design using a specified number of rods.

Copy another child's design (then have the child who copied make the next design).

Build a staircase (horizontally and vertically, going up and down).

Outline a simple design on graph paper and color it in using the rods to determine the colors.

Give children a design on graph paper and have them duplicate it with the rods.

Use smaller rods to measure the larger rods.

Make a repeating pattern with the rods.

COMMENT   Cuisenaire rods can be used at many different levels. They have the potential to teach higher-level skills such as addition, subtraction, and multiplication as well as more basic skills.

AREAS

GOAL   To improve shape/size concepts
To improve measurement concepts

OBJECTIVE   The child will cover the given shape with a variety of the building pieces.

MATERIALS   building pieces made of white poster board

shapes made of red poster board

PROCEDURE   Using a combination of building pieces, outline a variety of shapes on red poster board and cut them out. Then have the children cover the shape with the white building pieces as if it were a puzzle.

Increase Level of Difficulty

Materials   Make more shapes using different configurations of the building pieces. All building pieces equal 1, 2, or $1/2$ a square inch.

Procedure   Help children "discover" the relationship of the building pieces and use this information to figure out the area of designated shapes.

SAMPLE PIECES:

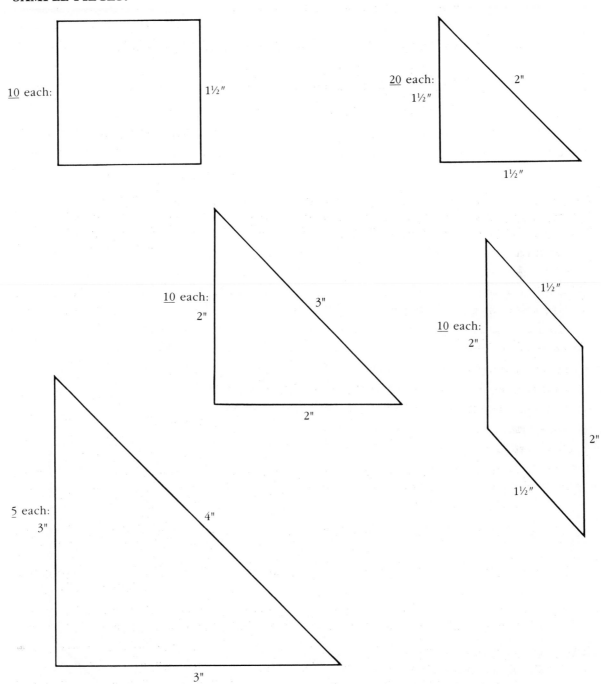

Decrease Level of Difficulty

Materials   Use only the 1″ square and triangle and shapes that can be made from them.

Procedure   Use the shapes as if they were a puzzle and count how many building pieces it takes to cover each shape.

COMMENT   This activity can be used at several different levels by varying the complexity of the shapes and the challenges you pose. You can teach measuring and area concepts and have children see the variety of ways they can use the pieces to cover the shapes. For children with visual and physical impairments, glue sandpaper to the shapes and put the materials in a jellyroll pan. This confines the area and makes the pieces less slippery.

SAMPLE SHAPES:

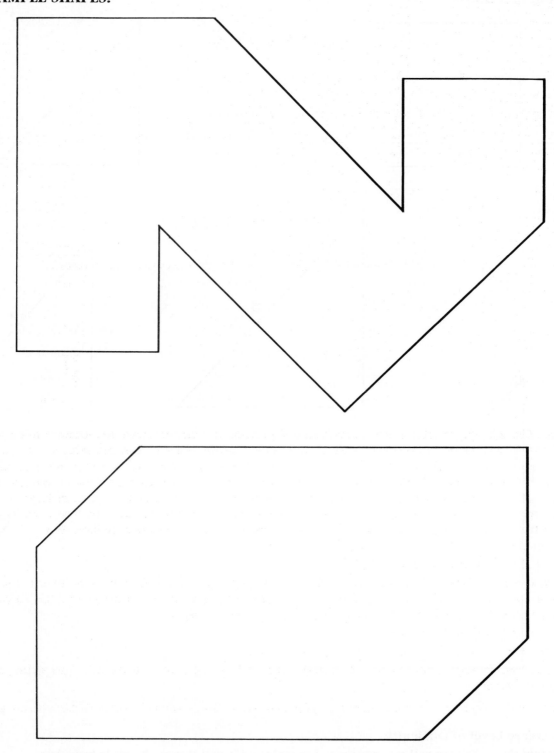

OBJECT SIZES

GOAL   To improve shape/size concepts
     To improve measurement concepts

OBJECTIVE   The child will order objects according to size.

MATERIALS   at least three different sizes of an object: measuring spoons, measuring cups, plastic glasses

     other objects that can be filled

     a water or sand table

½ cup   ¼ cup   1 cup   ⅓ cup

1 teaspoon   ¼ teaspoon   1 tablespoon   ½ teaspoon

PROCEDURE   Place sets of three-dimensional objects in the water or sand table. Ask the children to point to or give you the objects in order of size. Help children explore the relative sizes of objects through pouring and measuring. Give them examples for comparisons: "It takes four of the smallest cup to fill the big one." Arrange the objects in order of size (measuring cups are easy), and give the children another set to match to the first. When this has been mastered add a slightly different set to be matched. (Measuring spoons will do in this case.) Have the children arrange the sets from largest to smallest. Then stagger the arrangement. See if the children can remember the relative sizes by having them place the objects in the proper order again.

Increase Level of Difficulty

Procedure   Give children containers that are deceptive (a tall thin container that holds the same amount as a short fat one). Use a series of four, not three, different sizes. Encourage children to make predictions about relative volume and then to check if they are right.

Decrease Level of Difficulty

Materials   Use only two different-sized containers.

Procedure   Give children time to explore the objects and play with them by just filling and dumping them.

COMMENT   Change the materials the children measure. Use cornmeal, oatmeal, rice, beans, and so on.

THINKING SHAPES

GOAL   To improve shape/size concepts
     To improve classification skills

OBJECTIVE   The child will find or name objects in the room that are the designated shape.

MATERIALS   None

PROCEDURE   The teacher will think of objects in the room that are a particular shape. The children must guess the object she is thinking of. The teacher will answer only "yes" or "no" to questions.

TEACHER: I'm thinking of something in this room that is square.
CHILD: The record player.
TEACHER: No, the record player is square, but that is not what I'm thinking of.
CHILD: Is the square you are thinking of red?
TEACHER: Yes.

The process continues as the children make more guesses.

Increase Level of Difficulty

Procedure   When children can classify objects in the room by two-dimensional shapes, introduce three-dimensional shapes and their names (for example, cube, pyramid, sphere, cylinder). Add objects that are composed of more than one shape. Encourage children to narrow the field categorically before guessing specific objects.

Decrease Level of Difficulty

Procedure   Accept and support anything that is the right shape and ask the children to find more objects of that shape.

COMMENT   This is a good activity to share with parents to use in rooms that are unfamiliar to children, such as doctors' offices and hospitals. It gives familiar qualities to unfamiliar settings and helps time pass. For children with hearing impairments, or children who may not have mastered shape concepts, hold up a card with that shape or draw it on the chalkboard so the children are sure to be looking for the right shape.

Mathematics

PEOPLE SHAPES

GOAL   To improve shape/size concepts
To increase inclusion

OBJECTIVE   The child will be able to form a shape with the bodies of his classmates.

MATERIALS   Shapes drawn on a 5″ × 8″ card

PROCEDURE   Discuss shapes. Hold up a drawing of a shape and pick one child as "shaper." Have him choose the children he needs to make the shape and have them lie on the floor in the area he designates. If you don't have the space for this activity, the children can use wooden clothespins to build the shapes.

   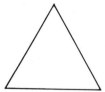

Increase Level of Difficulty

Materials   Larger and more complex shapes

Procedure   Have the child change the shape by adding or removing children.

Decrease Level of Difficulty

Procedure   Have children participate in the shape but do not choose them as the "shaper."

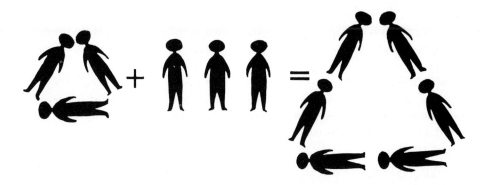

COMMENT   People Shapes allows all children to participate in a group experience. It uses both tactile and visual cues to teach shapes and sizes. It requires planning and abstract reasoning.

Mathematics

SANDWICH TRICKS

GOAL   To improve shape/size concepts
To follow directions

OBJECTIVE   The child will eat the designated shape.

MATERIALS   Sandwiches

PROCEDURE   Cut sandwiches into geometric shapes. Give each child a separate piece of a whole sandwich. Have the children put the sandwiches back together as if they were puzzles, and then direct them to eat the pieces shape by shape (square, triangle, large rectangle, and so on).

Increase Level of Difficulty

Procedure   Make more pieces of irregular shapes.

Decrease Level of Difficulty

Procedure   Cut sandwiches into fewer, simpler shapes.

COMMENT   Make the filling a sticky one, such as peanut butter, so the bread stays together (jelly and honey are pretty messy). It requires little fine motor manipulation and has a built-in reward system. Children with visual impairments can feel the sides of sandwiches to determine the shape: be sure to give them plenty of time. *Note:* Have children wash their hands before this activity.

Mathematics

BOXES AND MORE BOXES

GOAL   To improve shape/size concepts
To improve measurement concepts
To improve sensory integration

OBJECTIVE   The child will identify the boxes by size and label her relation to them.

MATERIALS   cardboard boxes of varying sizes

a large box (usually from an appliance)

PROCEDURE   Place small, medium, and large boxes in an open area. Encourage children to climb in and out of the small and medium size boxes. Some children may even enjoy "hiding" for a short time in larger boxes. Allow children to push and pull toys or other children around the area. Talk about size concepts such as small, medium, and large boxes and the objects that might be placed in each. Use language about spatial relations: in, out, in front of, behind, beside, and measurement terms. With a larger appliance box children may enjoy having their own private "house." Help them decide where the windows and doors should be placed, decide how to measure the height and area of each, and how large they should be.

Increase Level of Difficulty

Procedure   Encourage children to use the boxes in imaginative play, for example, making a train. Help them arrange the boxes in a sequential order by size. Measure the length of the train. See if children can build a tower with the boxes.

Decrease Level of Difficulty

Procedure   Support children's exploration of the boxes both verbally and physically. Place children in boxes if they need help.

COMMENT   This is a good outdoor activity in nice weather. It increases spatial awareness by using the large muscles of the body. Children with health and physical impairments can participate with their peers, and if their energy runs out they can be pushed in the boxes. Children will enjoy the creative aspect.

Mathematics

PICTURE SHAPES

GOAL   To improve shape/size concepts
To improve classification skills
To improve generalization skills

OBJECTIVE   The child will sort the pictures according to shapes.

MATERIALS   Pictures of common objects with definite geometric shapes mounted on cards (record, house, ice cream cone, bed)

PROCEDURE   Have the children sort the pictures according to shape.

Increase Level of Difficulty

Materials   Use more complex pictures with several shapes.

Procedure   Have children search for a particular shape in a picture containing several shapes.

Decrease Level of Difficulty

Materials   Pictures with less detail. Provide the shapes so the children can use them to place over the pictures.

Procedure   Encourage children to use the shapes to find a shape in the picture.

COMMENT   Activity requires visual generalization and application of knowledge of shapes to pictures of real objects.

Mathematics

SHAPE PICTURES

GOAL   To improve shape/size concepts
To follow directions
To improve reading readiness

OBJECTIVE   The child will connect the designated shapes using a crayon or marker.

MATERIALS   Dittos containing arrangements of various shapes (triangles, circles, squares). Within each arrangement, all the shapes of one type, when connected, should form a letter or shape.

PROCEDURE   Have the children connect the shapes with a crayon or marker and then name the design.

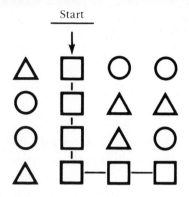

Directions: Connect the squares in order. What letter do the squares make?

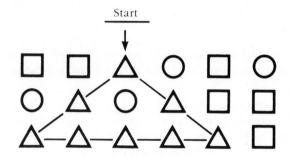

Directions: Connect the triangles so that they make a triangle.

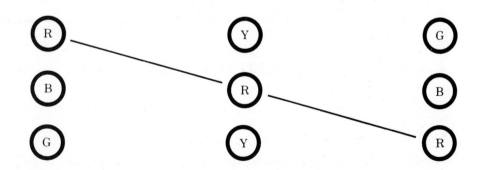

Directions: Connect the colors that will make a straight line.

Increase Level of Difficulty

Materials   Color the shapes in the design different, inconsistent colors. Use more shapes and a greater variety of them in the design.

Procedure   Make the directions more complicated: e.g., "Start at the upper right-hand corner (or designate it with a star). Count down one triangle and two circles. Connect this shape to the closest oval, then. . . ."

Decrease Level of Difficulty

Materials   Designs with fewer shapes and consistent shape and color patterns.

Procedure   Use simple one-step directions and be sure the children are keeping pace with you.

COMMENT   Be sure to have the children count the shapes and colors when they are finished. Interested children might graph this information.

NESTING CUPS

GOAL   To improve shape/size concepts
To improve eye-hand coordination

OBJECTIVE   The child will nest and unnest the cups.

MATERIALS   Stacking/nesting cups

PROCEDURE   Encourage the child to nest the containers and to make a tower with the cups. Talk about size, first using only the largest and smallest cups. Say, "Give me the biggest one." Gradually offer more choices.

Increase Level of Difficulty

Materials   Add a second set of nesting cups.

Procedure   Have the children order and match the two sets. Mix up the cups and take one away and have the child discover which one is missing. Use the concept of seriation (ordering large to small or small to large) and the vocabulary first, second, and third.

Decrease Level of Difficulty

Materials   Offer a small number of loosely fitting cups at first. (If the set has five cups take out the second and fourth ones.) Give verbal prompts as needed (i.e., say, "Put this cup in."). Gradually increase the difficulty by offering more cups.

Procedure   Offer the cups to the child nested together. Let the child play and discover what she can do with these objects. If the child doesn't pull them out of the nested position, show her how to do so. Let the child play and experiment by dumping and filling the cups with water, sand, cornmeal, and so on. Build a tower, encouraging the child to help. Let the child knock it down.

COMMENT   Rectangular cups don't roll away from children when they fall. When budgets are low, look at your kitchen. Pots and measuring cups teach children about increasing sizes and seriation.

BIG AND LITTLE PAIRS

GOAL   To improve shape/size concepts
To improve classification skills

OBJECTIVE   The child will pair the large and small objects.

MATERIALS   Pairs of objects, one large and one small:

tablespoon—teaspoon	large piece of paper—small piece of paper
adult shoe—child's shoe	large plate—small plate
large book—small book	
large bag or box to contain the objects	

PROCEDURE   Have children empty the box and place the large and small objects together in pairs.

Increase Level of Difficulty

Procedure   Encourage children to find other ways of classifying the objects (size, use, color, and so on). Have the children pair the objects using only touch (put a cover over the box). The child chooses one object and then must find its pair using only his hands.

Decrease Level of Difficulty

Materials   Choose the objects so that the large and small objects are the same color and different from other pairs.

COMMENT   There are many variations of this activity. For example, use cards and envelopes of different sizes or boxes and lids of varying sizes.

MEASURING TOOLS

GOAL   To improve measurement concepts
To improve classification skills
To make predictions

OBJECTIVE   The child will choose the appropriate measuring tool for an activity or event.

MATERIALS

timer	ruler	"diet" scale
hourglass	tape measure	bathroom scale
alarm clock	yardstick	balance scale
stopwatch	meter stick	paper/pencils

PROCEDURE   Place one group of measuring devices on a table with appropriate suggestions for things to be measured, timed, or weighed. Encourage children to use the tools. Discuss with children the efficiency of their choices, what worked, and what didn't work as well.

Increase Level of Difficulty

Procedure   Encourage children to record and graph their results and to make predictions about other measurements. Have them begin to order objects and events based upon principles of measurement.

Decrease Level of Difficulty

Procedure   Use fewer measurement tools and encourage children to explore the tools.

COMMENT   This is a good activity for children working in pairs. It can encourage inclusion as well as teach math concepts.

MEASURE IT

GOAL   To improve measurement concepts
To improve classification skills
To make predictions

OBJECTIVE   The child will predict how far he can throw particular objects.

MATERIALS

beanbag	tennis ball	ping-pong ball
sponges	small rubber ball	rubber rings
horseshoes	whiffle ball	crumpled paper
beach ball	12″ rubber ball	softball

PROCEDURE   Have a variety of objects for the children to throw. This is not a contest to see who can throw the farthest, so style of throwing is not important. Have the children help you draw a line or stake a string and then mark it at each foot with a tie. Have the children develop a base line (average throw) with the small rubber ball or a tennis ball. Have other children watch where the ball goes and then stand where it first hits. Determine how far it went. Then have the child who is throwing decide whether the next object will go farther or closer. Measure the distance and classify the objects after they are thrown. Have several children do this and compare the results. Help children understand how to make better predictions.

Increase Level of Difficulty

Materials   feather   balloon   towel

Procedure   Encourage children to choose other objects they might safely throw, make predictions, and then test them.

Decrease Level of Difficulty

Procedure   For some children this might simply be a motor activity with an understanding that it is easier to throw some objects farther than others.

COMMENT   A useful way of combining math, science, and motor skills.

Science

MY YARD

GOAL   To improve observational skills
To improve classification skills

OBJECTIVE   The child will identify at least five things.

MATERIALS   a yard of string for each child

small sticks or nails

magnifying glasses of different strengths

binoculars

PROCEDURE   On a warm, sunny, dry day cut pieces of string a yard long and tie one end to a stick or nail. Have the children push or pound these into the ground. Give each child a magnifying glass and have them explore their "yard." Their "yard" is a circle with a one-yard radius. At first you may have to help them see the little things: a blade of grass, an ant, dirt.

Increase Level of Difficulty

Materials   Pad and pencil

Procedure   Encourage children to list what they find and even map out the location. Use different degrees of magnification, and note what is seen. Note where the child is and repeat the activity in a different season.

Decrease Level of Difficulty

Procedure   Have children work in pairs. Point out specific objects to the children.

COMMENT   Be sure to draw the analogy between glasses and magnifying glasses. They are different devices to help people see better. If the ground is damp, have the children sit on something. Note: If any children are allergic to grass, these allergies are usually worse just after the grass has been cut.

Science

GOOP

GOAL   To improve observational skills
To improve cause-and-effect reasoning

OBJECTIVE   The child will explore the properties of cornstarch in its various states.

MATERIALS   water   tea

cornstarch   food coloring

beet juice   bowls or jellyroll trays

PROCEDURE   Have children mix approximately equal amounts of cornstarch and water to make goop. Allow children to experiment with the proportions and observe the results. If this is the children's first experience, leave the goop white. Later try adding some natural dyes like beet juice or tea (be careful, these can stain). Help children talk about the different and confusing states of the goop.

Increase Level of Difficulty

Materials   flour   sugar   water

Procedure   Use equal proportions of flour and water and compare the results to the goop. What happens with sugar and water? Help children learn about the different properties and reactions of materials that look similar.

Decrease Level of Difficulty

Procedure   Allow children more time to explore the plain goop.

COMMENT   Goop is edible and relatively easy to clean up. It is easily used on a bed tray, and it is clean. Goop requires little strength to manipulate and defies coordination. It is a soothing, yet intriguing media.

Science

ANT FARM

GOAL   To improve observational skills
To improve generalization skills

OBJECTIVE   The child will observe the ants.

MATERIALS   sets of two clear glass jars (one small enough to fit inside the other)

loose or sandy soil

sugar

water

ants

PROCEDURE   Put the smaller jar inside the large one, open side down. Fill the larger one with loose soil—don't pack it down. (You want to be able to see the ants, so you want the space relatively narrow.) Collect ants from one ant colony only for each jar (otherwise they may fight). Collect about twenty ants, put them in the jar, and screw on the lid. Once a week feed the ants a few drops of sugar water. Add a few grains of bird seed if you like.

Increase Level of Difficulty

Procedure   Make two ant farms and encourage the children to compare the two. Have them draw the configuration of tunnels. Encourage them to look up ants in reference books and learn about how they live and work.

Decrease Level of Difficulty

Procedure   Concentrate on the observation process. Point out what is going on in the ant farm.

COMMENT   Discuss the needs of animals to survive and how ants are both different and the same as other animals. It is possible to get commercially available ant farms, but the process of making your own is part of the children's learning.

Science

NATURE BOARD

GOAL   To improve observational skills
To improve classification skills
To improve cause-and-effect reasoning

OBJECTIVE   The child will identify and classify objects found.

MATERIALS   objects found on a nature walk   cardboard

glue   small bags

rubber gloves

PROCEDURE   On a nature walk, help the children pick up objects such as nuts, sticks, stones, leaves, twigs, and so on. Try to get at least two of each object. In addition to picking up natural objects, using gloves, pick up environmental pollutants as well—styrofoam, aluminum cans, plastic bags, cigarette butts. Put these in a separate bag. When you get back to the class, glue each of the natural objects onto a separate, small piece of cardboard. Put the "pairs" to these objects in a bag, and have children see if they can match the designated object. Have children try to remember where they found certain objects and why they might be there, for example, acorns and pine cones under trees. Classify the objects found in as many different ways as possible. Talk with children about pollutants and the problems they cause in the environment. Have them help figure out some solutions to these problems.

Increase Level of Difficulty

Procedure   Have children make a map of the nature walk and draw significant landmarks. Help them mark where objects were found and if possible glue some of the objects to the map.

Decrease Level of Difficulty

Procedure   Label objects for the child. While you are on the walk point out obvious relationships: "Look, you found a leaf. Let's look up in the tree and see if there are more like it. I think this leaf fell from this tree. This is called an oak tree. You have a green oak leaf."

COMMENT   Classifying objects that children have found makes them more relevant. It is never too early to begin environmental education.

Science

SINK OR FLOAT

GOAL   To improve observational skills
To improve classification skills
To improve cause-and-effect reasoning

OBJECTIVE   The child will state which objects will float and which will sink.

MATERIALS   water table, small plastic pool, or bucket water

paper with illustrations of sinking and floating

objects to put in the water

different shapes and weights of sinkers (that fishermen use) and floats

items from the classroom (paper, cardboard, blocks)

items from the kitchen (silverware, cups, egg cartons)

items from nature (bark, wood, seeds)

PROCEDURE   Fill a water table, small plastic pool, or bucket at least three inches deep and allow children to put objects in the water and to both play with them and observe them. Encourage children to make predictions and place objects that sink and float in separate groups.

Increase Level of Difficulty

Procedure   Encourage children to think about why fishermen use different kinds of sinkers (weight and shape). See if children can use floaters to make sinkers float. If they need other objects from the classroom, for example, a paper clip, penny, or pin, help them find the objects. Discuss where the sinkers are placed on the floater. Have them try variations. Have them categorize materials and try to generate principles for their classifications.

Decrease Level of Difficulty

Procedure   Encourage active exploration. Encourage children to place objects in the water in different ways (upside down, sideways). As they generate hypotheses, support their checking them out.

COMMENT   Always have an adult present when young children are near water. Have a variety of objects and repeat this activity with different items.

Science

COLOR CHANGES

GOAL   To improve observational skills
To make predictions
To improve cause-and-effect reasoning

OBJECTIVE   The child will mix water and food coloring and predict the color of the water.

MATERIALS
water	measuring cups
spoons	red, blue, and yellow food coloring
eye droppers	clear plastic glasses (about six per child)
large container	

PROCEDURE   Fill the glasses about half full of water. Give children food coloring and other equipment and allow them to experiment. Emphasize the vocabulary about specific colors as well as the relationship between the intensity of the color and the ratio of water and food coloring. Encourage children to predict what will happen before they mix colors. Have them count the number of drops used of each color. If children want to mix more colors have them use a large container, and at the end put all their colors in, observing the changes with each addition.

Increase Level of Difficulty

Materials   A set of sixty-four crayons of varying colors

Procedure   Using the crayons as a guide, have children pick a crayon and see if they can match it with food coloring. Encourage them to ask their peers whether or not the color matches and what to add if it doesn't.

Decrease Level of Difficulty

Procedure   Encourage color identification.

COMMENT   The activity can help children learn color names in a creative way as well as be a science project. Help generalize this experience to painting and using markers.

Science

GELATIN

GOAL   To improve observational skills
To make predictions
To improve cause-and-effect reasoning

OBJECTIVE   The child will state the changes that take place in the gelatin during the activity.

MATERIALS
fruit-flavored gelatin	ice cubes
boiling water	fruit
cold water	bowls
spoons	

PROCEDURE   Following the directions on the package, make gelatin with cold water. Then make another batch with ice cubes. Emphasize vocabulary like cold, hot, boiling, melt, thicken, powder, liquid, and solid. Add fruit at various stages in the thickening process and discuss sinking and floating. Plan to have the gelatin for snack or lunch.

Increase Level of Difficulty

Procedure   Compare making gelatin with cold water and with ice by timing both processes and predicting when the gelatin will be thick enough so the fruit floats instead of sinking. Make a chart showing how the children's predictions compare with what actually happens.

Decrease Level of Difficulty

Procedure   Concentrate on the vocabulary and the change of state of the gelatin.

COMMENT   Encourage children with visual impairments to stir the gelatin at various stages to learn more about the change from a powder to a liquid and the process of thickening as the gelatin turns to a solid. If you make a small batch for these children they can stir it with their fingers.

Science

POLLUTION

GOAL   To improve observational skills
To make predictions
To improve cause-and-effect reasoning

OBJECTIVE   The child will predict the color of the celery or carnation.

MATERIALS   2 sticks of fresh celery with leaves or white carnations
3 glasses of water
red and blue food coloring

PROCEDURE   Cut off the bottoms of celery sticks or carnation stems. Put a few drops of red food coloring in one glass of water and blue in a second. Leave the water in the third glass clear. Put one stick of celery (or carnation) in each glass. This can be done early in the day and checked at the end or checked the next day. Cut the celery and see how the ones in colored water are different from the one in fresh water. One needs only to observe the carnations to see the effects. The carnations may look beautiful, but it is important that children see beyond the visual effect. Talk with children about the concern about pollution in underground water. Tell them how it gets into the plants we eat. Help them learn about the principles of osmosis. Have them begin to think about ways of preventing pollution.

Increase Level of Difficulty

Procedure   Help children learn more about pollution and how it affects them. Talk about the implications of increasing populations and conservation. Help children generate ideas for actions that could be done at school and at home to decrease pollution.

Decrease Level of Difficulty

Procedure   Pollution is a relatively abstract concept, and children may learn only about the principle of osmosis. The implications of pollution may not be absorbed at this time.

COMMENT   Children need to learn about conservation at an early age. It is important to make such a global, abstract problem relevant to them.

Science

POPCORN

GOAL   To improve observational skills
To improve cause-and-effect reasoning
To improve measurement concepts

OBJECTIVE   The child will discuss how heat causes popcorn to change states and measure the distance from the popcorn popper to the designated piece of popcorn on the sheet.

MATERIALS   popcorn   salt   flat, double bed sheet
popcorn popper   bowl   measuring tape
butter or margarine

PROCEDURE   Place a popcorn popper in the middle of a clean sheet on the floor; have the children sit around the edge. Make popcorn in a forced hot air popcorn popper without a lid so the children can see the corn pop. Talk about the different senses. Visually compare a kernel to the fluffy popcorn (compare a few kernels that didn't pop, too). Feel the kernel and the popped corn. Have children close their eyes and listen to the pop and smell the popcorn. Obviously, taste the popcorn. Discuss the role of heat in the change. After the popcorn is popped move the hot popper away and have the children measure the various distances the popcorn has gone. Make additional popcorn and eat the popcorn with no additions, then with some salt and butter. Show how the butter, too, changes state when heated.

Increase Level of Difficulty

Procedure   Have children use different measuring devices to calculate the distance to a piece of popcorn; that is, use a tape measure for inches, their feet, hands, and so on. Chart the results.

Decrease Level of Difficulty

Procedure   Children may just enjoy the sensory aspects of the project.

COMMENT   Be careful to avoid accidents when popping corn with children nearby. The popper gets very hot. *Note:* It is possible for children to choke on a piece of popcorn. Learn the Heimlich maneuver—all teachers should know it.

Science

MAPS

GOAL   To improve observation skills
To improve measurement concepts
To improve computer skills

OBJECTIVE   The child will make a map of an area of a room.

MATERIALS

cardboard	water	paper
crayons	a container	masking tape
papier-mâché	string or yarn	

PROCEDURE   Have the children choose an area of the classroom (e.g., block, dramatic play) or playground and draw it on cardboard with crayons. Discuss with the children where things are in their drawing and how they decide where to put them. Make large graph paper for the children (1 inch equals 1 square foot) and use string or yarn to mark off the area the children are mapping in one-foot square sections. (If you are lucky you may have floor tiles that are one-foot square so this will be unnecessary.) Have them make another map.

Increase Level of Difficulty

Procedure   Now ask the children what in the area is flat and what should stand up from the surface (tables, swings, and so on). Use papier-mâché to have the children's maps reflect these contours. You can talk about relative size as it relates to both area and height.

Decrease Level of Difficulty

Procedure   Divide the area and paper into quarters.

COMMENT   This project is best done over the course of several days. They need not be consecutive.

Science

BUBBLES

GOAL   To improve observational skills
To improve cause-and-effect reasoning
To improve eye-hand coordination

OBJECTIVE   The child will blow bubbles and catch them.

MATERIALS   bubble wand   bubble mixture (5 cups water, $1/2$ cup Joy

pail   2 T. glycerin)

PROCEDURE   Have some children blow bubbles and other children try to catch or pop them. Encourage children to figure out where the bubbles will go based on the wind. Have them experiment with blowing hard and soft.

Increase Level of Difficulty

Materials   bubble-blowing rings   plastic six-pack holder   wire

bubble mixture

Procedure   Encourage children to make their own bubble wands. Help them observe the relationship between the wand and the size and number of the bubbles. Help them experiment with soap and how it reduces water tension, resulting in bubbles not droplets.

Decrease Level of Difficulty

Materials   straw   paper cup   bubble mixture

Procedure   Have children blow bubbles with a straw. Be sure children understand the difference between blowing out and sucking in.

COMMENT   This is a good activity on a warm day.

Science

FOOD LOTTO

GOAL   To improve classification skills
To improve generalization skills

OBJECTIVE   The child will match the sets of pictures correctly.

MATERIALS   A Lotto game with four sets of pictures of fruits or vegetables:

2 identical pictures of each fruit or vegetable

a picture of a whole fruit or vegetable as it grows (e.g., apple on an apple tree, squash on a plant)

a picture of a whole fruit (vegetable) to be matched with a picture of the same fruit (vegetable) cut in half

a picture of a whole fruit (vegetable) to be matched with a picture of the same fruit in a different state (e.g., apple/applesauce; orange/orange juice; pumpkin/pumpkin pie; corn on the cob/corn in a bowl)

PROCEDURE   Start with a traditional Lotto game in which children match the identical pictures. Then have the child match the other sets. This can be done individually or in small groups.

Increase Level of Difficulty

Materials   Choose more unusual fruits and vegetables (kiwi, star fruit, yard-long beans, and so on).

Decrease Level of Difficulty

Materials   Have the actual fruits or vegetables whole and cut up.

Procedure   Let the children first have the experience with the actual objects. Encourage children to look and taste the actual fruits or vegetables, then go on to the Lotto game.

COMMENT   You can draw the pictures yourself or find a parent or friend to do it. Otherwise, get seed catalogs. (Many people will willingly give you out-of-date ones, or you can write to a publisher for extras.) Two or three of the same kind are especially useful. While all children may have some trouble recognizing the source of less familiar food, this task may be especially difficult for children who live in large cities.

SORTING

GOAL   To improve classification skills
To improve generalization skills

OBJECTIVE   The child will sort common objects and classify them.

MATERIALS   three containers for each child

objects that can be sorted into two categories

OBJECTS	CATEGORY A	CATEGORY B
buttons	rough	smooth
buttons	two holes	four holes
silverware	forks	knives
silverware	big spoons	little spoons
shapes	circles	squares
shapes	oval	rectangle

PROCEDURE   Anchor three containers to a board or place them in a row. (Coffee cans with lids work well.) Vary the size of the can to the size of the objects to be sorted. Put the objects to be sorted in the middle container. Then have the children sort the objects into the two empty containers.

Increase Level of Difficulty

Materials

fruits	animals	furniture
vegetables	vehicles	kitchen utensils

Procedure   Have children sort the objects into categories and tell you the basis for their sorting. Then have them re-sort the same objects using different classes. Have them sort the objects into three categories.

Decrease Level of Difficulty

Materials   blocks   balls

Procedure   Use simple objects with obvious differences that are large enough to be handled easily and few enough so the task can be completed.

COMMENT   For children with visual impairments choose objects that are visually very different (black and white) or have tactile cues.

MAGNETS

GOAL   To make predictions
To improve cause-and-effect reasoning

OBJECTIVE   Before using the magnet the child will predict which objects will be attracted by the magnet and which ones will not.

MATERIALS   magnets of varying sizes, shapes and strengths

assorted small nonmetal objects

toothpicks   plastic clips

assorted small metal objects (not aluminum)

paper clips (large and small)   nails   washers

safety pins (large and small)   staples

shallow box of metal filings covered with plastic wrap

PROCEDURE   Give the children a variety of magnets and materials to experiment with. Encourage them to use the magnet both on the top and bottom of the box with metal filings. Ask them to sort objects according to the object's response to the magnet. As they begin to understand the idea, ask the children to predict whether or not specific objects will be attracted by the magnet. Have them discover objects in the room that are attracted to the magnet. Teach them to modify objects so that they will be attracted to the magnet (e.g., attach a paper clip to a small piece of paper).

Increase Level of Difficulty

Procedure   Encourage children to chart the results of their investigations. Have them explore the strength of different magnets by finding out how many paper clips each magnet can pick up. Introduce paper clips of different sizes and see how many of each size can be picked up. You might even try to weigh or balance the different sizes of clips. Again, graph or chart your results.

Decrease Level of Difficulty

Procedure   Allow more time for exploration.

COMMENT   Iron filings are often available from hardware stores that cut pipes. Encourage children to think about ways that magnets might be useful, such as picking up or containing paper clips. Then add a magnet to the end of a stick. Have children sit in a chair and use the tool as an extension of their arm to get things they can't reach. Have them try to pick up paper clips on the floor while sitting in the chair. This activity is an initial step in showing how some devices can help those with physical impairments.

Science

PLANTING

GOAL   To make predictions
     To improve cause-and-effect reasoning
     To improve generalization skills

OBJECTIVE   The child will help plant seeds, help put signs on the pots, and make predictions about how well each plant will grow.

MATERIALS

seeds (large)	water
potting soil	signs
large pots	paper (to graph results)
crayons	popsicle sticks marked at 1″ intervals

PROCEDURE   Plant seeds in three large pots with a popsicle stick beside each. Make signs to indicate the conditions under which the seeds will try to grow. Note that all plants need air and food. Have children count and mark the days on a calendar until the first sprout appears. Once they sprout, measure the plants each day, and then graph the results. Be sure to put several seeds in each pot, as some seeds may not grow even under ideal conditions. Choose seeds that are easy to handle and sprout quickly (a combination of rye grass and beans works well).

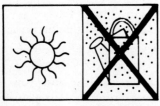

Sun   No water

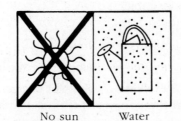

No sun   Water

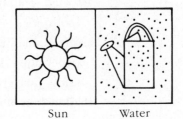

Sun   Water

Science must be a "hands on" experience for children. To understand how plants grow, children need to participate in planting, tending, and harvesting.

Increase Level of Difficulty

Procedure   Expand the concept of planting. Have children cut pictures out of seed catalogs and make a matching game by gluing several seeds to a card to match to the picture. Help children notice differences among the seeds. Plant some of the seeds in a pot or garden. Observe the plants at various stages and compare the resulting plants with the picture.

Decrease Level of Difficulty

Materials   lima beans (dried, soaked in water)

damp cotton or paper towel

plastic (see-through) glasses or large glass container

water   sponge

Procedure   Have each child plant several beans in a plastic container with the cotton or paper towel inside so they can see the bean from the side. This way they can watch the root develop. They can begin to understand that even if they can't see anything happening, things are going on under the surface of the ground. Add a new bean each day to help children see the differences. Be sure to keep the beans damp. When the seeds are sprouted, the sprouts can be planted and observed.

COMMENT   This project is best done in the spring as part of a general theme on plants and growth. It helps show variations in growth patterns. Send a sprouted seed home to a child who is absent for a long time and compare the growth between the school plant and the home plant.

SCRAMBLED EGGS

GOAL   To make predictions
To improve cause-and-effect reasoning
To improve computer skills

OBJECTIVE   The child will scramble an egg and eat it. He or she will also put the unbroken egg, the egg in the bowl, and scrambled egg in the right order.

MATERIALS   1 egg per child   cup   pepper

water   fork   electric fry pan

salt   teaspoon   spatula (metal)

PROCEDURE   Have a group of three or four children make scrambled eggs. At each stage of the procedure, have children predict what will happen. Allow each child to crack his own egg into a cup and stir it; add 1 teaspoon of water and salt and pepper if desired; stir; put it in an electric fry pan; scramble it with the fork; put it on a plate with the spatula. Then eat it for a snack with the other children in the group. When they have finished show them:

> an egg in the shell
>
> an egg beaten in the dish
>
> an egg scrambled

Have the children put these different egg states in the correct sequence and discuss the differences among them and the effect of heat on the egg. Help them see the analogy of selecting a disk, putting it in the computer and booting the system.

Increase Level of Difficulty

Procedure   Encourage children to look at the color of the yolk and see how the color changes as more air is beaten in. Have children beat with a fork, eggbeater, and whip it to see the differences in color and volume. Discuss the use of heat in cooking and what it does to different common foods. Encourage children to think about how the raw or unheated food is different.

> bread—toast   potato—baked potato
>
> raw carrots—cooked carrots   oatmeal—hot oatmeal

Decrease Level of Difficulty

Procedure   Help talk children through the sequence to remind them of the stages.

COMMENT   Give a play-by-play description of what the children are doing while they are doing it. It is good fine motor practice to pick out any broken eggshell by using part of the broken eggshell.

INPUT-OUTPUT

GOAL   To improve computer skills
To improve sequencing skills
To improve generalization skills

OBJECTIVE   The child will state at least one input and one output.

MATERIALS   chalkboard   chalk   outline of a person

PROCEDURE   Talk with the children about how they learn information. For example, how did they decide what to wear today? If they looked outside and saw the sun was shining that was visual

INPUT. If their mother told them what to wear that was auditory INPUT. That INPUT went into their Central Processing Unit (CPU) or their brain. They all came with clothes on; that is OUTPUT. Help children think about how they learn in terms of an INPUT–CPU–OUTPUT framework. Ask the children who is absent today. The children look around, INPUT, and in their CPU (brain) they compare whom they see with their memory of who is in the class. They process the information. Then they decide that Danny is absent—OUTPUT. Use the chalkboard to draw further illustrations for the children.

Increase Level of Difficulty

Procedure   Encourage children to design their own processors based on the principle of INPUT–CPU–OUTPUT. Help them think of simple machines that work on this principle (drinking straw dispensers, soda machines, jukeboxes, and so forth.) Now help children go a step further to the automatic teller at the bank and the computer at the fast-food restaurant. You may have to tell children that they must put money in the bank before they can take it out!

Decrease Level of Difficulty

Procedure   Start by using a simple machine such as a drinking straw dispenser or by making popcorn. Explain how pressing the lever is an INPUT, the movement inside the CPU causes the straw to fall, and the straw is the OUTPUT.

COMMENT   This is a basic introduction to the concepts of INPUT–CPU–OUTPUT, some basic computer terminology, and also good logical thinking. It is important for children to know that if they don't put anything in the computer nothing will come out. Beyond this, it is important that they learn that even if they use a software program somebody had to put all the information into the computer.

Computers

ROBOT-CONTROLLER

GOAL   To improve computer skills
To improve cause-and-effect reasoning
To follow directions

OBJECTIVE   The child will give commands that can be carried out by the teacher or another child.

MATERIALS   None

PROCEDURE   Have one child be the controller of a robot (another child or the teacher) and another be the robot. The controller's job is to command the robot. You should be the first robot. If the commands are unclear ("Robot walk") send back a message: "That does not compute. Robot needs to know whether to walk forward or backward or sideways." The feedback will help children expand their vocabulary and become more specific in their speech as well as gaining practice giving commands. The children take turns so that they get practice in both commanding and following directions. The children need to build the concept that the computer will not do anything unless the children give the commands. They also need to learn that the commands must be specific and that some commands "will not compute" so they need to find ones that will.

Increase Level of Difficulty

Procedure   Have children give two- and three-step commands at one time and increase the complexity of locational cues and numbers: "Take three steps to the right and then raise your hands and clap twice."

Decrease Level of Difficulty

Procedure   The robot could actually work like a toggle switch. If the child said "jump" the robot would jump until the child said "stop jumping." Especially in cases where the teacher is the robot you can lead the child into more complexity by the questions you ask. For example: "Shall the robot jump fast or slow?" "Shall the robot jump in place or around the room?", and so on.

COMMENT   The robot-controller can be modified to work in any situation in which someone is in charge and teaching another what to do. You could have an animal trainer in the circus, a dog (pet) obedience school, ground control to someone in a space capsule, a transportation maze where the navigator verbally, through remote control, steers the car (other child) through the roads, and so on. This activity is an excellent way for children to see the results of commands.

Computers

PORT-STARBOARD

GOAL   To improve computer skills
To improve generalization skills
To follow directions

OBJECTIVE   The child will both give and follow directions.

MATERIALS   red and green channel markers

red (right or starboard) and green (left or port) running lights (bracelets) for the children

string, yarn, or tape to lay out the channel

boxes with the tops and bottoms cut out for boats

PROCEDURE   Explain to the children that they are ships—large ships—and that the water is shallow and there is a lot of fog so they can't see. Because they are so big they have to stay in the channel or they will go aground. The only way they can tell if they are in the channel is if the red markers are always on their right. Because of the fog they cannot see very well so they must rely on instructions from the tower (control center) for directions to get home. At least one child is on the tower commanding the ships. Help them with some of the following:

Turn to starboard (right).

Turn to port (left).

Ahead full throttle.

Ahead half throttle.

Ship abeam (alongside).

Hold your course.

Increase Level of Difficulty

Materials   Make the channel longer with more turns and wide enough for two ships. Have one area where the channel splits or gets narrower. Put an obstruction across part of the channel.

Procedure   Have two ships in the channel and see if they can safely pass.

Decrease Level of Difficulty

Procedure   Have children work together. One child can be a tugboat towing another boat (child). The second child will get the listening experience and will follow the other child.

COMMENT   Port-starboard may seem like an added complication in distinguishing left from right, but if children keep checking their bracelet color with the channel markers it is not as complicated as it sounds. Children are often intrigued with the sea jargon.

Computers

BURIED TREASURE

GOAL   To improve computer skills
To improve generalization skills
To improve reading readiness

OBJECTIVE   The child will find the buried treasure on the first attempt.

MATERIALS   large flat box with top   sand, oatmeal, or rice

string or yarn   masking tape

9 small treasures   clay

marker

cards with coordinates on one side and a drawing of the treasure in those coordinates on the other

PROCEDURE   Using four pieces of string, divide the box into nine equal segments. Tape the string so it goes on top of the open box. In each segment put a small piece of clay to keep the treasure from moving around and stick the treasure in the clay. Add sand to the box, making sure the treasure stays in the designated segment. Divide the top of the box in the same way, using a marker to divide it into sections. Add a narrow section across the left side and the bottom: put the numbers 1, 2, and 3 on the left side and A, B, and C on the bottom. Give the children a card with a set of coordinates (2/B) and see if they can find the right treasure. Draw a simple picture of the treasure on the back of the card so they can check themselves.

Increase Level of Difficulty

Materials   Use the same system with a sand table or a much larger box so that there are twenty-four possible areas.

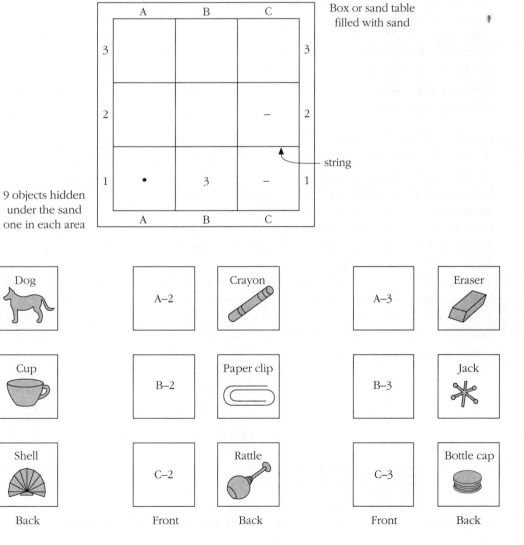

Procedure Have children find the treasures. Once they have the idea, bury the treasures and give them an 8½″ × 11″ ditto of the area marked off and have them chart the location of the treasures they found.

Decrease Level of Difficulty

Materials Divide the box into just four areas.

COMMENT This activity helps children learn to move in a systematic way between vertical and horizontal planes, a skill that is necessary not only for the computer but for copying off the chalkboard. It also helps children learn to read the coordinates of a graph.

Computers

MY KEYBOARD

GOAL To improve computer skills
To improve sequencing skills
To improve reading readiness

OBJECTIVE The child will make his name from the keyboard letters.

MATERIALS poster board   markers   Velcro

PROCEDURE Using the computer keyboard as a guide, make a keyboard out of poster board by using a large piece (12″ × 15″) for the base and smaller pieces (¾″ circles or squares) for the keys. Write the letters and numbers on the keys. Place four 15″ strips of Velcro across the base and attach Velcro to the back of each of the keys. Place the keys in a container and have the children place the keys on the keyboard in the correct order, using a keyboard as a guide.

Increase Level of Difficulty

Procedure This is a difficult task, but you might add some of the additional keys such as the return, shift, control, alternate, and delete. Choose keys that are meaningful in the software packages you use.

Decrease Level of Difficulty

Materials A guide strip with the letters or numbers for each row of the computer keyboard

Procedure Place the guide strip above the Velcro. At the beginning have some of the letters in place so that the children only have to find three or four missing ones. Increase the number of missing letters until the children can place all the letters.

COMMENT Whether or not your classroom has a computer, an activity such as this provides a good foundation in both computing and reading readiness.

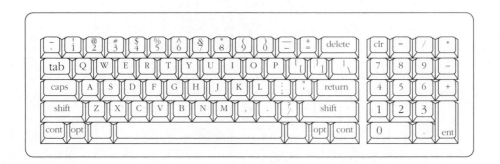

SPELL IT

GOAL   To improve computer skills
To improve sequencing skills
To improve reading readiness

OBJECTIVE   The child will "type" three words.

MATERIALS   keyboard from My Keyboard with letters and numbers and guide strips in place

poster board 3″ × 15″ with a Velcro piece 15″ long

basket with children's names printed on poster board

basket with words printed on cards or poster board

PROCEDURE   Have children find their name or a word they want to "type" and place it above the keyboard. The children can then take the letters off the keyboard and place them on the blank strip. Encourage children to replace the letters when they are finished. The guide strip is essential for this part of the process. Print words that children request and place them in the basket.

Increase Level of Difficulty

Materials   Put short sentences on cards.

Decrease Level of Difficulty

Procedure   Encourage children to work with a friend.

COMMENT   This activity does not require a computer and supports reading readiness skills.

Children can work together at computers.

FRUIT KABOB

GOAL   To improve computer skills
To improve sequencing skills
To improve eye-hand coordination

OBJECTIVE   The child will make a fruit kabob following the rebus picture menu.

MATERIALS   wooden skewers   cut-up apples   pineapple cubes
grapes   banana slice   picture menues

PROCEDURE   Design several rebus pictures (these are simply pictures designed for nonreaders that resemble international road signs) menues using varying amounts of fruit (1 apple piece, 3 grapes, 2 pineapple cubes, 1 banana slice) on a skewer or a repeating pattern of fruit (1 apple piece, 1 pineapple cube, 1 grape, 1 apple piece, 1 pineapple cube, 1 grape, and so on). Let children choose the menu they want and make it. They then eat the fruit kabob for snack.

Increase Level of Difficulty

Procedure   Increase the complexity of some of the menus by having additional fruits and more difficult patterns. Have a word menu as an alternative for children who can read.

Decrease Level of Difficulty

Procedure   Use fewer fruits and just one of each.

COMMENT   Children need practice selecting from a menu and interpreting rebus pictures. This procedure can be used for adding fruit to a fruit salad or making trail mix and other food projects.

CEREAL BALLS

GOAL   To improve computer skills
To follow directions
To improve measurement concepts

OBJECTIVE   The child will make the recipe following the picture directions.

MATERIALS   honey   measuring cups
peanut butter   large bowl
coconut   small bowl
cereal   mixing spoon
Write the recipe on large paper.

PROCEDURE

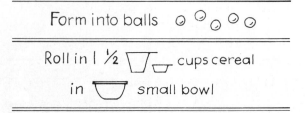

CEREAL BALLS

Mix ✎ in 🥣 large bowl
½ ☐ cup honey
½ ☐ cup peanut butter
½ ☐ cup coconut
½ ☐ cup cereal

Form into balls ○ ○ ○ ○ ○

Roll in 1 ½ ☐ cups cereal
in ☐ small bowl

Mix honey, peanut butter, coconut, and ½ cup cereal.
Put remaining cereal into cereal bowl.
Scoop peanut butter mixture out, form into balls, and roll in cereal. (½ cup dry milk can be added if children seem to need this.)

Increase Level of Difficulty

Procedure   Make this an individual activity by reducing the honey, peanut butter, coconut, and cereal to one tablespoon each and rolling it in $1/4$ cup of cereal at the end.

Decrease Level of Difficulty

Procedure   By encouraging children to take turns all children can participate.

COMMENT   Following sequential multistepped directions is an important computing skill. Using rebus pictures for illustration reinforces the concept as well. Give a play-by-play description of what you are doing. Be sure to use words that imply the sequence. ("First we are going to measure the honey. Second, . . . third, . . . ") Show children with visual impairments how to touch the containers to see if they are full if this is necessary.

Note: Be sure to check whether any children have allergies, as peanut butter is a rather common one.

Computers

ALPHABET KEYBOARD

GOAL   To improve computer skills
To follow directions
To improve reading readiness

OBJECTIVE   The child will connect the designated letters using a crayon or marker.

MATERIALS   dittos of the letters and numbers on the computer keyboard

a separate card for each letter of the alphabet and the numbers 0 to 9

PROCEDURE   Have the children draw lines between the letters and numbers with a crayon or marker as someone reads them after drawing them from a hat.

Increase Level of Difficulty

Procedure   Increase the pace of reading the letters and numbers, but not to the point that it is frustrating.

Decrease Level of Difficulty

Procedure   Have children draw their own numbers and letters from the hat so they can control the pace and match the letters before connecting them.

COMMENT   Another "off" computer activity that stresses keyboard skills. Children can connect the letters of their name. They can even color in the connecting shapes.

Computers

COMPUTER BINGO

GOAL   To improve computer skills
To follow directions
To improve reading readiness

OBJECTIVE   The child will place a marker on the designated letters.

MATERIALS   dittos of the letters and numbers on the computer keyboard

cards with a number and letter designation

| 1-Q | 2-W | 3-E | 4-R | 5-T | to | 0-P |
| 1-A | 2-S | 3-D | 4-F | 5-G | to | 0-; |

(and so on)

PROCEDURE   Have the children place a marker on each letter as the caller reads the cards after drawing them from a hat.

Increase Level of Difficulty

Procedure   Increase the pace of reading the cards drawn, but not to the point that it is frustrating.

Decrease Level of Difficulty

Procedure   Have children draw their own cards so they can control the pace.

COMMENT   Another "off" computer activity that stresses keyboard skills. Although structured like bingo, obviously all the children who follow the instructions accurately will "win."

References and Bibliography

Cliatt, M. J., & Shaw, J. (1992). *Helping children explore science: A sourcebook for teachers of young children*. Riverside, NJ: Merrill/Macmillan.

Davidson, J. I. (1990). *Children & computers together in the early childhood classroom*. Albany, NY: Delmar Publishers, Inc.

Harlan, J. (1992). *Science experiences for the early childhood years* (5th ed.) Riverside, NJ: Merrill/Macmillan.

Haugland, S., & Shade, D. (1990). *Developmental evaluations of software for young children*. Albany, NY: Delmar Publishers, Inc.

"Helping your child at home with arithmetic" (Series 1). (no date). Parent Brochures. Novato, CA: Academic Therapy Publications.

Hurth, J. (1985). *Microcomputers for early childhood special education*. Chapel Hill, NC: TADS.

Kamii, C. K. (1982). *Number in Preschool and kindergarten*. Washington, DC: National Association for the Education of Young Children.

Lamme, L. (1985). *Growing up writing*. Washington, DC: Acropolis Books, Ltd.

Nichols, W., & Nichols, K. *Wonder science: A developmentally appropriate guide to hands on science for young children*. Palo Alto, CA: Learning Expo Publishing.

Payne, J. N. (Ed.) (1990). *Mathematics for the young child*. Reston, VA: National Council of Teachers of Mathematics.

Schickedanz, J. A., York, M. A., Stewart, I. S., & White, D. A. (1990). *Strategies for teaching young children* (3rd ed.). Englewood Cliffs, NJ: Prentice-Hall.

Bibliography for Additional Reading

Mathematics

Baratta-Lorten, M. (1976). *Mathematics their way*. Menlo Park, CA: Addison-Wesley Publishing Co.

Baroody, Arthur J. (1987). *Children's mathematical thinking: A developmental framework for preschool, primary and special education teachers*. NY: Teachers College, Columbia University.

Barron, Linda. (1975). *Mathematics experiences for the early childhood years*. Columbus, OH: Merrill Publishing Company.

Berman, B. (1982). How children learn math: Rediscovering manipulatives. *Curriculum Review, 21,* 192–196.

Burns, M. (1975). *The I hate mathematics book.* Boston, MA: Little, Brown.

Burton, G. M. (1985). *Towards a good beginning: Teaching early childhood mathematics*. Menlo Park, CA: Addison-Wesley Publishing Co.

Charlesworth, R., & Lind, K. (1990). *Math and science for young children*. Albany, NY: Delmar Publishers.

Cooney, T. J., & Hirsch, C. R. (1990). *Teaching & learning mathematics in the 1990s*. Reston, VA: National Council of Teachers of Mathematics.

Copeland, R. W. (1974). *Diagnostic and learning activities in mathematics for children*. New York: Macmillan.

Copeland, R. W. (1984). *How children learn mathematics: Teaching implications of Piaget's research*. New York: Macmillan.

Cruikshank, D. E., Fitzgerald, D. L., & Jensen, L. R. (1980). *Young children learning mathematics*. Boston, MA: Allyn & Bacon.

Davidson, P. S. (1977). *Idea book for cuisenaire rods at the primary level*. New Rochelle, NY: Cuisenaire Company of America.

Davidson, T., Fountain, P., Grogan, R., Short, V., & Steely, J. (1976). *The learning center book: An integrated approach*. Santa Monica, CA: Goodyear.

Gelman, R., & Gallistel, C. R. (1986). *The child's understanding of number*. Cambridge, MA: Harvard University Press.

Harsh, A. (1987). Teach mathematics with children's literature. *Young Children, 42* (6), 24–29.

Holmes, E. E. (1985). *Children learning mathematics: A cognitive approach to teaching*. Englewood Cliffs, NJ: Prentice-Hall.

Kamii, C. K. (1985). *Young children reinvent arithmetic: Implications of Piaget's theory*. New York: Teachers College Press, Columbia University.

Kaye, P. (1987). *Games for math: Playful ways to help your child learn math, from kindergarten to third grade.* New York: Pantheon.

McCracken, J. B. (1987). *More than 1,2,3: The real basics of mathematics.* Washington, DC: National Association for the Education of Young Children.

Richardson, L. I., Goodman, K. L., Hartman, N. N., & LePique, H. A. (1980). *Mathematics activity curriculum for early childhood and special education.* New York: Macmillan.

Schultz, K. A., Colarusso, R. P., & Strawderman, V. W. (1989). *Mathematics for every young child.* Columbus, OH: Merrill.

Stenmark, J. K., Thompson, V., & Cossey, R. (1986). *Family math.* Berkeley, CA: Lawrence Hall of Science, University of California.

Stern, M. (1988). *Experimenting with numbers: A guide for preschool, kindergarten, and first grade teachers.* Cambridge, MA: Educators Publishing Service, Inc.

Stevenson, H. W., Lummis, M., Lee, S., & Stigler, J. W. (1990). *Making the grade in mathematics.* Reston, VA: National Council of Teachers of Mathematics.

Stone, J. I. (1987). Early childhood math: Make it manipulative! *Young Children, 42* (6), 16–23.

Zaslavsky, C. (1979). *Preparing young children for math: A book of games.* New York: Schocken.

Science

Butzow, C. M., & Butzow, J. W. (1989). *Science through children's literature: An integrated approach.* Washington, DC: National Science Teachers Assoc.

Carlin, A. A., & Sund, R. B. (1980). *Teaching science through discovery.* Columbus, OH: Merrill.

Cassidy, J. (1987). *The unbelievable bubble book.* Palo Alto, CA: Klutz Press.

Druger, M. (Ed) (1988). *Science for the fun of it: A guide to informal science education.* Washington, DC: National Science Teachers Assoc.

Foreman, G., & Kaden, M. (1986). Research on science education for young children. In C. Seefeldt (Ed.), *The early childhood curriculum: A review of current research* (pp. 141–181). New York: Teachers College Press, Columbia University.

Harlan, J. (1976). *Science experiences for early childhood years.* Columbus, OH: Merrill.

Herbert, D. (1980). *Mr. Wizard's supermarket science.* Washington, DC: National Science Teachers Assoc.

Iatridis, M. D. (1986). *Teaching science to children: A resource book.* New York: Garland.

James, J. C., & Granovetter, R. F. (1988). *Waterworks: A new book of water play activities for children ages 1 to 6.* Lewisville, NC: Kaplan Press.

Javna, J. (1990). *50 simple things kids can do to save the earth.* Kansas City, KS: Andrews and McMeel.

Johnson, C. M. (1987). *Discovering nature with young people: An annotated bibliography and selection guide.* Westport, CT: Greenwood Press, Inc.

Katz, A. (1986). *Exploring nature with your children.* Reading, MA: Addison-Wesley.

Levenson, E. (1985). *Teaching children about science: Ideas and activities every teacher and parent can use.* Englewood Cliffs, NJ: Prentice-Hall.

Link, M. (1981). *Outdoor education: A manual for teaching in nature's classroom.* Englewood Cliffs, NJ: Prentice-Hall.

McIntyre, M. (1984). *Early childhood and science: A collection of articles.* Washington, DC: National Science Teachers Assoc.

Neugebauer, B. (Ed.). (1989). *The wonder of it: Exploring how the world works.* Redmond, WA: Exchange Press.

Outstanding science trade books for children. (1987). *Young Children, 42*(6), 52–56.

Promoting science in your program: Use outstanding science books (1988). *Young Children, 44*(1), 72–73.

Ricter, B., & Wenzel, D. (Eds.). (1985). *The Museum of Science and Industry basic list of children's science books, 1973–1984.* Chicago: American Library Assoc.

Ricter, B., & Wenzel, D. (Eds.). (1987). *The Museum of Science and Industry basic list of children's science books, 1987.* Chicago: American Library Assoc.

Robinson, B., & Wilson, E. (1982). *Environmental education: A manual for elementary educators.* New York: Teachers College Press, Columbia University.

Shaffer, C., & Fielder, E. (1987). *City safaris: A Sierra Club explorer's guide to urban adventures for grownups and kids.* Washington, DC: National Science Teachers Assoc.

Sisson, E. (1982). *Nature with children of all ages.* Englewood Cliffs, NJ: Prentice-Hall.

Sprung, B., Froschl, M., & Campbell, P. M. *What will happen if . . . Young children and the scientific method.* New York: Educational Equity Concepts.

Ukens, L. (Ed.). (1986). *Science experiences for preschoolers: CESI sourcebook IV.* Washington, DC: National Science Teachers Assoc.

Williams, R. A., Rockwell, R. E., & Sherwood, E. A. (1987). *Mudpies to magnets: A preschool science curriculum.* Mt. Rainier, MD: Gryphon House, Inc.

Williams, R. A., Rockwell, R. E., & Sherwood, E. A. (1990). *More mudpies to magnets: Science for young children.* Mt. Ranier, MD: Gryphon House, Inc.

Woodard, C., & Davitt, R. (1987). *Physical science in early childhood.* Springfield, IL: Charles C. Thomas.

Ziemer, M. (1987). Science and the early childhood curriculum: One thing leads to another. *Young Children, 42*(6), 44–51.

Computers

Adams, D. M. (Ed.). (1986). *Computers and teacher training: A practical guide.* New York: Haworth Press.

Beaty, J. J., & Tucker, W. H. (1987). *The computer as a paintbrush: Creative uses for the personal computer in the preschool classroom.* Columbus, OH: Merrill.

Burke, W. (1986). *Computers in the classroom . . . What shall I do? A guide.* New York: Garland Publishing, Inc.

Campbell, P. F., & Fein, G. G. (1986). *Young children and microcomputers.* Englewood Cliffs, NJ: Prentice-Hall.

Clements, D. H. (1985). *Computers in early and primary education.* Englewood Cliffs, NJ: Prentice-Hall.

Clements, D. H. (1987). Computers and young children: A review of research. *Young Children, 43*(1) 34–44.

Haugland, S., & Shade, D. (1988). Developmentally appropriate software for young children. *Young Children, 43*(4), 37–43.

Hoot, J. L. (1986). *Computers in early childhood education: Issues and practices.* Englewood Cliffs, NJ: Prentice-Hall.

Hoot, J. L., & Silvern, S. B. (Eds.). (1988). *Writing with computers in the early grades.* New York: Teachers College Press, Columbia University.

Hyson, M. C., & Eyman, A. P. (1986). Approaches to computer literacy in early childhood teacher education. *Young Children, 41* (6), 54–59.

Muhlstein, E. A. (1986). *Using the microcomputer to enhance language experiences and the development of cooperative play among preschool children.* Cupertino, CA: Child Development Center, DeAnza College.

Nathan, J. (1985). *Micro-myths: Exploring the limits of learning with computers.* Minneapolis, MN: Winston.

Papert, S. (1980). *Mindstorms: Children, computers, and powerful ideas.* New York: Basic.

Sloan, D. (Ed.). (1985). *The computer in education: A critical perspective.* New York: Columbia University Press.

Taylor, R. (Ed.). (1980). *The computer in the school: Tutor, tool, tutee.* New York: Columbia University Press.

Chapter 25

Sensory Motor: Large Motor, Sensory Motor Integration, Small Motor

The first several years of life are characterized by a multitude of new motor behaviors. The first year sees rapid growth in motor development. The next several years are devoted to "fine-tuning" these motor skills. Ultimately, children participate in intricate motor processes. Much of what we consider to be motor development occurs as a result of experience and practice.

Having adequate motor abilities is important for young children. They learn from the sensations acquired through movement. The acquisition of new sensations occurs through active participation with the environment rather than through passive interaction. Because children with disabilities, like others, spend increasing amounts of time watching television, and additionally, may be overprotected, they may need extra encouragement and support to develop motor skills. They need to participate in activities that expose their muscles to demanding tasks. We must resist the temptation to do too many things for children with disabilities and must allow them to participate in enough resistance and power activities to develop strength.

Large Motor

To help children develop appropriate large motor skills, you need time, space, and the proper equipment. Climbing requires a tree with low branches (or a ladder) and a jungle gym. Children are often more capable **463** in this area than we are willing to allow them to be. Outside, children can creep in concrete or ceramic culverts. Inside, they need free floor space and barrels for this purpose. Incorporate this as part of an obstacle course. Encourage children to jump and hop. They can broad jump, jump over ropes, or play hopscotch as they incorporate rules into their play. Have balls for children to kick and throw.

Children's motor skills need to be progressively challenged. As their sense of balance improves, children can progress from walking, to walking on a line taped on the floor, to walking on a balance beam. You might even consider time for "power" walking. Support running activities, in games and also as an activity for its own sake.

You must provide space and objects for children to push, pull, carry, and lift to help children develop strength in the trunk area. Children need safe places to slide and swing. Skipping and dancing are part of large motor planning. Turn on the music and encourage children to dance either alone or together. This is not ballet; this is moving! There are some records that encourage children to exercise. Use these regularly, especially when you cannot go outside.

Encourage children to participate in games that require physical activity. Evaluate these to see how many children are active what proportion of the time. For example, "Duck, duck, goose" is an active game, but only for the two children who are "it."

Children need these activities year-round, day in and day out. There is real concern about the physical fitness of young children and the increasing number of them who are obese, a condition to which lack of exercise contributes.

Sensory Motor Integration

Sensory motor integration is necessary to run an obstacle course, to pick up tiny objects, to draw pictures, to cut with scissors, and to perform many adaptive activities such as buttoning and snapping. Reading, writing, arts and craft activities, and many sports are dependent upon the development and refinement of sensory motor integration.

Bissell and others (1988) list nine separate components involved in sensory motor integration: auditory processing, body awareness, coordinating body sides, fine motor control, motor planning, ocular control, perception of movement, perception of touch, and visual-spatial perception.

Auditory processing involves the ability to understand what is heard. It is not a process relating to hearing per se, but rather the ability to sort, remember, and sequence auditory information.

Body awareness requires the interpretation of sensations that come from the muscles and joints of the body, enabling you to know what position your body is in without visually scanning yourself.

Coordinating body sides is necessary for the development of a dominant hand and also for the hands to work independently of each other on a given task. That is, for one hand to hold a piece of paper and the other to cut it with scissors.

Fine motor control in the hands is necessary before children can be expected to use "tools" such as crayons, markers, or pencils.

Motor planning is the cognitive conceptualization of how a skill is performed that occurs before movement. Children need motor planning skills to figure out how to climb a tree or how to build a tower. It is particularly important in learning new skills.

Ocular control is the ability of the eyes to smoothly track objects. It underlies all activities requiring eye-hand coordination and is a necessary prerequisite for reading.

The perception of movement requires the processing of vestibular information originating in the inner ear. Children who don't process enough information about movement may have trouble maintaining balance and need to spend conscious energy just to sit in a chair. Those who process too much movement information may become overstimulated. Vestibular information helps to regulate attention as well as posture and balance.

The perception of touch involves both a protective aspect and a discriminative touch. The protective tactile system is what makes us withdraw our hand quickly from a hot surface. Children can either overreact or underreact to touch. Children who are hyposensitive may not feel pain from bumps and bruises and may not be able to manipulate materials well. Children who are hypersensitive may avoid tactile input by not participating in messy activities such as art or sand and water play. Such children are sometimes labeled "tactile defensive."

Visual-spatial perception is more than seeing. It involves assessing the relative distance between one's body and a particular object as well as between objects. The child with deficits in visual spatial perception may bump into objects and have trouble adjusting his gait to go down or up a step. Letter and number recognition may be difficult, and reversals common, for this child. Going from a vertical to a horizontal plane, such as copying from the chalkboard or the computer monitor, may also be difficult. These children need to establish spatial concepts through physical experiences (e.g., up, down, left, right).

Children who experience many problems in sensory motor integration to the point that it interferes with behavior and learning in the classroom may need to be referred to an occupational therapist. A teacher's awareness of the importance of observing sensory motor integration in children is an important first step. Regularly including activities that facilitate sensory motor integration can facilitate learning in this area.

Small Motor

Fine motor development involves the child's ability to use the small muscles of the arms, hands, and fingers for reaching, grasping, and manipulating objects.

Muscle and joint stability is a prerequisite for fine motor control. It is difficult for children to perform fine motor tasks such as writing without the necessary trunk stability. Developmentally, children need to progress through early patterns of grasping (whole hand) to voluntarily releasing before "tools" are useful. Developing strength in the whole hand grasp is done through such activities as hanging from bars and tree limbs and playing tug of war. Fine grasp involves the independent use of the fingers and the ability to use the thumb and index finger together to pick up small objects. Experience with finger foods, large crayons, and large wooden beads facilitates the development of these skills. Again, the children need to develop motor planning to pick up these objects precisely and to release them when finished. Catching and throwing beanbags and underinflated beach balls help develop these skills.

Sensory Motor Goals

To Improve Large Motor Coordination

To carry out activities smoothly, children need to practice large motor skills regularly so coordination increases. Children must be challenged with increasingly more demanding and complex activities to refine these skills.

To Increase Body Awareness

Children need to control their body and move in ways they desire. They need to know where their body is in relation to objects. Children must learn to vary their posture, strength, and force to meet required tasks. They need to evaluate tasks and determine which tasks are easy and which are difficult for them. All antigravity postures require body awareness: walking, running, cycling, skating, and dancing. These are dynamic activities. Children also need practice in static activities such as holding a position or an object without losing balance.

To Increase Physical Fitness

Children need to develop an interest in physical fitness from an early age. Although we think of young children as always being on the move, they often do not participate in activities frequently enough or for a long enough sustained time span to develop physical fitness. Activities that develop flexibility, strength, and endurance are necessary.

To Improve Sensory Motor Integration

Sensory motor integration involves the organization of the senses and muscles of the body to perform both gross and fine activities. Children need many and varied experiences to develop and refine these processes. Skipping, galloping, and riding a tricycle all require coordination with large muscles. Cutting, putting in puzzle pieces, and drawing also require sensory motor integration.

To Improve Motor Planning

Motor planning is the ability to think about, organize, and execute a sequence of movements. It is the first step in acquiring new motor skills. Motor planning occurs as children are given variations of familiar activities. Varying the sequence of familiar actions, such as in an obstacle course, also requires motor planning.

To Improve Small Motor Coordination

Children need opportunities to develop and refine reaching and grasping skills both for the hand itself and as a prerequisite for using the hand to manipulate tools such as silverware, crayons, and pencils. They need opportunities to strengthen their hand and finger muscles to allow ease in using tools.

To Improve Eye-Hand Coordination

Good eye-hand coordination is needed as a foundation for so many activities that it has been singled out as a particular goal. It is a requirement in most adaptive skills as well as many motor tasks, from using a pencil to catching a ball.

To Improve Adaptive Skills

The development of independent functioning and self-sufficiency is important not only as a motor accomplishment, but for the self-concept as well. Focusing on motor activities that promote autonomy serves both functions.

Teaching Strategies

For children with *communication* disorders, be sure to supply words for what they are doing in the motor area. Focus fine motor activities on those movements associated with speech, such as breath control and lip and tongue action, in addition to those necessary for visual discrimination, writing, and self-help. Help children increase their body awareness, particularly to learn when they are tense. Many speech problems increase with tension. Children can learn to voluntarily relax.

Children with *hearing* impairments are very dependent upon their motor skills for information. At the same time, they are likely to be challenged in this area, as the sense of balance is located in the inner ear and may be part of their problem. Consequently, they may have had limited opportunities at integrating auditory input with motor skills. These children benefit from extra help with activities that focus on body awareness and balancing. Noncompetitive games that require starting, stopping, and turning are great. Fingerplays are particularly good, as the child can be part of a group while refining finger movements that may be necessary for signing.

Children with *visual* impairments, just as with hearing impairments, are dependent upon motor skills and also have more limited opportunities for practice. They need to learn where they are and to develop safe ways of moving through unknown spaces. This requires sensory motor integration. These children often lack the visual aspect of sensory integration and may have to learn ways of compensating for, as well as refining, their residual vision. The refinement of fine motor skills will aid braille reading (if needed). Body awareness and motor planning are an integral part of orientation and mobility training. Creative movement can make these skills more enjoyable without being threatening. Children with limited vision need encouragement and a safe place to practice these skills. Outdoor activities may be a challenge. With temperature changes, glasses sometimes fog up, so have tissues handy to wipe them off. For children with low vision, watch for safety concerns. Be sure that paths for moving vehicles are well delineated and that there is a low fence around swings, seesaws, and other moving equipment so that children cannot accidentally walk into them.

Children with *learning disabilities* can use large motor activities as a way of releasing energy as well as to increase body awareness. Often children with learning disabilities have related sensory motor integration problems. It is critical that they develop trunk stability as a prerequisite for fine motor skills. As these children may not be good at these activities they may avoid them. Skills such as snapping, tying, and buttoning are adaptive behaviors skills that also promote sensory motor integration.

Children's particular *physical* impairments will determine to some extent their ability to participate in motor play and the strategies that will be most effective. Children whose lower body is most affected need to strengthen the upper body to allow them to use a walker or move from a wheelchair to the floor. To adapt activities to individual differences, use lightweight objects that are easily manipulated or materials that tolerate some degree of error but still work, such as blocks with bristles, which can be placed half on and half off and still stay, instead of blocks which must be placed perfectly to stay. Help children control the environment by putting smaller objects in jellyroll pans or trays with edges. Allow children time to participate.

Children with *health* impairments must develop as much strength and endurance as they can. Respect their limits, but encourage them to participate in gross motor play. Young children will rarely overextend themselves, but individualize programming so children can set their own limits. Opportunities for sensory motor integration are essential. Small motor activities are easily adaptable for quiet play. Children can use them to pace their day. Since they have probably spent a lot of time with small motor activities, try to think of variations and new materials that will keep them interested. Be aware of the weather, especially when it is windy or very cold or hot. These extremes may cause children to tire quickly. When feasible, try to have some quiet activities outside also.

Children with *emotional/behavioral* disorders can use large motor activities as a way of venting energy and participating in a group experience. Noncompetitive, loose organization allows you to individualize activities without focusing attention on a particular child. Children with disorders often have difficulty refining small motor skills. It is important that they be encouraged to use and develop these skills without being pushed to the point of frustration.

Children with *mental retardation* may not be as proficient as other children because their large motor development may be slower. Be sure to plan activities that are not too demanding. They must devote more time than other children to small motor activities. They need simple activities and lots of practice. Use relatively large objects with few pieces; program for success. Try to include as many self-help skills as you can.

Children with *multiple* disabilities will require adaptations depending upon the area that is most involved. In general, follow the strategies given above and combine them to meet the child's needs.

Sensory Motor Activities

Goal	Activity
To improve large motor coordination	Variations on Jumping
	Variations on Creeping
	Variations on Running
	Ladder Walk
	Obstacle Course
	Variations on Balancing
	Variations on Bouncing
	Variations on Rope Jumping
	Variations on Walking
	Variations on Hopping
	Variations on Rolling
	Target Bounce
	Picture Relays
	Variations on Throwing
	Fitness Course
To increase physical fitness	Fitness Course
	Balloon Badminton
	Circle Ball
	Variations on Jumping
	Variations on Running
To improve sensory motor integration	Hand Clapping
	Balance It
	Mirroring
	Variations on Tossing
	Barefoot
	Be the Body
	Foam
	Freeze
	Tense Me
	Feely Bag
	Draw It On
	Follow That Light
	Pick-a-Pair
	Variations on Jumping
	Variations on Creeping
	Ladder Walk
	Obstacle Course
	Variations on Balancing
	Variations on Bouncing

Goal	Activity
	Variations on Rope Jumping
	Variations on Walking
	Variations on Hopping
	Variations on Rolling
	Buttons
To improve motor planning	Variations on Creeping
	Variations on Running
	Ladder Walk
	Obstacle Course
	Variations on Balancing
	Variations on Bouncing
	Variations on Rope Jumping
	Variations on Walking
	Target Bounce
	Picture Relays
	Balloon Badminton
	Circle Ball
	Hand Clapping
	Mirroring
	Variations on Tossing
	Balance It
	Progressive Dress-up
To increase body awareness	Variations on Hopping
	Variations on Rolling
	Balance It
	Mirroring
	Barefoot
	Be the Body
	Tense Me
	Foam
	Freeze
	My Puzzle
	Be the Body
To improve small motor coordination	Buttons
	Progressive Dress-up
	Nuts and Bolts
	Picking Cherries
	Tools
	Lock Box
	Gameboard
	Feely Bag
	Draw It On
To improve eye-hand coordination	My Puzzle
	Caterpillars
	Pouring Rice
	Playdough Beads
	Target Bounce
	Variations on Throwing
	Balloon Badminton
	Lock Box
	Nuts and Bolts
	Variations on Tossing
	Follow That Light
	Tools
	Picking Cherries
	Gameboard
	Circle Ball

Goal	Activity
To improve adaptive skills	Lock Box Caterpillars Pouring Rice Tools Picking Cherries Progressive Dress-up
To follow directions	Tense Me
To improve sequencing skills	Caterpillars Playdough Beads
To improve number concepts	Playdough Beads
To improve size concepts	Nuts and Bolts
To improve classification skills	Pick-a-Pair
To improve generalization skills	Pouring Rice
To increase inclusion	Picture Relays Gameboard
To improve self-concept	My Puzzle

Large Motor

VARIATIONS ON JUMPING

GOAL   To improve large motor coordination
To improve physical fitness
To improve sensory motor integration

OBJECTIVE   The child will participate in various jumping activities.

MATERIALS   None

PROCEDURE   Have the children participate in the various styles of jumping.

Pairs jumping. One child faces another and they hold hands; they jump together to the count of ten.

Line jumping. Children jump forward and backward over an imaginary line a specified number of times.

Stair jumping. Children jump from a step to a line on the floor.

Long jump. Children jump forward for a distance from standing position.

Snake jump. Children crouch in squat position and jump up as far as possible.

Kangaroo jump. With feet together, elbows bent, and hands away from body children do knee bends and jump.

Rabbit jump. Children squat low on heels, palms down and fingers pointing forward, and simulate a rabbit jumping with feet coming forward between hands.

Mattress jump. Use partially filled air mattress; children jump forward and backward without falling. For additional safety, put mattress on a 5′ × 8′ rug with adult spotters.

Jumping jacks. Children do these exercises as in physical education classes.

COMMENT   A good energy release on a rainy day.

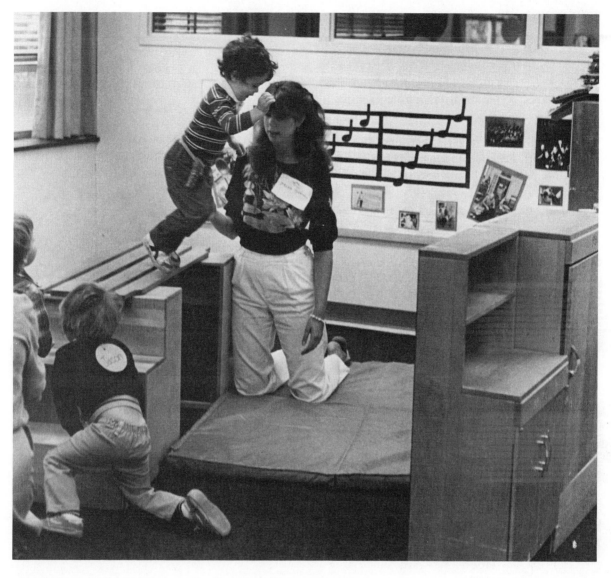

Children master a skill by practicing the skill and its variations.

Large Motor

VARIATIONS ON CREEPING

GOAL To improve large motor coordination
To improve sensory motor integration
To improve motor planning

OBJECTIVE The child will participate in the various creeping activities.

MATERIALS record or cassette player
record or cassette
materials for an obstacle course:

yarn	boxes	barrels
boards	chairs	hula hoops

PROCEDURE   Have the children participate in various types of creeping and crawling activities.

Turtle crawl. On hands and knees with a beanbag chair on top of the child (the chair looks like a shell over the child).

Texture crawl. Blindfold children. Have them crawl on a path of different textures (carpet squares, welcome mats, bubble packing, and so on).

Snake crawl. Slither with stomach on floor using only arms to pull.

Obstacle course. Creep through a course made of boxes or chairs, barrels, boards, and so on.

Yarn trail. Creep following yarn trails and have someone keep time for each child. Write the time down and have the child decide to do it faster or slower the second time.

Seesaw. Crawl up one side of a seesaw board, maintain balance as board tips down, and then crawl down the board to the ground (be sure to have an adult as a spotter).

Balance board. Crawl forward and backward on a board propped between two blocks.

COMMENT   Creeping is a basic skill, and the variations can be geared to the abilities of the individual children involved. When creeping outside, clear the area of harmful objects. Encourage the children to think about the different crawling and creeping experiences and what each feels like. Discuss with children when these might be a useful way to move. Have children participate in thinking up variations. Note: In crawling the stomach touches the ground; in creeping it is off the ground.

Large Motor

VARIATIONS ON RUNNING

GOAL   To improve large motor coordination
To improve physical fitness
To improve motor planning

OBJECTIVE   The child will run in a variety of ways.

MATERIALS   Materials to make a path

tape   yarn

rope   cones

string

PROCEDURE   Have the children run and try some of the following variations.

Run slowly without touching anybody.

Run quickly without touching anybody.

Run without touching anybody and stop on the signal.

Run and change direction on the signal.

Run as quietly as possible.

Run as noisily as possible.

Run as lightly as possible.

Run as heavily as possible.

Run, walk, run; see how long the children can alternate between the two.

Run slowly and talk to a friend.

Run a designated path.

Increase Level of Difficulty

Procedure   Increase the length of time and the distance children run. Increase the number of variations.

Decrease Level of Difficulty

Procedure   Decrease the length of time and distance children run and make fewer variations.

COMMENT   These variations help children refine skills as well as build endurance. Be sure to give children time to warm up and cool down. For children with *visual* impairments run slowly with the child holding your hand or that of another child. As confidence and skill is built gradually increase speed. This activity may be inappropriate for some children with *physical* impairments, but they can use their wheelchairs or a scooter with the signaled variations.

Large Motor

LADDER WALK

GOAL   To improve large motor coordination
To improve sensory motor integration
To improve motor planning

OBJECTIVE   The child will walk the length of the ladder as directed.

MATERIALS   Wooden ladder

PROCEDURE   Lay the ladder flat on the ground and have the children step into each square between the rungs. Have children walk from end to end with one foot on each side, first forward, then backward. (As children get older the ladder may flip, so test it first and have another child stand on one end if this is a problem.) Walk on the rungs of the ladder. (Walk on the balls of the feet; it hurts if you walk on the arches.) Put feet on the rungs and hands on the sides and cross the ladder (knees must be bent to do this).

Increase Level of Difficulty

Procedure   Have children play wheelbarrow using the spaces, sides, and rungs. Raise the ladder about six inches off the ground and use the variations given above. Repeat the procedure but make the ladder into an inclined plane by raising only one end. Be sure to have a spotter when you raise the ladder.

Decrease Level of Difficulty

Procedure   Hold the child's hand and serve as a spotter even when the ladder is on the ground.

COMMENT   Although seemingly simple, it requires a lot of concentration to complete these activities. They may be inappropriate for some children with *physical* impairments.

Large Motor

OBSTACLE COURSE

GOAL   To improve large motor coordination
To improve sensory motor integration
To improve motor planning

OBJECTIVE   The child will complete the obstacle course.

MATERIALS   barrels   boxes   boards
chairs   hoops   balance beam

PROCEDURE   Set up an obstacle course either inside or outside. The course may be simple or complex, depending upon the age and past experience of the children, but should require a variety of physical skills and should be long enough so that several children can participate at the same time. Use obstacles that require children to move over, under, around, and through them. Allow children to explore the course. When they are comfortable, make suggestions for specific actions.

Increase Level of Difficulty

Procedure   Have children go through the course blindfolded. Give them more complex activities to do such as picking up a beanbag or walking through a hoop while on the balance beam. Add music to determine the pace of movement.

Decrease Level of Difficulty

Procedure   Keep the course simple and relatively short or allow the children to stop in the middle. Use arrows if the course has options, and add line drawings of the necessary postures to get through the obstacle.

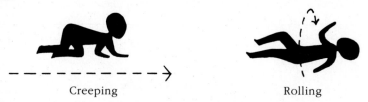

Creeping   Rolling

COMMENT   Use auditory cues for children with *visual* impairments to help them locate themselves on the course. Use a rope as a guide through the course and have sighted children do it blindfolded. Give children a play-by-play description of what they are doing so they begin to associate the activity with words. For children with *physical* impairments, adapt the course requirements or make the course in two sections, one of which all children can accomplish. Encourage children to time their trip through the course and see if they can complete it in a specified amount of time (it's not a race, it's a prediction).

Large Motor

VARIATIONS ON BALANCING

GOAL   To improve large motor coordination
To improve sensory motor integration
To improve motor planning

OBJECTIVE   The child will walk the length of the balance beam without help and following the directions given.

MATERIALS   Balance beam, 4″ wide

PROCEDURE   Have children walk across the beam in the following ways.

Walk forward, backward, sideways.

Walk forward turning at each end.

Walk holding an object (short pole) in hands.

Walk touching heel against toe.

Walk forward and backward without looking at feet.

Walk to the middle and touch the board with hand, then knee.

Walk to the middle and pick up a small object.

Walk to the middle and catch a ball.

Walk over a small object on the balance beam.

Increase Level of Difficulty

Materials   Use a balance beam 2″ wide and/or move the 4″ beam higher off the floor so that you can add one-foot dips.

After the children become proficient, curve the lines:

or:

Decrease Level of Difficulty

Materials   Use lines taped on the floor, then use lumber that is 6″ × 6″ × 8′ for walking board.

COMMENT   Dynamic balance is an important skill for children. Children with *visual* impairments will need some initial orientation. Some children with *physical* impairments won't be able to participate. However, they could use this as practice for following directions and perform the tasks in wheelchairs or on scooters.

Large Motor

VARIATIONS ON BOUNCING

GOAL   To improve large motor coordination
To improve sensory motor integration
To improve motor planning

OBJECTIVE   The child will bounce the ball in a variety of ways.

MATERIALS   8″ or 10″ balls

PROCEDURE   Have the children bounce the ball with one hand. Then encourage them to try these variations.

Bounce the ball low.

Bounce the ball higher.

Bounce the ball as high as their waist.

Bounce the ball with their right hand.

Bounce the ball with their left hand.

Bounce the ball alternating hands.

Bounce the ball fast.

Bounce the ball slow.

Increase Level of Difficulty

Materials   Use a smaller ball.

Procedure   Have children perform stunts between bounces such as clapping or turning around.

Decrease Level of Difficulty

Materials   Use a larger ball.

Procedure   Have children use two hands to bounce the ball.

COMMENT   This activity is designed to develop control and coordination, not speed and strength. It can be self-paced, and the variations can be developed on an individual basis to meet the child's needs. This is a good outdoor activity.

Large Motor

VARIATIONS ON ROPE JUMPING

GOAL   To improve large motor coordination
To improve sensory motor integration
To improve motor planning

OBJECTIVE   The child will participate in the various jumping activities using rope.

MATERIALS   Jump rope 12–15 feet long for 2–4 children

PROCEDURE   Have the children participate in the various styles of jumping using a rope.

Rope line. Children jump from side to side over length of rope, forward then backward.

High water. Two children hold a rope between them (loosely in hands). The third child attempts to jump over the rope forward, backward, sideways, and at progressive heights.

Snake. Two children hold a rope between them (loosely in hands) and move it back and forth on the floor like a snake. The third child attempts to jump over the rope. (Moved vertically it is like waves.)

Swing jump. Two children hold a rope between them and swing it back and forth. The third child jumps over the rope. When a child can do this successfully, turn the rope overhead.

Circle. Teacher or child is in the middle of a circle and turns with the rope so that each child must jump as it passes.

Run. Two children turn the rope between them and a child tries to run through without the rope's touching him.

Individual jump rope. A child turns the rope overhead and jumps with both feet, alternating feet.

COMMENT   These activities get progressively more difficult. Observe the children for their motor planning ability. Can they time jumps to the movement of the rope? Can they turn the rope smoothly? Encourage children to sing or say traditional rhymes as they jump.

Large Motor

VARIATIONS ON WALKING

GOAL   To improve large motor coordination
To improve sensory motor integration
To improve motor planning

OBJECTIVE   The child will participate in various walking activities.

MATERIALS   None

PROCEDURE   Have children participate in various types of walks.

Barefoot walk. Children walk on mud, sand, smooth rocks, and concrete surfaces and finally through a tray of water and describe the sensations involved.

Walking a line. Children walk a line forward and then backward keeping each foot on the line. Have children walk pigeon-toed, turning feet out as far as possible and crossing the front foot over the line each time.

Walking sideways. Children walk to the right one step at a time, crossing their left foot over their right foot. Reverse the step when moving to the left. If the children are in a circle or two circles the activity requires less space and can be done in the classroom. As a long line it can be more like follow the leader.

Ostrich. Children bend forward at waist, grasp ankles, and walk forward while keeping knees stiff and stretching neck in and out.

Duck. Children do a deep bend and place hands behind their back; they walk forward one foot at a time, but remain in bent-knee position.

Time walk. Have children walk a prescribed path and time them. Have them predict how long it will take them the next time and see how accurate their estimates are.

Discuss what ideas the children have for variations and how each walk feels to them; that is, could they do the walk for a long or short time and was it hard to keep their balance?

COMMENT   These are good rainy day activities and fun ways of moving from a large group experience to smaller groups.

VARIATIONS ON HOPPING

GOAL To improve large motor coordination
To improve sensory motor integration
To increase body awareness

OBJECTIVE The child will participate in the various hopping activities.

MATERIALS Hopping stones made of tiles or carpet squares

PROCEDURE Have the children participate in various types of hopping activities.

Hop on their left foot.

Hop on their right foot.

Hop as quietly as they can.

Hop as loudly as they can.

Hop as high as they can.

Hop as low as they can.

Hop as far as they can on each foot.

Hop in one direction as far as they can on one foot, and see if they can hop back on their other foot.

Hop and change feet.

Hop with a partner.

Hop as long as they can (time it, record it, and compare it to the next time).

Play a hopping game by having patterns of tiles set out and having the children hop on the tiles in an obstacle course fashion according to your directions. Play hopscotch.

COMMENT For two- or three-year-olds, hopping itself may be a challenge; for four- and five-year-olds, the more complex variations are fun.

VARIATIONS ON ROLLING

GOAL To improve large motor coordination
To improve sensory motor integration
To increase body awareness

OBJECTIVE The child will participate in the various rolling activities.

MATERIALS record or cassette player record or cassette
beach towel   pillow   ball

PROCEDURE Have the children participate in various types of rolling activities.

Log roll. Hands extended over the head, feet together.

Ball roll. Hands extended over the head, feet clasping ball.

Torpedo roll. Hands at sides of body.

Windmill roll. One hand above head, one at side.

Towel roll. Start at one end of a beach towel and roll up into it, then reverse and roll out.

Circle roll. Roll in circles while someone holds their ankles.

Downhill roll. Roll down a hill or incline.

Encourage practice in large motor skills.

Encourage the children to think about the different rolling experiences and how each feels. Discuss with children when rolling might be a useful way to move. Have children participate in thinking up variations.

COMMENT   Rolling is a good energy release as well as a strengthener for necessary large muscles. These rolls are good for rainy days or as outdoor activities on the grass. Be sure to clear the area of rocks or other potentially harmful objects.

Large Motor

TARGET BOUNCE

GOAL   To improve large motor coordination
   To improve motor planning
   To improve eye-hand coordination

OBJECTIVE   The child will bounce the ball on the target.

MATERIALS   tape   8″ or 10″ ball

PROCEDURE   Tape a target on the floor, large at first (3′ square). Have the children see how often they can hit the target and have their partner catch the ball. Have the children stand about three feet on either side of the target and bounce the ball to each other, hitting the target with the ball.

Increase Level of Difficulty

Materials   Use a smaller ball and/or a smaller target.

Procedure   Have children try to establish a rhythm to the bouncing by singing a song. Have children sit in chairs and play. After so many successful bounces have them move the chair back six inches.

Decrease Level of Difficulty

Materials   Use a larger ball (a beach ball for example, a little underinflated) and a larger target.

COMMENT   Have children see how often they can catch the ball and/or hit the target. This is good for the development of upper body strength. For children with *physical* impairments, if necessary, modify the size and weight of the ball. For children with *visual* impairments, use either a large ball or one that has a bell inside.

Large Motor

PICTURE RELAYS

GOAL   To improve large motor coordination
To improve motor planning
To increase social integration

OBJECTIVE   The child will participate in a team relay.

MATERIALS   8″ or 10″ ball   beanbag   balloon

cards showing different ways of moving the object

Using both hands pass ball over head of child *a*, between legs of child *b*, over head of child *c*, and so on.

Turn halfway around and pass.

Roll ball through legs.

Ball passes over head.

PROCEDURE   Show the children the drawings you have made and ask the children to demonstrate the movements. Divide the children into teams. Give each team a card and something to pass. Have the children perform the actions with the last person in line coming to the front when she gets the object. Then have the teams change cards and objects. As they are doing different activities with different objects they can feel team spirit but no one can win.

COMMENT   You can pick other objects and movements depending upon the age and skill of the children.

Large Motor

VARIATIONS ON THROWING

GOAL   To improve large motor coordination
To improve eye-hand coordination

OBJECTIVE   The child will participate in various throwing experiences.

MATERIALS   8″ or 10″ ball   15″–24″ wastebasket

tennis ball   hula hoops

cans

PROCEDURE   Have the children participate in various types of ball-throwing activities. Discuss the differences in skills required to throw large and small balls. Have the children try the following variations.

Throw the ball as high as they can.

Throw the ball as low as they can without hitting the ground.

Throw the ball as far as they can.

Throw the ball softly to another child.

Throw the ball in a high arc to another child.

Throw the ball into a round wastebasket from 2′ to 5′ away.

Throw the ball through the hula hoops from varying distances.

Increase Level of Difficulty

Procedure   Have children measure the distances they throw and make a graph, or count the number of times they can throw and catch a ball with another child. Using cans as a target, have children stand increasing distances away and try to knock the cans over.

Decrease Level of Difficulty

Materials   Use an underinflated beach ball.

Procedure   It is far easier to catch. It requires two hands to throw.

COMMENT   These activities are most easily done outside. Encourage children to play throwing games with others. For children with *visual* impairments use a ball with bells inside or a large ball.

Large Motor

FITNESS COURSE

GOAL   To improve physical fitness
To improve large motor coordination

OBJECTIVE   The child will perform the correct number of exercises at each station.

MATERIALS   Cards with a picture of the exercise to be done and the number of repetitions

5 bent knee sit-ups	10 knee lifts
4 toe touches	count to 15 running in place
3 push-ups	10 double leg jumps

PROCEDURE   Place cards around the room and have children go to each area and perform the activity. Vary the activities, the number of repetitions, and the task to meet the needs of the children you teach.

Increase Level of Difficulty

Procedure   Increase the number of activities, the number of repetitions, or choose more difficult activities. Have children keep a record so they can see how they improve over time.

Decrease Level of Difficulty

Procedure   Decrease the number of activities, the number of repetitions, or choose easier activities.

COMMENT   Children with *visual* impairments may need some coaching to do the activities, and some of the activities may be inappropriate for children with *physical* impairments. They will have to be modified depending upon the needs of the child.

Large Motor

BALLOON BADMINTON

GOAL   To increase physical fitness
To improve motor planning
To improve eye-hand coordination

OBJECTIVE   The child will hit the balloon with the racket.

MATERIALS   balloons   badminton rackets

string or net

PROCEDURE   Have children hit balloons (underinflated ones break less easily) with another child. As they become more proficient, add a net or string. Help them make predictions about how far or how often they can hit the ball. Explore the causal relationships between how hard they swing, the angle of the racket, and where the balloon goes. Help them swing overhand for high shots and underhand for low ones. Have children count the number of times they can hit the balloon back and forth.

Increase Level of Difficulty

Materials   Badminton bird

Procedure   Have children play using the bird instead of the balloon.

Decrease Level of Difficulty

Procedure   If children have difficulty with the racket have them hit the balloon with their hands. Then, hit it alone with the racket. Finally, hit it to a partner.

COMMENT   Balloon badminton can be played indoors or outside. It requires skill but not strength. Children can play sitting as well as standing.

Large Motor

CIRCLE BALL

GOAL   To increase physical fitness

To improve motor planning

To improve eye-hand coordination

OBJECTIVE   The child will hit the ball with her hands or feet.

MATERIALS   8″ to 12″ ball

PROCEDURE   Have the children in a circle on their stomachs facing the inside of the circle. The ball is in the center of the circle, and the children roll it to each other using two hands. As they tire have them hit the ball with only one hand, or kneel. The objective is accuracy not force.

Increase Level of Difficulty

Procedure   Play the game in pairs so there is less time to relax.

Decrease Level of Difficulty

Procedure   Children can sit on their bottoms and use both feet to hit the ball.

COMMENT   This activity strengthens the muscles of the upper back.

Sensory Motor Integration

HAND CLAPPING

GOAL   To improve sensory motor integration

To improve motor planning

OBJECTIVE   The child will duplicate the clapping patterns.

MATERIALS   record or cassette player   record or cassette

PROCEDURE   Have children clap in rhythm to a recording or a song you sing. When children can predictably do this, progress to a two-step sequence: clap hands, clap thighs, clap hands, clap thighs. (You can choose other body parts such as head, feet, shoulders.) Now make the pattern itself more difficult: clap hands twice, clap thighs twice, repeat. Or do it three or four times. Another variation is to have the children clap hands and then clap their left thigh with their right hand, clap hands, clap their right thigh with their left hand. (The object is to cross the midline of the body, not to be concerned about right and left.)

Increase Level of Difficulty

Procedure   Try clapping with a partner, repeating the patterns given for individual clapping. They are arranged in increasing levels of difficulty. That is, start clapping your own hands, slap partner's hand, clap your own hands, and so on. The most difficult pattern is clapping the partner's right hand with your left hand and vice versa.

Decrease Level of Difficulty

PROCEDURE   The clapping is given in order of difficulty. Simply plan to spend more time at the lower levels with some children.

COMMENT   Many traditional children's songs and games are enhanced by higher levels of clapping.

Sensory Motor Integration

BALANCE IT

GOAL   To improve sensory motor integration
To improve motor planning
To increase body awareness

OBJECTIVE   The child will balance the beanbag on the body part requested.

MATERIALS   Beanbags

PROCEDURE   Have children balance a beanbag on their heads. Encourage them to stand up and sit down, walk fast and slowly while balancing it. Then have them balance the beanbags using other body parts: shoulders, elbow, knee, foot. Have them get down on the floor, feet in the air, and balance it on the bottom of one foot and then catch it with their hands.

Increase Level of Difficulty

Materials

| books | paper plates | paint brushes |
| feathers | crayons | plastic glasses |

Procedure   Encourage children to experiment with balancing a variety of objects and have them predict how long they can balance each object, or whether or not they can sit down and stand up twice without its falling off. Have them choose additional objects to balance.

Decrease Level of Difficulty

Procedure   Give children feedback about their posture and hints about how to move to make balancing easier.

COMMENT   These activities require both static and dynamic balance and concentration.

Sensory Motor Integration

MIRRORING

GOAL   To improve sensory motor integration
To improve motor planning
To increase body awareness

OBJECTIVE   The child will mirror the movement.

MATERIALS   None

PROCEDURE   Have the children work in pairs facing each other. Tell them to pretend they are looking in a mirror. One child initiates a movement, and the other child mirrors it. This can be done to music, and the movements can get increasingly more complex.

Increase Level of Difficulty

Procedure   Make the movements faster and more subtle. Have a third child give feedback on the accuracy of the mirroring.

Decrease Level of Difficulty

Procedure   Choose carefully the children you match. Have the child start as the initiator of the movement; this is easier. Encourage the children to use slow, simple movements.

COMMENT   Mirroring requires the child to look at another child, not his own body to figure out what to do. For children with *visual* impairments, tie a 12″ string between the children's wrists and have them move gently to respond to the pressure on the string or to touch hands gently and move together.

Sensory Motor Integration

VARIATIONS ON TOSSING

GOAL   To improve sensory motor integration
To improve motor planning
To improve eye-hand coordination

OBJECTIVE   The child will participate in various tossing games.

MATERIALS

beanbag	tennis ball	ping-pong ball
sponges	small rubber ball	rubber rings
horseshoes	whiffle ball	crumpled paper
Velcro-covered ping-pong ball	cups	
targets	milk cartons	

PROCEDURE   Have the children participate in the various types of tossing activities listed below. Discuss how the activity feels, where they can safely throw objects and where they shouldn't, and which objects are harder to throw and which are easier. Allow them to add their own variations.

Texture ball toss. Use a sponge or texture ball (whiffle ball). The children begin with underhand tossing to a person close by. Gradually extend the distance and graduate to overhand throwing.

Basketball toss. Use a shoe box with the bottom removed. Tape it to the wall for an indoor game. Toss a tennis ball.

Dodge ball. Divide the class into teams and play dodge ball outside.

Ring toss. A variation of horseshoes with rubber rings, this game requires a different set of tossing skills.

Beanbag toss. Toss bags through large holes in a target or into empty coffee cans.

Paper toss. Crumple paper into balls and toss them into a wastebasket.

Tennis ball toss. This game becomes more difficult as the ball bounces; help children to cup hands together to catch the ball if it is low.

Milk carton toss. Use plastic milk bottles or cartons stacked in pyramids. Knock the structure down with a tennis ball.

Bucket toss. Use a bucket or wastebasket for catching balls. First set the bucket on the floor, then raise it on a chair or box.

Empty box throw. Place a bottomless cardboard box on its side on the ground or on a chair. The object is to toss a ball through the box without hitting the sides.

Tennis toss-back. Throw a tennis ball against a brick or cement wall and catch it before it bounces (an outside activity on a wall without windows).

Target toss. Use the Velcro-covered ping-pong ball and toss it at a target (with Velcro pieces attached). Vary the distance from the target and the size of the target.

Sponge toss. Make a cardboard target with holes of various sizes, or see if they can throw the sponges through suspended hula hoops. On a hot day you might throw wet sponges.

Ping-pong ball toss. Have children stand arms-width apart, toss a ping-pong ball, and catch it in a plastic or paper cup.

COMMENT   The variations strengthen the sensory motor component. The need to make adjustments and compensate makes the learning experience more than just a motor refinement. These activities are good both indoors and outdoors. Be sure to assign retrievers who take turns with the children tossing, and be aware of safety needs all the time.

Sensory Motor Integration

BAREFOOT

GOAL   To improve sensory motor integration
To increase body awareness

OBJECTIVE   The child will talk about how the various textures feel on his feet.

MATERIALS   Blindfold (a half-face Halloween mask with eye holes covered works well)

PROCEDURE   When it is warm enough, allow children to go outside barefoot. Ask them to describe the feel of sand, grass, mud, gravel, cement, wood, and so on. As the children walk in different areas, talk about how the feelings change underfoot: cold/hot, soft/hard, wet/dry, round/pointed, and so on. As children say things like "It hurts," try to help them figure out what properties of a substance make it hurt (i.e., sharp, hard, or hot). Bring samples of what was walked on into your class and have a discussion about the experience. Have the children feel the same substances with their hands and talk about the difference. Be sure to check the area in advance for broken glass or other objects which might injure the children's feet.

Increase Level of Difficulty

Procedure   Help children think about the design of footwear for specific movements on different textures. Bring in baseball shoes with cleats, golf shoes, running shoes, walking shoes, tennis shoes, hiking boots, swim fins, snow shoes, rubber boots, and slippers and have children decide why they were designed to be used on a particular surface.

Decrease Level of Difficulty

Procedure   Set up a structured area indoors or out with specific textures on a particular path. Let the children first both walk and look, then have them do it blindfolded.

COMMENT   Be sure to include the specific vocabulary that goes with the tactile experience. For children who may not be able to walk the path, encourage them to crawl and feel or use their hands to experience the textures.

Sensory Motor Integration

BE THE BODY

GOAL   To improve sensory motor integration
To increase body awareness

OBJECTIVE   The child will assume the same position as the cardboard body.

MATERIALS   cardboard (enough to cut out a child-size body)

scissors   brads

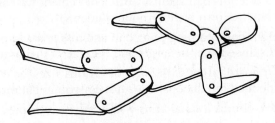

PROCEDURE   Cut the parts of a body out of cardboard and fasten them together at the joints with brads. Name the parts of the body. First, have a child lie on the body and assume its positions. Then stand the cardboard body up and have one child move the parts and another child either mirror the movements or copy them. Discuss the differences.

Increase Level of Difficulty

Procedure   Add additional body parts such as hands with fingers and feet with toes. Talk with children about the range of motion of joints. See how far their elbow joints will allow the forearm to move. Demonstrate the difference with the cardboard body. Show how the knee works as well. Talk about, and have children pretend their joints are "tight" and see what things are more difficult.

Decrease Level of Difficulty

Procedure   Name the parts of the body. For example, have the child point to both his arm and those on the cardboard body. Move one part at a time and have the child imitate.

COMMENT   Children rarely think about how their body works. This is a good way to make them more aware of it and to understand some of the problems children whose bodies work differently might have.

Sensory Motor Integration

FOAM

GOAL   To improve sensory motor integration
To increase body awareness

OBJECTIVE   The child will perform the designated activities.

MATERIALS   A piece of 4″ or 5″ foam or mattress

PROCEDURE   Put the foam on the floor, preferably in the center of a piece of carpet. Have the children walk, roll, jump, and so forth on the foam. Encourage them to experiment by doing these activities on the floor and then on the foam. Discuss the differences. Be sure to have spotters.

Increase Level of Difficulty

Procedure   Encourage children to perform more difficult tasks involving both dynamic and static balance. When they are successful, see if they can articulate how they compensated with their body.

Decrease Level of Difficulty

Procedure   Perform only simple tasks such as walking and initially hold the child's hand.

COMMENT   This is a very good rainy or snowy day activity.

Sensory Motor Integration

FREEZE

GOAL   To improve sensory motor integration
To increase body awareness

OBJECTIVE   The child will stop and maintain his position until he is unfrozen.

MATERIALS   Drum, gong, or record/cassette and record or cassete player

PROCEDURE   Have the children move around the room (walking, skipping, hopping, jumping, spinning). Play some music or beat a drum or gong, then stop suddenly. At the silence, the children should freeze in their position. As you unfreeze the children (by touching them), talk about the positions they are in. As a variation, have all the children melt to the ground before the music is started again.

Increase Level of Difficulty

Procedure   "Unfreeze" these children last. Encourage them to move in more difficult ways that will be harder to hold.

Decrease Level of Difficulty

Procedure You might initially call out "freeze" until they get the idea. Touch children who are having trouble balancing first.

COMMENT This is good practice in static balance. Use a visual signal such as flicking the lights or waving your hands for children with *hearing* impairments. Freeze can be played inside or outside.

Sensory Motor Integration

TENSE ME

GOAL To improve sensory motor integration
To increase body awareness
To follow directions

OBJECTIVE The child will tense and relax the designated body parts.

MATERIALS None

PROCEDURE Have all the children lie or sit on the floor. Sitting is easier at the beginning because both you and they can see better. Have the children make a tight fist or muscle in one arm and feel that arm with the other hand. Tell them that feeling is *tense*. Ask if they can squeeze harder and make it more tense. Have them hold it to a count of five. Then tell them to see how loose (relaxed) they can make that arm. Again have them feel it with their other hand. Discuss the difference in feeling. Encourage them to make the arm even floppier. Repeat with the other arm. On another day, do different body parts such as legs and face. Words like "tight," "loose," or "floppy" seem to work better than the words "tense" and "relax." Use your voice as a teaching tool to mirror both the tension and relaxation.

Increase Level of Difficulty

Procedure Move to other body parts, particularly the face and legs. See if the children can learn to isolate parts of their body and tense just the part requested. Can they tense their right fist and keep the left fist relaxed? This activity requires isolating the sides of the body.

Decrease Level of Difficulty

Procedure Have children tense and relax both arms and then both legs. You may need to touch the tensed part to see if the child understands the request.

COMMENT Before children can voluntarily relax, they need to learn the feeling of what relaxation is. Otherwise, they won't know what they are striving for.

Sensory Motor Integration

FEELY BAG

GOAL To improve sensory motor integration
To improve small motor coordination

OBJECTIVE The child will identify an object by feeling it.

MATERIALS several small bags

objects that can be identified by feel:

cups or glasses	cars and trucks
blocks	doll furniture
balls	dishes

PROCEDURE Make several large drawstring bags out of soft pliable fabric such as cotton knit or old sheets. Be sure the fabric is thick enough so that children can't see through it. Place an object in the bag and have the children feel through the bag to figure out what the object is. Use only one object per bag.

Increase Level of Difficulty

Materials   Use objects that have less distinct features.

Procedure   Choose objects that have to be felt systematically to be identified.

Decrease Level of Difficulty

Materials   A duplicate set of objects

Procedure   By having a set of objects available for the child to see you have narrowed the possible choices and made the task much easier.

COMMENT   Almost anything in your room that will fit in the bag and has obvious tactile features will do. For variation you can have children put their hand in the bag to feel what is there. This allows you to add items like a snake skin, feather, and others that are not easily felt from the outside. Watch out for sharp pointed objects.

Sensory Motor Integration

DRAW IT ON

GOAL   To improve sensory motor integration
         To improve small motor coordination

OBJECTIVE   The child will identify and draw the message.

MATERIALS   paper and markers

         cards with simple shapes, numbers, or letters

PROCEDURE   Have children sit one behind the other (four is a good number). Give the last child in line a card. This child draws the design on the card on the back of the child in front of him with his finger. This child repeats the process. The child in front draws the design on the paper with a marker. The children then compare the design drawn with the one on the card.

Increase Level of Difficulty

Procedure   Use more difficult designs or have a series of designs such as printing a simple word ("up") with the child guessing the word at the end. This can be done in pairs.

Decrease Level of Difficulty

Procedure   Tap numbers or use even simpler designs with only two children.

COMMENT   Draw It On is an interesting quiet activity that requires unusual concentration.

Sensory Motor Integration

FOLLOW THAT LIGHT

GOAL   To improve sensory motor integration
         To improve eye-hand coordination

OBJECTIVE   The child will make a light follow another light.

MATERIALS   Two flashlights

PROCEDURE   Make the room as dark as possible. Turn on two flashlights. Give one each to two children. Have one child make simple designs with the light on the wall, floor, or ceiling, and have the other child repeat the design.

Increase Level of Difficulty

Procedure   As the skills improve make the designs more complex and move the flashlight faster.

Decrease Level of Difficulty

Procedure   Keep one flashlight and move it slowly in a simple pattern for the child to follow.

COMMENT   This is a good activity for a dreary, rainy day. It can easily be done at home and is an interesting novelty for children who must remain in bed.

PICK-A-PAIR

GOAL   To improve sensory motor integration
   To improve classification skills

OBJECTIVE   The child will match the textures.

MATERIALS   Materials made of different textures:

cardboard	flannel	felt
sandpaper	sponge	nylon
corduroy	dotted swiss	wool
silk	ultrasuede	fake fur

PROCEDURE   Cut each piece of fabric in two pieces. Place one piece on a tray and the other in a feely bag or box. Ask the child to match the pieces.

Increase Level of Difficulty

Materials   Small pieces of sandpaper of different grades from coarse to fine

Procedure   Ask the children to put the sandpaper in order by grade and to match the pieces. Start with rather obvious distinction and work to more subtle gradations.

Decrease Level of Difficulty

Materials   Make the differences between materials obvious (e.g., use cardboard, fake fur, and nylon).

Procedure   Have fewer materials to choose among.

COMMENT   Have the children classify the textures in some way—woven/not woven, soft/hard, rough/smooth, and so on. Have them explain how they know they have a match.

BUTTONS

GOAL   To improve small motor coordination
   To improve sensory motor integration

OBJECTIVE   The child will pair the buttons.

MATERIALS   12 pairs of buttons (tactile differences)   a bowl or bag
   an egg carton or ice cube tray   a blindfold

PROCEDURE   Collect pairs of buttons that feel different from each other. Put one button of each pair in an egg carton or ice cube tray section and put the other in a bowl or bag. Have the children match up the pairs while blindfolded. (If children don't like blindfolds, put the buttons in a bag.)

Increase Level of Difficulty

Materials   Buttons that are smaller and more similar

Decrease Level of Difficulty

Materials   Buttons that are larger and more dissimilar

Procedure   Allow children first to match the buttons visually, then do it without looking.

COMMENT   This same procedure can be used with fabric, textured wallpaper discs, or small objects.

Small Motor

PROGRESSIVE DRESS-UP

GOAL   To improve small motor coordination
To improve motor planning
To improve adaptive skills

OBJECTIVE   The child will put on the designated clothing.

MATERIALS   Adult clothing:

sweaters	sweatshirt	pants	shirts
skirts	shorts	socks	shoes

PROCEDURE   Divide the clothing into three piles—tops, bottoms, and footwear. Put the piles in three different places. Have the children walk, jump, or skip to each pile, find and put on that article of clothing and then go on to the next pile until they are "dressed."

Increase Level of Difficulty

Procedure   Put all the clothing in one pile so the children have to determine the correct order. Add clothing that is closer to the children's actual size and add accessories such as gloves, ties, scarves, and hats. This could also be done as a relay.

Decrease Level of Difficulty

Procedure   Choose clothing without buttons, with cut-off sleeves, and be sure the clothing is oversized.

COMMENT   This is a fun way to practice adaptive skills.

Small Motor

NUTS AND BOLTS

GOAL   To improve small motor coordination
To improve eye-hand coordination
To improve size concepts

OBJECTIVE   The child will screw the correct size nut on the bolt.

MATERIALS   matching nuts and bolts   bowls

PROCEDURE   Put the bolts in one bowl and nuts in another. Provide a third bowl for the bolt with the nut on it. Use sizes of bolts that vary greatly, such as $1/4''$, $1/2''$, and $1''$. Encourage children to screw the nut on the bolt until it is tight.

Increase Level of Difficulty

Materials   Add washers and intermediate sizes of nuts and bolts.

Procedure   Blindfold the children and see if they can match the nuts and bolts by touch alone.

Decrease Level of Difficulty

Materials   Use wing nuts (they are easier to turn).

Procedure   Have fewer bolts to select from and choose the larger ones at first.

COMMENT   This activity is particularly good for developing rotational skills.

PICKING CHERRIES

GOAL   To improve small motor coordination
To improve eye-hand coordination
To improve adaptive skills

OBJECTIVE   The child will button the designated number of cherries.

MATERIALS   green felt   glue   needle

red buttons   scissors   thread

PROCEDURE   Sew ten red buttons on a piece of green felt within an outline of a tree. Sew or glue a second piece of felt that has been cut to look like a tree over the first piece. Cut slits where the buttons are. Ask children to make a cherry tree with six cherries (i.e., button six buttons) and so on. Children can "eat" the cherries as they unbutton the buttons.

Increase Level of Difficulty

Materials   Make the buttons smaller or irregular in shape. Make the button hole smaller. Sew on more buttons.

Procedure   Ask for increasingly higher numbers of cherries or even incorporate the activity into a simple word problem: Jane picked 3 cherries and Tara picked 1 cherry. How many did they pick altogether?

Decrease Level of Difficulty

Materials   Make the trees larger and buttons and/or the button holes larger.

Procedure   Ask for smaller numbers and sew fewer buttons on each piece of felt.

COMMENT   The buttons can be any color, as can the felt. The buttons can represent butterflies, birds, any fruit or vegetable, hidden faces, and so on. The activity also gives practice in number concepts.

TOOLS

GOAL   To improve small motor coordination
To improve eye-hand coordination
To improve adaptive skills

OBJECTIVE   The child will pick up small objects using tools.

MATERIALS   tub with sand or oatmeal   small objects

tongs   spatula

spaghetti spoon   pierced serving spoons

PROCEDURE   Place the small objects in the tub with the sand and have the child retrieve the objects using the different tools.

Increase Level of Difficulty

Materials   tweezers   needle-nose pliers   magnifying glass

small plate   tiny objects

Procedure   Have children pick up very tiny objects using the tweezers. Once these objects have been picked up, encourage children to explore them under a magnifying glass, turning them with tweezers.

Decrease Level of Difficulty

Procedure   Children can use their hands to find the objects in the sand, then add the spoon and finally more complex tools.

Sorting games combine classification skills and small motor development. The tongs provide a further challenge for small motor skills.

COMMENT   Children need practice using tools. To sustain interest you might have the children classify the objects, or give them a card and have them find a particular object that is hidden in the sand.

Small Motor

LOCK BOX

GOAL   To improve small motor coordination
   To improve eye-hand coordination
   To improve adaptive skills

OBJECTIVE   The child will perform all of the possible tasks.

MATERIALS   A busy board lock box

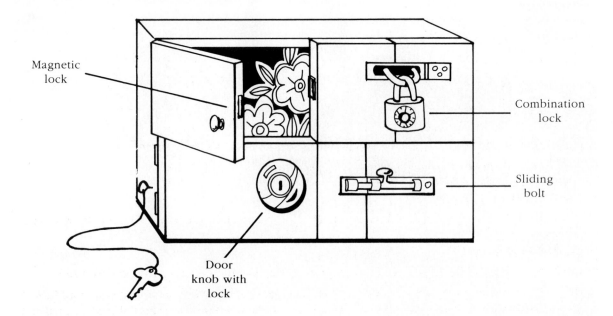

Magnetic lock

Combination lock

Sliding bolt

Door knob with lock

PROCEDURE   Make or buy some busy boards. All require fine motor skills, but some teach more needed skills and are more intriguing than others. My most successful one was a "lock box." It has a variety of locks and keys (attached by strings so they don't get lost). Include a combination lock to be really challenging. Put pictures inside so the children see something when the doors open.

Increase Level of Difficulty

Materials   Replace the magnetic lock on the lock box with another key lock that has cuts on both sides. Put the combination to the lock on the bottom of the box itself so the child must remember the numbers and direction of the turns.

Procedure   Request that children open the locks in a specific order or time them to see how quickly they can open all the locks.

Decrease Level of Difficulty

Materials   Choose a busy box that requires less skill.

COMMENT   After using the "lock box" busy box, children might be able to get into locked places if they had a key, but they might also be able to get out of a locked bathroom.

GAMEBOARD

GOAL   To improve small motor coordination
To improve eye-hand coordination
To increase inclusion

OBJECTIVE   The child will help make the gameboard and play the game with some of his classmates.

MATERIALS   a cookie sheet or jellyroll pan   magnets
string or 20–30 toothpicks   paper plate
glue   felt dots
black construction paper   brad

PROCEDURE   Have the children help make the gameboard by gluing the string or toothpicks to the pan in a ladderlike track. Use magnets as markers. You can make a variety of games in this way. To make a simple counting game, make a spinner out of a paper plate and use felt dots to signify the number of spaces to move.

Increase Level of Difficulty

Procedure   Encourage children to make a different game. Help them decide the rules and write them down.

Decrease Level of Difficulty

Procedure   Help children learn the concept of taking turns and playing a game with rules.

COMMENT   Children enjoy and learn a lot from playing games. Having them make the board themselves is an added bonus. The tactile cues allow children with *visual* impairments to have an added cue.

MY PUZZLE

GOAL   To improve eye-hand coordination
To increase body awareness
To improve self-concept

OBJECTIVE   The child will put the picture together.

MATERIALS   an 8″ × 10″ picture puzzle of each child
scissors or jigsaw

PROCEDURE   Take pictures of all the children in class. (Black and white is fine; color is expensive.) Keep a small picture for each child's locker or a class collage. Have an 8″ × 10″ enlargement of each child made. Laminate it or cover it with clear contact paper and glue it to heavy cardboard. Draw lines on the back and cut it with heavy scissors or a jigsaw. No matter how you cut it, it will fit back together. (Put the child's initials on each piece so the children can put the puzzles back together if they get mixed up.)

Increase Level of Difficulty

Materials   Cut the picture into more pieces.

Decrease Level of Difficulty

Materials   Cut the picture into fewer pieces. As the child becomes more skilled you can cut more pieces. Having a frame might make it easier for some children.

COMMENT   Point out the uniqueness and similarities of the children in the group. This activity can also be done with children's drawings, or you can buy blank puzzles that are cut and have children draw on them. These often have many pieces, however.

Small Motor

CATERPILLARS

GOAL   To improve eye-hand coordination
To improve adaptive skills
To improve sequencing skills

OBJECTIVE   The child will make a caterpillar in a designated pattern.

MATERIALS   Fabric pieces about 2" long of different colors and/or textures with a button on one end and a button hole on the other

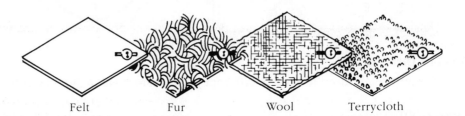

Felt   Fur   Wool   Terrycloth

PROCEDURE   Decide on the shape (or shapes) you want to use and cut shapes out of different fabrics (e.g., felt, leather, velvet, cotton, wool, terry cloth). Put a button on one end and a button hole on the other. Finish the edges so they don't ravel. (Felt is good to use because it doesn't have to be finished and you can just make a slit for the button hole.) Button the materials together in a sequence to make a caterpillar and have the children copy it.

Increase Level of Difficulty

Materials   Add hooks and eyes, snaps, and Velcro closures as well as varying the size of the buttons used.

Procedure   Increase the length and complexity of the caterpillar by varying both color and texture in the pattern.

Decrease Level of Difficulty

Materials   Use Velcro instead of buttons.

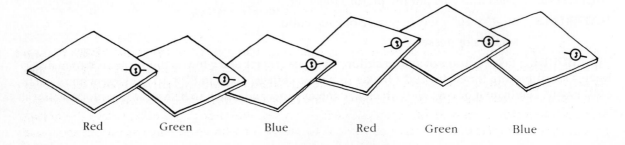

Red   Green   Blue   Red   Green   Blue

Procedure   Initially let children just practice buttoning or fastening the material together, then use a short color sequence of the same fabric instead of a textured one (red, green, red, green).

COMMENT   This activity provides good tactile feedback for children as well as some essential reading readiness and math skills. Encourage children to count the "links" in their caterpillar and even read *The Hungry Caterpillar* and build the caterpillar to reflect what he ate each day.

Small Motor

POURING RICE

GOAL   To improve eye-hand coordination
To improve adaptive skills
To improve generalization skills

OBJECTIVE   The child will pour the substances without spilling them.

MATERIALS   trays or jellyroll pans   rice, split peas, dried beans

pitchers   measuring cups

a large container   bowls

PROCEDURE   Put some containers on the jellyroll pans or trays and have the children practice pouring from the large to the smaller containers. Ask them to make predictions about the size relationships among the containers and how much each will hold relative to the others. Name the containers and their parts (handle, lip, pitcher, glass) as well as the sizes of the containers (1 cup, 2 cups, 1 quart) or help the children discover the relative relationships.

Increase Level of Difficulty

Procedure   Use liquids, at first in a water table, then at juice time. Be sure to include pouring liquid from a half-gallon container into a four-ounce glass.

Decrease Level of Difficulty

Procedure   Use containers that are closer in size and give more time for practice.

COMMENT   Self-confidence is gained through independence. On the other hand, it is no fun to clean up spills. Helping children learn to pour by using a non-liquid substance can build skill with less mess.

Small Motor

PLAYDOUGH BEADS

GOAL   To improve eye-hand coordination
To improve sequencing skills
To improve number concepts

OBJECTIVE   The child will make a bead necklace with a repeating pattern.

MATERIALS   1 cup cornstarch

2 cups baking soda

1-$\frac{1}{2}$ cups water (food coloring can be added if desired)

yarn for stringing

PROCEDURE   Mix ingredients. Cook until mixture looks like mashed potatoes and begins to form clumps. Turn onto a plate and cool. Knead when cool. Roll into a "snake" and cut off pieces (be sure these are large enough to allow for a hole) or roll out flat and cut into shapes with kitchen knife or small cookie cutters. Make holes for stringing by inserting a cut-off straw in each piece. Dry in sun or heat oven to warm. Turn oven off, then put beads in to dry. Flip over to dry other side. (The drying process may take a day or two.) Have children color the beads with water color markers if they have not yet been colored. Provide yarn for stringing. Taping one end of the string or dipping it in glue and allowing the glue to harden makes stringing easier.

Encourage children to design patterns that have two beads and repeat or three or four. Encourage them to count the number of patterns in the necklace.

Increase Level of Difficulty

Procedure   Have children measure the ingredients and knead the dough. Encourage them to make more complex bead patterns.

Decrease Level of Difficulty

Procedure   Have children color and string only one kind of bead or use a random order.

COMMENT   Children can participate in this activity at many different levels. The pattern can be one of color or shape or both. This is often an area where children with *learning disabilities* are challenged, and this activity is very reinforcing.

References and Bibliography

Ayers, A. J. (1987). *Sensory integration and the child*. Los Angeles, CA: Western Psychological Services.

Bissell, J., Fisher, J., Owens, C., & Polcyn, P. (1988). *Sensory motor handbook: A guide for implementing and modifying activities in the classroom*. Torrance, CA: Sensory Integration International Publishers.

Clark, J. E., & Humphrey, J. H. (Eds.). (1985). *Motor development: Current selected research*. Princeton, NJ: Princeton Book Company.

Gabbard, C., Leblanc, E., & Lowy, S. (1987). *Physical education for children: Building the foundation*. Englewood Cliffs, NJ: Prentice-Hall.

Luvmour, S., & Luvmour, J. (1990). *Everyone wins: Cooperative games and activities*. Philadelphia, PA: New Society Publishers.

Munro, J. R. (1985). *Movement education: A program for young children ages 2 to 7*. Newport News, VA: Munro-Drake Educational Associates.

Prudden, B. (1986). *How to keep your child fit from birth to six*. New York: Ballantine Books.

Prudden, B. (1987). *Fitness from six to twelve*. New York: Ballantine Books.

Stinson, W. J. (1990). *Moving and learning for the young child*. Reston, VA: American Alliance for Health, Physical Education, Recreation and Dance.

Young, S. B. (Undated). *Movement is fun: A preschool movement program*. Torrance, CA: Sensory Integration International Publishers.

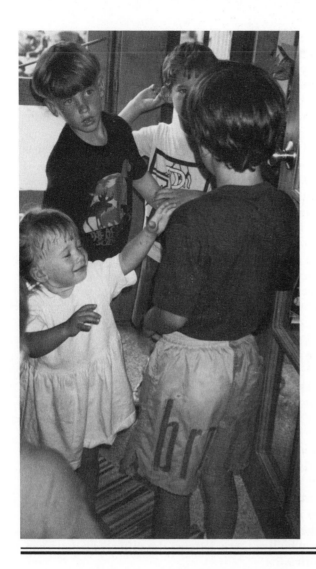

Social Awareness: Social Studies, Inclusion, Health and Safety

Social awareness for young children is designed to help them understand and function in the world in which they live. During their early years children are developing their sense of values and attitudes about themselves, other children, and adults in their family and community. They are developing their concept of self. It is important that they have a broad range of experiences and are exposed to people and materials without gender, racial, or cultural bias. People with disabilities must be portrayed accurately, including both their abilities and disabilities.

Social Studies

Social studies is an area for specific activities and learning, but also one where observation and modeling are important learning tools. Social studies is also taught through the informal organization and decision making of each day: deciding what to name the new goldfish, what to do when someone knocks down the blocks, and how to share special materials. This is all part of the social learning that occurs at this age.

As children and their families step into your classroom, they will learn something about how you teach social studies. They will look at the pictures and bulletin boards to see if they represent the culture and language of the children you teach. They will look at the books on display to see if they support an anti-bias approach, or if they reinforce racial and **497** gender stereotypes. They will evaluate the room to determine whether or not it allows diversity in play. As their eye wanders to the dramatic play area they will note whether the dolls represent the culture of the children in the classroom. They will look for the possibility of language differences, not only Spanish, but American Sign Language and braille. They might even note whether there are pictures and books about children with disabilities.

As children with disabilities are included in regular classrooms, it is important that they become more aware of the community around them. If they are to become part of the community, they will be expected to know not only about the specialists that are a part of their lives, but also about other community employees.

All children need to feel as though they are part of the class. It is important that they become aware of themselves both as unique human beings and as people who are similar to, as well as different from, others. Children can learn that they are all members of the class even though some of them are boys and others girls, some like art and others don't, and some wear glasses and others don't.

Children learn through social studies about the situational aspects of behavior. Behavior that is appropriate in one situation is not necessarily right in another. Shouting in the play yard is fun and suitable; shouting in the classroom is not.

Children in the process of learning to take turns wonder whether or not they will actually get their turn if they postpone it or let someone ahead of them. If they *do* lose their turn, they will be less likely to take turns in the future.

As children with disabilities are increasingly included in regular classrooms and community activities, it is important that they learn more about these environments. Start with your setting. Help children feel comfortable knowing their way around both indoors and out. Take short walks in the area. Focus some part of your curriculum on the community itself as well as communities in general—why we have them, what they do, and how they help the people who live there. Discuss the differences between rural and urban communities.

Field trips are one of the most common ways of making abstract ideas concrete to young children. Where field trips are impractical, resource people can be invited to visit. Resource media such as film, television, video tapes, records, or audio tapes can also be used.

Inclusion

From an early age children need to become aware of individual differences and learn to respect these differences. Children need to better understand how this diversity affects another child and how children can interact with each other in light of these diverse abilities. Ignoring differences is not effective. To begin with, children must become aware of others' situations. Stories can be useful, but children learn best by doing.

Examine your feelings about children with disabilities, children from different ethnic backgrounds, and your expectations based on gender to discover if you have personal values that might make working with children difficult. Check out your verbal language and body language to see if it reflects an anti-bias message.

As children begin to be aware of the ways in which they are different from each other, the skill of a sensitive teacher can help determine the long-term outcome of this awareness. Children look to you as a model. If you pity children with disabilities or are overprotective or condescending toward them, the children will react the same way. If you celebrate only holidays that a majority of the children participate in, then those who have different beliefs may feel excluded. If you always choose boys to go to the block area and expect girls to use the dramatic play area you are supporting stereotypic gender differences.

Awareness is important for *all* children. For example, a child with a physical impairment cannot be expected to have any more understanding of what it is like to have a visual impairment than any other child in your class. Children need help in learning to view events from others' perspectives early in life, without making judgments about whether that perspective is good or bad. Activities in the area of inclusion are not easy: they are rarely part of the everyday curriculum. They require special planning, thinking, and sensitivity on your part. They also have special payoffs, to you and to all the children in your class.

Provide an atmosphere where issues about race, gender, and disability can be freely discussed. Young children are very aware of differences (Wardle, 1987). Support diversity in your classroom through activities, materials, and program planning (Phillips, 1988). Children may need to be taught specific ways to handle people who stare or make unkind remarks. Find out how parents cope with these problems and support and expand on their techniques, or if necessary, support them in learning different ways of responding. Children may wonder how to talk to a child who stutters, or what questions it is appropriate to ask about a prosthesis. They will use your behavior as a model. Children may need to be taught specific skills in how to approach others. They will need help in finding roles to play and accommodations and adaptations that allow all children to play together.

Health and Safety

Health and safety are areas of study as well as states of being. When young children become aware of what it means to be unhealthy and have the knowledge and vocabulary to describe their symptoms, there is less likelihood of serious, undetected illness. When they have learned to recognize signs of danger and act appropriately, the environment will be less threatening to them. It is important for all children to refine their awareness and skills in these areas. Only children who are healthy and feel safe are free to enter into your program fully. Children learn basic health practices as part of a routine (such as washing their hands after toileting and before snack).

Common health concerns for children focus on infectious diseases (those that can be given to others), such as chicken pox, colds, and strep throat, and injuries that typically require first aid treatment. Children with infectious diseases are usually sent home or are kept at home until they feel well enough to participate in the program and are no longer a risk to the other children. Other than practicing good hygiene patterns there is little teachers can do to prevent illness. A good safety education program, however, can prevent injuries in the classroom and at home. Accidents are the leading cause of death for children under the age of fourteen. Common accidents for young children include falls, burns, eating small, sharp objects or poisonous substances, choking, smothering, getting into traffic, and water accidents.

Proper nutrition is an important part of being healthy. Infants come into this world preferring sweet over bitter or sour tastes. Too many sweets in the diet contribute to dental caries and to excess weight. As a teacher, your role is to choose snacks wisely, offering foods that are low in fat and salt and high in complex carbohydrates. As 22 percent of children's caloric intake comes from snacks (Rogers & Morris, 1986), choose them wisely. When you make snacks with the children as part of your programming, make sure they adhere to the same standards. Find ways of celebrating special events that do not always include cupcakes and candy.

Management of health-related problems is part of the programming for young children. Allergies are the most common chronic health problem of children. However, current concerns focus on developmentally appropriate drug and alcohol abuse prevention and AIDS programming as well.

Today, young children with AIDS or who are infected with the Human Immunodeficiency Virus (HIV) usually acquired it from their mothers, who used intravenous drugs or had partners who did. Because it is not always known when children are HIV positive, precautions should be taken to reduce the risk of infection. Two strategies are most effective: washing hands properly (running water, liquid soap, and disposable towels) and cleaning up soiled surfaces with bleach solution prepared daily (1 tablespoon bleach to 1 quart water; 1 to 10 ratio for cleaning blood spills) (New guidelines on HIV infection [AIDS] announced for group programs, 1989).

Social Awareness Goals

To Broaden Concepts of Families

Children start out very egocentric, believing that all children are like them and all families are like their families. They need to become aware of individual and family differences without making judgments that "different" is "bad." Learning about the functions of families and the roles they play, including an international perspective, is the beginning of citizenship.

To Increase Awareness of Roles People Play

When children enter school, they may have had little experience with adults other than their immediate family and caregivers. They need to broaden their experience with the roles that adults play as well as the authority structure that exists. They need information about the helping professions. Children can begin to learn which occupations sound interesting to them. People's occupations require different skills and preparation. They need a perspective on roles that presents neither gender nor racial bias.

To Increase Problem-Solving Skills

Living and working with others, children have to learn to compromise. Young children know about "yes" and "no" and "mine," but they need to be taught ways of taking turns, sharing, and developing rules that all can abide by. They also need to have some knowledge of exceptions to rules and why and how these exceptions are made. As we live in a world of diminishing resources, children need to learn about conservation and the interaction between people and their environment. (We use paper to draw. Paper comes from trees. If we use both sides of the paper we will have to cut down fewer trees.)

To Increase Inclusion

If this is the children's first school experience, they may have had little experience with peers other than siblings. Some children learn how to get along with each other easily, without conscious effort on the teacher's part; others need to be taught this just as much as they need to be taught math and language skills. Children may need to be taught specific skills to help them become part of the group, and special activities may need to be created that include all children in the group.

*To Improve
Self-Concept*

How a child feels about herself may influence the risks she is willing to take in trying out new materials and meeting new people. Children who have positive self-concepts evaluate information from that perspective; a bad experience is just that. Children with low self-concepts often have a difficult time differentiating between the bad experience and themselves.

*To Increase
Awareness of
Individual
Differences*

Children need to become aware of how others are both alike and different from them. They must learn to acknowledge, but not judge, others by these differences. The sensitivity must be taught through firsthand experiences with adult input to help clarify feelings.

*To Increase
Survival Skills*

Health and safety patterns must be conscientiously taught to young children. Children must learn to make good judgments about what is and is not safe for them to do. They must learn to think through the implications of actions *before* they decide to do something and then evaluate the consequences in terms of whether or not it is a safe thing to do. Children must be taught ways of compensating for their disabilities and be aware of ways to be safe and healthy.

**Teaching
Strategies**

Children with *communication* disorders can work on broadening their language skills through field trips, followed by language experience stories. This sequence supports both the social studies and language aspect of the experience. The language skills necessary for sharing and taking turns can also be emphasized. Field trips and resource people offer the opportunity for learning and trying out new vocabulary. Begin with listening skills and following directions: "Show me what you do when you see a red light." Next, work on vocabulary to go with the actions. As children learn to identify more body parts and more accurate ways of expressing feelings, help them become more specific in their speech.

Children with *hearing* impairments profit from firsthand experiences, followed in the classroom by visual aids to clarify and generalize these experiences. These children may need to be taught nonverbal ways of approaching other children, and others must be made aware that that is what is happening. At an early age, they need to have signs and words that are descriptive of feelings and body parts they cannot point to if they are to tell others how they feel. Safety procedures must be emphasized. Children must learn to recognize and respond quickly to visual signals of danger. They must be taught visual cues if they cannot hear the warning sounds of a car horn, fire alarm, or a shout.

Children with *visual* impairments must be exposed to role models who wear glasses and use other optical devices. They need to be encouraged to use the correctable vision they have and to learn the skills to explain to others why these particular devices help them. For those with little vision, the use of records and tapes can help them expand their social world. They are often more sensitive to auditory signals than visual ones. They may not see another child riding a tricycle toward them, the traffic light, or the swing in motion. They need to learn to use both their residual vision and their hearing to compensate. They need to work on labeling body parts and developing a vocabulary to explain how they feel. Children with limited vision need to use their sense of touch to determine if they have rashes or cuts or to tell if their hands are clean.

Children with *learning disabilities* must be encouraged to use a variety of solutions to problems: they have a tendency to get stuck. They require guidance and practice. The skills of taking turns and sharing are especially critical. They need practice responding appropriately to safety signals. Early childhood is a time when obedience is important and self-control must be stressed. Because the behavior of children with learning disabilities is variable, they are often unaware of how they feel.

Children with *physical disabilities* may not move as fast as others and need to refine skills of speed and distance for their own safety. If they have a prosthetic device or braces, they need to be aware of any irritation or pain that develops, or they might have to do without these aids until the irritation clears up. Children who lack sensation in some body parts must learn to deal with conditions they may not feel, such as sunburn, getting wet, and so on. Be sure to include children with physical disabilities on field trips. Use creative problem solving to increase all children's awareness of accessibility and what it means.

Children with *health* impairments may be aware of medical aspects of the community, but this knowledge should be expanded and put into perspective. These children often have recurring episodes of illness. They can help prevent some of these episodes by learning to recognize their symptoms and/or avoiding situations that are likely to cause them difficulty. This knowledge will in turn make them feel more in control and help them toward independence. They need to develop approach skills as well as methods of keeping in touch with peers when they cannot attend school (telephone, visits after school, and so on).

Children with *emotional/behavioral* disorders may have few social skills and perhaps even an unwillingness to approach others. The classroom and community need to become familiar and safe places for them. Do a lot of preparation for field trips as well as follow-up. Assign an adult to this child on a field trip. Children who are less responsive to the environment need more help in choosing clothing that is appropriate for the weather and in responding to safety cues. They may temporarily forget health and safety rules and may need reminders. Take care to keep these routines a stable part of the program.

Children with *mental retardation* can learn about their environment by building on familiar experiences. Begin with their immediate surroundings of family and school, then expand to the larger community. They may be less able than others at this age to evaluate situations relative to health and safety. Evaluate your classroom and see that the environment itself is safe. Start making good health and safety practices part of their routine; for example, wash hands after toileting and before eating and dress appropriately for the weather (this may mean telling children to take off their coats on a warm afternoon outside).

Children with *multiple disabilities* will require adaptations depending upon the area that is most involved. In general, follow the strategies given above and combine them to meet the child's needs.

Social Awareness Activities

Goal	Activity
To broaden concepts of families	Photograph Story
	Family Map
	Holidays
	International Snack
	Roles
	Animal Families
	Food Forms
To increase awareness of roles people play	Visitor
	Get Well Cards

Goal	**Activity**
	Our Town
	Medical Tools
	Patient in the Hospital
	Audiologist
	Eye Doctor
	Emergency Room
	Who Am I?
	Be the Teacher
	Library
	Cast It
	Photograph Story
	Family Map
	Holidays
	International Snack
	Roles
To increase problem-solving skills	No Words
	One More
	Charades
	Hands and Feet
	Who Has Been Here?
	Emergency Room
	Our Town
	Animal Families
	Who Am I?
To increase inclusion	I'm Thinking Of
	My Day
	Share Your Feelings
	Wheels
	From Your House to Mine
	Get Well Cards
	Audiologist
	Eye Doctor
	Who Am I?
	Our Town
	Library
To improve self-concept	Medical Tools
	Patient in the Hospital
	Be the Teacher
	Audiologist
	Eye Doctor
	Emergency Room
	I'm Thinking Of
	Share Your Feelings
	My Day
To increase awareness of individual differences	Cutting Cardboard
	Finger Spelling Lotto
	Muffles
	New Doll
	Noisy Tasks
	Sad
	Tired
	Tongue Twisters
	Voiceless Roll Call
	Who Is It?
	Foreign Languages
	Simulated Glasses
	Creepers

Goal	Activity
	Mittens
	Moving in the Dark
	Special Dolls
	Talking
	Slings
	Not to Eat
	Cast It
	My Day
	I'm Thinking Of
	No Words
	Hands and Feet
To increase survival skills	Not to Eat
	Seasonal Clothing
	Smell Cues
	Symptoms
	Traffic Sign Hunt
	Warning Sounds
	Stop and Go
	Warning Signs
	What Would You Do If?
To increase expressive language	Share Your Feelings
	One More
	Seasonal Clothing
	Smell Cues
	Symptoms
To improve listening skills	Foreign Languages
	Traffic Sign Hunt
	Warning Sounds
To follow directions	Be the Teacher
To improve reading readiness	Library
To improve measurement concepts	From Your House to Mine
To improve observational skills	Charades
	Simulated Glasses
To make predictions	Who Has Been Here?
To improve cause-and-effect reasoning	Food Forms
	Who Has Been Here?
	Stop and Go
	Smell Cues
	Traffic Sign Hunt
	Warning Sounds
	Warning Signs
	What Would You Do If?
	Wheels
	Seasonal Clothing
To increase body awareness	Hands and Feet
	Creepers
	Special Dolls
	Talking
	Moving in the Dark
	Mittens
	Symptoms
	Slings

Goal	Activity	Page
To encourage creative problem solving	What Would You Do If? Slings Cast It	

PHOTOGRAPH STORY

GOAL   To broaden concepts of families
     To increase awareness of roles people play

OBJECTIVE   The child will state at least two roles the person in the picture can play.

MATERIALS   Pictures of several familiar people, including teachers in your school and even you, in a variety of roles:

> a teacher with the children in the class
>
> an adult daughter with her mother
>
> a father with young children
>
> a sibling with brothers and sisters
>
> a wife with her husband
>
> a student taking a course

PROCEDURE   Use pictures of males and females. Be sure to include pictures of children and the roles they play. Note the similarities and differences among the roles that children and adults play. It is important at the beginning to use pictures of familiar people so children understand the concept of multiple roles.

Increase Level of Difficulty

Procedure   Use pictures of famous people and occupations: the President of the United States, astronauts, movie stars. All may be husbands, wives, sons, daughters, siblings, aunts, uncles, and so on.

Decrease Level of Difficulty

Procedure   Start with yourself and show the children pictures of you with them and with your family.

COMMENT   Children need to gain a perspective on adult roles. They need to see medical personnel and related service providers as playing other familiar roles. They also need to see that they themselves have many roles.

FAMILY MAP

GOAL   To broaden concepts of families
     To increase awareness of roles people play

OBJECTIVE   The child will make a map of his family.

MATERIALS   manila paper   crayons

     small circles and squares made from construction paper

PROCEDURE   Give children construction paper and tell them that they are going to make a map of their family. For this map, all the females in the family will be circles and the males, squares. Encourage children to decide who is part of their family and where they should go on the page. Have children designate in some way who the squares and circles represent. Be sure to allow for pets if children want to include them. They can put a boundary around the family, or not, as they choose. Some children may be part of more than one family and the map can represent this.

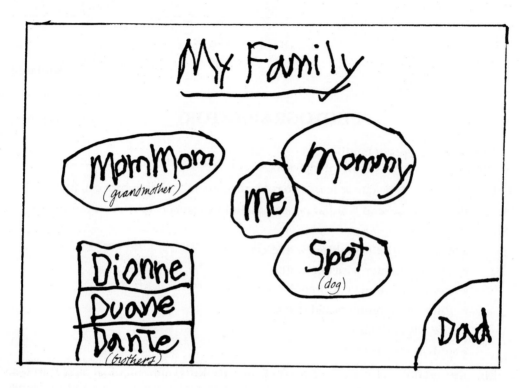

Family Map

Increase Level of Difficulty
Procedure   Encourage children to think more about families and how they are connected. Help them develop a key to show relationships among family members.

Decrease Level of Difficulty
Procedure   Help children identify family members and mark them. After you make the circles and squares, the children can put them on the page where they choose.

COMMENT   This activity helps children see different family configurations. It also can give you insight into the child's perception of her family. If possible, have children use small pictures of family members in the maps.

Social Studies

HOLIDAYS

GOAL   To broaden concepts of families
          To increase awareness of roles people play

OBJECTIVE   The child will share with the group how his family celebrates a special holiday.

MATERIALS   None (unless the child wants to bring in something)

PROCEDURE   Talk with children about how their families celebrate particular holidays. Then choose one or two children each day to act this out for the group. Include different holidays and birthdays. Be sure to discuss feelings, excitement, and expectations. Discuss how fine it is that families have different ways of celebrating as well as different holidays that are celebrated.

Increase Level of Difficulty

Procedure   Encourage children to have their parents or others come to talk about the holiday as well. Plan some special activities and snacks that support the learning experience.

Decrease Level of Difficulty

Procedure   Have several children talk briefly about important celebrations.

COMMENT   Be aware if there are children in your class who do not celebrate holidays. Find out from them and their families how they want to share this information with their classmates.

Social Studies

INTERNATIONAL SNACK

GOAL   To broaden concepts of families
To increase awareness of roles people play

OBJECTIVE   The child will taste the snacks.

MATERIALS   An international snack including:

flour tortillas	pupu
fondue	crepes
Irish soda bread	
pita bread	

PROCEDURE   As one activity for the day, make a snack that is not traditionally "American." Start with something that is familiar but borrowed, like pizza and tacos, and move on to less familiar foods. Discuss what the foods are made of and where they come from, then eat them. Use parents and grandparents as a resource.

Increase Level of Difficulty

Procedure   Have children help make the snack. As you make the snack talk about the foods used, the culture, and the people.

Decrease Level of Difficulty

Procedure   Start with foods that, although from other countries originally, are familiar to many of the children, such as tofu, pita bread, and crepes. Then work into foods that are increasingly different.

COMMENT   Help children think of differences without the implication of a judgment. Children will often participate in experiences at school with food that they would not try at home.

Social Studies

ROLES

GOAL   To broaden concepts of families
To increase awareness of roles people play

OBJECTIVE   The child will state at least three roles he has in the family.

MATERIALS   Flannel board and Pellon figures:

4 boys	2 women
4 girls	2 older men
2 men	2 older women

PROCEDURE   Have a group discussion about the variety of roles that children play. Use flannel board figures to help clarify these roles for the children. Explain such roles as:

brother/sister, stepbrother/stepsister	friend	grandfather/grandmother
boy/girl	cousin	
daughter/son, stepdaughter/stepson	man/woman	
nephew/niece	husband/wife	
grandson/granddaughter	father/mother, stepfather/stepmother	

Explain that one person can play many roles. Be sure to include all the relationships that children in your classroom might have. When the children have identified their various roles, describe roles to see if the children can guess whom you are talking about: "I'm thinking of a girl who has one sister who is younger than she is and no brothers. Who am I thinking of?"

Increase Level of Difficulty

Procedure   Increase the complexity of relationships you talk about. Include great-aunts, second cousins, and so on.

Decrease Level of Difficulty

Procedure   Start with roles that children are most familiar with.

COMMENT   All children have a variety of roles regardless of ethnic or cultural diversity. Discuss family change and roles that change with changing situations (marriage, husband–wife roles) and those that don't change (parental). Your mother is still your mother even if she no longer lives with your father. *Note:* This area may be sensitive for a child in whose family a dramatic change is occurring (divorce, death, birth, and so on).

Social Studies

ANIMAL FAMILIES

GOAL   To broaden concepts of families
To increase problem-solving skills

OBJECTIVE   The child will role play one member of an animal family.

MATERIALS   None

PROCEDURE   Create an animal family. Provide role-playing situations with this family at play. Include characteristic behaviors for the animals chosen. Include some misbehavior, sibling rivalry, or peer quarrels in the role play. Have the children make up endings for the situations. Help them form conclusions about the consequences of their actions. Talk about the similarities and differences between animal families and people families. Expand this idea to the environment where the animals live.

Increase Level of Difficulty

Procedure   Make the family more complex, include extended family members, make the situations more difficult so they include not only problems of relationship but the environment as well.

Decrease Level of Difficulty

Procedure   Have fewer family members, simpler problems, or give some children easier roles within the family group.

COMMENT   You can use this activity to solve some classroom problems. Role play can make it easier to address a particular situation without making it obvious. Then draw the analogy.

Social Studies

FOOD FORMS

GOAL   To broaden concepts of families
To improve cause-and-effect reasoning

OBJECTIVE   The child will identify food in different forms and state who in a family eats it in those forms.

MATERIALS   a variety of whole foods   a baby food grinder

baby food jars of the same foods   a knife

a scraper   a hot plate

a masher

PROCEDURE   Pick one or several foods (carrots and apples are traditional favorites, peaches and squash also work well). Have the children feel the food, whole and cut up into different shapes.

CARROT

whole   curls (cut long and thin and put in ice water)

pieces   cubes (cut at an angle)

coins

Put some of the carrots in a saucepan to cook. (It's fun to cook some whole carrots as well as the cut-up ones. Set a timer and have the children see which is softer after a specified time period.) When the carrots are cooked, experiment again with different forms:

whole   coins   mashed

purée (if you have a blender)

ground (in baby food grinder)

Compare these to baby food in jars. Discuss the taste of the different forms and how some are the same or almost the same and others different. Experiment by adding salt. Talk about who would eat the various forms (babies who don't have teeth, children getting permanent teeth, and people with braces or false teeth) and why (variety, need, or individual preference).

Increase Level of Difficulty

Procedure   Use less familiar foods and a greater variety of vegetables. Have a tasting party at the end.

Decrease Level of Difficulty

Procedure   Start with only one food and have children eat it in each stage (e.g., raw apple, cooked apple slices, applesauce).

COMMENT   Children may not be aware of what causes food to change. Explain to children what being on a "soft" diet means. Be sure to include the vocabulary about the states of food—soft, hard, crisp, mushy, and so on.

Social Studies

VISITOR

GOAL   To increase awareness of roles people play

OBJECTIVE   The child will state what the adult does in the community.

MATERIALS   None

PROCEDURE   Invite adults from the community to come into the class. Pick people who are comfortable with children. Have them talk briefly about what they do and answer the children's questions. Choose people who will broaden the children's understanding of the community, as well as reduce sex role stereotyping. For example:

photographer   Red Cross staff

businessman/woman   waitress/waiter

Welcome Wagon staff   male nurse

female medical doctor   female lawyer

plumber	female engineer
builder	real estate agent
construction worker	farmer
musician	computer programmer

Increase Level of Difficulty

Procedure   Have those children who are particularly interested follow up the large-group experience with a small-group discussion. The visitor can go into greater depth about the profession as well as answer additional questions. Follow this up by visiting the person at work as well as by dramatic play in the classroom incorporating that theme.

Decrease Level of Difficulty

Procedure   Start with occupations the children are familiar with. Keep the large-group discussion short.

COMMENT   Children often have a restricted view of the community. This activity can extend their understanding and make them feel more a part of the community. Be sure to include visitors who represent a variety of cultural and ethnic groups.

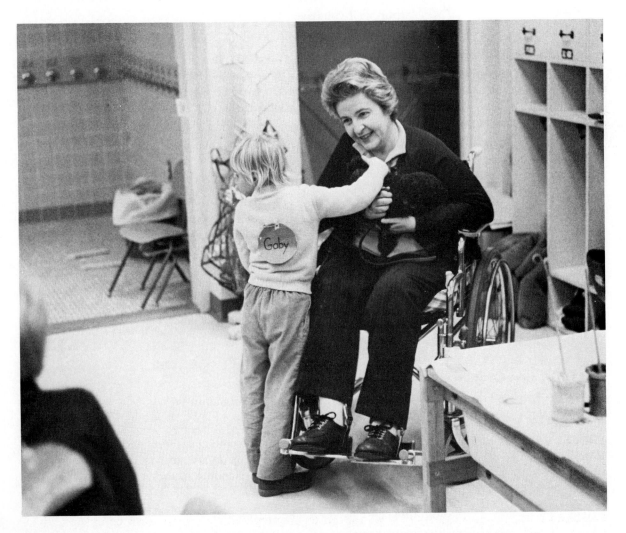

Classroom visitors offer opportunities for children to ask questions and learn about people in a safe environment.

GET WELL CARDS

GOAL To increase inclusion

To increase awareness of roles people play

OBJECTIVE The child will make a get well card for a classmate.

MATERIALS construction paper crayons or markers

PROCEDURE Have the children make drawings or paintings of their choice on a folded piece of construction paper. They can make either two pictures (front and inside of card) or one picture within a written message (dictated to teacher).

Increase Level of Difficulty

Procedure Talk with the children about the particular illness the child has and the kinds of activities that child particularly likes. Encourage children to write a message.

Decrease Level of Difficulty

Procedure Focus on the idea of sending get well cards.

COMMENT Make the first card for a specific child; then start a collection so you will always have a card to send when the occasion arises. After a while, the children may notice that certain members of the class are absent more often than others.

OUR TOWN

GOAL To increase inclusion

To increase awareness of roles people play

To increase problem-solving skills

OBJECTIVE The child will construct a block structure.

MATERIALS masking tape blocks and accessories

PROCEDURE In the block corner, use masking tape to map out a road and plots. Assign each child a plot and have them construct buildings. Ask children to decide what kinds of buildings (houses, restaurants, hospitals, firehouses, gas stations, apartments) their community needs and who is going to build them. Leave the construction style up to each child. Pose questions, such as, "Where would someone go if he got sick?" Expand the children's ideas if necessary. Emphasize group problem solving and a sense of community spirit.

Increase Level of Difficulty

Procedure Have the children help map out the roads and plots. Expand the block area and leave the structures up for several days. Allow the children to build additional structures and play in their "community."

Decrease Level of Difficulty

Procedure Decrease the number of building plots and more actively help children decide what they will build.

COMMENT This activity encourages children to play together, yet keeps firm boundaries about what is each child's territory if this is necessary. Use a variety of blocks from large, light ones to small, colored ones.

MEDICAL TOOLS

GOAL   To increase awareness of roles people play
To improve self-concept

OBJECTIVE   The child will match the equipment shown to the correct body part.

MATERIALS   Pictures of pieces of medical equipment and the parts of the body where these are most commonly used:

mouth: tongue depressor	arm: blood pressure cuff
throat: throat swab	eyes, ears, throat: small flashlight
knee: rubber hammer	lungs, heart: stethoscope
arm: intravenous system	bottom: needle and syringe

PROCEDURE   Have the children match the pictures of medical equipment to pictures of the appropriate body parts. This often leads to discussion about doctors and medical procedures.

Increase Level of Difficulty

Procedure   Discuss in more detail the equipment and how it is used. Include information on what doctors look for and why. Have a medical dictionary available so you can look up needed information.

Decrease Level of Difficulty

Procedure   Demonstrate how the tools are used on a child or doll. Begin with the most familiar ones.

COMMENT   Be sure to use the equipment the children in your class are most likely to encounter. This activity should help make all children's contact with the medical profession less frightening, and also help them realize that some of their classmates must see doctors more frequently than they do.

PATIENT IN THE HOSPITAL

GOAL   To increase awareness of roles people play
To improve self-concept

OBJECTIVE   The child will participate in the game and discuss the roles of the people the "patient" comes in contact with.

MATERIALS   None

PROCEDURE   Adapt the song "The Farmer in the Dell" to your specific purposes relative to the medical profession.

There's a child who is sick,
There's a child who is sick.
Hi Ho the Office O.
There's a child who is sick.

"There's a child going to the doctor" and "There's a child going to the hospital" can also be used. In the following stanzas, the child chooses someone to accompany him to the hospital (mother, father, grandmother, aunt), that person chooses the doctor, the doctor chooses the nurse (or specialists). Then:

They all stand together,
They all stand together.
Hi Ho the Office O.
Until the child gets better.

Increase Level of Difficulty

Procedure   Precede the song by talking about some of the various specialists and what they do. Include the speech and language therapist, occupational therapist, physical therapist, psychologist, family therapist, different types of doctors (pediatrician, neurologist, surgeon, and so on).

Decrease Level of Difficulty

Materials   Pictures of the specialists or significant equipment that is a clue to their job

Procedure   Have the children hold the picture or equipment (stethoscope, thermometer) as a clue.

COMMENT   Children encounter many members of the health profession, and this activity helps make the interaction fun rather than threatening. Let the children choose whom they want to include.

Social Studies

AUDIOLOGIST

GOAL   To increase awareness of roles people play
          To increase inclusion
          To improve self-concept

OBJECTIVE   The child will play the role either of the audiologist or the patient.

MATERIALS   Props for an audiologist's office:

        bells

        ear muffs

        a box with knobs

        buzzers

PROCEDURE   During group time, introduce the concept of an audiologist and what he does. Talk about how and why people get their hearing tested. Then explain that there is an audiologist's office set up in the dramatic play area. Use a box with knobs on it; bells, buzzers, or anything that makes noise; and ear muffs for earphones. Have the children "test" each other's hearing. They can raise a hand when they hear a noise.

Increase Level of Difficulty

Procedure   Erect a barrier so one child can't see what is happening and has to rely on sound to respond. Ask children to identify the sound.

Decrease Level of Difficulty

Procedure   Ask children to do a task, such as stack a circle on a stick, each time they hear a noise.

COMMENT   Use this activity to prepare all the children to have their hearing tested by a school nurse. Allow children for whom this is a common practice to take a leadership role and work through any feelings that they have about the procedure.

Social Studies

EYE DOCTOR

GOAL   To increase awareness of roles people play
          To increase inclusion
          To improve self-concept

OBJECTIVE   The child will play the role of either the eye doctor or the patient.

MATERIALS   Props for an eye doctor's office:

        vision chart (the chart the children will be tested with) or a similar homemade
           vision chart

card with a "three-legged table" to be matched to the chart (see illustration)

glasses   index card

frames   pointer

mirror

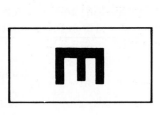

Card

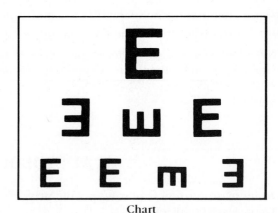

Chart

PROCEDURE During group time, discuss eye doctors and what they do. Explain that you have set up the dramatic play area as an eye doctor's office. Encourage one child to be the doctor and point to the letters, another to be an assistant and help with glasses and the testing process. Have the children match the card to the chart to become familiar with the procedure. Have them talk about these roles and how they feel about them.

Increase Level of Difficulty

Procedure Have children experiment with the relationship between distance and seeing, and have them find where in the room they can no longer see accurately. They can measure this distance.

Decrease Level of Difficulty

Procedure Concentrate on the matching aspect of this experience at a distance where you are sure children can see.

COMMENT Follow this activity with vision screening by a nurse or other qualified person. Eye Doctor teaches children how doctors help people see better and may also identify some children with vision needs.

Social Studies

EMERGENCY ROOM

GOAL To increase awareness of roles people play

To increase problem-solving skills

To improve self-concept

OBJECTIVE The child will play the role of either the doctor or the patient.

MATERIALS An emergency room set-up:

table	paper
chairs	pencils
bandages	lab coat

PROCEDURE Set up the dramatic play area as an emergency room. During group time, talk about the reasons for going to the emergency room: a broken bone, a bad cut or burn, as opposed to a headache or a cold. Talk to the children about what would be likely to happen: someone would ask for their name and insurance number, and they would have to wait. Also discuss what they could do while they wait, what the doctor might do, and the possibility that they would not know the doctor.

Increase Level of Difficulty

Procedure   Stress the importance of time, and how something that is life-threatening comes ahead of what is not, regardless of when you arrived.

Decrease Level of Difficulty

Procedure   Emphasize that you go here for an emergency and that the doctor will not be one you know.

COMMENT   The purpose of this activity is really to familiarize the child with a set of procedures so that the fear of the emergency room is not added to the medical problem if they should have to go. Try to have an element of realism as well as creativity. See this as a variation on the doctor's office, although the element of time, the reasons for going to the emergency room, and the other people in the waiting room are different.

Social Studies

WHO AM I?

GOAL   To increase awareness of roles people play
To increase problem-solving skills
To increase inclusion

OBJECTIVE   The child will act out in pantomime the role suggested by the hat.

MATERIALS   Characteristic hats:

firefighter's hat	fishing hat	baseball hat
police officer's hat	cowboy hat	baby's bonnet
hardhat	woman's hat	rain hat
stocking cap	football helmet	sunbonnet

PROCEDURE   Show the collection of hats to the children. Have them figure out what person would wear each hat and act out that person's role in pantomime. At first use hats that are specific to one role, then use some to broaden ideas; that is, a woman's hat could be worn by a mother, teacher, secretary, or lawyer. Talk about the characteristics of the hats that make them suitable for the people who wear them.

Increase Level of Difficulty

Materials   Similar hats from other areas and cultures

Procedure   Help children understand the efficacy of hats and how they are different based on where you wear them. Focus on the purpose of the hat. Look at the subtle differences among similar hats (football helmets, motorcycle helmets, and bicycle helmets) and help children understand why they are different.

Decrease Level of Difficulty

Procedure   Start with what children know. What hats do they wear and why? Then concentrate on hats of people who are familiar to them. Again, help them ascertain the purpose of the hat.

COMMENT   This activity is a different way of approaching community helpers because it uses one clue and leaves the rest to the child. Be sure to talk about the purpose of hats in general.

Social Studies

BE THE TEACHER

GOAL   To increase awareness of roles people play
To improve self-concept
To follow directions

OBJECTIVE   The child will imitate the teacher by giving directions to the children.

MATERIALS   None

PROCEDURE   During group time, pick one child to help you give instructions. Pick a routine that you have done frequently, such as the calendar or dismissing the class. Help him give specific directions: "All children who have plaid shirts may go to free play."

Increase Level of Difficulty

Procedure   Give children greater responsibility for a longer time. They might be the teacher and lead singing as well as the transition.

Decrease Level of Difficulty

Procedure   Have the child do part of the task, that is, you would dismiss about half of the children and she would have only part of the transition.

COMMENT   Children need practice in being in charge when they can be successful. It is helpful to talk about how they feel when other children are not attentive.

Social Studies

LIBRARY

GOAL   To increase awareness of roles people play
 To increase inclusion
 To improve reading readiness

OBJECTIVE   The child will pretend he is taking books out of the library and returning them.

MATERIALS   Props for a library:

　　　　　books　　　cards　　　　posters

PROCEDURE   Set up a library in your room with a collection of children's books that can be categorized by the pictures on the front; use books about the country, animals, people, and so on. Encourage children to look over the selection and ask for the books they want. Be sure some children are librarians and some borrowers.

Increase Level of Difficulty

Procedure   Have the children categorize the books by topical area of interest and mark them so they know the area. Encourage the other children to ask for books on specific topics. Talk with them about the role of a reference librarian. Encourage them to develop a system for checking the books in and out.

Decrease Level of Difficulty

Procedure   Have the children select a book and check it out. Be sure to provide time to look at the book.

COMMENT   Children need to learn to enjoy books from an early age. This activity provides an opportunity to be in control of the books and to make choices. It also helps children become familiar with library procedures.

Social Studies

CAST IT

GOAL   To increase awareness of roles people play
 To increase awareness of individual differences
 To encourage creative problem solving

OBJECTIVE   The child will put a cast on either a doll or a classmate.

MATERIALS   plaster tape (available at most drug stores)   water

scissors without points   dolls

broken chicken bone

PROCEDURE   Talk about broken bones: show one from an animal and talk about what a cast does for a bone. Set up the dramatic play area with plaster tape (just soak it in water to use it), a bucket of water, and dolls. First, have the children experiment with a doll. Then, if you want, have them put a cast on a thumb or finger. The cast will slip off, but you might feel more secure if you have some blunt-nosed fingernail scissors so you can cut off any stubborn ones. Discuss with the children that breaking bones hurts, but casting doesn't.

CONTINUATION   If most of the children put casts on their thumbs, you can make an art project out of decorating the casts.

Increase Level of Difficulty

Materials   X ray

Procedure   Bring in an X ray of a broken bone and show it to the children. Help them understand the purpose of the cast and why it is important that the bone be both set and cast.

Decrease Level of Difficulty

Procedure   Allow the children to explore the plaster tape as if it were an art medium.

COMMENT   You might warn parents about this project so they will know their child's thumb isn't really broken when he wears his cast home. It is possible that any child in your class may have to have a cast put on. Children who know how and why casts are put on and taken off are less fearful when they need an actual cast.

Social Studies

NO WORDS

GOAL   To increase problem-solving skills

To increase awareness of individual differences

OBJECTIVE   The child will state how he feels when others don't understand him.

MATERIALS   None

PROCEDURE   Have a discussion about how animals and people communicate without using words.

bees: dance to help other bees find honey

dogs: bark, wag tails

birds: chirp

people: gesture

Give one child in the class instructions for a task the group must perform. Have him get the other children to carry out the task without using words. Initially all the children could do the same thing—for example, go to the bathroom and wash their hands. As the children get better at this, you could give more difficult tasks.

Increase Level of Difficulty

Procedure   Give the children more difficult tasks.

Decrease Level of Difficulty

Procedure   Make the tasks easier and have a pair of children convey the message.

COMMENT   Discuss the differences between using nonverbal "language" and words, especially in relation to how long it takes to convey information without words. Lead this into a general discussion of communication and how difficult it is to express yourself when you don't know the right words to say. Point out examples of nonverbal body language people use.

Social Studies

ONE MORE

GOAL   To increase problem-solving skills
To increase expressive language

OBJECTIVE   The child will state at least four different possible solutions to a given problem.

MATERIALS   None

PROCEDURE   Make up hypothetical situations or use actual problems that have occurred in the classroom. The situations can relate to peer relationships, sharing materials, time with the teacher, and so forth. For example, if two children want the same toy, ask them for a solution, then ask, "What else could you do?" See if children can generate at least four different alternatives to consider. Don't give children solutions or judge their answers as inappropriate although they may seem outlandish to you. It is important that children learn to generate alternatives as a way of coping.

Increase Level of Difficulty

Procedure   Expand the scope of the problems. Help children evaluate the probable outcome of each solution and decide which they might try first.

Decrease Level of Difficulty

Procedure   Support all solutions and encourage children to help each other.

COMMENT   The more complex situations children are in the more likely they will need to find solutions to problems. They may need to try several options before they find one that works.

Social Studies

CHARADES

GOAL   To increase problem-solving skills
To improve observational skills

OBJECTIVE   Without using words, one child will act out his object or action for the other to guess.

MATERIALS   pictures of people, animals, or objects

pictures of someone doing something:

getting a drink	going outside
getting a cookie	getting in the car
putting on a coat	

PROCEDURE   Give the child a picture or tell him what he is to pantomime.

Increase Level of Difficulty

Procedure   Make the pictures more difficult. Include titles of books that children know. Teach them some of the codes that charade players have developed.

Decrease Level of Difficulty

Procedure   Give hints and suggestions to both actors and guessers until the children catch on.

COMMENT   Encourage awareness of nonverbal communications and how hard it is to communicate accurately without speech.

HANDS AND FEET

GOAL   To increase problem-solving skills
To increase awareness of individual differences
To increase body awareness

OBJECTIVE   The child will place the objects appropriately.

MATERIALS   flannel board

pictures of hands and feet

a variety of small pictures that will adhere to the flannel board:

keys	socks	gloves
spoons	boots	slippers
mittens	shoes	swim fins
rings		

PROCEDURE   Have the children pick a picture and place it on the flannel board near the hands or the feet.

Increase Level of Difficulty

Materials   Additional small pictures that will adhere to the flannel board that can show the function of the hands and feet as well:

lake	How do you get there?
puzzle	How do you do this?
pen	How do you write with this?

Procedure   Discuss what might be hard to do without hands and feet and how people compensate. Tie this into a dramatic play activity.

Decrease Level of Difficulty

Materials   Use real objects instead of pictures.

Procedure   Have children actually do the task.

COMMENT   If you have a child with a missing limb in your classroom, consult with her before choosing an activity like this one. Find out whether or not the child wants to show or tell others how she compensates. Children who have had broken limbs might want to share their experiences.

WHO HAS BEEN HERE?

GOAL   To increase problem-solving skills
To make predictions
To improve cause-and-effect reasoning

OBJECTIVE   The child will describe who would make the designated footprints and give a reason for his choice.

MATERIALS   A variety of footwear in different sizes and for different purposes:

baby shoes	high heels	sneakers
baseball spikes	hiking boots	roller skates

| ice skates | clogs | gold shoes |
| ballet slippers | toe shoes | riding boots |

water-based paint

paper (8½″ × 11″)

PROCEDURE Make footprints with the shoes by putting the bottom of the shoes in paint, then printing each one on a sheet of paper. (You might let the children walk or skate in them.) Make at least six footprints with each pair of footwear. Start by showing the children footprints that are about the size they would make. Ask them to arrange the prints as if someone were walking. Ask the children to describe the size of the person and where the person might be going. Have the children walk on the prints to see if the spacing is right; help them correlate the size of footprints with the spacing between footprints. Then help the children view the prints of specialty footwear and decide under what conditions they would be most useful.

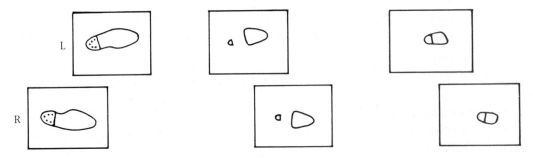

Increase Level of Difficulty

Procedure   Have a specialty footwear store in the dramatic play area; the children can describe the circumstances and activities they want shoes for.

Decrease Level of Difficulty

Procedure   First use only one type of shoe, differing only in size (for example, sneakers). Have children match the shoe to the print. gradually add the more specialized footwear.

COMMENT   Thinking skills are both challenging and fun. You might have children design shoes for various environments (swamp versus desert). Be sure to include shoes from a variety of places—moccasins, thongs, clogs, and so on. For added cues, use textured paint so the children can feel the prints as well as see them.

Inclusion

I'M THINKING OF

GOAL   To increase inclusion
To improve self-concept
To increase awareness of individual differences

OBJECTIVE   The child will guess the person or object.

MATERIALS   None

PROCEDURE   This is a variation of the game "Twenty Questions" but is used as a teaching tool to help children realize when they don't have enough information.

TEACHER: I'm thinking of someone with brown hair. Who am I thinking of?
CHILD: Me.
TEACHER: I could be thinking of you, but you can't be sure. Listen. I'm thinking of someone with brown hair and a plaid shirt. Who am I thinking of?
CHILD: Sam.

TEACHER: *I could be thinking of Sam, but who else has brown hair and a plaid shirt?*
CHILD: *Tom.*
TEACHER: *Listen then. I'm thinking of . . .*

Increase Level of Difficulty

Procedure   Make the clues more subtle to help children develop the skills of classification and observation. Give children two or more characteristics to consider at one time: "I'm thinking of someone who has blond hair, who loves to paint, and whose last name starts with J."

Decrease Level of Difficulty

Procedure   Take the game a step at a time and keep eliminating children. Make the clues obvious.

COMMENT   This activity is designed to create a sense of group belonging; children learn that they are all both similar to and different from each other. The activity is not demanding. Children can participate either verbally or nonverbally. Be sure not to pick out stereotypic characteristics; don't say, "I'm thinking of someone in a wheelchair."

Inclusion

MY DAY

GOAL   To increase inclusion
To improve self-concept
To increase awareness of individual differences

OBJECTIVE   The child will help the teacher plan a special event.

MATERIALS   None

PROCEDURE   Have a celebration on each child's birthday or some other designated day, and have the child help you plan for his favorite things. Be sure the choices are ones you can actually follow through on; do you want fingerpaint or easel paint provided, or are you willing to have either? Encourage the child to set up the dramatic play area, blocks, pick the snack; plan a parade, a picnic, and so on.

Increase Level of Difficulty

Procedure   Show the child the lesson plans you do and how you plan each day. Allow the child to participate in the process as you might a new student teacher.

Decrease Level of Difficulty

Procedure   Use your knowledge of what the child likes to make suggestions. Have the child choose between two alternatives rather than asking her to generate the ideas.

COMMENT   This activity is good for all children. It can be used to highlight their uniqueness and to help them develop a sense of belonging. Include their favorite activities (in some blend that is teachable), and try to indicate to the class why a child might choose certain activities and reject others.

Inclusion

SHARE YOUR FEELINGS

GOAL   To increase inclusion
To improve self-concept
To increase expressive language

OBJECTIVE   The child will share a feeling with his classmates.

MATERIALS   None

PROCEDURE   After the children have discussed feelings and expressions, ask them to share a feeling with the other children. For example, love. Some ways the children might share this are to hold hands, kiss, hug, say "I love you," and so on.

Increase Level of Difficulty

Procedure   Help children think of a variety of ways to share feelings, both verbal and nonverbal.

Decrease Level of Difficulty

Procedure   Support children in expressing feelings with their peers and knowing that they are valued members of the class. Be sure to give children the vocabulary they need to express their feelings accurately.

COMMENT   Sharing feelings is not usual in some cultures. At first older children might feel self-conscious doing this activity, but if you demonstrate and encourage them, they are usually willing to follow.

Inclusion

WHEELS

GOAL   To increase inclusion
  To improve cause-and-effect reasoning

OBJECTIVE   The child will state the function of wheels in moving objects.

MATERIALS   Pictures of familiar objects with wheels:

wagons	tricycles
roller skates	toy cars

PROCEDURE   Have the children discuss the function of wheels and encourage them to experiment moving on or using things with wheels. If you happen to have shelves on wheels, have the children compare moving those shelves with shelves not on wheels. When you are outside, keep the wheels of a tricycle or wagon from turning by putting something through the spokes and discuss how this affects its movement. Be sure to include a wheelchair. Talk about brakes as well.

Increase Level of Difficulty

Procedure   Help children experiment by using rollers to move objects. Encourage them to use a wheelchair on a ramp to see the difference in energy it takes to go up and to go down. (Be sure to have an adult with the child in the chair.)

Decrease Level of Difficulty

Procedure   Allow children to experiment with the wheelchair to see how it works.

COMMENT   Children can learn about the functions wheels play in moving and at the same time become more aware of the implications of using a wheelchair.

Inclusion

FROM YOUR HOUSE TO MINE

GOAL   To increase inclusion
  To improve measurement concepts

OBJECTIVE   The child will trace a path from his house to a classmate's.

MATERIALS   a simple laminated map of the community that includes the school and the children's houses (Each house should have a child's name or picture on it.)

  crayons

  tissue

PROCEDURE   Set the map on a table with several crayons beside it. Encourage the children to pick a friend and work together to trace a path from one child's house to the other child's house. Use the tissue to erase the crayon.

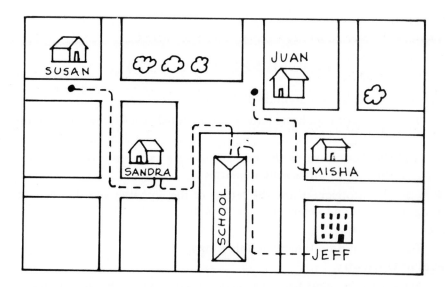

Increase Level of Difficulty

Procedure   Help children map out a walk or field trip. Encourage children to find alternative routes.

Decrease Level of Difficulty

Procedure   Start with a map of the classroom and have children use the map to go to a certain area.

COMMENT   This activity is a way of increasing children's understanding of their community and of what is near the school.

Inclusion

CUTTING CARDBOARD

GOAL   To increase awareness of individual differences

OBJECTIVE   The child will state his feelings about cutting the cardboard.

MATERIALS   scissors   cardboard (from the back of tablets)

PROCEDURE   Draw intricate designs on cardboard and have the children try to cut out the design. Given children's scissors and the coordination of children this age, this task will be difficult. Discuss how the children feel about not being able to accomplish this task and relate it to how hard it is for them to cut out even simple designs on paper. Discuss that some things are easy and some hard for all children. Talk about how it feels to do things that are hard. Ask, for example, how they felt while attempting the task: if they wanted to leave and do something else; wanted to get help from the teacher; wanted to talk to their friends; and so on. Have them talk about which things are easy and hard for each of them and how they can help each other do difficult tasks (don't do it for someone, don't tease, don't tell them to hurry up, and so on).

Increase Level of Difficulty

Procedure   Make the designs more intricate or time the children to see how quickly they can accomplish the task.

Decrease Level of Difficulty

Procedure   Use simpler designs.

COMMENT   This activity is designed to help children gain some insight into the frustrations that result from attempting a task that is difficult. Talk with the children about how they might feel if everyone else thought the task an easy one and they couldn't succeed.

FINGER SPELLING LOTTO

GOAL   To increase awareness of individual differences

OBJECTIVE   The child will match the letters of the alphabet with the appropriate finger spelling letters.

MATERIALS   Alphabet Lotto cards with Ameslan signs for each letter (example of signs in glossary of Chapter 11 on hearing impairment)

PROCEDURE   Make a Lotto game using the letters of the alphabet and the manual signs for those letters. Encourage the children to make the sign with their hands as they match the cards.

Increase Level of Difficulty

Procedure   Have the children finger spell their names.

Decrease Level of Difficulty

Procedure   Start with the signs that have some visual resemblance to the letters they represent (e.g., *c, d, i, l, m, n, o, v*).

COMMENT   This activity shows children another representation of language and a potential avenue of communication.

MUFFLES

GOAL   To increase awareness of individual differences

OBJECTIVE   The child will discuss how it feels to have trouble understanding speech while playing with others.

MATERIALS   ear muffs or cotton balls

record player and records   *or*

tape recorder and tapes

PROCEDURE   Set up the dramatic play area in the usual way. Have the children wear ear muffs or put cotton balls in their ears and tell them to whisper while playing instead of talking out loud. You can add to the effect by having a record or tape playing in the background to make it even harder to hear the speech. Follow this activity with a discussion at group time. Start your discussion by talking very softly while the music is playing. When the children get restless and frustrated, go back to your normal style. Talk about how hard it is to cooperate with others and to pay attention when you can't hear.

Increase Level of Difficulty

Procedure   Spend a whole day this way.

Decrease Level of Difficulty

Procedure   Shorten the amount of time children play this way.

COMMENT   Children can begin to better understand the implications of not being able to hear well.

NEW DOLL

GOAL   To increase awareness of individual differences

OBJECTIVE   The child will tell how he feels about the new doll.

MATERIALS   A child-size (4′) doll dressed in typical clothes

PROCEDURE   Bring the doll into the classroom and give it special privileges: Let it sit beside you during group time, point out how well it is dressed and how special it is, but don't let the children touch it for fear they will break it or get it dirty. When they are allowed to touch it, tell them how careful they must be. Have some "presents" for the new doll—clothes, books, and so on. Then discuss with the children how they feel about this new doll and its privileges and whether or not they want the doll to visit again. Discuss ways of dealing with these feelings.

Increase Level of Difficulty

Procedure   Have a baby visit. Discuss the good and bad points of new babies. Read stories on this subject. Discuss how having a baby is different from having a doll (more time-consuming, messier, and so on).

Decrease Level of Difficulty

Procedure   Shorten the discussion to the most obvious points.

COMMENT   Children appreciate a chance to talk about their feelings of neglect when they have a new sibling or a family member who has a disability.

Inclusion

NOISY TASKS

GOAL   To increase awareness of individual differences

OBJECTIVE   The child will state how it feels to work in a noisy environment.

MATERIALS   record and record player   *or*

tape and tape player

noisemakers

PROCEDURE   Have the children do some task that requires a lot of concentration (coloring intricate designs, lacing a paper plate). Tell them you want them to do this task as fast as they can without making mistakes. Time them (2 minutes is about right). Spend another 2 minutes in the same activity, either before or after, but provide as many distractions as possible: Turn the lights on and off; talk loudly to an aide; bang some things together; open and shut the door; stomp around; and so on. Have the children count how many holes they laced or squares they colored under each set of circumstances. You could graph the results for the whole class if you choose. Talk with the children about how easy or difficult it was for them to work with lots of distractions. Then explain to the class that for some children even small distractions prevent them from working well.

Increase Level of Difficulty

Procedure   Increase the importance of the task; be clear that it has to be completed in the specified time.

Decrease Level of Difficulty

Procedure   Focus on the experience itself and how each child felt.

COMMENT   Talk about distractions, such as the TV at home, traffic noise, loud music, and so on. Help children think back to this activity as a reminder of how difficult it is to work with distractions.

Inclusion

SAD

GOAL   To increase awareness of individual differences

OBJECTIVE   The child will draw a picture of a situation in which she felt sad.

MATERIALS   paper   crayons   markers

PROCEDURE   Have children make a book of drawings of situations in which they were sad (or angry, unhappy, or mad). When most of the children have had time to put in several entries, have a group discussion and talk about how children might feel if a lot of sad things happen at one time, how hard it would be to be happy, and how they might even be scared and expect sad things to happen. Talk about what children can do to make themselves feel better when they feel sad.

Increase Level of Difficulty

Procedure   Encourage children to talk in greater depth and to determine short- and long-term emotions. Have them discuss how the actions and reactions of others influence their response.

Decrease Level of Difficulty

Procedure   Focus on the most obvious situations.

COMMENT   This helps all children realize that everybody, including adults, has some "down" days.

Inclusion

TIRED

GOAL   To increase awareness of individual differences

OBJECTIVE   The child will name at least two activities he doesn't want to do when he's tired.

MATERIALS   None

PROCEDURE   Encourage children to run or jump very actively until they are tired (they could run or jump in place if the weather is bad). Then have them list the activities they wouldn't want to do right away (run more, climb fast, ride a tricycle, and so on) and those they would do (quiet activities like

Inclusion requires adaptability. A block under the table may be all that is necessary to participate in lunch time.

listening to a story or record). Talk about how children differ in how easily they get tired and how it isn't fun to play actively when you're tired.

Increase Level of Difficulty

Procedure   Encourage children to talk about the difference between what they don't want to do because of lack of energy and tasks they just don't like (cleaning their room, picking up in general, and so on). Ask them if they ever use being tired as an excuse. Do they ever not believe others in this situation?

Decrease Level of Difficulty

Procedure   Focus on the obvious differences.

COMMENT   All children know how it feels to be tired. They need to learn that others may feel tired when they don't. Encourage children to tell each other when they are tired and suggest things they can still do together.

Inclusion

TONGUE TWISTERS

GOAL   To increase awareness of individual differences

OBJECTIVE   The child will state how he feels after saying a difficult "tongue twister" fast.

MATERIALS   None

PROCEDURE   Teach children some tongue twisters, then encourage them to say them fast. This often results in both laughter and the realization that some things are difficult for all of us to say. For example:

The bootblack brought the book back.
Beth brought a big blue bucket of blueberries.
Big black bugs buckle and bulge beneath the big blue bundle.
Betty Balder bought some butter for her bread batter.
Greek grape growers grow great grapes.
Peter Piper picked a peck of pickled peppers.
Suzy sells seashells down by the seashore.
The sixth sheik's sixth sheep's sick.
Red roosters read riddles rapidly.

Increase Level of Difficulty

Procedure   Have children make up their own tongue twisters. It is good language exercise.

Decrease Level of Difficulty

Procedure   See if the children can say the tongue twister more slowly.

COMMENT   This activity promotes awareness and, done slowly, is an interesting way of practicing specific initial sounds.

Inclusion

VOICELESS ROLL CALL

GOAL   To increase awareness of individual differences

OBJECTIVE   The child will respond to his name in an appropriate way.

MATERIALS   None

PROCEDURE   Call roll, but mouth the names instead of speaking them out. Use your regular form for response. Discuss how difficult voiceless roll call is, especially how hard it is to keep paying attention.

Increase Level of Difficulty

Procedure   When the children get the idea, tell them voicelessly what activities are available and ask them to make choices.

Decrease Level of Difficulty

Procedure   Call on the children who will have the most difficult time near the beginning.

COMMENT   You may have to practice a bit before you are comfortable calling roll this way. Discuss with the children why it would be impossible for a child who is severely visually impaired to participate.

Inclusion

WHO IS IT?

GOAL   To increase awareness of individual differences

OBJECTIVE   The child will identify a classmate by touch.

MATERIALS   A blindfold

PROCEDURE   Blindfold one child and have him touch another child. You will have to give some guidance at first on the appropriate ways to touch another person. You might even guide the child's hand to feel the length of hair, type of shoes and clothes, facial features, and so on. Help the child by telling him what to feel for:

Let's see. Who has long, straight hair, and is wearing a long-sleeved blouse, a sweater that buttons down the front, a pleated skirt, knee socks, and tie shoes?

Increase Level of Difficulty

Procedure   Don't give the child any clues.

Decrease Level of Difficulty

Procedure   Choose a child to identify who has very obvious features or one that is a good friend. Have the child talk.

COMMENT   This activity gives children the experience of "seeing" with their hands as a child who is blind might. It also shows them some of the difficulties such children face.

Inclusion

FOREIGN LANGUAGES

GOAL   To increase awareness of individual differences
         To improve listening skills

OBJECTIVE   The child will be able to recognize when speech is in English and when it is not.

MATERIALS   None

PROCEDURE   Sing or play a record of a familiar song in a foreign language. Ask children what the words mean and discuss how some words are the same or similar in several languages. Then teach the English version. "Frère Jacques" is one of the most familiar songs; there are many holiday songs that are appropriate. Discuss with the children how hard it is to listen and pay attention when you don't understand.

Increase Level of Difficulty

Procedure   If there is a Spanish or French TV or radio station in your area, ask the children to listen to it, or use an audio tape of a foreign language. Help children become more aware of other languages and how difficult it is to learn another language but also how valuable.

Decrease Level of Difficulty

Procedure   Have children work on differentiating English from non-English. Use a variety of languages if possible so children understand that there are many different languages.

COMMENT   Encourage children to think about their dependence on language to communicate and what the problems are when you do not speak the language of the people around you.

Inclusion

SIMULATED GLASSES

GOAL   To increase awareness of individual differences
To improve observation skills

OBJECTIVE   The child will state what he sees using various types of glasses.

MATERIALS   glasses frames or sunglasses   gauze
half-face Halloween masks   cellophane
adhesive tape

To simulate visual conditions, you can use inexpensive sunglasses or the Halloween masks. When you cover the eye holes put the cellophane over the inside opening or make sure the sticky side of the tape faces outward.

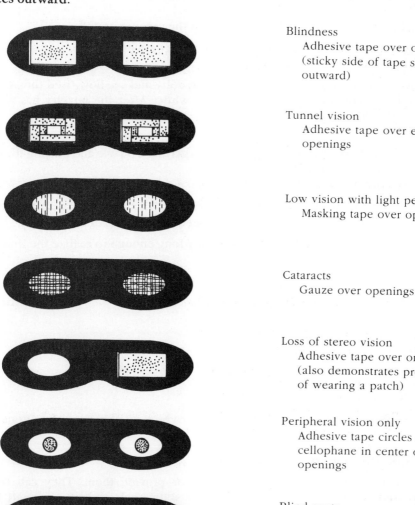

Blindness
Adhesive tape over openings
(sticky side of tape should face
outward)

Tunnel vision
Adhesive tape over edges of
openings

Low vision with light perception
Masking tape over openings

Cataracts
Gauze over openings

Loss of stereo vision
Adhesive tape over one opening
(also demonstrates problem
of wearing a patch)

Peripheral vision only
Adhesive tape circles on
cellophane in center of
openings

Blind spots
Small adhesive tape circles on
cellophane over openings

PROCEDURE   Have children talk about what they can and cannot see with the glasses. Encourage them to wear the glasses and then do what they usually do during the day. Talk with them about what is easy to do with the glasses and what is difficult.

Increase Level of Difficulty

Procedure   Encourage children to use magnifying glasses and binoculars and talk about the changes these make in what they see.

Decrease Level of Difficulty

Procedure   Have the children use the special glasses for only a short time. Talk with them about how it feels.

COMMENT   Have the glasses available for several days so that children can continue to experiment with them. Children can progress from being aware of what a particular visual impairment means to the implications this has for daily life.

Inclusion

CREEPERS

GOAL   To increase awareness of individual differences
　　　　To increase body awareness

OBJECTIVE   The child will move around the classroom on the creeper or dolly.

MATERIALS   Several creepers, mechanic's dollies, or anything on wheels, several inches from the floor and propelled by the children's hands and feet

PROCEDURE   Have the children explore the room from the dolly and see how tired they get, what they can and can't reach, and how their body feels after a while. After the novelty has worn off, discuss with the children the limitations involved in moving around this way.

Increase Level of Difficulty

Procedure   Ask children to perform specific tasks such as getting a puzzle and putting it together, getting something from the locker area, and so on.

Decrease Level of Difficulty

Procedure   Focus first on the mechanics of using a creeper. This may be a new and different experience for some children and they may not have developed the muscles to do this task.

COMMENT   It is important to have children stay on the dolly long enough to realize the limitations.

Inclusion

MITTENS

GOAL   To increase awareness of individual differences
　　　　To increase body awareness

OBJECTIVE   The child will state how he feels when trying to pick up objects with mittens on.

MATERIALS   mittens
　　　　　　　　a variety of small objects

PROCEDURE   Have the children bring mittens to school or provide them. They can be worn throughout the day or used just to demonstrate fine motor skills such as stacking small blocks, interlocking shapes, eating snacks, stringing beads, coloring, and so on. Have children discuss how they feel after the day's activities. If they take the mittens off, ask why and discuss how they felt before and after.

Increase Level of Difficulty

Procedure   Have the children wear the mittens for the entire day.

Decrease Level of Difficulty

Procedure   Allow the children to take off the mittens when they become frustrated. However, encourage them to put them on again when they change tasks.

COMMENT   Through this activity all children become more aware of how useful their fingers are. They also gain an appreciation of the difficulties faced by children with fine motor coordination problems.

Inclusion

MOVING IN THE DARK

GOAL   To increase awareness of individual differences
            To increase body awareness

OBJECTIVE   The child will show how he can move safely in the dark.

MATERIALS   None

PROCEDURE   Make up a story about a child who has to go some place in the dark and is afraid of hitting his head. Have the children think of ways he could move so that he won't be hurt, then demonstrate these.

Log roll

Crab walk

Hold hands in front

Duck walk

Hitch

Increase Level of Difficulty

Procedure   Create some obstacles the child has to go around or through to add interest.

Decrease Level of Difficulty

Procedure   Make it more relevant to the child; help him understand that he could get up in the night and it might be dark. See if he can learn some specific techniques for moving.

COMMENT   This activity helps children become aware of their heads in space and the need to protect them. It also illustrates the problem of moving when you can't see.

Inclusion

SPECIAL DOLLS

GOAL   To increase awareness of individual differences
            To increase body awareness

OBJECTIVE   The child will play with the dolls.

MATERIALS   To make a doll with hearing aid:

rubber or vinyl dolls	small plastic box (size proportionate to doll's size)	heavy needle
hearing aid		bias tape
ear molds	waxed thread	snap
bag to hold aid	plastic T-shaped plug (game parts are ideal)	felt

1. Heat the needle and make hole in doll's ear; enlarge with heated needle to accommodate the shaft of the plug.
2a. Make a hole in the shaft of the plug with the needle.
2b. Push the waxed thread through the hole in the shaft and knot.
3. Make holes in the box with the heated needle; open the box and insert ends of string through holes and knot.
4. Make slots in the top of the box with heated needle.
5. Cut rectangle of felt large enough to make bag for box, sew on three sides, leave top open.
6. Cut two strips of bias tape—one long enough to reach around the doll (side) and the other long enough to reach from the doll's waist in front over the doll's shoulders to the waistline in back doubled (top).
7a. Sew the side strip to one side of the bag.
7b. Sew one half of the snap to the other end and the other half to the bag.
7c. Sew the ends of the top strip to the top of the bag.
8. To assemble: Place box in bag on doll's chest; slip (top) bias tape strip over the doll's head; and wrap (side) strip around doll *through* loop made by (top) strip and snap on the other side.

To make a doll with casts:

flour paste	plastic bags
newspaper	1/2″ diameter dowel (or primary pencil if long enough)
paper towels	

1. Mix flour/water paste to a thin consistency.
2. Cover the area of the doll on which the cast is to be built with plastic.
3. Cover the plastic with 1 1/2″ strips of newspaper dipped in the paste mixture.
4. If applying hip/leg casts, after covering the plastic with one layer of newspaper, force the doll's feet apart and brace them with the dowel.
5. Continue to apply strips of newspaper until three layers have been applied and the dowel is covered.
6. Use 1 1/2″ strips of paper toweling to form a fourth layer.
7. Allow to dry at least two days.

To make a doll with leg braces:

tin (tuna or cat food cans work fine)	Velcro
leather	aluminum tubing
felt	paper fasteners
waxed thread	shoes to fit the doll
heavy needle	

1. Use tin snips to cut four strips of tin to the desired size (width and length).
2. Trim heavy rim from tin can.
3. Shape the tin around the doll's leg(s), thigh, and calf.

4a. Cut aluminum tubing to desired length. Flatten ends and drill two holes approximately $1/2$–$3/4''$ from the tip on each end.

4b. Place strips in position on the outside of the top band. Drill hole through tin to match the holes in the aluminum strips.

4c. Fasten strip to tin with paper fasteners.

4d. Repeat procedure for lower band but drill only one hole at the appropriate height from the bottom strip to secure the lower band. Secure with paper fasteners.

5. Wrap leather around the outside of both bands. Stitch in place using waxed thread. Leather should extend beyond the front edge far enough to overlap the ends.

6a. Cut felt and cover the inside of the band. Edges of felt should extend to cover the tin edges.

6b. Glue felt in place.

7. Sew Velcro to the ends of the leather to finish the closing.

8. Attach the braces to doll shoes with paper fasteners.

PROCEDURE   During group time introduce the doll to the group. Explain the doll's need briefly to the children. Then ask a child to take the doll to the doll corner to be included with the others. Encourage conversation about the doll, what it can and can't do as well as the other dolls, and how the children feel about the doll. Be sure not to make judgments if they don't like the doll. Some children probably won't.

Increase Level of Difficulty

Procedure   Make additional dolls and encourage children to see how they can interact together.

Decrease Level of Difficulty

Procedure   Support the children in exploring the dolls. Don't expect play until they are comfortable with how the doll works.

COMMENT   It is important that the dolls are attractive and don't appear to be broken. For example, don't use a doll with a missing arm to represent an amputee. It is just a broken doll and should be treated like one. Because children often use dramatic play to work through feelings and practice roles, these dolls offer children the opportunity to practice interacting with playmates who face different challenges. (Development of and directions for making dolls were provided by Marilyn Little, graduate student in Individual and Family Studies, College of Human Resources, University of Delaware, as part of her thesis requirements. Used with permission of Marilyn Little.)

Inclusion

TALKING

GOAL   To increase awareness of individual differences
To increase body awareness

OBJECTIVE   The child will state how he feels when others can't understand him.

MATERIALS   None

PROCEDURE   In a small group give a child a specific thing to say and then tell him how he has to use his mouth. For example:

Keep your teeth clenched while you talk.
Keep your lips closed.
Keep your tongue behind the lower teeth.

Have the children continue trying to make themselves understood until they experience some frustration and can empathize with the child who has a speech problem. Discuss how it feels to the child when others don't understand his speech.

Increase Level of Difficulty

Procedure   Help children focus on the function of the various parts of their mouths in speech. Help them specify how speech changes based on the parts of the mouth that they cannot use.

Decrease Level of Difficulty

Procedure   Demonstrate to the children the various ways of talking before asking them to do each one.

COMMENT   This activity can be varied by having an individual child talk into a tape recorder, then listen to himself. It is useful in helping children gain an understanding of speech problems.

Inclusion

SLINGS

GOAL   To increase awareness of individual differences
To increase body awareness
To encourage creative problem solving

OBJECTIVE   The child will state at least three things that are difficult to do using only one arm.

MATERIALS   A piece of material or scarf for each child, large enough to be made into a sling

PROCEDURE   During group time, talk about what it is like to have only one arm. (Some children are born with only one arm, others break their arms, and so on.) Have the children guess what things are difficult to do with just one arm, and encourage them to participate in activities in the dramatic play area with one arm in a sling. At the end of the period, help the children who participated to talk about the feelings and difficulties they had. Most children, especially younger ones, will become frustrated and take the sling off. That's fine, but be sure to use their experience of frustration to make your point.

Increase Level of Difficulty

Procedure   Put the child's dominant arm in the sling.

Decrease Level of Difficulty

Procedure   Put the child's nondominant arm in the sling.

COMMENT   This activity can increase children's perceptions of what kinds of adaptations having only one arm might require.

Health and Safety

NOT TO EAT

GOAL   To increase awareness of individual differences
To increase survival skills

OBJECTIVE   The child will state what substances are edible and which are not.

MATERIALS   A variety of substances, some edible (milk, peanut butter, nuts) and some not, (soap, playdough, sand)

PROCEDURE   Put the substances on a table and talk about which ones the children can eat and which ones might make them sick. Then talk about individual differences in things people can't eat. Children with allergies, for example, must avoid some foods. Mention the particular allergies of children in your class.

Increase Level of Difficulty

Procedure   Add foods that are eaten by animals (bird seed, dog food). Talk about the differences in what animals and people eat.

Decrease Level of Difficulty

Procedure   Start with obvious things that cannot be eaten, then include those that children often try. State the rules about how to decide what to eat.

COMMENT   Children must learn which food they can and cannot eat and that some children cannot eat some foods that are good for others. They may not be able to eat some food they really like. Discuss the temptation of "sneaking" these foods and the implications of that behavior.

Health and Safety

SEASONAL CLOTHING

GOAL   To increase survival skills
To improve expressive language
To improve cause-and-effect reasoning

OBJECTIVE   The child will state in what season various items of clothing are worn and why.

MATERIALS   articles of clothing or pictures of them

pictures of scenes of the four seasons labeled by season

PROCEDURE   Have the children sort the clothes or pictures into piles by season. Include fabric swatches to sort as well. Be sure to discuss why certain clothes and fabrics are chosen for different seasons.

SPRING	SUMMER	FALL	WINTER
long pants	swimsuit	long pants	snowsuit
sweater	shorts and sleeveless top	jacket	mittens
jeans	cotton	kneesocks	boots
flannels	eyelet	knit	fur
terrycloth	terrycloth	gabardine	wool
			velvet

Be sure to agree that some clothes for cool weather can be worn in spring or fall or all seasons. It is the reasoning that matters.

Increase Level of Difficulty

Materials   pictures of events that happen in various seasons

Procedure   Have children classify the events and also include appropriate clothing to be worn at the events. Add pictures of events to be classified as well.

SPRING	SUMMER	FALL	WINTER
trees bud	people swim	school starts	animals hibernate
birds build nests	people take vacations	leaves change colors	snow falls
wind blows		apples and pumpkins are harvested	trees drop leaves

Decrease Level of Difficulty

Procedure   Start with characteristic clothing from the season that you are currently in (a snowsuit in winter). Compare this to a swim suit. Start with the most obvious comparisons. Have the children try on the clothing and sort it into boxes. Make comments to support children's choices: "When you put mittens on, I can't see your hands. Mittens keep your hands warm."

COMMENT   This activity is an opportunity for children to talk about the predictability of seasonal change and how seasons are different in various climates. Children need to learn to be responsive to the weather as they choose their clothing. They can also learn about the protective quality of clothing. *Note:* This activity is only appropriate for places where there are four seasons. In places where there are rainy and dry seasons, that would be an obvious division. Relate the activity to the climate where you are.

SMELL CUES

GOAL   To increase survival skills
To improve expressive language
To improve cause-and-effect reasoning

OBJECTIVE   The child will state what the smell is, what the situation might be, and what to do after smelling the container.

MATERIALS   Small containers, each holding a cotton ball saturated with a familiar-smelling substance (paint, food, perfume, liquid smoke, and so on)

PROCEDURE   Have the children guess what the smells are, in what situations they would find them, and how they could respond. For example:

> paint, wet paint, don't touch
>
> food, mealtime, set the table
>
> smoke, danger, leave
>
> ammonia, cleaning time, pick up toys
>
> perfume, going out, say good-bye

A variety of behaviors is possible in all these situations. Support all appropriate behaviors and help children think of many different ways to respond.

Increase Level of Difficulty

Procedure   Increase the variety of smells under careful supervision. Where possible include smells of dangerous substances. Be very clear that these are dangerous and must be treated as dangerous. Obviously, this activity needs close supervision.

Decrease Level of Difficulty

Procedure   Tell children to smell and not to taste the substances, but use only substances that are safe to ingest.

COMMENT   Because of experience and visual association, small cues are meaningful to us, but they are not necessarily meaningful to children who have different experiences or those who have sensory impairments. These children may need to be specifically taught when a situation is dangerous. Some children are more curious and less cautious than others. They must learn that there are some things in the environment that it is not safe to experiment with, and that one cue about this is smell.

SYMPTOMS

GOAL   To increase survival skills
To improve expressive language
To increase body awareness

OBJECTIVE   The child will state what his symptoms are.

MATERIALS   None

PROCEDURE   Help the child develop the vocabulary to describe his symptoms and to give some information on the area and degree of the "hurt."

BODY PARTS	MEDICAL TERMS
tummy, stomach	vomit, throw up
head	dull pain

BODY PARTS	MEDICAL TERMS
arms, legs	sharp pain
knee, neck	sore
DEGREE TERMS	swollen, puffy
a little	dizzy
a lot	cut
small, little	blood, bleeding
large, big	hot, cold

Role play situations in which a child who is "hurt" tells you or another child what's wrong. Decide what to do in the case of various symptoms (dizzy—lie down; cut—wash it; swollen part—put ice on it; and so on).

Increase Level of Difficulty

Procedure   Help children learn more internal body parts as well as where they are located.

Decrease Level of Difficulty

Materials   Doll

Procedure   Use both the child's body and a doll to teach body parts. Role play the most likely events a child might encounter, for example, a cut or a stomachache.

COMMENT   This activity provides useful information for a child to have *before* he becomes ill. Be sure to include specific terms that children may need depending upon their impairment. Be sure that children understand that their objective is to be accurate, not creative.

Health and Safety

TRAFFIC SIGN HUNT

GOAL   To increase survival skills
To improve listening skills
To improve cause-and-effect reasoning

OBJECTIVE   The child will state what to do in response to each sign shown.

MATERIALS   story   traffic signs

PROCEDURE   This is an adaptation of the bear hunt. Start "walking" by putting your palms on your thighs in a rhythm.

Anyone want to go on a traffic sign hunt? OK, let's go. Close the gate (close with hand motions). We're coming to a corner. I see a sign (hold up a stop sign). What do you think it is? A stop sign! What do we have to do? (Stop. Hold up palms toward children.) OK, look both ways. (Look.) No cars. Let's cross the street. Hurry. (Increase beat of hand.) You don't wander across streets, but you don't have to run either. Oh, what's this? This is a railroad crossing sign. (Hold up.) See the tracks. Be very careful. Look both ways. Are the gates up or down? Listen, do you hear anything? Are there any lights flashing? OK, let's cross. Look again and let's go. Oh, there really are a lot of signs to look at when you go for a walk. What's this one? (Hold up yield sign.) What shape is that? What should we do? It's a little like a stop sign; we don't have to stop, just slow down (slow rhythm) and look around. If we see anyone, then we have to stop.

 Look, do you see anything? Hey, I see an elephant. Do we have to stop? Yep. The elephant has the right of way. We have to yield. Go very slowly. OK, he's gone. That was a nice rest. I wonder what other kinds of signs we'll see. Hey, that one has lights. It's green and yellow and red. What is it? (Hold up traffic light.) We have the green; now what do we do? We can go. I am beginning to get tired; how about you? No, well, ah, there is another sign. That's for a curve. Lean left or you'll get off the road. Do you think we're on a mountain? Let's slow down. Oh, what's that sign? (Hold up skull and crossed bones sign.) Danger. Let's get out of here. As fast you can, lean right, hurry back over the curve. Now, oh, there's the light; what color is it? Red.

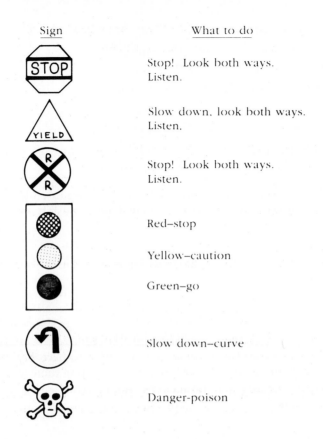

Sign	What to do
STOP	Stop! Look both ways. Listen.
YIELD	Slow down, look both ways. Listen.
RR	Stop! Look both ways. Listen.
(traffic light)	Red–stop
	Yellow–caution
	Green–go
(curve sign)	Slow down–curve
(skull and crossbones)	Danger–poison

Stop. OK, now it's green; let's go. There's the yield; is there anything coming? (Look.) We're OK, good, keep going. What will it be next? Oh, the railroad. Stop. Look. Listen. Any trains? Let's go. Hurry, oh, there's the stop sign; everybody stop. Look, let's go. Open the gate; shut it. Whee, it's good to be back here in our classroom.

Increase Level of Difficulty

Procedure   Add more signs, make the walk longer, and go faster.

Decrease Level of Difficulty

Procedure   Go over each sign with the children before you start the walk and be sure they know what to do. Make the walk slower and shorter.

COMMENT   Use your imagination and be dramatic. The children love it at the end when you go fast. This is good practice and yet fun. Children can participate at different levels.

Health and Safety

WARNING SOUNDS

GOAL   To increase survival skills
To improve listening skills
To improve cause-and-effect reasoning

OBJECTIVE   The child will state what he should do when he hears a specific sound.

MATERIALS   an audio tape with warning sounds   tape recorder

PROCEDURE   Make a tape recording of various warning sounds a child might hear and have him identify them. Include a broad range of sounds:

fire alarm	truck's beep (when backing up)
shouts of alarm	fire siren or whistle
police siren	bell buoy
car horn	fog horn
train whistle	calling a name
oven timer	"timber" (tree falling)
microwave timer	"fore" (golfers)
"watch out"	clothes dryer timer
smoke alarm	telephone sound when left off the hook

When the children can identify these sounds, have them name a sound and tell where they might hear it and what they should do when they hear it.

Increase Level of Difficulty

Procedure   Use more unusual sounds and ones that are more difficult to discriminate.

Decrease Level of Difficulty

Materials   videotape of objects making warning sounds

VCR

Procedure   Initially, show children a videotape of warning sounds and the objects making them. Talk about what the children should do in these circumstances. Start with the safety sounds they are most likely to encounter. Then use audio tape only.

COMMENT   Children need to depend upon their auditory cues for safety. This activity helps them determine what is happening in their environment whether or not they can actually see what is going on.

Safety rules can be taught at an early age. These children know where the tricycles can be ridden, and a barrier has been set up in case some children forget.

STOP AND GO

GOAL   To increase survival skills

To improve cause-and-effect reasoning

OBJECTIVE   The child will stop when red is held up and go when green is held up.

MATERIALS   Red and green pieces of paper

PROCEDURE   Adapt the traditional game of red light/green light by having the children walk when you hold up a piece of green construction paper and stop when you hold up a piece of red paper. Once children learn the process, increase the time between changes from red to green, and make some times very short so the children must pay close attention.

Increase Level of Difficulty

Materials   Yellow paper

Procedure   Using the same procedure, introduce the concept of caution to children. When holding up the yellow paper have them walk more slowly. Have a child be the traffic director and regulate the tricycles with the red, yellow, and green "lights."

Decrease Level of Difficulty

Procedure   Say the word "stop" with red and "go" with green.

COMMENT   Stop and Go is an important safety concept for all children to learn. Children need practice learning to wait for the signal to change as well as identifying the basic relationship between the color and what they should do.

WARNING SIGNS

GOAL   To increase survival skills

To improve cause-and-effect reasoning

OBJECTIVE   The child will demonstrate appropriate behavior when the sign is held up.

MATERIALS   Pictures of familiar warning signs (stop, yield, railroad crossing, one way, traffic lights, walk signals, and so on)

PROCEDURE   Introduce the various warning signs; be sure to include the ones near your school. Discuss with the children what the signs mean and what the children should do when they see them. Have the children role play situations. Use the signs outside in the play yard to direct traffic flow. Be sure to change the locations and directions frequently so children really do have to look. Follow this with a walk in the community and have children identify the signs.

Increase Level of Difficulty

Materials   Include more signs such as those that give information about places to camp, sleep, eat, and buy gas.

Procedure   Have children help make up signs to add to the play yard that include additional information about the area (swinging, no trikes, picnic area, and so on). Encourage children to think of significant ways of portraying the information they want to convey.

Decrease Level of Difficulty

Procedure   Focus first on the signs that are necessary for survival that the children are likely to encounter. Role play with the children while verbalizing for them what they are doing.

COMMENT   Obeying safety signs is necessary for all children. Those with sensory impairments may need specific help learning the cues; others may have difficulty waiting for the sign and readjusting when the signs change. This is an important experience for all children.

WHAT WOULD YOU DO IF?

GOAL   To increase survival skills
To improve cause-and-effect reasoning
To encourage creative problem solving

OBJECTIVE   The child will state four solutions to a problem.

MATERIALS   None

PROCEDURE   Think of a variety of problems a child might encounter and ask the children:

What would you do if
  you cut your finger?
  you smelled smoke or saw a fire?
  you broke a glass?
  you got lost?
  you fell down and couldn't get up?

The usual response will be to tell an adult. Support children in that response but continue to question the children: "What if there weren't an adult around?" Or, as the children solve the problem change the situation slightly: "I'd go outside." "What if the doors were locked?" Try to get children to think of as many solutions as possible, because in a true emergency, paths may be blocked. Discuss the implications of various solutions. Have children role play some of the situations.

Increase Level of Difficulty

Procedure   Call on children when the more obvious solutions have been suggested. Place some restrictions on them, such as not being able to speak the language, to see how they might help others solve the problem.

Decrease Level of Difficulty

Procedure   Call on less able children first.

COMMENT   It is especially important for children to know what to do if they are lost. In a real situation they would probably be scared as well. Having practiced solutions may help if the problem arises.

References and Bibliography

Hawkins, J., Lesliner, D., & Catalano, R. (1985). Childhood predictors and the prevention of adolescent substance abuse. *NIDA Research Monograph 56, Etiology of Drug Abuse— Implications for Prevention,* (pp. 75–126).

New guidelines on HIV infection (AIDS) announced for group programs (1989). *Young Children, 44*(1), 51.

Oyemade, U., & Washington, V. (1989). Drug abuse prevention begins in early childhood: (And is much more than a matter of instructing young children about drugs!) *Young Children, 44*(5), 6–12.

Phillips, C. (1988). Nurturing diversity for today's children and tomorrow's leaders. *Young Children, 43*(2), 42–47.

Rogers, C., & Morris, S. (1986). Reducing sugar in children's diets: Why? How? *Young Children, 41*(5), 11–19.

U.S. Department of Health & Human Services, Public Health Service (1987). *Report of the surgeon general's workshop on children with HIV infection and their families.* DHHS Publication No. HRS-D-MC 87-1.

Wardle, F. (1987). Are you sensitive to interracial children's special identity needs. *Young Children, 42*(2), 53–59.

Bibliography for Additional Reading

Cech, M. (1990). *Globalchild: Multicultural resources for young children.* Ottawa, Ontario: Child Care Initiatives.

Comer, D. (1987). *Developing safety skills with the young child.* Albany, NY: Delmar.

Derman-Sparks, L., & the A.B.C. Task Force (1989). *Anti-bias curriculum: Tools for empowering young children*. Washington, DC: National Association for the Education of Young Children.

Hale-Benson, J. (1986). *Black children: Their roots, culture, and learning styles* (rev. ed.). Baltimore: Johns Hopkins University Press.

Michaelis, J. U. (1985). *Social studies for children: A guide to basic instruction*. Englewood Cliffs, NJ: Prentice-Hall.

Seefeldt, C. (1989). *Social studies for the preschool-primary child* (3rd ed.). Columbus, OH: Merrill.

Saracho, O. N., & Spodek, B. (Eds.). (1983). *Understanding the multicultural experience in early childhood education*. Washington, DC: National Association for the Education of Young Children.

Yawkey, T. D., Dank, H. L., & Glosenger, F. L. (1986). *Playing inside and out: How to promote social growth and learning in young children including the developmentally delayed child*. Lancaster, PA: Technomic Publishing.

Chapter 27

Creative Arts: Art, Music, Creative Movement, and Dramatic Play

All children are creative. Some are more creative than others. Some children are more creative in one area than in other areas. As children feel the impact of the environment, the response they get to their creative efforts plays a large part in their creative development. Teachers have an important role in the development of creativity. They can actively support creativity or squelch it by concentrating only on the product that emerges.

As children get older they are increasingly rewarded for accurate convergent thinking. There are six chairs around the table. The child who counts "five" is wrong; the name of the color is red, not yellow; and so on. Children need to learn these facts. They also need to be supported in divergent thinking. The world is changing too quickly to predict the kinds of facts children will need in twenty years. They need to develop processes that allow many potential solutions and methods for figuring out how to solve problems. This approach to problem solving begins now. Children who know only how to acquire facts and who are rewarded for conformity and neatness may not be equipped to solve tomorrow's problems.

What is creativity? Creativity is a process of thinking, acting, or making something that is new or different. It doesn't mean that a person has to be the first one to produce a product, but it does mean it is a new experience for that particular person. For example, finger painting isn't new, but it can be a creative experience for a two-year-old as he explores the texture and qualities of finger paint. It can also be a creative experience for a **543** four-year-old as she experiments with new ways to apply the paint to the paper. A two-year-old and a four-year-old will work with finger paint very differently, but each can use it in a creative way.

The creative process can be thought of in two stages. The first is the thinking or idea stage. Children play with what they want to do in their mind. The second stage is the implementation stage. This is the "doing" stage. Children try out their ideas. This process is probably best thought of as a circular rather than a linear process, as children change what they have planned as they get feedback from the process.

Children gain many benefits when their creativity is fostered. This is a time when there are no right and wrong answers. Rewarding creativity helps develop a positive self-concept. It supports children's finding alternative solutions to problems and expressing their own ideas. Children learn to take risks to develop new skills and also learn about their own uniqueness.

As we look at children with disabilities it becomes clearer that as teachers we must support all children in developing nonconventional solutions to problems. Consider the quadraplegic artist who holds the paintbrush in her mouth, or Christy Brown, who typed a best-selling book with his left foot, or John Shaw Billings and Herman Hollerith who developed the 1890 Census Machine, the forerunner of the computer (NICHCY).

Teachers can support creativity in two major ways in children. The first involves supporting the creative process itself. The second involves providing the time, space, and materials necessary to foster creativity. Creative arts offer opportunities for individual participation as well as for being part of a group. A mural made after a field trip helps consolidate both the experience and group belonging. Participating in dramatic play involves learning about the roles of those in the community as well as negotiating with peers as to who plays those roles.

Art

Art for young children is messy, fun, and exploratory. It ranges from squashing sponges and watching how much paint drips to rolling and pounding playdough. It includes gluing paper, cloth, and macaroni to coloring or scribbling with water-based markers, chalk, or crayons. Art is actively engaging materials. It is not making something that looks like everyone else's. Nor is it gluing precut objects in the same place as everyone else. Art is an experience, a process. The best art may never hang on the refrigerator door. It may remain in the child's mind.

Art helps young children understand the properties of materials. Children's first response to any new medium is one of exploration. What can it do? What are the limits? What do I like to do with it? Curiosity abounds. Allowing children to explore these differences and helping them figure out the variables to test is far more useful than explaining to them that objects stuck with glue will stay when turned upside down, whereas paint is unlikely to hold objects together. They also learn that thin paint is more likely to run down a page than thick paint.

At about twelve months children can begin to do simple art projects. They will begin by exploring and experimenting with the media provided. They need to have a variety of experiences to abstract the important qualities of each medium. They begin to develop more purposeful activities around age two. We often call this the scribbling stage. This activity becomes more refined and starts to include patterns. By three, these patterns begin to have more structure and children are willing to tell you about them. The patterns are meaningful to them, but are rarely something you might recognize. Most three-year-olds are on the verge of developing the fine muscle skills and eye–hand coordination that is necessary for more purposeful drawing with a crayon. They still do better with large paintbrushes. Cutting with scissors is a difficult skill and probably should not be introduced until the child's fine motor skills are well developed, around age four. Children's pictures are now often recognizable.

With increasing age, products become more important, and this is the time when reinforcing the process is imperative. If children decide they don't draw well, they may decide not to draw. Some children will have better products than others. However, the process is still more important than the product.

To support art in your program you need to:

— Schedule time for children to paint, draw, glue, color, and use dough or clay each day.

— Do *not* provide a model for the children to copy. When children request a model, help them visualize what they want to draw and emphasize the process, not the product.

— Differentiate between art and fine motor development. Keep art activities for art. Teach academics like letter printing or coloring within the lines for other times.

— Show interest in what the children are doing and display everyone's original art work regardless of quality.

— Instead of asking "What did you make?", say "Tell me about your picture."

Art provides a lifelong means of expressing feelings and gaining enjoyment that is essential for all people. It allows children to be part of a group, while at the same time expressing their feelings and creativity without being judged as different or strange. Children can explore materials and express themselves in a visual form, and they can look back at past art work and see how they have changed.

Music

Music is enjoyable to most young children. It can be soothing or stimulating, it can promote social activity, and it can be used any time anywhere. Traditionally, music has not been integrated with the rest of the curriculum. It has been restricted to a "music period" and taught without any goal beyond the vague one of teaching children music. But music can be used to meet a number of educational needs. It can teach and/or reinforce skills that are part of other curriculum areas, such as recognizing colors and shapes, counting, and rhyming. Teaching goals must be specific and related to individual needs and differences. Music is fun, and it makes children want to use their bodies, their minds, and their creative energy.

Music is, however, a field in and of itself. It is a multisensory experience. Music can be used to foster learning skills without sacrificing the goals and objective of a music education program. Children can learn new words and develop memory as they recall songs or parts of songs from one time to the next. They can develop a sense of rhythm as they sing and listen to music.

Musical experiences need to match the developmental level of the child. At about one year children begin to become active participants in music. They clap and hit drums or xylophones in a purposeful way. From one to two children explore instruments and their properties. They like to dance, but they seem to dance for their own pleasure as they will often continue after the music stops (Mayesky, 1990). About age two children enjoy learning simple songs, especially those that include movement. Songs need to be short. By three children may have favorite songs and can recognize some tunes. They may want to add words or motions to songs for a new verse. Children have more concept of rhythm and how they can move to it. They can learn longer songs. By age four children can participate in singing games and more actively participate in selecting musical experiences. With increasing age children are able to sit longer and enjoy songs and dances that have rules (Mayesky, 1990). By seven or eight children can read the words to songs, and some become interested in more formalized music training.

The overlap of music and necessary listening skills is obvious. Children can learn to differentiate pitch, rhythm, and intensity. They need to remember the names of favorite songs as well as the word sequence of the music. Often songs have a motor action paired to the singing. As children become older they enter into some of the more visual aspects of music, such as visually discriminating the musical notes and symbols and then integrating this information into auditory output. Pairing music with movement can use both gross and fine motor skills and supports sensory integration. The mood of the music can set the pace for the movement. Music also supports language development. As children vocalize sounds and words, they may create new verses to familiar songs. Music is also a social experience. Be sure to include music of other cultures, folk music, and contemporary selections. As a creative experience, music allows free expression.

Music can be incorporated into your daily schedule or routine in a number of ways.

— Sing a song at a particular time of the day to let children know it is time to move to another activity. For example, at the time for clean-up, sing the same song every day and children are likely to join in both the singing and the clean-up. The tune can be simple such as:

Time to put the toys away, toys away, toys away.
Time to put the toys away, for another day.
(Sung to the tune of "Mary had a Little Lamb.")

— Play records or cassette tapes at a variety of times throughout the day. Children's songs will be enjoyed, but classical or popular tunes may be appreciated as well. Fit the music to the activity. Play quiet, relaxing music at nap time, and louder, bouncier music on a rainy day for dancing when children can't go outside.

— Sing simple songs throughout the day while pushing a child on a swing or giving a bath, for example. You can make up the words. Children especially enjoy having their name included in the song. Songs can be as simple as "Enzo is swinging, swinging, swinging." Even if you think you don't have a good voice, children will appreciate your efforts at singing and are rarely critical.

— You may want to set a special time aside for music with your older children. Most children enjoy combining music and movement with group games like the "Hokey Pokey" or "Ring Around the Rosie" or by singing songs with motions like "If You're Happy and You Know It."

— Most children enjoy experimenting with sounds. Help children make simple instruments which they can "play" while you sing or play records or tapes. Oatmeal boxes can be painted or covered with construction paper and decorated as drums. Shakers can be made from a number of scrap materials including "L'eggs eggs," which can be filled with dried beans and securely fastened with heavy tape. Even the youngest children enjoy pounding on a drum or shaking a shaker.

— If you play music throughout the day while other activities are going on, be sure that the child with a disability is not distracted by the music. Some children find it difficult to focus on even one activity and need as few distractions as possible. If this is the case, don't play music while other activities are going on. Instead have music at a time specifically for music.

Creative Movement

Movement helps children become aware of their body. This awareness in turn can help them express feelings and moods, improve self-control, and help them learn how to relax at will. It is important for children to relax, since many disabilities are worsened by tension. Children are frequently put in tension-producing situations, such as visits to doctors, physical therapists, and audiologists, or having to take batteries of tests. Movement exploration helps children discover ways to relax and to work off excess energy. Movement activities help develop rhythm and balancing techniques. (Putting one's arms out makes it easier to balance on one foot.) They can provide sensory integration and offer an opportunity for creativity and expression.

Creative movement is not a child-sized version of calisthenics with a "no pain, no gain" philosophy. It is the way young children learn how their bodies work. They acquire skills, knowledge, and attitudes that give them information about what is easy and what is difficult for them. Creative movement is a personal statement about one's inner self. This is what differentiates it from functional movement, which usually has a practical purpose such as running to get a ball.

Movement can be integrated with other activities, especially music, and done in small or large groups. It is important not to judge movements as being silly or awkward, and to see movement of all kinds as being equally appropriate for boys and girls. Avoid demonstrating movements as children may use this as a model and then movement is no longer a creative activity. Pair creative movement with poetry, literature, and science. Read *What Makes the Wind?* by Laurence Santrey and have the children be the wind on a warm beach or a winter blizzard. Have them move as a gentle breeze, a strong wind, a gale, and a tornado. Help children understand the life cycle of the butterfly by moving through each stage.

The more freely and easily children can move in their world, the more opportunities they will have for exploration and active involvement with materials of all kinds.

Dramatic Play

Dramatic play is spontaneous, self-expressive play through which a child can learn to understand himself and his relation to others and to the world around him. In dramatic play children construct a world in which they can make up for defeats and frustrations and experiment with different ways of working out fears, feelings, and uncertainties. Dramatic play can help a child with a disability grow in social understanding and cooperation; it provides a controlled emotional outlet and a means of self-expression. Because it involves the whole child—body, mind, emotions, and experience—dramatic play is an exciting curriculum area where much can be accomplished.

You, the teacher, can use dramatic play as an index to measure the growth and development of children. Through observations you can assess small and large motor coordination, speech development, social-emotional growth, and concept formation. There are developmental progressions in dramatic play; young children who have not had much experience playing with others often play alone. This is called solitary play. Regardless of age, all children participate in solitary play, but young children have that as their total repertoire. Next, children learn to participate in parallel play. That is, they play beside another child using the same materials but don't interact in a way that focuses on a cooperative venture.

As children grow older, they demonstrate increased language skills, attention span, and more complex play patterns. Children form loosely associated groups that have a purpose but are not well regulated as there is no leader and children seem to come and go at will, but while together they work on the same project (associative play). By the time children are about five they begin to play cooperatively. Groups are formed with a purpose, and members of the group are assigned various roles. Some division, however fleeting, of leader and followers appears. With increasing age, play becomes more imaginative, more complex, and begins to be governed by rules. Younger children (2 to 3) may pretend they are other people, such as favorite television stars, particularly superheroes, and are offended if they are called by their given name. They may also have imaginary friends who are brought to school and who are also an important part of play at home. I remember one such character, appropriately named "Mr. Nobody," who was frequently sat upon, and certainly spilled a lot of juice.

Play is an active form of learning. It provides children with the opportunity to try out new ideas and practice new skills. As children interact with materials, they can experiment with ideas and reorganize skill sequences. Without penalty they can practice skills that are necessary to their function as adults. They can try out roles and experiment with an adult world.

"Superhero" is a specialized form of dramatic play that occurs frequently in early childhood settings. Its appeal to children is obvious. The superhero is the epitome of good. Villains are just as clearly bad. Even more appealing, superheroes are powerful. They can take control of problems with their supernatural powers. They are always in control and they always win. Children who have little power in a world of adults identify with these characteristics.

Superheroes provide children with clear models and predictable themes for play. As with most dramatic play in early childhood, children start out with what they know the best: domestic scenes. Children cook, clean, care for younger children, leave for work and return, have visitors, and so on. They begin with roles they are most familiar with. The second theme is superimposed upon the first and involves a rescue mission. The baby is sick, someone has fallen and broken a leg, and the children focus their play around solving the problem presented. Once solved, a new "problem" is likely to occur. The third theme is sudden threat. A monster appears to carry off a victim, wild animals threaten to attack, and villains must be beaten off (Kostelnik, Whiren, & Stein, 1986).

Children re-enact these themes over and over again. The setting changes and with increasing age the play becomes more sophisticated, but the themes remain. The play itself, however, often is chaotic, violent, noisy, and difficult to manage (Kostelnik, Whiren, & Stein, 1986). It sometimes involves children who "don't want to play" as unwilling victims. It has some unquestionable advantages, but it needs firm guidelines to work for all the children in the class.

Blocks are another aspect of creative play that deserves special mention. A set of blocks is essential for the early childhood classroom. Blocks can be used in a variety of ways by children of varying ages. Infants enjoy reaching for and grasping them, toddlers like to knock down the towers you build, and preschoolers will enjoy the construction process.

Blocks support learning in a variety of other areas. Children learn about cause and effect relationships by knocking down block towers: when they hit the tower with their hand, the tower falls and makes a loud sound. They may want you to build towers over and over again as they test to see if the same thing happens each time.

Stacking blocks enhances fine motor development and concepts of spatial relationships. Initially, you may have to demonstrate stacking two blocks, then say, "Now it's Jillian's turn." This will also help children develop skills in imitation. Remember that larger blocks will be easier to stack, but they may be harder for small hands to manage. You will have to figure out what works best for an individual child. Stacking blocks in groups by size and shape on a low open shelf gives children a chance to practice shape and size sorting as they clean up.

Rotate the blocks available, sometimes using large cardboard blocks, unit blocks, and smaller blocks. Include odd-shaped blocks. Use a block to represent an object such as a car or a telephone receiver. Push the "block car" across the floor and say "beep-beep," for example. You can gradually build more complex structures to represent something else. Use different accessories to support pretend play in young children, such as cars, animals, or people. Combine the block and dramatic play areas.

As children make more complex structures, encourage them to work on them for more than one day. Have children design communities with blocks and accessories. Blocks allow children to obtain three-dimensional feedback about their ideas. They learn what to do when their building isn't complete and there are no more long blocks, and they learn about gravity. This is all hands-on learning. As they build together they learn about social relations and sharing.

Audio-visual equipment can be used both as a source of creativity and as a method of capturing creativity so that it can be shared or viewed at a later time. Consider videotaping a creative movement experience or the dramatic play area and then showing it to the children. Children can use simple cameras and record the events of a field trip with snapshots. Encourage children to record their voices and play them back, or record the group singing and then listen. Children are intrigued with media. Use them to encourage and support creativity.

To support dramatic play:

— Play with children to encourage their participation. Help them expand roles to allow more children to play.

— Take time to listen to the children.

— Instead of giving a direct answer to every question, occasionally ask children to make predictions: "What do you think might happen?"

— Allow children to find answers to their own problems as much as possible. Let them figure out why their building fell over and how to prevent its happening again. You might need to ask a good question that gets them thinking on the right track.

— Ask why and how questions, not questions that can be answered with a "yes" or "no." For example, "Why do you think that happened?" or "How did you make that?"

— Use simple open statements such as, "I wonder why that happened," to give children the opportunity to think and respond without putting them on the spot.

Creative Arts Goals

To Increase Art Concepts

Art is a process of creation. To develop art concepts children need to explore a wide range of art materials: those designed for drawing, brush painting, finger painting, pasting, modeling, and woodworking.

To Increase Music Concepts

Music can teach children to differentiate pitch, rhythm, and intensity. Children must remember the names and word sequence of favorite selections. As children learn to play instruments they learn causal relations—beating a drum hard makes a louder sound. With increasing age children experience some of the more visual aspects of music such as musical notes and symbols and integrate this information into auditory output. When music and movement are combined children can interpret music as they explore the relationship of music and movement. Children can express their feelings and moods through music.

To Encourage Creative Movement

In addition to becoming more aware of their bodies, children can, through movement, become a tree in the wind, a flower ready to bloom, or a fish swimming against the current. By actually acting out their interpretations of these events, they can learn about nature and themselves. Creative movement allows children to compare their body when it is tight and tense to when it is limp and relaxed and to compare an open, stretched position to a tightly curled position.

To Encourage Creative Problem Solving

Children need to look at situations creatively if they are going to find new solutions to some of the problems confronting humanity today. The process of seeking additional and nonconventional solutions starts in early childhood. Children with disabilities face challenges that others do not. They need to seek innovative solutions to keep themselves in the mainstream.

To Encourage Creativity

Creative arts focus on a process of thinking, acting, or making something that is new or different. Children don't have to invent a new idea; they just need to participate in an experience that is new for them. Encourage children to "do their own thing," not what another child does. Help them experiment with techniques, methods, and media.

To Express Feelings

Children first need to become aware of their feelings, label these feelings, and then find constructive outlets for expressing them. If these skills are learned as children they have lifelong usefulness. It is important for children to be in tune with their feelings and to develop socially acceptable ways of venting them.

Teaching Strategies

Children with *communication* disorders may become so absorbed in art that they forget their reluctance to talk as they discover they want to share their work with others. Music can provide a nonthreatening atmosphere for using expressive language. Through music, you can encourage children to attempt speech and to imitate other children and adults. Include songs and activities that concentrate on sounds that are difficult for them to produce. Creative movement allows children to participate without the need for speech and also provides the potential for increasing body awareness.

Through dramatic play children can practice situations before encountering them. They can use puppets, talk on the telephone, or dress up and pretend they are another person as they participate in situations that provide the opportunity for communication. They can learn the vocabulary of math and science while building.

Children with *hearing* impairments can refine visual skills while playing beside other children in a way that does not demand high-level language skills. They can learn by watching what others do and seeing what they make while still choosing and using materials in their own way. Music is primarily an auditory experience. For children with *hearing* impairments, depending upon the degree of loss, music activities must be adapted to include experiences that will be meaningful to them and allow them to participate. Include visual cues so the children can clap the rhythm, stamp their feet, and so on. Include hand motions or signs along with your songs so that these children will be able to be involved as well. Encourage them to watch the other children. Use a guitar or auto harp so the children can see the hand movements or arrange the piano so the child has a good view of your hands. Use creative movement activities that allow them to experience rhythm. Have another child or adult mirror-dance with them. As the sense of balance is located in the inner ear, these children's sense of balance may be impaired, and creative movement is an excellent opportunity for them to experiment with movement. Make music and movement a release for emotions, not an emotionally frustrating experience. Help these children act out situations they are likely to encounter. Use as many props as you can, and keep them realistic. Help children learn what to do in a given situation through dramatic play. Use accessories to set the mood for block building.

Children with *visual* impairments may need obvious boundaries for work on paper, such as a thick black line marking the outside of the paper, or a larger, high contrast piece of paper underneath the paper being worked on. As long as the emphasis is on process, there are few limitations on what these children can do. It is often useful to add textured materials to paint and playdough when possible. Three-dimensional materials such as clay and dough are particularly good because the children can feel the results. Music can be used to enhance listening skills and auditory discrimination. Moving to music is an excellent way to acquire body awareness, but be sure to have an area without obstacles. Give the children boundaries they can trust, such as two adults who can cue them when their movements are too large. Creative movement supports orientation and mobility skills. Children with limited vision must learn a variety of ways of moving safely. Have children move with partners. Use music to help them localize sound and distinguish one voice from another. Let them feel vibrations of instruments and voices. Sound will be vital in the life of these children, so use music to train their hearing. Children with visual impairments, like those with hearing impairments, profit from acting out situations and having realistic props. Be sure to keep the props in the same place so they will be easy to find. Use physical boundaries to delimit the block area, and put the blocks in a tub so the child can locate them easily. Show and tell the child the dimension of the blocks in the tub. Start with individual block building.

Children with *learning disabilities* find in art an emotional release and an opportunity to integrate the visual and tactile senses and make a creation that will not be judged by others as right or wrong. Make sure children understand what is expected of them. Give visual and movement cues to help them understand. Use high interest activities. Music can help improve sensory motor integration; adding creative movement helps children express emotions and increase body awareness. Use dramatic play to help children become more aware of roles and feelings. Help them express caring and happy feelings as well as sad, angry, and unhappy ones. As holidays and special events are often stressful for these children, playing them through may help. Encourage children to both build and knock buildings down. However, be clear that children may only knock down what they themselves have constructed.

Encourage children with *emotional/behavioral* disorders to use art as a way of expressing feelings. Strong feelings can be expressed through the use of bold colors, pounding clay, and tearing paper. Draining angry feelings in these ways helps the children keep themselves in control. Use music to help children relax (play soft music at rest time) and to release feelings (encourage them to beat a drum to express anger). Provide plenty of movement and large motor activities to help them express pent-up emotions. Movements that might at other times be thought unusual could at these times be allowed. As long as there is no right or wrong, these children can participate and learn about their body. Dramatic play can help children work through their fears and anxieties about specific issues. They may need your guidance to play with other children. If talking directly about situations produces anxiety, have the child dress up and pretend to be someone else or talk through a puppet. Blocks can be a solitary or group experience; there are no right or wrong buildings. Encourage children to use this area, but establish clear safety rules with both words and pictures.

Children with *health* impairments may express concerns and fears through art that they are unable or unwilling to express with words. When their large motor activities are limited, art can be used as an alternative way of releasing energy and emotions. Music can provide a good transition between home and school. Use slow music when children appear to be tiring. If a child is out of school for an extended period of time, send a musical greeting or a tape of new songs the children are learning so he can come back to school knowing the words and increase his feelings of group belonging. Help children use dramatic play to better understand their world and to play through situations that they may find scary. Because of many encounters with the medical profession, these children may be very competent at role playing and can provide leadership, while at the same time working through some of their feelings. Have a variety of sizes, shapes, and weights of blocks for them to choose from. Encourage children to make choices based on their image of what they plan to build and the energy it will take to build it.

Children with *physical* disabilities can use art to express feelings, increase body awareness, and practice necessary motor skills. The children can use this information to make changes while still moving at their own pace in an activity of their choice. The process can be one of experimentation and learning rather than drill and exercise. If children cannot move their legs, include some creative movement activities with everyone sitting. If children have limited control of their arms, have them stomp instead of clapping. During music and movement, be sure to provide assistance to these children so they feel included in the games. Have the child sit on your lap, for example, and gently guide her through motions to a song. Or carry the child as your partner while you play "Ring Around the Rosie." Help children "visit" some places that may not be accessible to them, or figure out creative ways of increasing accessibility. Large, light blocks may be the easiest for the child to work with, or some other variation such as those with bristles. You might even put sandpaper or fabric on blocks to make them less likely to fall.

Children with *mental retardation* can use art to practice fine motor skills; they can see and even feel how they are growing in this area. Through the manipulation of various art media, they can learn about color, shape, and size. These children need a lot of repetition to learn. Expect them to choose to sing one or two songs over and over. They may not show a lot of imagination in moving. If you use costumes, provide realistic ones. Start with large motor activities and encourage children to move their whole body by stimulating them with bold music. Gradually work on small motor skills. They may not have the most creative interpretations, but for them the practice of moving and the opportunity to be part of a nonjudgmental group is more important. Be sure to include familiar materials in the dramatic play area; begin the year with a housekeeping area to which you gradually add more materials or changes. Provide simple, realistic props. Blocks provide a great opportunity to practice skills and see the results of one's behavior. Help the child integrate this information by verbalizing what she has done: "When you put the block on top, you made the building higher."

Creative Arts Activities

Goal	Activity
To increase art concepts	Creature
	Crayon Rubbing
	Corrugated Collage
	Straw Painting
	Texture Paint
	Clay
	Stencils
	String Painting
	Torn Paper Flowers
	Hand Print Mural
	Texture Playdough
To increase music concepts	Mood Songs
	Rhythm Walk
	Conductor
	Reeds
	Bumblebees
	Clouds
	Bonnie
	Sequencing Songs
	Movement Songs
	Musical Colors
	Tempo
To encourage creative movement	Mood Songs
	Rhythm Walk
	Be It
	Rag Doll
	Body Maneuvers
	Tense Me
	Moving Colors
	Relaxation Stories
	Moving Balloons
	Movement Exploration
To encourage creative problem solving	Creature
	Crayon Rubbing
	Corrugated Collage
	Finger Puppets
	What Shall We Make?
	Tracing Pictures
	Body Maneuvers
	No Name

Goal	Activity
	Dentist
	Doctor's Office
	Shoe Store
	Connections
	Day Play
To encourage creativity	Straw Painting
	Texture Paint
	Clay
	Stencils
	String Painting
	Torn Paper Flowers
	Mood Montage
	Mood Colors
	Painting a Feeling
	Reeds
	Bumblebees
	Clouds
	Be It
	Weighty Movements
To improve self-concept	Hand Print Mural
	Mood Montage
	Mood Colors
	Painting a Feeling
	Conductor
	My Song
	No Name
	Circus
	Day Play
To express feelings	Mood Montage
	Mood Colors
	Painting a Feeling
	No Name
	Dentist
	Doctor's Office
To improve listening skills	Bonnie
	Musical Colors
	Sequencing Songs
To follow directions	Conductor
	Tense Me
	Moving Balloons
To improve classification skills	Texture Playdough
To improve cause-and-effect reasoning	Creature
	Straw Painting
	Texture Paint
	Texture Playdough
	Finger Puppets
	What Shall We Make?
	Reeds
	Shoe Store
	Connections
To increase body awareness	Tempo
	Movement Songs

Goal	Activity
	Rag Doll
	Body Maneuvers
	Tense Me
	Moving Colors
	Relaxation Stories
	Moving Balloons
	Movement Exploration
	Weighty Movements
	Circus
To improve sensory motor integration	Crayon Rubbing
	Mood Songs
	Rhythm Walk
	Bumblebees
	Clouds
	Bonnie
	Musical Colors
	Sequencing Songs
	Tempo
	Movement Songs
	Moving Colors
	Weighty Movements
To improve small motor coordination	Tracing Pictures
To improve eye-hand coordination	Corrugated Collage
	Clay
	Stencils
	String Painting
	Torn Paper Flowers
	What Shall We Make?
To increase inclusion	Hand Print Mural
	Finger Puppets
	My Song
To broaden concepts of families	Day Play
To increase awareness of roles people play	Dentist
	Doctor's Office
	Circus
	Shoe Store
	Connections
To increase awareness of individual differences	Tracing Pictures
	Movement Exploration

Art

CREATURE

GOAL   To increase art concepts
To encourage creative problem solving
To improve cause-and-effect reasoning

OBJECTIVE   The child will make a creature and describe the environment in which it lives.

MATERIALS   papier-mâché made with newspaper, wheat paste, and water (see below)

balloons

PROCEDURE   Tear the newspaper into very small pieces and pour a little boiling water over it. Stir until it forms a pulp. Cool. Then add about 6 tablespoons of wheat paste for every 2 cups of pulp. Mix first with a spoon, then with the hands. Let the children mold the papier-mâché into some creature-like form. Covering an inflated balloon with papier-mâché is a good way for the children to begin. Talk about this creature during the process so that the children think about how it moves (crawls, walks), what and how it eats, where it lives, and so on. See if they can adapt the creatures to the environment they create.

Increase Level of Difficulty

Procedure   When the creatures are dry, encourage the children to use the construction area to build an environment for them. Help children focus on adaptations people make to the environment: wheelchairs, prosthetic devices, and eye glasses are all adaptations.

Decrease Level of Difficulty

Procedure   Allow children to create the creature and then help them think of the environment it would be most adapted for.

COMMENT   Precede this activity by discussing people and animals and how they are adapted to their environments (a monkey's tail is for climbing; polar bears are white [protective coloration]; a cheetah is fast). Another good activity to precede this one is paper tearing, a great rainy day tension reliever. Keep the torn paper for the papier-mâché (encourage small pieces). The papier-mâché process is as much fun as the product.

Art

CRAYON RUBBING

GOAL   To increase art concepts

To encourage creative problem solving

To improve sensory motor integration

OBJECTIVE   The child will rub with a crayon on paper placed over textured articles to reproduce a pattern.

MATERIALS   paper   masking tape

thick crayons   objects with various textures

PROCEDURE   Talk about various surfaces that the children touch and how they would describe them (soft, furry, scratchy, and so on), then about surfaces that they see (shiny, hairy, has ridges or patterns), and then about the two combined (something that feels bumpy, looks rough). Demonstrate rubbing techniques to the children. Either have them go around the room and find their own textures to rub or provide a variety of textured objects on a table. Tape the corners of the paper to the table with the object under it. The tape keeps the paper from moving as the children rub. Write the names of the article rubbed on the other side of the paper. During group time, ask the children to look at the papers and guess what article was rubbed. (The name on the back helps for those "creative" rubbings.)

Increase Level of Difficulty

Procedure   Have children predict how a rubbing will look before they begin and then see if they were accurate.

Decrease Level of Difficulty

Procedure   Help children color the edges of objects first to determine their shape. Pick objects that have distinctive shapes as well as textures.

COMMENT   This requires little coordination, yet helps develop finger strength and sensory integration and gives the children feedback about how hard they are pressing the crayon.

CORRUGATED COLLAGE

GOAL   To increase art concepts
To encourage creative problem solving
To improve eye-hand coordination

OBJECTIVE   The child will make a collage on corrugated paper.

MATERIALS   a 6″ × 9″ or larger piece of corrugated paper (such as a box divider or packing separator)

a variety of yarns   glue or paste

cloth materials   Popsicle sticks

pipe cleaners

PROCEDURE   Have the children make collages with a piece of corrugated paper, some glue, and the materials to be glued. Help the children see that the glue goes naturally into the corrugations, where it is easy to glue the yarn, but where it is much more difficult to glue the cloth.

Increase Level of Difficulty

Procedure   As the children gain experience and better motor control, you might have them try doing this blindfolded. This becomes more of a sensory experience than an art activity.

Decrease Level of Difficulty

Procedure   Expect children to just experience the media.

COMMENT   The paper provides an interesting and challenging change. It gives children with visual impairments a definite tactile boundary as they work.

STRAW PAINTING

GOAL   To improve art concepts
To encourage creativity
To improve cause-and-effect reasoning

OBJECTIVE   The child will make a painting by blowing paint through a drinking straw.

MATERIALS   watery tempera paint

paper

drinking straws

PROCEDURE   Make very watery tempera paint. Put a small amount of paint on the paper and have the children create a picture by blowing the paint around on the paper with a straw.

Increase Level of Difficulty

Procedure   Have children predict where the paint will go. See if they can predict both the direction and distance.

Decrease Level of Difficulty

Procedure   Put a larger amount of paint on the paper and just have the children blow it toward the corners.

COMMENT   Children are often not aware of their breath and how they can control it. The activity provides a visual sign to help them control their breath. *Note:* As there is really very little paint on the paper it is unlikely that children will "drink" the paint, but many will try as they experiment. Use less paint and color the water with food coloring if children have difficulty with the concept.

TEXTURE PAINT

GOAL   To increase art concepts
To encourage creativity
To improve cause-and-effect reasoning

OBJECTIVE   The child will describe the texture of the paint.

MATERIALS   Add texture to easel paint with one of the following:

flour: lumpy (don't stir it too much)	sawdust: rough
sugar: shiny, grainy (use right away)	salt: shiny, grainy (table or Epsom salt)
syrup: sticky	sand: gritty
salad oil: oily	

PROCEDURE   Have the children experiment with various textures.

Increase Level of Difficulty

Procedure   Experiment with making different colors and different textures on the same day:

red: rough—sawdust

blue: oily—salad oil

yellow: lumpy—flour

Focus on the cause-effect relationship in the materials added and the resultant texture.

Decrease Level of Difficulty

Procedure   Allow the children to experiment. Focus on the process and verbalize the change in texture.

COMMENT   This activity provides both tactile and visual changes of a familiar substance.

CLAY

GOAL   To increase art concepts
To encourage creativity
To improve eye-hand coordination

OBJECTIVE   The child will mold the clay.

MATERIALS   dry clay   rolling pins
water   blunt knife

PROCEDURE   Make, or have the children make, clay from powder. Vary the amount of moisture with the strength and motor skills of the children (more moisture—easier to manipulate). Encourage the children to use rolling pins and blunt knives as well as hands to mold the clay. If you want, allow the clay to dry and paint it, or fire it in a kiln and paint it.

Increase Level of Difficulty

Procedure   Help children focus on a product that you will allow to dry and they can paint. Be wary of objects that are supposed to fit together when they dry. They rarely do. Have children paint the object after it is dry.

Decrease Level of Difficulty

Procedure   Allow adequate time for exploration. Use more water than usual. Look at the clay as an emotional release or a means for developing finger strength and coordination. Plan to put the clay back in the crock when the activity is completed.

COMMENT   Clay offers potential for many levels of development. Because playdough and plasticine are readily available we often forget about clay, but it has potential that the other media don't have.

Art

STENCILS

GOAL   To increase art concepts
To encourage creativity
To improve eye-hand coordination

OBJECTIVE   The child will make and color a stencil.

MATERIALS   construction paper (5″ × 5″)   scissors
cotton ball   colored chalk
crayons

PROCEDURE   Give the children several pieces of paper. Have them cut holes or designs in the paper. If they want a symmetrical design (for example, heart, flower, or person), it is easiest if they fold the paper in half first. After they have finished making the stencil have them use the colored chalk to color the opening or rub the colored chalk with the cotton ball, and working from the stencil paper to the center of the opening, have them color until they have a clear print. Crayons can be used in the same manner.

Increase Level of Difficulty

Procedure   Have children print a scene or make a card using this process.

Decrease Level of Difficulty

Procedure   Use tape or bits of adhesive to keep the stencil in one place as the children color it.

COMMENT   This activity is very adaptable to holidays. It allows children who want to plan for a special occasion the opportunity and those who just want to participate can do so as well.

Art

STRING PAINTING

GOAL   To increase art concepts
To encourage creativity
To improve eye-hand coordination

OBJECTIVE   The child will make a string painting.

MATERIALS   pieces of string, yarn, or cord of various thicknesses approximately two feet long
two or three colors of tempera paint in pie pans
paper

PROCEDURE   Give the children a variety of pieces of string, cord, or yarn, show them how to dip it in the paint, and allow them to make a design by applying the paint on paper with the string.

COMMENT   If very thick paint is used, the children will be able to feel the ridges the string makes. The children can also match the ridges to the thickness of string used. Help children identify differences in techniques: for example, holding string taut between two hands versus holding one end and swirling.

Increase Level of Difficulty

Procedure   Encourage children to use different thicknesses of string in the same picture and to compare different techniques.

Decrease Level of Difficulty

Procedure   Put the yarn or string through an empty spool to make it easier to grip.

COMMENT   This is a creative visual process and children can feel the picture when it is dry. If thick paint is used the ridges will be more apparent.

Art

TORN PAPER FLOWERS

GOAL   To increase art concepts
   To encourage creativity
   To increase eye-hand coordination

OBJECTIVE   The child will make a picture by tearing and pasting paper.

MATERIALS   a pot or vase of flowers   construction paper

   colored paper scraps   paste

   crayons

PROCEDURE   Show the children the flowers. Discuss the parts that make up the flower (stem, petals, leaves, and so on). Show the children how to tear and paste paper petals and other flower parts. (If flowers aren't interesting to the children in your class, make something that is.) Once the children know the technique, allow them the freedom to make *their* flower. Use crayons to complete details.

Increase Level of Difficulty

Procedure   Encourage children to both cut and tear the flowers and show them how to curl the paper around a pencil so that it curls away from the paper to give depth.

Decrease Level of Difficulty

Procedure   Have the children just tear the paper and paste it.

COMMENT   Tearing is a frustration release and is satisfying for children who have trouble cutting.

Art

HAND PRINT MURAL

GOAL   To increase art concepts
   To improve self-concept
   To increase inclusion

OBJECTIVE   The child will participate in a mural by making a hand print.

MATERIALS   paint   butcher paper

   paint brush   construction paper

PROCEDURE   Decide on the purpose for the mural. Will it be a get well card, part of a bulletin board display, or a thank you card for a past field trip? Have the children generate an appropriate message. Then take the mural to a separate table. Have children stop by and put on their hand print and name. Encourage the children to be creative with the hand print. Help them look closely at their hand and perhaps paint the palm one color and the area between each knuckle another. Supply additional small paper so children can try out their print first or make another project.

Increase Level of Difficulty

Procedure   Have children add fingerprints and look at both hand and finger prints with a magnifying glass. They might even personalize the prints.

Decrease Level of Difficulty

Procedure   Put the paint on a sponge and have children press their hand on the sponge, then print it.

COMMENT   The concept of printing is different from finger painting. For some children this will be new. This project is an easy one for children to participate in and, if hung on the wall, a reminder that all children are part of the class.

Art

TEXTURE PLAYDOUGH

GOAL   To increase art concepts
To improve classification skills
To improve cause-and-effect reasoning

OBJECTIVE   The child will classify the playdough as rough, smooth, soft, or grainy.

MATERIALS   Playdough made with flour, salt, oil (recipe follows)

PROCEDURE   Make playdough with:

7 parts flour to 1 part salt (1 tbsp. or so of vegetable oil)

2 parts flour to 1 part salt (1 tbsp. or so of vegetable oil)

Discuss the difference in texture.

Have the children help make the playdough so that they can see the difference in the quantities of flour and salt. Help them verbalize: the more flour, the smoother the dough; the more salt, the grainier it is.

Increase Level of Difficulty

Procedure   Vary the texture of the playdough; use 7 parts flour to 2 parts salt; 7 parts flour to 3 parts salt; 7 parts flour to 4 parts salt; 7 parts flour to 5 parts salt; and 7 parts flour to 6 parts salt to see how well the children can make tactile discriminations. Color code the different mixtures if necessary.

Have children classify the playdough by touch. Talk about uses for the different textures. Have children make other recipes by adding sawdust, sand, and so on. Use small quantities as some of the products might not be appealing.

Decrease Level of Difficulty

Procedure   Start with gross discrimination, then see if the children can make finer distinctions.

COMMENT   This activity helps develop and refine tactile skills. As children participate in the process of making the dough they can begin to understand the logic.

Art

FINGER PUPPETS

GOAL   To encourage creative problem solving
To improve cause-and-effect reasoning
To increase inclusion

OBJECTIVE   The child will make a finger puppet and use it in a group.

MATERIALS   papier-mâché made with newspaper, wheat paste, and water (see below)
balloons

PROCEDURE   Tear the newspaper into very small pieces and pour a little boiling water over it. Stir until it forms a pulp. Cool. Then add about 6 tablespoons of wheat paste for every 2 cups of pulp. Mix first with a spoon, then with the hands. Let the children mold the papier-mâché into some creature-like form.

After the children have molded their creation, have them insert their finger to make the finger hole. Wait for the puppets to dry and then have the children paint and dress them. Have children take them into the dramatic play area and use them together.

Increase Level of Difficulty

Procedure   Before starting, help children focus on what they want their puppet to do or be when the puppet is finished.

Decrease Level of Difficulty

Procedure   Have children create the finger puppet and then decide on the type of character it is.

COMMENT   Finger puppets require less manipulation than other puppets, and children have to supply more of the dramatic energy. They especially enjoy using a puppet they have created.

Art

WHAT SHALL WE MAKE?

GOAL   To encourage creative problem solving
To improve cause-and-effect reasoning
To improve eye-hand coordination

OBJECTIVE   The child will make an appropriate piece of doll's clothing.

MATERIALS

linen	corduroy	needles
wool	gabardine	patterns
gingham	knit	scissors
cotton	denim	pins
chiffon	velvet	tape
vinyl	fur	thread

PROCEDURE   Have patterns for doll clothes (be sure to have patterns appropriate for both boys and girls). Have the children choose a pattern, then pick the material to make the desired clothing. Help the children pin or tape on the pattern, cut it out, and sew up the seams with a large needle and heavy thread. Talk about their choices of material relative to the style and weather, when it will be worn, and so on.

Increase Level of Difficulty

Procedure   Encourage children to choose more difficult patterns and materials to work with. Add fasteners such as buttons, snaps, and hooks and eyes.

Decrease Level of Difficulty

Materials   Stapler and staples

Procedure   For some children just choosing the material and cutting it out will be enough. However, those who want to continue could staple the garment together or have a volunteer help with the sewing.

COMMENT   Encourage children to make up a story about the occasion for which the clothing will be worn.

Art

TRACING PICTURES

GOAL   To encourage creative problem solving
To improve small motor coordination
To increase awareness of individual differences

OBJECTIVE   The child will trace the shape with his fingers.

MATERIALS

paper	glue
crayons	sand

PROCEDURE   Have the children draw a simple shape (circle, triangle, square), pattern, or picture (kite, table, cup, balloon, maze) on heavy paper. Tell the children to put glue around the outline and then sprinkle sand on it. Point out where the sand stays and where it doesn't. When the glue is dry, shake off the excess sand and have the children trace the object with their fingers or lightly color in the object using the sand as a boundary.

Increase Level of Difficulty

Procedure   Have the children make several shapes or designs on the paper. Encourage children to trace the outline blindfolded and color the picture that way as well.

Decrease Level of Difficulty

Procedure   Put the sand in a large salt shaker so it is easier to control. Help children avoid ending up with puddles of glue that take days to dry.

COMMENT   Talk to the children about the tactile picture they have created. Help them think about how they could share this picture with a person who can't see.

Art

MOOD MONTAGE

GOAL   To encourage creativity
To improve self-concept
To express feelings

OBJECTIVE   The child will create a mood montage.

MATERIALS   pictures and/or magazines   scissors

crayons   paper

glue or paste

PROCEDURE   Give the children pictures, magazines, and crayons. Have them pick a mood or feeling, find pictures that match or create that mood, and paste the pictures on pieces of paper. They can use the crayons to personalize and finish the pictures.

Increase Level of Difficulty

Procedure   Encourage children to "write" a book on "The Many Moods of Me." Children can illustrate the moods as well as write about them.

The illustrations of the book should help set a mood too. Discuss some of the color stereotypes (fire engine red—hot; sky blue—cool; clean white—aseptic, sterile; and so on).

Decrease Level of Difficulty

Procedure   Use a big piece of paper for a wall mural that is a group project. Encourage active interchange among the children.

COMMENT   Encourage children to talk about their pictures. Help children become more aware of moods and some of the situations in which these moods may occur.

Art

MOOD COLORS

GOAL   To encourage creativity
To improve self-concept
To express feelings

OBJECTIVE   The child will choose an appropriate color theme for the picture.

MATERIALS   a short story

tempera paint or crayons

paper

PROCEDURE   Read (or tell) the class a story with a definite mood. Have the children draw pictures about the story in dark and/or light colors.

Increase Level of Difficulty

Procedure   Make the moods a bit more subtle. Have them consider the different reactions and moods of each character and how these might be portrayed.

Decrease Level of Difficulty

Procedure   Stick to obvious moods until children get the idea. Help them identify color clues in their environment.

COMMENT   This activity helps children learn to use visual environmental cues for information. It may also help children realize that all people have moods.

Encourage children to use art as a creative way of expressing their feelings.

PAINTING A FEELING

GOAL   To encourage creativity
To improve self-concept
To express feelings

OBJECTIVE   The child will paint a picture that depicts a feeling.

MATERIALS   paper

paint in vibrant colors and somber colors

PROCEDURE   Have a discussion about feelings. Talk about being happy, sad, angry, and scared. Have the children think of imaginary situations, or ones they might have been in, where these feelings are appropriate. You might read a story on emotions. (See bibliographies.) Then have the children choose an emotion they are going to paint (write it on the back of the paper they are going to use).

Be sure not to judge the children's pictures. Help children differentiate between feelings and behavior. It is OK to feel angry; it isn't OK to throw rocks.

Increase Level of Difficulty

Procedure   Encourage children to write or dictate a story to go along with a picture.

Decrease Level of Difficulty

Procedure   Once children have picked a feeling, help them think about the colors they might use in the picture, the size and tone of the picture, and what they might paint.

COMMENT   This activity creates an awareness of feelings and a sense that it is OK for the children to feel the way they do. It provides an avenue for expressing feelings. Once you have used an activity such as this you can refer back to it when children are having a difficult time. For example, "Do you remember when we read *Nannabah's Friend* and drew pictures about how lonely she felt? Do you think drawing your feelings would help today?"

MOOD SONGS

GOAL   To increase music concepts
To encourage creative movement
To improve sensory motor integration

OBJECTIVE   The child will move in a way that is congruent with the music (fast/slow, loud/soft, high/low).

MATERIALS   record, tape, or compact disc player

records   tapes   compact discs

PROCEDURE   Choose songs that have a specific mood: lullabies, jazz, rock, easy listening, as well as more traditional children's music. Have the children talk about the songs and the movements that might go with the mood of the songs. Talk about when they might want to listen to the songs. Have them sing a familiar song the "wrong" way (e.g., a loud, fast lullaby). Discuss how they feel while moving to music and why songs have distinctive moods.

Increase Level of Difficulty

Materials   Use songs that are not familiar to the children.

Procedure   Have children identify some of the musical characteristics that are used to create the mood. Help them identify how different instruments contribute to the mood.

Decrease Level of Difficulty

Materials   Start with only familiar, obvious songs until children get the idea.

Procedure   Help children focus on the mood of the music before they begin to move. Have them demonstrate what they will do. If necessary, help them expand their movements to better match the music.

COMMENT   Children learn to become more aware of their own moods and can perhaps match music to these as a way of learning to control them.

Music

RHYTHM WALK

GOAL   To increase music concepts
        To encourage creative movement
        To improve sensory motor integration

OBJECTIVE   The child will move in time with the beat.

MATERIALS   Drum or piano

PROCEDURE   Set up a path around the room (or outside) and have the children walk to the beat that you play. (If you don't "play," use a record or tape.) Vary the beat and see if the children change with you.

Increase Level of Difficulty

Procedure   Make the changes more quickly. Don't let the children see what you are doing. This takes away the visual cue. Sometimes beat slowly enough for their movements to become a balancing activity.

Decrease Level of Difficulty

Procedure   Warn the children before changing: "Listen, I'm going to change now. Is it faster or slower?" Be sure the children can see you and beat or play dramatically.

COMMENT   Instead of walking, children can participate in many different movement activities, including bouncing or tossing a ball to a partner; or children can become "statues" when the music stops.

Music

CONDUCTOR

GOAL   To increase music concepts
        To improve self-concept
        To follow directions

OBJECTIVE   The child will give (or follow) visual musical directions for a sound.

MATERIALS   None

PROCEDURE   Teach the children some of the simpler hand signals that musical directors use.

softer: palms toward the group (up and down)
louder: palms toward you (large gesture)
slow: waving slowly (circular)
fast: waving fast (circular)
expand: pass arm in front of body parallel to floor
staccato: cut in the air (vertically)

Your signals don't have to be the actual signals, but you and the children should agree on their meanings. Make a picture of the signal you agree to with the word written below.

Start with the teacher being the "director." Use words like me, me, me, me; la, la, la, la; see, see, see, see. Then go to two or more syllables. Names are always fun: *Ja*—expand (use horizontal hand movement), *mie*—staccato (vertical hand movement). As children learn the process let them take turns being the director.

Increase Level of Difficulty

Materials   rhythm band instruments   videotape of a concert

Procedure   Play the videotape and point out to the children the motions the conductor uses as he directs the orchestra. Encourage them to figure out what happens with each different motion. Then have the children use their instruments with a "conductor." Instruments are far more challenging to control than voices.

Decrease Level of Difficulty

Procedure   Be sure the children know the process before choosing them to be the conductor. If children are not comfortable or unable to make the hand motions, have them point to the cards that show the agreed upon hand signals.

COMMENT   Even if children just discover that the other children will start and stop on their hand signals they can have a positive experience.

Music

REEDS

GOAL   To increase music concepts
To encourage creativity
To improve cause-and-effect reasoning

OBJECTIVE   The child will make two horns of different pitches.

MATERIALS   plastic drinking straws   scissors

PROCEDURE   Make about 1 inch of a plastic drinking straw flat, creasing it so it stays that way. Using scissors, cut a *V* in that end. This becomes the reed. The children put this in their mouth behind their lips and blow. Encourage children to make several reeds of different lengths and see if they can discover the relationship between length and pitch. (The shorter the straw the higher the pitch.) Shorter straws are easier to blow.

Increase Level of Difficulty

Procedure   Have children make a series of tuned reeds. Arrange them by pitch. See if children can produce a song.

Decrease Level of Difficulty

Procedure   Help children make short straws and see if they can get a noise out of it.

COMMENT   This is fun to use in a class-made rhythm band.

Music

BUMBLEBEES

GOAL   To increase music concepts
To encourage creativity
To improve sensory motor integration

OBJECTIVE   The child will make a bumblebee.

MATERIALS   record, cassette, or compact disc player

"Flight of the Bumblebee" by Rimsky-Korsakov

black pipe cleaners   toothpicks

construction paper   glue

wax paper   crayons or markers

yarn: yellow and black, cut into strips

styrofoam balls

PROCEDURE   Write the word "bee" on the chalkboard. Find out what children know about bees. Help them add characteristics if necessary. Be sure to include information about bumblebees' flying. Listen to the "Flight of the Bumblebee." Talk about the music with the children.

Give the children the materials to make a bumblebee and encourage them to talk about the music while they make their bumblebee. Encourage the children to use the materials creatively. Whether or not the children's product looks like a bumblebee is not important.

Increase Level of Difficulty

Materials   Pictures of bumblebees

Procedure   Listen to the "Flight of the Bumblebee" again and have children pretend they are bumblebees and dance to the music. Talk in more detail about bumblebees and what they look like.

Decrease Level of Difficulty

Procedure   Describe only the most salient characteristics of bumblebees, and be sure to be supportive of any product the children make.

COMMENT   We rarely think about using classical music with young children, but some selections fit in well.

Music

CLOUDS

GOAL   To increase music concepts
To encourage creativity
To improve sensory motor integration

OBJECTIVE   The child will move as a cloud.

MATERIALS   record, cassette, or compact disc player
"Nuages" (Clouds) by Claude Debussy

PROCEDURE   Discuss clouds with the children. If possible go outside and have the children lie down on the ground and watch the clouds as they listen to "Nuages." Then have the children listen a second time and move as if they were clouds.

Increase Level of Difficulty

Materials   cotton balls   paste   construction paper
crayons, pencils, or markers

Procedure   Encourage children to make pictures of clouds and write about their feelings.

Decrease Level of Difficulty

Materials   *The Cloud Book* by Tomie DePaola

Procedure   Read *The Cloud Book* before playing the selection. Play only a portion of it if the children get restless. Then encourage them to go out and look at the clouds.

COMMENT   Children can develop another way of enjoying and thinking about nature.

Music

BONNIE

GOAL   To increase music concepts
To improve listening skills
To improve sensory motor integration

OBJECTIVE   The child will change positions on every other *Bonnie.*

MATERIALS   None

PROCEDURE   Sing the song "My Bonnie Lies over the Ocean" with everyone standing. Each time you sing the word *Bonnie,* if the children are standing, they squat; if they are squatting, they stand.

Increase Level of Difficulty

Procedure   Use other songs that have this repetitious quality ("The Ants Go Marching," move up on *hurrah,* down on *hooray*) and encourage the children to decide on other patterns of movements (e.g., raising and lowering their hands). If you sing, but don't move with the children, it is also more difficult.

Decrease Level of Difficulty

Procedure   Be sure the children have a good view of you and move dramatically.

COMMENT   This is a lot easier to do than it sounds on paper.

Music

SEQUENCING SONGS

GOAL   To increase music concepts
To improve listening skills
To improve sensory motor integration

OBJECTIVE   The child will remember at least three items in the sequence.

MATERIALS   None

PROCEDURE   Sing songs that require the children to remember a particular sequence. As you reach that part, pause to see if they can remember the sequence without your help. For example, when you sing "Old MacDonald Had a Farm," pause after "and on his farm he had a _____."

Increase Level of Difficulty

Procedure   Add more sequences for the children to remember.

Decrease Level of Difficulty

Procedure   Make pictures for the different words the children have to remember and hold them up as visual reminders. For "Old MacDonald" it would be pictures of the different animals.

COMMENT   Use additional songs, such as "This Old Man," "Where is Thumbkin?", "If You're Happy," "I Know an Old Lady Who Swallowed a Fly," and "Hush Little Baby," that have many verses.

Music

MOVEMENT SONGS

GOAL   To increase music concepts
To improve body awareness
To improve sensory motor integration

OBJECTIVE   The child will follow the motions stated in the song.

MATERIALS   None

PROCEDURE   Sing the song: "Put Your Finger in the Air." Once they know the song, help the children explore their bodies by putting their finger on their knee, cheek, shoulder, ankle, and so on. Then go on to various other combinations like "Put your nose on your shoulder, on your shoulder." In the third line, you need to be creative and have a rhyme in mind: "Put your nose on your shoulder, leave it there until you're older."

Other songs designed to increase body awareness include:

"Heads, Shoulders, Knees, and Toes" (Tune: "Oats, Peas, Beans")

"My Head, My Shoulders, My Knees, My Toes" (Tune: "Mulberry Bush")

"Where Is Thumbkin?"

"Clap Your Hands"

"The Hokey Pokey"

"The Wheels on the Bus"

"Eensey-Weensey Spider"

"Johnny Hammers with One Hammer"

"I'm Being Swallowed by a Boa Constrictor"

Increase Level of Difficulty

Procedure   Have the children sing these songs with their eyes closed.

Decrease Level of Difficulty

Procedure   Start with some of the shorter, easier songs. The repetition in the songs makes them easy for children to learn. Sing the song more slowly and dramatically. Or modify some songs.

Have children put an object (bean, checker, pebble) on the body part named "Put the bean on your knee, on your knee," and so on.

COMMENT   These songs teach body parts, use both auditory and tactile senses, and provide an opportunity to experience success and a sense of group belonging.

Music

MUSICAL COLORS

GOAL   To improve music concepts
To improve listening skills
To improve sensory motor integration

OBJECTIVE   The child will name the color and the shape he lands on.

MATERIALS   A variety of colored shapes, one for each child, mounted on cardboard and placed in a circle

PROCEDURE   Play music and have the children move around the outside of the circle of colored shapes. When the music stops, have the children sit on the nearest shape. Ask them to name the color and the shape. If you want to make this a game, eliminate those who do not know. Remove some of the shapes (probably the easiest ones) so that again the number of colored shapes matches the number of children, and start the music again. Continue until only one child is left. The longer the children last in the game, the more colors and shapes they know.

On the other hand, remember that if your goal is to teach these concepts by eliminating children who don't know, you limit their opportunities for learning. As a variation use numbers and letters instead of colors and shapes.

Increase Level of Difficulty

Materials   shapes in shades of colors (pink, violet, and so on)

more difficult shapes (oval, cross, trapezoid, and so on)

Decrease Level of Difficulty

Materials   Use simple shapes and primary colors

Procedure   Have children move like various animals around the circle.

COMMENT   This is an adaptation of musical chairs based on color/shape recognition but without the mad scramble: There is a place for everyone. As speed is not important, children with physical disabilities can play.

TEMPO

GOAL   To increase music concepts
To increase body awareness
To improve sensory motor integration

OBJECTIVE   The child will change the speed of his movements as the tempo of the music changes.

MATERIALS   Drum or piano

PROCEDURE   Have the children lie down on the floor, spaced so that they can stretch and not touch each other. As they are lying there, tell them that you want them to listen to the beat and move according to how fast or slow the beat is. They can move any body parts they want in any way as long as they remain in one place on their back. Start with a slow beat so you can watch and make comments to the children about their movements. Then abruptly go to a fast beat. If they move with you, get finer gradations to your changes.

Increase Level of Difficulty

Procedure   Change the beat more frequently and introduce some intermediate tempos. Also, vary the loudness and sometimes send confusing messages, that is, soft but fast or loud but slow. See if the children can focus on the tempo.

Decrease Level of Difficulty

Procedure   Warn children before you change the tempo.

COMMENT   This activity can be used to quiet excited children. Pace your periods of vigorous beat so that the children don't become too tired. Unless you want excited children, be sure to end on a slow tempo.

When musical instruments are available, children can experiment with sound while fine tuning their auditory discrimination skills.

MY SONG

GOAL   To increase music concepts
To improve self-concept
To increase inclusion

OBJECTIVE   The children will look at the named child while singing.

MATERIALS   None

PROCEDURE   Sing songs in which you can substitute the name of a child from your group, or adapt a song to include a name.

BINGO *There was a farmer had* *a son and Michael* *was his name—O.* *M-I-C-H-AEL* *M-I-C-H-AEL* *M-I-C-H-AEL* *And Michael was his* *name—O.*	*PAW-PAW PATCH* *Where, oh where is pretty* *little Sherry?* *Where, oh, where is* *pretty little Laura?* *Where, oh, where is* *handsome Juan?* *They're in the block* *corner, picking up blocks.*
HEY BETTY MARTIN *Hey, Jenny Gilbert* *tippy toe tippy toe.* *Hey, Dante Turner* *tip toe fine.*	*WHO HAS RED ON?* *G.L. has a red shirt,* *red shirt, red shirt,* *G.L. has a red shirt* *in school today.*

Increase Level of Difficulty

Procedure   Use songs that require the children to sing back a response such as "Here I Am."

Decrease Level of Difficulty

Procedure   Point to the child whose name you are singing.

COMMENT   These songs are great at the beginning of the year when children are getting to know each other. Also, use them when you are trying to get a group together and you have a few wanderers ("Hey, Railyn Turner, come join us").

BE IT

GOAL   To encourage creative movement
To encourage creativity

OBJECTIVE   The child will move his body to show how an object moves.

MATERIALS   Pictures of objects that move:

airplanes	windmills
trains	helicopters
birds	worms
kites	

PROCEDURE   Show the children the pictures and discuss how they might make their body move like the objects in the pictures. Encourage creativity by pointing out differences in the children's interpretations and by not making judgments.

Increase Level of Difficulty

Materials   Pictures of unusual objects or objects from other cultures

Decrease Level of Difficulty

Procedure   Point out salient characteristics of the objects that give hints to how it moves (fast, slowly, in air, on water, over land).

COMMENT   This activity requires children to integrate visual and auditory stimuli and translate them into active physical movement. Have an appropriate way to stop the children's movements: airport, train station, heliport.

Creative Movement

RAG DOLL

GOAL   To encourage creative movement
To increase body awareness

OBJECTIVE   The child will move in a loose, relaxed manner.

MATERIALS   Rag doll

PROCEDURE   Show the children a rag doll and demonstrate how it moves. Start with the children lying down and show them what happens to the rag doll when the legs and arms are lifted. Then go around the class and check out your collection of "rag dolls." Raise limbs an inch or two and see how floppy children can be. (Don't drop a leg very far or the children will tense!)

As the children learn to relax lying down, see if they can gain skill in locating just the muscles they need; that is, they can sit up while keeping their arms and head relaxed. Then have them try standing. Eventually add music.

Increase Level of Difficulty

Procedure   See if children can alternate between being floppy rag dolls to tense, marching, tin soldiers on your command. Call out to the children what you want them to be. Help children learn to relax specific body parts on command, for example, their left arm and right leg.

Decrease Level of Difficulty

Procedure   This activity is difficult for some children until they develop the feedback in the system. You may have to start "catching them relaxed" when you play slow music at rest time. Point out how relaxed they are and ask them to remember how it feels. Your goal is for them to relax voluntarily.

COMMENT   Tension increases pain, so anything you can teach children about relaxing is useful. It will be especially helpful to those who will be going through scary or painful medical procedures, but many children find *all* contact with dentists and doctors an occasion for tension.

Creative Movement

BODY MANEUVERS

GOAL   To encourage creative movement
To encourage creative problem solving
To increase body awareness

OBJECTIVE   The child will move in response to the directions given.

MATERIALS   None

PROCEDURE   Start by having the children follow some fairly simple directions. See if they can make their bodies as small as possible, then as large as possible (discuss the effect of a deep breath on this). Then have them crawl under a chair or stretch to reach something very high (a real object). Have them pretend they are crawling through a small hole or a tunnel that turns periodically; climbing up a steep, rock-faced mountain; walking on a high, thin wire; and so on.

Increase Level of Difficulty

Procedure   Introduce other factors for children to adapt to: The tunnel gets muddy; a wind comes up; they can't reach the shelf; they see a bear.

Decrease Level of Difficulty

Procedure   Have children begin by using a real obstacle course and then when they can still see the obstacle course have them go through it, imagining where they are. They may need to crawl next to it at first.

COMMENT   This is an opportunity for children to use their creativity, yet it is possible to incorporate some real problem-solving skills.

Creative Movement

TENSE ME

GOAL   To encourage creative movement
To increase body awareness
To follow directions

OBJECTIVE   The child will tense and relax the designated body parts.

MATERIALS   None

PROCEDURE   Have all the children lie or sit on the floor. Sitting is easier at the beginning because both you and they can see better. Have them make a tight fist or muscle in one arm and feel that arm with their other hand. Then tell them to see how loose (relaxed) they can make that arm. Again have them feel it with their other hand. Discuss the difference in feeling. Next move to the face and have them make their face "tight" ("tight" and "loose" or "floppy" seem to work better than the words "tense" and "relaxed"). Again, ask them to feel their faces, this time with both hands. They might even look in the mirror. Then have them see if they can relax by wiping away the tightness with their hands.

Increase Level of Difficulty

Procedure   See if the children can learn to isolate parts of their body and tense just that part: Can they tense the right arm and keep the right fist relaxed? This is more difficult.

Decrease Level of Difficulty

Procedure   Start with a more global approach where children are requested to tighten their whole body. Let the children feel your arm when you have it tense and then relaxed. Have them compare the arm that is tense with the one that is relaxed.

COMMENT   Before children can voluntarily relax, they need to learn the feeling of what relaxation is, otherwise they won't know what they are striving for.

Creative Movement

MOVING COLORS

GOAL   To encourage creative movement
To increase body awareness
To improve sensory motor integration

OBJECTIVE   The child will move in a way that expresses her reaction to the color.

MATERIALS   cards of various colors

pictures of objects of various colors

PROCEDURE   Hold up a color card and ask the children how the color makes them feel. Have them name objects that could be that color. Show them pictures of significant objects that are traditionally that color.

red: stop signs
        fire engines

orange: safety hats and vests

yellow: sun

blue: water

white: uniforms
        snow

green: grass
        trees

Then have them move creatively to the color cards as you hold them up. Note the differences in how children move in response to a color. There is no right or wrong interpretation.

Coordinate this activity with an art section on color. Add music to enhance the mood. Place colored cellophane over the projector and turn down the light to create a whole atmosphere of color.

Increase Level of Difficulty

Procedure   Help children think about why certain professions choose particular colors for uniforms. Have them decide what color they might paint the room and the implications of the room color on their behavior.

Decrease Level of Difficulty

Procedure   Use only the most obvious colors at the beginning.

COMMENT   Children, especially those with hearing impairments, often rely on visual cues to interpret mood. Color is often a clue to the behavior expected.

Creative Movement

RELAXATION STORIES

GOAL   To encourage creative movement
To increase body awareness

OBJECTIVE   The child will relax his body while listening to the story.

MATERIALS   None

PROCEDURE   Have the children lie down and shut their eyes. Tell them a story while they listen and relax. The actual content of the story may vary with what your class has done and the experiences your children are familiar with. An example follows:

There was a little boy who was tired, but he couldn't go to sleep; he had the wiggles. Every time a part of him was tired, another part would start to wiggle, and he'd giggle, and then he couldn't go to sleep. So he decided to tell himself a sleepy story. He started with his toes and said, "Toes, don't wiggle," but they kept wiggling. Then he said, "Toes, we're going to the beach and we are going to walk through so much sand that you'll be glad not to wiggle." And he walked and he walked and he walked and finally he was so tired that he sat down and his toes weren't wiggling. They were too tired. His ankles were tired and so were his knees. They felt heavy. Even his legs felt heavy. It just felt nice to be sitting down. Maybe even lying down. Oh, stretch out. . . . Umm. Rest your head back, get comfortable, close your eyes. . . . Oh, relax those tired feet again, all the way up the leg. Now your hip. Now your middle. Let your shoulders touch the floor if they want to; your elbows too. Now your hands. Uncurl your fingers. Even that little finger is heavy. Now let's check on the way back up. The wrists, elbows, and shoulders are all heavy and relaxed. Move your head up and lay it down; roll it a little to find a comfortable place. Open your mouth. Now close it. Yawn. Close your eyes. (Pause.) Breathe deeply. (Pause.) You're waking up. Roll your head, open your eyes. Sit up and wiggle just a little.

Increase Level of Difficulty

Procedure   As the children learn the process, increase the length of the pauses and incorporate some visual images. Make a recording of the story and encourage children to make up their own stories. Point out the relevant variables of pace and tone as well as content.

Decrease Level of Difficulty

Procedure   Begin by using this to teach body parts and lightly touch the parts as you talk or have someone else do that.

COMMENT   The relaxation portion of this is best spoken in a slow, placid monotone. At first, make your pauses short.

Creative Movement

MOVING BALLOONS

GOAL   To encourage creative movement
To follow directions
To increase body awareness

OBJECTIVE   The child will follow the directions given.

MATERIALS   Balloons (a variety of shapes and sizes)

PROCEDURE   Show the children several balloons, then blow them up. Talk about what happens if you do different things to a balloon (tie it in the middle and pinch off the end; blow it up until it pops, if you are comfortable doing this; let the air out fast, then slowly, stopping sometimes). Then have the children pretend their bodies are balloons. Talk them through the process of being blown up, then have them slowly let the air out. Have them let it out fast, and so on.

Increase Level of Difficulty

Procedure   Have small groups of children be one balloon by joining hands and being blown up and deflated together. Encourage children to be different shapes and sizes and have different things happen to them.

Decrease Level of Difficulty

Procedure   Be more illustrative in your directions: "I am blowing you up. You are getting bigger, and bigger. I'm almost out of breath. I don't think I can hold on any longer. I'm going to let you go. Whiz. You are getting smaller and smaller as the air goes out."

COMMENT   This activity allows energy release in a controlled way. You can regulate the pace by your directions.

Creative Movement

MOVEMENT EXPLORATION

GOAL   To encourage creative movement
To increase body awareness
To increase awareness of individual differences

OBJECTIVE   The child will move his body in response to directions given.

MATERIALS   None

PROCEDURE   Ask the children to move in unusual ways, such as:

Use any 3 parts of your body to move across the floor:
*   1 hand, 2 feet*
*   2 hands, 1 foot*
*   1 hand, 2 knees*

Hold your feet with your hands and pretend they are connected: How many ways can you move across the floor?
Can you move across the floor without touching your feet on the ground?

Increase Level of Difficulty

Procedure   After one child has responded to a request, see if other children can respond to the same request in a different way.

Decrease Level of Difficulty

Materials   Pictures of body parts

Procedure   Use pictures of body parts or demonstrate what specific parts can be used.

COMMENT   Given appropriate choices, children with physical disabilities may be very skillful in following the directions. With discussion, others may become aware of the problems of not being able to use one or more limbs.

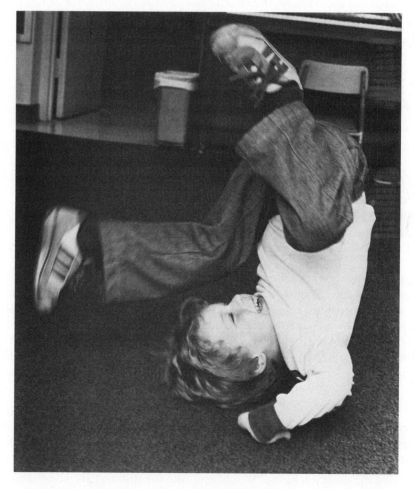

Children learn about their bodies by experimenting. For some children movement is easy and fun; for others it is difficult.

Creative Movement

WEIGHTY MOVEMENTS

GOAL   To encourage creativity
To increase body awareness
To improve sensory integration

OBJECTIVE   The child will follow the movements as directed.

MATERIALS   record, cassette, or compact disc player

records, cassettes, or compact discs

PROCEDURE   Talk to the children about the way they move. Talk about the weight of their movements. Ask them to stomp across the floor, then tiptoe across the floor. Have them label which was light and which was heavy. Have them demonstrate other heavy and light movements. Then have them combine heavy and light movements in a rhythmic fashion using heavy movements to accent the beat (light, light, heavy, light, light, heavy). Add music and see if they can accent the beat with their movements.

Increase Level of Difficulty

Procedure   Use dance music with a definite beat, such as a tango, and see if they can accent the beat with their movements. Be sure to use rhythm patterns that represent different cultures.

Decrease Level of Difficulty

Materials   Drum

Procedure   Count out the beats for the children as you use the drum for example ONE, two, three, FOUR, five, six, ONE, two, three, FOUR, five, six. Count slowly.

COMMENT   This activity emphasizes the rhythmic nature of movement, especially when it is paired with music. It shows children a repeating pattern that is not related to pitch or loudness.

Dramatic Play

NO NAME

GOAL   To encourage creative problem solving
To improve self-concept
To express feelings

OBJECTIVE   The child will suggest a name for the doll.

MATERIALS   A doll that has not been in the classroom before

PROCEDURE   During group time, show the children the doll. Explain that it is new to the room and doesn't have a name. Ask the children how they think you should go about naming the doll—not what, how. Note their suggestions; then suggest that if they want, they can play with this doll in the dramatic play area. (You may have to regulate the number of children that can be there at any one time.) At the end of the day the class can actually name the doll or make suggestions that will be finalized the following day. When the group meets again, talk about the method used to reach a decision as well as the decision reached. Then ask them about their own names and why they think their parents chose those names.

Increase Level of Difficulty

Procedure   As the doll can have only a limited number of names and nicknames, have the children discuss *how* they will decide on the name, in addition to participating in the naming process.

Decrease Level of Difficulty

Procedure   Give the children hints: "Would you like the doll to have your name?"

COMMENT   This activity can be used for a class pet or anything in the classroom that can be named.

Dramatic Play

DENTIST

GOAL   To encourage creative problem solving
To express feelings
To increase awareness of roles people play

OBJECTIVE   The child will play the roles of both dental office personnel and patient.

MATERIALS   Props for a dentist's office:

dental floss	cups of water	lab coat
tongue depressors	pretend drill	chair
cloth for around neck	small mirrors	table

PROCEDURE   Set up a dentist's office. Allow children to play the dentist, dental hygienist, nurse, receptionist, patient, parent of patient, and so on. Encourage them to talk about their concerns. Also talk about why it is important to go to the dentist.

Precede this with a trip to a dentist's office and follow it with some information on teeth and food. Talk about the care of the teeth and oral area as well as its function in speech.

Increase Level of Difficulty

Procedure   Support children in cooperative play and role taking. Provide them pictures and additional equipment. Encourage them to talk about the dentist and their feelings about going to the dentist's office. Add a listening tape of the sounds of the dentist's office. Emphasize the role of the dentist and that both men and women can be dentists.

Decrease Level of Difficulty

Procedure   Help children find an easier role. Assist them in exploring the materials.

COMMENT   Some children may not have been to the dentist's office. They might have many questions. For children who are fearful of trips to the dentist, this activity might help them work through some of their concerns. Be sure that all materials that are likely to be in children's mouths are clean and then thrown away.

Dramatic Play

DOCTOR'S OFFICE

GOAL   To encourage creative problem solving
To express feelings
To increase awareness of roles people play

OBJECTIVE   The child will pretend to be the doctor, nurse, or patient.

MATERIALS   Props for a doctor's office:

stethoscope	flashlight (without batteries)
syringes (without needles)	tongue depressors
dolls	lab coat

PROCEDURE   Set up the dramatic play area like a doctor's office. Have the children examine "sick" dolls and/or classmates. Be sure to include information on routine procedures, such as immunization and regular checkups, in addition to sick calls.

Increase Level of Difficulty

Procedure   Give children information on some of the different types of specialties in medicine. Talk about a pediatrician, surgeon, ophthalmologist, family practice physician, or allergist, and how you might need several doctors to handle a particular problem. Include the specialties that are most relevant to your classroom.

Decrease Level of Difficulty

Procedure   Allow the children to explore the equipment. It is sometimes useful to have the same equipment available for several days, as after initial exploration children participate in higher level play.

COMMENT   The doctor's office will probably be a familiar setting because most of the children will have been to the doctor for a checkup. Introduce this activity with a story or a visit from a doctor. Be sure to discuss why people go to doctors. You can expand this activity into a hospital set-up. Be sure to talk to the children about the differences.

SHOE STORE

GOAL   To encourage creative problem solving
To improve cause-and-effect reasoning
To increase awareness of roles people play

OBJECTIVE   The child will select and buy a pair of shoes appropriate for his stated purpose.

MATERIALS   Shoes for different purposes:

baseball shoes with cleats	walking shoes	shoes with steel toes
running shoes	clogs	baby shoes
high heels	winter slippers	golf shoes
ballet slippers	sandals	bowling shoes
toe shoes	boots	thongs
hiking boots		

PROCEDURE   During group time, discuss with the children the functions of shoes and how some situations require certain kinds of shoes. Have some examples and talk about how these shoes make it easier. Use obvious examples:

steel toes: won't hurt if something gets dropped on the toes
baseball cleats: get better traction running, less likely to slip
sandals: cooler

Once children have grasped the idea, have them use it in dramatic play to choose the shoes they need.

Increase Level of Difficulty

Procedure   Use the concept of shoes to help children think of a variety of ways in which we can adapt to changing situations.

Decrease Level of Difficulty

Procedure   Have children pair up the different shoes as they become mixed up either through play or your intervention.

COMMENT   This activity not only teaches the principles of buying and selling but also teaches specialized ways of coping with environments. For children with hearing impairments, add pictures of the places where the shoes might be used and have children match the shoes to the picture.

CONNECTIONS

GOAL   To encourage creative problem solving
To improve cause-and-effect reasoning
To increase awareness of roles people play

OBJECTIVE   The child will make one statement about what will happen when a connection is cut.

MATERIALS   string

8″ × 8″ squares of construction
paper of various colors

wide marking pen

tape

scissors

PROCEDURE   Pick a familiar place (e.g., the children's school) and draw a large picture of that place. Help the children think through the places in the city or services they are dependent upon. As each is mentioned, write the name on a piece of paper, attach string with a piece of tape, give this to a child, and secure the other end of the string to a central location in the picture.

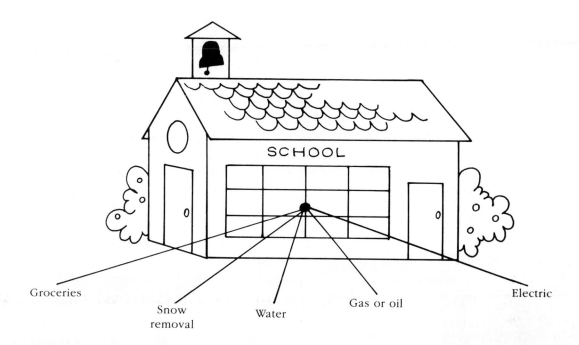

Talk about what each connection signifies. Then take a pair of scissors and cut one string (e.g., electric). Ask the children how the school would be different without electricity and what they could do to compensate: no lights—use flashlights or candles.

Increase Level of Difficulty

Procedure   Talk about different places and environments and how connections are not necessarily the same in all places.

Decrease Level of Difficulty

Procedure   In addition to cutting the string, explain to children the implications of what happened: "There is no water. What do we do if we are thirsty, have to go to the bathroom, and so on?" Help them experience the problem and generate possible preventive measures or solutions.

COMMENT   Children can think about their homes and talk about connections with their parents. It's important that children see the interdependency of services as well as the alternatives for services.

Dramatic Play

DAY PLAY

GOAL   To encourage creative problem solving
To improve self-concept
To broaden concepts of families

OBJECTIVE   The child will enact a sequence of appropriate activities.

MATERIALS   Props for the activities of a day:

kitchen   family room

bedroom   bathroom

PROCEDURE   Talk about the different times of the day and the activities that go with them. Set up centers designated as specific parts of the day and have the children rotate from center to center until they have completed a whole day. Have them play different roles (themselves, mother, father, sibling) and discuss who gets up first, what or who wakes them, and what they do first. Emphasize that family patterns are different.

Increase Level of Difficulty

Procedure   Focus on how families are different, yet each child gets to school. Different families have different patterns and routines.

Decrease Level of Difficulty

Procedure   Help children understand the part school plays in the context of their day. They may have many different placements before and after school, and these need to be acknowledged.

COMMENT   This activity can also be done with a small group of children playing different parts of the day and others guessing the part. If children are having difficulties adjusting to school, it helps them get a perspective on where school is in their personal sequence.

Provide a variety of clothes so that children can dress up and experiment with roles.

CIRCUS

GOAL   To improve self-concept
To increase body awareness
To increase awareness of roles people play

OBJECTIVE   The child will participate in at least one event.

MATERIALS   Props for a circus:

hats	balance beam
scarves	stuffed animals
costumes	mats

PROCEDURE   Encourage children to cooperate in developing circus acts using the props.

Read a story about the circus and talk about animal trainers, acrobats, tight-rope walkers, and so on. Be sure to have this activity if there is a circus in town.

Increase Level of Difficulty

Procedure   Encourage children to help organize the circus. Focus their interest on ordering the events, being sure everyone is included, making tickets, and so on.

Decrease Level of Difficulty

Procedure   Include some acts which are undemanding. Provide children with alternative roles if they are uncomfortable performing (e.g., handing out tickets).

COMMENT   Make sure that there are a variety of acts so all children can participate at an appropriate level.

References and Bibliography

Edge, N., & Hunter, T. (tape cassette). *Music is magic: Linking music and literacy*. Salem, OR: Nellie Edge Resources for Creative Teaching.

Haines, J., & Gerber, L. (1992). *Leading young children to music: A resource book for teachers* (4th ed.). Riverside, NJ: Merrill/Macmillan.

Hendrick, J. (1986). *Total learning: Curriculum for young children*. Columbus, OH: Merrill Publishing Co.

Jarnow, J. (1991). *All ears: How to choose and use recorded music for children*. New York: Penguin.

Kostelnik, M., Whiren, A., & Stein, L. (1986). Living with He-Man: Managing superhero fantasy play. *Young Children, 41*(4), 3–9.

Mayesky, M., Neuman, D., & Wlodkowski, R. (1985). *Creative activities for young children* (3rd ed.). New York: Delmar Publishers, Inc.

Mayesky, M. (1990). *Creative activities for young children* (4th ed.). Albany, NY: Delmar Publishers, Inc.

National Information Center for Children and Youth with Handicaps. (1989). Assistive Technology: *News Digest*. Washington, DC. Number 13.

Perry, J., Perry, I., & Draper, T. (1987). *Music and child development*. New York: Springer-Verlag.

Smilansky, S. & Sfefatya, L. (1990). *Facilitating play: A medium for promoting cognitive, socio-emotional and academic development in young children*. Gaithersburg, MD: Psychosocial and Educational Publications.

Tegano, D., Moran III, J., & Sawyer, J. *Creativity in early childhood classrooms*. Washington, DC: National Education Association.

Bibliography for Additional Reading

Bayless, K. M., & Ramsey, M. (1987). *Music: A way of life for the young child* (3rd ed.). Columbus, OH: Merrill Publishing Co.

Bergen, D. (1988). *Play as a medium for learning and development: A handbook of theory and practice*. Portsmouth, NH: Heinemann.

Berlfein, J. (1985). *A classroom with blocks* (Filmstrip). Washington, DC: National Association for the Education of Young Children. (NAEYC #820, $25.)

Christoplos, F., & Valletutti, P. J. (1990). *Discovering children's creative thinking through the arts*. Bloomington, IN: Phi Delta Kappa.

Day, B. (1988). *Early childhood education: Creative learning activities.* New York: Macmillan.

Hagan, J., Lewis, H., & Similansky, S. (1988). *Clay in the classroom: Helping children develop cognitive and affective skills for learning.* New York: Peter Lang.

Herr, J., & Libby, Y. (1990). *Creative resources for the early childhood classroom.* Albany, NY: Delmar Publishers, Inc.

Hirsh, E. (Ed.). (1984). *The block book* (rev. ed.). Washington, DC: National Association for the Education of Young Children.

McDonald, D. T., & Somons, G. M. (1989). *Musical growth and development.* New York: Schirmer.

North, M. (1990). *Movement & dance education: A guide for the primary & middle school teachers.* Plymouth, England: Northcote House.

Rogers, C. S., & Sawyers, J. K. (1988). *Play in the lives of children.* Washington, DC: National Association for the Education of Young Children.

The role of music in the education of special learners (1979). Englewood Cliffs, NJ: Silver Burdett Co.

Skeen, P., Garner, A. P., & Cartwright, S. (1984). *Woodworking for young children.* Washington, DC: National Association for the Education of Young Children.

Striker, S. *Please touch: How to stimulate your child's creative development through movement, music, art and play.* New York: Simon & Schuster.

Sullivan, M. (1982). *Feeling strong, feeling free: Movement exploration for young children.* Washington, DC: National Association for the Education of Young Children.

Wachowiak, F. (1985). *Emphasis art* (4th ed.). New York: Harper & Row.

Zavitkovsky, D. (1985). *Listen to the Children.* Washington, DC: National Association for the Education of Young Children.

Chapter 28

Activities for Infants and Toddlers: Language Arts, Discovery, Sensory Motor, Social Awareness, and Creative Arts

Activities for infants and toddlers are so different from those for preschool children that they are included in a separate chapter. Activities for infants are usually one-on-one experiences that are planned for a particular child. Infants, especially very young ones, have such a small repertoire of behavior that a single activity with slight variation can be repeated until the infant reaches another developmental level. For example, the activity "Books" can be repeated many times. One just reads a different book; the techniques are the same.

For purposes of clarity, I have decided that infants become toddlers at one year. In the objective for each activity the word "infant" indicates activities specifically designed for children under one year, and "toddler" indicates those designed for one- and two-year-olds. If the activity is appropriate for both, the words "infants and toddlers" are used.

These designations are also used to represent developmental levels, that is, infant activities are designed to be done lying or sitting. Toddler activities are designed for children who can walk. More importantly, toddler activities are for children who can choose what they want to do by going to it. As toddlers advance, move on to some of the activities designed for preschoolers and use the variations for decreasing level of difficulty.

Appropriate activities enhance learning and encourage independence in infants and toddlers. As you think about activities for infants and toddlers the most important consideration is matching the particular activity to the developmental level of the child you are teaching. Children need different activities at different stages of development to stimulate learning.

In general, materials that encourage active involvement of the child are best. Active involvement differs: Just looking might be active involvement for a very young child, but not for an older one. Young children need a wide variety of materials that serve the same purpose, as they have such a small repertoire of behaviors. For example, as children learn to walk they enjoy pull toys. You need to have many different toys that can be pulled or pushed.

For purposes of activity planning, infancy is divided into three groupings based on motor development. The motor requirements of an activity determine what activity is appropriate for which child. Infants from birth up to about five months of age do not have good antigravity skills. Therefore activities are designed for an infant who is lying either prone (on stomach), supine (on back), or in a supported sitting position. These **585** activities are also designed for older infants who are at this developmental level. At about five months of age, children need less support sitting (head control is greatly improved), and they are moving toward independent sitting. They show more independent exploration in their play. Their hands are now free to explore the environment. The third stage (about nine or ten months) is marked by some form of emerging mobility. The child can move independently by crawling, creeping, hitching, scooting, or perhaps walking.

Activity planning changes dramatically as infants move into toddlerhood at about one year. Toddlers can move purposefully around the room. Toddlers understand more than they can say, so planning involves offering children choices. Choosing is most easily provided for by having low, open shelves with safe toys that children can use. Young toddlers still play alone most of the time, but they may want to be part of a small group for a short time.

Older toddlers are interested in doing things for themselves. Although still playing alone most of the time, they can participate in organized group experiences, provided the groups are small and the time is short (about 5 minutes). Toddlers can throw and kick large balls and even walk backward. Their vocabulary is increasing rapidly. Fine motor skills are improving; they can use paints and brush and can scribble. They can participate in pretend play.

Underlying all programming for infants and toddlers, especially those with disabilities, is respect. Young children need activities that help them establish some control over their environment. This security builds a sense of efficacy and self esteem, difficult issues for infants and toddlers with developmental delays. To facilitate this development talk directly with the infant. Tell young children what is going to happen; even if the child cannot talk still consult with the infant before taking action and explain to the children the purpose of your actions (Ross, 1992). (You might ask the infant, "Are you ready to be picked up?" The child's nod or tensing might be your answer.)

Language Arts

Learning to talk is a major task for infants and toddlers, requiring listening skills and someone to listen to. As the infant is learning to talk he is also learning to use language as a way of internalizing and organizing information.

Listening and Speaking

Infants begin the process of learning to talk at birth. In the first few months of life infants are learning to distinguish different sounds; that is, noise versus the human voice. By one month of age, infants will respond differently to speech than to other sounds and even begin to show awareness of the different speech sounds that people make. Although young infants can hear speech sounds, they are not yet able to make them because they lack the muscle coordination for speech. By the time the infant is about a month old, she begins to practice sound formation by cooing and babbling by about four months. Talking to her and imitating the infant's babbling are good ways to foster language during this stage.

As infants begin to babble they also initiate verbal contact with others. Infants need verbal stimulation at this time. You can support language development by responding to an infant's attempts at conversation (babbling). Introduce new words, but take turns with her. Infants are continually learning how to say new sounds and eventually new words.

Language development next involves the toddler's learning the meaning of words. Helping toddlers build a vocabulary (children understand the meaning of many words before they are able to speak them) is an important goal (Segal, 1988).

Around a year, infants begin to form easy words from the sounds they have been babbling. Da-da-da-da becomes "dada" or "daddy"; ma-ma-ma becomes "mama" or "mommy." The sounds become meaningful and consistently applied. Other common first words are action words or words that the child hears frequently like cup, juice, bye-bye, or ball.

Usually those first words carry lots of meaning. For example, when a toddler says "ball," it is usually easy to understand from the situation whether he means "Get me the ball," "Catch the ball," or "Look what I found. A ball!" It is not until about eighteen months that toddlers begin to string words together, such as "Juice all gone," or "Daddy up!"

Toddler conversations are not the same as adult conversations, so you will need to continue to rely on situational cues for the meanings of toddlers' words. Children's language, as their other skills, develops at different rates. Some children are early talkers and some are not. Almost all children have problems with pronouncing certain sounds or words. Children developmentally cannot make all the sounds necessary for the English language until about age six or seven.

Offer infants and toddlers a wide range of experiences and talk with them during and following these experiences. Experiences as simple as a stroll around the block, a trip to the grocery store, or looking and touching a visiting pet are very important. Point out the flowers you pass on your walk, name the bananas as you place them in the grocery cart, and label the kitten's fur as "fluffy" while the children pet it.

Some ways of supporting language development are:

— Model good language skills when you talk with children.

— If a child mispronounces a word, repeat the word correctly in your next sentence. For example, if she says, "Here's a poon," you might say, "Oh, you found the *spoon.*"

— When giving toddlers a choice, encourage them to tell you which one they want, not just "yes" or "no."

— For very young children, point to what you are talking about so the children can learn the names of objects.

— Keep sentences simple but refrain from using "baby talk."

— Listen to what toddlers say. Having someone listen encourages their talking.

— Provide materials that encourage talking: toy telephones, puppets, books, and so on.

Reading

Very young children learn best from concrete experiences. They learn more about the concept of "apple" when they can see, touch, smell, and taste a real apple rather than when they just see a picture of one. However, when concrete experiences with objects are accompanied by appropriate books, learning can be further enhanced.

Programs specifically aimed at helping children become good readers when they are infants and toddlers are controversial. Indeed, programs that encourage parents to use an academic approach, such as letter and word flash cards with infants and toddlers, have been criticized for placing undue pressures on children and for not letting them "be children" and learn through play experiences. It is, however, appropriate to set the stage for reading, even with infants.

Read aloud to infants and toddlers. Have a daily time for reading. Infants enjoy sitting on your lap as you slowly turn the pages in a book and name pictures on the pages. The close physical contact provided is often as important as the book itself. Independently, toddlers may mouth or chew on books, attempt to turn the pages, squeal and slap pages, or carry books with them as they toddle about. Even such playful manipulations of books provide positive early experiences, which enhance learning language and preparation for reading.

When selecting books for infants and toddlers:

— Choose books with bright, colorful, appealing pictures.

— The simpler the pictures the better. Books with one picture per page are good for the very young.

— Encourage toddlers to talk about the pictures.

— If there are words, the language should be simple and brief.

— Select durable books. Many infant/toddler books are available with pages of heavy coated cardboard, cloth, or plastic.

— Expect toddlers to bring their favorite book to you to be looked at or read again and again.

Writing

In the area of writing, the major objective for toddlers is to introduce them to the concept of a written language and for them to understand that there is a connection between written and spoken words. Provide writing materials. With supervision, they love coloring and drawing on blank paper. You can introduce words informally as you write their name on their paper. (Say something like, "This says Tiki," each time you write his name.) As children begin to label their drawings, for instance, calling their scribbles a "ball," write their label on the paper whether or not it looks anything like what they say it is. This, too, will help children make the beginning connection between spoken and written words.

Discovery

Infants and toddlers need to learn about the world they live in. They need many real-life experiences as a foundation for concept development. From birth until about twenty-four months of age infants move from reflex-dominated behaviors to voluntary, planned responses to objects or events in the environment. For this learning to take place infants need to be actively engaged with their environment and must have a variety of experiences from which they can abstract ideas.

Adults need to provide opportunities for learning as well as the language labels that make these experiences more meaningful to children. This combination of experience and language is necessary for children to develop scientific and mathematical thinking. For example, the young toddler first learns that soft, green things outside are called plants. Later, he discovers that not all green things outside are plants, but can be other things such as cans, cars, trees, and so on. Further, he learns that there are different types of plants, some that you can eat, some that hurt, and some that look pretty. Later, the child learns that small, green things called plants outside are also called plants when inside. Finally, the child learns that different plants have individual names, which distinguish one plant from another. In each case, the child adapts previously learned information into a new category of information. He does this by experiencing his world with the support of adults.

Mathematics

There is no expectation that infants and toddlers will learn complex math skills, but rather, that they will be aware of numbers and the concept of counting. They will have heard songs and nursery rhymes that include numbers. They will be familiar with words that designate quantity and size.

With increasing age, toddlers can make size distinctions between what is big and what is little. They can put large pegs in pegboards as adults count them. They can sing counting songs. They may be able to "count," but it is unlikely that they will have number concepts at this age. They can do simple (three-piece) form boards and puzzles.

Science

Science for infants and toddlers involves investigating the world they live in. The process of learning to find answers is more important than the answers themselves. It is the basis for a way of thinking. For children this age, science is mostly informal; that is, it is nondirected, free investigation by the infant and toddler. The adult's role is to plan an intriguing environment that invites exploration.

Infants, beginning about four months, become fascinated with what objects do. Infants now explore materials to see what they can do. Previously, the goal was simply motor action. Now, an infant who "discovers" he can make a toy rattle will repeat the shaking action again and again to hear the rattle. This is the beginning of means-end behavior. This is also science.

Means-end describes the ability to use a means or procedure to achieve a desired end or goal, for example, pulling a string to get a ring that is out of reach. This behavior starts as trial and error in the middle of the first year, but becomes more purposeful by the end of the year.

To facilitate this learning infants need sound toys: shakers, bells, rattles, clackers. Show the infant the xylophone and help him make a noise with it. Give him spoons or blocks to bang. He needs a variety of toys and time to experiment. Include materials that involve cause-and-effect relationships: wind-up toys, "busy boxes," and Jack-in-the-boxes.

The first signs of the concept of object permanence begin about the middle of the first year. Object permanence is the knowledge that allows infants to remember that objects exist even when they are not in sight. Infants at this age will search for and may find a toy that is partially hidden. If the toy is completely hidden, the child loses interest and will not search for it. By the end of the first year the infant will search for objects that he sees you hide. However, if the object is not where he initially searched for it, he will stop looking. By the middle of the second year the infant searches beyond the initial uncovering place. He begins to search in new places for hidden objects. He must, however, still see the object hidden to know what to look for.

As infants and toddlers are developing the concept of object permanence, play games with them that involve forms of looking for objects and hiding and seeking. Drop objects and see if the child looks for them and then retrieves them. Hide toys for the infant to find, play peek-a-boo, disappear and reappear in the same or different places. Talk to the children when you are out of their sight.

By about age two the toddler can begin to solve problems in his mind, without going through the physical actions of the external problem-solving process. He can mentally represent objects and actions without needing to see them. He can invent new means to get objects, without relying on the trial and error process. He can find hidden objects that are identified verbally.

Between two and three toddlers begin to use mental representations and symbolic thought. Words become signifiers of objects and events. Toddlers can classify based on function. The child's play skills expand into more creative activities.

Infants and toddlers acquire information by experimenting with materials, objects, and events. Active learning experiences allow toddlers the opportunity to practice, refine, and revise previously learned skills. They need a safe environment, with materials that encourage exploration and experimentation.

Sensory Motor

Infants and toddlers need activities that encourage the development of large and small motor skills and provide opportunities for integrating these skills with sensory input. They need a variety of materials that encourage all types of movements and reflect a developmental progression for skill building.

Large Motor

Activities for young infants are designed to use the large muscles of the body, such as those in the neck, trunk, arms, and legs. These muscles are necessary for all antigravity postures, such as sitting, standing, and walking. They also are necessary to stabilize the body as finer movements are performed. The pattern in which they develop serves as a guide for matching activities to children.

— Infants gain head control first, then arm coordination, and finally control of their legs. Coordination of motor skills first develops close to the center of the body with control of the neck and the shoulders. Then control of body parts moves further away from the midline to the arms and, eventually, the fingers.

— The acquisition of more complex motor skills builds on simpler motor skills. A young child must acquire the ability to control his head before he acquires the ability to sit.

— The sequence of motor development is overlapping between skills. Mastery of one skill is not necessary before others can begin, although it does need to reach a functional level. Children begin to experiment with new motor skills as they are fine-tuning others.

— The development of motor abilities involves the breaking down of gross movements into finer, coordinated, and voluntary motor responses.

— Children differ in the rate at which they acquire motor skills, but the progression of development is the same.

Developing and using the large muscles of the body is one of the tasks of infancy and early childhood. The pattern of motor development dictates that gross motor development precedes fine motor development. Children who cannot pick up a large ball and lift it over their head cannot be expected to print their names recognizably, regardless of the amount of time spent practicing.

To support large motor development children need materials that encourage movement: soft, easily grasped balls, small riding toys, push and pull toys.

Small Motor

Fine motor development involves the child's ability to use the small muscles of the arms, hands, and fingers. Reaching begins with gross movements of the arm and progresses to directed, precise touching of objects. Grasping proceeds from swiping at and missing objects to accurately picking up small items.

Fine motor development has three concepts that underlie all skill maturity.

1. Initially the infant's hands are used palm down. As the wrist muscles strengthen, the hand can rotate so that he can accept objects with his palm up.

2. Skill development (reaching) occurs close to the midline of the body and slowly moves to the outer extremes.

3. The infant develops grasping skills first using the "little finger side" of the hand and hand pad. As hand muscle strength increases, this action moves to the thumb side. The child progresses from raking up objects with her whole hand to picking up objects with the tips of the thumb and index finger.

The development of fine motor skills is dependent on other related skills. Although vision is not a prerequisite for fine motor development, the ability to see objects motivates children and directs their reaching. Reaching is also dependent on the child's head and trunk control and adequate balance. Reaching is a prerequisite to grasping and picking up objects. An infant must be able to pick up and release objects for finer eye-hand coordination skills to develop.

Children need interesting toys to reach for and grasp. They need materials with pieces that fit together or stack, such as shape boxes, simple puzzles, blocks, and stacking rings. Also useful are materials that require pressure to put together or take apart, such as bristle blocks, rubber pegboards and plastic pegs, rubber puzzles, and "pop" beads.

Sensory Motor Integration

Motor skills are often used in conjunction with vision and hearing. In sensory motor integration both sensory and motor components of behavior are integrated in the brain to facilitate smooth movement and the ability to learn new skills.

Use materials with varied textures (textured rattles and blocks, fuzzy puppets, playdough made from different recipes) to facilitate sensory motor integration.

Social Awareness

Infants first need to develop self-awareness, then awareness of others and the roles those significant others play in their lives. First they learn about their family and caregivers. As they enter a group setting they must expand their awareness of roles of adults to include teachers. Likewise, they will need to develop methods of interacting with peers. Throughout this process they are learning about themselves.

Social Studies

Infants and toddlers gradually become aware of their near environment, their home and school setting, and then the community in which they live. They do this by taking short field trips around the school, going to the grocery store, and visiting others. They see people who look different than they do. They see adults performing many different tasks. Social studies helps children learn about the complexities of their environment.

Young toddlers will spend most of their social studies time re-enacting the adult roles that they are most familiar with and the situations that are meaningful to them. As children's awareness of the environment expands, these new roles will be incorporated into play. After a visit to a fire station, domestic play scenes may be interrupted by firefighters who are called to put out the fire.

Inclusion

For infants, social awareness begins with self-awareness. Adults can help infants develop self-awareness in a number of ways. For infants to interact they must be in a quiet, alert state: calm *and* aware of what is going on around them. In young infants this state only lasts for a few seconds or minutes at a time.

Some ways you can help infants develop self-awareness are:

— When the infant begins to stir from a nap, begin to talk in a soothing voice. Try to catch and maintain eye contact.

— When the infant cries, lift him to your shoulder, rub his back, and help him to focus on an interesting object or your face.

— As the infant notices his hands and has fun making them move, play a gentle game of pat-a-cake or peek-a-boo using the child's hands.

— When you are changing the infant, take the opportunity to develop body awareness by massaging her arms, legs, and feet with gentle pressure and light touches (adapted from Prudhoe, 1989).

With increasing age, self-awareness grows. Toddlers can tell you their name; they know the members of their family and their ethnic background. They learn where they live. Toddlers also become aware of ways in which they are similar to and different from others. They become aware of their strengths and limitations. They learn about themselves by the way others respond to them.

Toddlers who feel good about themselves can accept themselves as they are. They can also accept others, for social awareness also involves the child's growth as a member of a group. To be part of the group, toddlers must learn to share materials, take turns, listen at appropriate times, work independently, and also join the group.

Toddlers may need to learn new ways to be with adults when they enter an early childhood program. They must learn the different expectations of teachers and parents and understand the expectations of school versus home. They need to find ways of sharing adult attention. These are difficult areas of growth, especially for infants and toddlers with disabilities.

Include materials that encourage awareness of self and others, such as toys with mirrors, dolls, and puppets. Provide materials for cuddling, such as stuffed dolls and toys, as well as a cozy area to cuddle in.

Health and Safety

As children become more independently mobile, issues of health and safety take on new importance in the curriculum. As you venture out into the community with young children they will learn that red means stop, and that they must hold hands or a rope while crossing streets. Even before infants can walk you can begin to teach these concepts by verbalizing what you are doing as you push the stroller or pull a wagon: "The light is red. We have to stop until it turns green." "I'm looking both ways before we cross the street."

As children learn to label their body parts and become more aware of their bodies, they can take a more active part in their health care. Toddlers can learn some health routines early, such as washing their hands before eating and after toileting.

Creative Arts

Children are unique. Each has his own special way of being in the world; his own style of working, learning, and creating. Creativity is somewhat dependent upon the developmental level of the child and his past experience with media. That is, what is creative for infants is not creative for toddlers and what is creative for children who have never experienced a particular medium is not creative for children who have much experience with it. Creative experiences are usually unstructured opportunities for exploration.

Art

Art for toddlers is a sensory experience. They randomly make marks on paper. They may be just as interested in getting crayons out of the container or the tops off markers as they are in making marks. Because of their lack of concern about the product, the boundaries of paper are seen as arbitrary and are rarely acknowledged. Toddlers need large, sturdy crayons, chalk, and paint brushes. The paper, too, needs to be large enough to accommodate broad movements. Toddlers need to explore and use many different art media. They can paste collage materials and they can help tear them into pieces. They enjoy finger painting as well as using thick tempera paint, clay, or playdough. Toddlers are interested at first in exploring the medium itself.

At some point, children discover the connection between their movements and the marks on the paper. They are now in control. The product may not look different, but the experience is different for the toddler. The control is motivating. It is also generalized. If they know they made a mark on the page, they also know their finger made the hole in the dough. Although children differ, this usually happens around age three.

Music

Very young infants respond to quiet singing and rocking. It is soothing and sets the tone for sleep. When infants develop means-end behavior (beginning about four months), moving rattles and hitting bells are initial musical experiences. At about eight months infants can use tools to produce sound. They can hit the xylophone with a mallet or the piano with their fingers to produce sound. The toddler experiments with sound by hitting different instruments with different objects to discover different sounds. By about a year and a half toddlers enjoy music and dancing. By two they can learn simple songs and will want to sing them again and again. They like simple songs and nursery rhymes that you can sing or chant together.

Creative Movement

As movement comes more under the toddlers' control they begin to experiment. About age two they like songs with motions and moving to music. They do, however, need frequent breaks. They are not up to prolonged periods of strenuous movement. While movement is still being mastered children are not as free to be creative.

Dramatic Play

Young toddlers use dramatic play to consolidate adult roles that they are most familiar with. These are usually roles that revolve around the home. Child care, cleaning, and cooking are typical "housekeeping" themes. Toddlers also play through situations that are meaningful to them. One can often learn about the toddlers' feelings by watching and listening to their play.

Infant and Toddler Goals

Goals for infants and toddlers are broader and more general than those for older children.

To Increase Language Arts Concepts

Infants and toddlers need to have many opportunities to listen to adults talking to them. Their beginning babble and use of words needs to be reinforced. They also need exposure to reading and writing readiness activities.

To Increase Discovery Concepts	Basic scientific thinking begins in infancy. The process needs to be supported regardless of the accuracy of the information.
To Increase Sensory Motor Skills	The development of sensory motor skills is most rapid during infancy and toddlerhood. The skills emerge and are refined with practice during these years.
To Increase Social Awareness	Infants and toddlers need to develop self-awareness. This awareness expands into awareness of peers and the roles of other adults. It begins with the infants' near environment and expands into the community.
To Increase Creative Arts Concepts	Infants and toddlers need to have the opportunity to freely explore art media, move to music, learn simple songs, and play through familiar roles.
Teaching Strategies	Young children with *communication* disorders need experiences that help them to communicate more effectively. Teachers must give clear instructions, provide opportunities for conversation, and model good language skills. Books that are on the child's developmental level are always important.

Learn the gestures toddlers with *hearing* impairments use for communicating. Be sure to use hand signs, gestures, and body language while you talk with these children. Provide stimulation through their senses of vision, smell, touch, and taste. Establish eye contact before you begin interactions. Imitate the infant's sounds to encourage her continued babbling and respond enthusiastically to all vocalizations. Let the toddler feel your lips and throat vibrate as you talk or sing. Use a mirror often for the infant to watch herself make babbling sounds.

Infants and toddlers with *visual* impairments need high contrast materials (such as black and white combinations) to use their residual vision (if any). Offer stimulation through their other senses (sounds, smell, touch, taste). When you talk to the infant or imitate his babbling, let him feel your lips move. Help infants identify and locate the source of sounds they hear. Some infants with *visual* impairments rock themselves back and forth for self-stimulation. Distract them by providing them with an interesting activity or toy. Use words to tell the toddler what you are doing and pair words with motions or activities. For example, pair the word "up" with the action of picking up the child. Sensory activities help children learn the meaning of words when adults pair words with the way the materials feel. Be sure to tell toddlers the name of foods or drinks. They will learn what peanut butter is by the smell, texture, and taste of it, even if they can't see it.

It is unlikely that you will encounter an infant or toddler that is labeled as having an *emotional/behavioral* disorder or a *learning disability*. At this age a child with a severe disability in either of these areas would probably be classified as *developmentally delayed* or seen as having a communications disorder. Later testing would be necessary for classification.

For infants and toddlers with *physical* disabilities, provide toys to look at and listen to. Be sure to bring to the child objects that she can't get herself. Positioning is very important. Be sure to consult with the occupational or physical therapist for specific information.

You will encounter few children with *health* impairments, as these usually are not diagnosed this early.

The term *developmental delays* is used when a clear diagnosis is not possible, yet delays in one or more areas are apparent. Children with developmental delays will have very mixed characteristics at this age. It is useful to look at assessments to determine areas of strength and need.

Children with overall *developmental delays* need a great deal of repetition. Give short directions one step at a time. Offer challenging activities in small steps. Use demonstrations and modeling to help children learn. Encourage children for effort as well as for achievement. Expect children to have a very short attention span. Emerging language skills may be best encouraged with a short picture book with one picture per page, which you verbally label for the child. It is likely that developmental skills will be more difficult for children with developmental disabilities to master, and they will develop at a later time than they do with other children.

Activities for Infants and Toddlers

Goal	Activity
To increase language arts concepts	Books
	Dressing Books
	Feed the Face
	Food
	Hats Off
	My Book
	Puppets
	Telephone
	House
	Inflatable Animals
	Moving Like the Animals
	Cleaning House
	Dolls
	Mirror
To increase discovery concepts	Hidden Toys
	Big or Little
	Nesting Toys
	Noisy Rollers
	Rattle
	Shape Sorter
	Suction Cup Toys
	Take Apart Toys
	Blocks
	Dump and Fill
	Grab It
	Puzzles
	Whole-Piece Knobbed Puzzles
To increase sensory motor skills	Dressing Books
	Feed the Face
	Food
	Hats Off
	My Book
	Big or Little
	Nesting Toys
	Noisy Rollers
	Rattle
	Shape Sorter

Goal	Activity
	Suction Cup Toys
	Take Apart Toys
	Keys
	Mobiles
	Rolling Balls
	Teether
	Yarn Balls
	Inflatable Animals
	Moving Like the Animals
	Blocks
	Dump and Fill
	Grab It
	Puzzles
	Whole-Piece Knobbed Puzzles
	Cleaning House
	Dolls
	Mirror
	Washing Dishes
	Dancing
	Dress Up
	Painting with Water
	Print It
	Stick It
	Textures
To increase social awareness	My Book
	Puppets
	Telephone
	Cleaning House
	Dolls
	Mirror
	Washing Dishes
	Big Pictures
	Dog Walking
To increase creative arts concepts	House
	Dancing
	Dress Up
	Painting with Water
	Print It
	Stick It
	Textures
	Big Pictures
	Dog Walking

Language Arts

BOOKS

GOAL   To increase language arts concepts

OBJECTIVE   The infant or toddler will explore the book.

MATERIALS   Child's picture book (one picture per page)

PROCEDURE   Let the child explore the book while sitting on your lap or close by. Comment on the picture the child is looking at. For example, say, "Look at the bear. He is climbing a tree." If the child's attention continues, keep talking about the major details of the picture, pointing out colors and familiar objects. As soon as the child loses interest, stop.

Increase Level of Difficulty

Procedure   Open the book so two pictures are visible. Ask the child to show you the bear, for example. If the child points to the wrong picture, say: "Here's the bear. That is a cat." Place the child's hand on each picture as you are naming it. Later move on to having the child name the picture you point to. Look for chances to use the words in the book in your later verbal interactions with children. For example, say: "There's a cat. We saw one like that in our book." Choose books that have detailed pictures or those that show less familiar objects.

Decrease Level of Difficulty

Procedure   Place the child on your lap. Look at one page at a time. Name the picture. Encourage the child to touch or pat the picture. Ask the child to repeat the word or the first syllable of a more difficult word after you.

COMMENT   Children enjoy books at an early age, even if they can only attend to one picture.

Language Arts

DRESSING BOOK

GOAL   To increase language arts concepts
To increase sensory motor skills

OBJECTIVE   The toddler will point to the articles of clothing named.

MATERIALS   A book about dressing

PROCEDURE   Read the book while the child is sitting on your lap or near you. Name and point to the articles of clothing. Ask the child to point to the correct picture as you name each article. Then ask him to name the article of clothing shown in the picture and find the piece of clothing on himself if he is wearing that article. Discuss how the colors and styles he is wearing are different from those in the book.

Increase Level of Difficulty

Procedure   Have the child "read" the book. Then ask him to show you where each article goes. For instance: "Where do the shoes go? Yes, that's right! Shoes go on your feet!" Encourage the children to help undress and dress themselves as much as they are able during daily activities. For example, wait for younger children to push their arms and legs through their sleeves and pant legs. Encourage older toddlers to pull up socks and put on shoes. Talk and ask questions about their activity.

Decrease Level of Difficulty

Procedure   Use children's clothing and ask the child to point to part of himself or you that the clothing would cover. If necessary, give the child a choice. Then point to the picture and back to the clothing as you name each.

COMMENT   This activity fosters adaptive behavior as well as language development.

Language Arts

FEED THE FACE

GOAL   To increase language arts concepts
To increase sensory motor skills

OBJECTIVE   The toddler will put the tops in the designated opening.

MATERIALS   shoe box   paper   markers   tape or glue
tops from baby food jars or small blocks

PROCEDURE   Cover a sturdy shoe box with paper and draw a face on the front. Decorate the face. Then cut openings for the mouth, eyes, and nose. (Laminating the face or putting clear Contact paper over it increases its durability.) Demonstrate how the jar lids fit into the clown's mouth, eyes, and nose and encourage the toddler to try.

Increase Level of Difficulty

Procedure   Ask the child to put a lid in the facial part that you name. Ask the child to point to her corresponding facial part. Ask her to name the parts of her face as you point first to your face then to her face. Talk about how hungry the clown is today and count the number of lids the clown "eats." Have the child decide what the clown's favorite foods are.

Decrease Level of Difficulty

Materials   Increase the size of the holes in the clown.

Procedure   The child may not be ready to put items in, but may enjoy removing the lids from the shoebox.

COMMENT   This is a fun way to practice eye-hand coordination with the opportunity for a lot of language input.

Language Arts

FOOD

GOAL   To increase language arts concepts
To increase sensory motor skills

OBJECTIVE   The toddler will put the pictures of the food in the tub.

MATERIALS   laminated pictures of foods   tub with lid (slotted)

PROCEDURE   Put the lid on the tub and encourage the child to explore the tub. Demonstrate how to put "food" into slot, if necessary. Talk to the child about what food he is putting into the tub, especially foods that are most familiar to the child.

Have simpler books available so toddlers can look at books independently.

Increase Level of Difficulty

Materials   More laminated food pictures

Procedure   Ask the child to find a certain food you name: "Can you find the grapes?" Ask the child to name the picture he chooses to place in the tub. Have the child name foods at snack and meal time. When possible, give children a choice of foods to eat.

Decrease Level of Difficulty

Materials   Plastic food (fruits, vegetables, and so on)

Procedure   Take the lid off the tub and let the child put the plastic food in and take it out of the tub.

COMMENT   Food is a familiar and relevant concept to children. Using the pictures, however, is more difficult than using the food itself or a three-dimensional representation.

Language Arts

HATS OFF

GOAL   To increase language arts concepts
To increase sensory motor skills

OBJECTIVE   The toddler will put the hat on and take it off upon request.

MATERIALS   A hat for each child

PROCEDURE   Show the children your hat. Say: "This is my hat. Now it's *off*. I'm going to put it *on*." Put it on. Then tell the children to put their hats on and then take them off. Do this several times. Be dramatic!

Increase Level of Difficulty

Procedure   This activity can be used as a simple Simon Says game by just putting the hat on and off. That is, Simon says put your hat on. (Hats go on.) Take it off. (Hats should stay on.) Have children put the hat on another body part, for example, the hand, foot, or knee.

Decrease Level of Difficulty

Materials   Mirror

Procedure   Have the child stand in front of a mirror and put on and take off the hat. This way the child can see himself as you both model and give directions.

COMMENT   This activity involves both following directions and understanding the concepts on and off. Be sure to reinforce these concepts throughout the day by telling children that they are "on the cot" or that they just jumped "off the bench."

Language Arts

MY BOOK

GOAL   To increase language arts concepts
To increase sensory motor skills
To increase social awareness

OBJECTIVE   The toddler will make a book.

MATERIALS   sandwich-size plastic bags that zip closed

magazines	markers	construction paper	paste
yarn	rings	paper scraps	

PROCEDURE   Cut construction paper so that it fits inside the plastic bag. Encourage the children to draw or paste on the paper and then help them put it inside the bag. Write their name on one piece of paper and put that in a bag for the beginning of the book. Children can make as many or as few pages as they wish. Put each page in a separate bag. Put holes through the pages (and bags) and fasten them together with small rings or yarn.

Increase Level of Difficulty

Procedure   Encourage children to make more pages. Help them decorate both sides of the paper. They might have a theme for the book, such as color, and they could have a different color paper on each page and paste pictures of that color on the paper.

Decrease Level of Difficulty

Procedure   Support children in marking or gluing objects on the construction paper. You may have to put the pages into the plastic and make the book while the child observes, if his attention span is that long.

COMMENT   Children can enjoy looking at these books. Encourage parents to make similar books with pictures of family members or as a way of reminding children of a trip or special event.

Language Arts

PUPPETS

GOAL   To increase language arts concepts
To increase social awareness

OBJECTIVE   The infant or toddler will interact with the puppet.

MATERIALS   Duck and bunny puppets (or other animal puppets)

PROCEDURE   With the puppet on your hand, talk to the child and encourage the child to talk with the duck or bunny.

Increase Level of Difficulty

Procedure   Let the child experiment with putting the puppet on his own hand. Use the puppet to have a "conversation" with the child. Give the child time to respond.

Decrease Level of Difficulty

Procedure   Say, "I'm a duck. I say 'quack, quack'" or "I'm a bunny. I hop-hop-hop." Encourage the child to imitate sounds, words, or actions.

COMMENT   Encourage older children to use puppets with younger children. Talking with puppets may encourage peer interaction as well as foster development of language skills.

Language Arts

TELEPHONE

GOAL   To increase language arts concepts
To increase social awareness

OBJECTIVE   The toddler will "talk" on the telephone.

MATERIALS   Telephone

PROCEDURE   Make phone noise: "Ring, ring." Pick up the phone and hold to your ear and say, "Hello, it's for _____." Hand the phone to the child and encourage conversation. Praise any sounds or words made.

Increase Level of Difficulty

Materials   An additional telephone

Procedure   Using your telephone, ask the child simple questions, such as: "Hi, how are you today?" "What are you doing today?" "Did you eat breakfast?" "What did you have?" Allow child time to respond to each question. Give an answer, if the child does not respond, "Oh, yes, I had warm oatmeal to eat." Say "Good-bye" and that you will call again before the child loses interest.

Decrease Level of Difficulty

Procedure   Help the child explore the telephone. Show her how the dial turns. Model holding the receiver up to your ear and talking. Encourage the child to do the same. Guide her hands and fingers, if needed. Then allow the child to explore on her own.

COMMENT   Use blocks or tubes as a pretend telephone. Encourage two or three children to talk on the pretend telephones with some help from you.

Language Arts

HOUSE

GOAL   To increase language arts concepts
          To increase creative arts concepts

OBJECTIVE   The toddler will develop imaginative skills and increase language concepts.

MATERIALS   large doll house   dolls   furniture

          or build a "house" with blocks for this activity

PROCEDURE   Sit down with the child and encourage exploration of the doll house. Encourage imaginative play. Stimulate conversation with the child and talk about what is happening. Introduce new vocabulary while encouraging creativity.

Increase Level of Difficulty

Procedure   Lay the doll on the bed. Say: "He's tired. Go to sleep." Seat a doll at the table. Say: "Time to eat! I'm hungry." Encourage the children to imitate your actions and words. Ask a child what a particular "person" is doing in the house. Give directions, such as: "The boy looks sleepy. Can you put him to bed?"

Decrease Level of Difficulty

Procedure   Talk about activities in the house as the child plays. Talk about concepts like open and close, up and down, in and out.

COMMENT   Small people pieces are not recommended for children under age three due to concerns about choking. Choose doll house accessories and people that are too large to choke on.

Discovery

HIDDEN TOYS

GOAL   To increase discovery concepts

OBJECTIVE   The infant or toddler will find the toy.

MATERIALS   a small toy   a cloth

PROCEDURE   Get the child intrigued with a toy. Then cover the toy completely with cloth and encourage the child to find it. If the child does not find it, partly uncover the toy and again encourage the child to look.

Increase Level of Difficulty

Materials   An additional cloth

Procedure   Start with a toy that intrigues the child. Hide it first under one cloth then move it to the other, covering the toy completely. Initially, expect that the child will hunt under the first cloth and then perhaps go to the second.

Decrease Level of Difficulty

Procedure   Only partly cover toy with cloth. Encourage the child to find the toy. If the child doesn't attempt to get it, point to the toy and again encourage the child. If the child still doesn't get it, take the cloth off dramatically and say, "Here it is!" If the child is willing, play the game again.

COMMENT   Activities such as this help children develop the concept of object permanence.

Discovery

BIG OR LITTLE

GOAL   To increase discovery concepts
          To increase sensory motor skills

OBJECTIVE   The toddler will identify the big and little toys and put them in the appropriate places.

MATERIALS   objects that are large and small   two containers

dolls   books   cars   blocks   shoes

PROCEDURE   Put out the two containers and the toys to be sorted. Start with just one type of object, shoes. Tell the child that you want her to put all the big shoes in one container and the little shoes in another. Show her a shoe and say, "Is this big or little?" When she correctly identifies it, have her put it in the appropriate container. If she forgets which container is for big, remind her to look at the shoes already in the container.

Increase Level of Difficulty

Procedure   Have children sort two types of objects, such as, shoes and cars, into two containers. See if the children can then figure out additional ways to sort the objects (shoes by type, cars by color, and so on).

Decrease Level of Difficulty

Procedure   Coach the child by asking each time for information about size and the appropriate container. If necessary, work only on identification skills and omit the sorting.

COMMENT   Size and classification concepts are the foundation for many later skills.

Discovery

NESTING TOYS

GOAL   To increase discovery concepts
          To increase sensory motor skills

OBJECTIVE   The infant or toddler will pull the toys apart.

MATERIALS   Stacking/nesting cups

PROCEDURE   Offer the cups to the child nested together. Let the child play and discover what she can do with these objects. If the child doesn't pull them out of the nested position, show her how to do so. At another time, let the child play and experiment by dumping and filling the cups with water, sand, cornmeal, and so on.

Increase Level of Difficulty

Procedure   Encourage the child to nest the containers herself. Begin by offering a small number of loosely fitting cups. (If the set has five cups, take out the second and fourth ones.) Give prompts as needed. (Pointing, say, "Put this cup in.") Gradually increase the difficulty by offering more cups. Continue to provide some time for the child to play in her own way with the cups. Talk about size, using first only the largest and smallest cups. Say, "Give me the big one." Gradually offer more choices.

Decrease Level of Difficulty

Materials   Take out every other cup.

Procedure   Build a tower, encouraging the child to help. Let the child knock it down.

COMMENT   Nesting toys that are cubes are easier for young children, as they do not roll away from them as the cylindrical ones do.

Discovery

NOISY ROLLERS

GOAL   To increase discovery concepts
To increase sensory motor skills

OBJECTIVE   The infant or toddler will roll the toy to make a noise.

MATERIALS   Toy that makes noise when rolled

PROCEDURE   Encourage the child to explore the toy in various ways. That is, shake it or roll it to see if he discovers the relationship between his behavior and the noise the toy makes.

Increase Level of Difficulty

Materials   A variety of noise-making pull toys

Procedure   Toys may be pulled or pushed. Encourage the child to try different toys to listen for different sounds. Help him notice the different sounds, based on how quickly or slowly he moves the toy, as well as the noises made by the toys themselves.

Decrease Level of Difficulty

Procedure   Encourage reaching for and grasping the toy. Show the child what happens when you roll the toy, and then give the toy to the child. Encourage the child to imitate your actions.

COMMENT   Toys in this category support a variety of motor and cognitive skills and can be used at many different levels.

Discovery

RATTLE

GOAL   To increase discovery concepts
To increase sensory motor skills

OBJECTIVE   The infant will shake the rattle to make a noise.

MATERIALS   Rattle or toy that must be shaken or poked to make a noise

PROCEDURE   Shake the rattle and offer it to the child. Demonstrate how to shake the rattle or poke the toy.

Increase Level of Difficulty

Procedure   Tie a sturdy string onto the rattle and attach it to a high chair. When the toy falls off tray, encourage him to pull the string to get toy. Offer help if needed. You can also encourage the child to imitate your behavior with the object. For example, make two sounds and see if the child can make just two sounds. Make short or long sounds, loud or soft, and see if the child can follow your lead.

Decrease Level of Difficulty

Procedure   Help the child explore the toy or manipulate it for him so he can see and hear how it works. Talk about what you are doing and the relationship between what you do and the sound. Use a Velcro bracelet to help the child hold the rattle.

COMMENT   Use dolls, blankets, bottles, and other accessories that rattle or make noise for pretend play. *Note:* Use the string only with direct adult supervision. The child should not be left alone with string.

SHAPE SORTER

GOAL   To increase discovery concepts
To increase sensory motor skills

OBJECTIVE   The toddler will place the shapes in the correct places.

MATERIALS   Shape sorter

PROCEDURE   Present toy to the child and encourage him to lift the top off, remove the blocks, and then replace the top. Encourage him to place the blocks in appropriate holes. If needed, demonstrate how the shapes fit in the holes.

Increase Level of Difficulty

Materials   Shape sorter with more shapes

Procedure   Name the shapes and ask the child to put in the shapes you name.

Decrease Level of Difficulty

Materials   Shape sorter with fewer shapes

Procedure   Allow the child to put in and take out blocks from the container without the lid. Then cover one or two spaces with your hand or piece of cardboard or tape so child has fewer choices and can be successful more easily.

COMMENT   Help children learn about the shapes in their environment. Play a game by looking around your room for shapes that are round, square, or triangular. A doorknob, a ball, a book, and blocks are examples of items you may find.

Infants explore toys with their mouths as well as
their hands. For younger infants, toys that attach to
a surface with a suction cup may be less frustrating
to all.

SUCTION CUP TOYS

GOAL   To increase discovery concepts
To increase sensory motor skills

OBJECTIVE   The infant will purposefully move the suction cup toy.

MATERIALS   Toys with suction cups

PROCEDURE   Place the suction cup toy on a high chair or walker tray or other smooth surface where the infant can easily reach it. Encourage him to hit it to watch the movement and listen to the sound it makes.

Increase Level of Difficulty

Procedure   Move the toy in a pattern and see if the child can repeat your pattern. Use two toys with different sounds and move one of the toys and see if the child will imitate you.

Decrease Level of Difficulty

Procedure   Slowly move the toy in different directions so the infant can follow its movement visually. Gently guide the infant's arms from the shoulder to help him either reach and grasp toy or bat at it.

COMMENT   Toys such as these provide a variety of feedback to the young child. Once the child learns the underlying principle, he can use this toy independently.

TAKE APART TOYS

GOAL   To increase discovery concepts
To increase sensory motor skills

OBJECTIVE   The toddler will take the toy apart and put it back together.

MATERIALS   Toy that comes apart

PROCEDURE   Present the toy to the child to explore. If he doesn't take it apart on his own, show him how. Talk about the toy's body parts. Ask, "Where's his head?", and so on.

Increase Level of Difficulty

Procedure   Take off one part at a time, such as the head or tail. Encourage the child to replace that piece. Gradually remove more and more pieces for the child to replace or encourage the child to pull the toy apart himself. Help put the toy back together as needed.

Decrease Level of Difficulty

Procedure   Use the toy to stimulate language development while you do the more difficult taking apart and putting together. Ask the child, "Is this where the head goes?" Or ask the child to show you where the head goes and then you put it on.

COMMENT   This activity helps children think about body parts as well as part–whole relationships.

KEYS

GOAL   To increase sensory motor skills

OBJECTIVE   The infant will reach for and grasp the keys, crossing his midline.

MATERIALS   Plastic keys

PROCEDURE   Offer keys to the child to reach and grasp from different angles (up, down, right, left). Encourage feeling, looking, mouthing, and shaking. Try to get the child to reach across his midline to get the keys. (This can be encouraged by having the child hold a toy in one hand while you offer the keys.)

Increase Level of Difficulty

Procedure   Increase the distance the keys are from the child so that it is a long reach. Put the keys out of the child's field of vision and call, "Get the keys," so that he has to turn and reach.

Decrease Level of Difficulty

Procedure   Call the child's name and shake keys. Gently place the keys in the child's hand. Help the child mouth, look at, or shake keys, if necessary. Keep the keys close to the midline.

COMMENT   Any small toy that intrigues the child can be used.

Sensory Motor

MOBILES

GOAL   To increase sensory motor skills

OBJECTIVE   The infant will look at the mobile.

MATERIALS   Mobile

PROCEDURE   Secure mobile tightly on crib out of the child's reach. The mobile provides something interesting and visually stimulating for a child who cannot yet coordinate movements to reach and grasp objects. Place the mobile in different places on the crib every few days to encourage the child to look in different directions. Continue to interact with the child in the crib while you attend to other children. Talk to, look at, or help focus the child's attention on the mobile.

Increase Level of Difficulty

Materials   Change or rotate mobiles to keep child's attention.

Procedure   Remove the mobile when the child can reach for and grasp it. Mobiles are for infants to look at and can present a danger if the infant grasps and pulls them. Provide safe rattles or other toys when children are ready to use them.

Decrease Level of Difficulty

Materials   Choose a mobile with few details and highly contrasting colors.

COMMENT   Children enjoy the stimulation of a mobile.

Sensory Motor

ROLLING BALLS

GOAL   To increase sensory motor skills

OBJECTIVE   The infant or toddler will explore and roll the ball.

MATERIALS   Beach ball

PROCEDURE   While sitting on the floor, roll the ball towards the child. Encourage him to get the ball and examine it.

Increase Level of Difficulty

Procedure   Place the ball a few feet from the child who is sitting on the floor and pat the ball. Say, "Get the ball," as you encourage the child to crawl towards it. Roll the ball to the child and encourage him to roll it back. Sit behind him and help him roll the ball to another child. Provide smaller balls and toys of other textures for rolling. The child can experiment with rolling objects of different weights and sizes.

Decrease Level of Difficulty

Procedure   Take some of the air out of the beach ball so it is easier to grab. Hold the ball in the child's line of vision. Say, "Get the ball." If child does not reach for the ball on his own, put the ball in the child's hands.

COMMENT   Children need firsthand experience to discover that balls roll but cubes do not.

Sensory Motor

TEETHER

GOAL   To increase sensory motor skills

OBJECTIVE   The infant will "mouth" the teether.

MATERIALS   Teether

PROCEDURE   Encourage child to reach, grasp, and mouth teether. Say: "This is a foot (if teether is foot-shaped). Do those toes taste good?" Touch child's foot and toes and say: "Here's your foot. I have your toes!"

Increase Level of Difficulty

Procedure   Encourage the child to explore the teether in ways other than mouthing, such as banging, shaking, and throwing. Try to support the child in simple imitation skills. For example, put a foot-shaped teether in a big shoe. Take it out and encourage child to try to put it back. Tap the teether on a surface or clap while holding teether in one hand.

Decrease Level of Difficulty

Procedure   Gently guide the child's arm from the shoulder area to help grasp teether. Help grasp and mouth if needed. Talk to child and tell him about your actions as well as his.

COMMENT   This activity uses a natural form of exploration (teething) to interest the child and then expands on this activity.

Sensory Motor

YARN BALLS

GOAL   To increase sensory motor skills

OBJECTIVE   The infant or toddler will play with the ball.

MATERIALS   Yarn ball

PROCEDURE   Encourage the child to explore the yarn ball. Hold it so the child can grasp it. Encourage the child to transfer it from one hand to the other. (If necessary, model this behavior.) Take turns giving and receiving the ball with the child.

Increase Level of Difficulty

Procedure   Toss the ball into a container (empty wastebasket, clothes basket, cardboard box) and retrieve it. Encourage the child to do same. Use a sturdy cardboard tube and encourage the child to move the ball along the floor by pushing it. This activity encourages tool usage skills.

Decrease Level of Difficulty

Procedure   Let the child feel and touch the ball. Roll the ball on the child's arms, legs, and stomach. Name her body parts as you touch them. Suspend the ball from the crib or other frame. Encourage the child to move the ball with her arms or legs.

COMMENT   Yarn balls are extremely forgiving, easy to hold, easy to make, and washable, and they don't break objects when they stray.

INFLATABLE ANIMALS

GOAL   To increase sensory motor skills
To increase language arts concepts

OBJECTIVE   The infant or toddler will explore the toy.

MATERIALS   Plastic rabbit or other plastic inflatable animal

PROCEDURE   Offer toy to child slightly beyond his reach. Say, "Get the bunny." Allow child to explore the toy with hands and mouth. (Be sure to wash it if the child puts the toy in his mouth.)

Increase Level of Difficulty

Procedure   Encourage imitation by squeezing the bunny and then saying, "Now you do it." Talk about some of the bunny's body parts such as ears, eyes, and tail. Say: "I'm touching the bunny's ears. Can you touch the bunny's ears?" If child can squeeze bunny to make a sound, provide more complex objects for manipulation. Give him a busy box or cash register with buttons to push.

Decrease Level of Difficulty

Procedure   Call child's name and touch his hand with toy to catch his attention. If the child doesn't try to grasp toy, gently squeeze it to make a sound. Move the toy out of the child's line of vision and squeeze toy again. Say, "Where's the bunny?" and watch to see if child turns head.

COMMENT   Children sometimes need stimulation to encourage them to explore their environment.

MOVING LIKE THE ANIMALS

GOAL   To increase sensory motor skills
To increase language arts concepts

OBJECTIVE   The toddler will move like an animal.

MATERIALS   Pictures of familiar animals

PROCEDURE   See if children can identify the animals in the picture. Help them decide if the animals are large or small and how they move. Have the children move like they think the animal would move.

Increase Level of Difficulty

Procedure   Choose animals that are less familiar but have obvious movement patterns. Talk about the animals and where they live.

Decrease Level of Difficulty

Procedure   Make sure the children have enough space and encourage movement of any kind.

COMMENT   This activity helps children learn more about the world in which they live.

BLOCKS

GOAL   To increase sensory motor skills
To increase discovery concepts

OBJECTIVE   The infant or toddler will participate in block play.

MATERIALS   Blocks

PROCEDURE   Sit on the floor with the child and begin stacking blocks. Give the child a block and encourage him to join you.

Increase Level of Difficulty

Procedure   Let the child do most of the building. Provide other materials to extend the child's block play, such as cars or toy people. Begin to build simple structures such as roads and so on. Roads can be built easily by stacking blocks side by side and "driving" a car over them. Say, "Look! I made a road!"

Decrease Level of Difficulty

Materials   A few large blocks

Procedure   Let the child knock down the blocks you've stacked. Then encourage her to put one block on top of another. Praise any of the child's attempts whether they are successful or not.

COMMENT   Blocks have the potential for building both mathematical and creative problem-solving skills for young children. At this age, large, light blocks are preferable. Those made out of two milk cartons forced together with the triangular ends cut off are just fine.

Sensory Motor

DUMP AND FILL

GOAL   To increase sensory motor skills
To increase discovery concepts

OBJECTIVE   The toddler will fill the small container and then dump it.

MATERIALS   dishpans   rice   sand   oatmeal   beans

plastic measuring cups   measuring spoons

PROCEDURE   Put about two inches of rice, sand, oatmeal, or beans in a dishpan. Add a variety of cups and spoons. Encourage the children to fill up the containers and dump them.

Increase Level of Difficulty

Procedure   Have the children dump the contents from one container into another container. Help them establish a relationship with size and volume of contents.

Decrease Level of Difficulty

Procedure   Help the children explore the medium itself. If necessary, place his hands in the container and help him explore the medium. Encourage him to fill the container with his hands.

COMMENT   This activity is a precursor to pouring liquids and is a lot less messy. It has the potential for simple exploration as well as for building concepts about measurement and relative size.

Sensory Motor

GRAB IT

GOAL   To increase sensory motor skills
To increase discovery concepts

OBJECTIVE   The infant will grasp the block.

MATERIALS   Small blocks

PROCEDURE   With the child in a sitting position, hold a small block just outside of the child's reach and see if she will reach for it. If she does, offer a second and then a third to see what she does. Vary where you place the block for reaching. Sometimes place it close to the center of the child's body, sometimes more to the right or left so the child has to maintain balance while reaching.

Increase Level of Difficulty

Materials   A variety of blocks of different sizes

Procedure   Give the child two blocks of different sizes and have two blocks that match the child's for yourself. Hold up one block and say, "Show me one just like this." As the child is successful, gradually make the task more difficult by using blocks that are closer to each other in size.

Even very young infants are intrigued and aware of each other. Be sure to give these infants the opportunity to be together under your watchful eye.

Decrease Level of Difficulty

Procedure   Place the blocks close to the child's midline or preferred hand, if that has been established.

COMMENT   Some children need to be encouraged to reach and grasp. *Note:* Consult with the child's therapist to see if you should be placing the block in a particular position to stimulate reaching.

Sensory Motor

PUZZLES

GOAL   To increase sensory motor skills
           To increase discovery concepts

OBJECTIVE   The toddler will put the puzzle pieces in correctly.

MATERIALS   Wooden puzzle (1 to 6 pieces)

PROCEDURE   Encourage the child to remove and replace puzzle pieces. Label pieces as child uses them; encourage child to say name of each piece.

Increase Level of Difficulty

Procedure   Hide puzzle pieces in oatmeal, cornmeal, or another medium. Have child find puzzle piece and put it in correct place. Hide puzzle pieces around the room while the child watches. As he finds one, he replaces it and finds another. Provide a variety of whole-piece puzzles. When the child successfully completes several, try a simple interlocking puzzle with few pieces.

Decrease Level of Difficulty

Procedure   Play with easier shape-matching activities, such as shape sorters or puzzles with circles, squares, and triangles. Cover one side of the puzzle so the child has fewer spaces from which to choose.

COMMENT Sturdy wooden puzzles are a good early learning experience for toddlers. They provide the child with feedback about his movements yet hold up to his lack of precision.

WHOLE-PIECE KNOBBED PUZZLES

GOAL To increase sensory motor skills
To increase discovery concepts

OBJECTIVE The toddler will put the puzzle together.

MATERIALS Whole-piece knobbed wooden puzzles

PROCEDURE Have the puzzle available for the child to manipulate and experiment with on her own. If the child is not familiar with this type of puzzle, remove a piece by lifting the knob. Encourage the child to pick up the puzzle pieces.

Increase Level of Difficulty

Materials Puzzles with more pieces

Procedure Remove all puzzle pieces and have the child replace them. When the child can identify the puzzle pieces, ask her to replace the piece you name. Next, provide puzzles with individual pieces.

Decrease Level of Difficulty

Materials Puzzles with few pieces and simple shapes

Procedure If the child doesn't try to imitate, help her. Place her fingers on the knob and help lift the puzzle piece. Place all but one of the pieces in the puzzle. Then, ask the child to place the final piece. Offer help as needed, but be sure to let the child try to replace the pieces on her own first.

COMMENT This activity is the first step in helping children work with puzzles. The knobs help emerging small motor skills and provide variety in practicing these skills.

CLEANING HOUSE

GOAL To increase social awareness
To increase language arts concepts
To increase sensory motor skills

OBJECTIVE The toddler will use the house cleaning materials appropriately.

MATERIALS toy vacuum cleaner   broom   dust cloth
sponge   dust pan

PROCEDURE Let children "vacuum" the floor or rug. Encourage them to work together with the broom and dust pan. Talk about cleaning and how you are all helping to get the room cleaner.

Increase Level of Difficulty

Procedure Demonstrate how different cleaning tools work and help the child use the materials.

Decrease Level of Difficulty

Procedure Make vacuum sounds. Use different actions (such as several pushes and pulls, a long push, a twist around a corner) and encourage the child to imitate. Make path with tape or paper for child to follow around a room.

COMMENT Children often enjoy imitating the work of adults. As you don't really care how effectively the children are cleaning, you can concentrate on the process.

DOLLS

GOAL   To increase social awareness
To increase language arts concepts
To increase sensory motor skills

OBJECTIVE   The toddler will play with the dolls in a variety of ways.

MATERIALS   Dolls

PROCEDURE   Encourage the child to play with dolls in different ways. He may want to carry, cuddle, bottle-feed, sing to, or rock the baby. When he is ready, introduce new ways of playing with the baby in an appropriate way. Encourage two children to play together and talk about what each is doing with his baby and why. Encourage them to think about what the baby might want or need.

Increase Level of Difficulty

Procedure   See if the child can imitate more difficult skills, such as pretend feeding with a spoon, sprinkling powder or rubbing lotion on body parts, or combing the doll's hair. Help the child use his imagination with the doll. For example, have a pretend (or even real) tea party. Take the doll for walk in a wagon or stroller. Wash the baby in a small tub, using soap and a wash cloth, then dry the doll with a towel. Help the child develop adaptive skills by practicing undressing and dressing, not only himself, but also a doll. Remember undressing is a skill that comes before dressing.

Decrease Level of Difficulty

Procedure   Encourage exploration of the doll. Help the child to gently feel the doll's hair, eyes, and clothing, and to move body parts. Name body and clothing parts for the child.

COMMENT   Children may need to be taught caregiving skills. They are often more willing to practice adaptive skills in play situations.

MIRROR

GOAL   To increase social awareness
To increase language arts concepts
To increase sensory motor skills

OBJECTIVE   The infant or toddler will look at himself in the mirror.

MATERIALS   unbreakable mirror (about 12″)

PROCEDURE   Hold the child in your lap with a mirror in front so he can see himself. Talk about what he sees in the mirror: "Look, there's Josh! I see you!"

Increase Level of Difficulty

Procedure   Point to and name the child's facial parts when he looks in the mirror. Ask the child to point to or name facial parts, as he is able. Have him play imitation games in the mirror, such as opening and closing his mouth, patting his head, tugging his ear, and making silly faces!

Decrease Level of Difficulty

Materials   Large, mounted mirror

Procedure   Place child in front of large mirror where she can more easily see herself. Or, use the smaller mirror as an object to explore by looking and touching.

COMMENT   Children enjoy looking at themselves in the mirror. As many mirrors they encounter are too high for them to see in, this activity is a good way to show them what they look like.

WASHING DISHES

GOAL   To increase social awareness
To increase sensory motor skills

OBJECTIVE   The toddler will put dishes in and take them out of the basin.

MATERIALS   plastic dishes   basin   water (lukewarm)

PROCEDURE   Put objects in basin. Help the child explore the dishes. Encourage him to put the dishes in the basin, swish the water, and take them out. Talk about his actions. Ask him questions. Have at least two basins so that children can interact.

Increase Level of Difficulty

Procedure   Fill basin with small amount of water and add a small amount of soap. Let the child "wash" dishes. Add a sponge or handled scrubber for the child to wash dishes. Have several towels available to dry dishes. Encourage appropriate actions, that is, placing cups on saucers, pouring, and stirring the cup with a spoon. Have children sort utensils in storage unit. Encourage them to match items by color. Have children "set" the table and use dishes to serve snack.

Decrease Level of Difficulty

Procedure   Say "out" as you take a dish out and "in" as you put the dishes in. Physically guide child's hand, if needed. Say, "Good, you took it out!"

COMMENT   Even young children enjoy pretending with familiar objects. The lukewarm water is soothing.

DANCING

GOAL   To increase creative arts concepts
To increase sensory motor skills

OBJECTIVE   The toddler will dance to the music.

MATERIALS   record, cassette, or compact disc player   record, cassette, or compact disc

PROCEDURE   Play music for toddlers to dance to in their own ways. Use many different types of music. If toddlers don't dance, dance with them or pair them with other children who have the idea.

Increase Level of Difficulty

Procedure   Have the children listen for about a minute and talk about the beat and the concepts of fast and slow before they begin to dance. Add scarves.

Decrease Level of Difficulty

Procedure   Encourage movement of any type.

COMMENT   Moving to music is a lifelong skill.

DRESS UP

GOAL   To increase creative arts concepts
To increase sensory motor skills

OBJECTIVE   The toddler will put on the clothing.

| MATERIALS | hats | shoes | shirts | blouses | skirts |
| | dresses | pants | jackets | scarves | ties |

PROCEDURE   Encourage the children to dress up in the clothing. Talk with them about where they are going and what role they are playing.

Increase Level of Difficulty

Procedure   Encourage the children to play together with complementary roles.

Decrease Level of Difficulty

Procedure   Focus on the self-help aspect of the play and encourage children to put on and take off the clothing. Be sure clothing is large enough to go on easily.

COMMENT   Most toddlers enjoy a familiar level of pretend play.

Creative Arts

PAINTING WITH WATER

GOAL   To increase creative arts concepts
      To increase sensory motor skills

OBJECTIVE   The toddler will paint with water.

MATERIALS   2″ paint brushes   buckets   water

PROCEDURE   On a warm day, fill the buckets with water and encourage the toddlers to paint the sidewalk or house.

Increase Level of Difficulty

Materials   1″ brush

Procedure   Encourage the children to draw faces or pictures and then watch as the sun makes them disappear.

Decrease Level of Difficulty

Procedure   Support any type of tool use.

COMMENT   This is a clean painting activity. Children are free to experiment with the water and brush.

Creative Arts

PRINT IT

GOAL   To increase creative arts concepts
      To increase sensory motor skills

OBJECTIVE   The toddler will make a finger painting print.

MATERIALS   finger paint   washable table   finger paint paper

PROCEDURE   Put finger paint directly on the table (one color or two at most). Let the children finger paint directly on the table. You may have to model this behavior by showing the children how to get started. Encourage them to experiment. When they are finished ask if they want to print their painting. If so, put the paper over the painting and smooth your hand over the paper to print the painting.

Increase Level of Difficulty

Procedure   Have the children paint directly on the finger paint paper.

Decrease Level of Difficulty

Procedure   Concentrate on the finger painting process and don't print the pictures.

COMMENT   Finger painting is a messy activity. It requires aprons for the children and a pan of soapy water or ready access to a bathroom for handwashing.

STICK IT

GOAL   To increase creative arts concepts
To increase sensory motor skills

OBJECTIVE   The toddler will lick the stamps and put them on the paper.

MATERIALS   paper   stamps (free ones)   stickers   markers

PROCEDURE   Show the children how to lick the stamps to make them stick to the paper. Then encourage the children to lick them and put them on the paper. If there are other stickers and markers, they can use those as well. You may need to show the children how to take the stickers off the backing.

Increase Level of Difficulty

Procedure   Help the child draw a simple figure, such as a circle or triangle, and then put the stamps on the design.

Decrease Level of Difficulty

Materials   Larger stamps

Procedure   Larger stamps may be easier for the child to handle. Let the child participate in the process.

COMMENT   As you are sent stamps in the mail for advertising purposes, save them and let the children use them when you have a collection. Children may not have had much experience with stamps.

TEXTURES

GOAL   To increase creative arts concepts
To increase sensory motor skills

OBJECTIVE   The infant and toddler will explore the textures.

MATERIALS   Squares (6″) of different textured cloth

satin   cotton   wool   terry cloth   lycra

knit fabric   dotted swiss   fake fur

PROCEDURE   Put the fabric squares on the table. Let the children explore them. Gently rub a piece of fabric on your arm and talk about how it feels. Encourage the toddler to do the same. Stroke the fabric. Talk about its texture. Compare the fabrics.

Increase Level of Difficulty

Materials   Additional fabrics, some that are the same texture in different colors or patterns
Procedure   See if the children can classify some of the fabrics or match them by texture.

Decrease Level of Difficulty

Procedure   Gently rub the fabric on the infant's arms or legs. Talk about how it feels.

COMMENT   This activity increases children's awareness of different textures and builds language skills as they label the textures.

BIG PICTURES

GOAL   To increase creative arts concepts
To increase social awareness

OBJECTIVE   The toddler will mark the paper.

MATERIALS   large sheet of newsprint   water-based markers

large crayons   large chalk

PROCEDURE   Cover a table with the paper. Tape it down so it won't move. Be sure that each child has her own space to work in, with her own set of markers, crayons, and chalk. Encourage the children to work together and to talk.

Increase Level of Difficulty

Procedure   Make the picture part of a theme and have the children scribble something related to that theme. If the children desire, label the scribble and write what they say about it.

Decrease Level of Difficulty

Procedure   Support and accept any marks the child makes on the paper.

COMMENT   Leave the paper out long enough so that children can use it and then come back. Young children often leave an activity and return to it later.

Creative Arts

DOG WALKING

GOAL   To increase creative arts concepts
To increase social awareness

OBJECTIVE   The toddler will walk an animal.

MATERIALS   string   stuffed animals

PROCEDURE   Use the string to make a leash for the dogs (or other animals). Have one animal for each child who participates. Talk about taking the dog for a walk. Walk around the room or outside. (In reality, pull the animal with the string.) Talk about why you walk dogs and what you see on the walk.

Increase Level of Difficulty

Procedure   Make the walk a little longer and make more detailed observations. See if the children will really pretend with you.

Decrease Level of Difficulty

Procedure   Just expect the children to walk with the dog and not participate in the creative aspect of the play.

COMMENT   Don't forget to take off the leashes when you bring the dogs home. If you take an outside walk, be sure the animals are washable and expect to wash them.

References and Bibliography

Auerbach, S. (1981). *The whole child: A sourcebook.* New York: G. P. Putnam's Sons.

Cryer, D., Harms, T., & Bourland, B. (1987a). *Active learning for infants.* Menlo Park, CA: Addison-Wesley.

Cryer, D., Harms, T., & Bourland, B. (1987b). *Active learning for ones.* Menlo Park, CA: Addison-Wesley.

Cryer, D., Harms, T., & Bourland, B. (1988). *Active learning for twos.* Menlo Park, CA: Addison-Wesley.

Dmitriev, V. *Time to begin: Early education for children with Down syndrome.* Milton, WA: Caring, Inc.

Greenberg, P. (1991). *Character development: Encouraging self-esteem & self discrimination in infants, toddlers, & two-year-olds.* Washington, DC: National Association for the Education of Young Children.

Levy, J. *The baby exercise book: For the first fifteen months.* New York: Pantheon Books.

Prudhoe, C. M. (1989). Helping babies develop self-awareness. In P. L. Deiner, L. C. Whitehead, & C. M. Prudhoe, *Technical assistance: Information sheets for day care providers and families of children with special needs.* Unpublished technical report. Newark, DE: University of Delaware.

Ross, H. (1992). Integrating infants with disabilities? Can "ordinary" caregivers do it? *Young Children, 47* (3) 65–71.

Segal, M. (1988). *In time and with love: Caring for the special needs baby.* New York: Newmarket Press.

Index of Activities

Contents

Goal	Activity	Curriculum Area	Page
To increase expressive language	Sentences	Language Arts	375
	Synonyms	Language Arts	376
	Same and Different	Language Arts	377
	Never	Language Arts	377
	My Shoes	Language Arts	378
	Shoe Theater	Language Arts	379
	Ideas	Language Arts	379
	Divergent	Language Arts	380
	Bring Me	Language Arts	381
	Weekend News	Language Arts	381
	Peek Pictures	Language Arts	382
	Rhyming Words	Language Arts	383
	Telephone	Language Arts	384
	Object Hunt	Language Arts	384
	Interviews	Language Arts	385
	Body Sounds	Language Arts	398
	Share Your Feelings	Social Awareness	521
	One More	Social Awareness	518
	Seasonal Clothing	Social Awareness	535
	Smell Cues	Social Awareness	536
	Symptoms	Social Awareness	536
To improve listening skills	Magician	Language Arts	386
	Sounds of Silence	Language Arts	387
	Whisper	Language Arts	387
	Say It	Language Arts	387
	Listening Walk	Language Arts	389
	Noisy and Quiet	Language Arts	389
	Sound and Tell	Language Arts	390
	Sound Cues	Language Arts	391
	Noisy Steps	Language Arts	391
	Sound Eggs	Language Arts	392
	Water Tones	Language Arts	393
	Number Tapping	Language Arts	393
	Where Is It/Who Is It?	Language Arts	394
	Tape It	Language Arts	394
	Same and Different	Language Arts	377
	Rhyming Words	Language Arts	383
	Telephone	Language Arts	384
	Flannel Board Stories	Language Arts	399
	Letter Day	Language Arts	400
	Sound Bingo	Language Arts	400

Goal	Activity	Curriculum Area	Page
	Maps	Discovery	447
	Popcorn	Discovery	446
	Cereal Balls	Discovery	458
	Object Sizes	Discovery	435
	From Your House to Mine	Social Awareness	522
To improve observational skills	My Yard	Discovery	442
	Goop	Discovery	442
	Ant Farm	Discovery	443
	Nature Board	Discovery	443
	Sink or Float	Discovery	444
	Color Changes	Discovery	445
	Gelatin	Discovery	445
	Pollution	Discovery	446
	Popcorn	Discovery	446
	Maps	Discovery	447
	Bubbles	Discovery	447
	Hidden Objects	Discovery	431
	What Is It?	Language Arts	405
	Charades	Social Awareness	518
	Simulated Glasses	Social Awareness	529
To improve classification skills	Same and Different	Language Arts	377
	Never	Language Arts	377
	Bring Me	Language Arts	381
	Food Lotto	Discovery	448
	Sorting	Discovery	449
	Picture Shapes	Discovery	438
	Big and Little Pairs	Discovery	440
	Thinking Shapes	Discovery	435
	Variations on Blocks	Discovery	430
	Variations on Cuisenaire Rods	Discovery	432
	Measuring Tools	Discovery	441
	My Yard	Discovery	442
	Nature Board	Discovery	443
	Sink or Float	Discovery	444
	Measure It	Discovery	441
	Pick-a-Pair	Sensory Motor	488
	Texture Playdough	Creative Arts	561
To make predictions	Matrix	Language Arts	403
	Color Concentration	Language Arts	404
	Magnets	Discovery	449
	Planting	Discovery	450
	Scrambled Eggs	Discovery	451
	Measuring Tools	Discovery	441
	Variations on Cuisenaire Rods	Discovery	432
	Gelatin	Discovery	445
	Color Changes	Discovery	445
	Pollution	Discovery	446
	Measure It	Discovery	441
	Number Squares	Discovery	428
	Who Has Been Here?	Social Awareness	519
To improve cause-and-effect reasoning	Divergent	Language Arts	380
	Natural Sequencing	Language Arts	396
	Sound Eggs	Language Arts	392
	Water Tones	Language Arts	393
	Follow That Line	Language Arts	404
	Magnets	Discovery	449
	Planting	Discovery	450

Index of Subjects

Index of Names

Photography Credits